CLASSICAL AND MEDIEVAL LITERATURE CRITICISM

Guide to Gale Literary Criticism Series

For criticism on	Consult these Gale series
Authors now living or who died after December 31, 1959	*CONTEMPORARY LITERARY CRITICISM (CLC)*
Authors who died between 1900 and 1959	*TWENTIETH-CENTURY LITERARY CRITICISM (TCLC)*
Authors who died between 1800 and 1899	*NINETEENTH-CENTURY LITERATURE CRITICISM (NCLC)*
Authors who died between 1400 and 1799	*LITERATURE CRITICISM FROM 1400 TO 1800 (LC)* *SHAKESPEAREAN CRITICISM (SC)*
Authors who died before 1400	*CLASSICAL AND MEDIEVAL LITERATURE CRITICISM (CMLC)*
Black writers of the past two hundred years	*BLACK LITERATURE CRITICISM (BLC)*
Authors of books for children and young adults	*CHILDREN'S LITERATURE REVIEW (CLR)*
Dramatists	*DRAMA CRITICISM (DC)*
Hispanic writers of the late nineteenth and twentieth centuries	*HISPANIC LITERATURE CRITICISM (HLC)*
Native North American writers and orators of the eighteenth, nineteenth, and twentieth centuries	*NATIVE NORTH AMERICAN LITERATURE (NNAL)*
Poets	*POETRY CRITICISM (PC)*
Short story writers	*SHORT STORY CRITICISM (SSC)*
Major authors from the Renaissance to the present	*WORLD LITERATURE CRITICISM, 1500 TO THE PRESENT (WLC)*

ISSN 0896-0011

Volume 15

CLASSICAL AND MEDIEVAL LITERATURE CRITICISM

Excerpts from Criticism of the Works of World Authors from Classical Antiquity through the Fourteenth Century, from the First Appraisals to Current Evaluations

Jelena O. Krstović
Editor

Catherine C. Dominic
Denise Kasinec
Michael Magoulias
Associate Editors

An International Thomson Publishing Company

NEW YORK • LONDON • BONN • BOSTON • DETROIT • MADRID
MELBOURNE • MEXICO CITY • PARIS • SINGAPORE • TOKYO
TORONTO • WASHINGTON • ALBANY NY • BELMONT CA • CINCINNATI OH

STAFF

Jelena Krstović, *Editor*

Catherine C. Dominic,
Denise Kasinec, Michael Magoulias, *Associate Editors*

Matthew C. Altman, *Assistant Editor*

Susan Trosky, *Managing Editor*

Marlene S. Hurst, *Permissions Manager*
Margaret A. Chamberlain, *Permissions Specialist*
Susan Brohman, Diane Cooper, Maria Franklin, Arlene Johnson,
Michele Lonoconus, Maureen Puhl, Shalice Shah,
Kimberly F. Smilay, Barbara A. Wallace, *Permissions Associates*
Edna Hedblad, Margaret McAvoy-Amato, Tyra Y. Phillips, Lori Schoenenberger, *Permissions Assistants*

Victoria B. Cariappa, *Research Manager*
Frank Vincent Castronova, Eva M. Felts, Mary Beth McElmeel, Donna Melnychenko, Tamara C. Nott, Tracie A. Richardson, Norma Sawaya, *Research Associates*
Melissa E. Brown, Maria E. Bryson, Michele McRobert, Michele P. Pica,
Amy Terese Steel, Amy Beth Wieczorek, *Research Assistants*

Mary Beth Trimper, *Production Director*
Deborah Milliken, *Production Assistant*

Barbara J. Yarrow, *Graphic Services Supervisor*
Sherrell Hobbs, *Macintosh Artist*
Pamela Hayes, *Photography Coordinator*
Willie Mathis, *Camera Operator*

∞™ This book is printed on acid-free paper that meets the minimum requirements of American National Standard for Information Sciences—Permanence Paper for Printed Library Materials, ANSI Z39.48-1984.

Library of Congress Catalog Card Number 88-658021
ISBN 0-8103-4878-0
ISSN 0896-0011
Printed in the United States of America
I(T)P™ Gale Research Inc., an International Thomson Publishing Company.
ITP logo is a trademark under license.

10 9 8 7 6 5 4 3 2 1

Contents

Preface

Since its inception in 1988, *Classical and Medieval Literature Criticism* has been a valuable resource for students and librarians seeking critical commentary on the writers and works of these periods in world history. Major reviewing sources have assessed *CMLC* as "useful" and "extremely convenient," noting that it "adds to our understanding of the rich legacy left by the ancient period and the Middle Ages," and praising its "general excellence in the presentation of an inherently interesting subject." No other single reference source has surveyed the critical reaction to classical and medieval literature as thoroughly as *CMLC.*

Scope of the Series

CMLC is designed to serve as an introduction for students and advanced readers of the works and authors of antiquity through the fourteenth century. The great poets, prose writers, dramatists, and philosophers of this period form the basis of most humanities curricula, so that virtually every student will encounter many of these works during the course of a high school and college education. By organizing and reprinting an enormous amount of commentary written on classical and medieval authors and works, *CMLC* helps students develop valuable insight into literary history, promotes a better understanding of the texts, and sparks ideas for papers and assignments. Each entry in *CMLC* presents a comprehensive survey of an author's career, an individual work of literature, or a literary topic, and provides the user with a multiplicity of interpretations and assessments. Such variety allows students to pursue their own interests; furthermore, it fosters an awareness that literature is dynamic and responsive to many different opinions.

CMLC continues the survey of criticism of world literature begun by Gale's *Contemporary Literary Criticism (CLC), Twentieth-Century Literary Criticism (TCLC), Nineteenth-Century Literature Criticism (NCLC), Literature Criticism from 1400 to 1800 (LC),* and *Shakespearean Criticism (SC).* For additional information about these and Gale's other criticism series, users should consult the Guide to Gale Literary Criticism Series preceding the title page in this volume.

Coverage

Each volume of *CMLC* is carefully compiled to present:

- criticism of authors and works which represent a variety of genres, time periods, and nationalities
- both major and lesser-known writers and works of thc period (such as non-Western authors and literature, increasingly read by today's students)
- 4-6 authors or works per volume
- individual entries that survey the critical response to each author, work, or topic, including early criticism, later criticism (to represent any rise or decline in the author's reputation), and current retrospective analyses. The length of each author or work entry also indicates relative importance, reflecting the amount of critical attention the author, work, or topic has received from critics writing in English, and from foreign criticism in translation.

An author may appear more than once in the series if his or her writings have been the subject of a substantial amount of criticism; in these instances, specific works or groups of works by the author will be covered in separate entries. For example, Homer will be represented by three entries, one devoted to the *Iliad,* one to the *Odyssey,* and one to the Homeric Hymns.

Starting with Volume 10, *CMLC* will also occasionally include entries devoted to literary topics. For example, *CMLC*-10 focuses on Arthurian Legend and includes general criticism on that subject as well as individual entries on writers or works central to that topic—Chrétien de Troyes, Gottfried von Strassburg, Layamon, and the Alliterative *Morte Arthure.*

Organization of the Book

An author entry consists of the following elements: author heading, biographical and critical introduction, principal English translations or editions, excerpts of criticism (each preceded by a bibliographic citation and an annotation), and a bibliography of further reading.

- The **Author Heading** consists of the author's most commonly used name, followed by birth and death dates. If the entry is devoted to a work, the heading will consist of the most common form of the title in English translation (if applicable), and the original date of composition. Located at the beginning of the introduction are any name or title variations.

- A **Portrait** of the author is included when available. Many entries also feature illustrations of materials pertinent to the author or work, including manuscript pages, book illustrations, and representations of people, places, and events important to a study of the author or work.

- The **Biographical and Critical Introduction** contains background information that concisely introduces the reader to the author, work, or topic.

- The list of **Principal Works** and **English Translations** or **Editions** is chronological by date of first publication and is included as an aid to the student seeking translated versions or editions of these works for study. The list will focus primarily on twentieth-century translations, selecting those works most commonly considered the best by critics.

- **Criticism** is arranged chronologically in each entry to provide a useful perspective on changes in critical evaluation over the years. All titles by the author featured in the critical entry are printed in boldface type to enable the user to ascertain without difficulty the works being discussed. Also for purposes of easier identification, the critic's name and the publication date of the essay are given at the beginning of each piece of criticism. Anonymous criticism is preceded by the title of the journal in which it appeared. Publication information (such as publisher names and book prices) and parenthetical numerical references (such as footnotes or page and line references to specific editions of works) have been deleted at the editors' discretion to provide smoother reading of the text. Many critical entries in *CMLC* also contain translations to aid the users.

- A complete **Bibliographic Citation** designed to facilitate the location of the original essay or book precedes each piece of criticism.

- Critical excerpts are also prefaced by **Annotations** providing the reader with information about both the critic and the criticism, the scope of the excerpt, the growth of critical controversy, or changes in critical trends regarding an author or work. In some cases, these notes include cross-references to excerpts by critics who discuss each other's commentary. Dates in parentheses within the annotation refer to a book publication date when they follow a book title, and to an essay date when they follow a critic's name.

- An annotated bibliography of **Further Reading** appears at the end of each entry and lists additional secondary sources on the author or work. In some cases it includes essays for which the editors could not obtain reprint rights. When applicable, the Further Reading is followed by references to additional entries on the author in other literary reference series published by Gale.

Topic Entries are subdivided into several thematic rubrics in which criticism appears in order of descending scope.

Cumulative Indexes

Each volume of *CMLC* includes a cumulative **author index** listing all authors who have appeared in Gale's Literary Criticism Series, along with cross references to such biographical series as *Contemporary Authors* and *Dictionary of Literary Biography*. For readers' convenience, a complete list of Gale titles included appears on the page prior to the author index. Useful for locating an author within the various series, this index is particularly valuable for those authors who are identified with a certain period but who, because of their death date, are placed in another, or for those authors whose careers span two periods. For example, Geoffrey Chaucer, who is usually considered a medieval author, is found in *Literature Criticism from 1400 to 1800* because he died after 1399.

Beginning with the tenth volume, *CMLC* includes a cumulative index listing all topic entries that have appeared in the Gale Literary Criticism Series *Classical and Medieval Literature Criticism, Contemporary Literary Criticism, Literature Criticism from 1400 to 1800, Nineteenth-Century Literature Criticism,* and *Twentieth-Century Literary Criticism.*

Beginning with the second volume, *CMLC* also includes a cumulative nationality index. Authors and/or works are grouped by nationality, and the volume in which criticism on them may be found is indicated.

Title Index

Each volume of *CMLC* also includes an index listing the titles of all literary works discussed in the series. Foreign language titles that have been translated are followed by the titles of the translations—for example, *Slovo o polku Igorove (The Song of Igor's Campaign)*. Page numbers following these translated titles refer to all pages on which any form of the title, either foreign language or translated, appears. Titles of novels, dramas, nonfiction books, and poetry, short story, or essay collections are printed in italics, while those of all individual poems, short stories, and essays are printed in roman type within quotation marks. In cases where the same title is used by different authors, the author's name or surname is given in parentheses after the title, e.g. *Collected Poems* (Horace) and *Collected Poems* (Sappho).

Critic Index

An index to critics, which cumulates with the second volume, is another useful feature of *CMLC*. Under each critic's name are listed the authors and/or works on whom the critic has written and the volume and page number where criticism may be found.

A Note to the Reader

When writing papers, students who quote directly from any volume in the Literary Criticism Series may use the following general forms to footnote reprinted criticism. The first example pertains to material drawn from a periodical, the second to material reprinted from books.

Rollo May, "The Therapist and the Journey into Hell," *Michigan Quarterly Review,* XXV, No. 4 (Fall 1986), 629-41; excerpted and reprinted in *Classical and Medieval Literature Criticism,* Vol. 3, ed. Jelena O. Krstović (Detroit: Gale Research, 1989), pp. 154-58.

Dana Ferrin Sutton, *Self and Society in Aristophanes* (University of Press of America, 1980); excerpted and reprinted in *Classical and Medieval Literature Criticism,* Vol. 4, ed. Jelena O. Krstović (Detroit: Gale Research, 1990), pp. 162-69.

Suggestions Are Welcome

Readers who wish to make suggestions for future volumes, or who have other comments regarding the series, are cordially invited to write or call the editors.

Acknowledgments

The editors wish to thank the copyright holders of the excerpted criticism included in this volume, the permissions managers of many book and magazine publishing companies for assisting us in securing reprint rights, and Anthony Bogucki for assistance with copyright research. We are also grateful to the staffs of the Detroit Public Library, the Library of Congress, the University of Detroit Mercy Library, Wayne State University Purdy/Kresge Library Complex, and the University of Michigan Libraries for making their resources available to us. Following is a list of the copyright holders who have granted us permission to reprint material in this volume of ***CMLC.*** Every effort has been made to trace copyright, but if omissions have been made, please let us know.

COPYRIGHTED EXCERPTS IN *CMLC,* VOLUME 15, WERE REPRINTED FROM THE FOLLOWING PERIODICALS:

Comparative Literature, v. V, Winter, 1953 by University of Oregon. Reprinted by permission of Comparative Literature.—***Forum for Modern Language Studies,*** v. VI, January, 1970 for "Some Observations on the Status of the Narrator in Hartmann von Aue's 'Erec' and 'Iwein'" by W. H. Jackson. Copyright © 1970 by Forum for Modern Language Studies and the author. Reprinted by permission of the publisher and the author.—***German Life & Letters,*** v. XXX, 1976-77. Reprinted by permission of German Life & Letters.—***The German Quarterly,*** v. XLII, January, 1970. Copyright © 1970 by the American Association of Teachers of German. Reprinted by permission of The German Quarterly.—***The Germanic Review,*** v. XLVIII, November, 1973 "Christian Allegory in Hartmann's 'Iwein'" by J. M. Clifton-Everest; v. L, March 1975 for "Fallen Man in Hartmann's 'Gregorius'" by Frank J. Tobin; v. LVI, Summer 1981 for "Hartmann's 'Erec': Language, Perception, and Transformation" by S.L. Clark. Copyright © 1973, 1975, 1981 by Helen Dwight Reid Educational Foundation. All reprinted by permission of The Germanic Review and the respective authors.— ***Interpretation: A Journal of Political Philosophy,*** v. XIV, May-September, 1986. Copyright © 1986 Interpretation. Reprinted by permission of Interpretation: A Journal of Political Philosophy.— ***Journal of the American Oriental Society,*** v. 86, 1966. Reprinted by permission of Journal of the American Oriental Society.—***Medievalia et Humanistica,*** n. 12, 1984. Copyright © The Medieval and Renaissance Society 1984. Reprinted by permission of Medievalia et Humanistica.—***The Modern Language Review,*** v. 70, October 1974 for "Hartmann's Ironic Praise of 'Erec'" by D.H. Green. Copyright © Modern Humanities Association 1974. Reprinted by permission of The Modern Language Review and the author.—***Monatshefte,*** v. 80, Winter 1988. Copyright © 1988 by the Board of Regents of the University of Wisconsin System. Reprinted by permission of Monatshefte and the author.—***Neuphilologische Mitteilungen: Bulletin de la Societé Neophilologique***, v. LXXXIV, 1983. Reprinted by permission of Neuphilologische Mitteilungen: Bulletin de la Societé Neophilologique.—***PMLA,*** v. 94, May 1979. Copyright © 1979 by the Modern Language Association of America. Reprinted by permission of PMLA.—***Seminar,*** v. XIV, February 1978. Copyright © The Canadian Association of University Teachers of German 1978. Reprinted by permission of the Seminar.—***Speculum,*** v. XLI, January 1966. Copyright © 1966 by The Medieval Academy of America. Reprinted by permission of Speculum.

COPYRIGHTED EXCERPTS IN *CMLC,* VOLUME 15, WERE REPRINTED FROM THE FOLLOWING BOOKS:

Batts, Michael S. From "Hartmann's 'Humanitas': A New Look at 'Iwein'," in ***Germanic Studies in Honor of Edward Henry Sehrt.*** Frithjof Anderson Raven, Wolfram Karl Legner, James Cecil King, editors, University of Miami Press, 1968. Copyright © 1968 by University of Miami Press, Coral Gables, Florida. Reprinted by permission of the publisher.—Campbell, Mary B. From ***The Witness and the Other World: Exotic European Travel Writing, 400-1600.*** Cornell, 1988. Copyright © 1988 by Cornell University. All rights reserved. Used by permission of Cornell University Press.—Chadwick, Henry. From ***Boethius: His Life, Thought and Influence.*** Blackwell, 1981. Copyright © 1981 Basil Blackwell Publishers Limited 1981. All rights reserved. Reprinted by permission of the publisher.—Chadwick, Henry. From an introduction to ***Boethius: His Life, Thought and Influence.*** Blackwell, 1981. Copyright © Basil Blackwell Publisher Limited 1981. All rights reserved. Reprinted by permission of the publisher.—Chen, Yu-Shih. From ***Images and Ideas in Chinese Classical Prose: Studies of Four Masters.*** Stanford University Press, 1988. Copyright © 1988 by the Board of Trustees of Leland Stanford Junior University. Reprinted with the permission of Stanford University Press.—Crabbe, Anna. From "Literary Design in the 'De Consolatione Phiolophiae'," in ***Boethius: His Life, Thought and Influence.*** Blackwell, 1981. Copyright © 1981 Basil Blackwell Publishers Limited 1981. All rights reserved. Reprinted by permission of the publisher.—Duckett, Eleanor Shipley. From ***The Gateway to the Middle Ages.*** The MacMillian Company, 1938. Copyright © 1938, by MacMillian Publishing Company. Renewed 1966 by Eleanor Shipley Duckett. All rights reserved. Reprinted with the permission of the publisher.—Grant, Michael. From ***The Ancient Historians.*** Charles Scribner's Sons, 1970. Copyright © 1970 Michael Grant Publications Ltd. All rights reserved. Reprinted by the permission of the author.—Hart, Henry H. From ***Marco Polo, Venetian Adventurer.*** University of Oklahoma Press, 1967. Copyright © 1967 by the University of Oklahoma Press, Publishing Division of the University. Reprinted by permission of the University of Oklahoma Press.—King, K. C. From "The Mother's Guilt in Hartmann's 'Gregorius'," in ***Mediaeval German Studies.*** Institute of Germanic Studies, 1965. Copyright © Basil Blackwell Publishers Limited 1981. All rights reserved. Reprinted by permission of the publisher.—Kirby, Helen. From "The Scholar and His Public," in ***Boethius: His Life, Thought and Influence.*** Edited by Margaret Gibson. Blackwell, 1981. Copyright © Basil Blackwell Publishers Limited 1981. All rights reserved. Reprinted by permission of the publisher.— Latham, Ronald. From an introduction to ***The Travels of Marco Polo.*** Translated by Ronald Latham. Penguin Books, 1958. Copyright © Ronald Latham, 1958, renewed 1986. Reproduced by permission of Penguin Books, Ltd.—Lerer, Seth. From ***Boethius and Dialogue: Literary Methods in 'The Consolation of Philosophy.'*** Princeton University Press, 1985. Copyright © 1985 by Princeton University Press. All rights reserved. Reprinted by permission of the publisher.—Lewis, C. S. From ***The Discarded Image: An Introduction to Medieval and Renaissance Literature.*** Cambridge at the University Press, 1964. Copyright © Cambridge University Press 1964, renewed 1992. Reprinted with the permission of the publisher.—Liebeschitz, H. From "Boethius and the Legacy of Antiquity," in ***The Cambridge History of Later Greek and Early Medieval Philosophy.*** Edited by A.H. Armstrong. Cambridge University Press, 1967. Copyright © 1967 Cambridge University Press. Reprinted with the permission of the publisher.—Makin, Peter. From ***Provence and Pound.*** University of California Press, 1978. Copyright © 1978 by the Regents of the University of California. Reprinted by permission of the publisher.—Mallery, Richard D. From an introduction to ***Masterworks of Travel and Exploration: Digests of 13 Great Classics.*** Edited by Richard D. Mallery. Doubleday, 1948. Copyright © 1948 by Doubleday, a division of Bantam Doubleday Dell Publishing Group, Inc. Renewed 1975 by Copeland & Lamm, Inc. All rights reserved. Used with permission of Donald S. Lamm.— Olschki, Leonardo. From ***Marco Polo's Precursors.*** Johns Hopkins Press, 1943. Copyright © 1943, The Johns Hopkins Press. Renewed 1970 by Leonardo Olschki. Reprinted by permission of the Johns Hopkins University Press.—Patch, Howard Rollin. From ***The Tradition of Boethius: A Study of His Importance in Medieval Culture.*** Oxford University Press, 1935. Copyright © 1935 by Oxford University Press, New York, Inc. Renewed 1993 by Howard Rollin Patch. All rights reserved. Reprinted with permission of the publisher and author.—Rand, Edward Kennard. From ***Founders of the Middle Ages.*** Cambridge, Mass.: Harvard University Press, 1928. Copyright © 1928 by the President and Fellows of Harvard College. Renewed 1956 by Belle Pallmer Rand. All rights reserved. Excerpted by permission of the publishers and the author.—Reiss, Edmund. From ***Boethius.*** Twayne, 1982. Copyright © 1982 by G. K. Hall & Company. All rights reserved. Reprinted with the permission of Twayne Publishers, an imprint of MacMillian Publishing Company.—Watson, Burton. From an introduction to ***Su Tung-P'o: Selections from a Sung Dynasty Poet.*** Translated by Burton Watson., Columbia University Press, 1965. Copyright © 1965, renewed 1993 Columbia University Press, New York. All rights reserved. Reprinted with permission of the publisher.—Wilhelm, James J. From an introduction to ***The Poetry of Sordello.*** Edited and translated by James J. Wilhelm. Garland Publishing, Inc., 1987. Copyright © 1987 by James J. Wilhelm. All rights reserved. Reprinted by permission of the publisher.—Yoshikawa, Kojiro. From ***An Introduction to Sung Poetry.*** Translated by Burton Watson. Cambridge, Mass.: Harvard University Press, 1967. Copyright © 1967 by the Harvard-Yenching Institute. All rights reserved. Excerpted by permission of the publisher and the author.

PERMISSION TO REPRODUCE ILLUSTRATIONS APPEARING IN *CMLC,* VOLUME 15, WAS RECEIVED FROM THE FOLLOWING SOURCES:

Illustrations by Robert Browning from ***Justinian And Theodora,*** by Bayerisch Staatsbibliothek, Munich. Copyright © 1971 by Robert Browning, London, England. Reprinted with the permission of Bayerisch Staatsbibliothek, Munich. Illustration by Audrey Kursinski from ***Marco Polo's Asia: An Introduction to His "Description of the World" Called "il Milione",*** by Leonardo Olschki. Copyright © 1960 by the Regents of the University of California. Reprinted with the permission of Audrey Kursinski.

PERMISSION TO REPRODUCE PHOTOGRAPHS APPEARING IN *CMLC,* VOLUME 15, WAS RECEIVED FROM THE FOLLOWING SOURCES:

Photograph from ***The Poetry of Sordello,*** edited and translated by James J. Wilhelm, for Garland Library of Medieval Literature, Volume 42, Series A. Reprinted by permission of Garland Publishing, Inc., and ROGER-VIOLLET, Paris, France.

Boethius

c. 480-c. 524/526

(Full name Anicius Manlius Severinus Boethius) Roman philosopher.

INTRODUCTION

Characterized by Edward Gibbon as "the last of the Romans whom Cato or Tully could have acknowledged for their countryman," Boethius links the world of late antiquity with that of the Middle Ages. Although he is best known for the philosophical dialogue *Consolatio Philosophiae* (*Consolation of Philosophy*, c.524), Boethius is equally significant in the history of Western civilization for his transmission of Greek and Roman thought to later centuries. Scholars have argued that, without Boethius, the Medieval West would have known little of such subjects as Aristotelian logic and ancient musical theory. An important commentator on Greek philosophy in his own right, Boethius succeeded in forging for the first time a philosophical vocabulary in the Latin language, thereby providing the foundation for the achievement of later Medieval philosophy. For over one thousand years, Boethius's writings were viewed as part of the common cultural inheritance of western Europe and as a storehouse of all kinds of information about the nature of the world. Significant elements of the Boethian worldview are to be found in the works of such writers as Thomas Aquinas, Dante Alighieri, Geoffrey Chaucer, Thomas More, and William Shakespeare. R. W. Southern has written that "if Aristotle, in Dante's famous phrase, was the 'master of those who know,' Boethius was the master of those who wanted to know. He was the schoolmaster of medieval Europe."

Biographical Information

Boethius was born into one of the oldest and most notable aristocratic families in the western part of the late Roman Empire. After the last Roman emperor in the West, Romulus, was deposed in 476, Boethius's father, Aurelius Manlius Boethius, served the Ostrogothic ruler of Italy, Odovacar, in several high administrative positions. Around 488 Boethius's father died, and the young boy became the ward of the illustrious and highly cultivated Roman senator Quintus Aurelius Memmius Symmachus. Symmachus, who was to become one of Boethius's most important influences, is believed to have had a guiding role in the education of his charge. Although it is unclear exactly where Boethius received his instruction, by the time he reached manhood he was proficient in Greek and well-versed in philosophy and scientific thought. As a young man, Boethius entered into a successful political career, becoming a consul and senator in the year 510. In 522, the Ostrogothic king of

Italy, Theodoric, elevated him to the position of *magister officiorum*. Throughout his administrative career, Boethius devoted himself to intellectual pursuits, writing works on arithmetic, music, logic, and theology between the years 505 to 523. In 523, however, for reasons which still remain obscure, Boethius was implicated in a conspiracy against Theodoric and was imprisoned in Pavia. During his imprisonment he wrote the *Consolation of Philosophy*, a work concerned with the problems of evil, fate, and free will. At some point between the years 524 and 526 Boethius was executed.

Major Works

Scholars have divided Boethius's writings into four groups that include educational writings, logical writings, theological writings, and the *Consolation of Philosophy*. Written early in his career, the *De institutione arithmetica* (c.503) and the *De institutione musica* present translations of now-lost Greek texts on mathematics and music. While these are not original writings, they were of enormous importance in the foundation of the Medieval educational system. Similarly, many of Boethius's logical writings are translations of the works of such philosophers as Aristotle and Porphyry. Boethius wrote original commentaries on Aristotle's *Topics, Categories,* and *Interpretation*, as well as an important treatise, *De hypotheticis syllogismis*, which departs from Aristotle in its handling of linguistic concepts. Later in his career Boethius devoted his attention to bringing the rigor of ancient philosophy to bear on theological disputes within the Christian church. In five theological tractates, known collectively as the *opuscula sacra* (c.512-22), he analyzes such issues as the nature of the Trinity, the true, orthodox faith, and the contemporary Eutychian and Nestorian heresies. While these works have been praised for their original use of philosophical argument to defend orthodox Christianity, Boethius's masterpiece, the *Consolation of Philosophy*, has been commonly viewed as an ambiguous text, owing to the absence of any direct reference to Christianity in the work. Composed in the literary form known as Menippean satire, the *Consolation* contains alternating sections of poetry and prose and presents a dialogue between a grief-stricken narrator and the female personification of Philosophy. The narrative charts the progress from spriritual blindness to gradual enlightenment, as Philosophy clarifies the nature of evil in the world, the role of fortune in human affairs, the providence of God, and the existence of free will. The *Consolation* closes with an affirmation that everything which happens is in accordance with the will of God and that man is free to use his reason to conform to the divine will.

Critical Reception

Attention to the corpus of Boethius's writings has naturally focused on the *Consolation of Philosophy*. Edmund Reiss has maintained that it has "exerted a greater influence on Western thought and literature than any other book except the Bible." It was one of the first texts to be translated into European vernacular languages; in England alone, it appeared in versions by King Alfred, Chaucer, and Queen Elizabeth I. Additionally, there are powerful resonances of the *Consolation* in such works as Dante's *Divine Comedy*, Jean de Meun's *Romance of the Rose*, Chaucer's *Troilus and Criseyde*, and William Langland's *Piers Plowman*. In assessing his stylistic attainments, critics have occasionally faulted Boethius for failing to live up to the Classical Latin of Vergil and Cicero. Modern scholars, however, have tended to praise many of the poems in the *Consolation* and have asserted that in comparison with the ornate rhetorical excesses of his contemporaries, Boethius's lucid prose style is an impressive reflection of Classical literary values. Modern critics have also devoted increasing study to Boethius's theological tractates. While these works were a significant component of the intellectual heritage of such Medieval thinkers as John Scotus Erigena, Alcuin, and Aquinas, it is only in the twentieth century that they have begun to receive serious attention once again. Summing up the achievement of Boethius, Henry Chadwick has written that he "taught the Latin West to judge the validity of an inference, to be aware of the foundations of mathematics, and to envisage reason and revelation as related by very distinct ways of apprehending the mystery of God."

PRINCIPAL ENGLISH TRANSLATIONS

The Consolation of Philosophy (edited and translated by "I. T.") 1609

The Theological Tractates (edited and translated by H. F. Stewart and E. K. Rand) 1918

The Consolation of Philosophy (translated by Richard Green) 1962

The Consolation of Philosophy (translated by V. E. Watts) 1969

Boethius's De topicis differentiis (translated by Eleonore Stump) 1978

CRITICISM

Edward Gibbon (essay date 1776-88)

SOURCE: "Chapter XXXIX," in *The Decline and Fall of the Roman Empire, Vol. II,* edited by J. B. Bury, The Heritage Press, 1946, pp. 1226-249.

[*Gibbon's monumental* The Decline and Fall of the Roman Empire, *written between 1776 and 1788, is recognized as the finest work of history in the English language and a seminal text in eighteenth-century thought. In the following excerpt from that work, Gibbon appraises Boethius as "the last of the Romans whom Cato or Tully could have acknowledged for their countryman."*]

The senator Boethius is the last of the Romans whom Cato or Tully could have acknowledged for their countryman. As a wealthy orphan, he inherited the patrimony and honours of the Anician family, a name ambitiously assumed by the kings and emperors of the age; and the appellation of Manlius asserted his genuine or fabulous descent from a race of consuls and dictators, who had repulsed the Gauls from the Capitol and sacrificed their sons to the discipline of the republic. In the youth of Boethius, the studies of Rome were not totally abandoned; a Virgil is now extant, corrected by the hand of a consul; and the professors of grammar, rhetoric, and jurisprudence were maintained in their privileges and pensions by the liberality of the Goths. But the erudition of the Latin language was insufficient to satiate his ardent curiosity; and Boethius is said to have employed eighteen laborious years in the schools of Athens, which were supported by the zeal, the learning, and the diligence of Proclus and his disciples. The reason and piety of their Roman pupil were fortunately saved from the contagion of mystery and magic, which polluted the groves of the academy; but he imbibed the spirit, and imitated the method, of his dead and living masters, who attempted to reconcile the strong and subtle sense of Aristotle with the devout contemplation and sublime fancy of Plato. After his return to Rome and his marriage with the daughter of his friend, the patrician Symmachus, Boethius still continued, in a palace of ivory and marble, to prosecute the same studies. The church was edified by his profound defence of the orthodox creed against the Arian, the Eutychian, and the Nestorian heresies; and the Catholic unity was explained or exposed in a formal treatise by the *indifference* of three distinct though consubstantial persons. For the benefit of his Latin readers, his genius submitted to teach the first elements of the arts and sciences of Greece. The geometry of Euclid, the music of Pythagoras, the arithmetic of Nicomachus, the mechanics of Archimedes, the astronomy of Ptolemy, the theology of Plato, and the logic of Aristotle, with the commentary of Porphyry, were translated and illustrated by the indefatigable pen of the Roman senator. And he alone was esteemed capable of describing the wonders of art, a sun-dial, a water-clock, or a sphere which represented the motions of the planets. From these abstruse speculations, Boethius stooped, or, to speak more truly, he rose to the social duties of public and private life: the indigent were relieved by his liberality; and his eloquence, which flattery might compare to the voice of Demosthenes or Cicero, was uniformly exerted in the cause of innocence and humanity. Such conspicuous merit was felt and rewarded by a discerning prince; the dignity of Boethius was adorned with the titles of consul and patrician, and his talents were usefully employed in the important station of master of the offices. Notwithstanding the equal claims of the East and West, his two sons were created, in their tender youth, the consuls of the same year. On the memorable day of their inauguration, they proceeded in solemn pomp from their palace to the forum, amidst the applause of the senate and people; and their joyful father, the true consul of Rome, after pronouncing an oration in the praise of his royal benefactor, distributed a triumphal largess in the games of the circus. Prosperous in his fame and fortunes, in his public honours and private alliances, in the cultivation of science and the consciousness of virtue, Boethius might have been styled happy, if that precarious epithet could be safely applied before the last term of the life of man.

A philosopher, liberal of his wealth and parsimonious of his time, might be insensible to the common allurements of ambition, the thirst of gold and employment. And some credit may be due to the asseveration of Boethius, that he had reluctantly obeyed the divine Plato, who enjoins every virtuous citizen to rescue the state from the usurpation of vice and ignorance. For the integrity of his public conduct he appeals to the memory of his country. His authority had restrained the pride and oppression of the royal officers, and his eloquence had delivered Paulianus from the dogs of the palace. He had always pitied, and often relieved, the distress of the provincials, whose fortunes were exhausted by public and private rapine; and Boethius alone had courage to oppose the tyranny of the Barbarians, elated by conquest, excited by avarice, and, as he complains, encouraged by impunity. In these honourable contests, his spirit soared above the consideration of danger, and perhaps of prudence; and we may learn from the example of Cato that a character of pure and inflexible virtue is the most apt to be misled by prejudice, to be heated by enthusiasm, and to confound private enmities with public justice. The disciple of Plato might exaggerate the infirmities of nature and the imperfections of society; and the mildest form of a Gothic kingdom, even the weight of allegiance and gratitude, must be insupportable to the free spirit of a Roman patriot. But the favour and fidelity of Boethius declined in just proportion with the public happiness; and an unworthy colleague was imposed, to divide and control the power of the master of the offices. In the last gloomy season of Theodoric, he indignantly felt that he was a slave; but, as his master had only power over his life, he stood without arms and without fear against the face of an angry Barbarian, who had been provoked to believe that the safety of the senate was incompatible with his own. The senator Albinus was accused and already convicted on the presumption of *hoping,* as it was said, the liberty of Rome. "If Albinus be criminal," exclaimed the orator, "the senate and myself are all guilty of the same crime. If we are innocent, Albinus is equally entitled to the protection of the laws." These laws might not have punished the simple and barren wish of an unattainable blessing; but they would have shown less indulgence to the rash confession of Boethius that, had he known of a conspiracy, the tyrant never should. The advocate of Albinus was soon involved in the danger and perhaps the guilt of his client; their signature (which they denied as a forgery) was affixed to the original address, inviting the emperor to deliver Italy from the Goths; and three witnesses of honourable rank, perhaps of infamous reputation, attested the treasonable designs of the Roman patrician. Yet his innocence must be presumed, since he was deprived by Theodoric of the means of justification, and rigorously confined in the tower of Pavia, while the senate, at the distance of five hundred miles, pronounced a sentence of confiscation and death against the most illustrious of its members. At the command of the Barbarians, the occult science of a philosopher was stigmatized with the names of sacrilege and magic. A devout and dutiful attachment to the senate was condemned as criminal by the trembling voices of the senators themselves; and their ingratitude deserved the wish or prediction of Boethius, that, after him, none should be found guilty of the same offence.

While Boethius, oppressed with fetters, expected each moment the sentence or the stroke of death, he composed in the tower of Pavia the ***Consolation of Philosophy***; a golden volume not unworthy of the leisure of Plato or Tully, but which claims incomparable merit from the barbarism of the times and the situation of the author. The celestial guide, whom he had so long invoked at Rome and Athens, now condescended to illumine his dungeon, to revive his courage, and to pour into his wounds her salutary balm. She taught him to compare his long prosperity and his recent distress, and to conceive new hopes from the inconstancy of fortune. Reason had informed him of the precarious condition of her gifts; experience had satisfied him of their real value; he had enjoyed them without guilt; he might resign them without a sigh, and calmly disdain the impotent malice of his enemies, who had left him happiness, since they had left him virtue. From the earth, Boethius ascended to heaven in search of the SUPREME GOOD; explored the metaphysical labyrinth of chance and destiny, of prescience and free-will, of time and eternity; and generously attempted to reconcile the perfect attributes of the Deity with the apparent disorders of his moral and physical government. Such topics of consolation, so obvious, so vague, or so abstruse, are ineffectual to subdue the feelings of human nature. Yet the sense of misfortune may be diverted by the labour of thought; and the sage who could artfully combine in the same work the various riches of philosophy, poetry, and eloquence, must already have possessed the intrepid calmness which he affected to seek. Suspense, the worst of evils, was at length determined by the ministers of death, who executed, and perhaps exceeded, the inhuman mandate of Theodoric. A strong cord was fastened round the head of Boethius and forcibly tightened, till his eyes almost started from their sockets; and some mercy may be discovered in the milder torture of beating him with clubs till he expired. But his genius survived to diffuse a ray of knowledge over the darkest ages of the Latin world; the writings of the philosopher were translated by the most glorious of the English kings; and the third emperor of the name of Otho removed to a more honourable tomb the bones of a Catholic saint, who, from his Arian persecutors, had acquired the honours of martyrdom and the fame of miracles. In the last hours of Boethius, he derived some comfort from the safety of his two sons, of his wife, and of his father-in-law, the venerable Symmachus. But the grief of Symmachus was indiscreet, and perhaps disrespectful: he had presumed to lament, he might dare to revenge, the death of an injured friend. He was dragged in chains from Rome to the palace of Ravenna; and the suspicions of Theodoric could only be appeased by the blood of an innocent and aged senator. . . .

Edward Kennard Rand (lecture date 1928)

SOURCE: "Boethius, the First of the Scholastics," in *Founders of the Middle Ages,* 1928. Reprint by Dover Publications, 1957, pp. 135-80.

[*Rand was an eminent American classical scholar who, in addition to writing works on such authors as Vergil, Horace, and Ovid, provided one of the most influential twentieth-century accounts of Boethius, which appears below. Originally delivered as a lecture and reprinted later with minor alterations, Rand's overview of Boethius's life and career is placed within the political context of sixth-century A.D. Italy.*]

A century of barbarism had swept like a wave over Roman civilization, or dashed against its coasts, when there suddenly appeared the most thoroughgoing philosopher, and, with the exception of St. Augustine, the most original philosopher, that Rome had ever produced. Boethius must not be considered an altogether isolated phenomenon. He lived under an Ostrogothic king, whose capital was at Ravenna, or Verona, or Pavia; and yet Theodoric, like Odovaker before him, had brought law and order into Italy; he was far more true to the Roman ideal than various of his Roman predecessors had been. After his initial deed of treachery, the base murder of his rival, for which he had abundant sanction in the acts of various emperors before him,—in fact this sort of homicidal house-cleaning had become a species of Imperial good form,—Theodoric ruled wisely and well. He was a worthy precursor of Charlemagne, who admired him. Boethius, then, was not fighting single-handed. His philosophical endeavors were in keeping with the spirit of the age, that general movement toward peace and consolidation which set in after the confusions of the fifth century, and prevailed as long as Theodoric reigned. Theodoric was an Arian, but he had the support of the Catholic clergy in his contest with Odovaker; and, though we shall note that divergence on this theological issue had unpleasant political consequences, the beginning of Theodoric's reign saw all factions of the church and the state well united.

Once on a time, Boethius's ***Consolation of Philosophy*** was one of the hundred best books—one of those books that no educated man left unread. That was still the case in the eighteenth century, and had been so since the Middle Ages, in which period his influence was sovereign. As Morris puts it in the preface of his edition of Chaucer's translation of Boethius [Richard Morris (1868)], "No philosopher was so bone of the bone and flesh of the flesh of Middle-Age writers as Boethius. Take up what writer you will, and you find not only the sentiments, but the very words of the distinguished old Roman." This is true in general, and it is true in great and special cases, as is testified by the names of his royal translator King Alfred, Jean de Meung, Chaucer, and Dante. Boethius was a name with which everybody had to reckon. He is one of the Founders.

The mind of Boethius presents a problem. Was he Christian or Pagan? It is rather late, in the days of Boethius, for a Pagan to have a prominent political career. How many times must the historian record the "final triumph" of Christianity? In Boethius's last utterance, his ***Consolation of Philosophy***, the name of Christ is not mentioned, and the Holy Bible is not cited. At the same time, Boethius is apparently the author of certain theological tractates. Are these little works spurious? Or, as a Renaissance editor suggested [Glareanus], is the ***Consolation of Philosophy*** spurious? And if both are genuine, how interpret the latter work? Did Boethius in his dungeon throw over the petty complexities of theology and lapse back to Plato and Aristotle, the masters of ancient thought?

Answers have been numerous and diverse. First of all, we should take account of the political situation, and in particular, of the code of laws promulgated by Theodoric. This code is exceedingly severe. For instance, capital punishment was decreed for perjury and for the bribing of false witnesses in case the guilty party was of noble birth; if he was of low birth, the penalty was the confiscation of all his property. Here is the law against public informers, who had been a curse of the state ever since the days of Tiberius. "He who assumes the function of an informer as an ostensibly necessary act of public utility, . . . even so, in our opinion, ought to be thoroughly discountenanced and . . . in case his accusations cannot be corroborated he shall suffer death by burning." This ferocious law gave cold consolation to Boethius, as we shall see. As for Pagans, "If anyone be detected in offering sacrifice according to the Pagan rite, or if anyone be found practising the arts of a soothsayer or diviner, he shall suffer capital punishment. Anyone who is an accomplice in magic arts shall suffer confiscation of all his property, and if of high birth, be sentenced to perpetual exile, or if of low birth, suffer capital punishment." Not much inducement to be a Pagan in the days of Theodoric.

I have cited only one or two specimens, but they indicate the character of this remarkable piece of legislation. The only code more stringent that has come to my notice is one proclaimed by an undergraduate publication of Yale University not many years ago, which provided *inter alia* that cutting chapel should be punishable with death. I imagine that Theodoric before he got through was reminded of the wise Horace's maxim, "What profit vain laws without morals?" To put through a Constitutional amendment you must have the sentiment of the country behind you. Yet Theodoric meant to have his code enforced. At the end of it there is a vigorous statement that the laws apply to high and low, Romans and barbarians alike; the nobility is warned that there will be no respecting of persons. It is also stated that judges who cannot enforce the law shall at once report to the Emperor; "for provisions in the interest of each section of the empire," it is declared, "should be maintained by the central power."

Obviously Boethius, as man and office-holder, could not have been a professing Pagan in the days of Theodoric. But while outwardly conforming to the new faith, he might have mentally accepted something quite different, particularly after the orders of his royal master had landed him in jail. The standard historian of Greek philosophy, Zeller, can call "the noble Boethius the last representative of the ancient philosophy; for though he may have associated himself externally with the Christian Church, his real religion is philosophy." Even a Roman Catholic theologian, who presumably accepts Boethius's Christianity, assigns him a lowly place in the history of thought, as one of those who labored "merely to preserve what the past had bequeathed and to transmit the legacy to times more favorable for the development of Christian speculation." This is true so far as it goes: but it does not go very far.

The first thing that we note about Anicius Manlius Severinus Boethius is his noble lineage. The *Anicii* were an extremely important family in the fourth century and still earlier. The first Roman senator to be converted to the new faith was an *Anicius;* he is celebrated in Prudentius's poem against Symmachus. The *Manlii* take us back to the very earliest days of Rome, while the *Severini* are a branch of the *Severi,* who rose to imperial heights. From first to last, Boethius is an aristocrat, with a sense of *noblesse oblige*. He was born about 480 A.D., and must have attained distinction early in both scholarship and politics. Left an orphan at an early age, he became a protégé of certain eminent men, particularly of Symmachus, and he married the latter's daughter. The mention of *that* name takes us back to the fourth century and the leader of the Pagans. Boethius's father-in-law was a lineal descendant of Quintus Aurelius Symmachus the opponent of Ambrose, and bore his very names. The family had renounced Paganism; in fact Symmachus and certain friends of his, members of the most exclusive circle of the nobility, were now pillars of orthodoxy and foes not only of Paganism but of the Arian heresy; the importance of this fact will become clearer as we proceed. It is a natural state of affairs; in one age as in the other, the nobles upheld the tradition, whatever that happened to be.

We think of Boethius as primarily a philosopher, snatching the moments of contemplation from a busy life devoted to the state; but his youth may have been as sentimental and poetic as that of any youth. We know that pastoral verse was among his early efforts, and he also probably wrote elegies; not elegies in a country churchyard—elegies outside his lady's window. One feels a repressed emotion in Boethius. He has absorbed poetry, as Plato had done, only in a more sombre fashion; his prevailing mood is nearer to Dante's than to Plato's. He has not Plato's divine gift of comedy.

Boethius's political relations with Theodoric start at least as early as 506—possibly 504, the date of Theodoric's entry into Rome. The monarch found his advice useful on the most varied subjects. As mechanical expert, Boethius gave directions for the construction of a water-clock for Theodoric's brother-in-law Gundobad, king of the Burgundian . As musical expert, he selected a harper for the court of Clovis the Frank. As financial expert, he helped to convict the paymaster of the Guards of an attempt to cheat the men with light coin; some writers have inferred, with no real evidence at their disposal, that Boethius was in charge of the public mint. He had an eye out for financial affairs, at any rate, for on one occasion he prevented a cornering of the wheat market. In 510, he was elevated to the consulship. The year 522 was, in external pomp, the most distinguished of his life, for his two sons were the consuls, attaining that office, like him, at an extremely early age; it was natural that the panegyric on their inauguration should be pronounced by their illustrious father. In the following year, if not before, Boethius was created *magister officiorum,* a high position involving constant attendance upon the king. In the next to the last year of his life, Boethius received a quite unexpected honor, conviction for high treason. He was exiled to confinement in a dungeon at Pavia, and the next year, whether 524 or 525 is uncertain, he was put to death. The execution of his father-in-law, Symmachus, took place one year later. The exact place of the philosopher's confinement was the *ager Calventianus* (Calvenzano) between Milan and Pavia. Tradition has it that the Lombard King Luitprand transferred his bones, and those of St. Augustine, to the cathedral at Pavia. They can be seen there at the present time. I saw them on one eventful day at five o'clock in the afternoon, having visited the birth-place of Virgil at five o'clock in the morning.

Boethius's great plan was to translate both Plato and Aristotle for the benefit of the philosophically minded of his times, when the readers of the original Greek were getting fewer and fewer. Probably he had the same dismal feelings about the future that some Classical scholars have to-day. His fears were justified, for a period of about eight centuries came on, in which virtually nobody in the western world read the works of Greek literature in the original. But let us take heart. Perhaps eight centuries from now there will be another Renaissance of Greek.

Boethius's undertaking was a large one. Jowett had quite enough of an order with Plato alone. Boethius meant to translate all Plato and all Aristotle. Furthermore, his work was not to be a mere translation. In his day, and in all ages since, Plato and Aristotle have stood for opposite types of idealism, Plato for the transcendence of the ideal and Aristotle for its immanence. This is a rough and general statement, one which many would wish to refine, but if not quite true for Plato and Aristotle, it describes well enough what the Middle Ages regarded as Platonism and Aristotelianism. Now Boethius was one of those who were dissatisfied with the tendency to divide Platonists and Aristotelians. His ultimate purpose was to show that there is no essential difference between the two schools. His idea was not, as is sometimes set forth to-day, that Aristotle was a second-rate thinker who developed into ponderous systems what Plato preferred to leave as hints, patiently dogging his thoughts, a sort of metaphysical Boswell. Boethius would rather have accepted the memorable title that Dante conferred on Aristotle, "the master of those that know."

Boethius began his great plan with a comment on a work of Porphyry's, entitled *Introduction to the Categories of Aristotle*. This is a natural starting-point, a consideration of the nature of reasoning, of the problem of cognition or "epistemology," and of the method of reasoning. The text used by Boethius was a translation made by Marius Victorinus, which eventually proved so unsatisfactory that he threw it away, prepared a new one of his own, and wrote a fresh commentary. He was working out his plan on a large and leisurely scale. There is a striking difference between the two commentaries. The former is put in the form of a Ciceronian dialogue. Boethius and a friend called Fabius meet at a villa out of town on the Aurelian road, and hold their very abstract conversation, on a winter's night. Never had a dialogue been given such a setting; it suggests that the passion of these friends for the eternal verities was such that they forgot that it was night and winter. But the second commentary drops this conventional device, which Boethius had found difficult to maintain, and gives straight science without palliatives. His scheme of translation is something new, and exceedingly scientific. He fears, he tells us, that Horace would not relish his method, which is to render the most trivial phrases and particles *ad verbum;* thus there is something even for μὲν—δὲ (*quidem—vero,* or *quidem—autem*), while the Greek ὅτι is responsible for *dico—quoniam* in indirect discourse.

This carefulness on the part of Boethius led to the creation of a new vocabulary for philosophy, worked out step by step in the Middle Ages and appearing in something like a final form in St. Thomas Aquinas. It is a novel and elaborate diction, admirably suited for the need. Its history has never been adequately discussed, nor has Boethius's contribution to it received the attention that it deserves. The humanists of the Renaissance understood it, in their way. "Boethius was the first," remarks Georgius Valla, "to teach us to speak barbarian." Strange to say, I think Cicero would have approved the whole business. For Cicero was also concerned in creating new philosophical terms for new ideas, and he too declared that his method was to render those terms *ad verbum* in language that must have shocked the purists of his day and almost shocked St. Jerome. At least Jerome cites Cicero's authority for his own inventions in his rendering of the Hebrew Scriptures, and declares that the latter were far less numerous than the "monstrosities" that the master of eloquence had devised in writings of far less compass. Time has condoned these novelties. Who to-day would think of the words *quality* and *specific* as barbarisms? But nobody was audacious enough to say *qualitas* before Cicero or *specificus* before Boethius.

By helping to create a new philosophical idiom, Boethius performed a valuable service to the development of thought in the Middle Ages. There is also a passage in his commentary on Porphyry that has often been cited as the starting-point for the most important discussion that agitated the earlier period of scholastic philosophy in the Middle Ages. Boethius, after Porphyry, is speaking of the nature of universals and asks whether *genera* and *species* have a real existence? Do they subsist? And if subsisting, are they corporeal or incorporeal? If they are incorporeal, are they separate from sensible objects? He asks these questions in such a way that we can at least see that he is not a materialist. He implies his belief in the actual existence of abstract ideas. But on the issue that would enable us to class him as either Platonist or Aristotelian, he suddenly becomes silent. "'T is a lofty topic," he declares, "and one that requires further investigation." Of course, that was precisely the question with which philosophers in the early period of scholasticism started their disputations; the schools of realism and nominalism derive from the different answers given to it. Boethius's attitude of reserve—ἐποχή, or metaphysical neutrality—seemed rather cold-blooded to the fighting logicians of the twelfth century, and one of them, Godfrey of St. Victor, wrote a little poem about it.

> Assidet Boetius stupens de hac lite,
> Audiens quid hic et hic asserat perite,
> Et quid cui faveat non discernit rite,
> Nec praesumit solvere litem definite.
>
> (Sits Boethius quite stunned by this disputation,
> Listening to this and that subtle explanation,
> But to side with this or that shows no
> inclination,
> Nor presumes to give the case sure adjudication.)

As a matter of fact, Boethius's commentary on Porphyry was not the place to go into the matter, for the writer's immediate concern was logic and not metaphysics. Nor is it doubtful, I believe, when one looks at all the works of

Boethius, that he did definitely take sides on this issue.

After the two expositions of Porphyry, Boethius changed, or enlarged, or perhaps really first formed, his great plan. We must not imagine that he had settled all the details before he started on his first work, any more than that Plato's philosophy sprang from his mind full-armed, like Athene from the head of Zeus. Boethius now turned aside, or apparently turned aside, to write a book on Arithmetic. It is, I say, only an apparent deviation. He had come to the conclusion, it would seem, that to present Greek philosophy to his countrymen effectively, he had better lay the foundations by treatises on the liberal arts. For the work on arithmetic did not stand alone; it was followed by one on geometry, of which only portions remain, one on music, which we have almost complete, and probably one on astronomy. There was also a mechanical treatise after Archimedes, and something or other besides from Plato and Aristotle.

Just how much else he accomplished, we do not know. His purpose, once more, was to lead up to philosophical studies, and he had a great predecessor in this very undertaking—St. Augustine, who likewise, as we shall see, wrote treatises on the liberal arts. Those of Boethius became firmly embedded in the curriculum. The ***De Musica*** was a text-book at Oxford way down into the eighteenth century. Modern critics are dubious as to its usefulness for the study of music to-day. One of them remarks [R. H. Bosanquet] that "the very eminence of Boethius makes it a matter of regret that he ever wrote upon music," and an Oxford professor [Sir F. A. Gore Ouseley] declares that Boethius is "no more useful to a modern musician than Newton's 'Principia' to a dancer." We can only the more admire that stalwart Oxonian conservatism which prescribed "Boethius on Music" for so many centuries.

Those of my readers who are musicians may be interested to know what, according to Boethius, a real musician is. There are three classes of people, he explains at the end of his first book, who have to do with music—performers, composers, and critics. Those of the first class, like harp-players, flute-players, and organists, must be excluded from the number of real musicians, since they are merely slaves. Their function is concerned with mere action, production, and is as subordinate and slavish as is the material body compared to the mind. Even a good performer is nothing more than a good slave. Then there is the second class, the composers, who are impelled to music not by reason or philosophy, but by a certain instinct, or inspiration. The Muses are responsible for what they do, not they themselves. They too, therefore, must be counted out. There remains the third class, the critics. "They alone," he declares, "are the real musicians, since their function consists entirely in reason and philosophy, in a knowledge of modes and rhythms, of the varieties of melodies and their combinations, in short, of all the matters that I shall treat in Volume II, as well as of the achievements of the composers." I once asked a friend of mine, a musical critic of some note, what he thought of this doctrine. He replied that he thought that Boethius was considerably in advance of his time and of our own. I did not venture to submit Boethius's ideas to a performer or a composer.

Boethius did more with the Aristotelian part of his programme than with anything else; he finished his translations of the *Organon,* the works on Logic. When about halfway through this undertaking, he also busied himself with Cicero, perhaps because Cicero, no less than Aristotle, had written on the subject of *Topica;* Boethius, at any rate, wrote a work ***De Differentiis Topicarum***, in which he compared his two authorities. This is the same leisurely method that we noted before. It is a method not incompatible with the development of side-interests.

The final act of comparing and reconciling Plato and Aristotle, he never lived to accomplish. This is sometimes called a Neoplatonic undertaking, because certain Neoplatonists had felt that the breach between Plato and Aristotle could be healed. As I am concerned to prove that Boethius was not a Neoplatonist, I would point out that the idea is as old as Cicero. Cicero, no less than Plato and Aristotle, had a remarkable influence on Boethius, and doubtless helped him to his conclusion in this important affair. For with both Cicero and Boethius, it is Aristotle that is harmonized with Plato and not *vice versa.*

It was in the last dozen years of his life that Boethius wrote on a vastly different topic, or what one might imagine a vastly different topic, namely, theology. There are preserved under his name four brief but pithy letters, addressed, one to Symmachus and the rest to a mutual friend, John the Deacon, dealing with theological subjects of great contemporary importance. That to Symmachus is entitled "How that the Trinity is one God and not three Gods" (*Quomodo Trinitas unus Deus ae non tres dii*), and presents a specially vigorous criticism of the Arian heresy. No. II, addressed to John, continues this topic; it is entitled, "Whether Father, Son, and Holy Spirit may be substantially predicated of Divinity" (*Utrum Pater et Filius et Spiritus Sanctus de divinitate substantialiter praedicentur*). The last in the series, "A Treatise against Eutyches and Nestorius" (*Liber contra Eutychen et Nestorium*), takes up one of the great controversies of the age, the doctrine of the Person of Christ. Boethius upholds the orthodox view against the divergent heresies of Eutyches, who discarded the human element in our Lord's nature, and of Nestorius, who discarded the divine element. The little work, which was written most probably in 512, is one of the best contributions to the subject ever made. The definitions of *nature* and of *person* given by the author became classical and were constantly appealed to by the Schoolmen; "Nature," according to Boethius, is the specific difference that gives form to anything; "Person" is the individual substance of a rational nature. One eminent Oxford authority [C. C. J. Webb, *God and Personality,* 1919,] regards the latter definition as "still, perhaps, take it all in all, the best that we have." Among the mediaeval thinkers, I would call particular attention to John the Scot, who wrote a commentary on the theological *Opuscula* of Boethius, and had the latter's categories in mind in a way not yet explained when he composed his masterpiece on the *Division of Nature.*

In short, the character of this treatise is fully as philosophical as theological. The author's report of the council that received the letters of the Eastern Bishops on the two heresies does not read like the work of an ecclesiastic. The ecclesiastics present talked most glibly, he declares, but nobody knew what the talk was about. Boethius himself preserved a haughty silence. He looked about him like Ferinata in Dante's *Inferno,* "as if he had Hell in great despite." He feared, he says, quoting Horace, "lest I should be rightly set down as insane if I held out for being sane among those madmen." Methinks I hear the lashing of a humanistic tongue.

The philosopher is also evident in the title of the third letter—*Quomodo substantiae in eo quod sint bonae sint cum non sint substantialia bona* ("How Substantives can be good in virtue of their existence without being Absolute Goods"). If this piece had been separately transmitted as the work of the author of the ***Consolation of Philosophy***, and the other theological tractates had been all lost, nobody would have thought of questioning the authorship. As it is, it is part and parcel of this little collection, the genuineness of which has the best possible attestation in the manuscripts. To anybody who has read through, or read in sufficient extracts, Boethius's works on logic, the theological tractates seem altogether of a piece. It is the same mind here as there, only exercising itself in a different field, with the result that Boethius has started a new method in theology, the application of Aristotelian logic to Christian problems.

This was a fatal step to take, according to Dr. Paul Elmer More, who, in his admirable volumes . . . , is not altogether courteous to the scholastics, St. Anselm in particular, whose ontological argument for the existence of God he calls a nightmare of logic. He attributes the bad invention of scholasticism, not to Boethius, to whom he makes no reference at all, possibly including him in the general condemnation that he visits on the legalistic Romans, but to Boethius's eastern contemporary, Leontios of Byzantium. I would relieve the latter of the odium, for, so far as I can gather, Boethius published first. And I would invite the attention of Dr. More, and others of his way of thinking, to the results obtained by Boethius in his treatise on Eutyches and Nestorius, results that I am confident Dr. More would accept. I would also suggest that a better guide to the scholastics will be found in two works, one on "Natural Theology" (1915), one on "God and Personality" (1918), by the Oxford scholar Clement C. J. Webb, well known as an editor of John of Salisbury, and also—this is something to say—as profound a student of Plato at first hand as Dr. More himself.

Of course Boethius was not the first of the Christian thinkers to resort to Greek philosophy. This resort had been made ever since Christians had begun seriously to connect their faith with the great systems of the past. "As certain also of your own poets have said"—the beginning was made by St. Paul. "As certain also of your own philosophers have said"—this was the next step to take; it was taken, not only by St. Clement of Alexandria among the Greeks and Minucius Felix among the Romans, but by the Gnostic heretics before them, and, earliest of all, it would seem, by whoever wrote the prologue of the Gospel according to St. John. In St. Augustine, we have a thinker who had gone through all the schools and had formed his powers of thought by training in the ancient method. In one way, Christian theology is no different in kind from any thought that had preceded it. It is just as free and just as human. It works with the same categories. But it reckons with a new historical fact, the person of our Lord, and on the basis of that fact proceeds to revolutionize previous conceptions of the nature of God and of man. There have been similar epochs in the natural sciences, created by the discovery of new facts, like that of radium in chemistry, and that of the moving and decentralized earth in astronomy. After such an event, the mind of man works on in its former way, adjusting the new condition to the old.

Now, in this sense, Boethius's procedure was nothing novel. St. Augustine had resorted to Plato and Aristotle quite as frequently as he. In his tractate on the nature of the Trinity, Boethius modestly states that he is but following in the steps of his great precursor, St. Augustine. What is new is the creation of a system, the reduction of the terms of thought to Aristotelian logic, and the application of them to theological problems. Thus the problem of the Holy Trinity must come under Aristotle's ten categories, and the meaning of person and nature must be settled in accordance with Aristotle's treatment of definition and division. A whole new science of theological procedure has been worked out. Axioms are established to control the processes of thought. At the beginning of the treatise on the substantiality of good things, Boethius lays down certain axioms,—he adds that he is proceeding like a geometrician,—which shall govern the course of his reasoning. In brief, so far as method is concerned, the relation of Boethius to St. Augustine is not unlike that of Aristotle to Plato.

Another feature of the method introduced by Boethius is its recognition of a body of revealed truth which exists by its own right and does not absolutely need the help of the philosopher. But he can help; he uses the free power of reason to substantiate, or rather to corroborate, the doctrine of the Church. He is aware that he may fall into error in this attempt, and is willing to suffer correction from those who are more intimate with the implications of the revealed truth. Thus, at the end of his discourse on the Holy Trinity addressed to John the Deacon, Boethius says, "If I am right and speak in accordance with the Faith, I pray you confirm me. But if you are in any point of another opinion, examine carefully what I have said, and if possible, reconcile faith and reason." St. Thomas Aquinas could not have put it more clearly. The whole programme of scholasticism is already in Boethius. Everybody recognizes that he furnished the Schoolmen, in his translations of Aristotle's logical works, with the chief *corpus* of philosophical material that prompted thought in the first half of the Middle Ages. He also, as we saw, broached a problem that led to the formation of important schools of mediaeval thought. He likewise invented a new philosophic vocabulary, a development ever on the increase in the Middle Ages. But, most important of all, he illustrated, in these brief tractates, the application of logical method, as well as the new vocabulary, to theological problems, on the understanding that *fides,* the ultimate truth, may be supported by the free effort of the human reason. To this conclusion we are forced by the acceptance of the *Opuscula Sacra* as the genuine productions of Boethius. Prantl, in his well-known book of the history of logic, rightly caught the spirit of these works, and declared them the output of the incipient scholasticism of the ninth century. That was in the days when a scholar who valued his scientific reputation would not dream of attributing the *Opuscula Sacra* to Boethius. Now that we must attribute them to him, former accounts of the development of thought in the early Middle Ages must be extensively revised and the influence of Boethius be more carefully followed, not only in the works of John the Scot, but in various unpublished commentaries of the ninth century. The history of the great movement known as scholastic philosophy begins, not with the contemporaries of Abelard, but with Boethius. From one point of view, Boethius is the last of the Romans; from another, he is the first of the scholastics.

Among the theological tractates is one that I have not yet discussed, no. IV in the series, called by editors ***De Fide Catholica,*** but in the best manuscripts not called anything at all. The title ***De Fide Catholica*** defines its nature. It is a kind of expanded creed, with a glance at Old Testament history, the progress of the Church, and the most important heresies. These are the doctrines of Eutyches and Nestorius, of the Manichees, of Sabellius and of Arius, that is, the very issues that were exceedingly urgent in Boethius's day; the author calls all these false views the work of those who think "in carnal terms." I once wrote a doctor's thesis to prove that Tractate no. IV was not the work of Boethius; but as even doctors' theses are sometimes not infallible, I have deemed it expedient to recant. The style of the little work is different from that of the other tractates—but so is that of the ***Consolation of Philosophy***. Boethius, like Aristotle and St. Jerome, as we saw, and like many scholars and scientists to-day, cultivated an *esoteric* or technical style, intended for the inner circle of specialists, and an *exoteric* or popular style, intended for the general public. Distinguishing between faith and reason, Boethius applied the principles of the latter to confirm the doctrines of the former. He accepted, therefore, certain articles of the faith. Well then, why should he not have stated them? The fourth tractate gives us such a statement. He drew it up, I should imagine, to clarify his thought and to provide a basis for further procedure. He did not intend to publish it, and had not given it a title. But it might have been found with his papers after his death, and, very sensibly, added to his works; for it is a clear and admirably ordered account, not without touches of poetic intensity, and a dramatic scope which in the compass of a few pages takes the reader from the creation of the world through human history to the last judgment. The work is a little masterpiece.

We have seen enough, I believe, to put Boethius in his historical setting and to determine his intellectual attitude. He is a Christian humanist and, indeed, one of the most satisfactory representatives of Christian humanism that we have examined thus far. In temperament he is more equable and urbane than Augustine or Jerome, though he can exercise a humanistic tongue, and he is far more profound than Lactantius. In his day, the stirring conflicts of the fourth century with Paganism were over, and the church was more at liberty to assimilate the best of the past. Boethius was not only a philosopher but a man of letters, as we might not have known so well had it not been for his imprisonment, which occasioned the ***Consolation of Philosophy***. It is an ill wind that blows nobody good luck. In his philosophy, one may apply to him what Sidonius said of Claudian Mamertus: "He was a man of wisdom, prudence and learning; he was a philosopher all his days without prejudice to his faith." The mind of Boethius, like that of St. Augustine, was impassioned for the philosophic quest, in which he engaged without let or ceasing. It was his chief solace in life—*summum vitae solamen;* I am quoting, not from the ***Consolation of Philosophy,*** but from one of the logical works, "***On Hypothetical Syllogisms,***" written a dozen or more years before.

Philosophy is also for Boethius, as for Lucretius and Cicero and Lactantius, a patriotic act. In the busy year of his consulate, 510, he remarks, as he writes his work on the *Categories*,

> Although the cares of my consular office prevent me from devoting my entire attention to these studies, yet it seems to me a sort of public service to instruct my fellow-citizens in the products of reasoned investigation. Nor shall I deserve ill of my country in this attempt. In far-distant ages, other cities transferred to our state alone the lordship and sovereignty of the world; I am glad to assume the remaining task of educating our present society in the spirit of Greek philosophy. Wherefore this is verily a part of my consular duty, since it has always been a Roman habit to take whatever was beautiful or praiseworthy throughout the world and to add to its lustre by imitation. So then, to my task.

One might imagine that the speaker is Cicero. Boethius virtually declares that he is continuing the programme of his illustrious predecessor in the consular office, as the latter had announced it at the beginning of the *Tusculan Disputations*. Cicero had already introduced Greek philosophy into Rome, but much remained to do. Nor did Boethius live to achieve all, or half, of his impressive plan. He worked in a different way. His interests were more immediately philosophical; his method was more scientific. And yet in this passage, and in the style and in some of the substance of the ***Consolation of Philosophy,*** Boethius declares himself the successor of Cicero. We must add him to the list of Christian Ciceros of which we found the fourth century to be full. And we must conclude that Boethius, while the first of the scholastics, is also the last of the Romans. His worship of the eternal Rome is as devout as that of Cicero himself.

Such was his career,—and it is all of a piece,—up to the last year of his life. Then came the *peripeteia* of his fortune—his imprisonment in the dungeon at Calvenzano, and his death by execution. The reasons for his sudden downfall may never be accurately ascertained. He denied the charge of the informers that he was guilty of secret negotiations with the court of Byzantium. He indicates that he was also accused of the malevolent practice of the black arts. We may waive both indictments, the latter on the ground of common sense, the former from our belief in the integrity of Boethius. Why had Theodoric, then, come to regard him, after all his services to his monarch and the state, as a public enemy? I shall try to answer this question after we have taken a fleeting look at the ***Consolation of Philosophy***.

The ***Consolation of Philosophy*** is prison-literature, and prison-literature often takes the form of a theodicy. The solitary thinker, beginning with the sense of his own wrongs,—unless he is aware that his punishment is well deserved,—seeks justification somewhere. If the world does not give it, heaven will. The tyrant may win for a time, but the righteous knows that his own purpose is attuned to the everlasting purposes, which ultimately know no defeat. This is the way that proud spirits think the matter out; for them, the mind is its own place. It is not for them to weep and wail, to pine away or to end their lives in despair, but rather to justify the ways of God to men, and to know that they share in His victory. Besides Boethius, we may cite as examples Dracontius and Bunyan and Sir Thomas More. There is something of this fine despite of the present moment even in Ovid—little, I fear, in those other eminent exiles, Cicero and Seneca. But the blind Milton belongs in the company; his latter life was in a cell, though not one built of iron bars. I have recently come across an instance in the literature of our own ancestors. Mrs. Mary Rowlandson, who in 1676 was dragged from her burning house by the Indians and kept in captivity for twelve weeks, wrote a narrative of her experiences bearing the title, "The Soveraignty and Goodness of God."

This, then, is Boethius's starting-point. To whom should he look for help but to Philosophy, the guide and solace of his life from earliest youth? He thinks of her in personal terms. She is an allegorical symbol, and by the power of his imagination becomes something more. As Natura spoke to Lucretius, Patria to Cicero, and the divine Roma to Symmachus, Claudian, and, none the less commandingly, to Prudentius, so Philosophia visits the exile's dungeon, chases away the singing Muses from whom her favorite was seeking an ineffective consolation, and administers her own remedies.

Viewed simply as literature, this is a great work, "a golden volume," as Gibbon remarked, "not unworthy of the leisure of Tully or Plato." First of all, its simple and Ciceronian style is well nigh a miracle in view of the tendency of deliberate rhetoric toward that distorted ornateness that we note in Sidonius and other writers of the times. Further, in its composition, it represents an exceedingly skilful combination of several literary types. It is dialogue, of the kind that Plato and Cicero had made popular in philosophical treatises. It is a talk between Boethius and Philosophy from beginning to end. Philosophy is at first the good physician; she hardly expects her patient to answer back—but before long he gathers strength and takes his share in the argument. The work is also an allegory, so far as the person of Philosophy is concerned, and suggestive also of the allegories found in certain apocalypses, like the Shepherd of Hermas and the Poimandres of Hermes Trismegistus. This is not a mere device; Boethius's passion for the dry light of reason makes it natural for him to speak in personal terms. Philosophy steps into the scene by her own good right, and plays her part convincingly to the end. The work also belongs, as the title indicates, to ancient consolation-literature, of which Boethius knew abundant examples in Cicero, Seneca, and the poets. But it is also a kind of introduction or incentive to Philosophy, a πρτρεπτικὸς εἰς τὴν φιλοσοφιᾷν, like Aristotle's work by this title, and Cicero's *Hortensius*. As one reads on, however, the value of Philosophy needs no demonstration; nor do the nature and efficacy of her consolation. Both these elements are caught up in a higher purpose, which is, as I have explained, a theodicy of great power and scope. . . . To assert the eternal justice, it becomes necessary to solve the mysteries of divine unity and goodness, of fate and human freedom. The writer is setting forth all that he can see of life and time and eternity.

Finally, the structure of the work suggests yet another literary variety; for to vary the presentation, to break the flow of dialogue, a number of little poems are interspersed,—thirty-nine in all,—which now sum up the argument of the preceding prose section, and now themselves carry it on. They vary in poetical quality. Some are exceedingly good, some are only moderate, and a few are insignificant—that being the only way, according to the poet Martial, in which one can write a book. The metres of the poems are varied and skilfully wrought out. Boethius tries almost every metre going, and invents two or three new ones. This mixture of prose and verse at once classes the work as a *satura,* a literary form that has no equal for its Protean changes of contents throughout its lengthy history. Our English satire is only one moment in its career.

The circumstances in which the ***Consolation of Philosophy*** was written make the study of the writer's sources peculiarly interesting. We are given a clue, I believe, to the right way to examine the sources of any ancient author. Sometimes, after reading dissertations, let us say, on the plagiarisms of Virgil, one pictures the poet at a large desk on which ten or a dozen volumes of his more worthy predecessors are displayed, from whom he filches a line here, a half-line there, a quarter-line there, an epithet there, constructing in this way a painful mosaic or picture-puzzle. Virgil himself had answered this kind of criticism, if one would only hear him; when somebody charged him with stealing the verses of Homer, he replied that it was easier to steal the club of Hercules than a verse from Homer. He implied that the process of making great and Classical poetry which, like a liturgy, pays homage to tradition, is other than an act of petty larceny, or if conceived in the spirit of petty larceny, it inevitably pays the penalty of detection. Now in the case of Boethius,—and likewise in that of the exiled Ovid,—the thieving author had no wares from which to pilfer. Boethius laments, in tones too sincere to allow us to suspect a literary device, that his library had not been shipped to his prison. I will not deny that a few books might have come to him, but not so many as the patient investigators of his sources have tracked in the text of the ***Consolation of Philosophy***. For me the conclusion remains that this great work is not a thing of shreds and patches, of clippings and pilferings, of translatings and extractings, but springs from two main sources, *ingenium* and *memoria.* For the ancients had not lost the faculty of remembering. When a Virgil or a Boethius composed, he thought out a plan, wrote from the fulness of his own knowledge and his own inspiration, which depended in part on wide reading in the best of literature. His mind was mature and well stocked. He had something to say. He spoke as a prophet of the great tradition, but he added to its richness. He translated or half-quoted or borrowed a phrase to make his meaning clearer, to lend it distinction, or to summon the reader to inspect the past; and his product is more and not less original for this trait.

I am dwelling on this point, not only to save Boethius's reputation in general, but to refute a charge brought against him, I am sorry to say, by that great scholar Hermann Usener, whose golden little book, *Anecdoton Holderi,* is in other respects the best that has been done for Boethius in our times—or was until Klingner's recent work appeared. Usener pronounces unfavorably on the orginality of the ***Consolation of Philosophy,*** declaring it a tissue of two main sources of entirely different nature—one an Aristotelian passage, translated straight out of Aristotle's *Protreptikos,* the other a lengthy extract from a Neoplatonic work. These two sections were tacked together by Boethius, despite their incongruous nature,—and possibly Boethius was not original enough even to tack them together, but found them so united in some source, which he proceeded to translate. He then prefixed an introduction and interspersed throughout the work, as thus conglutinated, a number of sorry poems, which make a startling contrast to their context; for there one hears the voice of the ancients, but in them, that of a child of the sixth century.

I cannot attempt here a full refutation of Usener's hypothesis, but I should like you to bear it in mind as I sketch the contents of the ***Consolatio***; knowing how unoriginal it is thought to be, you may be better able to appreciate how original it is.

The writer begins with a disconsolate poem, in elegiacs—for it is a real elegy, unlike those of his young manhood; he now has some cause for lamentation. The Muses are sitting sadly about his couch, keeping his sorrow alive by their sympathy. Of a sudden, My Lady Philosophy enters, drives the false comforters from the cell and clears the air of sentimentality. At her bidding, Boethius describes the miseries which have befallen him, and thereby starts the question with which the metaphysical plot of this treatise begins—the nature of fortune, that ultimate principle which permits a good man to suffer. Philosophy declares that her fosterling is a pretty sick man; he is sadly in need of her remedy. In answer to his reproaches for her desertion in the hour of his need, she reminds him that he is not the first to suffer for the truth. Socrates, whose heritage the Epicurean and Stoic pretenders so sorely mistreated, Anaxagoras and Zeno among Greeks, Canius, Seneca and Soranus among Romans, were martyrs for philosophy—why should Boethius shrink from such a fate? There follows a fine and thoroughly characteristic passage on the contempt of evil, a kind of translation into metaphysics of the Horatian despite of the *profanum vulgus,* a sentiment to which Boethius was no stranger.

> Wherefore thou hast no cause to marvel, if in the sea of this life we be tossed with boisterous storms, whose chiefest purpose is to displease the wicked; of which though there be an huge army, yet it is to be despised, because it is not governed by any captain, but is carried up and down by fantastical error without any order at all. And if at any time they assail us with great force, our captain retireth her band into a castle, leaving them occupied in sacking unprofitable baggage. And from above we laugh them to scorn for seeking so greedily after most vile things, being safe from all their furious assault, and fortified with that defence against which aspiring folly cannot prevail.

If this is the voice of a child of the sixth century, it is either a pretty good century or a precocious child. And possibly both. He is not too young a child to have learned of the inorganic character of evil, and he knows how to transfer this metaphysical notion into poetical imagery in a dignified style. He has also read deeply enough in the history of philosophy to have selected as his favorite period the best of all periods, when metaphysics was the prime interest and thought had not slumped into ethics. Plato and Aristotle form a kind of philosophical orthodoxy, of which the later schools had preserved only broken lights. As Boethius expresses it, the mob of Epicureans, Stoics, and the rest usurped the inheritance of Socrates and Plato and tore fragments from the robe of Philosophy, each imagining that he possessed the entire garment. Here, as in other points to which I have called attention, Boethius is following the lead of Cicero. For Cicero is, in the best sense of the term, the first of the Neoplatonists.

Boethius then proceeds to enumerate his services to the state and to dwell on the injustice of his degradation; it is a brief *apologia pro vita sua.* How can the good fall so low, he ponders, while wicked men flourish like the green bay-tree; there is a great contrast between the world of nature, which obeys a just and unalterable law, and the world of man, which tosses in the perpetual and irrational changes of Fortune. This arraignment of the universal order starts the whole problem, for which, however, Philosophy has a solution ready. Her method, first of all, is to arouse in her patient a better mind, a spirit capable of receiving the cure which she can impart. She speaks of a "gentler remedy" which she will first apply, and catches at his persisting belief in Providence,—whose ways, to be sure, seem very dark,—as the one last spark from which his former ardor may be revived. The closing poem of the book pictures the clouded mind, from which the light of

Ivory diptych of Boethius's father, who was consul in 487.

reason should drive all the passions away.

The first book is the opening act in a metaphysical drama; it presents, in a pictorial form, and with a truer sense of the dramatic than Cicero shows in any of his philosophical dialogues, a speculative problem which the following books are to solve. The poems have something of the effect of the choruses in a Greek tragedy or the meditative passages in Lucretius. They give the reader an outlook, and a downward look from the height to which he has climbed by the steep path of the argument.

With the second book begins the "gentler remedy." It consists of an exposition of the essentially fickle nature of Fortune, whose only law is that of constant mutability. What was he to expect? Fortune's slave must follow Fortune's will; in fact, her very mutability is cause for hoping now. But this specious reasoning—which Philosophy herself had characterized as "Rhetoric's sweet persuasion"—fails to satisfy. She adds thereto the suggestion that the memory of past success should be a solace, and that, if Boethius will but lump his experience, he will find in the total more good than bad. The philosopher replies sadly with a sentiment that Dante and many others have echoed, that the memory of happier things is of miseries most miserable. But Philosophy enumerates the blessings that remian,—his wife, his sons, and Symmachus,—and by this simple appeal to human affection draws from Boethius the admission that some anchors still hold despite the storm.

Thus far Philosophy has treated the gifts of Fortune as absolute entities, absolute goods or ills. Encouraged by the symptoms of convalescence in her patient, she now advances a point in the argument; examining the so-called goods in turn, she proves that felicity is merely relative. This is part of the "stronger remedy"—and just here, according to Usener, begins the passage that Boethius translates from Aristotle's *Protreptikos*. But the preceding part is far more than an introduction; it is an important part of the whole argument, and, in my opinion, altogether of a piece with what follows.

Philosophy now analyzes various of the goods in turn,—riches, aesthetic enjoyment, fame,—with the result that all these are relative, depending for their significance on the personality with which they are connected. Indeed, Fortune is kind only when her fickleness shows the true nature of temporal gifts, discloses false friends, and thus, negatively at least, points the way to abiding human friendship and to the universal principle of love, the only source of absolute good. The finest part of this discussion is a passage on the evanescence of fame. Usener may well be right in believing that Aristotle had made similar remarks in his *Protreptikos,* but Cicero, whom Boethius quotes, is surely a direct model, and a reference to Ptolemy shows that Boethius did not confine himself to either Aristotle or Cicero. He sums up the idea in a sombre poem which various scholars who have forgotten their Classics think a harbinger of the mediaeval brooding over the transitory glories of earth.

> Who knows where faithful Fabrice' bones are
> pressed,
> Where Brutus and strict Cato rest?
> A slender fame consigns their titles vain
> In some few letters to remain.
> Because their famous names in books we read,
> Come we by them to know the dead?
> You dying, then, remembered are by none,
> Nor any fame can make you known.
> But if you think that life outstrippeth death,
> Your names borne up with mortal breath,
> When length of time takes this away likewise,
> A second death shall you surprise.

This, true enough, is in the spirit of Villon's *Ballade des Dames du Temps Fadis*, but it is also in the spirit of Cicero and Juvenal, of Ovid and Ausonius, and of the author of the *Book of Kings*: "Where is the king of Hamath and the king of Arpad, and the king of the city of Sepharvain, of Hena, and Ivah?" Melancholy meditation on the passing of the beautiful or the great is not confined to the Middle Ages.

The third book develops in positive form the reasoning which the second has negatively suggested. The opening sections, however, merely repeat the method previously employed. The various goods are again examined, with more detail, to be sure, than in the second book. They are first discussed in general, and then each is considered in turn—wealth, office, kingship, glory, nobility, carnal pleasures. The conclusion follows that the understanding of the false goods will lead us to the true. There certainly are traces of Aristotle apparent, but Epicurus is also mentioned and his doctrine of the *summum bonum* is briefly treated; Catullus is quoted; Decoratus serves as an illustration from Boethius's own times; the Roman praetorship is discussed; Nero, Seneca, Papinianus, and Antoninus are passed in review; and the argument is colored with personal touches, including a delicate compliment to the philosopher's wife and sons. In this section, therefore, while the writer is dependent on various thinkers of the past—here Aristotle notably—for some of his conceptions, he has combined diverse elements in an original fashion and fused the whole with his own personality.

The positive part of the "stronger remedy" appears in the latter portion of the book. The goods are subjected to a fresh analysis, this time to show their essential unity and their dependence on the ultimate principle of the good: *sufficientia, potentia, claritudo, reverentia, laetitia* have value and are worthy objects of human ambition, but only because they present different aspects of the *summum bonum,* the goal to which they lead. Man, therefore, should strive directly for this final idea of good, and not for the broken lights of it. But this source of all goods may be approached only by the way of prayer; so Philosophy prays to the Highest Good. The argument then turns to an analysis of the *summum bonum* and demonstrates its existence, its perfection, its unity, its inherence in God. Thus the idea of Good is identified with God, though the converse proposition, that God is nothing more than the idea of Goodness, does not follow; for the underlying conception of the divine nature is not idealism but personal theism—a step that neither Aristotle nor Plato (except for pictorial purposes in the mythological *Timaeus*) could quite take. But this God, though omnipotent, is incapable of one thing, evil, which is thereby pronounced non-existent. Dropping this utterance as a seed of further inquiry, Philosophy closes the book with a song on the "lucid source of good," illustrating her theme by a somewhat perverted application of the story of Orpheus and Eurydice that no lover, Browing, for instance, would approve.

The treatment has been most impressive in these last chapters; the argument moves with a majestic sweep to the conclusion, which, like that of the first book, may fairly be called dramatic. In this entire passage, Plato is much more prominent than Aristotle. He is quoted several times, and the poetic prayer is a kind of summary of the *Timaeus*. But Boethius goes beyond both Plato and Aristotle, as I have pointed out, in his acceptance of a personal theism. He invokes the authority of Plato for the need of asking divine aid before undertaking a great metaphysical quest, but while Plato calls on θεύς τε καὶ θεάς, Boethius prays to the very Being that he is attempting to prove, assuming, it would seem, that faith in deity must precede the endeavor to demonstrate its existence—*credo ut intellegam*. This proof, therefore, to quote again from the treatise on the Trinity, the philosopher does not discover, but corroborates something that "stands by itself on the firm foundation of Faith."

Philosophy's stronger remedy has now been administered; she has shown her patient that the source of all goods, and hence of the best fortune, is still at his disposal. There are some difficulties, however, still untouched—one in especial at which Philosophy has hinted at the end of the third book. How can evil exist in the presence of a Personal Good that is at once benevolent and omnipotent? At the opening of the fourth book, Boethius at once attacks this problem, which has been his chief perplexity all along, and the discussion of the nature of evil occupies the greater part of this book. Philosophy demonstrates that the good are always rewarded and the wicked always punished; in fact, the latter virtually cease to exist. It is, finally, the presence of mere brute chance, which intrudes after moral evil has been comfortably explained, that leads to larger issues, and, necessarily, to a new turning-point in the argument. The new question is hydra-headed, Philosophy declares: the proper answer to it involves the discussion of five distinct problems—the simplicity of providence, the chain of fate, chance, divine cognition and predestination, and freedom of the will. With the words, "Leading off, as it were, from a new starting-point," she approaches the first of these matters; precisely at this point, Usener sets the beginning of the Neoplatonic text. Surely the last part of the supposedly Aristotelian portion has been getting rather ethereal for Aristotle—and a bit too theological for Plato. Boethius is resorting to Plato and Aristotle as ever,—to the Stoics as well,—but he is thinking the thing out for himself in his own way.

"Leading off, as it were, from a new starting-point"—these words might indicate, as Usener thinks, that Boethius here takes up a fresh source; they might, however, simply mean that at this important turn in the reasoning a new method or line of thought is approached. Philosophy has been discoursing on human and physical evil; now, neglecting this aspect for the moment, she starts at the other end, at the divine simplicity where the thought of evil is out of question. Indeed, when we find Cicero [in *De Divinatione*] using the same words at a similar division of the argument, it becomes clear that Boethius is merely following his example.

Philosophy takes up the first two of the problems above mentioned, devoting to them the remainder of the fourth book. It is, after all, one problem, for the "simplicity of the divine providence" is but the inner aspect of which the "chain of fate" is the outer expression. Providence conceives, fate executes. Providence is simple, stable, eternal; fate is composed of multifold agencies, acts and shifts constantly, and is subject to time. Fate includes weather and the fortunes of men, which are thus indirectly of divine appointment. All, therefore, is done well, even by the apparently wicked, of whose moral temper only the all-seeing judge can be certain. Boethius reinforces his point by a witty quotation from Lucan, who, so far as I am aware, was not often read by Neoplatonists. God gives to each, Philosophy continues, good and bad alike, exactly the medicine that his cure demands; perhaps the prison, she intimates, is exactly what Boethius needed. Nor is there any escape from the Divine dispensation. One may leave the order in which one is set, but only to fall into another order. Love rules all, and nothing can exist unless it return to this love that gave it being. Thus all fortune is good, and the sage should be as eager for his trial as the soldier is for battle. Every Hercules has his labors, but if he endures, heaven is his reward.

Throughout this discussion, Boethius is reckoning with certain ideas of the Neoplatonists. They, too, distinguished between providence and fate, but went much more minutely into the sorts and kinds of fate and of the different entities that led in a definite hierarchy from the one omnipotent essence, which was too holy and abstract even to name, down to that evil substance, matter. Boethius, however, is not afraid to name the supreme essence; he calls it God, he remarks, in the good old-fashioned way. But he does not bridge the gap between God and his world by any elaborate series of graded abstractions—mind, soul, nature, and the rest. Fate is directly under the control of Providence, which is of the very heart of divinity itself, not a principle depending on it at third or fourth remove. And the Neoplatonic agencies of fate, including angels and demons and the influences of the stars, are all lumped together as possible manifestations of the *fatalis series,* the order of fate. Any contemporary Christian theologian would not have put it otherwise. That is to say, the intimate association of fate with the providence of the Deity, as well as the wholesale levelling of the Neoplatonic hierarchy, is tantamount to an attack on a cardinal feature of that system. And so, more significant still, is the assumption of a personal Deity in place of the ineffably transcendent Being, or rather Super-being, of the Neoplatonists.

At the beginning of the fifth book, we find Philosophy rather coquettishly changing the subject. The stronger remedy is now administered. Boethius has turned from the false goods to the true good, has seen that moral evil does not exist, and that even the shifts of fortune are part of the divinely appointed order of fate. What need of further argument? Still, though morally cured, the philosopher is not yet mentally illuminated as to the remaining questions bound up in the problem of fate, and insists now on the answers to these. With the discussion of chance, predestination, and freedom, the theodicy, and with it the full consolation, is brought to a close. I shall attempt to guide you no farther into Boethius's well-ordered thought. If he has not quite solved the problem of freedom, we may pertinently ask who has? His solution, at any rate, is in accord with Christian theology in its insistence on the two opposing and logically contradictory principles of human freedom and divine omniscience. Deity is personal and prayer is a vital act. "Wherefore fly vices, embrace virtues, possess your minds with worthy hopes, offer up humble prayers to your highest Prince. There is, if you will not dissemble, a great necessity of doing well imposed upon you, since you live in the sight of a Judge who beholdeth all things."

These stately words, with which the ***Consolation*** ends, are anti-Pagan in general and anti-Neoplatonic in particular. I need not further labor either of these points. The Pagans are constantly used; both method and material come from Plato, Aristotle, and the "plebeian" philosophers. The thinker reasons solely with his own powers, without any revelation, save that of Philosophy, who is naught but the idealization of his own intellect. But the result fits in neatly with the revealed truth of Christian theology. The latter is in the background of the thinker's consciousness. He is proving as much of *fides* as *ratio* will allow him. That explains why there is not a trace of anything specifically Christian or Biblical in the entire work; the assumption of any portion of faith in an endeavor of the unaided reason would defeat its very purpose. In similar fashion, though with a different goal in view, Minucius Felix . . . carefully excluded Biblical quotations and the very name of Christ from his Christian apologetic. On the other hand, there must be nothing in such a ***Consolation of Philosophy*** that contravenes the principles of the faith. One or two points—particularly Boethius's theory of creation—call for comment, but, in brief, there is nothing in this work for which a good case might not have been made by any contemporary Christian theologian, who knew his Augustine. Had Theodoric suddenly repented of his decision and the life of Boethius been spared, I can readily conceive that, after reconciling Plato and Aristotle, he might have gone on to harmonize the result with the doctrine of the Church, and thus have saved St. Thomas Aquinas his gigantic task, or, rather, have performed it in a different way.

But Theodoric did not repent. Boethius met his death. And not long after, so did Symmachus and John the Deacon, if he is the Johannes who had been elevated to the Papacy. The explanation of this *volte-face* on the part of Theodoric, I believe, is that the circle of Boethius, in particular, and the Senate, in general, formed the core of the Catholic conservatives who were bitterly opposed to his Arianism. This issue also had its political significance, for the Catholic conservatives were also the old Roman conservatives, and whether or not they were actually in communication with the Eastern Empire, they were only biding their time. Theodoric saw it all and struck suddenly,—and wisely for his own interests,—before the danger should come to a head. His ostensible charge against the accused was treasonable negotiation with the Eastern Empire; the actual reason could hardly be stated.

One of the mediaeval lives of Boethius states that he was called St. Severinus by the provincials. Those provincials were wise persons. So was Abelard, who stated that the noble Roman senator had fallen with Symmachus in that persecution in which Theodoric raged against the Christians. So was Dante, who placed the *anima santa* of the philosopher in the *Paradiso,* and spoke of his coming from martyrdom and exile unto that peace. The learned Bollandists of the eighteenth century in their *Acta Sanctorum* call Boethius *catholicissimus,* give him the title of saint,—St. Severinus Boethius,—and record his life with that of his friend Pope John on May 27. But no more recent publication, authoritative or unauthoritative, on the saints of the Church, so far as I know, ventures to include his name. I wish that someone influential with the Holy See would present a petition in favor of St. Severinus or St. Boethius, for, if I have stated the facts about him, the logic of the case seems inexorable. If he was put to death partly because of his defence of the Catholic faith against an Arian monarch, he suffered martyrdom; and if so important a person suffered martyrdom, he deserves canonization. Indeed, the honor might be given anyway to the first of the scholastics; or—a point that may appeal to His present Holiness, once prefect of the Biblioteca Vaticana—a certain saintliness attends a scholar who lost so fine a library and who yet could transport so much of it, inside him, to his dungeon-cell.

Howard Rollin Patch (essay date 1935)

SOURCE: "Imitations and Influence," in *The Tradition of Boethius: A Study of His Importance in Medieval Culture,* Oxford University Press, Inc., 1935, pp. 87-113.

[*In the following excerpt, Patch examines the impact exerted by Boethius on Medieval and Renaissance writers, including Dante, King James I of Scotland, and Sir Thomas More.*]

The most striking testimony of all to the power of the ***Consolatio*** appears in the attempt through many centuries to interpret its meaning in various adaptations and imitations. Something like this we have already observed [earlier], in varying ways, in King Alfred's rendering and the Provençal *Boece* and especially in Simund de Freine's *Roman de Philosophie,* where invention to a greater or less degree has certainly distinguished translation. Indeed on these terms it is hard to find much difference between Simund's work and the poem written by Henry of Settimello which we shall presently examine, except that Simund's *Roman* aims at keeping a little closer to the original. Most of the early versions are adapted in some fashion to their times, and even the later and fairly close translations introduce some measure of change in form or content. Simund tries to reproduce the scheme of the original; and it is fair for us to pay some consideration to the author's own purpose, as well as to take account of the traditional method of classifying these documents. In any case the moral to be derived from the material remains perfectly clear. The full extent of the influence enjoyed by the ***Consolatio*** is beyond our power to estimate.

This influence appears in a number of works where it would seem that the authors were inspired by Boethius mainly to appreciate the form of his treatise. The variety gained by a shift from prose to verse commended itself apart from his special purpose. The allegorical method, also, of setting forth a discussion of serious problems was particularly to the taste of the Middle Ages; and, although it was familiar in the works of Prudentius and others, surely it gained some of its popularity from the little book which became so widely known. The Socratic style too of dealing with problems in dialogue, of showing the "sic et non" by question and answer, was certainly less familiar through the works of Plato than in the pages of Boethius. Furthermore the content of the book permeated, as we have seen, the thought of men for at least a thousand years; and it found new expression in various forms, offering consolation for ills other than those specifically of prison and exile. At all times men have assumed the vocation to justify the ways of God to man; or, if they concede that at least part of the time human disobedience is at the root of suffering, they are likely to search for remedies in counsel not unlike those suggested by the ***Consolatio***. So Philosophy, if not always justified of her children, seems through the ages to have many of them.

The imitation of the form of the ***Consolatio*** in the mere alternation of prose and verse is not easy to identify. It is, for one thing, the manner of the *satura,* and it appeared earlier than Boethius in the exceedingly popular work *De Nuptiis Philologiae et Mercurii* of Martianus Capella. On the whole the ***Consolatio*** was perhaps more likely to be the instrument which effected the plan, especially where we find its metrical patterns reproduced; but absolute certainty in the matter is out of the question. With this proviso we may cite the *De Rectoribus Christianis* (855-859) of the poet Sedulius Scottus, who composed this regimen of princes for Lothar II, setting forth the duties of his monarch in this tactful way in twenty chapters, and managing at the same time to make a considerable display of his own learning. Here too belongs the Norman History in three books, intended by its author Dudo of St. Quentin (fl. c. 1000) to celebrate the Normans; but, more resplendent with learning than reliable historically, it introduces the Muses who sing in the measures of Boethius. Neoplatonic inheritance appears in the allegorical *De Mundi Uniuersitate* of Bernard Silvester (fl. xii century) on the creation of the Megacosmus and the Microcosmus, a sort of Christian *Timaeus* in which symbolic figures set forth the material. Natura complains to Nous that matter is still formless, and we then follow the beginnings and the process by which the universe receives its order, with every detail listed. The journey of Natura through the spheres and to the lower world to obtain the aid of Urania and Physis for the creation of man is dwelt on at length. In this complicated task Bernard has been obviously assisted by Martianus Capella, the *Somnium Scipionis* with the commentary of Macrobius, and Boethius.

It is significant to note that Adelard of Bath and Alanus de Insulis were pupils of Bernard. We have already referred to Adelard's *De Eodem et Diuerso,* a prose allegory with two passages in verse. In this treatise Philosophy appears with the Seven Liberal Arts, holds converse with Adelard, and disputes with Philocosmia (representing change and decay), whose handmaids are Riches, Power, Honour, Fame, and Pleasure. In the Second Book of the ***Consolatio*** Boethius had dealt with the "falsely seeming goods" of Fortune which these handmaids represent; now with Adelard they become "oppressed as if with shame" and can not "bear the gaze of the opposite seven," the Liberal Arts. Thus even as early as the twelfth century culture was supposed to weaken the hold of secular interests; salvation presumably comes by education! The Arts themselves may be ultimately derived from Martianus Capella, but the work is also richly indebted to Boethius. Incidentally we may also take note of the *Fons Philosophie* of Godfrey of St. Victor, written in the same period. According to this poem the author goes on a visionary journey past the seven poisonous streams of the mechanical arts to the mountain-spring whence flow the clear rivers of the Liberal Arts; and Boethius himself is mentioned along with the other great masters of philosophy who drink of the waters of Dialectic. He listens to the strife regarding Aristotelianism and Platonism, and the controversy between nominalists and realists, but according to Godfrey . . . shows no preference.

From the impulse derived from Bernard Silvester came the further transmission of things Platonic and Neoplatonic in the well-known writings of Alanus de Insulis, which have been often described. His *De Planctu Naturae* carries on the tradition of Martianus Capella and Boethius in its verse and prose, in which Dame Nature, elaborately described, bewails the unnatural vice of the time. She talks with the author, and the sins are discussed. Further symbolic figures appear, and the poet visits the house of Nature, wisely cautious, however, about daring to enter such intimacy. His *Anticlaudianus,* written entirely in verse, deals with the creation of man. In Nature's garden a meeting is held to discuss the project of making a perfect man, and Prudence, prompted by Reason, and assisted by her daughters the Liberal Arts, goes to heaven to obtain the soul. Nature makes the body. The house of Fortune, part dazzling with splendour, part in ruins, must be sought out for proper gifts from the fickle Goddess. The complications of the allegory only serve to furnish an abundance of material for later productions of the sort. Both works of Alanus were utilized by Jean de Meun in composing his *Roman de la Rose,* where the dwelling of Fortune appears again, and where borrowings of that kind are equaled only by the indebtedness to Boethius. Jean de Meun, as we have seen, was a close student of the ***Consolatio,*** which he translated and also rifled. In a similar way Chaucer used the French poet's work as well as that of Alanus, made his own translation of the ***Consolatio,*** and borrowed from Boethius. His *House of Fame* shows the benefit of hints received from the abode of Fortune in the *Anticlaudianus;* his *Parlement of Foules* takes much from *De Planctu Naturae.*

We cannot attempt here to indicate all the developments of this sort. The history of medieval allegory is as intricate as its plots. One other outstanding instance may, however, be briefly considered. The *Anticlaudianus* is also in part responsible for the Spanish *Visión Delectable* (1430-1440) written entirely in prose by Alfonso de la Torre. This ponderous narrative relates how Understanding, repelled apparently by the corruption of the world, seeks knowledge of the truth. Accompanied by Instinct he goes to a lofty mountain and comes to the abode of the Arts, from whom he gets instruction. One thinks immediately of the mountain-springs in the *Fons Philosophie;* and here too there is something of the tradition from Martianus Capella. At the top of Alfonoso's mountain are Truth and her three sisters: Nature, Wisdom, and Reason. This is the realm of the Earthly Paradise, and in this pleasant region dwell the Four Cardinal Virtues. It is to be noticed that Reason's height at times touches the heavens and occasionally she assumes normal stature, a familiar trait of Philosophia in the ***Consolatio***. The idea is older than that, however, although that is the probable source for its use in this instance, as well as with reference to Fortune in the *Roman de Fauvel* (where we find a long account of Boethius) and perhaps in the passage describing Fame in Chaucer's *House of Fame.*

But it is impossible to trace all the details of indebtedness. Works which show an alternation of prose and verse, in addition to the instances already discussed, might be further listed, and some will be mentioned in the course of this chapter; but the connexion of many with Boethius is tenuous. For example, the fourteenth-century *Voir Dit* of Guillaume de Machaut, in the tradition of love poetry with inserted letters in prose, almost certainly bears no relation to our theme. On the other hand, Dante's *Vita Nuova,* which reveals the many ways in which Beatrice became the poet's friend and guide and indeed his philosopher, is not entirely remote in substance. Still more remarkable is the parallel in the *Convivio,* where Dante gives some account of Lady Philosophy and several references to Boethius. After losing Beatrice, he set himself, he tells us, "to read that book of Boethius, not known to many, wherein, a captive and an exile, he had consoled himself." When he speaks of the book as not known to many, he refers perhaps to the knowledge of intimate understanding. In the *Convivio* as in the *Vita Nuova* and the ***Consolatio*** the prose interprets and expands on the verse; in this case indeed it becomes even a direct commentary. Dante's work inspired Boccaccio, whose *Ameto* shows a similar form, telling how the young hunter whose name furnished the title met Lia (faith) and was led by Venus to the awareness that it is love which teaches and reveals all things. In this instance, however, the verses as songs constitute a part of the narrative, which, though exalted in purpose, cannot quite lift its delicate feet from the solid earth.

Closer than most of the compositions just considered, however, are the works whose theme is in some definite way allied to that of the ***Consolatio***. Perhaps because their influence was restricted or their aim narrow, some of these are lost or difficult of access. The *Consolatio siue Laterna Monachorum* by Ekkehard of Aura (d. 1130) has not survived, but we are told that it was written in imitation of Boethius. Lawrence of Durham's *Consolatio de Morte Amici* (c. 1100-1154), in which Lawrence tells his troubles in prose and a Consoler replies in verse, remains in manuscript. The *Consolatio Nostri Exemplo* of Pier della Vigna [Petrus de Vineis] (1190-1249), minister to Frederick II and a man of great power in his day who fell into disgrace with Fortune and men's eyes, has not survived. On the other hand, the *Consolatio Theologiae* of the exiled Johannes of Dambach [Iohannes de Tambaco] (1288-1372) had enough popularity to be reprinted many times, excerpted, and translated, at least in part, into Dutch, Spanish, and English. In the original Theologia is accompanied by *Puellae* and *Milites.* The dialogue is conducted between a crowd of sufferers and the separate damsels who answer their complaints. In fifteen books of prose Johannes sets forth ample remedies for all disturbances of public and private peace. The causes of such disturbance are taken up systematically: adverse fortune, persecutions, injuries, exile, loss of friends, lack of exterior joy, silence, sadness, loss of freedom, physical defects, everything. Quotations from various authors, Augustine, Jerome, Gregory, Chrysostom, Cato, Seneca, Valerius Maximus, Boethius, and many more, afford the solution of all difficulties. Such a comprehensive work may have been in part inspired by Seneca; one wonders if there is any possible connexion between it and another essentially different compilation of remedies, that of Petrarch.

Not so close to Boethius in title, the prose *Synonyma de Lamentatione Peccatricis* of Isidore of Seville (c. 570-636) offers an undoubted parallel to the ***Consolatio***. This work presents a sort of dialogue between Homo, who bewails the age in desperate outbursts, and Ratio, who instructs and comforts him. The remedy for ills is to be found in the spiritual life and contemplation. About 1140 another Spaniard, Petrus of Compostella, wrote his *De Consolatione Rationis* in two books of alternating prose and verse in which the debt to Boethius is also obvious. Here Petrus sees the World in a vision as a maiden who lures him. Impelled by the Flesh and about to yield to World's charms, he beholds another gentle creature, Nature, who by showing him the wonders of created things leads him to perceive the indwelling spirit. Reason then appears leading the Seven Liberal Arts, berates the others, and gives Petrus an instructive discourse. Further complications follow which introduce material on divine prescience and human free will, and various religious and theological subjects. The point of the whole treatise is that God gave man reason to achieve understanding. The similarity of the allegory to Adelard's *De Eodem et Di-*

uerso is of course inescapable. Martianus Capella has contributed here as well as Boethius.

A more famous work, however, is the *Liber Consolationis et Consilii* in Latin prose of the thirteenth century by Albertano of Brescia. Anyone who has diligently read Chaucer's *Tale of Melibee* will remember the story of how Melibeus left his home one day, and on his return found his wife Prudence and his daughters beaten and wounded by three enemies. Husband and wife debate as to what should be done in such situation. In her counsel to her husband Prudence is as prudent as she should be, and learned as well. Perhaps it was her long-winded as well as edifying discourse in the face of present disaster that commended the "little treatise" to Chaucer's interest. Certainly the *cadre* of the story is unique. Yet in the idea of humiliation and the comfort supplied by the philosophical lady, one can see how the inspiration of Boethius was made practical, and a work of art translated in a sense from Boethius into entertaining mediocrity. A pleasant scene is that in which Prudence, according to Chaucer's version, "delibered and took avys in hirself" how she could solve their great difficulty. She proceeds to call in their adversaries and appeal to their better nature, touching on the benefits of peace and the harms of war. "And whan they herden the goodliche wordes of dame Prudence, they weren so supprised and ravysshed, and hadden so greet joye of hire that wonder was to telle. 'A, lady,' quod they, 'ye han shewed unto us the blessynge of swetnesse. . . . '" Thus may one achieve peace, domestic as well as foreign! This narrative Chaucer assigned to himself on the Canterbury pilgrimage, presumably for its sobering effect after the impudence of his *Tale of Sir Thopas*. He took it perhaps from the Latin of Albertano and certainly from a French translation sometimes attributed to Jean de Meun. A slightly different text of this French version was included in the treatise which the Ménagier of Paris wrote so delightfully for his young wife in 1392-1394 to prepare her for her second husband should she marry again.

Another work of consolation has been ascribed to the Spanish Pedro de Luna (c. 1328-1422), one time antipope Benedict XIII who was deposed by the Council of Constance. Something of the sort he may have written, as scribes and tradition testify. But the Latin text attributed to him is one of the compilations from Johannes of Dambach, with few differences from the original. Like the earlier treatise it has fifteen main divisions, in which most of the material is lifted bodily from Johannes with little rearrangement but without the allegorical framework. The scribe himself admits that the work may have been composed by someone in Pedro's behalf, and it is easy to imagine how people came to think that Pedro was responsible for such an anatomy of melancholies. His life was under great duress in the ecclesiastical upheaval of his day. His fame was widespread, however, and soon a Spanish translation of the book appeared. In this material, Boethius is not forgotten but often quoted as in the original, and in the Spanish preface is named as "el noble é costante baron."

In the same period Alain Chartier offered hope for the social situation in his uncompleted *Espérance ou Consolation des Trois Vertus* (published 1429), discussing in prose and verse the corruptions of the clergy and other ills, and offering the remedy of a more truly Christian life. Alain like many another blames Fortune for all that is wrong. Understanding (Entendement), who tells the author to have recourse to God, here performs the function assigned to Reason in some allegories; and Hope (Espérance) counsels Understanding to seek God's grace. Intellect, we infer, needs illumination. Social treatises of one sort or another are fairly common in the period, and often bear a slight resemblance to the ***Consolatio*** in the use of a figure like Reason or Sapience or Prudence vaguely parallel to Philosophia. Thus the *Songe de Pestilence* (1374-1377), written in prose and verse with a complicated allegory introducing Ratio, Sapience, Prudence, and various others, might be considered here. But the history of such figures in medieval literature is far from simple, and they cannot be derived from the personification in Boethius with any great likelihood.

Similarly the general motif of blaming Fortune for social or personal discomfort is enormously popular. Boethius showed the way in which it might be treated lyrically and even dramatically; he supplied numerous formulae for describing the goddess; he suggested proper remedies for vanquishing or annihilating her. It is hardly an exaggeration to say that in the ***Consolatio*** all the details of the conventional portrait of Fortune in medieval literature found a beginning. One cannot hope to stop her wheel; if the goddess cease to be fickle, she ceases to be Fortune; she puts one up, another down: ideas like these in great number were first expressed for the Middle Ages by Boethius, and then passed round in common currency. Thus we eventually get the rich collection of material, to take one example, in Machaut's *Remède de Fortune*. How significant it is that there Machaut says of the goddess:

> Mais Boëces si nous raconte
> Qu'on ne doit mie faire conte
> De ses anuis.

They never forgot who it was that so successfully gave Her Majesty away! Or we find debates between Fortune and some other personification—Virtue, Poverty, Love, and the like—for which the ***Consolatio*** really offers an initial impulse, like that of the (eleventh-century or earlier) *Altercatio Fortune et Philosophie,* a short but pithy affair in twenty-four distichs. Fortune claims the earth, but Philosophy offers heaven. Fortune rules things of the body; Philosophy, those of the soul. Fortune bestows the goods of life; Philosophy teaches how to discriminate between what is good and what is evil. And so on, almost an epitome of the discussion in Boethius! The Marquis of Santillana (in the early fifteenth century) presents a dialogue in Spanish verse in his *Bías contra Fortuna,* according to which Bías defends his poverty against Fortune and prefers the life of reason to her gifts. Fregoso's *Dialogo di Fortuna* (1521) sets forth in verse the power of the goddess and suggests a remedy in the instruction of Truth, incidentally touching on the problem of free will. But such matter is embodied in almost countless poems and treatises and longer or shorter works, in which Fortune causes tragedy or contends with Reason, Understanding, or some other figure. Personal troubles or social evil, the charge is the same. The theme is almost universal, and the lines of interrelationship among the documents that treat it are too involved for us to give a fair representation here of the way in which the tradition developed. Like Eustache Deschamps we know where it began:

> En Boece, de consolacion
> Trouverez-vous de Fortune l'assault,
> Ses blandices et sa decepcion. . . .

Against this tide of complaint rose the doctrine of moral responsibility in brief discussion or stern treatise or in the argument of the scholastics, which derives, at least in part, from the same astonishing source.

Among the books thus far described we have occasionally noticed one where the author was prompted to write because of his own sufferings in prison or exile. Pier della Vigna, who wrote the *Consolatio Nostri Exemplo,* was blinded and imprisoned, and eventually he committed suicide. He is the bleeding bush in Dante's *Inferno,* who tells how he formerly "held both keys" of the heart of Frederick II. Johannes of Dambach in his preface compares his own case with that of Boethius, telling us that he himself was "cast out from the place of his own home." Albertano of Brescia, we know, had been imprisoned in the conflict between the emperor and the pope, although it was several years afterward that he wrote his *Liber Consolationis.* Alberto della Piagentina, we recall, made his translation of Boethius when he was imprisoned at Venice. There are a number of other treatises which seem to have had similar beginnings. Alienated by the rapacious Berengar and his extremely disagreeable wife Willa, Liutprand of Cremona (d. 972) went into voluntary exile, and comforted himself by writing a history of his own times. The *Antapodosis* or "book of retribution," which he set down in prose and verse during 958-962, was composed partly to revenge himself on his enemies. It refers to Boethius, quotes him, and uses some of his metrical forms. The tone of Liutprand's work, however, entirely unlike that of the ***Consolatio,*** can hardly be described as free from envy, hatred, and malice. Its purpose is often to include the gossip of history. As the author himself declares:

> The aim and object of this work is to reveal, declare and stigmatize the doings of this Berengar, who now is not king but rather despot of Italy, and of his wife Willa, who because of her boundless tyranny is rightly called a second Jezebel, and because of her insatiate greed for plunder a Lamia vampire. Such shafts of falsehood, such extravagance of robbery, such efforts of wickedness have they gratuitously used against me and my household, my kinsmen and dependents, as neither tongue avails to express nor pen to record. Let this present page then be to them antapodosis, that is, repayment.

In a wholly different temper Hildebert of Lavardin (1056-1133) wrote his long poem *De Exsilio Suo* on the troubles of his harassed life. Tormented by problems of the clergy in the diocese of Le Mans, persecuted by William Rufus, and involved in strife with King Louis in the diocese of Tours, he was wearied but steadily urbane. He became a distinguished figure in the literary world as well as a most important Churchman. As a master of classical style he achieved a wide reputation, and his letters became familiar as models of their kind. Yet the world that he knew was filled with turmoil and with the disruption of human affairs that appears in his poem. Once, he tells us there, he was in good estate, and indeed thought it strange that all went so well:

> Mirabar sic te, sic te, Fortuna, fidelem:
> Mirabar stabilem, que leuis esse soles.

Then came the grievous reversal:

> Has ludit Fortuna uices, regesque superbos
> Aut seruos humiles non sinit esse diu.
> Illa dolosa comes, sola leuitate fidelis,
> Non inpune fauet aut sine fine premit.

Her countenance once bland was transformed. Now all is stormy and harsh. But the moral deduced nevertheless is that God actually rules everything:

> Ille simul semel et solus preuidit et egit
> Cuncta, nec ille aliter uidit agitque aliter.
>
> . . . . .
>
> Ipse manens, dum cuncta mouet, mortalibus egris
> Consulit atque ubi sit spes statuenda docet.

The allusion to the unmoved mover of the universe nicely gathers up a conspicuous theme of Aristotle and Boethius. M. Hauréau found in the work certain expressions alien to the spirit of the remoter antiquity. Perhaps diatribes against Fortune are not in general marked with what we think of as classical restraint, but Hildebert's poem has its own dignity none the less.

A more tempestuous outburst, written also in elegiacs, is the *Elegia de Diversitate Fortunae et Philosophiae Consolatione* by Henry of Settimello of the latter part of the twelfth century. The author, a priest, had been a man of some affluence in a worldly way, but now he has lost all his money and must go begging. He recalls the sufferings of others, including Boethius, and his plaint echoes the *Lamentations* of Jeremiah, which he must often have heard in the liturgy of Holy Week:

> Quomodo sola sedet probitas! flet, ingemit, aleph,
> facta uelut uidua que prius uxor erat.
> Cui de te, fortuna, querar? cui? nescio. . . .

The ironic turns here mark his bitterness. Whither, he asks, shall he fly? He cannot stand, and on his couch he suffers. Thus Fortune revolves men about on her wheel. In the second book a closer similarity to the ***Consolatio*** begins to be apparent. The author calls on Fortuna, who replies in self-defense. He attacks her in turn; and while the manner of the dialogue becomes less like that of Boethius as they exchange abuse, Fortune's account of herself is much in the vein of her imagined words in the older treatise. In the third book appears Philosophy, whose stature varies in the familiar way, and who is accompanied by the Seven Arts, a motif we have already found in Adelard's *De Eodem et Diuerso,* in the allegory of Petrus of Compostella, and in Simund de Freine's *Roman.* Philosophy rebukes the author for his blindness, and reminds him that Fortune only follows her accustomed method:

> Nonne meus Seuerinus inani iure peremptus
> carcere Papie non patienda tulit?
>
> Quid referam multos, quorum sine crimine uita
> uerbera Fortune non patienda tulit.

The examples of great men all remind us that Fortune brings tragedy in her train. Philosophy scolds the author roundly; in contrast one appreciates the measured restraint of her speeches in the ***Consolatio***. But, asks Henry, will things improve in this world: virtue goes into exile and vice triumphs; what chance is there of hope for better things? In the fourth book Philosophy offers her remedies. Strength of character is the cure for ill fortune; stand firm and be of good cheer; let Fortune go on as she likes; seek virtue, flee from vice, and trust in the goodness of God. With such counsel Philosophy bids farewell to the author, and he in turn ends the poem, taking gracious leave of the Bishop of Florence to whom it is dedicated. The work became popular; it was quoted, and furnished with a commentary. It had due influence on Peter of Eboli, who in about the same period wrote an elegiac poem on the campaigns of Henry VI and incidentally the maleficence of Fortune and the hope offered by Sapientia.

In 1276 Pierre de la Broche, a barber of Louis IX (better known as St. Louis) and a favourite of his son, was hanged for calumny of the queen, Marie of Brabant. In poetry at least his sufferings were attributed, one may say inevitably, to the caprice of Fortune. One lyric refers to him thus:

> J'oi l'autr'ier d'un homme moult forment reprochier
> Qu'il seut des esperons les granz chevaus brochier.
> Quant le senti Fortune de l'un des piez clochier,
> Si le fist trébuchier de plus haut c'un clochier.

> "The other day I heard of a man much reproached because he knew how to stick great steeds with his spurs. When Fortune caught him limping with one foot, she made him fall from higher than a clock-tower."

How perfectly the man was suited for a theme of this sort! If ever the sharp contrasts of the Middle Ages offered the right opportunity it was here in the case of this commoner and barber, raised to the position of minister to a king, and alas! plunged again into misery through the malice of Fortune! In this vein, if we may judge by the fragment left to us, was composed a dialogue conducted by Pierre with Reason and Fortune. There is no great originality in the piece except in the application of the theme to the present tragedy. Fortune, according to Pierre, has sold him riches and dignity only too dearly. Now all is turned to his harm. Reason announces that Fortune herself is at hand to speak in her own defense. The fickle goddess has her say, reminding Pierre of the condition from which she raised him and rebuking him for pride. It is his disloyalty to his earthly lord, she avers, that has brought him so low. In the exchange of speeches she accuses him of defaming the Queen; iniquity, she points out, has brought its own reward. Reason then pronounces sentence:

> Pierres, bien as Fortune oïe,
> Qui se desfent moult sagement. . . .

He has indeed heard Fortune, who defends herself wisely, and for his treachery he is doomed to receive suffering:

> Qui mal fet, ce dist l'Escripture,
> Mal trovera: c'est ma créance.

Seldom, in allegory at least, does Fortune come off so triumphantly with the support of Reason. All this follows no doubt the tradition of Boethius but only in a general way.

A similar motif runs through the Anglo-Norman poem of the early fourteenth century written by Edward II, or by a strong sympathizer, to lament his imprisonment. This begins as follows:

> En tenps de iver me survynt damage,
> Fortune trop m'ad traversé:
> Eure m' est faili tut mon age.
> Bien sovent l[e]ay esprové:
> En mond n'ad si bel ne si sage,
> [Ne] si curtois ne si preysé,
> Si eur(e) ne lui court de avantage,
> Que il ne serra pur fol clamé.

> "In the winter injury came upon me. Fortune too much has thwarted me. Luck has failed me all my life. Full often have I found it so: in the world is none so fair nor so wise, nor so courteous nor so highly prized, that, if luck does not run to his advantage, he will not be acclaimed as a fool."

Strikingly similar to this poem again, at least in some respects, is the fourteenth-century Middle English *Somer Soneday,* which also lays the blame on Fortune for a king's downfall. In the same connection one is inevitably reminded of Petrarch's consolation delivered orally to King John of France on the occasion of that monarch's liberation from an English prison in 1360. It was to be expected that Petrarch should attribute the misadventure to Fortune's caprice, but his suggestion was taken seriously and later he had to give account of himself for his use of such a pagan figure. One recalls as well his long treatise *De*

Remediis Utriusque Fortunae, which with the use of dialogue offers antidotes for the effects of good fortune as well as for those of bad. Here Ratio debates with Gaudium and Spes, on the one hand, and with Dolour and Metus, on the other. Hope of long life, beauty of body, intelligence, eloquence, virtue, sweet odours and songs are discussed, as well as imprisonment, losses, and other forms of distress. The book, which derives from Seneca as well as from Boethius, bears some slight resemblance to the *Consolatio* of Johannes of Dambach. It was widely known and ran through some twenty editions.

Many accounts of the rise and fall of kings on Fortune's wheel found favor in the Middle Ages, showing some trace of influence from Boethius. Even Boccaccio's *De Casibus Virorum Illustrium* should be mentioned, a compendious work in which we learn of a whole succession of royal tragedies as well as others. Here the story of Boethius himself appears, just before that of King Arthur. By this extraordinary production Chaucer was partly guided in his *Monk's Tale;* but in this instance the Knight, and perhaps Chaucer's own patience, cut the story short. Boccaccio's entire work, however, was translated into French by Laurent de Premierfait; and this version served as the basis of Lydgate's *Fall of Princes,* a monument of edification and re-edited of late as three solid volumes chiefly important to the antiquarian. It is an interesting feature that here Boethius is celebrated mostly as a social hero, although his writings and sanctity are recalled:

For comou*n* proffit he was onto the tou*n*
In mateeres that grou*n*did wer on riht
Verray protecto*ur* and stedfast champiou*n*
Agey*n* too tirau*n*tis, which of force & myht
Hadde in the poraille [the poverty-stricken]
  oppressid many a wiht
Be exacciou*n*s and pillages gun*n*e of newe
Vpon the comou*n*s, ful fals & riht v*n*trewe.

Guillaume de Machaut's *Confort d'Ami* was written in 4004 lines of octosyllabic couplets to console the King of Navarre, who had been imprisoned in 1356 by John of France. What the King has lost, says Machaut, were only the gifts of Fortune. Search the "livre de Boesse" to find out about that kind of thing!

So the catalogue may go on, with as little hope of finishing as Chaucer's *Monk's Tale,* full of sound and fury and occasionally poetry as well. When James I of Scots languished in an English prison, he took a book to read upon and pass the time away, and we may guess what it was:

. . . the name is clepit prop*er*ly
  Boece, efte*re* him þ*at* was the compiloure,
Schewing [gude] counsele of philosophye,
  Compilit by that noble senatoure
  Off Rome, quhilom þat was the warldis floure. . . .

who "Foriugit was to pou*er*t in exile." In his very sufferings Boethius found security:

And so the vertew of his youth before
  Was in his age the ground of his delytis:
Fortune the bak him *tur*nyt, and therefore
  He makith ioye and confort, þ*at* he quit is
  Off thei*re* vnsekir warldis appetitis;
And so aworth he takith his penance,
And of his vertew maid it suffisance:

With mony a noble resou*n,* as him likit,
  Enditing in his fäi*re* Latyne tong,
So full of fruyte, and rethor[ik]ly pykit,
  Quhich to declare my sc[e]le is ouer yonge. . . .

This is fine praise for a man dead, lo, these many years! In a remarkable poem, *The Kingis Quair,* from which these lines are quoted, the King tells of his own miseries, for which he spends much time blaming Fortune, just as Charles d'Orléans poetically inveighed against the same lady during his term of imprisonment in England. King James has a vision in which he sees the wheel on which the Goddess turns lovers, bringing them to good estate or to woe. It is a slippery affair, and many failed footing thereon, while some were whirled to an ugly pit beneath. Something of a debate on free will is introduced in a discourse conducted by Dame Minerva, who is not unlike Philosophy. This truly fine work inspired the *King's Tragedy* of Dante Gabriel Rossetti. It is also possible that *The Kingis Quair* was itself partly inspired by such a poem as Baudouin de Condé's *Li Prisons d'Amours.* The idea of a prison of love, however, in which Fortune constrains her victims, has doubtless at most a tenuous connexion with the story of Boethius. It would be interesting but impossible at the present time to follow the motif in its various literary forms—for example in Froissart's *Prison Amoureuse,* where, as with Machaut's *Voir Dit,* the narrative is in verse and the epistles in prose; but in most cases resemblance to the ***Consolatio*** is pretty remote.

Despite the claim of James I to have read the Latin original, we may suspect that the "Boece" which he pondered over in prison was Chaucer's translation. Certainly that was the book which was consulted by Thomas Usk, who, perhaps for shiftiness in politics and for siding with the young Richard II as against the Duke of Glouscester, tasted a prison term and was finally put to death for treason. He wrote his *Testament of Love* in self-defense, a book long assigned to Chaucer but identified as Usk's by the acrostic in the initial letters of the chapters. Brembre, who was executed for the same crime, was a friend of Chaucer's. In the *Testament* there are borrowings from the poet's works and a direct reference to his *Troilus and Criseyde.* The work is in many ways a strange production, somewhat cluttered and heavy. It is a "testament" in the sense of a confession of faith. The author represents himself in prison, bewailing his chance and lamenting the loss of his pearl, Margaryte, who symbolizes among other things divine grace and Holy Church. Once, we infer, he was suspected of Lollardry, but now he wishes to make his orthodoxy plain to every reader. Into his foul dungeon comes a lady, the seemliest and most goodly to his sight that ever appeared. She is divine Love, who like Philosophia, loves wisdom and sets Thomas right concerning his present distress and many incidental questions, including that of fate and free will. Thus "In this boke be many privy thinges wimpled and folde; unneth shul leude [ignorant] men the plites [folds] unwinde." Esoteric the book is indeed, or at least sometimes difficult to follow; Usk treats everything in full. Incidentally his search for his precious pearl seems once or twice reminiscent of the Middle English poem the *Pearl,* and throws a curious light on its interpretation.

Very different in the annals of prison literature, and altogether French in temper and framework, is *Les Fortunes et Adversitez de Jean Regnier,* which by its colophon is also entitled a *Livre de la Prison*. Jean Regnier, whose name appears in acrostic, was imprisoned 1432-1433, and in another work, a "Balade morale que le prisonnier fit," he gloomily uses the *Ubi sunt* formula to ask: "Ou est Boece et Chaton et Thobie?" *Les Fortunes et Adversitez* is a long complaint with lays interspersed, blaming Fortune and calling on God and the Virgin Mary for aid. Espérance sends Jean news that help will eventually come to him. He laments the evils that he beholds destined for France. Several ladies, for whom he makes lays, pay him a visit. Desconfort, leading in Despoir, comes to see him; but at last he is cheered by the sight of Réconfort, who is accompanied by Espoir, and who tells him the story of Job and also that of the penitent thief. Various balades are inserted for the great feast days, and serve an ornamental purpose. Jean takes long leave of the world:

> A Beauvais, droit devant sainct Pierre,
> Ou je suis enfermé en pierre. . . .

Did he see the magnificent wheel of Fortune on the wall of the parish Church of St. Étienne not far away?

But all this seems petty in its elegance. Fortune has a broader canvas than this to work on. The great Jean Gerson (1363-1429), Chancellor of the University of Paris, philosopher, champion of woman in the controversy started by Christine de Pisan, and notable Churchman who took a conspicuous part in the Council of Constance, suffered exile from France at the hands of the Duke of Burgundy. Ruthlessly Gerson had pursued with indictments certain followers of Burgundy because they were implicated in the murder of the Duke of Orléans. He carried the vigour of his onslaught even into the Council of Constance, where presumably he hoped that godly men would stand him in good stead; but the Council failed to lend him much support. In this humiliation he wrote a direct imitation of Boethius, his *De Consolatione Theologiae* in four books of prose and verse treating of the slings and arrows of outrageous Fortune. In a dialogue conducted between Volucer and Monicus we find discussion of the problem of God's will and human free will, the power of chance, and the hope to be discovered in goodness and God. Volucer in a general way represents the active life, and Monicus the contemplative. But why, asks Monicus, in obtaining consolation against the power of chance, against the empty felicity of the world would not that dialogue of Philosophy and Boethius suffice "which is composed in a style altogether elegant, brief and distinguished, containing most weighty doctrines." Volucer explains, however, that Theology is superior to Philosophy, as grace is to nature, or the mistress to her handmaid, the master to his disciple, eternity to time, intelligence to ratiocination, and the things which are not seen to those which are. The verse uses the metrical forms of Boethius, and the temper of the work is not unworthy of its spiritual ancestor.

One wonders, however, whether the ghost of Boethius was present at the Council of Constance. We remember the case of Pedro de Luna, competing for the highest position of all and completely frustrated therein, deriving his consolation at second hand through Johannes of Dambach. There were others, notably Theodorich Vrie and Jacobus de Teramo, who dealt with the corruptions of the Church in works touched by the influence of the original ***Consolatio***. In an *Historia Concilii Constantiensis* in eight books of prose and verse Theodorich Vrie presents a dialogue of Christ and his bride Ecclesia showing the evil inheritance the Church received from Cain, and incidentally referring to the grievous story of Pedro de Luna. Another name for the work is *De Consolatione Ecclesiae*. In his *Consolatio Peccatorum* or *Processus Beliali* Jacobus de Teramo gives us the burlesque account of the lawsuit in which Belial prosecuted Christ as an interloper in His harrowing of Hell. Here there is little reflection of Boethius except in the name. Incidentally, Gerson finally achieved the personal title of Doctor Consolatorius, which may have comforted him.

About a hundred years later an Englishman no less famous and of a quality not unlike Gerson's was writing a similar treatise in the Tower of London. In 1534 Sir Thomas More "made" his *Dyalogue of Comforte agaynste Tribulacyon* after he was imprisoned for refusing to compromise his religion to the advantage if not the respectability of Henry VIII. It was written for his children and his friends, and the martyr's courage appears in the playful tone with which some of it is conceived. It purports to be a translation through French from a Latin treatise composed by a Hungarian. In general character it bears more resemblance to Gerson's work than to that of Boethius, and indeed it quotes from another book of the great Frenchman. In three parts it offers the prose dialogue of Anthony and Vincent on the evils suffered in their poor country from the harsh and brutal Turk, who at times obviously carries suggestions of Henry of England and his policies. The suggestions, however, are not quite explicit. Thus with reference to religious difficulties More observes:

> . . . but if we tourne as they dooe, and forsake our Sauiour too, and then (for there is no borne Turke so cruell to christen folke, as is *the* false christen that falleth from the fayth) we shall stand in peril (if we perseuer in *the* trueth) to be more hardelye handeled, and dye more cruell death by our own countrey men at home, then if we wer taken he*n*ce and caried into Turkye.

The remedy for all ills, according to More, is to be found in religion. The philosophers of old are not quite adequate to help us; for they failed to refer "the finall ende of theyr coumforte vnto God." The charges against the Turk are unsparingly bitter, and one sees that the writer contemplates martyrdom serenely for the ancient faith in England. Four centuries after his death he has been canonized as a saint. It is a truly noble book, recently described by an authority on More as "one of his greatest works." It too is a worthy child of the tradition to which it belongs, in its dignity and also in its special type of humour not unlike the original ***Consolatio***. Very different is the temper of the *Spiritual Consolation,* written by Bishop John Fisher (also in the Tower) for his sister Elizabeth. Fisher was canonized with More. Although he knew Boethius, his work is only a brief and lugubrious complaint or plea for repentance.

At this point it may be interesting to recall a much earlier work by More, the *Wordes of ffortune to ye people: the Boke of the fayre Gentyl woman, that no man shulde put his truste or confydence in.* In this poetical collection, in stanzas of rime royal, the discourse of Fortune gives a conventional picture of her character and methods, omitting few if any of the motifs known to the tradition of her literature. But it is vividly managed for all that. The remedy for injuries received from the goddess is a familiar one: love virtue, it alone is free. Another document in much the same sort is the anonymous *Complaint against Fortune* in the Shirley manuscript, also in stanzas of rime royal, a little recalling the verses of Henry of Settimello though not deliberately reminiscent. Whoever wrote it holds converse with Fortune in the usual style:

> Fortune alas. alas what haue I gylt
> In prison thus to lye here desolate
> Art thou the better to haue [me] thus yspylt.
> Nay nay god wote. . . .

Rather uniquely Fortune here admits that the author is really guiltless of the crime that brought him to prison; but she insists unanswerably that he is punished thus for his other sins. The humble author offers a prayer to God to protect the Church and to make people virtuous.

We cannot follow in detail the manner in which Boethius was received at the Renaissance. In Italy the great Rienzi named a son after him. A century later Politian asks: "Who is keener in dialectic than Boethius, or subtler in mathematics, or more satisfying in philosophy, or more sublime in theology?" Girolamo Cardano (1501-1576), famous for mathematics and astrology, wrote a work in three books of prose *De Consolatione* urging that the true remedy for ills is found in the interior life: in the use of the mind and in the love of virtue. This was translated into English by Thomas Bedingfield, better known for his rendering of Machiavelli's Florentine History. Another English version of Cardano appeared about a century later. Like Sir Thomas More confined to the Tower, John Leslie (1527-1596), Bishop of Ross, composed a work called *Piae afflicti Animi Consolationes, divinaque Remedia,* which was later translated into French with another book of his, *Animi tranquilli Munimentum et Conservatio.* Bishop Leslie's crime was complicity in the attempt to restore Mary Queen of Scots to the throne of England, and he dedicated the work in its original form to her. It was he, in fact, who arranged to have the papal bull which deposed Elizabeth nailed to the door of the Bishop of London. Our afflictions, he holds, come from God and not from Fortune. The consolation which he offers is Christian doctrine, with the advice to be ever instant in prayer, and to fix one's desires on the eternal life. Thus, for different reasons, Bishop Leslie and Queen Elizabeth both seem to have derived some help from Boethius. The Belgian Justus Lipsius wrote his *De Constantia* (published 1583-1584), a treatise which belongs in the list of books which offer remedies for grief. Lipsius had suffered the loss of his property through pillage in the civil war in his country. The theme of his work, in two books, is that public as well as private ills derive from fate. Necessity, which comes ultimately from God, rules everything and permits no escape: "Necessitatis non aliud effugium est, quam uelle quod ipsa cogat"—the Renaissance method of saying "In His will is our peace." One must bow, accordingly, to what is inevitable. These ills are external. Charmingly cultivate your garden and seek wisdom. Thus did the stoic retreat within himself, while More had discussed the sins of fear and advised contemplation of the joys of heaven. Yet one may urge that something of both types of remedy is prompted by the original argument of Boethius.

So we might continue our study of the tradition, and Dr. Houghton in his unpublished dissertation has followed it in part in the seventeenth century. Prisoners in that period apparently consoled themselves in a similar way. The father of that Sir Harry Coningsby who translated the ***Consolatio*** was confined in the Tower and then in Peter House. Doubtless it was for this reason that the son was led to his task; in his preface he tells of his father's sufferings. So too Sir Richard Graham, Lord Preston, another illustrious translator, was sentenced to death for high treason, and spent due time in the Tower and in Newgate. Edward Barlow, priest and prisoner, entertained himself in jail by reading the ***Consolatio***. Some eleven hundred years, therefore, after the time of Boethius a natural impulse still led men in disaster or suffering to see a parallel to their own fortune in the story of the ***Consolatio,*** and to draw refreshment for their souls from its philosophy. This point is the more interesting when we recall the fact that Aristotelianism was on the wane at the time. Boethius must have held his own as a Platonist or as a moralist, or just for the good sense of his discussion.

Down through the centuries, then, a multitude of readers tried to render the ***Consolatio*** accessible to others in some form or other, perhaps in the attempt to utilize its effective scheme of presentation or again with the wish to preach its healing doctrine. Impressively in fact as well as in name it was a source of consolation. Boethius clearly stood for much more than an intellectual figure. Among men there are those who going through the vale of misery use it for a well, and the pools are filled with water.

Eleanor Shipley Duckett (essay date 1938)

SOURCE: "Philosophy in the Sixth Century," in *The Gateway to The Middle Ages,* The Macmillan Company,

1938, pp. 142-212.

[In the excerpt below, Duckett provides a general overview of Boethius's life and influence, asserting that "it was he who fanned the flame of conflict that was to occupy philosophical minds through all the Middle Ages - the struggle between Nominalism and Realism in their various forms."]

[Boethius's] ***Consolation of Philosophy*** has been the meat of souls in distress, of minds in doubt, of editors, commentators and students in mediaeval browsings, all down the years from the sixth century to modern times. It was every whit as popular in the Middle Ages as Martianus Capella's famous text-book on the Seven Liberal Arts, and reaped a far more varied harvest of readers; it is still studied in our times, largely because of its influence upon Chaucer. But it loses some of its interest if it be not seen first in the picture of its own century.

For the name of Boethius has been the centre of many problems, as many as the varied sides of his extraordinary genius. He was skilled in mathematics and in logic, he was a musician and a poet; he was, above all, learned in the philosophy of Greece and Rome. So far all is serene. From this point scholars have started in the examination-paper they have set themselves to answer. Was Boethius a pagan? Or a nominal Christian? Or a convinced champion of the Catholic Church? Was he a martyr to his religious or to his political creed? Or did he fall justly in punishment for treason against his King? Did he write the ***Theological Tractates*** which have been ascribed to him? Above all, did he compose that confession of the Catholic Faith known as ***Tractate Four***?

Theodoric's mausoleum in Ravenna (c. 526).

He was of aristocratic birth and tradition, of the great line of the Anicii, as his name tells. In 487, when he was about seven years old, his father held the consulship, but died not long after, and the boy, as he himself relates, was brought up and educated by the leading men of Rome. Very probably his guardian was Quintus Aurelius Memmius Symmachus, destined to be his chief friend and his father-in-law, whom he describes as "the richest glory of the human race." Symmachus had himself been consul in 485, and it was his daughter Rusticiana whom Boethius married. A worthy lady, it would seem. Boethius calls her "modest, singularly chaste and pure—in a word, the image of her father." Long afterwards she reappears in the pages of Procopius at that crisis in the Gothic War when the Romans were suffering agonies through Totila's siege of their city in 546. This was twenty years after her husband's death, and Rusticiana was living in Rome. She had spent all her resources in helping the worst cases of misery, and now with other Roman citizens and even senators was driven by sheer starvation to beg for a little bread and other necessities from the barbarian enemy. Dressed as servants or country folk they would knock at door after door of the Gothic visitors after these had entered the city in triumph, so pressed by hunger that they could feel no shame. But the Goths one day seized her and carried her before Totila, with the charge that she had bribed the Roman generals to allow her to overthrow the statues of Theodoric in revenge for the fate of her father Symmachus and her husband Boethius. Let her be put to death, they urged. It is to the credit of Totila that he did not permit his soldiers in the first flush of conquest to hurt her or any other Roman woman.

From his childhood Boethius was devoted to learning, and as he grew older was looked on as one of the rising men by intellectual and political circles in Rome and in Ravenna. Ennodius, in his *Instruction on liberal culture,* written about 511 for two young friends, Ambrosius and Beatus, speaks of him as a master and model for these disciples: "so young and yet he knows enough to teach."

More significant were three letters written to Boethius by Cassiodorus in the name of King Theodoric. Two are dated by Mommsen in 507 and show not only the high place Boethius had earned at the age of twenty-seven in the confidence of the King but also his achievements in intellectual work at this time. In one of them Theodoric asks him to send a water-clock to Gundobad, King of Burgundy, who has earnestly requested this favour. Cassiodorus writes thus for his royal master: "I know that you understand the inner workings of the arts which men commonly practice in ignorance, for your mind is packed full of learning. From afar you have entered the schools of Athens, you have united in your learning the toga and the pallium, you have turned into Roman doctrine the dogmas of the Greeks. Now, thanks to your translations, Pythagoras the musician and Ptolemaeus the astronomer are read in Latin; the arithmetic of Nicomachus and the geometry of Euclid are heard just as if their writers were Italians. Now Plato discusses theology and Aristotle treats of logic in the language of the Quirinal; you have even restored to the Sicilians their mechanician Archimedes in a Latin form. And more. It is you, Boethius, who have entered into the famous art of noble disciplines through the fourfold doors of learning."

The second letter asks Boethius to choose out a player on the harp, requested from Theodoric by Clovis, King of the Franks. Only Boethius could fulfil this office, writes the King, because he is skilled in music. The third, written at some time between 507 and 511, asks him to attend to a complaint from the infantry and cavalry of the Royal Household, who have been defrauded of part of their pay by receiving coins of illegal weight: "Let your sagacity, trained by your learned researches in philosophy, drive out this accursed falsehood from its partnership with truth." This request shows, it seems, that Boethius held at the time superintendence over the domestic payroll in virtue of the office of Count of the Sacred Largesses.

Lastly, Cassiodorus gives us another glimpse of Boethius in the fragment we still possess of his *Family History of the Cassiodori,* the little collection of short notices describing members of his own clan and some "learned citizens" who had distinguished themselves by their writings. Here we read that Boethius "held the highest offices, and was an orator deeply versed in both Greek and Latin"; that "in translating works of logic and in mathematical studies he was so distinguished that he equalled or surpassed the writers of antiquity."

In 510 Boethius held the consulship alone, and twelve years later, in 522, he had the supreme joy of seeing his two sons installed as consuls on the same day. There was a grand procession of Senators escorting the two young men from their home to the Senate House amid the shouting of the people who lined the streets. In the Senate House they sat in the famous chairs of their office while Boethius himself made an oration of praise and thanksgiving to Theodoric and earned great applause for his eloquence. Afterward in the Circus the crowd of citizens thronged around him as he stood between his two Consuls, repaying eager cheers of the public to the full by his splendid gifts of bounty. In the same year the King promoted him to be Master of Offices and his cup of political prosperity seemed full.

But even patriotic and public life was not so dear as the meditations of his study. In one of his works he tells his readers of his aim in writing: "If God grant it me of His power and grace, my fixed purpose is this: The whole of Aristotle's writings, so far as they shall be accessible to me, I will translate into Latin and interpret by a commentary in Latin. All the subtlety of the logical skill of Aristotle, all the weight of his moral philosophy, all the keenness of his physical science as contained in his writings, I will arrange in due order, will translate and illuminate in some sort by observations. Furthermore, I will translate and comment on all the dialogues of Plato. And after finishing this I would not disdain, indeed, to bring the philosophy of Aristotle and Plato into some kind of harmony, to show that most people are wrong in maintaining that the two disagree at all points; that, rather, in most matters, and these the most important, they are in agreement with each other. These tasks, if sufficiency of years and leisure be given me, I would accomplish with great advantage and also with much labour."

Of the work on Plato we possess nothing, and we may believe that the untimely death of Boethius entirely frustrated this part of the great plan. In the labours on Aristotle the work at least reached and included the writings on logic, in which Boethius was pre-eminently interested.

But first there must be preparation. He would approach his life-work through the "fourfold gates of learning." The sixth century was an age of compendious science, when students craved rather a view of universal learning, carefully and conveniently digested by some scholar, than the browsing for their own sake on the great works of antiquity. Were not these written by pagans? And, therefore, how could such avail for pilgrims following the star of Christianity through the dark desert of this present life? The development of the Christian life, whether in the world or, in its most prized degree, within the hermitage or the cloister, had driven from men's esteem the lingering joy of prose and poetry written by those who knew not the Catholic Church. Far better, surely, to absorb in comprehensive form and far swifter manner the cold substance of these heathen works, in order that the knowledge thus gained might be used for the glory of the Faith, not for the intellectual delight of the human mind.

Moreover, pagan ideals and Christian virtues were diametrically opposed. The old Latin tradition of independence, self-respect, and a sane enjoyment of this world's bounty could not be reconciled with a training in self-abnegation, in ascetic renunciation of temporal things for the fruits of eternity.

Already in the days before Christ the condensing of science in encyclopaedic form had been begun. In the welter and hurry of political life the rising statesmen of Caesar's Rome, who were also her students, had gladly turned to Varro's *Nine Books of Disciplines,* dealing with the seven liberal arts as we know them and in addition with medicine and architecture. The two last were omitted in the far more famous handbook of Martianus Capella, written in the fifth century under form of an allegory to describe the "Nuptials of Mercury and the Lady Philology." Here the seven liberal arts attend the bride as maids of honour, and each in turn expounds the principles of her department of learning. Neither was this book of Christian character, though perforce it was eagerly read by Christian schools for the training of scholars who were to argue with skill and reason for the faith within them.

Boethius, then, was in sympathy with his age when he

desired to educate young men in the liberal arts. We shall see later on that his friend Cassiodorus pursued the same ideal in the labours for education which filled his advanced years. But it was on the four arts which afterwards formed the higher division of culture among Renaissance scholars that Boethius chose first to write. The study of these would presuppose some acquaintance with the other three: the art of grammar, including literature, the art of dialectic, mainly concerned with logic, and the art of rhetoric, embracing composition both written and oral. To the influence of Boethius was due in great part the establishing in later days of the four arts of the higher course as an integral and fixed part of liberal education. It was to him, indeed, that we owe the famous name of this fourfold training: in arithmetic, music, geometry, and astronomy. "Among all the scholars in ancient days," he boldly declared, "who were renowned for reasonings of pure intellect as disciples of Pythagoras, it is certain that no one reached the height of perfection in the schools of philosophy except he had sought such noble prudence by what I may call a fourfold path (*quodam quasi quadruvio*). . . . By this fourfold path the student must travel whose mind, already endowed with promise, rises from the natural senses to the surer certainties of intelligence." The name "Quadrivium" thus runs back to Boethius.

He began his work naturally with a treatise on arithmetic, "the first-fruits of my labour," he himself tells us. It was dedicated to Symmachus, to whose fatherly criticism he earnestly commended his toil. There is little trace of originality in any part of the work on the "Quadrivium," and in this first section the source was the Greek mathematician, Nicomachus of Gerasa (probably the city in the Decapolis of Palestine). Some time between 50 and 150 A.D. Nicomachus had won lasting fame by his *Introduction to Arithmetic,* and he was the obvious model for one who, like Boethius, was no master in the field. So closely did Boethius follow his lead that scholars have not hesitated to call this Latin treatise a translation. And worse still, severe criticism has been dealt him for marring his rendering by the repeated omission of valuable portions of the original. He declared in the Preface that he was not "binding himself by the most narrow law of translation but was roaming freely in the path, not in the actual footprints" of his source, intending to condense parts of his material and in other parts to make small additions. This plan he carried out, though it is agreed that the additions were of little, if any, value to later generations; and his work only interests us here because through it many of his own countrymen, and the vast majority of students of mathematics in the Middle Ages, learned Greek principles of arithmetic.

The same is true with regard to music, on which Boethius wrote a treatise, ***De Institutione Musica,*** in five books, the last of which lacks eleven chapters in its present state. Music, he begins, holds its special power, not only over the intellect, but over the character and behaviour of men of every age of life and of every class and race. That, therefore, which is of such universal importance, for which humanity possesses a natural affection, must not only be enjoyed from without, but must be learned and understood in its inner rhythms and harmonies. It must be learned, moreover, as a philosophical and mathematical science. Of the three classes into which Boethius divided students of music: those who play upon instruments, those who compose tuneful melodies, and those who understand the theory and harmony of this subject, only the third class, according to him, really deserves the name of musician. Those who play musical instruments are but the servants of scholars of musical science in his view, and composers of tunes are led, not by speculation and reasoning, but by some natural instinct.

It was this stress upon music, as training in mathematics rather than as a practical art, which Boethius bequeathed to the Middle Ages. Martianus Capella had handed on the teaching of Aristides Quintilianus; Boethius summarized as best he could the wisdom in matters musical of Pythagoras, Claudius Ptolemaeus, Aristoxenus, and Nicomachus, whom he had used for his arithmetic. At times, it is true, he misunderstood his authorities, and so theoretical was his treatment that he tarried in his discussion to deal with matter long obsolete in actual practice. But this legacy of his was meat and drink to humanity long after his death, prescribed by statutes of Europe's Universities as part of their fixed course of higher learning.

The next treatise of Boethius in logical order, that on geometry, has enjoyed its own dispute. Scholarship has been divided as to whether two books on geometry which we still possess under the name of Boethius are really by him. The consensus of opinion now holds them spurious. That Boethius did translate Euclid into Latin we know from Cassiodorus, and, indeed, Greek scholarship was naturally his model; Roman experts were not interested in the theory of geometrical mathematics and only used the science for practical purposes of surveying land. The question of the authenticity of the extant work in two books is of interest in connection with that noted mathematician of the tenth century, Gerbert, afterward Pope Sylvester the second. For this work, whether genuine or spurious, contains information regarding the nine Hindu numerals. If it was Boethius who told of these, they must have been known to the western world in the sixth century, perhaps before. If Boethius did not write the books, it would seem that these numerals were not known to the Christian world, at least outside trading circles, before the time of Gerbert, who was well acquainted with them. Gerbert tells, in a letter written by him as Abbot of the monastery of Bobbio in 983 A.D., that he has found "eight volumes of Boethius on astrology, and also some splendid books on geometry." If these were the work of Boethius, as has been thought, Gerbert could have obtained his knowledge of the matters mentioned above from him, as this knowledge is found in no other European authority before the end of the tenth century. But that Boethius was not the author is the more likely theory.

No eight books of Boethius on "astrology," or, as we should call it, "astronomy," are extant, though from the importance which he attributes to the study of all four divisions of his "Quadrivium" it is highly probable that he did complete his introduction to philosophy by a treatise on this subject. We have seen, also, that Cassiodorus writes of a translation of Ptolemaeus the astronomer, made by Boethius from Greek into Latin.

We have now passed through the fourfold outer courts of mathematical science and can look at the more direct interests of Boethius in philosophy. Now, when he begins his labours in earnest, it is logic, above all, that attracts him. And, therefore, in accordance with his aim, he turns to the *Organon* of Aristotle. Here, again, problems have engaged students of his writings. Did he translate all or only the greater part of the *Organon*? And what knowledge did the Middle Ages have of his work?

For the benefit of those to whom the name of Aristotle is more familiar than his works, we may note that *Organon,* meaning "instrument" of scientific knowledge and argument, was the title given long after Aristotle's time to the collection of the following writings by him: *Categories; On Interpretation; Topics; Sophistici Elenchi; Prior* and *Posterior Analytics*.

From his own words we learn that Boethius was occupied with the *Categories* of Aristotle in the year of his consulship, 510. For he writes at the beginning of the second book of his Latin rendering of this work: "And if the burdens of consular office hinder me from devoting all my leisure and all my labour to these studies, yet to instruct citizens in this doctrine does seem to be part of a magistrate's care for the State. Nor should I deserve ill of my fellow-countrymen if, seeing that the vigour of early times transferred to this One City of ours the rule and governing of other states, I should at least do my part in informing the manners and morals of our City by the methods of Greek philosophy." Translation alternated with comment in the four books which Boethius gave to this task.

The *De Interpretatione* of Aristotle was translated and expounded by Boethius in two commentaries: the first, comparatively brief and simple, in two books; the second, intended for those who wished to go more deeply into the subject, in six books. The chief sources on which he drew in this second commentary were the Aristotelian scholars Porphyry, whom he calls elsewhere a "man of the highest authority," and Syrianus. He tells us, moreover, in the midst of the second work that he is making an abridged edition of it. If he ever did, it is now lost to the world. This second commentary is regarded through its learning and intellectual power as the high-water mark of the labours of Boethius on logic.

The influence of Porphyry lies also on another work of Boethius, which, again, took two forms. The first was a commentary on a translation which the rhetorician C. Marius Victorinus had made of Porphyry's *Introduction* (*Isagoge*) to the *Categories* of Aristotle. We are given to suppose in the beginning of this commentary that it is winter-time, and that Boethius and a student friend of his are enjoying a vacation in the "mountains of Aurelia." As the north wind howls outside the house they settle down comfortably before the fire to entertain themselves by trying to unravel the knotty tangles of dialectics. "Now we have made all our Christmas calls and done our duty to our families," young Fabius pleads, "can't we have a real holiday? Won't you please keep your promise and explain to me what that frightfully learned Victorinus meant in his translation of Porphyry's *Introduction*?"

So in those good old days Boethius and his undergraduate gladly whiled away two evenings in philosophical chat. The dialogue is given here in two books, one for each evening.

Not content with this exposition, some time afterward Boethius made a much longer commentary on the same *Introduction* of Porphyry. This time he accomplished five books of interpretation, and in his zeal for clearness and accuracy made for their basis his own translation of Porphyry's Greek. It was a very close and literal rendering and somewhat wounded his literary conscience, though his scientific mind felt that the charm of words must be ruthlessly disregarded in dealings with logic. His decision must have comforted many since his day! Continuous narrative in this work replaces the easier form of dialogue, and the interpretation is intended for students far more advanced than young Fabius. At its beginning Boethius maintains that logic is indeed part of philosophy.

One more labour of annotation remains for our Boethius. This is a commentary made by him on the *Topica* of Cicero, a work on rhetorical questions. The commentary, as we have it, is incomplete. Only five books and the greater part of a sixth are to be found, though Boethius states clearly elsewhere that he "sweated over his seven books." He aimed in this work to supplement another commentary on the same *Topica,* made by the same Marius Victorinus.

But Boethius was not only translator and commentator. We have a whole series of independent works of his, mostly dealing with his beloved logic: ***On the Categorical Syllogism***; ***An Introduction to Categorical Syllogisms***; ***On the Hypothetical Syllogism***; ***On Division***; ***On Topical Differences***. Originality, again, was not the chief characteristic of these books. So far as was possible, they harked back to Aristotle, to Porphyry, to Theophrastus, Eudemus, Themistius and Cicero. At the beginning of the ***On the Hypothetical Syllogism*** there are some pleasant words on the joy of sharing the fruits of one's research with a friend, though the friend addressed here is unknown to us. Nothing lay to hand in Latin on this difficult subject, and a clear-minded sympathy must have been gladness untold.

So much, then, for the Boethian logical *corpus* as we have it, duly certified. References in some of his extant works point to other writings of his, now lost to us, and still others have been wrongly listed under his name.

Before we discuss the appearing of the other parts of Aristotle's *Organon* in Latin translation, it will be necessary to turn for a moment to the tradition of Aristotle's works. Only two of his treatises on logic, the *Categories* and the *On Interpretation,* were in general use in the eleventh century, and these not in their original Greek, but in the translations of Boethius. These, and the original works of Boethius on logic, with the work done by him on Porphyry's *Isagoge,* and the books of Marius Victorinus, with, also, the legacies left to scholars by Augustine, by the Pseudo-Augustine, by Martianus Capella in his *Nuptials of Mercury and Philology,* by Cassiodorus and by Isidore of Seville, in writings which held most valuable matter from works of Aristotle, lost since the time of these borrowers, made up for this time the sum in practice of its library on logic. Two-fifths alone, then, of the *Organon* were known fully or generally to students during the lapse of centuries, as Abelard in his *Dialectica,* written about 1121, bears mournful witness. Subsequent scholarship described this two-fifths as the *Logica Vetus,* the "Old Logic." The remaining three parts of Aristotle's Organon—the *Topics,* the *Sophistici Elenchi,* and the *Analytics, Prior* and *Posterior,* were still in any complete form, either in Greek or Latin, generally unknown in the first two decades of the twelfth century.

We may trace to two sources the introduction, a little later on in this same century, of these remaining parts, called in distinction the *Logica Nova,* the "New Logic." One source centred in Toledo of Spain, whither Arabs had carried the writings of Aristotle in Arabic version. There, from about 1135 onward, scholars, attracted by this rich treasure, were busily engaged in translating many of Aristotle's works on logical and on physical science.

Yet before this time the "New Logic" had come into the hands of scholars in the West. Under the year 1128 we find inserted in the chronicle of Robert de Torigny, Abbot of Mont Saint Michel, a statement that "James the Clerk of Venice translated from Greek into Latin and annotated some books of Aristotle: namely, the *Topica,* the *Analytica* (*Priora* and *Posteriora*), and the *Elenchi,* although there was available an older translation of these books."

Is this older version that of Boethius, and, if so, what had become of it since it was made in the sixth century? And was the version of these three works which was used by the later Middle Ages the genuine work of Boethius himself?

Some critics are of the opinion that the version which was circulated in later mediaeval days as the work of Boethius was not really by him. James of Venice, they believe, was its author. On the other hand, the theory that the translation of these three books used by scholars of the twelfth century onward was, indeed, the genuine work of Boethius finds support from Charles Homer Haskins [in his *Studies in the History of Mediaeval Science,* 1927]. He has brought forward a piece of evidence from a thirteenth century manuscript in the library of the chapter of Toledo. This manuscript contains three different renderings into Latin of the *Analytica Posteriora:* one from the Arabic, and the one current under the name of Boethius, and another not found elsewhere, so far as we know. A preface accompanies this last version, in which we are told that the writer, whose name is not given, has been invited to make a translation of the *Posteriora.* "For the translation of Boethius which we have is incomplete and its text is bad. Moreover, professors in France say that although they do possess a translation and commentary by James, yet this translation is little used and they do not dare to employ it in their lectures." This was due, no doubt, to the difficulties of the poor text.

This Preface bears witness to the version of James of Venice, to a lack of its use, and to the existence of an older text, here definitely assigned to Boethius. From evidence given us by Boethius himself we may believe that he did translate the *Analytica,* as he twice refers to such a rendering, mentioning expressly both the *Priora* and the *Posteriora.* He also speaks repeatedly of his *"Analytics,"* in such terms as *in Analyticis nostris* and *in Analyticis diximus,* which seems to point to a commentary by him on this work, and he mentions a translation and a commentary made by himself for the *Topica.* Not one of these commentaries has come down to us, and there is no reference to either translation or commentary for the *Sophistici Elenchi* in any work assigned to Boethius. Since, however, as soon as the treatises of the *New Logic* gained currency in Latin form early in the twelfth century, they were regularly known under the name of Boethius, and since later writers, such as John of Salisbury, in quoting a Latin translation as "of Boethius" used a version similar in the parts quoted to that printed by Migne, we may think, not without reason, that we still have in the *Patrologia* the rendering, much corrupted in places, which Boethius made of the three works in question, in spite of the necessity of assuming that it was not used from the sixth till the twelfth century. Possibly it was discarded for this long period through discouragement on account of its bad text and through lack of interest in the higher branches of dialectic.

So much for the purely philosophical works of Boethius. As an original authority on logic he has little claim for renown. He founded no new school. He has even been blamed, with Martianus Capella and Cassiodorus, for much of the blundering of the logic of the Middle Ages. Yet his worth is inestimable for his tradition of Aristotle, both by direct translation and by quotation and interpretation in those "original" works in which he depended so greatly upon Porphyry and other Greek exponents of Aristotle. Without Boethius Aristotle would have been lost to the West in the Dark Ages before the revival of learning in the twelfth century. As we have seen, their knowledge of the "Old Logic" was derived in pre-eminent degree from his work; the introduction of the "New Logic" into the West was due at first, we may think, to his labours, reappearing after long lapse of time. As has often been remarked, he was the last of the Romans to hand on from his own familiar knowledge of their original the great wealth of the Greeks in science logical and mathematical; in a way worthy of his great predecessor Cicero he brings to an end the direct transmission by the Romans of their magnificent inheritance of culture. The barbarian races who occupied Italy knew no Greek and depended, when they know of things Greek at all, upon a Latin intermediary.

But, in his pre-occupation with Aristotle and logic, Boethius meant far more to Churchmen of the earlier Middle Ages than did Cicero. For logic, or dialectic, as it was commonly called, was a safe and valuable instrument for the Christian pilgrim in this naughty world. Study of pagan writings on other branches of philosophy, arguing of God and His dealings with men, of men and their dealings with one another, was regarded as waste of time, or worse, in this Christian era. Far better to elevate the soul, if not the mind, by studying and digesting the countless miracles laid to the credit of saintly prayers, or heroic deeds of austere life. The devil surely lurked in pages written on ethics and moralities by heathen philosophers, waiting to ensnare the unwary by his bait of delicate words. Logic was impersonal and far removed from charm of style. Moreover, it sharpened the intellect for battle against the adversaries of the Lord. A weapon was a weapon, whether used for good or for evil, and a Christian must fight well-armed. Further, this armour did not turn its edge inwards against him who used it; for was not Christianity based on ultimate truth?

In a far different way the same result obtained for the barbarian. Logic was far better suited for the young energy of the barbarian mind than the ancient refinements of matter and style of pagan classics. Here was something on which the "new man" could exercise his own mind in argument, easier than the effort of bringing his cruder thought into harmony with an ancient civilization already dead and gone. The subtle ponderings of Aeschylus on Divine justice, of Sophocles on human fate, the rebellious mind of Euripides, the intellectual searchings of Plato and the Neo-Platonists after God, did not specially concern the young students of Gothic and Frankish and Lombard blood, descended from men of practice and achievement rather than of meditation on mysteries. It warmed their blood to argue, as long as the argument was the chief thing rather than abstruse metaphysics.

In either case logic was a tool, whether of apologetics or of education. And Boethius fully deserved the gratitude of all future students, readers of the Latin tongue, for the care with which he shaped this Latin weapon of logic. Roger Bacon remarks in his *Opus Majus* that "alone of translators did Boethius thoroughly understand both the language into which and the language from which he was translating." To the philosophers of the Middle Ages it was one of his great services, and this time an original one, that he made most valuable additions in his translations from Aristotle to their Latin philosophical vocabulary and fixed the meaning in Latin equivalents of Greek philosophical terms.

The influence of the secular science of Boethius on mediaeval times is, indeed, a subject more meet for volumes than for paragraphs. The "Quadrivium" owed far more than its name to him. Its curriculum of education depended on his treatises, as did that of the preliminary "Trivium," the course of the three arts. Of these, whether in England, France or Germany, dialectic or rhetoric required Aristotle, translated or summarized by Boethius, or Isidore of Seville, borrowing from Boethius. In the fourfold courses, arithmetic, music and geometry required Boethius, together with Martianus Capella. In the early years of the thirteenth century the course for the Master's degree in Arts at Paris prescribed in Rhetoric the third book of the *Ars Major* of Donatus and the ***Topics*** of Boethius; later on we find the ***Divisions*** of Boethius prescribed together with the ***Topics***. At Oxford late in the same century candidates for the degree of Bachelor of Arts were required to have heard once the logical works of Boethius with the exception of the ***Topics,*** Book IV.

Again, Boethius was both food and stimulant to those who sat in the professorial seats of the mediaeval schools. He gave them both the words they used and the dialectical form of argument in which they expounded their matter by way of mouth or pen. Already in his works the *dubitationes,* the *quaestio,* the *solutio,* so beloved of Saint Thomas Aquinas and the Schoolmen, play their logical part. Already in the eighth century Alcuin was busy with him. He included Boethius among the writers he proudly listed as stacked on the shelves of the Library of his Cathedral School at York. He drew on Boethius in his dialogue, *On Dialectic,* a conversation with Charles the Great, who had called him to preside over his Palace School at Aachen. He taught his pupils there from this same source, and in the early years of the ninth century he instructed in Boethius his monks in the Abbey of St. Martin at Tours.

Among these was Raban, who carried his vast erudition to the School of Fulda in Germany, including his study of Boethius *On Arithmetic.* In Reims late in the tenth century Richer, of fame as chronicler, was listening to the mighty Gerbert disentangling dialectical knots of the ***Introduction*** and the ***Topics*** as explained by Boethius. We can imagine Gerbert ever and anon taking up his Boethius on Aristotle and on Porphyry as he passed from his teacher's chair at Reims to his abbey at Bobbio and finally to his Papal See in Rome. In St. Gall early in the eleventh century Notker Labeo was drawing crowds of enthusiastic listeners as he expounded Boethius on the mysteries of dialectic.

Perhaps most famous of all homes of training in dialectic in the eleventh century was the Cathedral School at Chartres, brought into renown by the labours of Fulbert, Bishop of Chartres, who had himself been Gerbert's disciple in liberal studies. Under him and under the three great Chancellors of Chartres who in the twelfth century in turn continued his work, Bernard of Chartres, Gilbert de la Porrée, and Thierry of Chartres, the courses of the *trivium* and the *quadrivium* as expounded by Boethius were carried on from day to day and hour to hour. Fulbert speaks [in his *On the Acts of the Apostles*] of Boethius as one "read in the secular schools" and quotes his poetry in company with that of Vergil himself. Gilbert de la Porrée imbibed so well the principles of Aristotelian dialectic in the current Latin mediaeval rendering, that of Boethius, as we may think, that he proceeded further to rival his master in his *Book of the Six Principles,* held afterward in the schools of logic a worthy successor to the Boethian treatises. Thierry of Chartres discussed through its Latin version all of the *Organon* of Aristotle in his *Library of the Seven Arts,* the two great tomes he bequeathed at his death for the guidance of future students in his Cathedral School.

The same fountain of Aristotelian dialectic, bubbling through the channel of Boethius, sparkled in the twelfth century in the Cathedral School of Notre Dame at Paris, established at the beginning of this period by William of Champeaux. Here and later on near Paris at Saint Victor were sown the seeds of the University of Paris as students flocked to hear William discussing thorny dilemmas; here the foundation was laid of that passion for logical precision which has always been characteristic of French studies in liberal arts. Here Abelard, already impatient to argue the points debated by his master, sat under William of Champeaux; here Abelard in his turn made Paris far more renowned as the centre *par excellence* of logical training. Hither John of Salisbury was drawn by Abelard's renown to study in his lecture-room. We can picture to ourselves the hungry desire of Abelard to learn more of Greek philosophy than the prevailing ignorance of Greek and the scanty volume of Latin translations available for himself and his students would allow.

But John of Salisbury could not be held permanently by logic alone, however sparkling. Chartres soon called him away from Paris to sit at the feet of Richard "l'Évêque" and of William of Conches, "second only to Bernard of Chartres in his rich store of literary learning." William himself wrote a commentary on Boethius's last work. The method of teaching at Chartres, John tells us, had been developed by Bernard, and he praises with enthusiasm its day's work with its alternation of literary exercise and religious devotion as laid down by the master. It was literature which John loved above all, and in his *Metalogicon* he rebelled against the passion for logic for its own sake which ran like fire in the schools of Europe of the earlier twelfth century. "Just as the sword of Hercules is of no use in the hand of a pigmy or a dwarf, but lays low all it meets like lightning in the hand of Achilles or Hector, so dialectic, if stripped of the might of other disciplines, is so to speak, maimed and useless. But if it be vigorous with their power, it avails to destroy all falsehood." Dialectic, then, or logic, which came to the same thing, must be firmly supported by a thorough training in her sister art of grammar, which, of course, involved long study of literature.

John knew his Boethius from end to end and his Aristotle both through Boethius and through other source, as the pages of the *Metalogicon* prove. As we have seen, he knew the whole *Organon* when he published the *Metalogicon* in 1159. He wonders why the *Topica,* the *Analytica,* and the *Sophistici Elenchi* of Aristotle have been so long lost to the world, and rejoices that the *Topica* has at length "been as it were raised from death or, at least, from sleep by some diligent and zealous student of our age to recall the erring and to open to its seekers the way of truth." Among the logical treatises of Boethius he especially admires the ***On Division*** for its "singular grace of vocabulary and nicety of expression." As Fulbert did, he quotes the verses of Boethius in company with those of Vergil, and calls Boethius "more excellent in faith and in knowledge of the truth." Yet the way of truth to John did not mean the disquisitions of Boethius on Aristotle as a substitute for straight translations of the text of Aristotle itself, and he blames bitterly those who rest on the inferior authority without striving to get as near as may be to the fountain head: "Against those who set aside the judgment of the ancients and dismiss the books of Aristotle, content for the most part with Boethius alone, many things could be said. But no matter, for it is pathetic to all men to see the imperfection of those who scarcely know anything, because they have spent their time and substance on Boethius alone."

But among the professors of these times Boethius had a yet deeper effect. It was he who fanned the flame of conflict that was to occupy philosophical minds through all the Middle Ages—the struggle between Nominalism and Realism in their various forms. The distinction between Aristotle and Plato had already been made by Cassiodorus in writing to Boethius: *Plato theologus, Aristoteles logicus*. The question turned for Boethius, as for later philosophers, on the reality of the existence of *genera* and *species*. Aristotle held that as universals and incorporeal they existed only in bodies apprehended by the senses; Plato believed that as universals they had a real existence apart from sensible bodies. Porphyry had refused to give judgment on this problem: "For it is a very deep matter and needs further enquiry." At first Boethius decided in favour of Plato and Realism, when he was writing his first commentary on Porphyry's *Introduction*. But later on he changed his mind. In the second and more learned commentary on the same work of Porphyry, after carefully pondering the doctrines of both Plato and Aristotle in this matter, he declared: "I have not thought it fitting to decide between their positions; it would need too deep probings into philosophy."

From this observation springs the picture given of Boethius in the twelfth century by Godefroi of Saint Victor. He is describing in rhymed verse the crystal streams of the seven liberal arts as distinct from the foul waters of mechanical sciences, and the progress of philosophical enquiry in the great figures of its history: Plato, Aristotle, Porphyry, Donatus, Boethius, Priscian. Here, then, Boethius sits hesitating between the claims of Aristotle and Plato:

> Assidet Boethius, stupens de hac lite,
> Audiens quid hic et hic asserat perite,
> Et quid cui faveat non discernit rite,
> Nec praesumit solvere litem definite.

The fire of conflict burned on merrily, fed by his doubt. Fuel was added in the eighth and ninth centuries, on the side of Aristotle by Raban, on the side of Plato by Johannes Scottus. Thence it flared up into the fierce conflagration which from the twelfth till the fourteenth century blazed in every great European school and set the disciples of Saint Francis and Saint Dominic to battle for intellectual truth.

Here, then, we have a tiny view of the work of "Boethius, last of the Roman philosophers," for the professors, for the secular thought of the Middle Ages. But only half of this famous description has yet been quoted. It concludes with "Boethius, first of the scholastics." The term implies the union in harmony of secular and spiritual learning and dates its rise from 787 when Charles the Great, in a letter to the Bishops of France, sounded the call for a revival of secular learning among her clergy. Clerical training in the seven liberal arts was diligently pursued in the Palace School of Aachen. From thence it slowly spread, till many Cathedrals possessed their own Schools, in which the courses of the "Trivium" and the "Quadrivium" were taught in subordination to the principles of the Christian creed. This called forth a new technique on the part of Catholic scholars, the using of secular learning for the confirming and the elucidating of Christian doctrine in the minds of thinking men at large. In this, once more, Boethius had already led the way.

The statement rests on his ***Sacred Treatises***: four, or, we may think with reason, five in number. Furthermore, on them hangs the belief that Boethius was a Christian, and, withal, an earnest adherent of his faith.

In the nineteenth century there was much scepticism as to the genuineness of all these writings. It was held that, as Boethius undoubtedly wrote the ***Consolation of Philosophy*** in uttermost stress and in the last crisis of his life without giving any direct evidence of a Christian belief, he could not have been author of a number of theological treatises dealing with this. Such feeling was strong enough to conquer the clear ascription to Boethius of four such brief works. The publication, however, in 1877 by Usener of that fragment from the *Family History* of Cassiodorus known as the *Anecdoton Holderi* has settled the question with regard to these four in the minds of all except the determinedly sceptical.

This fragment tells us concerning Boethius that "he wrote a book on the Holy Trinity and some chapters on dogma and a book against Nestor." Now Cassiodorus, as a contemporary and friend, must have known what Boethius wrote. Both internal evidence and the testimony of manuscripts have confirmed this view, and with belief in the authenticity of at least four of the five ***Theological Tractates*** extant under his name we may confidently look upon Boethius as a Christian philosopher and theologian.

How, then, does the philosopher who longed to harmonize Plato and Aristotle for the world of scholars approach the Queen of sciences? Exactly as we should expect, so far as these four treatises go, Numbers 1, 2, 3 and 5. Here he seeks another and an even higher harmony. At the beginning of the first one, known as ***On the Trinity,*** he writes to his father-in-law, Symmachus, to whom he dedicates the work: "I have long pondered this problem with such mind as I have and all the light that God has lent me. Now, having set it forth in logical order and cast it into literary form, I venture to submit it to your judgment, for which I care as much as for the results of my own research. You will readily understand what I feel whenever I try to write down what I think if you consider the difficulty of the topic and the fact that I discuss it only with a few—I may say with no one but yourself. It is indeed no desire for fame or empty popular applause that prompts my pen; if there by any external reward, we may not look for more warmth in the verdict than the subject itself arouses. For, apart from yourself, wherever I turn my eyes, they fall on either the apathy of the dullard or the jealousy of the shrewd, and a man who casts his thoughts before the common herd—I will not say to consider but to trample under foot, would seem to bring discredit on the study of divinity. So I purposely use brevity and wrap up the ideas I draw from the deep questionings of philosophy in new and unaccustomed words which speak only to you and to myself, that is, if you design to look at them. The rest of the world I simply disregard: they cannot understand, and therefore do not deserve to read. We should not, of course, press our inquiry further than man's wit and reason are allowed to climb the height of heavenly knowledge." And at the end a similar hope is expressed: "We must not in speaking of God let imagination lead us astray; we must let the Faculty of pure Knowledge lift us up and teach us to know all things as far as they may be known.

I have now finished the investigation which I proposed. The exactness of my reasoning awaits the standard of your judgment; your authority will pronounce whether I have seen a straight path to the goal. If, God helping me, I have furnished some support in argument to an article which stands by itself on the firm foundation of Faith, I shall render joyous praise for the finished work to Him from whom the invitation comes."

The keen desire to make trial of his long devotion to Aristotelian dialectic in its application to the mysteries of theology was natural, once we admit that Boethius was a Christian, whether he wrote these works in his eager youth or in his riper age. It is here that we see him as the forerunner of Saint Thomas and the Schoolmen of the thirteenth century in their passion to relate after their due order the things learned by men of natural reason and the things revealed to them from without of supernatural faith.

The scholastic method is already foreshadowed through the treatment in this first pamphlet of the doctrine "That Trinity is One God, not three Gods." After the aim of the work has been set forth, we find, next, a statement of the Catholic Faith regarding this doctrine; then a description of the scientific method of theological enquiry, based on Aristotle; then the application of this method to that particular doctrine.

The treatise ***On the Trinity*** was well known throughout the Middle Ages. Alcuin praised its author in the eighth century as "learned in tomes both philosophic and divine"; in the ninth Hincmar, Bishop of Reims, referred to it and to Tractates II and V in his *De una et non trina Deitate;* Johannes Scottus, the great Irishman who presided over the Palace School at Aachen in the time of Charles the Bald, and his pupil, Remigius of Auxerre, toward the end of the same century wrote commentaries on it and on others of these *Sacred Treatises.* In the twelfth century Abelard studied it, in the thirteenth it was in the hands of Albertus Magnus, and was made the subject of a special commentary by his great pupil, St. Thomas Aquinas [*Opusculum* LXIII]. Especially interesting is another commentary written by Gilbert de la Porrée, Bishop of Poitiers from 1142, "the one saint whom Bernard of Clairvaux unsuccessfully charged with heresy." Certain statements in this exposition of Boethius, ***On the Trinity,*** brought upon Gilbert the displeasure of the Church. He was tried before Pope Eugenius III at the Council of Reims in 1148 and discharged without punishment on his promise to satisfy his accusers with regard to the text of his book. John of Salisbury, who cites these theological works of Boethius in his *Metalogicon,* was present, he tells us, at the Council of Reims. We can picture him watching the fiery zeal of Saint Bernard there, declaring against Gilbert that in his Commentary on Boethius were found "certain things worthy of condemnation by the wise because they accorded not with the precepts of the Church or were unseemly by reason of their strange novelty of language." Gilbert was also roundly accused in Commentaries on the same work of Boethius written in this twelfth century by the "Pseudo-Bede," possibly Gottfried of Auxerre, and by Clarembaud, Archdeacon of Arras, himself a pupil of Thierry of Chartres.

In the sculptures which make beautiful the West, Front of the Cathedral of Chartres the Seven Liberal Arts are represented, together with their greatest exponents: Priscian, Aristotle, Cicero, Pythagoras, Nicomachus, Euclid and Ptolemy. At least, so experts have been content to believe. Boethius has not been discovered, perhaps, it has been thought, because of a shadow cast on his work by this Commentary of Gilbert de la Porrée. But Martianus Capella has not been identified there, either, and Saint Bernard himself defended Boethius.

The second of these ***Theological Treatises*** is also concerned with the Holy Trinity. It is dedicated to "John the Deacon" and was frequently known by that title. Attempts have been made without any definite result to identify this John with Pope John I (523-526) or Pope John II (533-535). He, whoever he was, exchanged letters with Ennodius and with Avitus, Bishop of Vienne in the fifth century. We have an interesting letter by him on the Baptismal Office, written at the request of Senarius, the friend of Ennodius, for his instruction. Boethius addresses this John with great respect at the end of this little work as one expert in the doctrine of the Church: "If my words are true and in keeping with the Faith I beg you tell me so. But if peradventure you disagree in any point, look carefully at what I have written and try to bring into harmony both faith and reason." Here again Boethius strikes the key-note of his purpose. The authenticity of this second treatise is attested, not only by superscription but by reference in later writers, as in Hincmar of Reims and St. Thomas Aquinas. The pamphlet is essentially logical in spirit, and its beginning tersely states its aim: "The question before us is whether Father, Son, and Holy Spirit may be predicated of the Divinity substantially or otherwise. And I think that the method of our inquiry must be borrowed from what is admittedly the surest source of all truth, namely, the fundamental doctrines of the catholic faith."

The third treatise, addressed to "the same," is equally logical in treatment. It is often referred to briefly as "The Hebdomads" of Boethius, since he writes to John at its beginning: "You ask me to state and explain somewhat more clearly that obscure question in my *Hebdomads,* concerning the manner in which substances can be good in virtue of existence without being absolute goods. . . . I confess I like to expound my *Hebdomads* to myself, and would rather bury my speculations in my own memory than share them with any of those pert and frivolous persons who will not tolerate an argument unless it is made amusing."

The meaning of the word "Hebdomads" has been variously explained: as the name of a society in which Boethius and his friends, such as John and Symmachus, and probably Cassiodorus, met periodically for philosophical discussion, or as a work in seven parts, after the manner of the *Hebdomads* of Varro. The scientific method is next introduced: "As is the custom in treatises on mathematics and other sciences I have set forth terms and rules throughout in developing my argument." Thus we have in orderly sequence the introduction, the statement of general principles, the *quaestio* or question in point, and, lastly, the *solutio* or conclusion, arrived at by means of the general principles laid down before. Saint Thomas Aquinas made also a detailed commentary on this work, which attracted him through this very scientific method.

More famous in antiquity was the fifth of these treatises, much longer than any of the others, a reasoned argument against the heresies of Eutyches and Nestorius. It, also, is dedicated to "John the Deacon, his revered Father, by his son Boethius." Boethius states at the beginning that he has lately been present at a meeting to hear a letter, no doubt the one sent in 512 by Eastern Bishops to Pope Symmachus asking for direction regarding these errors, and that the reading of the letter has stirred up a theological turmoil in his mind. No one else, however, of all who were present seemed to be worried, and he concluded with much disgust that they must all be very stupid! After thinking things over for a long time he has decided to write down his own conclusions and to submit them for judgment to this director of his mind in matters of faith. Once again he argues in logical course: First, the terms to be used, Person and Nature, must be defined; then the two opposing heresies, of Nestorius and of Eutyches, must be overthrown; lastly, what is of Catholic belief on this matter must be clearly set forth.

It is in this treatise that Boethius laid down his well-known definition of "Person," a definition finally accepted, after full discussion, by St. Thomas Aquinas and still regarded as valid: "Person is the individual substance of a rational nature." After the unfolding of the various points of attack against the heresy of Nestorius, that there were Two Natures and Two Persons in the Christ, and that of Eutyches, that in Him were Two Persons but only One Nature, Boethius finds the solution of the problem in the Aristotelian mean between two extremes: the belief in the One Person and Two Natures which is the creed of the Catholic Church.

We come now to the controversy which has so long centred in the fourth tractate, ***On the Catholic Faith***. For many years this has been held spurious, even after the fragment discovered by Alfred Holder spoke for the genuine authorship of Boethius in the case of the other four treatises, either by direct mention or by their indirect inclusion in "some chapters on dogma." The difficulties regarding No. 4 are both internal and external. From the point of internal evidence the great problems have been the simple style and content of the work, entirely different from the dialectical argument and scientifically logical form of the other four theological papers. We have here simply a plain statement of the Catholic faith, composed in easy language and popular manner. For this reason critics have suggested other authors: John the Deacon might have written it for one of his spiritual children; or another Severinus, possibly Saint Severinus of Noricum, who was, indeed, a missionary and not at all a philosopher. On the other hand, it is true that part of the fifth tractate is also written in plain style, that Boethius in his proven work was not always writing in scientific language. He wrote at times in simple and easy words; he wrote various kinds of verse in his ***Consolation of Philosophy***. The man, whom the four tractates we have discussed reveal as a firm Catholic, might well have been content on occasion to write a plain statement of his faith, perhaps for some unlearned friend. If he could aid the learned of his time by his dialectic, he might well have been willing to help some younger or less educated reader. Moreover, the words of Cassiodorus, "some chapters of dogma," suit this fourth treatise much better than either the second or the third, to which they are generally applied. So far as the theological content goes, the work could quite reasonably be dated in the lifetime of Boethius.

With regard to external evidence the MS. tradition dates back to the ninth century. If Boethius did not write the tract, it may have been sent to him by a close friend, such as John the Deacon, his Father in the Church, or by some other man with whom he was accustomed to talk of spiritual things. It would thus have been found among his papers at his death and published with them. We have such instances of the inclusion of the work of other men, as that of Marius Victorinus, in the *corpus* of Boethius. Serious ground for hesitation to assign it to Boethius comes from the fact that there is very little MS. evidence dating before the twelfth century for the author's name and the title of the work and that the paper holds no introduction, and no words of personal import at its end. All the other four treatises are expressly assigned to Boethius, either by name (I, II, V), or by the words "Of the Same" (III); all have a definite introduction, and all, except the third, some concluding words of a personal nature. Against this, various lines of defence have suggested that Tract IV might have depended, as one of a series, upon mention of the name of its author in the tracts preceding it in the same volume; or that Boethius himself deliberately omitted his name from this short composition. If it be spurious, it is difficult to see why it should have been inserted between Nos. 3 and 5, unless the ***Tractates*** were published in two parts. Much importance has been attached to the appearance of the words ACTENUS BOETIUS ("Here ends the work of Boethius") between Tractates III and IV in red capitals in the ninth century Codex Augiensis, inserted by the hand of the copyist or one of his assistants. This subscription, however, died with the copy, as this manuscript was not perpetuated. It may well have been due to a writer's error. Lastly, the lack of scholia and commentaries from which this particular tract has suffered may reasonably be explained by the eager interest of scholars in all matters of dialectic throughout the Middle Ages. A simple confession of faith hardly called for interpretation. This might explain its neglect by students like Abelard and Gilbert de la Porrée, though in the ninth century Remigius of Auxerre annotated all five tracts.

At least, MS. tradition does not render the authorship impossible, and it is pleasant to think that Boethius, as other learned men have done since his day, could lay aside his erudition to sum up his creed in the simple language of his own devotion, for the assurance of his own heart or the enlightening of some enquirer after God. His last words may be translated here as an indication of the character of the whole:

> There are, therefore, three truths by which ye shall know the Catholic Church throughout the world. All she holds, she holds either by authority of the Scriptures, or by universal tradition, or of special and particular custom. Of these, the authority of the Scriptures and the universal tradition of the Fathers bind her whole body; particular rules and special governances support and direct her individual parts, according to differing locality and the counsel deemed expedient by each. Herein now lies the one great hope of the faithful: the coming of the end of this world, when all corruptible things shall pass away, and men shall rise again for judgment, each to receive his merits and to remain for ever and eternally where he has deserved to be. This alone is the reward of blessedness, the contemplation of the Creator, so far as the created may be able to contemplate its Creator. Then shall the ranks of Angels be filled again from the number of the blessed in that City on high, whose King is a Virgin's Son. There unto men for their eternal joy and delight, for their meat and for their work, shall be His perpetual praising.

But it is time that we look back again to the life of Boethius the man, whom we last saw prospering magnificently as Master of Offices in 522. He was now a ripe scholar as well as statesman, renowned not only in Rome and Ravenna but in East and West, wherever the Roman learning and the Latin tongue were still esteemed. He was still in his forties and might confidently look forward to many further years of his beloved research and successful administration. His great aim of harmonizing the Aristotelian and the Platonic philosophy was in steady progress, though still far from its goal; Theodoric needed supremely the support of wise and cultured men, and all looked well on the outside for his future career.

Within, however, things were far from well. Theodoric, in spite of his honest strivings after *civilitas*, after harmony, peace, order and beauty in his composite kingdom, was, after all, a Goth and an Arian—in other words, a barbarian and a heretic. He was proud of his race and of the religion of his fathers. Boethius belonged to the aristocratic circles of Rome; he had been trained from his childhood in Greek and Latin culture; he was a steadfast adherent of the Catholic Church. Friction was inevitable, even if sternly repressed and never allowed to escape in disloyal word or act. As Boethius felt, so did his fellow-Senators, and Theodoric must have been nervously aware in his heart of the gulf which separated him from the nobler of his subjects. As time went on, the fair record of the greater part of his reign seems to have been darkened by fear and suspicion. This was natural enough. Yet there is no need for us to press forward the story that this King, so keen on toleration and justice for his citizens, of whatever blood or religious faith, now began to yield to the devil's machinations, ordering a Chapel of Saint Stephen on the outskirts of Verona to be destroyed and forbidding any Roman to carry weapons, even as much as a knife. Undoubtedly the time was a difficult one for Theodoric, and it did not help matters for him that the Pope who succeeded Hormisdas in 523, John the first, was resolutely opposed to tolerance of any deviation from the Catholic belief.

The King's irritation, at first somewhat vague, was sharply stimulated by change in the religious attitude of the Imperial government in Constantinople. The Emperor Justin the first, who had followed Anastasius of Monophysite tendency in 518, was himself an orthodox Catholic and was steadily urged on against all forms of heresy by his nephew Justinian, the power behind his throne. At this time Justin was meditating, if not already declaring, strict legislation against the Arians, even an edict that their churches in the East must be surrendered to the Catholic See. When the edict did come, Theodoric was enraged at such an affront to his own creed. But we may think that he had been disturbed in mind long before, suspecting that Catholics in Italy were secretly yearning toward Constantinople. No doubt they were attracted by the orthodoxy of the East and the stability of its Emperor, who held his throne by a right of tenure to which the Goth could not lay claim. No doubt even those who felt it their duty to support Theodoric as one who had deserved well of them and their country did sometimes turn eager eyes eastward toward the traditional Emperor of Rome and the supporter of their faith. The King in the West must have tossed at times by night on his bed, dreaming uneasily of this very thing.

On the other hand, the position of Boethius had its own point of danger. Among the courtiers of the King in Ravenna, ever ready to flatter and acquiesce in the royal will, he stood out, we may imagine, as a rock of uprightness and stern virtue. Public life for such men forms a target of attack, and we find Boethius lamenting afterward to his Lady Philosophy the hard fight he had fought in the cause of honour:

> Following, then, this authority (of Plato), I longed to transfer what I had learned at leisure in secret to the conduct of public administration. You and God, who has placed you in the minds of the wise, are my witnesses that nothing but the common aim of all good patriots brought me to public office. Thence have come to me grievous and implacable quarrels with wicked men, and in the free following of my conscience I have oftentimes right willingly given offence to the powerful by maintaining what is just.
>
> How often I have checked Conigatus when he was attacking the fortunes of some weak man! How often I have turned aside Trigguilla, Chamberlain of the King's Palace, from some wrong he had plotted, or even set into action! How often I have protected those unhappy men whom the barbarian greed was vexing with endless slanders unrestrained, though thereby I exposed my own authority to peril. Never did anyone drag me from justice to injustice. I sorrowed for the ruin of people in the provinces by private robbery and public taxation as deeply as the victims themselves. I took up the cause of Campania in a season of dire famine when hard and inexplicable terms of purchase seemed likely to bring about a lack of food there. I opposed the Praetorian Prefect, I fought the matter out before the King, I won my case, and such terms were not exacted. When the dogs of the Palace had already eaten up in greedy hope the wealth of Paulinus, a man of consular rank, I dragged him from the very jaws of those seeking to devour him.

At times, too, Boethius could be very outspoken. He writes of a certain Decoratus as a "right worthless rogue and a spy," though Cassiodorus sang the official praises of Decoratus for Theodoric. Ennodius, also, wrote to Decoratus as his friend. But Boethius declared roundly he never would hold office in company with such a man. The man, nevertheless, was Quaestor under Theodoric, and, we may think, in the very year in which Boethius languished in prison. Apparently his enemy flourished in his disgrace.

The stage was set, prepared for tragedy if only a sufficient argument should present itself. It came suddenly. Certain letters, sent by a Senator named Albinus or by his friends to the Emperor Justin at Constantinople, were intercepted in Italy by an official named Severus, a most zealous minion of the law, as it would seem. In these letters were words which were interpreted as conveying a treacherous desire for negotiation with Justin, a hinting at the "freeing of Rome" from the Ostrogothic rule. The discovery was promptly reported by Severus to the officer whose business it was to collect all information relevant to cases brought before the royal Consistorium, or Court of trial for persons accused of treason. The officer (*referendarius*) of the moment was named Cyprian, and he was serving under Boethius himself, the Master of Offices. It was a difficult matter for Boethius. He would

Philosophia visits Boethius in prison, from a tenth-century manuscript.

naturally be reluctant to press a charge against Albinus, a friend of his and a fellow-Senator; moreover, *ex officio* he was a member of the Court which would try the accused. We need not think that Boethius had had any hand in sending to Justin foolish letters of doubtful loyalty; such a course is in keeping neither with his scrupulous honesty both intellectual and moral nor with the sagacity which had raised him high in the King's counsels. But we may well imagine that he had keenly sympathised with Albinus and other Senators in a common desire to be ruled in those days from Constantinople rather than from Ravenna; he may possibly have known of correspondence with Constantinople.

At any rate, with or without the official consent of his superior, Cyprian referred the matter to Theodoric, who was at the time in Verona, and conscientious loyalty drove Boethius there at once to defend Albinus in his own person. We still have his words to Theodoric: "This accusation by Cyprian is false. But if Albinus did do this deed, then also I myself and all the Senate did it together with him. But the thing is false, Lord King."

His honesty was fatal to himself. For Cyprian after some hesitation, whether caused through his own reluctance or through fear of the consequences, went on to include his superior in the charge of treason, supporting the accusation, it was said, by evidence of false witnesses. It was certainly a shock for Theodoric to hear that two of the leading Romans, one of whom was his own Master of Offices, had been charged with treason against his throne. It was a greater shock to find good ground for fearing that members of the Senate, how many he did not know, were in league against him. In his angry mood he doubtless remembered that Justin had specially favoured Boethius in 522 when he allowed Theodoric to raise his two sons to the consulship. He may also have been told of a work which Boethius had lately published on the Catholic doctrine of the Trinity. Was there on foot a movement of the Catholic Romans to drive his race from the throne of Italy? The fact that the accusers of Boethius, Cyprian and others, were themselves Catholics did not allay this fear. Someone must suffer, and in his rage he seized the victim ready to his hand, this man so calmly confronting his royal power with bold words, and eagerly he lent ear to the proceedings in the Consistorium.

Boethius tells us something about accusation and accusers. On behalf of the whole Senate he withstood the charge of traitorous action, brought, as he says, against that Order by the King. On his own behalf he resisted the statement, very probably pressed by his subordinate officer, Cyprian, that he had tried to obstruct justice by preventing the presentation of evidence against the Senate. He resisted, further, the charge of "sacrilege," in which commentators have seen an accusation of magic practice, possibly drawn from the skill of Boethius in mathematics and astronomy. In passionate words he protested afterward his innocence to his Mistress, the Lady Philosophy, both for her own assurance and for the knowledge of men to come.

The accusers were Cyprian and also three other men brought forward as witnesses; Basilius, Opilio, and Gaudentius by name. Of Cyprian Boethius tells us, continuing the defence of his own public life: "I faced the wrath of Cyprian, the informer, lest unfair accusation should condemn Albinus, once Consul. Do I seem to have piled up sufficiency of grievous enmities against myself?"

Cyprian appears, however, in another light in two letters of Theodoric, in which his merits as *referendarius* are sung and he is admitted to the office of Count of the Sacred Largesses. This was in 524. Like Decoratus, he flourished in his opponent's fall. Special stress is laid on his loyalty to the throne of Italy; it is just possible that we may detect here a covert reference, by contrast, to Boethius and his recent accusation.

The characters of the other three accusers are more directly attacked by their victim. He declares, continuing the argument quoted above: "But I ought to have been safer in the hands of other men, I who through my love of justice reserved for myself no refuge among the King's courtiers. Yet who were the men who by their informing struck me this blow? One was Basilius, who had been banished from the King's service and was forced by his debts to lay information against me. Others were Opilio and Gaudentius, men sentenced by the King to exile because of innumerable acts of dishonesty. When the King heard that they would not obey this order and had fled to sanctuary, he proclaimed that if they had not left Ravenna by a certain day they should be driven out with branded foreheads. What could be more severe? And yet on that very day information against me was accepted from these same men."

Here also we have contrary evidence in two letters of Cassiodorus written for Athalaric in the year 527. Opilio was a brother of Cyprian and, according to Cassiodorus, equally loyal to Theodoric. The two letters tell of his rewarding by bestowal of the same office of Count of the Sacred Largesses. In one of them we may very possibly see a reference to the trial of Boethius, by this time matter of history; Cassiodorus had had special cause to be concerned about the fate of his fellow-citizen. His words here seem rather to be the cautious expression of one who really sympathized with his friend, now condemned and dead in disgrace, than indication of judgment that Boethius had been guilty. They also appear to contain an implicit warning to Opilio to watch his official steps. "You are going to enjoy," the royal letter runs, as penned by Cassiodorus, "all the privileges and emoluments which fell to your predecessors, and we pray that those who stand firm in their own deeds may not be shaken by any contrivings of slander. There was a time when even judges were troubled by informers. But you have no bad conscience. Lay aside fear, therefore, and enjoy the fruits of your honours." If this does refer in any way to the fate of Boethius, the word *delator,* "informer" or "spy," is certainly a daring one. It was the word used, as we have seen, of Cyprian, Opilio's brother, by Boethius himself.

There lies a strange contradiction in the thought that Opilio, whom Boethius could describe in 523 or 524, when he was writing his ***Consolation,*** as one guilty of innumerable frauds, punished with exile and threatened with branding, should three or four years later be honoured with office in the State. Apparently Athalaric and his Regent Mother chose the officers whose aid they desired among their Gothic subjects without looking too closely into their history under Theodoric. Cassiodorus, we may suppose, wrote his missives of congratulation as an official servant of the Crown without allowing his private conscience to overrule obedience to the sovereign for whom he worked.

The evidence was found sufficient to arrest Boethius and to cast him into prison at Pavia together with Albinus. He was also stripped of his high dignity, and Cassiodorus himself was made Master of Offices in his place. But the King in his anger went further. He stopped the hearing before the Consistorium and cast aside legal procedure by assuming in his own person the conduct of the trial at Pavia, after summoning thither the Prefect of Rome to assist him in judgment. State magistrates and Senators who composed this Court of Treason were relieved of all responsibility concerning the matter; this rested by his own determination with Theodoric. The Senate was so terrified of implication in the charge of high treason after hearing of the words of Boethius that it passed special decrees of compliance, declaring him guilty.

Meanwhile Boethius remained in prison, ignorant of all that was happening, till the royal deliberations ended in sentence of death and confiscation of property. We do not know much about these deliberations or even how long they actually lasted; according to Boethius himself forged letters formed part of the evidence. By the time the sentence was carried out in 524 he had endured nearly a year of captivity. Records differ as to his end. Our chief authority declares that he was transferred from Pavia to another prison in Calvenzano, near Milan, and was there put to death with torture: "A cord was tied round his head and drawn so tightly that at length his eyes burst from their sockets, and he was then despatched by a blow from a club." Fortunately the horrible record is placed in doubt by two other versions, which state: one, that he was beheaded, the other, that he was killed by a sword.

The sequel of Theodoric's quarrel with Constantinople is interesting. According to evidence of chronicle, when the edict against the Arians had been published, he sent for the Pope John himself, and when he arrived at Ravenna, curtly bade him get to Constantinople and obtain from Justin relief for those who did not desire adherence to the Catholic faith. The Pope went reluctantly, but was received at Constantinople with all honour. He obtained the relief, except that Arians already converted to Catholicism were not permitted to return to their former creed. On his return, however, he was received by Theodoric in an angry mood and was actually cast into prison, where he died shortly after. His funeral was carried out with great distinction, and he was subsequently enrolled among the Saints of the Church. An honourable exception among terrified Senators at this time was Symmachus, who, while Boethius was still alive in prison, "grieved for his injuries." His grief cost him dear. He must have shown it clearly; for he, also, was arrested and put to death in 525.

Remorse, we read, came quickly to Theodoric for these hasty acts of spleen. He is described to us by a contemporary writer as beset by fears of conscience, doubtless aggravated by the sickness which troubled these last days of his life. After recording the aristocratic birth and the high standing in the State of both Symmachus and Boethius, the narrative goes on:

> They were earnest disciples of Philosophy and foremost in love of Justice and they ministered of their substance to the need of many, both citizens and strangers. Thus they enjoyed great renown and brought to envy men of evil character, who with their lies persuaded Theodoric that the two were plotting revolution. So he slew them both and made forfeit their goods to the treasury. A few days later as he sat at dinner his servants placed before him the head of a great fish, and it seemed to him just like the head of Symmachus, lately killed. For it looked at him in a dreadful threatening manner with its teeth clenched on the lower lip and its eyes fixed in a grim and cruel stare. Sudden terror seized the King, and shivering with cold he hurried to his bed, where he buried himself in heap of blankets hastily brought by his servants at his call. The doctor, Elpidius, was summoned, and Theodoric confessed to him with tears the whole story of the crime he had committed; but his grief and pangs of conscience constantly tormented him till he died a little later. This was the first and the last wrong done by the King to his subjects in condemning both of these men without first trying their case as he was wont.

In years to come Boethius was honoured as a Martyr by the Church. Already in Paul the Deacon's *History of Italy* we read that while Pope John and his fellow-ambassadors "were tarrying to return from their mission to Constantinople, Theodoric, driven by the fury of his wickedness, slew with the sword Symmachus and Boethius, Catholic men," though we know that Pope John did not start for the East till after the death of Boethius. If Theodoric's fear of the alliance of Catholics in Italy with Constantinople and his vexation at the hostility toward the Arians of both the Pope in the West and the Emperor in the East can raise Boethius to the rank of martyr for his faith, then surely he merits a martyr's place. But since his prosecutors, Cyprian and the rest, were also Catholic, his trial could not actually have been based on religious grounds.

It is also true that a cult of "Saint Severinus Boethius" has continued down the ages, though here, again, it would be difficult to say how much the fame of another Severinus may be indirectly responsible for this, through confusion of persons. The Cathedral of Pavia still holds his relics, and the observance of his feast-day there on the 23rd of October was formally sanctioned by the Sacred Congregation of Rites in the year 1883.

To the days when Boethius lay in torment of suspense and discouragement we owe the best known of his works, the ***Consolation of Philosophy***. Many have asked why Boethius seemed to ask aid of philosophy rather than of his religious faith as he sat in the shadow of death, alone and imprisoned; many, as we have seen, have denied for this reason that he was a Catholic Christian at all. But surely a man's book need not show all his self. Boethius might well have written a treatise in like circumstances on mathematics or on music for the relieving of his mind while, unknown to the public of future days, morning and evening and at noontide he offered his prayers for the comfort of his soul and the keeping of his faith. He may well have wanted for years to write such a book, "In Praise of Philosophy," and have seized this time of enforced leisure, with the difference that she was now to stand forth as his friend in sorrow, as before in joy. There is nothing that is hostile to the Catholic religion in her counsel as given here. On the contrary, a man's faith might well find support from her reasoned argument.

To her, then, Boethius now turned, while the reserve of his inner soul in those last hours forbade the revealing of his colloquies with God. It may be that he desired further to use his knowledge of philosophy for the enlightening of others beset by problems like unto his own, men to whom the truths of religion would not so surely appeal. If this was his thought, he succeeded as he never dreamed. In the Middle Ages his book was read by all men, found everywhere, in places both sacred and secular. It trained the young, it comforted the old, it stayed the doubts of the vigorous and of the weaker brethren alike. Men, learned and simple, theologian and lay, marked and digested its pages for the sake of others as of themselves. Its pithy definitions gave food for argument to Saint Thomas Aquinas and the Schoolmen; its subtler passages gave thought to countless commentators. Already in the ninth century Asser, teacher of King Alfred, was busy at this work. In the same century Alfred made his famous version in Anglo-Saxon, the forerunner of translations into many other tongues. Among them those by Notker Labeo or his pupils into Old High German in the eleventh century and by the monk Maximus Planudes into Greek in the fourteenth, are perhaps of special interest for their language. Far better known is the prose rendering of Chaucer. He was ever devoted to his dear "Boëce," whatever he was writing, and especially in his tale of *Troylus and Cryseyde.* A little later came the translation of John Walton, and we may remember, also, a rendering by Queen Elizabeth of the year 1593. Among the innumerable recollections of Boethius in prose and poetry two shall be mentioned here: in English literature the brief summary of John Lydgate, in Italian the picture given by Dante. Lydgate wrote of him as slain for his faith:

> But touching Boys, as bookis specefie,
> Wrotte dyvers bookis off philosophie,
> Off the Trynyte maters that were dyvyne,
> Martyrd for crist and called Severyne.

Dante places him among the flaming spirits that make glorious music around the throne of God: "The sainted soul that from martyrdom and from exile came to this peace." His bones, as Dante told, were laid, long after his death, under the Golden Ceiling in Saint Peter's Church at Pavia.

And now to the book itself. It was written in a medley of prose and verse, such as Varro and Martianus Capella had used before and Bernard Silvestris of Tours and Alan of Lille were to imitate. Verse alternated with prose for the relief of the mind from application to logical argument, written in a variety of metres, with many traces of the influence of Seneca's tragedies. At times we find real poetry, at times mere versification. That Boethius was given to writing poems we know from his own and from other witness. The prose is clear and simple, easy to read, and of a Latin sufficiently pure and classical to cause no difficulty.

The relation of Boethius to his sources is, again, a matter of varying judgment. These sources are undoubtedly the teachings of the Stoics, of Plato and the Neo-Platonists, and of Aristotle, and yet these component borrowings have been transfused into a whole which bears a new and original impress from the mind of the author himself. We have here the tree of a philosophy rooted in ancient theory, bearing a fruit all its own. And so, while we see the matter of the *Timaeus* and of the *Gorgias,* the thought of Proclus and of Plotinus, the substance of the lost *Protrepticus* of Aristotle clearly in evidence, we see them through the mind of the Roman philosopher and thinker and man of this sixth century. And more. We see the pagan doctrines through the mind of one who knew in his own religious experience something of that philosophic contemplation of God which Christian men have always held as part of their inheritance. Philosophic reasoning here led Boethius to the contemplation of the Divine, nurtured him in its high thought, till in this same book he passed beyond its ken to the vision of the Personal God whence springs Christian belief.

At the beginning of the work we find him in the full misery of his changed fortune, suffering the torments of reflection in his prison while he ponders on his injuries and dreads worse to come. As he sits in this deep sadness, he is suddenly amazed by the vision of a Lady, familiar and yet strange to him. Her face is vigorous as of one in youth, yet it bears the thought of untold time; her stature seems to vary, now of human height, now rising high beyond man's gaze. She is clad in a robe that carries in its lower part the Greek letter *pi* to mark her skill in practical meditation, in its upper part the letter *theta,* denoting her knowledge of contemplative science in ways beyond reason or intellectual imaginings. Steps fashioned in her dress lead from the lower to the higher part; but her clothing is torn by the violence of men in snatching fragments for their use.

It is the Lady Philosophy. She quickly perceives the unhappy mood of her disciple, so different from the earlier promise of his philosophic studies; but she determines rather to aid him by remedies than to waste time in complaints. Gradually the mist of depression clears a little from the mind of Boethius, and he recognizes his Mistress and Healer, long known to his life.

Now Philosophy begins her mission of succour. She reminds Boethius of the heroes of adversity in past time, of Socrates, of Zeno, of Seneca. Such as they care nothing for tyrants or adverse happenings; for a mighty fortress of philosophy stands ever ready to receive them in the hour of their need. Thither they may retire and laugh merrily from within at those who run after vain trifles outside. Philosophic indifference is their sure armour, dreading nothing, desiring nothing that may chain them to earth.

At her bidding Boethius opens his sorrow; he tells her of his upright administration and the wrongs done him by false charges, wails that the good are afflicted and the wicked rejoice. In answer Philosophy grieves that he has wandered in his complaining so far from his native country, the land of soul's content in God, and sets to work to bring him back:

> If you truly remember your own native land, you know that it is not ruled by a democracy as the Athenians once were ruled. It owns
>
> *Unus Deus et Pater omnium,*
>
> Who rejoices in the multitude, not in the banishment of His citizens, Whose service is justice and perfect liberty. Are you ignorant of that most ancient law of your City, which ordains that none may be an exile who has willed to settle his dwelling within her? For there is no fear that he who is held safely by her rampart and fortifying should deserve to be an exile. But he who ceases to wish to dwell within her ceases also to deserve this.
>
> And so the sight of this prison of yours does not concern me so much as the look upon your face. Not the walls of your library at home with their adornment of ivory and crystal matter to me so much as the house of your mind. There I have gathered, not books, but my ancient doctrines, for the sake of which books are prized.

The complaints that Boethius has made are true enough, and far more might be said, the Lady continues. But in his present state of distress remedies, mild remedies at first, must be applied for his healing. One or two questions then bring out the real trouble. He remembers, indeed, that God is the source and ruler of all the world, but he has forgotten how and by what means God governs it. "Now I know," replies Philosophy, "another, yes, and the greatest cause of your sickness. You no longer understand your true nature. Now, then, I have fully discovered the reason of your bitterness and so the means to win your rescue. You are confounded through forgetfulness of yourself, and for this reason you have grieved as an exile, robbed of your possessions. You do not know what is the real end of things, and so you think that worthless and wicked men are powerful and happy. You have forgotten by what helm the world is guided, and so you think that Fortune veers now this way, now that, without control. These are grave reasons, not only for sickness, but even for death."

Yet there is still hope. For Boethius, even in this great unhappiness, still knows that the world is ruled by divine reason. From this tiny spark the fire of life shall again blaze up in him. From this starting-point Philosophy will build up her cure of instruction.

First, then, it is entirely wrong to think that Fortune has shown a new and strange side of herself to him. For she is changeable of her own true nature and has ever been so. Why, then, be surprised when she shows herself in her true self? Everyone who takes Fortune as mistress must accept her as she shall be, bound by her own character to alter at some time, however constant she may be for a long period: "You have given yourself over to the will of Fortune. Then you must submit to the ways of your mistress. Do you want to stop her revolving wheel? But, most stupid of mortals, it is no longer the wheel of chance if it stays unmoved!"

The arguments which Fortune might bring forward in her own defence are now reviewed and found just and reasonable from her standpoint. Of her own she gave, of her own she has taken away. The turning of her wheel is within her own right, to swing up and down as she will. Why should Boethius expect treatment different from that meted out to other men? Further, Philosophy recalls all the blessings which have fallen to him in life, both domestic and political. Not now for the first time has he suddenly come as a stranger upon the stage of this world. To which Boethius answers in that cry which meets us again on the lips of Francesca, tossed in outer darkness upon the wind of torments, the grief of Tennyson for Arthur Hallam:

> A sorrow's crown of sorrow is remembering
> happier things.

Yet, urges Philosophy, your wife still lives and your sons, dearer to you than your own existence. What man, moreover, that lives can boast of fortune that shall give to him unmixed joy, be it of wealth or ancient lineage or wife of children? He who is blessed in one respect ever cries for his lack in another, and no earthly happiness remains stable. The only true happiness of man is found within himself, the chief of his own possessions. While he remains ignorant of the ways of Fortune, he cannot rest in peace, fearing her fickle habit. And, come what may, earthly fortune must desert the soul at its passing from this world of time. Have not many men sought and attained happiness in the rejection of temporal fortune, deliberately choosing pain and torment, even death itself?

By this time the healing touch of Philosophy has begun to take effect in the sick soul, and she warms to her work with increased vigour of longing to expose the futility of false fortune. If a man's possessions are bad, she declares, they are but a trouble to him; if they are good, their goodness is inherently their own, not of the man who only possesses them from without. Beauty and riches can only adorn a person; they must always be external to his real self; and how can mere clothes or servants add to a man's inner store of blessedness?

> Other creatures, truly, are happy in their own

> possessions. But you, with mind made in the image of God, do you seek the adornings of your high nature from the lowest things, and do not understand how great wrong you do your Creator? He willed that the human race should excel all earthly creatures; you thrust your dignity down below the very lowest. For if it be granted that what each man holds as his Good is more precious than the man himself, then you rank yourself inferior to the cheapest things by judging them to be your Good. And this is only what you deserve. For human nature is such that it only rises above other things when it knows its own true character, but is cast down below the beasts if it ceases to understands itself. Ignorance of self is natural to other living creatures; for men it is a sin.

The same is true regarding honours and offices of the State, which are the source of great harm when held by bad men and are only of profit in the hands of good citizens by reason of the personal virtue of their recipients: "So it comes about that public offices do not magnify virtuous men, but virtuous men magnify their offices." This desire of fame and glory is the special weakness, however, of great men. Yet how foolish it is! Reflect, observes Philosophy, that only a quarter of the world is inhabited by men, and much of this is taken up by seas and marshes and desert lands where no one may dwell. Why should anyone want to show forth his renown in this "tiniest point of a point"? Reflect, also, that in this little space there are assembled many races of different languages, manners and views of life—how can one man's fame reach very far? And what seems splendid to one race will seem blameworthy to another.

This is true enough of life. It is even more true when we think of death, which brings oblivion to most men's work in course of time. And what of a man's fame when brought face to face with eternity? Do men expect or desire earthly renown after death? Truly, we believe that the soul lives on. But will she crave to be still entangled in the things of this unstable world?

Yet, sometimes, Philosophy allows, Fortune does deserve well of men, and this, strangely enough, when she frowns upon them. For here, in changing, she not only shows her true self, but she reveals to those whom she deserts what store of happiness is really theirs in the friends that remain steadfast, the most precious of riches.

By now, through this method of reasoning, interspersed with the relaxation of song, Philosophy has cleared away the outer débris that had choked entrance to the happiness still latent in her patient's soul. And so, after a brief moment of recollection for the gathering of her resources, she now approaches more nearly to his higher self. Now she will teach him what is that happiness which is the end and aim of all men: "And that is the Good which utterly satisfies its possessor. It is truly the Highest Good, containing within itself all good things. If any good were absent from it, it could not be the Highest Good, for something to be desired would still be left outside it."

Yet men in their blindness do not recognize their true joy, and seek lower blessings, vainly supposing these to be the perfect good which they are all trying to attain by false paths. So "like drunken men they cannot find their way home." Such lesser goods are worldly wealth, honours, power, glory and pleasures, all of which men seek by natural inclination. Not one of these in itself can satisfy. They are prone rather to create their own craving for further possession and to bring with them their own sorrows, as being each and in their total union incomplete and lacking the sum of all goodness. They are but parts divided off from that undivided good which is the real desire of mankind. And this undivided perfect good is perfect happiness, a joy which in itself contains all gifts which a man can desire, and will render him in lack of nothing: neither wealth nor power nor reverence nor fame nor any manner of content.

Where, then, are we to seek this ideal happiness? Before trying to solve this problem Philosophy stays to ask help from the Father of all. Her petition is put in form of a hymn, from which students in the Middle Ages were gladly to regain much of the teaching of the *Timaeus* of Plato, still lost to them.

The final search is now entered upon, with the premise that the existence of every imperfect postulates a perfect. If there were no standard of perfection, nothing could be imagined as imperfect, spoiled of previous perfection and corrupted by this corrupt world.

We start in the certainty that God is good. Moreover, as such, He must be the Perfect Good, since He is chief of all things. That He could not be if there were anything more excellent or older than He; for the perfect must have existed before the imperfect. He must be the Perfect Good in Himself; for otherwise He must have received the Perfect Good from a source greater than Himself, in which case He would not be Him whom reason acknowledges as God. God, also, as God, is the beginning of all things, and as such the Author of all good. But the perfect good is in itself perfect happiness; therefore, God is both perfect happiness and perfect goodness alike.

If, then, continues Philosophy, we learn to know perfect goodness, we shall learn to know God. Perfect goodness is found in the union of all blessings and gifts which severally would be incomplete in virtue. Perfect goodness, moreover, possesses the quality of wholeness; for anything that is maimed or incomplete is so far lacking in good. Perfect goodness, we may therefore say, is identical with wholeness, with one-ness, with unity. But everything craves that wholeness for itself, that soundness and completeness of its parts, which is unity. Therefore everything strives after perfect goodness, and this goodness is the goal and end of all things.

Boethius is then allowed to catch his breath while Philosophy sings a song, of interest for its Platonic doctrine that human learning is but a remembrance of light given to the soul before her descent to this earth.

Now at last the disciple recalls his former knowledge,

forgotten for the time under the burden both of the flesh in general and of his own sorrow in particular: that God rules the world and all within it by means of Himself, Who is Perfect Goodness. "He is, we may say, the rudder and the helm by which this world's body and its workings are kept stable and unspoiled."

From this there follows immediately another conclusion. Since all things of their own nature are striving after perfect wholeness, which is one-ness, which, as we have seen, is perfect goodness, or, under another name, perfect happiness, all things in following their natural desire must be really striving to find God.

Another thought also arises. Since God is all-powerful and can do all things, but is unable to do evil, we must conclude that evil is nothing and does not exist. This kindles a new spark of grief in Boethius, as he hears that evil is to be believed non-existent! So Philosophy leaves her logical instruction for a while to calm him in a song of Orpheus and Eurydice.

The listener, however, can hardly wait for the end, before he bursts out with the question: "Why, under God's rule, are wicked men powerful and good men lacking in power?" Philosophy answers that this is not true. Here he has touched upon a great matter, and its unfolding will lift him swiftly as it were on wings, to bear him once more to the native country of his soul.

We have seen, she begins again, that all men strive eagerly for happiness. As happiness is their chief good, both the virtuous man and the evil man strive equally after goodness, the one rightly, the other in mistaken fashion. Since, therefore, the virtuous man attains his object of goodness and the bad man fails, of necessity the virtuous possesses power and the bad lacks it. In proportion as a man's character is worse, so does he fall further short of his goal by his error of judgment, and so the more does he lack of power. He must either fall short through blind ignorance, weakest of qualities, or through frailty itself, in that he sees but is not able to compass that end of good which he really desires. No man, however, is wholly evil or he could do nothing at all. For evil is nothing, as we have said.

Further, we may argue thus: That all real power is to be desired, and that all desirable things are desired because of their goodness. But the possibility of committing crime is not desired because of its goodness, and accordingly the possibility of committing crime is not real power at all.

By these stages, therefore, we are brought to the conclusion of Plato in the *Gorgias:* "Only the wise are able to do what they want to do. The wicked are able to carry out their immediate pleasure, but they cannot fulfil their real desire. They do their pleasure and think to obtain the Good they desire by the things which please them. But they gain it in no sort at all, for the wicked cannot attain to happiness."

Now good and evil have opposite destinies, led thereto by their opposite qualities. Since goodness is the reward of the good, wickedness must be the reward of the bad. But, as goodness is happiness, so wickedness is misery. Therefore the bad man is miserable. And more. Since all that is exists in so far as it is whole, or, in other words, in virtue of its one-ness, and since the Perfect One-ness or Unity is the Perfect Good, therefore, all that exists is good. On the contrary, whatever has ceased to be good has ceased to exist; therefore, as evil has no existence, so bad men, in so far as they are bad, are not real men at all.

Presently Boethius, who is now feeling much better, sympathetically utters the pious wish that bad men had not this power of doing their imagined pleasure. Philosophy replies that this very power is in itself their punishment, since evil is misery. The bad man, indeed, who is punished is really happier than the bad man who escapes penalty. For penalty, in so far as it is just, is good, and, therefore, the bad man's badness is mixed with some proportion of good when he is bearing the penalty for his sin. On the contrary, the bad man unpunished is in a parlous state, for injustice is thereby added to his burden of badness. For this reason criminals should be brought to tribunals of justice, as sick men, even if unwilling, are brought to a doctor. Indeed, on reflection they ought to be glad to be punished that they may thus obtain something of goodness in their evil plight. Moreover, none should hate the wicked, but should rather regard them as sick souls in need of a physician. Hatred of the criminal is a sin against reason, seeing that crime is a disease of the mind.

Here the Lady Philosophy and her patient begin to find themselves in deep waters. For Boethius naturally wants to know why the good are punished and the bad are rewarded. Why do men sin here, in a world governed, not by chance, but by the Divine Will? Does God force men on to the destiny His foreknowledge sees awaiting them? The answer to this most difficult problem involves discussion of such weighty matters as the simplicity of Providence; the consequence of Fate; sudden accidents; the knowledge of God; predestination and free-will. Little time is now left to the two after so long talk. Yet Philosophy will try to treat of the question of Boethius in some brief sort.

From this point the colloquy takes a new turn, as its writer attempts some new step toward the harmonizing of the old, old connection in human thought between God's foreknowledge of man's destiny and the doctrine of man's predestination.

He begins with his famous definings of Providence and of Fate. They may best be given in a translation of his own words: "Providence is that very Divine Reason which is seated in the Most High Lord and disposes all things. Fate, on the other hand, is inherent in the things that are moved, and is the means whereby Providence intertwines all things in their own due order. Providence embraces all things alike, however different, to infinity; Fate moves things one by one, according to different places, forms and seasons. Therefore, the exposition of this temporal order of ours in one single view foreseen by the Divine Mind is Providence; the same view, when its various parts are arranged and displayed in their different times, is called Fate."

Whatever, then, the immediate agency by which things are done, "it is clear that Providence is the immovable and simple form of events that are to be; Fate is the movable intertwining and the order in time of the events which the Divine Simplicity has bidden come into being. Therefore, all things which are under Fate are also subject to Providence, to which even Fate itself is subject. Some things, indeed, under the will of Providence rise above the ordered sequence of Fate."

What, then, is chance? Here we find another definition of note in later times. "Chance is the unforeseen result of a combination of causes in acts done for some purpose." It is brought about by Fate emanating from Providence in accordance with the will of God.

This brings us to the final enquiry: whether men have free will or are constrained by necessity? The answer is unhesitating: human nature, in so far and in such degree as it is endowed with reason and guided by it, is, indeed, possessed of free will. But not, therefore, in equal measure. Supernatural and divine beings have clear judgment and pure will and efficient power for the carrying out of their wishes. Human souls are less free when they descend from the heavenly vision into bodies, still less when they forsake the light of reason through weakness or vice.

But God in his Providence foresees all things, embraced in one simple view. Then must not all that God foresees as going to happen, happen of necessity? And how can man be free to act as he would, caught in this chain of inevitable sequence? For we cannot believe that God sees uncertainty in His gaze, lest we bring down His foreknowledge to the level of human opinion.

The cause of this dilemma of man, Boethius asserts, rests on an initial error, "the belief that knowledge of things is only derived from the character and nature of the things themselves. The truth is just the opposite. Knowledge of each thing known depends, not upon its own character, but upon the varying faculties of those who know it." The different faculties, ranging from lower to higher—sense, imagination, reason, intelligence—know and understand things in a corresponding degree of gradually ascending power. The higher faculty includes in its knowledge of any object all the knowledge of the faculty or faculties below it in power; so that, finally, intelligence must be said to possess all the powers of apprehension owned by sense, imagination and reason together.

It would, therefore, be foolish of the lower faculties of knowledge, which can but grasp the sensible or the imaginable, to deny that reason has a higher power, seeing that it can grasp the universal. And in like manner it would be foolish of human reason to refuse to yield in comprehension to the Divine intelligence. For reason cannot by her own light see the things of the future which lie open to the mind of God.

If, then, we would understand somewhat of the knowledge of God, we must also understand somewhat of His nature. God is Eternal. And if we can understand in some degree the meaning of eternity, we shall know of the nature and thus of the knowledge of God. Eternity, we may say, is the whole and perfect possession at one and the same moment of everlasting life, whereas whatsoever lives in time is constantly passing from past to present, and so on to the future. There is nothing in time which can embrace at one and the same moment the whole space of its life: yesterday, today, and tomorrow. But that which at one and the same moment embraces and holds the whole plenitude of everlasting life, to which nothing of the future is wanting nor anything of the past is lost or gone, that rightly is called eternal. Of necessity the Eternal is always present and in possession of itself; of necessity it has present with it and before its mind the infinity of moving time.

It is true that the perpetual movement of temporal things by its constantly passing periods tries to imitate the infinite presentness of the unmoving eternity of the Divine Mind. But time, the perpetual, can never be eternity embracing all knowledge, past, present and future, in each moment of its consciousness. For we have observed that every judgment comprehends the things subjected to its knowledge by means of its own nature and comparative power. So the knowledge of God, being both Eternal and One, embraces in its one-ness, in its perfection, all things, that have been, that are, and that shall be, ever and always, at one and the same time. These things are in perpetual motion, while God, seeing all from beginning to end, is Himself unmoved, is unaffected by the passage of time. We may regard, then, His power not so much as foreknowledge, but rather as never-failing perfect alknowledge, surveying the plain of human experience in its totality as from some lofty height.

Why, therefore, should we think that those future things which the Divine Mind includes in its comprehensive grasp of all time are necessarily bound upon man's will, any more than we think that the things which men see every day must necessarily happen merely because men see them happening? We see the sun rise, and call it necessary; we observe other men walking, and call it voluntary. Neither event is constrained to happen just because we see it happen. So with God, Who sees, without compelling them, both the necessary and the voluntary things that shall be. For with Him present, past and future are all one.

This is the end of this meditation in captivity, and Boethius now places on the lips of his Mistress the thoughts that were staying his soul as he awaited, he knew not what, in those months before his death: "There remains, therefore, freedom of will unspoiled for men, and the laws are not unjust which hold out prizes and penalties for wills freed from all necessity. God ever abides in His foreknowledge, spectator on high of all things; and eternity, ever present to His vision, concurs with the judgment our actions shall gain for us, awarding prizes to the good and punishments to the wicked. Hopes and prayers laid up in God are not in vain; if they be rightful they cannot fail of fruit. Fight, then, against sins, cultivate virtues, lift up your mind to rightful hopes, stretch out to the highest your humble prayers. A great constraint toward good life is declared unto you, if you will not to deceive, in that you live before the eyes of a Judge Who beholds all things."

Cassiodorus, Ennodius, Boethius: these are the three last sounds from the train of Italy's culture before it plunges into the long tunnel of the Dark Ages. Flashes of light may occasionally illuminate its buried course, but they do little save reveal the darkness. Italy recked little of ancient culture in the time of Gregory the Great, and it was in Spain and in Celtic lands, in Ireland and in Britain, in Gaul nurtured by Ireland, that classical learning still found its lovers when these three were dead and gone. Even already, if the metaphor be not too strained, the rising cliffs that mark the tunnel's approach have cut off from these three much of the freshness and the radiance of the open horizon. Yet all three worked on in the twilight of Roman letters, fearing the coming night, hoping for a new dawn, if from the barbarians themselves. All refused to despair. There is something courageous even in the rhetoric of Ennodius; something higher, perhaps, than the careless blindness of Sidonius Apollinaris. Cassiodorus only retired when he felt he had nothing more to offer his country in political service; from his retirement and his old age he was to offer her a legacy far greater than any of his workings in active life. The scientific translations and commentaries of Boethius were to influence mightily the coming Schoolmen. But the work that influenced the world and is always connected with his name came from his prison, written without books, without scholars, in loneliness and weariness of life. These are strange things; yet not strange, to those who know the world's history.

C. S. Lewis (essay date 1964)

SOURCE: "Selected Materials: The Seminal Period," in *The Discarded Image: An Introduction to Medieval and Renaissance Literature,* Cambridge at the University Press, 1964, pp. 45-91.

[*Lewis was an acknowledged authority in the fields of Medieval and Renaissance literature, as well as an esteemed writer of fantasy and science fiction. In the following excerpt from a posthumously published work, he elucidates the extent to which the* Consolation of Philosophy *helped to shape the standard Medieval perception of human affairs.*]

[Boethius's] ***De Consolatione Philosophiae*** was for centuries one of the most influential books ever written in Latin. It was translated into Old High German, Italian, Spanish, and Greek; into French by Jean de Meung; into English by Alfred, Chaucer, Elizabeth I, and others. Until about two hundred years ago it would, I think, have been hard to find an educated man in any European country who did not love it. To acquire a taste for it is almost to become naturalised in the Middle Ages.

Boethius, scholar and aristocrat, was a minister to Theodoric the Visigoth, the first barbarian king in Italy and an Arian by religion, though no persecutor. As always, the word 'barbarian' might mislead. Though Theodoric was illiterate, he had passed his youth in high Byzantine society. He was in some ways a better ruler than many Roman emperors had been. His reign in Italy was not a sheer monstrosity as, say, the rule of Chaka or Dingaan in nineteenth-century England would have been. It was more as if a (popish) highland chieftain (who had acquired a little polish and a taste for claret in the French service) had reigned over the partly Protestant and partly sceptical England of Johnson and Lord Chesterfield. It is not, however, surprising that the Roman aristocracy were soon caught intriguing with the Eastern Emperor in the hope of delivering themselves from this alien. Boethius, whether justly or not, fell under suspicion. He was imprisoned at Pavia. Presently they twisted ropes round his head till his eyes dropped out and finished him off with a bludgeon.

Now Boethius was undoubtedly a Christian and even a theologian; his other works bear titles like ***De Trinitate*** and ***De Fide Catholica***. But the 'philosophy' to which he turned for 'consolation' in the face of death contains few explicitly Christian elements and even its compatibility with Christian doctrine might be questioned.

Such a paradox has provoked many hypotheses. As:

(1) That his Christianity was superficial and failed him when brought to the test, so that he had to fall back on what neo-Platonism could do for him.

(2) That his Christianity was solid as a rock and his neo-Platonism a mere game with which he distracted himself in his dungeon—as other prisoners in like case have tamed a spider or a rat.

(3) That the theological essays were not really written by the same man.

None of these theories seems to me necessary.

Though the ***De Consolatione*** was certainly written after his fall, in exile and perhaps under arrest, I do not think it was written in a dungeon nor in daily expectation of the executioner. Once, indeed, he speaks of *terror;* once he describes himself as doomed to 'death and proscription'; once Philosophia accuses him of 'fearing the bludgeon and the axe'. But the general tone of the book does not match these momentary outbursts. It is not that of a prisoner awaiting death but that of a noble and a statesman lamenting his fall—exiled, financially damaged, parted from his beautiful library, stripped of his official dignities, his name scandalously traduced. This is not the language of the condemned cell. And some of the 'consolations' which Philosophia addresses to him would be comically cruel mockeries to a man in that situation—as when she reminds him that the place which is exile to him is home to others, or that many would regard as wealth even those remains of his property which he has managed to save. The Consolation Boethius seeks is not for death but for ruin. When he wrote the book he may have known that his life was in some danger. I do not think he despaired of it. Indeed he complains at the outset that death cruelly neglects wretches who would gladly die.

If we had asked Boethius why his book contained philosophical rather than religious consolations, I do not doubt that he would have answered, 'But did you not read my title? I wrote philosophically, not religiously, because I had chosen the consolations of philosophy, not those of religion, as my subject. You might as well ask why a book on arithmetic does not use geometrical methods.' Aristotle had impressed on all who followed him the distinction between disciplines and the propriety of following in each its appropriate method. We have seen this at work in Chalcidius [earlier]; and Boethius draws our attention to it in his argument. He compliments Philosophia on having used 'inborn and domestical proofs', not 'reasons fetched from without'. That is, he congratulates himself on having reached conclusions acceptable to Christianity from purely philosophical premises—as the rules of art demanded. When, on the other hand, she draws near the doctrines of Hell and Purgatory, he makes her check herself—'for it is not now our business to discuss such matters'.

But why, we may ask, did a Christian author impose upon himself this limitation? Partly, no doubt, because he knew where his true talent lay. But we can suggest another, and probably less conscious, motive. The distinction between Christian and Pagan can hardly, at that moment, have been more vividly present to his emotions than that between Roman and barbarian; especially since the barbarian was also a heretic. Catholic Christendom and that high Pagan past to which he felt so deep a loyalty were united in his outlook by their common contrast to Theodoric and his huge, fair-skinned, beer-drinking, boasting thanes. This was no time for stressing whatever divided him from Virgil, Seneca, Plato, and the old Republican heroes. He would have been robbed of half his comfort if he had chosen a theme which forced him to point out where the great ancient masters had been wrong; he preferred one that enabled him to feel how nearly they had been right, to think of them not as 'they' but as 'we'.

As a result, the specifically Christian passages in the book are few. The martyrs are clearly referred to. In contradiction to the Platonic view that the Divine and the human cannot meet except through a *tertium quid,* prayer is a direct *commercium* between God and Man. When Philosophia, speaking of Providence, uses the words 'strongly and sweetly', from Wisdom viii. I Boethius replies, 'I am delighted with your argument, but much more by the very language you use'. But far more often Boethius is saying what Plato or the neo-Platonists would have confirmed. Man, by his reason, is a divine animal; the soul is fetched from heaven, and her ascent thither is a return. In his account of creation Boethius is much closer to the *Timaeus* than to Scripture.

Apart from its contributions to the Model ***De Consolatione*** had some formal influence. It belongs to the kind called *Satira Menippea* in which prose sections alternate with (shorter) sections in verse. From Boethius this descends to Bernardus and Alanus and even into Sannazaro's *Arcadia.* (I have often wondered that it has never been revived. One would have thought that a Landor, a Newman, or an Arnold might have turned it to good account.)

In Book I the appearance of Philosophia as a woman both old and young is borrowed from Claudian's *Natura* in the *Consulship of Stilicho* (II, 424 *sq.*). It will re-appear in the *Natura* of the French poem which Lydgate translated as *Reason and Sensuality* (line 334). She tells him, among other things, that we—we philosophers—must anticipate calumny, for it is our express purpose (*maxime propositum*) to displease the rabble. This towering vaunt, this philosophic *panache* which goes beyond mere indifference to mud-flinging and actually courts it, is of Cynic origin. Milton's Christ is infected with it, when he describes the common herd as people 'of whom to be disprais'd were no small praise' in *Paradise Regained* (III, 54). But poor Boethius is not yet ready for so high a strain; he is as deaf to it as a donkey to the harp—an image Chaucer appropriated in *Troilus*, I, 730. Everyone is now slandering him, though in reality his conduct while in office had been of flawless purity. He adds with almost comic inconsistency—Boethius the author here ruthlessly exposing Boethius the natural man—that his virtue was all the more admirable because he practised it with no thought of being admired. For, he adds, virtue is tarnished if a man displays it so as to get credit for it.

This modest maxim cuts right across the ideals of the Dark Ages and of the Renaissance. Roland unashamedly desires *los* as Beowulf desires *dom* or the heroes in French tragedy desire *la gloire.* It was often discussed in the later Middle Ages. Alanus knows it but agrees with it only up to a point. The good man should not make fame his object, but to reject it altogether is too austere (*Anti-claudian,* VII, iv, 26). Gower, on the other hand, applies it in its full rigour, even to knightly deeds,

> In armes lith non avantance
> To him that thenkth his name avance
> And be renomed of his dede.
> (*Confessio Amantis,* I, 2651.)

Boethius then passionately demands an explanation of the contrast between the regularity with which God governs the rest of Nature and the irregularity He permits in human affairs. This is made a central theme of Nature's 'complaint' in Alanus and of her 'confession' in Jean de Meung. Later still Milton is recalling, and no doubt expects us to recognise that he is recalling, this place from Boethius in one of the choruses of *Samson,* (667 *sq.*). The whole concept will seem less remote to some modern readers if they relate it to the Existentialist position that Man is a *passion inutile* and compares very unfavourably with the irrational or even the inorganic world.

With Book II we embark on that great apologia for Fortune which impressed her figure so firmly on the imagination of succeeding ages. Comments on good and bad luck and their obvious failure to correspond with good and ill desert may be expected in any period; but the medieval allusions to Fortune and her wheel are exceptional in their frequency and seriousness. The grandeur which this image takes on in the *Inferno* (VII, 73 *sq.*) is a reminder how entirely it depends on individual genius whether a *locus communis* shall or shall not be what we call 'commonplace'. And this, like a thousand inferior passages, is part of the Boethian legacy. No one who had read of *Fortuna* as he treats her could forget her for long. His work, here Stoical and Christian alike, in full harmony with the Book of Job and with certain Dominical sayings, is one of the most vigorous defences ever written against the view, common to vulgar Pagans and vulgar Christians alike, which 'comforts cruel men' by interpreting variations of human prosperity as divine rewards and punishments, or at least wishing that they were. It is an enemy hard to kill; latent in what has been called 'the Whig interpretation of history' and rampant in the historical philosophy of Carlyle.

At every point in this discussion we meet 'old friends'—that is, images and phrases which first became our friends when they had grown very much older.

Thus from Book II: 'The most miserable misfortune is to have been happy once.' Dante's *nessun maggior dolore* (*Inferno,* V, 121) and Tennyson's 'sorrow' crown of sorrows' leap to mind. 'Nothing is miserable unless you think it so.' We remember Chaucer's 'no man is wreched but himself it wene' in the *Ballade of Fortune* and Hamlet's 'There is nothing either good or bad but thinking makes it so'. We are told that we cannot lose external goods because we never really had them. The beauty of fields or gems is a real good, but it is theirs, not ours; the beauty of clothes is either theirs (the richness of the stuff) or the skill of the tailor—nothing will make it ours. The idea will turn up again unexpectedly in *Joseph Andrewes* (III, 6). Soon after this we hear the praises of the *prior aetas,* the primeval innocence pictured by the Stoics. Readers of Milton will here notice the *pretiosa pericula* which became his 'precious bane'. From this *prior aetas* came both the 'Former Age' of Chaucer's ballade and 'the old age' mentioned by Orsino (*Twelfth Night,* II, iv, 46). We are told that nothing so much beguiles those who have some natural excellence but are not yet perfected in virtue as the desire for fame. It is a maxim from the *Agricola* of Tacitus; it will later blossom into Milton's line about 'that last infirmity of noble mind'.

Philosophia proceeds to mortify this desire, as Africanus had done in the *Somnium* [Cicero's *Somnium Scipionis*], by pointing out how provincial all earthly fame is since this globe, by cosmic standards, is admittedly to be regarded as a mathematical point—*puncti habere rationem.* But Boethius deepens this stock argument by stressing the diversity of moral standards even within this tiny area. What is fame in one nation can be infamy in another. And anyway how short-lived all reputations are! Books, like their author, are mortal. No one now knows where the bones of Fabricius lie. (Here, for the benefit of his English readers, Alfred happily substituted 'the bones of Weland'.)

Adversity has the merit of opening our eyes by showing which of our friends are true and which are feigned. Combine this with Vincent of Beauvais' statement that hyena's gall restores the sight (*Speculum Naturale,* XIX, 62), and you have the key to Chaucer's cryptic line "Thee nedeth nat the gall of noon hyene' (*Fortune,* 35).

From Book III: All men know that the true good is Happiness, and all men seek it, but, for the most part, by wrong routes—like a drunk man who knows he has a house but can't find his way home. Chaucer reproduces the simile in the *Knight's Tale* (A 1261 *sq.*).

Yet even the false routes, such as wealth or glory, show that men have some inkling of the truth; for the true good is glorious like fame and, like wealth, self-sufficient. So strong is the bent of nature that we thus struggle towards our native place, as the caged bird struggles to return to the woods. Chaucer borrows this image for his *Squire's Tale* (F 621 *sq.*).

One of the false images of the good is Nobility. But Nobility is only the fame (and we have already exploded fame) of our ancestors' virtue, which was a good of theirs, not ours. This doctrine had a flourishing progeny in the Middle Ages, and became a popular subject for school debates. It underlies Dante's *canzone* at the opening of *Convivio,* IV, and the other place in *De Monarchia* (II, 3). The *Roman de la Rose* (18,615 *sq.*) goes beyond Boethius and boldly equates *gentilesse* with virtue. The English version at this point (2185-202) further expands its French original. *The Wife of Bath* reproduces Boethius more exactly (D 1154). Gower, like the *Roman,* identifies nobility with 'vertu set in the corage' (IV, 2261 *sq.*). One may be forgiven a smile when a (not otherwise very ignorant) author finds in this passage a proof that Gower expresses the feelings of the middle class which in his day was (as usual) 'rising into new importance'.

The argument now climbs to the position that the whole and perfect good, of which we usually chase only fragments or shadows, is God. In the course of proving this—though it needed no new proof either for Platonists or Christians—Boethius slips in, as axiomatic, the remark that all perfect things are prior to all imperfect things. It was common ground to nearly all ancient and medieval thinkers except the Epicureans. I have already stressed the radical difference which this involves between their thought and the developmental or evolutionary concepts of our own period—a difference which perhaps leaves no area and no level of consciousness unaffected.

Those who have once risen to contemplate 'the admirable circle of the divine simplicity' must be careful not to look back again to worldly objects. The moral is enforced by the story of Orpheus and his fatal backward glance at Eurydice, and this telling of that story was as widely influential as Virgil's. It is also of great structural importance in the ***De Consolatione,*** for Boethius himself, when Philosophia visited him in Book I, was indulging in just such a retrospection. Here, too, he reaches his highest point as a poet in the famous lines

> Orpheus Eurydicen suam
> Vidit, perdidit, occidit.

From Book IV: The doctrine of divine Providence, Boethius complains, rather aggravates than solves the real problem: why is justice—certainly 'poetic justice'—so unapparent in the course of events? Philosophia makes two replies.

(1) It is all justice. The good are always rewarded and the wicked always punished, by the mere fact of being what they are. Evil power and evil performance are the punishment of evil will, and it will be infinite since the soul is immortal (as philosophy, no less than Theology, asserts). The passage looks back to Virgil's hell whose inhabitants *ausi omnes immane nefas ausoque potiti,* 'all purposed dreadful deeds *and got their way'* (*Aeneid,* VI, 624). It looks forward to Milton who says of the wiser Pagans that 'to banish forever into a local hell . . . they thought not a punishment so proper and proportionate for God to inflict as to punish sin with sin' (*Doctrine and Discipline,* II, 3). And yet, pleads Boethius, it is very strange to see the wicked flourishing and the virtuous afflicted. Why, yes, replies Philosophia; everything is strange until you know the cause. Compare the *Squire's Tale* (F 258).

(2) That which 'in the citadel of the divine simplicity' is Providence, when seen from below, mirrored in the multiplicity of time and space, is Destiny. And as in a wheel the nearer we get to the centre the less motion we find, so every finite being, in proportion as he comes nearer to participating in the Divine (unmoving) Nature, becomes less subject to Destiny, which is merely a moving image of eternal Providence. That Providence is wholly good. We say that the wicked flourish and the innocent suffer. But we do not know who are the wicked and who are the innocent; still less what either need. All luck, seen from the centre, is good and medicinal. The sort we call 'bad' exercises good men and curbs bad ones—if they will take it so. Thus, if only you are near the hub, if you participate in Providence more and suffer Destiny less, 'it lies in your own hands to make your fortune what you please'. Or, as Spenser turns this passage, 'each unto himself his life may fortunize' (*F.Q.* VI, ix, 30).

The noblest descendant of this passage, however, is not in words. At Florence in Santa Maria del Popolo the cupola above Chigi's tomb sets the whole Boethian image of the wheel and the hub, of Destiny and Providence, before our eyes. On the utmost circumference the planets, the dispensers of fate, are depicted. On a smaller circle, within and above them, are the Intelligences that move them. At the centre, with hands upraised in guidance, sits the Unmoved Mover.

In the fifth and last book the argument is closer, and succeeding generations were unable to pluck out of it many isolated plums. But this does not mean that it proved less influential. It underlies every later treatment of the problem of freedom.

The conclusion of the previous book has left us with a new difficulty. If, as its doctrine of Providence implies, God sees all things that are, were, or will be, *uno mentis in ictu,* in a single act of mind, and thus foreknows my actions, how am I free to act otherwise than He has foreseen? Philosophia will not put Boethius off with the shift that Milton is reduced to in *Paradise Lost* (III, 117), that, though God foreknows, His foreknowledge does not cause, my act. For the question never was whether foreknowledge necessitates the act but whether it is not evidence that the act must have been necessary.

Can there, then, be foreknowledge of the indeterminate? In a sense, yes. The character of knowledge depends not on the nature of the object known but on that of the knowing faculty. Thus in ourselves sensation, imagination, and *ratio* all in their several ways 'know' man. Sensation knows him as a corporeal shape; imagination, as a shape without matter; *ratio,* as a concept, a species. None of these faculties by itself gives us the least hint of the mode of knowledge enjoyed by its superior. But above *ratio* or reason there is a higher faculty, *intelligentia* or understanding. (Long afterwards Coleridge reversed this by making reason the higher and understanding the lower. I postpone further consideration of the medieval terminology till a later section.) And Reason cannot conceive the future being known except as it would have to be known, if at all, by her; that is, as determinate. But it is just possible even for us to climb up to the intelligential level and get a glimpse of the knowledge which does not involve determinism.

Eternity is quite distinct from perpetuity, from mere endless continuance in time. Perpetuity is only the attainment of an endless series of moments, each lost as soon as it is attained. Eternity is the actual and timeless fruition of illimitable life. Time, even endless time, is only an image, almost a parody, of that plenitude; a hopeless attempt to compensate for the transitoriness of its 'presents' by infinitely multiplying them. That is why Shakespeare's Lucrece calls it 'thou ceaseless lackey to eternity' (*Rape,* 967). And God is eternal, not perpetual. Strictly speaking, He never *fore*sees; He simply sees. Your 'future' is only an area, and only for us a special area, of His infinite Now. He sees (not remembers) your yesterday's acts because yesterday is still 'there' for Him; he sees (not foresees) your tomorrow's acts because He is already in tomorrow. As a human spectator, by watching my present act, does not at all infringe its freedom, so I am none the less free to act as I choose in the future because God, in that future (His present) watches me acting.

I have so ruthlessly condensed an argument of such importance, both historical and intrinsic, that the wise reader will go for it to the original. I cannot help thinking that Boethius has here expounded a Platonic conception more luminously than Plato ever did himself.

The work ends with Philosophia thus speaking; there is no return to Boethius and his situation, any more than to Christopher Sly at the end of *The Taming of the Shrew.* This I believe to be a stroke of calculated and wholly successful art. We are made to feel as if we had seen a heap of common materials so completely burnt up that there remains neither ash nor smoke nor even flame, only a quivering of invisible heat.

Gibbon has expressed in cadences of habitual beauty his contempt for the impotence of such 'philosophy' to subdue the feelings of the human heart. But no one ever said it would have subdued Gibbon's. It sounds as if it had done something for Boethius. It is historically certain that for more than a thousand years many minds, not contemptible, found it nourishing.

H. Liebeschütz (essay date 1967)

SOURCE: "Boethius and the Legacy of Antiquity," in *The Cambridge History of Later Greek and Early Medieval Philosophy,* edited by A. H. Armstrong, Cambridge at the University Press, 1967, pp. 538-64.

[*In the following excerpt, the critic provides a survey of Boethius's importance in the history of philosophy, maintaining that the work of the Roman senator defines the point where antiquity ends and the Middle Ages begin.*]

When we try to draw a borderline between antiquity and Middle Ages, in order to define the point where the history of medieval philosophy begins, the work of Boethius comes immediately to our mind. The last Roman and the first schoolman, the two titles with which he is normally introduced, express in their combination clearly his position between the two periods. His link with the Middle Ages is obviously very strong. Translations of two treatises from Aristotle's *Organon,* his introductions for the beginners and his commentaries and monographs for the advanced student of logic, have deeply influenced the course of medieval thought. In this development the gradual absorption of the Boethian legacy remained an important aspect up to and including the rise of early Scholasticism in the twelfth century. Through all the centuries of the Middle Ages ***De consolatione philosophiae,*** the Roman senator's final account with life, was a standard book, stimulating discussions among scholars, and a source of spiritual strength in critical situations. Hundreds of manuscripts, originating from the eighth to the fifteenth century, prove the importance of the Boethian corpus of writings in the libraries of Western and Central Europe.

But the history of his influence in the medieval world shows clearly that the Roman interpreter of Aristotle was not himself a part of it, but rather an intellectual force radiating from a distance. In life and thought Boethius still belonged to Christian antiquity. There is no doubt that he and his contemporaries felt the possibility of the end approaching and certainly such foreboding had a stimulating influence on their studies and literary activities. At this time Italy was ruled by a Germanic king, and his Ostrogothic retainers represented the power in the state as a warrior class. Theodoric, in his attitude to learning, may appear rather similar to Charlemagne, if we do not compare them too closely. Boethius was favoured by the court for many years and reached finally a high position as *magister officiorum* in this society, in which military power and administration were divided between the Gothic swordsmen and the literary Romans. But Boethius, in contrast to representatives of learning in the medieval world was not only a layman—examples of this type existed still in the Carolingian period—but he did not write for the education and religious instruction of the Germanic society by their clergy; he expected his readers to come from the educated class of the landowning aristocracy, to which Anicius Manlius Severinus Boethius himself belonged by his family. Symmachus, his father-in-law, who had also been the mentor of his youth, was the great-grandson of the man who had pressed the claim to restore the altar of Victory to the council chamber of the Senate. At this time that meant conflict with Ambrosius in the name of belief in the classical tradition and in Roman greatness. The fifth century had brought about a definite change. The national pride of this class, the feeling of continuity with the past was still alive. But now they found their ancient ideal represented in the position of Rome as the head of the Christian world. They were eager to defend such aspirations against rival claims from Constantinople and in the secrecy of their hearts they refused to recognize the Gothic rulers as legal represen-

A sixth-century portrait head believed to be of Queen Amalasuntha, daughter of Theodoric.

tatives of the *res publica,* because of their adherence to a heretical creed, Arianism. Their zeal for orthodox belief had a background of Roman patriotism.

This social environment is relevant to the understanding of Boethius' thought. To the modern reader of his books he certainly appears as a trained scholar and man of letters. But he did not see himself merely as a professional writer, but rather as a late follower of Cicero, for whom literary activities were an appropriate occupation for the leisure hours which high office and politics allowed him. After 550 years he intended to complete the great task which the master of Latinity had started, to renew philosophical learning in his own mother tongue.

Boethius was conscious of the fact that his great predecessor in this task had already faced the problem of finding the adequate equivalents for Greek terminology in a language which had grown by describing the concrete world of an agricultural community not originally interested in the theoretical aspects of things.

This task was carried on in schools, where literature was taught as a part of rhetorical education. Martianus Capella offers examples for the period about 400. The patristic writers of the Latin Church from Tertullian to Marius Victorinus and Augustine did the corresponding work in the service of speculative theology. But it was finally Boethius who established the vocabulary of abstraction with which the schoolmen of later generations could do their work.

The programme by which the Roman senator in Gothic Italy intended to complete Cicero's work was very comprehensive. He planned to translate the whole Aristotelian corpus, as far as it was still available to him. In this way he hoped to bring all three sections of philosophy, logic, ethics and natural science, in their full range to his countrymen. The next step in his scheme was the translation of all Platonic dialogues as basis for a synthesis of Platonism and Aristotelianism. He wished to refute the majority opinion, that the two great teachers of Greek philosophy were opposed to each other in the essentials of their thought.

When, in consequence of a radical change of political conditions, Theodoric's will brought violent death to Boethius, while he was still in his forties, all his work in this field had been restricted to the logical doctrines of Aristotle; nothing lasting had been accomplished regarding the translation of the Platonic dialogues. But this does not imply any siding with Aristotle. His disinclination to define an opinion on an issue which to most people seemed to contain the essential difference between the two systems, is expressed in a clear refusal to declare one master right and the other wrong. We read this famous passage in two versions, which appear in the first and second edition of his interpretation of Porphyry's *Isagoge*, the introduction to the elementary concepts of logic. In the Greek text the question of the nature of species and genus had been raised; the alternatives are surveyed: either they are, as concepts, mere products of the human mind, or they exist, either as material or as immaterial beings. Their existence may be inherent in the things which are the objects of our senses, or they may be separate. Porphyry had refused to discuss this question, because it would have led him to an investigation beyond his literary purpose of writing an elementary book on philosophy. Boethius goes beyond the text he explains by refuting the objection that universal propositions are fictitious, because nobody can see them. Nobody would maintain that a geometrical line is the same kind of fiction as the centaur, a compound of man and horse. We think of this mathematical conception as of something outside corporal existence, but we are conscious of the fact that we have abstracted it from our sense experience. In the same way 'species' exists in the objects of our observation, from which we collect the impression of similarity between different things. This similarity becomes a thought in our mind and so a 'species'. When we go on to compare different species and find similarity between them, 'genus' arises in the same way as a mental phenomenon. While we observe the similarity in single things it remains an object of our sense experience; but when it leads to an act of generalization it is transformed into the mental process of understanding: species and genus are inherent in objects of observation. But as instruments in the process of understanding reality they belong to the sphere of the mind as separate entities.

Boethius concludes this chapter by stating that Plato went beyond this view when he maintained the existence of species and genus not only in the act of understanding, but in reality. Aristotle's opinion is identical with the doctrine Boethius himself was giving as further explanation to Porphyry's text. He did so because the *Isagoge* is an introduction to an Aristotelian treatise. But Boethius emphasized that by doing so he did not mean to give a judgement on the question as such, which must be decided on a higher level of philosophical reflection.

This abstention from a subject-matter which seemed to lie beyond the scope of the endeavour which the author has in hand, corresponds well with the carefully organized programme in which one stage of work was planned to follow the other in logical sequence. Boethius, while writing these paragraphs in his commentary to Porphyry, could not foresee that 600 years later the alternatives, which he had left side by side without definite conclusion, would form the centres around which the opposite views of realists and nominalists in the important debate on the nature of concepts would crystallize.

But the impact of Boethius' logical work on the development of Western thought is no product of historical chance. The bias of higher education towards rhetoric, which can be traced back to the sophist and the early Hellenistic period, had brought dialectic into the service of literary activities as a part of the trivium. The subject was planned to train the student in the shaping of a persuasive forensic argument rather than in methods for establishing truth scientifically. Boethius, as an author of textbooks on the liberal arts, avoided dealing with the trivium. He translated and compiled from the Greek in order to produce up-to-date Latin textbooks for the quadrivium, the mathematical sciences of numbers and bodies, of immobility and motion. The manuals on Arithmetic and on musical theory survived and had a long history in the schools. In connexion with these scientific interests he was also considered as an expert on a technical problem. Theodoric thought him well equipped by his studies to design a water-clock, which he wished to send to the Burgundian King Gundobad, his brother-in-law.

This attitude of mind, unusual in the Latin West, had also an influence on his extensive logical studies; they were taken out of their usual literary context and brought back to their original philosophical meaning of examining man's instrument for the understanding of his world. The function of higher education in the earlier Middle Ages was essentially to preserve a class of men capable of understanding Latin. The emphasis was no longer on speech-making but on the writing of letters and documents, but the general aim of rhetorical training, which had made logic a part of the trivium, remained valid. We shall see later how the existence of Boethius' logical writings in the libraries and their use in schools was fitted into this framework of education. But their potential force as instruments for the investigation of truth did not remain latent for ever. Their fuller assimilation during the eleventh century was a factor in the rise of the scholastic method, and prepared the way for the full understanding and use of the whole Aristotelian organon during the twelfth century.

. . . . .

The strongest reason for tracing the origin of scholasticism back to Boethius is derived from his application of Aristotelian terminology to the definition of trinitarian doctrine. Not only Carolingian scholars and Gilbert de la Porée, but also Thomas Aquinas wrote commentaries to his theological treatises, and E. K. Rand went so far as to say that Boethius was perhaps only prevented by his early death from anticipating in his own way the great synthesis brought about by the Dominican master of the thirteenth century. In our context we cannot attempt to define the position of Boethius in the history of theological thought by measuring the distance which separates the Roman author at the end of Antiquity from his commentator in the thirteenth century. But we must try to sketch the relationship between philosophy and Christian belief in Boethius' mind as a necessary presupposition for the understanding of the book ***De consolatione philosophiae,*** which, on the strength of its theistic piety and Christian ethics, became a medieval classic. It is well known that its author has avoided any formulation which would declare an exclusively Christian belief and any clear reference to biblical or ecclesiastical authority. As long as the authorship of the theological treatises was disputed, this character of his final confession could be explained by the assumption that Boethius had always been a Christian only in name in order to fulfil the legal condition for holding high office in Rome. But the discovery of a short fragment from a writing by Cassiodorus about the men of letters related to his own family, has barred this easy way out of the difficulty.

The situation in which the Roman senator and philosopher entered the field of theological controversy has been reconstructed by recent research. Between 513 and 519 negotiations were going on for liquidating the schism between east and west, which more than thirty years earlier had arisen out of controversies about the definition of the two natures in Christ. A complicating element in the dispute of doctrines was the appearance of an ethnic group of monks from the lower Danube who, in order to reconcile the monophysite opinion of the East with Roman teaching, pressed for the inclusion of the formula *unus de trinitate passus est* in any proposed agreement. To the subject of this dispute, which combined subtle questions of doctrine with problems of political control and power, Boethius contributed four short theological treatises in 512 and 522. They were a kind of experiment, in which he applied the philosophical concepts, to which he had dedicated his studies, in order to define more clearly and persuasively the doctrine, once proclaimed by the council of Chalcedon under the influence of Pope Leo I. In this way he gave his support to the programme on which his Roman circle under the leadership of Symmachus wished to establish unity between east and west. They were successful in 519, when, after the death of the Emperor Anastasius, the new Byzantine regime under the influence of the future ruler Justinian decided to give in to Rome on the question of doctrine.

Boethius' intervention in the dogmatic debate was encouraged by Augustine's interpretation of the Trinity in philosophical terms. Boethius uses the concepts of substance and relation, which he had discussed thoroughly in his Aristotelian studies, to explain the dogma. The divine *substance* represents unity, relation within this unity is the presupposition of Trinity.

An investigation of the concepts *natura* and *persona* leads to the definition that nature is the specific peculiarity of every substance, while *persona* is the indivisible substance of a *rational* nature. In this way philosophical terminology renders Nestorius' doctrine of the two persons in Christ meaningless. At the end of one of the three treatises which were dedicated by Boethius to the deacon John, he asks his clerical friend whether he thinks these arguments agree with the teaching of the Church. In case John should not be able to give such assurance, he is requested to work out, if possible, another and more correct rational interpretation of faith. Boethius is conscious of the fact that this philosophical inquiry about theological questions cannot go beyond a certain point, but he adds that such a borderline also exists in other fields.

He knows well that he comes to theology as an outsider, who sees an opportunity of applying the resources of his own field of study, and cannot expect anything like general recognition. But he feels strongly that his own philosophical approach gives him superiority over the average ecclesiastic, the figure that dominates the council discussions, which do not even touch the surface of the subject. He gives in one preamble a short report on such a meeting, where he fell silent, because the pretensions of the ignorant controversialists impressed him like madness. But the problem of defining the right position between the heresies of Nestorius and Eutyches made his mind work; finally he formed a logically organized argument, which he submitted to the judgement of John, his theological expert.

There is no sign that any form of conversion or of spiritual progress has led Boethius at this stage definitely away from philosophy, demoting his former studies to the stage of preparatory exercises. The concepts which he applies have not become for him mere reminiscences from the propaedeutics of his rhetorical school or from reading, which have led him on the way to the Church, to ecclesiastical duties or monastic vocation. He remains a man of the world who writes theological treatises. In this respect his mentality is different from that of the authors who represent our main sources for the history of religious thought in the Latin world of Christian antiquity and the Middle Ages. This peculiarity of Boethius' career may be relevant to the understanding of his intention in writing ***De consolatione philosophiae***.

.....

We summarize first the relevant facts about the circumstances which led to Boethius writing this book in prison, while waiting for Theodoric's decision on his own fate after his condemnation to death. The ecclesiastical settlement between Rome and Constantinople in 519 had removed a strong motive for the city aristocracy's loyalty towards the Gothic regime. But the situation in Italy did not deteriorate immediately. Three years later co-operation between Byzantium and Ravenna still seemed better than before. But in 523 the charge was raised against Boethius of having given support to a plot of Roman aristocrats with Constantinople to overthrow the Gothic dynasty; the judgement of a special court was confirmed by a frightened and compliant senate.

The story of the catastrophe is given without consideration for personalities in high position by Boethius to personified Philosophia in the first book of ***De consolatione***. The outbreak of open hostility against Arianism and its freedom of worship in the Byzantine empire came after the end of Boethius. But we can assume that Theodoric at the moment of his action against the senatorial group had already some information about the preparation for this turn of religious policy and its impact on the loyalty of the Romans. Under these circumstances the reunification which ended the conflict between Constantinople and Rome, a result which Boethius had tried to strengthen by his theological writing, took on a different and more sinister look. The ecclesiastical element in the political conflict which led to Boethius' catastrophe is the genuine core in the ancient tradition that Boethius died as a martyr.

The idea that philosophy is called in to help in mastering a grave misfortune suffered by the author himself did not represent the usual convention of shaping the literary genus of *consolatio*. Normally such tractates were dedicated to another person in distress. When Cicero, after the death of his daughter, retired for some time from public life in order to recover quietness of mind by philosophical reflections, he observed that nobody before him had done so. Cicero had been an inspiring influence for Boethius in the earlier stages of his intellectual career, and he remained also the most important example for his final retreat to philosophy.

The book is a great dialogue between Boethius and Philosophia. When a certain result is reached, the preceding section is summarized in the form of a poem, in which the author tries to adapt the metre to the contents.

The same literary form had been taken up a hundred years earlier in the pseudo-apocalyptic introduction to Martianus Capella's encyclopaedia. The aim of the whole work is to discover the motives of the human soul's alienation from its genuine self and to point the way back from shadow to truth.

Philosophia starts with the assumption that the man whom she finds in prison still believes in the power of divine providence to establish and preserve the cosmic order, but that he sees in his personal fate only the cruel work of Fortuna's varying moods. But there is no real change in the character of this power when a good time is followed by evil days. Every gift of fate which makes the external life richer, contains necessarily an element of instability and induces man to forget what gives its real value to human existence. This theme is developed with the examples and the framework which were readily available from antiquity in the popular ethics of the diatribe. This section reaches its final conclusion with the statement that the good things of the world can only be right if they are accepted as gifts from the divine creator. In this context the fundamental idea of Plato's *Timaeus* is introduced in the poem III m. 9 which praises the creation of heaven and earth, man and animals in the harmony of the elements, as a witness to the goodness without envy which defines God. The medieval scholars in their commentaries have often seen in this poem, in which modern analysis has traced the influence of pagan liturgical literature, the core of ***De consolatione***. It certainly offers the transition from the critical examination of secular values to theological ideas. The poem ends with a request that the divine creator may give strength to the human mind to find the way back out of the world to its origin.

The creation of the world by God means that there is no room for evil as a genuine reality, because there can be no being in opposition to divine providence. In defence of this optimistic interpretation against everyday experience, exemplified by Boethius' situation in the dungeon, Plato's argument in the *Gorgias* is used: there are evildoers in the world so powerful that they are beyond punishment. Nobody will stop their doings. But God has created man in such a way that evil itself is punishment, because it destroys the essence of the human soul and leaves only an empty shell.

This argument leaves unsolved the question why visitations, which are intended as chastisements for the criminal, strike the just man, who would prefer to continue his way of life undisturbed and in honour. This objection leads to the first of two metaphysical investigations on the structure of providence, which form the last part of ***De consolatione***. At this point Philosophy emphasizes that a new line of thought has to be taken up. The transient affairs of our life have their origin in the stability of divine nature and its lasting simplicity. This centre of all events is providence in its purity. When we turn our observation to the periphery and try to see the realization of God's will in the changing pattern of things, we use quite correctly the ancient term 'fate'. All the infinite variety and multitude of phenomena in macrocosmos and microcosmos are comprehended in providence, but fate is the instrument allocating to every individual thing its special place and its special moment in time. Divine providence knows neither the one nor the other type of differentiation. This hierarchical subordination of fate to divine will and the concepts by which they are contrasted points clearly to a Neoplatonic origin.

But this philosophical doctrine appears here in a very simplified form, which allows it to avoid any deviation from biblical monotheism. Boethius emphasizes in this context the irrelevance of all concepts which describe the forces mediating between God and the variety of experience. Man's life is placed under the power of fate, but he is nevertheless able to turn from the periphery to the centre and to approach God directly without the intervention of cosmic forces, and so to escape from the pressure of necessity into freedom.

This idea of freedom also remains the theme in the long investigation by which ***De consolatione*** is concluded. The objection is raised that God's infallible prescience, which is an undeniable aspect of his providence, must frustrate man's liberty to act according to his own decisions. The answer starts with some reflections on the causal effect of knowledge on the event which forms its object. When we see a charioteer in the circus drive his horse as he thinks fit so as to win the race, our observation of his activities will in no way restrict his freedom of decision. Prescience does not differ from observation of events in the moment when they happen, as far as the lack of causal effect is concerned.

Against this argument the objection is raised that prescience of an event, which possibly might not happen, cannot be classified as knowledge, but only as opinion, and would therefore be quite unacceptable as an aspect of divine providence. But to argue in this way would mean misinterpreting the character of divine prescience, which is determined by eternity as an inherent quality. The implication of this attribute is made clear by a discussion of its contrast, the time process, which recalls very much the corresponding passages in Augustine's *Confessiones*. It is impossible for the individual existence to comprehend itself as a whole in one of the fleeting moments through which it passes from past to future. If one believes in the infinity of time, as Aristotle did, eternity is only imitated, without its essential quality. The quietness of eternity is transformed into a movement which has no beginning and no end. Unchanging simplicity appears degenerated into an infinite variety. For this reason it is wrong to blame Plato, because in his *Timaeus* he has not linked the process of creation to a definite time. His critics are wrong when they assume that the Attic philosopher, in doing so, makes the world co-eternal with God. Their assumption presupposes that the difference between creator and creature can be measured by the duration of time, while in reality eternity can only be understood as something beyond and above the course of time.

For this reason the character of God's knowledge is not influenced by the fact that every human action is preceded by a moment of uncertainty, in which the freedom of choice is exercised. The degradation of knowledge to opinion cannot take place in God's eternity. For the same reason divine prescience does not interfere with the sequence of human decision and action, which runs its course as a part of the time process.

The conversion, from the dependence on Fortuna and her external goods, to God as the only final value, does not imply a surrender of human freedom to a power which predestinates everything by knowing it before it happens. In God's view there is no difference of before and after. So ends Philosophia's message to the prisoner.

. . . . .

The most controversial question raised by the book in the mind of readers was always about the religious tendency of Boethius' philosophy. The range of the modern solution is marked by two answers at the opposite ends. Rand, who had done a great deal of spadework for the understanding of Boethius' writings, does not admit any serious problem. For him the Christian spirituality of this theistic philosophy disperses any serious doubts about the author's faith and intention which the lack of quotations from the Bible and ecclesiastical writings might raise. Boethius has tried out how far unaided reason is able to approach religious truth. If Theodoric had spared his life, Boethius might have supplemented the ***De consolatione*** by a second book demonstrating the complete harmony between the religious conclusions of his reason with revealed truth. This assumption implies that the design of Boethius' ***De consolatione*** was dictated by a methodical consideration of the parallelism of reason and revelation, which would have anticipated the thought-form of medieval scholasticism. The other alternative was recently formulated by Professor Momigliano, according to whom Boethius abandoned Christianity at the end of his life and, under the pressure of his experiences, returned to philosophy as the pagan way to human salvation.

The principle that Christian truth can be proved by philosophical argument, without any recourse to ecclesiastical tradition, had been established by the apologists in their attempts to win over educated opinion outside the Church. Lactantius' discreet circumscriptions of Christian concepts in his first treatise *De opificio Dei* is a good example of the tactical purpose of this method of defending the faith. Boethius had certainly no reason to introduce Christian truth in such disguise, and the situation which determined his work excludes any idea that he might have had in mind a plan to redevelop the doctrinal contents of revelation in a second work parallel to ***De consolatione.*** That in his four genuine theological treatises he attempted to find philosophical expressions for the central doctrine of the Christian faith, when it seemed helpful for the ecclesiastical cause to do so, does not form any basis for the assumption that ***De consolatione*** was designed as the section on rational theology in a system of revealed truth.

On the other hand, we cannot well overlook the fact that for his final confession he selected those ideas from the philosophical tradition which expressed essential features of Christian spirituality and ethics. Augustine's theoretical world-picture was still near to his thought, although he avoided any application leading to definite ecclesiastical doctrine. It is difficult to imagine that in the sixth century a former Christian should have written such a work in order to express renunciation of his faith by identifying philosophy with paganism in his mind as Symmachus in the fourth century had linked rational theism with the traditional worship of the Roman people.

The assumption of a real break at the end of Boethius' life would have greater force if we had to accept the treatise called ***De fide Catholica,*** which summarizes the history of salvation in theological, not philosophical terms, as a genuine work expressing Boethius' attitude a few years before he wrote ***De consolatione***. The manuscript evidence allows for arguments on both sides. Differences of vocabulary and style between ***De fide*** and the four genuine treatises have been accounted for by the contrast in the subject-matter. But, while such differences can be easily understood in a case like that of Tacitus writing both the dialogue on the rhetor's education and the two small historical essays, it would be very difficult to find room for a purely theological composition in Boethius' intellectual career.

We saw that his literary activity in all periods of his life had centred around the task of preserving the legacy of ancient philosophy. His preference for the abstract problems of Aristotelian logic made any possibility of conflict between rational thought and the doctrines of Christian faith remote. When he used his intellectual equipment to give literary support to the cause of Roman orthodoxy and ecclesiastical unity, religious and patriotic motives were inseparably fused in the loyalty of his allegiance. We saw how this contribution to the unity of West and East by a prominent Roman aristocrat became politically suspicious at the moment when the future of the Gothic dynasty was menaced.

But we do not know whether the abstention from anything definitely ecclesiastical in doctrine and language was caused to some degree by the author's hope of turning his fate by giving the impression of philosophical neutrality to the Arian court at Ravenna. The very outspoken style of his political justification in book I seems, however, to contradict the assumption that such considerations of prudence played a predominant part in the shaping of ***De consolatione***. On the other hand, the feeling of deep disappointment with the attitude of the Roman senate is clearly reflected in the work. Boethius had once applied philosophy to theology, acting as speaker for this body, who now had forsaken him. This experience did not change his deepest conviction, the belief in the harmony of philosophy and religious faith, but it made him refrain from the treatment of such problems and the use of any terminology which could lead a man into the sphere of political controversy. It was certainly the purpose of ***De consolatione*** to show the way of liberation from entanglement in the strife for power. His limitation to the expression of his faith in theistic universalism allowed him to avoid all problems which had become issues in the conflict between individuals and groups. That he knew patristic writings which followed a similar course, especially the early dialogues of Augustine, made this attitude easier. Boethius could neglect the fact that his circumstances and motive were different from those of the Fathers of the Church. That he was able to undertake such a task in the way he did was made possible by his contacts with the Hellenic East; here lies the key to his entire achievement.

The assumption that he was once a student in Athens has been ruled out by the consideration that it was based on a *metaphorical* description of his renewal of philosophy in the eulogistic letter of Cassiodorus. A further hypothesis that he spent his youth in Alexandria, where his father would have held high office, cannot be firmly established and does not fit in very well with the documentation of Boethius' life and career. On the other hand, the evidence that the Roman senator's unique intellectual position can only be accounted for by an intimate contact with Alexandrian thought and learning is very strong.

We must admit, it seems, that we simply do not know the way by which the Roman aristocrat acquired his extensive knowledge of language, methods and doctrines characteristic of contemporary Hellenic scholarship: in any case, the results were of lasting historical importance.

The spirit of scientific inquiry was very lively in Alexandria during the late fifth and the first half of the sixth century. The principles on which the right understanding of nature must be based were subjects of eager discussion. John Philoponus, who disputed Aristotle's dichotomy of heaven and sublunar world and aimed at a uniform explanation of the cosmos in physical terms, was a younger contemporary of Boethius, but in no way the first who introduced such themes among the scholars of this late period of Greek Alexandria. When the Roman philosopher's scientific interest enabled him to emancipate logic from the purely literary scope of the trivium, he did so in harmony with the ideas prevalent in the Greek thought of his days. But recent research, especially by Courcelle, has proved that the contacts between Boethius and the leading teachers of the Alexandrian school have left much more concrete results. The Egyptian centre of philosophical studies had shown a strong tendency to concentrate its main effort on the textual interpretation of the two classical authors, Plato and Aristotle. This approach corresponded to the interest in the critical study of authors which was rooted in local tradition of long standing. Moreover, there was the influence of an important section among the pupils, who wished to supplement their Christian belief by a training in abstract thought. Their purpose could easily collide with the tendency in the development of Neoplatonic speculation of combining philosophy with the defence of Polytheism. The safest way to avoid such serious friction was the return to the objective task of explaining the classic masters. This situation led also to emphasis on Aristotelian studies, especially on his *Organon*; while the tradition of the Alexandrian school prevented any refutation of Plato in favour of his master pupil. It is obvious that the comprehensive programme for his life's work, which Boethius has drawn up, corresponds to the syllabus of Alexandrian studies.

But the most intimate influence of the Alexandrian masters can be traced in ***De consolatione***. The simplification of the hierarchical world picture, by which Boethius removed an important difference between the Neoplatonic theory of emanation and Christian monotheism, was already prepared for him by his Alexandrian sources. Here the theological interpretation of the demiurge in Plato's *Timaeus* by Ammonius allowed man to face God without mediating powers. The same author, a pupil of Proclus, had incorporated in commentaries to Aristotle's logical and scientific works speculations on the relationship of God's eternal decision to the fluctuations of fate, as well as the investigation on the compatibility of divine providence and human freedom which made it possible for Boethius to find an adequate expression for his Christian piety in purely philosophical concepts. Fifth-century Alexandria had also brought forth reinterpretations of Plato's *Gorgias*; the tendency of this dialogue corresponded closely to what ***De consolatione*** intended to teach about the relationship of human sin and happiness. While denying that the world's creation had happened in time, Boethius safeguarded an important axiom of theism by differentiating between God's eternity and the permanence of the world. By doing so, he accepted again a tradition from Alexandria as consistent with his own religion. His whole plan excluded the possibility of discussing in his context the Church's difficulty with a theory which would not allow the first two chapters of Genesis to be understood literally. In this way Boethius' discipleship to the Alexandrian school offered to later generations in a less sophisticated world stimulating but also puzzling problems.

Henry Chadwick (essay date 1981)

SOURCE: An introduction to *Boethius: His Life, Thought and Influence,* edited by Margaret Gibson, Basil Blackwell, 1981, pp. 1-12.

[*In the following essay, Chadwick surveys Boethius's career and achievement, maintaining that "he taught the Latin West to judge the validity of an inference, to be aware of the foundations of mathematics, and to envisage reason and revelation as related but very distinct ways of apprehending the mystery of God."*]

By writing the ***Consolation of Philosophy*** Boethius provided all educated people of the Middle Ages and the Renaissance with one of their principal classics, a work of both intellectual profundity and literary delight to be read not only in Latin by clerks in their study but also by laymen at leisure, and therefore often in the vernacular. The author, it is true, wrote some pages on Christian theology which are of the greatest consequence. But he did not write them as a theologian in the ordinary sense of the word; he is addressing himself only indirectly to a pastoral or 'political' situation in the Church, as a logician who thought there was some tidying up to be done in the ecclesiastical garden. He writes as a layman and has been loved by laymen. In its philosophical content the ***Consolation*** attracted commentaries from several medieval authors, not as momentous as the commentaries called forth by his theological tractates, but a significant sign of the seriousness with which men took his philosophical reflections on the dealings of providence with a world beset by so much evil. But the common experience of apparently purposeless evil has attracted all thoughtful readers to Boethius' pages. His stylistic grace and above all his radical analysis of the true sources of human happiness contribute to making the book one that still retains its place among the masterpieces and jewels of western literature. Boethius' English translators alone include King Alfred, Geoffrey Chaucer and Queen Elizabeth I, which is not a weak list of admirers.

Nevertheless, there is a certain isolation about Boethius. This isolation has perhaps become akin to neglect since the Renaissance. His world is the old world of antiquity with an intellectual framework dominated by Ptolemaic ideas about the world, by Aristotle's doctrines of substance and accidents, by a Platonic metaphysic setting asunder mind and matter, by Pythagorean ideas of mathematics and of musical proportion as the key to the structure of the cosmos. A sense of isolation is felt even during his lifetime. He had his intimate circle of friends: his father-in-law Symmachus to whom he felt himself to owe a profound intellectual debt; a Roman advocate named Patricius for whom he composed, late in his career, a commentary on Cicero's *Topics;* a learned deacon of the Roman church named John (probably, not quite certainly, to be identified with Pope John I, 523-6), who shared his enthusiasm for questions of logic; a Roman senator in the bureaucracy at Ravenna named Renatus, like Boethius fluent in Greek, who seems first to have collected a corpus of Boethius' dialectical treatises a year or two after his death. But it is a small circle, and the treatises on logic did not make him new friends. They contain a large number of unhappy references to contemporary critics who were altogether failing to see any value in his labours on Aristotle and suspected him of writing for ostentation rather than for use. These critics are evidently not barbarian Goths, but fellow senators. His writing was caviare to the general and pleased not the million.

Boethius was by temperament a man who liked to strike

out on his own. In all the fields that he touched he had some Latin predecessors. Apuleius anticipated him in writing a short guide to Aristotle's difficult treatise on *Interpretation.* It is likely that Boethius knew Apuleius' work, but he never mentions it by name. Apuleius also anticipated him in making an adaptation of the *Arithmetic* of Nicomachus of Gerasa, but Boethius sets about his own version of Nicomachus as if he had no predecessor. Marius Victorinus, the African rhetor of the mid-fourth century whose conversion to Christianity astonished high Roman society about 355, directly covered some of the ground that Boethius was to claim as his own. He made a translation of Porphyry's *Isagoge* or introduction (Porphyry did not explain what he was introducing, but in the sixth century it was assumed to be an introduction to Aristotle's *Categories*); a version, with eight books of commentary, of Aristotle's *Categories;* a version of Aristotle on *Interpretation;* a tract on the hypothetical syllogism; and a commentary on Cicero's *Topics.* Boethius acknowledges that Victorinus was the most eminent orator of his time, but loses no opportunity of drawing attention to Victorinus' blunders either in logic or in translation from the Greek. Nevertheless, it can hardly be accidental that the portion of Boethius' dialectical work which became most widely known covers much the same area as that laid down as the standard curriculum by Victorinus in the fourth century. Although Boethius succeeded in making careful translations, which were then given a further meticulous revision, of both *Analytics, Topics,* and *Sophistic Refutations,* the transmission of these last treatises is a thin line. Until the twelfth century they were little known or not at all.

Neither in his dialectical studies nor in his works on mathematics did Boethius claim to be original. For arithmetic he closely follows his Greek model in the Pythagorean Nicomachus of Gerasa. This study is intended as a preparation for the introduction to music, a much longer work dependent on Nicomachus and on Ptolemy. The ***Institutio Musica*** is transmitted incomplete in the manuscript tradition, which breaks off in the middle of a sentence half way through the fifth book. Originally the work must have run to six or seven books. The matter preserved follows the Platonic/Pythagorean tradition in preferring theory to practice and in discounting the potent criticisms of the Pythagorean tradition from Aristoxenus of Tarentum in the fourth century B.C. Aristoxenus insisted on the primacy of the ear over abstract mathematical theory. Boethius has to concede to Aristoxenus that the judgement of the ear has some claim to consideration. In making these concessions he follows Ptolemy's extant *Harmonics.* Ptolemy's book is likely to have been the model for his discussion (in the lost books at the end) of cosmic and human music; that is of the way in which harmonic ratios and exact proportionality are exemplified in the structure of the cosmos (e.g. the distance of the planets from the earth) and in the fitting together of the human soul and body. Boethius' introduction to music is not intended to assist in the practice of the art, and has been held to have done disservice to music by instilling into generations of readers the doctrine that the true 'musicus' is master exclusively of the theory, and that practical skills can be left to the inferior orders of society. That prejudice, however, is virtually universal among ancient writers on the subject. We need not put all the blame on Boethius. In the ***Consolation*** he tells us that listening to music meant much to him. He felt that music should not merely be used to express one's feelings when one is either sad or glad, and attributed to it the dignity of being a clue to the providential ordering of things.

In his logical treatises there stands one monograph which had special interest for him, namely, that on the hypothetical syllogism of the conditional form: 'if A, then B; but A, therefore B', or 'if A, then B; but not B, therefore not A.' The school of Aristotle had begun the investigation of the logic of conditional statements of this kind. The Stoics had taken the matter considerably further, treating the variables AB as symbols not (as in Aristotle) for terms but for entire propositions. Cicero took some notice of this Stoic logic, so that it was not bringing out matter of which the Latin world knew nothing. But Boethius' monograph is the most careful and detailed study in logic to come from his pen, and without it our knowledge of ancient propositional logic would be thin. To medieval logicians this treatise was not perhaps of the greatest interest. John of Salisbury regarded it without enthusiasm, but conceded that it was at least clearer than anything that Aristotle would have written on the subject, had he done so. In recent times modern logicians have shown a more benevolent interest in Boethius' work in this complex field.

John of Salisbury felt that some of Boethius' logical studies were too abstract to be of any use. There is no doubt that his expositions of Aristotle are academic and detached, but written with the conviction that they train the mind to detect fallacies. In his second commentary on Porphyry's *Isagoge* he utters the warning: 'Those who reject logic are bound to make mistakes. Unless reason shows the right path, the incorrupt truth of reality cannot be found'.

In the commentary on Aristotle's *Categories* he writes in pain of the threat to the survival of culture in his own time, and speaks of the imminent collapse of liberal studies unless drastic action is taken to preserve the values of the classical past. Knowledge is not only gained in the process of historical change; it is even more easily lost. Human culture can suffer impoverishment more readily than it can achieve enrichment. Hence Boethius' sweat and toil in his study to make available to the Latin world those works which the best philosophers of his age regarded as the proper ladder of true education. They were Neoplatonists and set action far below contemplation. Their educational ideal was relatively little concerned with politics or economics or even ethics (though Boethius' contemporary Simplicius wrote a commentary on the *Enchiridion* of Epictetus which must be reckoned a treatise on the moral life), but was directed towards what they called 'theoria', rendered by Boethius 'speculatio'. Under the heading of speculative philosophy they wrote of physics, i.e. the scientific study of the natural order; or of mathematics; or of metaphysics and 'theology'.

The late Platonists are schoolmen in the sense that they

approach Plato and Aristotle not simply as acute thinkers whose arguments could and should provoke continued independent thinking on the part of their readers, but as authoritative figures, masters of philosophical truth, whose metaphysical beliefs deserve to be received with respect and awe by their pigmy successors. It followed that distress would be caused if these authorities seemed at important points to be speaking with divergent or even contradictory voices. Plotinus' biographer Porphyry accepted Plotinus' view that in Peripatetic logic there is much of the highest value, but it concerns truth in this world of time and space. The ten categories, according to Plotinus, have a limited applicability to the realm of the Ideas in the intelligible world beyond time and space. So Porphyry set out to prove Plato and Aristotle to be concordant on fundamental questions and to be in disagreement only in secondary matters. This scheme was facilitated by treating Plato as the master guide to the mathematical and metaphysical world of unchanging truth, and Aristotle as the master scientist, moralist and political theorist who best understood terrestrial matters. It followed that Aristotle's *Metaphysics* needed a certain amount of careful exegesis to bring the doctrines of the book into a Platonic line. On one major point of confrontation, namely the kind of reality to be ascribed to universals such as genera and species, Porphyry was able to keep his authorities from discord simply by not making up his mind. In his second commentary on Porphyry Boethius follows a decisively Peripatetic line, in agreement with the Aristotelian master of A.D. 200, Alexander of Aphrodisias, viz. that universals can have a reality only in so far as there actually exist concrete particulars, independent of our minds, for which universal terms such as genera and species serve as a convenient classification system. Admittedly Boethius juxtaposes this with a much more Platonising statement, that the reality of universals can be discovered not by collecting and putting together a large number of instances, but rather by a negative way of abstraction from matter.

An analogous procedure appears in the treatment of the problem of 'future contingents', in Boethius' commentary on the ninth chapter of Aristotle's *De Interpretatione* and then in the last book of the ***Consolation of Philosophy***. The commentary deals with divine foreknowledge of events that might or might not occur in a wholly Peripatetic framework. Foreknowledge makes nothing to happen, even if it is God's. If the cosmos has in its structure a certain indeterminacy, then God knows indeterminate things as indeterminate. If he believed them to be certainly predictable, he would hold false beliefs (which is incompatible with the concept of God). God's knowledge of future contingents is therefore a true knowledge that the possibilities are open, and that while a great deal in the world may take place by necessary causation, this is not true of everything. So the commentary. But in the ***Consolation*** the profound influence on Boethius of Proclus of Athens is directly felt, and the answer to the same questions is now found in a Platonic framework: what is an open and uncertain future to us is certain to God who foreknows all things and in whose world an element of indeterminacy would appear to a Neoplatonist to be some kind of defect in the order of things. Therefore Boethius has to embark on his argument that in God there is no before and after, but everything is known in the simultaneity of eternity: 'interminabilis uitae tota simul et perfecta possessio' (V pr. vi. 4).

Both the mathematical treatises and the studies in Aristotelian logic are concerned with knowledge for its own sake, not because it may lead to some enlargement of the wealth of Italy. No doubt Boethius was not displeased when Theoderic invited him to design for the Burgundian king a sundial and a waterclock, or invited him to express a view about the proper exchange rate between the gold solidus and the absurdly devalued copper denarius, out of compliment to his mathematical distinction. His ***Institutio Musica*** won him an invitation to select a harpist to be sent to Clovis, in the simple hope that music might tame his dangerous aggressiveness on Theoderic's borders. No special public service was expected of consuls in the sixth century, and his service as sole consul for the year 510 (for which office he must have been appointed by the Eastern emperor Anastasius on the nomination of Theoderic) did not lay heavy governmental burdens on his shoulders. Consuls had to be rich and dispense vast munificence in donatives and in the provision of public spectacles. Even so, Boethius used the dignity of his office to oppose the prefect Faustus when, at a time of famine and high food prices, he proposed compulsory purchase of food from farmers in Campania at prices that would have left them destitute. Otherwise his consulship did not much bring him out of his study; he tells us that the duties of the office have done something to delay his commentary on the ***Categories***, a work which he sees as a civic duty.

Paradoxically it seems to have been an interest in theology and in the logic of the ecclesiastical *usus loquendi,* or 'tradition of talking', which did more than anything else to bring him out of his library.

Until the last three years of his long reign, Theoderic's regime in Italy was distinguished for its rare liberality. His toleration was extraordinary. It did not extend to sorcerers, Manichees, and those who offered pagan sacrifices. His dealings with the Jewish communities in Italy were marked by justice rather than by acts of positive encouragement. As a Goth he was an Arian king presiding over a self-consciously separate race whom he wished to keep apart from the Romans especially by enforcing a religious apartheid of Arian and Catholic. He cordially disliked conversions from Catholic to Arian or vice versa. The Catholic churches of Italy he treated with liberality and fairmindedness. When in 500 he visited Rome, he came to St Peter's 'as if he were a Catholic'. It was easy for the churches in Italy to look to him for protection, though an Arian, because from 484 until 519 there was a breach of communion between Rome and the Greek patriarchates, the Acacian schism, caused by Rome's indignation when the patriarch Acacius of Constantinople established communion with the patriarch of Alexandria on a basis other than that of the Council of Chalcedon (451) and without reference to Rome. The new basis for communion was the emperor Zeno's Henoticon, or 'reunion formula' which, without expressly censuring the Council of Chalcedon referred to it in very cool terms. After Zeno his successor Anastasius (491-518) upheld the Henoticon as the standard of orthodoxy in his dominions, and sought to remain 'above parties'. His toleration of the Monophysite critics of Chalcedon seemed unendurable to Rome, and various endeavours from either side to reestablish understanding and communion ended in abrasive exchanges, especially with Pope Symmachus (498-514) who had a schism on his hands at Rome and was very uncertain of himself. Symmachus' successor Hormisdas (513-23) reopened negotiations with Theoderic's consent, but no progress was made until suddenly in 518 Anastasius died and was succeeded by Justin I. Assisted by his nephew Justinian, Justin's policy was to reestablish unity with the West on any terms the Pope cared to specify, the ultimate objective being to encourage the church in Italy to look to Constantinople rather than to the Gothic king at Ravenna, and so to make possible the ultimate overthrow of the Gothic kingdom.

Theology, however, lay at the heart of the ecclesiastical controversy, the terms of which were bewildering to the Latin West. When about 513 a Greek bishop wrote to Pope Symmachus begging him to adopt a less anti-Greek attitude and to take initiatives to heal the schism, the Roman clergy and senators were filled with alarm to learn that this professedly Chalcedonian and pro-Roman bishop wished to affirm as orthodox not only the Chalcedonian formula that Christ, God and man, is known as one person *in* two natures, but also that he is *of* two natures. Boethius was present at the resulting tumult and felt that a logician had something to contribute to the clarification of the issue. After some long pondering (which may have lasted five years rather than five weeks), Boethius wrote the earliest of his theological tractates, the fifth, 'against Eutyches and Nestorius', the most original work on any subject that came from his pen. Its content manifests affinity with the positions advocated both at Constantinople and at Rome by a group of Gothic ('Scythian', because they came from the Dobrudja) monks led by Maxentius and Leontius. Maxentius was firm for the Chalcedonian 'in two natures', but wished to meet its critics by adding that there is 'one nature of the divine Word incarnate', that Christ is both *of* and *in* two natures, and that the incarnate, crucified Lord is 'one of the Trinity'. He explained that this last formula implies neither that God can suffer nor that there is plurality in the divine being. However, at Rome Pope Hormisdas was alarmed by such doctrines, perhaps especially for any hint of an implication that Chalcedon needed supplementation or qualification. The Pope's advisers were suspicious of any concession to Byzantine compromise. Boethius' fifth tractate shows that he thought otherwise. In essentials he supports Maxentius, whose formulae were also congenial to Justinian, though he would not be so imprudent as to say so before he had won the Pope's approval.

Boethius' classic definition of person as 'the individual substance of rational nature' is formulated with the eastern Christological controversy in mind. It had its sixth century critics as well as adverse comment from Richard of St Victor (*De Trinitate* iv. 21f.). Boethius was aware that the term 'persona' may be obscure, but is easier to use of human kind than of God, in which context its meaning becomes unclear.

The first tractate, ***De Trinitate,*** written for his father-in-law Symmachus, displays an Augustinian reserve towards the word 'persona' in the exposition of the doctrine of the Trinity. Father, Son and Spirit are one God, not three. Yet these three biblical terms are not describing accidental qualities of the one divine substance, since it is axiomatic that what God is, he has; there are no accidents in God. But Neoplatonic logic can help with its analysis of the relationship of identity and difference. When we say that x and y are 'the same', some distinction between them is necessary if the assertion is to be of interest. The language of Father and Son is that of relation, a word which implies otherness. But within the Christian Trinity, relation is that between equals and identicals, a kind of relation not to be found among perishable, finite things. The second tractate, for John the deacon, pursues the question further. The term 'Trinitas' is not a term of substance, but of relation. For John Boethius also composed his third tractate, in which there is no discussion of any point of Christian dogma, but exclusively of a problem in Platonic metaphysics: Plato teaches that the good transcends being. All that exists derives from the good, and its existence as such is a good. If an existent entity is good, is it good in the same way as the supreme Good is good, or is goodness something it has rather than something it is? Boethius follows Proclus in proceeding on a mathematical analogy. First establish the axioms and definitions, and then, like Euclid, ask what must necessarily follow.

Boethius' role as a 'boffin' in the discussions at Rome will not have passed unnoticed at Constantinople. In the year 522 Boethius' two young sons were nominated as consuls for the year, which can hardly have happened unless Boethius' name was being spoken of at Constantinople as a personage carrying weight in the pro-Byzantine interest at Rome. From 1 September, probably of 522, Boethius took up a major administrative post at Ravenna as Master of the Offices. He used his position to protect his friends and to frustrate the corruption of court officials. In short, he made many enemies. The storm broke when he was accused of suppressing damning evidence that the senator Albinus had engaged in treasonable correspondence with Constantinople to the danger of Theoderic's kingdom. For the harsh realities of political life Boethius was too much of an academic to survive.

But his long imprisonment at Pavia gave him the opportunity to write his greatest book, ***The Consolation of Philosophy***. From an apologia protesting his innocence of the charge he goes on to an analysis of human misery and happiness. In serious trouble one quickly discovers by pain and disillusionment who are one's real friends (I pr. viii. 6). How bitter is the sadness of remembering one's past happiness (II pr. iv. 1); perhaps an echo of Augustine's 'tristis gaudium pristinum recolo' in the *Confessions* (X xxi. 30). But Boethius reproaches himself, through the lady Philosophy who represents his better self, for his self-pity. Nothing is miserable unless thinking makes it so (II pr. iv. 18). Those who trust to the deceitful lady Fortuna have no right to complain when her proverbial wheel turns (II pr. viii). But from the middle of the third book, with its literary climax in the poem 'O qui perpetua', the vindication of providence moves into a Platonic key, and owes much to the writings of Proclus. In the first book Proclus' authority is recognised in passing in the quotation, taken from his commentary on the *Parmenides* (1056 Cousin): 'If there is a God, whence comes evil? But whence comes good, if there is not?' (I pr. iv. 30). Boethius tells his readers that for some time past he has been studying the arguments about providence and evil, and the many parallels with Proclus' three opuscula on this subject illustrate his reading there.

At the beginning of his monograph on the hypothetical syllogism he remarks that the study of philosophy has been the solamen of his life. Now in prison, perhaps with a few books brought by Symmachus or his wife Rusticiana, he must compose his confession of philosophical faith. It is a profoundly religious view of the nature and destiny of man, but it is notoriously not a Christian book. There is nothing of the remission of sins or eternal life or redemption. There are a number of tantalising, near-echoes of biblical texts; it is characteristic of the style of the book that they can be otherwise interpreted, except one, the citation of a phrase from the Wisdom of Solomon 8:1 in III pr. xii. 22-23 to the effect that God 'rules everything firmly and gently disposes them', where Boethius expresses delight not only at the content of the lady Philosophy's statement but also at the very words she uses ('haec ipsa verba'). It is, however, to be emphasised that the truth conveyed by this biblical citation is a matter of natural theology, not of revealed.

The ***Consolation*** does not read like crypto-paganism; that is to say, like a manifesto of the inner pagan religion of a man who now has nothing to lose and has torn the Christian façade aside. But nor does it read like crypto-Christianity; that is to say, expressing thoughts that are inwardly Christian but, by way of literary conceit, adopt the outward dress of a Platonic metaphysic. The essential shape of the ***Consolation*** is a Neoplatonic thesis that the imperfections of this world are allowed to facilitate the return of the soul to its origin in God. But it is not very easy to specify themes admitted by Boethius which are frankly inconceivable within a Christian scheme of thought. There is one emphatic assertion of agreement with the Platonic doctrine of the pre-existence of the soul: 'Platoni vehementer assentior' (III pr. xii. 1; cf. m. xi) in the context of Boethius' forgetfulness of his true destiny. But the transmigration of souls merely becomes an innocuous description of the different beasts that various types of wicked men come to resemble (IV pr. iii. 16-21, where the final clause 'uertatur in beluam' is quoted from Cicero, *De Officiis* iii. 20, 82). Porphyry would have said the same. But the point is that in this form a Christian vigilante would have found nothing to object to. There are no Platonisms in the ***Consolation*** that one cannot also find somewhere in Augustine, notably in the Cassiciacum dialogues written between his conversion and his baptism

The church of S. Apollinare Nuovo, Ravenna, completed by Theodoric in 519.

where Augustine experiments with a juxtaposition of Christianity and Neoplatonism. It is possible to draw up a considerable list of anticipations in Augustine's writings, though none where one can establish a verbal echo or the probability of a literary dependence. Perhaps the closest analogies occur in Augustine's *Soliloquies* which, like Boethius, speak of the wings of the soul; of the need to know your own self to be immortal, simple and uncompounded; above all, of the embodied soul's need to recover gradually its sense of true identity by a process of 'remembering' (*Solil.* i. 14, 24; ii. 1, 1; 20, 34f.).

This is not to say that Augustine is a source for Boethius' Platonism, but rather that the early dialogues may have offered him a model that he was glad to accept.

Nineteenth-century scholars used to contrast the Christian author of the *Opuscula* with the pagan author of the ***Consolation,*** and wove fantastic hypotheses that they were two different authors. Obsessions blinded them to the paradox of Boethius' most serious works: there is even more Neoplatonism in the *Opuscula* (except for the very different fourth, ***De Fide Catholica,*** whose diction is nevertheless wholly Boethian) than in the ***Consolation***. And the ***Consolation,*** though it contains nothing either specifically pagan or specifically Christian, is composed by a man who is throughout aware of Christianity, and is therefore adopting no philosophical positions that he has good reason to think incompatible with an Augustinian version of the faith.

Boethius' mind is restrospective, so far as its content is concerned, soaked in Plato and Aristotle and in their

Neoplatonic exegetes of his own time. Yet the opuscula and dialectical treatises injected an essential ingredient into the formation of scholastic theology and philosophy, and the music and arithmetic long remained to educate medieval men in matters of which they would otherwise have been remarkably ignorant. If tragedy had never overtaken him and if he had never written the ***Consolation of Philosophy,*** charged from start to finish with intellectual and moral passion, no doubt his influence on posterity would have been greatly reduced, but it would still have been far from negligible. He set the feet of western men on the ladder that ascends from practical philosophy (morality, politics, economics) to contemplative questions of pure and abstract truth, transcending objects of sense-perception. He taught the Latin West to judge the validity of an inference, to be aware of the foundations of mathematics, and to envisage reason and revelation as related but very distinct ways of apprehending the mystery of God.

Henry Chadwick (essay date 1981)

SOURCE: "Evil, Freedom, and Providence," in *Boethius: The Consolations of Music, Logic, Theology, and Philosophy,* Oxford at the Clarendon Press, 1981, pp. 223-53.

[*In the following essay, Chadwick provides a detailed analysis of the* Consolation of Philosophy, *exploring such features of the work as its combination of Platonic and Stoic philosophies and its treatment of the problem of evil and free will.*]

Since the Renaissance, and especially since the scientific revolution of the seventeenth century altered our understanding of the nature and structure of our environment, Boethius has come to seem a rather lonely and forgotten foreigner in a world grown strange. Yet something of that isolation belongs to him even during his lifetime, and never more so than in the near dereliction of the imprisonment during which he wrote the ***Consolation of Philosophy***. By common consent this remains one of the high masterpieces of European literature, translated since early mediaeval times into many languages; a work whose English translators alone include King Alfred, Geoffrey Chaucer, and Queen Elizabeth I; a dominant force (with Thomas Aquinas) in the making of Dante's mind. The ***Consolation*** is the work of a refined humanist scholar with a richly stocked memory, delighting in lyrical poetry and elegant prose, fascinated by logical problems almost to the point of obsession. In Theoderic's prison at Pavia he knew that his time was limited (iv, 6, 5), but he evidently had more than sufficient leisure to produce polished composition and a sophisticated structure. The work has a Virgilian quality in being almost a mosaic of subtle literary allusions. Joachim Gruber's commentary (1978) marks a signal advance in the identification of his literary echoes, but also makes it clear that he is not transcribing sources. This is not a man composing with a library of books open before him, but a very well-read mind which can recall a phrase from here or from there at will. His Latin is densely packed with concentrated argument; and the argument is carried on from the prose sections into the poems which he inserts, he says (iv, 6, 57), with the intention of lightening the reader's task with a difficult subject. The poems normally have subtle links with the prose sections that precede or follow them.

The method of mixing prose and verse had been practised by Martianus Capella and by Ennodius. The style was associated with the Greek, Menippos of Gadara in the third century BC, whose work is lost. But something of its nature can be deduced from Lucian of Samosata and from remnants of Varro's 'Menippean Satires'. A light touch is deliberately employed with a deeply serious purpose. Jerome (*Vir. ill.* III) mentions an otherwise unknown Christian named Acilius Severus who composed an autobiography, with the Greek title *hodoiporikon* or 'travel-book', cast in both prose and verse. Ausonius and Sidonius Apollinaris composed letters in the prosimetric form. It is probable that on Boethius the greatest influence is that of Martianus Capella, since his work also describes a kind of intellectual pilgrimage ending in heaven.

Among the writings that have been produced by men and women in prison awaiting the execution of a death sentence under tyranny, the ***Consolation*** holds a place of lasting preeminence, partly because of the two grand problems of innocent suffering and the reconciliation of divine providence with human freedom with which it deals, and partly because in this profoundly religious book there is an evidently conscious refusal to say anything distinctively Christian. The book is a work of natural, not of revealed, theology, and strives after a universal appeal to every man. Boethius' subject is the consolation not of theology but of philosophy. Throughout his life philosophy, and especially dialectic, has been the ruling passion of his mind. Now at the supreme crisis he asks what it may have to say to him, especially concerning providence and evil. The question of providence was a topic much discussed in the late Platonic schools. Boethius declares that he had studied the subject deeply (v, 4, I), a statement which answers the query of many rapid readers who wonder whether so elaborate and sophisticated a book could really have been composed in custody. We have already seen that his family had the resources to persuade his guardians to allow him a few books and papers should he have needed anything. The ground for his labours had already been prepared. The Alexandrian Platonist Hierocles had written at some length on the subject, while Proclus addresses himself to the issue both in his commentary on the *Republic* and in his three opuscula concerning providence. There is good reason to think these works familiar to Boethius. He will also have known Plotinus' two not wholly self-consistent treatises on the subject (ii, 2-3).

. . . . .

The ***Consolation of Philosophy*** begins in a low minor key with a sad poem echoing Ovid's *Tristia* and *Letters from Pontus*. A writer who recalls having once written cheerful verses (an allusion perhaps to the bucolic poem recorded among Boethius' works by Cassiodorus in the Anecdoton Holderi) is now compelled at the bidding of the Muses to embark on tearful songs of self-pity. But then a dreamlike vision follows in the ensuing prose section (a dream which is the ancestor of many mediaeval dream-poems). The lady Philosophy appears to comfort him. She has burning eyes; a face old yet fresh and young; her height, too, varying in appearance, at one moment of normal human size, but then reaching up to and passing through the very heavens. Moreover, her dress woven with her own hands (like Athene's *peplos* in *Iliad* 5, 734, a text on whose symbolism late Platonists liked to meditate) is of fine thread and decorated with two Greek letters, Pi below, Theta above, linked by ascending steps. This dress has been roughly torn by violent hands.

The Theta on Philosophy's dress may have been suggested to Boethius by a Theta on his own. The Carolingian theologian Prudentius of Troyes, in an attack on John the Scot's dangerous treatise on divine predestination, prefixes to each censured excerpt from John a Greek Theta 'because some have used this letter to mark those condemned to death' (*PL* 115, 1012AB). Accordingly a prisoner on whom the death sentence had been decreed was required to wear regulation prison clothing marked with the initial letter of *thanatos,* intended either to increase his sense of humiliation or to safeguard the executioners from mistaken identity in their victim. An early allusion to the practice occurs in one of the epigrams of Martial (vii, 37, 2) which establishes the certainty that this was Roman custom with condemned criminals. It seems to follow, then, that if Boethius was in the 'condemned cell' and wearing some old torn sacking inscribed with a fateful Theta, he is likely to have been enduring more severe custody than the mild house arrest sometimes claimed for him on the presupposition that so elegant and urbane a work as the ***Consolation*** can hardly have emerged from a dank subterranean gaol. Certainly Boethius' freedom to write shows that he was not (or not yet) consigned to the worst of dungeons at Pavia. A text in Augustine's *Tractates on St. John's Gospel* (49, 9) attests the variety of treatment accorded to prisoners, not all being confined in rat-infested cellars. (For a modern analogy one might think of the gradually deteriorating conditions, through many months of imprisonment, inflicted by the Pakistan government on Zulfikar Ali Bhutto, culminating in his execution under sordid circumstances.) Boethius' father-in-law Symmachus was still *caput senatus,* though no doubt treading delicately, and had more than enough resources to provide the prison officers with douceurs to persuade them to allow the poor convict a few books and writing materials. The mere survival of the text of the ***Consolation*** (where the embittered scorn for Theoderic's government is unconcealed) proves that members of Boethius' family were allowed some access to him, or the work would no doubt have perished in the gruesome fires of the torture-chamber to which Boethius was to be compelled to make his way. The impression which the text is intended to convey is that he is writing under physical conditions of some discomfort. He is far from his beautifully furnished library with its ivory and glass décor, but his mind is filled with its contents (i, 5, 6, cf. i, 4, 3). He is encumbered with a heavy chain round his neck (i m. 2, 24-7). This, however, is primarily a symbol of his earth-bound condition. It may be literal as well as symbolic; one cannot be sure, for his physical prison is simultaneously the counterpart of the Platonic prison of his soul from which he seeks liberation.

Philosophy's alphabetical symbols would be no mystery to an ancient reader. They represent practical and theoretical studies, that is the hierarchy of sciences already set out in Boethius' exegesis of Porphyry and again in scholastic form in his ***De trinitate,*** ascending through the inferior disciplines of moral philosophy, politics, and economics, up to the less practical, purer disciplines of natural sciences, mathematics, and theology. In a gesture strikingly paralleled in Augustine the lady Philosophy dismisses the Muses as lighthearted meretricious entertainers whose song and dance, as it were of the *commedia dell'arte,* are wholly lacking in sufficient seriousness to speak to the sick patient's condition. Let him look to Philosophy who has been his gentle nurse since his youth and who, through the books in his library, has taught him both human and divine things, the mysteries of the stars and the secrets of nature. With her he suffers in good company. For Philosophy has had its martyrs: Socrates, Anaxagoras, and Zeno of Elea among the Greeks; Canius, Seneca, and Soranus among the Latins. Indeed Boethius' philosophical studies have been made the ground for the accusation against him of *maleficium,* sorcery, or *sacrilegium,* in the pursuit of his ambitions.

Most of the first book consists of Boethius' political apologia; a long protestation of innocence written with contempt both for Theoderic's barbarism and for the cowardice of his fellow senators. But once he has all that off his chest, the lady Philosophy has stern rebuke to offer him. He has forgotten his true self altogether. His citizenship is not in the realm of the many, subject to the changes and chances of political life, but in that of the One, the single ruler and king of a famous Homeric line which Aristotle cites in a theological context in the *Metaphysics.* Obedience to his justice is liberty. (Seneca says that 'obeying God is liberty', *Beata vita* 15, 7; and Augustine coins the phrase 'in his service is perfect freedom', *Quant. An.* 34, 78.) Nothing can exile Boethius from the kingdom of God except his own choice. But the emotional misery he is enduring suggests to Philosophy that his physical exile mirrors his spiritual exile. He has forgotten the nature and destiny of man. Merely to answer the question 'What is man?' with the Aristotelian definition 'a rational, mortal animal', is to disclose a loss of awareness of one's higher self and of the guiding hand of providence in ordering the world. To know oneself in this sense is to be free from all the peaks and troughs of emotion, to drive out both joy and fear, hope and grief, and to see the path of truth in a clear light. Philosophy wants to recall him to what he has learnt from Plato's *Parmenides* about abstract being (i, 1, 10), to liberate him from his attachment to this world, and to make possible his return to God who is true being and goodness. But his present 'lethargic' condition means that the healing drugs have to be applied gradually. He cannot take too much medication all at once; a principle familiar to ancient medicine (as in Galen XII, 590 Kühn) which had long been applied by moralists to the therapy of the soul, as in Seneca, *Consolatio ad Helviam* 1, 2, or in the excerpt from Origen's Exodus commentary in *Philocalia* 27, 4-5.

The first book of the ***Consolation*** is limited, then, to diagnosis by his gentle physician. Consolation proper begins with the second book. The argument, however, stands less in the tradition of ancient consolation literature than in that of the *Protrepticus* or exhortation to philosophical conversion. It gradually ascends from a Stoic moralism to a Platonic metaphysical vision of the divine ordering of an apparently chaotic world. Book ii is almost wholly Stoic in its inspiration, with many parallels in Seneca and in the *Consolation to Apollonius* among the works of Plutarch. Cicero's *Tusculans* are also much used.

. . . . .

The Platonists and the Stoics were the two philosophical schools of ancient Greece in which there was a serious defence of belief in providence, though the two schools undertook their defences from very different premisses. For the Stoics there is no real distinction between providence and fate and the inexorable chain of causation. The cosmos rolls on its everlasting way as an interlocking, ineluctable pattern of cause and effect. Human freedom is largely an illusion of grandeur, for in principle it is scarcely distinguishable from animal instinct, though the Stoics vigorously (and to their critics unconvincingly) protested their belief in the freedom of the will. What they meant by this is an inward process of personal psychotherapy, in which each individual's task is to learn to bear himself nobly before the blows of outrageous fortune, to conduct himself with a strong sense of public duty however adverse the circumstances, and to accept the benefits of nature with gratitude. In a world of complex diversity everything has its place. Even bedbugs may have the beneficial effect of preventing one from the enervating effects of oversleeping.

The Platonists, on the other hand, began quite at the opposite end of the cosmic scale, namely with the transcendence of the divine realm. God must be exempted from the least responsibility for evil. Since the cosmos is held to mirror the ideal noetic realm above, some explanation is required for the fact that human experience of this cosmos produces pain and dissatisfaction. The Platonists offered a series of explanations: (a) evil is rooted in a misuse of free choice; (b) 'evil' is merely a relative term for a defect of goodness, for as one descends the hierarchy of being, one also descends in degrees of the good; (c) evil inheres in matter, the very principle of multiplicity and so also of flux and change. Under different forms and variations Platonic philosophers expanded on these themes, and all three explanations find a place somewhere in Boethius' theodicy.

Accordingly, the second book and the first sections of the third operate with Stoic themes in which comfort is discovered by reconciling onself to a world of determined inevitability 'Do not try to change things, but adapt yourself to the way things are', said the moralist Teles (p. 9, 8 f. Hense). 'If our free wills could change the world, each of us would need his own private world; we all desire different things, so the only power we possess is to adapt ourselves', says the Platonist Hierocles (*de Providentia,* in Photius, *Bibliotheca* 251, 465a 4 ff.). We have to take the rough with the smooth. Farmers have bad as well as good years, sailors stormy as well as calm seas. One cannot reasonably complain if that deceitful and fickle lady Fortune turns her wheel with her well-known caprice, and suddenly removes power and affluence (a reflection much like Seneca, *ep.* 107, 7 f.).

In the past Boethius has done pretty well with Fortune: taken into Symmachus' household when he lost his father, married to a chaste wife, nobly honoured by the nomination of his young sons to be consuls, able to display his munificence to the populace at the circus. He has been a remarkably lucky man. And is he not tempted to exaggerate the awfulness of his situation? Hitherto his family remains untouched. Symmachus himself, most precious glory of the human race, is unmolested so far. (Boethius is evidently aware that a threat is very possible.) Inverting a damnatory Ciceronian phrase from *Pro Cluentio* 72, Boethius praises his father-in-law as 'a man wholly made of wisdom and virtue'. He has been taken far from home, but his place of exile is home to those who normally live there (perhaps echoing Seneca, *ep.* 24, 17). But then Boethius turns upon himself with the realization that there is no crumb of comfort in looking back on a distinguished past that is now for ever lost. Echoing a phrase from Augustine's *Confessions* (x, 21, 30 'tristis gaudium pristinum recolo'), he laments that the worst of all miseries is to remember past happiness now irrecoverable (ii, 4, 1). Alas, the human condition is that all such benefits hang by a thin thread. The very best of good fortune cannot be free of anxiety. No man is so content as to be without some cause of irritation or worry. Those who have most end up by desiring the satisfaction of ever more insatiable needs. The truth is that nothing is miserable unless thinking makes it so. Happiness should not be sought in any external circumstances. One must learn to be self-possessed ('sui iuris', i m. 4, 16 from Cicero, *ep. ad Brut.* 24, 4), self-contained ('sui compos', ii, 4, 23; used of God in v, 6, 8). The comfort of one's body is a gift of chance. Only the soul is immortal, as those have known who have sought their happiness through sufferings and pain (ii, 4, 29; possibly but in no way necessarily, a reference to Christian martyrs). One has to build one's house upon the rock (ii, m. 4). This world's values are merely relative. What is prized by one nation is censured by others. Life is brief but dignity is even more shortlived. High office confers no moral virtue on the holder and is extremely dangerous to society when united with vice. The praetorship was once an office of high standing, but is now empty and is felt to be a heavy burden by the senators who have to hold it, while the 'prefect of the annona', once of supreme distinction but now fallen to be a mere distributor of food in the capital (Cassiodorus, *Variae* vi, 18, 1), has become the lowest form of senatorial life. Nothing is more precarious than posts of high honour. To hold them is like living under the suspended sword of Damocles (so already Cicero, *Tusc.* v, 21, 61-2). Remember Seneca offered a choice of suicides by Nero; or Papinian, prince of jurists, butchered by Caracalla (iii, 5). When the time comes for you to fall they cannot even allow you quietly to resign and retire and to surrender your wealth. Both past and very recent history offer many instances of kings whose felicity has changed to calamity (iii, 5, 2 'plena exemplorum vetustas' echoing Cicero, *Pro Archia* 14).

Moreover, honour's relative status is proved by its local character. A grandee of one place is a nobody somewhere else. Boethius refers to his study in Ptolemy and the astronomical geography of Macrobius' commentary on *Scipio's Dream,* which has taught him what diversity there is in the regions of the inhabited world. Great officers of state are of no account at all once they step outside the Roman world.

And what appalling indignities have to be endured by the seeker after office! If he is to gain support, he must cultivate people he dislikes or even despises, knowing they will be ready to betray him whenever it suits them. None can hurt more than someone who was once your familiar friend. At least by falling into serious trouble Boethius has the advantage of having quickly discovered who his real friends are. They are remarkably few.

When one is suffering innocently, it is a discipline teaching one how independent one has to be of the opinion of the multitude. If one's praise is merited, popular estimation is no true guide to one's value and adds nothing to a wise man who is a better judge of his own merits. (The remark recalls Aristotle's dry observation that the pleasure given to a wise man by an honour is to see that others have reached a conclusion long apparent to himself.) The moral virtue in innocent suffering is even greater if other people do not realize one is innocent (i, 4, 33). Under insults a true philosopher should remain silent. He may even forfeit his title to be a true philosopher if he speaks about his patience under abuse (ii, 7, 20); a Boethian dictum whence has sprung the proverbial saying 'had you kept silent, you would have remained a philosopher', *si tacuisses, philosophus mansisses.* Boethius' words may call to mind not only a saying of Epictetus (iv, 8, 15 ff.) but also the preface to the *Contra Celsum* where Origen thinks the silence of Jesus before mocking accusers a model for wise Christians to follow.

In any event the frailties of life apply to all. Rich men too feel the cold and will bleed if pricked. Death is the great equalizer (ii m. 7).

Adversity is paradoxically better for one's character than prosperity (ii, 8, 3). The supreme duty is to keep a clear conscience. That is to be liberated from the bonds of this earthly prison. The sentiment strikingly combines Stoic and Platonic themes (ii, 7, 23).

The concluding poem of the second book (ii m. 8) is a fine hymn of praise to the love that binds together the cosmos to prevent its disintegration. The various races, married couples, all manner of incompatibilities are held together by this cosmic force. How happy men would be if only the love by which the stars are ruled could reign in their hearts:

> O felix hominum genus
> Si vestros animos amor
> Quo caelum regitur regat.

The providential equilibrium of the diverse elements of the world, the *pugnantia semina* (which Boethius probably borrows from Martianus Capella i, 1, 3), is a characteristic Stoic theme which recurs elsewhere in other verse sections of the ***Consolation*** (iii, m. 2, 1-5; iv m. 6, 4-5). Latin poets before Boethius had rhapsodized on the subject of the love manifest in the bonds averting cosmic catastrophe (Lucan iv, 191 'sacer orbis amor'). In Paulinus of Nola (poem 27) the ties of intimate friendship reflect those which cement the entire universe together. From Posidonius onwards in the first century BC, this defence of providential order had ceased to be distinctively Stoic property, and was absorbed by Platonists. It can be seen in Apuleius. Accordingly the concluding poem of the second book is initiating the 'change of gear' which in the third book begins to move outside the Stoic conventions into the sketching of a Platonic metaphysic.

The first prose section of book iii announces Boethius' readiness for stronger medicines, bitter to taste, sweet once swallowed. But the shift is not explicit until the poem *O qui perpetua* (iii m. 9) which is both the literary climax of the ***Consolation*** and a major turning point in its argument. The first sections of the third book recapitulate Stoic arguments of the type predominant in the second book. Men seek happiness in external things: in riches, power, fame, pleasure, family ties, above all in friendship, which is a matter not of luck but of moral virtue. In this variety of goals all men agree in seeking what they believe to be their good. Even though we human beings are so earthbound, we nevertheless have some dim vision of our origin and therefore of our true end. But we mistake where happiness lies. Riches can never satisfy the avaricious; and the wealthy are miserable surrounded by envious people wishing to relieve them of their money so that they are less, not more independent. He who needs a bodyguard is hardly a free man (iii, 5). 'Nobility' means being praised not for your own merits but for those of your ancestors. Its one moral value is to impress you with a sense of obligation to live up to their ancient virtue (iii, 6, 9, echoing Aristotle, *Rhet.* ii, 15, 1390b 16 ff., and frg. 92). There is a proper pleasure in family life. But children can inflict such torment as to rob you of all happiness. It is impossible to locate the good in physical pleasures or in athleticism or in a beautiful body. Boethius cites a saying of Aristotle that to one gifted with second sight like Lynceus the beauty of Alcibiades would only contrast with the vileness within. A close parallel in Iamblichus' *Protrepticus* proves that directly or indirectly Boethius is drawing on Aristotle's *Protrepticus,* an exhortation to the study of philosophy extant only in fragmentary quotations. The correspondence between Boethius and

Iamblichus does not extend further, and therefore can be no basis for flimsy hypotheses about a wider indebtedness to Aristotle's lost work.

Boethius now begins to perceive 'through a narrow crack' (cf. iv, 4, 40) where the lady Philosophy is leading him. 'But I would prefer to learn more plainly from you' (reminiscent of *Phaedrus* 263a). In seeking happiness man wants sufficiency, power, fame, respect, pleasure; he discovers that these goods cannot be had separately, but only as a single package, as one substance (cf. Plato, *Protagoras* 329cd) which is extremely rare. The actual happiness men know is marked by acute imperfections and beset by transitoriness and mortality. The prose section (iii, 9) concludes with a direct reference to Plato's *Timaeus* which teaches (27c) that in even the least matter we do well to ask for God's help. This explicit mention of the *Timaeus* prepares the way for the masterly poem summarizing the doctrines of the first part of this Platonic dialogue. Nothing in it has a correspondence with the second half, but that was not available to the West in Latin. Proclus' commentary on the *Timaeus,* which he had certainly read, is also incomplete; it is uncertain that Proclus' exegesis covered much of the second half.

. . . . .

In the 38 hexameters of *O qui perpetua* Boethius fashioned an exquisite poem of petition to the Creator. It is a nodal point in the work as a whole, and Boethius knew it. An acute observation in the recent commentary by Joachim Gruber (1978) has noted that the various metres of the poems in the ***Consolation*** are grouped in an ordered and symmetrical structure round *O qui perpetua* which occupies a central position. This shows, in passing, that there is no good reason to embrace speculations that something is likely to have been lost at the end of the last book.

Boethius' ecstatic hymn is reminiscent of the Neoplatonic hymns on cosmic theology characteristic of Synesius and Proclus. The ideas of the hymn are derived both from Plato and from Proclus' commentary. This was established by Klingner (1921). The Creator, himself at rest, is cause of motion to everything (Proclus, *In Tim.* i, 396, 24 f., a theme going back to Aristotle's *Metaphysics*). Boethius will repeat this in prose at iii, 12, 37. God is moved to create by his own goodness (*Tim.* 29e), not by any external cause. In creating he realized a heavenly pattern, forming the cosmos in beauty and perfection (30b). Taking a theme also expounded in his ***Institutio musica*** (i, 2) Boethius says that God binds the world's elements together on mathematical principles, 'by numbers' (*Tim.* 31c 'analogia', or proportion). Thus he keeps the equilibrium of cold and hot, dry and wet (31bc). So also he binds the world-soul in its harmonious parts (*per consona membra*) and gives it a threefold structure (35ab; 37a), set in the middle of the cosmos (36e) to move all things (as Plato's *Laws* 896e, *Phaedrus* 245c). Proclus (*In Tim.* ii, 197, 16) says that the Creator 'divides the Soul among the various parts, fits together the diverse elements and makes them consonant with one another'.

This divided Soul is split into two, each part to move in a circle (*Tim.* 36bc) so as to return upon itself—a theme very dear to Proclus (e.g. *In Tim.* ii, 247-9). The Soul encircles a yet deeper mind (much as Proclus, *In Tim.* i, 403, 3 'soul dances round mind'), and so moves the heaven in a similar circle. From the mixture of the world-soul Plato's Creator brings forth (human) souls and inferior living beings (*Tim.* 41d expounded by Proclus iii, 246, 29 ff.). These souls are provided with 'light chariots' (41e), i.e. the astral vehicles of Neoplatonic speculation as stimulated by the Chaldean Oracles and perhaps also by Aristotle, *Gen. anim.* 736b 27 ff., which linked soul and body through a semi-material, semi-immaterial, starry pneuma.

Distributed like seed in heaven and earth (42d), the souls are then turned back by God towards himself (Proclus iii, 289, 29 ff.), like creatures attracted by fire.

The last seven lines of the poem sum up Boethius' petition.

Da pater augustam menti conscendere sedem. His language echoes the fourth-century poet Tiberianus (*da pater augustas ut possim noscere causas,* iv, 28) and perhaps Martianus Capella ii, 193 (*da pater aetherios mentis conscendere coetus*), but modified by a Vergilian reminiscence from *Georgic* iv, 228, 'sedem augustam'.

So he may discern the source of the Good if he now fixes his gaze on God and if the heavy cloudiness of the earthly body is dispelled. God is the clear heaven, a haven of rest to the devout. 'To see you is our end. You are our beginning, charioteer, leader, pathway, goal' (*Principium, vector, dux, semita, terminus idem*). The accumulation of substantives, which recalls the closing lines of ***De fide catholica*** (*delectatio, cibus, opus, laus*), is a characteristic mark of ancient hymns of praise, which finds echoes in the New Testament itself (e.g. John xiv, 6; xxii, 13). 'Deus unus et idem' is Augustinian (*City of God* vii, 9). Tiberianus iv, 7 f. has 'tu primus et idem postremus mediusque simul.'

. . . . .

A fragment of Aristotle's lost work 'On Philosophy' quoted by Simplicius (*In de Caelo* 288, 28-289, 15 = frg. 16) argues from the degrees of perfection in things up to God as the highest being we can think. A similar 'Anselmian' argument was deployed by Platonists known to Augustine (*City of God* viii, 6). So Boethius goes on to argue that the awareness of imperfection demonstrates the existence of an absolute perfection in comparison with which it is seen to be imperfect. The imperfections of the world can be arranged in a graded hierarchy of goodness and power, and this ascent presupposes an ultimate goal. All men share the notion that the first principle of all things is good (so Boethius, *Perih.* ii, 42, 3-6; *opusc.* iii, 93). Nothing better than God can be conceived (*nihil deo melius excogitari queat*), a definition going back ultimately to Aristotle in the piece cited by Simplicius, first found in Latin in Seneca, and common in Augustine (e.g. *De moribus* ii, 11, 24). Only the perfect good can be at the summit of the hierarchy of goods. By 'God', therefore, we mean the perfection of both goodness and happiness, and goodness is of the essence of happiness (iii, 10). The argument works with the same axioms as those of the third tractate.

For Boethius' Platonic ontology this is a demonstration with mathematical force, carrying a corollary that a perfectly happy man participates in the being of God and in this sense can be said to become a god. Augustine would not have regarded such language as intolerable.

Plotinus (i, 4, 6) says that happiness is found not in a piecemeal amassing of individually desired ends but in a unity. Boethius lays down that individual goods confer happiness only when experienced as a unity (iii, 11). This points to the truth that the supreme God is also the One. Hence a principal good desired by humans, animals, and even plants (for they flourish in the right habitat) is a wish to avert destruction and disintegration, that is the loss of unity. The will to subsist is the desire not to fall apart but to remain one. The argument appears in Proclus' commentary on the *Parmenides* (1199, 20 f.): 'Everything has an instinctive urge towards the One, and everything is what it is by a desire for the One.' A comparable point has been made by Boethius in his ***Arithmetica*** (i, 7). Accordingly we look for an infinite first cause which is a simple undivided whole, free of the limitation resulting from division.

. . . . .

The next poem (iii m. 11) is highly Platonic. The mind (*mens profunda* as in *O qui perpetua*) in its quest for truth has to turn back on itself. The doctrine appears in Augustine, *Conf.* vii, 10, 16. The body weighing down the mind does not altogether obliterate all light or the seed of the truth. Hence Plato's inspired Muse taught that knowing is recovering the memory of what was once known but has become forgotten because of the mists of corporeal existence. On passing into prose once more, Boethius emphatically endorses the doctrine of reminiscence, a belief accepted by the young Augustine (*Solil.* ii, 20, 35) also; for the lady Philosophy has been recalling him to truths that his mind once knew: 'Platoni vehementer assentior' (iii, 12, 1). But instead of a development of the Platonic doctrine of the soul, the argument turns away to the central problem of divine providence. The diversity of the different elements in the world threatens disintegration. Somehow providence checks the centrifugal forces of destruction. 'Whatever holds everything together is what I mean by God' (iii, 12, 25). Accordingly by 'God' we mean not only the supreme good but also the supreme power, a power so great that it is irresistible and yet is gently exercised by an infinitely good wisdom. With a turn of phrase Boethius thinks singularly felicitous, the lady Philosophy declares that 'There is a highest good which rules all things firmly and gently disposes them' (*est igitur summum, inquit, bonum, quod regit cuncta fortiter suaviterque disponit*). Boethius at once tells the lady how delighted he is not only by her conclusion but by the very words she has found to express it—'haec ipsa verba quibus uteris'. Now at long last he is ashamed of the folly that had so exquisitely tortured him.

Why should Boethius take such pleasure in 'haec ipsa verba'? The only natural answer is that the words come from the eighth chapter of the Wisdom of Solomon (*adtingit enim a fine usque ad finem fortiter et disponit omnia suaviter*), a text that Augustine had occasionally found congenial, and which was to mould the words of the great Advent Antiphon *O Sapientia,* of whose liturgical use our earliest evidence comes from Amalarius of Metz in the ninth century, but as a text taken for granted as long established in western churches. In the context of the ***Consolation*** the effect of Boethius' cry of pleasure at the very words is as if he were saying to Philosophy: 'Fancy you, of all people, knowing the Bible'. The point has an evidently direct bearing on the interpretation of the religious standpoint of the ***Consolation*** and on Boethius' disposition towards the Christian faith at the time of its composition in prison.

There are a number of other places in the ***Consolation*** where an allusion to a biblical text is possible. Only in the case just considered does it seem the one natural interpretation of Boethius' prose. The others are curiously tantalising possibilities. The poem iii m. 10 begins 'Huc omnes pariter venite capti/Quos fallax ligat improbis catenis . . . (*libido*)'—'Come all you who are bound captive by the wicked chains of earthly desire . . . ' It is more than a little reminiscent of Matt. xi, 28 f. 'Come to me, all you who are heavy laden . . . ' At iv, 1, 6 Philosophy likens good and evil men to precious and worthless vessels in a great house; this is distantly reminiscent of Rom. iv, 21 ff. and 2 Tim. ii, 20. According to i, 1, 9 the meretricious Muses choke the good harvest of reason with the thorns of passion. A reference to the parable of the sower looks possible (Matt. xiii, 22). In v, 3, 34 Boethius writes of God as *inaccessa lux.* Is it recalling the 'inaccessible light' of 1 Tim. vi, 16? Other allusions could be catalogued, but are less likely than those here cited. It is no doubt the case that if one reference is virtually certain, the probability of other conscious or unconscious reminiscences is much enhanced. Nevertheless, even if these allusions are correctly identified as recalling his reading of the Bible, it is significant that each is presented in so ambiguous a way that the allusion could be picked up only by a reader well acquainted with the New Testament. Moreover, the reference to the Wisdom of Solomon enforces a doctrine of natural theology, not revealed. There is nothing specifically Christian about the content of what is being maintained, even at the point where a citation of the Bible seems as good as certain.

. . . . .

The argument of Philosophy continues that if God is supremely good and powerful, he is the ultimate source of being. Indeed he is being (*esse*), and the imperfections of the graded hierarchy of being leading down from him are also, as one descends the continuum, the successive deprivation both of being and of goodness. Evil is deficiency of being, and therefore strictly nothingness. At this point Boethius betrays a little anxiety that the lady Philosophy begins to play a verbal game with him, when she says that 'Evil is nothing, since God cannot do it, and there is nothing he cannot do' (iii, 12, 29). The doctrine of the non-being of evil is language closer to Augustine (e.g. *Confessions* vii, 12, 18) than to Plotinus or Proclus, for whom evil has nothing absolute about it, yet has some relative existence. The lady Philosophy vigorously denies that she is playing a verbal game. Her argument appeals to no external authority, but is a deduction from positions which are granted. It rests on the affirmation of the perfect self-sufficiency of God, expressed in a quotation from Parmenides (8, 43 Diels), important to the Neoplatonists because of its citation in Plato's *Sophist* 244e. This self-sufficient perfection, like a sphere, turns the moving circle of things while remaining unmoved itself. Despite the lady Philosophy's overmuch protesting, the ordinary reader will sympathise with Boethius' feeling that the argument has suddenly begun to become a little esoteric. Philosophy, however, is here announcing for the first time a theme which will soon be orchestrated more richly and fully. And Boethius should not wonder that the argument rests not on authority but on reasoned inferences from the nature of divine perfection. Plato's *Timaeus* 29b teaches that words ought to have an affinity for the objects to which they refer; a Platonic text which played a prominent part in the discussions designed to reconcile Aristotle's opinion that names are a matter of convention with Plato's that there is that in them which corresponds to reality and is therefore 'nature'. Boethius' second commentary on *Interpretation* (ii, 246, 21 ff.) refers to this debate, and there is also an echo in Ammonius (*CAG* IV, 5 p. 154, 16 ff.).

Perhaps because he is conscious that the argument has grown heavy, Boethius lightens the reader's burden by a poem on Orpheus and Eurydice (iii m. 12). Like Orpheus Boethius has found that sad songs fail to assuage his grief. But unlike Orpheus he is determined not to look back in his upward ascent towards the supreme good. The verses move lightly from a phase of Vergil's to another of Horace's or Seneca's, and the unphilosophical reader is grateful for the relief of Boethius' touching *fabula*. At the end he finds that the underworld visited by Orpheus has become merged with the cave of Plato's myth in the *Republic*.

The fourth book opens with a very respectful protest by Boethius. This insubstantial evil may be demonstrated by pure intellect, but it is experienced as a painful actuality and outrage by the sufferings of humanity. If providence is good and powerful, how can evil go unchecked and unpunished?

The answer is a mixture of Aristotelian and Platonic themes. All men seek whatever they believe to be good. What evil men seek is what they imagine to be good. But it is the mark of evil men that they cannot succeed in their aim of achieving happiness for which true goodness is an indispensable constituent. They suffer a diminution of their humanity, and fall to the level of beasts (iv, 3). A poem on the tormented heart of a tyrant (iv m. 2) looks as if Theoderic is in mind. The passage developing the idea that evil men are like wild animals is as near as Boethius approaches to the Platonic notion of transmigration into animal bodies, a notion which was accepted by Plotinus, but rejected by Porphyry and Proclus. Proclus' commentary on the *Timaeus* (iii, 295, 30) has language close to that of Boethius here.

The poem iv m. 2 pictures a dreamlike flight of the soul, borne by Platonic wings, to a circuit of the heavens, from the height of which petty tyrants seem remarkably trivial.

Much of the philosophical argument in the first sections of the fourth book hangs on Plato's *Gorgias,* especially 466b ff. Plato reasoned that wicked men must be of all men most miserable if they succeed in their endeavours. For them punishment is a source of purgation and therefore of happiness (472e). The justice of their penalty confers a good upon them. So hereafter there will be a judgement of souls with harsh penalties for some, purifying mercy for others. The allusion could be Christian, but in the context is most unlikely to be looking beyond Plato's *Gorgias* 525b. Hierocles has an exposition of the doctrine in his commentary on the Golden Verses of the Pythagoreans (xi, 39-40 cf. xiv, 6; also Proclus, *In Tim.* iii, 236, 27; *In rem pub.* ii, 339-40).

So far as the moral problem of evil is concerned, the argument of the ***Consolation*** reaches its climax with the exegesis of the *Gorgias*. But from the poem of iv m. 4 onwards a subtle shift in the language takes place. Words like 'fate' and 'chance' begin to occur, and with the prose section iv, 6 there is an explicit switch from the moral scandal of apparently unpunished wickedness to the tangled problem of destiny and free will.

The shift is expressly and emphatically marked by Boethius as beginning a fresh approach to his problem. This is an echo of Cicero, *De divin.* ii, 101. (Hermann Usener, of all people, was responsible for the suggestion that at this point Boethius simply switches from one Neoplatonic source to copying out another.) Reflection shows that in altering his ground Boethius is not evading issues. He has first argued, with the Stoics, that we are given the opportunity of deriving profound moral benefit to ourselves and to society from having to live out our lives under adverse and precarious conditions. He has then argued that evil as such is a negative thing, a privation of perfection, a frustrating failure to fulfil powers; but evil can never exist on its own apart from the good, or the pain and the frustration could not be present. Boethius is in effect saying that many of the evils which hurt are unavoidable because the world in which we live, a world of natural incompatibilities and limitations and imperfections, could not be what it is without them. But is there even a small area where evils result from the misuse of free choice? He has followed the *Gorgias* in the paradox that evil men can find the happiness they too seek not by achieving their wicked ends but only by accepting just punishment which for some is purgation. The notion of an acceptance of responsibility is thereby inserted by implication. But there remains the burning question of misused freedom as a cause of evil, and therefore of the reconciliation of freedom with belief in an omnipotent providence. Boethius is surely right to see that unless he can disentangle the problems of freedom and determinism he will have left many loose ends in his argument.

. . . . .

The Neoplatonists from Plotinus onwards (*Enn.* iii, 3, 5, 14) distinguish between providence, which concerns the higher realm, and fate which is another name for the unalterable chain of cause and effect in this inferior and determined world. The theme is prominent in Calcidius' commentary on the *Timaeus* and in several other late Platonic philosophers. Accordingly Boethius proposes to make this distinction: to our inferior mind 'fate' describes that nexus of causation in the cosmos which operates immutably in indifference to our wills. How it works we do not exactly know. Perhaps, as some think, it operates through ministering divine spirits i.e. Platonic daemons; but Boethius avoids the word which Christian ears found offensive. The ministrations of 'daemons or angels' (either word being equally acceptable to a Neoplatonist) are mentioned by Proclus in his Commentary on the *Republic* (ii, 255, 19 ff. Kroll) and in his 'Ten Doubts concerning Providence' x, 62. Boethius also thinks fate may perhaps be the action of the world-soul or of the entire natural order or the consequence of control by the stars, a possibility countenanced in his second commentary on *Interpretation.* Augustine has comparable reviews of the possible ways in which the order of the world is maintained (*City of God* v, 9; *De trinitate* iii, 4, 9).

Fate, therefore, is subordinate to providence. But some things under providence are above fate. Boethius compares this to a number of spheres which move round the same centre, where the inmost sphere is most nearly stationary, the outermost fast moving. So also that which is closest to the first divinity (*primae propinqua divinitati*) is most free from fate. The further the distance from the first mind (*prima mens*), the tighter the grip of fate.

Augustine speaks of God as 'the supreme hub of causes' (*summus causarum cardo: De trin.* iii, 9, 16). The simile of the circle or sphere appears in several writers, e.g. Pseudo-Plutarch, *De fato* 569C, Plotinus (ii, 2, 1; iii, 2, 3; vi, 8, 18, 23), and Proclus, *Decem Dubit.* i, 5.

Boethius suggests, therefore, that as time is to eternity, so the circle is to its centre, and so is the moving interconnection of events in fate in relation to the unmoving simplicity of providence. This chain of events controls the stars, the constant equilibrium of the elements, the birth and death of living things, and the acts and fortunes of men (cf. Boethius, *Perih.* ii, 231). The constancy of causation depends on the immobility of the first cause. But from his high watchtower (*specula alta,* a Virgilian phrase for a Platonic idea) God looks out on the world and arranges what is best for each individual. Plotinus (iii, 2, 9) emphasises that great as the power of providence is, it is not so overwhelming that it reduces the individual to nothingness. Boethius' doctrine that there is a care even for the individual would be congenial to a Christian reader. But his sentence is set in a Platonic context.

To take providence seriously is to become aware that things do not happen as we expect or think right. 'Our Lucan' wrote that the conquering cause pleased the gods, the vanquished's cause pleased Cato (*Pharsalia* i, 128). So even things that seem perverse and wrong to us are nevertheless right. It seems monstrous to us when a man of holiness and virtue, *deo proximus,* is afflicted. In some cases providence protects such a person even from bodily sickness. Indeed, the lady Philosophy adds that 'someone more excellent than myself has said, 'The heavens built the body of a holy man'.' The hexameter is cited in Greek, and since Philosophy thinks its author superior even to herself, the conclusion that it is a quotation from the Chaldean Oracles, held in profound awe as the highest revelation by Proclus and other late Platonists, seems irresistible. (Thomas Taylor first made this observation as long ago as 1806 in his *Collectanea* p. 102, but his book has been disregarded by the learned. The line is accepted by Edouard des Places as fragment 98 in his recent edition of the Oracles.)

Often providence brings good men to the summit of power to beat back evil. But lest prosperity bring excess, felicity does not last long. Providence's most ingenious achievement is to use evil men to force other evil men to be good, if only from a desire to be unlike their vile oppressors. And God uses the natural course of events, or fate, to get rid of evil; a proposition which looks like a variant of 'while there is death, there is hope'.

The prose section iv, 6 is the longest in the work. It is followed by a poem of praise for the good order of the world in the heavenly bodies, the beauty of the ordered seasons, the love that holds everything together. Philosophy then teaches Boethius that all fortune is beneficent, whether pleasant or painful, either rewarding or exercising the good, punishing or correcting the bad. The correspondence between these words and Simplicius' commentary on the *Physics* ii, 6 (*CAG* IX, 361, 1 ff.) has been acutely noted by Courcelle. Similarly Hierocles, *In carmen aureum* 11. The book concludes with a poem, full of echoes of Seneca's tragedies, concerning the struggles of Agamemnon, Odysseus, and Hercules.

. . . . .

The fifth and last book contains Boethius' most intricate discussion of the logic of divine foreknowledge and human freedom, in which he resumes many of the themes of his second commentary on *Interpretation.* . . . It is not certain that the book is constructed from Ammonius' commentaries on *Interpretation* and *Physics.* But it goes without saying that the exegetical tradition of the Peripatetic and then Neoplatonic schools in expounding these two books by Aristotle is lying behind Boethius throughout the book.

In the first prose section, there is an express reference by the lady Philosophy to the teachings on chance of 'my Aristotle'. Chance cannot mean a random event as opposed to a process of causation, or it becomes a meaningless word. It is axiomatic that 'nothing comes from nothing' (Aristotle, *Metaphysics* Z 7), though it applies not to the originating cause but to the material ordered by it. A causeless event is a nonsense and a nothing. Aristotle defines chance as a coincidence which happens without being intended; that is, because of the coincidence of different processes of causation. (Boethius has already mentioned this understanding of chance in his commentary on Cicero's *Topics*.) Aristotle's views are expressed not only in the *Physics* (B 4-5) but also in the *Metaphysics* 1025a 14 ff. whence Boethius or the school tradition derived the illustration of a man digging in a field for another purpose and finding a treasure.

Both the Neoplatonists and the Christian Augustinian tradition treat freedom as a moral quality. No one is less free than the person dominated by vice. Freedom is attained by continual contemplation of the divine mind, lost when one slips down into the corporeal. The upward look is full of light, the downward of darkness. It follows that there are degrees of freedom (Proclus, *De providentia et fato* 48). Complete surrender to vice means a loss of capacity for rational deliberation (cf. Proclus, *In rem pub.* ii, 276, 8), lost in the fog of the cloud of unknowing (*inscitiae nubes*), alienated from God who is the true Sun (v, 2 and m. 2) who is, who has been, and who is to come (echoing Vergil, *Georgic* iv, 392 rather than Apoc. i, 8).

In the next section (v, 3) Boethius takes up the simple proposition of popular assumption: if God knows everything including all future events, then no human act is voluntary, and free will is an illusion. This proposition is rejected on the good ground that, from a doctrine of what God knows, nothing necessarily follows about the voluntariness of human action. What determines events is the nexus of cause and effect, not knowledge even in an omniscient power that can hold no mistaken beliefs without ceasing to be omniscient and therefore ceasing to be what we mean by God. The confusion here is seen by Boethius to lie in our all too human interpretation of divine foreknowledge as holding beliefs about acts in advance of their occurrence.

We think of the future as consisting of uncertain, contingent events: contingent in the sense that there are a number of possibilities, and for us they are open; it is not the case that any of them can be seen to be necessary. And 'necessary' itself is a slippery word; for some necessities are absolute, whereas others are conditional. That a man will die is absolutely necessary because man is a mortal animal. If you know someone is walking, then, if your belief is correct, it is necessary that he is walking; and if he is walking, he is going. Here necessity is conditional. We see how for Boethius necessity is being contrasted both with voluntary action and with the contingent event which happens but does not have to happen. Our wills are in the order of causes known to God.

The problem of God's foreknowledge of future contingents becomes criss-crossed with another difficulty; the relation of time to eternity. Boethius rejects the favoured solution of Alexander of Aphrodisias (*De fato* 30) and Calcidius (*In Tim.* 162) that God knows the uncertain future as uncertain, just as we do. He is not happy to think that temporal events can be the cause of an eternal knowledge. With Iamblichus and Proclus he affirms that the knowledge possessed by God operates on a different plane from human knowledge. For us events fall into past, present, and future time. God is outside time. For him the knowledge of temporal events is an eternal knowledge in the sense that all is a simultaneous present. Therefore to affirm God is omniscient does not entail that he holds beliefs about acts *in advance* of their being done; the temporality involved in the phrase 'in advance of' must be abstracted from the discussion. Without the abstraction of the temporality in saying 'in advance of', the logical circle leaves no escape. Eternity does not mean perpetuity (such as may be affirmed of the physical world), but the simultaneous and perfect possession of limitless life (v, 6, 4). Time, as Plato defined it (*Timaeus* 38a), is a moving image of eternity and because it is a moving image fails to attain to the nature of eternity; the present is a kind of likeness of the eternal, but differs in that it cannot be possessed permanently (v, 6, 12).

The last book of the ***Consolation*** is a remarkable discussion of an intricate problem. The moral problem of innocent suffering is set aside in favour of the logical analysis of the difficulties inherent in any belief in providence and human freedom. The third verse section of the fifth book reflects on the necessity of holding together two truths that appear in tension with one another (v m. 3). The hierarchical Platonist theory of levels of knowledge and apprehension leads Boethius to suggest that some of the logical difficulty is caused by the limitation of our minds, bounded by the experiences of time and successiveness. In this life we can live only each passing moment, and cannot grasp past, present and future together (v, 6, 2).

But even in our minds there are four levels: (a) of sense which we share with animate creatures unable to move like limpets; (b) of *imaginatio,* the power to form corporeal images shared with animals that have powers of movement; (c) *ratio,* possessed by man alone on earth; (d) *intelligentia* which is God's (v, 5). An individual object taken by itself is singular; but reason has the power to discern the universal of which the particular object is a specimen (v, 6, 36).

The last sentences of the ***Consolation*** reaffirm that belief in free will is compatible with belief in providence and in a transcendent divine knowledge in which there is neither before nor after. Therefore prayers and the practice of virtue are not vain. To act out your life before a Judge who sees all things is to know that there lies upon you a great necessity of integrity (*magna necessitas probitatis*). There Boethius' pen fell from his hand. The rest is silence. The work shows no signs of being incomplete. There is no discussion, admittedly, of the soul's immortality except for one observation (ii, 4, 28) that it is established by many proofs, and underlies the conviction of many whose happiness has been found through and in spite of pain and martyrdom. On the other hand, the theme of immortality is little discussed in the surviving Neoplatonic tracts on providence in Plotinus, Hierocles of Athens, and Proclus.

.....

From 900 to 916 the abbot of the Saxon monastery of Corvey (daughter house of Corbie near Amiens) was Bovo II, a man of wide culture. We have from his pen a commentary on the verse section 'O qui perpetua' (iii m. 9), and his prologue warns his monks against the dangers of Boethius. It is astonishing (he says) that a man who wrote such correct doctrine on the Trinity and on the person of Christ, works which Bovo studied in adolescence, should also have written the ***Consolation of Philosophy*** in which he is not only silent about the teaching of the Church but also wide open to philosophical and especially Platonic doctrines. That both the theological tractates and the ***Consolation*** come from the same pen Bovo regards as certain on ground of style.

Bovo was evidently right in observing the unity of style shared by the opuscula and the ***Consolation***. We have already seen the tractates other than the fourth to be even fuller of Neoplatonic logic than the last three books of the ***Consolation***; because of their dry logical character they have less personal religious feeling than the later work. To this last description the fourth tractate ***De fide catholica*** is an exception, with its emotionally charged confession of faith cast in terms of high Augustinianism, offering neither logical elucidation nor apologetic defence, but simply setting down what Boethius believes the content of the revealed religion of Christ to be. But here as in the other opuscula Boethius shows the same sharp clarity and brevity, and the same eye for what is salient. The non-theological diction is very characteristic of Boethius. Moreover, the disjunction between faith and reason, revelation and natural religion, is presupposed by ***De fide catholica***. It is sometimes suggested that there is anachronism in attributing such a notion to a man of the sixth century. In fact Boethius' master Proclus operates with much the same disjunction in treating the Chaldean Oracles as a transcendent source of divine revelation in verbally inspired form, towards which philosophy may aspire but which human reasoning could never have found unaided.

To affirm the authenticity of ***De fide catholica*** as the evidence of the language requires us to do is greatly to sharpen the question, Why does he exclude anything specifically Christian from the ***Consolation of Philosophy***? Although the answer that the ***Consolation*** is an expression of deep inward disillusion with Christianity has been given by distinguished Boethian scholars, I think reflection shows the evidence is against this view. No doubt it is possible to speculate that at the crisis of his life Boethius may not have received from the higher clergy at Rome or northern Italy the support that he might have felt entitled to expect. Certainly there would have been great danger in submitting intercession to the angry Theoderic on behalf of a man against whom there was a political charge of treason. If Boethius' friend John the deacon is rightly identified with the John who became Pope in the summer of 523, his feelings would have been intelligible if this trusted friend, with whom (as the third tractate shows) he had enjoyed many metaphysical discussions in the more advanced flights of Neoplatonic philosophy, found it impracticable or for the sake of the good of the Church impolitic to offer any effective plea for Boethius. But the presence of subtle biblical and perhaps even liturgical allusions in the language of the ***Consolation*** makes the apostasy interpretation unlikely. If the ***Consolation*** contains nothing distinctively Christian, it is also relevant that it contains nothing specifically pagan either. Its character recalls Andromachus' defence of the Lupercalia before Pope Gelasius that its ceremonies are 'neither pagan nor Christian'. Unlike Proclus whose *Platonic Theology* weaves an elaborate pattern to integrate the gods of polytheism into the structure of his metaphysical system, Boethius puts a distance between himself and polytheism. The sun, he says, gives light much inferior to the light of God's truth (iii m. 6, 3; cf. iii m. 10, 15 ff.; v m. 2, 1 ff.; iii m. 11, 8). To speak with Boethius of Socrates as having won a 'victory over unjust death' (i, 3, 6) evidently echoes Christian language, consciously or unconsciously. But the ***Consolation*** contains no sentence that looks like a confession of faith either in the gods of paganism or in Christian redemption. Not a word hints at the forgiveness of sins or the conquest of death through resurrection. Everything specific is absent, and probably consciously avoided. The ambiguity seems clearly to be deliberate. The work's intention is given by its title. Boethius is not in quest of consolation from divine grace in the remission of sins and the promise of eternal life to those redeemed through Christ. His doctrine of salvation is humanist, a soteriology of the inward purification of the soul. The ***Consolation*** is a work written by a Platonist who is also a Christian, but is not a Christian work.

Nevertheless, I think it a work written with the consciousness of Augustine standing behind the author's shoulder, so to speak. The argument that Boethius intended a Platonic confession of faith which he knew to be incompatible with Christianity fails against the observation that there is nothing in the Platonic themes admitted to the ***Consolation*** which one cannot also find accepted in the philosophical dialogues and the *Confessions* of the young Augustine. Even the mature works of Augustine, the *City of God,* the *Trinity,* and that neglected masterpiece the *Literal Commentary on Genesis,* offer many anticipations of Boethius' Platonism, especially as expounded in the last book of the ***Consolation***.

For Augustine also God is absolute Being, from whom descends the great chain or continuum of derived entities, each grade having slightly less being and therefore less goodness than the grade above, until one finally reaches the absence of being which is the negativity of pure evil. To ask the cause of evil is for Augustine to ask to see darkness or to hear silence (*Confessions* iii, 7, 12; *City of God,* xi, 9; xii, 7). For him the good is unity, evil multi-

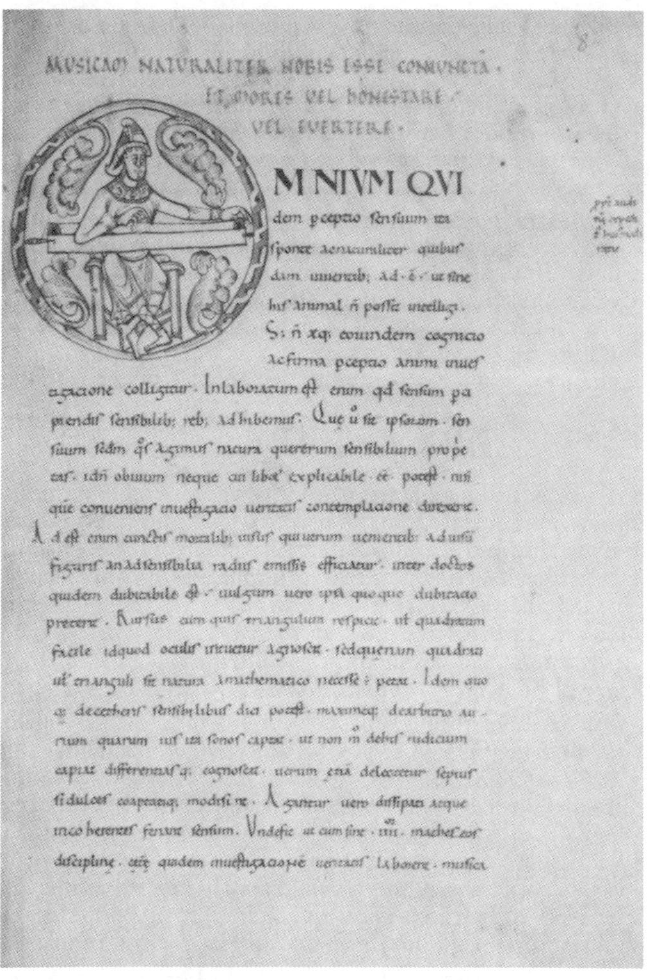

Medieval musical treatise showing Boethius at the monochord.

plicity and disruption (*Conf.* iv, 15, 24). Providence calls the rational creation to return to its true being and goodness which are one and the same (*City of God* xi, 28). Augustine confesses in the *City of God* (v, 5) that 'no philosophers are so close to us as the Platonists'. His discussion of divine foreknowledge and human free will (v, 9) begins with a reference to Cicero 'On divination', a reference which is evidently from memory since it is wrong, but which may well explain why in the ***Consolation*** Boethius also makes a similar reference in his own discussion of the subject (v, 4, 1). In what then follows Augustine mentions other matters familiar to the reader of Boethius: e.g. the interpretation of 'fate', *heimarmene,* as a name for the connected series of events that composes destiny outside the direction of human wills. Augustine differs from Boethius in thinking 'fate' a term with inappropriate associations. He knows about but is unsympathetic to the notion that fate rules lower things, providence higher. He is familiar with the Platonic view that our wills, to us creatures contingent and uncertain, are included among the causes whose outcome is certain to God; or with the view that chance is merely a name for an event whose causes are unknown.

Moreover, between the ***Consolation*** and Augustine's early philosophical dialogues there are a number of similarities: for example, the personification of philosophy (*Solil.* i, 1), though this is common enough and can also be found in Martianus Capella; the ejection of the Muses from a serious discussion (*C. Acad.* iii, 7; *De ordine* i, 24); the recognition that only a privileged few can attain the contemplative discernment of the divine order (*De ordine* ii, 24 f.; *C. Acad.* i, 1); the diagnosis of unphilosophical sensual life as a disease or a sleep (*De ordine* i, 24; *C. Acad.* ii, 16). All these points are no doubt common conventions, and do not add up to a demonstration of literary dependence. Nevertheless they help to show that in his Platonism Boethius is not necessarily turning away from Augustine.

Christine Mohrmann has drawn attention to the fact that much of the vocabulary in Boethius' two passages about prayer in the ***Consolation*** (v, 3, 34; 6, 47-48), with 'commercium, deprecari, supplicandi ratione, praesidium, mereor, porrigere', can also be found in early Latin collects of the ancient sacramentaries. We have too little pagan Latin liturgy to be able to assert that such language is distinctively Christian. One would expect such vocabulary to be neutral in itself. Nevertheless, so far as it goes, her observation gives a marginal reinforcement to the view that there is a latent awareness of Christianity beneath the surface of Boethius' text. Boethius writes with such artistry and 'artificiality' that we may be confident he does nothing accidentally.

Between Boethius and Augustine there are also many notable differences. Most important of these is the difference in the ways in which the two men speak of the relation between faith and reason: for Augustine, parallel and reconcilable ways of knowing the truth; for Boethius parallel ways which only meet at certain points where logic may help to clarify the confusions of popular or common usage. Boethius' vision of the cosmos is of a single great whole kept from disintegration by the goodness and power of providence, and one might expect him to affirm an optimistic view of the concord of faith and reason. In actuality there is much more of this kind of optimism in Augustine than in Boethius.

Nevertheless it must be a correct conclusion which calls Boethius a humanist in the classical sense of that word: a man positive to the values of great literature and philosophy wherever found, and especially in the thought of Plato and Aristotle. There is a certain sadness in the fact that because his fascination with logical problems so gripped the mediaeval schoolmen, the reaction against the schoolmen at the time of the Renaissance ended by making him unfashionable as well. Moreover, his picture of the world belongs to that 'Discarded Image' of which C. S. Lewis wrote. Nevertheless, this last Roman, whose gaze is so profoundly retrospective, transmitted a whole cultural world to his mediaeval successors. The finesse with which he composed his ***Consolation of Philosophy*** made it possible for Alcuin and many others to read the book as a Christian work. The book is an essay in natural theology apart from revelation; and the very possibility of that rests on Christian assumptions. The Christianizing readers have not been absolutely wrong.

Among all Boethius' writings the ***Consolation of Philosophy*** is rightly esteemed the climax of his achievement. The substructure that made it possible is seen in his other works on logic, mathematics, and theology, and it is only in relation to these other writings, and to his Neoplatonic masters, that the nature of his originality can be seen in clear outline. These other treatises came to be profoundly influential in mediaeval times. Alcuin and, after him, a thin line of Carolingian and later scholars found in Boethius' studies of the liberal arts and of dialectic a strength and resource which they badly needed. Without him their educational programme would not have made much headway. From the ninth-century commentaries were written to explain the obscurities of the theological tractates and of the ***Consolation***. From his dialectical and mathematical treatises Boethius' readers learnt precision and order. He taught mediaeval thinkers to examine first principles, to be careful in the use of words, to try to trace an argument back to its basic axioms and presuppositions. The principles of axiomatization in the third of the opuscula sacra created a foundation on which in the twelfth-century Alan of Lille would set about the task of constructing the whole of theology as a deduction from a single self-evident truth. Although cut off in his prime so that his grand ambitions to translate all Aristotle and Plato were never realized, he nevertheless succeeded to a remarkable degree in his prime endeavour to salvage major parts of Greek philosophical learning for future generations.

In the twelfth-century schools his influence reached its peak. His works became central to the syllabus of instruction, and strongly stimulated that thoroughgoing study of logic for its own sake which becomes so prominent a hallmark of the mediaeval schools. The *opuscula sacra* taught the theologians that they did not necessarily need to fear the application of rigorous logic to the traditional language of the Church. He made his readers hungry for even more Aristotle, and prepared the welcome given to the new twelfth century translations of the *Analytics* and the *Topics,* although his own versions were scarcely known at all. From the first of the *opuscula sacra* mediaeval philosophers learnt how to draw up a hierarchy of the sciences and to see the different departments of knowledge, now being pursued together in community as the newly founded universities set themselves to their common task, as an organized and coherent scheme in which the various parts could be seen to be rationally related to each other.

But the humanists of the Renaissance found themselves constricted by the number-games of his ***Arithmetic,*** by the Pythagorean indifference to musical practice of his ***Music,*** above all by the obsessive concern with logical niceties which came to give the mediaeval schoolmen an unhappy reputation. As the reputation of Aristotle declined, so also that of Boethius was bound to fall with him.

Only the ***Consolation of Philosophy*** came through with remarkably little of its power diminished. The work of a layman, it remained the loved reading of laymen, especially if (like Thomas More) they held high office and suddenly found themselves deprived of their sovereign's protection and favour. The masterpiece of Boethius still speaks in the twentieth century to those who grapple with the perennial problems of evil, freedom, and providence. His solution to the problems of divine foreknowledge, exploiting Iamblichus' idea that divine knowledge wholly transcends the successiveness of the temporal process, though retaining its modern advocates, raises difficulties of its own. But no one can read the last book of the ***Consolation*** without having a clarified vision of the nature of the question needing to be answered. The ideas with which Boethius was working already lay to hand in the discussions of the Neoplatonists. To lay his work side by side with theirs is to realize the independence of his critical judgement as he formulates his personal synthesis. Boethius permanently marked the western philosophical tradition by his doctrine that 'personality' has something to do with the unique quality of the individual. In the ***Consolation of Philosophy,*** as in no other among his writings, his own individuality stands out for all to see.

Anna Crabbe (essay date 1981)

SOURCE: "Literary Design in the *De Consolatione Philosophiae,*" in *Boethius: His Life, Thought and Influence,* edited by Margaret Gibson, Basil Blackwell, 1981, pp. 237-74.

[*In the following essay, Crabbe explores the literary influences on Boethius's theme and style, paying particular attention to the works of Ovid and Augustine.*]

I

Champion of Philosophy, orator to kings, theologian, poet, supreme logician: the achievements of Boethius compose a multicoloured garment. Yet just as the brief literary portrait supplied by Cassiodorus [in his *Anecdoton Holderi*] seems dulled by its omission of the ***Consolatio,*** so the sum of Boethius' other writings does not prepare us for this final work. True, each shade finds its place there, clearly discernible, indispensable to the complex weave of argument and theme. There is the breadth—and the depth—of erudition we should expect, the balance of control and composition. Yet the surprise remains. As literature all is of a different order, subsumed to a new and more vital purpose. Such urgency and creative independence hang strangely on this patient and methodical scholar, the meticulous translator and commentator who mapped out a lifetime's academic curriculum which he would not live to complete. For there came Pavia and the turn of Fortune's wheel: exile, prison, death. But before death, the ***Consolatio,*** the masterpiece, springing perhaps more clearly than any other work of antiquity directly out of the circumstances of its composition. Imminent death, it has been said, serves to concentrate the mind wonderfully. The real possibility of cold iron about the throat gave a new dimension to a Christian Platonist's understanding of metaphysical shackles.

To ask why and how Boethius wrote a masterpiece, instead of, or perhaps in view of its subsequent career as well as, a university text-book may go some way towards answering the equally fraught question of what exactly the ***Consolatio*** is. Imprisoned and despairing, Boethius receives a theophany, an apocalyptic vision. His former teacher Philosophy, an imposing figure with eyes ablaze and carrying sceptre and books, appears and chides him for his miserable state of mind. She diagnoses his problem and brings him gradually to recognize that it is his own distorted perception that has allowed temporal circumstance and mundane ill-fortune to affect him. Step by step as their talk progresses the quondam philosopher is re-educated; the arguments shift from the negative criticism of ephemeral values to a positive pursuit by means of reason of the 'summum bonum', which is found to consist in God. The whole culminates in a discussion of the problem of the existence of freewill in a universe governed by a supreme and prescient deity. To summarise thus briefly is to omit many of the work's more salient features, the majority of its difficulties and all its subtleties.

Attempts to define the nature and purpose of the book are bedevilled by its eclecticism in three respects: the genre, the figure of Philosophy and the details and direction of the philosophical arguments.

As regards genre, there is a surfeit of traditions within which to locate the piece, a welter of sources. Class it as a 'consolatio'. Courcelle has spoken aptly of a 'consolation for life' and the shift whereby the victim rather than the bereaved is comforted gives a twist to the theme of the desirability of death that does not easily find earlier parallels. In one sense it may fairly be called protreptic—what was in the pagan world since Aristotle's day an invitation to philosophy; in another sense a theological treatise without specific Christian allegiance, so that Rand [E. K. Rand, *HSCP* XV (1904)] and Courcelle [in his *Consolation,* 1967] are driven to use the phrase προτρεπτικος εὶς τὸν θεοŒν that is 'a protreptic towards God'. Both apocalypse and philosophical dialogue, yet not with every feature of either, in its consistent alternation of prose and verse the ***De Consolatione Philosophiae*** is clearly the most highly organised and polished 'satura' we possess; yet in style and much of its content it is poles apart from all other examples which employ this form. In short it parallels no genre precisely yet is like almost all.

Turn from the general to the specific and matters get worse. Philosophy's person and function have provided a battle ground for scholars. Is the inspiration for her elaborate portrait in the first prose section a pagan Athena or the Christian Sophia? Is the lady a literary artifice, a philosophical abstraction or personification or a goddess of revelation? Does the movement of her hand to Boethius' breast denote revelation, inspiration, diagnosis or healing? A strong case can and probably should be made for every view. The portrait is the source of the great group of metaphors which articulate the dramatic progress of the work, and all these aspects are to be developed in due course. Given that Philosophy expresses her scorn for the different schools of thought that snatch at her garment and come away merely with scraps, we may assume that Boethius intended a figure as comprehensive as a lifetime's reading might make it.

Details throughout the work, in both prose and verse passages, present similar difficulties. Times have changed since the ***Consolatio*** could be dismissed as a mere conflation, not necessarily original, of Aristotle's *Protreptic* with a neoplatonic source, done into Latin and interspersed with some rather indifferent verse, the whole being equipped with a 'Boethian' introduction of a book and a half. Even a perfunctory glance at recent treatments shows a different picture. The Plotinus expert may nail a source for a given phrase only to have it snatched by a champion of Proclus or Porphyry. On the other hand many will prefer to take the emphasis right back to the Platonic original. The enthusiast for Latin prose enters the lists next: something from Cicero's *Somnium Scipionis* or his lost *Hortensius,* a letter of Seneca perhaps, or one of his dialogues? And then there is always Augustine. We have yet to hear from the specialists in poetry: the omnipresent Seneca apart, surely a touch of Virgil, or Horace, Lucretius, Ovid, while the Hellenist retaliates with a parallel from a hymn of Synesius. Frequently everyone will be right. We must lay aside the residual, if declining, scholarly assumption that no late antique writer's acquaintance with classical authors extended much beyond select snippets from florilegia. Nevertheless how can it be legitimate to talk in terms of such a mosaic of sources and inspirations for a work whose author was incarcerated at Pavia under sentence of death without access to his library? One way out would be to assume some degree of literary fiction on the author's part about his circumstances. But such desperate measures are perhaps unnecessary, and in one sense unhelpful. Ultimately it may be that the explanation actually depends on those circumstances.

Roughly speaking, the detailed sources of the ***Consolatio*** boil down to three main constituents, Greek philosophy, Roman philosophy and Latin poetry, all areas in which Boethius was adept. Extensive knowledge of Plato, Aristotle and the Neoplatonic authors is clear already from the range and content of his previous works. His view was comprehensive rather than divisive, witness his avowed ideal, one shared by earlier Neoplatonists, of reconciling Plato's and Aristotle's philosophical systems. The master of logic's admiration for the Stagirite was complemented by the stronger appeal of Plato to the theologian and to the more concretely visual imagination of the poet. The Neoplatonic movement was not something set apart, rather a continuation and refinement of a tradition, with Proclus the most up to date modern commentator on an enduringly significant original. Klingner's view of Boethius as one who understood Plato 'Platonice', that is a Neoplatonist ('Platonicus') and a Platonist simultaneously is both acute and perceptive in this respect. Among the Latins, it was to Cicero and to Seneca that Boethius owed many features of his pleasantly anachronistic prose style as well as much of his philosophical vocabulary. Originality of thought had been the chief concern of neither writer. Cicero claimed to have invented a Latin vocabulary for philosophy as also for rhetoric and that his task was to transmit the gold of Greek thought to an untutored Roman world. Seneca's dependence on the Greeks is no less readily apparent. Boethius faced a similar task at a grimmer stage of Roman history. Instead of laying the foundations of a bright future, he had a salvage operation to perform: what might be preserved from a brilliant past for a dying civilisation as the dark ages fell. Christianity would survive, but its prospects in the west had little to do with those of the finer points of human reason. Nowhere is this more urgently apparent than in the ***Consolatio***.

The group of philosophical writings, both Greek and Latin, from which Boethius assembled his material and arguments, 'consolatio', protreptic and discussion of the nature of the soul, is a consistent one. It turns on the same questions of rejection of this world, the pursuit of the 'summum bonum', the understanding of man's existence and essence. Much of its metaphorical vocabulary is also common ground: imprisonment and freedom, exile and return, slavery and tyranny and the like. Bemoan the lack of his library as Boethius may, the range and subtlety of his manipulations of this large but related body of writings imply an ability to work without constantly referring to a small group of basic sources, but rather independently from a store of assimilated learning. This holds still more forcibly for the poems. An appreciation of the finest Latin poetry speaks for itself in the metra of the ***Consolatio***. Even without the testimony of Cassiodorus, the variety of forms attempted demonstrates that writing poetry was hardly a new departure for Boethius. Poems, merely by being metrical, are held more easily in the mind than prose. Many of Boethius' metra display a freedom of creative variation on his predecessors, exceptional at this late date, which would demand that he had much of Latin poetry by heart.

In this outline one figure is conspicuously absent: Augustine. I omit him deliberately here because there is some controversy over his importance to the ***Consolatio***. At one time Courcelle went so far as to doubt that Boethius had even read the early *Dialogues,* let alone taken note of them. My own view, in large measure shared by Silk [E. T. Silk in *HTR* XXXII (1939)], is that Augustine is crucial to the conception of the ***Consolatio***. For the present it is appropriate merely to remark that this sketch of Boethius' intellectual interests and equipment would require little adaptation beyond the removal of the latest century and a half of Neoplatonic refinements to apply equally well to Augustine shortly after his conversion.

II

Assuming that Boethius was capable of writing a work as complex as the ***Consolatio*** in such straitened circumstances, then his death-sentence, imprisonment and exile relate directly to the selection and treatment of his major sources. There are two obvious consequences and both bear on the immediacy of the composition. The first, on which I have touched already, is the imagery common to most of Boethius' philosophical mentors, above all those in the Platonic tradition, concerning the situation of the unenlightened soul, imprisoned by an earthly body and material circumstances, in exile from its true home, far from the light, without real freedom and at the beck and call of human tyranny. The Philosophy of the ***Consolatio*** is obsessed with these images and the task she sets herself is the release of her pupil's soul from their domination. Freedom, for the soul of the philosopher, she argues, is there for the taking. Chains and imprisonment, if they exist, are self-imposed. Even the final discussion in Book V of the relation of providence and freewill hinges on the question of 'libertas'. The constant repetition and manipulation of these themes as a significant part of the work's argument makes us unable to forget Boethius' actual circumstances. We are not meant to. It is not just the material world in general, but actual imprisonment and exile, perhaps even physical chains and certainly physical death towards which he must learn indifference in order to return to his former philosophical state. The paradox involved in the apparently identical nature of his physical and spiritual situation and the long struggle to establish the unreality of the physical prison and escape the reality of the mental chains provides the work's impetus. For once all the metaphors have become concrete and their validity is here put to the test.

Most of those authors of whom we are most explicitly reminded in the ***Consolatio*** share more than their metaphorical vocabulary with Boethius. Their biographies bear a striking resemblance to his own. This series of historical links has large consequences for the ***Consolatio***. We are required to picture Boethius sitting alone in prison mulling over his own predicament, measuring his own reactions to adversity up against those of his predecessors, and, with Philosophy's aid, finally outstripping them all. Ovid, Cicero, Seneca, Socrates and, in a rather different sense, Augustine: all play their part in this respect. Let us start with the three pagan philosophers. Philosophy herself draws her pupil's attention to two of them, Socrates and Seneca, in the group of those brought to disaster merely by virtue of a training in her school which set them apart from the interest of the wicked. She offers them as examples to account for Boethius' own fate and it is hard to imagine that Boethius himself had not compared his plight with theirs. This gives an insight into his thoughts in planning the ***Consolatio***. The pre-eminence of Plato is, as we have seen, scarcely surprising. Yet Plato implies also Socrates, and Socrates preferred a cup of hemlock to abandoning his beloved Athens for voluntary exile. The case of Seneca is more complex. Exile he had known and some of his writings at the time are perhaps not the finest testimonial to his strength of character. Nonetheless, he ranks as one of the foremost contributors to the genre of consolation literature. The majority of his philosophical writings, particularly the late ones, are deserving of respect. He tried, and signally failed, to educate the young Nero in clemency and philosophy. For some years he was one of the two most powerful men in Rome, apart from the emperor, and certainly the wealthiest. Yet the gift of his riches to Nero and his own philosophical retirement were not sufficient to avert the doom he saw approaching. The all too familiar invitation to suicide arrived from the palace and Seneca too went to his death at the hands of an erratic and uncivilised emperor. For Nero we can do worse than read Theoderic. Turning back to Cicero, of the three perhaps most akin to Boethius, a similar pattern emerges. Like Seneca, Cicero rose high in the land. More like Boethius he viewed his consulship as his supreme achievement and was the foremost orator of his day. He too had faced exile—and liked it little—political isolation and eventually, under the Triumvirate, death for political reasons. The climax of his personal misfortunes, something that Boethius did not have to face, as Philosophy trenchantly points out, was the death of his daughter Tullia. In this loss, combined with an enforced retirement from public life, must be sought the explanation of the extraordinary outpouring of philosophical writings between February 45 and November 44 B.C., many of them closely related to his own adversities. Several are particularly important here: the *de Consolatione* and *Hortensius* (both lost, the latter a close imitation of Aristotle's *Protrepticus*) and the *Tusculan Disputations* and *De Finibus,* both of which are in five books, a point of some importance to the ***Consolatio***.

Of the three figures so far mentioned, although Cicero's career is most closely parallel to its author's, Socrates, through the mediation of Plato and the Platonic school, emerges as the worthiest example in the ***Consolatio***. For although it is impossible to limit absolutely the importance of Cicero, Seneca or Platonism to any specific area in the work, it is fair to say that Cicero and Seneca receive by far their greatest weight in the consolatory and protreptic sections of the first two and a half books, and Plato thereafter. A parallel might be drawn here with the stairs which Boethius chooses to depict on Philosophy's robe, linking the π and the θ, *praktikeμ* and *theoμreμtikeμ*. This motif of ascent, which recurs frequently, is reflected in the general movement of the work as the vicissitudes of politics and the material world are left behind and the argument turns more positively to a pursuit of knowledge and enlightenment. The same applies to the three figures under discussion. Neither Cicero nor Seneca can be said to have confined their careers to philosophy, however considerable their contribution, or indeed ever to have achieved total indifference to the concerns of the world. In fact their very mixed interests are something of a mirror of Boethius before his downfall. Boethius, pondering his imprisonment in the light of the endeavours of his literary forebears in the face of adversity, came in the end to reject all but philosophical concerns. His ***Consolatio*** is the account of that journey. Small wonder that it is to Socrates, philosopher and nothing else, that the ascending scale proceeds.

III

There remain, of our original list of five, Ovid and Augustine: an unlikely pairing, yet paired they are at the start of the ***Consolatio,*** or rather set one against the other. Both require more detailed attention than the three pagan philosophical writers. To begin, like Boethius, with Ovid: two biographical points must be underlined. Ovid was the last and the youngest of the Augustan elegiac poets, and elegy in ancient tradition implied chiefly two things, the poetry of lament and that of love. Ovid's *Amores, Ars Amatoria* and *Heroides* fall into the second category, his *Tristia* and *Ex Ponto* into the first. Secondly Ovid ended his days in exile at Tomi on the Black Sea coast. He had been banished, as he repeatedly tells us in the two collections of elegiacs written there, for his salacious erotic verse, most notably the *Ars Amatoria,* and for some nameless 'error' or 'crimen' which was probably the more serious offence and may well have been political. Of all Latin writers composing and complaining in exile, Ovid was undoubtedly the most vociferous. Whether or not everything in the *Tristia* and *Ex Ponto* should in fact be taken at its lugubrious face value, Boethius saw little irony there, since it is in the guise of a despairing Ovid that he presents himself to us in the elegiac couplets of his opening metrum. Although both *Tristia* and *Ex Ponto* contribute to that poem, *Tristia* is the title we are intended to recall. Together with the Ciceronian *Tusculans* and *De Finibus,* the fact that there were also five books of *Tristia* undoubtedly influenced Boethius' decision to write five books ***De Consolatione Philosophiae***.

Boethius' singular treatment of Ovid in the first section acts as something of a guarantee for the view I have been expressing above of a hierarchy of reactions to adversity. If Socrates stands at the top, Ovid can scarcely be said to qualify at all. To all intents he has had his say by the end of the first metrum, before Philosophy has put in an appearance or her robe been mentioned. Clearly he is not fit to associate with her and there is no question of his ever ascending any philosophical stairs. The two are anathema to each other.

Nonetheless the introduction and almost instant dismissal of the muses of elegy, that is, of an Ovidian approach to the problem of distress, is of enormous consequence. The philosophical content of the opening poem is not impressive, but it could be urged that there is no single more significant piece in the whole work. Before introducing Augustine then, it will be well to give it close consideration.

Carmina qui quondam studio florente peregi,
I who made poems once with youthful zeal,

Flebilis, heu, maestos cogor inire modos.
Weeping, am forced to turn to grievous song.

Ecce mihi lacerae dictant scribenda Camenae
See now, the Muses, torn, dictate my words

Et ueris elegi fletibus ora rigant.
And with true tears Lament makes moist my lips.

Has saltem nullus potuit peruincere terror
These few at least no terror could dissuade

Ne nostrum comites prosequerentur iter.
To tread my road and give me company.

Gloria felicis olim uiridisque iuuentae,
They, once the pride of bright and happy youth,

Solantur maesti nunc mea fata senis.
Solace this old man's grief against his destiny.

Venit enim properata malis inopina senectus
Age entered, sped by sorrows, unforeseen;

Et dolor aetatem iussit inesse suam.
Grief gave command her years should stand in me.

Intempestiui funduntur uertice cani
White hairs upon my crown are out of season spread

Et tremit effeto corpore laxa cutis.
And over the worn-out body slack skin shakes.

Mors hominum felix quae se nec dulcibus annis
Happy of men a Death intruding not himself

Inserit et maestis saepe uocata uenit.
On joyous years yet swift to answer grief.

Eheu, quam surda miseros auertitur aure
Alas, with how deaf an ear he turns from wretched men,

Et flentes oculos claudere saeua negat!
How fierce declines to seal the eyes that weep!

Dum leuibus male fida bonis fortuna faueret
Whilst fickle Fortune smiled with trifling goods,

Paene caput trists merserat hora meum;
The hour of sorrow had near drowned my life.

Nunc quia fallacem mutauit nubila uultum
Now that, all cloud, she's changed her treacherous face,

Protrahit ingratas impia uita moras.
A thankless life draws out unwished delays.

Quid me felicem totiens iactastis, amici?
Friends, why did you boast my happiness so oft?

Qui cecidit, stabili non erat ille gradu.
The fallen man had never stood secure.

That there are many points of contact between Boethius' soliloquy and Ovid's exile poetry, particularly the programmatic poems which open individual books, will be clear to readers of the *Tristia* and *Ex Ponto*. The links are concentrated in the opening lines, with the poet's unwilling change of subject matter to the elegy of lament, with the chameleon-like sympathy and constancy of the Muses and their elegiac grief-stricken appearance. Premature old age and a death-wish are features common to both, although the discussion of Death's insensibility and uncertain temper belongs as much to the philosophical diatribe or indeed to the genre of 'consolatio' proper as to the Ovidian elegy. Ovid's pride in his earlier poetry, although it clearly exists, is somewhat tempered by the fact that some of it shared the responsibility for his misfortunes. The treachery of fortune is also found in Ovid, but at this point Boethius is laying the foundations for the elaborate portrait of that uncertain deity which will be painted by Philosophy at the start of book II in a passage designed to answer the opening of the first book. Further it should be noted that it was Ovid who transferred the use of 'comites' or 'amici', the standard source of advice to lovers in elegiac love poetry, to a key role in the *Tristia* and *Ex Ponto* in a consideration of the power of adversity to distinguish the true friends from the false. Underlying the final couplet of this metrum is the notion that, by their lack of judgement, Boethius' friends have also failed in their office. There is indeed more to the piece than a string of Ovidian tags applied to Boethius' own experience. The opening lines appear programmatic and should therefore anticipate the nature of the coming work. Yet anyone who takes the first poem as symptomatic of the ***Consolatio*** as a whole will be in for a rude awakening. Perhaps surprisingly, given his circumstances, but none the less certainly, Boethius is indulging in a display of cultivated literary wit that will extend some way into the work, and which is little short of playful. He has chosen to fuse several traditional topoi, or characteristic elements, of programmatic poetry, namely (i) the claim to ascend the literary scale from an inferior to a superior genre and (ii) the reverse, generally called 'recusatio', that is a refusal to write, either at all or in some expected genre, usually epic. Both types of 'recusatio' function as an apology, often specious, for the work in hand, and either personal grief or the advent of an inspirational deity is used to account for the poet's inadequacy in other fields.

Looking at the first metrum then, we are startled to find poetry at all beneath the dignified title ***De Consolatione Philosophiae,*** but the first line gives ground for hope. The hexameter, if one does not happen to be thinking of Ovid's *Tristia,* is a brazen conflation of two famous Virgilian passages which sum up their author's poetic achievements and look to the future. Virgil had ended the *Georgics* by stating that whilst Caesar was at war thundering as far as the Euphrates, he himself, a poet whom Naples nourished 'STUDIEIS FLORENTEM ignobilis oti', had written the *Georgics* and before them the *Eclogues* or *Bucolics:* 'CARMINA QUI lusi pastorum'. The four spurious lines prefixed to the *Aeneid* carry the story further. 'Ille ego', announces 'Virgil' 'QUI QUONDAM gracili modulatus auena/CARMEN': I wrote bucolic, then didactic, and now I proceed to epic. Given the Virgilian analogy we might reasonably infer two things from Boethius' first line, a backward reference to the 'carmen bucolicum' mentioned by Cassiodorus and an intention to follow his famous predecessor in progressing to higher things. The first inference is correct; about the second we are instantly disillusioned. The hexameter is answered by a pentameter. Elegy's status is low, far beneath that of 'carmina', whatever their nature. Boethius is sounding a retreat, writing a 'recusatio', rather than advancing. Worse still, the phrasing of the second line—whereby 'flebilis' (of Boethius) and 'modos' (of his verses) frame a line with 'maestos' at its centre—evokes not only elegiac lament but also the disreputable love elegy. Horace after all had played on the dual function of the metre by composing a mock funeral 'consolatio' to an erotic elegist in which he cruelly but accurately dismissed his victim's outpourings as 'weepy love poetry' in the phrase 'flebilibus . . . modis', and it is perfectly true that cheerful love elegies possess some scarcity value. Boethius' elegant allusion to the Horatian phrase with its pejorative undertones implies that he is well aware that even for a poet his current behaviour is pretty disgraceful. The role of the Muses in this moral collapse requires more attention than the mere listing of the plethora of Ovidian parallels. They dictate ('dictant') what Boethius writes and are therefore largely responsible for the abandoning of 'carmina', that is they function as the inspiring deities of the traditional 'recusatio', here with little independence of mind. Instead of water from Parnassus or even the rococo springs of an elegiac Venus, the best they can offer Boethius to wet his poetic whistle are what we take to be his own salt tears. The adjective 'true' applied to those tears may underline the seriousness of the grief but is probably also conciliatory, an attempt to draw some distinction between the present brand of elegy and the erotic variety. Apart from rather maudlin sympathy, Ovid's Muses can offer no real consolation for the unwelcome attendance of 'senectus' and 'dolor', merely an incitement to self pity, with the result that by the end of the poem Boethius is convinced that misery has been his since the day he was born.

But the programmatic section is not yet finished; rather it is about to be turned on its head. Whilst Boethius sits musing on this lament and committing it to paper, enter another lady, a rival claimant for his regard and, indeed, for his affections, whom at first he does not recognise. Philosophy's portrait is justly famous, but for the moment what concerns us is the contrast between her and the snivelling Muses of the first poem. Her gaze is clear and penetrating, her bearing queenly and her stature at times superhuman. She has woven her garment, learned associations and all, with her own hands. Any damage it may have suffered is not her fault but others'; it is dusky with neglect and there are holes where 'certain violent men's hands' ('uiolentorum quorundam manus') have torn pieces away. By contrast, we may well imagine from the adjective 'lacerae' applied to them that the Muses, in dressing the part of funeral mourners, have themselves torn their own garments as well as scratched their faces. Certainly they carry no symbols of learning or its sovereignty. This stately lady's reaction to the sight of the Muses dictating lugubrious elegy to her favourite pupil is a violent one. She is in no doubt as to the harm they can effect, increasing sickness, accustoming the mind to its illness rather than healing it. Now these 'stagey whores', these literary and lethal Sirens 'usque in exitium dulces' have dared to seduce one brought up in her own mysteries, not just a common 'profanus'. Out they must go, and out they do go, sadder than ever and covered in blushes, leaving Philosophy to get down to diagnosis and cure with the help of her own personal muses. We have arrived at the real 'recusatio' at last. Instead of an Apollo or a Cupid with accompanying muses finding some poet writing epic and insisting he pen elegies instead, Philosophy has caught her favourite protégé degraded to the composition of elegy, the lowest possible rung on the poetic ladder, and soon puts a stop to it by resubstituting her own interests.

It is worth noting that although this motif of 'recusatio' extends well into the prose sections of Book I, fundamentally it is more at home in poetry than in prose writing. Boethius, in a bold adaptation, has turned the question rather differently. He does not use it merely to ask 'What sort of poetry is appropriate?' but 'What sort of contemplation is worthwhile?' Ultimately neither form of composition is to be ruled out. For the present the expulsion of the Muses underlines the dichotomy between poetry and prose generally and poetry and philosophy in particular.

Philosophy's antipathy towards the Muses centres on the epithet 'scenicas meretriculas'. Were we to seek a poetic parallel for the expulsion of harlots, we would find only one poem, admittedly itself an elegy, but one remote from any literary concern. In one of Propertius' most famous elegies, his mistress Cynthia arrives home unexpectedly, purportedly from some religious festival, to discover her lover sharing his couch with a couple of very inferior prostitutes. Eyes ablaze (a point mentioned no fewer than three times), she kicks them out of the house. It is very likely that Propertius' witty and purportedly autobiographical piece made its contribution to Boethius' dramatisation of his own scene. However the idea that poetry plays the painted whore to Philosophy's virtuous woman is of great importance to the work as a whole. It finds its root in prose philosophical writing; the ultimate source for this scene is generally agreed to be Plato's banishing of the poets from the ideal state of his Republic. His decision was cited with approval by Cicero in his *Republic,* now lost, and in the *Tusculans,* where the peril involved in poetry that was 'dulcis' was stressed. Augustine does the same in the *De Civitate Dei* in a passage that forcibly underlines the connection of poetry with the stage. Boethius knew it from Plato as well as from both these Latin writers, since he prefaces his own ***De Musica*** with references to the very similar discussion of music that immediately succeeds it in the Republic. The stress in the ***De Musica*** on the inherent tendency of certain types of music to produce demoralising 'affectus' is closely parallel to Philosophy's analysis of the harm done by the Muses and fits well with her enduring hostility to any preponderance of the emotions over the reasoning faculties. To Boethius then, poetry and indeed the whole art of music was a dangerous affair, requiring rigorous discipline to make it safe.

On the other hand, if prose writers were more or less united in their disapproval of poetry, not all poets viewed philosophy as outside their purview. Even Propertius, insistently denying that he would ever abandon elegy for martial epic, could at a pinch consider an old age spent writing didactic poetry about natural philosophy. Horace also in later years abandoned the 'ludicra' of lyric verse for the moral philosophy of the *Epistles,* yet ironically still used the hexameter and so remained a poet. This Horatian riddle 'When is a poem not a poem?' applies the more forcibly to the Boethian Philosophy with her own private troupe of muses and a pair of servants, one called Music and the other Rhetoric. How can this paradox be upheld in the face of her extreme antagonism towards other poetic muses? Initially the question is generic. Some of the highest grades of poetry are closely related to philosophical concerns. The relationship has a strong historical basis in that in its infancy much natural philosophy used didactic poetry as its vehicle. Rhetorical theory viewed didactic dealing with τὰθεῖᾳ as the most sublime theme to which the poet might aspire and superior even to epic, which largely concerned itself with human affairs. Thus Philosophy's lament in the second metrum over the former achievements of Boethius in the field of natural philosophy describes a double collapse, in its most obvious application philosophical, but also poetical in a descent from potential didactic themes, possibly even the high peaks of astronomy, to the degradation of elegy. The literary notions of ascent and descent run roughly parallel to the Neoplatonic view of the soul's movement upwards towards enlightenment or downwards away from it which is to be expounded in Book III. Here at the start Philosophy can criticize Boethius' poetry quite as much as his state of mind.

IV

If poetry of a didactic nature, a fair description of most of the remaining metra in the ***Consolatio,*** might just gain admittance to a philosophical work, it remains none the less exceptional. We are still no wiser as to what exactly prompted Boethius to choose the satura form in the first place and then instantly to question its propriety. Why does he throw down the gauntlet quite so violently? The simple answer is Augustine; and it is to the profound influence of the bishop of Hippo on the ***Consolatio*** that we must now turn. He figured in the list of five whose lives bore some relation to that of Boethius, but this time the links are confined to the development of intellectual attitudes and their literary presentation rather than to specific events.

Augustine's views on poetry are important for the issues raised by the ***Consolatio***. We have seen that he shared Plato's doubts on the subject. Nowhere is this made so apparent as in the *Dialogues* composed in the country villa at Cassiciacum shortly after his conversion. If we leave aside the serious matter of Augustine's debates with his friends during that period of retreat, the dramatic background to the *De Ordine* is coloured by an intense argument on the subject of poetry. A young and talented friend Licentius is at the time engrossed in the composition of a poem about Pyramus and Thisbe. Augustine is eager to wean him from his Muses to the more profitable pursuit of philosophy. So passionately determined is he in this matter that we are presented with an unflattering self-portrait of a doctrinaire and sometimes almost brutally domineering Augustine that is lightened only by a slight element of teasing. Poetry, it would seem, is the Devil and all his works.

Yet Augustine himself was not immune to the charms of poetry, far from it. Even at that time he regarded half a book of Virgil as the appropriate lunchtime aperitif, and we know from the *Confessions* how deep an impression the tragedy of Dido and Aeneas had made on him as a youth. But unlike Plato, who also liked poetry and regretted the necessity of excluding it from his Republic, Augustine opposes Licentius' endeavours with something close to violence. In one sense then, Augustine's views contribute to the account of Philosophy's antagonism towards the Muses; in another we must think of Boethius (the author here, rather than the participating character) as taking up the cudgels on Licentius' behalf. Not only does he affirm that there is a place for the sweetness of poetry in a serious work, but also that philosophy and poetry can coexist to each other's mutual benefit. This is a step which Augustine cannot take. Licentius must leave poetry for a pure love whereby with the aid of philosophy the rational soul may be led to the 'uita beatissima'. Whereas for Augustine such a step involved the abandonment of poetic enterprise altogether, Boethius spends a good part of the ***Consolatio*** giving a practical demonstration that only its refinement is required. His teacher Philosophy may call her verses 'musici carminis oblectamenta', yet elsewhere she makes it abundantly clear that their function can be quite as serious as that of the more straightforward discussion and that anyway the rhetoric of the prose passages has an equal share in the work's decoration.

Yet it is the language of Augustine's hostility to poetry that concerns us most. Poetry, he says, builds a wall between Licentius and philosophy quite as solid as that which separated the two lovers Pyramus and Thisbe. This barrier proves to be a moral one, described in terms of spiritual adultery, and it brings us to the ladies in the case. It is a truism that the feminine gender of many classical abstract nouns fostered a natural inclination towards personification in literature. Philosophy herself has a lengthy pedigree in this respect. Already we have seen that Boethius, in setting her against the Muses, made effective use of this tendency. But the female opposition in his work is not confined to the Muses. The portrait of Fortuna at the beginning of Book II is painted in still more villainous colours: Boethius is languishing with desire for his former mistress, but the lady has transfered her affections. In Philosophy's opinion Fortune's various allurements come out of a jar; she is a hussy who leads men on and then leaves them in the lurch just when they think she is theirs. Boethius had known this perfectly well once and used to chase her from Philosophy's sanctuary. Inconstant in her nature, she but plays with men, and it is Boethius' own fault for choosing such a mistress ('domina') and bowing beneath such a yoke. Fortune views him as a mere slave who has no reason to complain at how she treats him. The metaphors throughout are those of love elegy, the image that of a real woman. There is much in common here with Augustine. In the *De Ordine* not only the subject matter of Licentius' poem, but the very fact of writing it belongs in the realm of 'foeda libido' as opposed to a 'purus et sincerus amor'. It is the pursuit 'modesta sane atque succincta' of liberal disciplines that produces lovers ('amatores') fit to embrace truth. God, that best and most beautiful husband ('coniunx ille optimus et pulcherrimus') seeks out souls worthy of the 'beata uita'. For the time being, says Augustine, let Licentius sow his wild oats among the Muses: when he has tired of them he may come to a better love. And indeed Licentius himself has already admitted that he thinks Philosophy more beautiful 'quam Thisbe, quam Pyramus, quam illa Venus et Cupido talesque omnimodi amores'.

Boethius, then, has much in common with Augustine in his treatment of Philosophy's rivals and errant philosophers. Unlike Augustine, and to a lesser degree the two other Latin panegyricists of Philosophy, Cicero and Seneca, he is remarkably restrained about casting Philosophy herself in the answering role of the truly desirable woman. Physician, wet-nurse, teacher, protectress, any other in the long list of common metaphors, yet this perhaps most frequent characterisation as the woman desired above all others, the unearthly love instead of the worldly, is played down to a surprising extent. It is still more surprising if two more passages of Augustine are adduced, the panegyric of Philosophy from the *Contra Academicos,* another of the *Dialogues* written during the days at Cassiciacum, and secondly the praise of Continentia from the *Confessions.*

In the first piece, Philosophy's face, as she appears to Augustine in a vision, is such as will turn a man from all earthly delights and make him flee to her beauty as a lover who is 'blandus et sanctus, mirans anhelans aestuans'. A fable follows speaking of Philocalia and Philosophia, love of beauty and love of wisdom, as sisters; and Licentius is there also represented as the lover of false beauty. Could he but see the true loveliness of Philosophy's face, 'quanta uoluptate philosophiae gremio se inuolueret'! All the complex symbolism of Boethius' description is absent; there is nothing but the two ideas of love and beauty. Nevertheless, in view of the mention of Licentius who figures so dramatically in the *De Ordine's* argument over poetry and philosophy in this passage of the *Contra Academicos,* there can be no doubt that Boethius' version was intended to challenge that of Augustine, nor indeed that he knew the *Dialogues* well. Of all Augustine's writings they would be the ones most calculated to appeal to Boethius' mind when he was writing the ***Consolatio***. They are presented as springing from study of Cicero's *Hortensius*, a work which exercised a great influence on the early part of the ***Consolatio***. (Indeed it is chiefly to these two later books that we must turn in any attempt to recover some of the lost Ciceronian dialogue.) They are also Augustine's most Neoplatonic writings, to a degree indeed for which he felt it necessary to apologise when reviewing what he had written in the course of a long life. He is particularly critical of the way in which he had treated Fortuna and the Muses almost as goddesses. Boethius had no such qualms, either about the validity of Neoplatonic ideas or the presentation of Philosophy as a goddess. His views are such as the newly converted Augustine might have approved. Where the latter parts company from him is in the passionate expression of personal feeling towards a personified Philosophy or for that matter towards the deity.

The same distinction between the two authors can be seen in the second Augustinian passage, that from the *Confessions.* The description of the vision of Continentia is a crucial element of that scene in the garden which was of such moment in the course of Augustine's conversion. By a characteristic paradox Continence is represented as the fruitful mother of many children, her joys, by her husband Christ. Sick and in torment, it is to Continence that Augustine finally turns in his protracted struggle against the temptations of the flesh. These he describes as trifles and vanities 'nugae nugarum et uanitates uanitatum', old girl friends of his ('amicae') who pluck at the garment of his flesh and whisper to him, asking—Will he send them away? Shall they never be with him again after their dismissal? Despite all his efforts, it is not until the vision of the chastely wedded Continence that he can shake them off entirely. Even during her admonitions Augustine says that he blushed because he still heard the murmuring of these 'nugae'. There follow the storm of penitent tears in the garden, the unexplained children's voices bidding him 'tolle, lege'—Take up and read—and the passage from Romans 13 which ends Augustine's doubts. He says that it was as if a light of certainty poured into his heart and all the dark shadows of doubting took flight: 'quasi luce securitatis infusa corde meo, omnes dubitationis tenebrae diffugerunt'. The whole account is strikingly like the arrival of Philosophy in Boethius. The clinging girl friends are adapted to become the Muses of elegy; Philosophy takes the place of Continence and her criticisms are directed more at the Muses than Boethius; likewise it is they who blush rather than the sinner. There is mention of tears again, but perhaps most striking of all is the final image of light out of the darkness. For when Philosophy wipes the blinded and deluded eyes of her pupil we meet the same image expanded over an entire metrum and into the start of the next prose as vision floods back again. It is hard to escape the conclusion that Boethius took the Augustinian conversion scene and fused it with those parts of the *Dialogues* discussed above as one of the major models for his own opening. If this is correct we are dealing with considerable literary pretensions on our author's part. There is one further scrap of evidence that would support the idea. Augustine calls the temptations that were his former 'amicae' trifles or playthings ('nugae'). In literature the word has a very specific significance. Catullus uses it to describe his poems in his dedicatory epigram to Cornelius Nepos. Horace calls his own poetry 'nugae', and on abandoning lyric for philosophical epistles, playthings ('ludicra'). Thus it fits well with the image of literary prostitutes and may have had some influence on the fusion of ideas in Boethius' adaptation. Augustine offered two paradoxes, an overwhelming passion that is both holy and lawful and a personification of Continence that is not barren; so Boethius makes his own plea in the ***Consolatio*** for a poetry that both serves and enriches philosophy.

V

Augustine and Boethius stand side by side in any treatment of early autobiography as the only Latin examples more concerned with matters spiritual than temporal. By and large Augustine figures as the author of a masterpiece, Boethius of an interesting curiosity. Certainly it is true that the intimacy and explicitness with which Augustine bares his soul has provided a more attractive model and more palatable reading matter to recent centuries than Boethius' intellectual dialogue. Nevertheless if the famous garden scene is indeed partly responsible for the later work, further consideration of the general relationship between the two seems desirable. I would like to suggest in what follows that Boethius was well aware that his ***Consolatio*** must inevitably challenge the *Confessions,* that he intended it to do so and that the similarities and contrasts between the two works give a clear insight into the very different mentalities of their respective authors, particularly with regard to their view of the appropriate relationship between man and God. On a small scale this had already been seen in the distinction between the two portrayals of Philosophy. Something of the sort applies throughout the two books.

It is simplest to begin with the use made of factual events. Like most autobiographies, they both contain a great many. Less usually, these facts are not central, but rather subordinate to the main purpose.

Augustine, writing in retrospect, charts events from his childhood till shortly after his conversion at intervals throughout the first ten books of the *Confessions* only in so far as they shed light on the development of his mind and beliefs. Events and people are on a par with the books that influenced him. If, as was often the case, they affected him deeply, they find their place. Otherwise they are left to one side. Boethius works differently. We are given the chief events of his life according to the lights of any Roman gentleman of affairs pursuing the cursus with such outstanding success as was possible under the Ostrogothic domination of the early sixth century. Political honours and activities emerge; something of his family, of his fine library and scholarly researches. Although Philosophy succeeds in eliciting further details about the behaviour of his friends as well as his enemies during the recent crisis, that is hardly the main purpose of the exchange. Instead it forms the basis of a discussion of 'amicitia' within the framework of 'consolatio'. Further, it underlines the purpose of all the factual information crammed into the early chapter where Boethius speaks at such length and with such bitterness: a practical demonstration of his deluded state; otherwise such details could hold no absorbing interest for him, nor we are to suppose, for his audience. Historians may be grateful that he chose to record the symptoms of the disease as well as its cure.

Briefly then, Augustine uses his own life to give some sort of historical framework to his steps backward as well as forward on the road towards the apprehension of the divine. Boethius prefers a division, lumping the terrestrial together at the start under the heading 'failure', before recording an intellectual ascent towards higher things. Consequently, we know almost nothing of the manner in which the earlier philosophical beliefs so painfully reacquired in the arguments of the ***Consolatio*** interacted with his career before his downfall. Rather the work has a linear development from the physical to the metaphysical, with the result that the explicit statement in Book V that Boethius was once so crassly practical as to undertake extensive researches into the question of providence comes as something of a shock to the reader.

Neoplatonism is a fundamental point of contact between the two works. Yet the manner of its introduction is very different. All the great metaphors are held in common and nowhere in Latin literature will the scholar find so striking a collection of the Boethian imagery of the earth-bound soul imprisoned, exiled, unenlightened, sunk in oblivion, together with its antithetical counterparts (ascent, freedom and the rest) as in the *Confessions* of Augustine. In Book VII, dealing with his own introduction to Plotinus, Augustine is at pains to list what he did not find in Neoplatonism, most notably trinitarian theology and a personal deity, yet he is far from underestimating the extent of his debt. It is in the great spiritual events and insights of Augustine's life that the Neoplatonic character of the writing is most heavily concentrated. We have already noted the metaphor of light and dark that closes the conversion scene. Two further examples must suffice. The first is the account of his extraordinary conversation with his mother, Monica, before her death. As they talk, both are taken over by an unparalleled spiritual exaltation and clarity, at the height of which their hearts seem briefly to touch the eternal Wisdom. The passage would read like Plotinus at his most sublime speaking of the ascent of the soul to unity, were it not for two things: the personal nature of Augustine's god and the fact that the experience is one shared between two human beings and springing directly from their reciprocal perception. A similar personal and individual approach to God also distinguishes my second example from pure Neoplatonism. In the first four chapters of the thirteenth book Augustine speaks of the nature of Creation and of the relation of Creator to creature: the dependent creature is forgetful of but not forgotten by his Maker. Memory is here linked with a turning, a 'conuersio' towards the Creator. There is a return to unity and perfection, a resolution of the dissimilitude between creature and Creator.

All these ideas are to be found also in the ***Consolatio,*** albeit in a far less personal vein, but I shall concentrate on that of memory, since it heads the discussion of Creation with which the final book of the *Confessions* opens. Creation occupies a position of comparable significance in the ***Consolatio***. The work's turning point, the shift from negative to positive argument, is the great central metrum III. ix, a poem which summarises much of the creation myth of Plato's *Timaeus*. Hitherto Neoplatonic ideas had been largely confined to the metra and to the metaphorical bulletins on the state of Boethius' mental health. Almost nothing of what follows that hymn is actually foreign to Neoplatonic thought, and the rest of Book III and most of Book IV are steeped in the tenets of the philosophy. But perhaps most striking in the passages immediately following the *Timaeus* poem, particularly the metra III. xi and xii and IV. i, is the stress on the theme of memory and forgetfulness. According to the Platonic doctrine of recollection or 'anamnesis' human knowledge consists in the regaining of what the earthbound soul had once known, but lost by its imprisonment in the body. The return of memory is therefore essential to the soul's ascent. The Neoplatonists laid particular emphasis on the idea of self-knowledge, the turning-in upon itself of the soul in order to arrive at a clear perception of truth without the distractions and confusions of a material world. This, in effect is the diagnosis of Philosophy: Boethius has somewhat forgotten himself, 'sui paulisper oblitus est', together with most of the things he once knew for certain. In the three poems I have mentioned it finds three very different modes of expression. The first is an abstract and highly metaphorical piece that draws all the associated images together to give a very precise account of the doctrine. Next comes a rewriting of the Orpheus myth, where the most dramatic moment, the point at which Orpheus turns back towards Hades, forgetful of his promise and concerned only with his Eurydice, is used to portray the failure of a soul in its ascent towards the light; finally the *Phaedrus* myth of the winged souls that have not lost their perception of the light is briefly adumbrated in an exhortation to Boethius to make use of the wings of Philosophy and return whence he came. In his ascent he will cease from his present forgetfulness and be no more 'immemor'. The significance of all this is not lost on Boethius. After the first poem he remarks that Plato's theory is correct but that exceptionally he has gone twice through the same process. He first 'forgot' when he put on mortal flesh with all its imperfections ('corporea contagione'), and for the second time when, bowed beneath the weight of grief ('maeroris mole pressus'), he lost what he had so far recollected. Here is one key to Boethius' conception of the work in relation to the *Confessions*. Augustine charts the journey to conversion, a process of anamnesis across the span of half a lifetime's searching. Boethius' tale is likewise anamnesis from start to finish, but he takes up the thread much later, when all has been won and then lost and is to be done again. The Orpheus myth becomes a self-portrait of a man who has bent his eyes once more to the depths from which he had almost emerged. But for him there are Philosophy's wings and he can turn again to the light and begin the long ascent. *Reconversion* is his theme and so he turns to Augustine's masterpiece both to imitate and to challenge.

Autobiography, anamnesis and conversion; there is another factor in common, this time one of design. Both books are very one-sided dialogues. Augustine rejects all intermediaries; his interlocutor is God. Boethius keeps God at a distance; Philosophy provides the link. It would be an exaggeration to say that Augustine does all the talking in the dialogue of the *Confessions* and Philosophy in the ***Consolatio,*** yet it is close enough to the truth to serve. Again, although both writers present themselves as failures, backsliders who need rescuing by divine intervention, Augustine writes in retrospect delivering a running commentary on events; the reader of Boethius must tread the road beside him, learning from Philosophy's arguments as they are presented.

This overall contrast is deliberate, but there is a complementary similarity. The *Confessions* employ two types of narration, the straightforward recounting of events and rather unusual direct addresses to the deity. The latter, particularly frequent at the start or finish of a book, take various forms, including that of prayer or prose hymn. Although arising often out of specific events, they interrupt the historical sequence and are delivered sub specie aeternitatis. Their chief function is to demonstrate that if Augustine did not always know what he was doing at the time, God has been directing his progress at every stage. This interweaving of narrative prose and emotional invocation occurs throughout the work, but there is a correlation between the level of Augustine's current perceptions and the isolation or otherwise of these addresses. They are rarer in the early stages and appear as interruptions in the narrative. Longer passages are found at the most significant moments in the author's life. By the time he arrives at the last confident philosophical books, his spiritual progress in understanding has so far increased that almost everything has become part of an address to God, almost a joint exercise in exposition.

The metra of the ***Consolatio*** are comparable. They contribute to the argument as it proceeds, yet take a wider view, with an authority outside and above the adjacent proses. They possess their own thematic design which spans the entire work. For example, many of the ideas of the later poems of Book III have been anticipated in the early metra of Book I. A certain unity and coherence result, in that the crucial issues are permanently before our eyes regardless of the immediate details discussed. There is an element of hindsight here that is comparable to Augustine's practice.

The disposition of proses and metra and also of speaker, quite apart from Philosophy's explicit comments on Boethius' needs for stronger or gentler remedies, enhance the work's dramatic design. Length and proportion of the prose and verse passages are particularly telling in this respect. The most famous example is the long prose IV. vi, where Philosophy proposes abandoning the pleasure of verse for a time because of the complexity of the subject under discussion. Fifty-seven sections later she notices that her pupil is flagging and offers him a draught ('haustus') of poetry to strengthen and refresh his mind. One more case must suffice. There are only two occasions in the work when Boethius delivers himself of a long speech and then launches without a break into the succeeding metrum. The fourth prose of Book I is disproportionately long, three times the length of any other in the book. The explanation is obvious: Boethius is giving a blow by blow account of his misfortunes and leaves nothing out; he does not even baulk at forty-eight lines of anapaestic hymn reproaching a god who can abandon mankind to the passing whims of fortune. Lest the point be missed, the narrating Boethius starts the next prose by saying that his prolixity had cut no ice with Philosophy: 'haec ubi continuato dolore delatraui', etc. By the time we get to Book V Boethius is strong enough to listen to lengthy arguments from Philosophy and is becoming very determined in his enquiries. Nonetheless the third prose is exceptionally long and both it and the following poem are given to Boethius. Gone is the bitter self-pity of Book I. In his philosophical zeal he passes from prose to the rhetorical questions of the poem. It is clear that the cure is almost complete. Clearly no precise correlation of method can be drawn between the two authors in this respect. But both may be said to employ the varied combination of two distinct types of writing to dramatic effect. Augustine's practice may have encouraged Boethius in developing his own.

The *Confessions* should be numbered among the most important influences on the ***Consolatio***. But Boethius' challenge is not purely literary. Rather he is concerned to draw attention to an area of fundamental disagreement. Already we have seen that he held differing views on poetry and that his expressions of enthusiasm, whether about Philosophy personified or about God, are muted by comparison with those of Augustine. Augustine thinks of God in terms of a personal relationship and his *Confessions* received embarrassed criticism on that account. Boethius' religion is the complete antithesis, coldly impersonal, abstract and theoretical to a degree, even when, for example, he is extolling divine amor. This may be brushed aside as simple difference of character, yet it offers a small insight into an old problem about the ***Consolatio***. Since Boethius was a theologian in his own right, why is there no explicit advocacy of Christianity in the work? We can evade the problem by saying that it would be inappropriate to the genre, or, better, that there is precious little evidence of pagan Neoplatonism either. Boethius has carefully avoided committing himself in either direction. More positively he has deliberately sought out the common ground between the two systems, especially in the matter of images. This is judicious, but an oddity remains.

One can ask another question. Is it at all likely that Boethius' commitment to Christianity ever bore the slightest resemblance to Augustine's? The answer will be a resounding 'no'. Augustine may have had a Christian mother, but his father was pagan, and every page of the *Confessions* declares that his conversion was anything but a foregone conclusion. He came late to it by way of a passionate intellectual search and a bitter emotional struggle. Boethius was probably brought up in a Christian household, without any great struggle or challenge in the matter, nor perhaps with any overwhelming enthusiasm either. He did not need his intellect to seek out an acceptable religion in the first place; rather he devoted his life to the pursuit of intellect pure and simple at a date when such a preoccupation was rare. The result was an isolationism that did not merely border on arrogance. He is Philosophy's star pupil in the ***Consolatio***. In the prologue to the ***De Trinitate*** he tells his father-in-law Symmachus that he can discuss the Trinity with no-one else. He dismisses the rest of the world as incapable of understanding his views and so not fit to read them. Although Boethius acknowledges a profound debt to Augustine in this work, the opinion that philosophy in the service of theology is a discipline to be reserved for an intellectual elite of two would hardly have met with his predecessor's approval. The ignorant mob that requires amusement to make rational argument palatable is castigated on several further occasions.

The *Opuscula Sacra* cannot be called 'religious works' in the sense that Augustine's writings can, implying a commitment to God that receives everything that the resources of reason can supply. Rather they are written by an enthusiast for the intellect to whom the personal aspect of religion would constitute a barrier to the raising of human reason to its ultimate heights. Thus, in the context of Boethius' other writings, the theological works are far from central. It is not that Christianity was meaningless to the author, simply that it did not mean the same to a Boethius as to an Augustine. Theology constituted a special challenge: it was particularly important to get it right. Yet the challenge remained abstract, another field for the exercise of a powerful intellect.

In the ***De Trinitate*** then, Boethius is excited by the philosophical problem involved. Despite a courteous appeal to God and a disclaimer on the possible limits of human reason in the last paragraph, the envoi to Symmachus which precedes it is much more telling: 'Enough has been said about the problem put forward for discussion. All that is needed now is the yardstick of your judgement as to the acuteness of my enquiry. The authority of your verdict will settle whether or not it runs a straight course to its conclusion.' The preservation and refining of reason, whatever its sphere, was Boethius' aim in life. That part of religion which might be apprehended by the pure intellect without recourse to the vagaries of speculation ('nulla imaginatione . . . simplici intellectu') did matter. It is a view of the sublime that is patterned on abstraction rather than on human relationships. By a paradox, the loss of the ability to perceive the true order and proportion of Creation, rather than the loss of faith in God, could and did touch him deeply. That is the root of his argument with Augustine; the ***Consolatio*** forms a moving record of the renewal of that perception.

Helen Kirkby (essay date 1981)

SOURCE: "The Scholar and His Public," in *Boethius: His Life, Thought and Influence,* edited by Margaret Gibson, Basil Blackwell, 1981, pp. 44-69.

[*In the following essay, Kirkby details the social and intellectual milieu of Boethius, describing him as "a man writing and acting consciously in the Roman tradition of*

Boethius protecting Paulinus, from a verse revision of the Consolation of Philosophy *(ca. 1380).*

his aristocratic ancestors, finding the origins of his intellectual pursuits in their traditions, moved to take up public office by their example, and losing his life in defence of what he saw as the most sacred Roman institution."]

I

Sometime in the mid-530s, Cassiodorus Senator embarked on a project to found a Christian school in Rome in co-operation with the pope, Agapitus. 'I strove with the most holy Agapitus, pope of the city of Rome, to collect subscriptions and to have Christian rather than secular schools to receive teachers in the city of Rome, that thereby the soul might attain eternal salvation, and the tongue of the faithful be adorned with a pure and completely faultless eloquence', he wrote later. His attempt proved to be a failure as a result of the turmoil which had been brought about by the war through which the Emperor Justinian hoped to reconquer Italy from the Ostrogoths. Cassiodorus lamented that his 'ambition was impossible to fulfil due to the raging wars and tumultuous fighting in the Italian kingdom'.

By the time Cassiodorus came to write of this episode in his earlier life, he had moved from Rome to his native Calabria where he had founded a double monastery at Vivarium (near the modern Squillace). There he wrote one of the works for which he is most famous, his *Institutiones,* a bibliographical guide for his monks to the library he had assembled there. 'I was driven to this resort out of divine love' he wrote, 'as there is no refuge for the affairs of peace in disturbed times, and thus with the Lord's aid, I myself in the role of teacher am providing for you these introductory books'. Maintaining intellectual contacts and getting information about scholarly works seemed in turn a hazardous and random affair in his isolation at Vivarium. 'It is said', he wrote to his monks, 'that St Ambrose too has composed a commentary on the Prophets in his usual elegant style. Up to the present, however, I have not in any way been able to find it; I leave the zealous search to you.' Happy discovery seems to play a large part in the acquisition even of apparently important works: 'I have discovered a certain anonymous annotated codex, conferred on us by divine foresight, which has discussed the thirteen Epistles of St Paul in a commentary that is not without excellence.' Still more fortunate was his chancing upon a work of Jerome: 'I have discovered a third codex of the Epistles of St Paul, which is said by some to contain the blessed Jerome's concise annotations.' He faces, too, the uncertainties of getting manuscripts from abroad, given the dangers, both natural and human, of their carriage from the remoter parts of the educated world. Talking of the acquisition of a North African commentary on the works of St Augustine, Cassiodorus writes in the *Institutiones,* with more than a hint of uncertainty, 'This codex, among others, ought, by God's grace, to be sent to you from Africa.'

However, such scholarly activity is incidental and not central to Cassiodorus' purpose at Vivarium. The focus of all the efforts of the community is the salvation of the individual soul: 'Let us with every effort, with every desire, with every exertion, seek to deserve through the Lord's bounty to attain to a gift of such quality and importance; for it is advantageous to us, beneficial, glorious, everlasting, a gift of such sort that death, change and forgetfulness cannot take away, but in that sweet fatherland, it will make us rejoice with the Lord in eternal exultation.' Whether this illumination is achieved through rigorous intellectual activity or through the practical labours of those simple monks who 'cultivate gardens and rejoice in the fertility of fruit trees', this attainment is the crown of the monastic life at which all his monks must aim. Here is the most important link which connects Cassiodorus to the western monastic tradition as represented by Cassian and his own contemporary St Benedict.

In the light of this preoccupation of his later life, it is worth remark that Cassiodorus' move to Vivarium marked the end of a highly successful public career in the service of the Ostrogothic kings. Following in the steps of his father, Cassiodorus achieved eminence in the most demanding of public offices, notably as quaestor and as magister officiorum, the most elevated civilian office. In this role he was largely instrumental in creating the image and arguably the policy of the Ostrogothic regime. The monument to this labour is his *Viriae,* a collection he made of the official letters written by him in the name of his royal masters, intended to be models of administrative practice for future generations. Though stylistically difficult to approach and often unjustifiably pedantic, this collection creates a strong impression of Cassiodorus as a man devoted to the public service, honoured by the high trust that has been placed in him and deeply devoted to the regime he serves. Given this evidence, some scholars have been tempted to see his move to Vivarium as a radical hiatus in his intellectual life, a complete 'conversio' from the life of the world to the life of the spirit. It is more valuable and, I believe, more accurate to see these two phases in his life as linked by intellectual preoccupations, common not only to aspects of his own life but also to the intellectual lives of his contemporaries. The evidence of the *Institutiones* is consistent with the idea that Cassiodorus saw the period of his life at Vivarium as one in which he could enjoy the pleasures of 'otium' in the tradition of the Roman aristocracy: a time of relaxation from the pressures of public life, in which he could both indulge his intellectual interests and advance in spiritual wisdom. Vivarium was for him the refuge from the affairs of the world that Cassiciacum had been for St Augustine and Tusculanum for Cicero. Cassiodorus' exhaustion at the strain imposed on him by events in the later years of his public life made such an intellectual retreat an increasingly attractive alternative. In his introduction to the *De Anima,* written at the end of his public career, he writes 'what kind of matters might I discuss, exhausted as I am, as I hasten so fervently to the end of my labour!' Cassiodorus' attempt to found a Christian school in Rome with Pope Agapitus indicates that the ideals of Christian education had been among his preoccupations during the years of his greatest public success. The *De Anima* reveals a sophisticated intellectual grasp of both the theological and philosophical problems of the definition of the soul which can only have been developed in times of leisure during his career of public service. At Vivarium, Cassiodorus was able to devote himself fully to issues to which during his public career he had only been able to give the attention, however intelligent, of the amateur.

In the *Institutiones* Cassiodorus presents a highly personal solution to the problems of synthesis between secular and Christian learning as an instrument in the spiritual life. In the fourth century the Christian Church had felt sufficiently under threat to see the armoury of secular learning as endangering its very survival; by the sixth its position was assured. The climate of thought which could produce the dreams of the fourth century saint and doctor of the Church Jerome was one alien to the earlier sixth century: as a punishment for Jerome's undue devotion to the pagan secular writers, God appeared to him sitting on the judgement seat declaring that Jerome was not a Christian but a Ciceronian; the warning put an instant stop to his illicit reading of such masters. The intellectual aristocracy of the sixth century by contrast were not always conscious of any fundamental antithesis between Christian and secular culture, though the traditions of literary expression might dictate a different sort of treatment for the two areas of thought. For Cassiodorus, as for Boethius, there was no moral conflict in an intellectual life that embraced Cicero, Aristotle, Plato and the early Greek philosophers as well as the theological problems of the soul and the Trinity. This was reflected in their social milieux: there was an easy interchange between the lay aristocracy and the higher clergy, most of whom were drawn from their own social ranks. Likewise the aristocracy would patronise and work alongside professional scholars of the traditional secular disciplines.

To set such men as Cassiodorus and Boethius against a more clearly defined background of the intellectual life of Italy in the period presents certain problems of evidence. Though such a study might begin with educational institutions in contemporary Italy, it should attempt to evaluate too the nature both of the intellectual life of the individual and of the contacts between intellectual groups where these can be discerned. The 'units' of intellectual activity in this period were personal contacts within a restricted intellectual circle. The most elusive factor is the unseen literary audience; to restrict this audience to an increasingly elite social group in the established centres—Rome, Milan, Ravenna—and to restrict it to individuals we can name or in some way identify is unrealistic. Some idea of the nature and extent of the literary audience in this period, the men who constituted the audience for example for Boethius' philosophical works, can be gained by looking at the intellectual projects undertaken by established scholars. The demands made of the reader in such works, and the assumption by the writer that a public exists for them, may cast light on the nature of an audience for which no other evidence is available.

II

The sons of the aristocracy in early sixth-century Italy followed much the same educational path as had their Republican and Imperial ancestors. The traditions of the secular schools of grammar and rhetoric remained vigorous, and we have illuminating evidence of pupils and masters working in these institutions in the leading Italian cities. This kind of education remained the common currency of the governing classes whether they went on to careers in public life or in the higher echelons of the Church.

In the preface to the *Institutiones,* Cassiodorus makes clear that he believed that it was the very success of secular schools in Rome that retarded the development of Christian educational establishments there: 'Since I recognised that there was an intense enthusiasm for secular learning (a great part of mankind believing that through this it would gain worldly wisdom), I was, I confess, deeply grieved that the Divine Scriptures had no public teachers, since secular authors were unquestionably honoured by very distinguished exposition.' An explanation for the success of the secular schools is easy to find in the continuing importance of the senatorial aristocracy in the administration and in public life, and in the maintenance of the Roman administrative system as a whole under the Ostrogothic regime. A study of the family history of Boethius and Cassiodorus in itself illustrates the continuing importance of the traditional aristocratic families in government: the fathers of both men had served in high office under Odoacer and Theoderic, Boethius' sons were consuls after him. There are numerous instances of the maintenance of the family tradition in government, and Cassiodorus underlines this feature of the Ostrogothic administration in the *Variae*. Rhetorical skills gained through traditional forms of secular education remained at a premium, for the same expectations were made of the senatorial aristocracy as a governing class as ever had been. To speak successfully before Theoderic could be a guarantee of royal favour and advancement: both Cassiodorus and Boethius profited from such a public display of their talents for oratory. Their sophistication, linguistic skills and foreign contacts maintained their value as ambassadors and negotiators with the emperor in Constantinople, and their economic position as landowners and substantial city dwellers underwrote their role as holders of the traditional offices. In the *Variae* Cassiodorus displays considerable concern that the traditional educational system in Rome should operate smoothly; to Symmachus, the father-in-law of Boethius, he commends the sons of one Valerian, who are to be detained in Rome for the sake of their education: 'Thus they achieve the advancement of their studies and the reverence due to our authority is maintained. No one can dislike Rome, for she can be called stranger to none, she is the fruitful mother of eloquence, the comprehensive temple of all the virtues'. In somewhat less florid language, he writes to the Senate on the subject of establishing fixed salaries for teachers in the secular schools of Rome: 'we have learnt, from the mutterings of certain men, that the teachers of Roman eloquence do not have definite rewards established for their work, and that by the corrupt dealing of some the payment assigned to the masters in the schools seems to be reduced.' The correspondence of Ennodius, bishop of Pavia, bears witness too to the pre-eminence of Rome as an educational centre for the sons of the aristocracy; Rome is for him the 'city friendly to liberal studies'. Ennodius is the central figure in a complex nexus of recommendation and patronage of young aristocrats who are seeking a liberal education; his circle is a microcosm of the interrelation of clergy and laity in the intellectual life of the period. His protégés include his own relations—even his errant nephew Parthenius ultimately goes to Rome to add polish to his education: 'Thus encouraged Parthenius, our sister's son, hastens to visit Rome in which learning has its birthplace.'

Though Rome is thus accorded the highest honour, it is scarcely surprising that in his correspondence Ennodius also attests to the vigour of the secular schools in Milan in this period. Much of the credit for this is accorded to the master Deutherius, for whom Ennodius has the highest regard: 'Thou pride of Italy, the upright man's most steadfast hope! thou torch and trumpet of the lawcourts, our emperor, farewell!' Outstanding among Deutherius' pupils is a protégé of Ennodius, Arator, who later went on to a distinguished career in the service of the Ostrogothic kings, and later still into the Church; Ennodius refers at length to his education in Milan, both under Deutherius and under Bishop Laurentius. We encounter Arator later on as a churchman giving public recitations of a poem he had composed on the Acts of the Apostles. Given in front of Pope Vigilius, the recitation was given on four separate days, due to the popular acclaim it received. Here a secular education is put to the service of the Church. On this evidence, and on that of the continuing importance of civic life, the vigour of the secular schools in the provinces may be assumed well into the sixth century. This applies particularly to the established provincial centres: there is no such evidence for the newly elevated administrative centre, Ravenna, which never pre-empts Rome's primacy in this, or any other, intellectual sphere. That Theoderic's court at Ravenna was to become a centre of learning is a concept found only in the most propagandist of works: the *Variae* of Cassiodorus and the panegyrics of Ennodius. Evidence for even private intellectual activity in Ravenna seems slight.

The *Variae* of Cassiodorus are indeed an outstanding instance of an educational project emanating from the Ostrogothic regime itself, and that largely on the personal initiative of Cassiodorus. In his preface to the work, he declares that he has made the collection with those in mind 'who are schooling themselves in eloquence for the service of the state' and for whom the letters will provide examples of correct usage. Here Cassiodorus has in mind not the governing aristocracy, but those involved in the administrative substructure which the persistence of the complex Roman administration in Ostrogothic Italy implied. These men cannot have been entirely unsophisticated, being involved in a highly complex and literate mode of government; perhaps Cassiodorus believes that such literary skills will become increasingly rare in the future.

III

Evidence for the intellectual activities of the individual, be he an amateur or a professional scholar, is in this period highly diverse but as a whole presents a remarkably rich picture. It is important for such a man as Ennodius, for instance, to establish contacts with and invoke the patronage of men powerful and highly thought of in intellectual circles. These contacts were further maintained by the web of correspondence; many of his letters solicit patronage for his intellectual protégés from such figures as Pope Symmachus and the patrician Faustus. This personal basis for intellectual contacts had its inevitable consequences: on the one hand, it was possible for outsiders—such as Ennodius himself who had come to Italy from Gaul, and for a poet such as Corippus going from North Africa to the court at Byzantium—to become fully integrated into the cultural life of the area; on the other, one suspects that this kind of contact led to a narrow and constricted view of the intellectual orbit. Thus Ennodius, in a famous letter in which he discusses the outstanding cultural figures of his time, cites some for whom there is no further evidence of intellectual stature, yet omits others who proved to be the most significant, and who are known to have been well thought of by their contemporaries, notably Cassiodorus himself.

In addition to such private correspondence, subscriptions to manuscripts produced or copied in the period are an extremely valuable source for its intellectual life. Subscriptions, commenting on the author and circumstances of the production of a manuscript, may cast light on the kind of people involved in this essentially isolated and private activity, whether amateur or professional. They give evidence of a vigorous tradition of editing and commenting on manuscripts in this period, and reflect both the traditional leisure pursuits of the intellectual aristocracy and the work of the professional scholar or scribe within an institutional framework.

Of those subscriptions that give evidence of work by professional scholars, one of the most interesting is that appended to manuscripts of the fifth century African writer, Martianus Capella, which runs thus: 'I, Securus Memor Felix, *vir spectabilis,* count of the consistory, rhetor of the city of Rome, have emended this manuscript from very corrupt copies, with my scholarly pupil Deutherius cross-checking the text, in Rome by the Porta Capena, under the consulship of Paulinus *vir clarissimus,* on the 7th day of March, with the aid of Christ'. Securus Memor Felix appears too in a subscription to a manuscript of Horace as an 'orator of Rome', a more lowly title than 'rhetor urbis Romae'. The Martianus Capella subscription may indicate that he had subsequently become the holder of the chair of rhetoric in the city. Unfortunately the dating of the manuscript to 534 probably precludes the identification of the Deutherius at work on this manuscript with the Milanese teacher known to Ennodius. The most interesting, if controversial, aspect of this subscription is Marrou's identification of the scholarly centre 'by the Porta Capena' with the unsuccessful Christian school in Rome which Cassiodorus attempted to establish with the help of Pope Agapitus. This suggestion is made largely on the basis of archaeological evidence: the knowledge that a library likely to have belonged to Agapitus was situated in this part of Rome.

Subscriptions give evidence too of the work of private, aristocratic scholars. In Rome, Vettius Agorius Basilius Mavortius (consul 527) is involved in the emendation of a volume of the *Epodes* of Horace. Here he is aided by 'the master Felix, orator of the city of Rome', whom we have just encountered; the amateur and professional scholar are seen at work here in fruitful cooperation. In his subscription to a manuscript of Virgil, Turcius Rufius Apronianus Asterius gives an impressive list of his public honours: *'vir clarissimus et inlustris,* formerly prefect of the City, patrician and ordinary consul'. Mentioned too in other subscriptions, Asterius seems to come from a well-known family which had risen to prominence in the fourth century, himself becoming consul in 494.

Yet perhaps the most interesting of the subscriptions giving evidence of aristocratic involvement in scholarly projects is that appended to a manuscript of Macrobius' commentary on Cicero, *Somnium Scipionis:* 'I, Aurelius Memmius Symmachus *vir clarissimus,* emended and clarified my manuscript in Ravenna with Macrobius Plotinus Eudoxius *vir clarissimus.*' That these two men, the former the father-in-law of Boethius, were interested in a work so intimately connected with the intellectual group surrounding their fourth century pagan ancestors has often been remarked upon. That they should undertake this work in Ravenna is also of interest: it is one of the few indications of such activity in the proximity of the Ostrogothic court. The very situation of the court in Ravenna must have attracted to the city the leading public figures of the day, if only temporarily in their capacity of men involved in government or as suppliants desirous to be so. That these men pursued their intellectual interests while in attendance at the court is fortuitous; this by no means implies that Ravenna was an intellectual centre in its own right. Two further subscriptions provide evidence for the scholarly activity in Ravenna of a fellow aristocrat, Rusticius Helpidius Domnulus, *vir clarissimus* and Count of the Consistory and possibly one of the correspondents of Ennodius. They are to a volume of Pomponius Mela and to an epitome of historical exempla probably based on the fourth-century collection of Valerius Maximus.

The Church, too, sponsored works by individuals on suitable texts. St Peter ad Vincula was the scene, in 544, of Arator's public recitation of his poem on the *Acts of the Apostles;* a description of this reading under papal patronage is added at the beginning of the manuscript. Such public recitation illustrates the persistence of this classical literary tradition, and its evident popularity speaks for an interested public for such a work in Rome at this time. One of the most striking subscriptions relating to a member of the clergy in the sixth century is in a manuscript of excerpts from Augustine produced in Naples late in the century. Peter, a notary of the 'holy Catholic Church' in Naples, had been instructed to correct the text by his bishop Redux; he writes that he completed his task as well as he could, although the Lombards were at that moment besieging the city. It was under the sponsorship of the Church that such traditional forms of scholarly activity were to survive.

IV

In this attempt to establish the nature and composition of the intellectual life of Italy in the early sixth century it becomes increasingly obvious that, given the fragmentary and circumstantial nature of the evidence, only part of the true picture can be filled in. Yet there must have been a wider, unknown, literary audience to maintain the degree of activity that can be observed among the well-known groups, and those producing scholarly and literary works must have been conscious of this audience. Take Arator's public recitation in Rome of his poem on *The Acts of the Apostles*. This attracted not only those 'most learned in letters' among the bishops and higher clergy, but also a crowd which included clerics, the lay nobility and a diverse group of 'the people', whose intellectual stamina cannot have been insignificant.

This wider audience may be discerned in the very nature of the projects which were undertaken: authors made natural assumptions about the capacity and interests of their intended reader. Boethius, in his programme of philosophical translation and commentary, was expecting to find not only an interested audience, but also one with the required level of technical knowledge, or he would not have embarked on what he saw as an intellectual crusade with such enthusiasm. Cassiodorus expected two different audiences: for his *Variae* the administrators of the future who might learn from his example, for the *Institutiones* the circle—limited both intellectually and numerically—of his monks at Vivarium. Indeed in the introduction to the *Variae* Cassiodorus expresses rigid views on distinguishing literary forms, in keeping with the subject matter or audience of a work. The conscious attempt to maintain a literary style among the intellectual elite, as seen in Cassiodorus and Ennodius, does not of itself imply an awareness of its erosion. The literary styles of the Late Antique world as a whole were extremely 'self-conscious': Augustine and Gregory of Tours, for instance, both argued that there must be a modification of the 'literary' language if educated men were to communicate with the Christian masses.

The question of an elite literary culture cannot, by the sixth century, be entirely divorced from that of linguistic skill, notably in Greek. Evidence for the knowledge of Greek among the upper classes is mainly in correspondence, as in that of Cassiodorus and Ennodius, and in the limited amount of translation work being undertaken. There is positive evidence only for a small group of Greek speakers, Deutherius, Amalasuntha, the daughter of Theoderic, Boethius, Symmachus and Cassiodorus among them. Yet we must assume that there were wider linguistic skills among those trading with the East or being sent there on embassies, notably therefore in the aristocratic and higher ecclesiastical circles, and in such professions as medicine. At the beginning of the sixth century the language of the administration and the law in Constantinople was Latin. With the increasing use of Greek in administrative circles in Constantinople, Greek ceased to represent for the West a 'disinterested culture' divorced from political life and became a practical necessity for those having political and administrative contacts with the Eastern court. The early sixth century may well be seen as a transitional period in this change in the status of the language, in which the fortunes of men such as Boethius, who had a profound interest in Greek culture, may be involved. Yet the link between knowledge of the Greek language, and interest in Greek culture may be overemphasised, as the example of Boethius himself illustrates.

The very fact that Boethius embarked upon an ambitious programme of translation of sophisticated philosophical works with highly technical commentaries, suggests that there was in Italy a potential audience with an interest in the technicalities of Greek philosophy, but not the linguistic skills to read the works in the original. Had Boethius intended his works for his own limited circle alone, translations of the texts might arguably have been unnecessary. 'If life and leisure are vouchsafed me for this task, I shall essay it on the grounds of its great usefulness,' he writes. Emphasis on the usefulness of his task supports the idea of a wider audience for this kind of work and warns us against equating interest in Greek culture with a knowledge of the language itself. For Cicero and for the fourth century scholar Marius Victorinus, with whom Boethius clearly identified himself in much of his intellectual life, there had evidently been an audience interested in their work of translation and commentary and eager for texts that would increase the accessibility of Greek philosophy to western readers. It is by no means certain that this audience had disappeared by the early sixth century.

V

Extravagant claims have been made for a so-called 'Hellenist Renaissance' in Italy in the early sixth century, of which Boethius and his father-in-law Symmachus are seen as the originators. 'It was the era of the triumph of Hellenism in Italy . . . Now it was Boethius, the great Hellenist, and his father-in-law Symmachus who enjoyed the favour both of the emperor and of the king of the Ostrogoths.' 'The real artisan of this renaissance in literature and science is Boethius. He had a clear consciousness that Hellenic literature alone could help to raise the level of studies in the West, and he tried to establish a Latin scholasticism similar to that which then prevailed in the Hellenic East.' 'We can conceive that Boethius' bold attempt to restore culture at Rome with the aid of Alexandrian philosophy met with lively opposition.' Such claims, made most eloquently by Pierre Courcelle, have been highly influential. They are born of the general trend of scholarly thought on the impulse of Boethius' intellectual life, and his role in contemporary culture: a man in splendid isolation, fighting against the engulfing forces of darkness and ignorance.

One of the clearest contemporary accounts of the intellectual achievement of Boethius is the biographical fragment by Cassiodorus, written shortly after his death:

> Boethius excelled in the highest honours and was a highly skilled orator in both languages, who praised King Theoderic in the Senate on the occasion of the consulship of his sons in a glowing speech. He wrote a book about the Holy Trinity and certain dogmatic propositions and a book against Nestorius. He also wrote a bucolic poem. Yet in his work of translation on the art of logic, that is dialectic, and in the mathematical disciplines he was of such stature that he either equalled or excelled the ancient authors.

Although all trace of the bucolic poem is lost, this estimate of the various aspects of Boethius' public and intellectual life accords with all the available evidence. It is particularly interesting that the estimate of his philosophical works, though glowing, implies no recognition of a novel intellectual movement, except in so far as this work was of an exceptionally high quality.

Boethius' rhetorical skills, his natural intellectual gifts, and the traditional importance of his family, brought him to the attention of the court, as did these talents in many other members of the senatorial class. It is these public qualities that are praised by Ennodius, when he writes to Boethius congratulating him on his appointment as consul in 510: 'This honour is bestowed on your lineage it is true, but—what is a greater distinction—your own worth demanded that it be bestowed on your person . . . You have distinguished yourself with the weapons of Cicero and Demonsthenes, and shown your superiority in both languages.' To this extent, Courcelle is right in claiming that Boethius 'enjoyed the favour of the King of the Ostrogoths'; little credence can however be given to claims for substantial royal patronage of intellectual activity, despite Cassiodorus' claim in the *Variae* for Theoderic's ambitions as a 'philosopher king'. The claims that Theoderic acted as an intellectual patron of Boethius rest on two letters in the *Variae,* where through the mouthpiece of Cassiodorus, he gives Boethius two commissions: one to organize the despatch of a water clock to the king of the Burgundians, the second when he asks Boethius, as one famed for his musical knowledge, to recommend a harpist to be sent to the court of Clovis, king of the Franks. These commissions may well have been conceived by Cassiodorus himself, who was fully aware of the range of Boethius' intellectual activity.

In the letter on the subject of the water clock, Cassiodorus refers not only to Boethius' treatises on music, geometry and arithmetic, but also to his translations of Greek philosophy undertaken, he writes, 'so that you might make Greek thought Roman'. There is no suspicion that such activities were a betrayal of what he himself had stood for throughout his public career; rather it is clear that Cassiodorus saw Boethius, as Boethius saw himself, as part of the long Roman tradition of translators and commentators on Greek philosophy, of which Cicero and Marius Victorinus formed a part. In the *Institutiones,* Cassiodorus places Boethius very firmly in this context. He writes:

> Victorinus the orator translated the *Isagoge:* the noble Boethius commented on it in five books. The same

> Victorinus translated the *Categories,* and also wrote a commentary on them in eight books. The *Perihermenias* the aforesaid Victorinus translated into Latin, and the patrician Boethius wrote an extremely detailed commentary on it in six books.

Given this sense of the continuity of the intellectual tradition, a distinctive 'renaissance' seems unlikely, and is a theme impossible to trace in contemporary sources. So too is the theme of the hostility to Boethius' intellectual activities, the 'lively opposition' so emphasised by Courcelle, the chief evidence for which he finds in Boethius' prefaces to his own works. But it may be that little reliance should be placed on the evidence that Boethius seems to provide in this respect. In the preface to the ***De Trinitate*** he addresses Symmachus thus:

> Wherever else I turn my gaze, I see either inert sloth or sly resentment. To cast one's theological discourse before subhumans like that—to be kicked around rather than understood—would only cheapen it. So I have distilled my thought in a few words, and concealed it in novel linguistic terms drawn from the heart of philosophy, so that you and I alone—should you deign to glance at it—may speak together.

Again, in the preface to the ***Contra Eutychen et Nestorium*** Boethius writes of his attendance at a church council, 'I must confess that I found it hard to bear; and being jostled by a crowd of ignorant men I held my peace, lest I should appear insane indeed, were I to try to make these madmen think me sane.' But we may ask how far Boethius is expressing a genuine feeling of isolation and how far merely utilising the traditional topoi of the Latin prose preface, one of which is the benevolence of the scrutinizer or dedicatee in contrast to the ill-will or lack of comprehension of other contemporaries.

That Boethius may well have been influenced by such a tradition is yet more evident in the letter to Symmachus which prefaces the ***De Arithmetica,*** where these various themes can be clearly identified. One such traditional theme is that of transferring part of the responsibility for the reception of the work to the shoulders of the dedicatee in order to silence criticism. Here Boethius calls on Symmachus' authority to silence criticism of his translation. 'Why should I seek to be rewarded further by anyone else's approval, when you, who are fluent in both languages, can by a mere utterance confound those ignorant of Greek, if indeed they have the nerve to express an opinion?' Tore Janson [in *Latin Prose Prefaces,* 1964] argued that such a theme in the prose preface had reemerged in the late fifth century, for example in the Gallic writers Sidonius Apollinaris and Claudianus Mamertus. Boethius employs it too in his preface to the ***Contra Eutychen et Nestorium,*** where he writes to John the Deacon, 'I turn away from such critics to you, to whom I am sending this little piece, slight though it is, for scrutiny and judgement. If you think it is sound, be so good as to file it with the other essays that have my name attached; if not, or if any passage should be cut or expanded or altered, please send me back these corrections to be entered in that form in my own copy.' A further theme is that of undertaking a work only at the request of the dedicatee or a number of suppliants; this is found in Quintilian, in the preface to Gregory of Tours' *History of the Franks* and in Cassiodorus' preface to the *Variae,* where his diffidence about undertaking the work seems more than usually unlikely: 'Since I had gained the esteem of educated men either by my reputation or the favours I had conferred—though by no real merit of my own—they persuaded me to arrange my writings . . . in a single collection, so that posterity might know in years to come the travails of the work which I undertook for the common good.' Boethius declares that he undertook the ***De Arithmetica*** only at the request of Symmachus; he refers to it as 'this work, which inquires into the devices of wisdom [and] depends on the judgement not of its author but of another.' Self-depreciation was, and continues to be, a common theme. Thus Boethius in his covering letter to the ***De Arithmetica***: 'You will confirm the first fruits of my toil with your most learned judgement.' Further sympathy is evoked by Boethius' description of the extent of his labours: 'The judicious reader will quickly appreciate how much effort this has cost me, and how many sleepless nights.'

This letter to Symmachus employs a number of the traditional topoi of the Latin prose preface, which a Late Antique reader would have recognised as belonging to a particular literary genre; he would not have accepted them at face value. So it is doubtful whether Boethius' prefaces can be used as evidence of contemporary hostility to his intellectual projects, the unique sympathy of those to whom he dedicated his work and his own reluctance to undertake it. The isolation of Boethius and his circle, the 'lively opposition' which they met, and the ignorance with which they were contending cannot be inferred from such evidence. Boethius, as well as anyone, understood how to express himself within the traditional structure of Latin prose, and had an exact sense of its meaning for the contemporary reader.

VI

Boethius' motives in embarking upon his intellectual projects were not as grandiose as has sometimes been argued: from the evidence which remains he cannot be regarded as having conceived a 'Hellenist Renaissance' on a significant scale. He saw his role as one of enriching the Latin intellectual tradition with the transfusion of Greek material, in the mould of many Latin intellectuals before him. He believed that he had an audience, interested in Greek culture if not skilled in the Greek language, and the opposition to such an enterprise (if indeed contemporaries recognised his intellectual activities as having the coherence this word implies) should not be overemphasised. Boethius' intention in his philosophical programme was, and this cannot be overstressed, a highly technical one, that of reconciling the philosophical schemes of Plato and Aristotle, and he himself makes no claim for it to have any greater significance than this. Yet we do have evidence for close links with Eastern intellectual circles. How significant were these contacts?

A contemporary Eastern intellectual with whom Boethius and his circle undoubtedly had contact was the grammarian Priscian, from whom Symmachus commissioned three works while on a visit to Constantinople. It is unlikely that this action can be invested with extraordinary political or intellectual significance; it was traditional practice for aristocrats to commission work from leading local scholars, in this case in an area where Symmachus as a member of one, that of reconciling the philosophical schemes of Plato and Arisand intellectual contacts. Priscian acknowledges this eminence in the preface to his *De Figuris Numerorum,* a study of the Latin debt to the Greeks for their numeral signs, which is dedicated to Symmachus. 'How fittingly has a favouring Fortune endowed you, O Symmachus, with the splendour of a matchless lineage, with every personal resource, with a shining moral preeminence, and a lively enthusiasm for good and useful learning!' He goes on to elaborate to Symmachus his view of the role of Greek culture in the West, as he does in the preface to his most famous work, the *Institutiones Grammaticae.* There he writes that he finds that 'the Latins have made their own every kind of learning, shining with the light of wisdom, that is derived from Greek sources'. To Symmachus he acknowledges that there are areas of study that the Romans have made peculiarly their own, and through which they may claim intellectual equality with the Greeks in contrast with the backwardness of other nations. The two other works commissioned by Symmachus deal with the influence of Greek culture on Latin in the study of metric forms and of rhetoric, where such an influence could scarcely be denied. None of this evidence suggests that Priscian recognised in the intellectual pursuits of Boethius and his circle anything more unusual than the interplay between the Greek East and the Latin West which had always been a feature of the cultural life of the Mediterranean, an interplay reflected in his own use of Latin for his technical works. That there is evidence that Priscian hoped for the political reunification of the Empire, a sentiment only expressed in a work of political propaganda, does not imply that his intellectual contacts had similarly political implications. To add substance to this picture of cultural osmosis between East and West in this period, we may cite a pupil of Priscian, Flavius Theodorus, who appears in a subscription to a manuscript of Priscian's grammatical works produced in Constantinople. Jahn identifies him with one Theodorus cited at the end of a manuscript of Boethius' logical works: THEODOR[VS] ANTIQARI[VS] QUINVNC PALATINVS. On the other hand Courcelle [in *Late Latin Writers and their Greek Sources,* 1969] argues that Boethius' cultural orientation was entirely towards the East, and to one school in particular, that of Ammonius of Alexandria. In this schema, Ammonius is the major intellectual source on which Boethius draws in the whole corpus of his writings. Curiously, Boethius never mentions his name. The form and content of Boethius' commentaries, the literary culture evident in the ***De Consolatione Philosophiae,*** the cosmology and theories of fate and providence which he discusses in the final sections of that work, even the complex nexus of faith and reason which is expounded in his theological tractates—all, argues Courcelle, have their origins in the writings and teaching of Ammonius. The textual and methodological comparisons between the works of the two men are highly technical, and beyond the scope of this study, but a few comments may be made on Courcelle's theory as a whole. Courcelle has succumbed to the temptation to place any Late Antique thinker within the confines of a distinct school of thought: in the case of Boethius, within the confines of a very particular and narrowly defined school, thus denying him any powers of independent thought. It may be a comforting intellectual framework, but it does Boethius a disservice. In remarking on sources that may have been common to the work of Boethius and the school of Ammonius, Courcelle seems to discount the possibility of an independent use of the same sources. He is inconsistent, too, in his interpretation of the silence of writers, here of Boethius and Cassiodorus, on their use of recent sources. The corollary to Courcelle's theories on Boethius' intellectual debt to Ammonius is his suggestion that its origin lay in Boethius having attended classes given by Ammonius as a young man, while his father was prefect in Alexandria. Courcelle himself admits that there is a 'lack of historical information on this point' yet persists in pressing his thesis. Such speculation is indeed open to considerable doubt: notably there is the question of whether the man who can be identified as prefect in Alexandria in the early 480s is indeed the father of Boethius. Even were this the case, the date later in the decade when he is known to have been back in Rome as Urban Prefect, and the dating of Boethius' birth certainly little before 480, would preclude the possibility of even an infant prodigy absorbing the highly technical intellectual programme of Ammonius and his followers while in Alexandria. Thus any sign of Ammonius' influence which may be traceable in the work of Boethius must surely be attributed to a common fund of sources rather than specifically to Ammonius as his philosophical master.

VII

Contemporary accounts of the fall of Boethius seem agreed on one fact, that it is not his contacts with Eastern intellectuals nor his interest in Greek culture that cause his downfall. The contemporary Eastern historian, Procopius, in his official *History of the Gothic War* describes both Boethius and Symmachus as learned, just and philanthropic men. Envious of such merit, their inferiors delated them to Theoderic, who put them to death, on the ground that they were plotting a revolt. There is evidence here for intellectual eminence, but no suggestion that the two men died as martyrs to the cause of unification with the East; such a theme might be expected from a propagandist in the position of Procopius were there even the suspicion that it was true. A later and Western source, the Anonymus Valesianus, tells a brief tale of lies and betrayal: on behalf of the whole Senate Boethius defends his fellow senator Albinus against the charge of having sent a treasonable letter to the Emperor Justin, asking for his intervention in the West. Boethius is subsequently imprisoned and put to death without a hearing.

Boethius' own analysis of the reasons for his fall accord with the view of the Anonymus Valesianus that he was punished for his defence of the privileges of the Senate and the freedom of action of its members. In his final testament, the ***De Consolatione Philosophiae,*** he writes: 'But you want to know the nub of the charge against me? I am charged with having desired the safety of the Senate. And as for the manner, I am alleged to have prevented an informer from lodging proofs whereby he intended to convict the Senate of treason.' How well this accords with an analysis of Boethius as a man writing and acting consciously in the Roman tradition of his aristocratic ancestors, finding the origins of his intellectual pursuits in their traditions, moved to take up public office by their example, and losing his life in defence of what he saw as the most sacred Roman institution!

Edmund Reiss (essay date 1982)

SOURCE: "Form and Method in the *Consolation,*" in *Boethius,* Twayne Publishers, 1982, pp. 131-53.

[*In the essay below, Reiss analyzes the structure, dialogue form, and interweaving of prose and verse in the* Consolation of Philosophy.]

Structural Patterns

Whereas linear progression is the most obvious structural pattern of the ***Consolation,*** this progression involves much more than a simple movement from a beginning to an ending, or a simple change of the narrator from despair to hope and from ignorance to understanding. As the work develops and consolation yields to instruction and to an awareness of truth, so simplicity yields to complexity—of thought, language, and structure. The five-book structure of the ***Consolation,*** where the subject of one book overlaps to that of the next, reveals a movement beyond the overall one that extends from Book 1, with its statement of the problem in terms of its effect on the narrator, to Book 5, with its detachment from the personal and its discussion of man's responsibility in a world governed by providential order. The fiction with which the work begins gives way to the presentation of truth itself. And though this process may be regarded as, on the one hand, an objectifying of that which had been presented subjectively, it may also be described as a moving from superficial appearance to essential truth, reflected by the narrator's looking into himself, a turning from external concerns to those at the heart of one's being.

It is not accidental that the so-called autobiographical parts of the ***Consolation*** are limited to the first two books. Similarly, the movement from emotion to reflection is mirrored by the movement from the initial emotional passage in verse to the final philosophical statement in prose. And beyond this, the alternation from verse to prose to verse and so on to the final prose passage necessarily entails a two-fold movement: on the one hand, the movement of the discrete forms, the narrative in the denotative language of prose and the songs in the connotative language of verse; and, on the other hand, the necessary interrelationship of these forms, the way the particular poem, for instance, stems from and leads to the prose passages around it.

The five-book structure of the work may also be seen revealing the traditional five-part division of oration that Boethius would have known from the *Institutio oratoria* of Quintillian. The structure first appears in the ***Consolation*** in microcosm, as Kurt Reichenberger recognized, as the controlling device of 1:pr.4, where the narrator delivers what amounts to an apologia for his life. Using the *exordium* (or *prooemium*), in which the speaker prepares the audience to be well disposed to his argument, Boethius has his narrator make the point that he has not deserved his misfortune; in the *narratio,* or recounting of the facts, he shows how he has always opposed injustice and worked for the common good; in the *probatio,* or proof, he states how he has been falsely accused; in the *refutatio* he rebukes his accusers and reaffirms his innocence; and in the *peroratio,* using eloquence and emotion, he relates his particular case to what he takes to be the state of the world: the innocent being overcome by the wicked. In terms of the rhetoric, the so-called personal details in this section of the first book—including the references to Basilius, Opilio, and Gaudentius, Boethius's false accusers—function essentially as *topoi,* or, as they were termed in Latin rhetorical tradition, *loci communes,* devices to develop the oration at hand.

Applying this five-part division to the ***Consolation*** as a whole, we may regard each book as equivalent to one part of a discourse, though we should realize that the discourse is finally that of neither the narrator nor Philosophy, but of Boethius the author. Book 1, the *exordium,* uses the narrator's particular condition to make the problem meaningful; Book 2, the *narratio,* states the facts of the narrator's good and bad fortune to examine the gifts of Fortune; Book 3, the *probatio,* demonstrates the nature of true happiness; Book 4, the *refutatio,* clarifies the nature of evil and the state of the wicked; and Book 5, the *peroratio,* makes clear man's responsibility in a world governed by Providence. The ***Consolation*** may be regarded in one sense as Boethius's demonstration of the uses of rhetoric and grammar, as well as a meaningful part of his educational program, coming after his study of the sciences of the *quadrivium* and the language of logic, and perhaps stemming from his treatises dealing with rhetoric, ***In topica Ciceronis*** and ***De topicis differentiis.***

At the same time, not only is the dialogue that Boethius creates between the narrator and Philosophy itself a form of drama, especially in Book 1, but the five-book structure of the ***Consolation*** may reflect the five-act structure of Roman drama. This structure may be found in the plays of Seneca, which are cited several times in the ***Consolation;*** and the basis for the structure is spelled out by Horace in his *Ars poetica.* Moreover, the change of the narrator from grief to serenity, seen in Book 3, the middle of the ***Consolation,*** may be understood to correspond to the *peripeteia,* or turning point, which, according to Aristotle in his *Poetics,* is central to the drama.

Beyond their relationship to oratory and drama, the five

books of the ***Consolation,*** divided unevenly into thirty-nine sections of alternating verse and prose, are organized so that the third book is the longest of all, the second and fourth the next longest, and the first and fifth the shortest. Book 1, with seven verse and six prose sections, is shorter than Book 2, composed of eight sections of each form, which is shorter in turn than Book 3, the central book, having twelve sections of verse and of prose. Book 4, composed of eight sections of each form, is likewise shorter than Book 3; and Book 5, with five verse and six prose parts, is shorter than Book 4. Such variations in length indicate a structure which may be described as X XX XXX XX X, and suggest that, along with the linear structure of the ***Consolation,*** there exists a ring structure emphasizing the dramatic center, Book 3, where the narrator changes from the despairing figure seen at the beginning and begins to pursue the *summum bonum.*

Ring structure also seems to be an especially pertinent way of describing how the thirty-nine poems are organized, though with these the organizing principle is not a quantitative, but a thematic or verbal, linking of parts. In this the first element is related to the last, the second to the penultimate, the third to the antepenultimate and so forth, resulting in a structure which may be described as ABCCBA. In the ***Consolation,*** though the actual arrangement of poems in each of the five books is more complex—and imprecise—than this simple statement would suggest, the arrangement itself may nevertheless be meaningfully described as ring structure.

In Book 1, the organization of the seven poems may be understood as follows. Poem 1, the introductory soliloquy showing the narrator's sorrow, stands apart from the other poems. Poem 2, which at the end tells of the mind's losing its light and man's being in chains, has as its counterpart m.7, which likewise shows the mind clouded and in chains. Similarly, m.3, relating the coming of light to man's eyes to the shining of the sun over all, may be linked to m.6, which, beginning with the rays of the sun—both poems refer to the *radiis Phoebi*—reexpresses the light-theme of the previous poem as the principle of order. And m.4, which celebrates the unmoved man, may be related to m.5, which invokes God as unmoved mover to make the earth stable.

In Book 2, the poems again seem to be organized into four pairs. Poem 1, on Fortune's ruling the world in disharmony, may be related to m.8, which emphasizes Love's ruling the world in harmony. Poem 2, on man's greed as boundless, contrasts with m.7, where man is seen as nothing in regard to the immensity of the universe and the fact of death. Poem 3, on change as a principle of the world, leads to m.6, on the instability of earthly empire. And m.4, on the need for man to lead a serene life, is generalized in m.5, on the need for man to return to the Golden Age. Here the emphasis on happiness (*felix*) at the end of m.4 is repeated at the beginning of m.5.

The ring structure of the poems in Book 3 is more complex because of Boethius's fragmentation of the false desires of man. Poem 1, which ends with man's finding truth, may be seen leading to m.12, which begins with man's seeking truth—now reexpressed as love. Moreover, as m.1 ends with man's shaking off his yokes, so m.12 begins with man's shaking off his chains. Poem 2, asserting the principle that everything desires to return to its home, may be joined to m.11, which calls for man to return to his home; here m.2 ends with the image of the circle (*orbem*), and m.11 begins with this image. The five poems represented by the short verses 3 through 7 may be understood to form a single unit in that they present man's false desires—wealth, high office, power, fame, and pleasure—and correspond to m.10, which shows man's release from these false desires. And m.8, detailing the blindness of man in pursuing false goals, leads to m.9, the prayer to God to reveal the *summum bonum* to man.

A similar joining of the separate parts would seem to be revealed in Book 4, but instead of being organized in terms of four groups of poems, it employs two groups. Poem 1, on ascending to the skies with the wings of Philosophy, has as its correlative m.7, on overcoming fortune and the earth, and on reaching to the stars. The four poems, from 2 through 5, are joined in showing man as an inadequate ruler, brought down by his vices to the level of beasts, perversely seeking to destroy himself in his ignorance of the proper order of things. The corrective to this group is m.6, where God the high king rules all, where man is brought up by God, where love banishes dissension, and where man understands the laws of God.

In Book 5, m.1, which presents the river guided by a higher law, may be related to m.5, that details the variety of life forms in the world, each likewise guided. Poem 2, citing Homer's picture of the sun shining on but not into the earth, may be echoed in m.4, with its statement of the Stoic view of images implanting the mind. In this book m.3, on man's being assured in his search for truth in God, stands in isolation, though at the same time, it may be regarded as coupled with the likewise-isolated first poem of Book 1, with its emphasis on the narrator's fall through his unsure foothold in this world.

The point of this ring structure is to provide an additional pattern of meaning to the ***Consolation***. Not accidentally, the climaxing poem of each book is in most instances the longest and/or most significant poem in the book, and the one that emphasizes love and harmony as principles of the universe which should be extended to man. The prayer to God of 1:m.5 emphasizes God's joining everything in harmony; the picture of the Golden Age in 2:m.5 stresses peace and harmony; the prayer to God the Creator in 3:m.9 amounts to a celebration of universal *concordia;* the hymn of praise of 4:m.6 emphasizes the mutual love (*alternus amor*) that holds everything in order, the *concordia oppositorum;* and the questions of 5:m.3 function as an assertion that man must discern the *connexio rerum,* the connections among all things, and, rather than break the bond of things through discord, should extend this bond to himself.

If these five key poems are likewise examined in terms of

ring structure, 1:m.5, which shows the narrator's improper prayer to God to provide for man the laws guiding the universe, and which reveals, as Philosophy says, the extent of his illness, easily leads to 5:m.3, the narrator's last speech, where he comes to a proper understanding of Truth, and in effect shows that he has been healed. Similarly, the harmony expressed in the picture of the Golden Age in 2:m.5 may be seen leading to the full statement of universal harmony in 4:m.6. The culminating, or central, poem, of the ***Consolation*** is then 3:m.9, the prayer to "the Father of all things" that celebrates and joins all of creation. More than a Platonic hymn to God, this important poem expresses perhaps not accidentally, such basic Christian elements as the Lord's Prayer and liturgical *Gloria*.

Along with linear and ring structure, we should also note the use of the circle as a structuring principle of the ***Consolation***. Expressed spatially as the celestial spheres suggesting cosmic order, the circle is also the thematic principle of return itself, man's turning back to God after his descent into the world of matter, parodied in the circling of the Wheel of Fortune, as seen in 2:m.1. In the final poem of the ***Consolation,*** 5:m.5, the image of man's raising his eyes to heaven not only refers back to man's looking downward to the earth, the image at the beginning of the work (1:m.2), it provides its corrective. Similarly, Philosophy's final admonition to man to lift up his mind in hope (5:pr.6) counteracts the despair pervading the initial poem of Book 1 and illustrates the change from complaint to affirmation seen in the course of the ***Consolation***.

Such relationships depend on our awareness of an earlier given. The affirmation of life and human dignity at the end of the ***Consolation,*** while contrasting with the emphasis on death and despair at the beginning, necessitates our reassessing this earlier position. Our being taken back to the beginning functions to transform the initial point. Moreover, just as Philosophy leads the narrator to God, so her final point in Book 5, that man lives in the sight of a judge who beholds all, gives meaning to her initial appearance, as the divine emissary who sees all and who provides for man.

Forms of Dialogue

This return, this completion of a circle, is actually effected through the dialogue between the narrator and Philosophy, the two characters in Boethius's drama. Although Boethius had employed the dialogue as a structuring form as early as his ***Dialogue*** on Porphyry's *Isagoge,* he here uses a complex blend of several kinds of discourses, including monologue, Socratic dialogue, and apocalyptic dialogue. From beginning to end, however, the ***Consolation*** is also a conversation, in which we are aware of the interacting of voices. Even when one voice is extended or dominant, as Lady Philosophy's voice so often is, the other frequently punctuates it. Didactic as the work is, it retains throughout a sense of voice as though what is at hand has a living presence. And even when the dramatic and personal are least present, the work gives the impression of being something other than an essay or even a lecture. Though at times the statement may be so extensive that we may tend to forget that it is speech, the lapse is but for a moment. In the last book, for instance, where the narrator's lengthy arguments about the necessary opposition of divine foreknowledge and human free will (5:3) are followed by an even longer reply by Philosophy, which offers a corrective to the narrator's position (5:4-6), we have little sense of conversation. But at the same time, Boethius insists that we differentiate the particular speakers and be aware that the first argument is but a jumping-off point for the second.

Boethius takes us from an awareness of the silent musing of the narrator at the beginning of the ***Consolation*** to speech and then back again at the end to an awareness of silence—there is no answer to Philosophy's last words. The initial and final speeches function as monologues that frame the entire work. The narrator's report at the beginning of his visit by Philosophy is balanced by Philosophy's final affirmation of universal justice. What happens is that the silent musing leads to a single voice which yields to two voices as the dialogue begins; then at the end this gives way to one voice again, which in turn leads to silence. Unlike the initial silence, the final silence suggests fulfillment. Now that speech has led to understanding and agreement, the need for words no longer exists.

As dialogue, the ***Consolation*** is obviously artificial: We recognize that it is actually the externalizing of an internal conflict. What Boethius does at the outset of this work may be meaningfully compared to what Augustine does at the beginning of his *Soliloquies*. There, after the narrator notes how for many days he has been seeking to know himself and the highest good, he suddenly hears someone speak: "whether it was myself or someone else from without or within I know not." When Augustine's narrator answers this voice, which he calls Reason (*Ratio*), the dialogue begins. So in the ***Consolation,*** the dialogue is a voicing of the feelings and thoughts existing within the narrator. Although Boethius externalizes these into contrasting positions represented by two characters, and creates two contrasting forms of language—the prose, denotative and analytic; and the verse, connotative and celebratory—the whole dialogue is less dialectic than didactic. Even though at the end, on the matter of reconciling God's foreknowledge and man's free will, we see something of an exchange of ideas, throughout most of the ***Consolation*** Philosophy is in the position of correcting the obviously erroneous views of the narrator, and of reaffirming accepted truth.

Although the kind of dialogue employed by Socrates in Plato's dialogues was well known in Latin literature, both in classical writings in the dialogues of Cicero and in Christian writings as early as the *Octavius* of Minucius Felix, Boethius's actual application of this kind of dialectic is only sporadic. The ***Consolation*** is more obviously a work of instruction and, more apparently, a protreptic, or *exhortatio,* to proper understanding. While perhaps to be understood in terms of Boethius's earlier protreptics, it leads to the study not of the preparatory *quadrivium* or of logic, but of philosophy itself, that which is at the end of

Ulysses and Circe, from Book IV of the Consolation of Philosophy, *in a late-fourteenth-century manuscript.*

the earlier studies. While as a protreptic the ***Consolation*** may be related to several Neoplatonic treatises, including those by Plutarch and Iamblichus, and while it may have had its impetus in the now-lost *Protrepticus* of Aristotle and the *Hortensius* of Cicero, it is finally quite different from all these works. As an *exhortatio* to philosophy, the ***Consolation*** is really an *exhortatio* to God, in which man is urged to seek the highest good.

Both monologue and Socratic dialogue should be viewed as part of a larger overall structure, that may be termed the sacred, or apocalyptic, dialogue. This is less the kind of discourse found at the end of the Book of Job, when God finally speaks to man, than that found in the apocryphal 2 Esdras, where a divine spirit reveals hidden wisdom to man. This kind of revelation became a genre at the end of the second century and was favored by both Christians and pagans, as may be seen in the extremely popular *Shepherd of Hermas,* as well as the Neoplatonic *Poimandres* of Hermes Trismegistes, where, as in the ***Consolation,*** a narrator numbed and immersed in his reflections is visited by a being of immeasurable height, signifying the highest Intelligence, who shows him a vision and then discusses with him various metaphysical issues. Closer to Boethius's lifetime are such other relevant examples of this genre as the *Soliloquies* of Augustine and the *Mitologiae* of Fulgentius, a Neoplatonic work more or less contemporaneous with the ***Consolation,*** that is likewise concerned with revealing the nature of divinity.

At the same time, we should note the significance of Boethius's making his instructor an allegorical personification and not a human figure, say Symmachus, thereby projecting a relationship of the sort he had created with Fabius in his early ***Dialogue*** on the *Isagoge;* or even Plato, thereby creating a human representative of philosophy. It is also significant that Boethius calls his instructor Philosophy and not Reason, or Intelligence, or Wisdom. Though containing reason, she is more than this way to truth; and similarly, she is not truth or wisdom itself; for in Boethius's view the personification of wisdom would have indicated God alone. Rather, the name Philosophy suggests both the way to truth and the end of the journey, in a sense as logic in Boethius's earlier writings was considered to be both a tool and a part of philosophy. And Boethius's understanding of philosophy in the ***Consolation*** is wholly in accord with his earlier definitions of it, as in the ***Arithmetic,*** when he writes that "philosophy is the love of wisdom," and as in his first commentary on the *Isagoge,* when he calls philosophy "the love and pursuit of wisdom and in some way the friendship with it." Philosophy should thus be understood as both the inclination toward wisdom and the expression of what is to be learned.

The Allegorical Principle

As an apocalyptic dialogue, the ***Consolation*** is necessarily an allegory. However, its allegory is "not a mere device" but rather a narrative principle. We are in fact aware of allegory from the beginning of the work with the mysterious appearance and description of Philosophy. Although we do not know whether or not her strange and contradictory appearance—both old and young, both of average height and higher than the heavens—is the product of the narrator's dulled perception, we soon realize that such details reveal the nature, scope, and purpose of philosophy itself. The point of her varying height, for instance, is obviously to show that philosophy pertains both to ordinary human existence and to the truth that is so far beyond man's ordinary understanding that he cannot hope to know it fully. Similarly, her dress further reveals her nature. The *pi* at the bottom of her dress and the *theta* at the top—probably indicating the first letters of the Greek terms for the two divisions of philosophy, *practica* and *theoretica*—make even clearer that Boethius means for his character to be understood as encompassing all of philosophy, while the link between the letters shows that it is possible to move from one to the other.

The unity of philosophy is reinforced, moreover, by the detail of the tear in her dress. All that is stated at first is that marauders had carried off pieces of the material, but we are told a bit later that after the death of Socrates, the various philosophical schools—what are called the "mob" of Epicureans, Stoics, and others—tried to seize philosophy for themselves. Though they succeeded in obtaining pieces of her garb, they foolishly thought these to be the whole thing (1:pr.3). Beyond representating a criticism of the ancient schools of thought after Plato, this allegory makes clear a major point of Boethius—that philosophy naturally battles the rash forces of folly. The narrator, the character Boethius, who has been one of Philosophy's staunchest supporters, should not be surprised at his predicament since wicked men have always tried to hurl down those who are concerned with truth. The unity of philosophy extends to the final detail in the description of the lady, the books and scepter she carries. These go beyond the different spheres of philosophy and focus on its twin roles. Through studying philosophy, man may reach wisdom; and through following its precepts, he may properly rule himself and his society.

The details of this description have been carefully emphasized by Boethius to achieve a certain purpose and to give a certain view of philosophy. But regardless of how vivid some of these details may seem, we should recognize their essentially traditional nature. For all of her individuality, Lady Philosophy is in a long line of allegorical personifications who instruct man, including the female instructors in the *Shepherd of Hermas,* Reason in Augustine's *Soliloquies,* and Nature—who is also both old and young—in Claudian's panegyric *On the Consulship of Stilicho* (early fifth century). Moreover, the depiction of wisdom as a female figure in general and as a beautiful, radiant goddess in particular expresses a convention which may be traced back to Plato's *Phaedrus* and which was well known in Latin literature from Cicero on.

Notwithstanding all of these analogous figures, the most likely source of Boethius's Philosophy is the nameless figure in Plato's *Crito* who, as Socrates reports, appears to him in a vision. Doubtless representing philosophy, this figure—like Boethius's character—is fair and comely and clothed in bright dress. While apparently making clear to the imprisoned Socrates the imminence of his death, she also seems to provide that which allows him to accept his death resolutely, just as Boethius's Philosophy teaches the narrator to accept his fall and to look beyond his personal misfortune. Moreover, it hardly seems coincidental that when noting how wisdom has always been threatened by the forces of evil, Philosophy focuses on the death of Socrates, which, while unjust, nevertheless represents a victory for her who, she says, was at his side (1:pr.3).

Not only does the description of Philosophy in the ***Consolation*** represent a way of regarding philosophy that would probably have been familiar to Boethius's audience, it seems likely that Boethius was relying on familiarity with the tradition. His allegory is not creating meaning; it is, rather, a way of referring to preexisting meaning. The fact that the narrator is unable at first to use the traditional and obvious details offered to recognize his visitor shows clearly how dulled he has become. Moreover, the initial contrast between the two figures is purposeful: Whereas Philosophy is calm and tranquil, the narrator is agitated and distraught; whereas her eyes are clear, his are full of tears; whereas she is ageless, he has moved from youth to old age; whereas she stands above him, he is fallen. In contrast with her brightness and vitality, his countenance is "sad with mourning, and cast upon the ground with grief" (1:pr.1). Her words, as may be seen in 1:m.2 in particular, concern the "perturbation" of the narrator's mind, which is "headlong cast/In depths of woe" and which has lost its light (1-2).

As Wolfgang Schmid first noticed, the condition of the narrator here is that of someone overcome by lethargy. According to a long tradition in which man's physical appearance is taken to be a sign of his spiritual condition, we may see that the narrator has fallen victim to lethargy, or sloth, which is the cause of the despair and mourning that occupy him totally. Regardless of whether or not the sickness detailed here represents the actual condition of Boethius after his fall, it functions in the ***Consolation*** as a symbolic expression of his spiritual condition.

The contrast between the narrator and Philosophy is but the first instance in the work of a blending of ordinarily disparate elements. Although we might think it incongruous that a figure from the familiar world of man should appear on the same plane as an allegorical personification, we should understand that this procedure is not unusual either in late classical writings or in the ***Consolation***. In fact, simultaneous linking and juxtaposing may even be regarded as the dominant method, if not the overall literary and philosophical principle, of the work, involving language, narrative details, literary structures, and philosophical ideas. It extends to the blending of the legendary and the historical, the fictional and the factual, and the personal and the traditional, and reflects Boethius's concern throughout the ***Consolation*** with relating the particular to the general and the individual to the typical. It is also the basis for the unusual mixture of prose and verse continued systematically throughout the entire work.

Prose and Verse

The prosimetric form of the ***Consolation*** necessarily relates the work to the Menippean satire—after the work of Menippus of Gadara (third century B.C.)—which had been Latinized as early as Varro's *Satyrae Menippeae* in the first century B.C. While *satura,* or satire, originally meant nothing more than a mixture or medley, in particular one of alternating prose and verse passages, in Roman literature it typically appeared in such works as the *Apocolocyntosis divi Claudii,* a lampoon of the dead emperor Claudius attributed to Seneca the Younger, and the bawdy and likewise comic *Satyricon* of Petronius—an author alluded to by Boethius at the end of his *Dialogue* on the *Isagoge.* Closer in spirit to the ***Consolation,*** and perhaps Boethius's actual source for the form, is the *De nuptiis Philologiae et Mercurii* of Martianus Capella. But notwithstanding the similarity in form of the ***Consolation*** and these antecedents, the "grave impressiveness" with which Boethius's work treats its passages of prose and verse removes it from these other instances of Menippean satire and raises the form to a position in literature it had never before attained.

Both the prose and the verse of the ***Consolation*** may be properly and meaningfully judged as literary language. While recognizing that Boethius's prose is hardly "the classical Latin of the Ciceronian age," we should recognize that it still offers "a simplicity, a restraint, a clarity of diction which are in very marked contrast to the overornate, diffuse and excessively rhetorical style" prevalent in the literature of the time. Indeed, Boethius's style may be regarded as "well nigh a miracle" in view of the tendency of contemporary writing toward "distorted ornateness." And it is hardly an exaggeration to say that Boethius in his prose is not only nearer than any of his contemporaries to the great age of Cicero, but "nearer than any of his predecessors had been for centuries."

The thirty-nine poems have not been so consistently praised over the centuries as the prose. Although offered by and large by Philosophy—and not by the narrator—to give a pleasant and welcome rest from the strain of following the arguments developed in the prose passages, they are more than diversions or decorations. Their function is to do more than intersperse the prose passages or enliven the instruction the narrator is receiving. Sometimes they summarize the argument of the prose; at other times they carry the discussion forward; and at still other times they comment on what is at hand, functioning, like the chorus in a Greek tragedy, to provide perspective for assessing the progress of the dialogue at hand. When the narrator is too weak to take the strong medicine of Philosophy, the poems provide relief; but as he becomes increasingly receptive to her words, they in turn become more complex. Although it has been suggested that as the argument becomes increasingly difficult, the verses occur less often, we should recognize that their connotative language is frequently more demanding than the relatively straightforward denotative language of the prose passages.

Widely different evaluations have been made of this poetry. An anonymous ninth-century critic felt that just as Boethius's prose was not inferior to Cicero's, so his verse was the equal of Virgil's; and in the Renaissance, Julius Caesar Scaliger spoke of these verses as "divine." In the nineteenth century, however, Hermann Usener was quite critical of them. Although he saw in the prose "a thinker of a greater time," he regarded the verse as the voice of "a child of the sixth century," an evaluation that led twentieth-century readers to affirm anew the power and poetic skill of the poems. Probably the most accurate view of the verses is still that of Rand [in his *Founders of the Middle Ages,* 1928]: "Some are exceedingly good, some are only moderate, and a few are insignificant—that being the only way, according to the poet Martial, in which one can write a book."

The thirty-nine meters themselves are so varied that they not only provide representatives of almost every meter known in the sixth century, they include two or three meters apparently invented by Boethius. But while they may represent a tour de force of prosody, we should realize that for Boethius the poems must be viewed in conjunction with the prose. The final poem in each book would seem to provide a transition to the next book. And the fact that all the books except the last end with a poem suggests that Boethius intended to move from verse to prose, and, moreover, to include in the ***Consolation*** precisely thirty-nine examples of each form—whatever the significance of this number may be.

Whereas the rational dialectic of the prose takes the form of catechism, syllogism, and dialogue, the verses, linguistically and functionally distinct, may be said "to constitute modes of knowing and discoursing alternative to those central to speculative philosophy." As Boethius makes clear, the operation of human reasoning has its limitations. Though higher than animal sensation, it is lower than divine understanding (5:pr.4), and rational discourse as the expression of this is likewise limited. Besides knowing through reasoning, man knows through remembering. Emphasizing the Platonic doctrine of reminiscence, where learning is viewed as a matter of recollection (3:m.11), Boethius points out that although man cannot foresee the future, he can remember the past. By doing so, he not only knows truth, thus becoming godlike, but he may also come to understand the perplexing disorder of the world. The recall of truth shares some meaningful similarities with the discovery of it by syllogistic argument: As the conclusion of a syllogism is implicit in its premise, so the object of reminiscence is contained in the memory. But Boethius emphasizes the differences by using prose as the language of rational discourse and verse as the language of recall, that which is appropriate for expressing history and myth.

To make this point is not to say that allusions to the past are absent from the prose sections of the ***Consolation***. Not only does Boethius cite classical authorities throughout the entire work, he also alludes to historical and mythological figures. In the prose, however, these allusions function mainly as points of reference in Philosophy's argument, whereas in the verse they are in effect expressions of the movement through time and space demanded of the narrator and Boethius's audience. The verses refer in particular to great figures from history and myth who provide models and warnings for man. From Roman history, Boethius singles out such figures as Nero (2:m.6; 3:m.4), Fabricius, Cato, and Brutus (2:m.7); and from myth he uses the story of Orpheus (2:m.12), as well as episodes from the stories of such heroes as Ulysses (4:m.3, m.7), Agamemnon, and Hercules (m.7).

The poems take the mind on journeys across time and space, insisting that it see what is beyond its immediate concerns, recall the past, and finally leave the earth behind and look to God. The verses are full of spatial references—equivalents, as it were, to the figures from history and myth—often based on the four elements—earth, air, fire, and water—and the four points of the compass (1:m.3-5; 2:m.4). Also they look to far off lands—Thrace (1:m.3), India, Thulé (3:m.5), Armenia (5:m.1)—and to the spectacular and exotic features of this world: to the mountains Vesuvius (1:m.4) and Etna (2:m.5), and to the rivers Tagus, Hermus, Indus (3:m.10), Tigris and Euphrates (5:m.1). And they even look beyond this world to the underworld (3:m.12) and to the heavens (4:m.1). In making the mind move back in time and across the earth and the universe, Boethius offers exercises of a sort that, on the one hand, make the torpid narrator come alive and cease musing on his personal troubles and, on the other hand, "set the memory going, turning over its riches until the desired truth is reclaimed."

The Philosophical Synthesis

While uniting such apparent alternatives as space and time, recollection and dialectic, and verse and prose, Boethius also extends the principle of synthesis to the philosophical content of the ***Consolation***. Although the work may well be described as remarkably heterogeneous, it, like Boethius's earlier writings, represents an amalgamation of classical thought. But rather than postulate different sources for different sections of the work—for instance, a Stoic section, an Aristotelian section, a Platonic section—we should recognize that regardless of where the seed of Boethius's thought originated, the "inspiring and sustaining spirit" of the ***Consolation*** is Plato, and the real unifying factor is late Neoplatonism.

To affirm the essential Neoplatonism of the work is not to deny the obvious Aristotelian influence. Not only does Philosophy once refer to "my Aristotle" (5:pr.1), she cites his ideas again and again. Besides showing the influence of treatises comprising the *Organon,* notably *On Interpretation,* the ***Consolation*** reveals that Boethius obviously knew well such other works by Aristotle as the *Nicomachean Ethics,* with its definition of happiness (3:pr.10); the *Physics*, with its definition of chance (5:pr.1); and *On the Heavens,* with its distinction between eternity and temporal duration (5:pr.6). But since Boethius had devoted the greater part of his work before the ***Consolation*** to translating and interpreting Aristotle, "it would be surprising"—as Helen Barrett realizes—if the ***Consolation*** did not show the influence of Aristotelian thought.

We must likewise acknowledge the general sense of Stoic resolution that permeates the ***Consolation***. It is hardly accidental that Philosophy, when identifying her martyrs, should single out Stoics (1:pr.3); and it may be significant that the Stoic thinker Seneca is, along with Cicero, the main Latin authority cited in the work. Moreover, Stoic ethical teachings, "strong and bracing" as they were, may well have had a special appeal to Boethius after his fall. But Stoicism was a major part of Boethius's cultural heritage, and the ***Consolation*** shows little Stoic influence on its particular ideas. In fact, Boethius is explicitly unsympathetic to the Stoic theory of the mind as a passive receiver of impressions (5:m.4), and he has little use for the Stoic theories of materialism, pantheism, and fatalism.

By far the greatest influences on the ***Consolation*** come from Platonic and Neoplatonic sources. Plato himself is at the heart of the work, and the *Timaeus* and *Gorgias* are notably significant. The *Timaeus* is the basis of the significant prayer to God in 3:m.9; and the *Gorgias* is the source of Boethius's solution to the problem of evil in 4:pr.2-3. But the bulk of Boethius's relationships to Plato are due to the influence of Neoplatonic intermediaries. Although it has been suggested that Boethius actually translated the *Timaeus,* he most likely knew the work as it existed in the commentary of Proclus; similarly, whether or not he knew the *Gorgias* itself, he certainly knew the commentaries of the Alexandrian Neoplatonists Ammonius Hermiae and Olympiodorus. Moreover, the *Enneads* of Plotinus may have provided Boethius with the framing principle of Philosophy's drawing up the mind of the narrator from earthly things, as well as with the identification of God as the highest good; Proclus certainly influenced Boethius's view of Providence and Fate; and Ammonius Hermiae influenced his distinction between the eternity of God and the perpetuity of the world, as well as his statement of the relationship between foreknowledge and free will.

To note these influences is not at all to suggest that the ***Consolation*** is a pastiche of earlier thought, or that, because Boethius does not produce a new philosophical system as such, he is "a mere collector" of the ideas of others. Rather, we must recognize that as with such earlier work as the ***Principles of Music,*** where he synthesizes several earlier views and authorities, Boethius uses the material in the ***Consolation*** to construct a new and autonomous work. And while it is most in harmony with the fundamentals of Neoplatonic thought, it is also in accord with the tenets of Christianity.

At the same time, the nature and extent of the influence on the ***Consolation*** of Christian doctrine in general and Augustinian thought in particular are not clear. In part, the problem stems from the accommodation by Christianity—and especially by Augustine—of Neoplatonism, and from the difficulty of isolating peculiarly Christian elements within this philosophical work. But it is not sufficient to say that whereas Boethius often echoes the Neoplatonists, "he studiously avoids any attempt to blend Christ with Plato." Whereas this evaluation may be correct in its recognition that the ***Consolation*** contains no overtly Christian doctrine, it is misleading in its implication that Boethius is not at all concerned here with the overlapping of Neoplatonism and Christianity. It is likewise misleading to say that both Christianity and Augustine "would of course be in the background of his mind and could not have been without influence on what he wrote in the ***Consolation***." The implication of this statement is that Christianity—like Stoicism—was merely part of the cultural heritage of the time and represented nothing special for Boethius.

Just as the affinity between Philosophy and Christ as healers—what Wolfgang Schmid calls *philosophia medicans* and *Christus medicans*—may be more than coincidental, so the similarity between certain issues of the ***Consolation*** and concerns of Christianity—for instance, the problem of evil—may not be accidental. And Augustine—who was very much troubled by the question of evil—may well have exerted a particular influence on the ***Consolation,*** not only on Boethius's method of allegory and dialogue but also on his thought. At times, as Antonio Crocco recognizes, "we sense clearly the presence of Augustine." And inasmuch as Boethius at the beginning of his ***De Trinitate*** openly cites Augustine as his authority, we may feel with Etienne Gilson that "one hardly risks being mistaken in saying that where the doctrine of the ***De consolatione philosophiae*** coincides with that of Augustine, the coincidence is not fortuitous. Even when he is speaking only as a philosopher Boethius thinks as a Christian."

But though cases have been made for a pervasive Augustinian influence, though the ***Consolation*** has even been presented as a sequel to Augustine's *Soliloquies,* and though the work has been thought to have its nucleus in Augustine's early dialogues, mainly the *Contra Academicos,* the arguments supporting this relationship are too frequently neither sufficiently clear nor persuasive. At the same time, however, arguments concerned with negating the possible Augustinian influence or with differentiating the thought of the two men have likewise been less than convincing. While on the one hand we may be left with a sense that, as Rand expresses it, "there is nothing in this work for which a good case might not have been made by any contemporary Christian theologian, who knew his Augustine," on the other hand we should also recognize that Boethius's accomplishment is finally rather different from Augustine's. We may get a sense of this difference by noting that Fortune and Fate, two terms in fact proscribed by Augustine, are fundamental to Boethius's argument.

The problem of establishing an Augustinian basis for the ***Consolation*** may be related to that of understanding Boethius's citation of authorities. Inasmuch as all of these are figures who lived before the first century A.D., the implication is that Boethius systematically omitted all references to later authorities, even though he clearly knew and used such writers as Plotinus, Porphyry, Proclus, and Augustine. Pierre Courcelle feels that this strange omission is due to Boethius's purposely citing only pagan authorities who lived before Christ. Having chosen as his fictional guide a figure representing Philosophy, Boethius could hardly have had her allude to Scripture or Christian theology, for such inconsistency would have amounted to "a fault of logic and of taste." Thus, when the narrator asks about the punishment of the soul after the death of the body, Philosophy acknowledges such punishment but says, "I purpose not now to treat of those" (4:pr.4). Moreover, argues Courcelle, Boethius purposely refrained from citing any of the Neoplatonists who lived after Christ—and who clearly influenced his thought in the ***Consolation***—because the figure of Philosophy he created is, in effect, the representative of Neoplatonic thought: "she is their own philosophy," that which they all have in common.

If this is indeed an accurate statement of Boethius's procedure, we should realize that it does not mean that the ***Consolation*** is thereby a celebration of Neoplatonic thought. Rather, Boethius may well have used philosophy in general and Neoplatonism in particular as a means of justifying the ways of God to man and of making man understand the need to return to God. The ***Consolation*** is without doubt "a theodicy of great power and scope." To assert divine justice in the face of obvious evil, Boethius had to face not only the helplessness and inadequate understanding of man but "the mysteries of divine unity and goodness, of fate and human freedom." Whether or not Boethius sets forth "all that he can see of life and time and eternity," we should recognize that these are indeed the concerns of his discourse.

What is important for Boethius is not to prove the existence of God or to define God. Rather, he intends, first, to show "the existence of a perfect Good which must be identical with God," and, second, to stress the workings of divine order in the universe—the term *ordo,* which describes the same reality as Providence and Fate, permeates the ***Consolation***—and the need for man to participate in this order by returning to God. This return, which is at the heart of both Neoplatonism and Christianity, is not only a major structuring principle of the ***Consolation,*** it is also a major theme. Representing the journey of the mind away from the world and back to God, it may be meaningfully described as a "conversion," in the literal sense of a turning around—here effected by means of philosophy; and the ***Consolation*** itself may be regarded as what Courcelle calls "a dual conversion in three stages," overseen by Plato. First comes knowledge of the self (Book 2); second, knowledge of the purpose of things (Book 3 to 4:pr.5); and third, knowledge of the laws that govern the universe (end of Book 4 and Book 5). The need for this conversion provides the ***Consolation*** with its subject which, though described as "human happiness and the possibility of achieving it in the midst of the suffering and disappointment which play so large a part in every man's experience," may more accurately be considered as the reaffirmation of the point and purpose of the universe and of man's place in God's creation: man's "loving participation in God's divine ordinance of the universe, informed by philosophical study."

The journey that comprises this "loving participation" involves understanding such distractions as Fortune and Fate. Fortune, though appearing in the first three books of the ***Consolation*** as above all harmful and detrimental to man, comes to be seen in the last two books as a principle related to Providence. Fortune—which Boethius distinguishes, initially at least, from Fate—is "merely an instrument in God's hand for the correction and education of man, and however harmful and capricious she may appear to his limited intelligence, she is really good in whatever guise she comes." Although Boethius's words may be thought to "constitute a polemical treatise against Fortune," it is clear that Fortune changes in the course of the ***Consolation*** from a mythological and allegorical figure to a philosophical concept. In making this revision of Fortune, Boethius is unique. Although Christian authorities had forbidden belief in the goddess Fortune and had even hesitated to employ the name itself, the ***Consolation*** not only addresses the issues of the nature of Fortune and its role in creation, it provides for the Western world the definitive way of regarding Fortune. In a similar demythologizing of Fate, a familiar figure in Greek myth and a popular folk deity, Boethius transforms this figure into a philosophical concept. And, following such Neoplatonists as Proclus, he links Fate with Providence and shows it to be subject to God.

Boethius's conception of God in the ***Consolation*** may likewise stem from various manifestations of deity in classical metaphysics. This God resembles Plato's Demiurge, Aristotle's Unmoved Mover, and Plotinus's One; He is the Supreme Orderer and the Highest Good, as well as Reality itself. While this conception is by and large Neoplatonic, it is also decidedly Christian inasmuch as it identifies God with Love. Perhaps, since God was not his subject any more than theology was, Boethius purposely refrained from limiting his principle of deity to that of any one religion or philosophical system. But at the same time it is clear that the God of the ***Consolation*** evades all of man's categories. As Gilson writes about Boethius's view, "when man has said all he can about God, he has not yet attained what God is."

For Boethius, what one can say about God applies less to God Himself than to His manner of administering the world. And God is finally best referred to as Love (*Amor*), the creative force and principle of harmony in the universe. This is the Love celebrated in at least five key poems as that which rules the sun and the other stars. While the notion of Love as a cosmic principle and a natural force may simply represent "that amalgamation of Greek and Christian thought which is so familiar to any reader of patristic texts," in identifying God as Love and Providential order as an expression of Love, Boethius "was probably inspired by the Christian faith and the spiritual climate of Christian reflection about the love of God." Moreover, in framing his discussion of the *summum bonum,* the central argument of the ***Consolation,*** with two poems on love—2:m.8 and 3:m.12—Boethius emphasizes that the highest good is not "an abstract cosmological force" but "an active outgoing love, descending from heaven to earth." This love is ideally common and mutual, embracing both God and man, who must recognize his need and responsibility to respond to it and participate in it. Man's desire for the good and his expression of this desire, his return to that which gave him being, are thus to be understood as manifestations of love, as well as of the search for truth.

Thomas F. Curley III (essay date 1984)

SOURCE: "How to Read the *Consolation of Philosophy,*" in *Interpretation: A Journal of Bible & Theology,* Vol. 14, Nos. 2-3, May-September, 1986, pp. 211-63.

[*In the following essay, written shortly before the critic's death in 1984, Curley analyzes the philosophical content, structure, and genre of the* Consolation of Philosophy.]

I. INTRODUCTORY

Boethius' ***Consolation of Philosophy,*** for centuries one of the most widely read and revered books in the West, is now little more than a historical curiosity. Most, but not all, educated people have heard of it; some have read it; very few seem to like it. But the reasons for the work's neglect are more significant than our common twentieth-century amnesia toward what one might term "the tradition". In the first place we are separated by a centuries-long tradition of philosophy from the intellectual context which gave rise to Boethius' synthesis of Plato and Aristotle. Minds such as Descartes and Kant have so altered the cast of western thinking that it is all but impossible, at least at first glance, to take Boethius seriously as a philosopher. What is more, the two dominant tendencies of twentieth century philosophy, the analytic school in England and America, and the continental schools of existentialism and phenomenology, are in radical disagreement with Boethius' most basic assumptions.

What, for instance, would A. J. Ayer, the author of a short and popularly accessible philosophic manifesto, comparable in scope to the Boethian text, make of the following exchange between the character Boethius and Dame Philosophy at the very beginning of the work:

> Tum illa: Huncine, inquit, mundum temerariis agi fortuitisque casibus putas an ullum credis ei regimen inesse rationis? Atqui, inquam, nullo existimaverim modo ut fortuita temeritate tam certa moveantur, verum operi suo conditorem praesidere deum scio nec umquam fucrit dies qui me ab hac sententiae veritate depellat (Bk. I, pr. 6, 3-4).

> (Then she said, "Do you think that this world is driven by reckless and haphazard chance or do you believe there to be any rational direction to it?" And I said, "But in no way would I think that such regular phaenomena are moved by reckless haphazard; rather I know that the creator god presides over his handiwork, and there will never be a day which might drive me from the truth of this opinion.")

Because Ayer dismisses metaphysical questions and answers as not only wrong but nonsensical, he could continue reading only on the assumption that he was perusing a text indicative of the philosophical errors of the past.

Likewise, what would Sartre, who in an accessible manifesto of his own defines existentialism as the conviction that existence precedes essence, make of the following argument in which existence is treated as a predicate like any other and derivable from the essence of the good:

> Quo fit ut, si in quolibet genere imperfectum quid esse videatur, in eo perfectum quoque aliquid esse necesse sit; etenim perfectione sublata unde illud quod imperfectum perhibetur exstiterit ne fingi quidem potest (Bk. III, pr. 10, 4).

> (Thus it happens that, if there should be seen to be any imperfect example of a given genus, it is necessary that there should also be a perfect example of that genus; for it is impossible to imagine whence that which is considered imperfect might come to exist, if the perfect is removed.)

In Sartre's case as well further reading could only proceed on the assumption that he was engaged in the merely academic exercise of becoming proficient in the history of philosophy.

Thus there exist significant intellectual differences to account for our neglect of Boethius' text and our failure to appreciate it. I suspect, however, that other equally important factors come into play. The ***Consolatio,*** in addition to being a work of philosophy, is also an intricately crafted work of literature: a dramatic dialogue between two fictional characters composed in alternating verse and prose. This blending of poetry and philosophy, categories we tend to keep strictly apart, is as great an obstacle to our understanding Boethius' intentions as is the incompatibility of his philosophical presuppositions with those of the twentieth century. We pay lip service to the clarity of certain philosophers' prose (that of David Hume and A. J. Ayer, for example) and to the wit and style of others' (Kierkegaard's and Nietzsche's, for instance); but in fact we believe that philosophic exposition is one thing, poetic invention quite another. We simply do not know how to read philosophy as poetry, or poetry as philosophy, which is precisely the response demanded by Boethius' text.

This distance from the work, both intellectual and aesthetic, clarifies the nature and limitations of Boethian scholarship in the last century. Modern research into the ***Consolatio*** may be dated from the publication in 1877 of Hermann Usener's *Anecdoton Holderi.* In this monograph the author dismisses the ***Consolatio*** as an unoriginal compilation of Aristotelian and Neoplatonic sources. Usener grants as Boethius' own an introduction (up through Bk.

II, pr. 4, 38) and the metra, which he rates very low; otherwise he sees the text as an amateurish pastiche of philosophical arguments better expressed elsewhere. On the one hand, Usener's approach was obviously determined by the twin tendencies of nineteenth century German scholarship: analysis and "Quellenforschung"; on the other, such blindness to the nature and merits of the text can only be explained on the basis of a deep lack of sympathy with Boethius' philosophic and poetic stance.

One might characterize twentieth-century scholarship on the ***Consolatio*** as constituting two possible responses to Usener's thesis: defense and illustration of the integrity and originality of the work or increasingly sophisticated investigation of the sources exploited by Boethius in the composition of his text. The first camp is led by E. K. Rand, who in 1904 ["On the Composition of Boethius' *Consolation Philosophiae, Harvard Studies in Classical Philology,* 15, (1904)] produced a thorough and reasoned rebuttal of Usener's point of view. His lead was followed by such scholars as Klingner and Reichenberger, who made considerable progress towards demonstrating the very complex structure of Boethius' work and the methods by which he made his sources his own. On the other hand scholars such as Courcelle, Silk, and most recently, Gruber, have brought the analysis of the influences on Boethius to the point where it is now clear that his command of his sources was extraordinary. If Boethius was a mere compiler, he was at least a compiler of the first rank.

Thus the result of the last century's researches into the ***Consolatio*** is, as often in the world of scholarship, the conclusion that the debate over Boethius' originality was a false question. It has turned out that in almost every line of both the prose and verse sections Boethius can be detected echoing, if not quoting, the literature and philosophy of the past; nonetheless it has become increasingly clear that he has shaped his material into a complex pattern of his own contrivance. The question then becomes, what are the dynamics of this curious work, so removed from us both philosophically and aesthetically. And in recent years a small group of scholars have begun to address this issue. L. Alfonsi has traced the relationship between the personal and the universal as dramatized in the dialogue between Boethius and Dame Philosophy. More recently still, F. Anne Payne [in *Chaucer and Menippean Satire,* 1981] has attempted to read the work as an example of Menippean Satire, while Anna Crabbe [in *Boethius: His Life, Thought, and Influence,* ed. Margaret Gibson, 1981] has sought the key to the work in its essential eclecticism which embraces and transcends the responses to adversity of such exemplars as Ovid, Cicero, Seneca, Socrates, and St. Augustine.

The problem with this trend of criticism is that its practitioners have either limited themselves to one aspect of Boethius' manifold text or have become tendentious in championing an idiosyncratic approach to the work. What has been most lacking is a comprehensive approach which takes into account both the philosophic and literary aspects of the work and seeks to demonstrate how they inform each other. This paper is intended, at least in part, to fill that gap.

Because the ***Consolatio,*** as many readers have pointed out, is so eclectic, I shall take this very eclecticism as my starting point and organize my argument around three aspects of the text's diversity. First of all, since the work is a philosophical treatise, it is necessary to clarify the structure and drift of its philosophical content. I shall not be concerned to label the provenance of this or that argument, a task largely completed by other more competent scholars, most notably, Gruber. I will, however, endeavor to make clear the structure into which Boethius has molded his Platonic, Aristotelian, and Neoplatonic materials. Second, since Boethius chose to cast his work in the form of a dialogue, the implications of this choice on the philosophical content must be gauged before a full understanding of the work can be achieved. To do so I shall have both to glance at the tradition of philosophic dialogue in antiquity, most importantly Plato and Augustine, and to uncover the dynamics of interaction between the character Boethius and Dame Philosophy. Finally, since the ***Consolatio*** is an example of that curious genre, Menippean Satire, it is incumbent on me at least to hazard a response to the question why Boethius chose to write a philosophic dialogue in the very artificial form of alternating verse and prose.

II. THE PHILOSOPHICAL CONTENT

The ***Consolation of Philosophy*** is essentially a dramatized therapy. Boethius is smitten with despair over his fall from fortune and Dame Philosophy endeavors to restore her pupil to a state of insight and calm. As first step on the way to Boethius' cure is the diagnosis which Dame Philosophy performs in Book I, prose 6. At the end of her examination of the patient, she summarizes his illness under three points:

> Nam quoniam tui oblivione confunderis, et exsulem te et exspoliatum propriis bonis esse doluisti; quoniam vero quis sit rerum finis ignoras, nequam homines atque nefarios potentes felicesque arbitraris; quoniam vero quibus gubernaculis mundus regatur oblitus es, has fortunarum vices aestimas sine rectore fluitare: magnae non ad morbum modo, verum ad interitum quoque causae (Bk. I, pr. 6, 19-19).

> (For since you have been confused by forgetfulness of your self, you have complained that you are in exile and dispossessed of your own goods; and since you do not know the purpose of things, you think that worthless and evil men are powerful and happy; and since you have forgotten by what means the universe is governed, you judge that these changes of fortune are in flux and without any direction: great causes not only of illness but of death as well.)

This passage is clearly meant to be programmatic for the structure of Books II through V. The second book is concerned with loosening Boethius' attachment to the gifts of fortune and, as Dame Philosophy repeatedly points out, Boethius' vulnerability to the rise and fall of fortune is occasioned by his lack of a sense of self:

> Quid igitur, o mortales, extra petitis intra vos positam felicitatem? Error vos inscitiaque confundit. Ostendam breviter tibi summae cardinem felicitatis. Estne aliquid tibi te ipso pretiosius? Nihil, inquies. Igitur si tui compos fueris, possidebis quod nec tu amittere umquam velis nec fortuna possit auferre (Bk. II, pr. 4, 22-23).

> (Thus, o mortals, why do you seek outside yourselves the happiness which is placed within yourselves. Error and ignorance are confusing you. I shall briefly demonstrate to you the essence of the greatest happiness. Is there anything more precious to you than yourself? "Nothing," you say. Thus if you should be in possession of yourself, you will be in possession of that which neither you would wish to lose nor fortune be able to remove.)

Thus Book II in its long discussion of the various gifts of fortune is in fact an attempt to restore to Boethius a strong sense of identity. Likewise, Book III seeks to make clear to Boethius the existence of the "summum bonum" which is the "telos" of all things. First by a kind of "via negativa" which demonstrates that wealth, fame, power, and pleasure cannot embody the highest good, and then in a more positive manner, Dame Philosophy elucidates the identity of God, the good, and happiness. Finally, Books IV and V seek as it were to justify the ways of God to man. The nature of the human self and of God as the goal of all things has been established in Books II and III; in these final two books the relationship between these two entities is depicted in all its complexity, as the dialogue ranges over such topics as theodicy, free will, determinism, and providence. Thus the most readily apparent structure of the ***Consolatio*** is the rather straightforward succession of three arguments calculated to address the three aspects of Boethius' illness as diagnosed in the first book: ignorance of self, of the "summum bonum", and of the relationship between the two.

But the situation is far more complex than these preliminary observations might indicate. As many scholars have pointed out, the mode or style of argumentation in the ***Consolatio*** changes as Dame Philosophy procedes in her exposition. F. Anne Payne's summary is a good example of such analysis:

> The names I give the four sections of her (i.e. Philosophy's) argument—Cynic (Bk. II-Bk. III, pr. 9), Platonic (Bk. III, m.9-Bk. IV, pr. 5), Aristotelian (Bk. IV, pr.6-Bk. V, m.I), and Augustinian (Bk. V, prs. 2-6)—are not intended to indicate Boethius' literal sources for these sections, but rather techniques and points of view to which the sections allude. The analogies between Lucian and the first section have already been discussed. The Platonic section begins with a paraphrase of Plato's *Timaeus,* and two proses of the discussion on evil contain a paraphrase of the *Gorgias*. The Aristotelian section ends with an allusion to Aristotle's definition of chance. The debate about the relation of foreknowledge and free will in the final section of the ***Consolation,*** which contains one indirect allusion to the *City of God* (Bk. V, pr. 4), is a debate always associated with Augustine.

The question then arises, how is this philosophic eclecticism rendered coherent?

One answer is that the ***Consolation*** may be seen as a succession of three increasingly lofty and comprehensive disquisitions on the order of the universe. In Books I and II, the ways of the world are viewed as they appear to the eyes of the unregenerate human soul, that is, under the aspect of "fortuna". In Book III, the way is opened up towards a clearer vision of the universal order, that is, under its aspect of "fatum"; and in Book IV, fate's determination of events is demonstrated with great rigor and detail. Finally, in Book V, the discussion seeks to rise beyond the merely human and rational point of view and to adumbrate God's own perspective on the universe, that "providentia" which is the viewpoint of the "nunc stans" of eternity. Thus, in addition to what one might term the "personal" structure of the work, that by which the text is organized according to the personal dilemma of Boethius, there is a second structural device, the cosmological, which articulates the text according to three aspects of cosmological order: "fortuna", "fatum", and "providentia".

Finally there is a third set of structures at work in the text, that which I choose to call the "epistemological" and which is the most important of all three structural systems. At prose 4 in Book V, in her attempt to explain divine providence, Dame Philosophy makes the following observation:

> . . . Omne . . . quod cognoscitur non secundum sui vim sed secundum cognoscentium potius comprehenditur facultatem (Bk. V, pr. 4, 25).

> (Everything which is known is understood not according to its own power but according to the capability of those knowing it.)

She then goes on to enumerate the four principal "faculties" of knowledge:

> Sensus . . . figuram in subiecta materia constitutam, imaginatio vero solam sine materia iudicat figuram; ratio vero hanc quoque transcendit speciemque ipsam quae singularibus inest universali consideratione perpendit. Intellegentiae vero celsior oculus exsistit; supergressa namque universitatis ambitum ipsam illam simplicem formam pura mentis acie contuetur (Bk. V, pr. 4, 28-30).

> (The senses judge of form embodied in underlying matter, the imagination judges of the mere form without matter; reason transcends even this latter form and by a universal meditation weighs the idea itself which is present in individual things. But the eye of intellection exists on an even higher plane, for it transcends the ambit of the universe and with the pure vision of the mind contemplates that simple idea itself.)

Although this hierarchy of knowledge is articulated only

towards the very end of the text, upon reflection it becomes clear that these four categories have provided a structural scheme for the work parallel to the two already described.

The fact that the work opens with Boethius writing an elegiac lament in which the physical details of his decay are dwelt upon:

> Intempestivi funduntur vertice cani
> et tremit effeto corpore laxa cutis (Bk. I, m.I, 11-12).
>
> (Prematurely white hair covers my head and the loosened skin of my weakened body shakes.)

indicates that he is mired in the material world, reacting to the universe mainly by means of his senses. As token of this first sensual stage of perception Dame Philosophy adapts herself to Boethius' capacities and responds to his condition in terms which he can comprehend, namely, those of touch. Thus she diagnoses Boethius' initial silence and causes him to recognize her for what she is, all by touch:

> Cumque me non modo tacitum sed elinguem prorsus mutumque vidisset, ammovit pectori meo leniter manum et . . . oculosque meos fletibus undantes contracta in rugam veste siccavit (Bk. I, pr. 2, 5-7).
>
> (When she perceived that I was not merely silent but mute and quite incapable of speech, she lightly touched my breast with her hand and with a portion of her garment drawn into a fold she dried my eyes which were overflowing with tears.)

The realistic detail of the phrase, "contracta in rugam veste", is very rare in the ***Consolatio*** and is appropriate only at this preliminary stage of "sensus".

In Book II Dame Philosophy begins to employ the next faculty in her epistemological hierarchy, the imagination. Whereas in the first book attention was focused on the particulars of Boethius' immediate situation, in the second book Philosophy leads her pupil towards a consideration of fortune in general, a step which can be taken only with the aid of imagination. The most striking example of this strategy occurs in prose 2 where Philosophy puts on the mask of "Fortuna" and interrogates Boethius on his claim to the gifts of fortune:

> Vellem autem pauca tecum Fortunae ipsius verbis agitare; tu igitur an ius postulet animadverte (Bk. II, pr. 2, 1).
>
> (I would like to discuss a few matters with you in the words of Fortuna herself. Therefore consider whether her claim is just.)

In fact Philosophy is here using one of the imagination's greatest achievements, the theater, to effect her own purposes. This recourse to the imagination is further underscored when, during her speech in the persona of Fortuna, she alludes to various works of the imagination such as legend, tragedy, and epic: . . .

> Were you unware of Croesus, king of the Lydians, an object of fear to Cyrus and then an object of pity, who, when handed over to the flames of the pyre, was saved by a miraculous shower of rain? And it has not escaped your notice, has it, that Paulus shed pious tears over the misfortunes of the Persian king, whom he himself had captured? What else does the shouting of tragedy bewail but fortune overturning prosperous kingdoms with a sudden blow? As a student, didn't you learn that "two jars, the one of evils and the other of goods" stand in Jove's threshold?

And throughout the book Philosophy constantly urges Boethius to imagine the situation of the rich man, the powerful man, the famous man, and so on, as means towards understanding the vanity of human fortune.

At the beginning of Book III the transition from "imaginatio" to "ratio" is signalled by the following statement by the character Boethius:

> O, inquam, summum lassorum solamen animorum, quam tu me vel sententiarum pondere vel canendi etiam iucunditate refovisti, adeo ut iam me posthac imparem fortunae ictibus esse non arbitrer! Itaque remedia quae paulo acriora esse dicebas non modo non perhorresco, sed audiendi avidus vehementer efflagito (Bk. II, pr. 1, 2).
>
> ("O greatest comfort of afflicted minds," I said, "how you have restored me, whether by the weight of your proposition or the delight of your singing, so that I do not think that hereafter I shall be unequal to the blows of fortune. Therefore, those remedies, which you said were slightly more bitter, not only do I not fear them, in fact I am strongly desirous of hearing them.")

The harsher remedies of strict reason are employed throughout Books III and IV to demonstrate the existence of the "summum bonum" and to elucidate its relation to the universe in general and to man in particular. In this section Boethius' borrowings from Plato are particularly frequent and particularly appropriate. The Platonic imagery of metrum 9 of Book III and the arguments drawn from the *Gorgias* in Book IV are incorporated into a rational explanation of the universal scheme of things. Furthermore, not only are the instruments of reason employed in this section, they are also reflected on in a critical way, in a fashion parallel to the criticisms of poetry to be found in Books I and II.

Finally, Book V constitutes an attempt to explain to the highest faculty of human understanding (ratio) the nature and scope of divine understanding (intellegentia). We have been led through the various stages of human knowledge: "sensus", "imaginatio", and "ratio"; Dame Philosophy now seeks to communicate to Boethius some indication of how the universe appears to the eyes of eternity. The exposition remains strictly rational in form, but because a real-

The crew of Ulysses and Circe, from Jean de Meun's prose version of the Consolation of Philosophy *(ca. 1500).*

ity beyond the humanly rational is being described, there is a religious, almost mystical, tone to Philosophy's speech, which breaks forth, for instance, in the final lines of the work:

> Magna vobis est, si dissimulare non vultis, necessitas indicta probitatis, cum ante oculos agitis iudicis cuncta cernentis (Bk. V, pr. 6, 48).

> (Unless you wish to pretend otherwise, a great necessity of acting virtuously has been pronounced to you, since you act under the gaze of a judge who discerns all things.)

Thus the philosophical content of the ***Consolatio*** is organized according to three different but parallel sets of categories. First of all Philosophy's exposition is structured to correspond to Boethius' particular situation: she first restores his sense of self, then points to the end or "telos" of things, and finally demonstrates the relationship between the individual human reality and the Alpha-Omega of the universe, God. Second, the content also falls into the three-fold division of "fortuna", "fatum", and "providentia". That is, the same cosmos is portrayed under three different lights: that of the human being as possessor of "sensus" and "imaginatio", that of the human as rational animal, and that of God as immediate and all-encompassing knower of the universe. Finally, these personal and cosmological sets of categories are set in relief by a four-fold epistemological structure: "sensus", "imaginatio", "ratio", and "intellegentia". The human being, as a human, has access to the first three modes of knowledge; the fourth can only be hinted at by the highest means at hand, namely, the rational.

The common purpose of all three sets of categories is to cure Boethius, to effect a conversion, or turning about, of his soul. The work is entitled a "Consolation"; it is in fact a "therapy". But it is a very different kind of therapy of the soul from that most familiar to us in the twentieth century, that is, psychoanalysis. Whereas in the contemporary analyst's office the patient does all the talking, in Boethius' prison cell Dame Philosophy is the principal interlocutor; and whereas modern analysis proceeds on the assumption that the higher faculties of imagination and reason are explicable in terms of unconscious drives and therefore reducible to the rank of "epiphaenomena" of "sensus", Dame Philosophy effects her cure of Boethius' soul by leading him upward from the senses, to the imagination, to reason, and at last points to the ultimate reality, "intellegentia". The problems and dilemmas of one level are resolved by proceeding upward to the next level rather than by descending backwards to a lower level. This procedure is most clearly set forth in the crucial step from "ratio" to "intellegentia". Boethius has just formulated his inability to maintain the seemingly contradictory propositions of "providentia" and human free will; Philosophy responds by stating that a higher vantage point must be reached before this contradiction can be resolved:

> Cuius caliginis causa est quod humanae ratiocinationis motus ad divinae praescientiae simplicitatem non potest ammoveri; quae si ullo modo cogitari quest, nihil prorsus relinquetur ambigui (Bk. V, pr. 4, 2).

> (The cause of this obscurity is the fact that the impulse of the human power to reason cannot reach the simplicity of divine foreknowledge; if this latter could in any way be conceived, absolutely nothing would remain unclear.)

Nonetheless, it is important to note that although Philosophy resolves the conflicts of one level by appealing to the next faculty up in the hierarchy, the lower and intermediate levels are not rendered insignificant in the light of "intellegentia" or "providentia". Rather, throughout the work Philosophy is careful to accommodate her mode of discourse to the condition of Boethius' soul. What is more, the whole process is based on the assumption that although a given level surpasses that below it, nonetheless that lower level is encompassed and perfected within the wider scope of the higher:

> Superior comprehendendi vis amplectitur inferiorem, inferior vero ad superiorem nullo modo consurgit. Neque enim sensus aliquid extra materiam valet vel universales species imaginatio contuetur vel ratio capit simplicem formam; sed intellegentia quasi desuper spectans concepta forma quae subsunt etiam cuncta diiudicat, sed eo modo quo formam ipsam, quae nulli alii nota esse poterat, comprehendit (Bk. V, pr. 4, 31-32)

> (The higher faculty of understanding embraces the lower; but the lower can in no way rise towards the higher. For sense perception is good for nothing apart from matter, nor does the imagination contemplate universal categories, nor does reason grasp the pure form; but "intellegentia", as if looking down from above, both perceives the form and also discerns everything which lies below, but in the same manner in which it comprehends the form itself, which was incapable of being known to any of the other faculties.)

It is precisely in this harmony of all aspects of the cosmos: of the human and the divine, of the temporal and the eternal, of becoming and being, of change and order, that the central point of the ***Consolatio*** as a work of philosophy lies. This harmony is not achieved through the blurring of distinctions, it consists, in fact, of a hierarchical articulation of the various aspects of the universe. The particular beauty of this hierarchy is that, although Philosophy insists on a strict protocol in the relation of lower to higher, nonetheless the lower is never completely jettisoned, rather it is embraced and validated within the context of the higher.

Thus Philosophy has a double task: to make manifest the divine order in the apparent flux of the world and to validate human striving within the order thus revealed. Thus double task is indicated by certain striking verbal echoes in the text. For instance, at the end of the first book, in which the interlocutors have been introduced and the nature of Boethius' illness has been diagnosed,

Philosophy gives her "alumnus" straightforward moral counsel:

> Tu quoque si vis
> lumine claro
> cernere verum,
> tramite recto
> carpere callem:
> gaudia pelle,
> pelle timorem
> spemque fugato
> nec dolor adsit (Bk. I, m. 7, 20-28).
>
> (If you, too, desire to discern the truth with clear vision and to make your way along the straight path, cast out joys, cast out fear, put hope to flight, nor let sorrow be present.)

This stoical warning against the power of the passions to cloud intellectual vision, appropriate to Boethius at this stage of dismay and self-pity, is turned on its head in the final sentences of Philosophy's disquisition on the harmony of divine "providentia" and human free will, where she insists on the validity of human striving within the context of divine order:

> Quae cum ita sint, manet intemerata mortalibus arbitrii libertas nec iniquae leges solutis omni necessitate voluntatibus praemia poenasque proponunt. . . . Nec frustra sunt in deo positae spes precesque, quae cum rectae sunt inefficaces esse non possunt. Aversamini igitur vitia, volite virtutes, ad rectas spes animum sublevate, humiles preces in excelsa porrigite (Bk. V, pr. 6, 44-47).
>
> (Since this is the case, human free will remains inviolate nor do laws unfairly propose rewards and punishment for wills freed from all necessity. . . . Nor are hopes and prayers, placed in God, in vain; as long as they are correct, they cannot be ineffectual. Therefore avoid vices, cultivate virtues, lift up your mind towards proper hopes, extend humble prayers on high.)

By way of summary, one might well point out that this central message of the work, the essential harmony between the microcosm and the macrocosm, is reflected in the relation among the three parallel structures of the work's philosophical content. The first structure is based on Boethius' three points of ignorance: of self, of the "telos" of things, and of the means by which the cosmos is governed, and as such may be termed the "personal". The second structure views the world under three aspects: "fortuna", "fatum", and "providentia", and can thus be properly labeled the "cosmic". The third structure, that of "sensus", "imaginatio", "ratio", and "intellegentia", is clearly epistemological and may be seen as the harmony of the first two structures, the personal and the cosmic. For the concerns of the microcosm, man can only be seen as in harmony with the laws of the macrocosm, the universe, when the possible epistemological relations between man and cosmos are defined, distinguished, and understood.

III. THE DIALOGUE FORM

But this philosophical content is couched in the form of a dialogue, and what is more, in the form of a very peculiar kind of dialogue. First of all, the setting, though deducible from certain scattered hints within the text, is never clearly indicated. Because Boethius at one point says to Philosophy

> Et quid, inquam, tu in has exsilii nostri solitudines, o omnium magistra virtutum, supero cardine delapsa venisti? (Bk. I, pr. 3, 3)
>
> (And why, I said, have you, O teacher of all virtues, descended from on high to enter into the loneliness of my exile?);

because at another point he gestures towards his surroundings with the rhetorical question

> Haecine est bibliotheca, quam certissimam tibi sedem nostris in laribus ipsa delegeras, in qua mecum saepe residens de humanarum divinarumque rerum scientia disserebas? (Bk. I, pr. 4, 3)
>
> (Is this the library which you yourself chose as your most fixed abode in my household, in which you often used to sit with me and discourse on the knowledge of things human and divine?);

and because at the end of his "defense" before Philosophy, as if before a court (Bk. I, pr. 4), he states

> Nunc quingentis fere passuum milibus procul muti atque indefensi ob studium propensius in senatum morti proscriptionique damnamur (Bk. I, pr. 4, 36).
>
> (Now about fifty miles away, unheard and without defense, I am condemned to death and proscription on account of my too great zeal on behalf of the senate.);

we infer that the setting is a prison cell, or some place where Boethius is being held under house arrest, at some distance from Ravenna, Theodoric's capital in Italy. And our ancient testimonia corroborate these hints within the text: it seems that Boethius fell from Theodoric's favor when he defended a fellow senator, Albinus, who was being prosecuted for treason. Boethius himself was soon accused of the same crime, tried and convicted in absentia, and executed in 524 A.D. Thus the reader is aware that Boethius is in prison, under sentence of death, alone, and in exile; but we are never told for how long or where Boethius has been imprisoned, nor when he expected to die, as we are, for instance, in the case of the most obvious model for Boethius' text, Plato's *Phaedo*. This vagueness of setting, with its associations of solitude, exile, alienation, and impending doom, is clearly meant to make identification with the character Boethius all the more easy. It renders him an everyman, lost and out of touch with his real self and purpose.

Now, the very mention of the "character Boethius" raises

the question: where is Boethius in the text? Our sources and the manuscript tradition assure us that the author of the *Consolatio* is indeed the historical Anicius Manlius Severinus Boethius, an orphaned member of the Roman senatorial aristocracy, who was adopted by the Symmachi and grew up giving every evidence of extraordinary literary and intellectual ability. He married the daughter of his adoptive father and had two sons by her. While pursuing a political career as a high official under Theodoric, he conceived the enormous project of translating the respective oeuvres of Plato and Aristotle, producing commentaries on them, and harmonizing the two systems of thought. In addition to the *Consolatio* there remain extant a few theological treatises, a textbook on music, and a translated introduction to Aristotle's *Organon*, which seems to represent as far as he progressed in his lifelong project before his early death. Thus "Boethius" is the author of the text. And because the text is such a highly wrought object, combining all manner of discourse in the alternating verse and prose of Menippean Satire, one can say something about the author based on the fact of the text. He must therefore have been extraordinarily learned, especially for this time. Not only does he exhibit a command of all possible Latin prose styles and meters, he also displays an acquaintance with Greek philosophy, not only with the Neoplatonism of late antiquity but with Plato and Aristotle as well, a phenomenon rare in an age when knowledge of Greek in the West had all but disappeared. In fact, the author Boethius stands as a lonely last citadel of the Greco-Roman tradition before western Europe enters definitively into what we rightly or wrongly term "The Dark Ages". Thus the first answer to the question of Boethius' presence in the work is that he is the author, heir by birth, breeding, and education to the twin tradition of ancient philosophy and literature.

But Boethius the author is not the only Boethius present in the text. Boethius the narrator of his encounter with Dame Philosophy and Boethius the character within that narration constitute two further personae of the author. This double aspect of Boethius within the text, as narrator and as character, makes for certain striking effects. Thus the work opens with an elegiac poem spoken in the first person:

> Carmina qui quondam studio florente peregi,
> flebilis, heu, maestos cogor inire modos (Bk. I, m. 1, 1-2).

> (I, who in my youthful zeal composed verses, am now forced tearfully to begin sad lamentations.)

The reader naturally assumes that the speaker is the author, especially since the voice contrasts its unhappy present with a pleasant past; but at the beginning of the first prose section one discovers that the voice pronouncing the poem was being quoted by the narrator-voice of the whole work:

> Haec dum mecum tacitus ipse reputarem querimoniamque lacrimabilem stili officio signarcm . . . (Bk. I, pr. 1, 1).

> (While I silently thought these things over with myself and inscribed my tearful lament by means of a stylus . . .)

These two passages, the first couplet of the metrum and the first clause of the prose section, taken together express the complexity of the Boethian presence within the text. First of all, the character Boethius has a past, a history which has brought him to the point of despair expressed in the opening elegy. Second, upon hearing the narrative voice at the beginning of the prose section, we realize that the character Boethius also has a future ahead of him, a development which will transform the character into the narrator. The distance to be traveled in the passage from the former condition to the latter is emphasized throughout the first book. Thus the narrator describes the character's elegy as a "querimoniam lacrimabilem"; likewise the narrator dismisses the character's defense and appeal to God (Bk. I, pr. 4 & m. 5) as mere barking:

> Haec ubi continuato dolore delatravi . . . (Bk. I, pr. 5, 1)

> (When I had barked all that with uninterrupted self-pity . . .)

Clearly the distraught and preoccupied character has a long way to go before attaining the firm calm of the narrator.

Finally, the emphasis within the text upon writing as opposed to speech serves a double purpose, illustrative of the relationship between Boethius the character and Boethius the narrator. On the one hand the description of the interaction between the elegiac Muses and the character expresses his passivity at this stage of despair: both the character and the narrator depict the Muses as dictating a discourse which Boethius merely copies down:

> Ecce mihi lacerae dictant scribenda Camenae (Bk. I, m. 1, 3).

> (Behold the mourning Muses dictate what I am to write.)

> Quae ubi poeticas Musas vidit nostro assistentes toro fletibusque meis verba dictantes . . . (Bk. I, pr. 1, 7)

> (When she saw the poetic Muses standing by my bed and dictating words to my tears . . .)

This passivity, whereby the character Boethius merely transcribes the words of others is strongly contrasted with the more active response demanded of Boethius by Dame Philosophy. After routing the elegiac Muses, her first action is to cure Boethius' blindness and dumbness, thus enabling him to become an active partner in the dialogue which will constitute his therapy (see Bk. I, pr. 2, 1-7, & pr. 3, 1-3). This transition from written poetry to spoken dialogue, parallel to the development of Boethius the character into Boethius the narrator, is reminiscent of the theme and dynamics of Plato's *Phaedrus,* which may well have been the source of this motif in the ***Consolatio***.

But it is important to note that in this dichotomy between written verse and spoken prose, the former element is not simply negated in the face of the latter. The fairly frequent mention of writing and its products (e.g. "stili officio" at Bk. I, pr. 1, 1, & "bibliotheca" at Bk. I, pr. 4, 3) reminds the reader that what he has before him is a written text. In particular the character Boethius' mention of a library surely draws attention to the fact that the text before us is a veritable library, an anthology of all available forms of discourse and philosophic arguments, a "library" which only an author, who had spent much of his life among books, could have composed. Thus in addition to underscoring the evolution of Boethius the character into Boethius the narrator, the motif of written poetry versus spoken dialogue also hints at the further evolution of Boethius into the author of the poem which is the ***Consolatio***.

To sum up the complex presence of Boethius in the ***Consolatio,*** one might say that the author of the text assumes the persona of the narrator in order to portray the story of the character. The character is pictured at the beginning of the text as indulging in poetry; the author of the text is obviously a poet, for the text itself constitutes a poem. But these two forms of poetry are very different and much of the dynamics of the ***Consolatio*** has to do with the process whereby Boethius the character develops to the point where he is identical with Boethius the narrator and foreshadows the figure of Boethius the author. In other words, Boethius must undergo the therapy of philosophy before he can handle narrative prose or imagistic poetry in other than self-destructive ways.

Thus the dialogue in the ***Consolatio*** must be viewed as taking place between the character Boethius and Dame Philosophy, as reported by the narrator Boethius, and as fashioned by the poet Boethius. What then are we to make of the other participant in the dialogue, Dame Philosophy? She is, first of all, the voice of being, eternity, and truth, in contrast with the character Boethius, the mouthpiece of suffering humanity, subject to the vicissitudes of time and the deceptions of appearance. That Dame Philosophy is the spokeswoman for eternity is clear not only from the fact that she guides the character Boethius towards an awareness of being in the midst of becoming but also from the description of her appearance in Book I:

> Astitisse mihi supra verticem visa est mulier reverendi admodum vultus, oculis ardentibus et ultra communem hominum valentiam perspicacibus, colore vivido atque inexhausti vigoris, quamvis ita aevi plena foret ut nullo modo nostrae crederetur aetatis (Bk. I, pr. 1, 1).
>
> (There appeared standing above my head a woman of a most dignified aspect, with eyes shining and piercing beyond the usual power of men, with a glowing complexion and inexhaustible strength, although she was of such an age that in no way could it be credited of our life span.)

That Dame Philosophy is both young ("colore vivido atque inexhausti vigoris") and old ("aevi plena") foreshadows her own disquisition on eternity in Book V, where "aeternitas" is defined as:

> interminabilis vitae tota simul et perfecta possessio (Bk. V, pr. 6, 4).
>
> (the completely simultaneous and perfect possession of life without beginning or end.);

that is, a state where all time is contemporaneous. Dame Philosophy's simultaneous youth and age clearly indicates that she embodies eternity's comprehension of all time.

But Dame Philosophy represents not only eternity but also a certain aspect of the character Boethius. This assertion is never explicitly made in the text, but the tradition of philosophic dialogue in antiquity, of which the ***Consolatio*** is the last great example, makes it evident that, when the character Boethius is in conversation with Philosophy, he is in some way talking to himself. At one point in the *Thaeatetus* Socrates describes the process of thinking as follows: . . .

> As a discussion which the soul maintains with itself concerning whatever it is considering. I'm sure I must seem a fool, but it seems to me that the soul, when it is thinking, is engaged in nothing other than talking with itself, asking and answering questions, making claims and denials. And when it comes to a decision, whether slowly or rushing to it quickly, and is in agreement and no longer differs with itself, we call this its judgment. So that I define the process of thought as discourse and judgment as a statement pronounced, not to another nor audibly, but silently and to oneself. But what do you think?

What Boethius has accomplished by introducing the persona of Philosophy is to dramatize this interior dialogue which is thought.

Both the Platonic and, as far as we know, the Aristotelian dialogues portrayed interpersonal dialogue and by and large the ancient tradition followed the same procedure. But in late antiquity there appear certain signs of a preoccupation with intrapersonal dialogue, that is, with thought. The phenomenon exists in Plato, as when Socrates stands meditating outside the house of Agathon (*Symposium* 174d-175b) or when his fellow soldiers take bets on how long he will remain standing, lost in thought (*Symposium* 220cd), but it is always portrayed from the outside, as a withdrawal of the person from interaction with others, never from the inside as a kind of interaction with one's self. However, in later works, such as Marcus Aurelius' *Meditations* . . . , where the author is both speaker and audience, and Plotinus' *Enneads,* which often read like a man thinking aloud, one sees the roots of a systematic portrayal of interior dialogue. A link between these first tentative ventures into the dramatization of thought and its full-blown accomplishment in Boethius is to be found in Augustine's *Soliloquia,* where the author recounts his dialogue with a personified "Ratio", who is explicitly stated to be both a divine figure and an aspect of Augustine himself.

Now if Dame Philosophy is in some way an aspect of Boethius himself, just what aspect is she? Since the author Boethius is the remarkably learned man he was, when he portrays himself as talking to himself, he does so by recording a dialogue between himself and the whole tradition of Greco-Roman philosophy, as he had learned and appropriated it. Thus Dame Philosophy, voice of eternity and aspect of Boethius, is also an image, or icon, representing the centuries-long tradition of thought of which Boethius is the end point. Not only does Dame Philosophy in the course of the dialogue avail herself of every conceivable kind of philosophic argument: Stoic, Platonic, Aristotelian, and Augustinian; but also our first encounter with her in Book I clearly indicates her role as image of the philosophic tradition:

> Vestes erant tenuissimis filis subtili artificio indissolubili materia perfectae, quas, uti post eadem prodente cognovi, suis manibus ipsa texuerat; quarum speciem, veluti fumosas imagines solet, caligo quaedam neglectae vetustatis obduxerat. Harum in extremo margine "Ɖ" Graecum, in supremo vero "È" legebatur intextum atque in utrasque litteras in scalarum modum gradus quidam insigniti videbantur, quibus ab inferiore ad superius elementum esset ascensus. Eandem tamen vestem violentorum quorundam sciderant manus et particulas quas quisque potuit abstulerant. Et dextra quidem eius libellos, sceptrum vero sinistra gestabat (Bk. I, pr. 1, 3-6).

> (Her clothes were made, by subtle craft, of the finest threads of an indissoluble material; and as I later learned from her own lips, she had woven them with her own hands. A certain duskiness of long neglect had darkened their appearance, as is often the case with images smudged with smoke. On the lower hem a Greek "Ɖ", on the upper border a "È" was to be read inwoven; and certain embroidered steps were to be seen between the two letters in the manner of a ladder, by which there was a means of ascent from the lower to the higher letter. But the hands of certain violent individuals had rent this garment and they had taken away those portions that each was able to. Finally, she carried books in her right hand, and in her left she held a scepter.)

Furthermore, Dame Philosophy's explanation of how her garments were torn betrays a critical understanding of the history of ancient philosophy, an understanding quite in accord with Boethius' own life-long task of reconciling the two fountainheads of the tradition, Plato and Aristotle:

> Cuius (Socrates' and/or Plato's) hereditatem cum deinceps Epicureum vulgus ac Stoicum certerique pro sua quisque parte raptum ire molirentur meque reclamantem renitentemque velut in partem praedae traherent, vestem quam meis texueram manibus disciderunt abreptisque ab ea panniculis totam me sibi cessisse credentes abiere (Bk. I, pr. 3, 7).

> When thereafter the Epicurean and Stoic crowd, and others, endeavored, each for his own part, to steal his (Socrates' or Plato's) inheritance and when they were dragging me away as if I were booty and I shouted and struggled against them, they tore the garment which I had woven with my own hands and they went away believing that I had yielded to them the whole garment, when in fact they had only snatched tatters from it.

Thus the figure of Philosophy, like the figure of Boethius, is also multifaceted: she is the voice of eternity, an aspect of Boethius, and a representation of the whole philosophic tradition. This refraction of the interlocutors into several aspects allows for a complex dramatic portrayal of the interior dialogue which is thought, a phenomenon which, from the outside, would appear as distant and opaque as the figure of *the abstracted Socrates*.

That Boethius, as heir to the gregarious tradition of ancient philosophy, which was almost always pursued in the context of human intercourse, be it the agora, the academy, the porch, or the garden, should be so cut off as to take refuge in the dramatization of thought, is perhaps the most poignant aspect of the ***Consolatio***. Comparison with the *Phaedo* will make this point quite clear. Although condemned by the city, Socrates is portrayed as engaging in conversation with family and friends as he prepares to drink the hemlock. In contrast, Boethius has to write his own swan song, for there is no one present to whom he can talk and who might preserve his memory. What is more, this solitude in prison and in the face of death is merely a concrete image of Boethius' essential solitude as someone who had digested and could manipulate the twin tradition of ancient philosophy and poetry at a time when Western Europe had all but forgotten the tradition and was plunging into the simplifications of popularized Christianity.

Now how does this peculiar kind of dialogue play itself out and how does it inform the philosophic content of the work? After the opening elegy the character Boethius falls silent until Philosophy loosens his tongue by her touch; in Book V, after expressing the paradox of maintaining both God's providence and human free will, the character Boethius again falls all but completely silent, while Philosophy delivers her disquisition on eternity which constitutes the end of the work. But these two discourses and their subsequent silences are very different from one another and the process whereby the character Boethius progresses from the former to the later is the history of his progress in the therapy of philosophy.

From beginning to end Boethius the character remains the spokesman for suffering humanity. He bemoans his fall from fortune in the opening elegy and presents his case before Philosophy and God, as if in a court of law, in prose 4 and metrum 5 of the first book. Thereafter, throughout the therapy which Philosophy applies, Boethius continues to insist on, to focus attention on, the plight of man in an apparently unjust universe. In response to Philosophy's prosopopoeia of "Fortuna", in which she challenges Boethius' claim to the gifts of fortune, the character Boethius replies:

Tum ego: Speciosa quidem ista sunt, inquam, oblitaque rhetoricae ac musicae melle dulcedinis tum tantum cum audiuntur oblectant, sed miseris malorum altior sensus est; itaque cum haec auribus insonare desierint insitus animum maeror praegravat (Bk. II, pr. 3, 2).

(And then I said, "Those arguments are indeed splendid and covered as they are with the honey of rhetorical and poetic sweetness they delight as long as they are being heard; but in the case of the wretched the sensation of misfortune lies deeper, and thus, when these arguments cease to ring in their ears, an innate sadness weighs down their mind.")

This elicits from Philosophy a list of the variety of good fortune Boethius has enjoyed, but he responds with the following reformulation of his sense of suffering:

Tum ego: Vera, inquam, commemoras, o virtutum omnium nutrix, nec infitiari possum prosperitatis meae velocissimum cursum. Sed hoc est quod recolentem vehementius coquit; nam in omni adversitate fortunae infelicissimum est genus infortunii fuisse felicem (Bk. II, pr. 4, 1-2).

(And then I said, "What you say is true, O nurse of all the virtues, nor can I deny the swift course of my prosperity. But it is just this very fact which troubles me even more when I look back, for in every adversity of fortune the most unhappy kind of misfortune is to have been happy.")

This in turn moves Philosophy to catalogue the benefits of fortune which Boethius, despite his misery, still enjoys; to which he replies:

Et haereant, inquam, precor; illis namque manentibus, utcumque se res habeant, enatabimus. Sed quantum ornamentis nostris decesserit vides (Bk. II, pr. 4, 10).

(And I said, "I pray that they (the "anchors" of father-in-law, wife, and children) continue to hold, for as long as they remain, whatever the situation is, I shall stay afloat. But you see how much has disappeared of my honors.")

Although he has made some progress:

Et illa: Promovimus, inquit, aliquantum si te nondum totius tuae sortis piget (Bk. II, pr. 4, 11).

(And she said, "we have made a little progress, if you are no longer completely dissatisfied with your lot.")

Boethius the character still insists that Philosophy take his immediate pain seriously.

Likewise, later in Book II, after Philosophy has made clear the vanity of worldly glory, the character Boethius objects that he sought office not for personal glory but in order to exercise virtue:

Tum ego: Scis, inquam, ipsa minimum nobis ambitionem mortalium rerum fuisse dominatam; sed materiam gerendis rebus optavimus, quo ne virtus tacita consenesceret (Bk. II, pr. 7, 1).

(Then I said, "You yourself know that ambition for the things of this world had very little hold over me; rather in the governance of affairs I sought the occasion whereby my virtue might not grow old, passed over in silence.)

To which Philosophy replies that this desire is the last weakness of noble minds, thus acknowledging, with reservation, the validity of certain human aspirations.

After Philosophy has demonstrated the relationship between the false goods of fortune and the true "summum bonum" in Books II and III, the character Boethius stresses his private suffering less and less; but all the same he still continues to focus Philosophy's attention on the apparent contradictions of the human condition. Thus at the opening of Book IV, after admitting the validity of Philosophy's arguments, he claims that the problem of theodicy remains unsolved:

Sed ea ipsa est vel maxima nostri causa maeroris quod, cum rerum bonus rector existat, vel esse omnino mala possint vel impunita praetereant; quod solum quanta dignum sit ammiratione profecto consideras. At huic aliud maius adiungitur; nam imperante florenteque nequitia virtus non solum praemiis caret, verum etiam sceleratorum pedibus subiecta calcatur et in locum facinorum supplicia luit (Bk. IV, pr. 1, 3-4).

(But that is precisely the greatest cause of my grief, that, although there exists a good lord over things, evils are able to exist at all or to go unpunished, which fact alone you yourself judge to be worthy of great wonder. But in addition to this there is something even greater, for, while evil rules and flourishes, not only does virtue go without rewards, but it is even cast at the feet of the wicked and trod upon and it suffers the punishments due to crimes.)

This insistence on taking a paradox of the human condition seriously elicits from Philosophy the Platonic arguments, derived from the *Gorgias,* by which good men are proven to be naturally happy, evil men naturally unhappy. And Boethius the character, while granting Philosophy's points, nonetheless maintains a human, down to earth, attitude towards the issue:

Tum ego: Fateor, inquam, nec iniuria dici video vitiosos, tametsi humani corporis speciem servent, in beluas tamen animorum qualitate mutari; sed quorum atrox scelerataque mens bonorum pernicie saevit, id ipsum eis licere noluissem (Bk. IV, pr. 4, 1).

(Then I said, "I admit and I do not consider that it is said wrongly that the vicious, although they keep the appearance of their human body, are nonetheless transformed into beasts with respect to the quality of their minds. But I would prefer that it not be allowed them that their fierce and criminal intention rage for the destruction of the good.")

Accedo, inquam, sed uti hoc infortunio cito careant patrandi sceleris possibilitate deserti vehementer exopto (Bk. IV, pr. 4, 6).

("I agree", I said, "but I strongly wish that, deprived of the possibility of accomplishing evil, they soon lack this misfortune.")

Tum ego: Cum tuas, inquam, rationes considero, nihil dici verius puto; at si ad hominum iudicia revertar, quis ille est cui non credenda modo sed saltem audienda videantur? (Bk. IV, pr. 4, 26)

(Then I said, "When I consider your reasoning, I think that nothing is more truly said; but if I revert to the judgment of mankind, who is there to whom these arguments would seem not only worthy of belief but even of hearing?")

Soon thereafter Boethius the character asks the decisive question, if the sun shines on good and bad alike, what is the difference between a cosmos ruled by God and a chaotic universe:

Minus etenim mirarer si misceri omnia fortuitis casibus crederem. Nunc stuporem meum deus rector exaggerat. Qui cum saepe bonis iucunda, malis aspera contraque bonis dura tribuat, malis optata concedat, nisi causa deprehenditur, quid est quod a fortuitis casibus differre videatur? (Bk. IV, pr. 5, 5-6)

("I would be less bewildered, if I believed that everything was mixed together randomly. But now the idea of a controlling god increases my bewilderment. Since he often apportions pleasant things for the good and bitter for the bad, but also bestows hardship on the good and their heart's desire to the bad, unless some cause is apprehended, what distinguishes this situation from pure chance?")

This question leads Philosophy into a discussion of providence, fate, fortune, divine predestination, and human free will which will occupy the remaining pages of the text and which represents the height of human understanding of the universe.

Finally, in Book V, first in prose (3) and then in verse (3), the character Boethius restates the human aspect of the work's central problem, how to reconcile divine providence and human free will:

Igitur nec sperandi aliquid nec deprecandi ulla ratio est; quid enim vel speret quisque vel etiam deprecetur quando optanda omnia series indeflexa conectit? (Bk. V, pr. 3. 33)

("Therefore there is no reason to hope for or to seek to avoid anything, for what might anyone hope for or seek to avoid, when an unchangeable order binds all objects of hope together?")

In the verse section he goes a step further and views the problem as one of epistemology:

An nulla est discordia veris
semperque sibi certa cohaerent,
sed mens caecis obruta membris
nequit oppressi luminis igne
rerum tenues noscere nexus?
(Bk. V, m. 3, 6-10)

(Or is there no contradiction between truths and are they firmly connected one with the other, while the mind, buried in the imperceptive limbs of the body, is unable to perceive the subtle interweaving of things by the flame of its buried vision?)

Taken together, prose 3 and verse 3 of Book V parallel prose 4 and verse 5 of Book I. In both passages the character Boethius first explains his dilemma in prose and then again in verse. In fact, the two verse sections are composed in the same meter (Anapestic Dimeter Acatalectic), a particularly striking coincidence, for verse 3 in Book V is the first time Boethius the character has spoken in verse since verse section 5 in Book I. The purpose of this parallelism is to demonstrate that from beginning to end the character Boethius continues to focus on the human point of view in contrast to Philosophy's tendency to view the issues at hand from the viewpoint of eternity. But while remaining the spokesman for humanity Boethius does change and develop. Whereas his formulation of the problem in Book I was personal and naïve, a performance which the narrator Boethius characterized as "barking", this formulation in Book V is intellectually sophisticated and motivated less by self-pity than by an honest bewilderment at man's epistemological position in the universe. What is more, this final articulation of the problem elicits the best Philosophy has to offer, her disquisition on eternity and its relationship to temporality, with which the work ends.

Let us now consider more closely by precisely what stages the character Boethius develops from the naïve self-centeredness of Book I to the intellectually sophisticated and emotionally balanced maturity of Book V. When Dame Philosophy appears and scatters the elegiac Muses, Boethius the character falls into a state of speechlessness. Upon receiving the healing touch of Philosophy he immediately recognizes her and expresses surprize that such an august personage should condescend to inhabit such lowly and ignoble environs. To which Philosophy responds, by listing many examples of martyrs to philosophy, that her devotees have always been subject to unjust suspicion and punishment. The first remark by the character Boethius neatly expresses his "problem", that which he must resolve before perceiving the cosmos correctly, namely, his inability to reconcile the reality of being, truth, and goodness with the reality of human suffering and ignorance. As Dame Philosophy will sum it up after performing her diagnosis: the character Boethius suffers from ignorance of self, of the end of things, and of the means by which the cosmos is governed.

At this preliminary stage of his therapy Philosophy insists on using mild remedies before proceeding to harsher medicines:

> Sed quoniam plurimus tibi affectuum tumultus incubuit diversumque te dolor ira maeror distrahunt, uti nunc mentis es, nondum te validiora remedia contingunt. Itaque lenioribus paulisper utemur, ut quae in tumorem perturbationibus influentibus induruerunt ad acrioris vim medicaminis recipiendam tactu blandiore mollescant (Bk. I, pr. 5, 11-12).

> (But since a great crowd of passions has settled upon you and pain, anger, and grief pull you in different directions, in your present state of mind stronger remedies are not yet appropriate for you. Therefore let us make use of milder ones for a while, so that those faculties, which have hardened into a tumor under the influence of disturbing passions, might, by means of a gentle touch, soften so as to become receptive to the power of stronger medicine.)

The effect of these mild remedies of poetry and rhetoric is to encourage Boethius to take his first step towards health by admitting that despite his immediate suffering Fortune has in general been kind to him. As Philosophy puts it:

> Promovimus, inquit, aliquantum si te nondum totius tuae sortis piget (Bk. II, pr. 4, 11).

> ("We have made some progress," she said, "if you are no longer completely dissatisfied with your lot.")

Shortly thereafter she judges that slightly stronger remedies may now be applied to her recuperating patient:

> Sed quoniam rationum iam in te mearum fomenta descendunt, paulo validioribus utendum puto (Bk. II, pr. 5, 1).

> (But since the good effects of my reasoning are penetrating into you, I think that I may now use stronger ones.)

And when Philosophy has reviewed all the gifts of fortune and demonstrated that they can neither really benefit nor harm Boethius in his essence, at the opening of Book III, in which she will clarify the difference between the false goods of fortune and the true good, Boethius states:

> Itaque remedia quae paulo acriora esse dicebas non modo non perhorresco, sed audiendi avidus vehementer efflagito (Bk. III, pr. 1, 2).

> (Therefore those remedies which you said were a little harsher, not only am I not afraid of them, in fact I am eager to hear them and earnestly beg for them.)

Thus for the first time he explicitly expresses his readiness to undergo the harsher stages of his therapy.

When Philosophy has definitively demonstrated the inadequacies of all fortune's gifts and is about to delineate the form of the true good, the following interchange takes place between the two interlocutors:

> Hactenus mendacis formam felicitatis ostendisse suffecerit; quam si perspicaciter intueris, ordo est deinceps quae sit vera monstrare. Atqui video, inquam, nec opibus sufficientiam nec regnis potentiam nec reverentiam dignitatibus nec celebritatem gloria nec laetitiam voluptatibus posse contingere. An etiam causas cur id ita sit deprehendisti? Tenui quidem veluti rimula mihi videor intueri, sed ex te apertius cognoscere malim (Bk. III, pr. 9, 1-3).

> ("Let the preceding suffice to show the form of false happiness; if you have clearly seen into it, the next step is to demonstrate what true happiness is." "And indeed I do see," I said, "that sufficiency cannot appertain to wealth, nor power to kingship, nor honor to office, nor glory to fame, nor joy to pleasure." "But have you also grasped the causes why this is the case?" "I think that I catch a glimpse as if through a slender crack, but I would prefer to learn more clearly from you.")

Here for the first time the character Boethius expresses a dawning ability to discern for himself, but he still needs the tutelage of Philosophy to attain full insight.

Later in Book III, when Philosophy has explained the nature of the true good and proclaimed that it is to be sought within and not without, Boethius again states that he can anticipate Philosophy's line of reasoning:

> Tum ego: Platoni, inquam, vehementer assentior; nam me horum iam secundo commemoras, primum quod memoriam corporea contagione, dehinc cum maeroris mole pressus amisi. Tum illa: Si priora, inquit, concessa respicias, ne illud quidem longius aberit quin recorderis quod te dudum nescire confessus es. Quid? inquam. Quibus, ait illa, gubernaculis mundus regatur. Memini, inquam, me inscitiam meam fuisse confessum, sed quid afferas, licet iam prospiciam, planius tamen ex te audire desidero (Bk. III, pr. 12, 1-3).

> (Then I said, "I am in strong agreement with Plato, since for a second time you remind me of those things, the memory of which I first lost through contact with the body, and then for a second time, because I was overwhelmed with the weight of grief." Then she said, "If you consider the points you have already conceded, it should not be very long before you remember what you recently confessed you did not know." "What," I said. "The means," she said, "by which the universe is controlled." "I remember," I said, "that I confessed my ignorance; but, although I already foresee the answer, I nonetheless desire to hear it more clearly

from your lips.")

Here, too, the character Boethius expresses his ability to see into the nature of things. Even more importantly, he has reached a level of self-awareness where he can accurately describe his condition as that of one who has twice forgotten the truth, that is, the ***Consolatio*** portrays not the education of a neophyte but the re-education of a lapsed philosopher. Boethius' increasing insight and self-confidence are expressed in the following passage, where for the first time he reasons for himself without the aid of Dame Philosophy:

> Mundum, inquit, hunc deo regi paulo ante minime dubitandum putabas. Ne nunc quidem arbitror, inquam, nec umquam dubitandum putabo, quibusque in hoc rationibus accedam breviter exponam (Bk. III, pr. 12, 4).

> ("Recently," she said, "you were of the opinion that in no way could it be doubted that this world is ruled by God." "Nor do I think so now," said I, "nor shall I ever think that it can be doubted, and I shall briefly lay before you the reasoning by which I came to this opinion.)

Finally, when Philosophy makes the bold assertion that evil does not, properly speaking, exist, Boethius the character is by now an active enough interlocutor to question her reasoning and to suggest that her argument might be circular:

> Ludisne, inquam, me inextricabilem labyrinthum rationibus texens, quae nunc quidem qua egrediaris introeas, nunc vero quo introieris egrediare, an mirabilem quendam divinae simplicitatis orbem complicas? (Bk. III, pr. 12, 30)

> ("Are you playing with me," I said, "by weaving an inextricable labyrinth with your arguments, so that now you enter where you exited, and now you exit where you entered, or are you winding some marvelous circle of divine simplicity?")

Thus by the end of Book III the character Boethius has reached the point where he is beginning to see things for himself and to take a more active role in the dialogue with Philosophy.

As I have already pointed out, the character Boethius in Books IV and V restates the central question of the ***Consolatio*** in more and more sophisticated terms and thus elicits from Philosophy progressively more sophisticated responses (see Bk. IV, pr. 1, 2-5, & Bk. V, pr.3-m.3). He remains a spokesman for the human point of view, but he is no longer plagued with blindness and dumbness; he can now manipulate and determine the direction of the discourse taking place between him and Philosophy. Thus at the opening of Book V he is confident enough of his abilities to insist that she discuss the question of chance despite her claim that the question is fraught with difficulty and is somewhat irrelevant to the progress of his therapy:

> Dixerat orationisque cursum ad alia quaedam tractanda atque expedienda vertebat. Tum ego: Recta quidem, inquam, exhortatio tuaque prorsus auctoritate dignissima, sed quod tu dudum de providentia quaestionem pluribus aliis implicitam esse dixisti re experior. Quaero enim an esse aliquid omnino et quidnam esse casum arbitrere. Tum illa: Festino, inquit, debitum promissionis absoluere viamque tibi qua patriam reveharis aperire. Haec autem etsi perutilia cognitu tamen a propositi nostri tramite paulisper aversa sunt, verendumque est ne deviis fatigatus ad emetiendum rectum iter sufficere non possis. Ne id, inquam, prorsus vereare; nam quietis mihi loco fuerit ea quibus maxime delector agnoscere. Simul, cum omne disputationis tuae latus indubitata fide constiterit, nihil de sequentibus ambigatur (Bk. V, pr. 1, i-7).

> (She had spoken and was about to turn the direction of her speech towards treating and explaining other matters. Then I said, "Your exhortation is proper and most worthy of your authority, but what you said before about the question of providence being tied up with many others, I now experience in fact. For I wonder whether you think chance exists at all and what sort of thing it is." Then she said, "I am in a hurry to pay the debt of my promise and to open up the way by which you might return to your fatherland. These matters, however, although useful to know, are nonetheless somewhat removed from the path of our undertaking and it is to be feared, lest, fatigued by side-tracks, you not be up to completing the right journey." "Have no fears at all," I said, "for it would be like a rest to become acquainted with those things in which I most delight. Likewise, since every side of your argument has been constructed with the strongest conviction, let there be no doubt about what follows.)

Thus we see that the character Boethius, by assuming the function of determining the course of the dialogue, instead of merely reacting to the initiatives of Dame Philosophy, is approaching the status of Boethius the narrator. What is more, by his restatement of the problem in epistemological terms in verse 3 of Book V, the only time he speaks in verse after verse 5 of Book I, the character Boethius also approaches the status of the author Boethius who can manipulate all kinds of discourse, both prose and verse, in the construction of the elaborate poem which is the text of the ***Consolatio***. So by the end of the work the character Boethius, while remaining the voice of the human condition, has nonetheless undergone a transformation from a passive and prostrate victim of fortune to an active and vigorous partner in the quest for the solution to the central human dilemma: how to harmonize being and becoming.

The character Boethius' silence in the last sections of Book V and the fact that the author Boethius has not framed his vision of Philosophy with a description of her departure have troubled many readers and have led some to suspect that the work is unfinished. But if my analysis of the development of Boethius the character is correct, the ending is no longer problematic; it is in fact the only

The goods of Fortune and Fortune's wheel, in Jean de Meun's prose rendering of the Consolation of Philosophy *(ca. 1300).*

possible satisfying conclusion to the work. Boethius the author has portrayed the evolution of the character Boethius into the narrator Boethius and has hinted at the further development of Boethius the narrator into Boethius the author of the text. Thus the voice of Philosophy at the end of the work, which had been contrasted with the human voice of Boethius the character and recounted by Boethius the narrator, is now seen to be one of the voices of Boethius the author. And what the voice says represents the successful completion of the work's central project, to harmonize being and becoming, for human hopes and prayers are validated within a universe under the strict determinism of God.

We have seen that just as Boethius' presence in the text is refracted into three facets: author, narrator, and character, so, too, does Dame Philosophy appear under three guises: the voice of being, an aspect of Boethius himself, and an image of the whole tradition of ancient philosophy. Likewise, just as the character Boethius undergoes a transformation in the course of his dialogue with Philosophy, so, too, does she undergo an analogous transformation from "Icon" to "Sybil". Furthermore, as I shall demonstrate, Philosophy's transformations are calculated to correspond to Boethius' specific capabilities at any given stage of his therapy.

The most efficient way of making clear the evolution of Philosophy's character is by reference to the epistemological structure of the work, whereby the text follows the progress of Boethius from "sensus" to "imaginatio", to "ratio", and finally towards "intellegentia". My claim is that Dame Philosophy adapts herself to each stage of this progress and thereby presents a different appearance to Boethius the character at each of the four levels of knowledge.

Thus in Book I, where the character Boethius is portrayed as mired in the realm of the senses, reacting to the blows of fortune in a merely personal way, Philosophy, in order to make herself apparent to Boethius, uses the only means he is prepared to understand, namely, the senses. Her first appearance is that of an icon, the imagery of whose person and raiment shadow forth her nature as it will unfold itself in the course of the dialogue. Furthermore, when she has put the elegiac Muses to rout and is faced with a dumb and blind Boethius, she again avails herself of the senses, in this case the sense of touch, in order to restore his powers of speech and sight (see Bk. I, pr. 2, 7). In addition to sight and touch, Philosophy also has recourse to the sense of hearing as a means towards reaching Boethius in his present condition:

> Itaque lenioribus paulisper utemur, ut quae in tumorem perturbationibus influentibus induruerunt ad acrioris vim medicaminis recipiendam tactu blandiore mollescant (Bk. I, pr. 5, 12).

> (Therefore let us make use of milder remedies for a while, so that those faculties, which have hardened into a tumor under the influence of disturbing passions, might, by means of a gentle touch, soften so as to become receptive to the power of stronger medicine.)

Here "tactu blandiore" obviously refers to the gentle touch of verse, which at this stage of Boethius' therapy is one of the principal means of care.

In the second book, where Philosophy seeks to lead Boethius from an exclusive preoccupation with his personal situation and to instill in him an understanding of the nature of fortune in general, she begins to exercise his faculty of imagination, which allows the human being to perceive the general form apart from its specific embodiment in matter (see Bk. V, pr. 4, 28). Thus Philosophy puts off her persona of icon and puts on that of Muse. This transformation is strikingly signaled in the second prose section of Book II, where Philosophy, in her attempt to reconcile Boethius to his lot, employs one of imagination's most powerful instruments, the theater, by playing the role of Fortuna herself. And in the course of her speech Philosophy as Fortuna alludes to various products of the imagination such as history, tragedy, and epic (see Bk. II, pr. 2, 11-13).

The transition from imagination to reason in Boethius' therapy and the analogous transformation of Philosophy from Muse to "Magistra" is clearly marked at the opening of Book III (see pr. 1, 1-3). Boethius describes himself as enchanted by the charms of Philosophy's poetic discourse, but also ready for the "somewhat harsher remedies" of pure reason. In her response Philosophy characterizes the nature of poetry and the function it has served in a philosophic therapy:

> . . . eumque tuae mentis habitum vel exspectavi vel, quod est verius, ipsa perfeci . . . (Bk. III, pr. 1, 3).

> (And I was expecting this condition of your mind or, what is truer, I myself brought it about.)

That is, she emphasizes the affective power of poetry to change moods and dispositions which was needed to render Boethius receptive to the stronger medicine of pure philosophy.

Thus throughout Books III, IV, and the opening sections of Book V Philosophy will play the role of a "magistra" instructing her "alumnus". Sometimes she delivers lectures in which she sets forth doctrines in a straightforward format (e.g., Bk. III, pr. 2, & Bk. IV, pr. 6, 7ff.); sometimes she questions her pupil so as to involve him in the process of reasoning (e.g., Bk. III, pr. 3, 5ff., & Bk. IV, pr. 7). At times, as we have already pointed out, Boethius himself comments on the argumentation, sets forth arguments of his own, and initiates new avenues of discussion. The purpose and effect of this process are concisely represented at the opening of Book IV, where Philosophy borrows Plato's image of the wings of the soul:

> Pennas etiam tuae menti quibus se in altum tollere possit adfigam, ut perturbatione depulsa sospes in patriam meo ductu, mea semita, meis etiam vehiculis

revertaris (Bk. IV, pr. 1, 9).

(And I shall attach wings to your mind by means of which it will be able to lift itself on high, so that, with all disturbance removed, you might safely turn back towards your homeland under my guidance, along my path, and by my conveyance.)

The image of wings and the insistent travel motif characterizes reason as a specifically human mode of knowledge. Since the human being is born into the realm of becoming, with its dimensions of time and space, the appropriately human mode of knowing must move from one point to another, must be forever in motion. But the ultimate goal of this movement is the "homeland", the realm of being and eternal rest. Thus "ratio", though it is a way towards the truth, is not the truth itself. This problem and its solution will constitute the conclusion of the work in the second half of Book V.

At the beginning of Book V Boethius the character changes the course of the dialogue by focusing on the question of chance, which focus in turn leads to the felt contradiction between the two concepts, divine providence and human free will. By redirecting the conversation and by articulating the paradox of maintaining seemingly contradictory propositions Boethius both displays his full command of the faculty of reason and shows up the ultimate limitations of that faculty, bound as it is by the human dimensions of time and space. Thus the "wings" of "ratio" have conveyed Boethius to the frontier of his "patria", but they are incapable of bearing him into the realm of eternal being itself. To effect this final step into the realm of the eternal Dame Philosophy undergoes her final metamorphosis: she takes off the mask of "magistra" and assumes the persona of Sybil, the mouthpiece of divine wisdom.

This change of Philosophy's role, and thus by implication of the role of the character Boethius, is represented by a sudden change in the nature of the dialogue. In the first half of Book V (through verse section 3) Boethius takes a very active part in the discussion; but once Philosophy begins to speak as a prophetess, propounding the ways of God to man, Boethius says little more than a perfunctory "yes" or "no". Throughout her dazzling disquisition on the four modes of knowledge, on the difference between "aeternitas" and "perpetuitas", in the analogous distinction between "providentia" and "praevidentia", and on the two forms of necessity, Philosophy speaks as an oracle revealing divine truth to a human audience. But as she herself says concerning the four modes of knowledge, the higher does not invalidate the lower, it merely subsumes and transcends it (see Bk. V, pr. 4, 24-39). Likewise, Philosophy as Sybil is not the negation of Philosophy as Icon, Muse, and Magistra; rather she is the culmination of her former roles, roles without which her pupil would never have progressed to a position where he is able to receive her divine teachings.

Thus, although at first sight Dame Philosophy might seem an unchanging, hieratic figure, an appropriate appearance for the mouthpiece of eternity, nonetheless her most important role in the dialogue is to constitute the second voice which makes the interior dialogue of thought possible and to serve as mediator between the character Boethius and the realm of being. This Hermes-like role, whereby Philosophy adapts herself to the capabilities of Boethius and interprets being to him in terms he is prepared to understand, that is, a power neither merely human nor fully divine which acts as intermediary between the two realms.

The epithets with which Boethius the character from time to time addresses his interlocutor underscore Philosophy's function as intermediary. Upon recognizing her for the first time Boethius refers to her as "nutricem meam" (Bk. I, pr. 3, 2), that is, as his nurse. Thus Philosophy is that power which oversees his growth, his transition from intellectual infancy to adulthood. After Philosophy's prosopopoeia of "Fortuna" in Book II, Boethius adresses her as "virtutum omnium nutrix" (Bk. II, pr. 4, 1), that is, as nurse of all the virtues. Thus Philosophy is now characterized not as Boethius' own private nurse but as a force nourishing all the excellencies of the human soul. This address represents a development in Boethius' understanding of his interlocutor: he no longer sees her merely from his own personal point of view. What is more, he aptly describes Philosophy, not as excellence itself, but as the nourisher of excellencies, much as in Plato, philosophy is not wisdom but the enamored pursuit of wisdom. At the opening of Book III, when Boethius the character claims that he is cured of his addiction to fortune, he addresses Dame Philosophy as "summum lassorum solamen animorum" (Bk. III, pr. 1, 2), that is, as the greatest comfort of weary souls. Thus Philosophy as a curative means is a figure whose function is essentially "demonic" or "hermeneutic", that is, to be the guide of the soul from one state to another, in other words, a psychopomp. Finally, in the first prose section of Book IV, Boethius addresses Philosophy as "veri praevia luminis" (Bk. IV, pr. 1, 2), that is, as guide to the true light. Here Philosophy's function as guide or intermediary is most clearly expressed: she is the way towards the light not the light itself.

This "hermeneutic" aspect of Philosophy was also signaled at the very beginning of the text, where the figures embroidered on her garments were described. The pi (the practical) and the theta (the theoretic) connected by a series of steps constituting a means of ascent from the former to the latter are clear images of Philosophy's role in the text. As mouthpiece of eternity and aspect of Boethius himself she . . . provides the means, the ladder, affording access to the higher realm from the lower. This ladder is the dialogue itself which conveys Boethius from the depths of humanity to the heights of divinity by means of discourses drawn from the whole tradition of Greco-Roman antiquity all calculated to correspond to Boethius' stage of receptivity at any given rung.

To summarize, therefore, the significance of the dialogue form of the ***Consolatio,*** one could say that, although firmly within tradition of ancient philosophic dialogue, Boethius' use of the genre is internalized to a degree which no previous practitioner of the genre had attained. This interiority reflects the alienation of Boethius the author, master of the tradition at a time when the tradition was in danger of being forgotten; but it also enables him to dramatize the only interaction available to him, interaction with himself. What is more, the dynamics of this interior dialogue allow him to achieve a great deal more than a simple portrait of intellectual alienation; they constitute a subtle and complex image of the individual human being's epistemological condition.

First of all, the three-fold persona of Boethius in the text: as author, as narrator, and as character, mirrors with remarkable accuracy the complexity of human self-identity. Every human being, whenever he or she pronounces the word "I", is involved in just this three-fold problem of identity. For instance, in the sentence, "I bought the paper this morning", the "I" first of all refers to the character who bought the paper within the story of that sentence. But the "I" also identifies that character with the speaker of the sentence, that is, with the narrator of the story. Finally the use of the word "I" suggests that elusive "I" which is beyond the "I" of the character and the narrator, which is always subject and never object, which determines what stories the narrator "I" will tell and in what manner. What Boethius has accomplished in the ***Consolatio*** is the depiction of the process of integrating these three aspects of "ego". As author he composes a text in which he, as narrator, tells the story of how he, as character, developed to the stage where he was capable of becoming both narrator and author. But it is important to note that Boethius never simply collapses the three aspects into an undifferentiated whole; rather he carefully articulates the drama whereby the three aspects interact.

Likewise with Dame Philosophy. Beyond the importance of any Platonic influence, such as Socrates' remarks in the *Theaetetus* concerning thought as an interior dialogue, the striking thing about Boethius' introduction of Philosophy as the second interlocutor in the dialogue is its accuracy as a depiction of the process of human thinking. We have all had, or nearly had, the embarrassing experience of being caught unawares talking to ourselves. The impulse to do so and the embarrassment at being observed to do so are both instructive. On the one hand, for a human being, to think implies the staging of a drama within one's self. The activity of thought can only proceed through the give and take of different voices, of different points of view. On the other hand, to be observed doing so, either aloud or silently as in the examples of Socrates in the *Symposium,* is to be considered somehow strange, either praeternaturally wise or a fool. This embarrassment is also significant, for clearly our human ability to think has as its basis our most characteristically human means of communicating with each other, language. Thus to talk to oneself, rather than to another, is in some way unusual or "unnatural"; it is the sign either of a great mind or of the failure to interact satisfactorily with our fellow humans. Thus what Boethius has accomplished by including the necessary second voice in any interior dialogue, and which had never been done quite so systematically before him, is the dramatization of the process of thought.

Now if the human "I" is three-faceted, it is natural to expect that the second voice, which we contrive in order to talk with ourselves, would also be three-faceted, depending on what aspect of the self the voice is felt to correspond to. And so it is with Boethius' Dame Philosophy. As the voice of eternity Philosophy obviously corresponds to Boethius as the author of the text, for both are in a position to comprehend the sequence of time and the expanse of space in an instantaneous and all-inclusive grasp. In a certain sense both stand outside the text: Boethius as fashioner of the story and Philosophy as the image of eternity which transcends all stories. Second, Dame Philosophy as the representative of the whole tradition of ancient philosophy can be associated with Boethius as narrator of the story. Both have a history: the narrator has his as character in the story he tells, Philosophy has hers as the history of the various schools of ancient philosophy, their rise and fall, and their interaction. Likewise both tell a story: the narrator recounts the progress of the character, Philosophy unfolds the whole content of Greco-Roman speculation in a sequential order corresponding to the progress of Boethius the character. Finally, Philosophy as an aspect of Boethius himself, as that second voice necessary for interior dialogue, clearly corresponds to Boethius the character. She converses with him throughout the text and adapts herself to his capacities at every stage of their conversation.

Thus Sartre, whom in my introduction I portrayed as pursuing the ***Consolatio*** merely for reasons of general education, should now be reading with greater attention, in fact, with a certain fascination. For, apart from whatever dogmatic biases Boethius may hold, he has, by means of the dialogue form of the work, taken great pains to depict the existential conditions of human thought and knowledge. On the other hand, I criticized F. Anne Payne for what I felt to be her tendentious characterization of the ***Consolatio*** as a text signaling the absolute relativity of all human discourse and understanding. By now I am in a better position to specify the terms of my disagreement. At one point in her study, *Chaucer and Menippean Satire,* she describes the final effect of the work as follows:

> There is no inevitable sequence in the subjects she (i.e. Philosophy) discusses (fortune, happiness, evil, providence and fate, chance, foresight and freewill), nor does Boethius ever reach his "home", the goal promised a number of times, partly because he keeps asking questions, partly because "home" for man is the recognition that he lives in time, that the dialogue will continue, that there will be insights, but no final answers.

First of all, there is indeed a clear and ordered sequence of subjects discussed, as I have demonstrated in my remarks on the philosophical content. Second, as Philosophy states very early in the work, Boethius' "patria" is a special kind of homeland, residence in which or exile from which is a matter of internal disposition not external necessity:

> An ignoras illam tuae civitatis antiquissimam legem qua sanctum est ei ius exsulare non esse quisquis in ea sedem fundare maluerit? Nam qui vallo eius ac munimine continetur, nullus metus est ne exsul esse mereatur; at quisquis inhabitare cam velle desierit pariter desinit etiam mereri (Bk. I, pr. 5, 5).
>
> (Are you unaware of that most ancient law of your home city, according to which it is declared illegal to exile whoever prefers to establish his residence there? For whoever is protected by its moat and walls, there is no fear that he should ever deserve to be an exile. But whoever stops wanting to live there, likewise ceases to deserve to do so.)

Thus, if I have rightly understood the dynamics of the dialogue, Boethius the character by the end of the work has evolved to the point where he is in fact properly disposed for entrance into the city. Third, the fact that Boethius the character insistently asks questions in his role as representative of the human condition does not prevent him from entering the city, indeed, the sophisticated nature of his final questions proves him ready to enter.

Finally, the claim that home for man is in time and that there are no final answers, though similar to certain strains within the ***Consolatio,*** is a great simplification of Boethius' stance. As a pupil of Plato, Boethius is accutely sensitive to the paradox that, although man lives in the "metaxy", that is, in the realm between pure being and utter nonbeing, a part of him is nonetheless nostalgic for another home in the realm of eternal, unchanging being. With rare exceptions the platonic tradition takes both sides of this paradox seriously with the result that at its best Platonism achieves a delicate balance of emphasis between the relativism and uncertainty of our human condition and the instinct for being, which, though never completely realized, it would be false to deny as characteristically human. Thus Boethius' refusal to depict true being in a straightforward and simplistic manner does not imply the denial of being as real, it merely represents a profound respect for the givens of the human condition, which "cannot bear very much reality". Although Plato and Boethius might fashion literary objects in which are portrayed various aspects of the human being's progress, or lack thereof, towards being, the great truth itself is always treated as a mystery, which, because it cannot be portrayed directly, must not be. Boethius, by his use of the dialogue form, exhibits an awareness, rare for a philosopher, that there is no such thing as a simple, declarative sentence, and then proceeds, informed by this awareness, to trace how one human being, cut off from all other human beings, might, in the drama of his own thought, approach being.

IV. THE MENIPPEAN-SATIRE FORM

But this highly wrought text has been elaborated in yet another fashion. Not only is the philosophical content structured according to three different but analogous sets of categories; not only is the work couched in the form of a dialogue between two multifaceted interlocutors; the text has also been cast in the highly artificial form of Menippean Satire, a medley of alternating verse and prose, which had enjoyed a long and various history before Boethius chose to appropriate it for his own purposes.

The genre seems to have originated with Menippus of Gadara, a Greek-speaking Syrian who flourished in the first half of the third century BC. He used the form of alternating verse and prose to write essays expressive of a Cynic's seriocomic attitude towards the world and mankind. It is unclear, however, exactly how the verse sections in his works functioned: they may have been original compositions or merely quotations from previous literature. Menippus was followed by his fellow Gadarean, Meleager, who produced a body of Cynic discourse in the Menippean form around BC 100. The genre was taken over into Latin by Marcus Terentius Varro (BC 116-27), who wrote 110 books of Menippean satires, of which some 600 fragments are extant and in which he mocked human foibles. In the first century AD Varro's lead was taken up by Petronius in the *Satyricon* and by "Seneca" in the *Apocolocyntosis*. Likewise, in the second century AD, Lucian of Samosate wrote a series of dialogues in which the Menippean influence is strong and in which "Menippus" himself sometimes appears as character. But, although Lucian shares Menippus' seriocomic stance, he does not choose to employ the format of alternating verse and prose to which Menippus had given his name.

The form then seems not to have attracted practitioners for almost three centuries; and when it reappears in the fifth and early sixth centuries AD, its characteristically cynic tone seems to have undergone a radical transformation. No longer is the genre used to poke fun at the pretensions and vanities of mankind; instead it is an aspect of the baroque complexity of composition characteristic of much of the literature produced in the Latin West during this period. Thus Martianus Capella (fl. c. 425) casts his highly elaborate allegory, *De Nuptiis Mercurii et Philologiae,* in the Menippean Satire form; and Fulgentius (467-532 AD) does the same in the first book of his collection of allegorical interpretations of classical myths, *Mitologiarum Libri Tres*. Thus by the time Boethius inherited the genre it had long lost its associations with the mocking tones of the Cynics and had taken on the status of a genre appropriate for the explication of lofty mysteries and expressive of the technical literary mastery of its practitioners. The question then arises, why did Boethius choose this strangely artificial form as medium for his ***Consolatio***?

The first observation to be made about Boethius' use of Menippean Satire is the systematic pervasiveness of alternating verse and prose throughout the text. Both his rough contemporaries, Martianus Capella and Fulgentius, employ the form only intermittently; furthermore, their use of verse appears merely decorative and at times gratuitous. In contrast, Boethius alternates verse and prose from beginning to end of the ***Consolatio*** and he endows verse with many important functions throughout the progress of the work. At times it serves to illustrate points made in the prose sections with the more vivid images of poetry (e.g., the metra of Book II); sometimes it actually advances the argument (e.g., metrum 3 of Book V); sometimes it is reserved for purposes less appropriately treated in prose, namely, prayer (e.g. metrum 5 of Book I & metrum IX of Book III); sometimes it serves to refresh Boethius the character between strenuous dialectical workouts (e.g., metrum 6 of Book IV). Finally, the effect of the verse sections in the ***Consolatio*** is analogous in many ways to that of the similes in the *Iliad.* In both works these respective devices interject aspects of reality not to be encountered in the stark settings of the main action. In the *Iliad,* the entire plot of which is restricted to the bleak plane running from the Trojan citadel to the sea, the similes afford glimpses of the natural world of plants and animals, and of the workaday world of humans at their domestic chores. Likewise in the ***Consolatio,*** all of which takes place within Boethius' prison cell, the verse sections continually present images of natural phenomena, both terrestrial and celestial, and sometimes refer to the characters of history and myth (e.g., metrum 6 of Book II; metrum 12 of Book III; metra 3 & 7 of Book IV). Thus, on first reading, the Menippean Satire format of the ***Consolatio*** appears more integrated than in other comparable works. But the question still stands, what end does Menippean Satire allow Boethius to achieve, which otherwise he could not have?

There existed throughout Greco-Roman antiquity an inveterate feud, which even in the fourth century BC Plato could refer to as a "certain ancient dispute", between philosophy and poetry. The most common expression of this tension was the repeated attack launched by philosophical critics against poetry as fictitious and false. As early as Xenophanes, most articulately in certain Platonic passages, and as late as Boethius, poetry is accused of beguiling the mind with dangerously deceptive fabrications. On the other hand, philosophy itself felt the strong pull of poetry; in fact, much of what we term ancient philosophy was composed as poetry, if not verse. For example both Parmenides and Empedocles chose to couch their thoughts in the heroic hexameters of Homer and Hesiod; Plato wrote philosophical closet dramas; Lucretius followed in Latin the example set by Empedocles; and Boethius chose the highly artificial form of Menippean Satire in which to compose his ***Consolatio***. A tension between philosophy and poetry is present throughout Boethius' text; but if my understanding of their interaction is accurate, the outcome of the feud is a draw.

Before proceeding I should forestall a possible confusion of terms. Menippean Satire is often defined as a potpourri of verse and prose, which is as good a definition as any. But when I speak of the relationship between poetry and philosophy in the ***Consolatio,*** I do not mean to suggest that Boethius has cast his philosophy in prose and his poetic aspirations in verse. The verse and prose sections are equally poetic, or literary; the philosophy is not to be found in any one specific mode of discourse but in the arrangement of the work as a whole. Thus, although the following analysis concentrates on the functions of the metra, much the same arguments could be applied to the variety of discourse to be found in the prose sections as well.

Verse in the ***Consolatio*** functions as a "pharmakon", that is, as a potent substance of mysterious, almost magical, properties, which can either cure or kill. Who applies the pharmakon and how it is applied are essential factors contributing to its eventual good or bad effect. Thus the whole work can be read, at least on one level, as the history of the right and wrong uses of this pharmakon which is verse.

The ***Consolatio*** opens with Boethius the character bewailing his fall from fortune in a poem firmly within the tradition of Latin elegy. Dame Philosophy then appears and scatters the elegiac Muses, but she immediately substitutes her own Muses in their stead:

> Quis, inquit, has scenicas meretriculas ad hunc aegrum permisit accedere, quae dolores eius non modo nullis remediis foverent, verum dulcibus insuper alerent venenis? . . . Sed abite potius, Sirenes usque in exitium dulces, meisque eum Musis curandum sanandumque relinquite (Bk. I, pr. 1, 8 & 11).

> ("Who," she said, "has allowed these theatrical bawds to approach this patient? Not only do they not tend him with any remedies, in fact, in addition, they feed him on sweet poisons. But off with you, you Sirens sweet even unto death, and leave him to be cared for and cured by my Muses.")

Thus verse is not viewed as essentially pernicious; its effects can be harmful or beneficial, depending on how it is used and by whom. And the first book of the ***Consolatio*** may be read as an account of how Philosophy removes verse from Boethius' hands and appropriates it for her own uses. After expressing his inability to perceive the hand of God in human affairs in the fifth metrum of Book I Boethius the character will not speak in verse again until the third metrum of Book V. Meanwhile Philosophy will wield verse in a variety of ways, all calculated to further the progress of Boethius' therapy.

The first use made by Philosophy of verse is what I shall term "the affective". Early in Book I, after giving the stoical advice to resist fortune (Bk. I, m. 4), Philosophy asks Boethius: . . .

> "Do you perceive these things," she said, "and have they penetrated your mind, or are you as an ass to the lyre?"

The implication is that in his present condition Boethius is incapable of receiving the healing truth of philosophy and the mention of the lyre hints at the instrument which will be able to effect the necessary change of heart, namely, verse. Accordingly, later in Book I, Philosophy describes her use of verse as calculated to respond to Boethius' emotional state:

Sed quoniam firmioribus remediis nondum tempus est, et eam mentium constat esse naturam ut quotiens abiecerint veras, falsis opinionibus induantur, ex quibus orta perturbationum caligo verum illum confundit intuitum, hanc paulisper lenibus mediocribus fomentis attenuare temptabo, ut dimotis fallacium affectionum tenebris splendorem verae lucis possis agnoscere (Bk. I, pr. 6, 21).

(But since it is not yet time for stronger remedies and the nature of minds is so constituted that they put on false opinions as often as they divest themselves of true ones and from these false opinions there arises a fog of disturbing passions which clouds the capacity for true insight, I shall attempt for a little while to disperse this fog with mild treatments of moderate strength, so that, with the shadows of false affections removed, you might be able to recognize the splendor of the true light.)

This affective use of poetry will prevail throughout Book II, in the course of which Philosophy appeals principally to Boethius' imagination. Even when Boethius himself complains of the ultimate inability of verse and rhetoric to alleviate deeply rooted sorrow (Bk. II, pr. 3, 2), Philosophy insists that at this stage of his therapy poetry is the most he can expect:

Et illa: Ita est, inquit; haec enim nondum morbi tui remedia, sed adhuc contumacis adversum curationem doloris fomenta quaedam sunt; nam quae in profundum sese penetrent cum tempestivum fuerit ammovebo (Bk. II, pr. 3, 3-4).

(And she said, "So it is, for these measures are not cures for your illness, they are merely certain comforts preparatory to the cure of your persistent pain. For when the time is right, I shall apply those measures which penetrate deeply.")

In Book III, a second, loftier use of verse comes into play, that which I choose to call its power to illuminate. Already in Book I, in the passage recently cited, Philosophy had hinted at the power of verse to reveal, to shed light on reality. This ability of verse to illumine is most effectively exercised in the central prayer to God as ruler of the cosmos:

O qui perpetua mundum ratione gubernas,
terrarum caelique sator, qui tempus ab aevo
ire iubes stabilisque manens das cuncta moveri . . .
(Bk. III, m. 9, 1-3).

(O you who govern the cosmos with constant reason, begetter of earth and heaven, who order time to proceed from eternity, and who, while remaining stationary, enable all things to move . . .)

This is the only verse section in the entire ***Consolatio*** to be composed in dactylic hexameters; which fact taken together with the poem's central position in the text indicates its status as the acme of verse's career in the work. Accordingly it presents a cosmology, derived in large measure from Plato's *Timaeus,* in terms of which the whole philosophical content of the second half of the text will be expressed. At the very heart of a philosophical treatise, designed to demonstrate the harmony of being and becoming, Boethius has placed a hexameter poem expressing the nature of God as beginning, middle, and end of all moving things:

. . . tu namque serenum,
tu requies tranquilla piis, te cernere finis,
principium, vector, dux, semita, terminus idem
(Bk. I, m. 9, 26-28).

(For you are the cloudless sky, peaceful rest for the good, the goal is to perceive you, beginning, conveyor, leader, path, end, all in the same being.)

But soon thereafter the status of verse as an instrument of philosophy begins to decline. Book III ends with a poem describing the descent into Hades of Orpheus in order to rescue Eurydice. The stated significance of the legend, to be found in the text of the poem itself, is that on the soul's voyage towards celestial truth it should not look back on terrestrial realities:

Vos haec fabula respicit
quicumque in superum diem
mentem ducere quaeritis;
nam qui Tartareum in specus
victus lumina flexerit,
quicquid praecipuum trahit
perdit cum videt inferos
(Bk. III, m. 12, 52-58).

(This tale concerns you who seek to lead your mind to the daylight above, for he who is overcome and bends his sight towards the Tartarean cave, loses whatever excellence he bore, when he sees the world below.)

But because Orpheus was a stock type of the poet in much Latin literature, I am sure that this description of a poet's failure to regain his wife is meant to suggest the ultimate inability of verse to grasp and keep whatever truths it might convey. Therefore, though not a definitive dismissal of verse from its employ under Philosophy, this poem does indicate the decreasing importance of verse as the therapy of philosophy advances.

Accordingly, in Books IV and V, verse will appear less frequently; nor is it insignificant that, whereas Book I began and ended in verse, Book V opens and closes with prose. Furthermore, Philosophy explicitly describes verse's diminished role at this stage of philosophic therapy. She prefaces a long lecture on "providentia" with these words

Quodi te musici carminis oblectamenta delectant, hanc oportet paulisper differas voluptatem dum nexas sibi ordine contexo rationes (Bk. IV, pr. 6, 6).

(But if the delights of musical song please you, you must defer this pleasure for a little, while I weave together lines of reasoning connected one with the other in strict order.);

and concludes the same lecture with the following remarks

> Sed video te iam dudum et pondere quaestionis oneratum et rationis prolixitate fatigatum aliquam carminis exspectare dulcedinem; accipe igitur haustum quo refectus firmior in ulteriora centendas (Bk. IV, 6, 57).

> (But I see that for some time now, burdened by the weight of the question and fatigued by the extent of our reasoning, you look forward to some poetic sweetness; receive therefore a draught, restored by which you might all the more firmly struggle onward.)

Verse is no longer characterized as affective or illuminating, as it had been in Books I-III; it is now merely restorative; it no longer works hand in hand with philosophy towards curing ignorance, it only serves as a rest stop on the arduous way towards truth.

But this is not the last word on verse in the ***Consolatio***. Since the fifth metrum in Book I Boethius the character has not once spoken in verse. Then suddenly, as just about his last words in the text at all, he breaks into verse (Bk. V, m. 3) before Philosophy launches into her disquisition on the four modes of knowledge, on eternity and perpetuity, on "providentia" and "praevidentia", with which the works comes to an end. In Book I Boethius had complained:

> Omnia certo fine gubernans
> hominum solos respuis actus
> merito rector cohibere modo.
> Nam cur tantas lubrica versat
> Fortuna vices? . . .
> Rapidos, rector, comprime fluctus
> et quo caelum regis immensum
> firma stabiles foedere terras
> (Bk. I, m. 5, 25-29 & 46-48).

> (You who govern all things with fixed purpose, it is only human affairs which you refuse to contain as ruler within the deserved measure. For why does slippery fortune turn such changes? Ruler, quiet the rushing waves, and with the same bond by which you control the great heavens, fix and stabilize the earth.)

In Book V he puts the matter as follows:

> Quaenam discors foedera rerum
> causa resolvit? Quis tanta deus
> veris statuit bella duobus
> ut quae carptim singula constent
> eadem nolint mixta iugari?
> An nulla est discordia veris
> semperque sibi certa cohaerent,
> sed mens caecis obruta membris
> nequit oppressi luminis igne
> rerum tenues noscere nexus?
> (Bk. V, m. 3, 1-10)

> (What discordant cause has undone the bonds of things? What god has established such contention between two truths, so that the same propositions, which, when taken one by one, are valid, should refuse to be joined together? Or in fact is there no discord among truths and they always firmly cohere one with the other, but the mind, buried in imperceptive limbs, is unable by the fire of its buried vision to discern the subtle interweaving of things.)

It is important to note that these final words of Boethius the character are couched in the same meter as the last verse he spoke in Book I (Anapestic Dimeter Acatalectic) and that this latter verse section poses essentially the same question as the former—what is the relationship between the realm of unchanging being and the unpredictably various world of humanity—but that it does so in less personal and emotional terms and with greater self-consciousness and epistemological sophistication.

I interpret this development as the last stage of verse's career throughout the ***Consolatio***. In the first book Dame Philosophy removed the "pharmakon" of verse from Boethius' hands much as a mother would take a potentially dangerous object from her infant child. Philosophy then proceeds to make use of that same "pharmakon" as one means among many in the course of Boethius' therapy. Thus, depending on the stage of therapy involved, verse fills more or less important functions. In the end, as token of his successful cure and new maturity, Boethius the character speaks in verse one last time, thus demonstrating his newly acquired ability to manipulate the "pharmakon" of verse correctly and beneficially.

Throughout its career in the ***Consolatio,*** verse, as well as the variety of prose styles, is judged according to the criteria of philosophy. As Dame Philosophy puts it at the opening of Book II:

> Adsit igitur rhetoricae suadela dulcedinis, quae tum tantum recta calle procedit cum nostra instituta non deserit cumque hac musica laris nostri vernacula nunc leviores nunc graviores modos succinat (Bk. II, pr. 1, 8).

> (Therefore let there be present rhetorical sweetness' power of persuasion, which advances along the straight path, only when it does not abandon our precepts and while, as a handmaid in our household, it sings measures now soft, now grave in its music.)

In this regard Boethius may be seen as coming down on the side of philosophy in its ancient feud with poetry, for the value of the latter is strictly determined by the canon of the former. But the situation is considerably more complex than this, for Menippean Satire, at least as Boethius handles it, is more than a simple alternation of verse and prose, it constitutes a veritable encyclopedia of available forms of discourse. Elegiac verse (Bk. I, m. 1), visionary literature (Bk. I, pr. 1, 1-6), allegorical literature (Bk. I, pr. 1, 7-11), didactic verse (Bk. I, m. 2), Cynic-Stoic diatribe (Bk. I, pr. 3), prayer (Bk. I, m. 5), forensic oratory (Bk. I, pr. 4, 2ff.), philosophic dialogue (Bk. I, pr. 6), and expository prose (Bk. I, pr. 5) are just some of the many genres included in this extraordinarily eclectic work. Thus the texture of the composition is one of great variety and one which displays its artificiality openly, almost proudly. That is, Boethius the author is consciously playing the whole gamut of ancient literary genres and he wants his reader to be aware of the fact. But again, to what end?

One answer, which does not really get to the heart of the matter, is that Boethius manipulates various forms of discourse according to a canon of propriety of form to content. Thus Boethius the character bewails his fall from fortune in the tones traditional to Latin elegy; Philosophy's first appearance is described according to the conventions of ancient vision literature and her rout of the Muses recalls the allegorical methods of a Prudentius; when presenting the case for his despondency Boethius the character speaks as if before a jury, employing the form and many topoi traditional to Roman forensic oratory; and so on throughout the work. Moreover this correspondence of medium to message is organized according to the same hierarchical structure which informs the philosophical content and shapes the progress of the dialogue. Thus the work opens with the character Boethius indulging in the lachrymose strains of elegy and closes with Dame Philosophy's disquisition on "providentia" couched in a lofty, almost oracular, prose reminiscent of certain such passages in Plato. The evolution from one mode of discourse to another follows the same progress from "sensus" to "imaginatio" to "ratio" and finally towards "intellegentia", which we have traced in other contexts. In this regard as well Boethius is clearly subjecting poetry to the demands of philosophy and in so doing he implicitly ranks poetry on a level lower than philosophy.

But the fact that the ***Consolatio*** itself as a text is essentially a poem, that is, a crafted fiction which Boethius the author presents to the reader as an obviously wrought object, has further implications. At the very core of the work, in the hexameter hymn to God at the exact middle of the central Book III (metrum 9), Dame Philosophy addresses a prayer to the fashioner of the universe. Throughout this poem God is depicted as crafting the "mundus", which is Latin for "cosmos", that is, the universe as an orderly structured whole:

> O qui perpetua mundum ratione gubernas,
> terrarum caelique sator, qui tempus ab aevo
> ire iubes stabilisque manens das cuncta moveri,
> quem non externae pepulerunt fingere causae
> materiae fluitantis epus verum insita summi
> forma boni livore carens, tu cuncta superno
> ducis ab exemplo, pulchrum pulcherrimus ipse
> mundum mente gerens similique in imagine
> formans
> perfectasque iubens perfectum absoluere partes
> (Bk. III, m. 9, 1-9).

> (O you who govern the world with constant reason, progenitor of earth and heaven, who order temporality to proceed from eternity, and while remaining stationary endow all things with motion, whom no external causes forced to fashion this work of inconstant matter but the innate idea of the highest good lacking all envy. You bring forth all things from the exemplar on high, yourself most beautiful wielding a beautiful world and shaping it according to a like image, ordering the perfect parts to complete a perfect whole.)

Then in Book V it becomes clear that not only is God's generation of the universe an act of "poiesis", his perspective on his creation is that of an observer viewing a work of art:

> Intellegentiae vero celsior oculus exsistit; supergressa namque universitatis ambitum ipsam illam simplicem formam pura mentis acie contuetur (Bk. V, pr. 4, 30).

> (But the eye of intellect exists on a higher plane, for transcending the circle of the universe it beholds the simple form with pure mental vision.)

To God's eye the universe does not appear as a history, that is, as a sequence of events, but as a poem, that is, as a wrought object capable of being immediately and completely perceived:

> Quod igitur interminabilis vitae plenitudinem totam pariter comprehendit ac possidet, cui neque futuri quicquam absit nec praeteriti fluxerit, id aeternum esse iure perhibetur idque necesse est et sui compos praesens sibi semper assistere et infinitatem mobilis temporis habere praesentem (Bk. V, pr. 6, 8)

> (Therefore that which equally grasps and possesses the whole fullness of life without beginning or end, and from which no future thing is absent nor has the past flowed by, that is rightly held to be eternal, and it is necessary that, possessed of itself, it is always present to itself and holds as present the whole infinity of moving time.)

Finally, the ***Consolatio*** closes with a vision of God as eternally fashioning and eternally contemplating his creation:

> Manet etiam spectator desuper cunctorum praescius deus visionisque eius praesens semper aeternitas cum nostrorum actuum futura qualitate concurrit bonis praemia malis supplicia dispensans (Bk. V, pr. 6, 45).

> (There also remains as spectator from above God who foreknows all things and the constantly present eternity of his vision is in accord with the future quality of our actions, dispensing as it does punishments for evils and rewards for good actions.)

Because within the text God is portrayed as a poet and his creation as a poem, the ***Consolatio*** as a poem assumes great significance. Although verse throughout the work has been criticized and subjected to the purification of philosophy, the goal of philosophy, which, in the Platonic tradition, is always a means and never an end, is the appreciation of the "supreme fiction" which is the cosmos. Thus just as God fashions the universe and contemplates his work of art, so too does Boethius the author fashion a text, the purpose of which is to guide the reader towards a perspective where he can view the world as God does, that is, as a poem. Therefore the critique and subordination of verse to philosophy within the text must be understood, not as the dismissal of an inferior technique, but as the castigation of the highest and most dangerous human capacity for not living up to its potential, for not constituting the human fiction which might adequately reflect God's supreme fiction. In the end, Menippean Satire allows Boethius to compose a kind of metapoem, that is, a poem freed from the conventional constraints of traditional literary genres, able to subordinate those genres to the demands of philosophy, and capable of reflecting on itself as an analogue to God's poem, the universe.

We have seen how the dialogue form of the work allows Boethius to portray the development of Boethius the character into Boethius the narrator; or, as Sartre might have put it, dialogue allows Boethius to portray the existential conditions of human knowledge. Likewise, Menippean Satire allows Boethius to present himself as a poet as opposed to a dogmatic philosopher. The implication of this strategy is that, unlike A. J. Ayer for instance, Boethius does not believe that philosophy's proper medium is a succession of simple declarative sentences but a highly wrought text, the many voices and tones of which interact so as to produce a pattern mirroring the complexity of the cosmos.

V. CONCLUSION

On the strength of the preceding analyses of the philosophical content, of the dialogue form, and of the format of Menippean Satire we can at last draw some firm conclusions as to how one might best approach the text, in other words, how one should read the ***Consolatio***.

On the one hand it is clear that we cannot treat the text as a straightforward philosophical essay or treatise, the elements of which, such as definitions, propositions, and arguments, are best understood when read most literally and as directly expressive of the author's intention. Thus, for instance, when Boethius the character concludes the opening elegy with the statement

> Quid me felicem totiens iactastis, amici?
> Qui cecidit, stabili non erat ille gradu
> (Bk. I, m. 1, 21-22).
>
> (Why, my friends, did you so often boast of my prosperity? He, who has fallen, proves that he was not in a secure position.)

we are not meant to assume that he speaks for Boethius the author, at least not as these words stand in their immediate context. Likewise, as we have already seen, when in the final metrum of Book I Dame Philosophy advises Boethius to cast out all hopes and fears, this exhortation cannot be simply accepted as Philosophy's last words on the subject, never mind as the opinion of the author, for the same character in the last sentences of the text will eloquently defend the validity of human hope (Bk. V, pr. 5, 44-48).

On the other hand to subject the text to a structuralist analysis or to deconstruction would be inappropriate, at least at this stage of our understanding, for both these methods arrogate to their practitioners a privileged position vis-à-vis the text and downplay or ignore the conscious craftsmanship, and thereby the intention, of the author. In the case of the ***Consolatio*** the foregoing pages will have given us good reason to suppose that whatever strategies we may tease out of the text were deliberately inserted by the author as elements in a larger construction. Thus, until we are confident that we understand the intended interaction of elements within the text and the intended implications of the text as a whole, it would be rash and wrongheaded to reduce the ***Consolatio*** to a set of structural categories or to a representation seeking to conceal or display its "difference". For example, the attentive reader will notice that the text on several occasions makes reference to the theme: "To every thing there is a season and a time to every purpose under heaven" (e.g. Bk. I, m. 1, 11; Bk. I, m. 6; Bk. III, m. 1). But to latch on to this motif as one element in an underlying structure or as evidence betraying an anxiety about the existence of an appropriate time would constitute a failure to appreciate both the generic status of the text—this "tempestivus" theme being one of the few elements which Boethius' ***Consolatio*** shares with more conventional examples of consolation literature—and the significance of this motif within the larger dialectic of time and eternity, order and chaos. I am not claiming that a structuralist or deconstructionist approach might not uncover some fascinating material; I am saying that the elaborate intricacy of the text should indicate to us that we are up against a master of construction and instill in us a healthy humility with regard to his work.

How, then, should one read the ***Consolatio***? I would respond that it requires both the mind of a philosopher and that of a poet fully to appreciate the dynamics and significance of the work. When confronted with the world the philosopher reacts by giving an account. The English word, "account", its Latin forerunner, "ratio", and the Greek archetype, "logos" all denote a rational explanation and further connote mathematical proportion. Thus the properly philosophic mode of discourse attempts to illumine reality by coming up, as it were, with a formula corresponding to the interaction of the elements of reality. On the other hand, the poet responds to experience by telling a story. This poetic response shares certain features with the philosophic: both attempt to represent reality and the consonance of certain English words, such as "to tell" and "to tally", "to recount" and "to count", suggests that in some ways the poetic story is a kind of philosophic account. But always present and operative in the telling of a story is the mode, "it is as if"; in other words, the poet's story, although meant to reflect reality, is always a consciously fabricated fiction.

Thus the "ancient disagreement" between philosophy and poetry is a family feud. The philosopher and poet, like Cain and Abel, like Eteocles and Polyneices, desire the same end, to represent what is, but their respective means, the account and the story, although they display a common concern for the orderly arrangement of parts within a whole, appear to be irreconcilable, for the philosopher's account cannot tolerate fiction and the poet's story ceases to function if read as a formula. As is true of all family feuds, the very likeness of the combatants renders the conflict all the more vehement.

Therefore the Boethian achievement and the response which that achievement demands are bold ones indeed, for they constitute nothing less than the reconciliation of philosophy and poetry. The various "stories" within the text (e.g. Boethius' elegy at Bk. I, m. 1 and his defense at Bk. I, pr. 4; Philosophy's prosopopoeia of Fortuna at Bk. II, pr. 2 and her retelling of ancient legends at Bk. III, m. 12, Bk. IV, m. 3, and Bk. IV, m. 7) are all subject and subordinate to a philosophic account expressed most clearly in the epistemological hierarchy of "sensus", "imaginatio", "ratio", and "intellegentia" (Bk. V, pr. 4, 24-39); on the other hand, that philosophical account is contained within the story of Boethius' encounter with Dame Philosophy: it is placed in a context, it is led up to by dialogue, and it is proferred not in the author's words but in those of a character within the story. The implication seems to be that to respond to reality merely as a philosopher or merely as a poet is insufficient, for being requires both an account and a story, and the tension between these modes must be endured. In the end the depiction of the universe as God's "supreme fiction" suggests a possible harmony between philosophy and poetry. Philosophy's account is required both to purge human fictions and to lead man towards God's perspective; but from this perspective the world constitutes a poem and must be read as such.

But what in practice does it mean to read a text with the dual focus of philosophy and poetry? The clearest response is to give a specific example. Thus it is very likely that the reader of this paper, and very certain that the reader of the ***Consolatio*** itself, will have realized by now that the central theme of the work is the question of the order and coherence of the universe. The question is not a new one, even for Boethius; but his means of addressing the question is novel.

The first formulation of the question is the character Boethius' distressed complaint in the middle of the first book:

> Omnia certo fine gubernans
> hominum solos respuis actus
> merito rector cohibere modo
>
> (Bk. I, m. 5, 25-27).

> (You who govern all things with fixed purpose, it is only human affairs which you refuse to contain, as ruler, within the deserved measure.)

His claim that order seems to reign over every aspect of the universe except that of human fortune is implicitly countered in the very next verse section, in which Dame Philosophy maintains that a universal order does obtain and that it is man's duty to conform to it:

> Signat tempora propriis
> aptans officiis deus
> nec quas ipse cohercuit
> misceri patitur vices.
> Sic quod praecipiti via
> certum deserit ordinem
> laetos non habet exitus
>
> (Bk. I, m. 6, 16-22).

> (God stamps the seasons, assigning each to its proper duties; nor does he allow the cycles which he himself has bound to be confused. Therefore whatever in its headlong course abandons this fixed order has no happy outcome.)

Here two opposing conceptions of man's position in the universe are simply juxtaposed. As Boethius the character sees it, mankind is in exile, because God's order does not extend to the realm of human affairs; while from Philosophy's point of view, man has exiled himself by failing to conform to the order inherent in the nature of things. What is important to note is that neither side of the question is guaranteed as the author's own; in fact, the entire ***Consolatio*** may be read as a dialogue between these opposing points of view.

Book II represents an attempt on Philosophy's part to convince Boethius the character not only that the gifts of fortune are not by right the possession of any human being but furthermore that the apparent flux of fortune in reality constitutes a kind of order:

> Constat aeterna positumque lege est,
> ut constet genitum nihil
>
> (Bk. II, m. 3, 17-18).

> (It stands firm and fixed by eternal law that nothing born stands firm.)

This law of change, according to which all sublunary creatures are destined to suffer highs and lows in the turn of fortune's wheel, when properly understood, no longer functions as the deceptive seductress, fortune's usual persona in philosophical texts, but as an effective teacher:

> Etenim plus hominibus reor adversam quam prosperam prodesse fortunam; illa enim semper specie felicitatis, cum videtur blanda, mentitur, haec semper vera est, cum se instabilem mutatione demonstrat (Bk. II, pr. 8, 3).

> (Therefore, I believe that bad fortune is of more use to mankind than good, for the latter, while it seems

propitious, deceives by means of the appearance of happiness, whereas the former is always true, for by its change it demonstrates its essential instability.)

This pedagogical power of fortune was foreshadowed and dramatized early in Book II when Dame Philosophy put on the mask of Fortuna herself in order to address Boethius' complaints (Bk. II, pr. 2, 1ff.). What is more, the paradox of change as the order of fortune gives rise at the end of Book II to the vision of "amor" as the principle of order in the universe:

Hanc rerum seriem ligat
terras ac pelagus regens
et caelo imperitans amor

(Bk. II, m. 8, 13-15).

(Love, which rules supreme in heaven, and which controls both land and sea, also binds this series of things.)

Thus we have the first response to Boethius' dilemma: the very fortune which he thought chaotic turns out to function according to a law proper to it, and the universe, seen in the light of fortune's law, is governed by a tensile harmony, best described as "amor". But again, one must remember that this description of universal order is not necessarily the author's opinion; instead it represents a calculated attempt by Dame Philosophy to communicate with Boethius the character on terms which he is capable of understanding.

This point becomes all the more clear when in Book III we see that certain aspects of this first conception of universal order are called into question. The first metrum of Book III reads very much like metrum 6 of Book I, both poems preach a proper order which it is man's duty to imitate; but in the very next verse section, #2, which seeks to describe the nature of this order in greater detail, certain troubling traits begin to emerge. Dame Philosophy opens the poem by stating her intention to sing of the means by which "Natura" governs the universe. There follow three examples illustrative of nature's ability to reassert herself despite the artificial interventions of humanity: the tame lion, who once he tastes blood, recovers his wild nature; the caged bird, who, though well fed by its human captors, breaks into song when it escapes to its natural haunts; and the tree, the top of which has been bent to the ground, snapping back straight up when released. In all three cases man appears as in some way not belonging to the nature of things, for the emphasis is on nature's capacity to maintain its own course despite human interference. In addition, all three examples bear associations of violence or ingratitude which might well instill in the reader a certain unease about the operations of nature. Likewise in the fourth and final example, and again in the concluding lines of the poem, the natural order described holds no place for man. The return of the sun every morning at dawn (11.31-33) is a process independent of man's control; and the concluding generalities about the "eternal return" of nature certainly suggest man's singularity in the larger scheme of things, for he is just that creature who seems unable to join his end to his beginning and thus to enter into the eternal round of nature:

Repetunt proprios quaeque recursus
redituque suo singula gaudent
nec manet ulli traditus ordo
nisi quod fini iunxerit ortum
stabilemque sui fecerit orbem

(Bk. II, m. 2, 34-38).

(All things seek out their proper cycles and everything rejoices in its own return, nor is any order handed down to anything, except that it join its beginning to its end and make a stable circuit of itself.)

Thus the natural order of things celebrated in the second book is here shown to have precious little to do with the realities of the human condition. What is more, the principle of "amor" no longer functions as it did in the final verse section of Book II, where it constituted a law or bond uniting the disparate contraries of the world. In Book II the turning of Fortune's wheel and the cosmic principle of "amor" were seen as counterbalancing man's lawless appetites, his eternal desire for more (Bk. II, m. 2); thus the book can end on a triumphant note of achieved harmony between order and desire:

O felix hominum genus
si vestros animos amor
quo caelum regitur regat

(Bk. II, m. 8, 28-30).

(O happy race of men, if the love by which heaven is ordered orders your minds.)

But in Book III nature's eternal return is suggested to be of little concern to mankind and consequently "amor" loses its status as a principle of order. When in the final metrum of Book III Orpheus attempts to rescue Eurydice from Hades, a human interference with the cycle of nature parallel to those described in the second metrum, he fails because his "amor" cannot bear to be constrained by Hades' "law":

'Donamus comitem viro
emptam carmine coniugem;
sed lex dona coherceat,
ne dum Tartara liquerit
fas sit lumina flectere.'
Quis legem det amantibus?
Maior lex amor est sibi

(Bk. III, m. 12, 42-47).

('We grant as companion to her husband this wife, bought for a song. But let one law hedge in this gift: it is not allowed to look back until he has left the infernal regions.' Who may impose a law on lovers? Love is its own greater law.)

Thus all that has happened in the progress from Book I to Book III is the attainment of a more intense and more sophisticated sense of man's disjunction with the universe. The realm of fortune and "amor" as described in Book II are in Book III shown up as in reality excluding all properly human aspiration. But of course this is not the whole picture; Boethius the author is not a Camus, he does not envision man as in an "absurd" relation with the world. What has been lacking throughout Books II and III is a sense of man's proper place in the universe; but the answer to this lack, which will be treated in detail in Books IV and V, has already been foreshadowed in the central verse section, #9, of Book III. There, in the context of a prayer, all that will become explicit in the disquisitions of the final two books, is succinctly summarized. Man does have a "homeland" but he is in exile from it and his reentry into it requires not only movement within one dimension, but the passage from one dimension to another. Likewise, it is possible to characterize man's place or homeland as the lack of a home, as his pilgrim status in the universe, but only with the proviso that man is on the way towards some very definite goal.

In Book IV the means of progressing towards this goal are mapped out with a certain precision. The significance of the wing imagery in the first verse section is elucidated not only in the arguments of the prose sections but, even more strikingly, in the measures of the verse sections. Thus in the fifth metrum the obstacle to man's return is declared to be, not distance, but ignorance, while in the sixth metrum the object of man's actual ignorance and potential knowledge is described in terms reminiscent of "amor" in Book II, but with certain all-important differences. God is portrayed as harmonizing the cosmos by means of "amor":

Hic est cunctis communis amor
repetuntque boni fine teneri,
quia non aliter durare queant
nisi converso rursus amore
refluant causae quae dedit esse
(Bk. IV, m. 6, 44-48).

(This is the love common to all things, whereby they seek to be contained within the boundary of the good; for not otherwise are they able to endure, unless, with love turned back full circle, they return to the cause which gave them being.)

But the relation between the principle of order and the ordered universe is profoundly different from that drawn in the final metrum of Book II. There the "amor" regulating the cosmos was depicted as immanent in the world itself, whereas here the principle of order is radically transcendent. The world, as before, is depicted as moving in eternally repetitive circles (Bk. IV, m. 6, 6-33), but, in contrast, the agent of order is exempt from this circularity, for he is exempt from all movement:

Sedet interea conditor altus
rerumque regens flectit habenas
rex et dominus, fons et origo,
lex et sapiens arbiter aequi,
et quae motu concitat ire
sistit retrahens ac vaga firmat
(Bk. IV, m. 6, 34-39).

(Meanwhile the lofty creator sits in control turning the reins of things, the king and lord, the fount and source, the law and wise arbiter of justice, and what he has put into motion, by pulling back, he brings to a halt, and he stabilizes what otherwise would wander.)

Thus by the end of the fourth book Boethius the character and Dame Philosophy agree that there is an order to the universe and, what is even more important, an order which makes sense to human beings and makes sense of human activity:

Ite nunc, fortes, ubi celsa magni
ducit exempli via. Cur inertes
terga nudatis? Superata tellus
sidera donat
(Bk. IV, m. 7, 32-35).

(Now go forth, heroes, where the lofty path of the great exemplar leads. Why, inactive, do you keep your backs free of burdens? The earth once overcome bestows the stars.)

What renders this order humanly satisfying, in a way which the order described in Book II was not, is the fact that it is in some way out of nature, just as man is in some way out of nature. But this very quality of transcendence is what makes this order so inaccessible to man, for if man is in one sense out of nature, he is even more obviously bound to nature. The expression of this dilemma and of the solution to it will constitute the content of Book V.

As I have pointed out in more than one context, metra 3 and 4 of Book V strikingly echo metra 5 and 6 of Book I. The metres of the respective poems are the same; in the first of each pair Boethius the character expresses his dilemma; in the second Dame Philosophy, somewhat obliquely, suggests a solution. The real and significant difference lies in the fact that the two poems in Book I represent the mere juxtaposition of two opposing points of view, whereas in verse section 3 and 4 of Book V Boethius first expresses his dilemma in intellectually sophisticated terms, terms which eventually elicit from Dame Philosophy the epistemological poem which is verse section 4 and in which she makes a strong case for the existence of the more active and creative mental faculties. In Book I Boethius says one thing, Dame Philosophy another; there is no attempt to harmonize their respective points of view, because it will require the whole process depicted in Books II, III, and IV before Boethius and Philosophy can, as it were, speak the same language. The various philosophical doctrines and arguments employed are important in and of themselves, but even more important is the process whereby a human interlocutor progresses to the point where he is on the verge of viewing his human condition from a radically different perspective, that, in fact, of eternity.

For the pair of poems in Book V portray Boethius as

making the decisive change of procedure from thought to critical thought and Dame Philosophy as completing Boethius' tentative venture into epistemology. Boethius first wonders why the universe is so constructed as to allow the paradox of divine providence and human free will (Bk. V, m. 3, 1-5) but immediately thereafter asks the more self-conscious and sophisticated question, is this apparent paradox merely the result of our limited powers of perception and reasoning? (Bk. V, m. 3, 6-10) The remainder of the poem is taken up with reflections on the peculiar mixture of knowledge and ignorance which is characteristic of the human mind. In the fourth verse section Philosophy continues these investigations into the workings of the human mind and claims that essential to an understanding of human mental activity is an appreciation of the mind's active role in perception, imagination, and reason. Thus in metrum 3 Boethius the character exhibits the mind's capacity for creative thought while in metrum 4 Dame Philosophy draws general conclusions from this one example as prelude to her revelation of the mysteries of eternity.

We see then that in the progress from Book I to Book V the question of the order of the universe is not handled as it might have been in an Aristotelian treatise. Instead of an exclusively rational account of the problem at hand, we are presented with a dialogue between two interlocutors who at first appear as polar opposites but who in the end complete each other's arguments. On the other hand, we are not merely presented with a story, as for instance in Hesiod's *Theogony,* of the rise of universal order; essential to Boethius' story are the various arguments contained within it and the over-arching epistemological hierarchy which structures it. By the blending of these two modes of discourse Boethius the author contrives not only to dramatize the process of thought, but even more significantly, to dramatize the emergence, on the epistemological level, or order itself. That is, Boethius not only gives an account, in fact several accounts, of order in the universe; he also tells a story about the revelation of order in the process of human thought. He seems to imply that it is inadequate merely to give an account without placing that account in the context of a story, or just to tell a story without subjecting it to the rigor of a philosophical account.

Thus poetry and philosophy, which we along with many in antiquity feel to be mutually exclusive modes of discourse, are here used to complement each other. Every story requires an explanation, an interpretation; and yet merely to explain, to interpret, or to give an account of, is by itself unsatisfying: every explanation must lead to another, better story if it is not to remain sterile. By constructing a text in which various stories are subject to the critical account of philosophy, in which various philosophical accounts are contained within a larger story, in which that larger story is structured according to an epistemological hierarchy, and finally, in which that epistemological hierarchy ushers in the vision of God creating and viewing his creation as a poem, by intertwining all these strategies Boethius manages not only to produce a subtly nuanced and delicately balanced depiction of the human condition, he also demonstrates what is required to make such a depiction possible, namely, the reconciliation of poetry and philosophy.

Early in the same century in which Cassiodorus composed his *Institutiones,* that model of perfection for the ossification of the Greco-Roman tradition under the aegis of the Christian cult, and in which Benedict produced his *Regula* in the rough and ready patois that spoken Latin had become in the sixth century as a guide to the practice of "holy ignorance", Boethius contrives a text which avoids the complementary pitfalls of merely academic erudition and religious ignorance, which, in fact, betrays on its author's part a mastery of the ancient tradition and an ability to handle that tradition creatively. Boethius himself was no doubt nominally a Christian: for all intents and purposes there was no other cult available in the Latin West; one could not hold official posts without being a Christian; and it is as certain as these matters can be that Boethius in fact wrote the theological treatises ascribed to him. But the fact that many scholars of the eighteenth and nineteenth centuries were convinced that Boethius the author of the ***Consolatio*** could not have composed Christian theological treatises together with the further fact that medieval commentators were by and large anxious about Boethius' orthodoxy, whether they expressed that anxiety in direct denunciation or by attempting to gloss over certain troubling passages, suggests that Boethius' Christianity, and thus his role in the transition from antiquity to the western European Middle Ages, is an unusual and complicated one.

There are echoes of Christian doctrine and of the Christian scriptures to be found here and there in the ***Consolatio,*** but the truly significant fact is that in the final analysis the text, though not anti-Christian, is profoundly non-Christian. Faced with his own mortality Boethius refuses to cut the Gordian knot by throwing himself onto the mercy of a God made man; rather he carefully traces the intricacies of that knot and produces a portrait of man, ignorant and hungry for wisdom, mortal and nostalgic for immortality. Although Christianity has on several occasions appropriated philosophy and poetry as handmaidens to revelation, it is nonetheless deeply suspicious of the artifices of poetry and impatient with the slow hard work of philosophy. Boethius, in contrast, works with and through these two modes of discourse and produces a philosophical poem, which serves as one of the few examples of "doing philosophy" available to the early Latin middle ages, and which provided a store of poetic strategies to be exploited by the likes of Dante and Chaucer. The question of Boethius' personal allegiance to Christianity is probably unanswerable and is certainly in bad taste—it is just not done among gentlefolk to force simplistic statements of belief or unbelief from one another. What we do know, what Boethius allows us to know is that, confronted with death, he chose to practice philosophy and poetry.

Seth Lerer (essay date 1984)

SOURCE: "Boethian Silence," in *Medievalia et Humanistica,* No. 12, 1984, pp. 97-125.

[*In the following essay, Lerer explores Boethius's notions of communication, dialogue, and rhetoric in the theological tractates and the* Consolation of Philosophy.]

Twenty years ago, in a landmark article, Joseph Mazzeo [in *Journal of the History of Ideas* 23 (1962)] identified St. Augustine's "rhetoric of silence" as the notable characteristic of his broader "attempt to assimilate classical rhetoric to Christian needs." Readers of Augustine long before Mazzeo recognized the Saint's attempted synthesis of Ciceronian rhetoric and Biblical narrative, and his contrast, expressed in *De Doctrina Christiana,* between the eloquence of words and the eloquence of things. But Mazzeo showed how the ideal of silence became for Augustine a method of communication between the spirit and Christ. "For Augustine all dialectic, true rhetoric, and thought itself were but attempts to reascend to that silence from which the world fell into the perpetual clamor of life as fallen men know it" (Mazzeo). Augustine also explored the processes of reading and writing as activities that, at their best, transpire in silence. One need only recall those famous moments in the *Confessiones* when the young Augustine finds Ambrose reading in silence (6.3), and when, at the moment of conversion, he takes up the Scriptures and reads silently to himself (8.12). Writing became a private experience for Augustine as well. He characterized the highest form of writing as "deliberations with myself when I was alone in your [i.e., God's] presence" (*Conf.* 9.4). The writing of the *Confessiones* itself becomes a process of turning away from the voices of men toward the inner voice of God and the self. In the great discussion of memory (10.8-21), Augustine shows how, by withdrawing into the self, the confession becomes a document written without the need of verbal or physical companionship.

Few readers of Boethius's "confession"—the ***De Consolatione Philosophiae***—have discovered a similar tension between true and false eloquence, or more precisely, between the virtuous rhetoric of silence and the vacuous inability to speak. The ***Consolatio***'s opening books call attention to and explain the prisoner's initial silence and his subsequent efforts at dialogue. The silence in this text is much different from Augustine's. While Augustine saw the fundamental spiritual movement as one of speech to silence, Boethius focuses on the essential propaedeutic to all philosophical speculation: public discussion. In the ***Consolatio*** silence can be an evil; it belies an ignorance of the most basic methods of communication and understanding. Reasoned eloquence, the old Ciceronian ideal, becomes the end toward which Philosophy directs the prisoner's voice.

This reading implies a notion of levels of discourse in the ***Consolatio,*** and one finds this notion explicitly stated in Boethius's logical writings. Briefly speaking, rhetoric and dialectic, for Boethius, were only preludes to philosophy. Following Aristotle rather than Plato, his dialectician persuaded through opinions rather than demonstrated through proofs. Under the rubric of dialectic, Boethius classed all forms of probable argument, including the topics, which were "the starting point of necessary arguments." Philosophical demonstration, however, was narrowly conceived in the logical writings as syllogistic reasoning. The philosopher employs necessary proofs, and "he differs from the orator and dialectician in their areas of inquiry, namely that for them it consists in ready believability, and for him in truth." The tension between belief and proof Boethius establishes in his logical writings also characterizes much of the dialogue between the prisoner and Philosophy. The following analysis illustrates how the rules of dialectic seldom meet the needs of philosophy.

The Boethian dialogue, then, may be said to begin at a level lower than the Augustinian confession. Augustine had, by this point, turned away from the public discussions of such early dialogues as *De Magistro,* and toward a private meditation conducted in silence. Boethius and his prisoner must begin truly at the beginning—with verbal facility, dialectical disputation, and reasonable eloquence—before embarking on philosophical speculation. Boethius's concern with the forms of communication, moreover, extends to a theory of writing, a theory embedded in the imagery of the ***Consolatio***'s opening books and stated in the prefaces to the theological tractates ***De Trinitate*** and ***Contra Eutychen***. As there are meaningful and meaningless forms of silence, and of speech, so there are comparable forms of writing. Boethius contrasts the vacuity of passive diction—writing down words received from without—with the virtue of active composition—turning into words ideas which come from within. In ***De Trinitate*** and ***Contra Eutychen*** Boethius presents a defense of silence similar to Augustine's, and he describes a process of philosophical writing which explains the prisoner's problems with his own writing at the ***Consolatio***'s opening. These elements in the tractates explain, perhaps better than any historical source, his condition at the dialogue's beginning and his place at the end of the autobiography Boethius fashioned through the prefaces to his other works.

I

Boethius opens ***De Trinitate*** with an appeal to private, rather than public judgment. The text he presents is very much a written structured document, "formatam rationibus litterisque mandatam" (set forth in logical order and cast in literary form). The word *mandare* signifies the formal presentation of a work, and it also appears at the beginning of texts to describe the physical activity of transferring thought into speech and writing. At the opening of the ***Contra Eutychen*** and the ***Consolatio*** Boethius uses the word to bring to the reader's attention the role played by writing in the formation of a literary argument. Boethius's concern with the linguistic character of his tract—its status as a verbal argument—is also clear in his use of the two components of classical topics theory: invention and judgment. "Offerendam vobis communicandamque curavi tam vestri cupidus iudicii quam nostri studiosus inventi". The text subscribes to the ordering principles of dialectic as outlined, for example, in Cicero's *Topica:* "Cum omnis ratio diligens disserendi duas habeat partis, unam inveniendi alteram iudicandi" (*Top.,* 6). Discovery is subject to constant appraisal by writer and reader, and Boethius offers the products of his *inventio* to the public exercise of judgment.

Boethius is apparently uneasy about writing down (*stilo commendo*) any thoughts, not merely because of the material's difficulty, but because of its fundamentally private nature. He creates a private discourse by successively excluding all possible audiences, including even the work's intended reader, Symmachus. Unlike the earlier, classical examples of the dedicatory trope, Symmachus is brought into the thought and writing of the work only to be dismissed later. If he remains the only possible audience for the work, his presence is imaginary, and it qualifies the kind of writing Boethius proposes. Symmachus becomes less and less the issue; he is no living participant in a dialogue, and Boethius is unsure whether he will read or even look at the words he has written. We see the writing of ***De Trinitate*** as a wholly internalized process. The question of the vulgar reader is but one aspect of this hermetically sealed discourse. Preservation of divine truth from the common or uninitiated had become, as is well known, a frequently articulated problem in late Antique thought. It is at the heart of Macrobius's familiar defense of fable and, ultimately, of the medieval term *involucrum:* the text wrapped in an allegorical cover. Boethius also devotes some time and effort to concealing his truths.

> Idcirco stilum brevitate contraho et ex intimis sumpta philosophiae disciplinis novorum verborum significationibus velo, ut haec mihi tantum vobisque, si quando ad ea convertitis oculos, conloquantur. . . .

But this sentiment differs markedly from the Macrobian ideal of the mysteries of fabulous narrative. Boethius writes not for fame, nor for applause, nor for the elect, but for the inner pleasure of discovery. His text develops from thoughts and long-pondered investigations; in effect, Boethius writes solely for himself. The divine light has informed the spark of his intelligence, and this Platonic image pinpoints the movement from thinking to writing ("Investigatam diutissime quaestionem, quantum nostrae mentis igniculum lux divina dignata est"). For Boethius, this is an image no doubt filtered through Augustine, and it suggests his concept of illumination and the doctrine of recall developed in *De Magistro* and elsewhere.

We may view the preface to ***De Trinitate*** as Augustinian in spirit, and the Saint's name in fact closes this section of the work. Boethius's writing manifests Augustine's idea of the "internal silent words by which the inner teacher, Christ, teaches us the truth" (Mazzeo). By adumbrating a doctrine of illumination within his spiritual autobiography, Boethius also recalls those moments in *De Magistro* when Augustine calls upon "not the speaker who utters words, but the guardian truth within the mind itself." Boethius chronicles the cognitive life of what Augustine called the "interior man" who deals in public words only to remind him of the truth that teaches privately. Yet, Boethius realizes that as long as he has chosen to communicate to the world of men, his method will be limited. With human language as his vehicle, he will be unable to express fully the spark of insight granted to him. Writing, like the other *artes,* is only one step on the ladder toward truth.

> Sane tantum a nobis quaeri oportet quantum humanae rationis intuitus ad divinitatis valet celsa conscendere. Nam ceteris quoque artibus idem quasi quidam finis est constitutus, quousque potest via rationis accedere. . . .

The *via rationis* is but a formal method which may teach us what to write or say, but not to think. Boethius's phrasing echoes the metaphor of the "way" taken from the theory of dialectic, and the notion of study as an ordered progress through basic stages to a higher goal. The imagery of *ars* as a *via* and of the *gradus* of study will reappear in the ***Consolatio***'s opening passages to characterize Philosophy's attempt to develop the prisoner's language skills and her attempt to direct his reason. Suffice it to say here, however, that the preface to ***De Trinitate*** brings to the fore Boethius's concern with his method's strengths and limitations, and it reveals his preoccupation with the problems of beginning a written work.

A similar concern opens the preface to ***Contra Eutychen***. Boethius initially notices the absence of an interlocutor with whom he can argue. Alone now, for whatever reasons, he sets down in writing, "mando litteris quae coram loquenda servaveram" (what I had been keeping to say by word of mouth . . .). The process of writing is again a private one, but here it becomes a way of filling the space of silence with written words. Boethius's autobiographical explanation of his beliefs in ***Contra Eutychen*** also explains the purpose of solitary, silent thought. Now, however, it is the silence of a man trapped in the babble of the ignorant. He reports a story of the Senate, where a letter was read aloud expressing unorthodox belief. This public reading engenders a flurry of vocal opposition, but the words of the mob are without insight into the complexity of the problem. In fact, they deny its obscurity, an act anathema to either Augustine's or Boethius's aesthetic and philosophical commitments to the pleasures of difficulty.

> Hic omnes apertam esse differentiam nec quicquam in eo esse caliginis inconditum confusumque strepere nec ullus in tanto tumultu qui leviter attingeret quaestionem nedum qui expediret inventus est. . . .

The crowd expresses itself in a noisy tumult incapable of investigating truth. *Inventio*—the process of reasoned, rational discovery—is denied them. They violate the order of argument and appeal to the whim of emotion. For all their clamor, their words are hollow.

Only Boethius, he tells us himself, sat apart from them, far from the man (i.e., Symmachus) he watched. Instead, "I kept silent (*conticui*)." He meditates to himself on the issue, and when insight comes to him, it is a totally private experience. He finds truth not by listening to the outer voices of others, but to the inner voice of himself.

The wheel of Fortune in a verse revision of the Consolation of Philosophy *(ca. 1380).*

His metaphor of sudden revelation must recall for us the Biblical statement of the accessibility of truth:

> *Boethius* Tandem igitur patuere pulsanti animo fores, et veritas inventa quaerenti omnes nebulas Eutychiani reculsit erroris. . . .
>
> *Luke, 11:9* Petite, et dabitur vobis; quaerite, et invenietis; pulsate, et aperietur vobis.

We may read Luke's injunctions as an appeal to forms of intellecutal and spiritual activity. The Bible and Boethius together advocate a *diligentia* rewarded with *sapientia.* Seeking, asking, and knocking receive their fulfillment in finding, receiving, and opening. *Inventio* now becomes a term of more than technical significance; it comes to represent the kind of mental activity missing in the Senatorial mob. The word's meaning transcends the arenas of public discussion to which it once had reference. Unlike the *indocti,* who fail to understand through debate, Boethius comes to knowledge through silent meditation. His activity in the ***Contra Eutychen*** is virtually the same as the Augustinian process of purposeful writing: "deliberations with myself when I was alone in your presence." Such internal disputations deny the need of any human and present companion, and this concept explains Symmachus's absence both from the remembered story of the Senatorial debate and from the written text of the ***Contra Eutychen*** itself.

For Augustine, what fills this absence is the eternal presence of God. For Boethius, with more immediate concerns here, what fills the space left by silence is writing: "semel res a conlocutione transfertur ad stilum" (the pen is now to take the place of the living voice). Boethius turns the process of composing back upon itself. As in the preface to ***De Trinitate*** and in Augustine, solitude and silence remove the writer in space and time from the noise of the multitude. Boethius turns away (*transeo*) from these external distractions to savor the eloquence granted by the mind alone. He has little concern for public judgment of his work, and like the author of the *Confessiones* may ask: "Need it concern me if some people cannot understand this?"

But Boethius differs from Augustine in a fundamental, structural way. Unlike the Saint, Boethius appears preoccupied with the problems of beginning his texts, and his overriding concerns with technique and method, combined with his autobiographical statements, make the problem of recording, rather than recalling, foremost in the reader's mind. Edward Said's remarks [in his *Beginnings,* 1975] on the relationship between an author's career and his attempts at beginning a new work express the problems implicit in the prefaces to the theological tractates and in the opening of the ***Consolatio***.

> [We may] take the author's career as wholly oriented toward and synonymous with the production of a text, especially if the author himself seems obsessively concerned with just that concern over technique or craftsmanship. A further implication is that the author's career is a course whose record is his work and whose goal is the integral text that adequately represents the efforts expended on its behalf.

Boethius creates the image of an author facing either a long gestation period for his work, or of the writer as a frustrated speaker, waiting anxiously for the opportunity to express his thoughts. The writing of ***De Trinitate*** can begin only after a long period of investigation: "Investigatam diutissime quaestionem . . . ". ***Contra Eutychen*** similarly begins after a lengthy time of reflection: "Anxie te quidem diuque sustinui . . . ". Both texts open with the decision to set down in writing (*mandare litteris*) for the present those thoughts which have occupied the past.

Boethius begins each work by confronting anew the difficulty of writing, and by giving it a place in the implied autobiography which stands behind its composition. Not only does he make reference to the work's place in his life; he also considers the present work's relationship to all his other writings. ***De Trinitate***'s preface reviews its author's continual difficulty whenever he attempts to transcribe what he thinks. The preface to ***Contra Eutychen*** begs the reader to measure the work against the corpus of Boethius's writings: "Quod si recte se habere pronuntiaveris, peto ut mei nominis hoc quoque inseras chartis". . . . Boethius's beginnings in the tractates establish what Said calls "relationships of continuity" with works already existing. The opening of the ***Consolatio,*** however, breaks with all other beginnings and makes itself something new and different from anything which has gone before. While the author of the tractates values the past, the prisoner of the ***Consolatio*** mourns it. Again, the author addresses the present effort to all his previous writings. But now, it is a relationship of contrast, rather than continuity. Here, the writer's silence is the fallen counterpart to the insightful, Augustinian rhetoric of silence. Rather than listening to his inner teacher, the prisoner hears only the Muses. Before he can ascend to that higher silence, he must first find his true voice.

II

From its opening, the ***Consolatio*** struggles with words and texts. Foremost in the prisoner's mind is not, as we would expect, his recognizable grief, but a deeper, less recognizable impediment: silence. He is no longer able to compose verses full of meaning and value; now his poem is but a hollow elegy for lost youth. He cannot invent his own words, but must silently take dictation from the Muses.

> Carmina qui quondam studio florente peregi,
> Flebilis heu maestos cogor inire modos.
> Ecce mihi lacerae dictant scribenda camenae
> Et veris elegi fletibus ora rigant.
> (1. m. 1. 1-4, . . .)

Reduced to a scribe, his role is passive, and the prisoner expresses a loss of moral and literary direction. He walks along a lonely *iter* of life (1. m. 1. 6) and his step falters: "Qui cecidit, stabili non erat ille gradu" (1. m. 1. 22).

The prisoner sits in silence, ready to record his lament when Philosophy appears: "Haec dum mecum tacitus ipse reputarem querimoniamque lacrimabilem stili officio signarem, adstitisse mihi supra verticem visa est mulier reverendi admodum vultus" (1. 1., . . .). Much has been made of the drama of her initial appearance, and even more has been said about the symbolism of her attire. I want to stress the strong and repeated use of imagery taken from linguistic education. Philosophy's dress is certainly a symbol of philosophical learning, but it is more. It is an imaginary book on whose literal margins (*margine*) are inscribed the Greek letters *pi* and *theta.*

> Atque inter utrasque litteras in scalarum modum gradus quidam insigniti videbantur quibus ab inferiore ad superius elementum esset ascensus. . . .

The flat, fallen *gradus* of the prisoner contrasts with the rising, vertical *gradus* of philosophical education. The meaningful markings of Philosophy's gown (the word *insigniti*) echo the meaningless marks Boethius made in silence (the word *signarem*). Through these verbal echoes Boethius creates a unified structure of imagery which explains the prisoner's initial silence and prepares us for Philosophy's opening words.

The word *gradus* is, of course, a commonplace metaphor for the struggle through life or education. Here, however, it signifies specifically a progress of verbal argument: the steps toward reason and belief effected through dialectical disputation and the mastery of invention and judgment. Three sources for the word—from Cicero, Augustine, and Boethius himself—illustrate the dialogue's opening concern with language, and they explain one aspect of the prisoner's inability to speak.

In the *Tusculan Disputations* Cicero summarizes the Socratic habit of inquiry as a method of understanding through discussion. In his review of the *Meno* (*Tusc. Disp.* 1. 57) Cicero places the idea of the *gradus* in a specifically dialogic context. When Socrates decides to question a young boy about geometry, Cicero analyzes the scene:

> ad ea sic ille respondet, ut puer, et tamen ita faciles interrogationes sunt, ut gradatim respondens eodem perveniat quo si geometrica didicisset.

The *gradus* comes to symbolize a path toward knowledge taken not through private speculation, but through public argument. As verbal activity, this movement stands in sharp contrast to the silent passivity of the prisoner's *gradus,* and it foreshadows the steps by which Philosophy will lead him in her method of question and response.

When Augustine appropriates this imagery in *De Magistro* he gives a specifically Christian resonance to the epistemological goal. Yet, the terms in which he analyzes his own dialogue with Adeodatus are primarily methodological rather than theological. The path toward a blessed life, he argues, may be directed, "gradibus quibusdam infirmo gressui nostro accomodatis perduci cupiam" (by truth itself through the stages of a degree suited to our weak progress). Here, the *gradus* represents a preliminary exercise, conducted at the comparatively low level of human discourse. While the force of Augustine's remark is to slight the method of open discussion as a mere *praeludo* to divine understanding, he nonetheless uses the word *gradus,* as Cicero had, to describe a uniquely verbal activity.

In his own writings on dialectic, Boethius adopted the word to characterize the study of argumentative forms. At the opening of Book Two of ***De topicis differentiis*** Boethius reprimands those students who would skip the necessary, early stages of study and proceed directly to its more advanced levels. To these impatient students he writes:

> Nam cum de differentiis topicis librorum titulum legerint omissis doctrinae gradibus statim finem operis attendunt.

Boethius's point throughout ***De topicis*** is that the topics are a system of argument rather than thought. They are, like the *via rationis* described in ***De Trinitate,*** a limited set of approaches to problems of judgment and belief. Such a system is bound by the limitations of ambiguity and obscurity found in human language; yet, as a regimen of study, the topics can lead to the threshhold of philosophy. As in Cicero and Augustine, the word *gradus* is linked with a method of public disputation. For these writers, the term represents a system of the study of language and the progress by which that study leads to understanding. When the word appears in the ***Consolatio***'s opening it complements the repeated images of silence, writing and speech; it highlights the failure and points toward the success of verbal expression. This process becomes the search for voice which is the controlling movement of Book One.

When Philosophy herself speaks, however, it is with a loud rhetorical flourish which banishes the Muses and which is designed to rouse the prisoner from his silence and lethargy. She understands his passive relationship to the Muses of poetry, and recognizes his silence for what it truly is:

> Quae ubi poeticas Musas vidit nostro adsistentes toro fletibusque meis verba dictantes, commota paulisper ac torvis inflammata luminibus. . . .

Again, Boethius gives structural unity to the opening passages through a series of verbal echoes. Philosophy recognizes that the Muses are dictating to the prisoner as he himself confessed: *verba dictantes* echoes *dictant scribenda.* Her first words boldly fill the empty silence in which the prisoner writes. In this context her banishment of the Muses can be read in a new way. Not only do they represent the vicious, vacuous music of a deranged mind; not only do they espouse, as David Chamberlain has noted, the *musica effeminita* guiding the prisoner's opening carmen. They are also a positive barrier to Boethius's search for his own voice. They render him passive and put words in his head, if not his mouth. They hinder the expression of his own self, that self he had forgotten. Philosophy's rejection focuses not on their absolute danger—for to a common man they do little harm—but on their effect on one of the learned, "reared on a diet of Eleatic and Academic thought." . . . Presumably, he was a man gifted with both reason and speech; and yet, he lies here, wasting his time on irrational poetry and staying dumb. Such a man, Philosophy laments in her first poem, sought and understood the workings of Nature, and could give voice to his understanding: "Naturae varias reddere causas" (1. m. 2., . . .). Her word *reddere* literally means the ability to give back in language, to translate or interpret from one language to another, or from symbols into speech. The word suggests that active quality now missing in the prisoner's silent transcription. Moreover, Philosophy sees into the prisoner's mind as he himself could not. She finds him lying *effeto mentis* (1. m. 2. 24., . . .). He had merely considered himself languishing *effeto corpore* (1. m. 1. 12., . . .).

We may pause here to compare the prisoner and Philosophy with the author of the tractates. Boethius showed how the writing of those works moved from inner knowledge to outer expression. The Muses did not dictate to him, and his literary activity, like Philosophy's initial appearance, uses signs and letters to present symbolically hidden truths. Both her gown and his text represent a kind of meaningful, virtuous use of language to ascend to knowledge. Thus, while ***De Trinitate*** and ***Contra Eutychen*** celebrate silence, the ***Consolatio*** condemns it.

The ***Consolatio***'s opening moves contrast the listlessness of the prisoner's laments with the power of Philosophy's eloquence. The emptiness of Boethius's opening poem is a foil for Philosophy's richly symbolic appearance. While the Muses have given the prisoner language, it is, strictly speaking, a "literal" language; it points only to human words. Philosophy favors a symbolic language: a language opaque to the uninitiated, one which must be interpreted and which ultimately points away from earth to heaven. The signs on her gown are not the kind of open, literal signs which explain themselves. They are the closed symbols which invite the mind's attention to a dimension of being which is not truly literal, not bound by words and letters. We cannot content ourselves with familiar explanations of Philosophy's symbols and her allegorical persona. Hers is an ostentatious symbolism which alerts us to its status *as* symbolism.

The tension between speech and silence develops further in the course of Book One. In *prosa* 2, Philosophy questions the prisoner's silence: "Quid taces?". . . . He appears stupefied by her appearance. But his silence is neither the dumbfoundedness of the visionary, nor the speechlessness of the awed, as Gruber [Joachim Gruber in his *Kommentar zu Boethius De Consolatione Philosophiae,* 1978] would claim. Rather, as Boethius himself tells us, it is a complex state. He is *tacitum, elinguem, mutum*: stripped of language, he has lost the ability to communicate in any form. When he can speak, through Philosophy's grace, he does not know where he is. The voice which returns to him is the oratory of the Senate: "An ut tu quoque mecum rea falsis criminationibus agiteris?" (1. 3., . . .). He considers himself still on trial for his crimes, still "in the dock" (as the Loeb translators put it), rather than in his library. When he finally gives vent to his anguish in 1. 4., it is through a classic, five-part oration defending himself against an imaginary accuser before a jury that is not there. The prisoner momentarily collects his thoughts ("ego collecto in vires animo," . . .), only to let out a flurry of thoughtless speech.

Kurt Reichenberger [in his *Untersuchungen zur literarischen stellung der Consolatio Philosophiae,* 1954] has analyzed in detail the forensic and rhetorical qualities of Boethius's extended speech, and it is not necessary to repeat him here. I do wish to stress the fact that this is pure oratory, replete with rhetorical questions, extended technical displays, and, in Reichenberger's words, "in dem gehobenen, oratorisch gefärbten Stil der Rede." When the prisoner has found a voice, it is like his opening poem transcribed in silence: language without meaning, or more appropriately, eloquence without wisdom. This speech also treats a form of writing similar to the prisoner's opening transcription. Midway through his tirade, Boethius asserts that he has written down the details of his accusation to be remembered by future generations: "Cuius rei seriem atque veritatem ne latere posteros queat, stilo etiam memoriaeque mandavi." . . . This writing, designed to preserve truth, merely perpetuates a lie. The truths of the affair are simply the facts, or a bill of particulars in a case of law. This is not the *veritas* of the philosopher, but simply a record of human events. By confusing truth with detail, the prisoner also confuses true memory with mere reportage. Boethius writes for public remembrance, and for vindication in the court of men rather than the eyes of God. This memory contrasts decisively with the proper philosophical or spiritual recollection which is one of the ***Consolatio***'s central goals. "You must remember what your native country is," Philosophy enjoins after this speech, "not one like that of the old Athenians," but the *patria* of the soul. . . . In his tirade, the prisoner travesties the Platonic relationship between remembering and forgetting which Philosophy addressed in 1. 2. ("Sui paulisper oblitus est; recordabitur facile, si quidem nos ante cognoverit," . . .). He reveals his forgetfulness by thinking that truth and memory may be wholly bound in the written letter, and by believing that to commit something to words (*stilo mandare*) is to commit it to eternity. In his overriding fidelity to *verba* rather than *res,* the prisoner admits that his case simply hinges on words. He claims to respond to the forgeries (the *falsa littera*) he is accused of writing. . . . While his opening *carmen* was an act of recording in silence, the prisoner's tirade becomes an act of recording performed through empty rhetoric.

That Philosophy is visibly unmoved by this bluster indicates the prisoner's misjudgment of his audience. After her broad, philosophical remarks on the prisoner's true forgetfulness and the condition of his spiritual exile, she returns to language. She analyzes his speech in terms taken explicitly from the theory of argument embodied in Boethius's own writing on the topics. Before she can engage him in a dialogue, she must descend to his level. The first indication of her shift in diction comes when she describes the library. As a *locus,* the library signifies the literal and figurative place of argument. She seeks a "storeroom of the mind" in which she has placed not physical books but the opinions they contain. By employing a diction taken from classical mnemonic theory, with its emphases on the *loci* and *sedes* of argument, Philosophy moves metaphorically into the prisoner's rhetorical world. She then summarizes his speech, separating and arranging the individual arguments by topic. She lists in order his accusations and comments on his forensic technique. Each statement is rhetorically signaled:

> De obiectorum . . .
> De sceleribus fraudibusque . . .
> De nostra etiam criminatione . . .
> Postremus adversum fortunam . . .
> in extremo Musae saevientis . . . .

Three sentences in a row open with the same *de,* and taken together with the following signals (*postremus, in extremo*) these devices call attention to Philosophy's deliberate display of her skill at *dispositio.* By organizing her remarks in this explicit manner, she offers herself as a model disputant. She is a master of both rhetorical form and psychological calm: "Illa vultu placido nihilque meis questibus mota". Hers is an ordered response which manifests itself through verbal perspicacity and mental tranquility. Philosophy highlights the prisoner's shortcomings and abilities as a debater and, in this way, justifies her cure. Grief has twisted his words, and she must use "milder medicines" to effect her treatment.

To correct his deficiencies as an arguer, Philosophy engages the prisoner in dialogue, and to do so, she begins her arguments in a dialectically technical way. She realizes that to move him away from opinions and toward truths—to effect her cure—she must begin at the level of probable disputation. After announcing the formal plan of question and answer which motivates their argument, the prisoner accepts.

> 'Primum igitur paterisne me pauculis rogationibus statum tuae men tis attingere atque temptare, ut qui modus sit tuae curationis intellegam?'
>
> 'Tu vero arbitratu, tuo quae voles ut responsurum rogato' [1. 6., . . .].

Their discussion properly develops from this point, with a commitment to dialogue at its basic level. The contract she proposes suggests that the dialectical method will dictate the form and pattern of their exchange. Echoing Boethius's own remarks in ***De topicis differentiis***, Philosophy had, immediately before (at 1. m. 6), foreshadowed discussion along the correct way. The *via* here, although a metaphorical usage, implies a methodological rather than a moral way.

> Sic quod praecipiti via
> Certum deserit ordinem
> Laetos non habet exitus
>
> [1. m. 6. 10-22., . . .].

This passage embodies the classical view of topical argument as an ordered way or method toward a proper goal. For the *ad Herennium,* technique (*ars*) was "praeceptio, quae dat certam viam rationemque dicendi" (1. 3), and this phrasing survives in Quintilian and Seneca. *Via* and *ordo* were the key terms in all classical definitions of correct argument. In ***De topicis,*** Boethius claimed that the topics point debaters to the path of truth ("viam quodammodo veritatis illustrat"), and he asserted that the study of topics promised "the paths of discovery" (*inveniendi vias*). In the opening of Book Two of ***De topicis,*** moreover, Boethius stressed how adherence to the proper order of study was essential before reaching the end: "Mihi autem necessarium videtur quod, nisi sit praecognitum ad ulteriora discentis animus pervenire non possit." The *ordo* of question and response, developed by Aristotle and praised by Cicero as the governing *gradus* of philosophical dialogue, stands behind Philosophy's commitment to dialectical discovery.

But the prisoner still has problems with method. He stubbornly adheres to the attitudes of a dialectician faced with a philosopher. Two examples from 1. 6. stand out. First, when asked about the governance of the universe, the prisoner can only reply: "Vix rogationis tuae sententiam nosco, nedum ad inquisita respondere queam." . . . Aristotle had permitted an answerer, if he did not understand, to say, "I do not understand." "He is not compelled to reply yes or no to a question which may mean different things." When faced with another, directly philosophical question, however, the prisoner's reliance on dialectical rules becomes his undoing. Philosophy questions his knowledge of himself as a man, and asks: "Quid igitur homo sit, poterisne proferre?" The prisoner replies: "Hocine interrogas an esse me sciam rationale animal atque mortale? Scio et id me esse confiteor." The question "what is man" had become, by Boethius's time, one of the classic examples of definition in dialectic. In his treatise *De Dialectica* Augustine had quoted the definition as if it were a commonplace, and in *De Magistro* Adeodatus voices a confusion similar to the prisoner's over the meaning of *homo.* Augustine is concerned here with the idea of a noun (*nomen*) and the concept of signification; his pupil mistakes the word for the object, and describes a man. In Boethius's own ***De topicis,*** the definition is held up as a more complete response than "two-legged animal capable of walking," just as, in *De Magistro*, "animal rationale mortale" is considered the *tota definitio.* "The question," Boethius writes in ***De topicis,*** "has to do with definition."

But Philosophy's question has little to do with definition. As Courcelle [Pierre Courcelle in his *La Consolation de Philosophie dans la tradition littéraire,* 1967] realized, with great florish, Philosophy does hearken back to an Aristotelian mode of argument: "Voilà donc le prix que Philosophie attache aux definitions logiques, telles que celle d'Aristote!" The point is not merely, as Courcelle would have it, that Philosophy calls attention to the spiritual inadequacy of the prisoner's response, nor that, in this dialogue, the author of the ***Consolatio*** reveals himself to be more than "un simple logicien." In failing to develop his answer philosophically (e.g., that man has a soul), the prisoner responds with a textbook answer; the idea of responding as a philosopher does not occur to him, and he remains trapped in a rudimentary habit of thought and expression. The scene has moral and methodological significance. In the context of Philosophy's own preparation for a technically accurate dialogue, the prisoner's response is another example of misdirecting his voice. As in the speech at I, 4, he has misjudged his audience.

From silence, then, the prisoner has progressed through florid rhetoric to a limited dialectic. He offers only examples of speaking and writing gone wrong, where silence is not a virtue but a vice. In the succeeding books, Philosophy will guide his expression through rhetoric and dialectic, but she must also educate him in the ways of writing. As we have seen, writing at its best becomes the natural process of the mind's independent investigation of truth. At its worst, it becomes the unthinking reflex of a man with no words of his own.

III

Book Two begins by commenting on the silence of Book One. About to speak, Philosophy is silent, and as she collects her thoughts, her "quiet modesty" does more to gain the prisoner's attention than any device of classical forensics.

> Post haec paulisper obticuit atque ubi attentionem meam modesta taciturnitate collegit, sic exorsa est [II, 1, . . .].

Her initial refusal to speak (*obticuit*) recalls Boethius's silent withdrawal from the noisy Senate in ***Contra Eutychen*** (*conticui*). Both characters meditate in quiet before voicing their knowledge or understanding. Just as Boethius had, in the tractate, abandoned the fruitless oratory of the forum, so Philosophy, for the moment, relinquishes her rhetorical skills. Philosophy also compares favorably against the prisoner in Book One. In his speech at 1. 4., he began by "collecting" his strength of mind (*collecto in vires animo,* . . .). As Gruber observed, Philosophy performs a similar activity as she *collegit,* or, "'sammelt' and ershlieât damit . . . die Aufmerksamkeit des Boethius." The similarities of phrasing compare Philosophy's calm with the prisoner's bluster, and contrast the ineffective use of rhetoric with the effective use of silence. Her quiet, unlike his, comes close to the ideal spiritual tranquility which grants the mind insight into itself and others.

The Book's initial concern with forms of expression colors Philosophy's opening remarks. In her first speech she summarizes the prisoner's relationship to fortune in terms of language. Different kinds of fortune, she claims, engendered different kinds of verbal responses. When the prisoner experienced good luck, he would "attack her [i.e., Fortuna] with firm language and chase her with arguments produced from our very sanctuary." . . . Bad fortune, though, has stripped the prisoner of his command of wisdom and eloquence. Philosophy implies that his inner, mental disturbance creates an outer, verbal incapacity. His present silence comes not from calm tranquility, but from agitated speechlessness.

Philosophy attempts to goad the prisoner into speech by creating an issue to which he must respond. She achieves her purpose by impersonating another character, Fortuna; if the prisoner will not respond to Philosophy's voice, perhaps he will respond to another. In his first words since the aborted dialogue of Book One, the prisoner appears to recognize the sham of Fortuna's rhetoric. After her long speech, Philosophy steps out of her imaginary role and back into the prisoner's forensic world. If Fortuna defended herself in this way, she asks, "you would not know what to reply" (2. 3., . . .). She now offers him a chance to speak: "Dabimus dicendi locum." The locus is an opportunity, but it is also a place or topic. The word signals a technical vocabulary at work, and enables the prisoner to reply in what appear to be his own terms.

> Speciosa quidem ista sunt, oblitaque Rhetoricae ac Musicae melle dulcedinis. . . .

Whereas Philosophy's music held an inner sweetness, Fortuna's is sugar coated. The prisoner's word (*dulcedinis*) echoes lexically and grammatically Philosophy's earlier term (*dulcedinis*). Once again, Boethius has one speaker repeat the words of another to demonstrate verbal ambiguity. The meaning of this word is bound by context and intention. The prisoner's recognition of the two kinds of sweetness is his first real insight of the ***Consolatio***. When he speaks, then, he initiates a process of discovery; yet, he has little to say throughout the book, save for an occasional assent (e.g., 2. 4., . . .), which in fact belies his own misunderstanding.

The prisoner opens 2. 7., however, by apologizing for his apparent pursuit of fame. His weak rejoinder contrasts with the rhetorical afflatus of his earlier defense in Book One, and the force of his latest remarks rests on a notion of unappreciated altruism.

> Scis ipsa minimum nobis ambitionem mortalium rerum fuisse dominatam. Sed materiam gerendis rebus optavimus quo ne virtus tacita consenesceret. . . .

Even in this modest excuse the prisoner belies a rhetorician's fear of silence. Whatever virtues he may have possessed found their expression in the Senate. His failure as a public man can be seen as a failure to move the public. When he voices his fear that his powers would "wither away silently," he expresses a limited, earthly concern with speechlessness. The higher, meditative quiet of Augustine or the tractates is absent from his mind. He thus reveals his own entrapment in a limited, human expression, while at the same time publically arguing for his dismissal of worldly ambition.

In her following arguments, Philosophy gives a broader relevance to the prisoner's condition. Glory cannot be immortal, she argues, for it is bound by reputation, and reputation is bound simply by words. Language and culture present barriers to the world-wide spread of human fame.

> Adde quod hoc ipsum brevis habitaculi saeptum plures incolunt nationes lingua, moribus, totius vitae ratione distantes, ad quas tum difficultate itinerum tum loquendi diversitate tum commercii insolentia non modo fama hominum singulorum sed ne urbium quidem pervenire queat. . . .

Cicero's argument that eloquence wisely used brings people together, fosters social mores, and establishes political unity must, I think, stand behind Philosophy's rebuttal of human fame. The fable of man in the state of nature which opens *De Inventione* posits a world in which men lived as savages until a great and wise man brought them together into an audience for his rhetoric and, in turn, into a community of civic life. Philosophy points out that language does not bring men together, except in very small groups. Rather it separates them into mutually incomprehending neighbors. As Gruber rightly noted, her phrasing *loquendi diversitate* echoes Augustine's idea in the City of God: "linguarum diversitas hominem alienat ab homine." Language alienates man from man, and written records, as Philosophy will argue, serve only to alienate man from his past.

While the prisoner had offered to preserve his case for future readers (1. 4.), Philosophy questions, "How many men famous in their own time are now completely forgotten for want of a written record? Though what is the value of such records themselves when they and their writers are lost in the obscurity of long ages". . . . Written records, like speech itself, have a limited spatial and temporal effect. The inscribed word cannot preserve a name for all eternity, she argues, and the prisoner's earlier claims now appear not only wrongheaded, but vain.

> Vos vero inmortalitatem vobis propagare videmini, cum futuri famam temporis cogitatis. Quod si aeternitatis infinita spatia pertractes, quid habes quod de nominis tui diuturnitate laeteris? . . .

Philosophy's suspicion of the power of the written word again recalls Cicero's view of writing as a social force, and of the written record as a source of knowledge about the past. At the opening of *De Inventione* Cicero reports how he began "to search in the records of literature for events which occurred before the period which our generation can remember." Historical writing served as a repository of public memory; it substituted for the oral mnemonics of an earlier era. Throughout his later dialogues Cicero repeated a concern for the power of the written word. It recorded historical acts, as in *De Inventione*. In *De Finibus* writing preserved Greek and Latin masterpieces for contemporary edification and imitation. In the *Tusculan Disputations* Plato's philosophical dialogues were themselves written documents. They preserved the structure of Socratic inquiry as well as the ideas embodied in the man's thought.

But it would appear to Philosophy that letters are not a blessing but a curse; they do not preserve the truth for the future, they merely ossify the past in obscurity. In the course of her polemic, Philosophy retells a famous story about philosophical silence to illustrate the limits of the prisoner's understanding and, more important, the difficulties she herself will confront in trying to put thoughts into words. When the bogus philosopher of the story—after quietly enduring his challenger's insults—replies "Now do you recognize that I am a philosopher," his taunter answers, "I should have, had you kept silent." . . . This ideal philosophical silence is a commonplace of Ancient thought, given a new resonance in Boethius's larger context of speaking and writing. The story serves to highlight the prisoner's early reliance on faulty rhetoric directed at a foolish audience. As Philosophy reminds him, "de alienis praemia sermunculis postulatis" (You ask for the rewards of the common chatter of other men. . .). For now, the alternative to vulgar chatter is philosophical silence. As Boethius illustrated in the preface to ***Contra Eutychen,*** the philosopher must remove himself physically and verbally from the crowd.

This imagery reinforces the commonly noticed visions of exile and loneliness throughout the ***Consolatio***. Languages separate man from his neighbors and distance him from his ancestors, and speech, rather than making him part of a community, makes him an exile in his own world and from his own past. In *metrum* 7 Philosophy restates the transitory quality of human language, and the mutability of writing.

> Signat superstes fama tenuis pauculis
>   Inane nomen litteris.
> Sed quod decora novimus vocabula,
>   Num scire consumptos datur?
> Iacetis ergo prorsus ignorabiles
>   Nec fama notos efficit
>
> [17-22 . . .]

Unlike Cicero, who would find companionship in Antique writers, Philosophy can only ask: "Do we really know the dead?" It is this characteristic of language to make something limited, or transitory, which hinders Philosophy's own exposition of her doctrine.

In her final prose statement of Book Two she questions the very vehicle of their dialogue. She expresses some trepidation at using a purely philosophical language, a language which makes no concessions to common opinion or to apparent credibility. How can the prisoner understand her thoughts when words constrain her arguments? "Nondum forte quid loquar intellegis" (2. 8.,. . .). She attempts to convey to him the wonderful paradox of the benefits of bad fortune, and she fears that, argued straightforwardly, her idea will fall beyond the prisoner's grasp: "Mirum est quod dicere gestio, eoque sententiam verbis explicare vix queo." . . . At issue here is the inability of *verba* to contain *sententia,* and of rational argument (*explicatio*) to express marvels. Up to now she has avoided the problem by relying on "milder medicines"—rhetoric and poetry—whose purpose was to soothe rather than to convince. But at this point she creates in the prisoner the expectation of understanding, and stimulates his reason and his voice.

By the opening of Book Three, still in silence, the prisoner finds a voice which can successfully initiate dialogue. The sweetness of Philosophy's last poem leaves him in expectant, attentive silence. For the first time in the ***Consolatio*** it is the prisoner who willingly breaks a silence without waiting for Philosophy's goad. His opening exclamation, "O," set apart from the rest of the sentence by an intrusive *inquam,* calls attention to the prisoner's vocal ability. He utters at first not a word but a non-verbal exclamation of joy. The long *O* of Philosophy's concluding verses, "O felix hominum genus" (2. 8. 28), must still ring in his ears as he echoes sound for sound.

But for all his eagerness, the prisoner fails to make an open commitment to participating in the dialogue. He wishes only to be a listener, even though this silence will be more virtuous than that of the previous books. Philosophy herself notices this new quiet ("Sensi cum verba nostra tacitus attentusque rapiebas," . . .), and she makes an attempt to describe familiar matters as a kind of propaedeutic to more difficult issues. She will try to point out in words—*designare verbis*—"a subject better known to you". . . . Her phrasing recalls her earlier inability to *verbis explicare;* but now, she will deal not in marvels but in commonplaces, not with goals of their inquiry but rather with its method. By explaining how they will proceed, Philosophy shows how the dialogue will move through human issues toward divine ones. Her remarks embody that sense of the *gradus* found at the ***Consolatio***'s beginning and in Boethius's writing on the topics: a moral and methodological rectitude which guides the *via rationis.*

From this point onward, the prisoner's silence is no longer that unique Boethian silence of the opening. When he fails to answer Philosophy's questions, or accedes to her authority, he appears simply as an incompetent student or a faltering dialectician rather than as a man stripped of language. Finally, when his own presence disappears from the dialogue altogether at the end of Book Five, we see the prisoner moving closer to the higher form of philosophical silence which demands no company save the self and God. I have argued here, however, that the ***Consolatio***'s beginning represents a search for voice; that the prisoner's character is less a physical presence than a verbal one; and that to change his character Philosophy must direct his speech. By using the images and metaphors of writing and speaking developed in his technical and theological works, Boethius gives the ***Consolatio***'s beginning a firm place in the development of his thought. By responding to Augustine's notion of a rhetoric of silence and to Cicero's views of oratory, Boethius gives his work a place in the history of ideas. In their meditations on the written word, Cicero and the Saint provide the vocabulary for Boethius's own reflections on language and silence in society. If he has created his personal rhetoric of silence, it is to understand and transcend the rhetoric of man.

Seth Lerer (essay date 1985)

SOURCE: "Language and Loss in Book Three," in *Boethius and Dialogue: Literary Method in "The Consolation of Philosophy,"* Princeton University Press, 1985, pp. 124-65.

[*In the following excerpt, Lerer analyzes the thematic and stylistic patterns of the third book of the* Consolation of Philosophy, *calling it "a book of transformations, as its poetry turns mythological narrative and Senecan tragedy into an almost religious cosmology, and its prose turns the language of Aristotelian dialectic into a suitable medium for philosophic inquiry."*]

The third book of the ***Consolation*** is perhaps the most philosophically rewarding and the most methodologically subtle of all the dialogue's sections. Containing the great Timean hymn (m.9), the long discourse on earthly goods (pr.3-9), the intricate Platonic arguments of prosa 12, and the enigmatic poem on Orpheus (m.12), the book challenges the prisoner's expressive and interpretive abilities. It is little wonder that the book has stimulated more criticism than any other part of the ***Consolation***. Most readers have found in it the heart of Boethius' Platonic thought and imagery. Structurally, the book has traditionally been seen as dividing itself, and in turn the work as a whole, in two. While the first section (prosae 1-9) appears to continue the Aristotelian dialectic of Books One and Two, the second section (metrum 9 to the end) points towards an explicitly Platonic epistemology. This Platonism may inform the concluding poem on Orpheus, as the hell-descent it portrays carries with it a mass of Platonic and Neoplatonic allegorical implications. The function of the metra themselves has also been understood as changing in the course of the book. From what one critic has called "a larger dialogue between rational argumentation and poetry," the poetry after "O qui perpetua" seems "relegated to the role of a moralizing chorus."

My reading of Book Three qualifies and takes issue with these earlier approaches. The opening prosae develop the relationship between dialectical and philosophical forms of argument explored in earlier books. The speakers come to talk more and more about the structure of their dialogue itself. Their discussion becomes self-reflexive, in that it is fundamentally concerned with elucidating its own method. It also becomes self-referring, in that key terms presume the reader's familiarity with their use elsewhere in Boethius' writings. I will explore these qualities by finding the sources for the ***Consolation***'s language in the technical vocabulary of the logical writings. Boethius' remarks on the relationship of probable logic to philosophical demonstration highlight one aspect of Philosophy's conversation with the prisoner. While she relies on proofs, he is content with opinions; while she addresses his mind, he responds through his senses. This tension motivates the text's dramatic progress, and Boethius' constant Platonizing of the dialectical terminology gives the discussion an added dimension.

If the ***Consolation***'s opening books represent the search for a voice through which the prisoner may learn to argue, then Book Three may be said to portray the search for a place towards which he must direct his energies. That place has been interpreted as the soul's home in the heavens, the *patria* towards which the mind returns after death. The prisoner's position thus places him in a state of loss or unfulfillment. He lacks the awareness of his future spiritual goal and a present intellectual direction. Philosophy's purpose in Book Three will involve directing his mind (metaphorically described as looking upwards) and developing his reason (methodologically depicted as learning how to argue). Images of loss, be they of purpose, direction, or meaning, permeate the book, from Philosophy's opening arguments on happiness, to the final poem on Orpheus' loss of Eurydice. As Philosophy herself puts it, the prisoner is menaced by psychological disturbances which create in him a feeling of emptiness or absence. Human desire, she argues, is motivated through an inner need to fill that absence with a spiritual beatitude. The longing for fulfillment or knowledge leaves man dependent on such earthly substitutes as wealth, fame, power, or sensory pleasure. These "external" ways to happiness are but bypaths on the path to the true good. Fulfillment will be gained, she argues, through self-sufficiency: through strength of mind and growth of spirit.

To this end, Book Three explores images of alienation and of the undeniable otherness which sets the self apart from the multitude. If the movement of the opening books was methodological, then in Book Three it is epistemological. The prisoner must come to know and to comprehend that process of knowing. In this sense, the book develops a vocabulary of wonder, both in the prose and the poetry. While Philosophy's arguments are calculated to eliminate admiration and foster comprehension, her poetry, especially the Timean hymn, is designed to inspire awe. Her poems turn nature into myth, for they figure forth the physical or psychological processes in literary narratives. Her poetry also contributes to the intellectual progress of the dialogue, embodying through its rhetoric and imagery the underlying order of rational inquiry.

Book Three is also the most obviously rhetorical of the ***Consolation***'s sections, for in it Boethius uses structures of form and imagery to call attention to his thematic concern with technique. It offers a counterpoint to the "rhetoric of silence" explored in the Augustinianism of the tractates, and it presents a more rigorous system of argument than the forensics of Book One. Close examination of the formal structures of metra 2, 9, and 12 reveals how Philosophy presents herself not only as a model disputant, but as a model poet and musician. Through these devices, her poetry directs the prisoner's mind away from his earthly cares and towards the inspired meditation of the kind Boethius experienced in the ***Contra Eutychen***. By filling the prisoner with a sense of wonder, she restores his emotional stability and points towards spiritual enlightenment.

I

After her initial commitment to describe in words the subjects familiar to the prisoner, Philosophy begins her extended analysis of human happiness in prosa 2. Like Boethius' own meditative process described in ***Contra Eutychen,*** Philosophy prepares for her speech by directing her vision and her voice away from external distractions and towards her own thoughts. As in the tractate, the process of introspection appears in visual terms. Boethius was concerned with watching Symmachus, and with seeking to discover in his expression a source for his opinions. Similarly, throughout the ***Consolation,*** the prisoner pays careful attention to Philosophy's countenance, from her opening look which fills him with awe (I.I.I) and her blazing eyes, to the gravity of her appearance at the opening of Book Four (IV.I.I). The movement of turning away from or towards something becomes the central image of Boethian meditation (as when he turns away from the mob in ***Contra Eutychen***), and it informs Philosophy's own injunction at the opening of Book Three for the prisoner to turn his eyes towards blessedness. Moreover, Philosophy's appearance contrasts with the fallen look of the prisoner at the dialogue's beginning. Just as she had sought to see into the prisoner's mind ("tuae mentis sedem requiro," 1.pr.5.6), now Boethius echoes her own words in describing her thoughtful countenance (". . . suae mentis sedem recepta," III.pr.2.1). Her inward preparation for rational argument also recalls the prisoner's misguided attempt to shape his own arguments before his oratorical outburst at 1.pr.4.

In this manner, Boethius uses one of the ***Consolation***'s prevalent metaphors to characterize Philosophy's intellectual virtue. From a purely technical standpoint, however, Philosophy's initial moves also correspond to the mental activity prescribed for a debater in Aristotle's *Topica.* Aristotle had outlined a three-step process for formulating and expressing an argument. First, the questioner must select the basis of the approach; second, he must frame and arrange his points in his own mind; finally, he must proceed to verbalize his argument to his partner. Philosophy's preparation describes her as a textbook disputant, where the order of the argument corresponds to the ordering of thoughts. Her behavior also conforms to Aristotle's suggested habits of philosophical inquiry. While both dialecticians and philosophers, he wrote, start from the same tripartite system of inquiry, the philosopher may prefer to begin questioning with familiar axioms, and his initial argumentative moves may seem to progress little from the given starting point. When Philosophy decides, therefore, to present in words things better known to the prisoner, she commits herself to a method of inquiry consonant with the Aristotelian rules for reasoned investigation. It is from this commitment to begin with familiar subjects that, as Aristotle claimed, syllogistic reasoning grows (in the Boethian translation, "ex his enim disciplinales syllogismi," . . .).

It is significant that Philosophy speaks metaphorically in her opening remarks, and that her images are securely grounded in the vocabulary of direction developed in Boethius' logical writings. In the ***In Topica Ciceronis*** Boethius credited Cicero with preserving Aristotle's method for finding arguments directly and without error. His own ***De topicis differentiis*** had developed the image of argument as a way through error into a controlling ethos of study. When Philosophy comes to characterize the human and cosmic order, she draws upon a dialectical vocabulary to make her concepts understandable to the prisoner. Her repetitions reinforce the sense of direction which returns the mind to its proper home.

> Mortal men laboriously pursue many different interests along many different paths, but all strive to reach the same goal of happiness. . . . And, as I said, all men try by various paths to attain this state of happiness; for there is naturally implanted in the minds of men the desire for the true good, even though foolish error draws them toward false goods.

In the course of her speech, Philosophy speaks more and more figuratively, developing her metaphors and similes into codes of behavior. She employes the imagery of vision to place before his eyes the range of human happiness. In a simile which recalls the picture of the wandering ignorant or the fickleness of fortune, she explains how the mind no longer knows the good, "like the drunken man who cannot find his way home." The symbolic drunkenness of the mind lost in sensory error contrasts with Philosophy's earlier claims for the sobriety of prudent caution. Boethius has built these figures from the language of dialectic, and he equates propriety of speech and thought with propriety of action. The strong moral sense of error is also figuratively transformed into a kind of incompleteness. The prisoner lacks a sense of home (a *domus* or *patria*), and his spiritual error creates a psychological condition of insufficiency or emptiness.

To this end, Philosophy, in her next prosa, questions the prisoner about his emotional condition. To his realization that at no time could he recall being free of worry, she asserts: "And wasn't it because you wanted something you did not have, or had something you did not want?" ("Nonne quia uel aberat quod abesse non uelles uel aderat quod adesse noluisses?") Her questioning establishes a tension between wanting and having, reinforced by the rhetorical pattern of her speech. She arranges her words chiastically, with parallel sequences: *aderat / addesse* answers *aberat / abesse*. At the heart of the prisoner's misery is a deep void, expressed as a lack of direction and fulfillment. To Philosophy, the action of desire becomes a longing to fill that emptiness: "So you desired the presence of the one, and the absence of the other?" As her argument develops, she delineates the relationship between the outer show of language, cheapened by time, and inner virtue. In characterizing the prisoner's condition of desire, she shows how such external qualities as language, wealth, power, and glory serve only to alienate man from man: to render hiim parasitic on the world rather than sufficient in himself. Fame, as she argued in Book Two, does not eliminate desire, it intensifies it. The fear of loss motivates worldly achievement, as the man enamored of earthly goods obsessively tries to guard them against theft. This activity, compounded by an equally compulsive appetite for personal ownership, creates insatiable need.

In formulating Philosophy's arguments, Boethius draws on his own view of the individual's relationship to the mob expressed in ***Contra Eutychen*** and adumbrated in the asides in his commentaries. His repeated use of the word *aliena* reinforces the split between the self and the other. Throughout the ***Consolation*** the word describes those external goods which, by directing man towards others, alienate him from himself. The language of the mob also appears in these terms. Like rumor and popularity, the common speech of men is vapid and meaningless, rendering man passively subject to a corrupting force. In Book Three Philosophy shows how public reputation and nobility depend on the perception of others. Like fame, nobility brings man into the confusion of other men, and the fame of others cannot redound to oneself. Together, these images restate the fundamental emptiness of fame and the vacuity of power.

Into this structure of imagery, Philosophy introduces the word *extrinsecus* to characterize spiritual and rational insufficiency. With its source in Cicero's and Boethius' dialectical writings, the word signals a discipline where belief takes precedence over truth. Because dialectic aims to convince, rather than demonstrate, it can employ *extrinseca argumenta* which depend on the authority of others for their credibility to the listener. In ***De topicis differentiis*** Boethius classes arguments from judgment under the heading of *extrinsecus*, and he clarifies their difference from philosophical demonstration.

> There remains the Topic which he [i.e., Cicero] said is taken from without (*extrinsecus assumi*). This depends on judgment and authority and is only readily believable, containing nothing necessary.

In the dialectical writings, *extrinsecus* is a term used to characterize an argument which derives its strength from outside opinion. In other writings, it is used metaphorically, to describe accidental qualities (as in ***De Trinitate***) or, in the ***Consolation*** itself, to refer to the power of God or the power of reasoning. God's grace is not received from outside, but is unique to and part of his nature. Unlike the transitory, extrinsic things of this world—which depend on perception for their value—God needs no outside assistance in governing the Universe. He remains the uniquely self-sufficient being of the cosmos. Towards the end of Book Three, the prisoner begins to recognize the structure of philosophical arguments in these terms, and he commends his partner: "And you proved all this without outside assumptions (*nullis extrinsecus sumptis*) and used only internal proofs which draw their force from one another." Central to his praise is his characterization of Philosophy as a philosopher; he virtually echoes his own earlier definition of ***De topicis differentiis,*** and reveals that, by the conclusion of Book Three, he has learned something of method, if not of doctrine. The imagery here is not designed to suggest, as some have claimed, that the prisoner praises Philosophy for arguing without need of outside, *Christian* arguments. It is specifically couched in the language of the logical writings, and it contributes to the larger structure of imagery which to this point has focused on

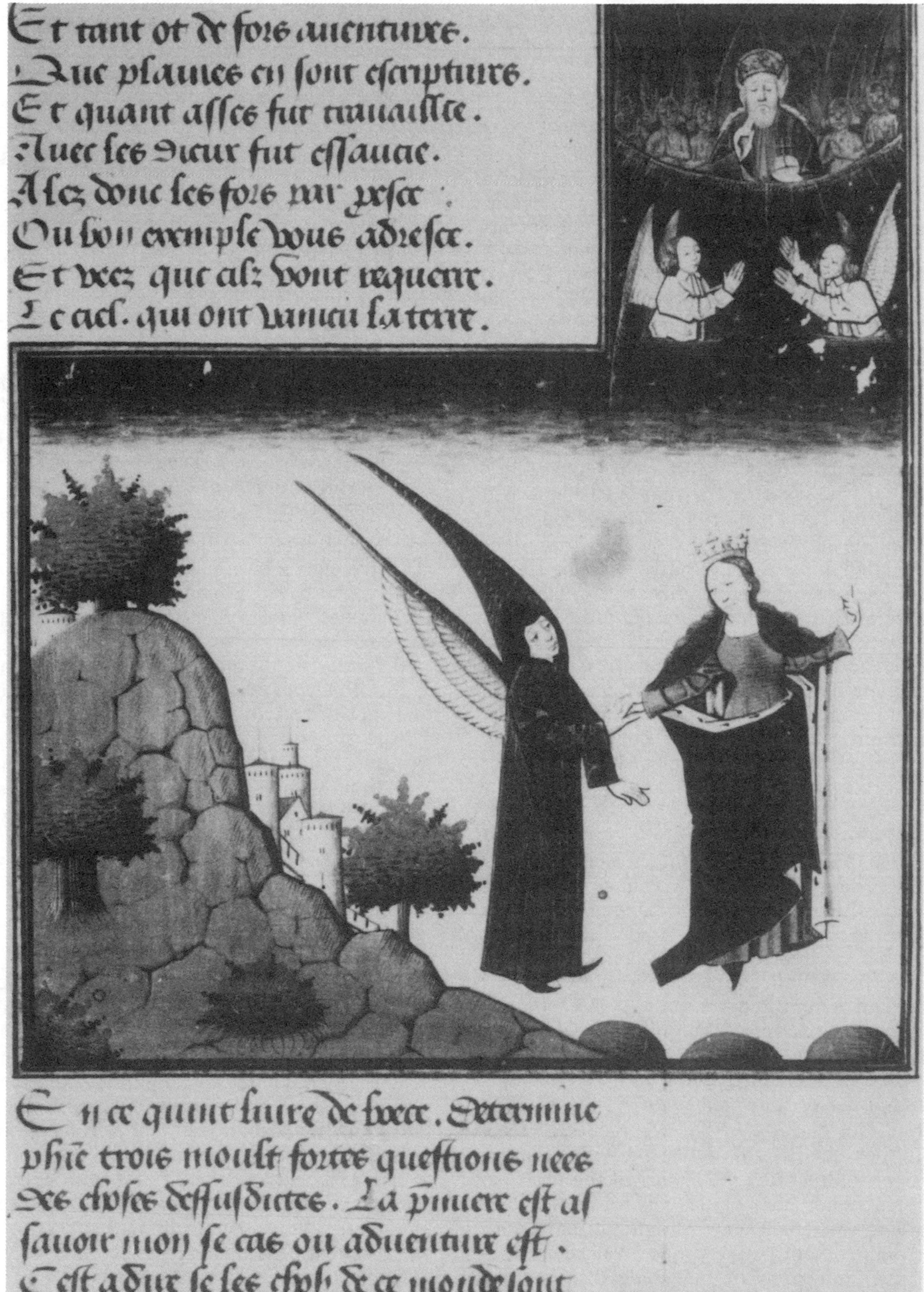
Et tant ot de fois aventures.
Que plaines en sont escriptures.
Et quant asses fut travaillee.
Avec les dieux fut essaucee.
Alez donc les fors par presce.
Ou bon exemple vous adresce.
Et vees que alz vont requerre.
Le ciel. qui ont vaincu la terre.

En ce quint livre de boece. determine philosophie trois moult fortes questions nees des choses dessusdictes. La premiere est a savoir mon se cas ou adventure est. Cest a dire se les choses de ce monde sont ou aviennent de cas ou daventure. La seconde est se franc arbitraige cest a dire franche voulente domme est. La tierce est. Se franche voulente domme puet

The ascent of Boethius.

interiority, propriety, and self-sufficiency.

II

Before the prisoner can recognize Philosophy's method for what it is, and long before he can attempt to imitate it, he must engage his teacher's arguments and learn to respond rationally. He has said nothing from the middle of prosa 3 to the beginning of prosa 9. When he begins to speak again, it is through a rhetoric of simple assents which reveal his apparent impatience with Philosophy's method and his lack of commitment to the proper order of inquiry. The concluding prosae of Book Three create the context for reflection and interpretation, as they continually take stock of the dialogue's progress. These prosae also develop the imagery of wonder which Philosophy had earlier used to describe the inability to express divine wisdom in human terms. For verbal discussion to progress, she must eliminate the sense of wonder in the prisoner, a wonder which had kept him in silent awe of Philosophy's implied truths. In the ***Contra Eutychen*** Boethius had marvelled at the truth revealed through private meditation ("unde mihi maxime subiit admirari . . . "). This emotional response resulted from the figurative opening of the door to knowledge, or from the experience of truth unmediated by public discourse. In the ***Consolation,*** however, where public discussion is but a propaedeutic to the revelation of enigmatic truth, arguments must proceed without amazement on the part of either disputant. Just as Philosophy had suppressed her own impending wonderment in order to proceed at the end of Book Two, so the prisoner must replace his sense of wonder with a sense of purpose.

Prosa 9 opens with Philosophy's explicit statement of procedure: "Up to this point, I have shown clearly enough the nature of false happiness, and, if you have understood it, I can now go on to speak of true happiness." In the Latin, the phrasing emphasizes the proper sequence of inquiry: ". . . ordo est deinceps quae sit uera monstrare" (III.pr.9.1). This prosa will explore the various ways of understanding, and it repeatedly expresses the action of knowing as a process of seeing. The metaphorical structures have moved from telling (from Philosophy's earlier desire to *explicare*) to showing. Philosophy now attempts to *monstrare,* and the prisoner responds that he sees, albeit imperfectly, the purpose of her arguments. "I see," he begins, and then qualifies his statement with an image which recalls, by contrast, the metaphors of the tractates: "I think I glimpse them [i.e., Philosophy's reasons] as it were through a narrow crack, but I should prefer to learn of them more plainly from you." At one level, the prisoner prefers to have Philosophy do his intellectual work for him. His desire to learn "more openly" (*apertius*) is a request to listen rather than to argue. At another level, the prisoner's statement illustrates the preliminary nature of dialogue, and it reveals the limitations of verbal explanation. In his request for a more open method of understanding, the prisoner hearkens back to the imagery of the tractates, where philosophical knowledge was wrapped in new and enigmatic terms, but also where truth itself could come revealed as through an open door. At the heart of the prisoner's imagery is a basic impatience with the slow moving method of question and response, and at the same time an awareness of the need for progressing through the steps of argument. He is not yet ready to see the truth openly, and his vocabulary here recalls the rhetoric of understanding reserved for the theological investigations of the tractates or the close of Augustine's *Confessions.*

The prisoner's impatience extends to his evaluation of his own abilities. By the end of prosa 9 he has agreed with much of what Philosophy has said, and he itches to inform her of the scope of his understanding. For the first time in the ***Consolation,*** the prisoner reformulates her arguments, and he registers his attention to their outer structure and their inner substance.

> But this is clear even to a blind man, and you revealed it a little while ago when you tried to explain the causes of false happiness. . . . And to show that I have understood you, I acknowledge that whatever can truly provide any one of these must be true and perfect happiness, since all are one and the same.

The prisoner's vocabulary revives the imagery he and Philosophy have developed to this point. Clarity appears in terms of sense perception, and even though the seeing is metaphorical, the prisoner's use of the blind man as his foil reinforces the notion of logical demonstration as a form of showing rather than explaining. He uses Philosophy's word *monstrare* here, and his term for explanation (*aperire*) echoes his own earlier request for philosophical revelation. The prisoner is also deeply concerned that Philosophy come to know something of his own interior state. He has understood her inwardly (*interius*), and he seems to exult in his discovery of a truth *sine ambiguitate.* He offers an attempt at pure philosophizing without the double edge of dialectic, and an attempt to move beyond that discourse in which, as Augustine noted, every word is ambiguous.

While Philosophy is proud of her pupil, she qualifies her praise. She makes clear that the prisoner still labors under opinion: that, while he may grasp the form of her argument, he is still incapable of complete understanding. "Your observation is a happy one," she states, "if you add just one thing." She focuses on an epistemological movement subtly different from the prisoner's, and the vocabulary shifts are important. While he attempted to *cognoscere,* she will show him how to *agnoscere.* I think the difference in these terms represents a difference between cognition and acknowledgment, or between the inner contentment of knowing and the outer expression of that knowledge through verbal activity. Again, Boethius distinguishes between things understood passively, as through listening or revelation, and things learned actively, as through public argument. This activity, however, will for the moment be postponed, as Philosophy offers in the Timaean hymn a poetic counterpoint to her prose argument. If her prose passages are calculated to eliminate wonder and foster verbal discussion, her poetry is designed to inspire awe and instill a reverent silence. As expressed in the visual metaphors of the Book, "O qui perpetua" directs the prisoner to look up to his heavenly goal, to see (*defigere, cernere*) not with the eyes but with the mind. In its use of the central figures of the ***Consolation***'s thought, the Timaean hymn recapitulates the movement of the dialogue, and it imbues the terms taken from dialectic with a new philosophical and cosmological significance.

The poem's indebtedness to the *Timaeus* and its commentaries is so apparently obvious, and so frequently stressed by critics, that few of its readers have cared to notice how the poem functions within the dialogue itself. Generations of the ***Consolation***'s readers have found in "O qui perpetua" a set piece of Boethian Platonism; next to Fortune's wheel, this is perhaps the most famous of all sections of the work. By restating the fundamental images developed by the disputants, the poem comments on the terms in which Philosophy and the prisoner characterize their method and their music. One example of this restatement appears at the poem's opening. God acts without external causes, and forms within himself an image of the good impressed on all creation. "No external causes impelled You to make this work from chaotic matter." This phrasing recalls the language of extrinsic arguments developed by Boethius and explored, in its moral dimension, throughout the ***Consolation***. It also looks forward to the description of God as sufficient in himself, and it will give to the conversation later in Book Three—where the prisoner praises Philosophy's arguments as containing *nullis extrinsecus sumptis*—a certain philosophical resonance. The poem's initial effect depends on recognizing its uniquely Boethian vocabulary. The hymn takes Philosophy at her word by developing her earlier ideas of musical and cosmic order. It enacts this recapitulation by transforming earlier mythological motifs into an abstract Platonic cosmology. In two earlier poems, II.m.8 and III.m.2, Phoebus had been a figure for celestial harmony. The regularity of sunrise and sunset in these poems confirmed one's expectation of and faith in the essential rightness of the system.

> . . . that Phoebus in his golden chariot brings in the shining day, that the night, led by Hesperus, is ruled by Phoebe, . . .
>
> (II.m.8.)

> Phoebus sets at night beneath the Hesperian waves,
> but returning again along his secret path he drives his
> chariot to the place where it always rises.
>
> (III.m.2)

In these metra the chariot symbolizes the process of travel and return. Phoebus and Hesperus appear as mythological representatives of day and night and of light and dark. In "O qui perpetua," however, the picture of Phoebus in his chariot becomes an image of the human soul's passage from heaven to earth and back to heaven. While the ideas expressed in the poem have their origins in Plato and Proclus, within the structure of the ***Consolation*** these lines resonate with earlier poetic treatments of the same image.

> In like manner You create souls and lesser living forms and, adapting them to their high flight in swift chariots, You scatter them through the earth and sky. And when they have turned again toward You, by your gracious law, You call them back like leaping flames.

The Phoebus narratives which described features of living in the world prefigure the condition of living in the cosmos. The human sight of the sun returning in its rosy dawn becomes the divine vision of the soul returning in its celestial fire. By Platonizing the story of Phoebus, Boethius creates a new philosophical context in which to re-read the earlier passages. His structure of imagery unifies the poetic sequences in the early books. In this framework, the Timaean hymn reads less as an isolatable expression of Neoplatonic thought and more as an integral part of the ***Consolation***'s progress.

The image of returning expressed in the lines above complements the theories of harmony which find thematic and structural expression both in the hymn itself and in Philosophy's earlier poem, "Quantas rerum flectat habenas" (III.m.2). This metrum foreshadows the metaphorical and structural patterns of the hymn, and points toward a theory of poetic composition embedded in the poetry. In III.m.2, Philosophy restates her moral and methodological aims. The opening lines reformulate her earlier injunction against the vicious muses of the prisoner's opening song, and she presents him with an example of music at its best.

> Now I will show you in graceful song, accompanied by pliant strings, how mightily Nature guides the reins of all things; how she providently governs the immense world by her laws; how she controls all things, binding them in unbreakable bonds.

The instrumental music she offers in this poem fosters wisdom and virtue, and the imagery of its opening lines associates the strings on which she plays with the bonds which unite all elements of the universe. Concord is both instrumental and cosmic, and even the formal structure of her verse mimes the metaphorical structure of her subject. The Latin is intricately woven in its syntax; internal and end rhymes complement the patterns of assonance; the first sentence, six lines long, suspends its agent *cantu* ("in song") until the very last word. Philosophy's elaborate display of technique exemplifies the poet as orderer and creator. Throughout this poem Philosophy uses structural devices to imitate her subject. In her description of the caged bird, she employs a self-conscious formal pattern to give new expression to the old Platonic idea, dubbed by Courcelle [Pierre Courcelle, "L'âme en cage," in K. Flasch, ed., *Parusia,* 1965], of "l'âme en cage." The bird shut in her cavernous cage suggests the Platonic image of the soul imprisoned in the body. In the final two lines of this description, anaphora marks the bird's vocal longing with a metrical pattern: "Siluas tantum maesta requirit, / siluas dulci uoce susurrat" (III.m.2.25-26). The poem's end brings the reader structurally and thematically back to its beginning. The sense of returning home in the last lines combines with the idea of order expressed in the first sentence. The ordered course is "that which connects the beginning to the end" (*quod fini iunxerit ortum,* 37). While this moral statement comments on the poem's structure as a whole, the text's final lines give a unifying conclusion through a pattern of repetition:

currum solitos vertit ad *or*tus.
Repetunt proprios quaeque recursus
redituque suo singula gaudent
nec manet ulli traditus *or*do
nisi quod fini iunxerit *or*tum
stabilemque sui fecerit *or*bem.

Through the repeated *or*-syllable, the ideas embodied in the poem's vocabulary are reified through sound, as well as sense.

The Timaean hymn appears as a complex restatement of the problems posed by this earlier poem, for it uses rhetoric and musical imagery to express its philosophical content. The expression of Timaean world harmony and the imagery of binding the elements develop the poetic and mythological material of the earlier poem into a statement of divine cosmology. The phrasing of "O qui perpetua" has been seen, in one critic's words, as offering "man a pattern of love and order by which to guide his own life." But these patterns also suggest imaginative structures: habits of mind which find their voice in virtuous metrics. Philosophy's language points to a poetry subject to the divine *ordo,* yet also governed by the speaker's own power. The self-reflexive qualities which the poem attributes to God are embodied in the verbal patterns of the text. As the mind of God turns inward from the world created in its own likeness, and as the soul turns inward to comprehend itself, so the text creates a system of self-reference through rhetorical echoes. As in III.m.2, the order of reason becomes the order of poetry.

"O qui perpetua" contains in its opening sentence a series of repetitions which establish the reflective patterning. It opens with what Gruber calls [J. Gruber, *Kommentar zu Boethius De Consolatione Philosophiae,* 1978], "der Relativstil der Prädikation . . . mit dem anaphorischen *qui . . . qui . . . quem.*" It then works through a rhetorical system of interlacement to reinforce God's impression of his own mind on the outer shape of creation. Using a limited vocabulary charged with meaning, the poem mirrors itself metrically and sonically, as creation mirrors creator. The entire text is punctuated by rhetorical parallels which mark the progress of the argument. Through antistrophe, Boethius repeats line endings (*cuncta moueri,* 3; *cuncta superno,* 6; *cuncta mouentem,* 13). Through anaphora, he restates the form of address in an almost litanizing way (*Tu numeris,* 10; *Tu triplicis,* 13; *Tu causis,* 18). The appearance of words for earth and sky sets up a chiastic pattern of echo and return.

terrarum caelique sator . . . (2)
. . . deducant pondera terras. (12)
. . . conuertit imagine caelum. (17)
in caelum terramque seris, . . . (20)

The concluding repetitions, "Da, pater, . . . / Da fontem . . . , da luce" (21-22), and, "tu namque serenum, / tu requies . . ." (26-27), bring the poem to an emphatic climax, directing the reader's mind away from the forms of God's work to divinity itself. The poem's final vision thus fulfills the prisoner's "eager longing" for the way to happiness.

The poetry thus differs from the prose in that it shows rather than argues. It is designed to instill wonder not simply by stating God's power but by presenting the poet's skills. The elaborate rhetorical patterns in poems such as III.m.2 and III.m.9 are an integral part of Philosophy's purpose; rather than the vacuous displays of the prisoner's early poetry, these technical flourishes enact the themes of the metra. They show Philosophy as a master of poetic diction, as well as of dialectical and philosophical argument, and her return to these systems of rational inquiry may come as something of an anticlimax to the prisoner and reader. In prosa 10 she returns to structures of reason from patterns of wonder. Even though the prisoner has seen (*uidisti*) the form of the good, he must use logical inquiry to understand its earthly counterpart. Now, Philosophy's commitment is to demonstrate (*demonstrare*) her truths. As in her earlier decision to "designare verbis," or to "explicare," her terminology signals a rational rather than a transcendental process. By directing the prisoner back to a system of questioning (her word *inquirendum,* III.pr.10.2) she restates the dialectical contract made in Book One. But, as before, the prisoner is unable to follow her arguments precisely and to fulfill his role in the discussion. Whereas his earlier failures revealed themselves either through silence or incomprehension, his problems at the close of Book Three are masked by a misguided self-confidence and an impatient readiness to agree with anything Philosophy says.

III

As the dialogue continues through prosae 10-12, the prisoner responds to Philosophy's arguments with a bold, confident series of assents. His ready responses voice a concern with the formal correctness of reasoning rather than an intuitive awareness of higher truths. Behind his assents lies the voice of Fabius from the early *In Isagogen,* and, as I will suggest, it has a strong analogue with the figure of Adeodatus from Augustine's *De Magistro.* At times, the prisoner's words read like a schoolboy's vain attempt to impress the master with his command of terminology and the intensity of his attention. "That is firmly and truly established," he avers on one occasion. Soon after, he answers, "I agree. Your argument cannot be contradicted." To another argument, he chimes, "Rectissime" (III.pr.10.16), and he asserts the impregnability of Philosophy's line of reasoning as proof of her claims: "I found your earlier arguments unassailable, and I see that this conclusion follows from them." In his desire to hear, rather than talk, the prisoner prefers the silent passivity of the pupil to the activity of the debater. He asks Philosophy to clarify her arguments through specific examples; he longs to hear her conclusion; he is waiting for the rest of her proofs.

> I wish you would explain this point by recalling what is involved.

> I understand the problem now and am eager to have your answer.

> There is no doubt about that, but you have not yet given me the solution.

The prisoner opens prosa II continuing his rhetoric of assent, and Philosophy now responds to his desire to know God by conceding to his brand of reasoning. Answering his earlier request for her to explain (*patefacere,* III.pr.10.29), she announces: "I will show you (*patefaciam*) this with certainty." As if to interject a bit of modesty, however, she qualifies her assertion and seems almost to request the prisoner to let the conclusions stand ("maneant modo quae paulo ante conclusa sunt," III.pr.II.4). But the prisoner will have none of these qualifications; her remarks *will* stand ("Manebunt," III.pr.II.4). His confidence in Philosophy's reasoning betrays that lack of doubt which has permeated the tone of his responses ("ne dubitari" is his favorite expression of agreement). Arguments still appeal to his all-too-human judgment and opinion. They are acceptable not because they are true, but because they are incapable of being challenged, doubted, or denied. The prisoner expresses positive assent in negative terms, and his phrasing reveals a habit of mind which relies on structures of belief rather than on proof. His diction reflects the fundamental subjectivity behind the ways in which he sees the world and follows Philosophy's arguments. His commendations of her rational coherence depend only on his *perception* of that coherence, as a language of seeming (e.g., in his term *videtur*) predominates. In short, for Philosophy, things are; for the prisoner, they seem to be.

By prosa 12, however, the dialogue begins to break down, and Philosophy must exhort the prisoner to maintain his side of the discussion. As before, the prisoner notices the manner and method of her speech at the expense of its meaning. In one case in particular, he is so taken with the beauty of her reasoning that Philosophy must stop the discussion altogether and reaffirm their contract. Both disputants develop an imagery of sweetness and delight which leads up to that moment of breakdown. Philosophy begins by noting that the highest good disposes all things sweetly. The prisoner responds:

> I am delighted not only by your powerful argument and its conclusion, but even more by the words you have used.

Most readers of this exchange have considered the prisoner's apparent delight to derive from the Book of Wisdom. For tescue considered this moment the most certain of all possible Biblical allusions in the ***Consolation,*** and many have argued that the prisoner's pleasure is the joy of recognizing the word of God. Whether Boethius puts the words of Wisdom into Philosophy's mouth, or whether this vocabulary was received second-hand through Augustine, Philo Judaeus, or others, is less important than the effect of the diction within the dialogue itself. Boethius presents this rational sweetness as an alternative to the dubious sweetness of Fortuna's rhetoric in Book Two. The prisoner himself had warned against the "specious sweetness" of her arguments, honeyed with music and rhetoric (II.pr.3.2). His words were also designed to echo Philosophy's praise of right rhetoric, whose sweet persuasiveness was only effective if it kept to the path of reason (II.pr.I.8). Now, in Book Three, the prisoner recognizes almost intuitively the elegance of reason and the kindly strength which, as Philosophy tells him, sets desire in its rightful place. The imagery has its counterpoint in the violent pictures of the tortured prisoner, the warring Giants, and the clash of arguments which Philosophy proposes. Taken together, these impressions of conflict and beauty figuratively restate the original system of question and answer which motivated the dialogue, and point towards the rewards of verbal struggle:

> You have read in the fables of the poets how giants made war on heaven; but this benign power overthrew them as they deserved. But now let us set our arguments against each other and perhaps from their opposition some special truth will emerge.

Unlike Boethius in the ***De Trinitate*** preface, where the writer's spark of reason was fired by solitary meditation, Philosophy applies the same, essentially Platonic, image to characterize public discussion. She establishes a complex metaphorical environment in which to reflect upon the dialogue's formal progress. In addition, she explicitly reminds the prisoner of his experiences as a reader, and her characterization here will have great importance for the interpretive demands which her poem on Orpheus will make on him.

In this context of imagery, allusion, and metaphor, it is significant that the prisoner responds to Philosophy also in a figurative way. He complains that she is playing games with him, losing him in an inextricable verbal labyrinth. His restatement of her procedure summarizes many of the central figures of thought developed in the ***Consolation*** thus far: the imagery of the way; the notion of philosophical wonder; the explicit use of mythological allusion in the mention of the labyrinth.

> You are playing with me by weaving a labyrinthine argument from which I cannot escape. You seem to begin where you ended and to end where you began. Are you perhaps making a marvelous circle of the divine simplicity?

Philosophy must convince him that it is no game (*minime ludimus,* III.pr.12.36), but a process grounded in a formal method and directed towards a vital truth. But her explanation sustains the metaphorical coloring of their discussion, as Boethius lets diction do the work of reason. The prisoner and Philosophy exchange the metaphors of inner and outer which they developed earlier. He praises her arguments for developing proofs not from outside but from within. Philosophy takes up his imagery, giving his argument precision and concentrating on its emotional effect.

> You ought not be surprised that I have sought no outside proofs, but have used only those within the scope of our subject, since you have learned, on Plato's authority, that the language we use ought to be related to the subject of our discourse.

As she adopts the prisoner's explication of her method, Philosophy places it in a stated Platonic context. The intrinsic/extrinsic dichotomy now has an epistemological purpose, and she builds her theory of knowledge out of the language of topical argument and the figurative expression of wonder. While her thought is clearly Platonic, and her Greek Presocratic, her diction is uniquely Boethian. The relationship between *res* and *verba* is calculated to confirm the prisoner's own intuitions. She invokes the authority of Plato and Parmenedes if only to make her truths believable to the prisoner. If it is the opinions of the wise he needs—as any dialectician would—then Philosophy is ready to provide them. Moreover, the prisoner should not wonder ("nihil est quod ammirere") at these truths, but accept them as sanctioned by their authors.

A similar problem arises in *De Magistro,* where Augustine must make clear to Adeodatus that the playful or taunting appearance of his questions is a systematic prelude to a more difficult form of investigation. In this dialogue, however, the figurative diction lacks the poetic resonance which it has for Boethius, and yet it offers an analogue to the ***Consolation***'s thematic treatment of formal structure. Midway through the discussion (*De Mag.,* VIII.21) Augustine recognizes the seeming formlessness of his line of questioning and the obscurity of his train of thought.

> But it is difficult at this point to say just where I am striving to lead you by so many circumlocutions. For it may seem that we are quibbling (*ludere nos*) and so diverting the mind from earnest matters with naive questions, or that we are seeking after some mean advantage.

Both the prisoner and Adeodatus confront a loss of rational and verbal direction. While it may seem that they are playing a game, Augustine shows his son the importance of their goal and the validity of their method: "But I want you to believe that I wish neither to have occupied myself with quibbles in this discussion, although we cannot afford to play if the matter is not viewed naively; nor to have labored for petty or unimportant ends." He entreats Adeodatus to follow their course, as argument becomes a *praeludo,* and not a *ludus,* which exercises the mind and develops the reason. When their dialogue begins again Adeodatus seems stunned to find Augustine asking him "whether man is a man." He takes *homo* to be the signified object, rather than the word, and in his confusion Adeodatus protests, "Nunc uero an ludas nescio" (VIII.22.29). Augustine has prepared for this moment, developing the language of game and providing the vocabulary in which his son can express his confusion.

By pausing in the dialogue to explain its purpose, Augustine raises the discussion of method to a statement of theme. He builds the reader's awareness of how discussion directs reason rather than perfects it. The imagery of the "way" and of the *ludus* in Boethius and Augustine, then, achieves three effects. First, it makes the formal constraints of dialogue a suitable subject matter. By taking the time to justify their method or defend their techniques, the speakers create an environment in which no outside excuses are necessary. They close off the world of the dialogue by making it uniquely self-referring. Second, these pauses create in the listener (either Adeodatus or the prisoner) certain expectations. They bring to the fore the hidden desire which motivates the soul, and they turn that desire into an interest in the process of discovery itself. Finally, the moments when dialogue collapses reveal the limits of human understanding and expression. While the prisoner seems lost in a tangle of language, Adeodatus is perplexed by the reference of a single word. Both these examples posit the relationship between the student's failure at formal argument and his relative success at adopting his teacher's phrasing. Where Boethius differs sharply from the Saint is in his use of a highly figurative language to recall the diction of poetry and to create, in the speaker, the sense of wonder associated with the transcendent poetry of Book Three. By denying the prisoner the opportunity to marvel, Philosophy distinguishes between the emotional effects of poetry and prose. She points him, instead, to a hermeneutic principle based on reflection and literally presented as a process of looking back. Augustine is seldom so concerned with reviewing in the *De Magistro.* He pauses to restate the formal constraints of the discussion, but his argument, and Adeodatus' remarks at the dialogue's end, stress a linear progress.

For Boethius, however, literary interpretation follows the same reflective patterns as the structure of the ***Consolation*** itself. The prisoner is constantly called upon to look back over the progress of his life and his discussion with Philosophy. As I have already shown, passages of the ***Consolation***'s poetry will recast earlier images from the text, and the prisoner and Philosophy will frequently echo each other to establish a unity of diction and a continual sense of repetition as the governing principle of the ***Consolation***'s composition. In the final poem of Book Three, Orpheus becomes a figure for the prisoner himself, for not only does his journey recapitulate the prisoner's early condition, but the very effect of the poem is designed to make the prisoner learn from the narrative. The following analysis of metrum 12 explores the ways in which Boethius rewrites earlier moments of the ***Consolation***'s text into this new mythological context. Like the Timaean hymn, the poem on Orpheus reviews the progress of the dialogue by drawing upon the diction, imagery, and narratives developed earlier in the work. Like the hymn as well, the poem is a "reading" of an outside text: here, not of Plato but of Seneca. Boethius recasts scenes from Seneca's *Hercules Furens* to measure the prisoner's progress and Philosophy's authority. The principle of rewriting which operated within the ***Consolation*** itself now operates on an outside text as well. Philosophy presents a poem to be read and interpreted; for its ultimate effect, however, Boethius relies on his reader's recognition of the Senecan "super-text" to his metrum, as we measure the prisoner, Philosophy, and the author of the ***Consolation*** himself as readers and rewriters of the tragic mythology which stand behind their words. In its presentation of musical ideas, its self-conscious metrical structuring, and its concluding moral, the poem takes as one of its subjects the formal problems of literary execution. By encapsulating the central hermeneutic movements of the ***Consolation,*** the text also comments on the process of loss and recovery characteristic of the prisoner's spiritual development.

IV

The parallels are clear between Orpheus and the prisoner at the ***Consolation***'s beginning. Both are oppressed by grief and are subject to those Muses who stifle reason and engender passion. In this and the opening metrum, the speakers contrast former happiness with present grief. The prisoner bemoaned his lost literary abilities (I.m.1.1-2), and Philosophy shows how Orpheus' grief also impedes the exercise of his poetic power.

> Long ago the Thracian poet mourned for his dead wife.
> With his sorrowful music (*flebilibus modis*) he made
> the woodland dance and the rivers stand still.

Through *flebilibus modis* Orpheus' songs, while they reorder nature and calm the beasts, fail to soothe the singer. The prisoner wrote tearful verses (*flebilis modos,* I.m.1.2), having taken dictation from the Muses. For both Orpheus and the prisoner, extreme grief comes to represent the loss of power and of poetry. Vocal imagery permeates both poems. Written in silence, it shows how his lament goes unheard: "Death . . . turns a deaf ear to the wretched." Death is a process of literal calling (*vocata,* I.m.I.14), as the poem details the prisoner's emotional and creative responses through specific sensory imagery.

In the poem on Orpheus repeated patterns of musical and vocal imagery also express artistic and psychological tensions by marking the movement of his song and the progress of his descent. Verbal parallels highlight the formal nature of the text and draw attention to the technical devices used to punctuate emotion.

> captus carmine ianitor (III.m.12.30)
> emptam carmine coniugem (43)

At the poem's opening, structural parallels again reinforce psychological problems. Orpheus' infelicity appears twice at the poem's opening:

> Felix, qui potuit boni (1)
> felix, qui potuit grauis (3)

In his opening carmen, however, the prisoner tried to objectify his unhappiness by placing the blame on friends (I.m.1.21). Both poems offer images of *felicitas* turned into suffering, as their speakers move from a language of music to a language of sensation. While Philosophy's poem stresses Orpheus' lost clarity of vision, the prisoner's poem concentrates on the opacity through which he discerns the world. The fog which obscures true vision oppresses the prisoner; his life is ruled by the clouded, cheating face of Fortune (19); his eyes will not close in death (16). For Orpheus, who could once behold the fountain of goodness, his gaze has turned to Hell and he is lost. Echoes mark the narrative movement:

> fas sit lumina flectere (46)
> uictus lumina flexerit (56).

In one brief line, Orpheus sees, loses, and kills his love, and with her dies his truth: "uidit, perdidit, occidit" (51).

Metrum 12 restates in mythological terms the literary and psychological condition of the prisoner. It also develops the philosophical diction expressed in the ***Consolation***'s poetry, and the Timaean hymn provides one foil for its opening image. In her final prayer, Philosophy had petitioned the mind to raise itself towards God, to wander by the fountain of the good (III.m.9.22-24). Orpheus, however, cannot look upon the *fons boni,* nor can he lift his vision to the light. He must face downward to darkness, for while Philosophy points desire towards Heaven, his passion leads him to Hell. The divine *serenitas* and *tranquillitas,* granted to the blessed in the Timaean hymn and effected in the speaker by prayer, are denied an Orpheus unsoothed by his own music. The phrasing which describes his *fervor* recalls the picture of the prisoner struck dumb by Philosophy's poetry at the opening of Book III, and this recollection highlights the relationship between music and emotion present throughout the ***Consolation***. Parallels in the Latin pointedly bring this out.

> cum flagrantior intima
> feruor pectoris ureret
> nec qui cuncta subegerant
> mulcerent dominum modi,
>
> (III.m.12.14-17)

> Iam cantum illa finiuerat, cum me
> audiendi auidum stupentemque
> arrectis adhuc auribus carminis
> mulcedo defixerat.
>
> (III.pr.I.I)

Central to these passages is the effect of music on the listener, and his ability to attend to the possibilities of meaning in song. Implicit also in these two passages is the difference between human and beastly reactions to music. True music addresses the soul directly and brings it into harmony with the heavenly concord. It is a limited music which affects only the passions and which charms the beasts without calming Orpheus' mind. The differences, then, between the prisoner at the opening of Book Three and Orpheus at its close depend for their effectiveness on a pattern of rewriting which give a unity to the reading of the ***Consolation***.

Such patterns of rewriting operate on the cosmological metra of Book Two, as well. The poem on Orpheus draws on the naturalism and mythology of the earlier metra to make figurative statements about man's place in the world. While Orpheus could once tame the beasts of the wood with his song, to retrieve his wife he must subdue the inhabitants of Hell. He had reshaped the natural order to his own will; the fearful are tamed, and the eternal torments of the damned stop for one brief moment. These images of music altering the natural and supernatural order stand as a climactic inversion of the thematic movement of the ***Consolation***'s poetry. The stable concord Philosophy praised in II.m.8 had kept the sea within its bounds and the land within its borders. The love which joined the married had bound the world—but now that bond is broken as Orpheus faces the *funera coniugis*. The sequence of naturalistic poems in Book Two, depicting the stability of a rural golden age and the trauma of an urban Roman past, established a controlling tension between order and chaos at the level of human civilization. The ideas of order developed in the poetry are instinctively perverted in the picture of Orpheus the poet. His abilities to transform the observed world into his own image comment on the creative power of the *vates*. As one critic has noticed, "the poem gives eloquent expression to the very impulse it is intended to curb," for it confounds the natural harmony of Philosophy's world view. In its illogic, the story presents a pervasive disharmony, from the breaking of the bonds of marriage, through Orpheus' fervor, and finally to the mad pursuit of the dead. The poem suspends the workings of necessity to admit the power of passion, if only to negate that power in the end.

In the image of Orpheus turning back, Philosophy incorporates the poem's interpretive key. Not only is her moral *not* to turn back towards earthly goods, but in it lies the complementary movement of looking back to review the prisoner's life. Her admonition presents the prisoner, and the reader, with a method of interpretation as well as a guide to behavior.

> This fable applies (*respicit*) to all of you who seek to raise your minds to sovereign day.

The word *respicit* here embodies one of the central metaphors of the ***Consolation***. It signifies the human contemplation of heaven or the enlightened contempt of the world. To *respicere* is literally to *re-spicere,* to "review" or "see again," and it signals the full exercise of rational abilities and the desire to review and interpret past events as guides for present behavior. When Philosophy notes that her fable itself *respicit* she means two things. First, she implies that the narrative looks back over the prisoner's progress to this moment. The poem itself points backwards to the worldly concupiscence which enslaved him, and forward to the higher day towards which he must direct his mind. Second, Philosophy enjoins the prisoner to interpret her fable. She prods him into activity, showing how the story retells his life and how he must act upon it. The poem is explicitly a *fabula,* and like the *fabulae* which had earlier illustrated the proper order of being (III.pr.12.24), it is designed to be read and interpreted. Like the fables of the Giants which the prisoner had read, the poem on Orpheus will become a text against which he can measure both the order of the world and the reordering of his own psyche. In turn, just as the Giants attempted to rule Heaven, so Orpheus made his bid to sway Hell. In their own ways, these fabled characters challenged the benign strength which controls earth and sky and which points the prisoner on his moral path.

Philosophy has to this point been directing the prisoner's interpretive abilities. She explicitly refers to his earlier acts of reading, and her monitory moral is as much a guide for the prisoner as it is for the reader outside the ***Consolation***'s fiction. The ways in which the poem on Orpheus rewrites earlier portions of the ***Consolation***'s prose and verse, moreover, signal a process of rereading and revision: the reader is, in effect, encouraged to return to earlier portions in the text to notice, not simple repetition, but subtle shifts in tone and emphasis. Through these structural devices, Boethius measures the progress of his prisoner; he also enables the reader to measure himself against the work's persona. These injunctions towards the end of Book Three also return the reader to the figure of the prisoner as a reader and writer expressed in the opening metrum. Read in the larger context of Boethius' self-styled literary career, and his development of a reading persona throughout his earlier works, these injunctions sustain the fictional construct at the heart of the Boethian corpus.

With these issues in mind, I now turn to what has long been recognized as the clearest source for the poem on Orpheus, Seneca's *Hercules Furens,* to show how Boethius rewrites not only his own text but that of another. The undeniable presence of Seneca's text behind Boethius' reveals, at another level, the activity of the prisoner as a reader, and it also gives a new facet to Philosophy's abilities as a writer of philosophical poetry. Orpheus appears in Seneca's play in an exemplary moral chorus anticipating Hercules' arrival on stage. Boethius adapts verbatim about one-third of Seneca's material (*Herc. Fur.*, 570-595), and his editing and expansions chronicle a reader's response to the meaning of Seneca's scene for the ***Consolation***'s prisoner.

Because the poem on Orpheus so consciously directs its purpose and phrasing to the earlier stages in the prisoner's development, Boethius naturally redirects the focus of Seneca's lines away from public grief and towards private loss. From the opening of his poem, Boethius makes Orpheus' own pain the subject of his verse, while Seneca continuously shifts the acts of grieving and weeping to other characters. In Boethius, it is the Thracian poet who mourns, while in Seneca it is the chorus of Thracian brides. Seneca stresses the power of Orpheus' music to tame the beasts, alter heaven, and soothe Hell. Boethius, however, concentrates on the ways in which Orpheus' music fails to soothe himself. His use of the word *dominus* to characterize Orpheus himself counterpoints the phrasing *dominos umbrarum* in both his own and Seneca's text. His usage reinforces a focus on the condition of Orpheus' mind, and directs the reader's attention to the inner workings of his character's psyche. Seneca continually points to the outer effects of Orpheus' music on an audience. In *Hercules Furens* it is the gods of Hades who weep; in the ***Consolation*** it is Orpheus himself. Whereas Seneca's Orpheus is admonished not to *respicere* and lose his wife, it is the prisoner whom Philosophy advises to look back, as the poem itself refers and reviews (*respicit*) his own life. Moreover, while Seneca's Orpheus is warned not to turn until he reaches daylight, it is Philosophy's metrum which directs the prisoner to seek the "higher day." Boethius' penultimate lines echo Seneca's introductory verses to the Orpheus chorus, and he thus contrasts the upper world towards which his hero strives with the higher daylight granted the mind in heaven.

To turn Seneca's Orpheus into a figure for the prisoner, Boethius' revisions have concerned tone and focus. He also redirects the doctrinal emphases of the play's chorus by altering the relationship of love and law in the legend. Both poems present Pluto's judgment as law, but while Seneca's *lex* is violated only by true love's hatred of delay, Boethius points directly at love's denial of all laws save its own (*HF* 582-598; ***Cons. Phil.,*** III.m.12.40-48). Boethius' description of the conquest of Pluto appears as a nearly verbatim quotation from the Chorus:

> Tandem, "Vincimur" arbiter
> umbrarum miserans ait
>
> (III.m.12.40-41)

> tandem mortis ait "vincimur"
> arbiter
>
> (*HF,* 582)

In transforming the motives of Hell's court, Boethius shifts the notion of judgment and authority away from individually empowered beings and towards a higher, abstract law. Within the structure of Seneca's play, Pluto's system of judgment—losophy, however, the "higher day" is lit not by the sun and stars but by the light of reason and the glow of heaven.

Book Three may be said to end in the way it began, with Philosophy commenting explicitly on the intent and method behind her dialogue with the prisoner. Her arguments in prose and her statements in poetry re-state phrases developed elsewhere in Boethius' writing, and her diction alerts the reader to sources in earlier literary and philosophical texts. Boethius creates unified structures of allusion in the Book: to his earlier remarks in the ***Consolation***; to his definitions and idioms of the logical writings; to the persona of the tractates and commentaries. In sustaining the figure of a reader and a writer, Boethius provides a guide for the ***Consolation***'s audience: they may measure themselves against the prisoner's progress and include themselves in Philosophy's final injunction; but they may also measure the prisoner against the corpus of Boethius' earlier works. These patterns of self-reference are also articulated in the dialogue's moments of pause and breakdown. By stopping to reflect on technique, the disputants make method their theme; they take as their subject the creation of the dialogue inscribed within the ***Consolation***'s text. In the poetry, rhetorical forms create structures of imagery which unify the metra into narrative sequences. Moreover, the prose dialogue itself frequently moves through figurative diction and allusive metaphor. Through these patterns of literary allusion and imagery, the ***Consolation***'s progress can be charted in ways which complement the straightforward and apparently linear movement of the dialogue's logic.

Book Three has an integrity of movement which reenacts the themes of returning, reviewing, and recapitulating in its very structure. A deep feeling of loss permeates the book, and it is only at its end that the prisoner witnesses the possibility of recovering a stability of mind and a strength of purpose. Book Three is also a book of transformations, as its poetry turns mythological narrative and Senecan tragedy into an almost religious cosmology, and as its prose turns the language of Aristotelian dialectic into a suitable medium for philosophic inquiry. The book gradually moves from literal explanations of method to figurative expressions of truth. While Philosophy begins with an attempt to explain her purpose in words, her final poem points towards a form of self-knowledge accessible only through individual meditation on literary symbols. The prisoner himself has been transported from a physical reliance on the impressions of his eyes and ears to a spiritual awareness granted the mind. He has moved from the limits of dialectic to an inkling of philosophic method, and his growth as a speaker and as a reader will inform the purpose of Book Four.

FURTHER READING

Chamberlain, David S. "Philosophy of Music in the *Consolatio* of Boethius." *Speculum* XLV, No. 1 (January 1970): 80-97.

Analysis of Boethius's ethical and metaphysical approach to music in the *Consolation of Philosophy,* which contrasts to his earlier treatment of the subject in *De musica.*

Coolidge, John S. "Boethius and 'That Last Infirmity of Noble Mind'." *Philological Quarterly* XLII, No. 2 (April 1963): 176-82.

Argues for a Boethian influence in John Milton's poem "Lycidas."

Coster, Charles Henry. "The Fall of Boethius: His Character." In his *Later Roman Studies*, pp. 54-103. Cambridge, Mass.: Harvard University Press, 1968.

Influential discussion of Boethius' imprisonment and execution, concluding that "we think that the cause of his fall was the reaction in Italy to the anti-Arian meausures of Justin."

Courcelle, Pierre. *Late Latin Writers and Their Greek Sources*, translated by Harry E. Wedeck. Cambridge, Mass.: Harvard University Press, 1969, 467 p.

Celebrated study of the cultural milieu of literature in

the period of late antiquity that contains excellent discussions of Boethius, Symmachus, and Cassiodorus.

Curley III, Thomas F. "The *Consolation of Philosophy* as a Work of Literature." *American Journal of Philology* 108, No. 2 (Summer 1987): 343-67.

Discusses the *Consolation* as an example of Menippean satire, maintaining that Boethius "required a form which would allow poetry and philosophy to play off of each other in order to define their relationship and to suggest a possible reconciliation."

Mohrmann, Ch. "Some Remarks on the Language of Boethius, *Consolatio Philosophiae*." In *Latin Script and Letters A.D. 400-900*, edited by John J. O'Meara and Bernd Naumann, pp. 54-61. Leiden: E. J. Brill, 1976.

Linguistic study of Boethius's greatest work, concluding that the philosohical treatise betrays the influence of Christian piety and liturgy, rather than that of Christian theology.

Olmsted, Wendy Raudenbush. "Philosophical Inquiry and Religious Transformation in Boethius's *The Consolation of Philosophy* and Augustine's *Confessions*." *The Journal of Religion* 69, No. 1 (January 1989): 14-35.

Examination of the tension between religion and natural philosophy in the thought of Augustine and Boethius. The critic concludes that "Boethius's religion supports the person who may be cut off from community, from friendship, from positive action. It provides a way for the solitary individual to overcome his isolation and understand himself to be in relation to all else that is."

Rand, Edward Kennard. "On the Composition of Boethius's *Consolatio Philosophiae*." *Harvard Studies in Classical Philology* XV (1904): 1-28.

Influential essay that overturned nineteenth-century assessments of the *Consolation*. The critic argues that the fundamental aim of the dialogue "is to make the language of philosophy approach as closely as possible to the meaning of faith; for Boethius was neither a Pagan, nor a cold eclectic, nor a dilettante reviser of others' texts, but the first of the scholastics."

Shiel, James. "Boethius's Commentaries on Aristotle." *Mediaeval and Renaissance Studies* IV (1958): 217-44.

Analysis of Boethius's methodology in transmitting Aristotelian logic to Latin Christianity, arguing that Boethius acted primarily as a translator, rather than as an original commentator.

Stump, Eleonore. "Boethius's Works on the Topics." *Vivarium* XII, No. 2 (November 1974): pp. 77-93.

Disagrees with Shiel's thesis (above), maintaining that Boethius's independent work on Aristotelian logic "is not just that of a translator . . . but that of an excellent philosopher as well."

———. "*Hamartia* in Christian Belief: Boethius on the Trinity." In *Hamartia: The Concept of Error in the Western Tradition*, edited by Donald V. Stump, James A. Arieti, Lloyd Gerson, Eleonore Stump, pp. 131-48. New York: Edwin Mellen Press, 1983.

Exploration of Boethius's Trinitarian theology as expounded in the tractate *De trinitate*.

Vogel, C. J. de. "The Problem of Philosophy and Christian Faith in Boethius's *Consolatio*." In *Romanitas and Christianitas: Studia Iano Henrico Waszink*, edited by W. den Boer, et. al., pp. 357-70. Amsterdam: North-Holland Publishing Company, 1973.

Explores Boethius's fusion of pagan and Christian elements in the *Consolation of Philosophy*.

Wiltshire, Susan Ford. "Boethius and the *Summum Bonum*." *The Classical Journal* 67, No. 1 (October/November 1971): 216-20.

Examines the philosophical, poetic, theological, and dramatic aspects of Boethius's presentation of the supreme good in life in the third book of the *Consolation*.

Wright, F. A. and Sinclair, T. A. "The Fifth, Sixth, and Seventh Centuries." In their *A History of Later Latin Literature: From the Middle of the Fourth to the End of the Seventeenth Century*, pp. 67-133. London: Dawsons of Pall Mall, 1969.

General discussion of Boethius's works and those of his contemporaries.

Hartmann von Aue

c. 1170-c. 1210

(Also spelled Hartman von Ouwe) German poet.

INTRODUCTION

Hartmann von Aue, with Wolfram von Eschenbach and Gottfried von Straâburg, is one of the three most prominent figures of the *Blütezeit* of Middle High German poets. In addition to love lyrics, Hartmann wrote secular and religious epics and is credited with introducing Arthurian legend into medieval Germany. His *Iwein* seems to have been especially widely read, and Hartmann's contemporaries emulated its elegant poetic style. Thematically, Hartmann attempts to reconcile the knightly values of the secular world with the asceticism of medieval religion; his oeuvre, which fluctuates between religious didacticism and secular humanism, reflects these countervailing commitments.

Biographical Information

Despite Hartmann's popularity during his lifetime, no historical records exist on which to base an extensive biography. What modern scholars know of his life has been largely gleaned from Hartmann's short autobiographical asides and from comments by other medieval poets. Apparently, Hartmann was born in Swabia and was of Alemannic heritage, but the 'Aue' of his name may refer to the town of Eglisau on the Rhine in Canton Zürich, or to Obernau near Rottenburg on the Nektar. A member of the lower nobility, he was educated beyond his social standing and probably received instruction in a monastery, perhaps Reichenau, where he became acquainted with the classics and the Bible, and became fluent in Latin and French. Hartmann was a *ministeriale*, a civil servant—he refers to himself as a "*dienstman*" ("vassal") and a "*rîter*" ("knight")—and although his lord's identity is uncertain, most recent scholarship identifies the Zähringer family as his likely benefactor. Hartmann probably wrote his *minnesangs* (love poems), *Die Klage,* and *Erec* about 1180, after which he started to explore more openly religious themes. Most scholars believe that the subsequent death of his lord inspired Hartmann to participate in a crusade, a type of atonement that Hartmann may have allegorized in *Gregorius.* Although historians disagree as to whether Hartmann was involved in the Third Crusade of 1189-90 or in Emperor Henry VI's crusade of 1197, Hartmann seems to have written *Der arme Heinrich* and *Iwein* upon returning. Literary references by Straâburg and Heinrich von dem Türlîn place Hartmann's death between 1210 and 1220.

Major Works

Although critics cannot indubitably date any of Hartmann's works, they generally agree on chronological sequence and divide his poetry into three major periods. Hartmann's early career produced the *minnesangs, Die Klage* (also known as *Das Büchlein*), and *Erec.* In the *minnesangs,* Hartmann explores a theme typical of the Middle Ages: that serving an inaccessible love interest is morally educative. However, in one of Hartmann's poems the subject considers leaving his unyielding mistress to seek a mutual love relationship among commoners; some critics cite this as the earliest example of *niedere Minne*, or common love. Hartmann's *minnesangs* also include three crusaders' songs (*kreuzlieder*), in which the crusade is a means of reconciling the dichotomy between God and the world. Such a fusion of apparent opposites is a common subject for Hartmann. *Die Klage* describes a similar attempt at reconciliation in an argument between *herz* ("heart") and *lîp* ("body"). Hartmann's most notable literary contributions, however, follow his lyrics. *Erec,* which Hartmann based on the *Erec et Enide* (c. 1165) of Chrétien de Troyes, appeared circa 1180, and with it, Hartmann introduced the classic bipartite form of the Arthurian epic into Germany. In *Erec,* a young knight loves his wife Enite so inordinately that he neglects his knightly duties. Only after realizing his error and regaining his honor in a series of adventures does he reconcile love and knighthood.

Gregorius and *Der arme Heinrich* comprise Hartmann's second phase, which is characterized by its strict religious didacticism. In *Gregorius,* which he may have drawn from the French *Vie du Pape Gregoire,* Hartmann portrays Gregorius, both born of and involved in incestuous relationships, who performs penance, is forgiven, and eventually rises to the papacy. *Der arme Heinrich* follows, and may have been drawn from the family history of Hartmann's lord. In *Heinrich,* an apparently flawless man is stricken with leprosy, indicating his physical and spiritual corruption. Drawing on the medieval belief that leprosy could be cured by the blood of a human sacrifice, Hartmann's protagonist befriends a young peasant girl who agrees to enact the cure. Heinrich prevents her death, however, and, apparently because of "*eine niuwe güete*" ("a new sense of charity"), is subsequently cured.

Iwein, a secular, Arthurian epic that is also based on a work by Chrétien, constitutes Hartmann's final literary period. Here, the protagonist neglects his wife in an inordinate quest for honor, only to realize that love and knightly duty must be balanced. Although *Iwein* continues themes typical of Hartmann's earlier works—some critics consider it a companion text to *Erec*—Hartmann's final secular epic is much more stylistically sophisticated.

Textual History

Hartmann's works exist in several manuscripts and fragments dating from the thirteenth to the sixteenth centuries, some in the original Middle High German, and some in Latin. Commissioned by Emperor Maximilian I and copied by his secretary, Hans Reid, between 1504 and 1516, the Ambraser Heldenbuch contains the only extant version of *Die Klage,* and nearly complete versions of *Erec* (of which the first several lines are missing), and *Iwein,* Hartmann's best preserved work. Hartmann's other works appear in various other manuscripts and fragments. His *minnesangs* are collected in three major manuscripts, all circa 1300: Die groâe Heidelberger Liederhandschrift, Die kleine Heidelberger Liederhandschrift, and Die Weingartner Liederhandschrift. Several manuscripts and fragments of *Gregorius* are preserved, all dating from the thirteenth to the fifteenth centuries. However, the prologue only appears in two of the manuscripts, and was possibly written by someone other than Hartmann. *Der arme Heinrich* appears only in thirteenth- and fourteenth-century Latin manuscripts and fragments. Despite their popularity during the Middle Ages, Hartmann's works were not translated into modern German until the mid-eighteenth and nineteenth centuries, and no English translations appeared until the twentieth century.

Critical Reception

Hartmann was highly esteemed by his contemporaries, most notably by Gottfried von Straâburg, Heinrich von dem Türlîn, and Rudolph von Ems. His style and elegant use of structure, which represented significant advances over his predecessors, were held as a standard of Middle High German writing. As evidenced by the many manuscripts and by the numerous tapestries and frescoes that depict scenes from his Arthurian epics, Hartmann's reputation seems to have rested primarily on *Erec* and *Iwein* during the Middle Ages, though some scholars considered them mere translations of Chrétien. However, *Der arme Heinrich* has become Hartmann's best known and most widely studied text in modern times. *Heinrich* has attracted the attention of such figures as Johann Wolfgang von Goethe, Henry Wadsworth Longfellow, Dante Gabriel Rossetti (who wrote a paraphrased version of the poem), and Gerhart Hauptmann (whose play, "Der arme Heinrich" [1902], is based on Hartmann's epic). In recent years, the critical study of Hartmann's entire oeuvre has flourished, emphasizing, among other aspects, his artistic revisions injected into Chrétien's text and the religious ideas inherent in his works. Rather than a mere translator of Chrétien, Hartmann is now considered an imaginative poet in his own right, a linguistic innovator of Middle High German, and a vital part of German literary history.

PRINCIPAL WORKS

POETRY

Erec c. 1180
Die Klage [*The Lament*; also published as *Das Büchlein, The Little Book*] c. 1180
Minnesangs [*Love Poems*] c. 1180
Gregorius c. 1187
Der arme Heinrich [*Poor Heinrich*] c. 1191
Iwein c. 1203

PRINCIPAL ENGLISH TRANSLATIONS

Henry the Leper (paraphrased by Dante Gabriel Rossetti) 1905
Old German Love Songs (translated by Frank C. Nicholson) 1907
Peasant Life in Old German Epics: Meier Helmbrecht and Der arme Heinrich (translated by C. H. Bell) 1931
Gregorius: A Medieval Oedipus Legend (translated by Edwin H. Zeydel and Bayard Q. Morgan) 1955
Erec (translated by J. Wesley Thomas) 1982
Iwein (translated by J. Wesley Thomas) 1982
The Narrative Works of Hartmann von Aue (translated by R. W. Fischer) 1983

CRITICISM

H. B. Willson (essay date 1958)

SOURCE: "Symbol and Reality in *Der arme Heinrich,*"

in *The Modern Language Review,* Vol. LIII, No. 4, October, 1958, pp. 526-36.

[*Willson is one of the most prolific Hartmann scholars writing in English. In the following excerpt, he insists that* Der arme Heinrich *attempts "the paradoxical mingling or fusion of the two spheres of the human and the divine without loss of 'substantial' identity by either," through the spiritual power of* caritas.]

If we discount the occasional misguided attempt to interpret Hartmann's ***Der arme Heinrich*** as basically pagan in spirit and outlook, it is true to say that its debt to medieval Christian thought has always been recognized. In recent years interpretation along these lines has advanced considerably. Nevertheless, it is doubtful whether all that Hartmann put into his poem has yet been extracted. To judge from the opinion of his contemporary, Gottfried von Strassburg, Hartmann enjoyed the highest reputation as a *tiutœre,* that is, as one who succeeded in conveying to his listener and reader the full depth of meaning inherent in the story he relates. Is the *meine* of ***Der arme Heinrich*** entirely clear to the poet's modern audience?

Certainly the poem, in spite of its slender form, has a fullness and richness of content extending far beyond the narrow canvas and context of the events described, and it has had its fair share of attention from critics. But what might be called its ulterior significance has not, we believe, been precisely determined. There is room for interpretation, so to speak, on a higher level than has so far been achieved. The superstructure has still to be erected. The work remains at best only partially integrated into its contemporary background, a background in which lay piety and 'mystical' symbolism play an important role. Many pointers to this ulterior significance may be found in recent criticism, but no coherent synthesis has yet emerged.

The basic formula governing this mystical content is, to put it simply, the paradoxical mingling or fusion of the two spheres of the human and the divine without loss of 'substantial' identity by either. This is, of course, the essential formula of mysticism itself. Fusion of the transcendental and the immanent may be observed in numerous forms and guises throughout the poem, and the ultimate validity of the analogical, and often paradoxical, symbolism employed is determined by it. Above all, it finds expression in the concept of *caritas,* which itself binds together man and man and man and God in mystical union. The apparent dualism between God and the world is resolved in the *caritas* which actuates the entire poem, though, at the same time, each sphere retains its substantial individuality. The first chord in this symphony of *caritas* is struck in lines 26-8:

man giht, er sî sîn selbes bote
und erloese sich dâ mite,
swer umb des andern schulde bite.

Needless to say, the central position in this 'caritative' scheme is occupied by the two major characters, Heinrich and the peasant maid who becomes the instrument of his redemption. As is made clear in ll. 29 ff., the hero of the poem is Heinrich, whose punishment for the sin of *superbia* takes the symbolical form of leprosy. But he is incomplete without his complement. Both he and the maid are essential to each other, and together they finally achieve a unity or fellowship in charity, which is symbolized by their union in wedlock at the conclusion of the poem. Because of this interdependence, the two partners are better treated as a whole, rather than as two separate individuals. Their respective portrayals must be considered in terms of their interaction.

Before this 'reconciliation' of the parts which make the whole can be realized, Heinrich must atone for the sin he has committed, for sin divides man from man and man from God. In the privileged possession and enjoyment of material wealth, in the fullness of youth and chivalrous honour, Heinrich can find no place in his life for God, Who has bestowed all these blessings upon him. He has many virtues, of which a comprehensive list is given in ll. 32-74. Yet the whole purpose of this catalogue is to show, not what he has, but what he lacks, namely, the highest virtue of all, the 'theological' virtue of *caritas,* without which all others are of no account. The passage is a clear echo of I Cor. xiii, for, although Heinrich has *milte,* which may seem to resemble charity, together with other merits, it profits him nothing. His virtues are bounded by the worldly horizon; love for God, the supreme degree of charity, does not figure in the catalogue:

daz herze mir dô alsô stuont
als alle werelttôren tuont,
den daz raetet ir muot
daz si êre und guot
âne got mügen hân.

(ll. 395 ff.)

Superbia and *caritas* are irreconcilable. Charity should be reciprocal: God has first manifested his love for Heinrich, but it has not been reciprocated. Accordingly, the punishment meted out is suited to the sin committed, even though Heinrich may not have been fully aware of his guilt. God's inexorable Old Testament justice takes its logical course. God is a jealous God. He demands love, not so much for his bounty towards Heinrich, but for himself. Heinrich's love is 'disordered'.

The parallels with Job (l. 128) and Absalom (l. 85) drawn by Hartmann have their obvious immediate significance. But, over and above this, the Old Testament context in which Heinrich's situation is viewed has a part to play in the wider symbolism intended. The Old Testament relationship between God and man is, in fact, the key to the higher-level interpretation required. As a result of the sin of *superbia* committed by its first parents, mankind incurred the punishment of leprosy of the soul. The human soul became disfigured, deformed, corrupted, losing its perfect resemblance to God, in whose image it was made. Its original 'simplicity' became mixed with 'duplicity', the duplicity of the serpent to whose counsels Eve gave ear. The generation of Adam and Eve was condemned to exile from paradise, the paradise of resemblance. The situation in which Heinrich finds himself is clearly representative of the situation of the whole of mankind under the Old Law. Heinrich's leprosy and consequent 'exile' from courtly society mirrors analogically this wretched human condition of dissimilitude, of sin and death.

The hero, by his own admission, is a *werelttôre*. Like Adam and Eve, he has impressed upon his soul an 'alien deformity' by attaching himself to mortal things, instead of to the immortal things which are in keeping with the soul's own immortality. Yet the latter's original purity and simplicity is not lost, but only obscured, and it has therefore a 'double cloak' of mortality and immortality, of similitude and its opposite, of divinity and sinful humanity, a whiteness of substance mixed with an 'accidental' blackness which is foreign to its nature. This paradoxical duplicity of the human soul since the Fall is fundamental to the portrayal of Heinrich and his relationship with the maid.

In this miserable state of sin, Heinrich is befriended and hospitably accommodated by the farmer and his family, whose charity expresses their gratitude for the benevolent patronage they have received from their lord. Above all, it is the maid, their daughter, who is the personification and incarnation of this charity. From the very moment of his entry into her parents' house, the maid is moved to compassion for the wretchedness of her lord and master. Charity, the gift of the Holy Spirit, inclines her to seek his company at all times. In her eyes he is essentially pure:

diu guote maget in leiz
belîben selten eine,
er dûhte sî vil reine.

(ll. 342 ff.)

Her love for him—for love it can and must be called—is disinterested, transcending the difference of rank between them. It is, from the very outset, selfless service extending far beyond the requirements of feudal allegiance. From this moment on, a companionate relationship, a *gesellechaft*, is established between the two. While others see fit to avoid his presence *ze rehter mâze* (l. 315), the maid proves that her love for him is without measure. The contamination of his leprosy has no power to keep her from him. In view of later developments, it is impossible to believe that her tender age and innocence alone cause her to behave in this manner. On the contrary, her whole attitude to Heinrich is symbolically conceived. In her eyes, he has a Christ-like quality, for she sees through the accidental blackness of sin to the whiteness and purity of his immortal soul, obscured though it may be. His potential 'perfection' arouses in her a compassion analogous to the compassion of the faithful towards the suffering Christ, who took upon himself the blackness of human sin in order to redeem mankind. Although Heinrich is human, and a sinner, he represents to the maid, by virtue of his original purity and the divine image in which he is created, a potential earthly analogue of Christ, the New Adam he has the power to become. Such is the nature and degree of her *caritas*. Like Mary, she chooses the better part and has the 'one thing needful'. The fact that she is a child and innocently pure would have little compelling significance were it not for the symbolism; in contrast to the 'potential' perfection (but actual sinfulness) of Heinrich, the maid herself is indeed actually perfect, an analogue of humanity in its original 'simplicity', before the transgression of *superbia*. She is untouched by worldliness:

ouch hât mich werltlîch gelust
unz her noch niht berüeret,
der hin zer helle füeret.

(ll. 690 ff.)

Because she has this symbolical 'simplicity' she is able to see Heinrich also in his original freedom from blemish, his purity of 'substance'. She neither fears nor despises his leprosy, though her greatest desire is to restore him to health. To her, he is supremely worthy of redemption. We do not, of course, imply that all this is in any sense to be psychologically interpreted, but rather that it is inherent in the *caritas*-symbolism of the maid's characterization and that her actions derive from the symbolical motivation of her *caritas*.

Significantly, Heinrich refers to the maid as his *gemahel*. This term indicates that their relationship is conceived as being of the most familiar kind (*heimlîch*, l. 340), but essentially spiritual in character. No carnal love is yet involved, a fact which underlines the spirituality of their bond. *Gemahel*, of which the Latin equivalent is *sponsus*, with all its pregnant mystical associations, cannot be dismissed lightly, however commonplace the context in which it is used may seem to be. Its force derives directly from the all-important part played by the *caritas*-concept in the poem. In the light of the high level of spirituality ultimately reached by their fellowship *gemahel* must be regarded as a most meaningful term. In short, he calls her his *gemahel* because her behaviour is motivated by *caritas*.

The compassionate love of the maid for Heinrich is, then, spiritual, and by virtue of this God-inspired, transcendental quality, it contains within itself a potentiality for complete self-sacrifice. The maid, when she hears that she has the necessary qualifications for the operation which alone will heal her lord, at once offers herself. Now is the time for her charity to reveal itself in the full measure of its sacrificial humility. In contrast to Heinrich's *superbia*, she humbles herself to assure him that his life is more valuable than her own (l. 926), the culmination of a display of humility which begins three years earlier. The symbolism associated with this readiness to offer herself to save the life of a fellow human-being needs the greatest possible emphasis. The maid in her purity and 'simplicity' is an analogue of Christ himself, who gave freely of his life-blood to save mankind. She is willing to shed her blood to save Heinrich, and, through him, mankind, since he represents humanity in its state of sin. She holds the power of redemption, which is spiritual and not of this world; it is inherent in her 'divinity', her similitude.

Only God, in the person of his Son, was pure enough to redeem the world; only the maid is pure enough to redeem Heinrich. Her *caritas* is his *caritas*.

The Christ-symbolism of the maid's portrayal must be followed to its logical conclusion, even though this may lead beyond what is actually described. In the event, her blood is not actually shed. But the symbol must be accepted as the Reality. Her naked body lying on the table, the sharpening of the surgeon's knife—these are potent symbols. They stand for the absolute Reality of the broken body of Christ on the cross and the shedding of his blood to save sinners. The beauty of her body, as Heinrich sees it (ll. 1241 ff.), is the beauty of his body as it hangs crucified. Heinrich's compassion for the maid, which actually effects his redemption, must be viewed against the background and in the symbolical context of Calvary. Symbolically, the maid dies, but is resurrected by the compassionate charity of Heinrich, operative for the first time. Heinrich's words,

> nu sach er sî an unde sich
> und gewan ein niuwen muot,
>
> (ll. 1234 f.)

express the sacramental paradox inherent in the situation. The maid, pure and innocent, beautiful in form, is to suffer the consequences of the sin which has deformed, not her body, but the body of Heinrich. Not he, but she, is to die. Her body, like the body of Christ, is to take upon itself this deformity and to suffer, though spotless, the pains of death. Thus, behind and beyond the physical beauty which Heinrich perceives with his eyes there lies the moral beauty attached to the Christ-symbolism, to which his heart responds, a moral beauty of which the wholly voluntary nature of the sacrifice, like the voluntary sacrifice of Christ, is the outward expression. In one sense, this willingness to give one's life for the sake of another is truly superhuman, but, at the same time, it also reveals the essential 'humanity' of the maid, a perfect humanity which is resemblance to God. Transcendental and immanent are inseparable.

The nakedness of the maid as she is about to be sacrificed is invested with further symbolical meaning of relevance to our present argument. It is said of her:

> schiere stuont sî âne wât
> und wart nacket unde blôz;
> sî schamt sich niht eines hâres grôz.
>
> (ll. 1194 ff.)

In her state of innocence she feels no shame at her nakedness, unlike Adam and Eve, who, having eaten of the forbidden fruit, knew that they were naked, and were ashamed. The maid knows no shame because she knows no sin. Nothing could be more clearly indicative of the wider symbolism than these lines.

The efficacy of the sacrifice is conditional upon its being voluntary, and it is clear why this condition is made. Heinrich, by his attachment to worldly things, against the 'better nature' of his soul, has enslaved his will. He has 'voluntarily' followed a sinful course. Harsh though this judgement may seem, it is nevertheless true, since any form of sin, whether it be witting or unwitting, is by definition enslavement of the will. Free-will is an integral part of the immortality of the soul, and can never be lost, but by the paradox of 'voluntary necessity' the soul becomes enslaved when the will consents to sin. Heinrich's leprosy, therefore, inasmuch as it is representative of sin, is a symptom of enslavement. If he is to be purified, free-will must be exercised. Thus the maid's free decision to sacrifice herself fulfills the essential requirement for the liberation of Heinrich and the repair of the damage inflicted upon him by sin. Her *caritas,* which is true freedom, has the necessary therapeutic property.

Owing to textual corruption in ll. 225 and 447, the other qualification (apart from maidenhood) required for the sacrifice has always been uncertain. Until comparatively recently it was more or less generally agreed that the doubtful word in both lines had the meaning of 'marriageable'. In spite of more modern suggestions to the contrary, we share this older view. The fact that in both lines one MS. (though not the same one) has a word meaning 'marriageable' (l. 225—B—*vrîebere;* l. 447—A—*manbere*) seems to be strong evidence in favour of this sense being required. Most commentators have assumed that both lines must contain the same word, since l. 447 is Heinrich's verbatim report of the Salerno doctor's remarks in l. 225. But this is not necessarily true. Heinrich may well have used a synonym. *manbere* is a synonym of *vrîebere,* and these two words we believe to have been in the original text, the former in l. 447 and the latter in l. 225. Moreover, it is quite clear that the maid is in fact marriageable at the time she offers to make the sacrifice, whereas she is unlikely to have been when Heinrich first withdraws to her parents' farm. Hartmann is evidently concerned to make this fact as obvious as possible. She talks as if the time had come for her parents to give her to a husband. She supposes her father to be wise enough to realize that she cannot remain with them for longer than two or three years at the most. If during that time Heinrich should die, they may be so impoverished that they could not provide a dowry. Far better that they should give her to Christ now, and so ensure Heinrich's survival and their own future prosperity:

> nu setzt mich in den vollen rât
> der dâ niemer zergât.
>
> (ll. 773 f.)

It will be noted that she asks for her parent's consent even for the mystical marriage. In other words, at this stage her parents might be expected to renounce their claim to her as their exclusive property and give her away in marriage. When she speaks these words she is certainly marriageable, and much is made of the fact. Why, then, this emphasis on marriageability, and if, as we believe, it is intended to show beyond all doubt that she has the qualification referred to in ll. 225 and 447, why is marriageability so important for the sacrifice? There seems to be only one answer: while she is still under her parents' *huote* she has no rights of her own, and therefore cannot make a free decision. All responsibility for her actions rests with her parents. If she is to cease to be their property, her parents must give up their legal authority over her, which they do for the sake of Heinrich:

> wir wellen ir durch iuch entwesen.
>
> (l. 986)

The legally precise meaning of *sich entwesen* here has escaped the attention of commentators. Her parents are giving up their right to absolute control over her. She is to be betrothed to Christ to ensure Heinrich's recovery, since only if she is so betrothed can she attain the supreme degree of *caritas* needed to effect his cure. As soon as she is betrothed, although not yet married, she becomes a *wîp:*

> ich bin ein wîp und hân dic kraft:
>
> (l. 1128)

Now she is legally entitled to make a decision which will not be her parents responsibility. As we have said above, free-will must be exercised if Heinrich is to be saved. The maid must be able to show that her love is neither servile nor mercenary, but wholly disinterested. Only if this is the case will the sacrifice be effective, since the highest degree of *caritas* is required, not only to attain mystical union, but also to cure Heinrich. Only in this way can her blood acquire the redeeming efficacy of Christ's blood. She derives her power from the 'authority' of him to whom she is betrothed.

The maid's yearning for mystical union is given considerable emphasis by Hartmann. If, on the one hand, she is to be regarded as a 'redeemer' so also, on the other hand, does she herself long to be united with her Heavenly Bridegroom, the original Redeemer. Although it may not appear to be the case at first sight, these two aspects of the maid's portrayal are completely harmonious. They are complementary aspects of the same *caritas*. . . . Her whole speech to her parents (ll. 663-854) is inspired by the Holy Spirit (ll. 863 ff.), and the gift of the Holy Spirit is *caritas*. The devastating logic with which the maid presents her case transcends her own natural powers of reasoning and proves that a Higher Wisdom guides her. In insisting that she must place *triuwe* to herself above all other forms of loyalty and love she follows the advice of St. Bernard:

> In acquisitione salutis nemo tibi germanior unico matris tuae. Contra salutem propriam cogites nihil. . . . Quidquid se consideration offerat, quod non quoquo modo ad tuam ipsius salutem pertinet, respuendum (*De Consideratione,* II, 3; *P.L.* CLXXXII, 746).

Her determination to brush aside all obstacles to her salvation, cruel though her apparent lack of consideration for her parents may seem to us, is fully consistent with her violent passion for the mystical marriage. In 'considering' herself above all else she is guided by a mystical logic which sees no contradiction between love of self and love of God in the state of similitude. Only dissimilitude creates an opposition between the two. By virtue of a wisdom greater than her own the maid knows that the only true love of self is love of God above all else. In this context the word *triuwe* expresses, as adequately as any M.H.G. word can do, the full content of *caritas.*

No contradiction exists, therefore, between the maid's *caritas* towards Heinrich and her *caritas* towards herself, which is identical with love of God. Both are the gift of the Holy Spirit. Love of one's neighbour and love of God are inseparable one from the other (I John iv. 20-1). Consequently, in terms of the wider symbolism, the portrayal of the pure maiden in her mystical longing for eternal bliss is an indissociable part of her function as the redeemer of Heinrich.

When the maid discovers that, after all, she is not to be allowed to make the sacrifice, her disappointment takes the form of an unseemly outburst of anger. This reaction is inspired by the same *caritas* as that which determines her attitude to her parents while they still remain unreconciled to her decision. The mystical love of the Bride for her Beloved is essentially a violent love. . . . The maid's infringement of the law of *mâze* proves that she loves without measure. The same lack of measure is shown when she tears off her clothes in preparation for the sacrifice (l. 1193). As we saw earlier, her *caritas* for Heinrich was without measure, and of necessity, since it is the same *caritas,* which we have also just seen to be the case. The maid loves *ardenter,* with a love which demands fulfillment. In her anger she accuses Heinrich of fear:

> ir wâret alle iuwer tage
> und sît noch ein werltzage!
>
> (ll. 1319f.)

She herself knows no fear, since fear and *caritas* are incompatible; she has the full confidence in God's readiness to reciprocate her love. But her faith in Heinrich is shattered. He has failed to come up to her expectations. Paradoxically, it is Heinrich who seems afraid, though it is she who is about to suffer death.

This introduction of the element of fear is the culmination of a sustained attempt by Hartmann to focus attention upon that emotion. For example, in ll. 999 ff., Heinrich is said to be in a state of *zwîvel* as to whether he should accept the maid's offer of sacrifice or not. She, in her turn, accuses him of *verzagetheit* and sheds tears of *vorhte*. Later, in ll. 1111 ff., she is said to be *ein teil verzaget* because she fears that the doctor's *zageheit* will prevent the operation from taking place. This continual play on *verzagen, zwîvel,* and *vorhte* (with the further play on their antithesis, *triuwe,* in l. 1114) is more than mere coincidence. It is intended to show that, in the situation of the maid's proposed sacrifice, the obstacle which must be surmounted is fear. While fear is operative, *caritas* cannot achieve its aims. The maid has no fear for herself, but her enterprise cannot succeed until all fear and doubt, real or imagined, in others upon whom she depends is removed. Love and fear are deliberately placed in antithetical relationship, whether implicitly or explicitly, and the importance of *caritas* is thereby given greater emphasis, just as in I John iv. 18: 'Timor non est in caritate, sed perfecta caritas foras mittit timorem, quoniam timor poenam habet: qui autem timet, non est perfectus in caritate.'

The paradox, of course, is that the hesitation of both Heinrich and the doctor is not the result of fear, but of *caritas!* When the former refuses to allow the sacrifice to proceed he proves that he is indeed transformed and reborn, of the Spirit. His transformation is expressed in his compassion for the maid, which itself is the outward sign of his redemption from sin, leading directly to the miraculous cure performed by God and his return to courtly society from exile. Compassion for the suffering of a fellow human-being is *caritas*. Its highest form is active participation in the sorrows of the crucified Redeemer, the Word made Flesh. Just as the maid displayed *caritas* in participating in the misery of Heinrich, so also does Heinrich participate compassionately in the symbolical sacrifice of the body of the maid. Her love awakens in him a reciprocal love. By showing his *caritas* towards the maid as she lies on the operating table he shows his love for God in the Person of Jesus Christ, his Son. The change from the Old to the New Law is achieved through the co-operation of Heinrich and the maid in mutual *caritas* and by the co-operation of both with the Grace of God, his supreme *caritas*. Transcendental and immanent are again reconciled.

On the highest level, Heinrich's malady is cured by God, who extends the Grace of his Holy Spirit to both partners. Both receive God, the maid, a chaste soul, as a Bridegroom, Heinrich, an infirm soul, as a Doctor. When the latter approaches God in true charity, he reveals himself not as a jealous God, but as a God of tender love and mercy. The Old Testament situation gives place to the new situation of Christ's coming.

In this new context, the maid and Heinrich are united with each other and with God in an all-embracing *caritas* relationship. The completeness of the union is illustrated by the fact that Hartmann describes the experience through which they have come as a test in which both have been tried and proved by God:

> sît er [cordis speculâtor] durch sînen süezen list
> an in beiden des geruochte,
> daz er sî versuochte
> rehte alsô volleclîchen
> sam Jôben den rîchen. . . .
>
> (ll. 1360 ff.)

The symbolical significance of *versuochen* is patent: Adam and Eve succumbed to temptation and brought sin into the world. Christ passed the supreme test and triumphed over sin and death.

Further symbolical detail may be observed in the description of their homecoming. Heinrich's friends set out to meet them a three days' journey away—a 'vestige' of the three days between the death and resurrection of Christ—and:

> sîn geloupten niemens sage
> niuwan ir selber ougen.
>
> (ll. 1392 f.)

One is reminded that similar doubts were entertained as to the truth of Christ's resurrection, and that those who doubted hurried to the tomb to see for themselves. On arrival they saw with their own eyes that the miracle had indeed been performed. So also did Heinrich's friends witness a miracle:

> si kurn diu gotes tougen
> an sînem schoenen lîbe.
>
> (ll. 1394 f.)

His restoration to health and vigour and youthful beauty had taken place. Furthermore, the maid also is involved:

> ezn wart nie freude merre
> dan in beiden was geschehen,
> dô sî hâten gesehen
> daz sî gesunt wâren.
>
> (ll. 1406 ff.)

Both are 'delivered', Heinrich from the malady of sin and the maid from death. Both are 'resurrected' and have new life in Christ. Together they have overcome sin and death through compassionate charity:

> dô erzeicte der heilec Krist
> wie liep im triuwe und bärmde ist,
> und schiet sî dô beide
> von allem ir leide. . . .
>
> (ll. 1365 ff.)

The sinister words *media vita in morte sumus* (ll. 92-3) have lost their meaning. By contrast, life has emerged from death. The whole glorious truth of redemption shines forth from these lines.

No more fitting conclusion could have been found than the marriage between Heinrich and the maid who has helped him to salvation:

> nu sprâchens alle gelîche,
> beide arme und rîche,
> ez waere ein michel fuoge.
>
> (ll. 1509 ff.)

No more suitable word than *fuoge* could have been used to express the true harmony and concord characteristic of the union of these two persons once so contrasting. All differences of rank and birth have been transcended in the unity of *caritas* which they have attained. Heinrich returns to the courtly world; the maid enters it as his chosen wife. Their marriage, far from being a romantic, conventional ending, is one of the most momentous symbolical events in the whole poem, and without its symbolism Hartmann's message remains largely unintelligible. As we have said, after Heinrich's rebirth in charity a new situation arises, symbolizing the new situation in human affairs occasioned by Christ's coming. The marriage springs naturally from this new situation. Heinrich and the maid are in a state of grace. Their salvation is assured. The new life which they are about to begin will be a foretaste of beatitude:

nâch süezem lanclîbe,
dô besâzen sî gelîche
daz êwige rîche.

(ll. 1514 ff.)

In so far as mystical union is attainable in this life, the maid has achieved it in the short-lived ecstasy of her sacramental, symbolical sacrifice, as a result of which she redeemed Heinrich and at the same time attained the highest degree of her fellowship in charity with him. This fellowship, and the marriage which springs from it, is an *analogia entis* of the union with the Heavenly Bridegroom himself. It is sacramental, not merely in the usual liturgical sense, but also by virtue of its symbolical validity as a union in *caritas*. As we have also said, their relationship is, in the first instance, of the spirit. That it should now become also of the flesh raises no problems of reconciliation between the spiritual and the carnal, as long as the supremacy of the former over the latter is maintained, that is, as long as *caritas* itself remains the bond which unites them. And, since the New Law is operative, *caritas* will so remain; the antinomy between the spiritual and the carnal is disposed of in the new situation in which God is made Flesh and becomes reconciled with the world. It follows, then, that there is no incompatibility between the maid's carnal union with Heinrich and her hoped-for union with Christ, but rather a continuity, since the former is spiritualized and transfigured. The full content of *trûtgemahel* now reveals itself. Heinrich, the maid, and Christ are all three united in the sacramental embrace of *caritas*. The divine image in Heinrich has been revealed; both he and the maid have resemblance to God in as perfect a sense as can be achieved here below. There can be no question of the maid having to reconcile herself to her apparent loss of quick salvation: she automatically becomes reconciled, in more senses than one, in the greater Reconciliation. For this reason we hear no more of her anger after Heinrich has been cured.

In the course of this article we have tried to piece together into a coherent whole the symbolical detail in ***Der arme Heinrich*** and to view it in terms of a mystical synthesis. The central position occupied by *caritas* has been stressed often enough before, and indeed, its importance is obvious even to the non-specialist reader. But what has been lacking is insight into its full implications and its integrating function, probably because of the extreme breadth of meaning with which it is invested in medieval Christian thought. Its applications and aspects are numerous. It solves all contradictions and oppositions. It is one of the most, if not *the* most, comprehensive and universal of religious terms, and for this reason, if for no other, its potentialities for symbolical reference are unlimited. It lies at the very heart of the Christian message. ***Der arme Heinrich*** is a song of love, and its *meine* is as comprehensive and universal as the *meine* of *caritas*, which may be formulated as: the fellowship of God and sinners reconciled. . . . The consolation it offers is the consolation of the world: however wide and deep may be the gulf opened up between man and God by sin, *caritas* has the power to bridge it. On earth, as in Heaven, this law is eternally valid.

Bell on the secular and religious themes in Hartmann's poetry:

The poet's thoroughgoing change from the worldly material of the Arthurian epic to the religious legend and then back again is a remarkable one. It doubtless reflects the cross-currents of his soul, which embraced a whole world of conflicting moods. The opposition between secular and religious forces, which moved this whole age, left its mark upon Hartmann's life and works. He never overcame the conflict in his nature between the worldly and the religious elements, nor was he able to weld these elements harmoniously in his writings.

Clair Hayden Bell, in an introduction to Peasant Life in Old German Epics: 'Meier Helmbrecht' and 'Der Arme Heinrich', *Columbia University Press, 1931.*

Hugh Sacker (essay date 1961)

SOURCE: "An Interpretation of Hartmann's *Iwein,*" in *The Germanic Review,* Vol. XXXVI, No. 1, 1961, pp. 5-26.

[*Sacker has written several critical studies of Medieval German literature, including* An Introduction to Wolfram's "Parzival" *(1963). In the following essay, Sacker insists that, in* Iwein, *Hartmann did not portray Arthur's court as the symbol of virtue, but rather made changes to the Chrétien story in order to depict ironically a moral code that differs from that professed by the narrator and the characters.*]

Iwein's story is set against the background of Artus' court. This court has usually been understood to represent the poet's ideal of chivalry, which the hero symbolically quits when he is disgraced and to which he is symbolically readmitted when he has finally proved his worth. Support for this view is found in the many statements of the narrator and his characters, who unanimously proclaim the Round Table as the very flower and touchstone of chivalry, a pattern of comment which is set by the opening twenty lines of the work. Yet it seems to me doubtful whether these statements are borne out by the events themselves. If one took as a criterion the *actions* of the various members of the Round Table (and not the statements made about them), one might well conclude that this company consisted of a weak and passive king, a number of well-intentioned but quite useless knights—whose seneschal Keii is not even well-intentioned—and Gawein: a hero whose great abilities are perpetually misdirected. On closer inspection it would, I think, appear that what renders this company so ineffectual is its preoccupation with its own honor—as is most clearly shown in the episode of the rape of Ginover: Artus hands over his queen to an unknown knight (Meljaganz) simply to save his own reputation; the knight carries her off simply to test his honor against that of the Round Table knights; these are all defeated by him, except Gawein—and it is Gawein's absence on this rather footling adventure which prevents his saving both Lunete from the stake and a whole family from rape and murder at the hands of the giant Harpin.

Now Hartmann has been criticized for being concerned only with the form, not with the subject-matter of ***Iwein***—de Boor even suggests that translation from the French had become for him "Zeitvertreib müssiger Stunden, nicht mehr Auseinandersetzung mit sich selbst und den Fragen des Daseins" [*Geschichte der deutschen Literatur* (1958)]—but it is noteworthy that Hartmann has elaborated both Chrétien's initial praise of Artus, in which the King's high honor is proclaimed, and the episode of the rape of Ginover, which demonstrates the futility of the excessive concern of the King for his honor. The possibility therefore exists that Hartmann's formal modifications, if not necessarily evidence for the struggles he fought with himself and the problems of existence, do at least serve to clarify, as well as slightly alter, the meaning of Chrétien's story—and that this meaning resides to some extent in a conflict between generally accepted views (as expressed by the narrator and the characters) and the lessons of experience.

To consider this interpretation at all, even in principle, one must admittedly assume that the meaning of a work is not necessarily adequately expressed in the statements of the narrator, but that the events themselves furnish as important a guide to the meaning as do the narrator's comments. Both are elements of the total work, and if the implications of the events are at variance with the comments of the narrator, then that is a fact which should be taken into account when investigating the nature of the work—and need not necessarily be regretted. It may perhaps indicate that irony plays a more fundamental role in the whole genre of Arthurian romance than has hitherto been recognized. Even the possibility that the poet consciously identified himself with the narrator (a possibility that cannot be proved or disproved without external evidence) is not of importance, if it is the implicit meaning of the finished work that one is investigating and not the intention of its creator.

It is with these considerations in mind that I propose to attempt an interpretation of Hartmann's ***Iwein,*** beginning with the story told by Kalogreant in the first eight hundred lines of the work.

At the start this story is itself held up by a curious incident which provides a first pointer to the unsatisfactory elements in Arthurian society. Of the half-dozen knights gathered for story-telling, none sees the approach of the Queen except Kalogreant, who jumps politely to his feet to receive her. For this he is roundly scolded by Keii, whose custom is to begrudge any honor which falls to another (108-112) and who claims that since the remaining knights sat still, Kalogreant should have done so too. The Queen rebukes Keii, and there the matter very nearly ends, but not quite. The significant detail which remains is that, although the Queen states that nobody pays any attention to Keii's mockery which indeed, since he only mocks at the best knights, is tantamount to praise, yet in the event Kalogreant is sufficiently put out by it to refuse at first to proceed with his story. Admittedly the Queen wins him round, but his reluctance makes it plain that he at least is not so impervious to Keii's mockery as the Queen's remarks might lead one to expect. Nor is this an isolated motif: Iwein himself, after he has defeated Ascalon, pursues and kills him primarily to escape Keii's mockery (1062-74). The scorn of one whom nobody respects (in Hartmann's work Keii is even more freely criticized than in Chrétien's) thus appears as one of the driving forces of Arthurian society—possibly as the principal driving force, for Keii is seneschal at Artus' court. That he should hold this position is a fact which causes even the narrator some concern, though the narrator explains that, if Keii's tongue disgraces him, he is redeemed by his valour (2565-74). But this valor itself brings Keii only ridicule, as is most evident when his fellow knights leave him hanging by the neck from the branch of a tree which caught him when he was unhorsed by Meljaganz (4670-94). To have such a man as seneschal is to make the jester the master of ceremonies: Keii is both laughed at by the other members of the Round Table and feared by them; he represents the ridiculous extreme to which they approximate, which they take as their model and yet despise for its absurdity. But as Kalogreant's story is only the prelude to the main story, so this theme is only lightly touched on at this stage.

That the adventure which Kalogreant eventually relates is presented as the type of an Arthurian adventure (apart possibly but not necessarily from its outcome) is brought out in Hartmann's version by the manner in which the *theory* of adventure is emphasised: Kalogreant rode out seeking *aventiure, gewafent nach gewonheit* (261, f.), he received hospitality from a knight who had never previously entertained a stranger *von dem er haete vernomen daz er aventiure suochte* (376, f.), and he gave the famous definition of adventure to the unprepossessing creature he found herding wild animals in the wood:

> ich sprach "ich wil dich wizzen lan,
> ich suoche aventiure."
> do sprach der ungehiure
> "aventiure? waz ist daz?"
> "daz wil ich dir bescheiden baz.
> nu sich wie ich gewafent bin:
> ich heize ein ritr und han den sin
> daz ich suochende rite
> einen man der mit mir strite,
> der gewafent si als ich.
> daz priset in, ersleht er mich:

gesige ich aber im an,
so hat man mich vür einen man,
und wirde werder danne ich si.

(524-537)

Kalogreant is an armed knight and he rides seeking another armed knight who will fight with him. Whoever kills the other, wins glory. Indeed he may then be considered a man.

This primitive and brutish code of behavior never appears to be questioned by Kalogreant; yet it follows by less than fifty lines upon the definition which the man of the woods has given him of his own attitude to strangers:

Ich sprach "bist übel ode guot?"
er sprach "swer mir niene tuot,
der sol ouch mich ze vriunde han."

(483-5)

Unlike knights, this wild herdsman does not seek to do anyone harm just for the sake of glory—and it is nicely ironical that Kalogreant, who would be thought a man if he killed a fellow knight, does not recognize the humanity of such a creature (486-8). For the reader, even if not for Kalogreant, these contrasting attitudes raise the question: does the uncouth woodsman, who exercises such easy control over his animals and who hurts no one who does not hurt him, possess certain positive qualities which Kalogreant, the perfect courtier, lacks? It is a question to which an answer is given, not in the future history of Kalogreant, who eventually returns to his starting point, but in that of Iwein, who progresses beyond it.

Meanwhile the wild herdsman, who knows where adventure is to be found even if he has not previously heard it defined, sends Kalogreant to the well with detailed instructions. From these and from later episodes it appears that the act of pouring water on the perforated stone above the well is interpreted by the lady of the land as a dire threat to herself, against which she needs to be protected by a champion. At present the lady, Laudine, is married to Ascalon, who wholeheartedly shares her attitude and fights off all who are attracted to the adventure at the well. By this means he effectively prevents strangers from intruding upon his married life and, but for the provocation offered to the outer world by basin and well, it might be thought that husband and wife were self-sufficient. But in view of this provocation, which is presented as an integral part of the scene, I do not think their position can be considered as stable; moreover Ascalon's attempt to impose stability by fighting off all knights who respond to the challenge of the well only leads ultimately to his own death. There is thus a real problem implicit in Kalogreant's adventure, a problem of whose existence the wild herdsman is aware, but which he is content to leave to others to solve, which furthermore can only be solved by someone capable of overpowering Ascalon.

Both Ascalon, until long after his death at Iwein's hand (2274), and Laudine, until her marriage to Iwein (2421), remain anonymous. This anonymity confirms the general impression that they are not (at this stage) presented as whole people, anymore than for instance the wild herdsman is, but are confined to specific functions, Ascalon I suggest to that of male protectiveness, Laudine to that of female provocation and vulnerability. As it were instead of names, they have associations, Laudine with the well (e.g. 1823-30, 2058-61), Ascalon with the forest around it (*des selben waldes herre,* 1001, cf. 716). Associations of males with trees, females with wells, suggest a Freudian type of symbolism, made particularly interesting in this case by the special relationship of the well to one most unusual tree:

kalt unde vil reine
ist der selbe brunne:
in rüeret regen noch sunne,
nochn trüebent in die winde.
des schirmet im ein linde,
Daz nie man schoener gesach:
diu ist sin schate und sin dach.
si ist breit hoch und also dic
daz regen noch der sunnen blic
niemer dar durch kumt:
irn schadet der winter noch envrumt
an ir schoene niht ein har,
sine ste geloubet durch daz jar.

(568-580)

This lime-tree, which is not subject to the change of the seasons but shields the well from rain, sun, and wind all the year round, is I suggest indicative of the primarily protective nature of Ascalon's love for Laudine. That, however, neither she nor her husband is altogether content with such a love seems to be indicated by the basin, which hangs down from a branch of the tree over the well as an invitation, or challenge, to strangers (581-97).

Kalogreant accepts this challenge but proves no match for Ascalon, who unseats him at the first encounter and makes off with his horse. Without his horse Kalogreant is too weak to carry his armour, which he accordingly takes off—and is thus exposed by his pursuit of adventure as rather less than a knight. He returns on foot to the castle of the man who had never before entertained a guest seeking adventure, where he meets as generous a reception as the first time. It is a suggestive return, the only one of its kind in a story in which each castle may be interpreted as a station of a man's spiritual pilgrimage through life. The only parallel is Iwein's return to the well; but whereas that indicates his determination to make good a previous failure, Kalogreant's return to this unadventurous castle indicates a retreat to a previous station after failing to arrive at the next. Resolving not to attempt such feats in future, Kalogreant further retreats from here to Artus' court—where he joins a company of knights who, at least so far as their exploits in this particular work are concerned, all, with the single exception of Gawein, in all their adventures meet with similar failure.

Not so Iwein. True, he shares at this stage Kalogreant's chivalrous code, as is made plain by his instant resolve to avenge his cousin's defeat, and by his following the identical course to the well. But what distinguishes him is his *vrümekeit,* revealed in his ability to win the battle with Ascalon and so to face the consequences of success in his chosen way of life: they are not at all what he looked for, and before he learns how to cope adequately with them, he has to emancipate himself from the society in which he grew up and from its values; to start again as it were from scratch, and to develop an independent outlook and an inner strength of his own. The significance of the "Vorgeschichte" (the story of Kalogreant which precedes that of Iwein) derives to a very large extent from this contrast between the one knight who returns to and is finally absorbed in Artus' court and the other who, in spite of repeated contacts, gradually withdraws from this court: a contrast full of implications both for Arthurian society and for Iwein himself.

In one important respect Iwein's eagerness to escape Keii's mockery leads him to transgress the Arthurian code: after wounding Ascalon mortally, he pursues him *ane zuht* (1056), desperately anxious to have either a corpse or a prisoner to prove his victory. This may be an indication that Iwein's passions are not entirely subordinated to the conventions of courtly behavior; if so it helps to explain his later development. Anyway he fails in his immediate objective, for the dying man escapes into his castle, while Iwein, ignorant of the secret of its approach, has his horse slain under him by the fall of the first portcullis and is himself trapped between this portcullis and a second one which Ascalon lets down behind him. The one portcullis cuts off Iwein's retreat, so that one might say that his unchivalrous pursuit of Ascalon has made it impossible for him to return to Artus' court, the other prevents his storming the castle and gaining access to Laudine by force. He is trapped as it were between two worlds, and in this trap he would die, slain by Laudine's followers, were it not for a hitherto unmentioned aspect of his character and for the intervention of a hitherto unmentioned person.

Iwein's survival is due neither to his prowess, by which he overcame Ascalon, nor to the passion which soon awakes in him for Laudine, but to the consideration which he once showed for Laudine's lady-in-waiting, Lunete. This young lady, like Ascalon and Laudine, remains for some time anonymous; and during this time her role is as clearly defined as theirs: she contributes to their single-minded preoccupation with warfare and sex the elements of reason and morality. She saves Iwein out of gratitude because he had once honored her with his greeting when the other Arthurian knights, distressed by her *unhövescheit* (1189), failed to do so; and she overcomes Laudine's aversion to the man who killed her husband by arguing that Laudine's own safety depends on her marrying precisely this man. Later, when Iwein fails Laudine, Lunete's morality is impugned (cf. *triuwe* 5249-58); finally, at the end of the whole work, the reconciliation of Iwein and Laudine is attributed to her reason (cf. *sin,* 8149-55). Meanwhile the importance of her role is emphasised by the fact that she too has a symbol: near the well and the lime-tree stands a chapel, a chapel associated with no one else in the work except Lunete, who is imprisoned in it when her *triuwe* is doubted, and is later apparently normally to be found there at prayer (5884-7).

The relationship between Laudine and Lunete is a major feature of the story: what dominated Ascalon and now engages Iwein is an uneasy feminine alliance between instinct (sex and insecurity) on the one hand, and control (reason and morality) on the other. At this stage Laudine represses her anger at Iwein in order to marry him (cf. *zorn,* 2062): Lunete's reason combines with Laudine's obsessive insecurity to overcome the latter's feelings of outrage. In consequence Iwein receives the impression that a similar sort of rational control reigns in Laudine's country as in that of Artus (note that Laudine, in accepting Lunete's reasoning that the victor in a fight must necessarily be the better man [1954-61], is accepting the code propounded by Kalogreant). Only when Lunete herself curses Iwein at Artus' court does he begin to have doubts, and only after he has integrated the instinctive and the rational elements in his own nature does he regain Laudine at the end of the work (for his *zorn* see below). Moreover it is suggestive that by that time Lunete has come closer to Laudine by giving way to anger (4136-52), while Laudine has turned to Lunete's special province of prayer (8023-5). But this is to anticipate.

The marriage between Iwein and Laudine rests initially on a very crude foundation. Iwein is moved primarily by the sight of Laudine's beauty, and makes no effort to find out anything else about her before marrying her; her beauty takes him out of himself (1331-9), and that is enough. Laudine on the other hand never so much as catches sight of Iwein before she falls in love with and resolves to marry him. Indeed she marries him in a sense not in spite of but because he killed her husband, and thus demonstrated his superior ability to defend her:

> si gedahte "mit mime libe
> mac ich den brunnen niht erwern:
> mich muoz ein biderbe man nern,
> ode ich bin benamen verlorn.
> weizgot ich laze minen zorn,
> ob ez sich gevüegen kan,
> und enger niuwan des selben man
> der mir den wirt erslagen hat."
>
> (2058-65)

Moreover, Laudine is convinced she has chosen rightly when Iwein does in the event successfully defend the well against Artus' knights (2670-82). The crudity of the situation is expressed laconically by the narrator on the occasion of the wedding ceremony:

> hie huop sich diu brutlouft sa.
> des toten ist vergezzen:
> der lebende hat besezzen
> beidiu sin ere und sin lant.
>
> (2434-7)

It is a passage which appears all the more striking since in the immediately preceding lines the narrator has generalized in a most high-falutin manner on the qualities required in a husband and wife to make a satisfactory marriage, and has concluded with reference to that of Iwein and Laudine: *daz was allez waenlich da* (2433). But Lunete has just previously reminded us that *wan* is not *warheit* (1960 f., cf. 2670-3)—and events very quickly show that this particular marriage is as yet quite inadequately based.

Ever since he first saw Laudine, Iwein has been torn between love for her and concern for his own honor (cf. 1519-38); until he is actually married, love gains the upper hand, but then Artus and his knights reappear on the scene and Iwein, frightened by Gawein's interpretation of the story of Erec, takes a year's leave from his wife so as to attend to the claims of honor. In urging this course on his friend, Gawein is acting like a true bachelor and member of a bachelor society (in ***Iwein*** at least, none of the Round Table company is married except Artus himself, and the limitations of his marriage are revealed by the episode of the rape of Ginover), and the only alternatives he can see for Iwein are to continue in his former honorable way of life—*wir suln turnieren als e,* he says (2803)—or to succumb altogether to the shame of domesticity. The possibility of finding a new sort of honor in marriage, the implications of Iwein's new position as king of a country instead of just another knight errant, never occur to Gawein at all. Moreover, his love for Laudine has as yet made so little impression upon Iwein that he enjoys his renewed bachelor existence to the extent of temporarily forgetting his wife and overstaying his year's leave.

There is of course a positive aspect to Iwein's desertion of Laudine: she had primarily wanted a protector, not a husband (1909-16); convinced by Lunete that this was not possible, she agrees to Iwein's taking Ascalon's place but clearly still thinks of him chiefly as a protector (cf. 2935-9, and 2191-9 where he is even dressed in Ascalon's clothes); had Iwein therefore not run away, his marriage might have degenerated into one of the Ascalon type. On the other hand, the solution he proposes is no more satisfactory: if he had his way, marriage would involve him in no responsibilities at all, but his wife would just be one more trophy of his buccaneering career, taken down from the shelf occasionally to be dusted and shown to his friends. Laudine's one great contribution to their mutual development is her refusal of this solution; however compulsive is her need for protection, she would rather risk life alone than be treated like a concubine (3167-73, 3190-2). And Iwein rises to this challenge—for it is precisely those qualities in Laudine which Ehrismann [in his *Geschichte der deutschen Literatur*] takes as evidence of her fairy ancestry, her "Seelenlosigkeit" and "unnatürliche Schroflheit," that force Iwein to reconsider his position, and that bring about the breakdown which demonstrates in spite of previous appearances *sin groziu triuwe sines staeten muotes* (3210 f.). This essential *triuwe* reveals itself in the seriousness with which he takes his disgrace, in his inability to shrug it off or blame it on his wife, and in the persistence with which he seeks to win her back, being content neither with a return to the single state nor with the prospect of a second, perhaps easier marriage; but without Laudine's harshness, Iwein's latent *triuwe* might never have come to the surface at all. A dependence upon the Arthurian code in which he has been educated, excessive in one whose abilities have taken him into a sphere where its regulations do not apply, has thus brought Iwein not honor but disgrace—and so he goes out of his mind. This breakdown is the turning point in his life, providing the opportunity, of which he makes full use, to start again from the beginning, to learn to live in accordance with experience instead of with precept. (Some idea of the significance of this breakdown for Iwein may be gained by comparing the lives of historical figures who have found new strength in critical breakdowns and recreative illnesses: St. Paul, St. Francis, Goethe, Lincoln and others.) Iwein's new start is suggested by his nakedness, his rejection of precept by his flight from the Arthurian circle. He reverts to a wild state, being compared by the narrator to a Moor (3348), a comparison which recalls the wild herdsman, who also resembles a Moor in Hartmann's version (427); and at first Iwein takes what he needs for survival by force: a bow and arrows to hunt with. Then, however, he learns by experience the basic premise of social living: that cooperation is advantageous. The hermit helps him from fear, he helps the hermit in return—and the standard of living of both is raised. He begins now to resemble the wild herdsman in behavior as well as in appearance.

Iwein recovers his senses when a lady (*diu vrouwe von Narison*), who needs his help, finds him asleep and goes to some trouble to cure him. The cure is affected by rubbing him with a magic ointment made by Feimorgan, a motif of some importance in ***Erec,*** but one which is not elaborated in ***Iwein***. Yet one point has special interest: the lady instructs her lady-in-waiting to rub the ointment on Iwein's head alone, and not to waste it by rubbing it all over him. The assumption is that he suffers from brain-fever (*hirnsuht* 3427) and from nothing else. But the lady-in-waiting gets carried away and anoints Iwein *allenthalben über houpt und über vüeze* (3476 f.): is there possibly a connexion between the "waste" of attending to his body as well as his mind and his later refusal to be sensible and marry the lady of Narison, his insistence instead on returning to the wood—where he immediately establishes contact with the animal world? In any case when he has freed the lady from the attacks of her neighbor, Count Aliers, this is what he does; rejecting the chance he is offered of re-establishing himself in the sort of society he has left on new and easy terms, Iwein returns, voluntarily now, to the isolation of the forest (in which, however, he now in his sanity keeps close to the main roads)—and there finds two animals fighting.

This is the second time in the story that Iwein is confronted by the animal world. The first time he had seen a wild man in charge of animals, had expressed surprise and gone his way; this time he intervenes himself, and it depends on him whether the lion or the dragon should triumph. That this world is as yet strange to him is revealed by his twofold uncertainty: he does not know which animal to help, nor whether, if he helps the lion, it will then turn on and rend him. But he decides to help the "noble" beast and chance the outcome (3846-53). It is a fateful decision, determining his whole future: he kills the dragon, the lion kneels before him, and it is stated that the two will remain together till death. With the single exception of the battle with Gawein, all Iwein's future fights are fought against powers of evil and are won with the lion's help; indeed he becomes known as "the knight with the lion." The lion thus plays an important part in the story, and so if the story as a whole has a meaning, the lion must contribute to this. Yet [in his *Hartmann von Aue: Studien zu einer Biographie* (1938)] Sparnaay writes of Chrétien's presumed introduction of it: "Die Aufnahme des Löwen geschah wohl ohne tieferen Grund. Chr[étien], der Meister in der Kunst der Erzählung, erblickte in ihm ein wirksames Mittel das Interesse der Zuhörer zu fesseln." This judgment is not supported by a study of the role of the lion, which will I think be seen to suggest, not necessarily a more profound intention on the poet's part than simply to capture the attention of the audience, but certainly some more profound effect obtained in the event by the lion's presence in the finished work.

The first fact revealed about the lion, that it is the enemy of the dragon, is not directly helpful, since no further details are given in the work about this dragon. Its mythological associations, however, suggest an evil and destructive nature which, as will be seen, would contrast the dragon significantly with its enemy the lion and give a point to Iwein's choice between them. The lion's "nobility," which distinguishes it from the dragon, is traditionally, and probably correctly, taken by scholars as referring in the first place to its aristocratic lineage (in mythology); but it is not nobility of birth that characterizes Iwein's lion, but nobility of behavior: its boundless gratitude to the man who saves its life, its acceptance of a normally inconspicuous role in everyday affairs, together with the passion it shows for defending its master's life when this in turn is threatened, the fact that its intervention always results in innocent sufferers' being saved from violence and injustice, these characteristics mark it out as a highly moral being, as a vital support for human society and not a threat to it. At the same time, as *der wilde lewe* (3921), it is very much an animal: it was found in a forest it takes no part in purely social activities, and, above all, it fights in a ferocious and most unknightly fashion. Yet if it is an animal, the lion is also in some sense a part of the character in the work known as "Iwein," for the name "Iwein" is, after this episode, the equivalent of the phrase "the knight with the lion"; moreover, the role the knight plays in society, indeed his very survival depends on his association with his lion. A knight, in this work, is a highly educated human being, a lion is an innately moral animal; King Artus' court is full of knights, the wild herdsman has control over animals—but only in Iwein are both aspects of human nature integrated. King Artus' knights aim high but achieve nothing, the wild herdsman's animals dissipate their strength in fighting each other, only Iwein is willing, able and available when needed to right wrong and save the innocent from the onslaught of evil.

Once Iwein has recovered his senses and teamed up with his lion, he returns directly—but unconsciously (3923 f.)—to the well. Thus forced by "chance" to remember and face up to his past, he nearly goes mad again and does faint and almost get killed by his own sword as he falls from his horse: a minor episode which reveals his present vulnerability. (The lion's dependence upon Iwein is illustrated by his resolve to kill himself too if his master is dead.) But Iwein recovers—and proceeds to indulge in an outburst of self-pity, lamenting the day he was born. When Lunete speaks to him, he doubts whether she can possibly suffer as much as he does, and when it comes to a recognition, he announces himself as *Iwein der arme* (4213); indeed he threatens to commit suicide before Laudine's eyes, so as to make her realize how much he has suffered for love of her (4227-46). This lapse into despair is the consequence of Iwein's total acceptance of his failure, as a result of which he has isolated himself from his fellows and can find in himself nothing to live for; and he is rescued from it by accepting, with no thought of doing himself any good whatever, the need to act on behalf of others. Although now he believes that when he has rescued Lunete he will kill himself, when the times comes no thought of suicide in fact remains: the blind motif, like many other blind motifs in Middle High German literature, has a definite function.

This first adventure which comes the way of Iwein and his lion is ultimately of his own making: when he stands by Lunete and saves her from death, he is justifying her faith in him, proving by his consideration for her that he is the man she thought him, demonstrating that he is not, as she proclaimed him at Artus' court, *triuwelos*. But it is only with Lunete, not also with Laudine, that Iwein reestablishes a relationship at this point; for his part, he is still too unsure of himself to approach his wife unbidden, and she, who as a result of his defection has repudiated Lunete, repudiated, that is, her alliance with morality and reason, and has withdrawn into her hard core of now unsatisfied sex, is incapable even of recognizing in the knight with the lion her rejected husband Iwein: a fact which is inadequately explained by the nature of medieval armor, and causes even the narrator some astonishment (5456-8). At this stage accordingly it is with the chapel (in which Lunete is imprisoned) and not with the well that Iwein is actively engaged (cf. 5145-7).

Before Iwein saves Lunete, he meets with another adventure—for he stays overnight at a castle which is being terrorized by a giant, Harpin. This giant is characterized, like other mythological giants, by the belief that might is right: in the attempt to force the daughter of the house to marry him, he has already slain two of her brothers and he proposes on the following morning to hang the remaining four whom he has taken captive; moreover he has lost any human feeling he may once have had for the girl, and threatens now that when he does get hold of her he will hand her over to the lowest fellow in his retinue (4492-7). He might be described as the giant of Rape. The question then arises: why does Iwein have to slay precisely this giant before he can free Lunete?

The giant's situation is similar to Iwein's in that each has suffered a rebuff from the lady of his choice, but their reactions to this situation are totally opposed: Iwein withdrew into himself, the giant attacked his lady and her family. Now, however, Iwein has once more found himself at the well and he has to decide how to behave when faced by Laudine: it is one thing to have resolved in the isolation of the forest to support the lion and not the dragon, but apparently before he can act in concert with his lion in the situation which concerns him most vitally, Iwein has first to overcome, as it were in a nightmare, the alternative possibility. Only when he has encountered (just in time) the giant of Rape and killed him, is Iwein free to save Lunete from the stake—and then to proceed on his way even though Laudine has not recognized him.

It is at this point that the episode of the rape of Ginover is recounted—to explain why no help is forthcoming from Artus and his knights. The issue is raised by Iwein, who clearly has up to now thought that, however unsatisfactory Arthurian counsels have proved in his particular case, at least the Round Table can be counted on to ensure the triumph of innocence and justice in the world at large (4510-19). But he learns that he is mistaken: at least in this story, it is not "society" that upholds the moral order, but the efforts of a particularly gifted and suffering individual. In case it is objected that I am reading something into this episode that is not there, that for instance the only reason Gawein has to be otherwise engaged is to give Iwein a chance to distinguish himself, I should like to stress two points. First, Gawein and the Round Table need not have been mentioned in this connexion at all by either Chrétien or Hartmann: Iwein encountered this adventure and so it was his; there is no sense in the reference to Gawein unless a comparison is to be drawn. (Gawein is not mentioned in the following adventure of the imprisoned maidens.) Second, there is a marked contrast between the adventure which detains Gawein and that from which he is detained: the one is a matter of honor—or rather of reputation—the other of life and death. And again this need not have been so: had Gawein been engaged in an equally vital and bloody encounter, then any comparison which might have been drawn would not thus have turned out to his disadvantage. But since the medieval poets did in fact mention Gawein at this point and did explain his absence in this particular way, it is surely up to the reader to make a comparison and draw the appropriate conclusion.

It has long been recognized that Iwein's success in returning in time to save Lunete in spite of the difficulties occasioned by Harpin's late arrival, provides a contrast to his earlier unnecessary failure to return punctually to Laudine; the contrast may perhaps be expressed as a development from a self-centered carelessness—delight in his own successes made him forget his wife—to a full awareness of all aspects of a very complex situation. Significantly, he now feels compassion, a new element in the story: *nu erbarmt ez sere den riter der des lewen pflac* (4740 f.); but even compassion for his host's family does not make him forget Lunete. Nor for that matter does concern for others, whoever they may be, occupy him to the exclusion of concern for himself; in a most interesting speech he states: *ezn giltet lützel noch vil, niuwan al min ere* (4874 f.), and argues that if impersonal considerations would justify the sacrifice of Lunete to save a whole family, his own *triuwe* (4902), which is particularly involved in her case, will not. Furthermore, although also for the first time in the story Iwein is moved by consideration of his duty to God, even this is not exclusive; on the contrary it is made plain that human ties also matter to Iwein, that he wishes to serve Gawein, the maternal uncle of the girl threatened by Harpin, equally with God (4861-8). Possible the conclusion may be drawn that Iwein succeeds in meeting all obligations partly because he is aware of them all; he leaves the issue to God (4889-92), and all turns out for the best.

The three battles in which the lion participates, against Harpin, against the three brothers who threaten Lunete, and, in the course of the following adventure of the imprisoned maidens, against the two giants who kill off all suitors for a particular girl's hand, may profitably be discussed together. In all three battles Iwein begins fighting alone in proper knightly fashion, but because of unfair odds and the unchivalrous tactics of his opponents he is soon threatened with defeat, and then the lion intervenes in his own wild way—and Iwein and the lion together win another victory over evil. But the details of this pattern vary considerably, and are particularly revealing for the development of the relationship between lion and knight. Whereas before the first combat the giant is unaware of the threat presented by the lion (who behaves more as though he were a sheep 4815-7), and Iwein himself does not seem to expect help from it, before the second the three men request the lion's removal and Iwein has high hopes that it may succor him (5167-74), and before the third its menacing appearance is unmistakable:

> unde als si den grozen leun
> mit sinen witen keun
>
> bi sinem herren sahen stan
> und mit sinen langen clan
> die erde kratzen vaste . . .
>
> (6687-91)

Nowhere else is the lion described like this: apparently its support of Iwein becomes more openly threatening as battle follows battle; nor can anything prevent this support, although before the second combat it is removed to some distance and before the third locked up in a shed. Correspondingly, Iwein's conscious acceptance of his lion gradually increases: it is only after the first combat that he thinks of identifying himself by reference to the lion (5123-6), and even during the second he remains very detached about its support—*ern sagtes ime danc noch undanc* (5404)—until it gets wounded; then Iwein takes into himself something of its savagery (*zorn!*), and quickly defeats his adversaries:

> ouch tete hern Iweine we
> daz er den lewen wundech sach.
> daz bescheinter wol: wander brach
> sine senfte gebaerde,
> von des leun beswaerde
> gewan er zornes also vil
> daz er si brahte uf daz zil

daz si gar verlurn ir kraft
und gehabten vor im zagehaft.

(5414-22)

Iwein subsequently rides away, cradling the wounded lion on his shield, and the two of them are put to bed in the same room to recover. Finally in the third combat Iwein saves the lion from death, thus confirming their mutual interdependence (6769-71), and the narrator suggests afterwards that Iwein is now invincible precisely because he has brought his lion through unharmed:

nu wer moht im gedreun,
do er gesunden sinen leun
von dem strite brahte?

(6867-9)

The implication is perhaps that it is only when the courtly knight totally accepts and loves his animal nature that he is secure—and (it may be added) is in a position, after one further episode, to return (together with his lion) and make peace with his wife.

There comes a break in the narrative after Lunete has been liberated: Iwein and his lion are left resting while the background of the next adventure to come his way is sketched in. As in the preceding case, the main adventure frames a second one of a rather dreamlike quality—note the strange way in which Iwein's girl companion fades in and out of the picture during their stay at the intervening castle—but because of the complexity of this inner adventure I do not propose to consider it until both beginning and end of the one which frames it have been discussed. The outer adventure rounds off the account given in the work of Iwein's relations with the Round Table society, and the obvious and principal deduction from it is that for its proper functioning this society needs Iwein more than he needs it: the adventure begins by Iwein being sought out to prevent injustice being done at the Round Table and, when he has accomplished this, it ends by his stealing away from there to seek happiness elsewhere. Although the nature of the dispute is such as one might expect Artus' knights to solve unaided—for no lion is required to decide between the claims of two sisters over their inheritance—it is only after Iwein's intervention has thwarted the triumph of injustice that Artus uses his wits and resolves the feud satisfactorily. (Previously the odds were weighted in favor of the hard-hearted elder sister cf. 5746-54, 6924-8, for Gawein agrees to champion her simply because she asks him, without any regard to the rights and wrongs of the case at all—an approach whose impersonality is emphasised by his deliberate assumption of anonymity [5676 f.]).

The sister who is in the right is able to find her way to Artus but, perhaps because she is both weak and stupid, she fails altogether to find the knight with the lion. However, a cousin of hers takes up the trail and proves to be of very different caliber, struggling on in a storm through the wild forest at night till, helped by God (5798), she arrives at the castle where Iwein and the lion fought their first fight together, and follows his course from there, station by station, to find him at last recovered from his previous adventure. (Such a girl might be thought a fitting mate for Iwein, but she disappears later as quietly as she first came on the scene, any further development being perhaps precluded by Iwein's lack of interest in sleeping with her on the way, 6574-83—a motif which links up the intervening adventure to be discussed separately). Iwein's reply to her request for help is revealing of his present attitude to adventure:

swem mins dienstes not geschiht
und swer guoter des gert,
dern wirt es niemer entwert.

(6002-4)

This philosophy transcends both that of Kalogreant, who sought profit at others' expense, and that of the wild herdsman, who expressed a passive friendliness to those who did not harm him; moreover Iwein's calm statement of a qualification—*und swer guoter des gert*—contrasts him possibly with Artus, who lacked the independence to stand by a similar condition, and certainly with Gawein, who is at present committed to championing a lady whom he knows to be in the wrong (7621-30).

Iwein leaves the lion behind when going to fight an Arthurian battle: since his opponent is abiding by the rules, he will do so too. In consequence the combat drags on all day without result. In spite of all the asseverations of its seriousness, it is by comparison with Iwein's other fights nothing but a game, as is made particularly clear from the interval in the middle, when the combatants prefer to rest for a time rather than disgrace themselves by fighting feebly on (7242-50). The stupidity and tediousness of this pointless and inconclusive duel between friends is expressed appropriately in the longwinded conceits, combining perfection of form with fatuity of content, with which the narrator supplements and to some extent replaces a description of the fighting. But the battle is not altogether in vain: Iwein's willingness and ability to meet Gawein on his own terms produces a situation in which Artus is able and willing to execute justice: apparently if society's stupidity can be held in check, it may in the end rise to a simple occasion of this sort. Nevertheless virtually our last impression of the knights and ladies of the Round Table is of their headlong flight for safety when Iwein's lion comes bounding to join him afterwards (7727-39): a comic touch of powerful suggestiveness.

On the first night of Iwein's association with the girl who leads him back into the Arthurian world, he meets an adventure (the so-called Pesme Avanture) which Lachman thought intrusive and at least at first reading better omitted; I myself find it not only indispensable but possibly the most intriguing part of the whole work, partly because, while linking up at many points with the rest, it yet eludes total assimilation into the interpretation offered here and thus demonstrates how inadequate this is.

In its lighter aspects this adventure may well be compared with the earlier one involving the lady of Narison; but whereas there Iwein's disregard of the conventions in which he had been brought up seemed abrupt, uncertain and even compulsive, here it is calm and considered, and conveys an impression of maturity. His unconcern over ridicule, whether coming from a servant whose *schalkheit* is reminiscent of but even more marked than Keii's (6238-82, cf. 845 and 1530), or from this servant's master (6639-43), contrasts with Iwein's own earlier behavior as well as with that of Kalogreant and Artus. His disinclination for adventure (6620-38), together with his acceptance of and success in it when it cannot be avoided, distinguishes him further not only from Arthurian figures but also from the lord of *der Juncvrouwen wert* who, like Kalogreant, was inspired by an immature longing for adventures beyond his capacity (6328-31). In his case the consequence of this was that thirty maidens a year were sold into bondage. (That Iwein should be able to release these maidens and so undo this consequence of their lord's immaturity indicates how far he himself has progressed.) Further there is a development from Iwein's panic in his first adventure with the lion, when he feared that the giant would fail to arrive in time for him to save Lunete, and the unhurried way in which, in Hartmann's version only, Iwein can, after fighting the two giants, wait for all three hundred ladies to feed up and still escort them home, without being unduly worried about arriving in time for his combat with Gawein. Lastly there is the emphasis on the compassion Iwein feels for the ladies and on his reliance on God—only before fighting giants is he ever recorded as going to mass (4821, 6587-91)—an emphasis without parallel in the work and one which sharply distinguishes this serious combat from the Arthurian one which frames it.

These more or less incidental points do not, however, illuminate the core of the adventure, nor suggest an explanation of why Iwein encounters it just when he does; to achieve these aims a consideration of the basic situation obtaining at this particular castle is needed. It is presided over by a lord and his lady and their very beautiful daughter. Young knights who arrive at the castle have to fight two giants: if the knights lose, they are put to death; should one win, he will receive the daughter's hand in marriage. These giants thus stand between the daughter and her suitors; they represent the exact opposite of Harpin, the giant of Rape, and might be described as the giants of Parentalism: the girl leads an idyllic life at home, but is unable to break away. There is however a complication, for the lord of *der Juncvrouwen wert* was permitted to trade his life for thirty maidens a year; these are exploited in a disgraceful fashion in a separate part of the castle and will only be freed if the giants are slain. They are thus also prisoners of the two giants, but they represent the seamy side of these giants' activities, for if the daughter's life is apparently one of bliss, theirs is unmistakably one of misery.

In general terms I would suspect that the parallel with Harpin provides the clue for understanding Iwein's encounter with these giants. What I suggested there was that, in killing Harpin, Iwein was resisting the temptation to force his attentions on Laudine. But by turning his back on Laudine he has abandoned her to a virtually single state, a state which in her case is dominated by an obsessive desire for protection for her well. By defeating the giants of Parentalism, Iwein is perhaps overcoming the temptation to leave his wife in this state. Before this (double) adventure support for Lunete meant retreat from Laudine, after it, support by Lunete helps Iwein win Laudine; a progression which is I think only intelligible with reference to the calm way he deals with the giants who dominate this castle.

The suggested analogy between the situation at this castle and Iwein's own position does not, of course, amount to an identity, a fact illustrated by the necessity for Iwein not only to resolve this castle's problem but also to keep himself from too personal an involvement: he kills one of the giants but allows the other to survive (6791-4), frees the three hundred enslaved maidens but refuses to marry the daughter. Nor was this decision easy, for the girl attracted him considerably, and only his constancy to Laudine prevented his falling in love with her (6497-6516). That this inner adventure resembles the one which frames it, in that both show Iwein helping others without depending on them, seems clear, but I am not certain to what extent the situation at the castle may throw light on the underlying truths of Arthurian society, nor do I clearly understand the relationship between the three hundred maidens and either the castle or the Round Table.

The concluding scene of the work resembles in many ways Iwein's first approach to Laudine, but this time he knows what he is doing in in threatening her position (7790-7804), and his violence (*gewalt* 7804) now has an unambiguously positive function. Moreover, as a result of his earlier reconciliation with Lunete, she is able both to persuade her mistress to look for help to "the knight with the lion" (5554-62, 7993-8005), and further to compel her to face the truth that this is no other than her husband Iwein. A reconciliation between husband and wife is thus achieved, and one feels that their marriage has better prospects than before; but Hartmann is too sophisticated to let the reader assume that there are no further difficulties in store for them. At the time of their marriage, as has already been stated . . . , the narrator makes some general reflections about the qualities required for married happiness and adds *daz was allez waenlich da,* the emphasis resting on *waenlich.* Now at the moment of reunion he makes a parallel series of reflections clearly reminiscent of the earlier one (though both subtler and more complex), and then adds once more *daz was hie allez waenlich sit* (8148). He then mentions Lunete, the importance of whose role is stressed by her inclusion here, and finally concludes:

> ez was guot leben waenlich hie:
> ichn weiz ab waz ode wie
> in sit geschaehe beiden.
> ezn wart mir niht bescheiden
> von dem ich die rede habe:
> durch daz enkan ouch ich dar abe
> iu gesagen niuwet mere,
> wan got gebe uns saelde und ere.
>
> (8159-66)

The future fate of Iwein and Laudine is thus neatly left undecided. It is not even stated that they enjoyed *saelde und ere,* those notorious catchwords which run right through the work from the opening sentence. And this omission appears to be in keeping with the tenor of the whole: at the beginning the narrator makes a categorical statement about life—*swer an rehte güete / wendet sin gemüete, / dem volget saelde und ere*—and illustrates it with reference to King Artus. But the body of the work reveals that only when Iwein draws away from the ideals of the Round Table, does he achieve a measure of inner peace, marital harmony, and service of others; and so at the end categorical statements about him are avoided—and instead there just remains the faintly ironical prayer that at least God may grant us *saelde und ere.*

To avoid misapprehension, may I say in conclusion that the interpretation offered here is not intended to be in any way definitive. In my opinion Hartmann's ***Iwein*** will support any number of partial interpretations and will never adequately be paraphrased by any of them. What I have hoped to show in this essay is that if we start from the assumption (which medieval scholars have been strangely reluctant to make) that ***Iwein*** is an autonomous work of art and that consequently the meaning of every one of its parts (a) is of the greatest importance and (b) depends exclusively on its relationship to the other parts, then we are rewarded by discovering the whole to be both more complex and more profound than has usually been thought. The assumption is admittedly too extreme to be maintained dogmatically on all occasions, but as a working principle for those engaged on the interpretation of any work of art it cannot be recommended too highly. For what we need above all is a principle which will prevent us from too easily reducing the unique creation of an unusually gifted human being to the commonplace of either his contemporaries' or our own trivial experience. Background information, be it historical, social, linguistic, literary or whatever, can only furnish *suggestions* as to the possible meaning of the various elements in a work of art, suggestions which should never be accepted as binding (no matter what arguments about the force of tradition, the pressure of social circumstances, or anything else be advanced to the contrary) but should be tested rigorously against the unique finished work and, if inadequate, should be modified, or rejected altogether. Nor does the fact that Hartmann's ***Iwein*** is more or less a translation of Chrétien's *Yvain* in the least affect this method of procedure. Either the translation has become a work of art in its own right or it has not, and this we can determine only by examining it independently.

J. Knight Bostock (essay date 1961)

SOURCE: An introduction to *Der arme Heinrich* by Hartman von Ouwe, fourth edition, edited by J. Knight Bostock, translated by Erich Gierach, Basil Blackwell, 1961, pp. xvii-xl.

[*In the following excerpt, Bostock examines* Der arme Heinrich *in light of the Medieval (platonic) belief that each person is naturally suited to a particular order of existence.*]

All serious literature which is the product of a sophisticated culture, such as that of the thirteenth century, is the expression of the moral philosophy of its time, and it is often impossible to grasp an author's intention without some knowledge of contemporary thought. Many of the ideas and even much of the language of the courtly poetry cannot be understood without a knowledge of contemporary religious literature such as the sermons of Berthold von Regensburg, of didactic works such as *Der welsche Gast* by Thomasin von Zerclære, and of legal codes such as *Der Schwabenspiegel* and *Der Sachsenspiegel.*

According to mediæval philosophy everyone was called to a particular manner of life which was his 'order' (*ordenunge*). The peasant was called to the plough, the monk to his asceticism and the knight to his elaborate conventions which made severe demands on his energy and strength of character. It should be understood that the knightly ideals were not, as is sometimes imagined, inconsistent with the teaching of the Church, for the Church

Miniature depicting Hartmann von Aue as a knight, from the Grosse Heidelberger Liederhandschrift.

never demanded renunciation of the world except from the select few who had the vocation. The sin lay in failure to conform to the moral law of one's own order.

Hartmann himself had a definite didactic purpose fully in keeping with the laboriously achieved harmony and balance of his literary style. In each of his four narrative poems he describes the career and moral development of a type of character familiar to the society of his age. All his heroes and heroines have to overcome a fault which arose from excess of one particular virtue or set of virtues and prevented them from attaining the ideal of courtly life, namely that perfect harmony and balance, called in the language of the time *diu mâze*. Thus Erec and Enîte had sinned against the laws of knightly good breeding by allowing their devotion to one another, which in itself was a good thing, to become excessive and thereby to cause them to neglect their duty to society. Both had to find their way back to the right way of life through hardship and sorrow (*arebeit*). Iwein was at first lacking in restraint and good breeding both as a warrior and a lover. Laudîne allowed her passion to overcome her courtly moderation. Both had to find their way to *sælde* and *êre*. Gregorius had been proud to excess, preferring the glitter of the world to the humble asceticism of the monastery, and when he learnt of his unwitting crime, his reaction was wrath, not humble repentance. He was pardoned after long penance and found the solution of his problems in his return to the Church, which had always been his true vocation. His mother, who sinned twice, took the veil immediately when the second sin was discovered. The second sin would have been avoided if she had not attempted to do penance for the first without renouncing her position in the world. Her Heinrich also had sinned. He had had all the accomplishments of the perfect knight in perfect proportion (ll. 32-74), only he had lacked humility (ll. 383-411). His reaction to the divine punishment was wrath (ll. 146-62). He tried earthly remedies in vain (ll. 163-232), for he still lacked humility and therefore insight into God's purpose. His acceptance of the position was the action of a well-bred knight (ll. 233-60), until he suddenly realized his folly in resisting God's will (ll. 1241-56). Then he was healed by grace. He was redeemed by his own submission to the will of God, and recalled to his ordained walk of life, namely knighthood made perfect, not only in respect of the worldly qualities which he had possessed before his trial, but by Christian humility. Though his call was of a lower order than that of Gregorius, namely the normal life of a married man, not the ascetic withdrawal from the world, it was, as stated above, a call recognized by the Church. Retirement from the world was only for the few.

Her Heinrich's redemption was brought about in the orthodox Christian manner, namely by submission to the will of God, for which he was rewarded by a miracle. At first sight the process appears obscure, nevertheless the action develops quite consistently. After Her Heinrich's attempts to find a cure had failed, he had accepted the position (ll. 233-60). This was not enough, because, although he realized that he was being punished for his false pride (ll. 383-406), he merely accepted defeat and gave no sign of real repentance (ll. 453-58). This did not come until he was forced to undergo a severe temptation, when the maid offered herself. At first he yielded to her urgency (l. 1011), but later the sound of the surgeon's knife on the grindstone and the sight of her beauty (l. 1233) working on his latent virtues of pity and *triuwe* converted him to complete self-abnegation and the final realization of God's will (ll. 1243-45). The significance of Hartmann's reference to the beauty of the maid has been disputed. The true explanation . . . [is]: Beauty in the Middle Ages was associated with dignity and costly apparel. There was no aesthetic significance in naked beauty. Nudity was a disgrace, and tolerable only in connexion with martyrdom. It was not her naked physical beauty, but the sight of her lying naked and bound in the conventional attitude of martyrdom which moved Sir Henry to repent of his purpose. His marriage also was not a matter of love and desire, but of deliberation. It must be regarded against the background of the teaching of the mediæval Church. As Heinrich had no call to enter a monastery, it was his moral duty to marry and, as he explains (ll. 1493-1508), no one could be more suitable than the maid. It was not necessary for Hartmann to explain further. Her Heinrich is now a perfect example of *diu mâze,* a perfect knight living the normal worldly life of a married man. There is one remarkable omission: Hartmann does not mention any children of the marriage.

The problem of the maiden is less clear. It is not enough to regard her case as one of perfect humility and self-sacrifice rewarded even during her life on earth. As ***Erec, Gregorius*** and ***Iwein*** each present a pair of sinful human beings finding their way to salvation through *arebeit,* it is reasonable to expect that the maiden in [***Der arme Heinrich***] should also have to redeem herself from an excess of virtue which had become a fault. It is difficult to see what fault she had committed. She had been inspired by God to serve Her Heinrich in his illness and to offer her life for him (ll. 693-98, 859-64, 1158). Even her lapse of manners when her sacrifice was frustrated by Her Heinrich was due to the belief that God's will was not being done (ll. 1281 ff.). There was, indeed, a certain amount of selfishness in her offer, for she expected to obtain salva-

McConeghy on the impact of Hartmann's *Iwein:*

Considering the influence of ***Iwein*** on modern literature, one quickly sees that Iwein does not share the fame of a Parzival, a Tristan, or a Lancelot. Iwein's lion and the harmonious resolution of his marital problems with Laudine have been no match for the search for the Holy Grail or the illicit love affairs of Tristan and Isolde, Lancelot and Queen Guinevere. But, to judge from the large number of extant manuscripts, the adaptations of the story in other languages and other art forms, and the number of references to ***Iwein*** by German poets of the thirteenth and fourteenth centuries, the tale enjoyed great popularity in the Middle Ages.

Patrick M. McConeghy, in a preface to Iwein *by Hartmann von Aue, Garland Publishing, 1984.*

tion very easily thereby (ll. 1144-49, 1160-67), but Hartmann has not developed the theme. His conclusion appears to be that God does not always intend us to escape the temptations of life. The maiden, like Her Heinrich, was ordained to live a normal human life, but with her character formed unusually early. Hartmann has not detailed her emotions when she found that she was destined to be not a martyr but an earthly wife. To have done so would have introduced at the close a new theme which would have entirely changed the character of the poem. Having told his story of repentance and forgiveness, Hartmann concludes as quickly as possible.

The peasant and his wife also are perfect examples of their type, as Her Heinrich is of his type: the man physically strong, honest, respectful to his lord and grateful for favours received, and the wife diligent in her duties. They have, as married couples should have according to the teaching of the Church, several children. They sacrifice their child as soon as they realize that it is God's will, and are duly rewarded (ll. 1437-1445) for their *leit* and *arebeit* (ll. 1029-30).

H. B. Willson (essay date 1962)

SOURCE: "Love and Charity in Hartmann's *Iwein*," in *The Modern Language Review,* Vol. LVII, No. 2, April, 1962, pp. 216-27.

[*In the following essay, Willson explores the ethical and stylistic influences of Medieval Christianity on Hartmann's* Iwein.]

In ["Sin and Redemption in Hartmann's *Erec*," *Germanic Review,* xxxiii (1958),] I set out to prove that Hartmann's ***Erec,*** in spite of its 'worldly' theme, is constructed on the basis of an ultimately religious formula, a formula which lies at the very heart of Christianity itself, namely sin and redemption. What is true of ***Erec*** holds good also for its complement, ***Iwein,*** which indisputably reveals a similar structural analogy with Christian reality. ***Iwein*** is also a 'worldly' poem, but nevertheless betrays the strong influence of the contemporary theological background in its fundamental pattern, ethical outlook and stylistic technique.

The transgression of Erec, as is well known, is his failure to fulfil his chivalrous obligations to society immediately following his marriage to Enite: *er verligt sich.* In the article referred to it was suggested that this mirrors the disordering of love which constituted the first sin of mankind, a turning away from love of God to love of self. Erec and Enite indulge too freely in love for each other, excluding completely their fellow human beings, a form of love which conflicts with the wider love-concept of *caritas,* that is, ordered love, whether in relations with the opposite sex, with one's fellows, or with God. Their *minne* is in direct opposition to *caritas;* ideally and 'ordinately' it should be harmoniously integrated into it, as indeed later happens, when both Erec and Enite redeem themselves and display *triuwe,* that is, *caritas,* in its highest and purest form, both towards each other and towards their fellows. Needless to say, this also means that they eventually reorder their relationship with God.

Iwein, on the other hand, *verrittert sich.* Far from spending too much time in the company of his newly won wife, Laudine, he forgets his promise to return to her after one year of knight-errantry. Yet, in spite of this absolute contrast between the relationships of the two heroes with their wives the same question is posed: how is a knight to preserve the balance between his love for his wife and his love for humanity (and therefore God), the latter a cardinal chivalrous and Christian virtue? The disturbance of this balance in either direction leads to disordered love, self-love, to a situation where *minne* (in the sense of love between the sexes) and *caritas* are mutually exclusive. Ordered love results when a knight's relations both with his wife and with his fellows are inspired by *caritas,* with which sexual, carnal union is by no means incompatible. In fact, ideal sexual relations must have a caritative basis. Love without charity is no love at all.

Before we proceed to consider in detail how all this is illustrated in ***Iwein*** it would seem desirable to repeat what was said in the ***Erec*** article, namely that the analogies and correspondences to be discerned are not, and cannot be expected to be, exact. Differences of detail between the *ordo* of the *maere* and the *ordo* of Christian historical and ethical truth are numerous. The two orders are not one and the same; their relationship is one of unity in diversity. But such differences of detail do not invalidate the analogical symbolism.

Iwein's *sich verrittern* to the extent of not returning within the promised time constitutes a breach of *triuwe* to Laudine. He loves adventure without measure. In his inordinate desire for knightly honour and fame he forgets her, fails to consider her feelings, is without *compassio* and *caritas,* in contrast to Parzival, who carries Cundwiramurs in his heart wherever he goes. Moreover, Iwein also shows little *caritas* towards his fellows. This is clearly revealed as soon as he has defeated and killed Ascalon, that is, even before he is *ungetriuwe* to Laudine. For the grief of Laudine he has a form of *compassio,* but it is hardly disinterested, for he has fallen in love with her. But for her courtiers, who have lost a generous lord, he has absolutely none, in spite of his words to Lunete, which are at once contradicted:

> die rede meinder niender so:
> wan ern gaebe drumbe niht ein stro,
> ob si mit glichem valle
> da zehant alle
> laegen uf den baren,
> die da gesinde waren,
> ane diu vrouwe eine.
>
> (1439 ff.)

His *caritas* is merely feigned. He is so concerned with his own awakening sexual love that he has no room in his heart for common humanity. In fact, his whole way of life, until his recovery from madness, shows a conspicuous lack of *caritas*. Although we hear little about his exploits during his year or more of adventure, we may presume that they are not of the same caritative order as those he undertakes later. Thus, when he is denounced by Lunete at Arthur's court, he is *ungetriuwe,* lacking in *caritas,* in both senses, to Laudine and to his fellows. In spite of the fact that his sin is largely one of omission it is of the utmost gravity, and he becomes a social outcast as much for the one form of *untriuwe* as the other. The two are inseparable, since *caritas* is the all-important factor in human relationships.

Iwein's departure from Arthur's court in disgrace is the beginning of a period of alienation, which takes the striking form of madness and nakedness in the forest, wholly removed from courtly environment. For his sin he has forfeited the 'paradise' (*ein wunschlebn*—1. 44) of courtly life and that of wedded bliss with Laudine. In religious terms he is in a state of absolute 'dissimilitude', a state clearly expressed in the poet's own words:

sus twelte der unwise
ze walde mit der spise,
unze der edele tore
wart gelich eim more
an allem sime libe.
ob im von guotem wibe
ie dehein guot geschach,
ob er ie hundert sper zebrach,
gesluoc er viur uz helme ie,
ob er mit manheit begie
deheinen loblichen pris,
wart er ie hövesch unde wis,
wart er ie edel unde rich
dem ist er nu vil ungelich.

(3345 ff.)

He is as unlike an ideal knight, his true self, as could possibly be imagined. This contrast between his former and his present mode of existence is given full emphasis; the pointed analogy with the situation and condition of mankind after it lost the paradise of similitude with God is conveyed with striking effect. The word *ungelich* summarizes the whole passage. Iwein is now *unwise,* just as the folly of man was demonstrated in original sin. Yet he is an *edele tore,* and here, too, the religious parallel is not far to seek: in spite of the Fall the soul of man retained its original nobility; this, because of the essential divinity of the human soul, can never be lost. Man is made in the image of God. On the other hand, Iwein is said to be *sin selbes gast* (3563), which again closely parallels the religious conception of the soul having become estranged from its true self as a result of sin, of having taken on an alien deformity. Iwein becomes like a Moor; his *similitudo* is not with a paragon of Christian chivalry and with the God who inspires that chivalry, but with something totally alien to these.

The passages describing Iwein's madness contain, significantly, a number of trinity or unity-plurality formulae which contribute powerfully to the symbolism. For example, in 3363-4 we encounter, *drie vrouwen da er lac, wol umb einen mitten tac,* where *dri* and *ein* occur in close proximity. With this may be compared *diu eine vrouwe von den drin* in 3369. Lines 3395 and 3433-5 may be placed in the same category. Furthermore, the lines:

ir höfscheit under ir güete
beswarten ir gemüete,
daz si von grozer riuwe
und durch ir reine triuwe
vil sere weinen began,
daz eim also vrumen man
diu swacheit solte geschehn
daz er in den schanden wart gesehn.

(3387 ff.)

are also meaningful. In them we hear echoes of the Crucifixion: Iwein is a man of sorrows, with whom those who have *triuwe* cannot fail to suffer; he excites *compassio,* just as the body of Christ on the cross in its *passio,* the quintessence of *compassio* and *caritas,* arouses *compassio* and inspires *caritas.* Shortly before this the word *wunde,* a key-word in Christian symbolism, is used (3379). To be sure, Iwein is not Christ, but only a *vrumer man* in a shameful condition, but he is made in the image of God. To redeem the shameful condition of man, the 'dissimilitude' he had brought upon himself by his own sin, Christ, God the Son, took on human form and was *in den schanden gesehen.* Iwein has sinned, whereas Christ did not sin, but rather suffered for the sins of man, but for all his divine perfection, his *schande* on the cross was the direct result of sin. The Fall of man and his redemption by God made man are complementary to each other. Through mystical dialectic the opposites of God and man are reconciled, becoming inseparable. These lines thus contain a typical *analogia entis,* forming a small part of the wider *analogia entis* of the poem itself.

The salve which restores Iwein to sanity has also an unmistakable symbolical function. The maiden who applies it (one of three) has received strict orders from her mistress to use it economically. It must be applied locally. What remains she must bring back, for it may be *maneges mannes heil* (3452). But the maid has so much *compassio* for Iwein that she applies it all over his body, and particularly *über houpt und über vüeze,* using up the whole box in the process. The analogy with the Gospel story of Mary, the sister of Martha, at once suggests itself. She, too, anointed Jesus' head and feet with the costly ointment of spikenard, and 'wasted' it; she was blamed for doing so, since it might have been used to help the poor. It would not be too much to say that this motif has a mainly symbolical justification. Once again, Iwein is not, of course, to be identified with Christ, yet he is the object of the maid's *caritas,* and she wastes the ointment on him, just as Mary wasted the ointment in her excessive love for Christ, an action which met with his full approval. The better part chosen by Mary is, moreover, traditionally used in mystical writings as a symbol of *caritas* in the highest degree. Both in the Gospel and in the ***Iwein*** passage the mystical formula *diligere sine modo,* love without measure, is present. Later the maid is required to explain to her mistress why she has used up the whole box, and is forced to lie. But Hartmann assures us that the lie is wholly excusable, a *gevüege* and *guote lügemaere* (3679-90). This bears a strong resemblance to Isolde's ordeal by fire in Gottfried's *Tristan*. . . . The words of reply used by the mistress are also symbolically suggestive:

si sprach 'heil und unheil
diu sint uns nu geschehen:
der mac ich beider nu wol jehen.
den schaden suln wir verclagen,
des vrumen gote gnade sagen.

(3682 ff.)

They contain the same mystical paradox as the Death and Resurrection: through *gotes gnade* the *unheil* of the one, the penalty for the sins of mankind, gives place to the *heil* of the other, namely salvation and redemption. *Caritas* turns loss into gain.

Finally, the maid's anxiety to remain hidden from Iwein in his nakedness also finds its analogue in the Fall of man, who, having eaten of the fruit, knew that he was naked and was ashamed. In other places, too, Hartmann makes use of this motif with symbolical intent. The whole episode of the salve, in fact, is full of suggestive, meaningful analogies with well-known religious contexts and symbolic imagery. The very miracle-working salve itself, though obviously of fairy-tale origin, is sacramentally conceived. It is of the same order as many other supernatural elements of the Christian background; it is Christian 'magic'. Iwein is cured miraculously, by the miraculous 'magic' of *caritas,* of which the salve is the symbol, and which transcends nature by virtue of its divine origin.

After his restoration to sanity, or, as one might say, his re-birth, Iwein begins a new series of knightly adventures. In all these demonstrations of his prowess he is actuated, not by the mere desire for fame and glory for himself, but by *compassio* and *caritas*. Not long after his recovery he rescues a lion from a serpent, as a result of which the lion becomes forever after his faithful companion and servant. Iwein overcomes his *zwivel* (3864) as to which beast to assist against the other by deciding in favour of the more noble of the two. The lion, far from turning and attacking him when it is no longer concerned with the serpent, as Iwein feared it might, miraculously transcends its own nature by showing gratitude and a form of *minne* (3873) more suited to a human being of exemplary Christian virtue. The designation of the serpent as being the less noble of the two has much in common with the biblical conception of the same creature as the symbol of evil, the instigator of the sin of Adam and Eve. Analogically speaking, Iwein is the saviour of the lion, whose exemplary reaction is everything that it should be. Iwein's *caritas* arouses a reciprocal *caritas* in the lion, which is displayed in its constant and unswerving *triuwe* to its saviour. Throughout the rest of the poem it 'suffers with' Iwein. This *caritas* of a dumb animal receives particularly striking expression when the lion sees Iwein *wounded* and *bleeding* after he has been pierced by his own sword while falling off his horse in a trance, brooding over his unhappy fate. The lion is filled with *compassio,* and believing Iwein to be dead, is about to commit suicide, in order to share his *passio,* when Iwein appears *lebende* (3956) before him in a kind of analogical resurrection. The words *brot* and *win* in 3907 add to the religious flavour of this whole episode, in which Iwein's 'perfect love' casts out his fear of the lion and inspires a miraculous reciprocal love in the animal he saves. Their subsequent *geselleschaft* is essentially a caritative one.

While still lamenting his misfortune Iwein comes upon Lunete imprisoned in a chapel awaiting death. She has incurred the disfavour of Laudine for having persuaded her to marry the faithless Iwein, and has failed to find a champion for her cause in the time allowed. Paradoxically, her *triuwe* to her lady, as she sees it, has been interpreted as *untriuwe* by Laudine. Iwein catches sight of Lunete looking out *durch eine schrunden* (4020), a typical mystical motif ultimately derived from the Song of Songs, and used by both Hartmann and Wolfram. Though in great distress himself Iwein has immediate *compassio* for the far greater trouble of Lunete, of which he is the direct cause. His is the *untriuwe* for which she is soon to pay the penalty. In his new caritative frame of mind he has no hesitation in deciding that her life must not be sacrificed for his sake; rather must he be prepared to die for her if necessary, in a combat where the odds are three to one against him. The central motif of *caritas* in this episode is reinforced by another series of number formulae. *dri starke man* is followed closely by *zwene* (4085-7), *zwene* occurs again in 4092, 4101 and 4106. *dri* appears in 4103, *dri* and *ein* together in 4108, *dri* in 4110, followed by *ein* in 4111. A little further on the play on numbers begins again: 4174 shows *dri,* 4150 *ein* and 4151 again *dri.* 4152 contains *vierzec,* 4160 *sehs,* 4162 and 4177 both *zwen.* This constant repetition of numbers, particularly of *dri* and *ein* in close proximity, is not coincidental, but a rhetorical illustration of mystical dialectic, of the reconciliation of the antitheses of unity and plurality. External and formal though this may seem, it is nevertheless an important part of the symbolical and analogical whole. Further Christian echoes are heard in Lunete's words, spoken when Iwein reveals himself to her:

mirn mac nu niht gewerren,
sit daz ich minen herren
lebende gesehen han.
ez was min angest und min wan
daz ir waeret erslagen.

(4267 ff.)

Her redeemer lives. Yet she gives no really convincing reason for believing that he was not *lebende,* merely assuming this to be so when she failed to find him at Arthur's court. The words have, once again, a symbolical rather than a logical justification, like so much else in medieval life and thought. Resurrection imagery is plainly in evidence.

After leaving Lunete, with a promise to return to champion her, Iwein comes to a castle whose lord is being sorely oppressed by a giant, and his *compassio* is again aroused. If the giant presents himself in time to allow Iwein to keep his appointment with Lunete's oppressors he will gladly engage in combat with him. But as time goes by and the giant does not appear, Iwein falls prey to *zwivel:* should he remain and abandon Lunete, or should he depart without having liberated his host, in order to be sure of arriving in time to champion her? It does not seem possible for him to do both. He appears to be faced with a problem of irreconcilable antitheses: one form of *caritas* seems to exclude the other. The poet brings the 'dialectic' of the situation into clear focus:

ich darf wol guoter lere.
ich weiz wol, swederz ich kiuse,
daz ich an dem verliuse.
ich möht ir beider gepflegn,
ode beidiu lazen under wegn,
ode doch daz eine,
so waer min angest kleine:
sus enweiz ich min deheinen rat.

(4876 ff.)

Iwein therefore asks God, in his divine *caritas,* to provide a solution to problem in which the dialectic of the world is of little avail, to bring unity where there appears to be only plurality:

nu gebe mir got guoten rat,
der mich unz her geleitet hat,
daz ich mich beidenthalp bewar
so daz ich rehte gevar.

(4889 ff.)

His request for help is answered; the giant appears, directed, as it were, by God's almighty hand:

nu schiet den zwivel und die clage
der groze rise des si da biten. . . .

(4914-15)

Through God's help Iwein is able to perform two acts of *caritas,* which had seemed to be mutually exclusive. The irreconcilable antitheses have been reconciled in a unity transcending dialectic. *Caritas* is above logic, solving all contradictions.

On arrival at the chapel for the second time Iwein finds Lunete bound and stripped of all but a smock, awaiting death. She despairs of salvation, but

do si sich missetroste
daz si nu niemen loste,
do kom ir helfaere,
und was im vil swaere
ir laster under ir arbeit,
die si von sinen schulden leit.

(5161 ff.)

Once again his *compassio* is aroused at the sight of her misery. He places his trust in God and her innocence. Lunete's companion-maids pray for their *spile,* the *vil getriuwe* Lunete (5215). There follows more unity-plurality symbolism as Iwein addresses his adversaries:

waz von diu, sint iuwer dri?
waent ir daz ich eine si?
got gestuont der warheit ie:
mit ten beiden bin ich hie.
ich weiz wol, si gestent mir:
sus bin ich selbe dritte als ir.
dar an lit, waen ich, groezer kraft
dan an iwer geselleschaft.

(5273 ff.)

Iwein himself is three-in-one, being aided by God and Truth. This is a real trinity, a more perfect unity than that of his three individual opponents, and has therefore greater power. The words *got, warheit, kraft* and *geselleschaft* add to the symbolism inherent in the numbers.

After his triumph against odds, the overcoming of plurality, Iwein's *erbarmen* is further displayed at the sight of the misery of the maidens who have been given as hostages to the giants:

nu erbarmet in ir ungemach:
er siufte sere unde sprach
'nu si got der süeze
der iu vrouwen büeze
iuwer unwerdez lebn,
und ruoche iu saelde und ere gebn.

(6407 ff.)

In a *boumgarten* he finds an old couple with their daughter, who is said to be so beautiful that

si mohte nach betwingen mite
eines engels gedanc,
daz er vil lihte einen wanc
durch si von himele taete. . . .

(6500 ff.)

Before the Fall of man the rebel angels also *taten einen wanc von himele!* Iwein's *staete* and *triuwe* are put to the test, but, in spite of the great temptation, his love for Laudine renders him proof against the charms of any other woman. He is unlikely to commit once more the sin of 'disordering' his love, as did the rebel angels and our first parents. By his victory over the giants the hostages are freed from diabolical domination. The *boumgarten,* we note, is a virtual Garden of Eden.

Iwein's final combat is on behalf of the maid whose elder sister is determined to take the whole of their dead father's possessions for herself. Unknown to him his opponent is to be his very close friend, Gawein. Beforehand Arthur tries to arrange a *suone* between the two girls, but without success. The issue can only be resolved by battle. The underlying paradox of this conflict is repeatedly stressed by Hartmann. Two very dear friends, linked by *caritas,* are about to engage in a fight to the death. As it would seem, the quarrel of the two maidens can only be settled in favour of one or the other, according to whether Iwein or Gawein should prove to be the better man. The dialectic of battle, hatred and enmity cannot reconcile two opposing parties; only *caritas* can bring this about. The limitations of such dialectic are made clear in a long passage which begins at 7015, containing frequent play on the antitheses *minne* and *haz*. It seems impossible, according to all the rules of dialectic, that *minne* and *haz* should ever be reconcilable, yet on this occasion the two live together in the same confined space:

ez dunket de andern unde mich
vil lihte unmügelich
daz iemer minne unde haz
also besitzen ein vaz
daz minne bi hazze
belibe in einem vazze.
ob minne unde haz
nie me besazen ein vaz,
doch wonte in disem vazze
minne bi hazze
also daz minne noch haz
gerumden gahes daz vaz.

(7015 ff.)

Two opposites are apparently united in one. Hartmann offers to explain to his audience how such a reconciliation is possible:

nu wil ich iu bescheiden baz
wie herzeminne und bitter haz
ein vil engez vaz besaz.

(7041 ff.)

They are in ignorance of each other's presence:

diu unkünde was diu want
diu ir herze underbant;
daz si gevriunt von herzen sint
und mit gesehnden ougen blint.

(7055 ff.)

This, then, can hardly be termed a true reconciliation. It is a paradox still to be resolved.

Somewhat further on a similar play on words of opposite meaning is to be observed. This time *borgen* and *gelten* are contrasted and mingled (7147 ff.). In fact, throughout the whole combat Hartmann draws upon all his resources of rhetorical skill to focus attention on its importance. As long as the encounter lasts neither of these two famous warriors can defeat the other. The problem still appears to be insoluble; a deadlock has been reached. Once again Arthur tries to effect a *suone* between the two girls, but the elder will make no concessions whatever. She is totally lacking in *caritas,* giving concrete proof of her *superbia*. The younger, on the other hand, possesses in full what her elder sister lacks. She has so much *compassio* for Iwein and Gawein that she asks for the fight to be stopped. Neither of these two noble knights shall sacrifice his life for her; she would rather forego her portion. But Arthur refuses. He cannot approve such a solution: *caritas* must be mutual and reciprocal. If the *superbia* of the elder sister were allowed to triumph complete disorder would result, as it did when the angels and man turned away from God in *their superbia*. And Arthur is the defender of order (*sin hovereht*—7341).

When it becomes too dark to see the fight is broken off, and there follows an exchange between the two combatants in which paradox is once again the dominant feature. Iwein begins by saying that although the day has always appealed to him more than the night, he now finds the latter more congenial. For him, black has become white and white black. He dreads the next day, for

got enwelle michs erlan,
so muoz ich aber bestan
den aller tiuresten man
des ich ie künde gewan.

(7415 ff.)

He respects, even loves, his enemy. Gawein is of exactly the same mind:

wir gehellen beide in ein.
herre, ir habent mir des verdigen:
unde hetent ir geswigen,
die rede die ir habent getan
die wold ich gesprochen han.
daz ir da minnent, daz minn ich:
des ir da sorget, des sorg ich.

(7432 ff.)

He tells Iwein his name, and at once

beide truren unde haz
rumten gahes daz vaz,
und richseten drinne
vreude unde minne.

(7491 ff.)

Reconciliation has taken place, a *concordia discordantium* is achieved. The love they bear towards each other as friends transcends the hatred imposed upon them by their duty towards the parties they champion. No further conflict between them is possible. Arthur then insists that the elder sister agree to divine the inheritance, which decision she is forced to accept, albeit from fear of the consequences, and not out of *caritas*.

There is no more significant episode in the whole poem than this drawn battle. It is a dialectical and rhetorical showpiece; the two branches of the Trivium work together in close association to produce the effect required, that of a precarious balance between two extremes, *caritas* and *superbia,* love and hate, order and disorder, light and darkness. As long as the battle lasts *caritas* cannot assert itself to bring matters to a harmonious conclusion. Both warriors are moved by *caritas* to fight each other on behalf of the maidens, but their *caritas* toward each other, which would, under normal circumstances, have prevented them fighting at all, is blinded by thier unawareness of each other's identity. Love without knowledge is no more effective than knowledge without love. The *superbia* of the elder sister is the root cause of all the trouble. But the antithesis is resolved through mutual recognition, revelation. Plurality gives place to unity, two become one in friendship once more, a reunion which leads to a reconciliation between the two sisters, however reluctant the one may be. Throughout, the poet excels himself in rhetorical subtlety of a kind admirably suited to and illustrative of the thought-content, itself so closely resembling the fundamental pattern of Christian truth.

Though Iwein and Gawein are now reconciled they nevertheless continue fighting, as it were, in words, each one insisting that he has lost the fight. The paradox remains, but the transcendent unity is patent, for it is now a friendly battle:

> sus werte under in zwein
> ane losen lange zit
> dirre vriuntlicher strit. . . .
>
> (7590 ff.)

Each is now concerned to humble himself before the other, which is a clear indication of their mutual *caritas,* since *humilitas, compassio* and *caritas* are inseparable.

After Arthur has given his decision and the matter has been settled once and for all, Iwein's lion appears, to the terror of the onlookers. But Iwein calms their fears with the assurance that this is no ordinary lion, but one with *caritas:*

> ern tuot iu dehein ungemach:
> er ist min vriunt und suochet mich.
>
> (7738-9)

Once again fear and love are contrasted and the greater power of the latter is affirmed. The word *vriunt* underlines the symbolism inherent in the figure of the lion, to which we have referred above.

By this time Iwein has fully proved his ideal chivalrous manhood. *Caritas* is his cardinal virtue. His relations with his fellows have been ordered in charity, and now the greatest problem of all awaits solution: the reordering of his relations with his wife Laudine. This supreme reconciliation must be achieved before the narrative can be completed. But it is a difficult problem, since Laudine's attitude towards Iwein is still most unfriendly. He goes to the fountain and calls forth the tempest, which is of such magnitude that *er die liute alle gar verzwivelen tete* (7824-5). Here the word *verzwivelen* is a measure of the situation, which might well give rise to despair: the fountain has no defender, and Iwein and Laudine are hopelessly divided from each other. But this is to reckon without the *caritas* of Lunete. Her only desire is that these two conflicting parties shall be reconciled (8065-6). Lunete is the faithful 'paranymph', whose *caritas* never fails throughout. Through her *list,* which is the measure of her measureless love, the two estranged spouses are reunited.

As so often elsewhere, Hartmann makes frequent use of paradox in his final solution. Laudine expresses the wish that the knight who slew the giants and saved Lunete were there to defend the fountain, without knowing that this same knight is, in fact, the challenger; in other words, she would like to have the fountain defended by its present challenger against himself! Lunete tells her that he will only come to help if she, Laudine, will promise to do everything in her power to assist him to regain his wife's *hulde.* Laudine swears that she will do so, again without realizing that she is the wife and Iwein the husband concerned. Thus husband and wife are, and are not, husband and wife; challenger and defender are, and are not, one and the same. Nothing could be more typical of the mystical way of thought than this 'similitude in dissimilitude'.

When Laudine sees that she has been outwitted her reaction is a natural one: she has every right to be angry. But she is bound by the terms of the oath she has sworn, and must comply, if she is not to become *ungetriuwe.* Thus she formally agrees to take Iwein back. The latter then asks her forgiveness for his *untriuwe:*

> vrouwe, ich habe missetan:
> zware daz riuwet mich.
> ouch ist daz gewonlich
> daz man dem sündigen man,
> swie sware er schulde ie gewan,
> nach riuwen sünde vergebe.
> und daz er in der buoze lebe
> daz erz niemer me getuo.
>
> (8021 ff.)

The formality of Laudine's consent to take Iwein back into her favour, imposed upon her by the oath, receives substance as soon as he has begged her forgiveness and repented of his sin, and his act of humility calls forth a reciprocal humility in her:

> Her Iwein, lieber herre min,
> nu beget genade an mir.
> von minen schulden habet ir
> grozen kumber erliten:
> nu wil ich iuch durch got biten
> daz ir ruochet mir vergebn,
> wand er mich, unz ich han daz lebn,
> iemer mere riuwen muoz.
>
> (8122 ff.)

Thus the two become reconciled: *sus wart versüenet der zorn* (8136). The *minne* of Iwein and Laudine is now a true fellowship, no longer in opposition to *caritas,* but in full harmony with it and partaking of it. Both have repented and been forgiven. Iwein has displayed his *caritas* in numerous situations, and through it he has regained a state of grace after his fall. His self-love was, as we have seen, in direct contradiction to *caritas,* leading to the separation of the two lovers. The *caritas* repeatedly shown by Iwein after his rebirth itself partakes of the divine *caritas* which is the essence of God in Three Persons, and which God demands from man in return, if he is to be redeemed. Only through *caritas* can antitheses be reconciled and the love of Iwein and Laudine be reordered. *Caritas* is law, order and measure, and without it Iwein could never have fitted himself to receive once again the *genade* and *hulde* of his wife. Through his acts of *compassio* and redemption he has himself been redeemed. His *geselleschaft* with Laudine has been re-established on a new basis, blessed and favoured by God. In the analogical sphere, the order of the story, the *hulde* of Laudine and of courtly society represents the ideal from which he has fallen away, just as in the sphere of Christian reality this ideal is God, for whose *caritas* man displayed a selfish disdain, and yet was, paradoxically, saved from damnation and the domination of the devil by this same *caritas* made flesh. The union of God and man was broken because the latter did not reciprocate the love of God and so lost the paradise of similitude. The relationship became disordered. God and man were reunited, order was re-established, when, paradoxically, God joined his divinity with sinful humanity, the two opposites co-operating in a 'communion of wills and a conformity in charity'.

Appropriately, Hartmann ends his poem with a tribute to Lunete, whose *triuwe* played a prominent part in bringing about this great reconciliation:

hie was vrou Lunete mite
nach ir dienesthaften site.
diu hete mit ir sinne
ir beider unminne
braht zallem guote.
als si in ir muote
lange hate gegert.
ir dienest was wol lones wert:
ouch waen ich daz sis also gnoz
daz si des kumbers niht verdroz.

(8149 ff.)

Her caritative efforts in the role of 'paranymph' (*ir dienesthafter site*) have been supremely worth while. The three *gesellen* enter upon a new life together in a union closer and more lasting than they have previously achieved. The unity of this blessed trinity is preserved by mutual *caritas,* just as *caritas* preserves the Unity of the Supreme and Blessed Trinity of God in Three Persons.

Thus it may be seen that in Hartmann's ***Iwein,*** as in his other three epics, the universal Christian love-concept of *caritas* is the dominant idea, the integrating force upon which the whole action depends, and that it reconciles with itself even carnal love. Any interpretation which fails to acknowledge this must fall lamentably short. Though the narrative moves on a 'worldly' plane it cannot be divorced from religious truth, for the love of God is immanent in all creation. It is precisely in the reconciliation of the carnal and the spiritual that the message of the poet lies. For Hartmann and his contemporaries all love stems from and participates in divine love. It would be altogether wrong to imagine that, since Hartmann was a poet, and not a theologian, he was necessarily unfamiliar with the fundamentals of Christian education and could never have had the knowledge and subtlety we have claimed for him. Though such matters may seem technical and even esoteric to the modern mind, they were nevertheless an essential part of the intellectual climate of Hartmann's age, which is characterized by lay piety, without which the courtly ideology and the literature arising out of it are unthinkable. The ideals cherished are unity, harmony, reconciliation and love.

K. C. King (essay date 1965)

SOURCE: "The Mother's Guilt in Hartmann's *Gregorius,*" in *Mediaeval German Studies,* The Institute of Germanic Studies, 1965, pp. 84-93.

[*In the following excerpt, King examines Hartmann's language in* Gregorius *in order to explore the extent to which Hartmann found Gregorius and his mother culpable for their incestuous relationships.*]

Discussions of the problem of guilt in ***Gregorius*** have usually centred on Gregorius himself; this is neither surprising nor without justification, for the *mare* is in fact about him, *von dem guoten sundare.* It is possible that an agreed solution might be achieved in this way, although there are still serious disagreements . . . but it should not be forgotten that there is another prominent actor in the story, who is called by the hero himself *ein schuldec wîp,* and a discussion of what constitutes her guilt could possibly help to throw light on Hartmann's intentions in the question of guilt in the whole work.

It is generally accepted that the church would have considered Gregorius and his mother free of guilt in their incestuous union, because of ignorance . . . , but it is not generally accepted that Hartmann was writing in accordance with the orthodox tenets of the church, although some critics maintain it, or assume it. On similar grounds it can be maintained that Gregorius is innocent in the eyes of God at his birth, although his mother experiences anxiety on that account. In the case of the mother the situation is different in that she is not only a party to the union with her brother, but knows it at the time, and Hartmann expresses himself quite explicitly (line 604) through the mouth of the old retainer to the effect that she had sinned and that that sin should be atoned. She is conscious that she has done a great wrong and willingly submits to the privations which are imposed on her as part of her atonement; so much would appear to be clear and generally accepted, but she breaks down in a state of mind approaching despair, expressing the view that all she has done has been in vain, when she learns that she had again committed incest. If one argues . . . that Gregorius is innocent, because ignorant, it is difficult to see why similar arguments should not be used for the mother, who was just as ignorant (*vür einen gast enphie si ir kint,* 1935), although this does not appear to have been done in detail. Possibly because it may have been felt that the mother at least was not entirely free of blame, in that she did not take what might seem to have been the obvious precaution of asking for more information about the cloak when she recognized the material (lines 1939 ff.). . . . Others have in their various ways sought to find a pattern behind her 'blindness', and it would be possible to argue a case that on the arrival of her son she shows an unseemly readiness to break her vow not to marry and to remain the 'bride of Christ'. Thomas Mann, for example, has devoted considerable care to the analysis of the mother's motives on the sight of the 'stranger' and would appear to wish to present her as still feeling pleasure at the remembrance of her sinful union with her brother; if that is so, one could almost regard the second union as a continuation of the first. Hartmann's views at this point in the story do not always appear clear to us nowadays, although they might well have been clear to his contemporaries, and there are points which need further discussion.

One thing, however, must be stressed first, and that is the way the poet presents his material. All concerned with the first incest are deeply distressed by it, and all three subject themselves to heavy penance, and accept the necessity of it, but, although the brother dies in the course of it, it is nowhere indicated that that which has been done cannot be atoned and that his death is in any way a punishment, or retribution, for his sin: he dies of a broken heart. When, later, mother and son realize the nature of their union, their horror is such that the mother is in danger of falling into the unforgivable sin of *desperatio,* from which extreme she is saved by her son's admonition and the son himself withdraws to do penance which in its intensity can only be described as beyond the normal power of men. They do this when they discover that *sî aber versenket was / in den vil tiefen ünden / tœtlicher sünden.* There is no reason to doubt the reliability of the text here, nor the meaning of the word *aber,* and so one is forced to the conclusion that Hartmann is here saying that the mother has sinned twice—which seems obvious, but it conflicts with the view so often expressed that what she did was not a sin in the eyes of God, because she did not know what she was doing. That Hartmann meant this is confirmed by the first words of the 'epilogue' (3961 f.), where he speaks of the two sinners and their *grôzer schulde* in terms which do not say expressly, but most certainly make that the obvious inference, that they had together committed a great sin. Lines 2602/3 point in the same direction.

If one allows proper weight to the poet's words, which he repeats and emphasizes, one cannot escape the conclusion that the mother has sinned greatly, and that she has sinned twice. As her first incest is called a sin, and as her despairing outburst is made immediately after the discovery of the second there can scarcely be any reasonable doubt that Hartmann intended his hearers to regard these two incestuous unions as the two sins which had to be atoned, unacceptable as such a view must be to those who hold the view that the poem was written according to the orthodox teaching of the church. In order to reconcile with this the obvious fact that Gregorius himself has sinned and is forced to atone for his sin(s), attempts have been made to discover a sin which he knowingly committed, so that he can be held guilty. This has not been done in the same detail in the case of the mother, although commentators have drawn attention to passages which could be interpreted in this way. For a proper understanding of Hartmann's work, however, such an investigation ought to be made, for, as indicated above, both mother and son are held by the poet to be involved together; and it should be carried out strictly in accordance with the text of the poem. The poem is not long, and much of it consists of action, and consequently there is not much room for the discussion of the motives of the characters. This can have the result that these motives may at times appear to be inadequately explained; but on the other hand any such inadequate psychological motivation may be simply because the poet was not interested in developing that aspect. . . .

Such considerations are not absent, however, and the first thing that readers notice is that Hartmann draws attention to the conflict in the young girl's mind when she is aware of her brother's intentions, whether she should prevent the devil's will being fulfilled or whether she shall risk their *êre* by screaming, and that she resolves it by not taking the step to stop her brother. She is therefore held guilty for putting worldly considerations before those of God. Against this must be put the further comment (639 ff.) that *enheten si niht gevürhtet got* they would have put up with the contempt of the world rather than suffer the bitterness of parting. . . . The apparent discrepancy is perhaps not serious, for her first, wrong decision was not a considered one, but was made in very difficult circumstances: the person in whose care she had been placed and whom she had regarded as her protector betrayed her trust in him. As if to exonerate her, Hartmann stresses that she lacked experience of such emotions and did not know against what she should be on her guard and therefore allowed him his way (345-50). The actual intercourse took place almost without her knowledge, for she was disturbed in her sleep. Further, the poet used two significant epithets, both pointing in the same direction: *daz einvalte kint,* which is clear in meaning, and *diu reine tumbe,* which is less clear; . . . [it means] something like 'the girl who was just simply young and inexperienced', without any implication of 'purity'. By referring to her as the *guote* in line 394 Hartmann implies that he regards her as 'innocent' as a person, but he leaves us in no doubt that she is afterwards conscious of having committed a heinous sin and that he himself also regards her deed as heinous; the point of this being that he presents the deed as arising out of the active will of the devil and not out of the sinfulness of the girl.

A modern reader, approaching the work with all the equipment of modern psychological analysis, cannot fail to notice what will appear to some the utter stupidity, not to say the criminal negligence of the mother in not asking for details about the cloth when she recognizes it; Thomas Mann has in fact dwelt at some length on it and it would appear that he would regard her suppression of her suspicions as symbolic of her continuing lustful thoughts of her brother, in that she did not in fact really try to suppress anything at all, rather the contrary. The cloth and the whole appearance of the stranger reminded her pleasingly of her love for her dead brother, and she transferred this love, as it were, to the stranger. No doubt, the trait could be used as such a symbol, but it is far from clear that Hartmann was in fact using it for that purpose. One might even go so far as to say that the line *daz ermante sî ir leide* (1954) points in just the opposite direction: she was reminded of the painful past and out of fear of that past suppressed any incipient thought which might bring it back into her mind. The great point at issue here is that if she acted out of the consideration that this was something which reminded her pleasantly of an aspect of her past one cannot but say that her thoughts were sinful and that this would lay a great element of guilt at her door for what happened afterwards; if on the other hand her motive was to suppress anything which reminded her of it she was at least acting in a way which was quite understandable, and consequently the further step should not be regarded as in any way the result of any guilty step or consideration on her part. Why, then, it will be asked, did Hartmann introduce this motive if he only wished to draw attention to something which was to be suppressed? The answer is not easy. It could of course have been the result of his source, and, try as one may, one cannot avoid the fact that Middle High German literature bristles with cases where the authors are at pains to deal with awkward situations arising from their faithful adherence to their sources; but it is perhaps not necessary to have recourse to that argument here. Gregorius was of high birth, and it was one of the aims which his mother had in mind when she prepared the tablet to make that known, and it was in the same spirit of pride in their courtly background that she tried to protect her son as well as might be from the rigours of the exposure by covering him with the very best material that she had available. The 'courtly' significance of the cloth is confirmed by the act of the abbot in having clothes made from it for Gregorius when he makes him a knight (1642/3); that the abbot should have preserved the material as carefully as he had the money is no more than a fully conscientious following of the injunction he received from the tablet. Seen from this point of view it is quite natural that Gregorius should have arrived in his mother's land wearing these clothes, and if one accepts that one must also admit that it is only natural that she should recognize them. This would mean that there is no special significance, such as for example Thomas Mann seemed to see, in the incident of any guilt on the mother's part. . . . One could perhaps go even further and say that the fact that she does not pursue the matter further is to be interpreted as an indication that not only did she not recognize her son—that is expressly stated—but that the possibility of it being her son simply did not occur to her. This should not be pressed too far, but if such a possibility can be entertained it should at least serve as a warning against attaching too much significance to such features as these, which the author does not develop and which may even be blind motives to which he does not attach great importance.

This reference to her promise to do penance leads on to the consideration of the remaining action, or omission, for which she would be held responsible, or guilty. . . . If there really had been . . . an injunction on her to remain celibate because of her sin, the case against her would be strong; but it is not at all clear that this had been imposed on her. In the first place it must be noted that the old retainer—and he is the only one who does give the couple any advice—is by no means too harsh in his judgement: he agrees with the brother that it would be best if he left the country and enjoins him to go on a crusade, hoping that he will return, but assuring him of God's blessing if he dies in the course of it. . . . He is quite precise in his advice to the sister, in saying that she should not withdraw from the world; on the contrary she can better atone for her sin by conducting the affairs of the realm and doing good to the poor. While, presumably, she is preparing to undertake these responsibilities, a further blow befalls her, the news of the death of her brother. As Hartmann presents it this is the signal for many a magnate to seek her hand in marriage, and the combination of the two things leads her to the decision not to marry. He does not say that her motive was the personal one of loyalty to her brother, but equally certainly he does not say that it was out of penitence for her great sin; one can only say that to judge by the point in the story at which the motive is introduced there are good grounds for considering the personal one as the more likely. In view of the clear statements of the affection of the two, this is also psychologically defensible. One thing however is clear and that is that there was no express command from the counsellor that she should never marry.

Another inescapable fact is that, as a result of her refusal to marry, one of the suitors laid waste her lands; and it is at this juncture that Gregorius arrives and offers, potentially at least, the hope of rescue. In line 1882 it is expressly stated that the lady was pleased at the arrival of the stranger, although she had not yet seen him, and so cannot know who it is, and there can be no grounds for doubting that her pleasure was due to the prospect of it being someone who could rescue her from the importunate suitor and the realm from the siege. The relief of the courtiers was no less great, and from their point of view, after the stranger had shown his mettle in single-combat, the obvious course was to reward him suitably and to secure the position of their realm by persuading their lady to offer him her hand in marriage. They support their argument by telling her that she would be doing better, both in the eyes of the world and of God, if she were to take a husband and have an heir; in the circumstances she would have to have an extraordinary strength of character if she were to continue to abide by her self-made resolution. . . . Hartmann adds his own expression of approval [in lines 2221-4].

If one regards her actions from this point of view, some of the references to God which have caused editors difficulty appear less surprising. Immediately after her decision to marry there is at least the suggestion that what she does is done in the name of God: *alsô daz sî ez in gote tete*. . . . From one point of view she is acting 'in the name of God', in that she is acting in the interests of her subjects; and lines 920-23 would confirm that Hartmann regarded the delivery of the realm as of importance and that its delivery (by Gregorius) was an act of God.

The trend of this whole argument has been to exonerate the mother from blame and from personal responsibility for the sins which undoubtedly are committed and have to be expiated, and it has been conducted almost exclu-

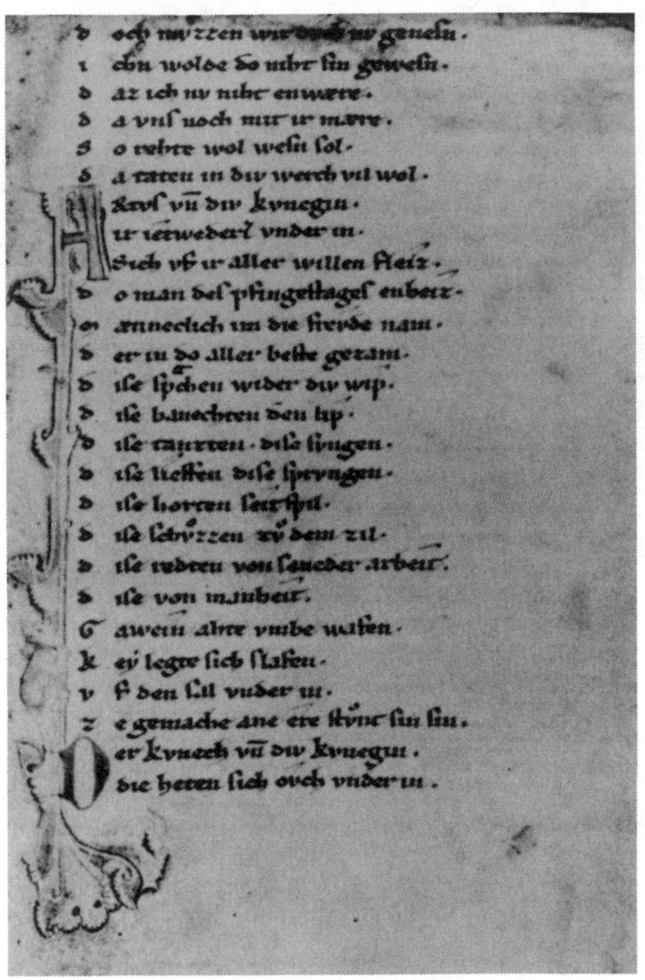

Lines 53-78 of Hartmann's Iwein, *from a Medieval manuscript.*

sively by reference to the text of the poem. That is not necessarily a virtue, for a poem is a product of its time and consequently a due consideration of the intellectual and spiritual background is necessary for a proper interpretation of it, but in the case of ***Gregorius*** it is by no means clear that there is any *prima facie* case for thinking that Hartmann was concerned with any particular problem of the time. It is, for example, fairly common for critics today to argue that medieval German poets were particularly concerned with the *ordo*-idea and the problem of those who were not content to remain 'in that state of life, unto which it shall please God to call' them. These ideas have been applied to ***Gregorius*** . . . but it is difficult to see with what justification they can be applied to the mother; she is of noble birth, her father is anxious that she shall be instructed and thus able to maintain her position in the courtly world, and the old retainer gives his opinion that she should retain an active rôle in the world, and this can, on the death of her brother, only mean that she shall conduct the affairs of the state. It is while doing so that she falls into the temptation to marry the stranger who is then revealed as her own son. It would be wrong to suggest however that Hartmann intended to depict in the mother an ideal woman, any more than he intended, in portraying the secular life of Gregorius, to set him up as the ideal man, but it is intended to suggest that he did wish to present the mother as a 'good' woman (he does actually use the epithet *guot* [394]), as a woman who was seduced into sin and who then, to all intents and purposes unaided, for years tried desperately to atone for what she had done. The one thing which does not fit readily into this picture is her behaviour on the arrival of the stranger who looks [to be] their rescuer. Her first reaction (1882/3) is entirely in accordance with the pattern of correct behaviour, but this 'statesmanlike' interest seems soon to give way to a personal one, in that she wishes to see him after hearing of his *zuht* and *vrümecheit*. When she does see him it is made clear by Hartmann that this is in fact a 'personal' interest, namely he appealed to her as man does to woman; which, given the circumstance that she has been told not to withdraw from the world, cannot be condemned. Nor does Hartmann seem to condemn it, for four lines later he again uses the epithet *guot* of her; what he does condemn is the application in this particular instance. He who had betrayed Eve had brought together, in circumstances which could hardly occasion any other than the given reaction, two people who had been for long at pains to do their best in the circumstances in which they found themselves. Personally their attitude to one another was beyond reproach, *wande sie wâren berâten / mit liebe in grôzen triuwen* (2254/5), but like so many things in the world *daz nam einen gahen val*.

It must no doubt be admitted that there are features in the behaviour of Gregorius's mother which may still appear inconsistent, or even psychologically not entirely satisfactory, although it might be possible on the other hand for a trained psycho-analyst to find a reconciling formula. Even if that were possible, however, it is doubtful whether much would be gained, for until we have good evidence that Hartmann was interested in a scientific, psychological analysis of the characters and the problem of incest we must be cautious of interpreting his work from such a point of view. To judge from the plan of his story he would not appear to have set much store by such considerations; certain events are clearly of the utmost importance for his purpose, such as the parting of the brother and sister and the casting off of the child, the life in the monastery, etc., and he dwells at length on these. On the other hand, the transitions from one to the other, such as from the monastery to the land of his mother, are dismissed with the utmost brevity, one might almost say with an utter disregard for verisimilitude. Hartmann's intention would appear to be to concentrate attention on the things which did happen, rather than on the strange circumstances by, or through, which they were caused. Opinion continues to differ on whether the dreadful deeds which occurred in the story are due to weaknesses of character in the hero; and in the case of the mother too there is not the evidence to justify any more positive conclusions. They both act in a way which not only seems justified to them in the circumstances in which they find themselves, but which is also in accordance with an acknowledged way of life; nevertheless they both fall into sin, and sin of a particularly heinous nature, namely incest. Hartmann's purpose is not to criticize the behaviour of either mother or son, nor, particularly, the mode of life which could lead such 'good' people into such sin; it is to show that where there is true repentance forgiveness is never impossible.

H. B. Willson (essay date 1966)

SOURCE: "*Amor Inordinata* in Hartmann's *Gregorius,*" in *Speculum,* Vol. XLI, No. 1, January, 1966, pp. 86-104.

[*In the following essay, Willson interprets* Gregorius *with regard to the doctrine of original sin and the opposition between ordinate and inordinate love.*]

Hartmann's ***Gregorius*** is concerned largely with the vicissitudes of a man who is the product of an incestual relationship between brother and sister. These, it is made absolutely clear, begin at the very moment of his birth and are the direct result of it. How, then, does the poet intend this highly abnormal sexual relationship to be viewed, and what inferences can be drawn from it with regard to the hero's own guilt and atonement? In recent years a number of attempts have been made to interpret the poem and in particular to assess the guilt of Gregorius himself, but no clear agreement has been reached. It is possible, however, that a reexamination of the case, starting from the parents' incest, which has such dire consequences, may lead to a better understanding of the poet's intentions.

In his description of the events leading up to the conception of Gregorius, Hartmann gives special prominence to the fraternal love of his father for his mother while they are still only brother and sister. On his death-bed their father laments the fact that he has not made adequate provision for his daughter. He frankly confesses that this was *unväterlîch getân* (242) and in his belated compassion for her he commends her to his son's love and care, with the injunction that his brotherly love must compensate her for his own lack of fatherly love (262). The intentional contrast of *unväterlîch* and *bruoderlîchen* concentrates attention on the bond of family union, the need for love and affection between those of the same flesh and blood. In this case the need is particularly great, since an imbalance must be rectified: the daughter has been unfairly treated and is all the more deserving of the love and compassion, the *caritas,* of her brother. The father having fallen short in this respect, the brother should make up, or atone, for his failure.

This he does in full measure:

Nû daz disiu rîchiu kint
sus beidenthalp verweiset sint,
der juncherre sich underwant
sîner swester dâ zehant
und phlac ir sô er beste mohte,
als sînen triuwen tohte.

(273 ff.)

Both children are now orphans, and the brother is determined to carry out his father's wishes and to show the utmost *triuwe* to his sister, his fraternal love for her. He at once gives concrete proof of this love by giving her everything she could possibly desire and making her as happy and comfortable as he can. He seldom leaves her side, even sleeping so close to her that each can see the other. No one can say of him that he is not treating her as a *getriuwer bruoder* should. This love is reciprocated in even greater measure on her side (282 ff.). She loves her brother as much as a sister could and should.

An ideal state of affairs thus obtains. Both children show complete obedience to their father's wishes. They show their love for him and for each other, a love that is right, seemly, and proper. It is "ordinate," conforming in every respect to the ideal *ordo* of fraternal love. Their behaviour is exemplary. But this happy state, stemming from their ordinate behaviour, becomes the envy of him who, in his *hôchvart,* first perverted the Divine Order itself with his disobedience, and, in his *nît,* disturbed the order of paradise (305). He sets himself the task of turning their happiness into sorrow by perverting the brother's love:

an sîner swester minne
sô riet er im ze verre,
unz daz der juncherre
verkêrte sîne triuwe guot
ûf einen valschen muot.

(318 ff.)

The word *verkêren* occurs in both 316 and 321, and in each case it expresses the idea of perversion, a change from an ideal state of affairs to its very opposite. This is clearly shown in the two contrasts *vröude-ungewinne* and *triuwe guot-valschen muot.* On the one hand is *ordo,* that which is good and right, and on the other *inordinatio,* the perversion of order.

By his intervention the devil does indeed succeed in disturbing the existing order of the brother-sister relationship. The former is led astray by his perfidious advice, so that

beidiu naht unde tac
wonte er ir vriuntlîcher mite
dan ê waere sîn site.

(342 ff.)

His *missetât* is that he is being even more friendly to her than had been his custom. The irony of the word *vriuntlîcher* underlines the *inordinatio.* Before very long the devil's victory is complete:

dô si begunde wachen,
dô hete er si umbevangen.
ir munt und ir wangen
vant si im sô gelîmet ligen
als dâ der tiuvel wil gesigen.

(370 ff.)

In this very meaningful section of the poem the devil is

referred to by name no less than eight times, while on two further occasions he is *der durch hôchvart und nît versigelt in der helle lît* (305) and *der hellehunt* (333). Hartmann is obviously determined to place a heavy load of responsibility for this turn of events fairly and squarely on his shoulders. His desire to create disorder is made very clear: he is the evil counsellor, whose perverted will triumphs. He it is who causes the father of Gregorius to show too much love for his sister:

> dâ was der triuwen alze vil.
>
> (396)

It will be noted that the poet here uses the same word for the inordinate sexual love of the brother for the sister as he does for the ideal and very proper fraternal love he had shown her previously, namely *triuwe,* and that it is clearly ironically meant. Again irony is used to emphasise *inordinatio*. In this context, excessive *triuwe* is an infringement of the *ordo* of *triuwe*. The limits of love between brother and sister have been overstepped; such love is inordinate because it is immoderate. The brother shows *unmâze* in his *triuwe* to his sister, since order is measure. He loves her without measure, but, ironically, this kind of measureless love is not the way to compensate for his father's deficiency of love for his daughter.

The influence of the mediaeval *ordo*-concept is thus very apparent, and it is also evident that *mâze,* and therefore order, upon which Hartmann lays such strong stress in his chivalrous romances ***Erec*** and ***Iwein,*** is also of fundamental importance in ***Gregorius***. The *missetât* which determines the entire course of action of the poem is that of inordinate love—*amor inordinata*—, at least if Hartmann's text is anything to go by. The birth of the hero is the direct result of inordinate love, a perversion of the *ordo* of fraternal love. It is not what their father had hoped for from them to rectify his own deficiency of love.

Hartmann's insistence on the role played by the devil as the instigator of this disorder is thus full of meaning. The devil rebelled against God in his *superbia,* preferring himself to his creator. To make matters worse, in his *invidia* of the happiness of man in paradise, he tempted Adam and Eve to disobey God and to show a similar preference for themselves. Original sin was committed; the love of our first parents became disordered, like that of the devil himself, that is, it was directed towards a lower object, themselves, in preference to a higher object, namely God. The hierarchy of values was perverted by this subordination of the higher to the lower. Since Hartmann refers directly to the *hôchvart* and *nît* of the devil, for which he was consigned to hell, the analogy of the temptation of the father of Gregorius with the original temptation in paradise at once suggests itself. His *missetât* is analogous to original sin. Brother and sister live in a paradise-like state, which excites the envy of the devil.

The doctrine of original sin assumes that, as a result of their inordinate love for themselves, Adam and Eve became prey to concupiscence and cupidity, the inability of the will to control the desires and passions, their animal instincts. Their nature became vitiated by sin. Love—the will—can be either good or bad, ordered or disordered, according to the end. The right will is good love, perverse will is evil love. *Amor inordinata—superbia*—is thus not only original sin itself, but the consequence of it, in that it implies man's continuance on the evil course of rebellion against God, of perversion of the order of values. Although this conception of ordinate and inordinate love applies to all the desires and appetites of man, it is significant that for St Augustine (and through him for mediaeval Catholic thought in general) one of the most important forms of cupidity, or *libido,* is that associated with sexual intercourse. This is so because the genital organs, unlike other organs in the body, are not subject to the control of the will, a result of original sin. Had sin not occurred, in other words if paradise had not been lost, the procreation of children by sexual intercourse would have remained under the control of the will and would have been neither shameful nor lustful. But sin brought with it *libido* in the sexual sphere and carnal concupiscence, which involves the parts of the body which are shameful (since the Fall), became the instrument by which sin was transmitted from generation to generation. There is, therefore, a clear connection in Augustinian thought between the original disobedience and sexual love, particularly when indulged in for its own sake, the lustful pleasure it gives. The one, original, form of *amor inordinata* leads to the disorder represented by the *libido* of sexual pleasure. *Cupiditas, concupiscientia,* and *libido* are all *amor inordinata* and the consequence of *amor inordinata*.

The analogy between original sin and the sin of the parents of Gregorius depends on this connecting link. The sexual relations between brother and sister are a particularly gross form of concupiscence, due to evil will, first of the devil and then of the brother who listens to his advice. They are a manifest perversion of sexual love itself, in the ordinate sense of marriage, for brother and are sister not, and never could be, married, and a child from such a union is unthinkable. It is made quite clear too, that the action of the brother is not controlled by the will, but is a clear case of *libido*. Furthermore, Gregorius' parents resemble Adam and Eve in that they are, as it were, of the same flesh.

Yet a child does spring from this union, and he is therefore especially heavily burdened with the sin of his parents, which is transmitted to him through their inordinate act, and although this applies, in the case of original sin, to every human being since the Fall, it is obvious that if he had been born in normal wedlock, or even if he had been illegitimate, in the ordinary sense, the symbolical force of the motif would have been greatly reduced. The antithesis between the brother and sister relationship and that of man and wife is irreconcilable, and a combination of these two opposites is an unmistakable indication of *inordinatio*. Inevitably, the parents not only bring shame and humiliation upon themselves through their inordinate conduct, but they also expose their child, from the very moment of his birth, to the scorn and contempt of the community into which he is born. For this reason he must be cast out, as were Adam and Eve, from paradise. Although he has not committed this sin himself, it is clear that he must at once begin to feel its effects. His mother says:

ouch ist uns ofte vor geseit
daz ein kint niene treit
sînes vater schulde.
jâ ensol ez gotes hulde
niht dâ mite hân verlorn,
ob wir zer helle sîn geborn,
wand ez an unser missetât
deheiner slahte schulde hât.

(475 ff.)

She speaks the truth: he has not lost *gotes hulde,* as later events prove, nor was he responsible for his parents' misdeed. He does not bear their sin in that sense. But what his mother does not say is that although her son has committed no sin of his own he is, nevertheless, *heir* to their sin, just as they were heirs to original sin (if they had not been, they would not have sinned themselves), and that this legacy of original sin has been transmitted to him by themselves, just as Adam and Eve transmitted original sin to all their progeny. Every child born of carnal union is burdened with sin, in spite of its own innocence of sin. How much more striking is this in the case of Gregorius, the love of whose parents was so clearly perverted! Although Adam and Eve had a good will and a good nature before sin, their nature and their will, together with that of all their descendants, became evil and vitiated. In the case of Gregorius this undeniable fact is underlined by the analogy with the Fall itself in the inordinate love of his parents. He is *geborn mit alsô grôzen sünden* (689), the product of a perverted act, and is thus predisposed to sin by nature as a result of that act, which itself symbolises by analogy the Fall of man. This is confirmed by the reference to his *süntlîche sache* (2283). That this is different from the *schulde diu ûf sîn selbes rücke lac* (2290) is clear from the distinction made in the passage, since he has committed incest himself by this time, but there can be no doubt that this second incest cannot be dissociated from that of his father and mother. This does not mean that he could not have avoided his own incest, or that this is a special punishment for his parents' sin, but it does mean that, sinful by nature, he was likely to commit sin himself and so needed to be especially vigilant in order not to do so. The sin transmitted by his parents might well be perpetuated by him, since he is the son of his parents.

That his mother is fully aware of the dangers facing him is evident from the words she inscribes on the *tavel.* [In his "Zur Frage der Schuld in Hartmanns ***Gregorius,***" *Euphorion* LVII] K.C. King has performed a valuable service in drawing special attention to the fact that the sense of these words, so relevant to the problem of guilt or innocence, is not altogether clear. As he rightly says, it is sometimes difficult, owing to the frequent use of the preterite subjunctive by Hartmann, to tell whether a clause is merely conditional, or whether it contains a request or command. The precise punctuation is also difficult to establish. Nevertheless, it seems possible to determine from the context which sense is the more appropriate. The essence of the matter is whether the inscription is meant as an injunction to Gregorius to do certain things when he is old enough to read it, or whether his mother merely hopes that her words will act as a warning to him and that he will take the good advice she is offering him. The latter seems more likely.

King's criticisms of Nobel and Schieb have some justification: although the mother does send a *message* to Gregorius, as the former says (the inscription is intended for him to read), the word "Bitte" is less apt. She merely tries to ensure that all the conditions are present for his reading of the tablet. The rest, she hopes, and has been led to believe by her Christian faith, will follow. She enjoins the finder to have her son christened and to pay for his upbringing with the gold (740-742), and if he happens to be a Christian, to increase its value for him. He is to keep the tablet for him and teach him book-learning, that is, to read and write, so that, if he ever grows up to be a man, he will actually read for himself the writing on the tablet and discover all that happened at the time of his birth (743-751). If these conditions have been met, and if he actually reads the inscription, then, his mother sincerely hopes, he will not fall prey to *superbia* (*sô überhüebe er sich niht*—752). She can hardly see how he could. As King says, a full-stop is desirable after *niht.*

His mother's idea is surely clear enough: if he reads about his shameful birth he could hardly become proud, since he will have nothing to be proud of. Rather will he, of his own accord, show humility, the virtue which leads to *compassio* and *caritas,* and therefore to God. He will know his own misery. On this depends all that follows, and it follows naturally and inevitably. The mother goes on to say that if he does avoid pride, that is, if he becomes "thus good" (*alsô guot*—753), so that he turns to God (754-755), then he will repair, or atone for (*buozte*), the sin of his father, counselled by his *triuwe* i.e. his *caritas.* Likewise he will also remember his mother in his prayers, because all these things spring from turning to God, which is avoiding *superbia* and thus showing *caritas.* He will become good himself by turning to God in this way (the way of *caritas,* which is the only way) and will thus atone for his parents' sin. His love for his parents will counsel him to pray for them both and to try to ensure that God forgives them, because he will have first shown his love for God.

It will be seen, therefore, that 753-760 state that once he has avoided *superbia* and shown its opposite, *humilitas* (as he should do once he learns of his birth), he will be, by definition, a good man, which means that he will have turned to God, since *superbia* is equivalent to turning away from Him. Turning *to* God is avoiding *superbia* and showing humility, which leads to *caritas. Alsô* thus refers back to the preceding line: *überhüebe er sich niht* and *alsô guot daz er ze gote sînen muot wenden begunde* stand in parallel, linked by *alsô.* But *alsô* also points forward to *sô* (756), since turning to God, *caritas* and showing love and compassion for his parents are all one and the same.

What Gregorius must do first and foremost, therefore, is to profit from his reading of the tablet, recognize his own misery, and show humility; *compassio* and *caritas* will follow. He will prove his love for God and his neighbour, which is turning to God. His behaviour will be ordinate and he will thereby re-order the perversion of his parents. At all costs he must not be proud, perpetuating in his own pride the original sin of pride born in him. Everything hangs closely together, depending on the choice Gregorius makes between pride and humility when he learns his birth, a choice which must be his own. The danger is that he will take the wrong road, and if he does, the rest will not follow, since he will not have *caritas* and so will not be able, however hard he may try, to show love for God and his parents. *Superbia* and *caritas* are mutually exclusive; you cannot both turn *to* God and away from Him. Thus his mother does not need to *ask* him to show his love for his parents; she knows he will once he has avoided *superbia.* But she does need to ensure that he finds out how he was born, since this will give him the knowledge he requires of his own misery and the opportunity to show humility. This is her message to him.

The miraculous recovery of the child from the waves by the two fishermen is, of course, indicative of the interest shown by God in his fate and a striking example, as Hartmann says, of the *genâde* of Him who also saved Jonas from the sea. He was in the care of *unser herre got der guote* (929-930). The sacramental content of this passage emerges in the significant detail of *drî-ein* in 933-935, followed by a similar unity-in-plurality formula of *zwei-ein* in 939, repeated in 944-945. God is deeply involved in all this, and has seen fit to extend his help to Gregorius in his plight. In spite of the sin of his parents, reflected in his own birth, Gregorius is not deserted by God, but given the opportunity to survive and redeem their sin, as his mother, in her faith in God and His power to work miracles, hoped that he might. In the safe custody, first of the poor fisherman, to whom he is entrusted by the abbot for six years, and later of the abbot himself in the monastery, there is no reason why he should not grow up to be a man and read the inscription on the tablet. God's concern for him is further demonstrated in that except for *unsers herren minne* the abbot would have never known about the foundling at all (1019 ff.). God thus gives ample proof of His *caritas* towards Gregorius and it is up to him to reciprocate it when he is old enough to make up his own mind.

The upbringing of Gregorius, too, seems to be exactly what is required and what his mother had hoped for. Not only is his actual survival and development to manhood assured, but he seems likely to be in a position to make the right choice when the time comes, and so re-order the *inordinatio* of his parents. God sees to it that the path to this goal is made smooth for him, since he is still under His *huote*. In fact, of the child Gregorius it might be said that 'he grew and waxed strong, filled with wisdom, and the grace of God was upon him'. He was obedient to his master's will (1167-68) and inquired diligently after things that are good to know (1169 ff.), outstripping those who, by virtue of their age, should have been ahead of him. God allows *vrouwe Saelecheit* and *der Wunsch* to bestow their blessings on him (1235 ff. and 1263 ff.). He had all the virtues and, in addition, health and beauty. Above all

> er suochte gnâde unde rât
> zallen zîten an got
> und behielt starke sîn gebot.
>
> (1260 ff.)

Thus, because of God's interest in him and love for him he has become, by his fifteenth year, a paragon of goodness and a devoted servant of Him to whom he owes everything. As yet he knows nothing of his sinful origins, the one serious gap in his considerable body of knowledge. Then as a result of a *wunderlîch geschiht* (1289), in which he accidentally does an injury to a playmate, the son of his foster-mother, he learns that he is a foundling. The effect on him of this newly-acquired piece of knowledge is that he feels shame and wishes to hide away somewhere where no one can humiliate and mock him. Distant echoes of the Fall, and perhaps also of Cain and Abel, may be heard here: the new knowledge gives rise to shame at the "nakedness" of his state as a foundling, just as the knowledge of their actual nakedness gained from the tree of knowledge itself produced shame in Adam and Eve. Cain was the son of Adam, just as Gregorius is the son of his parents, who, as we have seen, are analogous to Adam and Eve in their inordinate love, and, like Cain, Gregorius does harm to (though does not kill) his foster-brother.

The abbot, confronted with this precipitate decision to leave the monastery with which Gregorius has been associated for so long, nevertheless recognises that, in spite of this association, and however indebted to God he may be for his happy life, he has, like all human beings, freedom of choice. Of all the blessings God has bestowed on him free-will is the greatest (1436 ff.) He has a right to choose for himself, but at the same time he should not, in his *tumber zorn,* do anything he will regret later (1450 ff.). He must not forget to show love for himself, and in the abbot's opinion he will not be serving his own interests best by leaving the monastery.

Gregorius admits that he is angry and that this is due to his immaturity, but confesses his inability to control his anger:

> nû ist mir mîne tumpheit
> alsô sêre erbolgen,
> si enlât mich iu niht volgen.
>
> (1484 ff.)

But anger (*ira*) is a cardinal sin, and in showing it Gregorius behaves inordinately. His passions are no longer under the control of his will, which is in fact no longer free. He is in a state of perturbation of mind and in this state cannot exercise free-will. His wisest course would therefore be to follow the advice of the abbot. But he is so deranged by the shame of the knowledge that he is a foundling that he has an irresistible urge to compensate at all costs for this blow to his pride (the pride that is born in him as a result of original sin). Since he is not the fisherman's child, a condition which he has never questioned in any way, he begins to wonder (the proud wish being father to the thought) whether he might not be of knightly parentage. He tells the abbot that he has always felt that, had he been born into that *ordo,* he would have liked to be a knight. Now that he does not know what his origins are he is ready to "over-compensate" and to see knighthood as his true destiny. The abbot has *daz süezeste leben daz got der werlde hât gegeben* (1507), but it is only for those who have chosen it *ze rehte,* that is, because it is right and ordinate for them. The *unmâze* of his *tumber zorn* is such that he no longer thinks clearly: he "reasons" that because he does not know whose son he is this must mean that the religious life is not his *ordo.* This does not follow at all, yet it is his reason for wanting to leave the monastery! The use of *wille* (1512) recalls that, as we have seen, his will is disordered to the extent that he cannot use it freely. He believes that he is exercising free-will in leaving the monastery, but actually his choice to become a knight is not the choice of a will free to do as it wills, but is a result of his *zorn,* which has control over his will.

The abbot, in his wisdom, knows this for what it is, and tries even harder to convince Gregorius that if he continues on his present course, he will be guilty of yet more inordinate behaviour. In his *superbia,* of which his immoderate anger is an indication, he will show that he prefers the world to God:

swer sich von phaffen bilde
gote gemachet wilde
unde ritterschaft begât,
der muoz mit maneger missetât
verwürken sêle unde lîp.
swelch man oder wîp
sich von gote gewendet,
der wirt dâ von geschendet
und der helle verselt.

(1517 ff.)

He, the abbot, has chosen him to be a *gotes kint* (1527). The matter could not be more clearly stated: the abbot means that Gregorius' *muot* is now turned away from God and not towards him as his mother hoped it would be. Those who turn away from God are guilty of perversion and run a grave risk of ending up in hell. Such behaviour is inordinate love, first committed by Adam and Eve and then by Gregorius' own parents. The opposition of *sich von gote wenden* and *den muot ze gote wenden* (as phrased by his mother on the *tavel*) is fundamental: the one is *superbia,* the other *caritas,* the one evil, the other good, the one voluntary enslavement of the will, the other freedom. Hence the abbot's call to Gregorius: *durch got bekêre dînen muot* (1516), that is, forget your desire for worldly things, which is pride, and come back to God.

But Gregorius does not see it in such a clear light. He believes, and says, that if a man follows the vocation of knighthood with *mâze* (1532), that is to say, ordinately, no one has a better chance of prospering, both in this world and the next. By the "measure" of knighthood Gregorius clearly understands everything that is best and noblest in chivalry, as indeed is expressed in the words *gotes ritter* (1534), and, to do him justice, this is certainly an ideal worth striving for, as we know from Wolfram's *Parzival.* But whether it is better for Gregorius, given his origins and upbringing, than being what he contemptuously calls a *betrogen klôsterman* (1535), is another matter. The abbot, at least, does not think so. He is aware of the difficulties and dangers to which Gregorius would be particularly exposed because of his total lack of experience. How could he practise the calling ordinately? It is much more likely that he would fall lamentably short and that he would not be able to realise the ideal of a *gotes ritter.* Does he really know what this means? Does he know that knighthood carries with it, in its *hôher muot,* a grave risk of *superbia,* and that therefore humility is a prerequisite of a *gotes ritter,* a virtue he does not possess? He needs to be protected against his own ignorance.

The reaction of Gregorius to the abbot's plea is most revealing. He is convinced that he could learn to be a knight, since he is still young, and he tells the abbot that

sît der stunde
daz ich bedenken kunde
beidiu übel unde guot,
sô stuont ze ritterschaft mîn muot.

(1569 ff.)

The echo of the Fall is loud and clear: when Adam and Eve disobeyed, they ate of fruit of the tree of knowledge of good and evil. Since Gregorius has had a knowledge of good and evil, his *muot,* he says, has been in the direction of knighthood, which is away from God! He goes on to say that whenever he was forced to read books, his mind was on jousting (1582 ff.). He was never so happy as when he imagined himself on a horse in knightly combat. It is no wonder that this is Greek, not German, to the abbot (1625)! The boy to whom he had devoted so much loving care in the monastery was all the time wishing that he were a worldly knight. Yet he should not been have surprised: this urge to fight and to distinguish himself is inseparable from his heritage of original sin. It is *superbia* born in him. At the same time it is clear that it is unlikely that Gregorius ever allowed this urge to assume such violent proportions as to make his life in the monastery a misery, as he suggests it did—until he heard that he was a foundling. Only then did he begin to think seriously of knighthood as an alternative way of life. The *tumber zorn* he felt at being so humiliated has enormously increased this inborn *superbia* to the point where he can no longer hold it in check. Such *ritterlîche gir,* as Gregorius himself calls it (1622), is in itself a sign of *unmâze,* the *unmâze* inherent in his *zorn.*

The abbot's reply to this, that he is *des muotes niht ein klôsterman* (1636), shows that he recognises that the present state of mind of Gregorius is not conducive to humility and that he is out of place in the monastery. At this stage no advice from him or anyone else seems likely to bring about the rectification of his will. The tendency to *inordinatio* born in every man has clearly asserted itself. Since his *muot* lies inexorably in the direction of knighthood, the abbot can only hope that God will give him good fortune (1638).

Thus Gregorius becomes a knight, with the reluctant consent of the abbot, but the latter, alarmed at the ever more inordinate attitude of Gregorius, is even more anxious to protect him from his *superbia* and so offers him wealth and a wife if he will stay with him (1641 ff.). But Gregorius will accept no compromise. He is full of *hôher muot* and has no desire for *gemach* (1675 ff.). He will not follow in the footsteps of Erec. His *superbia* again shows clearly when he says he is confident that he can force *diu Saelde* to bow to his wishes (1697ff.). Like the young Parzival, Gregorius thinks he knows all there is to be known about chivalry and that he is capable of becoming a perfect knight without any help from anyone, least of all God. He brushes aside the advice of the abbot, so lovingly given. In his whole speech (1675 ff.) he makes no mention of God, who is to be left behind in the monastery. But, as Parzival's story makes abundantly clear, a knight cannot achieve the peak of chivalrous perfection without earthly advisers and without God. However firm may be his resolve to realise the ideal, however *unverzaget* he may be, it is *superbia* to imagine that he can do it alone. The path Gregorius proposes to take, in his *tumpheit,* is certain to lead him into further sin. Such a path leads him away from God, and he can only avoid sin by turning to Him.

In face of this *superbia* the abbot can only do one more thing (which in any case he is pledged to do), namely reveal to him the dreadful secret of his birth. He hopes this may shock him into a state of humility. Gregorius receives the news with mixed feelings: he is bitterly grieved that he was born so "inordinately," but he is overjoyed to find that he is of noble stock (1747 ff.). He feels sure that he has lost *gotes hulde,* and asks the abbot how he can possibly regain it (1779 ff.), but is not disposed to accept any responsibility for his parents' sin and shows no *caritas* whatsoever towards them. He does not seem to realise that such an attitude is in itself *superbia;* it is completely selfish. In reply to his request for advice, the abbot tells him that if he persists in choosing knighthood,

> sich, sô mêret sich diu kraft
> dîner tegelîchen missetât
> und enwirt dîn niemer rât. . . .
>
> (1788 ff.)

He has not yet irreparably lost *gotes hulde,* but is in danger of doing so if he does not change his course. He has indeed a part in his parents' sin, namely the very *superbia* he is now showing. This is the sin in which he was born, which is transmitted from generation to generation as a result of original sin, just as his parents had a part in the sin of Adam and Eve. He will perpetuate it daily if he carries on as he is doing, in a direction opposed to God, just as his parents perpetuated the inordinate love of Adam and Eve. The only way to avoid further sin is to show humility.

But Gregorius rejects this advice, after having asked for it, and gives further proof of his *superbia:*

> 'ouwê, lieber herre,
> jâ ist mîn gir noch merre
> zuo der werlde dan ê.
>
> (1799 ff.)

Gir zuo der werlde, like *ritterlîche gir* earlier, could not be more meaningful. This, of all things, is hardly likely to regain for him *gotes hulde.* It is a clear affirmation of *superbia, amor inordinata,* of *unmâze.* Now that he has rejected the abbot's advice, and obviously does not intend to show the humility the reading of the tablet was meant to produce in him, the latter can only leave the rest to God, hoping that He in whose image Gregorius is made will guide him (1806 ff.). This reference to man as being made in the image of God is yet another link in the symbolical chain. Gregorius is reminded that on the one hand he still possesses freedom of will by virtue of being made in the image of God, but the implication is also that, paradoxically, he has lost his similitude to God by allowing his will to become enslaved to sin, the sin of *superbia* which first enslaved the will of man and turned him from God. He can only regain similitude through *caritas* and *humilitas,* i.e. by turning back to God. His misguided self-reliance will not achieve this.

Yet the clear opposition of ordinate and inordinate love is undoubtedly the unifying formula and principle underlying [Gregorius], as it is of Christianity itself, and, unless it is recognised, the guilt of the hero and his parents cannot be properly understood.

—***H. B. Willson***

By his decision to turn away from God, expressed in this proud reliance on his own powers, Gregorius has therefore done nothing to restore the order perverted by the sin of his parents. There is not a trace of humility in his behaviour. He has perpetuated in himself their sin of inordinate love. The continuity of sin which runs from Adam and Eve through his parents to himself remains unbroken. *Inordinatio* is self-perpetuating and cumulative. The abbot has every reason to warn him that he will without doubt daily commit this sin of pride, the power of which will increase. In fact, he will never stop sinning so long as he shows pride. The abbot then tells the sailors to allow the winds to take Gregorius' ship where they choose, praying to God that He may guide it. God's answer to this prayer is to send the ship to his own mother's country, which proves that He is not exactly pleased with the behaviour of Gregorius and is not prepared to extend His grace to him any longer. He is now on his own, by his own choice, and he must turn back to God before He will help him as He used to do before Gregorius elevated himself above his Creator and benefactor. But if he goes on in this way, he cannot fail to fall deeper and deeper into sin, since his own resources are severely limited and he is exposed to the snares of the devil. The "free" choice he has made precludes any attempt by God to force him to turn back to Him.

Now that Gregorius is no longer under God's *huote,* the devil, in fact, comes into his own again. There is no impediment to his increasing beyond measure the disorder inherent in Gregorius' abandonment of God in his proud espousal of knighthood. This he does by arousing a mutual sexual attraction between Gregorius and his mother (1960 ff.), which would not have happened if Gregorius had not left the monastery. It is the same counsel, says Hartmann with significant emphasis, which led Eve to turn away from God, a reference which shows that the theme of the Fall of man is still highly relevant. The devil's two unfortunate victims, however, have no notion of what he has planned for them. Gregorius himself is concerned only to gain chivalrous fame by relieving his mother of the siege to which she is being subjected. This he succeeds in doing, displaying great knightly prowess, which only adds to the irony of the situation, since he is proud of his own achievements. He has, without doubt, made excellent use of his own powers, but has excluded God. Since he has no humility, even the service he does his mother cannot be regarded as having sprung from true *caritas,* for *caritas* cannot exist without *humilitas.*

The fear of the *lantherren* that their lady might again be troubled by the unjust arrogance of her enemies (2196) prompts them to advise her to marry. As Hartmann says, they thought they were giving her the very best advice (2222 ff.). Marriage is the best form of life God has given to the world. How could they possibly know that it was the devil's will that such a marriage should be contracted (2246). Only he knew that, however ordinate such a marriage might appear to be, the partners in it were mother and son. A marriage of this kind would be inordinate in the highest degree and therefore entirely to his liking. It is also noteworthy that, although the mother of Gregorius had steadfastly refused to marry since her husband's death, reserving her love for God—*einen starken helt, den aller tiuristen man der ie mannes namen gewan* (873-4)—, she now decides to put her faith in human aid, rather than in God. Like Gregorius her son, she thus turns away from God, after having turned to Him, and is therefore guilty of *superbia,* although her decision is made *in gote* (2228).

The married life of Gregorius and his mother was for a time *wünneclîch* (2260), a paradise, as it were, but suddenly, we are told,

> daz nam einen gaehen val.
>
> (2262)

Once again the Fall of man is recalled by a clearly audible textual echo. Just as the sexual union of his parents was *amor inordinata,* so also is the carnal love between Gregorius and his mother, in spite of the ironical fact that it has apparently been sanctified by marriage. The ironical contrast between this and an ordinate marriage, between appearance and reality, is indicative of *inordinatio.* One incest has led to another; the product of the first has committed the second with one of those who so inordinately produced him. Brother and sister become man and wife; the sister becomes the mother of the brother's son; the son becomes the husband of his mother. These close family and marital relationships, in which ordinate love should be the binding force, are all perverted. Ideally and ordinately, love between persons should be reconciled with love for God, but because the human relationships themselves are perverted those of the participants in them with God are also disordered. This remains true in spite of the fact that Gregorius and his mother are not aware that they are committing incest. The love of their marriage, which would never have been contracted if they had not turned from God, is perverted love.

Although the married life of Gregorius is described as blissful, he has, nevertheless, still one cause for sorrow, namely the knowledge of his sinful birth. When he reads about this on the tablet each morning in his *kemenâte,* his joy turns to deep distress (2377 ff.). But it is a sorrow which is neatly confined to a short space of time, whereas his mother had hoped that he would think about it *zaller stunde* (756). It is also kept within the private bounds of his *kemenâte.* Such *mâze* is clearly inordinate, since the measure of *caritas* is without measure. The paradox is intentional. Hartmann is deliberately playing on the concepts of order and measure in association with *caritas:* what seems to be ordinate, because it is "measured," is not always so. The essence of *caritas,* its order and measure, is that it cannot be limited in this way. Only when both Gregorius and his mother discover that they are mother and son does the former's sorrow become without measure (*er was in leides gebote*—2607), but this lack of measure is not a sign of *caritas* either, since his *superbia* once again asserts itself. It is not the sorrow of *compassio.* When he finds that he cannot confine his sorrow within such narrow limits, he shows anger towards God (2608), just as he had shown anger when told he was a foundling.

A crucial stage has been reached: apparently both Gregorius and his mother have fallen prey to the devil. Both have turned away from God in their *superbia,* their inordinate love, and to the mother, at least, there seems no way back to Him. She expresses her conviction that *der heize gotes zorn* has fallen upon her and that she cannot escape the pains of hell (2665 ff.). She is *verzaget;* her *desperatio* is patent. She has completely lost her faith in God's love and is indeed in grave danger, though not for the reason she thinks, for, as Hartmann makes clear in his prologue, the greatest sin of all is *zwîvel* (56 ff.). Not her double incest but her despair places her in danger of hellfire, for, however inordinately one may behave one may, through penitence, return to God and enjoy His grace and mercy if one does not despair of His love.

The sight of his mother in despair effects a sudden and

truly miraculous transformation in Gregorius himself. Whereas shortly before he had angrily blamed God for their plight, without accepting any responsibility for what had happened, now he gives proof of his innate and acquired chivalry and of his Christian charity. The knight Gregorius does not despair; instead his *unverzagetheit* reveals itself. He places his trust in God, encouraging his mother by assuring her that she can regain God's love through penitence, which is to show humility before Him and acknowledge one's sins, in fact, to turn to Him. More than this, he provides an example by resolving to take a similar course of action himself (2595 ff.). Now, for the first time, his own *unverzagetheit* leads him, not away from God, but towards Him. It no longer appears as a servant of his *superbia,* but of *caritas* and *humilitas*. The quality of courage, so indispensable to the successful pursuit of knighthood, serves him in good stead. He is well on the way to becoming, paradoxical as it may seem (since he is about to cease the actual pursuit of knighthood as such), a *gotes ritter*. This decision by both Gregorius and his mother to do penance is thus the first step in the direction of ordinate love, for God, for each other, and for their fellows, the *caritas* which God is ever ready to reciprocate to penitent sinners who have humbly realised that He forgives them and can help them when they can no longer help themselves, in fact when they have renounced *superbia*. God is once again in His right and ordinate place in the hierarchy of goods, the *Summum Bonum* who should be loved above all else.

From the above it may be seen that ***Gregorius*** is emphatically not a condemnation of chivalry as such. Knighthood is only inordinate when it is practised without humility. It is therefore not necessarily a sin to enter the profession, even if this should mean leaving a monastery, but to leave a monastery out of *superbia* and to enter knighthood in that state of mind is undoubtedly sinful. It will almost certainly lead to further sin, an increase of *superbia* and therefore of *inordinatio*. He who leaves a monastery is likely to fall prey to *superbia,* if he has not already done so. Because of the *hôher muot* associated with knighthood it is much more difficult to show *diemuot* as a knight than it is in a monastery, where humility and charity are part of the training and environment. But humility and charity *can* be attained in knighthood if *unverzaget mannes muot* and *êre* do not produce *superbia,* and chivalry of this ideal kind is no more and no less meritorious in God's eyes, since it implies turning towards Him in ordinate love, than is a blameless religious life. This is the true *ordo* of chivalry, as *Parzival* teaches. The same lesson is taught in ***Gregorius***. Its hero undoubtedly attains the ideal of a *gotes ritter*. Although he is ultimately chosen to be pope and so does not return to the actual practice of knighthood, he nevertheless shows true manly courage in enduring his penance and humility, and love in submitting to His will. When he becomes pope he gives further proof of his love for God and his neighbour, of his *triuwe,* in his benevolent pastoral care. One does not need, implies Hartmann, to wear a suit of armour, ride a horse, and carry arms to be a *gotes ritter*. In this way he transcends the apparent antithesis between the worldly and the religious, between clerical and lay. But in the case of Gregorius the lay calling of knighthood was not the way to become a true knight, although he might still have reached this goal by that road if at some point he had had a change of heart and turned to God in humility, as did Parzival with the help of Trevrizent. But then Parzival had not had a religious upbringing, nor had he the same shameful origins. Gregorius especially needed to show humility to compensate for the sin of his birth; and so in his case to enter knighthood out of *superbia,* leaving the monastery where he had already been taught the value of humility, was hardly the best course for him to take.

[In her "Schuld und Sühne in Hartmanns *Gregorius* und in der frühscholastischen Theologie," *Zeitschrift für deutsche Philologie* LXXVI] Nobel has seen very clearly that *superbia* is responsible for the unhappy consequences of Gregorius's decision to become a knight. She says: "Die Sünde, vor der die Mutter ihn warnen will, ist die *superbia,*" and gives some most relevant references to the theological background. His decision is wrong because it springs from "innerer Abkehr von Gott." She then goes on to say that although there is no actual law of the Church which stipulates that a man should do penance for the sins of his parents, there is nevertheless the New Law of *caritas* and the love of children for their parents, which should have caused Gregorius to do penance for his. Here everything depends on the word "Busse": if by it is meant that Gregorius should have stayed in the monastery and undertaken a stringent course of self-castigation, then nothing could be further from the truth. In this sense it is quite incorrect to say that "Gregorius ist durch seine Geburt zur Busse für seine Eltern verpflichtet. Er entzieht sich ihr und fällt damit in Schuld." This is only true if "Busse" is taken in the sense of "atonement through his own life of *caritas,*" thus restoring the order perverted by his parents. MHG *büezen,* as is well known means "to amend, make better, repair." As we have seen, the reason why he does not do his best to repair the damage caused by his parents' sin (*büezen*) is that he himself falls prey to *superbia*. If he had not shown *superbia,* the New Law of *caritas* would have operated in him. *Superbia* is the guilt (or sin, whichever word we choose) of Gregorius. Almost everything he does before his decision to do penance, in the strictest sense, for his own sins, is already a manifestation of *superbia*. This being so, it makes little difference whether incest is or is not strictly punishable in terms of Church Law, or whether it is excusable if it is committed unwittingly. In this case it follows from *superbia* and is a particularly horrifying consequence. *Superbia* is an undeniable sin. As King points out, Hartmann makes it clear that in his view and in the view of Gregorius and his mother, both incests are to be regarded as sinful. This is so because they are, both actually and symbolically, inordinate love. The *ordo* of love is perverted by them, as it first was, and always is, by *superbia,* and in this Hartmann is on the safest possible theological ground. Gregorius has, in and by his *superbia,* perverted the order of love, just as his parents did before him, and as Adam and Eve, counselled by the devil as they also were, did before *them*. Leaving the monastery, failing to do his best to restore the order perverted by his parents, committing incest with his mother, not any one, but *all* these are sinful precisely because they are the consequences of *superbia* and cannot be dissociated from it.

Through the first 2750 lines of ***Gregorius,*** then, there runs an unmistakable thread of continuity, the continuity of sin, the accumulation of *inordinatio,* its persistence in the human individual and from generation to generation. Over the whole lies the dark shadow of the Fall. The devil and his works are ever-present, reminding the audience that he is the author of perversion and that, having once tempted man to sin and disobey God, he is able to do it over and over again with similar success if man does not turn to God for help. No interpretation of the poem can be adequate unless it acknowledges the fundamental importance of *superbia* and its opposite *caritas.* Actual and symbolical reference is frequently made to the first transgression, and its genealogical continuity is reflected in the repetition of the incest-motive in two generations. Neither Gregorius nor his incest can be considered apart from his parents and their sin; it is, significantly, with his mother, that is, with the previous generation, that he commits his own incest. But his parents' guilt has already been transmitted to him long before his sexual relations with his mother; it lies in his sinful nature, as I have tried to show. That he does not know what he is doing when he marries her does not alter the fact that if he had not taken up the worldly vocation of knighthood, seeking in its pride a cure for his own feeling of shame and revelling in its honour and glory among men, he would never have married his mother, a marriage which, it should not be forgotten, was the reward for his chivalrous exploits. The penance he undertakes is thus fully justified by his previous inordinate behaviour, culminating in incest with his mother. The devil would have been powerless to ensnare him if he had shown humility, and this he would have done by taking the abbot's advice and remaining in the monastery. For his own inordinate love he must now *büezen* in the strictest sense, namely castigate himself for seventeen years chained naked to a rock. The lack of measure he shows in this self-castigation is the measure of his *humilitas* and *caritas,* his "ordinate" love for God.

The importance of the opposition of *amor ordinata* and *inordinata* in ***Gregorius*** has been almost completely overlooked in earlier interpretations of the poem. This is surprising, in view of the fact that the very nature of incest as an abnormal and perverted form of human love might have provided a clue to its significance as a symbol of *amor inordinata* in the wider, more comprehensive Christian sense, the sin of *superbia,* particularly as *superbia* is of such obvious relevance in ***Gregorius*** (*so überhüebe er sich niht*!). Yet this clear opposition of ordinate and inordinate love is undoubtedly the unifying formula and principle underlying the poem, as it is of Christianity itself, and, unless it is recognised, the guilt of the hero and his parents cannot be properly understood. Hartmann could scarcely have chosen a more effective symbol than incest to underline the perversion represented by inordinate love, whatever may be the form it takes in man separated from God by sin.

Michael S. Batts (essay date 1968)

SOURCE: "Hartmann's *Humanitas*: A New Look at *Iwein,*" in *Germanic Studies in Honor of Edward Henry Sehrt,* Frithjof Andersen Raven, Wolfram Karl Legner, James Cecil King, eds., University of Miami Press, 1968, pp. 37-51.

[*An English educator specializing in Germanic studies, Batts has written and edited several studies of German literature, including* Die Form der Aventiuren im Nibelungenlied *(1961) and* Gottfried von Strassburg *(1971). In the following excerpt, Batts argues that, in* Iwein, *Hartmann attempts to formulate a doctrine of* aventiure *("adventure") that opposes Arthurian convention.*]

Past interpretations of Hartmann's ***Iwein*** have been to a considerable extent based upon a comparison both with his earlier ***Erec*** and with Chrétien de Troyes' *Yvain.* The view that ***Iwein*** is a counterpart to ***Erec*** finds some justification in the passage in which Gawain introduces the warning example of Erec, in order to persuade Iwein to leave Laudine, but the comparison results in undue emphasis being placed on Iwein's defection. This leads in turn to a clouding of the deeper issue, which is not, as most critics would have it, simply the problem of reconciling knight-errantry with partnership in marriage. On the other hand, the comparison of ***Iwein*** with the *Yvain* of Chrétien directs undue attention to those passages which are markedly different from the source and leads to a neglect of those parts of the poem which seem to follow the original closely. The degree of stress laid on individual scenes is thus not determined by the context of Hartmann's poem but by extraneous criteria.

The difficulty of arriving at a satisfying interpretation of the poem on these bases has been compounded by the problem of Hartmann's style, for whilst there is general agreement as to its polished perfection, there is no common consent as to the inferences which are to be drawn from this quality. The very clarity and suavity with which Hartmann writes, supported, it must be added, by a literal interpretation of his introductory *deprecatio,* have been viewed by some as demonstrating that the poet composed ***Iwein*** without in the least being concerned with the theme of his work.

In recent essays on ***Iwein*** there has been an appreciable and welcome tendency to move away from traditional source comparison and the comparison with ***Erec,*** to pay also less heed to the problems of chronology and to textual minutiae. Critics have taken a new look at ***Iwein*** with a view to assessing the meaning of the work on its own merits and not as a companion-piece to ***Erec,*** a whimsical pastime of old age, or an exercise in translating flippant French into sober German. Attention has been directed to the deceptive quality of the style, to the deep and purposeful irony which is now seen as such a marked feature of the work and a feature indicative of concern rather than disinterest. Studies have also been made of the characters and situations of ***Iwein*** in order to demonstrate their symbolic (rather than superficial) significance. With these new approaches one may not always be in agreement, in particular with the suggestions as to Hartmann's use of symbols, but the aims are laudable and the attempts instructive, however much one may wonder where the methods will eventually lead.

In particular one wonders about the use of irony in ***Iwein***. The quality of irony is its very intangibility; the nature of its expression is such as often to conceal the real meaning beneath an imperturbably urbane pronouncement of the contrary. Who then is to decide what is irony and what is not? The modern critic, accustomed to dealing with so-called levels of irony, is not unnaturally disposed to find similar qualities in medieval works, but surely this is wrong. It is true that one may expect levels of meaning in medieval works, written as they were for an audience for whom the three or fourfold method of exegesis was a commonplace, but it is misguided to suppose a type of sophistication which relies upon ambivalence of standpoint, between, say, author, narrator, and characters. Such an approach is possibly appropriate in an age where the relativity of truth can be a subject for discussion, but not for the Middle Ages, when there was only one truth. Truth then could be expressed in varying ways, and varying levels or degrees of understanding could be inherent in one work, but the truth was in the fable as such rather than in the mode of expression. The aim of this essay is to derive a basic understanding of the meaning of the work from a study of the fable, from an analysis of the individual episodes and their relationship one to another. The question of symbolism will be omitted and also the problem of irony only touched upon, since knowledge of irony depends in this work almost entirely on *a posteriori* knowledge of the fable.

We may take as a concrete example Kalogreant's famous definition of *aventiure* . . . :

ich heize ein riter und han den sin
daz ich suochende rite
einen man der mit mir strite,
der gewafent si als ich.
daz priset in, ersleht er mich.
gesige aber ich im an,
so hat man mich vür einen man
und wirde werder danne ich si.

(530-37)

This statement has been justifiably held to be ironic, but the question: at whom is the irony directed, may be variously answered. Kalogreant could be indulging in self-irony or in irony at the expense of the wild man of the woods, or else Hartmann could be ironical at the expense of his characters or of his audience. In fact, it is clear from what follows, that Kalogreant believes in this definition, but that it is for Hartmann a false definition. The irony is made evident by the incongruity of the following action. The brave Kalogreant (after overcoming his terror of the *Waldmensch*) is frightened almost to death by the storm he calls up and then attempts to avoid the battle on the grounds: "wan er was merre danne ich"! Finally, he is neither victorious nor slain, but simply and ignominiously defeated. His vanquisher fails even to treat him as an equal (which would have meant death by Kalogreant's definition) but rather as a child. At this point one may still take the matter lightly, as Kalogreant does, until it is seen that Iwein also subscribes to the same false conception of *aventiure*. The real irony of this situation and of this definition of *aventiure* becomes steadily more apparent as the work proceeds and provides more and more evidence of the futility of this conventional view, and as we follow Iwein's progress towards a sounder, more humane concept.

This false view of what constitutes *aventiure*—the very essence of chivalry—dominates the first part of the poem, and it is the problem of attaining to a more valid concept that is subsequently the main theme, rather than the problem of reconciling *aventiure* (of no matter what nature) with connubial concord. The earlier scenes, which are often passed over except as material for the consideration of the character of Keie, all point toward a general acceptance by society (including Iwein) of a code of behaviour based on Kalogreant's definition. Keie has lashed Kalogreant with his tongue for his ostentatious behaviour, for his apparent attempt to gain recognition for his courtliness by rising on the approach of the queen. Later Keie rails at Iwein for wishing to rush to avenge the defeat of Kalogreant and restore his and the court's honour. It is noteworthy that in both cases when the queen upbraids Keie for his vindictiveness, Kalogreant and Iwein partly defend Keie, even though their reasons for this are not couched in the most complimentary of language ("ouch ist reht daz der mist / stinke swa der ist"). Kalogreant has, however, already done what Keie accuses Iwein of doing, for Kalogreant had, after being well dined and of course in the presence of the host's charming daughter, made known his great desire for *aventiure*. This speech accords then very ill with his subsequent actions. Iwein, for his part, by now planning to steal away ahead of the others and claim the adventure for himself, is behaving precisely as Keie had accused Kalogreant of behaving. It is not the desire to restore the family honour, but rather the desire to outshine others, coupled later with the fear of ridicule should he fail, which is the main motive for Iwein's behaviour. The only difference between Kalogreant and Iwein at this point is one of degree: Iwein is not afraid (he is in any case forewarned), and he is superior in skill of arms.

The stages by which Iwein wins Laudine require little discussion here. The lack of moderation in his love is in itself not important, since the power of *minne* was irresistible and total, but one aspect of its expression is not without significance. Iwein has already killed Askalon *ane zubt*; under the influence of his love for Laudine, says Hartmann:

. . . ern gaebe drumbe niht ein stro,
ob sie mit gelichem valle
da zehant alle
laegen uf den baren,
die da gesinde waren.

(1440-44)

Such a statement merely underscores Iwein's lack of humanity at this stage. Essentially, Hartmann motivates Laudine's abrupt change of heart and husband with the necessity of defending her land—a motive which would then have had considerably more influence than one might now tend to suspect—and follows this up with emphasis on the inexplicable and irrational quality of *minne*. His motivation is more practical than that of his predecessor, but his supposed embarrassment with the episode need not for that reason be so overly stressed.

The turning-point in the story is Iwein's departure from his wife, and it is here that the comparison with ***Erec*** is most revealing but at the same time most damaging to the argument that ***Iwein*** is a counterpart to the earlier work. Erec has no thought of leaving his wife and sins by over-indulgence in love and consequent neglect of his knightly duty. Iwein likewise has no thought of leaving Laudine, and this far he may be likened to Erec. But, Iwein has every intention of defending the well (and has, in fact, already successfully done so) and would thus have ample opportunity for maintaining his prowess. Furthermore, Iwein is persuaded quite against his better judgement to leave Laudine. The other example (aside, that is, from Erec) which Gawain introduces in order to support his argument, the example of the so-called *Krautjunker,* is somewhat problematic. The figure of the *Krautjunker* could perhaps be cited as an example of the danger of over-estimating a passage which is not in the source. Hartmann may well have thought it necessary to delete Gawain's rather flippant claim in Chrétien's work that he is justified in persuading a friend to do something he himself would not do, but it is difficult to believe that Hartmann's Gawain could suppose Iwein would become such a caricature. The portrait is so extensive and so overdrawn that one suspects Hartmann is attacking a type outside the poem rather than making a direct contribution to the matter in hand. Be that as it may, the essential point is that Iwein is *persuaded* to leave his wife and thus differs radically from Erec since his error is occasioned by the desire to eschew error.

In succumbing to Gawain's persuasiveness, Iwein is submitting again to the pressure of public opinion, for Gawain is motivated purely by fear of the ridicule which his friend might incur should he neglect his knightly duty. His assent is thus in some way similar to his ignoble act in murdering Askalon, at which time he had also given way to the thought that he might be mocked by Keie, should he return without evidence of his success. Gawain's act seems also to throw doubt on the value of friendship, which Hartmann elsewhere stresses strongly, and this adds weight to the view that both of them are conforming to social pressures, to conventional codes, rather than trusting to their own judgement. In all of this there is no evidence whatsoever to support the view that Iwein's adventurous spirit is the cause for his leaving Laudine.

Iwein's failure to return on the appointed date is similarly motivated; that is to say, it is again Gawain rather than Iwein who is made responsible:

Man sagt daz min her Gawein in
mit guoter handelunge
behabte und betwunge
daz er der jarzal vergaz.

(3052-55)

Hartmann thus largely exonerates Iwein both from the fault of leaving his wife and from the fault of failing to return. He further follows this passage with a definite emphasis on Iwein's loyalty to Laudine and to his being entirely at odds with himself. The extent to which he is divided in his mind is indicated in his behaviour before the arrival of Lunette:

in begreif ein selch riuwe
daz er sin selbes vergaz
und allez swigende saz.
  Er überhorte und übersach
swaz man da tete unde sprach
als er ein tore waere.

(3090-95)

In effect, Iwein's behaviour prior to his public disgrace serves not only to stress his loyal devotion but also to suggest his dissatisfaction with himself and with his activity in the past year. At all events, it is clear from the setting that Iwein has completed the first stage of his development. He has returned to Arthur's court, outwardly at the peak of his success but inwardly divided. He is aware of his transgression and is already behaving as the *tore* he is actually to become.

The completeness of Iwein's inner self-estrangement is demonstrated outwardly by his nakedness, his total abandonment of society and social practice; he is reduced to below even the level of the *Waldmensch.* By tearing off his clothes, however, he has stripped off the skin, as it were, of his former self, and his rebirth is thus possible as a man now untrammeled by social obligations from his past life. This rebirth is signified by his being anointed from head to foot and his donning new garments. An almost complete break has been made with his past, which now seems to have been a dream, but which was actually a period in which he lived as in a dream-world rather than in reality. All that he carries over with him into his new life, aside from his own innate qualities, is his love for Laudine.

Iwein's first act after restoration to health is to defend the Lady of Narison against Count Aliers. His conduct shows not only that his knightly prowess is unimpaired, but also that his love for Laudine is undiminished, for he is able to disregard the clear indications of favour given him by the Lady of Narison. In the subsequent conflict between the lion and the serpent, Iwein is not bound by gratitude as he had been to the Lady of Narison, but rather only by his innate nobility of character, which leads him to defend the accepted symbol of courage and loyalty against the symbol of evil. A sense of gratitude is now demonstrated by the lion, which attaches itself to Iwein and thus becomes the living image of his character.

The most striking evidence of the intimate association of

Thirteenth-century fresco depicting Iwein proposing to Laudine.

character between Iwein and the lion is provided by the scene at the well, when the lion attempts suicide out of grief over the apparent death of Iwein. This act is prevented, but it foreshadows the subsequent turn of events, for Iwein now finds Lunette imprisoned in the chapel and undertakes her defence. That is to say, he now risks his life for someone who previously has done him the greatest service. To what extent the well may represent the female principle is something which cannot be discussed here, but it is significantly associated with Lunette, and Hartmann is concerned with the idea of women as initiators and as a source of charity (in the strict sense of the word). Lunette herself is, if not the prime, at least the most obvious example. At this point she is instrumental in diverting Iwein from thoughts of self-destruction and in putting him, if only temporarily, on the path to Laudine. It thus becomes evident that this second visit to the well marks an important point on Iwein's second journey back to Laudine.

The defence of Lunette is almost prevented by Iwein's involvement in another conflict, namely in the defence of Gawain's sister and her family against the giant Harpin. In both conflicts Iwein has a personal interest and is consequently greatly dismayed by the late arrival of Harpin. The difficulty is resolved at the last moment, but it is made clear to Iwein that life is precarious, that much may depend upon timely appearance, and that the plans of mortals can only mature with the aid of providence.

After the successful defence of Lunette, Iwein again comes to Laudine, but he will not now discover himself to her. The reason is obscure, since he has been able to right the wrongs he has done and gain in the process enhanced reputation as a knight. He furthermore claims that he is estranged from his wife without fault on his part:

> miner vrouwen hulde:
> der mangel ich ane schulde.
>
> (5469-70)

Although therefore he has previously admitted having been at fault, there must now be a deeper cause for his anxiety to remain unknown to his wife and to the world at large, and for his adoption of the pseudonym of the knight with the lion. This can only mean that Iwein has become aware of deeper problems, that he will now place himself deliberately in the service of humanity at large, as he had intervened at personal risk but without personal involvement in the battle of the lion and the serpent. In other words: his concern is now no longer restitution but self-fulfillment.

In the following series of adventures, adventures under the sign, so to speak, of the lion, Iwein's love for Laudine remains unchanged. The danger in these episodes is greater and the temptations are also greater, but the examples of selflessness, which he meets are correspondingly more impressive. The maiden who asks him to champion the younger daughter of the late Count of the Black Thorn is such an example, for she is in no way related and under no obligation to the interested party; only her innate charity has led her to undertake the onerous task of finding Iwein. When she finally does find him, he expresses his new-found humanitarian philosophy in the simple words:

> swem mins dienstes not geschiht
> und swer guoter des gert,
> dern wirt es niemer entwert.
>
> (6002-04)

Later, when it is apparent that the two opponents (Iwein und Gawain) are great and noble champions, the younger sister is prepared to renounce her just claim to the inheritance rather than risk that either of the two be killed.

Into this episode is inserted the *Pesme Aventiure,* Iwein's battle with the giants, which forms a counterpart to the Harpin episode in the first series. Here too Iwein finds an example of unselfishness, for, although the townspeople would willingly see the giants defeated, they are sufficiently convinced of their invincibility to wish to frighten Iwein away, rather than let him face the risk.

With the return to Arthur's court and with the successful conclusion of the battle with Gawain, the scene is set for Iwein's third and last journey. Having first come deliberately and confidently to the well, having later returned there by chance with thoughts of suicide, he travels a third time to the well, in despair now but also in humility. His act in calling up the storm is not so much one of revenge or destructiveness; rather it is an act of desperation because he feels he has now accomplished something, he is now worthy of Laudine, but he is unable to find his way back to her. Once again Lunette appears at the well, and she now arranges the forced reconciliation. This reconciliation, like the original marriage, has been seen as an embarrassment to Hartmann, as an unavoidably forced dénouement, but it should be borne in mind that medieval formalism required in any case that Iwein make the same journey again. The manner in which the reconciliation is brought about resembles the original arrangement of the marriage, and in both cases the motivation is the same. Laudine must perforce accept Iwein, but is then moved by her underlying love to do so willingly. At the close of the poem this acceptance is further motivated by her feeling of having herself been guilty in some degree.

The structural finesse of this work is striking; the most notable feature is the parallelism of the related series of adventures. Iwein makes the journey from Arthur's court via the well to Laudine three times in all, each time in a different degree of awareness, first as in a dream, then newly awakened, finally in full consciousness. . . .

In addition, the two series of adventures which begin after the second visit to the well are related to the episodes of the Lady of Narison and the lion. . . .

Important is namely not only why and how Iwein fights, but also how the situations which occasion his intervention are brought about. It was claimed earlier that the false concept of *aventiure* as laid down by Kalogreant and unthinkingly subscribed to also by Iwein is the basic theme, and that the fable portrays Iwein's progress toward the realisation of the inhumaneness and ineffectuality of this code. Iwein's path takes him through a series of adventures which reveal individually the weaknesses of the chivalric code and stress the precariousness of human existence. . . . Concomitant with this development there is a progression from the ironic portrayal of the earlier part to the more sharp satire on the knightly code in the later part.

Consider, for example, how rare is the adherence to the "accepted" code of behaviour. Count Aliers, when his love is rejected, resorts to force of arms to obtain the Lady of Narison. In his other various encounters Iwein is never on an equal footing with his opponent again until he meets with Gawain. Even if one excludes the giants as *sui generis* uncourtly, nevertheless Iwein is forced to fight not one but three adversaries in a supposedly official trial by combat to determine Lunette's guilt or innocence. Hartmann is surely ironical when he says before this battle that God would be unable to refuse to come to Iwein's aid when asked by such delightful maidens (Lunette's friends). In fact, it is the lion that intervenes and saves the situation—and to what extent may one hold the lion to represent divine providence?

As for the question *why* Iwein has to fight, we must recall that he opposes Harpin because no other champion could be found at Arthur's court, Gawain having been called away on a wild goose chase; which brings us to the question of the rape of Guinevere. Arthur had at first not acceded to Meljakanz' demand and relented only under the pressure of public opinion. His weakness results in his wife being carried off by Meljakanz, who does not feel himself bound by the usual code; on the contrary, he makes mock of it and is stronger into the bargain, since he is able to defeat all the knights, all, that is, except Gawain.

If the consequences of the abduction of the queen are not serious, the same cannot be said of another example of the one-sided adherence to the supposedly accepted code of behaviour. The tragic situation of the maidens in the *Pesme Aventiure* derives directly from the foolishness of their overlord in riding out for *aventiure,* for he conflicts with those stronger than himself but not bound by the same code. The outcome is, strikingly enough, no great misfortune for him, but very great hardship for the maidens as his subjects. It is the innocent who suffer, as Gawain's sister and her family would have suffered had not Iwein been available to assist them.

The *reductio ad absurdum* of the chivalric convention is provided, however, undoubtedly by the manner of solving the dispute between the two sisters—the second example of an official trial by combat. The elder demands of Gawain—fresh from his rescue of the queen and concerned about the Harpin episode—that he represent her, and he, though apparently unwilling, for he refuses to allow his engagement to be made public, is unable to refuse. Both he then, and the king, know where the right lies but are unable to alter the course of events. It is given to Iwein to champion the rightful cause but in so doing he fights his dearest friend. The crowning absurdity is, however, the lack of any result—absurdity that is from the strict point of view of tradition, for Gawain should have been defeated. Indeed the battle would have continued, were it not that Iwein and Gawain in recognition of the situation both admit wrongly their defeat. And even at this point the king is still incapable of making any decision and has to resort to subterfuge in order to bring about a proper solution.

It is evident from the manner in which *aventiure* is first defined and then exemplified that Hartmann questions the validity of the conventional view of the basis of chivalry. The original definition of *aventiure* is primitive and leads to absurdly comic, but also to tragic situations. The humour of the Kalogreant episode vanishes when Iwein is led under the same circumstances to murder an innocent man defending his own lands. The humour of the Meljakanz episode cannot hide the fact that it could have had tragic consequences for Gawain's relatives. Above all the episode of the maidens demonstrates what great suffering can be inflicted upon entirely innocent people by unthinking adherence to conventional shibboleths. For the world is full of wickedness and full of people who refuse to recognise the knightly code of behaviour. Indeed, it is apparent that acceptance of it hardly extends beyond the confines of Arthur's court and that his knights are themselves completely ineffectual.

This ironic or at times sharply satirical portrayal of the chivalric world does not necessarily imply that Hartmann feels it is valueless, but neither does he attempt to design an improved form of social order. His concern is not with the community as a whole but with the individual, and to this extent his ***Iwein*** contrasts with Wolfram's *Parzival,* although there are remarkable similarities in the personal development of the protagonists. Against the background of the *Minnroman,* which has been reduced by Hartmann largely to the function of a framework, we are shown how a knight is misled by unreflecting acceptance of a

Scherer on Hartmann's poetic development:

In his ***Ereck*** Hartmann von Aue carried description to the extreme of absurdity. His description of Enite's horse occupies about five hundred lines. In ***Iwein*** he laid aside this bad habit, and this later poem is a model of epic style. Situations and habits of life are fully described, but never so as to become wearisome and always in connection with the main action. Battles are no longer pictured in set formulas, but with due regard to their special characteristics. But the representation of the inner life is always the chief interest with Hartmann. While ***Ereck*** still showed at times a want of refinement, ***Iwein,*** on the contrary, is a model of good taste and elegance. Again, while in ***Ereck*** the diction is rough and unequal, in ***Iwein*** the language has attained the highest level of perfection, and readily fulfills all that the poet demands of it. The narrative is smooth and flowing, and all exaggeration is avoided.

W. Scherer, in A History of German Literature, *translated by F. C. Conybeare, Charles Scribner's Sons, 1899.*

misunderstood and misapplied convention and continues to act in a manner incompatible with his real self, until his dream world is shattered. Thrown back at first to the animal level, Iwein must make his way back into society with eyes opened to the realities of life. Before meeting Laudine for the second time he has already experienced enough in his own life and seen enough of life around him to realise that the world is full of suffering and that the attitude represented by Kalogreant does nothing to alleviate but, on the contrary, much to cause or augment such suffering.

The true basis for knighthood is not then Kalogreant's definition, which is basically inhumane. Even the philosophy of the natural man, the *Waldmensch,* is superior, for he says:

> . . . swer mir niene tuot,
> der sol ouch mich ze vriunde han.
>
> (484-485)

This, however, is only a passive philosophy and inadequate as a basis for knighthood. Knighthood requires active participation in the world, an active defence of the oppressed and the suffering. It is for this reason that Iwein proceeds on his way, unrecognised and unaided, after providing restitution for his original shortcomings. He has perceived that the true basis of knighthood is a selfless service of humanity, an humanitarian ethic which precludes adventure for adventure's sake and commands intervention wherever there is genuine need. . . . Society itself is not improved at the end of the poem, but this is not Hartmann's concern. Acceptance and conventionalisation by society of the supposed essence of an idea render that idea a superficial and at bottom "heartless" code. The danger lies in the force which convention exerts over the individual as member of a social order. Hartmann shows how such an individual incurs guilt in unthinkingly adopting such a false convention, but how he is enabled through his experience and his suffering to attain to a genuine and meaningful *humanitas,* genuine since it stems from the true nature of man and meaningful because appropriate to a knight in his function as:

> . . . der nothaften vluht,
> ein schilt siner mage.

W. H. Jackson (essay date 1970)

SOURCE: "Some Observations on the Status of the Narrator in Hartmann von Aue's *Erec* and *Iwein,*" in *Forum for Modern Language Studies,* Vol. VI, No. 1, January, 1970, pp. 65-82.

[*Jackson was an English-born scholar of Germanic and comparative literature and the author of* The Literature of the Middle Ages *(1960) and* The Anatomy of Love: The Tristan of Gottfried von Strassburg *(1971). In the following essay, he compares the narrative strategies of* Erec *and* Iwein *and concludes that* Iwein *represents a more mature narrative technique.*]

In both his romances, Hartmann the poet dramatises the process of telling in the figure of Hartmann the narrator, a speaker at times poring over the internal situation of the poem, at times turning away to present himself to the audience. There are, however, significant differences between ***Erec*** and ***Iwein*** in the narrator's attitude toward his tale and his audience.

The many back references of the type *als ich iu gesaget hân* (453) in ***Erec,*** which are not always necessary as reminders even in oral delivery, are not just signs of clumsy technique, but part of the narrator's general purpose in this work, which is to draw attention explicitly to his presence and to his procedures: repeatedly he tells us what he has said and what he is going to say, e.g. weaving into his list of the guests at Erec's wedding feast seven lines of the type "now I shall tell you" or "now I have told you" (1902, 1939, 1941, 1954, 2073, 2086, 2113). He tells us he is working from a source, but he also explicitly selects, for instance by saying (at times ironically) that he will be brief and tell only what is relevant (1446 ff., 2129 ff., 4299 ff., 5223 ff., 7429 ff., 7450 ff., 7476 ff., 7573 ff., 7591 ff.). Thus we are recurrently made aware of the narrator's oratorical activity, and that we are hearing a tale that has been passed on to him, but in recounting which he makes his own decisions as to what is important, i.e. the narrator makes it clear that the audience depends on him for its view of the story, that the audience must trust him. And since he intimates a vast amount of background knowledge, ranging from information about Guivreiz (4299 ff.) to a familiarity with Lucan (5216 ff.), we accept him as a reliable authority.

The audience itself is frequently dramatised in ***Erec,*** for instance by the figure of *ratiocinatio,* as the narrator answers questions which the dramatised audience puts directly, or which the narrator anticipates (e.g. 5153 ff.,

5386 ff., 6554 ff., 7106 ff., 7144 ff., 7207 ff., 7643 ff., 7680 ff., 8745 ff., 8775 ff., 9169 ff.)—a device which emphasises the narrator's authoritativeness and is characteristic of his eagerness to leap from the preterite tense in which he records the action into the present tense of interplay with his audience. . . . [In ***Erec***] nowhere is the narrator closer to his dramatised audience than in the description of Enite's horse and saddle (7286-7766). Judged from the standpoint of an aesthetic which views the poem as an autonomous artefact whose every part should be functional to some purely internal system that leaves no place for a personal relationship between poet and public, this description would have to be regretted as tediously digressive. But interplay with an audience is part of the poet's aesthetic purpose in ***Erec***. The work has a clear social orientation in the light of which this passage is aesthetically legitimate precisely because the narrator is here less concerned to present a situation that is important for the internal action than to control the responses of his real audience by presenting his relationship with the dramatised, imagined audience as one of friendly interaction, with the narrator in dialogue with his audience, advising his friends to stay *hie heime* (7637) and accept his word, assuming the pose of *ein tumber kneht* (7480) but quickly showing his superior knowledge (7493-7525), ready later to reprove his audience by withholding information when the time is not yet, in his view, ripe for revelation (7826 ff.). Rarely in German literature before Hartmann can a narrator have assumed quite such explicit control over his material, and probably never before has the sheer process of telling assumed quite such an explicit status within the work, as a personal relationship between narrator and audience, as it does in ***Erec***.

The narrator appears in a different light in ***Iwein***. He is less ready than the narrator of ***Erec*** with explicit references to his oratorical and organising activities, he brings fewer formulae of the type "as I have said" and fewer reflections on his aesthetic procedures: he does not, for instance, parade his learning by telling us that he has much information which he is withholding for reasons of brevity, so that we are less often aware on reading ***Iwein*** than we are on reading ***Erec*** of the narrator as a man with a large store of knowledge that he could pour out if he had the time. In general, the narrator of ***Iwein*** uses the first person singular less often than does the narrator of ***Erec,*** and he addresses his audience less often explicitly in the second person: in the 10192 vv. of ***Erec*** (i.e. including the Wolfenbütteler Fragment) I count 142 occurrences of the narrator's first person singular (as pronoun alone or with a verb), whilst the 8165 vv. of ***Iwein*** have 71 occurrences; in ***Erec*** the narrator addresses his audience in the second person on 125 occasions, in ***Iwein*** on 26 occasions; and the first person plural is used in the narrator's voice (either as editorial we, or to embrace narrator and audience) 24 times in ***Erec*** as against nine times in ***Iwein***. Statistics can lie, but these are telling figures. The audience is dramatised as speaking to the narrator only once in ***Iwein*** (7027 ff.), at least four times in ***Erec*** (7106, 7493 ff., 7826, 9169 f.); and whereas the narrator of ***Erec*** puts some thirty questions, many of which are really the audience's questions to which he supplies an answer (see above), the narrator of ***Iwein*** puts only eight questions to the audience in his own voice, of which seven are purely rhetorical questions closely linked to the action and not implying much audience participation (1262, 2416, 3735ff., 6867 ff., 6939 ff., 6980, 7279 ff.). The public space in which the narrator is in open interplay with a dramatised audience is indeed narrower in ***Iwein,*** and moreover the narrator of ***Iwein*** presents his story more scenically than the narrator of ***Erec,*** with less summary in his own voice: direct speech takes up a higher proportion of ***Iwein*** (52.7% of the work) than of ***Erec*** (31.4%) and this contributes to the dominance of scene; there are fewer descriptive passages in ***Iwein*** and these are more functional to the unfolding of plot and theme, and played less explicitly towards the audience than the descriptive passages of ***Erec,*** which are exploited strongly in terms of the relationship between narrator and audience; and . . . the narrator's reporting of his characters' thoughts and feelings is more often backed up by visible gestures of the characters in ***Iwein*** than in ***Erec***.

It should be emphasised that these are differences of degree. Hartmann has not yet set about the task of eliminating the privileged narrator! But our observations point already to a certain retreat of the "intrusive" personal narrator as we pass from ***Erec*** to ***Iwein***. As a voice speaking in oral delivery, or imagined by a silent reader, the narrator is present throughout the works, but the narrator of ***Iwein*** is in less sustained rapport with a dramatised audience within the work than is the narrator of ***Erec,*** and he asks us less often to take his word on trust, he appears to place us more directly before the actions, the words, even the thoughts of the characters, inviting us to form our own judgement: *daz mugent ir kiesen, ob ir welt* (***Iwein,*** 2570). The narrator has become more questioning, less self-confident in his telling.

The shifts in the narrator's mode of presentation from ***Erec*** to ***Iwein*** are rich in implication for a purely stylistic approach to Hartmann's works: it may well be, for instance, that in working on ***Iwein,*** Hartmann was thinking more in terms of written literature than he was with ***Erec,*** where his narrator is so conscious of speaking to an audience. But in the context of the current debate on the *meine* of ***Iwein,*** the question of the narrator's status as ethical judge of the action has particular relevance, and it is chiefly to this question that the remainder of this paper will be devoted.

Predominantly in ***Erec*** one unambiguous ethical judgment is presented within the work as adequate to assess a given phase of the action, and on the main lines of the action the narrator guides our ethical sympathies firmly in his own voice. All the relevant characters, even the defeated Iders (1244 ff.), agree that Erec has acquitted himself well in his first combat, and the narrator places him clearly in his own voice as *der guote* (1056)—but he also forewarns us of the lovers' *verligen* by telling us of their intense desire to "spend a night or two together" (1857-1886). Erec's courtiers regret his *verligen* (2974 ff.), and the narrator records Erec's *wandelunge* (2984) in his own (the narrator's) voice with a firmness of judgement that does not allow us to consider a less critical interpretation of the hero's preoccupation with the marital bed: we are not allowed to contemplate the possibility of some moral nobility in the hero's abandonment of society for love, a possibility that Gottfried von Strassburg will present as a very real one when *his* lovers live *ane liute* (*Tristan,* 16849). Similarly in the *Joie de la curt* episode the narrator unambiguously approves Erec as *der guote* (9366) and places us against Mabonagrin (*sô mordic was sîn hant,* 9023!), and even Mabonagrin welcomes his defeat as a release (9583 ff.), so that the conflict between his values and Erec's is perfectly resolved not by a compromise, but by Mabonagrin's accepting the values of Erec—and of the narrator. Conflicts between valid norms are only incidental in ***Erec,*** and when Enite has to choose between keeping her promise to her husband and saving his life, the narrator (e.g. by referring to her *triuwe,* 3143) leaves us in no doubt as to which is the superior obligation. On the important issues, everyone is in agreement in ***Erec,*** and when the work has been devised with such ethical clarity, the narrator's task as judge and guide is relatively simple.

Iwein is already, as it were, a romance of the second generation in which the new conventions are subject to more critical scrutiny, and ***Iwein*** has a greater diversity of ethical perspectives: a literary convention of Arthurian *âventiure* as the pursuit of personal *êre* clashes with the demands of social reality as Askalon (who condemns Kalogrenant as *triuwelôs,* 712) and Gawein (who has only praise for Iwein's success, 2879-2904) express radically different views on the ethical legitimacy of unannounced provocations of the storm; and Laudine is caught between the duty of respect for her dead husband and the duty to find a new protector quickly. Even the apparently sound new chivalric norm of proffering aid to those who ask is open to criticism when it leads to Gawain's defending an unjust cause; in the resulting combat Iwein is placed (implicitly) between the demands of chivalric friendship which call on him to admit defeat (7561 ff.) and the obligation to fight on in defence of a just cause; and the kingly virtue of adhering to vows causes some embarrassment when it leads to the abduction of Arthur's wife (4579 ff.). The course of events in ***Iwein*** indeed demonstrates just how inadequate some of the general ethical norms of courtly literature are as a guide to conduct in specific situations, and certainly ***Iwein*** is an ethically complex work in which actions are judged from more than one standpoint. The high incidence of direct speech and hence of scene rather than summary is, in part, a formal reflection of this ethical complexity as Kalogrenant, Askalon, Lunete, Gawein, Laudine, Iwein all give voice to norms and pass judgements in their words, all emerge as "disguised narrators" expressing fragments of the poet's whole truth [W.C. Booth, *The Rhetoric of Fiction* (1961)]: even a figure of such minor consequence for the unfolding of plot as the woman who tells Iwein of a young knight's pursuit of *âventiure* (6320 ff.) can carry much weight as a spokesman for the poet's critique of chivalry. Already in ***Erec,*** of course, the narrator's commentary is by no means the poet's whole truth, for the poet does use his characters to impose his views, but as he passes judgement more often in ***Iwein*** than in ***Erec,*** by the "indirect" means of his characters' words, so the narrator's commentary covers even less of the ground; and whereas the narrator of ***Erec*** can rely on a central norm whereby to judge any one turn in the action, the narrator of ***Iwein*** is at times placed between a variety of voices not always in agreement and he not only covers less ground, but is also less consistently authoritative than is the narrator of ***Erec*** in judging the action ethically in direct commentary in his own voice. However, generalisation about the narrator's status as ethical judge is apt to merge into distortion when we consider ***Iwein,*** for his commentary varies in reliability and decisiveness from phase to phase in the unfolding of the action.

The narrator's ethical commentary in his own voice on Iwein's killing of Askalon and his sudden love for Laudine is remarkably scant and oblique. He refers in general terms to Iwein's *triuwe* (2427), but only after providing privileged inside views of his thoughts which place the hero in a critical light: the discrepancy between Iwein's public dismissal of Keii's taunts (856 ff.) and his private fear of just these taunts (1062 ff., 1530 ff.) seems calculated to arouse critical detachment in the reader and to cast doubt on the validity of Iwein's motives in attacking and killing Askalon. But the judgement is only implicit. The narrator's much debated *âne zuht* (1056) suggests more explicit disapproval, but the judgement is based on the means of pursuit, whilst at the moment of the combat the narrator turns away from the action and towards the audience with one of those technical reflections frequent in ***Erec*** but rare in ***Iwein***. Already in ***Erec*** the narrator refused to describe a lady's *roc* on the pretext that he lacked an eye-witness authority (8946 ff.), but that was a gratuitous piece of humour on a trivial point. In ***Iwein*** the narrator's technical reflections carry more weight, and his refusal to report the combat because of lack of an eye-witness authority (1029-1044) is surely ethically motivated, is a means whereby the narrator keeps himself and his audience distanced from the action at a point where it is anything but exemplary. The device of diplomatic ignorance is here used to avoid explicit condemnation of the hero. With regard to Iwein's love, the narrator praises his hero as a faithful host to *vrou Minne* (1585 ff.), but since *vrou Minne* will later be characterised as less than ladylike when she tells Hartmann to "shut his mouth" (3013) and since the narrator will later refer to her as the cause of Iwein's degeneration to a naked fool (3249 ff.), such praise seems double-edged. Indeed, the narrator remains bemusedly detached from the enslaved lover type throughout the work, and even before his praise of Iwein the lover, he has taken pains to show how his compassionate words contrast with the less noble thoughts of a man who, because of his love, would not give *ein strô* if all Laudine's courtiers fell dead (1432-1445). By such revelations of a discrepancy between appearance and reality the narrator seems systematically to be undermining our faith in Iwein, the knight and lover. But the criticism still remains implicit. The reader has to supply the explicit judgement. And when the marriage between Iwein and Laudine is finalised, the narrator says that it was *michel vuoge* (2417). Just when are we to take him seriously? In what direction is he guiding us?

It is significant that he closes his account of the first phase of Iwein's career, at another point of some ethical delicacy, with a further reflection on the material of his delivery, the exchange with *vrou Minne* in which he professes his failure to understand a literary commonplace (2995 ff.) and maintains that he is speaking not out of personal opinion but at the command of *vrou Minne* (2984 ff.) and in dependence on his source (3025 ff.). The narrator of ***Erec*** presents himself as one fully competent to understand the main lines of the action, and when he shows his wisdom on matters of love (e.g. 2364 ff., 3691 ff., 9169 ff.), we sense that the *poet* is speaking directly to us. But the narrator's commentary in the early stages of ***Iwein*** (up to v. 3028) is characterised by the recurrence of statements which cast doubt on his ability to understand the action, or which suggest that he is not convinced of the truth of what he is saying: he refuses to describe Iwein's combat because he "lacks an eye-witness" (1029 ff.), he says he cannot understand Laudine's and Iwein's exchange of hearts (2995 ff.), his qualifying *waenlich* of v. 2433 suggests doubt as to whether Iwein's and Laudine's married state is really so secure, he reports only as hearsay that the wounds of love last longer than those of sword and spear (1549 ff.) and says only "we are told" that a corpse will bleed in the presence of the killer (1355 ff.). Even when he comes out into the open with a firm *ich weiz* (1875), he "knows" only that women always change their minds out of *güete,* a clearly unreliable piece of knowledge which, if taken seriously, says more for his politeness than his acumen, and which will in any case be implicitly retracted when he describes a woman as *diu unguote* (5663) and tells how she changes *her* mind not because of *reht* and *güete* but under pressure of *gewalt* and *vorhte* (7704 ff.). Such apparent reliance on the views of others, however, such statements of doubt, limited understanding and bland politeness build up to a pattern which leads to our not accepting the narrator's every word as a direct statement of his own belief, still less as an expression of the poet's views.

Recent Chaucer criticism has shown that the medieval poet does not always identify with his narrator, and a discrepancy between the views of the poet and the words of the narrator is especially clear in ***Iwein*** when the narrator professes in vv. 2995 ff. an ignorance that cannot possibly be shared by the poet. But elsewhere (e.g. when he develops the allegory of *minne* and *haz,* vv. 7041 ff.) the narrator shows a literary expertise that cannot easily be reconciled with his failure to understand a commonplace in vv. 2995 ff., and at this point two lines of interpretation are open to the reader. Either we take the narrator in ***Iwein*** as a consistently portrayed ironist who only pretends to be ignorant on occasion. Or (and this I find a more satisfying interpretation) he is not dramatised as a psychologically and intellectually thoroughly consistent persona, nor is his standpoint wholly and consistently separate from that of the implied poet; i.e. he is not a unified "character" like the persons within the action, he is not dramatised as consistently wise, foolish, or ironical. Hartmann's ***Iwein*** does not yet sustain the purist point of view . . . , and I read the narrator in this work as speaking from various standpoints. Like Chaucer, Hartmann as, I think, still (even in ***Iwein***) too much the court poet facing a present audience to detach himself constantly from and reflect consistently on his narrator, but at the same time Hartmann the poet does not constantly identify with his narrator, he has already discovered some of the advantages to be gained from a separation of poet and narrator: at times Hartmann the narrator is the implied poet speaking directly, at times he is a series of masks worn, or poses imaginatively assumed in the process of writing (and mimed in oral delivery) by the poet, at times he speaks wisely, at times he is distinctly limited in knowledge, and it is an important task of interpretation to assess just when the poet is speaking directly and when, and to what end, he is wearing a mask in ***Iwein***. (The poet's oscillating between identification with and distance from his narrator is, I think, reflected in the fact that the narrator refers to Hartmann the poet in the third person in the prologue [***Iwein*** 28, cf. ***Gregorius*** 171 ff. and ***Der Arme Heinrich*** 1 ff.], which might suggest that the poet thinks of the narrator as a separate person, but in the body of the text the narrator is also addressed as, precisely, Hartmann [***Erec*** 7493, 9169; ***Iwein*** 2974, 2982, 7027], so that, if Hartmann the poet thinks of his narrator as a separate person in his prologues, he also forces a narrator in oral delivery to play the role, or roles, of *Hartmann* in the body of the text.) This might seem a complicated way of reading a work often praised for its clarity, but recent opinion suggests that ***Iwein*** is not, after all, quite so simple a work; moreover, what seems complicated to readers nurtured on later modes of narration may well have been self-evident to Hartmann's contemporaries.

However, whether we take the irony at any one point in ***Iwein*** as a product of the narrator's own ironic sensibility, or as lying in a discrepancy between Hartmann the wise poet and Hartmann the narrator who is dramatised for the immediate purpose as lacking knowledge, the important fact remains that this irony at times produces a disparity between the literal meaning of the narrator's comments and the views of the implied poet, and renders the narrator's commentary in the early stages of ***Iwein*** sufficiently ambiguous to provoke the opposed interpretations of those who see Iwein as still blameless when he marries Laudine and those who see him, with more justice, as already subject to the poet's criticism. Hartmann the poet is indeed dramatising Hartmann the narrator in this part of the work (up to v. 3028) in a variety of roles, now as a diplomatic ironist (1029-1044), now as an intellectually fallible first person singular who does not have complete control over and will not accept personal responsibility for the tale (2971-3028), and he is inviting us to think critically at those points where the narrator professes doubt, limited privilege, limited understanding: when the narrator says he cannot report on Iwein's combat because the hero was too *hövesch* (1040) to boast of his deeds, the poet is assuming a mask of politeness to launch ironic criticism by the device of an incongruously placed adjective, and when Hartmann the narrator says he cannot understand the workings of *vrou Minne,* the poet is providing a burlesque criticism of that enslaving love which the narrator seems not to understand.

Iwein's killing of a knight out of pure self-interest and his sudden, over-powering love for Laudine run against the values of Hartmann, the humane moralist. So much, I think, emerges from a reading of ***Iwein,*** without reference to Hartmann's other works. But the poet had ample reason to bring in the narrator's voice an ironic and to some extent ambiguous criticism. Firstly, by explicitly condemning Iwein in the narrator's voice as a murderer, he would have openly laid a charge against the hero so grave as to be capable of answer only in a work with the religious depth of a *Parzival,* whilst by keeping the criticism ironically oblique he reconciles it with the spirit of fantasy and comedy which largely determines the framework of the action in ***Iwein***. (The aesthetic congruity of criticism by irony and burlesque is, perhaps, especially evident in the development of the love theme). Moreover, the very fact that all the characters involved quickly accommodate to the situation created by Askalon's death encourages the poet to keep his narrator's criticism oblique, for a basic stance of Hartmann as narrator in his romances is his reluctance to criticise his central characters openly in his own voice when he lacks corroboration from reliable characters within the action. The narrator in Chrestien's romances comments less often than the dramatised Hartmann, but he is more willing to reveal the weaknesses of his heroes explicitly and on his own authority: for instance when Chrestien's Erec faces Guivret the narrator comments on his rashness (*Or fera Erec trop que fos, / se tost conuistre ne se fet,* 4968 f.), but Erec shows no awareness of having erred, whilst Hartmann reverses the situation, not even hinting at criticism in the narrator's voice, but bringing a speech in which Erec himself condemns his own *tumpheit* and *unmâze* (7007 ff.). Hartmann's sternest criticism is indeed brought preferably in direct speech, especially in the heroes' self-indictments (which are calculated to encourage self-criticism in the audience), whilst Hartmann the narrator tends to praise and justify his heroes in his own voice, is quick to assume the role of eulogist or defence counsel rather than impartial judge of his heroes in explicit commentary. The resulting stance of politeness in narratorial commentary is perhaps even more sustained in ***Iwein*** than in ***Erec*** and is an important reason why we cannot accept the narrator's direct commentary in Hartmann's romances as necessarily the poet's most important truth, a truth which also includes the moral criticism of the heroes' self-indictments. In criticising Erec's *verligen* the narrator does not need to abandon his stance of politeness, for he can simply agree with the reliable authority of Erec's court (and even here he strains at a gnat to praise Erec in vv. 2954 ff.), but since all the characters in ***Iwein,*** with the exception of the quickly forgotten Askalon, come to accept Iwein's killing of Askalon and his sudden love for Laudine, the narrator no longer has such an authority inside the action to lean on in open criticism, and distaste has to be registered in his commentary by a process in which criticism is implied by superficially polite words or protestations of ignorance. The irony of a disparity between the narrator's words and the poet's views in the early stages of ***Iwein*** is, in brief, the means whereby Hartmann the poet adjusts his humane idealism to an action part fantastic, part tragi-comical, and the means whereby he resolves the paradox of his position as both moral critic and polite eulogist of his hero's behaviour. It is an irony that leaves us with far more interpretative work to do than we have on reading ***Erec***.

Of the first 3028 vv. of ***Iwein,*** 1875 are in direct speech (or record thoughts as if they were direct speech, e.g. 911 ff.) whilst only 1153 are in the narrator's voice, and in these 1153 vv. the narrator addresses his audience explicitly in the second person ten times (1031, 1045, 1107, 1135, 1361, 2565, 2570, 2582, 2716, 2989), throws out two rhetorical questions (1262, 2416) and three times includes himself and his audience in the first person plural (50-56, 1355, 1586). The sequence of events from the account of Iwein's overstaying his leave up to his return to Arthur's court (3029-6894) occupies 3866 vv., of which only 1686 are in direct speech (or record thoughts as if they were direct speech) as against 2180 in the narrator's voice, but in this section, although he says almost twice as much as he did earlier in his own voice, the narrator addresses his audience explicitly in the second person only seven times (3031, 3036, 3102, 3309, 3928, 4429, 5700), twice implicitly addresses the audience by rhetorical question (3735 ff., 6867 ff.) and only once links himself with his audience as *wir* (5969 f.). This shift towards more summary in the narrator's voice and this fall in the number of times he dramatises the audience by direct address are only crude statistical reflections of a change in the narrator's attitude: he is, in this section, in closer sympathy with and has firmer control over the human situation of the poem. . . . But we need to distinguish between various kinds of distance in the relations of narrator, reader (or audience) and action. The dominance of scene in the early stages of ***Iwein*** brings the reader close in physical perception to the words and gestures of the characters, but at the same time the narrator remains at a distance by reminding us that the *âventiure* is of another's making (3025 ff.) and by his protestations of doubt, limited understanding, etc. And the irony of the narrator's commentary also keeps the reader at a certain critical, ethical distance from the action. The particular manner of the narrator's presentation in the early stages of ***Iwein*** thus brings us close to the action in physical perception, but keeps us ethically distanced. In vv. 3029-6894 the narrator reminds the audience of the remoteness of the action in time, e.g. by referring to a legal practice as obsolete (5429 ff.), and he remains detached from Iwein's love in so far as it is an enervating, sense-robbing force: he again reports the pain of love only as hearsay (5196 ff.) and humorously expresses surprise that Laudine, carrying as she does Iwein's heart, fails to recognise him (5456 ff.). But he is no longer detached from the action in so sustained a manner as he was earlier, rather by comparing Iwein's foreboding to his own experience he brings himself and his audience close to the hero:

im wîssagete sîn muot,
alse er mir selbem ofte tuot:
ich siufte, sô ich vrô bin,
mînen künftegen ungewin:

sus nâhte im sîn leit.
nû seht wâ dort her reit
sîns wîbes bote, vrou Lûnete. . . .

(3097 ff.)

The *her* of v. 3102 places narrator and audience spatially with Iwein and, together with the psychological comparison, effectively concentrates the energy of the narrative by reducing our emotional distance from Iwein when he is about to be accused; again at the end of the maiden's long search for Iwein the narrator brings himself and his public close to the action by comparing it to his own desired experience (5968 ff.). There are, in this section of ***Iwein,*** no technical reflections comparable with vv. 1029 ff. and 2971 ff. which placed the narrator (in different ways) at a considerable distance from the action. The brief references to a source (3052, 4861, 6456) do not suggest the narrator's doubt as to its veracity, and his earlier signs of lacking control over the action give place to a tone of greater authority as more of the action is recorded by summary in his own voice. The absence of technical reflections and the paucity of direct references to an audience make us less aware than we were earlier of being detached from the action, we are rather drawn into the human situation of the poem as the narrator records, for instance, the maiden's search for Iwein (5777-6012) and the meeting between Iwein and the maiden who would have tempted an angel (6471-6568) with a richness of mood and atmospheric detail that would be untypical of ***Erec,*** where the network of relations between narrator and audience in the public space of the work prevents the development of sustained "Stimmung" within the action.

Iwein's ethical situation is presented with less ambiguity in the present section of the work than it was earlier. Criticism of Iwein has already been suggested in the narrator's commentary, and now Lunete brings an open accusation. Her reference to a disparity between Iwein's *wort* and his *muot* (3125 f.) brings as explicit condemnation that discrepancy between appearance and reality which has already provided implicit criticism in the narrator's voice, and her condemnation of Iwein as the cause of Laudine's *laster* and *leit* (3132, 3135) and as *triuwelôs* (3183) because of his failure to return and protect Laudine's *lant* (3158) echoes Askalon's indictment of Kalogrenant as *triuwelôs* because of the *lasterlîchez leit* of his provoking the storm (712 ff.)—an indictment which also reflected on Iwein. Lunete is, indeed, a reliable spokesman for the poet's criticism of Iwein, she does not only accuse from the limited standpoint of herself and Laudine (from which standpoint Iwein's transgression is trivial, a mere overstaying of his leave which he himself already regrets, vv. 3084 ff.) but, without knowing it, is part of the poet's broader strategy; and the fact that a character inside the action launches so powerful an accusation when the narrator points at the same moment to the hero's *triuwe* (3089, 3210) is characteristic of the way in which Hartmann prefers to set about moral criticism of his main characters in ***Iwein***. Having experienced the full weight of Lunete's charge, Iwein undergoes that pattern of symbolic death and regeneration which is central to all Hartmann's narrative works, and as he emerges as an exemplary character, demonstrating the *triuwe* of social responsibility and erotic fidelity, so the narrator, whose earlier praise was systematically qualified and turned to irony, can now place his hero without irony or ambiguity as *biderbe unde guot* (4860), *ein hövesch man* (6856), and his ethical commentary on the hero's adventures becomes more decisive and more acceptable, at face value, as the poet's truth than it was earlier.

Indeed, Hartmann's presentation of the hero's journey of chivalric penance suggests that the narrator's attitude towards tale and audience is ethically conditioned in ***Iwein*** in that he is least liable to deflect from a close reading of the internal situation of the poem, and draws his audience into closest emotive contact with the action precisely when the action is most clearly exemplary. This tendency of the narrator is seen in reverse when Iwein returns to Arthur's court to face Gawein. Just as Iwein's killing of Askalon is judged from more than one standpoint in the work (he is *triuwelôs* if we judge from Askalon's angle, blameless according to Gawein), so the combat between Iwein and Gawein is open to more than one judgement: can we fully endorse Gawein's defence of an unjust cause? but on the other hand can we really condemn him for (presumably) having trusted the elder sister? Chivalric idealism presupposes trust in human relationships, and trust seems to have placed the flower of Arthurian chivalry in the wrong. A perspective opens up here which, if rigorously explored, would reveal the difficulty, indeed (given human nature) the impossibility of perfectly implementing in social reality the chivalric ideal of defending justice, for who is to say what is just? Hartmann senses the problem when he has Iwein say that he will help anyone who asks *in good faith* (6003), which is certainly a sounder attitude than that of Gawein, whose readiness to help all *vrouwen* (4275 ff.) seems dangerously uncritical. But the question of trust remains. What evidence does Iwein have that he is committing himself to a just cause? Only the sweet words and the appearance of the messenger (6064 ff.). In this case, Iwein's trust is justified by events, but as the action of ***Iwein*** shows, words and appearances can deceive: Iwein, too, appeared trustworthy to Lunete (3119 ff.), and the knight who took Arthur's wife away seemed to be a man *der betelîchen biten kan* (4574). In his commentary on the combat the narrator does not explore the problem of trust raised by Gawein's position. It is not his wont to discuss ethical ambiguities openly. He simply registers distaste at the prospect of the possible death of a fine knight (6932 ff.) and follows up immediately with another refusal to dwell in detail on a combat (6939 ff. cf. 1029 ff.). For the only time in ***Iwein*** the audience is dramatised as speaking when the narrator interrupts his account of the first charge to exchange words with his audience (7015 ff.), then the combat is again interrupted as he develops a metaphor over 100 vv. (7125-7227) with a plethora of conceits and maxims that smacks of irony of overstatement. Perhaps this rhetorical panache (which is more characteristic of the style of ***Erec*** than of the rest of ***Iwein***) is intended partly to echo the military skill and sporting decorum of the combatants, but it is also part of the pattern initiated with the narrator's first direct address to his audience in vv. 1029 ff., it is a leap out of the action and into the public space of the poem motivated by the narrator's ethical distaste for the situation within the action. But whereas the audience was kept at a distance from Iwein's first combat by the narrator's diplomatic ignorance, and from the workings of *vrou Minne* by the narrator's appearing as a simpleton, the narrator now keeps his audience distanced from the combat between friends by resolving it into formalistic aesthetic play.

Having turned away from a situation of some ambiguity, the narrator of ***Iwein*** never recovers quite the commitment to the action which he showed in his account of Iwein's deeds of *triuwe*. It is characteristic of the voices of agreement in ***Erec*** that the last word of direct speech is a universal "*âmen*" (9951), and typical of the narrator's control over the action that he ends with a full 170 vv. of summary in his own voice before his closing prayer (9954 ff.). There is no doubt in the narrator's voice as to his ability to judge his heroes' destiny, no questioning concern with emotional detail, but a decisively authoritative telling by which the narrator firmly circumscribes our response. He does not pretend to have invented the story, but he refers to his source with evident conviction that it is *diu wârheit* (10039), and if he does not lay claim to complete omniscience, he convinces us, by professing ignorance of the names of the guests at Erec's coronation feast (10061 ff.), that what he does not know is in any case hardly worth reporting. The narrator has all the relevant information, information which allows him to place the heroes (as is the case in ***Gregorius*** and ***Der Arme Heinrich***) finally in heaven, and not for a moment does he suggest in this robust final summary that there might be other evidence on the basis of which a conclusion might be reached that differs from his. The narrator of ***Iwein,*** by contrast, keeps up direct speech almost to the end, showing Iwein's and Laudine's reconciliation in a detailed scene of sentimental comedy that raises another ethical question: are we to believe Laudine, whose plea for forgiveness implies that she has incurred some guilt (8122 ff.), or Iwein, who says she is blameless (8133 ff.)? Typically, the narrator leaves the matter open and hurries to the end with less than 30 vv. of summary. Even here he does not firmly direct our attitude toward his characters. His praise of marriage is couched in a long conditional sentence and qualified for the particular instance by the adverb *waenlich,* just as his earlier reference to Iwein's and Laudine's married bliss was conditional and qualified (8139-8148 cf. 2426-2433)—whereas the narrator of ***Erec*** was convinced of his heroes' progress (see ***Erec,*** 10119 ff.), the narrator of ***Iwein*** seems unsure, with this delightful self-quotation, whether much advance has taken place in Iwein's and Laudine's partnership. As the dramatised Hartmann closes (before his brief final prayer) with one of his familiar stances of limited knowledge, saying that he cannot report what happened later because his source runs out at this point (8160 ff.), we are left with the impression of a narrator who does not have full control over his heroes' destiny, who is detached from the human situation of the poem and who is unwilling to do more than surmise on his own authority. Such an open ending is uncharacteristic of the courtly romance as a genre and is, in the case of ***Iwein,*** more than a gratuitous rhetorical device. Again, it is a question of distance. The narrator of ***Erec*** is convinced of the exemplary truth of his story and confident that he can "tell everything", and if he remains constantly at some distance from the internal situation of the poem (though the distance varies), it is because of his sheer delight in interplay with his audience; the narrator of ***Iwein*** takes less delight in such interplay, and if he remains always at some distance from the action (though the distance varies more sharply than it does in ***Erec*** from phase to phase in the work), it is because he is less confident than the narrator of ***Erec*** that he has all the relevant information, and also less convinced, when he comes to look back on the entire story, of its exemplary truth.

The *Nibelungenlied,* a late product of the heroic tradition, provides an apt point of contrast on which to close. The narrator of the *Nibelungenlied* never fills out even a single strophe with commentary in the first person singular, his ethical judgements are sparse and he tends frequently to include himself with his audience in the first person plural. He appears as an anonymous transmitter of a traditional *maere* who does not regard his personal views as sufficiently important to be recorded at any length. The tale is everything, the teller of little consequence. Nor am I conscious of the mind of an individual poet manipulating this self-effacing, but very effective narrator for purposes of some deep irony. With the rise of the courtly romance, however, we can trace the emergence in German secular literature of individual minds no longer transmitting patterns with the continuity of spirit that links the *Nibelungenlied* (despite all the differences between epic and lay) with the *Hildebrandslied,* but reflecting critically on the material: in Hartmann's romances, the narrator is named, he expresses personal views, . . . and our relationship with the narrator becomes a larger and more complex part of our experience of the work. The courtly romance is less individualist, still more bound to a suprapersonal rhetoric than the tradition of the novel, but the narrator of ***Iwein*** is already a rather different figure from the narrator of ***Erec,*** and the narrators of Gottfried's *Tristan,* Wolfram's *Parzival,* Ulrich von Zatzikhoven's *Lanzelet* are yet different travelling companions guiding us along yet different lines: the narrator of *Lanzelet* often records his hero's doings with a moral *insouciance* that would trouble the dramatised Hartmann; the narrator of Gottfried's *Tristan* has neither the sustained, bantering humour of the narrator of ***Erec,*** nor does he ever appear as quite such a simpleton as the dramatised Hartmann in his conversation with *vrou Minne,* and he will penetrate more deeply than both into the psychology of his characters; and (to point to only two features in so rich a poet as Wolfram), the dramatised Wolfram will strike up in *Parzival* a closer relationship with his hero than does Hartmann, and he will be a more explicit polemicist, far less committed to a rhetoric of politeness.

The masks which come between the words of the narrator and the views of the implied poet are less easily penetrable in ***Iwein*** than in many other works of the period, the narrator is no longer such a simple dramatisation of the implied poet as he was in ***Erec***. . . .

—*W. H. Jackson*

The dramatised Hartmann has a fairly consistent, thought not strongly individualised personality in ***Erec***: he displays his learning, he is a humorist, he has a fair grasp of moral problems. We cannot accept the narrator as simply the biographically real poet in Hartmann's works (though it is easy to take purism too far in distinguishing between narrator and biographically real poet), but the biographically real Hartmann is probably of less interest to most readers than the implied poet. Even in ***Erec*** the narrator's explicit commentary does not cover the implied poet's whole truth, which is also recorded in symbol and direct speech, but if the narrator's commentary is less complex than the poet's whole truth in ***Erec,*** it nevertheless expresses the broad outlines of this truth: the implied poet's concern with the degrading and inspiring power of love is explicit in the narrator's commentary (e.g. 3691 ff., 9171 ff.), and the poet's control over the action is recorded when the narrator reminds us that we are returning to the main theme (1838 f.), refuses to tell something out of place (7826 ff.), and summarises so powerfully at the end. On the main points, I would contend, Hartmann the narrator is, in ***Erec,*** Hartmann the implied poet speaking directly to reader and audience. The narrator of ***Iwein*** is not less liberal with the first person singular, he also presents a less consistent image. He speaks in many different roles: he is a courtier polite to women, but he also points to the guile of a woman; he professes remarkable ignorance on love's psychology, but he also speaks at times as a literary expert and an experienced, much travelled man. It is certainly more difficult to assess the narrator's tone of voice in ***Iwein*** than it is in ***Erec*** (and even, perhaps, than in Gottfried's and Wolfram's works), and this difficulty has to be faced as an important one: when he says *des tôten ist vergezzen: / der lebende hât besezzen / beidiu sîn êre und sîn lant* (2435 ff.), is he making a neutral statement of fact, or directing irony against the one who killed and those who quickly forgot, or is he even, perhaps, reminding us, in a half-humorous way, that we are in a fictive world where "real" human emotions have to dance to the tune of the action? There is no one simple and "correct" answer to this question of the narrator's tone of voice; the dramatised Hartmann is, I think, sufficiently open to interpretation in ***Iwein*** for readers of different persuasions legitimately to make their peace with his voice in different ways at many points. The masks which come between the words of the narrator and the views of the implied poet are less easily penetrable in ***Iwein*** than in many other works of the period, the narrator is no longer such a simple dramatisation of the implied poet as he was in ***Erec,*** and the narrator's commentary contains less of the poet's whole truth: Lunete's indictment of Iwein is more drastic in tone than any accusation laid against Erec, whilst the dramatised Hartmann is, on the surface, perhaps even more polite towards his hero in ***Iwein*** than in ***Erec,*** which suggests a larger disparity in ***Iwein*** than in ***Erec*** between the poet's full moral analysis and the narrator's explicit commentary; similarly there is a larger intellectual disparity between the position of the implied poet and the professed position of the narrator in ***Iwein*** than in ***Erec,*** as the poet's control over his characters' psychology and over the intricate development of plot contrasts with the narrator's protestations of limited knowledge and his reluctance to report on his own authority. Moreover, on the basis of extrinsic evidence, we know that when Hartmann the narrator says he can only report what has been told to him, he is not expressing the position of Hartmann the poet, who made many alterations of detail to Chrestien's *Yvain* and effected a large change in the indictment at Arthur's court. These discrepancies between the words of Hartmann the narrator and the whole truth of Hartmann the poet suggest the presence in ***Iwein*** of a large and complex strategy of the poet, only a small part of which is recorded in the direct commentary of Hartmann the narrator. The stylistic ob-

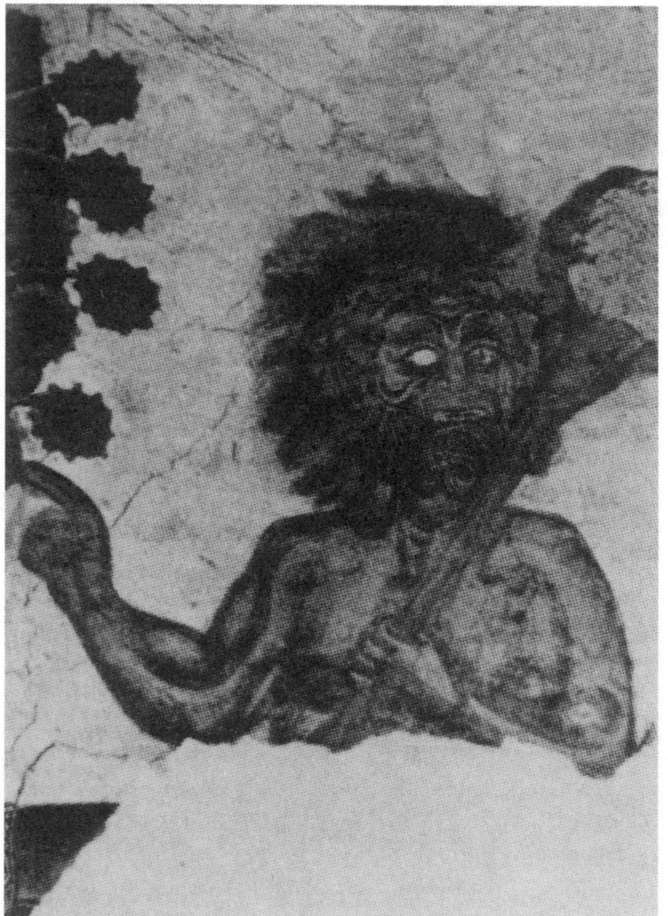

Thirteenth-century fresco depicting the wild man of Iwein.

servations of the first part of this paper can here be placed in a broader context of values. By sending his first romance into the world with a narrator who tells of love and chivalry with such authority, Hartmann the poet is registering a clear vote of confidence in the new ideals, their comprehensibility, their relevance to the public whose responses he so firmly controls. In ***Iwein*** the poet presents, by ambivalent symbolic commentary (the wild herdsman, the fountain) and by his elaboration of detailed scene and dialogue, more evidence about human behaviour and human values than he did in ***Erec,*** he expresses judgements from more standpoints, he thinks more critically about love and chivalry, and by equipping his second romance with a narrator who assumes a variety of stances and whose commentary is thinner, less authoritative more questioning than that of the dramatised Hartmann in ***Erec,*** he invites his public to form a more nuanced and a more independent judgement of the evidence than he did in ***Erec.***

H. B. Willson (essay date 1970)

SOURCE: *"Triuwe* and *Untriuwe* in Hartmann's *Erec,"* in *The German Quarterly,* Vol. XLII, No. 1, January, 1970, pp. 5-23.

[*In the following essay, Willson explores the relationship between Erec and Enite, insisting that Hartmann uses the characters to elucidate elements of Christian love.*]

In that part of ***Erec*** which begins with the *sich verligen* of the hero and heroine and ends with their reconciliation Hartmann von Aue tells us a great deal about his conception of how love should be ordered, particularly in his characterization of Enite. In its turn this vitally significant central section throws considerable light on the *joie de la curt* episode which marks the culmination of the hero's knightly career.

When she hears how people feel about their behavior, Enite is very distressed and blames herself for what has happened: "ouch geruochte si erkennen / daz daz ez ir schult waere" (3007-08). But she resolves to suffer "wîplîchen," because she dares not repeat others' criticisms to Erec himself for fear of losing him: "Êrecke entorste siz niht klagen: / si vorhte in dâ verliesen mite" (3011-12). Nevertheless, he does hear from her own lips what his courtiers are saying, since she gives utterance to her sorrow when she believes him to be asleep, thus unintentionally causing a situation she was too frightened to bring about of her own free will. Although she would like to see matters improve, her will is inhibited by fear. Because she loves him so much that she is afraid to lose him, she does not voluntarily make known to him how others view their conduct and give him the opportunity to make amends. It is by accident, not by her design, that he actually does find out. Fear inhibits the full and free expression of her love for him. That love is not yet ordered, since perfect love casts out fear. Yet he does hear it from her and does ultimately make amends; but before that happens he proves that his love for her is also lacking in order.

Enite's fear, clearly shown in her behavior at this point, is again stressed when she promises to obey Erec's order not to speak to him: "dise kumberlîche spaehe / muoste si geloben dô, / wan si vorhte sînen drô" (3103 ff.). Again she is afraid, this time that if she does not comply he may implement his threat to kill her. In both these instances Enite's fear stems from her conviction that as a dutiful and loving wife she must not only love her husband but also honor and obey him. This is what the marriage bond means to her, her *triuwe* towards him as his wife. If she does not observe this *triuwe* he will not be obliged to show *triuwe* towards her, whatever form this may take. As she sees the contract between them, he has a right to demand this obedience from her as proof of her love.

But the conflict between love and fear in Enite reaches its climax when, on a number of occasions, Erec's life is in danger. Each time the poet leaves his audience in no doubt that because of her inordinate fear of Erec's wrath she has an agonizing choice to make. When three robbers lie in wait for them, Enite sees them before Erec does, precisely because she is riding on ahead, as she has been ordered to do. She tries to warn Erec of the danger by signs, but he does not understand what she means. She must therefore speak to him if she is not to lose the dearest husband a woman ever had (3138-39). Since she cannot see the best way out—for such a decision a woman's heart is "ze kranc" (3166)—she asks God for help in her *zwîvel* and at once the thought comes to her mind that it would be better for her to die through warning Erec of the danger than for him to die because he has not been warned. They are of unequal worth: she is inferior to him in this respect and it would therefore be inordinate if he died and she lived (3167 ff.). She therefore looks round at him "vorhtlîchen" and says to him:

> sich ûf, lieber herre, / ûf genâde verre / wil ich dir durch triuwe sagen / (dînen schaden enmac ich niht verdagen): / dir sint ritter nâhen bî / die dir schadent, mugen si, / unser herre ensî der dich ner. (3182 ff.)

In other words, her *triuwe* to her husband makes her speak, although earlier she had been afraid to disobey or dishonor him by criticizing him, because she believed that in so doing she would not be showing *triuwe* and *minne* towards him and would lose him on that account. She is still afraid, but her love overcomes her fear, now that Erec's very life is at stake. The courage to show her love has been given her by God Himself, who is the essence of *caritas.*

A situation has arisen which has made it plain to Enite that there is more than one way in which she can show *triuwe* to her husband, and that this virtue can be displayed at different levels, not all of which have equal ethical value. Whereas earlier she feared to lose him by disobeying him, now she might well lose him if she *obeyed* him, which is not the objective she wishes to achieve. To save him and keep him she must disobey him, whatever may be the consequences to herself. Although this disobedience may appear to be *untriuwe* it is in fact a higher order of *triuwe* than that she would show him if she remained silent, which under the circumstances would be *untriuwe*. By showing this higher order of love Enite orders her love for Erec. It is clearly the poet's aim to draw special attention to this apparent paradox and to the fact that God, the God of Love, helps Enite to resolve it, in other words, to overcome her *zwîvel*.

Unfortunately for Enite, Erec chooses not to recognize for what it is, this higher order of love shown by his wife. Although she maintains that she only spoke out of *triuwe*, to save his life, he insists that she has been at fault in disobeying him. In response to her plea for forgiveness he does not carry out his threat to kill her, but he does nevertheless punish her by forcing her to be his *kneht* and look after both their own horses and those they have captured, which for her is an "ungelernet arbeit" (3281). Her *ordo*, the *ordo* of nobility to which she belongs, is perverted by this treatment; and the fact that Erec creates this *inordinatio* proves that he has not yet ordered his love for Enite, while by contrast the suffering and humiliation brought upon Enite by this perversion of her *ordo* is a sign of the *ordinatio* of her love for Erec.

Erec's conception of the *triuwe* he expects from his wife and the *triuwe* she actually shows him in this situation are thus very different from each other. The latter transcends the former. Enite's love is, as it were, above the "law" of Erec's "commandment." When they start out on their journey Erec uses the word *gebot* (3094), and when she disobeys, the verb *verbieten* occurs four times: 3239, 3246, 3255, and 3257; *gebot* occurs again in 3287. In Erec's view, Enite must keep his "commandment" in order to show her love for him; when she breaks it (*brechen:* 3241) she breaks the law and order of love he has prescribed for her. The analogy with the Old and the New Law seems to be suggested. Enite's love is, analogically speaking, the new law which transcends the old law of Erec's commandment. Its "caritative" quality is proved by her willingness to risk death in order to save his life. It is therefore no coincidence that in chiding Enite for her disobedience Erec should mention the fact that women have always done what they are forbidden to do:

> swaz man in unz her noch / ie alsô tiure verbôt, / dar nâch wart in alsô nôt / daz sis muosten bekorn. (3245 ff.)

where an insistent echo of Eve's original disobedience of God's commandment in paradise may be heard. Since that time it has been the (fallen) nature of women to disobey commands:

> swaz ein wîp nimmer getaete, / der irz nie verboten haete, / niht langer si daz verbirt / wan unz ez ir verboten wirt; / sô enmac sis niht verlân. (3254 ff.)

Women will not do a thing as long as they are not forbidden to do it, but if they *are* forbidden to do it they cannot stop themselves from doing it. Erec then goes on to say that he will not take full vengeance on her by killing her, but: "enkumt iuz niht ze heile" (3270). Here there seem to be echoes of the jealous God of the Old Law, who promises to take revenge on those who break His commandments, and of salvation in the word *heile,* in spite of the fact that "enkumt iuz niht ze heile" literally means only: "it won't do you any good." As Erec says, he *is* avenging himself partially ("an einem teile"; 3271) by making her do the work of a groom. This is her punishment for "sinning" against him. Seen analogically, 3270 may mean: "it will not gain you salvation."

On the second occasion when Erec's life is in jeopardy they are waylaid by five robbers and Enite is faced with exactly the same problem. She solves it in exactly the same way. She realizes that if she allows the man who has made her a wealthy queen to die:

> sô muoz von untriuwen / mîn *sêle* verderben / und von rehte ersterben / gelîche mit dem lîbe. (3367 ff.)

and this in spite of the fact that he is now treating her as a menial! If she allows him to die it will be the height of ingratitude, i.e., *untriuwe*. Again the religious background is clearly indicated: If she does not show *caritas* she will deserve to be condemned to hell. This would be right and proper and ordinate (*von rehte*). She therefore again appeals to God for help and at once decides to speak. She looks round at Erec, saying: "herre, durch got vernim mich: / bewar ez oder man sleht dich" (3380 ff.). Once again, when Erec has defeated these five, he scolds Enite for her disobedience, but she insists that her *triuwe* made her speak (3415). Nevertheless, she humbly asks his forgiveness "durch got":

> nû vergebet mir diz durch got: / zerbriche ich mêr iuwer gebot, / daz rechet dâ zestunt. (3422 ff.)

If she breaks his commandment again he must take revenge upon her, but she hopes that this time he will show grace and forgive her, as God forgives penitent sinners. As on the last occasion, she escapes with her life, but is given another five horses to look after. She accepts this new burden with humility ("diemuot": 3453) and goodness (3449), although it is patently inordinate behavior on the part of Erec to treat her in this way: "swie verre ez wider vrouwen site / und wider ir reht waere" (3445). Her humility and goodness are in fact proof of her ordered love for Erec and turn her *leit* into *liebe* (3450 ff.). She suffers gladly for love.

The *triuwe* of the robbers to each other is in complete contrast to the *triuwe* of Enite to Erec. One of the first three says to his fellows:

> nû sult ir herren sîn gemant, / daz iu diu triuwe sî erkant, / waz wir under uns gelobet hân. (3203-4)

They have a solemn agreement among themselves to share the spoils and they respect their oath to each other. This *triuwe,* honor among thieves, is thus ordinate in the sense that they are bound together by a promise given and are prepared to keep their word, unlike Enite, who keeps breaking the promise she made to Erec not to speak to him. But in terms of the higher order of *caritas,* love for one's fellow men, their behavior is of course completely inordinate. They have *triuwe* to each other, but it is *untriuwe* to Erec and Enite, or to anyone else who passes that way. Although the actual word is not used, a similar bond of *triuwe* exists between the second group of robbers. They have a "geselleschaft under in" (3300), and are pledged to share their gains, not only among themselves, but also with the first group. They, too, are prepared to observe their code of behavior. But it is very clear that their *triuwe,* being so narrow and restricted, is just as disordered in terms of the much wider order of *caritas,* love for *all* men.

Immediately following the encounter with the second group of robbers Erec and Enite are met by a page who feels compassion for them in their "arbeit" (3514) and most courteously expresses the opinion that it would be ordinate ("gevüege unde reht": 3523) if they came back with him to his master's castle to receive hospitality from him. Erec thanks him for his *caritas* ("minne": 3562) and, having no money, offers him the choice of a horse as a reward. The page again shows compassion, this time specifically for Enite, by asking to be allowed to look after the horses; but Erec refuses to permit this, since he wishes to continue to inflict punishment upon her. The contrast between his treatment of the page and that of Enite is very striking: he recognizes the ordered love of the former, but still fails to realize the high order of love shown him by his wife. In view of clear reference to the virtues of compassion and charity in this episode, the selfless love for other human beings shown by the page, it would seem very likely that the fact that he is said to be carrying "brôt gewunden . . . in eine tweheln wîze" and "ein kandel . . . mit wîne" (3492 ff.) is not entirely coincidental. The words *brôt* and *wîn* are repeated, closer together, in 3535-36, and occur yet again with *vleisch,* all in one line, in 3554: "vleisch brôt unde wîn." A strong Eucharistic echo is to be heard, as well as one of the Incarnation, thus underlining the *caritas* of the page. If this is not an analogical reminiscence of Christian truth, it is difficult to see why Hartmann should have found it necessary to refer three times to the food the page was carrying. Once would have been enough.

In spite of the cruelty of her husband, who seems to have no conception of the love she feels for him and the lengths to which she is prepared to go to prove it, Enite yet again displays her *triuwe* to him by saving him from the count, the master of the page, who becomes so enamored of Enite that he wishes to take her away from Erec by force. The count's whole relationship with Erec and Enite is characterized by *untriuwe* and *valsch.* The first indication of this disordered love is the phrase "wider sînen triuwen" (3669), and then Hartmann goes on to say: "untriuwe riet sînen sinnen / daz er dar sô kaeme / daz er si im benaeme" (3675 ff.), and that it was "wider dem rehte," i.e., inordinate behavior, that he should want to take Erec's wife away from him. But the reason is made very clear: his *untriuwe* is the result of the power of "minne" (3691-92), which has deprived him of his right senses (3693). He is in "der minne stricke" (3694). In his case, therefore, *triuwe* and *minne* are opposites, whereas in the case of his page they are synonymous. Of the count Hartmann says that he was not "staete" in keeping his *triuwe* and continues:

> wan in vrou minne betwanc / ûf einen valschen gedanc, / daz er dem vil biderben man / sîn wîp ze nemenne muot gewan. (3718 ff.)

Because he has such excessive love for Enite he is *ungetriuwe* and *valsch;* he cannot reconcile his *minne* with *caritas* towards his fellow human beings. In the toils of this perverse, inordinate love for Enite he comes to her and shows her what appears to be compassion for her in her plight (3757 ff.), offering her a much better and more ordinate life than that she is living with Erec, in other words, a life more in conformity with her hierarchical *ordo,* that of the nobility. But since he is without *triuwe,* i.e., *caritas,* his compassion is itself false and inordinate, for *caritas* and *compassio* are ordinately inseparable from each other.

Faced with this situation, Enite decides to use "schoenen list" (3842) and promises to marry him. She says she will disarm Erec during the night and the count may then come and take her away from him in the morning. But instead of keeping her word to the count, which she has sworn to do on oath (3901 ff.), Enite warns Erec in time and Hartmann praises her for so deceiving and outwitting the count: "vrouwe Ênîte was ein getriuwez wîp" (3943). But in order to warn Erec she has to speak to him again, that is, disobey him, and she therefore again asks God for His help and then goes to Erec:

> ir triuwe ir daz gebôt / daz si ze sînem bette gie / und bôt sich vür in an ir knie / und sagete im die rede gar. / von vorhten wart si missevar. (3993)

As before, she is afraid, but her love overcomes her fear. Her *triuwe commands* her to break his commandment, since her law of love transcends his.

In this scene the poet shows clearly how Enite not only chooses for the third time to display a higher order of *triuwe* towards Erec than she would have done if she had obeyed him, but also how the display of this *triuwe* is at one and the same time a display of *untriuwe* towards the count, who himself is showing *untriuwe,* disordered love, towards Erec and Enite. She lies to him and breaks her solemn promise, which in most circumstances would be regarded as highly inordinate, un-Christian behavior, but here it is fully justified by the high order of her *triuwe* to Erec. It is in effect an expression of that *triuwe.* Just as the *triuwe* she would show to Erec if she obeyed him is of a lower order than that she shows by breaking her vow of silence and warning him in each case of danger, so also is the *triuwe* she would show to the count by keeping her word to him of a lower order than that she shows to Erec by breaking her promise to the count and deceiving him. That is why Hartmann says of Enite: "diu hete den grâven betrogen / und âne sünde gelogen" (4026-27). According to the *ordo*-concept, a higher order must always take precedence over a lower. Enite's lying and deceit is *schoener list* and is entirely ordinate behavior. It is absolutely necessary for her to show this cunning in order to counteract the *untriuwe* of the count, just as it is necessary for the Christian to use cunning to outwit the devil, who is himself full of guile.

But still Erec gives Enite no credit at all for this high order of love and again reproaches his wife for her disobedience. He tells her that if she does not obey him he will certainly kill her, although he has so far spared her life. Enite promises not to disobey him again, but breaks her promise almost immediately when she hears the count approaching with his men in pursuit. Here Hartmann is at pains to point out that the warning was just as necessary as before, because Enite had no armor on and could therefore see and hear better than her husband (4150 ff.). Her *triuwe,* says the poet—and the paradox is clear—caused her to show *unstaete* in breaking her *gelübede* to Erec. Then, after Erec has disposed of the count and put his men to flight, Hartmann says:

> nû verweiz er vrouwen Ênîte daz / daz si sîn gebot sô dicke brach. / sîn zorn wart grôz und ungemach / und unsenfter dan ê. nû gelobete si / daz siz nimmer mê vürdermâl getaete: / daz enliez si aber niht staete. (4261 ff.)

Again she is *unstaete* in breaking her oath, but not in the sense that she fails to show a higher order of *staete* (or *triuwe*) towards Erec. On the contrary, she is being absolutely constant and true to him.

In these episodes which show Enite's disobedience of her husband and her deception and betrayal of the count, the poet draws particular attention to the paradox and contradiction inherent in the Christian ethical approach. This paradox and contradiction derives from the fact that the virtue of *triuwe,* love, may be associated with different orders, and that behavior which conforms to one order of *triuwe,* in other words, is ordinate in terms of that order, may be inordinate in terms of another order, one of the two orders being superior to the other in the hierarchy of ethical values.

This conflict of orders is even more strongly emphasized in Enite's behavior after Erec has fallen unconscious from his wounds and she believes him to be dead. She behaves, in fact, in an inordinate manner, at least in the courtly sense, by tearing her hair and clawing at her body (5760 ff.). It is not seemly and proper for noble courtly ladies to behave in such an undignified way. Yet at the same time Hartmann says that she did this "nâch wîplîchem site" (5762), by which he means that such emotional outbursts are characteristic of the *ordo* of womanhood. Normally, in a *courtly* environment, this *natural* tendency of women to show strong emotion is controlled in accordance with the higher measure (*mâze*) of courtliness, the restraint and decorum of a noble courtly *lady*. But here Enite's lack of courtly measure and order, in other words her conformity with the apparently lower order of her natural womanliness, is, paradoxically, more ordinate than if she had shown restraint, since it is the expression of her ordered love for Erec. She fails to be true to her courtly *ordo* of a *vrouwe* because she is being true to Erec. The measure and order of her *triuwe* is its lack of measure.

The apparent paradox becomes even more striking in the words: "vrouwe Ênîte zurnte vaste an got" (5774). She is so griefstricken at losing Erec, as she believes, that she turns her wrath upon God, which is the absolute summit of *inordinatio.* Yet she is angry with God because of her highly ordinate love for Erec! Since, according to God's law, a man and woman should be united in one flesh, she should not be separated from Erec, and so she asks Him in His compassion to send death to her so that they *can* be united. If God keeps them separated He will be behaving inordinately, that is, breaking His own law and order of *triuwe.* But God does not listen, because it is not His will that she should die. No wild animals are sent to devour her, as she demands, and her own direct appeal to Death to give her his love falls on equally deaf ears. She realizes that it is a perversion of order for a woman to ask a man for his love, but justifies the perversion by stressing how much she needs that love:

> vil lieber tôt, nû meine ich dich [now I love you]. / von dîner liebe kumt / daz ich alsô verkêre den site, / daz ich wîp mannes bite. / nâch dîner minne ist mir sô nôt. (5886 ff.)

But this inordinate behavior, the reversal of the roles of man and woman in the wooing relationship, is, of course, a further sign of the high order of her love for Erec, since by becoming the "wife" of Death she will be united with her husband, or so she believes. Both instances of *inordinatio,* her anger with God and her unseemly expression of love for Death, show how much she loves Erec.

Since her appeals have no effect, Enite decides to take the law of God into her own hands and kill herself with Erec's sword. There could be no greater proof of her *triuwe* to Erec, her *caritas,* than this eagerness to die in order to join him, but at the same time to kill herself would be a breach of God's law and therefore inordinate in Christian ethical terms. She would not be showing her love for God and obedience to His will if she did so. Fortunately (for Erec is not, of course, dead), she is prevented from carrying out her intention by Count Oringles, whom God, in His compassion for Enite in her plight, sends for precisely this purpose, namely to be her "savior":

> den hâte got dar zuo erkorn / daz er si solde bewarn. / er kom von sînem hûs gevarn. / ir ze heile reit er durch den walt. (6123 ff.)

The analogical implications of *heile* are clear. In her tirade against God Enite refers constantly to His lack of compassion for her, implying *inordinatio* on His part, *erbarmen* or its derivatives occurring on numerous occasions. Yet God does show compassion, not by allowing her to die but by saving her from suicide and forgiving her for her anger with Him and attempt to defy His will, in the full knowledge, as God of Love, that her *inordinatio* towards Him springs from her ordinate love for Erec. Hartmann brings out this paradox in a most masterly way, making it very clear that it is resolved by God Himself, who has compassion for Enite in her suffering.

Apart from the strong emphasis on *compassio* in association with God, shown in the almost endless repetition of *erbarmen* and its variants, this episode describing the inordinate, "measureless" grief of Enite has other religious associations and reminiscences of the *Heilsgeschichte*. For example, Enite accuses Death of lack of *bescheidenheit,* the ordinate courtly virtue of discrimination, in taking the life of a man so worthy as Erec, while allowing others to live who do not deserve to do so. Some "vil boeser râtgebe" (5924 ff.) is advising him to pervert order in this way. This is a clear echo of the evil, that is, inordinate, advice given by the devil to Eve in paradise, which brought about the *inordinatio* of the Fall of Man. The word *gevellet* is used immediately afterwards (5934) and then Enite goes on to say:

> unheiles wart ich geborn, / wande nû hân ich verlorn / beide sêle unde lîp, / als von rehte tuot ein wîp / von sô groezer missetât, / diu ir man verrâten hât / als ich mînen herren hân. (5940 ff.)

This suggests the evil advice given to Adam by Eve (*verrâten*) and the death of the body resulting from the Fall, a first death leading to the second death of the soul if man does not repent and turn to God. Literally, Enite feels that she has betrayed her husband by inadvertently drawing his attention to his *sich verligen* and so deserves both these deaths. On that accursed day she destroyed her "heil" (5955-57). She accuses herself of stupidity ("unwîses muotes": 5966), the stupidity shown by all those who listen to "des tiuvels rât, / dâ von ir heil zerstoeret wirt" (5971-72). The echo of the Fall is very clear. Yet, unlike the love of Adam and Eve, Enite's love is *not* disordered, although she may think so.

Her speech of self-condemnation continues in the same vein. Her invocation of her father and mother (5974-75), suggesting analogically the father and mother of mankind, is followed almost immediately by the phrase "swaz von got geschaffen ist" (5988), suggesting the creation, after which Enite says that God has condemned her body ("verteilet an dem lîbe": 5997), though she does not yet know what He will do with her soul. Twice the word *unsaelic,* suggesting loss of salvation, appears (5992 and 6006). Then follows the reference to the transplanting of a linden tree into a garden, in which the words "garten" (6010), "boumgarten" (6017), "obezboume" (6018) and "obez" (6023) suggest Paradise and the fruit of the Tree of Knowledge, the eating of which led to the Fall. Enite then says: "und möhte die werlt erbarmen / mîn vil grôzer ungeval" (6033), analogically recalling the compassion shown by God in saving fallen man, and: "sô hât got doch / mînen lîp sô unsaelic getân" (6037-38). These insistent echoes of original sin, of the *Heilsgeschichte,* are closely linked with the fundamental opposition of the ordering and disordering of love, since man's love was disordered at the Fall.

Although Count Oringles is sent by God to be Enite's "savior" from suicide, this function nevertheless contains within itself an inherent paradox, as is clearly shown by what follows. He saves her from death and is extremely kind and sympathetic towards her, commending her for the *triuwe* she is showing to her husband (6227), but he nevertheless advises her to impose a measure on her grief: "doch habet irs genuoc getân" (6228). In his opinion she is showing too much, that is, inordinate, grief; one should keep one's sorrow within bounds. He then offers to compensate her for the "loss" of her husband by marrying her himself. She will become queen of his land and: "nû wirt iu wol schîn / daz iu iuwers mannes tôt vrumt / und iu zallem heile kumt" (6267 ff.). Her husband's death will turn out to be to her advantage (*heil*). The religious analogy is clear: the death of Christ turned out to the advantage (*heil*) of mankind, and although the count does not know it, and does not, of course, mean it in this sense, Erec's "death" and subsequent "resurrection" will indeed bring "salvation" to Enite.

It thus emerges that Count Oringles, though he was her "savior" from death, has now become her "tempter." He is trying to persuade her to impose a measure on her ordered, but measureless love for Erec, in other words, to control the *inordinatio* of her grief and show love for him, Oringles, instead. But this would be to disorder her love for Erec, which Enite will not do, dead though he may seem to be. She rejects all the count's advances, saying that she will be neither *his* wife, nor the wife of anyone else, unless God gives her back her own husband (6293 ff.). When the count, impatient to have her for himself, has made preparations for the marriage and she is actually given to him, she still refuses to cooperate and swears:

> ê erwel ich daz ich der erde / mit im bevolhen werde. / ich hân immer manne rât / sît mir in got benomen hât. (6416 ff.)

God has taken Erec away from her and she now bows to His will, but she would rather die than marry another man. She cannot forget her "lieben gesellen" (6436). Again she shows inordinate grief, which the count advises her to moderate ("mâzen": 6444), in other words to order, but of this grief Hartmann says: "ir klage was vil staete" (6442). Her *constant* grief is indeed a sign of her *staete* and *triuwe* towards Erec, in spite, or rather because, of the fact that it is, as the count says, lacking in *mâze,* measureless.

Oringles then points out to Enite how her situation has improved now that she has exchanged Erec for him. The word he uses is "verkêret" (6461), which can mean a change for the better or for the worse. In the latter sense it is, of course, equivalent to the Latin *perversio*. As the count sees it she is much better off, but from Enite's point of view order has been *perverted* by her marriage to him. The passage is remarkable for its strong dialectical character: the count lists a series of no less than eleven contrasts between Enite's former life with Erec and her life as it will be with him. Then she had nothing, now she has everything. But for Enite, because of her inordinate love for Erec (which is, of course, ordinate at the higher level), the reverse is true; then she was happy, now she is unhappy. When she was being treated as a menial by Erec, her apparently inordinate situation was ordinate, since she was proving her ordered love for him; but now that she is being treated as a noble lady by the count, the apparent *ordinatio* of her situation is in fact the very opposite. When she vows that she will not even eat unless her "dead" husband eats first (6512 f.), the count becomes so enraged at what he believes to be her stupidity ("tumpheit": 6505) at hoping for a miracle, the "resurrection" of Erec, that he loses control of himself, showing just how foolish and unseemly he himself can be:

> nû enmohte der grâve mê / im selben meister gesîn, / er entaete sîn untugent schîn: / sîn zorn in verleite / ze grôzer tôrheite / und ûf grôzen ungevuoc. . . . (6515 ff.)

Having earlier warned Enite not to behave inordinately, he himself now behaves in the most immoderate and inordinate way possible by striking her and drawing blood.

The courtiers are appalled by this display of *inordinatio* and reproach him for it, just as Erec's courtiers were shocked by his inordinate *sich verligen,* but the count is undeterred, claiming that a husband has the right to do whatever he wishes with his wife, since she is his property. Nevertheless, although it is undoubtedly true, in terms of Christian ethics, that a husband has a right to expect obedience from his wife (cf. Colossians III.18), it is also true that, in the chivalrous ideology, knights are expected to honor and revere ladies. Oringles is, in fact, committing the same fault as did Erec when he mistreated Enite because she disobeyed him. Although the conduct of both Erec and Oringles may appear ordinate, in the sense that both have a right to expect compliance from their wife, it is in fact not so, because the behavior of the wife concerned, namely Enite, springs from a higher order of *triuwe* than that she would have shown by obeying. The poet continues his play on the opposition of *ordo* and *inordinatio* by showing how Enite demonstrates the ordinate quality of her love for Erec through the *inordinatio* of her behavior under the punishment meted out to her by the count: her *klage* becomes *ungevüege* and she screams loudly, which is "wider dem site" (6567-68), in other words, a perversion of the order of womanly courtly behavior. But in spite of the pain she is suffering, her *passio,* as it were, Enite will not yield to the count's demands, hoping that he will kill her so that her wish to be united with Erec will be fulfilled. This is proof of her *caritas.*

The "awakening from the dead" of Erec, his analogical "resurrection," as I have termed it [in "Sin and Redemption in Hartmann's *Erec,*" *Germanic Review* XXIII (1958)] is yet another example of the poet's fondness for the contrast of order and disorder. The happening is apparently inordinate, in that Erec is presumed dead and awaiting burial; for him to come to life again would appear to be a perversion of the natural order of things, and the reaction of the courtiers is therefore an appropriate one. They think they have seen a ghost and in their panic-stricken flight they completely pervert courtly order. They show no *zuht* whatever (6625). Hierarchical order is turned upside down, laymen going in front of priests and the servant preceding the master (6626 ff.). The *ordo* of knighthood is perverted as they cringe under benches in a most cowardly and undignified way ("wider ritter rehte": 6647). And yet, says Hartmann, their flight is "âne schande" (6666); such normally inordinate behavior is excusable if one sees a ghost. By contrast, the reaction of Enite is the very opposite. She is overjoyed at her husband's appearance. The "miracle" she hoped for has come to pass. She has no desire to flee, but is delighted to see the "dead" man (6682). Her love has completely cast out fear. The ordered *triuwe* she has shown him has been rewarded by this apparently inordinate resurrection of her husband from the dead. She herself is again saved, this time from the count by the "resurrected" Erec, who at last shows his ordered love for her.

When the episode of the journey of Erec and Enite, in which the latter gives such convincing proof of her ordered love for her husband, is seen in all its far-reaching implications, a great deal of light is shed on the *joie de la curt.* Here Erec becomes the "savior" of Mabonagrin and his wife, showing that his love is now ordered in *caritas* after his reconciliation with Enite and the adventures he successfully performs. Mabonagrin promised his young wife that he would remain in the *boumgarten* with her until he was defeated in combat. Because he loves her so much he will not break that promise (9494 ff.). He does not want to be "triuwelôs" (9451). Although he did not realize, when his wife asked him to promise to do anything she wanted, that she would demand anything he would not like to do, his conception of *triuwe* and *staete* is such that he will not refuse her anything at all, and he is convinced that she would do anything he asked of *her* (9497 ff.). For Mabonagrin, an ordinate marriage relationship consists in the union of both partners ("gesellen": 9514), not only in the physical sense ("lîp": 9513), but also in the sense that both want the same thing ("muot": 9515). If there is not this unity and harmony the marriage is inordinate ("ungevuoge": 9518). This is undoubtedly the right and ordinate conception of a Christian marriage, and yet in this case order is being perverted.

The perversion lies in the fact that the situation is the product not of Mabonagrin's will, but of the will of his wife ("wille": 9526), which is inordinate. The husband, not the wife, should decide what is to be done, but Mabonagrin has failed thus to conform to the *ordo* of his manhood. His *triuwe* towards her is therefore inordinate, particularly since what she requires him to do is itself inordinate, namely to stay with her in the garden and neglect his duties to his fellows, to cut himself off from people ("liute": 9448). He himself says to Erec that he has not chosen this life of his own free will, since there is no one who likes to see people more (9445 ff.). His *triuwe* to his wife in keeping his promise is therefore of a lower order than that he would have shown to her and to his fellows if he had broken that promise, fulfilling his ordinate courtly and knightly duties. Like Erec, Mabonagrin has *sich verlegen.* Both he and his wife disorder their love, and what is more, as I have pointed out [in "Sin and Redemption"], they disorder it in a *boumgarten* which his wife calls "daz ander paradîse" (9542), in other words a garden analogous to Eden itself. Both he and his wife are ignorant of the nature of true, ordinate love for God, their fellows and each other, which ignorance is the cause of their "sinful" behavior. Their "unequal" union, in which there is a lack of balance between them, her will dominating his, is not a union in *caritas.* It is therefore fully in keeping with the underlying analogical symbolism that Mabonagrin should have been tempted to sin by a woman, his wife, and that he does not resist that temptation. The analogy with Adam and Eve, where Eve tempted Adam to disobey God and show a lack of *caritas* towards Him, is plain. Mabonagrin's wife makes her husband obey *her* will, not that of God, which would have been to show *caritas* to his fellows, and therefore also to God Himself.

In three different situations, then, the poet makes the telling point that the highest order of love can only be shown by breaking a solemn promise given to another person: Enite's promise to Erec to obey him, her promise to the count to desert Erec and marry him, and Mabonagrin's promise to his wife to stay with her in the garden. The paradox is fully intended: *untriuwe* and *unstaete* (virtually synonymous in the sense of failure to keep one's word) are in fact *triuwe* and *staete* of a higher order than the apparent *triuwe* and *staete* which would have been shown if the promises had been kept. Such is the paradoxical nature of Christian *caritas,* the highest order of love, on which the poet wishes to lay so much stress. Wolfram von Eschenbach is equally fascinated by it, if not more so: Parzival fails to ask the all-important question on his first visit to the Grail castle because he does not realize that he must behave inordinately (i.e., behave with *unzuht,* even *untriuwe,* by asking a question in polite company and so disregarding the advice of Gurnemanz, which his mother had said he must follow) in order to display the highest order of *triuwe,* namely *compassio* and *caritas.* This is what the *Parzival* prologue, with all its bewildering antithetical play on *triuwe* and *untriuwe, Staete* and *unstaete,* is all about.

To summarize: in drawing special attention to the apparent paradox of *triuwe,* which may often be *untriuwe* in terms of another *ordo,* Hartmann wishes to show that the highest order of love, *caritas,* love of God and one's neighbor, knows no measure or order but its own. The measure and order of God's love for man, as shown in the Incarnation, Crucifixion, and Resurrection, His *compassio* for fallen humanity, are without measure, and so also should be the reciprocal love of man for God and his neighbor. This is the message the poet conveys to his audience through the highly meaningful analogical symbolism he employs, gradualistically reconciling the respective orders of the religious and the secular. The message is incomprehensible without reference to the gradualistic concept of *ordo* underlying medieval Christian thought.

It has been the purpose of this article to give as much detailed *textual* evidence as possible to support the thesis that the "secular" narrative of Erec has very close links with the medieval Christian religious background and that the guiding principle behind this is that of *analogia entis.* Through this principle the two separate "orders," the religious and the secular, God and the world, are brought together in an overall unity. Although the one sphere is superior to the other in grade or hierarchy, it is not wholly divorced from it, but linked with it through this very hierarchial gradualism of the *ordo*-concept. In other words, God is infinitely "higher" than the world, but is not cut off from it. His "nearness" to man is a direct result of the *caritas* which emanates from Him. This is why the text of ***Erec*** analyzed above provides so many echoes of Christian truth and why the ordering of love is of such central importance. If the poem is read and understood purely in its "down-to-earth" *literal* sense the major part of the significance it held for its medieval audience is lost to the modern reader. Not only this, but the whole artistic purpose of the poet is misunderstood. It was undoubtedly his intention to impregnate his text with as much analogical reference to Christian truth as his powers of imagination allowed him to do, and he expected his ultimate success or failure as a poet to be dependent on the extent to which he achieved his aim, namely: "mit rede figieren der âventiure meine."

J. M. Clifton-Everest (essay date 1973)

SOURCE: "Christian Allegory in Hartmann's *Iwein,*" in *The Germanic Review,* Vol. XLVIII, No. 4, November, 1973, pp. 247-59.

[*In the following excerpt, Clifton-Everest examines religious didacticism in* Iwein *and insists that Iwein, in pursuing a chivalric ideal, allegorically represents the quest for Christian virtue.*]

In [*The Rise of Romance* (1971)] E. Vinaver speaks of the "common intellectual origin of the interpretative nature of romance on the one hand and of the exegetic tradition on the other." Scriptural exegesis is what he has in mind. He argues that the formal education of the twelfth century romancers involved a great deal of training in biblical exegetic method, since such techniques constituted an important part of the *trivium.* His implication is that the romancers composed their own works with a conception of the narrative literary art profoundly influenced by the exegetic practice of the time, particularly as regards the relationship of story and meaning (*matiere* and *sen*).

In considering Hartmann, a writer of undeniable education, such an insight may be of some service. His ***Iwein*** shows such a diversity of interpretative potential (as is evidenced by the burgeoning secondary literature on the subject) that any contribution to the general problem of "meaning" in such a work can only be most welcome. . . .

A good deal of allegory has been uncovered in ***Iwein,*** and much more apparently awaits only the proper understanding of the clues, which are often immediately recognizable as such, even if their immediate interpretation defies us. In a group of articles H. B. Willson has brought to light a body of religious allegorical meaning. . . . But Willson sets out to analyse the text, or parts thereof, with regard to specific themes, and it remains to establish in how far the points he reveals are part of a consistent and organic allegory. Elsewhere, the traditional view that courtly romance treats the world of secular ethics, or even a special chivalric ethic, has for long somewhat impeded research into the religious content of ***Iwein***. In Germany itself, despite earlier groundwork, only very recently has the idea of a spiritual Christian meaning in the work begun to receive cautious acknowledgement.

In the story of Kalogreant's encounter with the grotesque *waltman* and of his abortive adventure at the magic fountain, Willson shows a plethora of allusion to the Creation of the World and of Man, and to Man's Fall in the Garden of Eden. Comparison with Chretien's *Yvain* at this point reveals that Hartmann gives special emphasis to this religious allegory. Whereas Chretien's *vilain* is herdsman to a collection of "tors sauvages et espaarz," Hartmann's wild man is the master "aller der ticre hande die man mir ie genande" (v. 405f.), and the unquestioned authority he has over them is particularly stressed. This treatment of the passage by Hartmann serves to underline the parallel with *Gen.* I,26: " . . . let them have dominion over the fish of the sea and over the fowl of the air and over the cattle and over all the earth and over every creeping thing that creepeth upon the earth." If the *waltman* is accordingly taken to represent natural, unfallen Man, it is further appropriate to the allegory that he leads directly (i.e. directs Kalogreant) to the magic fountain, where the latter's offence allegorically represents the Fall. At first all Nature protests violently at this introduction of Sin into the paradisiacal world, temporarily marring its perfect beauty (e.g. the birds are silenced), demonstrating its protest in that most violent of natural phenomena, a thunderstorm. In fact Nature seems intent on destroying the cause of Sin, and would have succeeded but for God's mercy towards Man— "wan daz mich der gotes segen vriste von des weters nôt, ich waere der wîle dicke tôt . . ." (v. 654ff). If the offence against Askalon individually is the unethical devastation of his lands, it is significant nevertheless that the primary act is the offence against nature which gives rise to the human offence: for many twelfth-century thinkers the essence of Sin is the action contrary to Nature—such considerations are no more than an indication of the sort of complex and subtle allegory the work may contain, and they cannot unfortunately be followed up here.

The tale of Kalogreant has proved something of a stumbling-block for critics in the past; its only apparent connection with Iwein's story was to provide him with a mixed and rather confused motivation for his own visit to the fountain. But seen in the light of its allegorical significance, Kalogreant's adventure is the essential prehistory to Iwein's, and a vital clue to the meaning of the latter. Moreover, Iwein's mixed motivation now becomes nothing but the literal depiction of the mixed moral nature of Man since the Fall.

I can find no adequate *textual* evidence for the assertion that Iwein's prompt vow to avenge Kalogreant's dishonour is to be seen as morally irresponsible, an assertion that seems to spring from the wish to find a sufficient literal wrong of Iwein's to justify his own later dishonour. Hartmann gives no hint of disapproval, and even Keii, past master at spotlighting others' weaknesses, does not question the desirability of revenge, but only Iwein's capacity to carry it out. To avenge dishonour is expected of a knight. For the allegory it is essential above all to consider the implications of Iwein's being victorious in his effort. We may see in his desire to revenge the Fall the innate desire of Man to overcome the fact of his sinfulness and to live a good life: the *Will* itself to overcome Sin is already a partial victory, for man is not totally given over to sinfulness while he essays to do good. The wish to be virtuous is moreover not dependent on the Christian religion (which, allegorically speaking, Iwein does not yet have), a fact the Middle Ages could see demonstrated in the classical world; Iwein's victory corresponds in this sense to the moral philosophies of classical writers that were held up as worthy examples in the twelfth century. Yet the limitations of these pagan writers in Christian eyes is also significant. Iwein, instead of going to Askalon with a formal challenge to fight after the customary forty days, as would be the proper and obvious thing to do, in fact undertakes precisely the same devastating adventure as his predecessor, thereby incurring guilt himself. A procedure that is so inappropriate from a realistic point of view may easily be explained allegorically. In the very act of attempting to overcome Sin, Man inevitably commits it, for it is intrinsic to his nature. Accordingly, in his adventure at the fountain, Iwein demonstrates the problematic moral quality of Man, a combination of the wish to do good and the inability to escape from Sin. Admittedly, we should in addition note his heeding of Keii's taunts, his desire for public approval; this association of Sin with the *vanitas mundi* is a favourite theme of Hartmann (cf. his two legends).

The true prize of Iwein's victory seems at first to be Laudine, the reward of his goodness in endeavouring to be virtuous. The argument advanced for giving him this prize is that he is the only person available for, and capable of, defending the fountain (v. 1889ff.), the only force existing to fight sinfulness. Of course Iwein has largely failed in this duty, but his own sin is temporarily overridden for practical reasons. There is no alternative to Man as master of God's creation.

But since Iwein is imperfect, and cannot truly deserve the ultimate prize of goodness, we need not wonder at the mere "technischer Defekt" which sets off the enormity of his downfall [Willson, "Inordinatio in the Marriage of the hero in Hartmann's *Iwein,*" *Modern Philology,* 68 (1971)], for it is enough to show to Laudine his imperfection, and that is sufficient to bar him from her. The denunciation by Lunete is in some sense his own personal Fall, when he is brought to realize his own sinfulness and its vast consequences. The nature of the Fall is precisely this awakening to knowledge of Good and Evil acquired from eating the fruit. In the same way the awareness of Good, and of the supreme position that was to have been Man's in the creation is a crucial part of the tragedy of human sin; Man must have some inkling of God if he is ever to aspire to return to him. Hence, perhaps, the necessity for Iwein's prior "winning" of Laudine. But, for the present, he is seemingly forever cut off by his imperfection from everything that matters to him, a loss that is by definition without an equal.

Along with his other deprivations, Iwein loses his God-given reason, rushing senseless into the forest, though even here God's kindness is extended to him (v. 3261ff.). This state of affairs, which I shall discuss later, is concluded with the cure effected by the Dame von Narison, an episode for which Willson points out the striking parallel to the anointment of Christ by Mary, sister of Martha. But I believe this to be more than simply an example of *caritas* or an indication of Christlike characteristics in Iwein. The name Christ, "anointed one" carries its meaning over into the sacrament by which man becomes a "member of Christ": anointment with water (baptism) admits one to Christianity, and gives thereby the chance of ultimate redemption. It is this "baptism," this Christian chance that Iwein here receives.

However, more is necessary for Christian salvation than the mere opportunity that baptism represents: one must also pursue the Christian life of goodness and justice, following Christ's example of humility and charity. It is from this point of view that Iwein's subsequent anonymity and selflessness in his ensuing adventures must be judged. First he rescues his own rescuer, the Dame von Narison, from her aggressor. But this is no act of charity, though doubtless his Christian duty required it of him. He has not yet *voluntarily* chosen the Christian way of life. This act of will he performs in the episode of the lion.

The most obvious explanation of the lion-adventure has been particularly slow to find acceptance: T. Cramer still argues strangely that, since the serpent clearly stands for the devil, the lion principally stands for *Recht*. But, as A. T. Hatto points out, the usual antagonist of the devil is Christ himself, who is commonly represented by a lion in the medieval bestiaries in a tradition going back to the *Physiologus*. M. Wehrli, at last, sees the lion "unter anderm als Christussymbol" ["Iweins Erwachen," *Formen mittelalterlicher Erzählung: Aufsätze* (1969)], whereby it might be incidentally pointed out that the other equivalents he mentions (*triuwe, recht*) can comfortably be fitted into an organic allegory as important aspects of the figure of Christ. The occurrence of this adventure in ***Iwein*** is not unique in arthurian literature. In the French *Quest del sainte Graal,* composed some forty years after ***Iwein,*** it is the virtuous Grail-knight Perceval who, espying a serpent and a lion in fight, hastens to aid the latter as being "of a nobler order than the serpent" (cf. ***Iwein,*** v. 3849). In the subsequent exegesis, on which the French writer seems throughout more intent than the story, it is explained to Perceval that he has espoused the cause of Christ against his enemies. Surely Iwein is doing just that: all the unselfish acts he subsequently performs are but the continuing results of this decision to fight evil with the usual moral weapons of Christianity, and the lion accordingly assists him "zaller sîner nôt, unz si beide schiet der tôt" (v. 3881f.), just as Christ does help those all their life who serve his cause.

This allegorical role of the lion is thereafter maintained with convincing consistency. Returning by chance to the magic spring, Iwein is overcome with grief and remorse at the memory of his sin, such that he *falls* swooning to the ground. The lion, believing him dead, prepares to commit suicide out of sheer *herzeleide* (v. 4004), but Iwein revives just in time to prevent this and to take example from the lion's selfless pity. The compassion of the lion at the "Fallen" state of Man (Iwein's guilt being the cause of his grief) and its readiness to sacrifice itself for him, represents quite clearly Christ's ready sacrifice on the cross for the sins of men. The self-sacrifice of Christ should inspire men to take on themselves the consequences of their sinfulness by attempting to make amends: this is precisely what the lion's act prompts Iwein to do:

> sit ich mirz selbe hân getân,
> ich solts ouch selbe buoze enpfân
> (nû gît mir doch des bilde
> dirre lewe wilde,
> daz er von herzeleide sich
> wolde erstechen umbe mich,
> daz rehtiu triuwe nâhen gât);
> sît mir mîn sclbes missetât,
> mîner vrouwen hulde
> unde dehein ir schulde,
> ân aller slahte nôt verlôs,
> und weinen vür daz lachen kôs
>
> (v. 3999ff.)

He is then accordingly at once granted the chance to recognize and offset some of his guilt, namely its adverse effect on others, by his defence of Lunete. Tellingly, the lion is at first forbidden to participate in the fight: Iwein must first show himself fully prepared to take on alone the consequences of his guilt. But when he has shown this, and is hard-pressed, the lion nevertheless rushes to the rescue: Man must show the Will, but can achieve nothing without God's help.

In all his other battles too, with the exception of the last fight with Gawein, he is dependent on the lion for his success. Fighting with Harpin, the lion brings him immediate victory because of the goodness of his cause. At the castle of the three-hundred maidens, the lion is initially once more forbidden to join the battle with the two *tiufelsknehte,* but gnaws a way out of its prison to help him in his just cause: however powerful the forces of Evil, God finds a way of helping their adversaries. In his battle with Gawein we may ascribe Iwein's lack of *military* victory precisely to the absence of the lion. But what matters here is not that sort of victory, but rather that Iwein should publicly identify himself as the knight with justice on his side. His is a moral victory, for all the onlookers agree he was fighting for a righteous cause.

At the same time he is at last publicly identified as the *riter mittem leun,* whose identity had hitherto been a mystery at Arthur's court. This brings us to the theme of humility, a Christian virtue no less important than charity, the emphasis on which has perhaps caused the other some neglect in considerations of this work. After discovering his sinfulness, Iwein must rid himself of the identity of the old, proud Iwein who was so anxious to see his victory acclaimed, and find a new one: he must cast off the Old Adam and put on the New Christ. The initial stage of this change is represented by his madness, when his total ignorance of who he is shows the complete lack of identity consequent on the loss of the old sinful one. With the coming of his Christianity in the cure episode, the new, good Christian identity is born and requires only to be developed and proven. After his departure from the Dame von Narison, he reveals his old identity to nobody (with the necessary exception of Lunete) until he has publicly demonstrated his virtuousness at Arthur's court. But in constructing a new identity and reputation as "der riter der des lewen pflac" he is only establishing himself as the "knight for Christ." Although in such an allegorical form charity and humility are not altogether separable, we should not lose sight of the humility entailed in this *incognito,* beside its obvious selflessness. The renunciation of any personal glory that may accrue to him through his deeds plainly relates to his earlier desire for public recognition of his achievement.

That he appears reluctant to fight with the two giants at the castle of the three-hundred maidens is surely a further display of selfless humility: the adventure is presented to him by the *wirt* as a chance to win a beautiful wife and lands—apart from his early ready promise to help the maidens, we only see his reaction to the adventure through his replies to the *wirt*—but he declines to fight on such terms, and only eventually agrees because he is given no alternative. When victorious, he still refuses the prize even in the face of threats, insisting that the only reward be the benefit of others, i.e. the freeing of the maidens. This sort of Christian altruism is now the essence of his chivalry. He is not even aware of being kind, only of the duty of selflessness: hence his reply to the request for *gnade* in the cause of the daughter of the Graf vom swarzen dorne:

> er sprach "ichn habe gnâden niht:
> swem mîns dienstes nôt geschiht
> und swer guoter des gert,
> dern wirt es niemer entwert."
>
> (v. 6001ff.)

But the most allegorical indication of this adoption of a new object for his chivalry lies in another passage that has been sadly neglected. In the battle to exonerate Lunete the lion is severely wounded and is soon incapable of walking. Iwein prepares a bed of moss in his shield and carries the lion to where it is restored. To read the allegory we need only reverse the shield: Christ's cause in the world is wounded and suffering, and so, in order to show that he has dedicated himself to its defence and cure, Iwein bears its emblem on his shield, just as the crusading knights bore the Cross on theirs, in token of their dedication to the Holy War. Literally the lion is carried inside the shield; allegorically it is "auf dem Schild getragen" in the manner normally understood. Such a chivalric emblem naturally gives further weight to the completely new identity of Iwein as the *Knight of the Lion,* for the fully-armed knight is only identifiable by the emblem he carries.

Enough has been said to establish a *prima facie* case, at the very least, for treating Iwein's career as a piece of allegory, though of course many of the problems involved cannot even be mentioned here. Other large sections of the work remain as yet unexplained, though it is often possible to see a suitable position for them in the overall allegory. I shall conclude with a brief look at three such fields—the figure of Laudine, the arthurian court, and the idea of chivalry itself.

As has already been suggested, Laudine, as the exclusive conscious personal objective of Iwein's quest throughout his later career, appears to represent the supreme reward of human endeavour. This must be a religious symbol of course, though only a full allegorical interpretation of her role could possibly establish whether one may understand by it anything so precise as the Grace of God, or Eternal Life. It is surely relevant to this that on both occasions Iwein gains access to her *hulde* through the intercession of a virgin, and that his final reinstatement involves an act of forgiveness on her part. He describes this forgiveness as "mîner vreuden ôstertac" (v. 8120), the allusion to victory over Death strongly suggesting the notion of eternal life.

But most interesting for Hartmann's allegorical style, and at first most disconcerting, is the fact that Laudine is criticised most explicitly by the poet. How can this be reconciled with her use as a symbol of divine reward? The answer may lie in a clear distinction between literal and allegorical meaning: she is criticised purely as a real woman, which does not necessarily give grounds for inferring criticism of her allegorical acts. She is declared to be irrational (v. 1863ff.), and it is implied that her marriage to Iwein is impetuous, both of which qualities are commonplace criticisms of female nature in medieval literature. In fact her treatment is very similar to that of the maiden in ***Der arme Heinrich,*** whose readiness to undergo self-sacrifice for her lord, giving him the salutory example of selflessness is symbolic of Christ's crucifixion, while her realistic feminine ire at the frustration of her plan is plainly the object of Hartmann's moral censure, as is perhaps also her impetuous eagerness to escape the proper rigours of human life. Certainly the didactic content of ***Iwein*** is not restricted to allegory, but may be found, where appropriate, throughout, in the poet's comments on literal events, just as the *sensus historicus* of biblical texts is not necessarily purely narrative, but also includes direct theological and moral statement.

The problems of Arthur's court and the chivalric ideal are

Gottfried von Strassburg's praise of Hartmann in *Tristan* (c. 1210):

Hartmann von Aue, ah how he colors and adorns his tales through and through—both without and within—with words and with meaning! How he pinpoints exactly the meaning of the adventure of his speech! How clear and how pure are his crystalline words—and they will always remain so! They approach one decorously and are pleasing to one who has the proper spirit. Whoever is capable of comprehending good language well and correctly, that one must grant the man from Aue his garland and laurels.

Gottfried von Strassburg, in his Tristan *(c. 1210), quoted and translated by Francis G. Gentry, in "Hartmann von Aue's* Erec: *The Burden of Kingship,"* King Arthur through the Ages, *edited by Valerie M. Lagorio and Mildred Leake Day, Garland Publishing, Inc., 1990.*

plainly closely related. In the allegory I have outlined, the chivalric life appears to represent the human quest for a virtuous life. Kalogreant's unsatisfactory description of the pointless aims of *aventiure* to the *waltman,* revealing his inadequate conception of knighthood, is to be associated with his following disgrace, which takes the form of a defeat in chivalric combat. In contrast to such faulty chivalry, Iwein has a worthy objective in his knightly adventure, so that his victory is at first a quite proper one (vv. 1045-1050), though when he then pursues the mortally wounded Askalon for selfish reasons, it is condemned as unchivalric—*âne zuht.*

After his denunciation, Iwein loses his knighthood, discarding all its trappings to become a mere animal (v. 3234ff.). Since his Fall is allegedly irrevocable, there is no longer any purpose for him in rational existence, any moral effort would be pointless. So he becomes blind to morality (ern ahte weder man noch wîp, v. 3225), a subhuman creature of pure instinct (cf. v. 3320ff.), until the bestowal of Christianity gives him a new chance of moral orientation. He dies, to "be born again in Christ," and immediately on his recovery he is aware once more of his chivalric calling (v. 3517f.).

The episode of the lion borne on the shield, and indeed the whole of Iwein's series of adventures plainly supports this view of the allegorical significance of knighthood; the compassion and selflessness required of Iwein in the adventures of his knight-errantry are typical for the virtues required generally of Christian men.

From this position it would seem appropriate to see in the arthurian court the allegory of human society on earth, striving for virtue in its pursuit of chivalric ideals. Society has its sinful temptations, such as to worldy vanity, demonstrated in the successful insinuations of Keii, and it is most significant for the type of Hartmann's religious-moral thought that, to achieve true moral success, one must part company with worldly society. Parallel to the sojourn of Gregorious on the rock, and to the withdrawal of Heinrich to the forest-farm, Iwein's moral fulfillment takes place in a life of studied anonymity, and, but for his symbolic lion, of solitariness, remote from the pleasures of Arthur's court. His failure and his consequent dehumanization drive him from this worldly society which seeks good, but in a lonely moral struggle for something higher, he incidentally regains a place there. That he deserves; but Laudine's favour he can never deserve, for Man is inescapably sinful, though it can be, and is, granted by forgiveness.

In view of this apparent allegorical use of the world of chivalry and its ideals, we should perhaps give more qualification to bald statements that ***Iwein*** is a "worldly" poem, and consider carefully the justification of treating its moral lessons as relating to the ethics of chivalry. K. Ruh's question as to why Hartmann returned to courtly romance after apparently turning away from it to the world of religious legend, which in his view "muâ weiterhin offenbleiben" is surely answered in part at least by assuming primacy for the author in the religious content of ***Iwein*** ["Zur Interpretation von Hartmanns Iwein," *Philologia Deutsch: Festschrift W. Henzen* (1965)]. However sceptical one may feel towards specific points in an allegorical interpretation of the work, or however personally reluctant one may be to see the delightful fantasy of the work as principally a story of human sin and redemption, it can hardly be denied that there is little, if any, moral didacticism in it which applies in any other than a universal human way. The selflessness and compassion which Iwein learns to show are also a part of the lesson of ***Der arme Heinrich:*** only the unrealistic literal form of his adventures (e.g. combatting preposterous giants) is specifically knightly.

But just as Iwein's career brings success and recognition in the dual worlds of Ladine and Arthur, a reconciliation of the divine and the secular so dear to twelfth century hearts, so Hartmann has effected a reconciliation in literature, using the temporal delights of chivalric romance in all its popularity, as sugar for a religious didactic pill apparently no less deeply felt and urged than were his two legends. Presumably he felt he might achieve more by using the form his audience preferred, and the popularity of ***Iwein*** in the Middle Ages testifies that he did not miscalculate in one respect.

D. H. Green (essay date 1974)

SOURCE: "Hartmann's Ironic Praise of Erec," in *The Modern Language Review,* Vol. 70, No. 4, October, 1974, pp. 795-807.

[*The Schroeder Professor of German at Cambridge University, Green has written several books and articles on medieval German literature, including* Irony in the Medieval Romance *(1979) and* The Art of Recognition in Wolfram's "Parzival" *(1982). In the following excerpt, Green suggests that irony in the narrator's comments renders* Erec *a criticism of the courtly ideal.*]

The merest suggestion of irony in connexion with Hartmann von Aue is likely to invoke immediate rejection on the grounds that he, of all poets of the courtly period, was so idealizing in his style and so serious in his didacticism that to seek for any reservations of criticism in his attitude is mistaken in principle. If anywhere in his work, we may hope to find critical reservations in his legends where . . . doubts about the absolute claims of the courtly ideal have a justified place and may therefore involve the use of irony. My purpose will be to suggest that such irony occurs not merely in the two legends, but also in the romances, more especially in ***Erec*** where at one point, under the guise of what appears to be superlative praise, Hartmann is in fact subtly insinuating criticism of his hero.

The technique of suggesting blame at the moment of praise is certainly no stranger to the poet's two legends. In ***Der arme Heinrich,*** for example, the prologue (verses 1-28) leads over to a *laudatio* of the hero (29-81) which, for all its length and pile-up of superlatives, is swiftly undermined by the mention of Heinrich's *Hôchmuot* (82 f.), by the uncomplimentary comparison with Absalom (84-90) and the ascetic reminder that *media vita in morte sumus* (91-6). Of the nature of this *laudatio* there can be little doubt, for the positive qualities which the poet bestows so generously on Heinrich are precisely the virtues which any knight with secular responsibilities might be hoped to possess. In a first approach we are told of his noble birth and riches, of his equality with princes and of his *êren,* but these qualities are then specified in greater detail: he has forsworn all dishonesty and boorishness, his worldly honours are unsurpassed, he possesses the gift of youth and of bringing joy to all, he is a model of loyalty and good breeding, a refuge for those in need and a protection for his kinsmen, generous, honourable and helpful, skilled in love poetry, deservedly renowned, courtly, and wise. Some of these qualities may be reconcilable with Christian virtues (honesty, loyalty, generosity, and helpfulness), whilst others are, within the context of a legend, either neutral (youthfulness, a source of joy) or even downright suspect (worldly honours, love poetry, courtliness). This spread of qualities suggests clearly enough that the *laudatio* is conceived in secular, courtly terms, so that when the blow falls and Heinrich is cast from *werltlîcher wünne* (79) and humbled, this divine intervention (compare verses 116 and 120) strikes down a man who is none other than a model of all that the courtly world held dear. This is not to say that Hartmann ascetically rejects all courtly values as necessarily flawed, but rather that, as he later makes clear (1430 ff.), these values are no secular absolutes but must be seen as gifts of God. This is not expressly stated in the *laudatio,* and it is this unvoiced criticism, lurking behind the surface brilliance of his many virtues, which is more relevant to the position in which Heinrich finds himself. His virtues really are virtues and the panegyric is literally true, but much more important is the devastating, but unspoken criticism which this passage conceals. Only retrospectively are we allowed to suspect that the reference to worldly honours (57) and worldly pleasure (79) may not be such unqualified goods in the Christian legend as they are in the courtly romance.

A similar undermining of apparent praise also occurs in Hartmann's other legend, although he uses this technique differently in his ***Gregorius*** by repeating it on several occasions. The brother and sister who later become the hero's incestuous parents are sketched in positive terms in their affection for one another and in the joy they share (296: *man enmac in anders niht gejehen, / er enphlæge ir alsô wol / als ein getriuwer bruoder sol / sîner lieben swester. / noch was diu liebe vester / die si im dâ wider truoc. / wünne heten sî genuoc*). Here again this *laudatio* (however brief) is placed at a very critical point, since it is immediately followed by the temptation scene so that we are shown the short-lived vanity of this idyll just as effectively when the devil intervenes in this case to bring about their fall (303 ff.) as when God strikes Heinrich with the punishment of leprosy. Even more telling than this clash between idyll and fall is the manner in which Hartmann forewarns us of what is to happen. With Heinrich it was the easily overlooked adjective *werltlîch,* but in this case it is the passage introducing the *laudatio* which hints to us how we are to read what follows. We are told that brother and sister were close in all things and rarely apart (the narrator even gives his approval to this, 291: *daz gezam vil wol in beiden*); but then is added *si wâren ungescheiden / ze tische und ouch anderswâ* (292 f.). The unspecific *anderswâ* is then suspiciously restricted in the next sentence (294: *ir bette stuonden alsô nâ . . .*) and, alerted now to what may be at stake, we recognize that the phrase *ze tische und ouch anderswâ* indirectly refers to the legal double formula 'bed and board'. The ironic force of *anderswâ* must therefore colour our reading of the apparently innocuous love between brother and sister, so that this supposedly laudatory passage is by now preparing us for the catastrophe soon to come.

A more prolonged eulogy is given when Gregorius is described in the perfection of his youth (1235-84). He has been formed by *vrouwe Sælecheit* herself and is accordingly handsome and strong, loyal, kind and patient, skilled and well-bred, not given to anger, but adept in making and keeping friends, moderate, willing to learn and generous, bold and cautious as the occasion demanded, experienced beyond his years and far from rash, and never needing to be ashamed of his behaviour. Lest this seem too good to be true (as in the case of Heinrich), the poet then expressly adds that Gregorius never lost sight of God (1260: *er suochte gnâde unde rât / zallen zîten an got / und behielt starke sîn gebot*) and that Perfection itself (*der Wunsch*) fashioned him with God's approval. Yet despite this string of superlatives we are given a glimpse that all is not as it seems to be, when the narrator shows us Gregorius as those around him at this stage see him, since, as with the young Tristan when he first comes unknown to Marke's court, people find it difficult to believe that one so perfect should be the son of the fisherman who has brought him up (1273-7) and regard it as a pity that he should not be of noble birth (1278: *ez wære harte schedelîch / daz man in niht mähte / geprîsen von geslâhte*). With that they have of course unwittingly hit upon the truth, so that through their eyes we have been shown that there are dimensions to this description that elude us, as they do Gregorius himself since, when he learns the facts of his birth, he feels completely alienated from his former self (1403: *ich enbin niht der ich wânde sîn*). This suggestion that he has lost his bearings has wider implications, however, since it introduces the scene in which Gregorius decides to seek knightly adventures, a decision which takes him, in disastrous ignorance of himself, to incest with his mother. This is the narrative reality so soon to be disclosed after this extensive *laudatio*—again, none of these admirable qualities protects him from what providence has in store for him and his virtues are simply irrelevant to this testing, but the slight element of doubt in this eulogy prepares us for what is to come.

Hartmann employs the same method (praise on the brink of disaster) as the catastrophe draws closer. When Gregorius's quest for adventure leads him to the conventional situation where he offers his services to a besieged lady, this typical motif of the romance is called into question by the fact that the lady is his mother. We are informed of this in advance (1935 ff.), so that the lines in which the growth of their mutual attraction is sketched are undermined for us in a way not true of the normal romance (1955: *nû behagete im diu vrouwe wol / als einem manne ein wîp sol / an der nihtes gebrast: / ouch behagete ir der gast / baz danne ie man getæte*). The laudatory words *sol* and *baz danne ie* suggest that events are following the usual ideal course, whereas we know that this is far from being so, that the Devil is again at work (1960-62) and that Gregorius's praiseworthy striving for chivalric renown (1967 f.) is mocked by the situation in which he finds himself, naïvely believing that God has simply conducted him to an opportunity to prove his chivalric worth (1868: *sô bin ich rehte komen. / daz ist des ich got ie bat / daz er mich bræhte an die stat / dâ ich ze tuonne vunde* . . .). Similarly, when mother and son marry, their happiness is first conventionally summed up in hyperbolic terms (2251: *ez enwart nie wünne merre / dan diu vrouwe und der herre / mit ein ander hâten, / wande si wâren berâten / mit liebe in grôzen triuwen*), but then destroyed in a one-line narrator's forecast (2256: *seht, daz ergie mit riuwen*), just as Gregorius's ideal qualities as a ruler, the gifts of justice and liberality (2257: *er was guot rihtære, / von sîner milte mære. / swaz einem manne mac gegeben / ze der werlde ein wünneclîchez leben, / des hâte er gar des wunsches wal*) are similarly undercut (2262: *daz nam einen gæhen val*) in terms that recall Heinrich's fall from courtly grace.

Repeatedly Hartmann has made use of this ironic technique, praising perfection on the brink of disaster, in both his legends, implying thereby that courtly qualities, however praiseworthy in their own limited sphere, are no absolute values and have no bearing on the testing which the hero of a Christian legend has to undergo. This point has been briefly made in [U. Pörksen's *Der Erzähler im mittelhochdeutschen Epos: Former seines Hervortretens bei Lamprecht, Konrad, Hartmann, in Wolframs Willehalm und in den 'Spielmannsepen'* (1971)], whose author has however made the further comment that this procedure is not employed by Hartmann in his Arthurian romances. I do not believe this judgement to be correct and wish to look more closely at a passage where Erec, victorious at his wedding tournament before he returns in triumph to Karnant, is also praised in superlative terms:

> Êrec der tugenthafte man
> wart ze vollem lobe gesaget.
> den prîs hete er dâ bejaget,
> und den sô volleclîchen
> daz man begunde gelîchen
> sîn wîsheit Salomône,
> sîn schœne Absolône.
> an sterke Samsônes genôz.
> sîn milte dûhte si sô grôz,
> diu gemâzete in niemen ander
> wan dem milten Alexander.

Pörksen has seen in this an example of straightforward praise—having nothing in common with the ironic praise of the legends—and others have agreed with him on this. Erec's achievement is here related to an ideal model not just once, but four times in quick succession. Is this meant as emphatic praise, fit for this climax at the end of the first part of the work, or are we meant to feel that the narrator may be protesting a little too much? Are we to take this praise as the narrator's opinion, or are we to detect his distance from what persons in the narrative think about Erec (*man begunde gelîchen* or *sîn milte dûhte si sô grôz*)? In short, are we to read these lines literally or ironically?

A first point to make concerns the division of Hartmann's narrative into two structurally similar parts (conflict, adventure[s], return to Arthur's court), for this has important ironic implications for the first part: the subsequent course of events (the crisis at Karnant) shows that Erec's 'crowning success' at the close of the first part was only superficial, provisional, incapable of meeting the demands made on it. If Erec's success were as complete as it seems to be at this stage, then his *verligen* would have been impossible and there would have been no subsequent narrative. The very existence of a second part must therefore lead us to view the appearance of success in the first part with some reservations. This also has a wider literary implication, since the first part is constructed essentially on the pattern of a fairytale (a young hero of noble birth challenges an opponent whom nobody has defeated before, gains victory and the hand of a poor, but noble maiden), so that the climax of this part (Enite is acknowledged as the most beautiful and Erec as the bravest at Arthur's court, both marry and 'live happily ever after') seems to be the conventional ending of a fairytale. But it is here that Hartmann disappoints our expectations (and ironizes the happy ending of the fairytale), since this marriage, far from being the happy conclusion of the narrative, leads quickly to a crisis and jeopardizes all that has gone before. The climax of this first part is therefore a false climax, any praise of Erec at this point is shown by subsequent events to be ironic praise, either untrue or irrelevantly true. Several considerations lead to the conclusion that the latter is the case here: Erec is indeed all that is said of him, but what is said is incomplete and conceals another truth about his position.

In the first place, we can be sure that Hartmann is ready to bestow ironic praise on his hero in the context of Karnant, for he does this three times in quick succession, thereby drawing attention to his procedure. After he has just mentioned Erec's neglect of chivalry because of his marriage, he hastens to add that he nonetheless generously provided his followers with the means to attend tournaments themselves (2954: *dô Erec fil de roi Lac / ritterschefte sich bewac, / der tugende er dannoch wielt, / dâ er sich schône an behielt, / swie er deheinen turnei suochte, / daz er doch beruochte / sîne gesellen alle gelîche / daz si vil vollecîche / von in selben mohten varn. / er hiez si alsô wol bewarn / als ob er selbe mit in rite. / ich lobe an im den selben site*). There is something forced about this eulogy, as if Hartmann had found it difficult to find a positive point to make, since the context into which this praise of a detail is inserted is hardly flattering to Erec: his behaviour cost him his *êre* (2969 f.) and he brought disgrace on his court (2989 f.), a judgement which is confirmed by those who had once praised, but now blame him (2985-8) and which is expressed in deeds as his vassals, heedless of his liberality in equipping them for tournaments but not taking part himself, desert his court (2977-9). We are to judge this scene in the same way as they do and recognize that Erec's generosity towards them is much less significant than his own inactivity. To praise him over a trivial detail merely highlights the more important point where he certainly merits no approval. That this praise is meant ironically is confirmed by the recurrence of ironic praise in the immediately following passage describing his followers' reaction to Erec's *verligen* (2974: *des begunde mit rehte / ritter unde knehte / dâ ze hove betrâgen*). The words *mit rehte* tell us that these followers' reaction has the narrator's approval (we are therefore justified in seeing this episode in the same light as they), but also that praise of these knights amounts to criticism of the lord whose behaviour scandalizes them, just as praise of Erec's generosity drew attention to his failure to set them a chivalric example. Finally, soon after this, Hartmann sums up the judgement of the court on Erec's downfall (2980: *wan ez enhâte wîp noch man / deheinen zwîvel dar an, / er enmüeste sîn verdorben: / den lop hete er erworben*). The use of *lop* here to describe a negative reputation (*verdorben,* cf. *schande* in v. 2990) is clearly ironic, but no more so than to praise Erec for a minor virtue whilst withholding any condemnation for a major offence. Three such cases of ironic praise in short compass are a clear indication that the Karnant episode has ironic implications in the poet's eyes and suggest the possibility that he may have prepared the way for this by similarly praising Erec instead of blaming him just before the crisis of Erec's *verligen.* The passage with which we are concerned comes barely 100 lines before this *verligen*—does it likewise convey blame under the appearance of praise?

We can approach this problem first through the figure of Absalom . . . For the Middle Ages he was a conventional prototype of human, especially masculine beauty (compare II Samuel 14. 25) and it is this which Hartmann has in mind in comparing Erec with him in respect of *schœne.* But this positive aspect is only part of the picture, since the biblical figure is himself complex: Absalom was beautiful, but he also killed his half-brother (II Samuel 13. 1 ff.) and rebelled against his father, David (II Samuel 15. 1 ff.), so that he could come to be regarded as a typical rebel. This figure was therefore a Janus-like *topos* and could be fittingly employed in ambiguous situations whenever an author wished to suggest negative features behind positive ones or to indicate that certain virtues are irrelevant if they are not backed up by other qualities. This is precisely what Hartmann does in the case of Absalom in ***Der arme Heinrich,*** where he praises the hero's virtues at the opening, just as he praises Erec's at the close of the first part of the romance. But just when he reaches his climax (80: *er was vür al sîn künne / geprîset unde gêret*), Hartmann mentions the *hôchmout* which led to his fall and compares him with Absalom (84: *an im wart erzeiget, / als ouch an Absalône, / daz diu üppige krône / werltlîcher süeze / vellet under vüeze / abe ir besten werdekeit*). It is because this eulogy of Heinrich concealed the pride which led to his fall that he can be compared with Absalom. If we apply this Janus-reading to the eulogy of Erec, this does not mean that Erec must be guilty of the same sin as Heinrich and Absalom, but rather that Absalom is a figure of human achievement on the brink of disaster. This is confirmed by the similar situations in which Heinrich and Erec are depicted. Heinrich is praised at length (50-81), he is compared with Absalom (85), he is struck by the disaster of leprosy (112 ff.), whilst Erec is praised in terms which include a comparison with Absalom (2811-21), but this comes immediately before his fall, the *verligen* at Karnant (2924 ff.). The conventional figure of Absalom serves therefore as a warning that Erec's positive features have their ambiguous implications too, for they protect him against a fall as little as Absalom's beauty shielded him. The comparison with Absalom suggests that Hartmann is about to turn the coin and show us the reverse side of Erec's apparent success.

There is a parallel to this use of ironic ambiguity in the English romance, *Sir Gawain and the Green Knight.* At an early stage of the narrative the poet describes Gawain's heraldic device, the pentangle, and its allegorical significance: it symbolizes the hero's chivalric ideal (*trawpe*), a meaning which the poet advances on the authority of Solomon himself (625 f.). But Solomon is drawn into the story as an exemplar on a second occasion at the conclusion when Gawain, convinced of his moral failure (brought about by the wiles of the lady of the castle), attacks womankind at large and lists Solomon as a traditional example of a man brought low by women (2414 ff.). It is noteworthy that Solomon, who had previously acted as the patron of the pentangle, the emblem of Gawain's perfect loyalty, should reappear here, after the hero's failure, as an example of the imperfection of fallen man. In this respect the English romance and Hartmann's ***Erec*** have much in common. The English poet compares Gawain with Solomon with regard to their common quality of loyalty, but belatedly we realize that the comparison goes further than we had suspected, that both are also victims of the wiles of women. Hartmann compares Erec with Absalom with regard to beauty, but Erec is also in the same situation as Absalom, he is on the brink of declining from his apparently perfect peak of success. Both poets use irony to suggest more than is immediately apparent to us, they entice us into a state of false security—which we share with the hero.

The parallel with *Sir Gawain* has suggested that Solomon, like Absalom, could also be regarded as an ambiguous exemplar in the Middle Ages, as a prototype of good and evil. Yet Hartmann also compares Erec with Solomon and other figures, so that it is necessary to look at these further prototypes and consider their implications for Erec's situation. All four are conventional prototypes in medieval literature and they can also be frequently mentioned together. Commonly, the three biblical examples occur together as prototypes of respective qualities and although this group is the basic medieval pattern, examples are not restricted to three figures (we also find two or four, as with Hartmann) or to biblical figures only (they can be replaced by classical counterparts). Or we find a mixture of biblical with classical figures, as with Hartmann. In other words, Hartmann's comparison is quite conventional within medieval literature, but what we have to ask is whether he is employing this topos conventionally or devoting it to ironical purposes (as in his parody of the fairytale convention at the close of the first part).

To be convinced of the presence of irony we need to be shown a common feature, shared by Solomon, Absalom, Samson, Alexander, and also by Erec, exposing them all to Hartmann's criticism, even at the moment when he appears to be praising the first four for their separate qualities (wisdom, beauty, strength, generosity) and Erec for possessing all these attributes together. We find this clue in the reference to the negative example of Solomon in *Sir Gawain,* for Solomon, despite his wisdom, fell victim to his concubines and committed the sin of idolatry (I Kings 11. 1 ff.). Yet this is true also of Absalom, whose beauty made him fit to be a victim of the omnipotence of love and who therefore belongs to the 'slaves of love' so frequently invoked in medieval literature. Samson, as the victim of Delilah, also fittingly belongs here—he is a favourite example with the Church fathers and with all secular poets who wish to moralize on the power of love, especially useful as a warning to warriors and therefore relevant to Erec's neglect of his chivalry. Finally, Alexander is included here because of his experience with Candace, his dalliance with her can be compared with Samson's with Delilah, or his fate as a victim of women can be compared with Absalom's. Similarly, Samson and Solomon can be compared because of their identical weakness in the same kind of situation. These four figures therefore all share this one feature: they were all enslaved by love and by a woman. Yet this is precisely what Hartmann's narrative, within 100 lines of this eulogy of Erec, is about to depict in the case of Erec, namely his *verligen* at Karnant. In other words, Erec may be wise like Solomon, beautiful like Absalom, strong like Samson, and generous like Alexander, but in addition, and again like them, he is weak before the power of love and his fall will be brought about (unwittingly) by a woman. The force of Hartmann's comparison goes much further than we first suspect and covers a negative feature common to Erec and these positive exemplars. Behind this praise, behind this comparison with such worthy figures there lurks Erec's failure, still invisible to us, but soon to be revealed. This passage prepares the way by its use of irony.

If this is so, then Hartmann must implicitly qualify and relativize this eulogy of Erec's achievement at this turning-point in the narrative, because only by thus undercutting it can he account for Erec's fall from grace. It is the merit of [*Studien Zum Stil von Hartmanns Erec*] by R. Endres to have shown us that the poet accomplishes this with regard to two of the qualities for which Erec is praised at this point (his *wîsheit* and *milte*) by making use of two methods: by prompting us to ask what are the actual exploits which qualify Erec for such praise (so that he insinuates the further question as to whether this praise is indeed justified) and by the contrast between this praise at the close of the first part and the crowning eulogy of the hero at the conclusion of the whole work (if the latter outshines the former, then again we are led to question whether the superlatives used on the earlier occasion are at all apposite, at least at this provisional stage in Erec's career). Hartmann does in fact imply that the early praise of Erec at the wedding tournament is superficial and external—perhaps because his achievement at this point is still only superficial and external, if not in the eyes of the world which lavishes such praise upon him, then at least to the omniscient poet who alone knows of his hero's true potential.

It is in this passage that the quality of *wîsheit* is attributed to Erec for the first time, but the comparison with Solomon is made expressly as a result of the *prîs* which the hero has won for himself (2813: *den prîs hete er dâ bejaget, / und den sô volleclîchen / daz man begunde gelîchen / sîn wîsheit Salomône*). In other words, because he has gained *prîs,* he is praised for his *wîsheit.* But for what reasons has Erec gained *prîs,* what are the occasions when his exploits lead others to praise him? This occurs for the first time when he unhorses five knights in the preliminary skirmish on the eve of the tournament (2452: *vil wol wart er geprîset dâ*); then he gains renown because he is heavily engaged in this skirmish, being the first on the field and the last off (2473: *Êrec den prîs gewan / des âbendes ze beiden sîten;* 2485: *im was des âbendes geschehen / dâ von er prîs bejagete*); when on the following morning Erec quickly disposes of fifteen spears in preliminaries this again brings him renown (2519: . . . *waz Êrecke wære geschehen / zêren und ze prîse;* 2536: *sus machete er im vriunde mê / und stuont ze prîse baz dan ê*); and the same is true when, in the main tournament, he unhorses many knights and drives the opposing side back almost singlehanded (2805: *vil sêre prîste Êrecken daz, / wan er hâtes êre*). In short, it is through his strength, bravery, and knightly skill that Erec gains *prîs,* and his *wîsheit* is therefore praised. But this can only mean that Hartmann is interpreting this *wîsheit* that Erec displays purely by externals ('skill') and heightens the superficiality of this judgement by his purposely inept comparison with Solomon's *wîsheit* (where the word must mean something very different, such as 'wisdom, justice'). By means of what is revealed as an unjustified comparison with Solomon's ideal wisdom Hartmann points up the restricted nature of Erec's *wîsheit*.

This can be confirmed by another consideration. Hartmann praises Erec at the end of the first part (with what I take to be dubious, relativizing praise), but then again at the close of the romance when Erec gains his final, lasting success, where such qualifications are no longer relevant. Whereas at the end of the first part Erec's *wîsheit* was restricted to one line only (2816) and was displayed in externals, at the close of the whole work it is described over fully thirteen lines (from 10085, *er tete sam die wîsen tuont,* down to 10097) and is specifically seen at its profoundest level as consisting in the right relationship between Erec and God (10086: *die des gote genâde sagent / swaz si êren bejagent / und ez von im wellent hân*). If *wîsheit* therefore attains its full proportions only in this concluding passage, this implies that it was still deficient and restricted when it was first applied to Erec, at any rate far removed from the Solomonic wisdom with which the poet compared it in what is now revealed as an unjustified exaggeration which served rather to raise our doubts.

Something similar is true of another ideal attribute of Erec, his generosity. This is applied to him explicitly for the first time at the end of the first part by the comparison with Alexander (2819-21), but if again we look for evidence to support this claim we find nothing but the fact that, at the tournament, Erec was not interested in booty and gave away the horses he had won from his defeated opponents (2615: . . . *wande er den mântac / maneges ros erledegete dâ. / diu liez er von der hant sâ, / daz er ir deheinez nam, / wan er dar niene kam / ûf guotes gewin;* 2634: *als er von dem rosse gesaz, / ein soldier nam daz / und seite ims genâde unde danc;* 2704: *daz dritte ros gap er hin. / harte schœnen gewin / hete sîn gesellescaft begân. / des âne in niht enwære getân;* 2783: *nû erbeizete von rosse sâ / der tugenthafte Erec / unde gap daz enwec*) . . . What is more, it is also modest by comparison with Hartmann's praise of Erec's generosity at the end of the work, where his *milte* has acquired the dimensions of Christian charity towards the poor (9980: *dô er von dem hove schiet, / dô trôste er nôtige diet / die sînes guotes ruochten, / und ob siz nimmer gesuochten, / nâch iegelîches ahte / und als erz haben mahte*). This contrast, serving to put Erec's earlier *milte* in its proper place as an admittedly positive quality, but one which still falls far short of his potential, is confirmed by the reaction of other people. The beneficiaries of Erec's generosity with the horses simply thank him on the secular level and spread his good name abroad (2711: *des wart im dô genâde gesaget / und gezam si deste mêre / ze sprechen sîn êre*), but at the end of the work this is raised to a metaphysical level as those who receive his gifts now bless him and entrust his *êre,* but also his soul, to God (9986: . . . *alsô daz si einen gemeinen segen / mit triuwen tâten über den degen, / daz got sîner êren wielte / und im die sêle behielte*). This heightening of Erec's praise at the close of the work does not have the effect of belittling his earlier achievement in any absolute terms, but it does show how this earlier achievement (and the praise bestowed upon it) fell short of Erec's own potentialities, as realized later in the narrative. It is part of Hartmann's ironic technique to reveal this falling-short to us by an apparent praise of his hero at this premature stage.

One other point may best be treated by comparing Hartmann with Chrétien. The French author has a similar passage at the corresponding point in his narrative (2266-70) which makes essentially the same point as in the German version, but then, a little later (just after the couple have returned to Erec's kingdom), he applies his ironic technique to Enide as well. He does this in a similar way, first by praising her at length (2413-33), but then by leading over immediately to Erec's *recréantise* for her sake (2434-42). Chrétien indeed goes so far as to say that there was no blemish in Enide (2420: *Onques nus ne sot tant d'aguet, / Qu'an li poïst veoir folie / Ne mauvestié ne vilenie*) and that nothing bad could hence be said of her (2430: *De li nus rien ne mesdisoit; / Car nus n'an pooit rien mesdire*). This is certainly an intentional overstatement, allowing us to see that the truth is otherwise, for when Erec immediately falls into his *recréantise* his knights are not slow to place the blame on Enide, as she herself realizes (2559: *Et por ce m'an poise ancor plus / Qu'il m'an metent le blasme sus; / Blasmee an sui, ce poise moi, / Et dïent tuit reison por quoi, / Que si vos ai lacié et pris / Que tot an perdez vostre pris, / Ne ne querez a el antandre*). As with Erec, Enide's superlative praise is later revealed as unfounded, but the illusion is more quickly dispelled here since we are now on the actual brink of the crisis. Indeed, Chrétien's sudden switch from his panegyric of Enide to Erec's *recréantise* (2434 f.) is part of his ironic shock effect.

Hartmann, however, has no such passage of ironic praise of Enite. Instead, he transfers Chrétien's example to Erec, whose status he therefore undermines twice. Hartmann's second passage occurs fairly soon after his first, after his couple have left Arthur's court and have returned to Erec's kingdom. The poet now recapitulates his earlier praise of Erec, compressing it into two weighty lines (2924: *Êrec was biderbe unde guot, / ritterlîche stuont sîn muot*), but now that the crisis is rapidly approaching he quickly adds his vital qualification (2926: *ê er wîp genæme / und hin heim kæme*). There follows a description of his *verligen* and we quickly realize the deficiency of this short eulogy, as we may not have done in the case of the earlier passage praising Erec's virtues. Hartmann differs from Chrétien therefore in giving us two passages apparently in praise of Erec at this point, but in reality pointing out his moral shortcomings as a knight. The reason for Hartmann's change is clear—unlike Chrétien, he does not attribute any major guilt to Enite and, in any case, his theme is the progression of Erec from *verligen* to his final and lasting success, so that his criticism and irony are fittingly directed against Erec alone. At any rate, by switching this second passage from Enite to Erec the German poet shows that the technique of ironic undercutting possesses critical implications for him, a realization that the person concerned has fallen short of Hartmann's ideal of chivalry. There is therefore no essential contradiction between his idealistic didacticism and his use of irony in passages like these.

In ***Iwein*** too we find the ironic use of praise to hint at a forthcoming disaster (so that this technique is by no means confined, as Pörksen suggests, to Hartmann's legends), but this time the praise is bestowed not on an individual, but on the supposedly happy marriage which is celebrated by the couple at the end of the first part of the romance and which, as in ***Erec,*** is about to be overshadowed by the dissension between Iwein and Laudine. None of this is expressed bluntly when the narrator adopts his guise of panegyrist during the marriage festivities (2426: *an swen got hât geleit / triuwe und andern guoten sin, / volle tugent, als an in, / und den eins guoten wîbes wert, / diu niuwan sînes willen gert, / suln diu mit liebe lange leben, / den hât er vreuden vil gegeben. / daz was allez wænlich dâ*). Just when all seems to be well (and should be well, according to the conventional fairytale pattern), doubts are insinuated (and it is part of this same procedure when, only two verses later [2435 ff.], the dead husband is tactlessly allowed to disturb the appearance of harmony). Doubts are raised whether the conditions mentioned as necessary for marital happiness are to be fulfilled: with Iwein because his *volle tugent* has hardly been displayed in his brutal killing of Askalon, with Laudine because a readiness to comply with her husband's wishes (*diu niuwan sînes willen gert*) is hardly prominent among her virtues. These reservations are confirmed by the syntactical structure of these lines, for they are made up of a lengthy generalizing statement, consisting of three conditional clauses and a concluding main clause of one line (2432), so that the conditions which have to be met outweigh the statement of fact. Furthermore, this suggestion of doubt overshadowing certainty is then carried over to the concluding one-line statement which is meant to reassure us that all is as it should be (*daz was allez wænlich dâ*), where the adverb betrays the narrator's refusal to commit himself. Nor are we left in doubt for long, for the disagreement between Iwein and Laudine which soon comes about tells us that the narrator was a shrewd judge of the situation in hinting at such reservations when eulogizing their married state.

Although Hartmann employs this technique both in his legends and in his romances, it is certainly not a monopoly of his, as can be shown by a passage in Wolfram's *Parzival* . . . If Hartmann ironically inserts a panegyric at the point when all seemed perfect, but which was really on the brink of his hero's downfall, we may expect to find a comparable example in Book VI, containing the scene in which Parzival's renown is both confirmed by his admission to the Round Table and destroyed by Cundrie's accusation. This is in fact the case with the long eulogy of his renown and beauty (311, 9-29) which seems to promise that his knightly strivings are at last crowned with success. In saying that Parzival's nobility offered no disappointment (311, 9: *als mir diu âventiure maz, / an disem ringe nieman saz, / der muoter brust ie gesouc, / des werdekeit sô lützel trouc*) the narrator is implying an agreement between character and renown which seems to justify his acceptance by Arthur's court and the favour which he immediately finds there (311, 29: *Man und wîp im wâren holt*). The rest of this panegyric concentrates on the hero's beauty, however: it is so pure and so much like a mirror that it has the power to compel ladies to constancy and banish all thought of *zwîvel*. These are high claims indeed, but is there anything about them to suggest that, as frequently with Wolfram's hyperbole, they are purposely so inflated as no longer to be fully credible? Here the context of this passage offers guidance. Parzival has just been admitted into Arthur's circle, but although Arthur is fully aware of the new member's exploits and renown the first words he addresses to him show that for him the mirror of Parzival's character is not completely unclouded (308, 12: *ir habt mir lieb und leit getân*). The same point is taken up and clarified by Guinevere's similarly mixed reception (310, 27-30), for she finds it necessary, in the act of kissing Parzival, to forgive him his killing of Ither. This is the shadow which is cast over this scene: we know of Parzival's guilt and must wonder whether he merits such absolute praise. These reservations are then strengthened by what follows as well, since the narrator's eulogy passes over to the arrival of Cundrie (311, 30: *sus het er werdekeit gedolt, / unz ûf daz siufzebære zil. / hie kom von der ich sprechen wil* . . .) and her violent tirade against the hero. Here if anywhere is revealed doubt about the claim just made of him (*des werdekeit sô lützel trouc*), for the Round Table's expectations on behalf of their new member could not be more rudely shattered than by her criticism. Where the favour which he found with Arthur's court seemed to set the seal of social approbation on his *werdekeit,* Cundrie sees only a reputation based on falseness (317, 16: *an prîse ir sît verdorben;* 318, 1: *Nu ist iwer prîs ze valsche komm*). Where the court saw Parzival's beauty and drew positive conclusions from this as to his character, Cundrie can only curse his false appearance (315, 20: *gunêrt sî iwer liehter schîn / und iwer manlîchen lide*) and draw an insulting contrast between him and herself (315, 24: *ich dunke iuch ungehiure, / und bin gehiurer doch dann ir*). Where the narrator, in introducing his apparently perfect knight to Arthur, idealized him even in nearly angelic terms (308, 1: *Dô truoc der junge Parzivâl / âne flügel engels mâl / sus geblüet ûf der erden*), Cundrie undermines the expectations raised by such flattery in showing that, for her, Parzival is rather a fallen angel and destined for hell (316, 7: *gein der helle ir sît benant / ze himele vor der hôhsten hant*). Like Hartmann, Wolfram carefully places his highest praise just before the hero's downfall, thereby accentuating the dramatic impact of the crisis and employing irony to induce in us a sense of false security which parallels that of the hero. With both authors the bipartite structure of the Arthurian romance (a first part where all seemed to lead to fairytale success, followed by a second part where all had to be won again) assisted them in their task and made of the eulogy at the end of the first part a critical turning-point. In this the romance follows a pattern close to, but different from Hartmann's legend, for in ***Der Arme Heinrich*** praise of the hero introduces the work, with no preceding narrative, whilst in ***Gregorius*** the repeated use of ironic praise at intervals underlines the sense of an inescapable testing by providence, but weakens any possible turning-point. It is because these romances hinge upon such a point that the irony of praise placed precisely there is even more effective than in the case of the legends.

If this technique of ironic praise is more widespread than has been suspected in the past, it would be fitting to conclude with one piece of evidence from the rhetorical handbooks which suggests how well known it was to the classical and medieval theoreticians. By this I mean that some of the rhetorical definitions of *ironia* illustrate it by the example of apparent praise when in reality blame is meant (or vice versa). Classical grammarians quote in this context the reproach made to Venus by Juno in the *Aeneid,* where her criticism is couched in what seem to be laudatory terms (*Aeneid,* IV. 93 f.). Iulius Rufinianus refers to this passage when defining irony (ñùí ßá *est figura sententiae, laudis et orationis et magnificandi, / non sine derisu in contrarium tendens*), whilst Quintilian quotes ironic praise from Cicero in his definition (*et laudis assimulatione detrahere . . . concessum est*) and Isidore of Seville draws on figures from Roman history (*ironia est, cum per simulationem diversum quam dicit intellegi cupit; fit autem . . . cum laudamus eum quem vituperare volumus*). In the thirteenth century an Italian teacher of rhetoric still conceives irony in the same manner, as criticism purporting to be praise (*Yronia enim est plana et demulcens verborum positio cum indignatione animi et subsannatione . . . Ceterum vix aliquis adeo fatuus reperitur qui non intelliget si de eo quod non est conlaudetur*). The vernacular authors considered in this essay did nothing other than what was recommended in the rhetorical handbooks when they voiced their criticism obliquely, but they exploited the potentialities of this technique to the full when they used it at so telling a position in the romance as the hero's first success, so soon to be revealed as deceptive and no more than provisional.

Frank J. Tobin (essay date 1975)

SOURCE: "Fallen Man and Hartmann's *Gregorius,*" in *The Germanic Review,* Vol. L, No. 2, March, 1975, pp. 85-98.

[*In the following excerpt, Tobin explores* Gregorius *with regard to the Augustinian view of original sin that formed the "mainstream of religious thought" during Hartmann's life.*]

Among the numerous attempts to interpret Hartmann's ***Gregorius,*** it has generally been recognized that seeing the story against a background of the religious thought of the age, whether this be the refined speculation of the theologians or the simpler, pastorally directed sermons, enriches and gives added precision to our understanding of the hero's fate. Sometimes this relationship of theology to literature has been conceived in a rather wooden fashion, as though Hartmann were using refined theological concepts and illustrating them in the structure of the story. This approach has rightfully drawn the wrath of others who object to putting ***Gregorius*** into a theological strait jacket. Still, most critics assume that exploring the relationships of theology to the story increases the yield of an interpretation far beyond what is possible by applying a strict *werkimmanent* approach. One religious teaching which has been frequently mentioned by critics in regard to ***Gregorius*** is the doctrine of original sin. Although many are convinced that seeing the story against the background of this doctrine renders it more intelligible, no study of ***Gregorius*** has really explored just what precisely the teaching concerning original sin was at this time, what it implied concerning man's nature, and how it is this more specific doctrine of original sin with all its ramifications that produces a rich yield for the interpreter.

If we intend to relate ***Gregorius*** to theological thought contemporary to it, we first ask what the sources were for Hartmann's knowledge of theology. Perhaps [in his *Über Hartmann von Aue. Drei Bücher Untersuchungen* (1971)] Schönbach was a bit overzealous in tracing parallels between Hartmann and a vast array of theologians. Certainly one may not conclude from this that Hartmann actually knew the works of all these theologians, but a solid familiarity with the mainstream of religious thought cannot be denied. . . . On the other hand, it seems improbable that Hartmann was aware of current questions that were providing impulses for new thought among professional theologians, especially in France. His lack of precision in religious terms and his apparent lack of concern in the question of what brings about the *reconciliatio* in the sacrament of penance—a central issue in the theology of the time—leads one to believe that Hartmann, though steeped in theological tradition, was ignorant of or unconcerned with strict contemporary theology. In view of all this, a reasonable approach would seem to be to present the essentials of the doctrine of original sin as it existed at the time in the conservative mainstream of tradition-oriented theology without belaboring refined differences between individual theologians. This is what one sees reflected in vernacular sermons. Augustine had been largely responsible for the development of this doctrine and it was taken over with little change by most of the theologians and compilers of the twelfth century. The presentation of the Augustinian view as found with only minor modifications in the *Sentences* of Peter Lombard is typical. . . .

Since Augustine's discussion of original sin and its effects provided the basis for early medieval anthropology, and since the influence of his views was increased through the writings of the early scholastics, it should not be surprising if we were to find them reflected in ***Gregorius,*** which is basically the story of a man's fall and redemption, whatever one might think about nuances of interpretation. Already in the prologue, . . . certain lines gain significance when viewed in the light of original sin. Thus in urging himself the necessity of penance, Hartmann says that even a man who keeps himself as pure as Abel, the medieval prototype of man needing redemption only because of the stain of original sin, does not do too much in doing penance to gain eternal life (26-32). Only the assumption that a man free of actual sin still has guilt, can take these lines out of the realm of exaggeration and rhetoric and give them serious meaning. Also, the emphasis on the guilt of the hero (52-53) becomes more intelligible if it is taken as at least including guilt arising from his situation and not just conscious guilt for personal actions. The last twenty years of scholarship concerning ***Gregorius*** have made it clear enough that such personal guilt is not that obvious. Finally the whole tone of the prologue with its emphasis on man's sinfulness, his need for penance and God's grace, and the power of evil is full of Augustinian pessimism regarding man.

Even a cursory inspection of the body of the narrative reveals striking parallels between Gregorius and man afflicted with original sin. The nature of the hero's birth puts him at a great disadvantage. Through the sin of his parents and no fault of his own he contracts a stain which must influence his life in essential ways. The incestuous relation of brother and sister caused by carnal lust demonstrates by an extreme example that it is concupiscence inseparably connected with conception which stains one from birth. When the abbot shows Gregorius the tablet which tells him of his origin, he replies:

> "ouwê, lieber herre,
> ich bin vervallen verre
> âne alle mîne schulde.
> wie sol ich gotes hulde
> gewinnen nâch der missetât
> diu hie vor mir geschriben stât?"
>
> [1779-1784]

The obvious contradictions between *vervallen verre* and *âne alle mîne schulde* and between the almost despairing question of how God's friendship can be gained and the hero's personal innocence regarding the *missetât* can only be resolved in this cultural context by seeing Gregorius as fallen man laden with guilt through no act of his own. . . .

A closer look at the story reveals the repeated occurrence of passages which reflect twelfth-century concern with original sin, fallen nature, guilt, and responsibility. Is Gregorius bound up in the guilt which his parents incur in conceiving him? The sister seems to answer the question clearly in the negative:

> ouch ist uns ofte vor geseit
> daz ein kint niene treit
> sînes vater schulde.
> ja ensol ez gotes hulde
> nicht dâ mite hân verlorn,
> ob wir zer helle sîn geborn,
> wandez an unser missetât
> deheiner slahte schulde hât.
>
> [475-483]

In the light of these lines . . . it is certainly wrong to assume . . . that Christian dogma maintained that the guilt of the fathers was incontrovertibly visited upon their children. However, the context of these lines compromises their being taken as the final word in the matter. They are preceded by the sister's asking her brother to find help so that even if the two of them lose God's favor their child might not be lost with them (469-74). If the offspring clearly has no share in the sin, why is help or counsel needed? Thus the *ouch ist uns ofte vor geseit* which introduces the idea that their child does not share their guilt can best be taken as representing the second of two views on the matter, and thus the whole question is left up in the air. Since whatever advice they receive and the measures they adopt for the birth of their child concern only his welfare in the forum of public opinion, these lines remain a *blindes Motif* for the story. Their whole function can be seen as being to raise the question of the theological effects of the parents' sin on Gregorius without providing any answer. Thus it is clear that our attention is being purposely drawn to this question. So, too, after Gregorius is born, when the mother, the vassal and his wife must decide what to do with the child, the whole question is put in terms again reflecting concern for its eternal salvation which has been put in danger by the sins of its parents and the circumstances of its birth. The beautiful child "'. . . waere schedelich verlorn: / nû waere aber ez geborn / mit alsô grôzen sünden, . . .'" (686-89). Again they act only to save the public reputation of mother and child, but the terms in which his fate is discussed, though perhaps ambiguous, force the attention of the audience to this same area of the child's involvement in supernatural guilt. Both these passages call to mind not only the question of the guilt of children for their parents' sins but also on a symbolic level, Adam's sin and the fate of fallen man. Also, since Gregorius falls into the same sin of incest as his parents, it may well be that the story supposes a wide-spread knowledge of the dictum that God punishes those who imitate the sins of their fathers.

Concerning evidence of the vitiating consequences of Adam's sin in the hero, it must be admitted that in contrast to the case of his parents concupiscence is not greatly emphasized. Nevertheless, it can be seen to be a contributing factor on both sides in bringing about the incestuous union of mother and son. All the more striking are the manifestations of ignorance which brings ruin to the hero and his mother. Gregorius' ignorance, like that of his Greek prototype, is of a very essential kind. It is ignorance of his own identity. Although the plot requires that the hero be ignorant about his individual identity, Hartmann's story, like that of Sophocles, is also making a statement about his protagonist's ignorance of his own nature as man. And since the story goes to great lengths to point out the outstanding personal qualities of the hero (1235-1272) and dwells especially on his unusual capacity for acquiring knowledge (1173-1200), his ignorance can best be taken as a characteristic inherent in his nature rather than as a shortcoming of a particular individual.

Gregorius' path from ignorance to knowledge progresses through different stages. In the first stage he passes from false knowledge to not knowing when he overhears the words of his foster mother and discovers "ich enbin niht der ich wânde sîn" (1403). The shame of learning that he is a foundling fills him with an overpowering desire to flee to a land where no one knows "wie ich her komen bin" (1419). Even at this early stage in his conversation with the abbot the pattern of his life as a knight and ruler are clear. By hiding his shameful origin and relying on his own ability he will succeed because he has the necessary *kunst* and *sin* (1420-21). The abbot urges him not to act rashly and to remain there, but the young man refuses to consider this and admits that it is a certain impetuous blindness (*tumpheit*) that will not let him do so. Then we learn that Gregorius intends to act on the most optimistic implication that can possibly be inferred from his ignorance. He may well be noble and thus eligible for knighthood.

The abbot dubs the young man a knight before revealing to him that he is of noble birth. Perhaps this is a flaw in Hartmann's tale. Certainly the abbot puts off this revelation of his nobility and fortune in order to keep him near the monastery. Another result of this delay, however, is that Gregorius, when confronted with the fact of his supposed poverty, twice confidently states that he can make it on his own and men will praise him all the more for it. Full of optimism and self-confidence because of his talents, he is unaware of the irony of his words when he says "ich trage si alle samet hie, / die huobe die mir mîn vater lie." (1695-1969) His inheritance is quite different from what he thinks.

The next step in his passing from ignorance to knowledge comes when the abbot presents him with the tablet and his fortune. In view of the devastating revelation concerning his origin it strikes one a bit odd that Gregorius can react so joyfully to the news of his noble birth, though he does show equal sorrow for the shameful aspects of his origin. Typical of his basic attitude, however, is that the main effect of the tablet is to reaffirm his desires of a knightly life. The shameful side of his origin can be attended to in private. It need not affect his whole life. However, he does feel the necessity of removing the last bit of ignorance concerning his identity and vows to be *iemer varnde* "'. . . mir entuo noch gotes gnâde schîn / von wanne ich sî oder wer'" (1804-1805). He claims to want to know the truth about himself. Yet the search is conveniently forgotten once he has achieved his knightly aspirations. Thus, this final ignorance has to be overcome by *gotes gnâde* working through chance and the curiosity of the servant girl. Gregorius has given up striving to overcome it by his own efforts.

Gregorius shares with all men the duty of finding out the truth about himself, of seeing his nature as it really is. He willingly accepts the discovery of his nobility, but this is only half the truth. Up to and during the confrontation with his wife-mother after she has discovered the tablet, he is still fiercely asserting his noble birth and bids that one not delve any deeper (2587-2588), as he himself has not done. He will neither admit to the world nor draw the consequences from the fact that he was conceived in sin. His blindness to the full truth of his nature and especially his neglecting to overcome the ignorance concerning who he really is are incriminating facts. While the hero's condition cannot be termed a clear case of willful ignorance, neither does it exculpate him. Rather it seems closest to that gray area of ignorance . . . as not mitigating the guilt in a substantial way. This explanation is the only one possible if one is to take the narrator seriously when he says of the happily married knight that he " . . . erkande niht der schulde / diu ûf sîn selbes rücke lac, / die er naht unde tac / mit sîner muoter uopte, / dâ mite er got betruopte" (2290-94).

Since the abbot introduces the concept of free will (*vrîe wal*) into his long debate with Gregorius (1439), we are justified examining how it functions in the story and whether it shows the effects of original sin. Werner Schwarz has devoted a whole article to free will in ***Gregorius*** [i.e., "Free Will in Hartmann's Gregorius", *Reiträge,* 89 (1967-68)]. However, he does not take full advantage of the concept by explaining it in its total theological context. Quoting Augustine, Schwarz sees man's free will committing a sin through an *aversio a Deo* which is a *conversio* to a worldly life. This is what Gregorius does in leaving the monastery against the advice of the abbot that whoever leaves the monastic life will lose his soul (1517-25). Gregorius, who is apparently without vows and thus under no clear obligation to stay, counters this argument well saying that it is better to be a *gotes ritter* than a *betrogen klôsterman* (1534-35). Certainly the abbot's views must be given considerable weight when one considers who he is and how much space Hartmann reserves for them out of all proportion to the French source. But the question which Schwarz does not clearly answer is why Gregorius in becoming a knight by this very action turns away from God. What in the decision makes it evil? The decision to become a knight in itself does not imply a turning away from God. If the concept of free will is reduced to mean man's ability to choose between two or more possibilities, it does not take us very far in an interpretation unless one can explain why the choice made is an *aversio a Deo*. Gregorius is not conscious of sinning. How can man freely sin without knowledge that he is doing so? Schwarz answers that the power of the devil is great. But does not such power as a cause for man's sinning cancel free will?

Only if one sees the doctrine of free will in its larger theological context, i.e., imbedded in the Augustinian teachings on original sin, can one answer these objections. If we assume for the moment that Gregorius' decision to become a knight is, for reasons to be subsequently specified, morally wrong and involves him in guilt, then in the view of free will prevalent at the time, grace was not aiding the act of the will and hence the will was not free *ad bonum* but in its unaided condition is in the state of *non posse non peccare* and only free *ad malum*. And if Gregorius is from this point on separated from grace, then any future action he performs, no matter what his intention or how good it may seem, is evil and increases his separation from God. This is exactly the position taken by the abbot:

> gestâstû bî der ritterschaft,
> sich, sô mêret sich diu kraft
> dîner tägelîchen missetât
> und enwirt dîn niemer rât.
>
> [1787-1790]

Later this prophecy is fulfilled as Gregorius goes about his knightly tasks and even prays daily that his parents may find God's favor and is quite oblivious of his own ever increasing guilt (2288-94). Thus Gregorius exemplifies well the helpless position of *non posse non peccare* in which fallen man finds himself.

The underlying assumption of the assertion that Gregorius' will was in the state of *non posse non peccare* is, of course, that God withheld his grace from his actions even though the hero himself indicates that he acts with God in mind (*durch got und durch êre,* 2070) in his knightly activities. If, as Schwarz maintains, Gregorius' leaving the monastery was an *aversio a Deo,* it must be shown why this is so, since Gregorius was under no obligation to remain. And if no action of the hero is wrong in itself, then we must look for an attitude in the hero which would hinder God in bestowing his grace.

To discover this false attitude we can best return to the theme of ignorance which permeates the material Hartmann chose, since the hero's basic disorientation clearly is that he does not know who he is. His mistaken notion of himself and what he can accomplish are spelled out in the long discourse with the abbot. There he shows a strong sense of self-reliance and confidence in his ability to overcome all difficulties through his own inborn qualities and efforts.

> 'sîtz mir nû sô geziuhet
> daz mich diu Saelde vliuhet
> und ich niuwan ir gruoz
> mit vrümigkeit gedienen muoz,
> dêswâr ich kan si wol erjagen,
> si enwelle sich mir mê versagen
> dan si sich noch versagete
> der si ze rehte jagete.
> sus sol man si erloufen,
> mit kumber saelde koufen.
> dâ enzwîvel ich niht an,
> wirde ich ein rehte vrumer man
> an lîbe und an sinne,
> ich engediene wol ir minne.'
>
> [1697-1710]

This, then, is the hero's fundamental mistake concerning who he is. Like the original denier of the fallen nature of man, Pelagius, Gregorius is convinced that *saelde* can be achieved by human efforts alone. Although he undertakes his chivalric actions *durch got* as well as *durch êre,* he is oblivious to the utter necessity of divine help and man's complete dependence on it. He does not recognize that human activity left to itself cannot work for good. Since he is blinded by the ignorance of his fallen nature to the limitations of this same nature, and since this attitude makes cooperation with grace impossible, the only avenue open to divine action is that Gregorius' earlier wish be ironically fulfilled: that *gotes gnâde* reveal to him who he really is.

Hence it becomes clear why the decision to leave the monastery and become a knight, though not immoral in itself, can in the case of Gregorius be termed an *aversio a Deo.* Based as it is on a culpable blindness concerning his real nature, it betrays in him an attitude of pride and arrogance. He embarks upon a knightly career with the idea that God will be at best a help as he endeavors to attain *saelde* through personal talent and effort. Not until he is overwhelmed by the horrible truth about where his own efforts have taken him does he acknowledge what the terrible revelation of his true identity makes unequivocably clear. Man is utterly dependent on God's grace. Any other attitude is pride.

One does not have to search far to discover why such a theme was appropriate to Hartmann's literary surroundings. The hero's idealization of the knightly existence which bursts forth in the dispute with the abbot, his extolling the hero who by great personal prowess overcomes great obstacles to attain *saelde* is, of course, the universal subject matter of the knightly romance. The hero left to his own resources succeeds in the quest and brings about his own happiness. The basic assumptions of this view of man are what we find being questioned here. Gregorius' life from the time he leaves the monastery until he becomes the ruler in his mother's land is a classic example of the knightly success story. After clearly enunciating the ethical principles governing knightly conduct to be followed in attaining the knightly goal, Gregorius proceeds to put them into practice. After overcoming the oppressor, he marries the lady in distress and becomes ruler of the land. In his own mind and according to the ethos of the courtly romance he has thereby attained *saelde.* What becomes evident in the discovery of his incestuous marriage is the ambivalence of this term. What is *saelde* within one frame of reference reveals itself as shame and misery when the total situation becomes clear. Within the framework of the knightly ambit, Gregorius has through his own efforts attained happiness. But the knightly order does not exist in a vacuum. It is dependent on the all-embracing divine order of which it is a mere part. Its system of ethics must not conflict with the universal moral order. In other words, since the knight is a man, the knightly ideal will only prove firm if it is constructed according to the true nature of man. Hartmann here shows that this has not been the case. Man cannot achieve happiness by relying on his own abilities and therefore neither can the knight. Such happiness is only apparent and based on ignorance. The discovery of the true state of affairs shows the true nature of man and what he accomplishes when left to himself. The knight, like all men, must rely totally on God's help in order to attain *saelde.*

This theme of man's utter dependence on God is stressed in other ways in the story. As in the case of Moses, putting the infant Gregorius out to sea is a gesture of complete trust in God and of admission that his aid is necessary if the child is to be saved. It is an admission of the insufficiency of human effort to handle the situation. God responds to this gesture of submission by taking the infant into his protective care, becoming its *amme* until it reaches the land which God had chosen (929-38). When Gregorius leaves the monastery as a young knight, he imitates this gesture by leaving the direction of his ship's

Thirteenth-century fresco depicting Iwein mortally wounding Ascalon.

path to the winds, bidding God to choose the way (1825-36). This time the results of the gesture are ambivalent because the motivation behind it is ambivalent. Because of his concept of knighthood, Gregorius is letting God choose merely the battle ground where he, Gregorius, will prove himself. God does choose where Gregorius' knighthood will bear fruit, but it is only by the unexpected bitterness of the fruit that the young knight is really helped. Finally, by placing himself *ûf den stein* and by having himself chained so that he is powerless to help himself Gregorius shows that he has comprehended to a heroic degree the necessity of complete submission to and dependence on God. Here, as in the first instance, God responds clearly and confirms the correctness of his attitude unequivocally.

Seeing the hero as fallen man also brings more clearly into focus the function of the tablet as the symbol of his true identity, of who he really is. The basic information it contains is the circumstances of his birth, that he is both noble and stained as the product of sin, and that he should lead his life accordingly. When the abbot first confronts him with the tablet, he reacts by building his knightly future on the news of his nobility and thinks that the shameful side of his background can be dealt with in private as something affecting his life only accidentally. However, when his wife-mother shows him the tablet and thus a second time informs him who he is, the knowledge allows for only one course of action: penance and submission. While the hero is purifying himself *ûf dem stein,* the tablet was left in the shack where he had spent the night at the fisherman's. Although the shack had shortly thereafter been burned to the ground and the area allowed to grow wild, Gregorius insists that it be found before he leave for Rome. Gregorius' wild and weakened body gives little evidence of the high favor in which he now stands with God. But the tablet proclaiming who he is, when found, shines miraculously resplendent as it was when first fashioned. This moves all who are present to proclaim that Gregorius is truly *saelic,* a judgment which the narrator shares (3740).

More than one critic has censured the excessive amount of attention given to the question of the hero's guilt in secondary literature, stating that the story intends to focus on the supreme power of God's grace. This is certainly true. And yet the implications of this statement are also important for understanding the story. If Augustine's many writings on God's readiness to help man have earned him the title *Doctor Gratiae,* it must also be admitted that this emphasis on God's grace in bringing about man's salvation was necessary because of the low estimation in which he held man's ineffectual efforts to work for good. Only in a similar context can the story of Gregorius be considered the story of the all-conquering power of divine grace. It is so because it is also the story of fallen man.

F. P. Pickering (essay date 1976-77)

SOURCE: "The 'Fortune' of Hartmann's Erec," in *German Life and Letters,* Vol. XXX, No. 2, 1976-77, pp. 94-109.

[*Pickering is an English scholar whose books include* Literatur und darstellende Kunst im Mittelalter *(1966;* Literature and Art in the Middle Ages, *1970) and* Essays on Medieval German Literature and Iconography *(1980). In the following excerpt, he asserts that, typical of chivalric romances generally,* Erec*'s storyline exemplifies an essentially Boethian view of history as fortune.*]

. . . I have contended that it is the Boethian view of history as fortune which is reflected in virtually all works of medieval narrative literature, even in Wolfram von Eschenbach's *Parzival,* a grail romance, and in Hartmann von Aue's ***Gregorius,*** a so-called 'courtly legend'. The two authors undoubtedly show a deep concern for the salvation of their respective heroes; they nevertheless as laymen tell and gloss their stories in terms of medieval fortune doctrine. . . .

Hitherto, anticipating greater difficulties elsewhere, I have restricted myself to the bald assertion that a typical romance of chivalry can only be Boethian. Here, taking ***Erec*** as example, I hope to show that it is—and not vaguely so, but as Boethian as the literary genre and the identity of the hero allow. A statement of the case in general terms would run as follows. Chivalric (Arthurian) romance is not concerned with universal history, the Christian faith, or even in any real sense with the Church and its sacraments, institutions, or history. Any allusions must fall to the account of characterization (e.g. of the hero) or be descriptive of a generally Christian world; they are not story. It is therefore not Augustinian, though anyone so minded could doubtless write an Augustinian gloss on the hero's progress to perfection. Chivalric romance (for instance ***Erec***) is, however, equally not concerned with the destiny of nations, or real or imaginary peoples; at most the idea is present that dynasties make history (Erec is 'fil de roi Lac' and succeeds Lac), but this does not shape the stories, which are those of individual heroes, each of whom succeeds in the end, achieving a personal *fama.* The hero goes out of set purpose into the unknown in search of *âventiure,* to be tried in a series of chance encounters. He readily accepts hazards known to be impossible, even for the bravest. But as each hero in turn is for the duration of his own story the bravest, the fortune (*sælde*) which he 'has' must hold. Success brings the recognition which (conventionally) Arthur's court alone can bestow. The consummation of the hero's career, now completed as story, is a state of 'happiness ever after' (i.e. until death), shared with the heroine. The final setting is often the hero's home country, in Erec's case an inherited kingdom. In an epilogue the poet may confidently assert hero and heroine now to be in heaven, their souls saved.—How, it may well be asked, can a story following such a course reflect a Boethian view of *history?* Is it not, as the handbooks say, simply the rationalization of an original fairy-story (*Märchen*)? That is precisely the point I seek to make. Hartmann's final rationalization falls within—well within—the entirely rational scheme of secular history which the Middle Ages had from *De Consolatione Philosophiae.* What other norm for story was there? Hartmann treated Erec's case, as any other schooled writer would have done, 'normally'.

How does this claim fare, however, when tested, not against such a general statement but against the ten thousand lines of Hartmann's text? All I can say at this stage is that I have reconsidered ***Erec*** in such a light and find Hartmann *at least* as concerned to deal adequately with Erec's fortune (*sælde*) as he is to illustrate his knightly prowess and pay homage to chivalric ideals, or to criticize the 'Minnedienst' of the Red Knight (Mâbonagrîn), Erec's final opponent. Erec is, in other words, successful, not because he is or becomes in the course of his trials a perfect knight with a social conscience, and so deserves his success. He succeeds because he takes his chances, and because he recognizes when the moment has come to risk the gambler's throw, all or nothing! That is a statement requiring immediate expansion. Putting his trust, as always, first in God, Erec dares to be brave when bravery will not suffice without fortune. He puts his fortune to the test, and, 'by the grace of God', wins. (Good fortune is ultimately in God's gift; it is reward, but it is not in any strict sense earned). Does such an emphasis on *fortune* suffice to make ***Erec*** a 'Boethian' work? I have already made qualifications to which we now turn.

We clearly need to consider what modifications of the Boethian philosophy of history were required to match the reduced scope for serious historical thought dictated by the two premises 'world of King Arthur' and 'story of Erec'. (There are of course compensatory enlargements of scope for fantastic story). Moreover, we must make due allowance for the prejudices and the milieu of Hartmann and his aristocratic audience, their shared belief, for instance, that God was disposed to favour them and their kind, their *mores:* he too was courtly (*hövesch*). The full Boethian hierarchy of historical forces (God, providence, fate, fortune, man's free will) is thereby almost automatically reduced, or is reducible, to the following: a courtly God, fortune (in the abstract, or personified as Dame Fortune), the personal fortune of Erec, and Erec as man. Let us start with Erec himself. Is it primarily as a knight that Erec first fails: 'Erec verligt sich'? Or is it as a man, who, forgetting his true nature, as moral philosophy would put it, wallows in sensuality until he is shamed by the reproach (*itewîz*) which such conduct earns him? Merely to rationalize a fairy-story as a tale of knighthood, it would surely have sufficed to show Erec content after marriage with the domestic life, a stay-at-home. One could of course say that here, as in the description of Enite's horse and saddle (and on several occasions) Hartmann opts for rhetoric, and that the full treatment of 'sloth' has Erec's completely unmanly behaviour as its consequence:

sîn site er wandeln began.
als er nie würde der man,
alsô vertreip er den tac.

(2934-6)

Erec's scrambles to get from bed to the dining-table (where he authorizes his knights to keep their engagements: 'ich lobe an im den selben site', 2965) and to Mass, preserve only tenuous links with his kind and with his obligations. His reaction when corrected is also all-too human rather than chivalric, from wounded pride. But in time his true *manheit* (manliness and knightly courage) reasserts itself, and, God so willing, the fortune (*sælde*) which was Erec's from the cradle . . . prevails. In the end he may, to a late twelfth-century audience, have appeared to deserve his final success, despite the unnecessary trials to which he subjected Enite. More important is the fact that his individual fortune survived his period of complete unworthiness. Sentimentally we may, with Hartmann, wish to attribute his timely recovery to Enite's patience and loyalty. Arthur's court (Hartmann is narrator) was more perceptive: it attributed Erec's success to Dame Fortune (*vrou Sælde*). . . .

As for the complete Boethian hierarchy of historical forces, man and fortune are clearly active in ***Erec,*** but what has happened to divine providence and fate? (Providence is timeless; its projection in the created world of time is fate.) The answer has, I think, to be that providence was not available, and that fate was not needed. I argue as follows. We have reached the point where we must (at last!) distinguish between history-writing proper and story-telling, between the imperial historian Otto of Freising (or for that matter the policy-maker Reinald of Dassel and the propagandist Archpoet) making claims concerning the divinely inspired (providential) mission of Frederick Barbarossa, and Hartmann entertaining his public with the 'romantic' exploits of Erec. It would surely have been the height of impiety seriously to suggest a divine purpose manifesting itself through the career of Erec or any other of Arthur's knights. As for fate, the concept itself was in Hartmann's day still indispensable in a completely systematic moral philosophy—in the always contemporary *De Consolatione Philosophiae,* for instance, and in Alain of Lille's *Anticlaudianus*. The whole chain of causation could indeed be referred to as *ordo, lex,* or *series fatalis*. But Augustine's strong deprecation of the use of the term was evidently remembered; *fatum* could on etymological grounds be held to mean the word spoken by God (thus Augustine and Isidor), but one should always refer to the will of God, not to fate. This was theologically correct; it was equally a welcome solution for writers and speakers of all kinds, whether for deliberate statements involving religious conviction or for even the most casual expression of Christian 'fatalism', as in the modern ultimate reduction of *deo volente* to 'd.v.'. That leaves little room for either the term 'fate' or the discrete idea. Even so, expression had occasionally to be found for the lot to which an individual is content to resign himself. . . .

From the foregoing remarks it is evident that in chivalric romance the expression 'the will of God' will rarely be a direct reference to the God of Christian faith and dogma. That is indeed the case in ***Erec***. Even at his devotions in church the hero prays for no more than the favour (*genâde*) of God, the bestower of success in combat. Much more regularly reference to God's will serves as the proper (or merely formal) preface to a more carefully worded attribution of cause to fortune (*sælde*) or chance (*geschicht*), both of which are manifestations of God's will. The former remains, as it had been in antiquity (classical and Germanic) and still is, an idea of some complexity. It is an outside force governing the course and outcome of human affairs, particularly change (*wehsel*); it is also a 'charismatic' quality of leaders of men and of individual heroes—they 'have' fortune. Chance, as the unforeseen coincidence of courses of action undertaken independently, determines the circumstances in which fortune (in either sense) comes into play. For all these basic ideas—God's will, fortune, chance—there are, of course, in medieval Latin (the language of the poets' schooling) and in the vernaculars, more or less synonymous expressions and a range of grammatical possibilities which ideally one would wish to distribute and define. I have no such ambitions.

With that observation I conclude my argument that Hartmann's Erec is as Boethian as the genre and the identity of the hero allow. It remains to adduce the textual evidence. . . .

The unanimous verdict of Arthur's court on Erec's crowning adventure—his triumph of *Joie de la curt* and his signal efforts on behalf of the eighty widows whom he had rescued from their enforced sojourn at Castle Brandigân—is that this could not have happened had *vrou Sælde* (Dame Fortune) not assisted his nurse when he lay in the cradle:

wan daz vrou Sælde ir stiure
gap sîner ammen diu sîn phlac
dô er in der wagen lac,
sô enmöhtez nimmer sîn geschehen.

(9899-902)

Does Hartmann's treatment of Erec's *sælde* in the story up to that point make this somewhat emotional acclaim (the sudden appearance of eighty widows was a sensation, 'ein vremdiu sache', 9903 f) also his own verdict? The following outline account of Hartmann's development of the theme suggests strongly that it is.

The first reference to Erec's *sælde* comes, it must be admitted, bewilderingly early. Hartmann introduces Erec as 'fil de roi Lac, / der vrümekeit und sælden phlac' (ll. 2f). This is, I think, merely a formula meaning that 'things have gone well for Erec so far; here he is, equerry to

Arthur's queen, his story now starts'. Erec's story starts in fact with a humiliating encounter with a dwarf, a *leit* that will be avenged in the defeat of the dwarf's master Îdêrs at Tulmein in the sparrow-hawk contest. With what hopes does Erec approach this, his first real test? He hopes that God may give him increase of *heil* (139, cf. 496). He is wished *gelücke* (657) by Duke Îmâîn. 'Luckily' (see 751) he was also wished *heil* (753) by the onlookers before the contest. [Note: *heil* is not *sælde* but may contribute to it, see below]. Erec then fights with borrowed and antiquated arms, not expertly, for he is still inexperienced, but 'sam er wuote' (859), until, having caught a glimpse of Enite, he feels the strength of two men (939). He is victor. He himself attributes his victory to *sælde* (973), but it is interesting that Hartmann is satisfied with 'Êreck sô wol gelanc' (1296), and that Arthur's court rejoices only at his *gelücke* (1302); the queen was 'sîner âventiure vrô' (1528); all praised his *manheit* (1311). So far then, only Erec senses that *sælde* (clearly fortune) favours him.

Erec's next testing is not in *âventiure,* but at a regular tournament organized by Gawain, as his contribution to the festivities associated with the wedding of Erec and Enite at Arthur's court. It is to take place in three weeks' time. Erec approaches this engagement with great circumspection, aware of his inexperience ('wan er vor der stunde / turnierens nie begunde', 2252 f) and, no doubt, of his new armour. He does not presume to carouse (*giuden*) with other knights ('er enwolde sich niht gelîchen / einem guoten knehte', 2383f. in the context of 2378-90). This earns him a high opinion among the knights who pay their courtesy calls. Hartmann's comment is:

in minnete allez daz in sach.
er tete alsam der Sælden schol:
man enspræche im anders niht sô wol.

(2401-3)

Erec's behaviour, namely his self-restraint as a test under approved auspices approaches, is 'such as Fortune requires' of a prospective favourite. When early the following (Sunday!) morning his competitors are still in their quarters attending to spit-and-polish (2407-10), Erec is out doing trial runs with two other early risers. He does well—why?

zwô genâde vuocten im daz:
sælde und grôze werdekeit,
die hâte got an in geleit.

(2437-9)

Hartmann has now committed himself: *gratia Dei* Erec has *fortuna* and *virtus*. Erec also excels at the *vespereide,* the fuller practice session on the eve of the tournament (2452-75). Surely, one would think from these indications, Erec's quite outstanding prowess in the actual tournament must earn him open acclaim in terms of his *sælde.* That is not the case. King Arthur, hearing on the morning of the contest that Erec has been out for fifteen spear-casts (he has also been to chapel, but Arthur is not aware of this), rebukes his knights for their sluggishness and says 'good luck to him! it's his for the asking' ('got gebe im heil swenne er sîn gert', 2531), and indeed Erec performs, according to Hartmann, 'on that one day even better than Gawain' (the gist of 2720-63). But there is no direct reference to Erec's *sælde* from any quarter. Instead, quite extravagant—and at first sight irrelevant—praise is showered on Erec by all who have seen him on and off the field:

. . . man begunde gelîchen
sîn wîsheit Salomône,
sîn schæne Absolône,
an sterke Samsônes genôz

(2815-8)

—not to mention Alexander, with whom Erec is compared for his *milte.* But *are* the comparisons irrelevant? Though I doubt whether Hartmann did better than to stumble on it, he found in the clichés 'wise as Solomon' etc. a means both of describing Erec at a moment when everything seemed to be going in his favour, *and* of foreshadowing a calamitous fall from grace. The fall from grace is a concealed *tertium comparationis* in the likening of Erec to Solomon, Absalom, Samson, and Alexander, for Hartmann knows that after the tournament Erec will repair with Enite to Destregâles—and to bed! (Hartmann remembers Absalom as a prototype when he deals more explicitly with the fall of Lord Henry in ***Der arme Heinrich,*** 11. 82-9.) The comparison is, in the event, belied by Erec's career, for his *sælde* survives, or at any rate chance brings him back to the path—'der Saelden wec'.

The true path to *sælde* (fortune) is what Erec claims to have been seeking all along—not mere *âventiure,* which is *unmâze* (7012-23). He chances upon it after taking what to his companion and friend King Guivreiz was the wrong route at a fork in the road (7811—906). This leads to the final testing of Erec at the *âventiure* (still *âventiure!*) of *Joie de la curt.* Despite all advice Erec argues his decision to accept the challenge as follows:

'ich weste wol, der Saelden wec
gienge in der werlde eteswâ,
rehte enweste ich aber wâ,
wan daz ich in suochende reit
in grôzer ungewisheit,
unz daz ich in nû vunden hân.
got hât wol ze mir getân
daz er mich hât gewîset her
dâ ich nâch mînes herzen ger
vinde gar ein wunschspil
dâ ich lützel wider vil
mit einem wurfe wâgen mac.'

(8521-32)

In his assurance that he has found *der Sælden wec* Erec is alone. Hartmann uses every means further to isolate his hero by enlarging on the alarm of Enite and the fears of well-wishers. He suggests even an element of arrogance and vainglory in Erec's behaviour. The latter's words 'got hât wol ze mir getân' border on presumption; he assures Enite as he takes leave of her that his victory is certain ('swenne mich der muot iuwer mant, / sôst sigesaelic mîn hant', 8868 f). For a reliable interpretation of Erec's words and behaviour at this juncture one should probably recall

Hartmann's earlier remark: 'er tet alsam der Saelden schol'. He has made his decision to risk 'lützel wider vil' in the gambler's throw. The rest follows: the words expressing confidence and resolve, and the composure and restraint required by one who puts his fortune to the test. With the words 'herre, alsô got wil' to his host, Erec retires for the night (8589 f). The following morning he attends Mass and prays earnestly that he may survive (8636-40), breakfasts frugally, drinks 'sant Jôhannes segen' at leave-taking (8651 f) and arms himself for combat with the Red Knight. He is victorious. I think we may take it that Hartmann endorses the verdict of Arthur's court. . . . Wolfram von Eschenbach was less reticent. Of his hero Parzival he writes: ' . . . den ich hân brâht / dar sîn doch saelde het erdâht' (827, 17 f).

A few further points remain to be made about *Sælde, sælde* and *sælic,* before we consider *sælekit*. The successful pursuit of fortune is necessarily the prerogative of the hero of any given story: Erec has *sælde,* and in due course brings it to fulfillment. And Enite? She triumphed *sælecliche* (1381) at the beauty-contest (part of the sparrowhawk adventure), and she no doubt shared Erec's fortune (and fall from grace) until the estrangement. But when Erec has so cruelly made her his groom and accumulated eight horses, Hartmann attributes her ability to bear the hardship to Dame Fortune and God's courtesy:

wan daz vrou Saelde ir was bereit
und daz diu gotes hövescheit
ob mîner vrouwen swebete, . . .
sô waere kumberlîch ir vart:
des wart diu vrouwe wol bewart.

(3460-67)

In her trials and near-despair Enite can only think of herself as *unsælic* or *sældenlôs* (3357, 5992, 6006, 6038), indeed, she was born to be unlucky: 'unheiles wart ich geborn' (5940). With the reconciliation comes a renewal of *sælekeit* of the married state. Incidentally, nobody argues more urgently that fortune favours Enite than the completely deluded Count Oringles. The *wehsel* (a marked change of fortune) that will follow marriage to him (6251-61, 6270, 6486 f, 6499) should be sufficient proof, he thinks, of her *sælde.*

Arthur's court knows *sælde,* it will be recalled, as an almost permanent state of being—as such it is probably *felicitas.* It is occasionally threatened by intruders, but always assured and even augmented by the exploits of Arthur's knights. For the duration of Erec's story there are, however, after the awkwardness with the dwarf, no real threats. Hartmann, who knows and says often enough that *sælde* (fortune) is God-given, seems to have no difficulty in accepting the convention of romance that, in addition to being *sælic* itself, Arthur's court recognizes *sælde* and accords due praise and honour to those blessed with it. In that sense it 'bestows' *sælde.* With that goes the corollary that merely to be admitted to Arthur's court is a measure of good fortune. We noted above the fortunate case of Erec when he was still a newcomer: he later offers the following words of encouragement to Cadoc, who on his way to Arthur's court was waylaid and mercilessly scourged by giants:

swer ez dâ gevürdern kan,
der wirt schiere ein saelic man.

(5686 f)

Sælde is of course cordially wished, e.g. at leave-takings (3598, 5709). A final point: Hartmann waggishly says of an otherwise unimportant wedding-guest (Gimoers of Avalôn): 'des saelde enwas niht kleine, / wan er minnete ein feine' (1930-34)—a case not envisaged by the moral philosophers!

Sælekeit is occasionally interchangeable with *sælde* (4242, 6130, 6713 f, 9591); it is generally 'happiness'. When 'wished', it carries, expressed or understood (9670, 5709), the qualification 'lasting'. It is then the equivalent of *fortuna manens* or (earthly) *beatitudo,* the latter being the highest good according to *De Consolatione,* Book III. An important passage enlarges as follows on the parting wishes of the *spilliute* at the wedding of Erec and Enite:

Êrecke und vrouwen Ênîten
wunschten si aller saelekeit.
diu was in doch nû bereit
lange unde manec jâr.
ir wunsch wart vollecliche wâr,
wan zwei gelieber wurden nie
unz ez der tôt undervie,
der allez liep leidet
sô er liep von liebe scheidet.

(2203-11)

The happiness will last 'lange unde manec jâr', but end with death. This is in accordance with the teaching of *De Consolatione:* lasting happiness is impermanent. Consideration of this instructive passage gives, however, little guidance to the interpretation of Hartmann's first description of Enite (323-41)—'her beauty' and her *sælekeit:*

ir lîp schein durch ir salwe wât
alsam diu lilje, dâ si stât
under swarzen dornen wîz.
ich waene got sînen vlîz
an sî hâte geleit
von schoene und von saelekeit.

(336-41)

God's favour manifests itself in Enite's beauty and, I think, 'grace' (or Enite is 'well-favoured').

. . . In ***Erec*** I find no word which in itself means 'fate'. The only character who both resigns himself to his fate and finds words to express his sentiments is Koralus, Enite's father. The victim of predatory attacks by enemies and now living in dire poverty, he says:

nû hât got über mich
verhenget swes er wolde . . .
daz wil ich von gote hân.

(535-39, cf. 601)

He continues, echoing the words of Hannah's prayer (Canticle of Hannah in I Sam. ii. 7):

des gewaltes ist alsô vil,
er mac den rîchen swenne er wil
dem armen gelîchen
und den armen gerîchen.

(540-3)

These words suit the patriarchal figure whom Hartmann describes (275-80). He has none the less kept his arms by him, and lends them to Erec.

One may wish to read fatalism into the words of the accident-prone knight Keiîn ('nû enmac doch daz nieman bewarn / daz im geschehen sol', 4801 f), or more certainly those of Enite in her overlong lament at Erec's 'death':

dâ vür enhoeret dehein list,
man enmüeze im (*sc.* God) sînen willen lân.
der muoz ouch an mir ergân:
ich muoz et unsaelic sîn.

(5989-92)

Misfortune is the lot 'dealt' (*verteilet*) to her, she thinks (see 5985-6007 and compare 6037-41). There is, of course, in romance no room for fate as 'doom', or for a fate which has to be defied.

[*Heil, gelücke,* and (*wol*) *gelingen*] seem in ***Erec*** to be almost interchangeable expressions. I see no gaps for the insertion of the lexicographer's wedge, or in the case of *gelücke* / *gelingen* of the etymologist's. By contrast with *sælde* they seem to refer primarily to success on a single occasion; they may indicate that the hero has *sælde*. There are no 'sacral' overtones to *beil,* and only in the context of prayers may we assume that hopes of 'salvation' are expressed. Its general meaning is 'safety', 'safe outcome'. Of the hero, and of any other worthy, it may be predicated that he has *beil* or *gelücke,* or that 'im gelanc' or 'geschach wol'. In this connection Erec's encounter with Guivreiz le pitîz, king of Ireland, is instructive. In Hartmann's long account (4277-610) there is no express reference to the hero's *sælde.* (He has known *sælde* and will later chance upon *der Sælden wec.* Erec's victory over Guivreiz is a turning-point). Guivreiz, though a dwarf, is a highly reputable and doughty fighter, and has hitherto had hitherto had *gelücke* (4305) in many a combat:

dar umbe man noch von im seit
daz im an sîner manheit
unz an den tac nie misselanc.

(4308-10)

He is able to engage Erec only after provoking him. The outcome will be *beil* (4343), he says: 'as God wills', favourable to the one or the other. Since neither combatant was a coward, says Hartmann, strength (Erec is already wounded) and *beil* will decide the issue. The term in Hartmann's use must cover the *gelücke* of Guivreiz and the at least potential *sælde* of Erec, see 4382-7. As for Erec's victory: 'dô Êrecke alsô gelanc' (Hartmann 4463), 'dâ ist iu wol gelungen an' (Guivreiz 4519). Guivreiz refers in his words specifically to Erec's success in making him his 'man', and if his vanquisher is 'ein edel man', Guivreiz will not deem himself unsuccessful (4528-34).

A prefaced reference to God's will does not materially affect the meaning of *beil* (139, 2531, 4343, 6126) or *gelingen* (140, 1265).

[Time, Chance, and opportunity] are of course interlinked and cannot be separately (or fully) illustrated. Towards the end of the romance, Hartmann—and his hero, Erec—seem increasingly to be concerned with time (*zît*), both the appropriate time (for weeping, rejoicing etc.) and time in relation to chance circumstances and opportunity, let us say 'kairos': the recognition of the favourable moment. . . .

As for time in relation to freely undertaken commitments, Erec—unlike Iwein—has no difficulty in keeping appointments. His promise to return within three days from his pursuit of the dwarf (in the event, from the sparrow-hawk contest)—'failing sickness' ('ob ich vor siechtuome mac', 143)—requires no final dash to Arthur's court. Tension results rather from the author's manipulation of the unplanned movements of hero and heroine (they travel *wîselôs,* 'without a guide'), and of various assailants who have no particular reason to be abroad at the time, particularly in the tale of Enite's trials. The possibilities are comically or tragi-comically exploited. There is the timely escape from the inn to dupe the amorous count (3644-4100), and then in the episode of Enite's attempted suicide, the entirely fortuitous arrival, willed by God, of Oringles. Hartmann stays Enite's hand to give her time to curse the sword (responsible for Erec's death'), and to allow Oringles to take in the scene on which he has chanced—and to misread all the signs. He believes himself favoured and acts on the strength of this *wân.* Everything is in fact under control: 'got hete den gewalt und er den wân' (6351).

As for chance (*geschicht*) itself, it is so fixed in Hartmann's mind that chance is willed by God that he can be specific in a prayer: 'nû müeze got gesenden / disen ellenden / . . . ros dâ sî ûfe rîten' (6698-700). God restores to Erec his own horse which a *garzûn,* unaware of the need of the moment, has brought out to water and hands over without comment. This, says Hartmann, proved Erec's *sælekeit* (6713 f).

Insufficient attention has been paid, I think, to the gambler's throw as a simultaneous challenge to all the forces which may govern man's destiny—God, fate, and fortune—to side with him. Erec rejects all 'wise' advice to forego the adventure of *Joie de la curt.* He ignores it as he also ignores omens ('ern was dehein wetersorgaere', 8128; 'er enphlac deheiner spaehe', 8135). He puts his trust in God (8147 f) and in his own conviction that his decision is right (8119-23); he was consequently 'sorgen vrî' when he put his fortune to the test. . . . Note the emphasis on God's will and the favourable time and cir-

Heinrich von dem Türlin's aside in *Die Krone* (c. 1220):

I know very well that it would be excessive and by no means praiseworthy if I were to name the splendid company that was with Fortune's child, King Arthur, as I have often read in the ***Erec*** that a Swabian poet has given us. For this reason I have included those not listed here, of whom Master Hartmann perhaps knew nothing. Maybe he reported as truth a false story that could have been invented by some deceitful man whose nature it was to tell only lies. Yet Hartmann could not be easily harmed by a two-tongued man who from the back attacks one with vicious gossip and from the front washes off the disgrace, because the poet was fully competent.

Heinrich von dem Türlin, in his The Crown: A Tale of Sir Gawein and King Arthur's Court, *translated by J. W. Thomas, University of Nebraska Press, 1989.*

cumstances—'genaedeclîchiu dinc':

got hât wol ze mir getân . . .
ich vinde gar ein wunschspil
dâ ich lützel wider vil
mit einem wurfe wâgen mac.
ich suochtez unz an disen tac:
gote lop, nû hân ichz vunden
dâ ich wider tûsent phunden
wâge einen phenninc.
diz sint genaedeclîchiu dinc,
daz ich hie vinde solh spil.

(8527-38)

Erec goes on to explain his reasoning to his host at Brandigân: great honour will be the prize. His host accepts the validity of his argument, whereupon they 'call it a day': 'nû gân wir slâfen, des ist zît' (8579).

As for the fight, and the inspiration which sustains the contestants, these are properly treated under more conventional headings, chivalry, honour, love etc. . . .

Virtually the only God known to the Arthurian world of Hartmann's ***Erec*** is the 'courtly' God who looks after knights in their perilous exploits and governs their chance encounters. It is the same God to whom private prayers are offered in 'church'. There are, it is true, passages where Hartmann remembers that the Church is 'spiritual':

mit dirre rede si kâmen
dâ si messe vernâmen
von dem heiligen geiste:
des phlegent si aller meiste
die ze ritterschefte sinnent
und turnieren minnent.

(662-7)

(cf. 'mit vrouwen Êniten er kam / dâ er messe vernam / in des heilegen geistes êre, / und vlêhete got vil sêre / daz et im behielte den lîp, 8636-40.) Of the 'messe' as such, we hear once that Erec did not leave until after the blessing (2501), no more. As for officiating and supporting clergy, if one excludes a bishop 'von Cantwarje ûz Engellant' at the wedding of Erec and Enite (2125), they are at best 'diu phafheit' (9751), at worst 'such bishops, abbots and priests as could be got' (or 'rustled up'?: 'swaz man der mohte berîten', 6342-5). The God and the church of the Arthurian world in Chrétien's *Erec* are to nothing like the same extent disestablished. Chrétien has, it is true, no patience with clerics at festive gatherings; but when he deals with the Mass, he remembers not only the Holy Spirit but also procession, altar and the crucifix before which Erec kneels (700-5 and 2374-8). In short, if one allows Hartmann's opening lead that God is 'courtly', all the rest follows, and Erec's faith in his God-given fortune was not misplaced. I prefer the more strictly Boethian interpretation. Erec's real concern is his fortune. His religious observance is 'courtly'.

Frank Tobin (essay date 1978)

SOURCE: "Hartmann's *Erec:* The Perils of Young Love," in *Seminar,* Vol. XIV, No. 1, February, 1978, pp. 1-14.

[*In the following excerpt, Tobin examines Erec and Enite's relationship in light of its influence on Erec's knightly duty to pursue adventure.*]

Through comments of the narrator and the reactions of the hero's own court Hartmann has supplied us with a basic interpretation of ***Erec***. Out of love for his wife Erec has neglected his courtly duties to society and has failed to pursue knightly activity. This has brought dishonour to his court (2966-98). At the end of the story when he returns to Karnant after a series of successful knightly endeavours, he reaps the praise of the narrator by living ever after a life correctly balanced between his duties to his wife and to knighthood (10, 119-24). Just in case we have missed the point, Hartmann has Gawein admonish Iwein about the dangers of *verligen* with specific reference to the fate of Erec. Certainly Hartmann cannot be accused of overestimating the interpretive abilities of his audience! And yet these 'messages' in the text may have the opposite effect—that the reader looks upon the whole narrative simply as a corroboration of the message. Thus Ruh aptly warns us [in his *Höfische Epik des deutschen Mittelalters* (1967)] that the narrator's comments do not do justice to the richness of Hartmann's narratives. Nor should Gottfried's much quoted words about the clarity of Hartmann's diction lead us to infer that he valued a certain naive simplicity in the content of Hartmann's art. After all, his main praise is reserved for the latter's ability to enrich the 'maere beid uzen unde innen / mit worten und mit sinnen,' and to fashion 'der aventiure meine.' The simple interpretation given the story by Gawein would hardly have appealed to the sophisticated Gottfried.

Because of the fine efforts of the past few decades, Kuhn's introductory statement in his ['Erec' in *Dichtung und Welt im Mittelalter* (1969) that ***Erec***] 'steht, trotz aller Arbeit, die man schon auf ihn verwendet, im ganzen nicht sehr überzeugend vor uns—wenn man es recht besieht sogar mehr wie ein Machwerk' is no longer true in its full application. Yet there are aspects of the story which still need explanation. One of these is what, over and above the basic message already mentioned, the narrative has to say about the relationship between the hero and his wife. Probably everyone agrees . . . that the series of *aventiuren,* which make up the bulk of the narrative, serve to test the *Liebesgemeinschaft* of Eric and Enite. General agreement disappears, however, when one asks, especially regarding Enite, what flaws necessitate the testing of the relationship. Moreover, secondary literature is remarkably silent when it comes to showing in any detail exactly how the *aventiuren* carry out such testing. It is the purpose of this study to bring some clarity and perspective to the first question and to offer some specific approaches to answering the second.

However, before we begin searching the text for flaws in the protagonist and his wife which might render the corrective experience of the *aventiurenweg* necessary, a brief consideration of narrative structure can provide orientation. It is generally recognized that the better Arthurian narratives in general and all of Hartmann's narratives (with ***Der arme Heinrich*** showing a slight variation) reveal the following structural pattern: 1 / rising action, 2 / happiness achieved, 3 / catastrophe, 4 / second rising action, 5 / stable happiness achieved. The first rising action and attainment of happiness demonstrate admirable qualities in the hero, but the ensuing catastrophe indicates he has not yet achieved the ethical level which the author envisions as the ideal. The first rising action and resulting happiness as well as the persons achieving it can be seen in retrospect as embodying clichés. This is a fact arising from the very structure being employed. To consider the main figures as static entities throughout the narrative who undergo no improvement is to accuse the author of not recognizing the nature of the structure he has chosen.

In ***Erec*** both hero and heroine, though the action up to the moment of crisis shows them to possess remarkable and endearing qualities, are little more than courtly stereotypes that need to be called into question. Erec overcomes the dishonour done to him by great physical prowess in defeating Iders. His success is motivated by the standard thoughts of shame endured and Enite's beauty (930-9). In fairy-tale fashion he gains a bride and through superior knightly ability raises her from a lowly condition to queen. He experiences the *de rigueur* exchange of hearts with her at the tournament (2358-67) before excelling again in knightly combat. Finally he enters into his inheritance and rules justly.

Enite's rise is no less cliché-ridden. Her adverse situation is unable to hide her stunning beauty. She complains bitterly when things are going badly for Erec in his contest with Iders. She is shy and child-like in public (1320). After finally being clothed in accordance with her beauty and goodness upon her arrival at the court of Artus, she captivates the hearts of all, as well she should, and receives in the kiss from Artus the ultimate confirmation of her womanly perfections. During the tournament she looks on and is proud when people praise her husband. She fears losing him but decides that she prefers having a *degen* for a husband to an *arger zage* (2628-51). Thus, she attains her rags-to-riches success through stunning beauty and a stereotype show that her heart is in the right place.

What is true of them in general is equally valid for their relationship to each other. Whatever specific reasons for their fall can be adduced, or whatever guilt can be determined, the events and their implications show that their *Liebesgemeinschaft,* too, had not risen beyond the level of a cliché. For the sake of clarity we shall follow first Enite and then Erec from the moment of crisis and along the path of *aventiuren,* examining what these tell us of their attitudes towards each other and how these attitudes are shown to change.

While the failings of Erec which cause him to leave Karnant are evident, Enite's possible guilt and her role on the journey are more ambiguous, as the disagreement among critics shows despite their unanimous praise of her. Kuhn mentions in passing the possibility of her being tinged by a kind of 'objective' guilt arising from her existence as a woman but gallantly balances this with an unqualified defence of this perhaps most appealing of Hartmann's female characters. Wapnewski pronounces her free of all guilt and remarks that only the boundlessness of her love could be considered a flaw [*Hartmann von Aue* (1967)]. Hrubý, in . . . ["Die Problemstellung in Chrétiens und Hartmanns ***Erec,***" *Deutsche Vierteljahresschrift für Literatur wissenschaft und Geistesgeschichte,* 38 (1964)] sees the *aventiurenweg* as a *Prüfungsfahrt* for Enite as well as for Erec, but in a more negative vein regarding the heroine asserts that, although Hartmann generally suppresses the notion of guilt regarding her, she shows a lack of humility in uttering the complaint which led to their journey, as she herself later recognizes. Tax's ["Studien zum Symbolischen in Hartmanns ***Erec***. Enites Pferd, *Zeitschrift für deutsche Philologie,* 82 (1963)] combines an appreciation of her exemplary position with a note of severity. Like her husband she was guilty of concupiscence in her love. Thus the gold that she always was needed purification. [In "*Triuwe* and *Untriuwe* in Hartmann's ***Erec,***" *German Quarterly,* 43 (1970)] Wilson also speaks of inordinate aspects in her love for her husband that become evident especially in her neglecting to inform him freely of his sorry condition and of that of his court in Karnant. Ruh, who shares the opinion of Kuhn and Wapnewski that Enite is without subjective guilt, answers that since the husband was clearly dominant in medieval marriages, Enite is not obligated to criticism, nor should such be expected from her. Diverging markedly from these lines of thought is Cramer's view [in "Soziale Motivation in der Schuld-Sühne-Problematik von Hartmann's ***Erec,***" *Euphorion,* 66 (1972)] that Enite's poverty is a social flaw with metaphysical implications which has to be compensated for before her marriage to Erec can rest on a secure foundation.

In attempting to deal with this diversity of opinion we can best begin by again considering a fact of the basic plot structure. As Cramer has noted, Enite, contrary to custom, accompanies her husband on his journey. One reason may be that, just as she has witnessed her husband's shame, so should she witness his efforts to erase it. Also we are later clearly told that Erec's purpose in commanding her to accompany him was to test her (6781-2). Whatever Erec himself conceives the exact nature of this test to be, the very fact that she must go along and be exposed to the dangers of the journey does indeed, quite apart from her husband's intentions, test her and force the articulation of her personality, so that the Enite of the end differs greatly from the newly crowned queen of Karnant. The narrator's reference to gold purified in the fire states this well (6785-6). On the journey Enite does not just observe but participates in most of the action in essential ways, influencing events and being influenced by them. Thus, because of the very mechanics of the literary form employed, Enite and her relationship to her husband must undergo development. That she accompanies Erec does not of itself indicate guilt in the heroine. However, if we admit that in becoming a queen she has not developed beyond a cliché, it becomes clearer why Enite's role in this narrative is quite different from that of the platonic idea of *frouwe* in the love lyric or of the perfect but static ideal woman represented by Condwiramurs in *Parzival*. What Kellermann has noted [in "L'adaptation du roman d'Erec et Enide de Chrétien de Troyes par Hartmann von Aue," *Mélanges de lange et de lìtterature du Moyen Age et de la Renaissance, offerts à Jean Frappier* (1970)] about the differences in the hero between the French and the German version—that Hartmann's Erec, though a unified character, is unfinished—is equally true regarding the heroine. She is largely an unformed personality, and her love for Erec has not taken on clear definition. Hartmann, in contrast to his source, presents us with a girl whose charm lies mainly in her naiveté. But this endearing quality is not without its problems. What has to be clarified is: What concrete form will her total and simple love of Erec take when confronted by a situation which renders its expression problematic? This, rather than her guilt or innocence, seems to be the central question concerning Enite, if we take our cue from her actions in her dilemma in Karnant and on the *aventiurenweg*. Before their journey her love is complete but amorphous. The moment of crisis demonstrates the defects of such love. Through the *aventiurenweg* her love will take on form, allowing it to function correctly in difficult situations.

Hartmann's sympathetic treatment of Enite during the catastrophe should make us wary of judging her too harshly. When she hears of the evil talk going on about Erec and the blame being put on her for his inactivity, she is saddened, 'wan si was biderbe unde guot' (3003). She acknowledges her own guilt in the matter (3007-8), which has caused benevolent critics to protest that this is a magnanimous gesture on her part rather than reflecting the true state of affairs or to explain the guilt as objective, i.e., arising out of her very existence as a lovely and desirable woman. But does not her position as Queen of Karnant demand that she be aware from the beginning of the effect of her marital love on the kingdom? This is of course a lot to expect from someone of such limited experience, but the fact remains that she gives much evidence of not being equal to her role. She does not dare to speak lest she thereby lose her husband (3011-12). Here Hartmann adds an interesting detail (absent in Chrétien) to the bedroom scene where Erec first learns of his wife's discontent. He devotes seven lines to a description of how the sun, 'daz er [sunshine] ir [Erec and Enite] dienest muoste sîn' (3017), illuminates the room, 'daz si sich mohten undersehen' (3022). There follows immediately the description of how Enite begins to ponder their unhappy situation and emits her fateful sigh. These lines can hardly be viewed solely as realistic description. Certainly mention of the sun serves to fix this central scene concretely in our minds, but its more proper function seems rather to be to emphasize that the couple see each other and their true situation with new clarity. This causes estrangement. Instead of two hearts beating as one, we see Enite at first try to deny her true feelings and speak only in the fear that her husband would otherwise accuse her of *ander dinge* and in the hope that it might still his anger (3038-49). She handles the situation badly, fulfilling her obligation to tell her husband his true condition, yet doing so only under duress and unwillingly. This ambivalence puts their relationship in jeopardy.

In attempting to determine to what extent the author thinks Enite to have failed in her duties or to have incurred guilt, we should consider on the one hand how humanly attractive he has made her, and on the other hand how through the instrumentality of her husband he returns her to the station she had before the sudden rise in her fortunes. She again becomes her husband's groom and remains so until her trials are past. Thus on the *aventiurenweg* both she and Erec make fresh starts to earn goals already dubiously in their possession.

Since Erec is clearly the protagonist of the piece, we should not expect to be able to explain all the events of the journey in terms of Enite or in terms of Erec's relationship to her. The *aventiuren* clearly function also in other ways as, for example, to restore Erec's knightly honour. Regarding Enite, however, one basic pattern occurs repeatedly in which she is forced into the same dilemma she faced but did not resolve in the bedroom in Karnant. This fact forces us to reflect on the nature of the *aventiurenweg*. The allegorical nature of *Joie de la curt* has been recognized for some time. What has not been fully appreciated is that there are definite allegorical aspects to the entire journey. In the case of Enite, who was unable to cope with clear *ethical* danger to her husband in Karnant, the recurring dilemma is one involving imminent *physical* danger. The robber episodes illustrate this well and should, even without the corroboration of later episodes, dispel any doubts about whether or not the author thinks Enite was under obligation to admonish her husband in Karnant.

In both robber episodes her lover and husband is in great danger and, as earlier, Enite alone is aware of it. Here, too, because of the command of silence she risks losing the favour of her lord (and physically her life!), if she speaks. This time, however, she freely and selflessly chooses to warn him and take upon herself whatever risks are entailed in protecting him. What she could not bring herself to do in the case of an ethical danger to her husband, namely, risk their *Liebesgemeinschaft* in order to make him aware of danger, she does here and thus shows that any complaints she may have uttered were not based on selfish thoughts of damage to her own honour because of his inactivity, but solely for his good.

Certain changes Hartmann has made in adapting Chrétien's version of the robber episodes give added indications as to how he wished the episodes to be understood. First of all, in the second robber episode Chrétien has Erec become aware of the robbers before Enide but feign ignorance in order to force her to speak. Hartmann's Erec engages in no such manipulation. Both times he really is dependent for his well-being on his wife's ability to perceive the danger. Hartmann also emphasizes Enite's utter dependence on her husband. Both times (only once in Chrétien) she is singled out by the first robber as his coveted booty. Thus her warning and Erec's prompt and successful response are absolutely necessary to protect her from certain shame and physical harm. Chrétien has his worldly-wiser Enide recognize and remark on this fact. Hartmann's heroine in keeping with her naiveté and selfless devotion seems totally unaware that in saving Erec she is saving herself. In this respect, too, the parallelism between the physical order and the previous ethical situation can hardly be missed. These episodes make clear to the reader, even if the hero and heroine still remain oblivious to the fact for different reasons, how intricate the bonds are which hold them together and how mutually dependent they are for their very existence.

The first episode with a count, besides repeating the pattern of the dilemma, serves to test Enite in a very direct way. In marrying Erec she had exchanged hardship for social prominence. Would she betray her love for another meteoric rise? As in the previous *aventiuren* she acts solely for the good of Erec, even if this should bring disadvantage and danger to her. Earlier, marrying Erec and raising herself socially were one and the same action. Here they are opposites. Thus the episode further clarifies and articulates her love.

The first Guivreiz episode, the interlude with Artus, and the saving of Cadoc are concerned mainly with aspects of Erec's knighthood and, aside from reinforcing points already made, yield little to increase our understanding of the problems of Erec and Enite's union. Not until Enite's complaint, when she supposes Erec to be dead, does their union again assume central importance. The function of this *klage* has been misunderstood by some critics, whose use of it for interpretation reveals a weakness in method. The underlying assumption of these critics is that the correct interpretation of events is expressed by a character in the story. If this assumption is dangerous in general (and, where true, often indicative of a lack of artistry on the part of the author), how much more so in the case of a woman who is beside herself with grief and contemplating suicide. Yet Hrubý in an otherwise sound and valuable piece of scholarship makes this assumption when he concurs with Enite's self-accusation that she is responsible for Erec's death because her sigh was the occasion for the journey, that she has thereby lost body and soul, and that the dissatisfaction which caused the sigh was the work of the devil (5940-73). Cramer on the other hand sees in her dark figure of the tree unable to change its nature by transplantation the confirmation of his thesis that Enite's guilt consists in her poverty. Her attempt at self-destruction, prevented not by any change of heart but only by the timely arrival of Count Oringles, does not deter Willson from characterizing her love for Erec as *caritas*. If one accepts some of her statements as expressing the intention of the work, is one not bound to accept all such statements as truth unless there is some clear indication to the contrary? Are we, then, also to assume she is correct when she charges God with a lack of mercy or when she blames Erec's sword for his death with the implicit assumption that the danger involved in knightly deeds make them evil? Rather than seek the answer to the guilt question in these anguished laments, we would do better to see in them the confused and contradictory yet eloquent verbal expression of Enite's all-consuming love for Erec which she has already shown so often in deed. Despairing because of his apparent death, she gives clear evidence through behaviour shocking to proponents of *mâze* and theologians of just how absolute her love is and just how dependent she has made her existence on Erec. If the *klage* has interpretive value over and above this, it might be sought in determining whether God seems to accept the offer she makes when she wishes to let Erec's life depend on the quality of her love:

unde habe ich mînen man,
sît ich in von êrste gewan,
verworht an ihtes ihte
mit muote oder von geschihte
alsô daz ez niht wol gezimt,
ob mir in dîn gewalt danne nimt,
daz selbe reht vinde ich mir,
wan ichs von rehte danne enbir.
enhân aber ich des niht getân,
des soltû mich geniezen lân:
herre, sô erbarme dich
durch dîne güete über mich
unde heiz mir in leben.

(5808-20)

The Count Oringles episode is clearly the turning-point for Erec and Enite in the perfecting of their relationship. Cramer's characterization of it as 'ein Geflecht von symbolisch zu verstehenden Handlungen und Gesten' is very apt. However, because he considers Enite's poverty together with Erec's failure to see its social and metaphysical implications in marrying her to be the basic cause of their problems, Cramer misses much of the significance of the scene. True, for Enite it represents a third chance (Erec and the first count being the first two) to improve her social position through marriage. But when Cramer sees in her refusal the symbolic reparation for the wrong connected to her marrying Erec, he must overlook her stated reasons for now refusing. She does so not out of any sense of the social impropriety such a marriage would entail, but solely because her devotion to Erec transcends death and renders union with any other man impossible. The absolute *triuwe* she has shown with almost monotonous regularity in every trying circumstance triumphs here one final time and, by removing any question concerning her relationship to Erec, leads to the reunion of the couple.

In contrast to Enite there is no need to comment on Erec's purpose in embarking on the *aventiurenweg.* To understand how it changes his attitude towards his wife, we must first briefly examine his relations to her up to the catastrophe. Their marriage, like the persons themselves, rests upon the questionable foundation of fairy-tale or Arthurian clichés. The promise of marriage is incidental to Erec's primary purpose of gaining revenge on Iders. Enite is a pawn to be raised to social prominence in return for the use of desperately needed armour (511-24). At this point her beauty or personal qualities are of secondary concern. Later, however, mutual passionate desire does emerge; and just before the wedding the secret thought of each is 'jâ enwirde ich nimmer vrô, / ich engelige dir noch bî / zwô naht oder drî' (1873-5). From all indications Erec has not gone beyond exploring this aspect of their marriage up to that fateful day when the sun casts its disturbing light into their bedroom and Enite sighs:

> . . . wê, dir, dû vil armer man,
> und mir ellendem wîbe
> daz ich mînem lîbe
> sô manegen vluoch vernemen sol.
>
> (3029-32)

The complaint is couched in such a way that to Erec's ears the reasons motivating it must remain uncertain. Since she had not intended to be heard, her words might well have been prompted by contempt for him or by egotistical self-pity. His immediate reaction, though his refusal to comment directly leaves some ambiguity, can hardly be interpreted otherwise than as an expression of extreme irritation at his wife. The ensuing ill-treatment of her, the command to silence, and the separation *toro et mensa* coupled with the later remark that he was attempting to determine 'ob si im waere ein rehtez wîp' (6782) indicate the gravity of the doubts he has concerning her which must be settled before they can resume their marriage.

The *aventiurenweg,* besides serving as a means for Erec to re-establish his knightly honour, is therefore a means for Erec to come to recognize just how much of a *rehtez wîp* for him Enite is. However, just as with Enite, the journey has also for him an allegorical aspect. The antagonists, at least those in the episodes we have examined concerning Enite, can be shown to embody attitudes present in Erec himself. In overcoming these adversaries Erec overcomes symbolically deficiencies in his attitude towards Enite which, along with his doubts, must be dealt with before their marriage can rest secure.

In besting the robbers, who consider Enite as booty to be won through combat, Erec symbolically divests himself of the assumption implicit in his business transaction with Koralus that she is a prize to be won by overcoming Iders. That any real change in attitude here remains slight is clear from Erec's continued ill-treatment of her, while his tirade against her as an Eve, who only really finds a deed interesting when it has been forbidden (3238-58), shows that he continues to think of her largely in clichés. The *minne* which Enite arouses in the first count and which the narrator reminds us can be a force for evil as well as good (3691-705) resembles Erec's passion for Enite. In the case of both men *minne* is the cause of reprehensible behaviour. The triumph over the count indicates a victory over merely impulsive or raw *minne.*

The morality of Enite's lying to the count is glossed over by the narrator who says did it *âne sünde* (4026), and perhaps we should follow suit rather than raise it to the dignity of a problem. However, her fabrications do seem to contain some hidden truths about the ambiguity of her position. In her first story she goes beyond the facts in claiming for herself neither *geburt* nor *guot,* and she maintains that she suffers Erec's treatment *mit rehte* (3810-12). When she sees that this approach does not deter the count, she reverses her story and claims to be of higher station than her companion, who had taken her as a mere child *mit liste* and is therefore an outcast from his own land (3868-84). As we have seen, there is some justification for the hardships she is suffering. And yet her present situation and her husband's absence from his land are due in part to his taking her, hardly more than a child, and putting her in a position of responsibility she was not ready to assume. The count, when his party has caught up with the fleeing couple, repeats the charge that Erec had taken her from her father. He continues: 'ez möhte an dirre vrouwen / ein tôre wol schouwen / daz si iu niht enist ze mâze' (4188-90). To Erec this stinging rebuke should contain a ring of truth since Enite has just proved again and immediately following a repetition of his command to keep silent under pain of death that her *triuwe* to him is unconditional and complete by warning him for the fourth time of approaching danger. However, his lingering ambivalence towards her reveals itself during their flight at the end of the episode. The flight is motivated by fear for his wife (4116). Yet almost immediately he repeats his command of silence under pain of death (4130-2).

If the examples of the robbers and the first count as reflecting something that Erec must overcome in himself do not appear completely convincing, the symbolic identity of Erec with Oringles seems unmistakable. Once Oringles has convinced himself of Enite's noble birth and has decided with the approval of his court to marry her, he is impervious to criticism of his haste or to the thought that the intended bride could react to his plans with anything but joy. Any other response would be unrealistic and show ingratitude. Erec, who has shown no great ability to think through and beyond the clichés around him, very probably fell into the very human syndrome of thinking that Enite's criticism, especially after all he has done for her, is ingratitude. The accusations of Oringles against Enite fit perfectly the facts surrounding Erec's winning of Enite and could well be thoughts going through the mind of

Erec after the *sûft* and on the journey:

hiute wider gester
sô stât iuwer dinc doch ungelîch.
ê wâret ir arm, nû sît ir rîch:
vor wâret ir niemen wert,
nû hât iuch got êren gewert:
ê wâret ir vil unerkant,
nû sît ir gewaltic über ein lant:
ê in swacher schouwe,
nû ein rîchiu vrouwe:
vor muostet ir ûz der ahte sîn,
nû sît ir ein mehtic graevîn:
ê vuoret ir wîselôs,
unz iuwer saelde mich erkôs:
vor wâret ir aller genâden bar,
nû habet ir die êre gar:
ê litet ir michel arbeit,
dâ von hât iuch got geleit:
vor hetet ir ein swachez leben,
nû hât iu got den wunsch gegeben:
vor muoste iu vil gewerren,
nû lobet unsern herren
daz er iuchs hât übertragen
und lât iuwer tumbez klagen:
ê lebetet ir âne êre,
der habet ir nû mêre
dan dehein iuwer lantwîp.

(6469-94)

He then strikes her and counters criticism with the remark that he can do what he wishes with her since 'si ist mîn und ich bin ir' (6546). This is hardly the context for such a formulation of what marriage is and shows that Oringles, like Erec, is completely unaware of the mutual aspect of the rights and duties implied in it. Enite endures this ill-treatment, which parallels the hardship Erec has forced her to suffer, willingly and, as always, out of love for Erec.

As in Karnant, it is again Enite, bewailing her fate, who raises the unconscious Erec to action. With every possible doubt about her *triuwe* removed, the new Erec . . . slays the last bit of the old Erec. Again we have the pattern of an 'existential' interdependence in which Enite occasions Erec's action which in turn saves them both. That the scene has its primary significance in this symbolism seems very probable when one realizes that on the 'real' level Erec perpetrates brutal murders out of all proportion to the baseness of the victims. Yet the episode is perhaps most memorable for being one of the great comedy scenes in medieval literature. The episode closes with the pair both seated on Erec's horse and Enite giving directions to her disoriented husband. They are closer now than if Enite were riding in proper fashion on her own horse. Erec no longer protests her speaking to determine the direction of their journey. Willingly he listens to her and is thus able to lead them both out of certain danger.

The Oringles episode removes the last traces of doubt Erec has concerning his wife and allows him to conquer those last failings of his own which have undermined their union. By their celebration of love after the brief interruption of the second encounter with Guivreiz they reaffirm that all difficulties have been completely resolved. The noble dwarf's presentation of a horse to Enite during the recuperative stay at Penefrec elevates her to the position she has merited and erases the wrongs she suffered as Erec's groom. The nature and length of the description which Hartmann, far surpassing his source, devotes to this marvellous animal and its trappings serve to raise the heroine to epic stature and to provide her with a fitting mount on which to ride beside her husband to their final triumph in *Joie de la curt*.

Concerning this final *aventiure* which confirms the couple in their roles as exemplary heroes we can add only one dimension to the clear and convincing interpretation given by Kuhn. As he has pointed out, we are presented with an allegory in which the correct form of *minne,* a *minne* which unites one with one's fellow men, conquers the wrong idea of *minne*. Because of the insight and experience which their journey represents, Erec, relying on Enite's love, can conquer Mabonagrin and can restore the joy of the court. Despite the fact of allegory Hartmann's portrayal of the episode is more vivid than what has gone before. The charm of the garden and its inhabitants when combined with the ghastly sight of the eighty poles capped with the heads of the defeated knights has an aura of eerie horror that is extremely functional. It is not just a false notion of *minne* that the hero overcomes. Rather it is exactly that *minne* which they had practiced in Karnant, here heightened by being shown as it would be if extended to its ultimate conclusions. In the garden *minne-dienest* means the ruthless destruction of anything which could interfere with the exclusive demands of love. This is just a logical extension or caricature of Erec's neglect of social duties out of love. The woman, who by her possessive love moves Mabonagrin to perform these terrible deeds in defence of that love, is just an extension or caricature of Enite who refuses to criticize Erec lest she 'lose' him. In *Joie de la curt* the insidious implications of the love in Karnant become manifest with fearful clarity. Not until *Joie de la curt* are we shown how much was at stake when Erec and Enite set out on the *aventiurenweg* to confront and conquer the problem of their *minne*.

S. L. Clark (essay date 1981)

SOURCE: "Hartman's *Êrec:* Language, Perception, and Transformation," in *The Germanic Review,* Vol. LVI, No. 3, Summer, 1981, pp. 81-94.

[*In the following essay, Clark outlines Hartmann's portrayal of Erec's maturation.*]

For much of Hartmann's ***Êrec,*** the protagonist is characterized as a man plagued by one or another form of disorientation; an examination of the narrator's justifications for Êrec's frequent perceptual failures opens up a profitable avenue of approach to the work's thematic structure. Throughout the poem, the narrator repeatedly calls attention to the hero's unfamiliarity with his surroundings (ll.250, 4277, 4623, 5288, 6737, 7808), his non-recognition of opponents (ll.459, 4468ff.), and his general unawareness of impending dangers (ll.3123, 4150ff.). In several instances the narrator appends a disclaimer that attempts to minimize Êrec's failings on the grounds of physical unaccountability; thus, it is Ênîte who notes the three robbers before her husband becomes aware of them, and she does so, on Hartmann's account, merely because "si verre vor reit" (l.3124). Similarly, it is Ênîte who is able to ascertain the lecherous count's intent, because she is simply sitting at some distance from her husband:

> . . . si sô besunder
> an dem tische sâzen
> und ensament niht enâzen.
>
> (ll.3731-3733)

Perhaps the most curious disclaimer comes in a narrative intrusion that approaches a rationalization. Ênîte hears the approach of a "michel her" (l.4148) and warns Êrec, at which point the narrator hastens to note:

> nû endarf niemen sprechen daz:
> 'von wiu kam daz diu vrouwe baz
> beide gehôrte und gesach?'
> ich sage iu von wiu daz geschach.
> diu vrouwe reit gewaefens bar:
> dâ was er gewâfent gar,
> als ein guot ritter sol.
> daz gehôrte er noch gesach sô wol
> ûz der îsenwaete
> als er blôzer taete.
>
> (ll.4150-4159)

The reader's immediate response is that this is a fairly sound piece of reasoning, medieval armor being what it is. Yet, upon closer consideration, several difficulties arise, the paramount of which is: all of Êrec's opponents are armed as well, and yet they are cast as being more perceptive than he is, in that either they spot him before he sees or hears them, or they are often engaged in active pursuit of him. Moreover, none of Êrec's opponents sends out a woman as a kind of advance guard, as Êrec does. If knights were so hampered by the perceptual limitations of their martial gear, each knight would have a woman to act as an early warning system, much as a shark has a pilot fish as part of its defense system. Thus, the narrator's explanation, rather than settling the matter, as it ostensibly sets out to do, raises the thematically central issue of perception in an impelling way and causes the reader to examine instances in which Êrec's perceptual abilities are limited or lacking, whether this is due to physical unaccountability or innate insensitivity.

In the cases where Hartmann shows Ênîte operating perceptively while at a distance from her husband, the author cannot be implying that close physical proximity to the dangers threatening his wife would make Êrec a more perceptive individual, for it is when Êrec and Ênîte are in greatest moral danger, as he succumbs to uxoriousness early in the romance, that he is most unaware—and she particularly aware—of the dangers such "gemach" (l.2967) presents. Similarly, in the companion "Scheintod" scene, Êrec is near his threatened wife, to be sure, but is for the greater part of the scene oblivious due to his unconsciousness. Quite clearly, the deciding factor cannot be physical proximity, but rather the consciousness of danger, a consciousness that entails the correct interpretation of perceptions and results in actions which can rectify a situation. The Êrec at the very beginning of the romance possesses this consciousness, and he wisely perceives danger and acts prudently to avoid physical confrontation when he is unarmed; he is significantly described by Hartmann as being "blôz als ein wîp" (l.103). But Êrec, in acquiring a wife and lover, lapses. Over the bulk of the romance that occurs after Êrec has won Ênîte, Hartmann will chart the process whereby the hero is transformed from a man who cannot perceive correctly and, as a result, is often portrayed as morally and physically disoriented, to a man who, in gaining an understanding of the extremely perceptive woman he has taken to wife, is no longer "wîselos" (ll.250, 6480), that is lacking direction and lacking wisdom.

Êrec's journey, during which he comes to perceive and acknowledge his wife's "triuwe," proves to be a highly organized series of challenges, rather than a random sequence of adventures. All are challenges which treat some aspect of the associations between perception, thought, speech, and actions. In effect, Êrec is placed into situations where he is uncertain about the outcome and is even at times physically lost, so that he can learn through trial and error to exercise right perception, thought, speech, and action in order to extricate and orient himself. His wanderings in the dangerous physical landscape mirror his mental restlessness and uncertainty concerning the words spoken to him by his wife, and his battle encounters stand out like signposts in his spiritual journey: each presents him with a challenge, positive or negative, to which he must respond properly. Over the course of the romance, Êrec is brought, by way of negative example, to consider the implications of rash decision (his own resolution to use his wife as bait for robbers and thieves), unconsidered word-giving (Mâbonagrîn's pledge to his wife), and precipitous action (Oringles' physical and verbal abuse of Ênîte). And he is given positive *exempla* of prudent behavior in the heightened perception and wise counsel of Gâwein, Guivreiz, Ênîte's father, and especially his own wife, who speaks words of wisdom which Êrec hears but initially cannot comprehend. Each of the adventures which befall Êrec teaches him and, at the same time, tests him in the translation of accurate perceptions into knowledge and, in turn, into sensible speech and action, so that the Êrec who repeatedly enjoins his wife to silence when she dares to give him information vital to his survival becomes a man who learns that it is wise to employ a variety of responses, now speech and now action, to individual situations, and who protects his wife from, rather than exposes her to, danger. In order to examine the implications of the transformation of the hero, it proves most illuminating to consider Êrec's changing attitude toward language, which serves as a mediator, on the one hand, between one's knowledge, so directly dependent on perception, and, on the other hand, one's speech, that vocalization which so often precedes action.

Hartmann's most obvious concern with language is couched in terms of a speech/silence dichotomy, ranging from his frequent employment of variations on *sagen/ verdagen* as couplet rhymes—for the repeated rhyme-pair placement serves as a particularly effective way of focusing on an important opposition—to the scrupulously presented debates that rage in Ênîte's mind, debates whose subject treats the question of whether or not to speak, and whose resolution breaks the silence. In fact, it is no oversimplification to state that the very plot hinges upon the presence and absence of speech, as well as on the perception and interpretation of language. To be sure, it would be rare to find a medieval romance that eschewed dialogue, but ***Êrec*** proves to be unusual in its use of dialogue as a thematic concern as well as a plot facilitator. In ***Êrec*** are raised questions not only about the suitability of speech at certain times but also about speech as a fitting vehicle for thought and as an adequate expression of intent.

Each of Êrec's adventures contains one if not more significant interchanges concerning the use, value, or suitability of speech. Êrec, "der wort wîse" (l.2521), is, in the early part of the romance, often cast in the role of one who demands information ("saget ir rehte wer ir sît" [l.1086]) or who admonishes others to remain silent when their words are foolish ("sult ir stille dagen" [l.577]); and it is Êrec who responds prudently to the maiden's encounter with the alternatively verbally abusive and stubbornly taciturn dwarf, of whom Hartmann writes:

> daz getwerc enwolde ir niht sagen
> und hiez si stille dagen
>
> (ll.44-45)

Clearly, Hartmann's intent here in presenting Êrec's encounter with the dwarf, over and above his decision to follow Chrétien's model, is to create an encapsulated portrait of Êrec against which the audience can judge the hero later in the romance, and it is a portrait that heavily stresses Êrec's wisdom with respect to speech and action. First of all, it must be noted that the fundamentals of the opening sequence are startlingly like those of Êrec's later adventures. A woman rides forth into an unknown situation, while Êrec initially remains at a safe distance, albeit at the queen's behest. This is not at all unlike Ênîte's testing dangerous waters for her husband; and the maiden, like Ênîte, bears the brunt of the consequences. Here, however, Êrec quickly perceives the danger, the ugly nature of the strange knight, and the necessity of his intervention, and caps this knowledge with a speech that stresses his eagerness to know even more:

> Êrec dô ahten began,
> der ritter enwaere dehein vrum man,
> daz er ez vor im vertruoc
> daz sîn getwerc die maget sluoc.
> er sprach: 'ich wil rîten dar,
> daz ich iu diu maere ervar.'
>
> (ll.66-71)

Êrec's attitude stands in sharp contrast to his subsequent lack of desire to know the nature of the dangers facing his wife, as she alerts him to the presence of robbers and as he rebukes her for her admonitory speeches. Furthermore, it proves significant that Êrec's request to the dwarf is one for speech (l.76), reiterating the maiden's request for knowledge, which was summarily met with a demand for silence (ll.44-45). Êrec's request is countered by a rude enjoinder to silence ('lâ dîn klaffen sîn [l.83]) and an incorrect assessment on the dwarf's part: "ir ensît niht wîse liute" (l.88). The narrator, however, shortly thereafter notes that Êrec acted prudently ("wîslîchen" [l.100]) in postponing conflict until he is armed. Êrec returns to the queen and in a lengthy monologue (ll.113-143) recounts the events, interjects his perception and interpretation of them, and details his anticipated reactions to them. The composite portrait of the protagonist thus reveals Êrec to be a man who perceives, thinks, and acts wisely and who here relies on the capacity of language to communicate, for he both requests speech of the dwarf and readily lets the queen be privy to his thoughts of revenge (ll.135-137). Unlike the man he will become, the Êrec at the romance's outset is not averse to letting others know what is on his mind, and, moreover, he is positively talkative in comparison to either the maiden or the queen.

In addition, the reader is shortly thereafter accorded a rare glance into Êrec's thoughts in a short interior monologue. One recalls that Êrec has taken refuge in what he mistakenly assumes to be a deserted house.

> er gedâhte: 'mîn dinc daz vert nû wol,
> wan ich in einem winkel sol
> belîben hinne unz an den tac,
> sît ich niht wesen baz enmac.
> des gan man mir doch âne strît:
> ich sihe wol daz ez oede lît.'
>
> (ll.264-269)

It is not only an unusual glimpse into Êrec's consciousness of his situation—he will not have another interior monologue until nearly 8,000 lines have passed (ll.8147-8153, when his thoughts are given as a prayer to God)—but it is also important that Êrec here makes what will be for him a characteristic misperception. Just as he will later not recognize the full value of his wife, so he here is unaware of the presence of inhabitants in what he takes to be an abandoned house; in each instance he takes control of, or occupies, before he has full information on the nature of the person he loves or the house he enters. In this scene, once Êrec has recognized his mistake, one finds the hero portrayed primarily positively, for he addresses Koralus (l.302) and later requests information (ll.447-450) and advice (ll.479, 495) from the old man. It is Êrec who comments upon Ênîte's caring for his horse and offers to do it himself (ll.344-346), an attitude diametrically opposed to that which he adopts later in the romance when he demands that Ênîte care not for one but for many horses. Moreover, it is Êrec who convinces Koralus that his words are "vür ernest" (l.565) about wanting to marry Ênîte, and it is Êrec who admonishes her father to silence about the matter of Ênîte's poverty:

'ir armuot hoere ich iuch klagen:
der sult ir stille gedagen.
ez enschadet iu niht gegen mir,
wan ich ir guotes wol enbir.'

(ll.576-579)

Throughout Ênîte has been surprisingly taciturn, having been limited to one obedient phrase ("herre, daz tuon ich" [l.322]), which stands in direct contrast to her later speeches. Here the reader simply does not know her thoughts; attention is focused on those of the man and on his willingness to communicate them: "ich sage iu wie mîn muot stât" (l.501). In fact, Ênîte is given no recorded speech until her fateful outburst:

si sprach: 'wê dir, dû vil armer man,
und mir ellendem wîbe,
daz ich mînem lîbe
sô manegen vluoch vernemen sol.'

(ll.3029-3032)

The reader is told that she laments as Êrec fights Îdêr (ll.802, 852), but the overall impression of a non-verbal Ênîte is confirmed in the vignette which occurs after the clash in which Êrec wins the sparrow hawk:

in ir schôz leite in
daz kint vrouwe Ênîte
ze ruowe nâch dem strîte.
ir gebaerde was vil bliuchlîch,
einer magede gelîch.
si enredete im niht vil mite:
wan daz ist ir aller site
daz si zem êrsten schamic sint
und blûc sam diu kint.

(ll.1317-1325)

That Ênîte's one pre-outburst thought to which the reader is party is also Êrec's thought raises interesting implications. Hartmann notes:

ir beider gedanc stuont alsô:
'jâ enwirde ich nimmer vrô,
ich engelige dir noch bî
zwô naht oder drî'

(ll.1873-1875)

The thought is unblushingly sensual, and it suggests that Ênîte is perceiving herself as the sexual being Êrec sees her to be. In fact, Êrec's initial interest in her is aroused solely by her beauty, and he frankly counters Îmâîn's cordial offer of better clothing for Ênîte with a cool statement concerning what he feels is worth noting in a woman:

'er haete harte missesehen,
swer ein wîp erkande
niuwan bî dem gewande.
man sol einem wîbe
kiesen bî dem lîbe
ob si ze lobe stât
unde niht bî der wât.'

(ll.643-659)

Lîp in Middle High German is, to be sure, a loaded word, but, given Êrec's subsequent tendency to uxoriousness and Ênîte's repeated association with horses, frequent icons for lust and the flesh during the Middle Ages, it is reasonable to assume that Êrec's interest is with 'lîp' on the literal, rather than on the abstract, level. His is an interest shared by the Arthurian court, which, after one dazzled glance at her person, selects her as "die schoenste" (l.1742). Her physical beauty even makes a self-professed lover out of the narrator, who affects inability to do justice to an account of her beauty:

vil gerne ich si wolde
loben, als ich solde:
nû enbin ich niht sô wîser man,
mirn gebreste dar an
solh sin ist mir unkunt
ouch hât sich manec wîser munt
in wîbes lobe gevlizzen,
daz ich niht möhte wizzen
welhen lop ich ir vunde,
ezn sî vor dirre stunde
baz gesprochen wîben.
si muoz von mir belîben
ungelobet nâch ir rehte,
wans gebrist mir tumben knehte.
doch bescheide ichz sô ich beste kan
und als ichz vernomen han,
sô was ûzer strîte:
ez was vrouwe Ênîte
diu aller schoeniste maget
diu ie, sô man saget,
in des küneges hof kam.

(ll.1590-1610)

That such a beautiful woman should have any thoughts other than sensual ones (ll.1873-1875) or concern for her spouse's physical safety (ll.802, 852) comes as a shock both to Êrec and, for that matter, the reader, who has heard what Êrec has to say and is aware that he does in fact think (ll.264, 582, 931, 1872, 2249, 2254, 2545, 2788) but who has found Ênîte to be decorative but essentially vacuous. If the reader is unprepared for Ênîte's subsequent portrayal as an extremely verbal wisdom figure, one can readily imagine Êrec's astonishment at getting much more than he bargained for in the person of Ênîte. And just as Ênîte begins to think and talk, Êrec reverts to minimal use of language and, with one exception over thousands of lines (ll.3004-6711), to thoughtlessness, both in the sense that he is not reported to have thoughts and in the sense that he exhibits reckless disregard for the physical person he previously so cherished. The exceptional thought ("gedanc" [l.4239]) that Êrec does entertain is a prayer to God that *he*—there is no reference to Ênîte—might be delivered without harm "von disem lande" (l.4235). Êrec, who is led by "der wec" into "ein unkundez lant" (ll.4277, 4278), needs Ênîte to escape, but he is not able to perceive the full extent of this need nor is he capable of expressing it now. And he will only orient himself in the physical landscape once he knows Ênîte on more than the carnal level.

Hartmann emphasizes the sudden glimpse into Ênîte's inner thoughts expressed vocally much more than does his predecessor Chrétien. Chrétien, like Hartmann, makes much of his heroine's beauty, but his Enide's beauty is said to be surpassed by her wisdom; she is "sage," and the careful reader is thus prepared for her prudent assessment of her husband's lapse, her reasonable commentary, and her wise actions as they journey through the forest. Moreover, Chrétien sets the stage for such wisdom, in that every character in his romance is judged according to his or her wisdom or folly. Hartmann, however, prefers the sharp disjunction between silence and language in his portrayal of Ênîte, probably because of its effect on an audience; Ênîte's verbal transformation is so unexpected that the reader has an opportunity to see her through Êrec's shocked and angry eyes. Êrec, who had been oblivious to the court's talk that had gone to the point that his wife heard it (ll.2999 ff.), suddenly apprehends: "dô vernam Êrec die rede wol" (l.3033). His immediate response is a speech studded with language terms ("saget" [l.3035]; "klaget" [l.3037]; "gelougent" [l.3038]; "lât die rede stân" [l.3039]; "die rede" [l.304]; "sagen" [l.3042]; "klagen" [l.3043]; "verswigen" [l.3044]) and capped with a terse "der ist genuoc getân" (l.3052). His reported speech thus is a talk about talking and not talking about language and silence, and thus sets the stage for the many debates on the wisdom or folly of speaking out that occur in the romance. Êrec's immediate response, too, involves a verbal deception and this is the first time that he employs a less than straightforward manner. As Êrec becomes taciturn and bids Ênîte to do likewise, he becomes covert as well in his actions; he secretly dons armor (ll.3064 ff.), leaves instructions with the cooks that dinner is to be ready upon his return (ll.3088 ff.), and gives out that he "wolde rîten ûz kurzwîlen" (ll.3061-3062). The change in Êrec is not only signalled by Hartmann's overt comments that it has occurred (ll.2931-2934, 2966-2967, 2984) but also by his sudden command to his wife that she should don "daz beste gewaete" (l.3056). Êrec, who earlier self-righteously and in front of Ênîte spurned fine garb for his wife, now attempts to tell her through his command to dress well just how little he values her person.

Êrec does not value Ênîte not only because he feels that she does not value him, but also because she speaks, albeit reluctantly, words of reproachful wisdom which he simply does not want to hear. She possesses a heightened sensibility toward perception, as is witnessed in the court's derogatory assessment being filtered through her consciousness and, after thought (ll.3004, 3024), to Êrec. Yet it initially seems as if she has made one drastic misperception, for "si wânde daz er sliefe" (l.3026). Since it is "nâch ir site" (l.3013) to make love in the middle of the day, one would expect Ênîte to be relatively experienced at determining such a basic fact as whether her husband is sleeping or not. Rather, in allowing Ênîte such an outburst, Hartmann seems to be indulging in a relatively sophisticated deception on Ênîte's part. In a sense, Ênîte behaves as if Êrec cannot hear her and in fact depends upon it, so that in vocalizing her thought she anticipates no danger of its being heard and yet seeks that very feeling of possible danger. Her speech is not an involuntary slip but rather the logical culmination of her thought ("da begunde si denken an" [l.3024]), for Hartmann will later examine the thought/speech linkage in Ênîte's interior monologues and in her voiced lament and suicide attempt. Furthermore, subsequent events bear out the necessity of Ênîte's misperception concerning her husband's "sleeping" state; there are times when misperception brings benefits, just as the pair will learn that there are times when it is wise to lie. True wisdom, as the concept is developed in Hartmann's ***Êrec,*** entails the development of varied responses to situations and looks toward the greater good to be attained, rather than to the sometimes correct and sometimes flawed responses to individual situations. Thus, here Ênîte makes what appears at first glance to be an error of judgement but what is seen in the final analysis to constitute a necessary, if chastizing, function of wisdom. The ultimate wisdom of Ênîte's speech act lies in its results, for both Êrec and Ênîte learn that actions have consequences, that wisdom is an active virtue that must be cultivated, and that unpleasant but necessary experiences must be undergone in order to correct unconsidered behavior and rash action.

Ênîte, in effect, communicates to Êrec an unpleasant truth which he does not wish to hear, as shown by the fact that his immediate response is a perverse attempt to muzzle the reproachful voice that has expressed this truth. And he begins to engage in a series of contradictory actions which serve to reveal how complex is the truth which Ênîte speaks. One must first question the degree to which Êrec understands Ênîte's words. Hartmann states, "dô vernam Êrec die rede wol" (l.3033), but one does not find Êrec mulling over in his mind the words his wife has spoken; as noted earlier, Êrec suddenly stops having reported thoughts. Indeed, Hartmann makes at this point an assessment of what will be characteristic of Êrec for the bulk of the romance:

> dô enwas aber niemen
> der sich des mohte verstân
> wie sîn gemüete was getân.
>
> (ll.3077-3079)

Since we do not know the contents of Êrec's mind, we cannot with any certainty ascertain just how much of Ênîte's message Êrec has in fact understood. Hartmann's companion-piece, ***Îwein,*** affords an interesting insight, however, with respect to the reception of language, and it is one which can be directly applied to Êrec's situation. One recalls that Kâlogrenant engages in a verbal sparring match with Keiî—ironically, over whether or not the former should speak—and delivers a last admonitory salvo before he tells his tale:

> 'man verliuset michel sagen,
> man enwellez merken unde dagen.
> maniger biutet diu ôren dar:
> er nemes ouch mit dem herzen war,
> sone wirt im niht wan der dôz,
> und ist der schade alze grôz,
> wan si verliesent beide ir arbeit.

der dâ hoeret und der dâ seit.
ir muget mir deste gerner dagen,
ichn wil iu deheine lüge sagen.'

(ll.249-258)

The situation is eerily akin to that of Êrec and Ênîte, except that Kâlogrenant incorporates the roles of one who tells something of significance and one who requests silence before telling. While it is Ênîte who makes a remark of significant import, it is Êrec who demands silence from the one who makes the remark. In Kâlogrenant's case, it is silence that is first requested before the statement of importance is made. And yet Kâlogrenant's very enjoinder to silence is fraught with importance for the cases of Êrec and Ênîte, for it details levels of perception that may throw light on the problem marriage in ***Êrec***. Quite clearly one may have ears and yet not perceive anything more than "der dôz" (***Îwein,*** l.253), and Êrec's immediate response to Ênîte's words of wisdom seems to be precisely that.

Yet it is in a further sense that Kâlogrenant's words may prove applicable to Êrec's and Ênîte's situation. As noted, Kâlogrenant both requests silence and then speaks words of import, while these roles are shared—and presented in reverse order, as Ênîte speaks and Êrec demands silence—by the Arthurian couple in ***Êrec***. This breaking up of the roles is more than a device to further plot; it suggests that the reader is dealing with a collective entity in the persons of Êrec and Ênîte. Together, the couple forms one entity, so that the several and related functions of perception, thought, speech and action are parceled out variously to each member of the couple and, indeed, can be seen to shift over the course of the romance. This is not at odds with the prevalent idealized concept of marriage in the Middle Ages, where the husband and wife form one entity, although this oneness is couched in the divided and weighted terms of the hierarchical stance of the husband to the wife and, abstractly, the soul to the body, the spirit to the flesh, and the reason to the will. In ***Êrec*** this concept of the unity of man and wife is explicit in Ênîte's long lament when she thinks her husband is dead and addresses God:

' . . . aller werlde ist erkant
ein wort daz du gesprochen hâst,
und bite dich daz dûz staete lâst,
daz ein man und sîn wîp
suln wesen ein lîp.'

(ll.5823-5827)

Moreover, the idea that two form one informs ***Êrec*** on several levels, not the least of which is the narrative level, where the husband and wife are seen to split up functions between themselves, so that Ênîte perceives, thinks, and speaks when Êrec primarily acts. She counters Êrec's demands for silence with its opposite, speech, and meets his rashness with her hesitant consideration. On a more abstract level, Ênîte comes to function as a voice of reason to Êrec's willfulness, so that she tempers his headlong actions with admonitions, and his lust with her moderation.

But, most importantly, the concept of Êrec and Ênîte seen as a composite entity by Hartmann draws its credence from the division of language functions which the author employs in ***Êrec***. In fact, the movement of the hero toward *mâze,* so often seen as one of the keys to the romance, finds its reflection in the interplay of language and silence on the part of Ênîte and Êrec. Êrec, initially so prudent in his speech and actions, is succeeded by an Êrec who not only cannot temper his rashness but who also imposes silence upon one whose words were for his benefit, and, ultimately, by an Êrec who can learn from admonitions and who can frame words—and situations—to his benefit. Correspondingly, Ênîte's garrulousness and verbal perspicacity are in their ascendance when Êrec's are at their nadir, so that her wisdom is seen to consist in her ability to translate her perceptions into knowledge and, in turn, speech, while Êrec remains his most unaware and taciturn. Similarly, Ênite is portrayed as being speechless when Êrec is seen to be wise and, correspondingly, most vocal at the outset of the romance; as he lapses into lustfulness, she becomes increasingly more vocal, until Êrec finally has access to the wisdom and loyalty/love expressed by her repeated outbursts concerning his safety. At that point Êrec begins to take over many of the perceptual functions previously fulfilled by his spouse, so that by the end of the romance he is often seen as recognizing danger before Ênîte does, and so that her reported speech dwindles and finally disappears, just as his perception and vocalization increase. The key, then, to the balance between the two halves of the married entity, that is, between Êrec and Ênîte, is the balance between language and silence, sifted through the awareness of what is prudent behavior. The turning point, of course, is the bedroom scene, in which Ênîte is so startlingly vocal and Êrec so surprisingly speechless. Here Êrec has ears but cannot hear in the fundamental sense, and Ênîte must repeat her admonitory/revelatory speeches over the course of several adventures until the significance of her words penetrates Êrec's consciousness and he stops misperceiving her.

In each of these adventures Ênîte is forbidden "ze sprechenne ir munt" (l.3099) or to report on "swaz si vernaeme/oder swaz si gesaehe" (ll.3101-3102, reiterated in ll.3963 ff). Hartmann's perception-to-language association is strengthened by word pairs:

vil drate si hin umbe *sach,*
zÊrecke si mit vorhten *sprach*

(ll.3378-3379, my italics)

als si sînen ernest *sach*
und daz erz von herzen *sprach*

(ll.3838-3839, my italics)

and by the meticulously set forth chains of command by which Ênîte perceives, then inwardly debates concerning language or silence (*[ge] sagen / [ge] [ver] dagen* in ll.3146-3147, 3184-3185, 3374-3375) and then speaks. Êrec does not have access to the workings of her mind, although the reader does, but he does receive explicitly the conclusion to which he will eventually come: that

Ênîte exhibits *triuwe*. In her very first infraction of Êrec's gag rule, Ênîte tells Êrec her motivations:

'wil ich dir *durch triuwe* sagen
(dînen schaden enmac ich niht verdagen)'
(ll.3184-3185, my italics)

Yet it appears that he does not hear her very well, for in his subsequent reproach he does not even mention the issue of her motivations but instead concentrates on what he perceives to be her characteristically female, perverse disobedience (ll.3238-3257). Êrec is given the truth but either will not recognize it or simply, through selective hearing, does not perceive it.

Ênîte's second outburst does not mention *triuwe,* but she urges Êrec "durch got" (l.3380) to listen to her, and the reader knows that she speaks because she fears that on account of "untriuwen" (l.3367) something might happen to Êrec. The reader also notes Ênîte's conclusion in her interior monologue:

'ich waene ez solde verdagen.
en*triuwen* niht, ich sol imz sagen.'
(ll.3374-3375, my italics)

Clearly, *triuwe* is at the heart of Ênîte's actions, and it dictates whether she speaks or, in fending off the lecherous count's advances, dissembles. Yet even when Ênîte reiterates to Êrec that she has again acted "durch triuwe" (l.3415), Êrec once more does not listen to what he hears and promptly saddles her with the care of the horses, an apt indication of his perception of her, as noted earlier.

At this point Hartmann interjects the sequence in which "ein knabe" (l.3491) is presented as an accurate perceiver (his phrases are studded with "mich dunket" [ll.3520, 3523, 3532]) who assesses the couple's situation at a glance (l.3510 ff.) and who speaks to Êrec concerning his mistreatment of Ênîte, only to receive a curt reply: "Knabe, daz sult ir lân" (l.3590). The boy is further cast in the role of a wisdom figure when he communicates his experience with Êrec and Ênîte to his lord, who, struck with Ênîte's beauty, begins to ruminate ("gedâhte . . . manecvalt wart sîn gedanc" [ll.3669, 3672]) until Hartmann announces:

der enwas dar an niht staete,
wan in vrou Minne betwanc
ûf einen valschen gedanc.
(ll.3717-3719)

Once again Êrec is shown to be unperceptive of the count's desire for and actions toward Ênîte ("dô enhete Êrec deheinen wân" [l.3727]), and he is virtually taciturn, snapping at the count concerning the fact that he and his wife are obviously dining apart: "herre, mîn gemüete stât alsô" (l.3745). Êrec here is not only a man of few words but also one whose utterances do not communicate anything that might be illuminating to a situation that puzzles another person. The count's ensuing discussion with Ênîte reflects the perception/language nexus we have been examining throughout this work. The count essentially misperceives Ênîte and, significantly, misperceives her in a way in which Êrec also misperceived her. He, like the Êrec who visited the impoverished household of Ênîte's parents, sees "armuot" (l.3765) and "lîp" (l.3759) to the exclusion of Ênîte's deeper nature, which encompasses *triuwe*. The count is a flatterer who speaks the truth concerning Ênîte, although he is not aware that he does ("und ist daz ir sô wîse sît" [l.3782]). Ênîte is indeed wise enough to realize that what the count cannot gain by "rede" (l.3837), he will take by force, and, since her devotion is to Êrec rather than to foolish consistency, she wisely shifts her tactics and contrives a "list" (l.3842) whereby she can extricate herself and her spouse from the dangerous situation. Her following speech to the count thus becomes a marvelous combination of lies and truth that bears close examination.

Ênîte begins with a disclaimer that is oddly reminiscent of her father's words to Êrec when the knight asked the aged man for his daughter's hand. Koralus, it will be recalled, perceives Êrec's request as a "spot" (l.532), a "schimph" (ll.546, 559) and a "wân" (l.558). Ênîte virtually echoes her father as she addresses the count:

si sprach: 'ich waene iu ernest ist.
herre, enzürnet ir niht:
wan iu der rede unnôt geschiht.
ez was zewâre mîn wân,
ir hetet die rede durch schimph getân.
wan ez ist iuwer manne site
daz ir uns armiu wîp dâ mite
vil gerne trieget
(ich entar gesprechen: lieget),
daz ir uns vil ze guote
geheizet wider iuwerm muote.'
(ll.3843-3853)

She later assures him: "ich wânte diu rede waere iuwer spot" (l.3891), thus further echoing her father. The linkage between Koralus' reactions and his daughter's dissembling speech is further heightened in the fact that Koralus is discussing, after all, Êrec's winning of Ênîte, which is the very subject Ênîte raises with the count:

'vil rehte wil ich iu bejehen
wie mich von êrste mîn man
im ze wîbe gewan.
ichn bin im niht genôzsam:
mînem vater er mich nam,
wan der ist waerlîche
edel unde rîche.
in des hof er dicke reit.
nâch kinde gewonheit
lief ich dâ hin unde her.
eines tages spilte er
mit uns. dô schein wol daz kint
lîhte ze triegenne sint,
mit liste er mich vürs tor gewan.'
(ll.3865-3878)

Her lie is all the more successful because it contains several truths: children *are* easily duped; Êrec *did* ride into

Ênîte's parents' house; Ênîte's father *is* noble and *is* now, through the efforts of Êrec, "rîch." Yet Ênîte, described earlier as a child (ll.309, 331), is hardly a "tor" (l.3878) but rather in the later and ironic assessment of Oringles, a "wunderlîchez wîp" (l.6160) who, through acute perception and wise thought, can transform bad situations into good ones. She accomplishes this end here through the giving of a double-edged counsel to the count, so that he concludes, "iuwer rât der ist guot" (l.3937) but the reader knows that it is this advice which will save her husband.

It is not enough for Hartmann to note that "vrouwe Ênîte was ein getriuwez wîp" (l.3943) who acts "durch triuwe und durch güete" (l.3961); he reports another of her interior monologues in which she debates the same issue, language and silence, but here couched in terms of "lîp" (l.3986) or "tôt" (ll.3983, 3992). The issue of choice ("kiesen" [l.3992]) surfaces, but "triuwe" (l.3993) decides the issue, and her silence is broken. Swift flight saves Êrec and Ênîte, leaving an enraged count to argue over language, silence, and information with their host, reported in one of Hartmann's characteristically peppery exchanges of one-liners. Here, too, Hartmann draws, in the count's subsequent lament, an ironic parallel to Êrec, who has already been noted to have similarities to the count in his essential misperception of Ênite. The The count cries out:

> . . . 'mir enwas êre
> niht ze teile getân,
> daz ich sus verlorn hân
> daz schoeniste wîp durch gemach
> die mîn ouge ie gesach,
> vremde oder kunde.
> vervluochet sî diu stunde
> daz ich hînaht entslief.'
>
> (ll.4087-4094)

He appends to this assessment, which applies equally well to Êrec, a statement of thematic importance, a statement of a principle of which he and Êrec are both instances:

> . . . 'swer sîne sache
> wendet gar ze gemache,
> als ich hînaht hân getân
> dem sol êre abe gân
> unde schande sîn bereit
> wer gewan ie vrumen âne arbeit?
> mir ist geschehen vil rehte.'
>
> (ll.4096-4102)

The count's attitude of regret nevertheless conceals truth important for an understanding of the romance—*gemach* does lead to danger—but there is no evidence that he profits from the wisdom of his words, for he is shortly thereafter depicted by Hartmann as misassessing Êrec's relationship to Ênîte, largely because he believed Ênîte's trumped-up tale (ll.4172 ff.). At this point the reader notes in Êrec's reaction to the count's speech a correct evaluation of the content of the words: "ir habet gelogen" (l.4203). And this is not the first instance of a changing attitude toward perception, assessment, and language on Êrec's part, for Hartmann allows Êrec to have his first accurate consideration of a matter in a long time. One would think that it is belaboring the obvious to have Êrec understand, "er weste wol, man rite im nâch" (l.4119), but it is a clear indication that Êrec is coming to see consequences of actions and to prepare for contingencies.

Êrec's progress is not without lapses, as Hartmann demonstrates when he allows Êrec to be aware that he will be pursued and yet unaware of the actual approach of his pursuers (ll.4139 ff.), with the result that Ênîte once more gives voice to her perceptions immediately after Êrec has forbidden her to do so. There is no reported dialogue interchange as she breaks her word in the scene, and even Êrec's delayed reproach is not given in recorded speech (ll.4258-4267). But Êrec is clearly on the road to wisdom, for after Ênîte warns him of his next assailant's approach, Hartmann states: "dô wart im aber ir triuwe erkant" (l.4319). Finally Êrec starts to regain his former perceptual acuity; he hears Guivreiz's "wort" (l.4325) and realizes that, much as he would like to avoid it, there is going to be a fight (ll.4378-4379). It is during this fight that Ênîte's cry is succeeded by Êrec's correction ("vrouwe, iuch triuget iuwer wân" [l.4429]) and his rapid defeat of Guivreiz, labeled "der wenige man" (l.4436). The overcoming of the dwarf subtly hearkens back toward Êrec's poor treatment by Îder's dwarf but also looks ahead to a renewed, more open Êrec. Êrec and Guivreiz exchange names, and Êrec becomes positively talkative in response to Guivreiz's requests for information, although he does not react favorably toward Guivreiz's suggestions concerning his need for medical attention (ll.4616 ff.), a reaction which will have grave consequences in the not so immediate future.

Êrec's wounds afford yet another opportunity for Hartmann to present situations in which perception and language are seen as the cornerstones upon which right action is laid. One recalls that Keiî, "der quâtspreche" (l.4664), comes upon Êrec, assesses his situation, and announces, "ich sihe wol, ir sît sêre wunt" (l.4629). Keiî is, pure and simple, a good perceiver, and it is no coincidence that he will later recognize Êrec by his voice (ll.4854-4857) and that he, unlike Êrec, is familiar with the physical terrain through which he rides ("der künec Artûs mîn herre enliget hie niht verre" [ll.4629]). Keiî may be perceptive, but his downfall comes in the transfer between his perceptions and his thoughts on his perceptions, and, accordingly, his words and deeds will be flawed:

> alsô daz er vor *valsche* was
> lûter sam ein spiegelglas
> und daz er sich huote
> mit *werken* und mit *muote,*
> daz er immer *missetaete.*
> des was er unstaete,
> wan dar nâch kam im der tac
> daz er deheiner triuwen enphlac.
> sô enwolde in niht genüegen
> swaz er *valsches* gevüegen
> mit allem vlîze kunde

mit *werken* und mit *munde:*
daz *riet* elliu sîn ger.
(ll.4642-4654, my italics)

Keiî's mistake comes, then, when he uses language unwisely ("herre, lât die rede sîn" [l.4679]) and attempts to act, by trying physically to bring Êrec to court. Êrec soon reduces Keiî, "der quât*spreche,*" to "ein sac under dem rosse" (ll.4730-4731) and later elicits from him useful information concerning Keiî's point of origin and the circumstances surrounding Keiî's borrowing of Gâwein's horse. Êrec refuses to give Keiî his name, however, but Keiî deduces ("kiesen" [l.4856]) Êrec's identity from his voice. There remains yet another point to be considered in this Keiî episode, for Keiî, who announces to Êrec that he is "unwîse" (l.4827) concerning his opponent's name, is still seen to have the admirable quality of wisely telling what he knows, of detailing his encounter with Êrec, even though he must be aware that it will only reflect detrimentally on him:

Keiîn hin ze hove reit
und twanc in des sîn wârheit
daz ers doch niht verdagete
wan daz er rehte sagete
sîn schemelîchez maere,
wiez im ergangen waere . . .
(ll.4836-4841)

Finally, Keiî's brush with Êrec results in the greater good that Gâwein is able to effect, through his recognition ("erkande" [l.4908]), consideration ("gedâhte" [l.4935]), and true perception of Êrec's situation (ll.4984-4985). Like Ênîte, Gâwein must resort to a "list" (l.4998), arrived at after thought ("erdâht" [l.4998]), in order to insure Êrec's physical safety and ease. Êrec himself expects nothing until he sees the peripatetic court, which maneuvers with ease in a landscape in which he is continually disoriented:

ouch erkande er si wol,
wan er si dicke hete gesehen.
(ll.5041-5042)

His immediate reaction to Gâwein is an echo of his reproaches to Ênîte's counsel:

'ir enhabet niht wol an mir getân.
her Gâwein, diz ist iuwer rât.
nû hân ich iuwer missetât
selten alsô vil vernomen.
daz ich dâ her bin komen,
das was mir vil ungedâht.
ir habet mich übele her brâht.'
(ll.5045-5051)

Yet Gâwein *has* acted in Êrec's best interests, as had Ênîte, so the issue becomes one of whether Êrec can know what is good or bad for himself. In this sense Gâwein and, to a far greater extent, Ênîte function as a type of cerebral warning system for Êrec, who is primarily depicted as a man of action. As wisdom figures, Gâwein and Ênîte provide the admonition, moderation, and correction which the often rash Êrec requires, and it is these two characters who must endure Êrec's "zorn" (l.3049 for Ênîte; l.5068 for Gâwein) and who must nevertheless speak words that he may not wish to hear:

'waz mac ich nû gesprechen mê?
wan sol ich iuch beswaeret hân,
daz hân ich doch durch guot getân.'
(ll.5077-5079)

Old habits die slowly for Êrec, as Hartmann depicts him, so that Êrec takes two steps down the road to wisdom, only to retreat one step. Having been tricked by Gâwein, even though it is for his own good, Êrec lapses into taciturnity in his overnight visit at Arthur's court. While Ênîte is reported to be verbal with Ginovêr:

dâ wart vil wîpliche
von in beiden geklaget,
vil gevrâget und gesaget . . .
(ll.5107-5109)

Êrec exchanges no dialogue with those who "entwâfenten in" (l.5122) and is portrayed as being perceived ("vil schiere kam diu künegîn in klagen unde schouwen" [ll.5129-5130]) rather than as being a perceiver.

Êrec is, however, shown to be thinking ("dô hügete er wider ûf die vart" [l.5249]), and his insistence on departure, thought by the court to be a mistake ("diz dûhte si alle missetân" [l.5273]) proves to be fortunate, since, despite the fact that he does not know where he is going (emphasized in ll.5288-5290), his path leads him to where he is most needed and where he can exercise his atrophied perceptual skills. Thus, Hartmann allows Êrec to perceive before Ênîte: it is Êrec who "hôrte . . . eine stimme" (l.5297) and who queries the grief-stricken maiden (ll.5339 ff.); and it is Êrec who sets about to free a man who is as silent, although for different reasons, as Êrec was at a certain point in the past:

er was geslagen unz ûf daz zil
daz er des bluotes was ersigen
unde nû sô gar geswigen
daz in schrîens verdrôz.
(ll.5417-5420)

Hartmann's intent is to show how Êrec's verbal skills are being honed throughout this *âventiure* to save the tortured knight, so that our protagonist is demonstrated to be wise in the manner in which he manipulates language. He speaks before he acts, first requesting information (ll.5436 ff.) and then resorting to verbal deception ("dannoch redete er mit listen" [l.5458]) with the giants who assess him, quite wrongly, to be "tump" (l.5448). Moreover, in order to indicate the giants' relative lack of wisdom, Hartmann gives to them an aspect of disregard for language that hearkens directly back to Îder's dwarf's retort to Êrec, when he barked: "lâ dîn klaffen sîn" (l.83). Here one giant significantly attempts to silence Êrec with the statement: "dîn klaffen ist mir ungemach" (l.5477). Furthermore, the fact that this entire exchange is to reflect in some way Êrec's path to wisdom is stressed in Hartmann's giving the reader an oblique glimpse into Êrec's motivations; he must act to save the knight even though such action involves raising the giants' ire ("zorn" [l.5493]). Like Ênîte and like Gâwein, he must risk *zorn* if he is to accomplish anything that is for the greater good. Having defeated the giants—and it should be recalled that the Êrec in the earlier part of the romance had a bad enough time of it with dwarfs—Êrec further demonstrates his perceptual abilities by locating the wounded knight, whose horse had stayed with him during the previous fracas, despite the fact that Hartmann intones:

> . . . niemen kunde gesagen
> wâ er im ze vindenne wart.
>
> (ll.5573-5575)

A positive transformation is brought about as Êrec restores the wounded man to his lover ("sus wart ir herze ein lûter glas" [l.5623]), and Êrec speaks at length with the pair concerning their and his identities, gives advice ("diz ist mîn rât" [l.5676]), and caps his performance by moving confidently through the once confusing landscape in order to rejoin Ênîte.

It is not merely the unusual physical effort that exhausts Êrec, for his verbal exertions have also been exceptional. Now "der halptôte man" (l.5730) lapses into silence, and it is no coincidence that Ênîte becomes again most vocal:

> von jamer huop diu guote
> ein klage vil barmeclîche,
> herzeriuweclîche.
> ir wuof gap alsolhen schal
> daz ir der walt widerhal.
>
> (ll.5743-5747)

Such is the shifting balance between the characters of Ênîte and Êrec that Ênîte now reproaches God for his "zorn" (l.5779) and calls him to task for giving her such a bad example of his consideration of her ("wie swachez bilde" [l.5783]). In the final analysis, Êrec's "Scheintod" will have instructive benefits, but Ênîte now is in the position Êrec was when he was made party to his wife's assessment of his situation: something is happening, but the person to whom it is happening cannot, for lack of perception or foresight, see its ultimate good consequences, so clouded are the perceptions by the present pain.

Ênîte is so prostrated by grief that she proposes the solution of being devoured by animals. Here Hartmann's skill is such that he couches even this possibility in terms of wisdom and perception. Ênîte calls upon "ir tier vil ungewizzen" (l.5844) and then suggests that they would be "wîse" (l.5850) to feed upon her and her spouse. Yet the romance's landscape, earlier portrayed as teeming with dangerous creatures, both human and otherwise, cannot produce an animal who sniffs the bait Ênîte so readily offers ("daz dehein tier ez vernaeme" [l.5858]). Clearly, there are times when even lack of perception, like verbal deception, is wise, if greater good is to be attained. Moreover, Ênîte may lapse too, as she does here, and the greater wisdom of God will hold life-threatening dangers in abeyance while Ênîte calls upon God and, later, Death, whom she accuses of providing bad examples (l.5917), as she earlier did God, and of giving bad advice (l.5924). Her verbal recklessness increases to the point that she assesses herself incorrectly regarding the speech act to-

Wedding feast of Iwein and Laudine, from the murals at Schmalkalden, c. 1250.

ward Êrec that resulted in the current situation:

> 'ich tete als die tôren tuont,
> unwîses muotes . . . '
>
> (ll.5965-5966)

Hartmann's point is not that Ênîte was a fool, but rather that here she is not able to perceive herself wisely and that here she falls victim to the problem that afflicts Êrec: lack of foresight. She cannot see any benefits down the weary road she travels, and neither, in fact, can Êrec until that path leads him to Mâbonagrîn's castle, at which point Êrec is given an example of his own former situation in terms that he cannot help but understand. Then he can state confidently:

> 'ich weste wol, der Saelden wec
> gienge in der werlde eteswâ,
> rehte enweste ich aber wâ,
> wan daz ich in suochende reit
> in grôzer ungewisheit,
> unz daz ich in nû vunden hân.
> got hât wol ze mir getân
> daz er mich hât gewîset her'
>
> (ll.8521-8528)

Êrec's path leads him to strife in the "boumgarte" (l.8700), and it is strikingly appropriate that the next topic upon which Ênîte focuses in her protracted lament is her "bilde" (l.6031) of the fruit tree in the "boumgarten" (l.6017). Ênîte interweaves her "boumgarten" *exemplum* with thoughts of her own childhood, so that she first thinks of her parents:

> 'ouwê liebiu muoter
> unde vater guoter!
> nû ist iu ze dirre stunt
> mîn grôzer kumber vil unkunt.'
>
> (ll.5974-5977)

She then develops the transplanted tree idea and finally announces:

> 'des sol man bilde kiesen
> an mir vil gotes armen.'
>
> (ll.6031-6032)

The reader must ask what it is about that orchard that one must perceive, so that Êrec must go to it in the form of Mâbonagrîn's challenge and Ênîte must refer to it in her *exemplum*. In a very fundamental sense Êrec's ultimate *âventiure* will involve Mâbonagrîn precisely because Mâbonagrîn, like Êrec, took to wife "ein kint" (l.9476) with a remarkable physical personage (ll.9469 ff.), a woman who used language to work changes upon her husband, although in a fashion diametrically opposed to the manner in which Ênîte uses language to effect positive changes. Thus, in Ênîte's lament over her supposedly dead husband one finds a compelling reversion to the circumstances surrounding her betrothal to Êrec. She states that her parents do not know now the circumstances in which she finds herself, and what she implies is that she did not know *then* in what circumstances she was to fall. Thus, in marrying, it is not only Êrec who does not know the full nature of his bride (Ênîte as wise) but also Ênîte who does not know the full nature of her husband (Êrec as a man who will lapse and then become wise).

But in order to bring Êrec to the point that he can undergo the crucial "Joy of the Court" adventure, Hartmann must first detail the essential waking of Êrec's consciousness, and he does so in a sequence that gathers its shape from the use and abuse of language. One recalls that Ênîte's voice, "vil lûte schrîende" (l.6084), resounds through the land so that the Count of Limors hears it ("gehôrte" [l.6140]); "ir stimme vernam" (l.6142) and prevents Ênîte from acting upon her "wort" (l.6110) to commit suicide. That the count is in some way to mirror Êrec's previous predilections becomes apparent in his first words to Ênîte, where he addresses her, as did the imperceptive, mocking Êrec, as "wunderlîchez wîp" (l.6160). He goes on to characterize her as "daz schoeniste bilde" (l.6164) that exists, and the reader suddenly apprehends that this is the crux of the matter: Ênîte's first impression is that of an exterior without an interior, so that thoughts and speech she might have come as a surprise. She is, moreover, a "bilde" in the sense that she becomes an image for those who see in her what they themselves are; if lustful and occupied with the flesh, they perceive her primarily in terms of lust and the flesh. And finally, looking back to Ênîte's own "bilde" (l.6031) of the tree, one may state that men do not see her in the sense of an instructive example; she is a "bilde" in the sense that characters can learn from her wisdom. She is beauty, to be sure, but beauty, as St. Augustine noted, must be *used* and not abused. Thus, Ênîte's cry,

> 'des sol man bilde kiesen
> an mir vil gotes armen.'
>
> (ll.6031-6032)

proves to be a thematically loaded statement: Ênîte simply *is,* and the essential issue is *how she is perceived.*

That the count of Limors misperceives Ênîte is emphasized throughout. Hartmann characterizes him as a man who hears only the advice he wants to hear from his advisers, in other words that he marry Ênîte (ll.6205 ff.), and one who promises unnecessary transformations from "armuot" (l.6262) to richness, which Ênîte, being already rich, does not need. Moreover, perception is again viewed as bound up with language, so that most of the count's energies are occupied in silencing Ênîte and much of her time is spent lamenting; the one who will ultimately triumph is seen as verbal, while the one who is held by even his retainers to be "toerlîch" (l.6532) is seen urging silence (ll.6420, 6458), accusing her of folly ("tumbez klagen" [l.6491]); "iuwer tumpheit" (l.6505), and delivering a blow, out of foolish anger ("sîn zorn in verleite ze grôzer tôrheite" [ll.6518-6519]), to Ênîte on the appropriate—and only—part of her body that offends him: "an den munt" (l.6579). The count of Limors, like Êrec, not only wishes to silence the reproachful voice which he hears but also essentially misperceives the owner of that voice, for he rationalizes Ênîte's lament as coming from "ein kint" (l.6451). Children, on Hartmann's account in ***Êrec,*** cannot be expected to be verbally accountable for themselves; they are easy to trick, and, implicitly, they are to be seen rather than heard. If Ênîte is to be perceived as a child, then these are the kinds of mistakes that will be continually made about her. And the physical punishment that the enraged count of Limors metes out to her is virtually the chastisement due a child, received with horror even by his retainers. One must note here yet another ironic parallel between the count and the lapsed Êrec with respect to courtiers' reactions, in the count's angry speech to those who verbally question his treatment of Ênîte:

> 'ir herren, ir sît wunderlich,
> daz ir dar umbe strâfet mich
> swaz ich mînem wîbe tuo.
> dâ bestât doch niemen zuo
> ze redenne übel noch guot,
> swaz ein man sînem wîbe tuot.
> si ist mîn und bin ich ir:
> wie welt ir daz erwern mir,
> ich entuo ir swaz mir gevalle.'
>
> (ll.6540-6549)

In essence, Oringles feels that no one has the right to question what goes on between a man and his wife, and this mirrors Êrec's own stance as he angrily reacts to his own court's assessment of his preoccupation with Ênîte. Judging by Êrec's learning process over the course of the romance, such an attitude toward one's wife signals that the count is about to be re-educated.

The education process for the count of Limors begins with Êrec's hearing Ênîte's cry and ends with swift death from Êrec, who now knows fully how to transform his perceptions into right action. Curiously, Ênîte's final outburst, which is her penultimate recorded speech (the ultimate is ll.6946 ff., where she again aids Erec's physical well-being), makes reference again to the ambiguous term *lîp,* but she employs it in a manner different from that of the lapsed Êrec or the count of Limors. She shrieks:

> ' . . . wê mir vil armen wîbe!
> waere mîn geselle bî lîbe,
> diz bliuwen waere vil unvertragen.'
>
> (ll.6584-6586)

Lîp, for Ênîte, is more than a beautiful or handsome form; it is life. And in Êrec's hearing these precise words, Hartmann draws the audience's memory back to the scene in which Êrec was physically *bî lîbe,* in the sense that he was lying in his wife's arms, but could not appreciate her words of wisdom. Ênîte's words both catapult him into the series of adventures and help extricate him, just as Ênîte's wise guidance will accompany him on the path he does not recognize (l.6737). Hartmann's comment on a physical event is an apt assessment of a spiritual process: "wan si in den wec lêrte" (l.6746).

The change in Êrec is most apparent in sheer perceptual response. He hears Guivreiz's approach, alerts Ênîte and is even prepared to wrestle an opponent if need be (l.6884); but Ênîte's wise intervention halts conflict. Moreover, Êrec begins to be a more considerate man, in the sense that he thinks more and in the sense that he treats others more favorably, as is evident in his speech with the newly recognized Guivreiz. One recalls that Guivreiz regrets having wounded Êrec, and Êrec replies with words that demonstrate the extent of the lesson he has learned:

> Êrec sprach: 'des sult ir gedagen
> und ûz iuwer ahte lân.
> ir enhabet an mir niht missetân.
> swelh man toerlîche tuot,
> wirts im gelônet, daz ist guot.
> sît daz ich tumber man
> ie von tumpheit muot gewan
> sô grôzer unmâze
> daz ich vremder strâze
> eine wolde walten
> unde vor behalten
> sô manegem guoten knehte,
> dô tâtet ir mir rehte.'
>
> (ll.7007-7019)

In effect, Êrec has learned to look at himself through others' eyes and has, in the process, absorbed something about the nature of wisdom.

Having learned, Êrec must now teach, and Mâbonagrîn, who represents an unregenerate Êrec, is the pupil on whom Êrec can test his wisdom. That Mâbonagrîn is a formidable opponent can be determined by Guivreiz's reluctance to talk about the nature of the "Joy of the Court" challenge as well as by his subsequent advice not to accept the challenge the affair offers. To understand Guivreiz's counsel we must assess him in light of two other wisdom figures who employ speech either to prevent or to correct mistakes. Îmâîn, Gâwein, and Guivreiz all serve in both capacities in offering counsel to Êrec, who does not avail himself of their advice. Îmâîn and Gâwein see situations which can be rectified (Ênîte's shoddy dress and Êrec's weakened physical condition, respectively) in order to prevent further unpleasant situations from developing. Guivreiz counsels Êrec to avoid confrontation with Mâbonagrîn (ll.8479, 8510, 8582); but here Êrec is wise to ignore Guivreiz's "rât," since fighting Mâbonagrîn will rectify a bad situation. The difference between the interpretations of Êrec's constant refusals to abide by Îmâîn's, Gâwein's, and Guivreiz's counsel lies in the fact that Erec is wrong to refuse Îmâîn's and Gâwein's prudent advice and is right to spurn Guivreiz's suggestion. Îmâîn and Gâwein rightly perceive and assess situations, and Êrec's refusal to take their advice is shortly thereafter rectified by an action of the Arthurian court: if Êrec will not take advice to clothe his wife properly, then the queen will have to do it; and if Êrec will not come to the court to rest, then the court will simply have to pack up its Round Table (ll.5019) and come to him. Guivreiz, however, is not described as a good perceiver; one recalls that Hartmann notes concerning Guivreiz's assessment of his opponent Êrec:

Jackson on Hartmann's style:

That [Hartmann] is clear and precise is true. The often turgid passages of early German writers are lacking, and he reproduces beautifully in German the language of Chrétien. It must be confessed, however, that compared with Wolfram and Gottfried he is unexciting. His rhyming couplets often seem to jog along somewhat wearily and, in spite of his undoubtedly more sensitive perception of courtly values and the true meaning of knighthood, we would have to grant supremacy to Chrétien had Hartmann been his only imitator in German.

W. T. H. Jackson, in The Literature of the Middle Ages, *Columbia University Press, 1960.*

der herre gedâhte: 'er ist verzaget,
sît er sîne arbeit klaget.'

(ll.4366-4367)

By virtue of the fact that Êrec "klaget," Guivreiz comes to a false conclusion, that his opponent is "verzaget," and it may be that some lingering vestige of this assessment explains Guivreiz's reluctance to speak (l.8390) of the matter of the "Joy of the Court"; Hartmann seems to imply this in his description of Êrec as "ein unverzageter man" (l.8425) who listens to Guivreiz's "rat" (l.8412) and sensibly disregards it. Guivreiz, who earlier held his guest to be "einen zagen" (l.4420) and was summarily defeated, once again misperceives Êrec's abilities. The example of Guivreiz is, nevertheless, instructive for Êrec—and for the reader—because it economically shows the process on which Hartmann focuses at length in Êrec's and Ênîte's relationship: the linkage of perception to knowledge, knowledge to speech, and speech to action. At each stage in the movement from perception to action, there is a possibility of a breakdown in the form either of a cessation or of an incorrect move. Where Guivreiz errs is on the essential level of perception. In perceiving Êrec as a coward he makes a mistake. Because Guivreiz's first perception is inaccurate, he rashly challenges Êrec, who protests, "ich enhabe iu niht getân" (l.4361). Guivreiz is trounced, but Hartmann goes on to show his audience that Guivreiz may argue differently the second time around but will make essentially the same mistake in his assessment of Êrec's chances against Mâbonagrîn. Since Guivreiz's assessment is inaccurate, his counsel is faulty. Moreover, he must be urged to speak and tell what he knows to Êrec, who urges:

'nû war umbe tuot ir daz
daz ir sô lange mich verdaget
daz ir mirs niht ein ende saget?'

(ll.7991-7993)

Here one finds an Êrec eager for knowledge and desirous of speech, an Êrec who digests and thinks about what information he finally wrings from Guivreiz (ll.8121, 8147, 8294, 8350, 8400), and an Êrec who is not, as Mâbonagrîn assesses him to be, a "tumber gouch" (l.9044) who acts "toerlîch" (l.9030). Thus, Êrec at the end of the romance stands in direct contrast to his mentor, Guivreiz; Êrec is seen to act "als die wîsen tuont" (l.8633), and Hartmann shows this to consist not only of his accurate perceptions and physical actions but also of his receptivity to language and thought, while Guivreiz is seen at the romance's end to be physically inactive, verbally reluctant, and perceptually inaccurate.

In disregarding Guivreiz's counsel, Êrec enters into battle with an opponent who possesses faults he once had and into a situation that allows him to demonstrate his new-found wisdom. Accordingly, before the battle one finds Êrec actively questioning (ll.8368, 8446), thinking (ll.8294 ff., 8350 ff.), and, yes, exhibiting prudent temerity (ll.8619 ff., 8633 ff.) that stands in contrast to his former rashness. Moreover, he waxes loquacious in his comforting speech to Ênîte (ll.8839-8873) in which he voices his dependence upon her (especially ll.8864-8867). During the battle his perceptions are heightened and his thoughts return again and again to Ênîte (ll.9183, 9230); the reader sees that the man who could previously not think of adventure because he was so occupied with his wife has been transformed into a man who is now able to have adventures while being mindful of his wife. Finally, after the battle, the reader hears the man who formerly preferred to be "von den liuten" (l.2950) telling Mâbonagrîn how nice it is to be in society: "wan bî den liuten ist sô guot" (l.9438).

There remains the question, though, of how much Mâbonagrîn has learned from Êrec, who has obviously learned considerably. A reckless, albeit triumphant note creeps into Mâbonagrîn's speech when he cries: "nû var ich ûz und swar ich wil" (l.9589). This is as precise a reflection of Êrec's own earlier actions as one can imagine, for did not Êrec leave his court with a similar compulsion and lack of specific direction? The key to understanding Mâbonagrîn's intent may lie in his wife's assessment of their physical situation as "daz ander paradîse" (l.9542). The Fall of Man, which entails the theme of knowledge, accompanies the exodus from Paradise, and Paradise can only be attained again through the redemptive acts of the second Adam, Christ. Having sinned, man must work to repent from sin and must be aided in this task. One finds in ***Êrec*** resonances of this process, so that the sense remains that Mâbonagrîn, who rashly gave his word and then was shocked at what his wife said, may have to travel the same difficult road by which Êrec has come to "daz ander paradîse" (l.9542). Optimism remains, however, for the reader has seen Êrec make that journey, with setbacks and disappointments, until Hartmann can finally say of him: "er tete sam die wîsen tuont" (l.10085). The inner transformation is further reflected in the fact that Êrec, who is repeatedly noted by the narrator to be in unfamiliar territory or even disoriented, suddenly has no difficulty in getting home to Karnant. Once Êrec knows *who* he is, that is, part of an entity with Ênîte, he knows *where* he is. In this manner, each adventure serves as a type of signpost on Êrec's road, so that as the adventures' shared features impress themselves on his consciousness,

Êrec orients himself with respect to proper perception, thought, speech, and action.

Winder McConnell (essay date 1983)

SOURCE: "*Sacrificium* in Hartmann von Aue's *Der arme Heinrich,*" in *Neuphilologische Mitteilungen: Bulletin de la Société Néophilologique,* Vol. LXXXIV, No. 2, 1983, pp. 261-68.

[*In the following excerpt, McConnell explores the proposed sacrifice of a virgin in* Der arme Heinrich *and posits that reference to such a pagan ritual skews interpretations that consider* Heinrich *to be strictly Christian in outlook.*]

On the surface, Hartmann von Aue's tale of the sinner, ***Der arme Heinrich,*** appears to be a fairly straightforward example of a miracle legend, a tale heavily imbued with religious didacticism, a message, perhaps, to the German nobility of 1195 concerning the efficacy of God's grace extended towards a repentant sinner. It is a tale of contrasts: Heinrich, the protagonist, is depicted as a knight endowed with all of the virtues a representative of his caste could desire. He is of high Swabian lineage, a man who enjoys the utmost respect among his peers, a paragon of knightly excellence who, we are told, lacked nothing but who also did not exceed the bounds of moderation: "im enwart über noch gebrast." At the pinnacle of worldly success he is struck down by leprosy, echoing the theme of *memento mori:* "mêdiâ vîtâ/in morte sûmus" (vv. 92-93). No explanation is given at this point for Heinrich's affliction. There follows simply a sermon-like compendium of contrasts, the narrator emphasizing the transitoriness of this world, that happiness often turns to sorrow, that we are all quite vulnerable beings. It is not until verse 120 that we learn of the direct connection between God and Heinrich's ailment. His leprosy is to be understood as a type of punishment. In verses 113 and 115 we have been informed that those who live in worldly splendor are not viewed kindly by God. The critics have felt obliged to provide these verses with an interpretative addendum: it is not the fact that one enjoys the pleasures of this world that is damnable, but rather that one does so without constantly remaining aware of the source of such riches. While these verses would seem to contain something of the message of Cluny-inspired asceticism, the conclusion of the work, which finds Heinrich enjoying even greater splendor than he had done before his affliction, points less to self-denial than to world affirmation. Heinrich's *superbia,* then, has its origins in his lack of spiritual consciousness, in his tendency to take things for granted, in his failure to observe the *ordo* of existence, that God is the beginning and end of all things. It remains for him to pass through the stages of *contritio, confessio* and *satisfactio,* a type of initiation process, in order to emerge at the conclusion of the work as an individual cognizant of God's grace and benevolence, of the fact that he owes everything to the Almighty. The lesson seems simple: the world's pleasures, its material riches and benefits, may be both accepted and appreciated, provided that one remains aware at all times of their ultimate source.

Problems arise, however, when we examine the plot in detail. While the author saw fit to compare Heinrich's fate to that of Job, the manner in which Heinrich finally attains salvation has little indeed to do with that of his Biblical counterpart. Superimposed upon the story of the sinner is the narration of the obligatory blood-sacrifice. Had Hartmann wished merely to demonstrate the "way" of the sinner to genuine realization of his culpability, to eventual repentance and subsequent salvation through the grace of God, it might well be queried why this tale of blood sacrifice had to be included. The way of *contritio, confessio* and *satisfactio* requires no such ritual. It is, then, the question of *sacrificium* in ***Der arme Heinrich*** which deserves further attention, for a closer examination of this aspect of the work may allow us to view Hartmann's intentions from a considerably different perspective than that normally presented.

Heinrich is informed by a number of people (as implied through verses 165 to 168) that his disease can be cured. No indication is provided at this point as to how that might come about, but the information serves to raise Heinrich's spirits. Obviously encouraged by the advice of laymen, he journeys to Montpellier where the doctors maintain that he is incurable. Not satisfied with this answer, he proceeds to the capital of the medical world in the Middle Ages, Salerno. Here he is informed by the best physician he can find that he could indeed be cured, but that he will remain afflicted. Two points of information provided by the doctor are of particular significance for our study: 1. Heinrich cannot be restored to good health unless God wishes to serve as his physician (vv. 203-204); 2. he can be cured if he can find a maiden who, of her own free will, will agree to sacrifice her heart's blood for him (vv. 230-232). It is impossible to underestimate the significance of these statements for the work as a whole, for they demonstrate the dichotomy between Christian theology and pre-Christian ritual that prevails throughout much of the rest of the tale. The advice given by the physician is . . . quite contrary to the traditions of Salerno and the medical expertise to be found there. There can scarcely be any reconciliation between views of such radically different nature. Heinrich, at least, should find the suggestion revolting and certainly contrary to his religious beliefs. Instead, we are told that he recognizes the impossibility of finding someone who would willingly die for him and loses hope that he may ever be cured. This is, of course, tantamount to saying that he subscribes to this non-Christian solution, even though he may consider its practical implementation to be impossible. Furthermore, at no point in ***Der arme Heinrich*** does the protagonist really refute his faith in the viability of this ritual, despite the fact that he does, at one point, express some doubt as to its effectiveness. All that transpires from this point on up to the "sacrifice scene" in the doctor's chamber occurs against the backdrop of the ritual and the belief in its effectiveness, provided the necessary conditions can be met. All of the figures in the work share this belief. Neither Heinrich, nor anyone else, asserts that such a "solution" is intolerable, as well as unbelievable, at best an old-fashioned superstition, at worst a flagrant denial of a basic Christian principle. The fact that there is no refutation of the ritual of blood-sacrifice suggests that Hartmann did not necessarily accord it great importance in theological-ethical terms.

Heinrich secludes himself at the home of one of his peasants after having been ostracized by his peers and the rest of society. His host eventually inquires into the possibility of a cure for the disease, expressing wonder that his lord was unable to find a satisfactory solution in Salerno. Heinrich's confession that he has been justifiably punished by God for his transgression, namely, not having accorded God his due (v. 392), loses much of its effectiveness as a true indication of repentance due to the manner in which he wallows in self-pity. He relates what the master physician had told him about the necessity for a sacrifice, and bemoans the unlikelihood that he will ever find such a girl. No mention is made of God's intervention which was, however, the first possibility stated by the doctor in Salerno. Once again, there is no reflection, by either person, on the significance of the proposed "solution." Heinrich's failure to distinguish between theology and superstition (or, possibly, pagan ritual) may be attributable to his egocentric attitude, his inclination to consider anything which may alleviate his condition, but it does not explain why the peasant has nothing to say about a suggestion which must, at the very least, be blasphemous, even to one accustomed to hearing rather than interpreting Christian dogma.

Closer examination of the attitude of the peasant family towards the proposed ritual demonstrates the extent to which belief in the efficacy of this rite has pervaded the work and its figures. The reaction of the peasant and his wife to their daughter's suggestion that she sacrifice herself for Heinrich is essentially what one would expect of parents. They rebuke her for having no idea of what death is all about, for talking like a child, but we note that there is not the slightest indication that they in any way repudiate the effectiveness of the "solution." It is, furthermore, because they do believe that Heinrich can be cured by her death that they eventually accept their daughter's arguments in favor of her sacrifice. The subsequent events in Salerno are predicated on the belief of *all* of the participants that this is a viable solution. The maiden will save Heinrich and, consequently, preserve the comparatively pleasant life-style of her family. She will simultaneously attain the Holy Kingdom and thus freedom from the cares and temptations of this world. Her renunciation of the latter and her enthusiasm to attain the next world are, in fact, so adamant, so laden with allusions to her union with Christ, that her parents ascribe her "wisdom" to the intervention of the Holy Ghost:

> si begunden ahten under in
> daz die wîsheit und den sin
> niemer erzeigen kunde
> dehein zunge in kindes munde
> si jâhen daz der heilic geist
> der rede waere ir volleist. (vv. 859-864)

They are convinced that God has imbued her with the spirit to talk in this fashion (v. 874). This is, of course, simply what *they* believe, but once again the reader feels obliged to query how even simple peasants can actually fail to see the discrepancy between Christian theology and pre-Christian ritual, how they could possibly believe that the Holy Ghost would condone ritual sacrifice of the sort advocated here. After all, Christ's sacrifice itself was meant as a one-time gesture, signifying the absolution from sin, and occasioned by the absolute *caritas* of God's son. To be sure, the peasants are indeed simple, and certainly not given to theological speculation, but the dichotomy between Christianity and heathen ritual is here so blatantly obvious that one could expect them at least to notice it. It is also astonishing that for one so anxious to attain the pinnacle of Christian experience, the maiden is so obvious to the travesty against the Christian *ordo* which she is about to commit. Contrary to what the narrator states in verse 903 ("Des vreute sich diu reine maget"), the "purity" of the girl, at least from a theological point of view, is quite problematical. The initial hesitation on Heinrich's part to accept the girl's offer of self-sacrifice is rooted in his doubt that she, as a child, would possess the stamina to go through with her proposal, not in any moral or religious considerations. His acceptance of her offer serves to underscore the fact that Heinrich is still very much guilty of *superbia*. By setting out for Salerno with the maiden, Heinrich demonstrates at least tacit belief in the efficacy of the pre-Christian ritual.

The physician's preparations for the sacrificial act have some of the characteristics of a cult ritual. The girl is to be disrobed, bound to a table, her heart cut out and the blood used to cure Heinrich. The act itself is to take place in a chamber, hidden from Heinrich's view. Precisely how the blood is to be used (sprinkled upon the flesh or, more likely, drunk) is not stated and is, for our purposes, irrelevant. The significance of the blood is that it is held to possess the power to heal or rejuvenate. Once again, it is remarkable to find God referred to in conjunction with the ceremony. The maiden, fearing that the physician may lose heart and refrain from performing the act, encourages him to proceed so that Heinrich may be healed and she herself may gain the crown of heaven: "getrûwet ir mînem herren/sînen gesunt wider geben/und mir daz êwige leben,/durch got daz tuot enzît" (vv. 1152-1155).

Of particular note are verses 1209 and 1210 in which we are informed that the physician picked up "ein scharphez mezzer daz dâ lac,/des er ze selhen dingen phlac." I do not believe this can be understood simply as an allusion to the "normal" function of the knife in a surgical sense. Hartmann may have intended to use the phrase "selhen dingen" in an ambiguous manner, and it is certainly possible to interpret it, within the present context, as an indication of the doctor's (priest's?) familiarity with the ritual, a sign to Hartmann's readers that this is an experienced cult figure, one of the initiated, who has performed similar "sacrifices" in the past.

Heinrich's intervention to prevent the death of the maiden is regarded as a manifestation of his growing awareness of his place within the *ordo,* a result of sincere reflection upon his own sins, and as an example of his own *caritas,* demonstrated toward the girl. This does not mean, however, that he has become entirely convinced that her sacrifice would indeed prove fruitless, despite the fact that in verses 1252 and 1253 he expresses some doubt as to the possible outcome: "und ouch dar zuo niene weist/ ob dich des kindes tôt ernert." Furthermore, any interpretation of Heinrich's intervention on the maiden's behalf as a sacrifice of his own, motivated by *caritas,* must be predicated on the idea that Heinrich did believe he was turning his back on a possible solution to his predicament. Critics who view Heinrich's action from this perspective are Hartmann's best audience, for they have allowed themselves, as undoubtedly his contemporaries did, to be "captured" by the narrative.

At this point of deep reflection, as Heinrich acquires a refreshingly new attitude towards himself and his relation to God, it cannot help but surprise us that he evinces no real thoughts on the matter of human sacrifice itself. As he leaves Salerno with the maid, the belief that her sacrifice would be a viable means of healing his affliction has not been refuted. The doctor has certainly had no change of heart with regard to the effectiveness of his proposed measures; there is no sign of conversion (away from such a superstition), nor is there a proclamation of any sort to the effect that this act was quite contrary to the religious tenets of the crime.

I have hitherto stressed what I consider to be the clear dichotomy in ***Der arme Heinrich*** between (pagan) superstition and ritual sacrifice on the one hand and Christian dogma or faith on the other. The two are, from a theological point of view, incompatible. There have been attempts, however, to reconcile the two poles, most notably by H. B. Willson, in an article entitled, "Ordo and the Portrayal of the Maid in ***Der arme Heinrich,"*** [*Germanic Review,* 44 (1969)] Willson compares the maid's will to sacrifice herself with the sacrifice endured by Christ, a comparison I find to be quite unwarranted. The analogy appears to be based on a misinterpretation of John XV, 13 ("Greater love has no man than this, that a man lay down his life for his friends"), as well as the girl's actions or the motivation which lies behind her desire to die. Willson queries: "Has she not *caritas,* the virtue which is supreme in the Christian ethical code? Is she not willing to lay down her life for another?". . . . It is by no means clear that *caritas* remains the primary motivating force behind the maiden's actions up to the point of sacrifice. There is, in fact, considerable evidence to demonstrate that her own salvation ranks foremost in her mind (note, in particular, verses 681-812, and also 1290ff.). Even if this were not the case, her alleged *caritas* would be overshadowed by her *superbia* in believing that she, not God, holds the key to Heinrich's deliverance from leprosy. This would be tantamount to viewing the disease merely as a physical malady when it is . . . also an allegorization of Heinrich's spiritual failing. The analogy between Christ and the maiden proposed by Willson is unfounded and the fact that he himself recognizes the latter's *superbia* makes his comparison all the more problematical. Willson claims that "in spite of the analogy between her proposed sacrifice and that of Christ, she cannot be placed on the same level as the latter." I would attribute more significance to this statement than Professor Willson himself may be inclined to do. It is precisely because the maiden can never be placed on the same level as Christ that the proposed sacrifice loses any validity one might accord it as an analogy to Christ's *passio.* The death of Christ precludes any further sacrifice by a human for the sins of his fellow man. . . .

The motif of blood-sacrifice is out of place in a work purported to convey a theological message, unless the motif is totally refuted within the tale, which is not the case in ***Der arme Heinrich***. It is also unacceptable from a medical point of view, and runs counter to all of the traditions associated with Salerno. . . . Everything which transpires within the physician's chamber in Salerno contradicts the basic concepts of medieval medical practice and the tenets of the Hippocratic Oath. We are dealing here not with Christian reality, but rather with pre-Christian, pre-scientific superstition.

The motif of blood-sacrifice is well documented in the Middle Ages. It can be found in the Sylvester legend, wherein Kaiser Constantine must decide whether or not to allow the sacrifice of a child in order that his health may be restored, and in the *Queste del Saint Graal,* in which the sister of Perceval sacrifices herself by opening her veins for the sake of her royal mistress who is afflicted with leprosy. The healing and rejuvenating power of blood is an old belief and is mentioned by Pliny; it is also referred to in Exodus and Leviticus. I would suggest that Hartmann made use of it within his tale because of its potential for the narrative, as an effective means of stimulating the interest of his readers, not because it had any significance from a theological or medical perspective. What theological implications one may wish to associate with the motif are purely secondary. ***Der arme Heinrich*** is simply not, in the first instance, a theological work. It is written . . . according to the needs of the narrative, and is not intended as a conveyor of inherent "ideas," as a depiction of a purification procedure for Heinrich. The tale is based on the concept of fictional fallacy, and its effectiveness rests on the ability of the reader to accept the idea of blood-sacrifice as a viable means of restoring Heinrich to health. The legitimacy of such means is never at issue.

To maintain that ***Der arme Heinrich*** is primarily non-theological in nature, a tale basically world-oriented rather than an example of theological didacticism, is to ascribe less importance to the gradualistic rehabilitation of the chief protagonist within the tripartite Lombardian framework of *contritio, confessio,* and *satisfactio* than is normally the case. An over-emphasis of the theological aspects of the work leaves too many loose ends of no minor significance. In his preface to *Pygmalion,* George Bernard Shaw remarked that "great art can never be anything else" but didactic; and there is, to be sure, a lesson included within ***Der arme Heinrich,*** but it would be a mistake to regard all of the components of the work as indispensable to its formulation. The narrative may be regarded profitably within its own context; it is, in fact, its own justification. That the clear dichotomy between Christianity and pre-Christian superstition in ***Der arme Heinrich*** is never resolved may make the work unacceptable as a theological tract, but it in no way impairs the effectiveness of its narrative. The contrary is, in fact, the case.

William C. McDonald (essay date 1988)

SOURCE: "Aspects of Time in Hartmann's *Der arme Heinrich,*" in *Monatshefte,* Vol. 80, No. 4, Winter 1988, pp. 430-43.

[*In the following excerpt, McDonald argues that Hartmann employs a characteristic time motif in his* Der arme Heinrich *in order to emphasize the transformation of the hero from his fall from grace to his eventual redemption.*]

Time is part of the fabric of the plot in each of the narrative poems of Hartmann von Aue, and chronological sequence enhances our understanding of events. In ***Erec, Iwein, Gregorius,*** and ***Der arme Heinrich*** (hereafter abbreviated as ***AH***), Hartmann demonstrates a keen awareness of the flow of time, relating the adventures of his protagonists in a linear manner within a time continuum. Despite the obvious differences in the concerns of these works, a consistent philosophy of time emerges. The main characters, bound to time and mortality, endure finite periods of erroneous living in the world, suffering, and expiation. In time—both in the figurative and temporal sense—they undergo spiritual growth and regeneration in their search for self-understanding. To illustrate the learning process, Hartmann calls on the full resources of chronology, exploiting the sinful past, the transformed present, and the promised bliss of eternity. Time is not a negative force but rather an agent for organizing experience. It is also an artistic medium through which a moral lesson is conveyed.

Given the importance Hartmann attaches to time sequences, it is surprising that his treatment of temporality has received little attention. Scholarship on Hartmann's conception of time has not progressed materially in the three decades since the appearance of Cornelia Grisebach's . . . ["Zeifbegriff und Zeitgestaltung in den Romanen Chrétiens de Troyes und Hartmanns von Aue"]. Chronology has in fact all but disappeared from a critical discussion eager to analyze the narrative structures and social implications of his poetry. The present study aims to close a gap in research by examining ***AH*** from the perspective of time. The vantage point chosen provides the groundwork for a reading of the poem, which, while generally confirming the *opinio communis,* reveals that the pattern of time is an unjustly neglected means of access to interpretation.

Before investigating in depth the aspects of chronology in ***AH,*** we should note that its precise time scheme is the most difficult to reconstruct among Hartmann's poems. A subtle reflection of this status is perhaps the amount of time ***AH*** takes to unfold, which sets it apart from the other narratives. The poem occupies a middle position between the hurried Arthurian tales and ***Gregorius,*** whose plot develops over decades. If we look beyond the divergences in total elapsed time, ***AH*** shares temporal features with Hartmann's stories. The narrator of ***AH*** states expressly that Heinrich remained at the homestead of a peasant for three years (351), while suffering from leprosy. The period of time is structurally close to that in the other poems, inasmuch as the hero spends a year or more in personal failure or atonement. Since Heinrich's three years are marked by humiliation and suffering rather than in the development of the fault itself, in contrast with the Arthurian romances, ***AH*** shows affinity to ***Gregorius*** with regard to time.

Even with this explicit reference to time, "driu jâr" (351), the reconstruction of the temporal horizon of ***AH*** is by no means easily realized. For the narrator cloaks timekeeping in willful opacity, as I hope to demonstrate. He avoids referring to the duration of Heinrich's period of suffering after his sojourn of three years, for example, and he remains silent on the length of time Heinrich was leprous before taking refuge on the farm. "Three" is therefore both explicit and emblematic, the latter meaning aided by the traditional religious signification attached to the number. The number "three," it is agreed, is key to the interpretation of ***AH.*** The triplicity of the narrative pattern is vividly evoked by the changing epithets given Heinrich—*herre, arm, guot.* If an aesthetics of number is accepted, then Hartmann, in juxtaposing plot, story divisions and a time signal according to a common denominator, confers chronology itself with a religious dimension. The time element becomes a theological statement: by virtue of years spent in overcoming the effects of human flaw, the contrite hero becomes an illustrative paragon for the audience of the poem. As seen in the case of Heinrich and the maiden, time is required for revelation, and all sins, however grave, can be forgiven in due time.

The plot outline of ***AH*** allows for brief recapitulation, for which purpose I borrow T.L. Markey's [summary in "Word as Motif and 'Der arme Heinrich' as Model," *Colloquia Germanica,* 15 (1982)]:

> For no apparent reason, a knight of good family . . . is afflicted with leprosy, a disease that resulted in social rejection and symbolized the wrath of God, the victim of which was regarded as unclean, unwhole. To be cured, he is informed that he must obtain the blood of a marriageable virgin willing to die for him. The knight retreats from society to the isolated homestead of one of his yeoman farmers . . . By divine intervention, the farmer's daughter, a marriageable virgin, agrees to die for the knight. The killing is stayed as the knight is miraculously cured, and he marries the girl who saved him.

From this sketch it is evident that Hartmann arranges his story chronologically. The tale unfolds in linear time, and the episodes are linked sequentially. The reader (or listener) is aware of the continuous flow of time even when the characters reflect on events that transpired in the past, for the flow of memory in these retrospective scenes illuminates present action and attitudes. Regret for time past is a necessary condition for the heightened state of existence that self-awareness brings.

Following the scholarly clerical tradition, Hartmann articulates his method in the prologue (1-28). He claims to have found a written source for ***AH,*** which he sets forth. The poem is a mixture of the saint's life, fairy tale, courtly romance and story of a penitent. Analogues are everywhere to be seen, sometimes for fragments of the plot, but no exact literary parallel to the story itself has been uncovered. (It is safe to assume that his source, or sources, were not dependent on a scheme of discernible time, as for instance is true of ***Iwein,*** which concerns the consequences of punctuality.) The passage directly following the prologue identifies the *maere* (29) as one concerning a feudal lord living in Swabia (30ff.). With this precise designation Hartmann defines his narrative space, setting the story in a place that can be geographically verified.

The adoption of an aspect of mimetic reality in spatial rendering is coupled with the observance of a continuous time scheme. Event follows event in logical and connected sequence. The story takes place in the unspecified near present. Thus situated in "knightly" time, ***AH*** relates a temporal existence that is subject to causality. Undeviating narrative progression is traceable: the noble protagonist falls from grace and, as a consequence of spiritual progress, is delivered. The reader follows the course of action with no difficulty. Instances of shifts from the past to the present (a form of the retrospective narrative) are invariably handled from a consistent viewpoint and do not provoke reader disorientation.

The time line of the poem is dominated by the past tense, the preterite befitting a finished (historical) recreation. Hartmann exploits the full range of tenses, however, using the present, the present with future implication, the present perfect, and the past perfect tenses. The present tense occurs with various functions. First, it is proverbial, frequently with religious overtones: "Man giht, er sî sîn selbes bote . . . " (26). Second, it is the agency of translation for a Latin hymn with direct relevance to the story: "daz diutet sich alsus, / daz wir in dem tôde sweben . . . " (94f.). Third, the present is the tense for narrative intrusion and authorial commentary: "als alle sîne gelîchen tuont" (136). Fourth, it is, in passages of dialogue and monologue, the medium for personal reflection and self-analysis: "als alle werlttôren tuont" (396); "dû hâst einen tumben gedanc" (1243). And finally, again in conversation, the present tense appears when the maiden wins the consent of her parents to sacrifice herself for Heinrich (544ff.). In summary, Hartmann switches to the present for immediacy, both of word and deed, embedding each in the framework of the narrative past. Therefore, although the story is past-oriented, the present intrudes to reinforce the validity and contemporary relevance of ***AH***. An example of the interaction of past and present is Heinrich's dialogue with the peasant, in which, entering the field of memory, he takes a despondent backward glance at his failed attitudes and behavior. In their conversation the past and present interweave, actually intersecting at the point where Heinrich begins to accept his punishment. Then the knight uses the present perfect tense, an effective means of conveying the fact that his suffering is not yet complete, but unremitting: "Ich hân disen schämelîchen spot / vil wol gedienet umbe got" (383f.). We observe that the condition of leprosy itself, extending over two thirds of the story, is presented both as a temporal and narrative device.

The plot is logical, straightforward, and unfolds diachronically. That the serial conception of time is a deeply embedded construct is shown by the relation of temporal directionality to the story proper: its artistic coherence rests on the perception of the protagonist's decline and recovery as a continuous, successive process of personal transformation within an objective time sequence. Simultaneously, however, Hartmann initiates a calculated play with the verifiability of temporal events, manipulating and distorting the dimension of time to the degree that one can speak of a paradox. For, although the tale progresses chronologically from event to event, it systematically withholds explicit and quantifiable indicators of the passage of time. Because of the wealth of temporal references and the seriatim time of the story, the reader has the impression that a discernible time scheme exists. There is actually time consciousness but little temporal specificity—the majority of sequences lack verifiable parameters, detail is scant and points of transition blurred. Blocked off from the necessary temporal details, the reader is compelled to adduce units of time, and the chronology must be worked out on the basis of inference. Hartmann therefore sets up a tension between his lucid plot, his proverbial translucent and unadorned style, and his subjective intervals. It will not do to characterize the temporal structure in ***AH,*** as Grisebach attempts, with the single phrase "die Zeit (wird) metaphorisch verwandt." Time is present in the metaphoric sense, but Hartmann's treatment of time is more complex than she suggests. Measurable chronology has a marginal function in the poem, and Hartmann shows a benign, almost irreverent attitude toward it.

AH is, as observed, replete with time indications. Only three of these are wholly articulated, however, and since each refers to the number "three," a play with numerical meaning and the time scheme is strongly suggested. Hartmann maintains continuity and orders time according to three, a numeral silhouetted against the backdrop of otherwise shadowy temporal scaffolding: first, Heinrich's three years of seclusion at the peasant's farm (351); second, the maiden's three days of decision, in which she gives an oral defense of her resolution to sacrifice herself (459ff.); and finally, the relatives' three-day journey to receive Heinrich after his cure (1391). This last is a particularly good example of Hartmann's attitude towards narrative history. While giving a time interval, three days, he simultaneously renders the time span imprecise, and therefore indeterminate, by the addition of the vague qualifier *wol:* "wol drîe tage." How long was the journey? (Similarly, "si kusten ir tohter munt / etewaz mê dan drîstunt," 1417f.)

The choice of the number "three," invested as it is with deep symbolic and typological meaning, expresses Hartmann's selective attitude toward time. Temporal specificity is more apparent than real and indicates no precise calendrical demarcation. The narrator mentions years of withdrawal from the world to stress that suffering over an extended period of time is necessary to Heinrich's healing; he speaks of days to suggest how concentrated and intense were the maiden's attempts to sway her parents; and he again refers to days to demonstrate the efforts Heinrich's relatives exerted to greet the healed knight. Apparent disclosure of temporal detail turns out to be Biblical triplets and outlines of the passage of time—years and days. This represents a symbolic point of view on chronology, a perspective reliant on holy numbers and allusion. A world in time thus transcends time and becomes both a realm of fiction and of higher truth.

That Hartmann strives for this effect is clear from the knight's words of insight, uttered at the moment when the maiden is ready to sacrifice herself: "Swaz dir got hât beschert, daz lâ allez geschehen. / ich enwil des kindes tôt niht sehen" (1254-56). He continues: "gotes wille müeze an mir geschehen!" (1276). These phrases, showing a unity of will with God's intentions, are in the present tense, active voice, and in the optative. By the very grammar of his presentation, Hartmann thus invests these sentiments with validity not bound to a specific moment in time. An act of compassion in the narrative past, the refusal of sacrifice and the acceptance of his condition, is so structured as to make it prototypically current.

To sum up, Hartmann positions his triadic date-frames in a network of chronological sequence that depends on bifurcation: the time markers both articulate and render enigmatic the determination of time. Temporal indications are therefore hermetic signs and a technique of manipulation that prohibits the objective placing of events in time. One discerns this pattern of nonspecific references first in the adverbs and adverbial phrases, which are prominent carriers of the time scheme in ***AH***.

The adverbs chosen point to the movement of time. But they leave precise temporal segments unspecified, and therefore make them inaccessible to the reader. For instance, Hartmann uses (with frequency of occurrence in parenthesis) *drâte* (3), *schiere* (6), *schierest* (1), *selten* (2), *vor der zît* (1), *vor kurzer stunt* (1), *vür dise stunt* (2), *zallen stunden* (1), *zallen zîten* (1), *zehant* (7), *ze jungest* (2), *zestunt* (1), and *zuo der selben stunde* (1). To cite examples of time words in context, Heinrich "shortly" learns that the doctors cannot heal him ("vil schiere," 176); God "immediately" makes Heinrich and the girl whole ("zestunt," 1369); and Heinrich tells the Swabians that, as they know, he was repugnant to all until "quite recently" ("vor kurzer stunt," 1476). In each of these instances the general effect is the transmission of information on time. But the placement of temporal designations alongside equally fuzzy time intervals makes time elusive as a measureable commodity.

Another tactic with similar force is the omission of temporal markers where the narrative calls for them. For example, the time span in which Heinrich's transgressions transpired is unclear; he contracts leprosy at an unspecified time; he suffers for an indeterminate time before going to the farmer's home; he makes trips at uncertain junctures and of ill-defined duration; the date of Heinrich's healing after this stay on the farm is vague; and only these words appear when the community decides on the propriety of his marriage to the maiden: "hie huop sich ein michel strît" (1468). In this last, one encounters the further paradox that an adverb of place, *hie,* communicates a (vague) unit of time, "then." The result of these consistent deletions of temporal specificity is that the length of time between most events is open to interpretation. Faced with remote or absent signs of duration, the reader must construct his own chronology of the story.

A less obvious but equally important mechanism for blurring time is the particles. Hartmann most frequently employs the temporal marker *dô,* which is an adverb of time and a subordinating conjunction with the various meanings "then," "at that time," and "when." *Dô* figures prominently in medieval German poetry, both as an epic formula for introducing single events in chronological sequence and as a syntactical indicator of narrative transition. It has a similar function in medieval saints' lives, which draw on the techniques of Biblical narrative. Characteristic of scriptural usage are the connectors "then," "at about that time," "after a time," "after some days," and "after many days," which Robert Alter has labelled ambiguous, formulaic time indicators [in his *The Art of Biblical Narrative* (1981)]. Hartmann therefore portrays temporal experience with a rhetorical device firmly grounded in Scripture that leaves time limits devoid of verifiability.

It is evident from the manuscripts that the scribes—or the poet himself—wish to focus attention on *dô,* where it appears in large initials some fourteen times. Two scribal divisions coincide with prominent narrative segments. Once *dô* indicates the onset of leprosy (75), which at the same time sets the plot proper into motion. And another time it allows us to penetrate Heinrich's self-awareness. Beset by despondency and self-loathing, he realizes that he is repugnant to his fellow creatures and is unwilling to suffer patiently like Job (133). In both sections, considerations of measurable time have a subsidiary part in relation to the demands of narration. *Dô* serves to establish that time has passed, that is, it allows for the perception of linear progression. But the word *dô* at the same time conceals the specific period of time elapsed.

In ***AH*** *dô* becomes a *Leitwort,* appearing some fifty times as an introductory signal and almost thirty times in other positions. One of these places is the conclusion of the verse, most frequently as a rhyme for *vrô* and *unvrô* (for example, 509f.). It therefore mirrors the emotional tenor of the episodes in which it is placed. An example of *dô* in the initial position (including an appearance in mid-position) is the account of Heinrich's resolution, after the attempted sacrifice of the maiden, to return home:

> *dô* der gnâdelôse gast
> sîne maget wider kleite
> und den arzât bereite
> als er gedinget hâte
> *dô* vuor er alsô drâte
> wider heim ze lande,
> swie wol er *dô* erkande
> daz er dâ heime vunde
> mit gemeinem munde
> niuwan laster unde spot:
> daz liez er allez an got
>
> (1342-52)

This passage has a stylistic counterpart in and a temporal relationship to the scene almost immediately following, when Christ intercedes to perform the miracle of healing:

> *dô* erkande ir triuwe und ir nôt
> cordis speculâtor . . .
> *dô* erzeicte der heilic Krist
> wie liep im triuwe und bärmde ist
> und schiet si *dô* beide
> von allem ir leide
> und machete in dâ zestunt
> reine unde wol gesunt
>
> (1356-70)

The episodes cited, interwoven with and carried by clusters of the word *dô,* are connected by the fabric of chronology already explored, namely causal efficacy but unspecific borders of time. The reader is asked to accept a narrative logic and momentum, according to which one event follows another in a span inadequately accounted for by the poet. Without knowing when the initial *dô* in such a pattern sequence occurred in time, it is impossible to ascertain what interval is present between the repeated signals of chronology. *Dô* therefore contributes materially to the ideology of narrative form in ***AH,*** assuming a subversive function as it works at cross-purposes with the verifiable continuity of the storytelling.

The result of these manipulations of chronology, especially of the miraculous entrance of Christ ("dô erzeicte der heilic Krist"), is the face of a world frozen in timelessness, at once inside and outside time. Time is inadequate in the face of heaven. Since Christ can enter time at will, the force of divine intervention in ***AH*** is to call into question the pertinence of man's experience in time and the attempt to chart it. Of what significance is the calculation of time or temporal precision, Hartmann seems to ask, if time itself is malleable and brought to virtual stasis by the design of providence? In obviating the distinction between the eternal and the temporal, Hartmann offers direct access to the way in which he posits reality in the poem. He sketches, exploiting the form and essence of religious narrative to the fullest, a timeless realm informed by the idea of eternity.

Just prior to the episode on Christ's healing power, another particle appears which operates contrapuntally with *dô, nû:* "Nû hete sich diu guote maget / sô gar verweinet und verklaget . . . (1353f.). *Nû,* in the meanings "now" and "now that," also functions as a recurrent time indication; I count almost fifty appearances. It occurs most frequently in the line-initial position and marks off sections of the story. Like *dô, nû* serves as an introductory signal with a type of structural-technical function, and although it is a word-motif reiterated for the purpose of narrative progression, it, too, lacks temporal specificity. One may regard *dô* and *nû* as a syntactical and chronological pair applied as an interconnective device: "then" and "now."

Two passages illustrate the correlation of *dô* and *nû.* The first concerns Heinrich's self-accusation, conveyed in dialogue form with the peasant. Expressing his sorrow, the knight dates the time spent in self-deception and presumption with the temporal marker *dô* ("dô nam ich sîn [God] vil kleine war," 393ff.). He contrasts this sinful past with *nû,* his current miserable existence ("nû versmâhe ich den boesen," 412ff.). Specific theological motivation resides behind the pair: *dô* indicates the remembered time of the sin of self, and *nû* is the present, a period of constant suffering. Heinrich's sorrow for the past and the penitential-like analysis in the scene with the peasant signal his budding self-knowledge.

Outlined by the temporal points "then" and "now," Heinrich's dawning insight becomes full contrition and acceptance of God's will at the place of intended sacrifice. The narrator conveys the change in the hero's attitude through verses interpenetrated with indications of time:

> *nû* sach er si an unde sich
> und gewan einen niuwen muot:
> in dûhte *dô* daz niht guot
> des er *ê* gedâht hâte
> und verkêrte vil drâte
> sîn altez gemüete
> in eine niuwe güete
>
> (1234-40)

Dô is set in relation to *nû,* but now the latter is contrasted with a further time reference, *ê* ("formerly," "before," "previously"). The elaborate word play here witnessed is prefigured in an earlier description of the leprous knight's reception by humanity:

> dô man die swaeren gotes zuht
> gesach an sînem lîbe,
> man unde wîbe
> wart er dô widerzaeme.
> *nû* sehet wie genaeme
> er *ê* der werlte waere,
> und wart *nû* als unmaere
> daz in niemen gerne sach
>
> (120-27)

The three, *ê, dô* and *nû,* operate reciprocally, creating a syntactic framework and a verbal symmetry as much spiritual as it is temporal. The relationship of the three is iconographic, reflecting as it does the temporal anchor to which *AH* clings, the number "three."

The passage cited above on Heinrich's conversion (1234ff.) is so typical that it can serve as a resumé of the dimension of time in the poem. Vague temporal designations (*ê, dô, nû*) link time segments and suggest orderly chronological progression, but are calculated so as to make moments in time mystifying. Each represents contrastive stages, or blocks, of time: "formerly," "then" / "when" and "now." Crucial, both from the narrative and theological perspective, is the opposition of the "foregoing" and the "ensuing." Judging the audience's narrower knowledge of elapsed time to be tangential, the poet and his narrator focus on states of existence that are exemplary, and thus eternal. Eternity is explicitly introduced at the conclusion of the story in verses set off by still another obscure chronological segment:

> nâch süezem lanclîbe
> dô besâzen si [Heinrich and the maiden] gelîche
> daz êwige rîche
>
> (1514-16)

AH is timeless at its core, as the portrayal of temporal experience with vague time references suggests. Time is everywhere in the story, and thus we expect Hartmann to account for it adequately. Instead we learn that time is a literary device, concurrently linear and horizontal, offering a view of eternity. Still, with due allowance for the theological implications of the story, it would be incorrect to identify Hartmann's dominant concern as the changeless and achronological state after life on earth.

Grisebach therefore overstates the case when arguing that the time indications converge predominantly in the "Gegensatz von Zeit und Ewigkeit." The fragility of human existence interests the poet greatly; likewise, his spiritual perception of history is undeniable. But allusions to the temporal character of man's experience, for example, the narrator's remarks on the instability of the world (97-100), should not obscure the fact that Hartmann effects a reconciliation between time and eternity in the practical example of the protagonists. He locates the meaning of time in moral action, prescribed and aided by heaven.

Both Heinrich and the maiden are forced to come to terms with the world, to deal with its laws and forces. Their successful struggle to realize their essential nature speaks strongly against a thorough depreciation of secular time and space. If anything, the moral example offered by the knight and the girl demonstrates that, in spite of the mutability of earthly things, there is human capacity for insight and understanding. For lives such as these, led in conformity with divine will, the reward is eternity. Time for Heinrich and the maiden is the revealer, not the destroyer.

Still to be explored is the effect of Hartmann's use of narrative expansion and contraction on the dimension of time in *AH*. The story proceeds at a variable rate, or rhythm, according to which certain episodes appear in sketchy, skeletal form, while others enjoy an inflated depiction. Narration is compressed and distended, with the result that the importance of an event has an ill-defined connection to textual proportions and the passage of time. For instance, the long, overland journey to Salerno is condensed, occupying only six verses (1049-54), whereas the encounter between the maiden and her parents is dilated, two nights' confrontation consuming over 400 verses (459-902). One of the scenes punctuated by the unequal distribution of tempo and textual significance is central to the story line: Heinrich's moral transformation is described in some twenty lines of text (1221-40), thus making it one of the shortest episodes in the poem. Throughout, the forward movement of the plot is interrupted at certain junctures—characteristically during dialogues and monologues, where time is almost suspended. The theoretical justification for this free play with chronology and the time sense of the reader emerges only gradually. By juxtaposing static moments with compressed, rapidly recounted ones, the poet is able to underscore the relativity and ultimate inscrutability of units of measurement.

To illustrate the nature of these dilations and contractions, the speeding up and slowing down of dynamic rhythm, we may cite two examples. The first is the full journey sequence to Salerno:

> Sus vuor engegen Salerne
> vroelich und gerne
> diu maget mit ir herren.
> waz möhte ir nû gewerren
> wan daz der wec sô verre was
> daz si sô lange genas?
> dô er si vol brâhte
> hin . . .
>
> (1049-56)

These condensed verses presuppose a lengthy passage of time, certainly of weeks, but there is no way of telling how long the trip actually took. The narrator accelerates the movement of the action, eliminating topographic and temporal details and allowing the lines to serve as a bridge from one episode to another. Over this bridge time traverses a silent route. The narrative interest lies with the girl's readiness for sacrifice, which is a thematic and moral concern. In organizing *AH* along thematic lines, Hartmann anticipates a technique seen later in Sir Thomas Malory. . . .

The dialogue between the maiden and her parents (490-854), through which she successfully persuades them to allow the sacrifice, is the counterpart to the journey to Salerno. The father and mother use a specific time indicator to indicate how long the extended discussion lasted:

> ez ist hiute der dritte tac
> daz si uns allez ane lac
> daz wir ir sîn gunden
>
> (981-83)

The reader immediately perceives a depiction of time set

in contrast to the rest of the poem. The narrator amplifies the scenes with spirited arguments and counter-arguments in the present tense and charts actions and reactions. He thereby illuminates the motives of the characters. Action is deliberately delayed and circumstances are reported concretely, in moment-by-moment sequence. . . .

What is one to make of the fact that the narrator alters his method of reporting the passage of time, as entire conversations, which profit of judicial oratory, appear verbatim? One conclusion is the elevation of the maiden above the status of a minor character. Time bends to the girl, virtually standing still for her. From the attention that she attracts and the attitude towards temporality that she activates in the story, it is certain that the revealed truth about her actions and emotions engages the poet. She is not precisely equal to Heinrich in narrative importance, but each endures ordeals and each is "healed" by a God who controls human affairs (1367-70). Second, the narrator's exhaustive rendering of scenes with the maiden is both a means of limning the characters according to strategic positions and a retarding element. The narrative pace grows leisurely, and time becomes subservient to the exchange of opinion itself, which anatomizes the themes of renunciation of the world and salvation through human sacrifice. To what extent, Hartmann seems to ask, do her motivations—which arise in a brief but lavishly detailed time span—derive from private goals? Third, the two narrative devices observed actually coalesce in a consistent attitude toward chronology. There is logical coherence, whether the narrator abbreviates or amplifies episodes, or whether he accelerates years or distends days and hours. For all human events are subject to the ceaseless and irreversible flow of time. The depiction of such progression, as ***AH*** demonstrates, need neither be mechanical nor slave to uniform literary proportions. Time is a flexible medium, manipulable as an agent of narrative concentration and religious insight.

Scholarship on ***AH*** has not been able to account for the aberrations of symmetry. The discursive passages, the fluctuating rhythms bringing a conscious lengthening and shortening of time in their wake, and the inconsonance of the narrative significance of episodes with their verse count appeared at first sight random and meaningless. Recent research on time concepts in medieval poetry brings to light the method Hartmann employs, which places ***AH*** in a line observable already in saints' lives and carried forth in the *Cid* (ca. 1140) and Chaucer's *Troilus and Criseyde* (1380-86). The distinctive attitude toward time observed here is labelled "psychological" and "dramatic chronology."

The technique is one of focus. Time is used, in a pattern of gradation and climax, to create emotional effects and to heighten audience expectation. Common to poems drawing on this branch of chronology are compressed or distended intervals of action, time suspension or delay, and the number "three" as a structural signifier. Consequently, it is impossible to read such works on a strictly chronological level. The oscillation between focused and unfocused time, between static and dynamic scenes, between continuity and discontinuity has of course direct bearing on the reader's ability to discriminate—his sense of time betrays him. This is not crucial, however. Following the conceptual apparatus sketched, queries on the duration of time are essentially unimportant, inasmuch as they do not elicit responses indicating proportion and hence the significance of individual episodes.

Applying these findings for the first time to ***AH,*** one can state that Hartmann is concerned with putting events in temporal sequence, but his time scheme aims for more than an ordering of events. He neither states the circumstances of time with equal compression (when time is specified), nor does he attempt to give uniform concentration to episodes. The measurement of time is secondary, because the poet is primarily interested in a thematic treatment permitting exposure of attitudes and placing the accent on the moral implications of word and deed.

In dialogues the brevity of time elapsed is directly proportional to narrative intensity, which suggests that Hartmann deliberately correlates a short time span with close scrutiny of action and reaction, motivation, cause and effect. . . . This concentration on psychological effects permits Hartmann to explore and dramatize the consequences of vivid passions. Unexpectedly, perhaps, his examination of the maiden's attitudes against the backdrop of temporal manipulation proves to be a technique of refutation. For once her clever argumentation and the emotional state generating it are laid bare, the ground is removed from under her. She is not allowed to pass at will to eternity. Perhaps the very fact that her decision for sacrifice occurs in a concentrated period of time is a sign of faulty vision. She is required in any event to live—like Heinrich—in a world that holds out the promise of the final dissolution of time, even as it opposes passive waiting for death or eagerness for it.

FURTHER READING

Boggs, Roy A. "Hartmann's Erec." In *Innovation in Medieval Literature: Essays to the Memory of Alan Markman,* edited by Douglas Radcliff-Umstead, pp. 49-62. Pittsburgh: Medieval Studies Committee of the University of Pittsburgh, 1971.

Compares Hartmann's *Erec* with its French source, the *Erec et Enide* of Chrétien de Troyes, concluding that Hartmann made significant changes to the story in order to depict more thoroughly Erec's character development.

Gentry, Francis G. "Hartmann von Aue's *Erec*: The Burden of Kingship." In *King Arthur Through the Ages,* edited by Valerie M. Lagorio and Mildred Leake Day, pp. 152-69. New York and London: Garland Publishing, 1990.

With a consideration of Arthurianism generally, explores the leadership qualities and knightly virtues that Hartmann stresses in Erec.

Green, D. H. "The Reception of Hartmann's Works: Listening, Reading, or Both?" *The Modern Language Review* 81, Pt. 2

(April 1986): 357-368.

Questions whether Hartmann intended and expected his writings to be read by literate members of the higher classes, recited without a written source, or read aloud (from manuscript) to an audience.

Keller, Thomas L. "The Relationship between Hartmann von Aue's *Klage* and His Lyric Poetry." *The USF Language Quarterly* XXIII, Nos. 3-4 (Spring-Summer 1985): 44-48.

Compares Hartmann's *Die Klage* with his *minnesangs,* insisting that *Die Klage* represents a more mature philosophy of love that breaks distinctly from the strict courtly ideals voiced by his early lyrics.

Lamse, James. "Hartmann von Aue's Crusade Poem '*Sweth frowe sendet ir lieben man*' (MF 211, 20): A Pre-Condition for the Journey." In *Itinerarium: The Idea of Journey,* edited by Leonard J. Bowman, pp. 76-93. Salzburg: Institut für Anglistik und Amerikanistik, 1983.

Examines the motif of the journey as exemplified in the three crusade poems (*kreuzlieder*) of Hartmann's *minnesangs.*

McConeghy, Patrick M. "Women's Speech and Silence in Hartmann von Aue's *Erec.*" *PMLA* 102, No. 5 (October 1987): 772-83.

Argues that, although *Erec* may initially seem to endorse the male pursuit of higher social status and the relative silence and passivity of women, Hartmann may actually consider an active female to be requisite for knightly success.

Simon, Paul. "The Underrated Lyrics of Hartmann von Aue." *The Modern Language Review* 66, No. 4 (October 1971): 810-25.

Examines the characteristic structure and organization of Hartmann's poems and evaluates his contributions to the *minnesang* tradition generally.

Tobin, Frank J. Gregorius *and* Der arme Heinrich: *Hartmann's Dualistic and Gradualistic Views of Reality.* Bern and Frankfurt: Verlag Herbert Lang, 1973, 112 p.

Studies Hartmann's shorter narratives, exploring the reconciliation of opposites—especially God and man—in *Gregorius* and *Der arme Heinrich.*

Willson, H. B. "'Marriageable' in *Der arme Heinrich.*" *Modern Philology* 64, No. 2 (November 1966): 95-102.

Critiques Hartmann's portrayal of the maid in *Der arme Heinrich* in order to understand the criteria by which she is judged a proper sacrifice.

———. "Kalogreant's Curiosity in Hartmann's *Iwein.*" *German Life and Letters* XXI (1967-1968): 287-96.

Explores the ethical implications of *Iwein* in order to understand Hartmann's conception of knighthood.

Marco Polo

1254-1324

Italian merchant and traveller.

INTRODUCTION

A Venetian merchant, Polo was among the first travellers to the East to provide an account of that region in a Western language. His narrative, *The Travels of Marco Polo,* met with skepticism and disbelief upon its circulation, as the region had only previously been written about in legends such as those of Alexander the Great, and by William of Rubrouck, a French Franciscan friar who wrote a missionary's account of his trip to Mongolia upon his return to France in 1255. Many of Polo's previously unsubstantiated observations and claims were, however, confirmed by later travellers and his work is now regarded by most scholars as the first accurate description of Asia by a European.

Biographical Information

Polo was born in Venice in 1254 while his father Nicolo and his uncle Maffeo were away on a trading voyage during which they first met Kublai Khan, the Emperor of Mongolia; they did not return to Italy until Polo was about fifteen years old. The elder Polos had been instructed by the Khan to solicit the Pope for Christian missionaries to be escorted back to the Emperor's court. The Polos were forced to wait until 1270 for a new pope, Gregory X, to be elected due to the failure of the cardinals to name a successor to Pope Clement IV following his death in 1268. Polo, now about seventeen years old, accompanied his father and uncle to Mongolia following the trio's presentation of the Khan's request to Pope Gregory X. After reaching the Khan's court and being employed in his service for a number of years, the Polos desired to return to Italy. The Khan was unwilling to release the merchants from his service, but complied with their request when they agreed to travel to Persia to escort a princess betrothed to the Khan's grand-nephew. The Polos completed their mission and then began their journey home, arriving in Venice in 1295 after a twenty-four-year absence. Soon after his return, Polo was appointed to command a ship in the war between the city-states of Venice and Genoa. His fleet was defeated and he arrived in Genoa as a political prisoner on October 16, 1298. Polo was released from prison in July of 1299. He lived in Venice until his death at the age of seventy.

Textual History

While he was in prison, Polo had dictated his account of his travels to a fellow prisoner, Rustichello. Scholars believe that Polo's original manuscript was translated, copied, and widely circulated following his release from prison in 1299. The language of the original manuscript is unknown and a topic of much debate. In 1320, Pipino made a Latin translation of Polo's *Travels* from a version written in an Italian dialect, implying that this dialect version was Polo's original. Giovanni Battista Ramusio, an Italian geographer whose edition of Polo's work was published in 1559 in a collection of travel accounts known as *Navigationi et viaggi*, believed that the original manuscript was written in Latin. Others have maintained that Polo's work was written in French or Franco-Italian. Another source of contention among critics regards the role played by Rustichello in the writing of *Travels.* Some critics argue that Rustichello copied a draft already completed by Polo, or transcribed the work as Polo dictated it. Others believe that Rustichello served as a collaborator and editor, rewording Polo's phrasing and adding commentary of his own. The manuscript regarded by many critics as the most complete is a French version known as *fr. 1116,* published by the French Geographic Society in 1824. Some critics have contended that *fr. 1116* is a true transcript of Polo's dictation to Rustichello, but other scholars such as N. M. Penzer have argued that it does not represent a direct copy of Polo's work, asserting that another manuscript (referred to by Polian scholars as *Z*) may antedate *fr. 1116.* Other groups of Polian manuscripts studied for their authenticity and their relation to the original manuscript include the Grégoire version, which critics have suggested is perhaps an elaborated version of *fr. 1116;* the Tuscan Recension, an early fourteenth-century Tuscan translation of a Franco-Italian version of the original manuscript; and the Venetian Recension, a group of over eighty manuscripts which have been translated into the Venetian dialect. *Travels* was first translated into English by John Frampton in 1579. In the nineteenth century, scholars such as William Marsden, Henry Yule, and Luigi Benedetto began to publish revisions of the work that utilized information from several manuscripts to produce a more comprehensive edition of *Travels.* Since the original manuscript of *Travels* has never been recovered, the search for the version most directly descended from it continues.

Major Works

Polo's *The Travels of Marco Polo,* his first and only known work, provides readers with a detailed description of late thirteenth-century Asia. The work includes an account of Nicolo's and Maffeo's first journey to the residence of Kublai Khan; geographical descriptions of the countries between the Black Sea, the China Sea, and the Indian Ocean; and historical narratives about the Mongolian Empire's rise and expansion. Polo's *Travels* also relates the author's personal adventures and his association with Kublai Khan. Polo's tone throughout the narration is that of a commercial traveller reporting what he has seen and heard. He employs the same straightforward style in discussing his own experiences as he does when he relates hearsay, which he identifies as such. Polo focused his observations on aspects such as trade, political and military structures, religious customs relating to marriage and burial of the dead, and the architecture and layout of cities. His matter-of-fact tone in the narrative emphasizes the presentation of facts over the discussion of theories or ideas.

Critical Reception

Polo's first critics, the friends and relatives to whom he verbally related his journey, refused to believe what they considered to be outrageous exaggerations or pure fiction. Yet Polo's story was appealing for its entertainment value and was rapidly copied and distributed following its initial transcription. His account did not gain credibility until after his death, when further exploration proved many of his claims. Some modern critics have faulted Polo for omitting certain subjects from the narrative: for example, Polo never mentioned tea, the practice of binding women's feet, or the Great Wall, all of which were unheard of in Europe. Polo's defenders have countered that since the merchant had lived in Mongolia for twenty-four years, subjects that would seem strange or exotic to Europeans had become commonplace in Polo's life. Others have contended that such omissions could also have been made consciously or accidentally by translators of the work. *Travels* is often criticized on stylistic grounds as well, for instance for shifting back and forth between first and third person narration, but scholars attribute many such faults to the numerous times the work has been translated and copied. Although many critics assess *Travels* as simply a merchant's pragmatic account of his stay in the East, some, like Mary Campbell, maintain that the work offers the authority of first-hand experience and argue that its value extends beyond providing enjoyment through vicarious experience in that it transforms the myth of the East into reality.

PRINCIPAL ENGLISH TRANSLATIONS

The Travels of Marco Polo (translated by John Frampton) 1579

The Travels of Marco Polo, the Venetian (translated and edited by William Marsden) 1818

The Book of Ser Marco Polo (translated and edited by Henry Yule) 1871

The Travels of Marco Polo (translated by Aldo Ricci from the Italian edition by L. F. Benedetto) 1931

Marco Polo: The Description of the World (translated and edited by A. C. Moule and P. Pelliot) 1938

The Adventures of Marco Polo (translated by Richard J. Walsh) 1948

The Travels of Marco Polo (translated by Robert Latham) 1958

The Travels of Marco Polo (translated by Teresa Waugh from the Italian edition by Maria Bellonci) 1984

CRITICISM

John Frampton (essay date 1579)

SOURCE: "The Epistle Dedicatorie," in *The Travels of Marco Polo,* edited by N. M. Penzer, translated by John Frampton, The Argonaut Press, 1929, pp. 1-2.

[*In the following dedication to his 1579 translation of* The Travels of Marco Polo, *Frampton states his reasons for committing the manuscript to print in English.*]

To the right worshipfull Mr. Edward Dyar Esquire,
Iohn Frampton wisheth prosperous
health and felicitie.

Having lying by mee in my chamber (righte Worshipful) a translation of the great voiage & lõg trauels of *Paulus Venetus* the *Venetian,* manye Merchauntes, Pilots, and Marriners, and others of dyuers degrees, much bent to Discoueries, resorting to me vpon seuerall occasions, toke so great delight with the reading of my Booke, finding in the same such strange things, & such a world of varietie of matters, that I coulde neuer bee in quiet, for one or for an other, for the committing the same to printe in the Englishe tongue, perswading, that it mighte giue greate lighte to our Seamen, if euer this nation chaunced to find a passage out of the frozen Zone to the South Seas, and otherwise delight many home dwellers, furtherers of trauellers. But finding in my selfe small abilitie for the finishing of it, in suche perfection as the excellencie of the worke, and as this learned time did require, I stayed a long time, in hope some learned man woulde haue translated the worke, but finding none that would take it in hand, to satisfie so many requests, nowe at last I determined to sette it forth, as I coulde, referring the learned in tongues, delighted in eloquence, to the worke it selfe, written in Latine, Spanish, and Italian, and the reste that haue but the English tong, that seeke onelye for substaunce of matter to my playne translation, beseeching to take my trauell and good meaning in the beste parte. And bethinking my selfe of some speciall Gentleman, a louer of knowledge, to whome I mighte dedicate the same, I founde no man, that I know in that respect more worthy of the same, than your worshippe, nor yet any man, to whome so many Schollers, so many trauellers, and so manye men of valor, suppressed or hindred with pouertie, or distressed by lacke of friends in Courte, are so muche bounde as to you, and therefore to you I dedicate the same, not bicause you your selfe wãt the knowledge of tongues, for I know you to haue the Latine, the Italian, the French, and the Spanishe: But bycause of youre worthinesse, and for that I haue since my firste acquaintaunce founde my selfe without any greate deserte on my parte, more bound vnto you than to anye man in *England,* and therefore for your desert & token of a thankefull minde, I dedicate the same to youre worship, moste humbly praying you to take it in good parte, and to bee patrone of the same: and so wishing you continuaunce of vertue, with muche encrease of the same, I take my leaue, wishing you with many for the cõmon wealths sake, place with aucthoritie, where you maye haue daylye exercise of the giftes that the Lorde hathe endowed you withall in plentifull sorte. From my lodging this .xxvj. daye of Ianuarie .1579.

Your worships to commaunde,

IOHN FRAMPTON.

The Quarterly Review (review date 1819)

SOURCE: "Marsden's Marco Polo," in *The Quarterly Review,* Vol. XXI, No. XLI, January-April, 1819, pp. 177-96.

[*In the following review, the anonymous critic praises Marsden's edition of Polo's book, provides an overview of the author's life, and comments on the accuracy of the narrative.*]

'It might have been expected,' Mr. Marsden says, 'that in ages past, a less tardy progress would have been made in doing justice to the intrinsic merits of a work (whatever were its defects as a composition) that first conveyed to Europeans a distinct idea of the empire of China, and, by shewing its situation together with that of Japan (before entirely unknown) in respect to the great Eastern ocean, which was supposed to meet and form one body of water with the Atlantic, eventually led to the important discoveries of the Spaniards and Portugueze.' At length, however, we need not scruple to assert that ample justice has been done to the character and reputation of this early oriental traveller; and that the name of Marco Polo stands completely rescued from that unmerited reproach which, in an age of ignorance, was wantonly heaped upon it, and which five centuries have not been sufficient entirely to wipe away; at least, according to Mr. Marsden, who tells us there are still those 'who declare their want of faith, and make the character of Marco Polo the subject of their pleasantry.'—There may be such 'persons;' but we should be somewhat less tender of their cavils and scruples than Mr. Marsden, and manifest very little of that consideration which he has vouchsafed to shew them, by undertaking his 'translation and commentary,' as he tells us, 'with the view of removing from such *candid and reflecting minds* any doubts of the honest spirit in which the original was composed.'

For ourselves we can safely say that, on every occasion where we have found it necessary to refer to Marco Polo, either for the corroboration of some fact, or to trace back the progressive geography of Asiatic countries, we never found cause to call in question the fidelity and veracity of this early traveller; on whom, perhaps not quite appropriately, Malte-Brun has not hesitated to bestow the appellation of 'the creator of modern oriental geography—the Humboldt of the thirteenth century'—We say, not quite appropriately, because Carpin and Rubruquis preceded him into Tartary; and he has no claim either to science or philosophy, with both of which the modern traveller is so eminently gifted. He was however a man of observation, of sound judgment, and discretion; and, like the 'Father of History,' whom he most resembles, always careful to separate the knowledge acquired by his own experience from that which was communicated to him by others. Mr. Marsden, we think, has succeeded in removing every unfavourable impression; and we augur confidently that, from this time, the reputation of this noble Venetian will be considered as fully established, even by those on whom the translator has bestowed the unmerited compliment of composing so elaborate a work for their conviction.

It is not a little remarkable that, while Mr. Marsden was preparing his work in England, no less than three Italian publications on the life and travels of Marco Polo were in preparation in Italy—one by the Cavaliere Baldelli at Florence, another at Rome, and a third, the only one that has yet appeared, by the Abbate Placido Zurla, who had already published a short account of our traveller in a work brought out in numbers at Milan, under the name of *Vite e Ritratti d'Illustri Italiani,* in which was given a pretended portrait of Marco Polo, but which is proved by Mr. Marsden to be altogether fictitious.

Judging from the scanty additional materials interspersed in Zurla's work, we are not led to form any very high expectation of the other two which are to follow; few if any new lights, we fear, are likely to be produced from the hidden stores of Italy. The plan of Zurla is radically defective; he has not only analyzed but absolutely anatomized his author—cut and hacked him into fragments, and mixed them up with so many extraneous scraps of his own, that even if Marco Polo himself were to rise from the dead he could not possibly recognise his own work—in short, it is no longer the travels of Marco Polo, but a collection of dissertations on the geography, natural history, customs, &c. of Eastern Tartary and China, preceded by a biographical notice of the author and his family.

Mr. Marsden has adopted a very different, and, in our opinion, a much more judicious plan in the conduct of his work: by preserving the author's narrative entire, he has exhibited Marco Polo in his true shape and proportion, unchanged in all respects, except that of his English dress. We were indeed persuaded, before we opened the volume, that no one was so well qualified to do justice to the merits of the illustrious traveller, as the learned and accurate historian of Sumatra. His residence on that island, which is largely spoken of by Marco Polo under the name of Java Minor, first gave him, he says, occasion to examine the narrative relating to it; 'and it has since,' he adds, 'been my unceasing wish that the elucidation of its obscurities should engage the attention of some person competent to the task of preparing a new edition from the best existing materials, and of illustrating it with notes calculated to bring the matter of the text into comparison with the information contained in subsequent accounts of travels and other well authenticated writings.' This task, fortunately for the literary world, he has himself undertaken, and accomplished with that success which was to be expected from so able a writer. Gifted as he is with an extensive knowledge of the customs, character and languages of most of the nations of the east; acquainted, from long residence, with most of their productions; possessing a library well stored with oriental literature; and having ready access to the best collections that Great Britain affords;—with such advantages, superadded to a well regulated mind, and a sound and discriminating judgment, we had a right to anticipate a work of no ordinary merit, and we have not been disappointed. The Translation is as close as the idiom of the Italian and English languages would admit, without being obscure; and the 'Notes' will be found to contain a vast mass of information, partly derived from personal knowledge, and partly from the best authors who have written on the various subjects which are brought under view.

In the choice of a text for his translation, Mr. Marsden was led to give the preference to the Italian version of Ramusio, who, indeed, of all compilers, may be considered as the most accurate. In the English language we had few editions of the work, and none that could be read with satisfaction. The first, by John Frampton, was printed by Ralph Newberry in 1579. Of this very rare book, entitled 'The most noble and famous Travels of Marcus Paulus, no less pleasant than profitable, &c.' Mr. Marsden observes, 'the style is remarkably rude, and the orthography of foreign names incorrect; but with regard to the matter of the text, it is by no means defective.' A second English version may be found in the 'Pilgrimes' of Samuel Purchas, in which, as usual, this industrious collector has taken great liberties with the text, and committed great mistakes. Yet this version, as Mr. Marsden observes, has served as the basis of that given by Dr. Campbell, in his edition of the collection of voyages and travels, first published by Harris in 1704; for the use of which work, he tells us, the language was modernized and polished, without any reference to the Italian or the Latin for correction; so that all the faults, excepting those of style, were suffered to remain, whilst some mistakes imputable to the modernizer have been superadded: such, for instance, as that in which it is said of a certain causeway in China, that 'on both sides are great *fences,*' instead of *'great fennes'* (fens), as it stands in Purchas; the word being *'palude'* in the Italian. Under these circumstances it will be readily conceded to Mr. Marsden that 'a new translation of Marco Polo's travels was wanting to the literature of our own country.'

The 'Notes' however are the most important part of the volume; and the plan of placing them at the end of each section, from which they are respectively referred to by figures in a consecutive series, beginning with No. 1, and continued to No. 1495, is perhaps the most convenient for the reader that could have been adopted. Many are of considerable length, and each of them illustrates some point in the text. Of the 781 pages of which the volume consists, the notes occupy, we should suppose, not less than two-thirds.

With such a variety of matter before us, it would be idle to attempt any thing like an abstract, however abbreviated; and unfair to select any particular note as a specimen of the whole. We shall therefore confine ourselves, principally, to a brief sketch of the life and travels of this illustrious Venetian. A great part of the matter is furnished by the traveller himself; the rest is chiefly taken from Ramusio. We had hoped that the Abbate Zurla, his countryman, might have been able to supply some additional information from the several manuscript collections of ancient records which are known to exist in the libraries of Italy, but this is not the case; and we fear, as we have already observed, that all the materials of any importance which relate to the Polo family are already before the public. The only advantage which this writer seems to have over Mr. Marsden is that of having apparently seen the manuscript chronicle of Frà Jacopo de Aqui, belonging to the Ambrosian library in Milan, which contains some account of the life of Marco Polo, but of which Mr. Marsden had no other knowledge than what is conveyed in a note of Amoretti, in his account of the voyage from the Atlantic to the Pacific by Cap. L. F. Maldonado, which note in fact contains all, or nearly all, that is mentioned by Zurla, personally relating to our traveller.

Andrea Polo de S. Felice, a patrician or nobleman of Venice, had three sons, Marco, Maffeo, and Nicolo, the last of whom was the father of our author. Being merchants of that wealthy and proud city, they embarked together on a trading voyage to Constantinople, where, as Mr. Marsden has shewn, they must have arrived in 1254 or 1255. Having disposed of their Italian merchandize, and learned that the western Tartars, after devastating many provinces of Asia and of Europe, had settled in the vicinity of the Wolga, built cities, and assumed the forms of a regular government, they made purchases of ornamental jewels, crossed the Euxine to a port in the Crimea, and, travelling from thence by land and water, reached at length the camp of Barkah, the brother or the son of Batu, grandson of the renowned Gengiskhan, whose places of residence were Sarai and Bolghar, well known to the geographers of the middle ages. This prince is highly praised by oriental writers for his urbanity and liberal disposition, and the traditional fame of his virtues is said still to exist in that quarter. The confidence which the Italians wisely shewed, by placing their valuable commodities in his hands, was repaid with princely munificence. They remained with him a whole year, when hostilities breaking out between their protector and his cousin Hulagu, the chief of another horde of Tartars, Barkah sustained a defeat, which compelled the European travellers to seek their safety in a circuitous route round the head of the Caspian, and through the deserts of Transoxiana, till they arrived at the great city of Bokhara.

It happened, during their residence here, that a Tartar nobleman, sent by Hulagu to his brother Kublai, made that city his halting-place. From motives of curiosity, he desired an interview with the Italians, with whose conversation he was so much pleased, that he invited them to the Emperor's court, with an assurance of their meeting a favourable reception, and an ample recompense for the trouble of their journey. The difficulties of their return homewards, on the one hand, and the spirit of enterprize, on the other, with the fair prospect of wealth, prompted a ready compliance; and recommending themselves to the Divine protection, they set out towards the farthest corners of the east; and after a journey of twelve months reached the imperial residence of Kublai. They were received most graciously by the Grand Khan, who was very inquisitive into the state of affairs in the western world, and so well satisfied with their answers, that he determined to send them back in safety to Italy, accompanied by one of his own officers, as his ambassador to the see of Rome, professedly with the view of prevailing on the Pope to supply him with preachers of the gospel, who might communicate religious instruction to the unenlightened people of his dominions; though Mr. Marsden supposes that political considerations might have been the predominant object. Their Tartar companion soon fell sick, and was left behind. But the imperial tablet was a safe passport; and at the expiration of three years they reached Giazza, or Ayas, in Lesser Armenia, and arrived at Acre in 1269.

Here they learned that Pope Clement IV. had died in the preceding year, and the legate on the spot advised them to take no further steps in the business of their embassy until the election of a new pope. They therefore made the best of their way to Venice, where Nicolo Polo found that his wife, whom he had left with child, was dead, after producing a son to whom she had given the name of Marco, out of respect for the memory of her husband's eldest brother, and who was now in his fifteenth or sixteenth year. 'Such,' says Mr. Marsden, 'were the circumstances under which the author of the "Travels" first makes his appearance.'

Two years having passed away without any election, in consequence of the factions that prevailed in the sacred college, the Venetian travellers resolved to return secretly to the legate in Palestine, and young Marco accompanied them. By his Eminence they were furnished with letters to the Tartar emperor; but just as they were on the eve of departure, advice was received at Acre of the choice of the cardinals having fallen upon the legate himself, M. Tebaldo di Piacenza, who assumed the name of Gregory X. Our travellers were now supplied with letters-papal in a more ample and dignified form, and dispatched with the Apostolic benediction, together with two friars of the order of Preachers, who were to be the bearers of the new pope's presents. On reaching Armenia, which they found in the hands of a foreign enemy, the two friars were so terrified by the apparent danger, that they declined proceeding farther, and resigning to the Polos the care of the presents from the Pope, returned to Acre.

Mr. Marsden traces without difficulty the route of our travellers into the country of Badakshan, where they remained twelve months, on account perhaps of Marco's illness, which, he tells us, was cured by removing his residence from the valley to the summit of an adjoining hill. They crossed the great ranges of mountains named in our maps Belut-tag and Muz-tag, and acquired a knowledge of Kashmir and other countries on the borders of India. They ascended the elevated and wild regions of Pamer and Belór, on their way to the city of Kashghar, belonging to the Grand Khan, and the usual resort of the caravans. From this place they proceeded to Khoten, and traversed the dreary desert of Lop or Kobi, in a tedious journey of thirty days, passed Tangut and Sifan, and came to Kan-cheu on the western extremity of the Chinese province of *Shen-si*. Remaining here for some time, to give notice, as usual, to the Grand Khan of their arrival, he commanded that they should be immediately forwarded to his presence, at his expense, and with the attentions usually shewn to foreign ambassadors.

Their reception was highly gratifying; the emperor commended their zeal, accepted the presents of the pope, and received with all due reverence a vessel of the holy oil from the sepulchre of our Lord, that had been brought from Jerusalem at his own desire, and which he concluded, from the value set upon it by Christians, possessed extraordinary properties. Observing young Marco, and learning that he was the son of Nicolo, he honoured him with his particular notice, took him under his protection, and gave him an appointment in his household. 'It is impossible,' Mr. Marsden observes, 'for those who have read the account of Lord Macartney's embassy not to be struck with the resemblance between this scene and that which passed at Gehol in 1793, when Sir George Staunton presented his son, the present Sir George Thomas Staunton, to the venerable *Kien-Long*.'

Young Marco soon became distinguished for his talents, and respected by the court. He adopted the manners of the country, and acquired a competent knowledge of the four languages most in use. He was employed by his sovereign in services of great importance in various parts of China, and even at the distance of six months' journey; he made notes of what he observed, for the information of the Grand Khan; and it is to these notes, undoubtedly, that we are indebted for the substance of that account of his travels which, after his return, he was induced to give to the world. Distinguished as he unquestionably was by marks of the royal favour, one instance of it only is recorded by him, and that incidentally and with great modesty. A newly appointed *Fu-yuen,* or governor, of Yang-chen-foo, in the province of Kiang-nan, being unable to proceed to his charge, our young Venetian was sent to act as his deputy, and held the office during the usual period of three years. That his father and uncle were also partakers of the monarch's regard is evident from his subsequent unwillingness to be deprived of their services: for when seventeen years had elapsed, and the natural desire of revisiting their native land began to operate upon their minds, all their endeavours to prevail on the emperor to consent to their return were ineffectual, and even drew from him some expressions of reproach. 'If the motive of their projected journey,' he concluded with saying, 'was the pursuit of gain, he was ready to gratify them to the utmost extent of their wishes; but with the subject of their request he could not comply.'

It was their good fortune, however, to be relieved from this state of impatience and disappointment in a manner wholly unexpected. An embassy arrived at the court of Kublai from a Mogul-Tartar prince named Arghun, (the grand-nephew of the emperor,) who ruled in Persia. Having lost his wife, he sent to the head of his family to solicit from him another wife of his own lineage. The request was readily granted, and a princess was selected from amongst the emperor's grandchildren, who had attained her seventeenth year. The ambassadors set out with the betrothed queen on their return to Persia; but finding their route obstructed by the disturbed state of the country, after some months they returned to the capital of China. Whilst they were in this embarrassed situation, Marco Polo arrived from a voyage which he had made to some of the East India islands; a communication took place between the Persians and the Venetians, and both parties being anxious to effect their return to their own country, it was arranged between them that the former should represent to the Grand Khan the expediency of availing themselves of the experience of the Christians in maritime affairs, to convey their precious charge by sea to the gulph of Persia. The emperor assented, and fourteen ships, each having four masts, were equipped and provisioned for two years. On their departure from his court, Kublai expressed his kind regard for the Polo family; and extorting from them a promise that, after having visited their friends, they would return to his service, he loaded them with presents of jewels and other valuable gifts. They took their route by Hainan, the coast of Cochinchina, Malacca, across the bay of Bengal, and by Ceylon, the celebrated peak on which is particularly noticed, as is also the pearl fishery. They sailed along the western coast of India, and finally, after eighteen months, reached Ormuz in the Persian gulph; having lost six hundred of the marines and two of the Persian noblemen on the passage. Whether this fleet ever found its way back is very doubtful; and its fate was probably less interesting at the court of Pekin, on account of the death of the venerable Emperor Kublai, which took place in the beginning of the year 1294.

On the arrival of the expedition in Persia, information was received by our travellers that the Mogul king Arghun had died some time before; that the country was governed by a regent who was suspected to have views on the sovereignty; and that Ghazan, the son of Arghun, was on the frontier with a large army, waiting for a favourable opportunity of asserting his right to the throne: to this prince they were directed to deliver their royal charge. 'Of her reception and subsequent fortunes,' says Mr. Marsden, 'we know nothing; but as Ghazan distinguished himself so much by his virtues as to make the world forget the defects of his person, (he was very diminutive,) we may presume that she was treated with the respect and kindness that belong to the character of a brave-man.'

Having thus accomplished the object of their mission, the Venetians repaired to the court of the regent, at Tauris, where they remained nine months reposing themselves from the fatigues of their long and perilous travels, and probably, as Mr. Marsden observes, realizing or investing more conveniently some part of that vast property which they had brought with them from China. Having procured the necessary passports, they proceeded on their journey homewards, passing Trebizond on the coast of the Euxine; 'from whence, by the way of Constantinople and of Negropont, or Eubœa, they finally, by the blessing of God, (as they piously acknowledged,) in the full possession of health and riches, arrived safely in their native city of Venice. This consummation of their memorable labours took place in 1295, (a date in which all the copies agree,) after an absence of twenty-four years.'

> Up to this period (continues Mr. Marsden) our narrative of the adventures of the Polo family has been framed from the materials, however scanty, which Marco himself had directly or indirectly furnished. For what is to follow, we must principally rely upon the traditionary stories prevalent amongst his fellow citizens, and collected by his industrious editor Ramusio, who wrote nearly two centuries and a half after his time. Upon their first arrival, he says, they experienced the reception that attended Ulysses when he returned to Ithaca. They were not recognised even by their nearest relations; and especially as rumours of their death had been current and were confidently believed. By the length of time they had been absent, the fatigues they had undergone in journies of such extent, and the anxieties of mind they had suffered, their appearance was quite changed, and they seemed to have acquired something of the Tartar both in countenance and speech, their native language being mixed with foreign idioms and barbarous terms. In their garments also, which were mean and of coarse texture, there was nothing that resembled those of Italians. The situation of their family dwelling house, a handsome and lofty palace, was in the street of S. Giovanni Chrisostomo, and still existed in the days of Ramusio, when, for a reason that will hereafter appear, it went by the appellation of *"la corte del Millioni."*

Of this house possession had been taken by some persons of their kindred, and when our travellers demanded admittance, it was with much difficulty that they could obtain it by making the occupiers comprehend who they were, or persuading them that persons so changed and disfigured by their dress, could really be those members of the house of Polo who for so many years had been numbered with the dead. In order therefore to render themselves generally known to their connexions, and at the same time to impress the whole city of Venice with an adequate idea of their importance, they devised a singular expedient, the circumstances of which, Ramusio says, had been repeatedly told to him when a youth, by his friend M. Gasparo Malipiero, an elderly senator of unimpeachable veracity, whose house stood near that of the Polo family, and who had himself heard them from his father and his grandfather, as well as from other ancient persons of that neighbourhood.

With these objects in view, they caused a magnificent entertainment to be prepared, in their own house, to which their numerous relatives were invited. When the hour of assembling at table was arrived, the three travellers came forth from an inner apartment, clothed in long robes of crimson satin reaching to the floor; such as it was customary to wear upon occasions of ceremony on those days. When water had been carried round for washing hands and the guests desired to take their places, they stripped themselves of these vestments, and putting on similar dresses of crimson damask, the former were taken to pieces and divided amongst the attendants. Again when the first course of victuals had been removed, they put on robes of crimson velvet, and seated themselves at table, when the preceding dresses were in like manner distributed; and at the conclusion of the feast, those of velvet were disposed of in the same way, and the hosts then appeared in plain suits resembling such as were worn by the rest of the company. All were astonished at what they saw, and curious to know what was to follow this scene. As soon, however, as the cloth was removed and the domestics had been ordered to withdraw, Marco Polo, as being the youngest, rose from table, went into an adjoining room, and presently returned with the three coarse, thread-bare garments in which they had first made their appearance at the house. With the assistance of knives they proceeded to rip the seams and to strip off the linings and patches with which these rags were doubled, and by this operation brought to view a large quantity of most costly jewels, such as rubies, sapphires, carbuncles, diamonds, and emeralds, which had been sewn into them, and with so much art and contrivance, as not to be at all liable to the suspicion of containing such treasures. At the time of their taking their departure from the court of the Grand Khan, all the riches that his bounty had bestowed upon them were by them converted into the most valuable precious stones, for the facility of conveyance; being well aware that in a journey of extraordinary length and difficulty, it would have been impossible to transport a sum of that magnitude, in gold. The display of wealth, so incalculable in its amount, which then lay exposed on the table before them, appeared something miraculous, and filled the minds of all who were spectators of it with such wonder, that for a time they remained motionless; but upon recovering from their ecstacy, they felt entirely convinced that these were in truth the honourable and valiant gentlemen of the house of Polo, of which at first they had entertained doubts, and they accordingly exhibited every mark of profound respect for their hosts.

Well vouched as this anecdote is, and, in our opinion at least, perfectly accordant with the spirit of the age, Mr. Marsden is incredulous of it, because (as he says) it betrays a mixture of vanity and folly quite inconsistent with the character of grave and prudent men, which in the preceding part of their lives they appear to have uniformly sustained; and he is therefore disposed to attribute the story to the fertile invention of their contemporaries, or to the succeeding generation, who seem to have regarded the travellers in no other light than as heroes of romance, and not unfrequently made them the subject of ridicule. Of this the reader must judge for himself;—but Ramusio proceeds to state, that no sooner was the report of what had taken place spread about the city of Venice, than numbers of all ranks, from the nobles down to the mechanics, hastened to the dwelling of the travellers, to testify their friendship and good will. Maffeo was honoured with a high office in the magistracy. To Marco, the young men resorted to enjoy the pleasure of his conversation; and as all he told them concerning the imperial revenues, the wealth and the population of China, was necessarily expressed in millions, he acquired amongst them the surname of *Messer Marco Millioni*. Ramusio adds that he has seen him mentioned by this name in the records of Venice, and that the house in which he lived (even down to the time he wrote) was commonly termed, *'la corte del Millioni.'* Sansovino, however, in his 'Venetia Descritta,' attributes the popular appellation to the immense riches possessed by the Polo family at the period of their return. The Ambrosian manuscript of Jacopo de Aqui does the same; and Apostolo Zeno, on the authority of M. Barboro, corroborates the prevailing opinion.

Not many months after their arrival in Venice, according to Ramusio, but according to others two years after this event, intelligence was received that a Genoese fleet, commanded by Lampa Doria, had made its appearance off the island of Curzula, on the coast of Dalmatia; in consequence of which a Venetian fleet put to sea under the orders of Andrea Dandolo. Marco Polo, being considered as an experienced sea-officer, was appointed to the command of one of the gallies. The Venetians were defeated with great loss; Dandolo was taken prisoner, and Marco Polo, who belonged to the advanced division, in bravely pushing forward to the attack, was wounded and compelled to surrender. He was conveyed to a prison in Genoa, where he was visited by the principal inhabitants, who did all they could to soften the rigour of his captivity. His rare adventures were here, as well as in his own country, the subject of general curiosity. It may readily be supposed that the frequent necessity he was under of repeating the same story would become irksome, and, 'fortunately,' says Mr. Marsden, 'for the promotion of geographical science to which it gave the first impulse, he was at length induced to follow the advice of those who recommended his committing it to writing.' With this view, he procured from Venice the original notes which he had made in the course of his travels, and which had been left in the hands of his father. Assisted by these documents and by his verbal communications, the narrative is said to have been drawn up in the prison by a person named Rustighello, or Rusticello, a Genoese, according to Ramusio, who was in the daily habit of passing many hours with him in his place of confinement; or, as others suppose, a native of Pisa and his fellow prisoner.

A strong difference of opinion has existed among the editors of this extraordinary narrative, as to the language in which it was originally composed; but Mr. Marsden thinks that the preponderance of authority and argument is in favour of its having been a provincial, probably the Venetian, dialect of Italian; and the reasons which he brings forward in support of this opinion are certainly not lightly to be passed over. Ramusion, however, from whom almost all the particulars of the life of our traveller are collected, and who, from his general accuracy, is himself a host, asserts that it was first written in Latin, by Rusticello, in which language, even so late as his own time, the people of Genoa were accustomed to record their ordinary transactions. He adds, that a translation of it was afterwards made into the common Italian, or *'lingua volgare,'* with transcripts of which all Italy was soon filled; and that from this it was re-translated into Latin, in the year 1320, by Francisco Pipino of Bologna, who, as he supposes, was unable to procure a copy of the original. But where, it may be asked, if all Italy was filled with copies, could be the difficulty of procuring one in Bologna? Ramusio accounts for Marco Polo not dictating his narrative in the vulgar tongue by observing that, in the course of twenty-four years absence, the Polos had forgotten their native speech, and presented 'un non so che di Tartaro nel volto e nel parlare, avendosi questi dimenticata la lingua Veneziana.' But the same argument would apply with equal force to the Latin language, the disuse of which for the same period (for they could not have had any occasion for it in China) was full as likely to estrange it from their memory, as their native language. The question indeed is not of paramount importance; but Mr. Marsden's arguments for an Italian original appear to us to overturn all the assertions in favour of a Latin prototype.

The imprisonment of Marco was the occasion of much affliction to his father and uncle, as it had been their wish that he should form a suitable matrimonial alliance, on their return to Venice. All attempts to procure his liberation by offers of money failed, and they had no means of conjecturing even the duration of his captivity. Under these circumstances, finding themselves cut off from the prospect of heirs to their vast wealth, it was agreed that Nicolo, although an old man, should take to himself a second wife.

Marco, however, after a captivity of four years, was released from prison; and found, on his return to Venice, that his father had added three sons to the family, whose names were Stefano, Maffio, and Giovanni. Being a man of good sense and discretion, he did not take umbrage at this change of circumstances, but resolved also on marriage. He had two daughters, Moretta and Fantima, 'which,' says Mr. Marsden, 'from their signification may be thought to have been rather familiar terms of endearment, than baptismal names.' On the death of his father, Marco erected a monument of hewn stone to his memory, which, Ramusio says, was still to be seen, in his days, under the portico in front of the church of St. Lorenzo, on the right hand side in entering; as to himself, his countrymen have been most unaccountably silent. His will is said to be dated in the year 1323, from which, without pretending to much accuracy, Mr. Marsden conjectures our celebrated traveller to have reached somewhere about the age of seventy years.

It would be extraordinary indeed if, considering all the circumstances under which the travels of Marco Polo were written, many faults, both of commission and omission, were not to be found in them. The greater part have been selected by Mr. Marsden for elucidation in his notes, and for vindicating the character of his author, in both of which he has been eminently successful. Of the former class of imputed faults, the most conspicuous are,—l. The relation of miracles pretended to have been performed on various occasions; on which it may be observed generally, that every body believed, in those days, in divine interference: our traveller, however, vouches for no miracles on his own knowledge, but only repeats what he had been told by the inhabitants of the places where the traditions were current. 2. An apparent belief in the efficacy of magical arts; but this was the common weakness of the times, and none were exempt from its influence. 3. The descriptions of animals out of the ordinary course of nature 4. The statements of the extent and population of the cities in China; 5. of the dimensions of the palaces; 6. of the magnificence and number of bridges; 7. of the military forces; and 8. of the amount of the imperial revenues. When to these statements, given in *millions,* was added the extraordinary story of the *black stones* used for fuel, it is not to be wondered at that, for centuries after his death, he should be branded as a writer of romance.

The prominent faults of omission are accusations of modern times; and they are such as Mr. Marsden is disposed to consider as less excusable, if really imputable to himself, and not to the loss of a part of the work, or to the omissions of transcribers. We do not however conceive that any vindication of the author's character is at all necessary on this head, even if the probability was not apparent, that they may have been owing to both these causes. Where is the traveller who has been careful to note down every thing that fell under his observation? Manners and customs, and new and singular objects of nature and art, however strange for a time, become familiar from long residence, and unless noted down while the impression of their novelty was strong on the mind, may well be supposed to escape the subsequent attention of the narrator. We can scarcely suppose that Homer was unacquainted with the Pyramids of Egypt any more than with the city of Thebes and its hundred gates, yet no mention is made of the former, while he familiarly speaks of the latter. Herodotus describes the Pyramids from ocular inspection, but never once alludes to the great Sphinx.

If, however, we may rely on the chronicle of De Aqui, his contemporary, Marco Polo has himself fully accounted for any omissions that may appear in his narrative. So little credit, says this writer, did he obtain, that when he lay on his death-bed, he was gravely exhorted by one of his friends, as a matter of conscience, to retract what he had published, or at least to disavow those falsehoods with which the world believed his book to be filled. Marco indignantly rejected this advice, declaring at the same time, that, far from having used any exaggeration, *he had not told one half of the extraordinary things* of which he had been an eye-witness. Let it be recollected too that his book was dictated in a jail at Genoa from loose notes sent to him from Venice, and we shall not be surprized at a few omissions of objects or customs however remarkable. The most important of them belong to China, in which country the greater part of his time was passed. His enemies particularly notice,—his silence with respect to the Great Wall—to the cultivation and general use of tea—to the preposterous fashion of bandaging the feet of female children in order to render them small and useless through life—and to the employment of wheel carriages impelled by wind. We may at once discard the last of these, as we believe they are confined to a particular district of the province of Petchelee, and have rarely been seen by any stranger. The other three were certainly familiar to him: he must have seen and even crossed the Great Wall, though at a place perhaps where it is only a mound of earth; but the most perfect and finished part of it is not more than sixty miles from Pekin, and it is there so very similar in construction to that of the walls of the capital and of most of the cities of China, as to cease possessing that attraction which, at first sight, it undoubtedly boasts. Some authors have speculated on its being built subsequently to the time of Marco Polo; and a missionary of the name of Paolino da San Bartholomeo (in a work published at Rome) has boldly fixed on the fourteenth century as the date of its erection:—he might, with equal probability, have asserted that Julius Cæsar invaded Britain in the fourteenth century.

The article of tea has supplied an almost universal beverage to the Chinese from time immemorial, and appears, by the early annals of the empire, to have then, as now, contributed to the revenue; it is mentioned by the two Mahommedans who visited China in the ninth century: the cramping of the ladies' feet too has been a custom from a time 'to which the memory man runneth not to the contrary.' These things must therefore have been well known to Marco Polo, though he has omitted them in his narrative.

But it has been the fate of this early traveller not only to be charged with faults of commission and omission, but to have other matters ascribed to him of which he makes no mention, and of which indeed he could have no knowledge. Thus nothing is more common than to find it repeated from book to book, that gunpowder and the mariner's compass were first brought from China by Marco Polo, though there can be very little doubt that both were known in Europe some time before his return. Indeed there is good evidence that the use of the magnetic needle was familiar here long before he set out on his travels; for Alonzo el Sabio, king of Castile, who, about the year 1260, promulgated the famous code of laws known by the title of 'Las siete Partidas,' has (in the preamble of ley 28, titulo 9, partida 2,) the following remarkable passage: 'E bien asi como los marineros se guian en la noche escura por el *aguja,* que les ès medianera entre la piedra è la estrella, è les muestra por do vayan, tambien en los malos tiempos, como en los buenos—otro si, los que han de anconsejar al Rey deben siempre guiar por la justicia.'—'And as mariners guide themselves in the dark night by the needle, which is the medium (medianera) between the magnet and the star, in like manner ought those who have to counsel the king always to guide themselves by justice.'

Now it is obvious that the monarch would not have availed himself of the happy comparison of the office of a faithful counsellor to the magnetic needle, if that instrument had not been generally in use, at the period when he wrote; but how long before that period it had been known, and applied to the purposes of navigation, it may be difficult, perhaps impossible, to ascertain. There were in those times no philosophical journals, no literary gazettes, no reviews to communicate such intelligence to the world; and we are indebted for the little information which has come down to us, to incidental notices by authors not writing expressly on the subject. Thus Guyot de Provins, who is supposed to have lived about the year 1180, evidently alludes to the magnetic needle in the following verses:—

> Mais celle estoile ne se muet,
> Un art font, que mentir ne puet,
> Par la vertu de la mariniere,
> Une pierre laide et bruniere,
> Ou li fers volontiers se joint,
> Ont si esgardent le droite point,
> Puis qu'une aguille ont touchié,
> Et en un festu l'ont couchié
> En l'eue le mettent, sans plus,
> Et le festus la tiennent desus:
> Puis se tourne la pointe toute,
> Contre le estoile.

Jacobus Vitriacus, bishop of Ptolemais, who died at Rome in 1244, and who composed his Historia Orientalis between 1220 and 1230, after his return from the Holy land, says—'Valdè necessarius est *acus* navigantibus in mari.' He had himself made more than one voyage by sea. And Vicentio of Beauvais (Vicentius Bellovacius) observes, in his Speculum Doctrinale, 'Cum enim vias suas ad portum dirigere nesciunt, cacumen *acus* ad adamantem lapidem fricatum, per transversum in festuca parva infigunt, et vasi pleno aquæ immittunt.' Bellovacius died in 1266; how long before his death the above was written we know not. In another passage he seems to hint that the Arabians were the inventors; but this is very improbable: had they possessed the compass when they traded so largely to China in the ninth and succeeding centuries, they would not (as they did) have crept along the shores of the bay of Bengal, of Cambodia, and Cochin-china; besides, the name they gave to it (*el bossolo*) leaves little doubt of the source from which it was derived. The route pursued by Marco Polo from the head of the Yellow Sea to the Persian Gulph affords a strong argument against any knowledge of the compass by the Chinese in the thirteenth century; to say nothing of his silence concerning this wonderful instrument, while he so minutely and accurately describes the four-masted vessels on which he and his retinue embarked.

Many other authorities might be quoted to shew that the magnetic needle was in common use among the mariners of Europe before the middle of the thirteenth century. It was indeed then a rude and simple instrument, being only an iron needle magnetized, and stuck into a bit of wood, floating in a vessel of water; in which inartificial and inconvenient form it seems to have remained till about the beginning of the fourteenth century, when Flavio Gioia, of Amalphi, made the great improvement of suspending the needle on a centre, and enclosing it in a box. The advantages of this were so great, that it was universally adopted, and the instrument in its old and simple form laid aside and forgotten: hence Gioia, in aftertimes, came to be considered as the inventor of the mariner's compass, of which he was only the improver. The Biographia Britannica mistakes the period of Gioia's death for that of his birth; he lived in the reign of Charles of Anjou, who died king of Naples in 1309. It was in compliment to this sovereign (for Amalphi is in the dominions of Naples) that Gioia distinguished the north point by a fleur-de-lis. This was one of the circumstances by which the French, in later days, endeavoured to prove that the mariner's compass was a French discovery: but to what discoveries will not our ingenious and ambitious neighbours lay claim, after their late attempts to appropriate that of the steamengine, and still more recently that of Mr. Seppings's most important improvement in the construction of ships of war!

That Marco Polo would have mentioned the mariner's compass, if it had been in use in China, we think highly probable; and his silence respecting gunpowder may be considered as at least a negative proof that this also was unknown to the Chinese in the time of Kublai-khan. Be this as it may, there is positive proof that the use of *cannon* was unknown, otherwise our travellers would not have been employed by the emperor to construct machines to batter the walls of Sa-Yan-Fu. There is nothing in the history of these people, nor in their 'Dictionary of Arts and Sciences,' that bears any allusion to their knowledge of cannon before the invasion of Gengis-Khan, when (in the year 1219) mention is made of *ho-pao,* or fire-tubes, the present name of cannon, which are said to kill men and to set fire to inflammable substances: they are said too to have been used by the Tartars, not by the Chinese, and were probably nothing more than the enormous rockets known in India at the period of the Mahommedan invasion. It is clear that Roger Bacon, who died in 1294, was acquainted with the composition, and even with some of the effects of gunpowder, for it is recorded in those of his works which have come down to us. It would, however, be difficult to connect his discovery with the application of it to the purpose of war, by a people apparently unacquainted with the labours of the English friar. The Moors, or Arabs, in Spain, appear to have used gunpowder and cannon as early as 1312. In the Cronica de Espana by Abu Abdalla, it is said that, 'el Rey de Granada, Abul-Walid, Ilev consigo al sitio de Baza una gruessa máquina, que, cargada con *mixtos de azufre, y dandole fuego, despedia con estuendo* globos contra el Alcazar de aquella ciudad.' And in 1331 when the king of Granada laid siege to Alicant, he battered its walls with iron bullets, *discharged by fire* from machines: this novel mode of warfare, adds the annalist, inspired great terror,—'y puso en aquel tiempo grande terror una nueva invencion de combate, que, entre las otras máquinas que el Rey de Granada tenia para combatir los muros, Ilevava pellotas de hierro *que se lanzaban con fuego.*'

It is stated in the *Cronica de Don Alonzo el Onceno,* cap. 273, that when Alonzo XI. king of Castile, besieged Algeziras in 1342-3, the Moorish garrison, in defending the place—'lanzaban muchos *truenos* contra la hueste en que lanzaban pellas de fierro muy grandes.' That the *truenos* (literally *thunders*) were a species of cannon, and fired with powder, is clear from the following passage in the same Chronicle,—'Los Moros que estaban en su hueste cerca de Gibraltar, des que oyeron el ruido de los trueños, e vieron las afumadas que facian en Algecira, cuidaron que los Cristianos combatian la ciudad.' Mariana mentions the circumstance of the inhabitants defending themselves by '*tiros* con polvora que lanzaban piedras;' and adds that 'this was the first instance he had found of any mention of the use of such arms.'—vol. vi. The celebrated battle of Crecy was fought by Edward III. in 1346; and Hume, on the authority of Villani, says that the English had cannon, but not the French; it is, however, worthy of remark that, although Villani was a contemporary, yet he composed his history in Italy, and therefore could only speak from hearsay; whereas Froissart, also a contemporary, residing in France, and almost an eye-witness, makes no mention of cannon, although he describes the battle very particularly; and Thomas of Walsingham, who wrote more than three centuries before Hume, and who not only gives a very detailed account of the battle, but even specifies by name the arms and weapons used by the English—*gladios, lanceas, secures, et sagittas*— makes not the slightest mention of the *bombarde,* nor of the *pallotole di ferro che saettavano.* The French were beaten by the English as completely at Crecy as they were at Waterloo; and their national vanity might have spread the report of the English owing their victory to the advantage of cannon, with as little foundation in fact, as they ascribed their defeat at Waterloo to the entrenchments and fortifications of Mont St. Jean.

In vindicating our traveller from the charge of not mentioning what did not exist in China when he was there, we have been tempted to lay before the public some facts, which, though probably known to those who are much read in the early literature of Spain, may yet be new to such of our readers as are not familiar with what noble language, or have not access to the sources from which we have drawn our information. For this we look to their usual indulgence, though we feel at the same time that an apology is necessary for the digression to which it has led us.

To return to our traveller. With all the apparent improbabilities, defects, and inconsistencies of the narrative there is still enough in it to convince the most sceptical of its general accuracy; while the numerous descriptions and incidents afford, as Mr. Marsden justly observes, unobtrusive proofs of genuineness; among others may be enumerated, the state in which the bodies of persons destroyed by the hot wind of the desert are found—the manufacture of inebriating liquor from the infusion of dates—the tradition prevailing in Budakshan, of the descent of its princes from Alexander of Macedon—the gigantic figures of idols in a recumbent posture—the description of the *bos grunniens,* or *yak* of Tartary—the figures of dragons in Kataian or Chinese ornament—the periodical residence of the emperors in Tartary during the summer months—the commencement of the Kataian year in February—the ceremony of prostration before the emperor or his tablet by word of command—the ascent to the top of Adam's Peak, in Ceylon, being effected by the assistance of iron chains—the burning of coal, before-mentioned, and a great variety of other matters utterly unknown at the time, but which have since been found to be perfectly correct. These indeed are now familiar to most readers: but all the other subjects of which the author treats, and which are not so generally known, are elucidated and explained by the erudition and research of Mr. Marsden; who has added, by his edition of Marco Polo, another treasure to the stock of oriental literature worthy of his distinguished reputation as a linguist and a geographer, and highly meriting a place on the shelf of every library, public and private.

Thomas Wright (essay date 1854)

SOURCE: An introduction to *The Travels of Marco Polo, the Venetian,* edited by Thomas Wright, translated by William Marsden, George Bell & Sons, 1890, pp. ix-xxviii.

[*In Wright's 1854 introduction to his revision of William Marsden's translation of* The Travels of Marco Polo, *Wright offers an overview of Polo's travels and discusses the history of Polo's manuscript.*]

So much has been written on the subject of the celebrated Venetian traveller of the middle ages, Marco Polo, and the authenticity and credibility of his relation have been so well established, that it is now quite unnecessary to enter into this part of the question; but the reader of the following translation will doubtless be desirous of learning something more about the author than is found in the narration of his adventures. We are informed by the Italian biographers, that the Polos were a patrician family of Venice, but of Dalmatian extraction. Andrea Polo da S. Felice had three sons, named Marco, Maffeo, and Nicolo, the two latter of whom were great merchants in a city where the profession of commerce was anything but incompatible with nobility. They were probably in partnership; and about 1254 or 1255, they proceeded on a voyage to Constantinople, between which city and Venice the commercial relations were at this time very intimate.

Under the stern rule of the Tartar monarchs, the interior of Asia, knit together in one vast empire, was far more accessible to strangers than it has been since that empire was broken up; and many European merchants and artisans proceeded thither to trade, or to find employment at the courts of the different princes of the race of Jengiz. The two brothers, Maffeo and Nicolo, learning at Constantinople that a market for certain costly articles was to be found among the Western Tartars, purchased a valuable stock of jewellery, and with it crossed the Euxine to a port in the Crimea; and travelling thence by land and water, reached at length the court or camp of Barkah, the brother or the son of Batu, grandson of Jengiz-khan, whose places of residence were Saraï and Bolghar, well known to the geographers of the middle ages. After turning their jewels to good account, they were preparing for their return, at the end of twelve months, when their plans were interrupted by hostilities between Barkah and Hulagu, his cousin, the chief of another horde or army of Tartars, who, in consequence of their approach from the eastern side of the Caspian, were then denominated Eastern Tartars, but were principally Moghuls, as the former were Turki, or natives of Turkistan. They are said to have crossed the Oxus, on their march from the headquarters of Mangu-kaan, in the year 1255. By the defeat of Barkah's army which ensued, and the advance of his opponents, the road to Constantinople was cut off from our travellers, and they were compelled to take a circuitous route, which led them round the head of the Caspian, across the Jaik and Jaxartes rivers, and through the deserts of Transoxiana, till they arrived at the great city of Bokhara.

During their stay there, it happened that a Tartar nobleman, sent by Hulagu to Kublaï his brother, came thither, and in an interview with the two brothers, was so gratified with hearing them converse in his native language, and with the information he derived from them, that he invited them to accompany him to the emperor's court, where he assured them of a favourable reception, and an ample compensation for the labour of their journey. Recommending themselves, therefore, to the Divine protection, they prosecuted their journey towards what they considered to be the extremity of the East, and after travelling twelve months, reached the imperial residence. The manner in which they were received by the grand khan is told in the following narrative. He determined upon sending them back to Italy, accompanied by one of his own officers, as his ambassadors to the see of Rome,—professedly with the view of persuading his Holiness to supply him with a number of preachers of the Gospel, who should communicate religious instruction to the unenlightened people of his dominions, but more probably to encourage a hostile spirit amongst the princes of Christendom against the soldan of Egypt and the Saracens, the enemies of his family. They accordingly set out on their return; but in the early part of their journey, their Tartar companion fell sick, and was left behind. With the assistance, however, of the imperial tablet or passport with which they were provided, and which commanded respect and insured them accommodation in all the places through which they passed, they made their way homewards, and at the end of three years reached the port of Giazza, or Ayas, in Lesser Armenia. Here they embarked for Acre, then in the possession of the Christians, where they arrived in the month of April 1269; and on landing, received the first intelligence of the death of Pope Clement IV., which happened in November 1268; and it was recommended to them by the legate on the spot, to take no further steps in the business of their embassy until the election of a new Pope. This interval they thought would be most properly employed in a visit to their family, and for that purpose they engaged a passage in a ship bound to Negropont and Venice. Upon their arrival, Nicolo Polo found that his wife, whom he had left with child, was dead, after giving birth to a son, to whom she had given the name of Marco, in respect for the memory of her husband's eldest brother, and who was now advancing towards the age of manhood. In consequence of the long delay in the election of a Pope, our two Venetians became impatient; and, apprehensive of incurring the displeasure of their employer, after having resided two years in Italy, they returned to the legate in Palestine. On this occasion they were accompanied by young Marco, then in his seventeenth or eighteenth year. Taking letters from the legate to the Tartar emperor, they embarked for Ayas; but scarcely had they got under weigh, when advice was received at the former place of the choice of the cardinals having at length fallen upon the legate himself, M. Tebaldo di Vicenza, who assumed the name of Gregory X. He immediately recalled the two brothers, and gave them letters papal in a more ample and dignified form, and sent them, along with two friars of the order of Preachers, who were to be the bearers of his presents. These transactions took place about the end of the year 1271, at which period the northern parts of Syria were invaded by the soldan of Egypt; and such was the alarm caused by his approach to the borders of Armenia Minor, that the two friars were deterred from proceeding, and returned for safety to the coast. The Polo family, in the meantime, prosecuted their journey to the interior of Asia, in a north-easterly direction, undismayed by the prospect of dangers they might have to encounter. Of their particular course few indications are given, but it must evidently have been through the Greater Armenia, Persian Irak, Khorasan, and by the city of Balkh into the country of Badakhshan, amongst the sources of the Oxus, where they remained twelve months. This long detention might have been occasioned by the necessity of waiting for a large assemblage of travelling merchants, under an adequate escort, preparatory to crossing the great ranges of mountains called in maps the Belut-tag and Muz-tag; but it may also be accounted for by the circumstance of Marco's illness at this place. Their road now lay through the valley named Vokhan, from whence they ascended to the elevated and wild regions of Pamer and Belôr, on their way to the city of Kashghar, which belonged to the extensive dominions of the grand khan, and is known to have been a principal place of resort for caravans. They next proceeded to Khoten, a town of much celebrity, and afterwards through places little known to geographers, till they reached the desert of Lop or Kobi, which is circumstantially described. This being traversed in a tedious journey of thirty days, they entered the comprehensive district of Tangut, and passed through the country of those whom the Chinese call Sifan or Tu-fan, as well as the strong place named Shacheu, or the town of the sands. From thence the direct road is to So-cheu, at the western extremity of the province of Shen-si. This place is within the boundary of what is now China proper, but was then, as well as the city of Kan-cheu, considered as belonging to Tangut. At Kancheu they experienced another long delay, which our author briefly says was occasioned by the state of their concerns. From Kan-cheu, it would seem that they took the road of Si-ning (just within the nominal line of the Great Wall, which on that side was built of sandy earth, and had mostly fallen to decay), leading through the heart of the province of Shen-si, and directly into that of Shansi. In the capital city of this latter, named Tai-yuen-fu, it was that the grand khan, who in the early part of his reign is known to have made it his winter residence, received notice of their arrival in his dominions; and as their account says, that at the distance of forty days' journey from that place, he sent forward directions for preparing everything necessary for their accommodation, we may understand this to mean, that upon his coming to the western part of China, and hearing of the detention of his Italian messengers at Kan-cheu, he commanded that they should be immediately forwarded to his presence, at his expense, and with the attentions usually shown to foreign ambassadors.

The reception given to them by the emperor was as favourable as they were justified in expecting. After the customary prostrations and delivery of the letters, they were desired to relate all the circumstances that had taken place in the business of their mission, to which he condescendingly listened. He commended their zeal, and accepted with complacency the presents from the Pope, and with reverence a vessel of the holy oil from the sepulchre of our Lord, that had been brought from Jerusalem at his desire, and which he concluded, from the value set upon it by Christians, might possess extraordinary properties. Observing young Marco, he made inquiries respecting him; and being informed that he was the son of Nicolo, he took him under his protection, and gave him an appointment in his household. In this situation he adopted the manners of the country, and acquired a knowledge of the four languages most in use. He thus became a favourite with the grand khan, who employed him on services of importance in various parts of the empire, even to the distance of six months' journey. On these missions he availed himself of every opportunity of examining into the circumstances of the countries he visited and the customs of their inhabitants, and made notes of what he observed, for the information of the grand khan, whose curiosity on such subjects appears to have been insatiable; and to this habit of taking notes it is that we are indebted for the substance of that account of his travels which, after his return, he was induced to give to the world. On the occasion of the inability of a member of one of the great tribunals, who was nominated Fu-yuen, or governor, of

A mosaic portrait of Marco Polo by Francesco Salviati (1510-53).

the city of Yang-cheu-fu, in the province of Kiang-nan, to proceed to his charge, Marco Polo was appointed to act as his deputy, and held this high office during the usual period of three years. Marco's father and uncle were also partakers of the monarch's regards; and in one instance, immediately after their arrival at his court, they were eminently useful to him, in suggesting to his officers the employment of certain projectile machines, or catapultæ, and superintending their construction, thereby contributing in an essential manner to the fall of the strong and important Chinese city of Siang-yang-fu, which had resisted the efforts of his besieging army for upwards of three years.

When about seventeen years had elapsed from the arrival of our travellers within the territories of the grand khan, the natural desire of revisiting their native land, notwithstanding the splendid advantages of their situation, began to work forcibly upon their minds, and the great age and precarious life of the grand khan determined them to effect their purpose with as little delay as possible. The grand khan refused absolutely to part with them, until an accidental circumstance gave them the opportunity of gratifying their desires. An embassy happened about that time to arrive at the court of Kublaï, from a Moghul-Tartar prince named Arghun, the grandson of Hulagu (and consequently the grand-nephew of the emperor), who ruled in Persia. Having lost his principal wife, who was a princess of the imperial stock, he sent this deputation to his sovereign and the head of his family, to solicit from him a wife of their own lineage. A princess was accordingly selected from amongst his grandchildren, and the ambassadors being satisfied as to her beauty and accomplishments, set out with her on a journey to Persia, with a numerous suite to do honour to the betrothed queen; but after several months' travelling, found themselves obstructed by the disturbed state of the country through which their route lay, and were obliged to return to the capital. In this dilemma, Marco Polo arrived from a voyage to some of the East Indian islands, and laid before his master the observations he had made respecting the safe navigation of those seas. The ambassadors, when they heard this, put themselves in communication with the Venetian family; and upon its being understood that they had all a common interest, each party being anxiously desirous of effecting their return to their own country, it was arranged between them that the Persians should urgently represent to the grand khan the expediency of their availing themselves of the experience of the Christians in maritime affairs, to convey their precious charge by sea to the gulf of Persia. His reluctant consent for their departure was thus obtained, and preparations were made on a grand scale for the expedition. When the period of their departure was at hand, the monarch addressed the Polo family in terms of kind regard, and required from them a promise that after having visited their own country and kindred, they would return to his service. He at the same time gave them authority to act as his ambassadors to the principal courts of Europe, furnished them with the passports necessary for their protection and accommodation in the countries acknowledging his sovereignty, and made them presents of many valuable jewels.

In the details that are given of the voyage, there is but little that personally regards our author. The first place at which they appear to have touched (if the expedition did not in fact proceed from thence in the first instance) was the port of Zaitun, in the province of Fo-kien, supposed to be either Tsuen-cheu, or the neighbouring port of Hia-muen, by us called Amoy. Passing by the island of Hainan, they kept along the coast of Anan, or Cochin-China, to the adjoining country of Tsiampa, which Marco Polo informs us he had previously visited in the year 1280. Mention is next made of the island of Java, although it is evident from the circumstances that they did not touch there, and also of two uninhabited islands near the coast of Kamboja. From the latter they steered for the island of Bintan, near the eastern entrance of the straits of Malacca. From this place they made a short run to the north-eastern coast of Sumatra, in one of the ports of which they were detained five months, waiting for a favourable season to pursue their voyage across the bay of Bengal.

After passing some of the smaller islands, they visited Ceylon, and from thence they crossed the narrow strait, to the southern part of the coast of the peninsula, called by our author, in imitation of the Arabian and Persian writers, the country of Maabar, which must not be confounded with Malabar. In his subsequent route, it is difficult to determine which of the places mentioned in his narrative he visited, and which he describes from information gained from others.

At Ormuz, in the Persian gulf, the course of his description may be considered as brought to a close; and there is every reason to infer that the Chinese expedition, after a navigation of eighteen months in the Indian seas, terminated at that place.

Upon the arrival of the expedition in Persia, information was received by our travellers that the Moghul king Arghun, for whose consort the princess had been intended, had died some time before (1291); that the country was then governed by a regent or protector, who was supposed to have views to the sovereignty; and that the son of the late king, named Ghazan, who afterwards became much celebrated, was encamped, with a large army under his command, on the northeastern frontier of the kingdom, towards Khorasan, waiting, as it appeared, for a favourable opportunity of asserting his rights to the throne, for which his extremely diminutive figure was thought to have rendered him unfit. To this prince they were directed to deliver their royal charge; and, after having done this, they repaired to the court of Arghun, at Tauris, where for nine months they reposed themselves from the fatigue of their long travels. Having received from him the customary passports, which they found the more necessary, as the unpopularity of his government occasioned tumults in the country, and rendered strong escorts indispensable, they proceeded on their journey homewards, taking the road of Arjis on the lake of Van, Arzerrûm, and the castle of Baiburt, and reached the city of Trebizond on the coast of the Euxine; from whence, by the way of Constantinople, and of Negropont or Eubœa, they finally arrived in their native city of Venice in 1295, after an absence of twenty four years.

Up to this period our narrative of the adventures of the Polo family has been framed from the materials, however scanty, which Marco himself had directly or indirectly furnished. For what is to follow, we must principally rely upon the traditionary stories prevalent amongst his fellow-citizens, and collected by his industrious editor Ramusio, who wrote nearly two centuries and a half after his time. Upon their first arrival, he says, they were not recognised even by their nearest relations, the more so as rumours of their death had been current, and were confidently believed. By the length of time they had been absent, the fatigues they had undergone in journeys of such extent, and the anxieties of mind they had suffered, their appearance was quite changed, and they seemed to have acquired something of the Tartar both in countenance and speech, their native language being mixed with foreign idioms and barbarous terms. In their garments also, which were mean and of coarse texture, there was nothing that resembled those of Italians. The situation of their family dwelling-house, a handsome and lofty palace, was in the street of S. Giovanni Chrisostomo, and still existed in the days of Ramusio, when, for a reason that will hereafter appear, it went by the appellation of "la corte del Millioni." Of this house possession had been taken by some persons of their kindred, and when our travellers demanded admittance, it was with much difficulty that they could obtain it by making the occupiers comprehend who they were, or persuading them that persons so changed and disfigured by their dress, could really be those members of the house of Polo who for so many years had been numbered with the dead. In order, therefore, to render themselves generally known to their connexions, and at the same time to impress the whole city of Venice with an adequate idea of their importance, they devised a singular expedient, the circumstances of which, Ramusio says, had been repeatedly told to him when a youth by his friend M. Gasparo Malipiero, an elderly senator of unimpeachable varacity, whose house stood near that of the Polo family, and who had himself heard them from his father and his grandfather, as well as from other ancient persons of that neighbourhood.

With these objects in view, they caused a magnificent entertainment to be prepared in their own house, to which their numerous relatives were invited. When the hour for assembling at table was arrived, the three travellers came forth from an inner apartment, clothed in long robes of crimson satin reaching to the floor, such as it was customary to wear upon occasions of ceremony in those days. When water had been carried round for washing hands, and the guests desired to take their places, they stripped themselves of these vestments, and putting on similar dresses of crimson damask, the former were taken to pieces, and divided amongst the attendants. Again, when the first course of victuals had been removed, they put on robes of crimson velvet, and seated themselves at table, when the preceding dresses were in like manner distributed; and at the conclusion of the feast, those of velvet were disposed of in the same way, and the hosts then appeared in plain suits, resembling such as were worn by the rest of the company. All were astonished at what they saw, and curious to know what was to follow this scene. As soon, however, as the cloth was removed, and the domestics had been ordered to withdraw, Marco Polo, as being the youngest, rose from table, went into an adjoining room, and presently returned with the three coarse, threadbare garments in which they had first made their appearance at the house. With the assistance of knives, they proceeded to rip the seams, and to strip off the linings and patches with which these rags were doubled, and by this operation brought to view a large quantity of most costly jewels, such as rubies, sapphires, carbuncles, diamonds, and emeralds, which had been sewn into them, and with so much art and contrivance, as not to be at all liable to the suspicion of containing such treasures. At the time of their taking their departure from the court of the grand khan, all the riches that his bounty had bestowed upon them were by them converted into the most valuable precious stones, for the facility of conveyance. The display of wealth, so incalculable in its amount, which then lay exposed on the table before them, appeared something miraculous, and filled the minds of all who were spectators of it with such wonder, that for a time they remained motionless; but upon recovering from their ecstasy, they felt entirely convinced that these were in truth the honourable and valiant gentlemen of the house of Polo, of which at first they had entertained doubts, and they accordingly exhibited every mark of profound respect for their hosts.

Of the degree of credit due to this anecdote, vouched as it is, the reader will form his own judgment; but, be this as it may, Ramusio proceeds to acquaint us, that as soon as an account of the scene just described was spread about the city of Venice, great numbers of the inhabitants of all ranks, from the nobles down to the mechanics, hastened to their dwelling, in order to have an opportunity of embracing them, and of testifying their good-will. Maffeo, the elder brother, was honoured with an office of much importance in the magistracy. To Marco the young men resorted, to enjoy the pleasure of his conversation. Finding him polite and communicative, they paid him daily visits, making inquires respecting Cathay and the grand khan; and to all of them his answers were so courteous, that each considered himself as personally obliged. In consequence, however, of their persevering curiosity, which occasioned frequent repetitions of the amount of the imperial revenues, estimated at ten or fifteen millions of gold ducats, as well as of other computations regarding the wealth and population of the empire, which were necessarily expressed in millions also, he at length acquired amongst them the surname of Messer Marco Millioni, or, in the modern orthography, Milione. "By this appellation," Ramusio (who was himself high in office) adds, "I have seen him mentioned in the public records of this republic, and the house in which he lived has, from that time to the present, been commonly termed, 'la corte del Millioni.'" It must at the same time be remarked, that Sansovino, in his "Venetia Descritta," attributes the popular application of this surname to the immense riches possessed by the Polo family at the period of their return to their own country. In this sense the French apply the term "millionnaire" to a great capitalist.

Not many months after their arrival in Venice, intelligence was received that a Genoese fleet, commanded by Lampa Doria, had made its appearance off the island of Curzola, on the coast of Dalmatia; in consequence of which a Venetian fleet, consisting of a superior number of galleys, immediately put to sea under the orders of Andrea Dandolo. To the command of one of these, Marco Polo, as an experienced sea-officer, was appointed. The fleets soon came in sight of each other, and an engagement ensued, in which the latter were defeated with great loss. This event is said by some writers to have happened on the 8th of September, 1296. Amongst the prisoners taken by the Genoese, besides Dandolo himself, was our traveller, who belonged to the advanced division, and bravely pushing forward to attack the enemy, but not being properly supported, was compelled to surrender, after receiving a wound. From the scene of action he was conveyed to a prison in Genoa, where his personal qualities and his surprising history becoming soon known, he was visited by all the principal inhabitants, who did everything in their power to soften the rigours of his captivity; treating him with kindness as a friend, and liberally supplying him with everything necessary for his subsistence and accommodation. His rare adventures were, as in his own country, the subject of general curiosity, and the frequent necessity he was under of repeating the same story unavoidably became irksome to him. He was, in consequence, at length induced to follow the advice of those who recommended his committing it to writing. With this view he procured from Venice the original notes he had made in the course of his travels, and had left in the hands of his father. Assisted by these documents (of which he speaks on more than one occasion), and from his verbal communications, the narrative is said to have been drawn up, in the prison, by a person named Rustighello or Rustigielo, who, according to Ramusio, was a Genoese gentleman with whom he had formed an intimacy, but, according to the manuscripts, a native of Pisa, and his fellow-prisoner; and we finally learn from the French text, which is now known to be the original, that this Rustigielo was Rusticien de Pise, a well-known medieval writer, who made a compilation in French of the romances of the cycle of king Arthur. The Travels of Marco Polo are said to have been written, and the manuscript circulated, in 1298.

The imprisonment of Marco was the occasion of much affliction to his father and his uncle, and the more particularly as it had long been their intention that he should form a suitable matrimonial alliance upon their return to Venice. Their plans were now frustrated, and it became daily more uncertain what the duration of his captivity might prove, as all attempts to procure his liberation by the offer of money had failed, and it was even doubtful whether it might not terminate only with his life. Under these circumstances, finding themselves cut off from the prospect of having heirs to their vast wealth, they deliberated upon what was most proper to be done for the establishment of the family, and it was agreed that Nicolo, although an old man, but of a hale constitution, should take to himself a second wife.

It happened at length, after a lapse of four years, that Marco, in consequence of the interest taken in his favour amongst the leading people in Genoa, and indeed by the whole city, was released from his captivity. Upon returning home, he found that his father had by that time added three sons to the family, whose names were Stefano, Maffeo, and Giovanni. Being a man of good sense and discretion, he did not take umbrage at this change of circumstances, but resolved upon marrying also, and effected it as soon as he found a suitable match. By his marriage, however, he had not any male descendant, but only two daughters, one of whom is said to have been called Moretta, and the other Fantina, which from their signification, may be thought to have been rather familiar terms of endearment, than baptismal names. Upon the death of his father, as became an affectionate and pious son, he erected a monument to his memory, of hewn stone, which, Ramusio says, was still to be seen in his days under the portico in front of the church of St. Lorenzo, upon the right hand side as you enter, with an inscription denoting it to be the tomb of Nicolo Polo, who resided in the street before mentionèd. Respecting the age to which our author himself attained, or the year in which his death took place, his countrymen have not given us any information, nor, as it would seem, was any endeavour made at an early period to ascertain the facts. Sansovino, the most elaborate historian of their city, observes only, that "under the passage to the church of St. Lorenzo, which stands on one of the islets named Gemelle, lies buried Marco Polo, surnamed Milione, who wrote the account of 'Travels in the New World,' and was the first, before Columbus, who discovered new countries;" on which expressions we may remark, that independently of the geographical ignorance displayed, there is room to conjecture (if Ramusio be correct) that he has confounded the tomb of the father with that of the son. In the chronicle of Jacopo de Aqui it is reported, that when upon his death-bed he was exhorted by his friends as matter of conscience, to retract what he had published, or at least to disavow those parts which the world regarded as fictitious, he scorned their advice, declaring at the same time, that so far from having exaggerated, he had not told one half of the extraordinary things of which he had been an eye-witness. His will is said to have been dated in the year 1323; in which case his life may be supposed (without pretending to accuracy, but also without the chance of material error) to have embraced the period between 1254 and 1324, or about seventy years.

With regard to the other members of the family, Marco, the eldest of the three brothers, appears to have died before the departure of Nicolo and Maffeo for Constantinople; and it was with the intention of doing honour to his memory, that the wife of the former, in the absence of her husband, gave to her son, our author, the name of his deceased uncle. Of the three children of Nicolo by the second marriage, one only, Maffeo, lived to have a family. This consisted of five sons, and one daughter named Maria; and, as all the sons died without leaving issue, she, upon the death of her last surviving brother, who likewise bore the name of Marco, inherited all the possessions of their father. With this event, which took place in 1417, the family became extinct in the male line, and the illustrious name of Polo was lost. The heiress married into the noble house of Trivisino, eminently distinguished in the *fasti* of the Venetian republic.

The book of the Travels of Marco Polo, containing so much that must be attractive to all classes of readers, became extremely popular during the three centuries which followed his death, and was reproduced in almost every European language which could boast of a literature; manuscripts are very numerous, independent of printed editions, and they differ very much from each other. From this latter circumstance, the choice of a text for translation is not a question of easy solution. Marsden, assuming that the book was originally written in Italian, translated from the text printed by Ramusio, who seems to have taken some liberties with his original. Since Marsden's time, several more critical editions of Marco Polo, in different languages, have appeared. In 1827, an Italian text, from an early manuscript, superior in authority to that of Ramusio, was published by Count Baldelli Boni. The manuscript appears to have been of the fourteenth century. Previous to this publication, in 1824, the Society of Geography of Paris, in the first volume of its Recueil de Voyages et de Mémoires, had printed from manuscripts of the fourteenth century two texts of Marco Polo, of a class which had not before been examined very critically, one being in Latin, and the other in French. Neither of these texts is very well edited, but they are of considerable importance, especially the latter, in relation to the literary history of the Travels of Marco Polo.

It has been, I think, most satisfactorily demonstrated by M. D'Avezac, that the original text of Marco Polo, which came from the traveller's own dictation, was written in the French language. I will give the reasons on which this judgment is established in the words of M. D'Avezac himself, as he has stated the question in a postscript to some remarks on the Relation of Plan du Carpin, in the Bulletin of the Society of Geography for August 1841. "The observations we have just made," says this able geographer,

> having led us to recur to certain passages of Marco Polo, we have had occasion to remark again, in the Italian and Latin texts, some of those gross blunders arising from verbal equivocations, of which the only possible explanation is found in recognising them as the work of unskilful translators from a French text; an argument already invoked by Baldelli, and which must have struck any man who made a comparative examination of the different editions of this famous relation. After the chapter devoted to Tangut in general, and before that which contains the description of its capital, are three chapters treating successively of the provinces of Camul, Ginchintalas, and Juctang, in the latter of which we find this passage: 'Et la grant provence jeneraus où ceste provence (Juctang) est, et ceste deux (Camuel et Ginchintalas) que je vos ai contés en arrieres, est appellés Tangut.' In the version of Ramusio this is rightly translated: 'E la gran provincia generale nella qual se contiene questa provincia et altre due provincie subsequenti, si chiama Tanguth.' But Ramusio professes himself to give a corrected text, whereas the celebrated manuscript of La Crusca, published by Baldelli, and the manuscript of Pucci, of which he gives the various readings, have: 'Ella e grande provincia, ha nome *Jeneraus,*' etc.; thus proving that the Italian translator of 1309 took the French adjective *ieneraus* (*generalis*) for a proper name of a province, as he had on another occasion taken the adverb *jadis* for a proper name of a king! A mistake equally curious, and into which, as far as we know, all the translators, old or modern, of Marco Polo have fallen, occurs, and is repeated many times, in the recital of the war of Prester John against 'un rois qe fu appelés le roi d'or.' Marsden has justly observed that this denomination must have been the translation of the Chinese name of the dynasty of Kin, or Altoun of the Moguls, since these words mean *or* (gold) in French. But it is evident that if a French translator could write that the monarch Kin was 'appelé roi d'Or,' it would be absurd to translate in Italian, 'un re chiamato Dor,' or in Latin, 'unus rex qui fuit vocatus rex Dor.' Evidently the translators took the French appellation in the genitive, *d'or,* for a proper name. Moreover, to all the motives given before by Baldelli, by M. Paulin Paris, and by ourselves, to demonstrate that the original

text of the relation of Marco Polo was written in French, we can add the authority of a formal testimony, which we have already communicated to the Society of Geography, and which we are astonished not to have found cited by our predecessors. But, which is still more surprising, this testimony was known to the learned Abbé Lebeuf, and cited by him in his 'Dissertations sur l'Histoire ecclésiastique et civile de Paris,' without his being aware of its importance, or apparently suspecting that it related to the illustrious Venetian; he says simply—'Un nommé Marc, qui avait été envoyé en Tartarie et aux Indes, fit en français un livre des Merveilles de ce pays là, que Jean d'Ypres, en sa chronique, dit qu'il possédait.' Now, this 'nommé Marc' was Marco Polo himself; and Jean d'Ypres said so, not in an obscure mention, lost in the midst of matters foreign to those which might awaken the attention of the reader to so remarkable a declaration: far from that, the chronicler expressly devotes a chapter to treat 'De Legatis Tartarorum ad Papam missis;' and there he says in full: 'Nuntii qui venerunt erant duo cives Venetiarum, nomine dominus Nicolaus Pauli et frater ejus dominus Maffeus Pauli,' etc. Then he relates their return from the East, and adds: 'Dominusque Nicolaus Pauli filium suum, viginti vel circiter annorum, juvenem aptum valde, nomine Marcum Pauli, secum adduxit ad Tartaros.' After this comes the history of their embassy, and this recital terminates with the following passage: 'Marcus Pauli cum imperatore retentus, ab eo miles effectus, sed et cum eo mansit spatio viginti-septem annorum; quem Chaam, propter suam habilitatem in suis negotiis, ad diversas Indiæ et Tartariæ partes et insulas misit, ubi illarum partium multa mirabilia vidit, de quibus postea librum *in vulgari gallico* composuit, quem librum mirabilium cum pluribus similibus penes nos habemus.' And the man who wrote this is the same Jean Lelong, of Ypres, abbot of St. Bertin at St. Omer, who translated from Latin into French the relations of Hayton of Armenia, of Ricold de Montecroce, of Oderic of Friulia, of William of Boldensel, and of John de Cor, archbishop of Solthânyeh; he was the man of his time the most profoundly acquainted with the various travels into the East, and whose testimony ought to carry the greatest authority in this matter.

With the new importance which is thus given to the French text of Marco Polo, I hope that my learned friend will not let us wait long for a new and perfect edition of it, one which will be worthy of himself, and of the language in which it forms so interesting a monument.

Since the appearance of the editions already mentioned, two others have appeared which are worthy of notice. An edition of the old German version, edited by August Bürck, in 1845, and an Italian edition by Vincenzo Lazari, in 1847. Singularly enough, neither of these editors appears to have been aware of the direct evidence of John d'Ypres to the fact of the original text having been written in French, although it had been so publicly stated by M. D'Avezae several years before.

Most of the editions I have mentioned contain long and learned dissertations on Marco Polo's travels. It was the original intention, in the present edition, merely to reprint the text of Marsden's translation, with a selection from the notes. Marsden's notes are rather lengthy, and a good part of them consists only of repetitions of statements and authorities in support of the credibility of Marco Polo's narration; and as this question in now more generally understood than it was in Marsden's time, these corroborations are no longer necessary. When, however, I came to compare this translation with the new editions of the text, I found that it was desirable to give it a general revision, comparing it with the texts published more recently. All the texts differ so much from one another, that it is not easy to form anything like a perfect text from them; but a comparison enables us to correct some of the dates, names, distances, &c., which were evidently wrong in the text that Marsden followed; to set right one or two mistakes into which he fell from his want of knowledge of the medieval literature of Western Europe; and to restore passages which had been lost from the texts he used. The supplementary chapters added at the end of the present volume are translated from the early French text. From the historical dates to which some of these refer, they may have been an addition to the original compilation of Marco Polo's Travels, and, from the peculiar phraseology in which they are written, they seem to have been translated into prose from a narration in verse. This phraseology is sometimes so diffuse, that I have found it necessary to compress it in the translation, especially in the descriptions of battles, which are almost copies of one another. . . .

Henry Rawlinson (review date 1872)

SOURCE: "Yule's Edition of Marco Polo," in *The Edinburgh Review,* Vol. CXXXV, No. CCLXXV, January, 1872, pp. 1-36.

[*In the following excerpt, Rawlinson praises Yule's translation of Polo's book, noting that he blends several earlier texts in his edition in order to best present "what the author said, or would have desired to say."*]

The publication of Colonel Yule's Marco Polo is an epoch in geographical literature. Never before, perhaps, did a book of travels appear under such exceptionally favourable auspices; an editor of a fine taste and ripe experience, and possessed with a passion for curious medieval research, having found a publisher willing to gratify that passion without stint on the score of expenditure; and the result being the production of a work which, in so far as it combines beauty of typography and wealth of illustration with a rich variety of recondite learning, may be regarded as a phenomenon in these days of thrifty and remunerative book-making. Nor is it a slight praise thus to pronounce Colonel Yule's edition to be a great success; for never, perhaps, has there been a more difficult book of the class to expound than Marco Polo's travels, since his great prototype, Herodotus, recited his history at Athens. Every page is a puzzle; every chapter contains strange names which it is hard to recognise, strange stories which it is harder still either to believe or to explain. And, indeed, when we remember Marco Polo's personal character, and the peculiar circumstances under which his very extraordinary experiences were reduced to writing, our wonder must be, not that there is so much requiring illustration in this account of his Eastern travels, but rather that the narrative should be in any degree intelligible—and especially that a commentator should have been found with the knowledge, the ingenuity, and the perseverance requisite to place the book in a really attractive form before the reading public of the nineteenth century.

The attempt has often been made before to bring Marco Polo into notice. According to a list, indeed, compiled by Colonel Yule, and given in the appendix to his work, twenty-seven different editions of these travels have been published in various European languages during the last four centuries; and although the majority of such editions have been mere reproductions or translations of a faulty text without any serious effort at emendation or explanation, still in some instances—as in the Italian editions of Baldello-Boni, of Lazari, and of Adolfo Bartoli—sound and able criticism has been exerted, by which Colonel Yule has duly profited; and moreover, in two particular instances—the English edition of Marsden, published in 1818, and the French edition of Pauthier, published in 1865—illustration has been added of a comprehensive, if not a very scholarly, character. Marsden's edition of Marco Polo, an honest and unpretentious work, represents the knowledge, or rather the want of knowledge, of 'Sixty Years since.' Pauthier's edition, with very much more of pretension, is hardly an improvement on Marsden in regard to the historical or geographical illustration of Western and Central Asia; though it must be admitted that his Chinese learning stands him in good stead, and has enabled him to furnish many valuable extracts from original sources, relating to Eastern Asia, in support or explanation of Marco Polo's own notices. At any rate, we think the general impression will be, on comparing the baldness and inaccuracy of previous editors with the stores of solid, as well as curious, information poured forth by Colonel Yule with an unsparing hand, that the edition we are now considering was imperatively called for.

The story of Marco Polo's book is told with much liveliness and effect in Colonel Yule's introduction. This introduction, indeed, which extends to 160 pages, and is of a very miscellaneous character, forms, we think, in a literary point of view, the most important, as it certainly forms the most interesting, portion of Colonel Yule's two portly volumes. Besides ample dissertations on such general topics as the state of the East in the thirteenth century, the jealousies and wars of Genoa and Venice, a digression on the war-galleys of the Middle Ages, &c. &c., it comprises all that can be recovered of the personal history of the Polo family, of the individual travellers, of their appearance, their character, and their objects; their singular reception at Venice on their return from the East after twenty-four years' absence, which reads, as has been said, like a chapter from the Arabian Nights; their subsequent adventures; Marco's participation in the great defeat of the Venetians at Curzola; his captivity at Genoa, and dictation of his memoirs to a fellow-prisoner, Rustician of Pisa; and finally, it suggests how Rustician's notes, jotted down in the 'Lingua franca' in which they were probably communicated, were enlarged, and amended, and annotated, either by Marco himself, or possibly by his uncle Maffeo, who had been his companion throughout his travels; and how from these original notes the various texts were formed which are now extant in seventy-five different manuscript copies of a more or less authentic character.

It is clear that Marco Polo, with little or no preliminary education, must still have possessed considerable natural abilities, since on his arrival at the Mongol court he acquired without difficulty the current languages of the country together with four different modes of writing (probably Mongolian, Ouigour, Persian, and Thibetan), and further ingratiated himself with the Emperor, so as to be employed by him on confidential affairs of state in preference to the officers of his own household; but it is equally clear that he fully shared in the credulity and superstition of the age; and although Colonel Yule does not scruple to avow his 'entire confidence in the man's veracity,' no one can doubt but that Marco was disposed to exaggeration in his phraseology, and indulged in a very high colouring in all his descriptions. He seems, indeed, mainly to have risen into favour with the Emperor from his skill in bringing back sensational reports of the wonders which he saw when employed on deputation in strange countries—such reports contrasting agreeably with the dry matter-of-fact relations of the ordinary commissioners; and we may well understand that it was this proneness to extravagant talk, this habitual indulgence in 'travellers' tales,' which gave him the nickname of 'Master Millions' among his countrymen, and which in fact discredited his general authority. The process of dictation, it may also be suggested, is of itself unfavourable to a very rigid accuracy of description. In telling his stories *vivâ voce* to Rustician, as he paced the floor of his prison cell at Genoa, he may be forgiven if he occasionally warmed up his flagging memory by a few free touches of lively rodomontade. That he did not designedly invent or falsify is all, we presume, that Colonel Yule contends for; and for this qualified acquittal there is ample authority in the contemporary evidence that when Marco was asked by his friends 'on his death-bed to correct the book by removing everything that went beyond the facts, he replied, that he had not told *one-half* of what he had really seen.'

Colonel Yule has allowed himself the fullest latitude in his adoption of a text. He calls his text 'eclectic,' which means that he has selected from several types the readings and expressions of which he approves, and has omitted those of which he disapproves. The basis of his translation is the same text which was used by Mons. Pauthier, and which is supposed to represent the version made from Rustician's barbarous 'patois' into French of the period, during Marco Polo's life, and subject to his own curtailment, correction, and revision; but he has not slavishly followed this version, of which there are exemplars at Paris, at Berne, and at Oxford. He has admitted variant readings of names, and many 'expressions' of special 'interest and character' from Rustician's original notes, published by the Geographical Society of Paris in 1824; and also in some instances he has borrowed from other versions that were made from that text (apparently during Marco Polo's lifetime), first into Italian, and then into Latin—Pipino's Latin text, under date A.D. 1320, being the type of this class of MSS.; and finally, he has introduced between brackets, as indicative of their supplementary character, a very large number of additional paragraphs, some of the highest interest and importance, which bear internal marks of emanating either from Marco Polo or his uncle, but which are only known at present from their being included, without comment or explanation, in Ramusio's famous posthumous translation in Italian, which was published in A.D. 1559, nearly 240 years after Marco Polo's decease. It is hardly perhaps consistent with the strict canons of criticism thus to blend several texts into one, culling the best passages of each, and correcting false readings or tedious repetitions *à discrétion*; but the result is certainly to the advantage of the general reader; and if a thorough dependence can be placed on the knowledge and judgment of the editor, there will be also felt an assurance that the 'eclectic' text presents what the author said, or would have desired to say. This, at any rate, is what Colonel Yule has aimed at, and we are bound to say that we think on the whole he has been successful.

George P. Marsh (essay date 1875)

SOURCE: "The Book of Marco Polo," in *The Nation,* New York, Vol. XXI, No. 530, August 26, 1875, pp. 135-37, 152-53.

[*In the essay that follows, Marsh discusses Yule's edition of Polo's book and comments on the traveler's "reputation for veracity" as well as his collaboration with his fellow prisoner Rustichello, here called Rusticiano.*]

When Marsden published his learned edition of the Travels of Marco Polo in 1818, it was supposed that he had so nearly exhausted all the possible sources of illustration of his author that future editors would find little or no matter for new commentaries. And when in 1865 Pauthier gave to the world a substantially authentic text for the old traveller's narrative, under the title of Le Livre de Marco Polo, and astonished European scholars by an imposing display of Chinese and other recondite lore, accomplished critics expressed a similar opinion with respect to his labors. But in the first edition of an English translation which appeared in 1871, the learning and diligence of the distinguished Oriental geographer, Colonel Henry Yule, brought to the elucidation of Polo's meagre, fragmentary, and confused recital a great amount of interesting and valuable material, which, though not inaccessible to earlier editors, had remained undetected until his patient and comprehensive researches brought it to light. The four years which have elapsed since the original publication have enabled our editor to incorporate in a second issue a large stock of new explanatory and supplementary matter, both from existing sources, which even he had overlooked, and from the journals and private communications of very recent travellers in the wild theatre of Polo's wanderings.

But Colonel Yule's rectifications and augmentations of our knowledge of the *terra incognita,* no insignificant portion of which had remained untrodden by any European foot save the Polo's until the present day (we may almost say, hour), are by no means wholly borrowed from the reports of others. His long personal familiarity with the East had qualified him to comprehend and interpret much that had proved unintelligible to former students, and he has given proof of rare discrimination in reconciling and harmonizing many apparently conflicting statements in his text by judicious choice between different readings, by happy conjectural emendation of corrupt passages in the manuscripts, and by illustrations and supplementary contributions from his own ample stores of knowledge, as well as often from quite unexpected quarters. Colonel Yule modestly disclaims any extraordinary amount of linguistic attainment, but few professional scholars, even in these days of polyglot study, read as many tongues as he, and in his felicitous translations from quaint and obscure or equivocal originals (which may well earn for him the compliment of *grand translateur,* anciently bestowed upon Chaucer), in his verbal criticisms, and especially in his new and ingenious etymologies, he has exhibited a linguistic sagacity which would have placed him in the first rank of philologists if he had chosen to devote himself to language with as much zeal as he has done to geography. We will not anticipate the judgment of the learned by suggesting that Colonel Yule has given further evidence of his knowledge and command of the dialect of his author, in the concoction of the curious "manuscript in the old French tongue of the early fourteenth century," quoted in the preface to his second edition; but in any case, the reader who, supposing himself a proficient in that "old French tongue," denies the genuineness of the manuscript, will show no mean amount of attainment in that respect if he is able to adduce good *linguistic* grounds for questioning its authenticity.

While linguists are many, truly genial geographers have always been few, and the most adventurous and even learned travellers—such, for example, as Manning, whom Charles Lamb vainly endeavored to dissuade from a journey to "Independent Tartary"—often want the power or the inclination to turn their observations to any real scientific account. It is therefore fortunate for the cause of knowledge that Colonel Yule has chosen to exert his rare gifts in a comparatively unattractive and unambitious field of labor, and contented himself with arranging around Polo's slender and disjointed carpentry a mass of binding, covering, and decorative joiner-work, which has compacted it into a coherent and harmonious whole, instead of rearing an independent monument to his own literary reputation out of original materials. The compositors' rule, oftener preached than practised, is: "Follow *copy,* even if it go out at the window." The commentator must stick to his author with like fidelity, though he lead him to the antipodes. Hence, in a case like the present, the arrangement of his illustrative and supplementary matter can be neither alphabetical nor chronological, nor even strictly topographical, and, to borrow an illustration from an art in which Colonel Yule is an adept, his architecture, though not wanting in unity of design or in symmetry of detail, must be of the Arabo-Gothic rather than of the Grecian type. At the first view, therefore, the book in its present form has not the aspect of a philosophical whole, and in fact we are not yet able to co-ordinate scientifically the scanty geographical secrets of the impenetrable East, which thus far have been more or less dimly revealed to us. But what is possible in this respect has been most ably done by our editor, and it is by no means unmerited praise to say of this new redaction of the book of Messer Marco Polo, that it has certainly done much more to illustrate the wanderings of the Cathaian traveller than any—we are tempted to say than all—of the threescore editions which had preceded it. Indeed, as a repository of our existing knowledge of 'Cathay and the Way Thither,' it comes very near realizing the ideal prefigured by a former publication of Colonel Yule's under that quaint but attractive title.

He has, however, by no means confined himself to the illustration of Polo's itinerary, which could have no great interest except for geographical specialists. His enquiries embrace a vast range and variety of subject, natural, civil, and religious history, political economy, social institutions, manners and customs, commerce, curious questions in literature and art, directly or indirectly connected with the nature and life of the vast countries lying between Venice and the uttermost East, or bordering on the routes followed by the three Polos in their whole periegesis and their intermediate journeys. This wide scope of research has given opportunity for many learned disquistions and erudite excursuses, which Colonel Yule's spirited treatment and pleasant style have rendered attractive, and he has thus accomplished the difficult task of making even a commentary in a high degree both instructive and entertaining.

The introductory matter, text, and annotations fill two octavos of about 600 pages each, of which the narrative, though printed in large type, composes not much more than a quarter. Fifty closely-printed pages are occupied with a singularly complete and commodious verbal and real index, wisely arranged under a single alphabet; the form, type, paper, and mechanical execution of the book are unexceptionable, and the pictorial illustrations numerous and well designed and engraved. In short, the author and publisher have evidently spared neither pains nor cost to make these volumes as conspicuous for their material good taste, elegance, and convenience as for their literary merit.

The Book of Marco Polo has given rise to more questions difficult of solution than any work of the same nature which has ever appeared. For example, the personal veracity and general accuracy of the traveller, the possibility of tracing his routes and identifying his localities, the reason for certain strange omissions to notice remarkable objects, facts, and customs with which Polo, supposing his narrative to be true, must have been familiar, such as the great Chinese wall, the mariner's compass, gunpowder, the art of printing, the general use of tea, and the like, which we should suppose could not fail to strike very powerfully the attention of an intelligent European of the thirteenth century; then the critical doubts as to the form and language of the original text, and whether there may not have been a later and more complete recension than any of which manuscripts have yet been found—all these Colonel Yule has ably discussed, and to many of them given satisfactory answers, though there remain some of which no sufficient resolution has been suggested. One of the most important of these, next to the fundamental problem of Marco's sincerity and honest purpose of speaking the truth, comes under the last head—that, namely, of the possible existence of a fuller recital of the traveller's observations than that of which alone old copies are known to us. Ramusio's Italian text, published about the middle of the sixteenth century, contains a considerable number of weighty passages which do not occur elsewhere. Are these fabrications, or are they taken from a more complete narrative drawn up by Polo at a later period, and under more favorable circumstances than that taken down in French, from his oral recital, by Rusticiano or Rustichello di Pisa, his fellow-captive in prison at Genoa? Many critics have rejected these additions as spurious, less on the ground of improbability or internal evidence of unauthenticity, than because Polo himself is known to have recognized the text of Rusticiano (in which they are not found) as authoritative, as no manuscript copies are known from which Ramusio could have borrowed them. Colonel Yule, for reasons which it seems difficult to resist, believes that they are in great part "supplementary recollections" of the traveller noted down at a later period of his life by way of illustration or complement to some copy of Rusticiano's manuscript; and we may add what, perhaps, should have been said before, that our editor is firmly persuaded of Polo's strict veracity and honesty of purpose.

The neglect of Polo to mention noteworthy points which could not possibly have escaped the observation of one who travelled so emphatically with his eyes open as the Venetian, is not so easily dealt with, and, after all, we cannot do better than to ascribe the omissions, in a general way, to the peculiar circumstances under which Polo's narrative was communicated to his companion in captivity. It was written in a crowded prison, where, as Cervantes says, "todo triste ruido tiene su habitacion" (every doleful sound hath its abiding-place), and of course in the midst of innumerable interruptions and distractions. Many years had elapsed since the period of the earliest journeys, and Marco had neither journal nor notes to refresh his memory, or indeed, so far as we can see, any motive for deliberately recording observations which might, under the circumstances, prove revelations of important commercial secrets to the rivals and enemies of his country. These considerations account for many imperfections. But we, being unhappily of the guild of bookmakers, think ourselves authorized to treat this as a question of our competence, and to theorize a little on the composition of Rusticiano's book. We shall therefore, *pace* Colonel Yule, enter into some perhaps heretical, and possibly even not altogether novel, speculations on the technical authorship of the work.

According to Rusticiano, the two, being together in prison, said to each other: "Go to, now, let us make a book,"

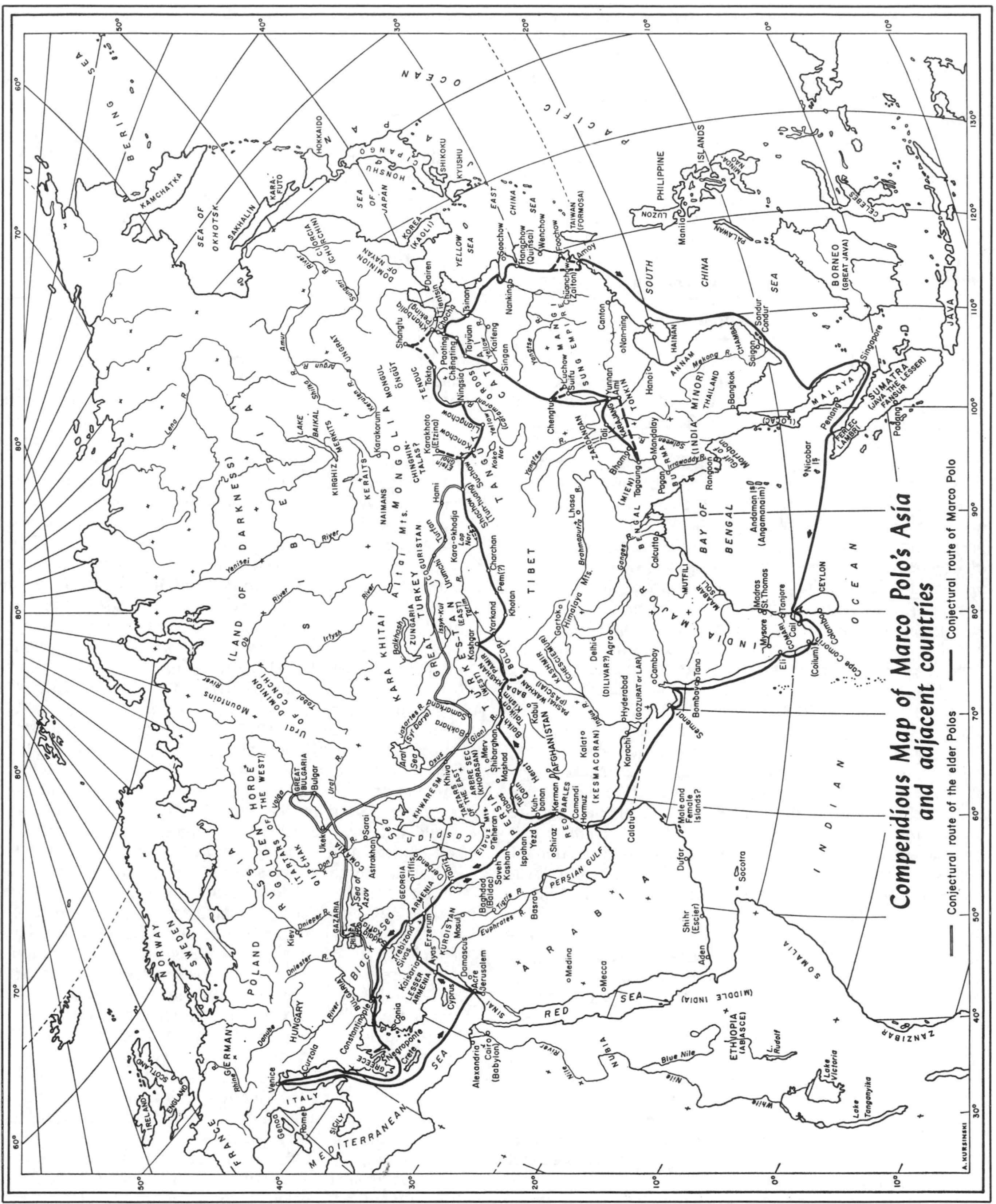

A comprehensive map of the Polos' travels, devised by Leonardo Olschki and drawn by Audrey Kursinski, integrating Marco Polo's geographic nomenclature with medieval and modern names.

and thereupon Polo dictated, and Rusticiano as amanuensis wrote, this now world-famous story. This account of the origin of the work has generally been accepted as satisfactory, but let us consider the probabilities. There is no apparent reason why Marco, who, educated as a merchant, certainly was able to write, should have dictated his narrative to a scribe instead of penning it himself; the first person is rarely used in the recital, which has much more the air of a hearsay report than of a copy from formal dictation; it is too unmethodical and *décousu* to be accepted as a deliberate history of travel and observation. It is written in French, not the vernacular of either party, Marco being a Venetian, Rusticiano a Pisan; and, considering where and how Polo spent the years of his youth and early manhood, it is hardly probable that he even knew French. It is therefore a translation, not an original redaction, and as it is much more strongly marked by Italic words and idioms than Rusticiano's other works in French, the communications from which it was derived were probably made in Venetian, Marco's household speech, or in that of Rusticiano, Tuscan, which at that time, A.D. 1298, had already acquired recognition as the *lingua comune* of Italy. Now Rusticiano was a professional writer, or, to describe him more accurately, a writer by trade. He would have been the Anthony Munday of his time, a regular bookseller's hack, had he not lived before the halcyon days when, to the infinite advantage of literature and the unfailing solace and comfort of "unprotected" authors, the process of evolution, development, or natural selection had unfolded that latest form of literary organism—the modern bookseller. Rusticiano combined in himself the functions of author, editor, and publisher, "three single gentlemen rolled into one," and he found it convenient to live on the product of other men's brains rather than on the growths of his own. So he translated, revised, compiled, abridged, and supplemented for publication or republication such good matter as he "became possessed of by finding." The marvellous relations of Messer Marco might very naturally strike him as excellent raw material for a new book, especially as the prison library was probably not very rich in *materia prima* for literary elaboration. Hence, under correction, it seems to us very probable that Rusticiano, upon his own mere motion, and not as the scribe of Polo, jotted down what struck him most in the conversations with which they whiled away the dreary hours of their long confinement. He wrote the story in French, because French was his professional language, and was indeed employed as best suited for general circulation by many a better man than himself—as, for example, Brunetto Latini and Canale, the one a Tuscan, the other a Venetian. We may suppose, then, that in Rusticiano's text we have not what Marco would deliberately have dictated as a history of his adventures, but so much of his oral narratives, delivered rather in the form of *yarns* than in a consecutive recital, as the "gaping soul" of Rusticiano understood or misunderstood, remembered, and thought good to record; and we may fairly ascribe many of Polo's otherwise unaccountable reticences and discrepancies to a want of intelligence, judgment, and memory in his reporter. Nor is the fact that Polo subsequently recognized Rusticiano's patchwork as authentic, by giving away copies of it, in the least inconsistent with this theory. Polo, once at liberty, and returned to his merchandising and other cares at Venice, would naturally have other things to do, in restoring his affairs, deranged by his absence, and setting his house in order, than to write a book, and he would gladly avail himself of Rusticiano's labors to spare himself a toil, for which, as a busy man and "no scholard," he had neither leisure nor stomach. He virtually said to the curious world: "Take this; ye get no more of me"; and we must thankfully accept this summary, such as it is, not only as the one source to which we owe nearly all we know of Polo and his wanderings, but as a memorial, without which, as our editor suggests, even the name of the Venetian Ulysses might have utterly perished.

Polo's reputation for veracity was by no means high in his own time. Not only was he known as "Squire Million" to the street (or rather canal) boys of Venice, but he is complimented with that sobriquet in legal documents of the period. Copies of his recital, indeed, were multiplied; but, probably on account of the general distrust of his reports, he seems to have produced little general impression on the European mind of his own or even of succeeding centuries. Mandeville, whose descriptions sometimes so nearly coincide with Polo's as to have suggested the idea that his book is made up of plagiarisms from Marco and other voyagers, never mentions Polo. Even Dante does not appear to have had any knowledge of him; he is not referred to in the Dittamondo of Fazio degli Uberti, or, so far as we have observed, by the compilers of any of the encyclopaedic works of the fourteenth century, or by Froissart, fond as he was of fable and tales of adventure; and Col. Yule does not find Marco to have been freely used by any writer of that period except the author of the romance of *Baudouin de Sébourg*. On the other hand, Chancer, who, we believe, does not name Polo, was evidently acquainted with his travels, and, as Col. Yule pointed out, borrowed the name of his hero Cambuscan from that of Chinghiz Kaan, who figures so largely in Polo's history. But Chaucer was a fabulist, and would not have respected or quoted Polo the less if he had supposed all his reports to be quite fictitious. De Barros, so far as we have been able to discover, refers to Polo only once, and then barely to correct an error respecting Prester John into which the traveller had fallen, nor can we find any mention of him in Clavijo, in Pietro della Valle, or in Coryat. It is curious that while Milton's imagination was evidently fired by Messer Marco Millione's notices of the "barbaric pearl and gold" which "the gorgeous East with richest hand showers on her kings," and his poems are pervaded with the *prestige* of Oriental life, Shakspere nowhere gives any indication of a knowledge of Polo's travels, scarcely even of an acquaintance with the strange world that forms their theme. But Shakspere, long before Pope, was of opinion that the "proper study of mankind is man," and Polo's Paynims were as simply men and only men as the most home-bred of the dramatist's countrymen. With him the accidents, the outward circumstance, the integuments of humanity were nothing, and under his scalpel the moral and intellectual dissection of the Englishman showed an organization not differing from that of the Tartar. Shakspere, therefore, had nothing to learn from Polo, and the material splendor of the East had no attraction for his eyes. Besides, Shakspere was a contemporary of Raleigh, whose search for El Dorado, following the Spanish conquests in America, had turned the minds of Englishmen in another direction. The old half-superstitious reverence for the East was neutralized, and men were coming to believe that not the morning star, but Hesperus, indeed, "bringeth all good things."

Helen P. Margesson (essay date 1892)

SOURCE: "Marco Polo's Explorations and Their Influence upon Columbus," in *The New England Magazine,* Vol. VI, No. 6, August 1892, pp. 803-15.

[*In the following excerpt, Margesson briefly comments on the influence Polo's narrative had on Christopher Columbus.*]

While Columbus never directly mentions Polo, his hopes and fancies and the deeds of his late years are wholly incomprehensible if he had no acquaintance with the writings of the great Venetian. In a Latin version of Marco Polo, printed at Antwerp about 1485, preserved in the Columbina at Seville, there are marginal notes in the handwriting of Columbus, and he may have become familiar with the work while living in Lisbon, through the cosmographer, Martin Behaim, a native of Nuremburg, where it was published extensively. The recent invention of printing had begun not only to diffuse literature more widely, but to reduce the price of manuscripts; and in a country actively engaged in exploration, as was Portugal at this time, Columbus had uncommon opportunities for the study of a book which certainly appears to have had an almost fatal ascendancy over his mind. It is known that he had indirect knowledge of the Eastern traveller through a correspondence with the learned physician and mathematician, Toscanelli. Columbus's first letter from the latter was a copy of one previously sent to a canon of Lisbon, who, by order of Alfonso V., had asked the Italian doctor if there were a possibility of a voyage to the west as well as to the south. This letter is little more than an extract from Marco Polo, but, according to Ferdinand Columbus, it was the means of giving Christopher courage to pursue his plans of discovery. Toscanelli wrote of the territory of the Khan and of its great cities, especially of Quinsay, and tells how, two hundred years before, ambassadors had come from Cublai to the Pope. This, of course, refers to the mission intrusted to the elder Polos, which Marco relates in his book. There was also a brilliant description of the wealth and power of the East. Accompanying the letter was a chart on which were the distances between Lisbon and Quinsay, and between the imaginary island of Antilla and Cipango. This first epistle was followed by a second, repeating the tale of kingdoms full of spices and jewels. "It made the Admiral still hotter for his discovery," says Ferdinand Columbus. It seems to be conceded that these two letters of Toscanelli, founded on the writings of Marco Polo, had the greatest possible influence on the mind of the Western explorer. . . .

C. Raymond Beazley (essay date 1906)

SOURCE: An introduction to *Dawn of Modern Geography: A History of Exploration and Geographical Science, Vol. III,* Oxford at the Clarendon Press, 1906, pp. 1-14.

[*In the following excerpt, Beazley provides an overview of the surge in geographic exploration that occurred from the mid-thirteenth to the early years of the fifteenth century—providing context for Polo's explorations.*]

Our conquest of the world we live in has a long history; in that history there are many important epochs, eras in which a vital advance was made, wherein the whole course of events was modified; but among such epochs there are few of greater importance, of deeper suggestiveness, and of more permanent effect than the century and a half [1260-1420] in which we gradually embark upon the oceanic stage of our development. For, in relation to man's knowledge of the earth and his exploration of the same, it is now that we reach the end of the overland philosophy of European expansion, it is now that we turn to another element to give us that final triumph which seems denied on *terra firma.* The Geographical history of the later mediaeval time is in many ways like its Constitutional, Literary, or Religious history—a record of brilliant achievement and still more brilliant hope, chequered by disillusion and disaster. Just as the noble ideals and promising experiments of political reformers, of Classical or Christian idealists, experience during these years the extremest alternations of confidence and despair; just as the 'perfect' Parliament of 1295 leads on to the New Monarchy; just as the struggles which cement the states of Modern Europe take in their later phases a peculiarly repulsive character, and the creative work of a Philip Augustus or a St. Louis has to be completed in such a gloomy and sordid struggle as that of the Hundred Years' War;—so in the annals of European expansion we find the work of earlier time is only perfected in suffering. The pioneers of Christendom cannot be roused to the effective exploration of ocean highways, of sea-routes to Cathay and the Indies, save by the ruin or ruinous decay of their influence upon the older land-routes of commerce; by the disappearance of the earlier, civilized, Islam; by the destruction of well-nigh all the Levantine outposts of Latin Christendom; by the paralysis of Byzantine power; by the break-up of the Mongol empire; by the conversion of the Western Tartars to Islam; and by the consequent revival, for an indefinite future, of the chief enemy of Catholic Civilization.

But before this final disenchantment has taken place, before the traders, missionaries, and statesmen of the 'Roman' World are confronted with the wreck of their most cherished castle of fancy, we have to notice an amazing series of efforts for the development of a genuine world-intercourse from Atlantic to Pacific, across the length or longitude of the Old World, mainly conducted by overland paths.

By the side of this we propose to consider the contemporary enterprises, spasmodic and transitory as they often are, in the way of maritime exploration. These enterprises, it is true, do not assume decisive importance in World-History till after the collapse of the wider overland commerce, when Prince Henry of Portugal imparts permanence, continuity, and comparative rapidity to the hitherto feeble cause of Atlantic discovery. But, at all events, they reveal, for the first time in the long life of mankind, some of the mysteries of the Sea of Darkness: they lift the veil from the Azores, the Canaries, and the Madeira group; they begin the search for an African coast water-way to the treasure-houses of Asia. The finding of that waterway is a decisive event in the European conquest of the outer world; the discovery of the Atlantic Islands contributes almost as much as the Portuguese advance along the Cape route towards the American revelation; here, as elsewhere, the earliest stages of a great movement are by no means the least suggestive, the least important, or the least deserving of study.

Once more, we hope to show how in scientific advance (as in oceanic exploration) the later Middle Ages frequently offer a noteworthy contrast to the decline and decay so often associated with their name; how in the midst of so much *débris* of a dying world we have here the first-fruits of a new and living one; and how the coming victories of our race, revealing the full extent and character of the world-surface, and surpassing in one hundred years the work of the preceding thousand, are prepared for by the invention of nautical instruments, and the execution of the first true maps.

The comparative importance of overland routes, of continental travel and traffic, has rarely been so great as in the earlier Middle Age, when the peoples of the future, the Christian races of Europe, were almost wholly deprived of the free use of the sea, by their own superstition, ignorance, and barbarism, by the growth of Islam, and by the heathen pirates, rovers, and conquerors of the North. In the Central Mediaeval time, Christendom, though full of expansive energy, relies mainly on land routes for its penetration of the outer world. While, even in the post-crusading period, the maritime side of European activity is far from having reached that preponderance which it attains with the discoveries of Bartholomew Diaz, of Christopher Columbus, of Vasco da Gama, and of Ferdinand Magellan—discoveries which bring with them the Modern World in geography and international history, just as the labours of Erasmus, of Luther, and of Loyola bring with them the Modern World in culture and religion. From the close of the fifteenth century to the age of railways, the overland intercourse of mankind is decisively subordinate to that oversea.

In the time now before us—the later thirteenth century, the fourteenth, the earliest fifteenth—we are, it is true, approaching modern conditions, but we have not yet reached them. We are still considering, for the most part, Continental developments of our civilization; we have not wholly left the age of caravan tracking, river navigation, and coast sailing; we are still far from the freedom and rapidity of movement which even the sixteenth century is able to realize. We are still in a time when the overland journey from the Crimea to Peking can be made with greater safety and in far less time than the sea voyage from the Persian Gulf to the Fokien ports and the mouth of the Yangtse Kiang. Yet even in the lifetime of Marco Polo, Genoese seamen venture into the Atlantic and push far along the West African coast in search of the Indies; the purely oceanic Azores are partially discovered—the Madeira group is sighted—the Canaries are repeatedly visited—by contemporaries of Petrarch and Boccaccio; the first use of the magnet by Italian seamen, the first accurate coast-charts of Italian pilots and captains, date at least from the closing decades of the thirteenth century and the opening decades of the fourteenth.

The Crusading Movement, the greatest collective enterprise of Latin Christendom, ends in military failure; but long before the fall of the Frankish States in the Levant, the non-military effects of the Crusades are proving themselves of higher value than the political conquests originally planned. And among these effects none is of higher value than the widening of our commerce and geographical outlook consequent upon the sacred wars. From the time of the Latin settlements in Syria, the expansion of Europe, the Christian discovery of *terra incognita,* are much more closely linked with the advance of trade than ever before; in the same way, the maintenance of the Crusading States in the East Mediterranean basin more and more devolves upon the maritime and commercial powers:—with the rise of the Mongol Dominion in Asia, the trade, the faith, and the mental outlook of our ancestors seem alike destined to a momentous extension.

Nor is it merely an appearance, a might-have-been. The history of the formal intercourse between the Mongol world and Western Christendom, initiated by Innocent IV and John de Plano Carpini, covers a period of more than 120 years (A.D. 1245-1368); and in this time, Tartar Eur-Asia—from the Black Sea and the Polish frontiers to the Pacific and the edge of the Siberian forest belt—is traversed in various directions by European preachers, traders, diplomatists, soldiers, and adventurers,—by men of Italy, France, Spain, Hungary, and Germany. Nor is it merely traversed. A very creditable and fairly exact knowledge of High Asia and of the Far East is obtained and embodied in written descriptions, in oral tradition, and in maps: the *Books* of Marco Polo and Friar Odoric (of 1298 and 1330); the *Merchants' Handbook* of Pegolotti (of c. 1340), and the *Catalan Atlas* (of 1375) are but the chief of many works in which a Roman Christian of the fourteenth century could find a reliable body of information and a fairly truthful delineation of great part of China and Indo-China, of India proper, of the Indian Archipelago, and of Upper Asia.

In this premature, but ever-memorable development of continental intercourse, the earliest figures are those of diplomatists, such as Carpini and Rubruquis; the greatest figures are those of merchants such as the Polos; in its later history we find European progress in Asia associated more and more intimately with trade-enterprise; it is evident throughout, to any one who looks below the surface, that commercial interests are the underlying and essential fact. But, on the surface, missionary activity often arrests our attention more sharply with its romantic daring, its brilliant triumphs won at so vast a distance from home, its pathetic and fascinating literary memorials. The experiment of winning Asia by Mongol alliance, of establishing regular communication,—ecclesiastical, mercantile, and diplomatic—between Western Europe and the Heathen Lands beyond the Islamic World was tried,—and failed; but none the less it illuminated a page too often soiled by baseness and smeared by dullness; and there are few brighter chapters in later Mediaeval history than those which tell of the journeys, schemes, successes, and failures of the Christian Pioneers in Asia. For Monte Corvino and Odoric in China; Jordanus in India; Pascal in Central Asia; the Polos alike in Turkestan, in Mongolia, in Cathay, in the Archipelago, in the Deccan, and in Persia; the Franciscans martyred near Bombay, near Lake Balkhash, or near Astrakhan; the merchants who follow out the commercial routes from Trebizond, the Don estuary, or the Gulf of Scanderoon, to the Pacific; the statesmen who weave a network of Roman bishoprics over the Orient, and dispatch so many Legations to the Court of the Grand Khan—all do something to redeem from reproach a time which, however often misconceived and depreciated, yields in essential import to no part of the Middle Ages.

In reality, while the fourteenth century draws on, the mediaeval stage of Human Development is beginning to pass away,—as the Papacy sinks into that Slough of Despond which we associate with the 'Babylonish Captivity' at Avignon, the Great Schism, and the fruitless efforts at reform by Oecumenical Councils; but as the mediaeval sun declines, it rests upon a splendid failure, and the beginnings of a more splendid triumph. The arms, the commerce, the religion of the Catholic nations, after an heroic struggle, are defeated in their frontal attacks upon the East; but in this struggle, Europeans acquire much of the knowledge essential to ultimate success; and, by the longer sea routes, they accomplish the outflanking and surmounting of every obstacle.

Italian, Catalan, Castillian, French, and Portuguese seamen share in varying degrees the credit of the first advances in this Oceanic field of action. And as in land travel, so in maritime; the Republics of Italy, both in theory and practice, are the leaders and teachers of the Christian states. Even as the Florentine Dante is the first great name in the new literatures of the West, so the Genoese Dorias and Vivaldi and Malocelli are the first to resume the old Phoenician and Norse enterprise in the Atlantic. And even as commercial ambitions are the most fruitful incentive to the land-exploration of the thirteenth and fourteenth centuries, so the earliest European venture in search of a water-way to the Indies is inspired by the unfulfilled desire to 'bring back useful things for trade.' The same practical purpose which takes the Polos from Venice to the Court of Kublai Khan encourages Mediterranean seamen from the other side of Italy to challenge the timidity, inaction, and superstition of so many generations.

The first age of Atlantic exploration (from about 1270 to 1340) is purely Italian; the second (from the middle of the fourteenth century) is marked by the gradual co-operation of other Europeans, especially from the coasts of Spain and France. Mariners from Catalan harbours, and especially from the Balearics, like the Genoese of fifty years before, seek for mercantile gain beyond the furthest known; they set out in 1346 to find the alleged River of Gold on the African coast, beyond Cape Bojador; with the like object, the conquest of new markets, French adventurers attack the Canary Islands in 1402; it is doubtless with similar hopes that unknown explorers (almost certainly Italians) add the Madeira group and the Eastern members of the Azorean Archipelago to the map of the *Terra Habitabilis* before 1351. With the commencement of the third maritime period, that of continuous, state-aided enterprise, led by a royal prince (Henry of Viseu), and prosecuted as a vital national interest by an organized Christian nation (that of Portugal), we have passed out of the Mediaeval and entered the Modern time. The 'Dawn of Modern Geography,' in the strict sense of the words, ends with the first voyages of the Infant's captains.

Down to the close of the twelfth century the Scientific Geography of Christendom is at best a feeble thing, markedly inferior to that of Islam (itself the somewhat slavish disciple of Greek thought), frequently a prey to the most absurd misconception and the most childish fable, and rarely aiming at anything higher than the reproduction of purely traditional methods and results. But when the Northmen and the Crusades have once thoroughly aroused the vital energies of the leading Christian races, they begin to expand in mind as well as in empire, and by the time of Prince Henry, a Portuguese can say 'our discoveries were not made without foresight and knowledge. For our sailors went out well taught and furnished with instruments and the rules of *astrology* and geometry, things which all mariners must know.' There is no exaggeration here: for compass, astrolabe, timepiece, and chart are all in use among South European seamen before the close of the fourteenth century.

A venerable tradition ascribes to Amalfi the introduction of the magnet among Western seamen; but the first mention of the 'ugly black stone' in Europe can be traced to the English monk Alexander Neckam and the French satirist Guyot de Provins, who both mention it about the time of the Third Crusade, not as the secret of the learned, but as the guide of mariners. And in spite of the astonishment produced half a century later in the mind of Brunetto Latini by the polar properties of the mysterious object, we cannot doubt that what was known to Roger Bacon, to Jacques de Vitry, and to Raymond Lull, as well as to Scandinavian poets and Moslem merchants of the thirteenth century, was employed by many Christian seamen of the Mediterranean when the Genoese made their first voyages in the Atlantic.

Amalfi did not introduce the magnet into Christendom; but 'Flavio Gioja' or some other citizen of that once adventurous republic which filled so large a part of the void between two great ages of civilization, the Classical and the Crusading, may have brought the magnetic needle into more general use by fitting it in a primitive compass. That it had reached such general use by the opening of the fifteenth century, at least among the ocean-faring seamen of Portugal, is clear from Prince Henry's exhortations to certain laggards among his earliest explorers.

Good maps were as valuable for true progress as good instruments; and here the close of the thirteenth century witnessed a momentous revolution. At a time when most European cartography was still half mythical, when map-designs were often rather picture-books of zoological and theological legend than delineations of the world, strictly scientific coast-charting begins with the Mediterranean 'Portolani.' The earliest existing specimen is of about 1300; but the type which then appears (with the *Carte Pisane*) must have been for some time in process of elaboration; and it is probable that examples of such work, dealing with sectional areas of shore-line, at least inside the Straits of Gibraltar, may yet be discovered from the time of the last Crusades. These plans of practical mariners are a refreshing contrast, in their often almost modern accuracy, to the work of other schools, from the most ambitious classical compositions (in Ptolemy's *Geography*) down to the wildest productions of mediaeval fabulists. Careful survey-work of this kind was apparently unknown to the Helleno-Roman world, as much as to the native Moslem civilization. The ancient *Peripli* were sailing directions, not drawn but written, and the only Arabic Portolan yet found is a copy of an Italian one. It was probably in North-West Italy that this kind of work originated, though very early traces of Portolan draughtsmanship may be found in Catalan lands; and long after the Italian leadership in exploration and commerce had begun to pass away, Italian science still controlled cartography; thus, among the early Portolani, the vast majority (413 out of 498) were executed by the countrymen of Marco Polo. At the same time we must recognize that an important minority of the leading fourteenth-century Portolani, such as the 'Dulcert' of 1339 and the magnificent 'Atlas' of 1375, are of Catalan authorship.

The first true maps constitute an important chapter in the history of our civilization; they mark the essential transition, in world-delineation, from ancient to modern, from empirical to scientific, from theory to practice; but they are only just beginning to receive adequate recognition. For they 'never had for their object to provide a popular and fashionable amusement'; they were not drawn to illustrate the works of classical authors or famous prelates; still less did they embody the legends and dreams of chivalry or romance; they were seldom executed by learned men; and small enough, in return, was the acknowledgement which the learned made them when their work was incorporated, by the geographical compilers of the sixteenth and seventeenth centuries, in pompous atlases of far inferior merit.

The continental or Asiatic travel, the maritime or Atlantic exploration, and the scientific advance of the later Middle Ages are the chief subjects of the present volume: the first may be said to supply the *matter,* the attractions and rewards, of European expansion; the others provided the *form* in which success was reached, the art of navigation, a working knowledge of oceanic conditions.

And the one was as much needed as the other. Human enterprise did its work so well because of a reasonable hope; men crept round Africa in face of the Atlantic storms because of the golden East beyond. That East (as we have noticed) had first been adequately revealed to Europe by the merchants and missionaries, the diplomatists and adventurers, who had followed the Crusading armies to Syria, and had then crept onwards to Cathay and the Indies. Thus inspiring certainty had been imparted to what had long been a tradition, but had remained, for all practical purposes, outside Latin experience; thus to European cupidity had been opened the greatest of earth's material prizes; thus had the true terrestrial paradise been pointed out to Western ambition. It was worth some labour to reach the treasuries of the Orient, once those treasuries were clearly located and verified; however long and toilsome, a sea path, free from all perils but those of nature, became more and more attractive as land routes were more and more endangered and obstructed. And once mistress of the South Asian trade, Christendom, already wielding the fighting power of the West, might hope to crush its old enemy Islam between two overwhelming forces, hammer and anvil—might dream of the control of the entire world.

The Pilgrim-Travel of Greek and Roman Christendom during the later mediaeval centuries does not call for any special notice in this place; though full of quaint and curious incident, it has no longer, as in the 'Dark Ages' or pre-Crusading period, a typical and vital character. Even more than in the Crusading time it has ceased, except perhaps among the Russian people, to be representative of Christian expansive activity. But in the number and position of those who take part in it, and in the character of their memoirs, we may still find enough of value and interest to compel a rather detailed survey.

Commercial enterprise, on the other hand, has now ceased to be merely the theme of one section of our subject; it pervades the whole. Mercantile conceptions are everywhere; the philosophy of utility is beginning to rule; in the material ambitions of commerce we find the mainspring of the chief outward movements of the time. . . .

N. M. Penzer (essay date 1929)

SOURCE: An introduction to *The Travels of Marco Polo,* edited by N. M. Penzer, translated by John Frampton, The Argonaut Press, 1929, pp. xi-lx.

[*In the following excerpt, Penzer provides a detailed analysis of the history of the Polian manuscripts.*]

The existence of an Elizabethan translation of the Travels of Marco Polo will probably come as a surprise to the majority of readers. This is not to be wondered at when we consider that only three copies of the work in question are known to exist, and that it has never been reprinted.

The very rarity of the book would be of itself sufficient excuse for reprinting it, but in the present case there are other considerations which make its appearance little less than a necessity.

In the first place, its value to students of Elizabethan literature is self-evident. Bearing this in mind, I have made no attempt to alter the spelling in any way, nor have I marred the charm of the narrative as known to contemporary readers by the insertion of unsightly notes. These are relegated to the end of the volume. The original head- and tail-pieces have also been preserved, together with sixteenth-century capitals.

In the second place, the translation, made by John Frampton from the Castilian of Santaella, originates in a MS belonging to the Venetian recension, one of the most important of all the Polian recensions. Its editing, therefore, should be of considerable interest.

Then again, the recently issued work of Prof. Benedetto, to which we shall return later, has so largely helped to unravel the tangled skein of Polian texts, that it is now necessary to reconsider afresh many of our long-accepted theories.

Finally, thanks to the recent surveys carried out in Central Asia and Mongolia, we are able to trace the itineraries with a much greater degree of accuracy than before, and although many queries still remain, some of the blanks have been filled in, and a few of the old mistakes rectified.

John Frampton

Apart from what Frampton tells us about himself in the Prefaces to one or two of his translations, we know nothing whatever about him. From these we learn that he was resident for many years in Spain, and that on his return to his native country about 1576, employed his leisure in translating several works from the Spanish. His knowledge of the language was very extensive as a comparison of the original with any of his translations will show. He must have worked hard during the first few years after his return to England, as between 1577 and 1581 six separate translations made their appearance.

His first work seems to have been an English rendering of Nicolas Monardes' *Primera Y Segunda Y Tercera Partes de la Historia Medicinal de las Cosas que se traen de nuestras Indias Occidentales que siruen en Medicina,* printed at London in 1577 by William Norton "in Poules Churche-yarde," under the title of *Joyfull Newes out of the Newe Founde Worlde wherein is declared the rare and singular vertues of diverse and sundrie hearbes, trees, oyles, plantes and stones, with their aplications, as well for phisicke as chirurgerie, . . .*

It was dedicated to Sir Edward Dyer (d. 1607), the Elizabethan courtier and poet, as was also *Marco Polo* and another of his translations, on China, to be mentioned later. A welcome reprint of *Joyfull Newes* has recently (1925) appeared in the Tudor Translations Series, edited by Stephen Gaselee. In his Introduction, the editor draws attention to a most interesting point: that it is by no means unlikely that to John Frampton is due the first interest taken in tobacco in England, leading shortly to the actual importation of the first smoking implements and the plant itself by Ralph Lane and Francis Drake.

To Monardes' description of tobacco, Frampton has added an account given him by Jean Nicot himself relating how, when French ambassador at Lisbon in 1559-61, he became acquainted with the new discovery and sent seeds to his Queen, Catherine de' Medici. An abstract of the actual report sent to France follows, in which we read of "the smoke of this Hearbe, the whiche thei receave at the mouth through certain coffins [paper cases of conical shape], suche as the Grocers do use to put in their Spices."

Thus nine years before Ralegh received the "herba santa" from Drake, a full description of it had been published in London by Frampton. A second edition, with some additions, came out in 1580, and a third edition in 1596.

His next work appears to be unrecorded, except in the *Registers of the Company of Stationers of London.* See Arber's *Transcript,* Vol. II., where we find that Henry Bynneman obtained a license on March 10th, 1578, for, *A brief Declaracon of all the portes. creekes. baies. and havens conteyned in the west India. the originall whereof was Dedicated to the mightie Kinge Charles the V Kinge of Castile.* I know of no copy in existence to-day. It was copied by Ames and Herbert, *Typographical Antiquities,* Vol. II.

In January 1579 Frampton finished writing the Dedication of his *Marco Polo,* so we may assume that it appeared in the early spring of that year. We shall return to a full discussion of this work later. . . .

Santaella

Rodrigo Fernández de Santaella y Córdoba was born in 1444 at Carmona, twenty-six miles north-east of Seville. Nothing is known of his early life, and we first hear of him in 1467 when he was presented with a fellowship of theology at the College of San Clemente de los Españoles at Bologna by the Archbishop and Chapter of Toledo. The fellowships lasted for eight years, so we may assume that Santaella remained at Bologna until 1475. After taking his degree as Doctor of Theology and Arts, he preached before Sixtus IV at Rome in 1477, in the presence of Innocent VIII.

Meanwhile Isabella had been recognized as heiress to Castile, and in 1469 had married Ferdinand of Aragon. The "Catholic Kings" were proclaimed in 1474, and soon after Santaella returned to Spain and embarked on his career of ecclesiastical preferment.

In 1499 his *magnum opus* appeared, the *Vocabulario Eclesiástico,* dedicated to the Illustrious Catholic Queen.

It went through no less than thirty editions, which are duly recorded by D. Joaquin Hazañas y La Rua, whose work, *Maese Rodrigo, 1444-1509,* is practically my sole authority for these few remarks on Santaella.

His *Sacerdotalis instructio circa missam* followed later in the same year, and the *Manual de Doctrina necesario al visitador y á los clérigos* in 1502.

In 1503 his Castilian translation of *Marco Polo* was published. In his Preface Santaella tells us that he was prompted to undertake the work since he realized its importance and no one had come forward to do it. It had already been printed in German, Latin, Venetian and Portuguese, and Santaella wished to see it in his native tongue. He also tells us that his library contained the treatise of Nicolò de' Conti, another Venetian, whose travels largely confirmed the narrative of Polo, and because of this fact he determined to include a translation in his work, "porque como nuestro señor dixo por boca de dos ó tres se confirma mas la verdad."

As is related on a later page the Polo MS used by Santaella is now preserved in the Biblioteca del Seminario at Seville. Subsequent editions appeared in 1507, 1518, 1520 and 1527, the last three being posthumous.

It is unnecessary here to enumerate the subsequent publications of Santaella. They consisted chiefly of sermons and other ecclesiastic writings of a similar nature, and are fully catalogued by La Rua.

On Sept. 12th 1502 Hurtado de Mendoza, Cardinal of Seville, had died, and Santaella was made "Visitador" for the whole of the see. On June 3rd 1503 the Chapter divided the Archbishopric into four sections, that including the city of Seville and Triana falling to Santaella. The vacancy was filled by Don Juan de Zúñiga, who made his entry into Seville on May 13th 1504, but he died on July 26th of the same year. The esteem in which Santaella was held is shown by the fact that at the death of Zúñiga, he was nominated "Provisor" during the interregnum, the next Archbishop, Fray Diego de Deza, not arriving at Seville till 1506.

For some years past Santaella had been deliberating on the founding of a university at Seville, and on June 13th 1503 the site was purchased for 4700 *maravedis*. A Bull, pointing out the necessity for a local university for the benefit of scholars and poor clergy studying in Seville, was approved by Julius III. Santaella's idea seems to have been to create a College for ecclesiastical studies, as well as a general university. In 1508 he obtained another Bull by which the College was united with three other benefices in order that medicine might be taught, and the whole establishment placed on the same footing as the university of Salamanca.

Santaella died on Jan. 20th 1509, and was buried in the chapel of his college. In 1771 the Colegio Mayor, as it was called, was separated from the university, and by 1847 hardly one stone remained upon another.

Thus the illustrious Archdeacon of the Realm, Maese Rodrigo Santaella, was almost completely forgotten, when the Rector of the university conceived the idea of erecting a statue to its founder.

This statue, more than life-size, was unveiled on Dec. 10th 1900, and stands in the great court of the university.

Having thus briefly given a short account both of Frampton and Santaella, we can pass on to a consideration of the extant texts of the Travels of Marco Polo.

THE MANUSCRIPT TRADITION

Previous to 1928 it would have been practically impossible to have written anything new about the numerous Polian texts, unless it had been to have given more detailed accounts of the leading MSS already briefly described by Yule.

Early last year, however, the eagerly awaited work of Prof. L. F. Benedetto *Marco Polo: Il Milione* made its appearance in Florence, and for the first time the MSS were properly classified and arranged in the respective groups to which they belong.

But this is only a small portion of the work that Benedetto has accomplished. He has not only increased the Yule-Cordier list of MSS from 78 to 138, but has discovered a copy of one that contains many of the passages used by Ramusio, the origin of which was not previously known. I shall return to this later.

All this forms the first part of Benedetto's work; the second half contains the text of the most famous MS of all, fr. 1116, correctly edited for the first time with textual notes and important passages from other MSS. In order to derive the full benefit afforded for the elucidation of the complicated mass of MSS, it is necessary to study both parts in conjunction.

As is only to be expected in research of this nature, it is impossible to find proofs for every statement, and in the reconstruction of lost originals there is plenty of scope for what amounts to little less than pure guesswork.

I have never been able to understand exactly why Yule discarded fr. 1116, which he owned to be the best text, in preference for those used by Pauthier which were much inferior. His excuse that the awkwardnesses and tautologies in fr. 1116 prevented its use hardly seems sufficient to debar a scholar from attempting to overcome those difficulties.

But Yule was no paleographist; he was a commentator, and a very great commentator; just as Cordier was a bibliographer. Benedetto, on the other hand, is both a philologist and a paleographist, and only such a scholar can give us the thread that will guide us safely through the labyrinthine intricacies of Polian manuscript tradition.

As a close study of the works of these scholars is a *sine qua non* for every student of Marco Polo, it is to be regretted that Benedetto has not used Yule's chapter enumeration for facilitating reference, in addition to his own.

Owing to the fact that Benedetto's work is limited to only six hundred copies, that it is in Italian, and that its high price places it quite outside the reach of students, I make no excuse for giving here some account of the different groups of MSS as now first classified and described by him, together with such further information or comments as my own reading has suggested.

We will consider the MSS under the following headings:

1. The Geographic Text (fr. 1116).
2. The Grégoire Version.
3. The Tuscan Recension.
4. The Venetian Recension.
5. Ramusio's Version and the ante-*F* phase.

I. *The Geographic Text (fr. 1116).*

As is only natural, Benedetto first discusses the precious MS at the Bibliothèque Nationale, Paris, fr. 1116 (formerly 7367). It was published in 1824 by the French Geographical Society, since when it has been known as the Geographic Text. Benedetto refers to it as *F.* Although that letter also includes all French MSS (twenty in number) in this group, fr. 1116 is its only complete representative. We know little of its history, except that it is supposed to have come from the old library of the French kings at Blois. It is round this MS that scholastic controversy has chiefly centred, and since the appearance of Yule's *magnum opus* we have been perfectly content to accept the view that in fr. 1116 we have a direct representation of what Marco Polo dictated to his fellow-prisoner in Genoa.

In the light of Benedetto's new evidence we find that we have to reconsider the whole question. In the end we shall see all our pet theories destroyed, with little hope of settling points concerning the early history of the book until various new lines of research have been exhausted to their utmost.

At first sight this may seem a hopeless position, but one thing is certain, and that is that we can never hope to clear up the history of any important work until we know what data we have to work on, and are satisfied that such data are arranged in their correct order, each separate item in its proper place. This, then, is the achievement of Benedetto. He has brought order into chaos. We are now in a position to ascertain what the MS tradition can teach us, and once we are on the right path there is no telling what headway may be made in the future.

Our discussion opens in the prison at Genoa, where Polo's fellow-prisoner, a Pisan, is called in to help in the writing of the narrative. The name of this man is shown definitively to be Rustichello, instead of such forms as Rustician or Rusticiano. It was natural to suppose that he had been chosen by the Genoese authorities because of his reputation as a writer of French Arthurian legends. Scholars have, therefore, been at pains to compare the style of fr. 1116 with that of his other works. They have considered (Yule especially) that the language of fr. 1116 is much more crude, inaccurate, and Italianized than that of Rustichello's other romances. This supported the theory of Polo's dictation, which, it was said, clearly betrayed itself in the halting style of the narrative.

Benedetto, however, after comparing numerous passages of fr. 1116 with portions of Rustichello's other works, has found practically identical phrases and idioms, some of which clearly betray the same hand. From this he argues that the same care and diligence that produced the romances also produced fr. 1116—in other words, that Rustichello did not copy down at Polo's dictation, but produced fr. 1116 (or rather a version of which that manuscript is a descendant) after a prolonged and detailed study of all the notes with which Polo supplied him. Polo was no trained writer, and, moreover, would not trust himself to present his story in a style acceptable to Western ears after his prolonged absence in the East. Here was a professional story-teller ready to hand! What more natural than to allow him to "write up" the work, after supplying him with all the necessary information! As Benedetto puts it:

> Compito espresso di Rustichello dev' essere stato quello di stendere in una lingua letteraria accettabile quelle note che Marco, vissuto così a lungo in oriente, non si sentiva di formulare con esattezza in nessuna parlata occidentale. Abbiamo intravisto abbastanza com' egli, assolvendo un tal compito, sia rimasto fedele allo stile ed alla visuale dei romanzi d'avventura. Ma non possiamo dire nulla di più.

Thus the style of fr. 1116, with all its "story-teller" mannerisms, does not necessarily betray dictation, but rather the usual style of a professional romance writer, who saw in Marco Polo a King Arthur come to life! Moreover, as regards the Italian words, we find quite a large percentage of them in fr. 1463, a MS which we *know* was not dictated. I may note in passing that Ramusio, in the Introduction to his version (to be discussed later), neither states that Polo *dictated* his work, nor that *a Pisan* had anything to do with it. He says that Polo was "assisted by a Genoese gentleman" who "used to spend many hours daily in prison with him," and helped him to write the book. It has always been taken for granted that facts had become muddled, and it was Rustichello the Pisan to whom reference was made. Now Benedetto argues with considerable skill that fr. 1116 must represent only a later copy of the original Polo-Rustichello compilation. Might it not be possible that Ramusio, so correct and reliable in other points, is also correct here—and that one of the numerous Genoese, who without the slightest doubt *did* visit Polo, became very friendly with him, and helped in the editing of the work, *in addition to Rustichello*?

However this may be, the fact remains that we must no longer regard *F* as the one and only direct and immediate descendant of the original Genoese text. Nor must we imagine that all subsequent recensions can be traced back to *F*. As will be seen later, they originate in lost prototypes dependent on lost MSS which we must regard as brothers of *F*. The Cottonian Codex Otho D. 5 at the British Museum, fragmentary though it be, is of importance in proving that the Franco-Italian recension was diffused, as well as all those MSS dependent on purer French texts.

2. *The Grégoire Version.*

A detailed study of this version has led Benedetto to believe in the existence of a lost version, F^1, very akin to *F*, but containing just those differences necessary to the production of an elaborated version (the lost *FG*) from which the Grégoire group is descended. In order to prove that *FG* is *not* a revision of *F*, as hitherto believed, it is necessary to determine the exact status of F^1 and to reconstruct it as far as possible.

This can be done chiefly by comparing the existing types of *FG* with *F*. This will show that *F* does not possess all the points necessary to produce *FG*—some of the *lacunae* should be different, and certain passages should be much more detailed. Thus the *FG* group must come from a MS similar to *F*, but certainly not *F* itself. This lost MS is Benedetto's F^1. *F* and F^1 can, therefore, be regarded as brother MSS.

We now examine *FG* as a separate group. Yule only knew of five MSS while Benedetto has been able to add another ten. He divides *FG* into four sub-groups, A, B, C, and D. These again are subdivided into single MSS which are closely connected. Thus B has seven subgroups, of which B^1 and B^2 are closely related. So also B^4 and B^5. B^3 differs slightly from these two latter, while B^6 and B^7 form a more collateral branch. By arranging the MSS in this way a genealogical table can gradually be built up.

I might note in passing that Pauthier's "A" type, which formed the basis of his, and Yule's, translation, consisted of A^1; his "B" type of A^2; and his "C" of B^4. B^3 and B^4 (to which now must be added B^5) are especially interesting, as they bear the curious certificate of one Thibault de Cepoy, on which Pauthier placed such great importance. It appears that Thibault was a captain in the service of Philip the Fair. After beginning as valet and squire, he rose to the rank of Grand-Master of the Cross-bow men. He then entered the service of Charles de Valois, Philip's brother, who sent him to Constantinople to substantiate his claim to the throne on the grounds that his wife, Catherine de Courtenay, was the daughter of Philip de Courtenay, titular Emperor of Constantinople. Thibault left Paris on September 9th 1306, and proceeded to Venice, where he concluded a treaty of alliance in December, 1306. During his stay there he met Marco Polo, who in August, 1307, presented him with a copy of his book, inscribed as "the first copy of his said Book after he had made the same." After Thibault's death, his son Jean made a copy of the book, which he gave to Charles de Valois. He also made other copies for those of his friends who asked for them.

The three MSS mentioned above thus describe in the Note attached to them Polo's gift to Thibault, and how copies of it came to be distributed in France.

The great importance that Pauthier attached to these MSS on account of the Note has long since been proved quite unjustifiable. Although Yule realized this, he still made Pauthier's MSS the basis of his own translation.

Benedetto has entirely discredited the Note and will not even allow Thibault to give his name to the group at all. He points out that it is impossible to believe that no copy of Polo's work should have been made until 1307. Certainly it is, but where is the evidence to prove it *was* made in 1307? Perhaps it had been written in 1299, and Polo had kept a copy by him for any important presentation such as this. Or, on the other hand, there may be something in Langlois' suggestion when he says: "Mais, avant 1307, Ser Marco avait dû faire à bien des gens semblable politesse, peut-être avec des protestations analogues qu'il la faisait pour la première fois. . . ."

Benedetto credits Grégoire with being the founder of this group because his name appears on two of the MSS (A^1 and A^3), while the date of the work is given as 1308 on the grounds that "this present year 1308" appears on another of the MSS (D). I cannot feel convinced, however, that Benedetto has proved his point in preference to accepting the original Thibault copy as the earliest extant MS of the group.

As I have already mentioned, *FG* is subdivided into four main groups. Among these, A^2 is the beautiful MS fr. 2810 at the Bib. Nat. containing 266 miniatures, of which 84 belong to the travels of Marco Polo, occupying the first 96 folios of the MS.

3. *The Tuscan Recension.*

At the commencement of the fourteenth century a Franco-Italian version of the original Genoese prototype was translated into Tuscan. It must have been very similar both to *F* and F^1, and can therefore be called F^2.

We possess five copies, which Benedetto has called TA^{1}-^{5}. Of these TA^1 is the famous MS II. iv. 88 of the Bib. Naz. at Florence, better known as the *Codex della Crusca*.

The other copies are at the Bib. Naz. Florence (TA^2, ^{5}); the Bib. Nat. Paris (TA^3); and the Bib. Laurenziana (TA^4).

The Tuscan group contains two other versions which must be mentioned. The first is a Latin one (Bib. Nat. lat. 3195) in which the Tuscan translation is corrupted by Pipino's version (to be mentioned later).

It was this text which formed the basis of H. Murray's English translation in 1844. It was published in 1824 by the French Geographical Society in the same volume as fr. 1116.

The second is a free *résumé* of *TA* found in the *Zibaldone* attributed to Antonio Pucci (d. 1388), the Florentine poet.

Owing to the differences found in the sub-groups of *TA,* it is necessary to utilize them all in attempting to restore the prototype of *TA*. Although *TA*1 is the oldest codex, it is incomplete (as also *TA*2) and less close to *F* than the others.

When we have restored *TA* as best we can with the help of all the sub-groups, we find that we have a complete text save for the omission of certain historic-military chapters and some minor details. It is of assistance in revising certain corruptions in *F,* as some of the *lacunae* in fr. 1116 could not have existed in *F*2 from which *TA* is descended.

4. *The Venetian Recension.*

This group is of the utmost importance, and contains over eighty MSS. In order to fully appreciate the extensive ramifications of its sub- and sub-sub-groups, it is necessary to study the genealogical table given by Benedetto.

It is, moreover, of particular interest to us, as it contains the Spanish version of Santaella, the English translation of which is reprinted in the present volume. A glance at the table referred to above shows that the primitive Venetian codex is represented by five MSS (*VA*1-5). Although *VA*3 and *VA*4 are the only complete ones, *VA*1 is by far the most important, as it consists of the Casanatense fragment (Bib. Cas. 3999), which is a direct descendant from the prototype which served as the source of Fra Pipino's famous version. The great fame that this version achieved from its first appearance, and the eulogistic manner in which Pipino referred to his sources, led to the popular opinion that the Venetian version was nothing less than Polo's original! Consequently, the Pipino texts are more widely distributed than any others. To the previously known twenty-six MSS Benedetto has added another twenty-four. These fifty must be supplemented by seven more in the vulgar tongue, besides a very large number of printed versions. Nearly all the important European libraries possess one or more Pipino MSS. There are several copies in the British Museum, while others will be found at Oxford, Cambridge, Glasgow, and Dublin.

Of particular interest is the MS which once belonged to Baron Walckenaer. Benedetto describes it correctly as being in a volume containing other matter, including a version of the *Mirabilia* of Jordan de Sévérac. He regrets that its present locality is unknown, and conjectures that it has probably found its way to America. Both Yule and Cordier had previously made similar statements as regards the MS itself, yet only last year my friend, the Rev. A. C. Moule, "discovered" it properly catalogued and indexed at the British Museum!

When scholars and bibliographers can pass over such fully recorded MSS, we can the more easily imagine that many unknown Polian treasures may still lie in European libraries *wrongly* catalogued, or not catalogued at all.

The fame of Pipino's version is well attested to by the numerous translations of it which exist—in French, Irish, Bohemian, Portuguese, and German. The French translation exists in two MSS, one at the British Museum (Egerton, 2176), and the other in the Royal Library at Stockholm. The Irish version is that in the famous "Book of Lismore," discovered in such a romantic manner in 1814. The Bohemian version forms part of Cod. III, E. 42, in the Prague Museum, and dates from the middle of the fifteenth century. Benedetto considers, however, that the MS is copied from a still older Pipino text. The Portuguese translation was printed at Lisbon in 1502 (reprinted 1922).

The first printed Latin text appeared about 1485, while a second edition (1532) was included in the famous collection of travels known as the *Novus orbis regionum ac insularum veteribus incognitarum*. It was edited by Simon Grynaeus, but actually compiled by Jean Huttichius. The text is corrupt, and has been considered by many to be a retranslation from the Portuguese of 1502.

There were several editions of the *Novus orbis*—1535, 1537, and 1555, as well as translations—German (1534), French (1556), Castilian (1601), and Dutch (1664). Apart from this, Andreas Müller reprinted the Latin in 1671 on which was based the French translation in Bergeron's *Voyages faits principalement en Asie* (1735).

The text of Ramusio (to be more fully discussed shortly) can be regarded as based on a version of Grynaeus, so that it is fundamentally a Pipinian text.

Apart from Pipino's version (*P*) and also that of an anonymous Latin writer (*LB*), a group of six Tuscan translations of the Venetian (*TB*1-6) must be added. This Tuscan group in its turn gave rise to a German translation (*Ted.*) and another Latin one (*LA*).

We now turn to a group based on a MS similar to that which gave rise to the Tuscan group. It consists of two distinct sub-groups, the first of which comprises: (*a*) a fifteenth century Venetian MS at Lucca (Bib. Governativa, No. 1296), and (*b*) a Spanish version from a Venetian codex, translated into English by John Frampton in 1579.

The second is also of importance as it consists of a mass of MSS and printed texts based on the early Venetian edition of 1496.

The Lucca MS is a paper codex of seventy-five pages, containing a brief epitome of Odoric besides the text of Polo. On the verso of the last page we are informed that it was completed on March 12th 1465 by one Daniele da Verona. The Spanish (Castilian) version of Santaella was taken from a MS of 78 folios, without pagination, which once belonged to the Biblioteca del Colegio Mayor de Santa Maria de Jesus at Seville. After the separation of the College and University in 1771 it entirely disappeared, and was given up as lost. Years later it was discovered with a number of papers in the garret of an old building belonging to the College, and is now preserved in the Biblioteca del Seminario of Seville. The manuscript is described by La Rua as a quarto volume, written in two inks, in contemporary binding, somewhat deteriorated by the action of the weather. It contains 135 chapters (as in the present translation), and was completed on Aug. 20th 1493. All Santaella's editions are of extreme rarity, and it is hard to say for certain how many there were, or even to be sure of the date of the first edition.

As far as I can ascertain, the first edition was that described by Salvá (*Catálogo de la Biblioteca de Salvá,* Vol. II. No. 3278), and published at Seville on May 28th 1503. There is a fine copy at the British Museum (C. 32. m. 4.) which has been fully described by Yule (Vol. II. p. 566). An edition of 1502 is mentioned in some detail by Don Fernando Colon, but as he gives the same printers and exactly the same date for the completion of the work (May 28th) as in the 1503 edition, it would seem that an error has been made.

The work was reprinted at Toledo in 1507, and, after the author's death, at Seville in 1518 and 1520, and again at Logroño in 1529. This latter edition is also at the British Museum (G. 6788), and for all we know may be the actual copy used by Frampton. The excessive rarity of the work fully justifies such a possibility.

Turning, now, to the second sub-group, we find a large number of Venetian MSS and printed texts all based on the edition printed by Sessa in 1496. This edition was derived from a MS which, like the Lucca, began with an epitome of Odoric. Owing, however, to a large *lacuna* after the first folio, it has not only been sadly reduced, but the first chapters of Marco Polo itself have also suffered heavily.

Apart from these mutilations, and the fact that in places the text is abbreviated and somewhat corrupt, the early Venetian printed edition is identical with both the Lucca text and that of Santaella.

Without going further into the relationships of the various branches of the Venetian recension, we will pass on to Ramusio and the earlier connected MSS.

5. *Ramusio's Version and ante-F phase.*

In 1550 the first volume of a collection of travels appeared under the editorship of one Gian Battista Ramusio, an illustrious member of a noble Italian family of Rimini. In 1556, another volume (Vol. III) was issued, while Vol. II, containing Ramusio's account of Polo's travels, did not appear until 1559—two years after the editor's death.

Other editions of the *Navigationi et Viaggi,* as the collection was called, soon followed, and the "Ramusian Recension" of Marco Polo took a unique place of honour in Polian tradition.

Ramusio was a good scholar, and enjoyed a great reputation for learning and critical research. His chief pursuit was geography, and he is believed to have opened a school for its study in his own house at Venice. In fact, everything we know about him compels us to treat his work with the utmost consideration and credence, as he fully justifies his title of "the Italian Hakluyt." Bearing this in mind, we can more readily appreciate the disappointment with which Yule had to record the absence of those MSS from which Ramusio had obtained certain parts of his information. Turning to the volume itself, we find that in a letter to his friend Jerome Fracastoro, Ramusio speaks of his sources, clearly indicating Pipino's text as well as another *di maravigliosa antichità.* Although Ramusio's text was at first ignored, its great importance has been gradually established, until, with Benedetto's discovery of *Z,* it is a *sine qua non* in helping to trace the earlier stages of the history of the book. At the same time, he admits that it is a composite text—*sbocco a tradizioni già sicuramente corrotte*—and therefore cannot be used as a basic text, especially when compared with *F.* Benedetto would analyse the Ramusio text as containing: (a) Pipino as the original and principal base; (*b*) three other MSS, *V, L,* and *VB*; (c) the newly discovered MS, *Z,* which corresponds to the Ghisi codex mentioned by Ramusio himself.

The history of the Milan copy of *Z,* so far as it is known, is very interesting. It is taken from an old lost Latin Codex Zeladiano, copied in 1795 by the Abate Toaldo to complete his collection of Polian documents. The original of this copy must be identified with the MS *cartaceo in-*80, *del sec. xv.,* mentioned by Baldello-Boni, who says it was left by the will of Cardinal Zelada to the Biblioteca Capitolare of Toledo. A close inspection of *Z* shows it to be a Latin version of a Franco-Italian codex, distinctly better than *F.* But, as we shall see later, *Z,* as represented in the Milan MS, is by no means complete.

The first three-quarters of *Z* seem like an epitome of a much fuller text, but after Chap. 147 *F* is faithfully followed, while the additional passages point to a pre-*F* codex, which must have been considerably more detailed than *F.* Benedetto suggests that the copyist of *Z* began with the idea of a limited selection of passages, but gradually became so interested in his work that he eventually found himself unable to sacrifice a single word.

A point of prime importance with regard to *Z* is that it clearly betrays Polo's mode of thought, showing that, as far as it goes, it is a literal translation of an early text now lost. This is also supported by the fact that the names of peoples and places appear in *Z* in less corrupted forms than in *F* or subsequent texts—*e.g.,* Mogdasio, Silingi, etc.

The various indications of *Z*'s anteriority to *F* suggest a subsequent suppression of certain passages by a copyist or by the cumulative work of several copyists. A large percentage of these passages occur in Ramusio, while some are found in *Z.* In those cases where *Z* only resembles an epitome, we must conclude that Ramusio had access to a text closer to the archetype of *Z* than *Z* itself. We can call this text *Z*1. We can, therefore, agree that if *Z,* as represented by the Milan text (Y. 160 P.S.), can account for unique passages only in the latter part of Ramusio, it is not unreasonable to conclude that he had a complete *Z* text before him (*Z*1), and took all the unidentified chapters in the first half of his book from it. The discovery of the archetype of both *Z* and *Z*1 would doubtless help to settle the question.

We now come to *V, L,* and *VB*. They can be looked upon as coming somewhere between *F* and *Z*. They are of value because they occasionally contain passages neither in *F* nor in *Z*.

V is a curious Venetian recension (Staatsbib. Berlin, Hamilton 424a) which has undeniable echoes both of a Franco-Italian and a Latin text. It contains about thirty unique passages, and was undoubtedly used by Ramusio. *L* is an interesting Latin compendium represented in the four following codices: Ferrara, Bib. Pubb. 336NB 5; Venice, Mus. Corr. 2408; Wolfenbüttel, Bib. Com. Weiss. 41; and Antwerp, Mus. Plantin-Mor. 60. They are practically identical, and represent the best compendium of Marco Polo extant. Its Franco-Italian origin is proved by the survival of certain expressions which, not being understood, have been retained unaltered. It was probably used by Ramusio, though this cannot be said for certain.

Taken together, *V* and *L* must be regarded as closely related to, but distinctly a sub-group of *Z*1 and *Z*.

VB is a Venetian version (Donà della Rose 224 Civ. Mus. Corr.) differing from any of the Venetian recensions we have already discussed. Two copies exist: one in Rome (Bib. Vat. Barb. Lat. 5361) and the other in London (Brit. Mus. Slo. 251). *VB* shows signs of a Franco-Italian origin, and in two cases contains details ignored by *F*, but preserved by *Z*. On the whole, however, this is the worst of all Polian texts, and it is a pity that Ramusio used it at all.

To sum up, we must not blind ourselves to the undoubted defects of Ramusio. Here is a man who has selected a distinctly ragged garment (*P*), with the intent to make it look new by the addition of various patches (*Z, V, L, VB*). Some of the patches are of very good material, but others are frayed and badly put on, and, moreover, not always in the best places. They do not harmonize well with the cloth to which they are sewn. In some cases they have been trimmed a little, but then again we find in other cases that our repairer has added extra pieces of his own.

Thus altogether, while the finished article contains much material, it does not approximate in any way to a complete and original garment.

In spite, however, of all this, Ramusio remains an essential source in the reconstruction of the richer text by which *F* was preceded. It has continually been assumed that from time to time additions were made to the original work of Polo. The researches of Benedetto clearly show that, on the contrary, as time went on, impoverishments have occurred.

Z gives occasional bits of folk-lore and details of intimate social customs; so also does the *Imago Mundi* of Jacopo d'Acqui (D. 526 Bib. Ambros.) called *I* by Benedetto. It may be that the church censored some of this material, for in the *Z* passages we have caught a glimpse of Marco Polo as the careful anthropologist, and how can we determine what curious and esoteric information was originally supplied to Rustichello? We do not find it hard to believe that there may well be some genuineness in the passage of Jacopo d'Acqui when he says in Polo's defence: "And because there are many great and strange things in that book, which are reckoned past all credence, he was asked by his friends on his death-bed to correct the book by removing everything that was not actual fact. To which he replied that he had not told *one-half* of what he really had seen."

The gradual decadence of the original text as proved in the cases of *FG, TA,* and *VA* must also have occurred in the stage anterior to *F*. The discovery of *Z*, the study of *V* and *L*, the analysis of Ramusio, and the reference of certain elements to the lost Ghisi codex all seem to point to the fact that *F* was preceded by more conservative and more exact copies. *Z, V,* and *L* not only help to bridge the distance from *F* back to the original Genoese archetype, but also prove the richness of the latter and its gradual impoverishment. They show as well, that each of the three phases (*Z, V* and *L, F*) is dependent on the same original Franco-Italian text. Thus, apart from restoring the lost passages of *F*, they also bear witness to its unique importance and authenticity.

Having thus briefly surveyed the five main groups into which, thanks to Benedetto's labours, we can now divide the Polian texts, it will be as well to summarize the conclusions:

(1) Fr. 1116 of the Bibliothèque Nationale is the best Polo MS that has come down to us.

(2) It does not represent a direct copy of the Genoese original, but is a later version, which, together with its three brother manuscripts, *F*1,2,3, is described from a common Franco-Italian MS of earlier date, now lost.

(3) From *F*1,2,3 were derived respectively the lost prototypes of the Grégoire, Tuscan, and Venetian recensions (*FG, TA, VA*).

(4) Of these *VA* is the largest and most important, Santaella's Castilian version being made from a MS in one of its sub-groups.

(5) There was an ante-*F* phase, as yet only represented by *Z, L, V* and *VB*.

(6) Ramusio based his version on Pipino, with additional help from all the MSS of the ante-*F* phase, as mentioned above. He also used one or more other MSS, at present undiscovered.

(7) The most complete account of Polo's travels, therefore, consists of fr. 1116 as a base, supplemented by Ramusio, together with a few unique passages from other MSS.

In a 1929 letter to E. Denison Ross, Aldo Ricci discusses the style of his translation of L. F. Benedetto's version of *The Travels of Marco Polo*:

Quite apart from the question of the texts Yule used for his version, his style of translating does not seem to me perfectly satisfactory, alternating as it does between archaisms and forms and expressions redolent of the fairy tale. Doubtless Yule intended by means of the latter to reproduce the ingenuousness of the author, but surely the ingenuousness of Marco Polo is not that of the child, and still less that of the grown-up telling a tale to children, which is the impression Yule so often leaves on one. It is, of course, a purely literary ingenuousness, so to speak, the inability to express oneself clearly at a time when a vernacular prose style did not yet exist, and on the part of a person who was by no means a "clerk." But the mentality is naturally far from being that of the child, except perhaps in the sense in which the middle ages are popularly considered childish.

After making several experiments, I have come to the conclusion that the only really legitimate way of translating Polo is to be as literal as the difference between the two languages will allow. In this way his mentality, if I may say so, is allowed to speak for itself, and his constant visible effort to express his meaning—which is extremely interesting from so many points of view, both literary and psychological—is in no way disguised. For this same reason I also believe that Yule was ill-advised in compressing and even suppressing so many passages and sentences of repetitions, not to mention the "formulae" at the end of chapters which he often passes over.

Aldo Ricci, in E. Denison Ross's introduction to The Travels of Marco Polo, *translated by Aldo Ricci, George Routledge & Sons, 1931.*

E. Denison Ross (lecture date 1934)

SOURCE: "Marco Polo and His Book," in *Proceedings of the British Academy,* Vol. XX, 1934, pp. 181-201.

[*In the following excerpt from a lecture delivered before the British Academy, Ross gives a brief account of Polo's journey and his narrative, and introduces several new theories regarding Polo's manuscript.*]

The outstanding geographical event of the thirteenth century was the discovery of the overland route to the Far East. The silk of China had long been known to the West, but the route by which it travelled was unknown, for European merchants had not ventured beyond certain Asiatic ports, whither the silk, like other Oriental wares, was conveyed by caravan.

It was an Italian, Plano Carpini, who first penetrated to the court of the Great Khan of the Mongols in 1245, and it was another Italian, Marco Polo, who at the end of the same century gave to the world the first full account of China in a Western language and 'created Asia for the European mind'. People were now to learn that a distant land which they imagined full of desert solitudes and strange monsters actually had a highly developed civilization of its own. In the fourteenth century further news of the Far East was brought or sent to Europe by other Italians, notably by Odoric of Pordenone, Marignolli, and John of Monte Corvino.

It was the sudden invasion of Central Europe by the armed hordes sent out by Chinghiz Khan at the beginning of the thirteenth century that gave the Western world its first introduction to the people of the Far East, and had it not been for this invasion Europe would no doubt have long continued to remain ignorant of China.

By 1240 the Mongol armies had reached Hungary and Upper Silesia, and no combination of European princes was able to withstand their advance. The whole of Europe was seized with the Mongol terror, and Matthew Paris, writing at St. Albans under the year 1238, tells us that for fear of the Mongols the fishermen of Gotland and Friesland did not dare to cross the North Sea to load their boats at Yarmouth, and that consequently herrings were so cheap and abundant in England that forty or fifty were sold for a piece of silver even in places far inland.

In 1241, after defeating the troops of Poland, Moravia, and Silesia under Duke Henry II of Silesia near Liegnitz, the Mongols withdrew even more unexpectedly than they had arrived, purposely destroying everything in their path to show that they were retiring of their own free will. [In a footnote, the author adds: "Some writers have suggested that this Mongolian army under Subutai withdrew because news had been received of the death of the Great Khan Ögedei, and that this event rendered necessary his presence at Karakorum. However, the battle of Liegnitz took place on 9 April 1241, and the death of Ögedei did not occur till 11 December. Subutai after the battle of Liegnitz joined Batu in Hungary, and both generals returned to Mongolia in the following year."] Fear was now replaced by curiosity, and men began to wonder whether the Mongols might not be a possible ally against the Saracens, i.e. the Mamluks of Egypt, who alone of the powers of Islam had withstood the Mongol invader. The strange legend of Prester John, an all-powerful monarch possessed of fabulous wealth, both king and Christian priest, had been current in Europe for nearly a hundred years; his kingdom had never been located, and it was thought that he possibly reigned in the distant land of the Mongols.

It was such hopes and beliefs, no doubt, that led Pope Innocent IV to send Plano Carpini, an Italian Franciscan, to visit the Great Khan in Mongolia. He set out in 1245, and in 1247 he returned with discouraging letters from Küyük Khan, whose investiture he had witnessed. Plano Carpini was then nearly sixty years of age and very stout. Insufficiently clothed and badly nourished, he had to make the three months' journey from the Volga to Central Mongolia at the rapid pace of the Mongolian ponies.

This mission was followed by another, that of William of Rubruck, a native of French Flanders, also a Franciscan, who carried letters from St. Louis of France to Mängü Khan. [In a footnote the author adds: "He was in Palestine with St. Louis, King of France, in 1251, and it was this king who sent him on his journey, which took place between 1253 and 1255. His book ranks in interest very close to that of Marco Polo."]

Another Italian, John of Monte Corvino, at the age of fifty penetrated into southern China just as the Polos were returning to Venice, with the object of preaching the Gospel to the Chinese, including the Nestorians, whom he regarded as little better than pagans. The Pope, at length realizing the fine work he was doing, made him Archbishop of Pekin with patriarchal authority; churches were established in various other cities; and Roman Catholicism was spread under the immediate patronage of the Great Khan. Many accounts of the work of Archbishop John have been preserved in letters written from Cathay. He died in 1328.

Another Italian, Friar Odoric of Pordenone, whose travels have been reprinted many times, set out for Pekin in 1316, returned to Europe at the beginning of 1330, and died in 1331. His book is comparatively small in compass, but is full of interesting details, and it is remarkable that he mentions many customs among the Chinese which are not referred to by Marco Polo, such as the binding of women's feet, allowing the finger-nails to grow long, and fishing with cormorants.

Marco Polo's journey to the Mongol court was due almost to an accident. His father and uncle, who were Venetian merchants, had already in 1260 found their way to the court of Kubilai Khan only because the disturbed state of the Near East made it impossible for them to follow their usual route home from the Crimea. Kubilai received them well, and entreated them to go back to Italy and to return to him bringing a hundred Christian priests—for the Mongols were always willing to give Christianity a hearing. After many delays they set out on their second journey in 1271 accompanied by the youthful Marco Polo, but by only two priests, whose courage failed them when they had travelled but a short distance.

The Polos started from Acre in November 1271, and it is possible that while there they may have met Edward I of England and Rustichello, who were both in Acre at that time. I shall refer later to Rustichello. The Polos proceeded to Hormuz at the mouth of the Persian Gulf, with a view to going to China by sea, but they abandoned this plan for various reasons, and continued their journey across Persia in a north-easterly direction. Their route from Acre to Hormuz lay through Kaisariya, Sivas, Erzinjan, Erzerum, north of Lake Van, Tabriz, Sava, Kashan, Yezd, and Kerman.

I mention these details because Yule and others held the view that the Polos passed through Mosul and Baghdad [*The Book of Ser Marco Polo,* edited by Sir Henry Yule, and revised by Henri Cordier, 3 vols., third edition, London, 1926]. Mr. Penzer has, I think, given good reasons for doubting this, and I myself find it hard to believe that Marco could have given such meagre accounts of these two cities had he himself seen them [*The Most Noble and Famous Travels of Marco Polo,* edited by N. M. Penzer, 1929]. Mosul especially must have called forth his admiration, for this city, which lies along the right bank of the Tigris, is one of the most lovely in the East. The waters of this river are here of Mediterranean blue, and the view of the city from the bridge is a sight never to be forgotten. No traveller, of course, in those days could have guessed that the mounds which lie on the opposite bank cover the once great city of Nineveh. Baghdad at the end of the thirteenth century was probably not looking its best, and the Tigris, which flows through it, is here the colour of mud. The city itself had in 1258 been almost destroyed, but not entirely, by Hulagu, who wished to retain it for himself and had even restored some of the Abbasid buildings.

From Hormuz the Polos proceeded by way of Sava, Kashan, Yezd, Kerman, Tabas, Tun, Kain, Herat, Balkh, across the Pamirs to Kashghar, thence via Yarkand, Khotan, Lop Nor and Tun-huang (Shachau) to Kaipingfu, the summer residence of the Great Khan.

The elder Polos no doubt returned to China because they had promised to do so, though their failure to secure the hundred priests might reasonably have exempted them from their promise. They could scarcely have foreseen that on their return the Great Khan would wish to keep them in his kingdom indefinitely. They actually remained in China seventeen years. We do not know whether during this time the two elder Polos had any fixed occupation, but it is certain that Marco was in the service of Kubilai and that he at any rate entertained very little hope of ever returning to Europe.

The accident which eventually enabled them to leave China was the request on the part of Arghun, the Mongol Il-Khan of Persia, for a Chinese bride. The Tartar envoys who had come on this mission refused to return overland on account of the disturbed state of Central Asia, and, having decided to return by sea, they begged Kubilai to allow the three Polos, as belonging to a maritime race, to accompany them. Their return journey by sea lay through the Straits of Singapore and Malacca; skirting the Nicobars they touched southern Ceylon, Cape Comorin, the western coast of India, Mekran, and finally Hormuz. The voyage took over two years, and over six hundred of the company perished on the way, but fortunately not their precious charge. When they finally arrived in Persia in 1294 they learned that Arghun had died three years previously, and so they married the Chinese princess to his son Ghazan. Instead of returning to China, as they had no doubt assured Kubilai they would, the Polos now found their way back to Italy via Trebizond and the Black Sea.

It was in the year 1295 that the Polos returned to Venice. We next hear of Marco in 1298 as a prisoner in Genoa, from which it may be presumed that he took part in the Battle of Curzola, which was fought on 7 September of that year, and that he was among the prisoners who arrived in Genoa on 16 October.

According to Ramusio [*Navigationi et Viaggi,* 1559] it was mainly in order to save himself the trouble of continually repeating his adventures to his fellow prisoners and the local gentry of Genoa that Marco Polo first thought of making a book. It seems certain that the original version which he drew up in Genoa was considerably longer and fuller in detail than any single version that has hitherto been discovered.

Now, with regard to the compilation of Marco's Book, it is quite obvious that no man could possess a memory sufficiently strong to enable him to recall so many strange names and facts extending over a period of twenty-four years. It is perfectly clear from many passages in his Book that he was in the habit of keeping notes: he tells us, for example, that he was sent on various missions by Kubilai Khan and that on his return he furnished reports which delighted the Emperor, and it is more than likely that he preserved copies of these reports. We cannot, of course, say whether he also kept notes on matters which would be of interest to European readers, who in those days knew nothing at all about China. In the first *proemio* of Ramusio's edition, to which I shall refer again later, we read that had Marco Polo imagined that he would ever be permitted to leave China he would have kept a far more elaborate journal; and seeing that it was a mere accident that eventually gave the Polos an opportunity of leaving the country, in the circumstances one wonders why he kept one at all. But we can well imagine Marco passing some of the long voyage to Persia in writing a journal.

The contents of the Book may be divided into four more or less distinct categories.

First of all there is the account of the first journey made by Marco's father and uncle to Kubilai's summer residence in Mongolia and their return to Venice. This narrative he of course received from his father and uncle. Not all of their narrative was included in this part of Marco's Book, for he probably derived from the same source his account of Russia and of those parts of Central Asia which were visited by the Polos on their first journey but not on the second.

Secondly, we have a geographical description of as much as Marco knew of the world lying between the Black Sea, the China Sea, and the Indian Ocean. Thanks to the researches of scholars we have to-day a fairly clear notion of the routes Marco actually followed, and of the places he described from hearsay but could not himself have visited. There can, I think, be little doubt that none of the Polos ever set foot in Mosul, Baghdad, Aden, or Abyssinia. It must be remembered that Marco's object was to describe the wonders of the then unknown world, and not to lay claim to have been everywhere himself. The title of the earliest French version of his Book is Le Divisament dou Monde. It has been well observed by Benedetto that 'Marco Polo wished to give to Europe a comprehensive picture of the Asiatic world; to make the occidentals realize that beyond the steppes and the mountainous regions a wonderful and intense life was palpitating, where they had hitherto imagined only solitude and monsters. . . . This book is a synthesis, an inventory of the wealth of the Orient.'

Thirdly, we find scattered throughout the work Marco Polo's personal adventures and his relations with the Mongol Emperor.

Fourthly, there are the historical narratives connected with the rise and growth of the Mongol Empire. These details must obviously have been based on notes taken on the spot by Marco either from books or from his learned Chinese friends.

Let us now return to the prison in Genoa, where Marco is said to have drawn up his Book with the help of others. It naturally suggests itself that the citizens of Venice must have been quite as anxious as those of Genoa to hear everything that Marco had to say, but no mention is made of his attempting to do for the Venetians what he did for the Genoese. Marco arrived in Genoa with the rest of the prisoners on 16 October 1298, and yet we are expected to believe that in the short interval between that date and his release from prison in July 1299 he had composed the whole of his Book. Unfortunately we do not know how soon after his return to Venice Marco Polo put to sea, or what he was doing between his return to Venice in 1295 and his setting out in a galley to fight the Genoese. I suggest that during those three years he spent much time in telling his adventures and in reviewing and adding to his notes. By 1298 he possibly had already the plan of a book in his mind.

Now according to the opening chapter of the oldest French version (the Geographic Text) he employed a writer of Arthurian romances named Rustichello of Pisa, his fellow prisoner, to remodel (*retraire*) his narrative, and according to Ramusio, for this purpose he sent to Venice for the notes and memoranda which he had brought with him from the East. If it is permissible to suppose that Marco Polo, before setting out to fight the Genoese, had made a more or less complete draft of his Book in his own Venetian dialect, the notes he is said to have received from Venice may have included not only the materials he had brought from China but this draft of his narrative, which Rustichello presumably proceeded to translate into his own peculiar French, without making changes in its structure.

In talking to those of his fellow prisoners who were not Venetians or to the local Genoese who visited him in prison Marco may have found difficulty in making himself understood, and Yule suggested that Marco the Venetian and Rustichello the Pisan communicated with each other in a kind of pidgin French, just as two Chinese from different provinces talk in pidgin English. Rustichello's written French is poor stuff, but it is certainly more like French than the jargon in which Marco Polo recounted his adventures. At that period Latin was the literary language *par excellence,* and the only vulgar dialect which had attained any literary dignity in Europe was French. An Italian *volgare* was on the point of being established by Dante, but Brunetto Latini, his master, spoke of French as *la parleure la plus delitable,* and wrote his *Tesoro* in that language.

Marco Polo had spent twenty-four years in the East, for the most part in China. Ramusio believed that on his return to Venice Marco had lost the habit of his own vernacular, and had become as much a foreigner in speech as he and his father and uncle had become in appearance and dress. Had he been a solitary wanderer during all those years it is conceivable that he should have forgotten his mother tongue, but it seems unlikely that these three strangers in a strange land should have conversed with each other in any language but their own Venetian. Had Marco Polo written his Book without external help he would no doubt have written in the Venetian dialect.

It has not, I think, ever been suggested that there may have come out of the prison in Genoa more than one original of Marco Polo's Book. Why should not others have done what Rustichello did? If he changed Marco Polo's notes into Franco-Italian some other fellow prisoner might have reproduced them in Latin or some Italian *volgare.*

Let us then picture Marco Polo with his Venetian rough draft before him, surrounded by fellow prisoners and visitors, who, anxious to take down as much as they understood of his story, each wrote in the language that suited him best. Such a situation would surely account for the similarities and discrepancies of the various versions. There are, however, strong arguments against such a theory, the most notable of which is the outstanding authority of the Geographic Text. Moreover, the discrepancies in the text of various early manuscripts are easily accounted for by the carelessness of scribes.

The same thing happened in the case of the Report of Odoric of Pordenone, and Yule suggested 'that the practice in multiplying copies of such works was not to attempt verbal transcription, but merely to read over a clause, and then write down its gist in such language as came uppermost. Yet why (he adds) should a practice have applied to these narratives different from that which applied to the multiplication of the classics?'

Supposing Marco Polo's rough draft in Venetian Italian were already completed, the work which remained for Rustichello was to change Marco's language into his own romantic French much flavoured with Italian. On his own account he can only have added, as Benedetto says, 'formule di transizione, battute di dialogo, moduli descrittivi di battaglie, facilmente riconoscibili alla loro fissità convenzionale. La sua inerzia creativa di fronte alla stesura di Marco si rivela chiaramente là dove l'opera è rimasta un semplice abbozzo.' This last sentence, which I take to mean that Rustichello employed little creative energy when dealing with Marco's model, seems to bear out the theory that Marco had prepared a text of his own. We may therefore suppose either that Marco dictated his Book, or that he handed to Rustichello his own complete rough draft in the Venetian dialect. Everything seems to point to the latter alternative. We must always bear in mind that Marco was writing a description of Asia and not merely a book of travels.

Ramusio tells us that within a few months of the appearance of the original (which he believed to have been in Latin) 'all Italy was full of copies and translations into "our vernacular", so greatly was this history desired and longed for by all'. This was no doubt the case, but it is strange that within so incredibly short a space of time the original and any complete copies that might have been made of it had been supplanted by translated, distorted, and abridged versions. Surely it would be easier to account for the discrepancies among the manuscripts, the rareness of Rustichello's version, Ramusio's belief that the original was in Latin, and such-like matters, were it possible to suppose that several different versions came out of the prison in Genoa.

The famous manuscript of Rustichello's version, known as the Geographic Text, which is itself by no means complete, exists to-day only in one copy in Paris and in one fragment in the British Museum which, however, differs very much from the Paris MS.

The most popular version during the fourteenth and fifteenth centuries was Pipino's Latin translation made *c.* 1320 from an Italian version. Pipino, in another of his works, tells us that his translation was made from the Lombard dialect. Actually his version corresponds to a well-known Venetian recension. Pipino himself says that he made his translation for the Reverend Fathers of his Order 'since it pleases my masters to read it in Latin rather than in the vernacular'. Ramusio states that Pipino was unable to find a copy of the Latin version, but Pipino nowhere says so himself; and indeed speaks of the Italian version which he translated in such a manner as to have led some to suppose that it was Marco Polo's original. Pipino does not mention Rustichello, but some Venetian versions do so; so also does the Spanish, which is derived from Pipino's Latin.

Marco Polo died in 1323, and at the time of his death there must have existed many different recensions in Latin, French, and the Italian vernaculars. There seems, however, to be no evidence that Marco showed any interest in the fate of his Book, and yet one cannot help believing that he himself possessed a copy of the complete text, whether that of Rustichello or some other. The 'de Cepoy' legend (contained in some Grégoire MSS.) which says that Marco in 1307 gave a copy of his book to a French envoy in Venice does not bear close inspection.

Benedetto published his monumental work on Marco Polo in 1928. In its preparation he discovered in the libraries of Europe eighty hitherto unknown manuscripts, and thanks to his untiring labours those now known to us number no less than one hundred and thirty-eight. Almost all may be grouped in one or other of two main categories, namely, those resembling Rustichello's text, and those related to certain Italian versions utilized by Ramusio, including of course Pipino's Latin translation. But according to Benedetto they all descend from a prototype which was already far removed from the original.

Ramusio prefixed to the Book two *proemios* or forewords. . . . The first opens with the well-known address to the 'lords, princes, dukes, marquises, barons', with which so many texts begin. The second is a statement prefixed by Fra Pipino to his Latin translation, which is somewhat freely translated into Italian by Ramusio. In his preface, which is addressed to his friend Hieronimo Fracastoro and is dated 7 July 1553, Ramusio says:

> And having found two *proemios* at the beginning of this book, which were originally composed in Latin, one of them written by that gentleman of Genoa, a great friend of the said Messer Marco, who helped him to write and compose in Latin the voyage while he was in prison; the other by a preaching friar Pipino of Bologna, who, not being able to lay his hands on a copy of the Latin version (for nowadays this 'voyage' is only read in the vernacular), turned it into Latin in 1320—I do not wish to fail to reproduce both for the greater satisfaction and contentment of my readers, so that they together may serve as a more complete preface to the said book.

Ramusio based his Italian edition (which was published in 1559, two years after his death) mainly on Pipino's Latin text, although he knew it to be only a translation. Ramusio states that he also made much use of another Latin version contained in a manuscript of 'marvellous antiquity' lent him by his friend Ghisi, which he obviously at one time believed to represent Marco Polo's original. [In a footnote, the author adds: "The passage in which this statement occurs was, however, omitted from all subsequent editions of Ramusio. It is hard to account for the omission of this striking passage; it is possible that Ghisi himself requested the printer (Giunti) to delete it from the second edition."]

This Ghisi manuscript which was consulted by Ramusio has never been traced, but it was no doubt closely related to a Latin version of which an eighteenth-century transcript of a manuscript once belonging to Cardinal Zelada was found in Milan by Professor Benedetto, and is now known as Z. This version was indeed known to Baldelli Boni, but Benedetto was the first to recognize its importance, although it is very much abridged in the earlier chapters. It obviously derives from a Franco-Italian version superior to the Geographic Text; on the other hand it contains no less than two hundred passages not met with there. Of these, three-fifths are also to be found in Ramusio, showing that Ramusio had before him a very similar transcript.

Z, although more complete than any other known text of the second half of the Book, is very much curtailed in the first part. On this account it is unlikely that it was identical with the Ghisi manuscript, for Ramusio could hardly have regarded a version so incomplete at the beginning as Marco Polo's original. It is important to know that the abridgements in the early part of Z are referred to specifically by the translator or transcriber as being intentional. If we place side by side corresponding passages in the Geographic Text of Rustichello and Z, the latter certainly gives the impression of being a translation from the former.

My object in these pages has been to give the adventures of Marco Polo's Book rather than those of Marco himself. Nothing new is likely to be discovered about the man, but so strange is the history of the Book that any day a new document may be forthcoming to dissipate the cloud of mystery that has always surrounded it. With regard to the problems connected with Marco Polo's journey, fresh light is constantly being thrown on these matters by scholars and travellers, and it may be safely asserted that every new discovery goes to emphasize and confirm the amazing reliability of Marco Polo's narrative.

In unravelling the great mystery attaching to Marco's Book it is important to dispose of all possible theories, in order that the ground may be clear for discussion on the basis of firmly established data. I myself have considered carefully three such theories, none of which have, so far as I am aware, been suggested before, namely:

1. Whether Marco Polo had prepared a complete draft of his own Book.
2. How closely the Ghisi manuscript was related to Z.
3. Whether more than one version of Marco Polo's notes issued from the prison in Genoa.

In spite of all the devoted labours of scholars like Yule and Benedetto no final solution of the problem has yet been attained, and it is this circumstance which has emboldened me to put forward the foregoing suggestions.

RAMUSIO

I feel that in connexion with Ramusio's famous version of Marco Polo an opportunity is offered me of giving a brief notice of this great Italian scholar, whose name is perhaps not so well known in this country as it deserves.

Giambattista Ramusio was born in Treviso in 1485, educated in Venice and Padua, and died in 1557. He spent forty-three years in the service of the State of Venice as Secretary to the Council of Ten or to various ambassadors. During his travels he took the opportunity of learning French and Spanish.

In 1523 he began to collect materials for his great book of Navigations and Voyages, of which three volumes eventually appeared, although four had been contemplated. The whole work contains seventy-seven voyages. During the sixteenth century four new editions appeared, and two more at the beginning of the seventeenth, but the work has never been reprinted since 1613.

Richard Hakluyt published his *Principal Navigations* in 1589, thirty years after the appearance of Ramusio's second volume. Hakluyt's volumes were mainly concerned with English travellers. Samuel Purchas, who continued Hakluyt's work, included many of Ramusio's travellers in his *Hakluyt Posthumus,* which was published in four volumes in 1625-6. Both collections have often been reprinted, and in 1846 the famous Hakluyt Society was founded. Ramusio has not fared so well in his native country, but I understand that there is a project on foot to issue an entirely new edition of his collections in Italy.

Ramusio prefixed introductions to all his travellers, and these, though not always accurate, are of great interest. In his introduction to Marco Polo he tells us many curious things, which bear witness to his wide reading. For example, with regard to the first part of Marco's Book, dealing with the voyage made by Marco's father and uncle to the court of the Khan of the Tartars and later to that of the Great Khan, he says: 'I would never have understood that voyage if good fortune had not recently placed in my hands a part of a Latin translation of an Arabic work composed over two hundred years ago by a great Prince of Syria called Abilfada Ismael.' This note is of considerable interest, as giving an indication of the earliest translation into Latin of a work of which no translation appeared in print until 1650.

The devotion which Ramusio inspired in his publisher Tommaso Giunti is attested by two beautiful tributes to Ramusio written by Giunti. One of these appeared in the first edition of vol. ii, and the other in subsequent editions. . . .

J. Homer Herriott (essay date 1937)

SOURCE: "The 'Lost' Toledo Manuscript of Marco Polo," in *Speculum,* Vol. XII, No. 4, October, 1937, pp. 458-63.

[*In the following essay, Herriott discusses the superiority of a fifteenth-century Polian manuscript believed to have been lost.*]

In 1559 the first attempt at a critical edition of Marco Polo appeared in Venice in a volume entitled Secondo volume delle Navigationi et Viaggi nel quale si contengono l'Historia delle cose de Tartari, et diuersi fatti de loro Imperatori, descritta da M. Marco Polo Gentilhuomo Venetiano, et da Haiton Armeno. The first volume of this collection of travels had been published in 1550, and the third volume in 1556. The editor of the series, Giouan Battista Ramusio, delayed publication of the second volume, since he was in search of additional materials to be incorporated in the work. Death overtook him in 1557, and, owing to a fire in the Giuntine presses, the volume was not issued until two years later.

In a long letter in the Introduction, dated July 17, 1553, Ramusio, dedicating the volume to Hieronimo Fracastoro, points out the importance of his edition of Marco Polo. He states that for many years, owing to numerous scribal errors, the work had been deemed a fairy tale, but that travelers in the East, especially the Portuguese, during the preceding hundred years had been discovering provinces, cities, and islands bearing the same names that Marco had attributed to them. [In a footnote, the author comments: "Ramusio exaggerates. It was of course due to the marvellous and unusual elements in Marco's narrative that little credence was given to his veracity."] He, for his part, wishes to purge the text of its many errors, and to offer to the public a critical edition based on several manuscripts.

In the opinion of Ramusio, some of the manuscripts which he utilized were copied in the first half of the fourteenth century. In a passage in which he deplores the unfaithfulness of the texts of contemporary editions of Marco Polo he goes so far as to declare that these manuscripts, more than two hundred years old, are 'perfettamente corretto' (*sic*). Then, on the next folio, when he cites the port of Soldadia mentioned by Marco in his Prologue, he says that several very old manuscripts, written more than a hundred and fifty years previously, had fallen into his hands.

For the third time he refers to his sources in a passage which offers us more details. He believes that Marco first wrote his work in Latin and that it was soon translated into Italian. However, copies of the former had not all been lost. A friend of his of the Ghisi family possessed a copy 'di marauigilosa antichità,' perhaps made directly from the original manuscript of Marco Polo. This friend permitted him to use the interesting old manuscript in the preparation of his edition.

Among the manuscripts that Ramusio utilized he found two prologues to Marco Polo. One of these was written by Marco and his friend in the prison at Genoa; the other one belonged to the Latin redaction of Pipino. Ramusio stated that the latter, unable to find a copy of the Latin original, had translated the Italian recension into Latin in 1320. Unwilling to omit either prologue, Ramusio places them both at the beginning of his critical edition.

Many editors of Marco Polo in the following centuries were convinced of the superiority of Ramusio's text.

From an illumination in the fourteenth-century Oxford manuscript of the Book of Ser Marco Polo; *the Polos are pictured presenting letters from Pope Gregory X and holy oil from Jerusalem.*

Hardly fifty years had passed when Samuel Purchase, rejecting the Latin manuscript which was bequeathed to him among the papers of Hakluyt, turned to the more copious and lucid text of Ramusio. He explained his reasons for doing so in his usual euphuistic style studded with puns and plays upon words:

> I found this Booke translated by Master Hakluyt out of the Latine. But where the blind leade the blind both fall: as here the corrupt *Latine* could not but yeeld a corruption of truth in *English,* Ramusio, Secretarie to the *Decemviri* in *Venice,* found a better Copie and published the same, whence you have the works in manner new: so renewed, that I have found the Proverbe true, that it is better to pull downe an old house and to build it anew, then to repaire it; as I also should have done, had I knowne that which in the event I found. The *Latine* is Latten, compared to Ramusio's Gold. And hee which hath the *Latine* hath but *Marco Polo's* carkasse or not so much, but a few bones, yea, sometimes stones rather then bones; things divers, averse, adverse, perverted in manner, disjoynted in manner, beyond beliefe. I have seene some Authors maymed, but never any so mangled and so mingled, so present and so absent, as this vulgar *Latine* of *Marco Polo;* not so like himselfe, as the Three *Polo's* were at their returne to Venice, where none knew them. . . . Much are wee beholden to *Ramusio,* for restoring this *Pole,* and Loadstarre of *Asia,* out of that mirie poole or puddle in which he lay drouned. [Samuel Purchase, *His Pilgrimes,* 1625].

In 1871 Sir Henry Yule brought out the first edition of his monumental work The Book of Ser Marco Polo. For his translation he chose two texts, Paris *Bib. Nat.* MS. *fr. 1116,* published by the Geographic Society of Paris in 1824, and the Pauthier redaction. He either interpolates within brackets in his text additions of Ramusio, or he gathers them together and forms a chapter apart. He expresses his confidence in Ramusio in the following words: 'The picture in Ramusio, taken as a whole, is so much more brilliant, interesting, and complete than in the older texts, that I thought of substituting it entirely for the other.'

He then points out circumstances peculiar to Ramusio's text which have been proved authentic in the nineteenth century and which must be ascribed to Marco. Among these are the prevalence of goitre at at Yarkand; the crossing of the yak with the common cow; the preying of wolves on the wild sheep on the Pamir plateau where piles of wild rams' horns are used as landmarks in the snow; the subterranean irrigation channels in Persia; the art of refining sugar in China introduced from Egypt; the water-tight compartments in the hulls of junks; the uprising of the Cathayans against Kublai's Mohammedan minister Ahmad; the vermilion seal of the Great Khan on paper currency. However, Yule is searching for the text nearest the original and he hesitates to include that of Ramusio, the language of which is too literary for Marco.

In 1928, under the patronage of the city of Venice, appeared the magnificent volume Marco Polo, Il Milione, edited by Professor L. F. Benedetto of the University of Florence. Benedetto realized that the root of the Polian problems in so far as the text is concerned lay in the troublesome passages of Ramusio. Therefore he searched throughout Europe, and succeeded in bringing to light sixty unknown manuscripts to be added to the list of some eighty recorded by Yule. He then examined Ramusio's text, collating it with all the newly discovered manuscripts. Many of the puzzling passages in Ramusio were found to have their counterpart in a Latin manuscript, unfortunately an eighteenth-century copy of a mediaeval Toledo manuscript. The copy was made in 1795 by order of Giuseppe Toaldo who was a collector of Polian manuscripts. At present it is in Milan, *Biblioteca Ambrosiana* MS. *Y P S,* paper, 32X22, and contains 211 folios.

In a note at the beginning of the copy, Toaldo expresses his appreciation of the kindness of Cardinal Zelada in lending him the Toledo codex, and he cites the names of the papal legates who brought it to Italy. He also explains that the Latin of the original was very corrupt and that the transcription was made with great difficulty due to the obscurity of the text.

Benedetto, carefully analyzing the methods employed by Ramusio in editing his work, is convinced that the Toaldo copy is a descendent of the manuscript 'da marauigliosa antichità' belonging to the Cà Ghisi. Not only does he find in the new manuscript the counterpart for almost all of the perplexing passages of Ramusio but also many additional passages not found elsewhere. Sir E. Denison Ross, editor of the English translation of Benedetto's text states that until the Toledo manuscript is forthcoming 'the Milan copy must be received with a certain amount of caution.'

The Toledo manuscript was described briefly in 1827 by Count Baldelli Boni, and for more than a century no further information concerning it has come to light. It is not listed among the manuscripts of the Biblioteca Capitolare of Toledo cited by D. José Octavio de Toledo in his incomplete catalogue of the manuscripts and books belonging to the Cathedral. Benedetto in his search for Polian manuscripts was unable to glean any information concerning its whereabouts.

However, the 'lost' manuscript is still there, now properly shelved *N°8°-49-20.* It is written on paper, octavo, and contains 135 folios varying in length from 24 to 30 lines. It dates from about the middle of the fifteenth century. The title page is found on fol. 1^r and was written at a period much later than the text, probably in the eighteenth century. It contains the following title: 'Marcus Paulus Venetus de diuersis hominum generibus et diuersitatibus Regionum Mundanarum. Vbi inuenies omnia magna, Mirabilia et diuersitates Armenie Maioris, Persarum, Tartarorum, et Indie, ac aliarum Prouinciarum circa Asiam, Mediam, et partem Europe. Compilat. in Carceribus Janue Anno MCCXCVIII' (cf. Plate I). Fol. 1^v is blank but in the margin at the top of fol. 2^r is the incipit also written in a later hand: 'Incipit liber domini Marci Pauli Veneti' (cf. Plate II).

Below these words the text proper begins: 'Domini imperatores reges duces marchiones comites milites et burgenses et omnes gentes qui vultis agnoscere diuersa hominum genera et diuersarum regionum mundanas diuersitates accipite hunc librum.' The text ends in the middle of fol. 135ʳ: 'Et cum inceperamus de mari maiori nos penituit ponere in scriptis quare multi sciunt et ideo descedemus ab ipso etc. Finis. Explicit liber domini Marci Pauli.'

Although the copyists who transcribed the Toledo manuscript were little versed in paleography, the Toaldo manuscript is a fairly good reproduction. Benedetto found it necessary to make emendations in numerous passages where the scribes clearly showed unfamiliarity with certain symbols; at times he leaves passages unsolved. The Toledo manuscript clears up doubtful passages, and offers a correct reading for those which are incomprehensible. Benedetto, utilizing his basic text *fr. 1116* and Ramusio, is usually right in his emendations. When the scribes have completely ignored the symbols he expands 'suba' to 'substantia,' 'altius' to 'alterius,' etc. At times the scribes have resolved incorrectly the symbols, and he corrects 'magron' to 'magistro,' 'de extranea' to 'dextraria,' etc. Among the passages that Benedetto does not understand is one on fol. 29ʳ: 'quedam bestia parva que magnitudinis est gaxelle in unius campe.' The Toledo manuscript has on fol. 18ʳ 'id est unius capre' instead of 'in unius campe,' and the meaning becomes clear.

The Toledo manuscript has some three hundred marginal notes which illustrate the special interests of the scribe. More than half of the notes refer to religions or religious subjects. Several notes indicate that he was interested in studies and learning:

> fol. 5ʳ: 'studia ipsorum sunt in lege Macometi in negromantia phisica astronomia geumentia et phisonomia'
> fol. 16ᵛ: 'gentes sapientissime sunt et student in artibus lib[er] alibus'
> fol. 42ʳ: 'hic sunt magni philosophi et medici.'

Especially is he interested in medicine:

> fol. 30ʳ: 'stercus etiam humanum est utile et operatur contra venenum quod facit stercus caninum'
> fol. 63ᵛ: 'vinum hoc liberat tropicos et tysicos.'

Unusual customs, strange facts, and marvellous accounts of men and beasts call for numerous notes:

> fol. 4ʳ: 'aqua quedam est que solummodo in quadragessima producit pisces'
> fol. 42ᵛ: 'quedam ciuitas girat miliaria centum habet duodecim milia pontium pro maiori parte de lapidibus'
> fol. 62ʳ: 'non potest stella tramontana videri'
> fol. 63ʳ: 'isti faciunt simios apparere homines'
> fol. 64ᵛ: 'homines habentes caudam'
> fol. 81ᵛ: 'habent aliquos religiosos qui viuunt CL annos et CC.'

Finally the scribe is not without wordly interests. Descriptions of palaces covered with gold, rich merchandise, precious stones and woods, and oil wells stir his imagination and merit a note on the margin:

> fol. 3ᵛ: 'nota quod nascitur hic oleum ex quodam fonte'
> fol. 55ᵛ: 'coperiunt palatia de auro . . . perule rubee . . . quum sepelitur homo ponitur in ore vnam perulam'
> fol. 65ᵛ: 'omnes silue de arboribus magni ualoris'
> fol. 66ʳ: 'nascuntur garofalli et nuces Indie'
> fol. 67ʳ: 'hic nascuntur rubini, zafini, topatii, amantiste, granate . . . rubinus mirabilis'
> fol. 124ʳ: 'hic inueniuntur peles magni valoris.'

The eighteenth-century scribes who copied the Toledo manuscript erroneously interpreted the abbreviated form of *'nota'* as 'uero' or as 'non.' Consequently many of the marginal notes are incomprehensible. Benedetto, at a loss to understand their meaning, does not touch upon them.

Aside from the fact that Toaldo states that he borrowed the Toledo manuscript from Cardinal Zelada, there is ample internal evidence to prove that our manuscript was the original. And, although the Toaldo manuscript is a rather good copy, especially as emended by Benedetto with the help of other manuscripts and editions, there is, I believe, a sufficient number of errors in the transcription to warrant that the Toledo manuscript should hereafter be referred to as *Z* and the Toaldo copy as *Z'*.

Manuscript *Z* of Toledo then contains many passages of Marco Polo not found in any other mediaeval manuscript. Some of these passages were translated by Ramusio who had at hand a more complete manuscript of the same family, *Z'*, probably the Ghisi manuscript 'di marauigliosa antichità.' There is to our knowledge only one copy of *Z*, which was made by Toaldo in 1795. The latter manuscript was discovered by Professor Benedetto in 1927, but owing to its late date, has been looked upon with a certain amount of caution. *Z* in addition to solving the obscure and incomprehensible passages of *Z'* places a stamp of authority on most of the newly unearthed passages as edited by Benedetto. It brings us one step nearer to the original text and must be utilized by future editors of Marco Polo.

Eileen Power (essay date 1938)

SOURCE: "The Immortal Marco," in *The New Statesman & Nation,* Vol. XVI, No. 400, October 22, 1938, pp. 606-07.

[In the following essay, Power discusses Polo's popular and literary reputation, arguing that his work is "a masterpiece of reporting."]

I once knew a master at a famous public school (which shall be nameless) who was under the impression that

Marco Polo was a kind of game. I did not question his qualifications for imparting culture to the young, for he had in his day been a noted blue and, as the saying goes, first things come first. But I have been reminded of him by the almost simultaneous appearance of the first two volumes of a magnificent edition of Marco Polo edited by Professors Moule and Pelliot . . . , and of the travesty of the great traveller's "adventures" released by Hollywood. It seems an appropriate occasion on which to speculate upon the reason why of all medieval travellers (and the adjective might almost be omitted without detracting from the truth of the statement) Marco Polo enjoys the most widespread fame and is, indeed, a household word to may who would be hard put to it to describe what he did and when and why he did it.

The reasons for his popular reputation are less obvious than might be imagined. It would probably be true to say that of all the great travellers of history Marco Polo is the one who has put least of his personality into his book. As an individual he emerges far less clearly than the fat friar William of Rubruck, who preceded him across Central Asia, or than the inimitable Ibn Battutah, who travelled in the East a little later. Their vivid autobiographical touch is entirely missing from his impersonal pages, for (in spite of Hollywood) "the adventures of Marco Polo" are precisely what he did not write. It is not always remembered that the account of the Polos' journey appears as a mere preface to a long book, occupying no more than nineteen out of the 232 pages of Mr. Moule's new translation, and very rarely does a word of their history appear in the rest of the work. As Mr. Moule says, he succeeded only too well in his resolve not to describe their journeys after that first summary statement. Even his description of routes and means of locomotion is completely impersonal; he does not say whether he went on horseback, by carriage or by canal barge. "In Cathay and the South-West," Professor Moule points out, "One sometimes rides; but from Giogiu to Zaitun one always and only goes."

Such a *tabula rasa* has allowed modern invention to make what it will of Marco the man and the popular picture shifts between the lineaments of a superior commercial traveller and those of a hero of romance. There is more foundation for the former than for the latter; a merchant he was and, faced with all the marvels of the East, a merchant he remained. Consider the material objects which he chose to bring back with him after seventeen years spent in the most advanced civilisation in the world; a specimen of yak's hair, the dried head and feet of a musk deer and the seeds of a dye plant (samples which might interest some enterprising firm on the Rialto); a few presents from Margate in the shape of a three-bladed sword, a Tartar collar and the like; and for the rest jewels, portable wealth in its most universal and conventional form and the normal stock-in-trade of Messrs. Polo Brothers. Here is a man who could have filled his pockets with movable type and forestalled the printing press by nearly two hundred years, but he fills them with diamonds and rubies instead. No painted scrolls are lovingly unpacked in the Cà Polo, no paper money, not even a pound of tea; only things which everyone knows already and which can readily be exchanged for cash by experienced jewel merchants. It is the baggage of a business-man; and it may be added that all the additions to our knowledge of Marco Polo's character which the late Professor Orlandini's researches among legal documents have brought to light, go only to strengthen the impression of a hard-headed and somewhat grasping fellow, who quickly contrived, upon his return, to concentrate most of the family fortune in his own hands, pursued his nephews with the full rigour of the law for debt, and left nothing to his kinsmen in his will. The greatest of travellers is an object lesson for all who think that civilisations have only to be in contact to learn from each other, irrespective of the nature of the contact. Barons and military gentlemen fighting crusades in Palestine no doubt bring back some silk and a bottle of scent for their wives and Damascus steel for themselves and (if very intelligent) put up a windmill the better to grind their corn and their peasantry. But they do not install bathrooms in the castle and, as to the learning of the Arabs, it is not until professional scholars from Europe take to attending lectures in Toledo that the Greek inheritance once more finds its way to the West. Culture flows through human filters and some filters let through one thing, some another. As with the Near so with the Far East, during the brief period in which the West established direct contact with it. The merchants and missionaries who went there in the thirteenth century transmitted only what they were qualified to transmit.

Here, then, is a merchant whose personality, so far as it can be judged at all, is not particularly attractive, who is obviously without imagination and sometimes dull and who, even if he does not deserve the harsh judgment that "he looked at everything and saw nothing," at all events left out a great deal that we should dearly like to know. His reputation in his own day is easy enough to understand, but why, with so many hundreds of more exciting travel books between then and now, does the fame of Marco Polo still stand four square? Because when all is said and done, he deserves it. To begin with he deserves it for the sheer drama of his own adventure, which, bare of all personality and of almost all detail, and compressed into a brief preface, is nevertheless such a good story that it explodes like a firework in the mind of any reader. Three men from the West making their way to the vast and hidden empire at the other end of the world, travelling all over the fabulous East, remaining for seventeen years in the service of the Great Khan and then returning as escorts to a princess; this is a perfectly first-class plot. It hooks the imagination, and that the imagination of modern readers is still very ready to be hooked by adventure in the East any publishers' book list will show. Mr. Peter Fleming and Mlle. Maillart have only to make a much less spectacular journey across Central Asia to-day to have all the lending libraries stocking their books. The bare skeleton of Marco Polo's story is worth a dozen other tales with frills on them.

And not only is it a first-class story, but Ser Marco invested his description of the world with all the qualities of his defects. Happily he had no imagination. When the Venetians nicknamed him Marco Million it was rather a mark of their incapacity to believe in the teeming populations and wealth of the East than of his own exaggeration of them. He had travelled more widely than any traveller of his day among peoples who before his time had been entirely unknown to Europe. He was a chief among them taking notes, and it was from his notes (sent from Venice to his prison in Genoa) that he dictated his book. He gives a description of what he himself saw. What he knew from hearsay he repeats as hearsay, and it is notable that all the tall stories are in the passages of hearsay and not in the passages of description. He was the honest commercial traveller. What he had to sell, first to Kublai Khan, then to his contemporaries and finally to posterity was not his imagination, but his observation. He was a man of great intelligence within his limits, and his limits were not narrow. It is no use complaining that he left out all the higher aspects of civilisation, which would not pass through the filter of his practical mind. We have only to compare his book with the marvels of Mandeville to realism what a masterpiece of reporting he has left us. He is a godsend to economic historians, because he sets down just the things that interest them, the aspect of cities, the organisation of communications, the trade of each area and every sea, the life and work and customs of rich and poor. It is the air of sheer everyday reality which Marco Polo contrives to give to his picture of the thirteenth century East which, no less than the stark drama of his personal story, has given him his abiding fame.

Leonardo Olschki (essay date 1943)

SOURCE: "The Literary Precursors," in *Marco Polo's Precursors,* The Johns Hopkins Press, 1943, pp. 1-15.

[*In the following essay, Olschki explores the influence of the poetic history of Alexander the Great on Polo's book.*]

Until about the middle of the thirteenth century, when the first missionaries set out "ad Tartaros," there prevailed in the Western world a profound and persistent ignorance of Central and Eastern Asia, an ignorance partially mitigated by a few vague and generic notions in which remote reminiscences of distant places and peoples were mingled with old poetic and mythical fables. The Tartar invasion of Eastern and Central Europe in 1241 did not alter or even correct the conventional image of Asia popularized by poems and legends. On the contrary, this bloody and destructive clash of the Mongolian and the Christian worlds left the latter just as ignorant of the physical and human aspects of Central and Eastern Asia as these Oriental peoples were of European civilisation. No actual experience of warriors, travellers and traders contributed to the clarification of geographical and ethnological details concerning those regions known only by persistent erudite and literary traditions. At that time even such bookish and superficial knowledge of the interior of Asia was confined to the limits of the world known to the ancients. The territories lying beyond the Caspian Sea, the Oxus, the Indus and the Ganges still appeared as the land of the Seres (the people referred to by Pliny), or as the Biblical kingdoms of the Magi and of Gog and Magog.

Commercial exchange contributed but little towards a practical knowledge of so many lands known only by more or less fantastic names. Recent studies and discoveries have proved, for example, that during the Middle Ages Chinese textiles found their way westwards where the technique of their manufacture and their ornamental designs spread throughout the Moslem and Christian worlds. Merchants journeyed over the same two routes used by the traders of Roman times: either across the China seas, India, the Persian Gulf, and Mesopotamia, or else by the continental routes to Persia through the desert of Gobi and Sinkiang, over the Pamir passes and through Western Turkestan. This commercial intercourse, however, was always indirect and was brought about by intermediaries of diverse origin who spoke many different languages. Hence it would be a mistake to suppose—what has indeed been widely accepted as a fact—that exchange of goods implied also an exchange of culture. In this respect, the only detailed information handed down by the ancient world regarding the far East and its inhabitants is most instructive. It passed unaltered from the books of Pliny and Ammianus Marcellinus into mediaeval texts in the vulgar tongue intended for the laity. These texts represent the geographical conceptions of traders, travellers and sailors or of the public at large much better than the contemporary Latin literature of an erudite character. A typical work of this kind is the famous *Trésor* written in France by the Florentine scholar and diplomat, Brunetto Latini.

In accord with the Latin authors mentioned above, he relates that "beyond the immense solitudes and uninhabited lands of the East . . . beyond all the dwellings of men, are a people called Scir or Seres, who, from leaves and the bark of trees which they subject to the action of water, make for themselves a woolen material with which they clothe their bodies. These people are peaceful and live amicably together among themselves, refusing the company of other peoples." "But our traders," continues the narrative, "pass over one of their rivers, where, on its further shores, they find all manner of merchandise. Without speaking, they examine the merchandise and decide by looking at it the price of each piece. And when they have seen it they take away what they wish, leaving in the place of each article its equivalent value. In this wise the natives sell their wares, neither do they desire little or much of ours."

This narrative is significant as it accounts, in a form more symbolic than actual, for the mystery which shrouded the origin of such precious merchandise, despite centuries of commercial intercourse and some political and religious contacts with the contemporary rulers of Central and Eastern Asia. It shows us through the story of mute exchanges how the acquisition of exotic goods did not at all imply an attainment of geographical knowledge or a broadening of cultural horizons. The Romans of the Imperial epoch imported silk at the price of its weight in gold but they had no exact idea of its origin or method of manufacture. Silk was considered to be a vegetable substance obtained, like linen or hemp, through a process of soaking in water or, as Vergil (*Georgics,* II, 121) and Pliny

(*Hist. Natur.*, VI, 54) affirmed, a species of finest vegetable wool found hanging on trees which the Seres combed and gathered.

In spite of the extensive silk production in the Middle East, in Italy and France, the ancient fables continued to be divulged through didactic treatises of this kind. Similarly, in the time of Marco Polo, the sea-ports and warehouses of Egypt, Syria, the Black and the Caspian Seas were peopled with Italian merchants, many of whom, like the Polo family, had established themselves permanently. But it seems that the extensive commercial activity of these traders was not equalled by a corresponding alertness and fruitful curiosity as to the nature of the countries and peoples who provided them with merchandise.

Certainly not one of them felt the need of relating to his contemporaries what he knew. We may even suppose that in their lively competition, not infrequently conducted by force of arms, the Eastern merchants of all creeds and races were more prone to tell idle stories about the queer peoples whom they had seen than to describe their lands with their customs and produce. It was easy to surround with legends of the marvelous and mysterious the far-fetched origin of the strange goods in which they traded. Such were the pearls, spices and precious stones which were prized, not only for their rarity and price, but also for the secret virtues they were supposed to possess, that is, their therapeutic and magic qualities.

Thus we may believe that the mediaeval traders contributed rather to the tenacious persistence than to the suppression of these fabulous reports. Before Marco Polo, no one ever knew exactly whence these treasures came or how they were obtained. Notwithstanding the data furnished by him, and, nearly forty years later, by the Florentine trade agent Balducci Pegolotti, about the products of distant Asiatic countries, old illusions maintaining the secret of their origin continued to be evoked for a long time. This tendency was corroborated by a literary tradition which preserved unaltered the ideas and notions handed down by the ancients with regard, not only to the unexplored lands of Asia, but also to those regions more accessible to geographical and commercial experience. Merchants and mariners, for the most part illiterate men, shared these notions as they were related in popular treatises on science and history, intended, like the *Trésor* of Brunetto Latini, for the instruction of the people, and for reading aloud in churches and public squares.

These texts represent the stationary period of mediaeval general culture, in which late Hellenistic literary doctrines, inherited from classical antiquity, propagated and fixed in the minds of men their notions of the Far East and of the regions bordering on it. It was mainly through poetry and only accidentally through the authority of erudite tradition, that the general public of that age, as well as the merchants and sailors, became acquainted with the natural and human aspects of Asia. Such people knew nothing of the original geographical and ethnological conceptions of Ptolemy, Strabo, Pliny, Pomponius Mela, Isidor of Seville and other leading authors in these fields. No authentic or reliable information about China, India and the Turkish peoples of Central Asia filtered through to the Western world from the most meager, confused and indirect accounts of Arab geographers and of Jewish travellers. Thus, lasting fantasies of poetical imagination and old legends of obscure origin sought to satisfy the intense curiosity of mediaeval society about the distant countries from which it expected both the most coveted goods and the most destructive invasions. To the Occidentals of the Middle Ages the kingdom of darkness, of fables and of marvels lay beyond the last storehouses of Italian and Greek merchants, and hence to the North in the hinterlands of the Sea of Azov, to the East in Transcaucasia, and in Armenia—that last, heroic and unhappy bulwark of oriental Christianity.

Whatever was known of the Moslem and pagan territories lying beyond the limits of Western geographical experiences was drawn almost exclusively from the fabulous deeds of Alexander the Great, as related in the popular poems of the twelfth century and in the new versions of these that appeared in the thirteenth century and even later. The vogue for such romances was enormous and wide-spread, to such an extent that the popularity of the great Macedonian surpassed that of any other hero or sovereign of antiquity. It was sufficient that the boy Marco Polo raise his eyes to the figure of Alexander the Great, on the north façade of St. Mark's, and see there the hero carried up to heaven by griffins, to recall to his mind the well-known stories of the "Merveilles du Désert," the Fountain of Youth, the prophesies of the Sun-and-Moon trees placed at the limits of the earth; of the marvelous palaces of Persia and India; of Brahmans and Gymnosophists; of the fabulous, strange and monstrous peoples inhabiting the borders of the world; of magic forests and the fantastic beasts which peopled them. His memory would recall all the fascinating legends which Greek biographers of the first centuries of our era had grouped around the figure of Alexander the Great, the conqueror who was the pupil of Aristotle and the victim of his own "desmesure."

Associated with the pagan traditions of the marvels of the East was the Biblical imagery of the fabulous lands of gold; incense and myrrh. These were to be found near the terrestrial Paradise whence flowed rivers, such as the Oxus and the Ganges, and which marked the furthermost eastern limits of geographical knowledge. The name of the Biblical river Geon is referred to in Marco Polo's book as the Oxus of the feats of Alexander. Similarly, the recollection of his adventures serves to identify the topography of those parts of Central Asia visited and described by the Venetian traveller. When he reached the northern frontiers of Persia and was among the Badakshan mountains, the Moslems of these localities repeated to him the self-same tales of the exploits of the Macedonian which, together with the imaginary enchantments of Asia, had inspired the bards of France and Italy. In fact, in journeying from Venice to the extreme limits of Bactriana, Marco Polo found himself still within the limits of the ancient world. Within its boundaries the figure of the Macedonian was, for the Christians of the West and for the Moslems of Asia alike, the outstanding representative and the only universal exponent of ancient expansion and civilisation.

It is unnecessary here to study exhaustively the reason why the figure of Alexander the Great remained throughout vast territories inhabited by heterogeneous peoples the common symbol of human greatness for so long a time and through so many historical vicissitudes. We can only suppose that this singular good fortune depended upon the fact that this imaginary biography, written in Greek by the Pseudo-Callisthenes, between the second and the third centuries of our era, was translated not only into Latin whence it found its way into the popular romances, but also into Armenian, Persian, Syriac and Ethiopic, becoming thus the common possession of all mankind. The person of the Macedonian who was the central historical figure in narratives of varied adventures; the partly real and partly fanciful topographical background of his deeds; the numerous fables set forth in the romance; the tendency to stress his moral character, the quantity of notions which owed their inspiration to him—these were all contributing factors to the universal and lasting diffusion of his name. Furthermore, we should take into consideration the fact that the earlier Greek romance of the Pseudo-Callisthenes abounds in Oriental motifs, which, in a new literary form, were thus restored to the peoples among whom they had originated.

Nevertheless, all this would not be sufficient to explain the vitality which the Alexandrian tradition, literary in origin and character, had in both the Christian and the Islamic worlds. The continuity and persistence of this partly historical and partly fabulous tradition does not depend upon intrinsic circumstances alone, but upon its transfusion into new civilisations which were heirs of the old. Two facts have sealed and confirmed his extraordinary and age-long glory. The first is the enthusiastic mention of Alexander made at the beginning of the first book of Maccabees, as the sovereign who "went through to the ends of the earth, and took spoils of a multitude of nations," thus initiating his Christian myth in that biblical book which most resembles the mediaeval "chansons de geste." Furthermore, the Koran has exalted his glory equally in a sort of transfiguration which remained connected with the wonders and mysteries of the East.

The persistent and universal vitality of this historical figure, twice praised in sacred writings, served to perpetuate a mass of geographical fables which baffles every attempt at rational correction as the result of practical experience. It was impossible to dissociate even the empirical image of Asia, derived from travels and exploration, from the legendary figure of Alexander, sketched by poetic imagination. This, then, is the reason why, despite commercial intercourse, diplomatic relations and direct contacts between the West and the East in peace and in war, everything relating to that continent appeared and persisted in the form of fables, as of a Utopia surrounded by poetic mystery.

The literary image of Asia was so deeply rooted in the mediaeval culture that it determined the character and the structure of Marco Polo's book. Although he had in mind composing a description of Asia on an empirical basis, it is incorrect to interpret this attempt as a result of Marco's scientific intentions. He dictated the Milione not so much for the information of travellers, traders and cosmographers, as mainly for the enjoyment of his contemporaries who eagerly yearned for this kind of pleasant instruction in an epoch of prevailing didactic interests in culture and literature. In fact, the first part of the book contains a sequel of entertaining and edifying stories dealing with the wonders of Bagdad, the legend of the Magi, the Old Man of the Mountain and his artificial Paradise, the *Arbre Sec* and sundry anecdotal details more or less connected with the authentic and the poetic history of Alexander the Great. Thus, later on, the story of the Nestorian Unc Khan is fused with the legend of Prester John and narrated rather as a fairy-tale than as an historical event. The Tartar expedition against Japan is described in the characteristic style of contemporary romances of chivalry, while the entire description of insular and continental India bears the marks of the traditional accounts which transformed those regions into a land of wonders, marvels and teratology.

Thus all the positive and practical information offered by this book on the basis of personal experience and observation appears in a tidy and elaborated frame of tales of wonders of Hellenistic, biblical and Islamic origin. This circumstance determined the prevailing literary character of the book even independently of the collaboration of Rustician, a professional writer. From this point of view, the title sometimes given to the book in mediaeval manuscripts and old editions as a "livres des merveilles du monde" appears quite justified and in accordance with the intention of the author and the interpretation of the public.

In spite of its exceptional character and of the rich and varied details of an objective and reliable kind which it contains, Marco Polo's book is still connected in its essential scheme with the old tradition of Asiatic imagery created and propagated by the poetic history of Alexander the Great. Mandeville's forgery represents a further step and the literary conclusion of this development of a fantastic geography, supported, rather than destroyed, by the results of new discoveries and explorations. The same interrelations between authentic reports and literary motifs which contributed to the success of these standard geographical works of the Middle Ages determined the cosmographical conceptions of Columbus and his interpretation of reality in the New World.

Richard D. Mallery (essay date 1948)

SOURCE: An introduction to *Masterworks of Travel and Exploration: Digests of 13 Great Classics,* edited by Richard D. Mallery, Doubleday & Company, Inc., 1948, pp. 3-12.

[*In the following excerpt, Mallery discusses the appeal of Polo's* The Book of Marco Polo *in the context of the travel narrative genre.*]

Travel narratives, through the ages, reflect the character and predilections of the era in which they are composed. Very often they help to determine the special character of the age. They appeal, of course, primarily to that sense of wonder which is found, to a greater or less extent, in all periods. What we know of the fascination exerted upon young and old by the *Arabian Nights* helps us to recapture the mood in which our forefathers read or heard read The Book of Marco Polo or the *Travels of Sir John Mandeville*. In the long run, travel books have always had an important educational value, but before men could develop a serious study of geography or history, their sense of wonder had to be awakened.

Travel books of the early centuries, like the most popular poetry, were therefore essentially romantic in their fostering of an interest in the remote, the unusual, and the faraway. Much formal literature of the fourteenth century was didactic and moral, but our first great poet Chaucer shows in his work the close relation between the traveler's tale and literature. The *Canterbury Tales* are told by pilgrims, who were the characteristic travelers of the Middle Ages. The Knight had journeyed widely, not only in Christian lands but among the infidels. His son, the young Squire, told a romantic tale of Cambuskan, full of magic rings and mirrors and flying horses, and set in the land of Kublai Khan. Whether or not Chaucer was exclusively influenced in the writing of this tale by The Book of Marco Polo, it has now been definitely proved that the narrative of the Venetian merchant with which our collection opens was known to him. In his capacity as a customs official he came into frequent contact, of course, with travelers from remote places, and he himself had journeyed across Europe to Italy, where he met men who were experiencing the first stirrings of the great awakening that we have called the Renaissance. Chaucer's own conceptions of geography were, naturally, those held generally in the Middle Ages. Modern geography did not begin until the rediscovery of Ptolemy a generation or so after Chaucer's death, and we should not look to the English poet for ideas and conceptions too much in advance of his time. His eager curiosity, however, is probably symptomatic of the age that is opening, and the prominence given to romance in his poems shows his awareness of the taste of his day.

It is only natural that the narrator of a travel book should adapt his style to his audience. As we read [travel narratives], we become increasingly aware of the fact that more often than not the author is trying to provide something other than mere entertainment. Obviously, the man who has lived through exciting or unusual times will not be averse to presenting himself as the center of attraction in the narrative. He knows that the reader, young or old, will want to identify himself with the narrator and live through his experiences vicariously. Such awareness may lead the author to adopt a pose or it may lead him to attempt to influence the character of the reader through moral precepts. In any event, this power he feels will color his narrative. We shall probably never know how much of the glamour of Marco Polo's narrative was the result of his desire, conscious or unconscious, to vindicate himself in the eyes of those doubting countrymen of his who had nicknamed him *Il Milione*. The reports of Columbus show the Admiral constantly torn between his own desire to explore the new lands and his haunting sense that he must satisfy his employers. Like Ralegh later, Columbus has to flatter his readers with stories of vast wealth when his own inclinations are often bent toward more ultimately significant things than gold. Many of the early narratives of life in North America, such as those of Captain John Smith, for example, are attractively worded advertisements designed to spur colonization. Captain James Cook, in the eighteenth century, and Alfred Russel Wallace, in the nineteenth, make clear their sense of obligation to science, and Dr. Josiah Gregg often subordinates his own personal interests to the interests of trade and commerce. David Livingstone was a missionary even when he was an explorer, but he seemed aware that his readers must first be interested in colonizing Africa before anything could be done toward suppressing the iniquitous slave traffic. The reading public, in other words, had always to be taken into consideration.

We have observed that the "common reader" is the ultimate judge of literary honors. The fate of travel books is bound up, therefore, with the rise and development of the reading public. It is impossible to estimate the part played

An excerpt from *The Travels of Marco Polo the Venetian* (1298)

PROLOGUE

Ye emperors, kings, dukes, marquises, earls, and knights, and all other people desirous of knowing the diversities of the races of mankind, as well as the diversities of kingdoms, provinces, and regions of all parts of the East, read through this book, and ye will find in it the greatest and most marvellous characteristics of the peoples especially of Armenia, Persia, India, and Tartary, as they are severally related in the present work by Marco Polo, a wise and learned citizen of Venice, who states distinctly what things he saw and what things he heard from others. For this book will be a truthful one. It must be known, then, that from the creation of Adam to the present day, no man, whether Pagan, or Saracen, or Christian, or other, of whatever progeny or generation he may have been, ever saw or inquired into so many and such great things as Marco Polo above mentioned. Who, wishing in his secret thoughts that the things he had seen and heard should be made public by the present work, for the benefit of those who could not see them with their own eyes, he himself being in the year of our Lord 1295 in prison at Genoa, caused the things which are contained in the present work to be written by master Rustigielo, a citizen of Pisa, who was with him in the same prison at Genoa; and he divided it into three parts.

Marco Polo, in The Travels of Marco Polo the Venetian, *translated and edited by William Marsden, revised by Thomas Wright, Doubleday & Company, Inc., 1948.*

in earlier centuries by the oral transmission of tales of travel. The reading public was of course at first a "listening" public, but so limited was the sphere of activity of the average man in the Dark Ages, so restricted were his horizons, that even though stories of far-off places must have been eagerly heard, we can make no useful generalizations about travel literature until we reach the sixteenth century. Education spread slowly to the masses as urban centers developed. With all its disadvantages London in the lifetime of Shakespeare was a stimulating place, full of bustle and excitement. As the nerve center of commerce and trade it kept men alert, and the flood of pamphlets, with their elaborate and inviting title pages, was a constant inducement to education.

With the growing prosperity of the middle classes in England there came new opportunities for men, formerly provincial in their outlook, to come in contact with the other peoples of the world. The sailors and merchants who thronged London were ordinary men. No longer was it the "gentlemen" only who traveled abroad. These ordinary persons were impelled to tell of their experiences, and when they wrote their narratives they wrote for persons like themselves. Most of the accounts gathered by Richard Hakluyt are of this sort. By and large the authors are content to give a straightforward narrative, unembellished with poetic flourishes and marked by an almost complete absence of literary consciousness. The authors know instinctively that the plain recital of great deeds in remote parts of the earth is more fascinating than fiction and that the very bareness of the narrative will do much to waken the average Englishman to a sense of sharing in the achievement of his nation. The appeal of Hakluyt's *Voyages* is the appeal of a great national epic. The plays and poems of the vibrant Elizabethan age give further expression to the growing sense of exhilaration felt by the average man after the defeat of the Armada, and the works of Shakespeare and his fellow poets betray the immense debt of the authors to the travel books of the day.

By 1600 the average man in England was, however, more often than not a member of one of the many religious groups loosely classified as Puritan. By and large, the Puritan looked with disfavor upon the arts, including literature. Reading, he felt, must be, if not specially pious or moral, at least "useful." So it is that the didactic note assumes more prominence. Having to a great extent divorced religion from life, especially from business life, the Puritan turns his attention to foreign trade. The seventeenth century, consequently, is an age in which the first excitement over new lands is replaced by a more intelligent interest in settlement and colonial enterprise. Purchas, the successor of Hakluyt, is a journalist who knows his public. In his collection of voyages he stresses the double motive of converting the heathen and deriving profit from colonization. Such a combination was irresistible to the pious tradesmen of England, who invested large sums in the Virginia Company and other groups of "adventurers."

So absorbing was the business of settlement in America that there was little time for further exploration toward the west. The French, it is true, pushed west through Canada, but the great discoveries of the missionaries were buried in the annual reports known today as the *Jesuit Relations*. Until Anson, Dampier, and Cook returned from their first voyages to the Pacific, there is little to record in a volume such as ours beyond the fact that geography as an exact science was emerging as the foundations of empire were being laid.

Books dealing with travel and exploration are inevitably bound up with the progress of geographical discovery. As we have already noted, such books reflect the era in which they are composed and show the changes that gradually develop through the ages in the goals sought by explorers and travelers as well as the changes in motives and methods.

When Rome fell to the barbarians, the Dark Ages ensued. The geographical knowledge of the ancients passed to the Arabs and was thus effectually removed from Christian Europe until the Renaissance. Although the ancient conception of the sphericity of the earth was never wholly lost, popular conceptions often took strange forms in the Dark Ages. Such traveling as was done consisted of pilgrimages or commercial voyages. In the north of Europe, the Vikings inherited the old trade routes of the Frisians and greatly extended them, pushing their activities south to the Mediterranean and west to Iceland and Greenland. Some knowledge of the extensive activities in the Atlantic must have reached Europe, but the preoccupation of the Church with the Crusades, combined with an understandable fear of the unknown, relegated news of the first discovery of America to the realm of fanciful legend. One must also keep in mind the fact that much of this early navigating was kept secret for reasons of trade monopolies. Irish chronicles and Icelandic sagas provide us today with what little we know of the activity of the Vikings in the north Atlantic, but it is safe to say that these literary accounts were too detached from the main currents of Western medieval thought to exert much actual influence. Columbus may have known of the Viking colonies in America, but he was primarily interested, not in traffic in furs, walrus tusks, whale blubber, and fish, but in reaching the wealth of Marco Polo's Cathay.

Far to the south, the Vikings came into contact with the extensive and orderly empire of the Arabs, whose merchants traded by land from Spain to India and by sea with China. With the conquest of Central Asia by the Mongols, the path to China was opened to Europeans and soon the magic word *Cathay* was on the lips of layman and priest alike. Ordinary men and women marveled at the luxuries that reached them on the Venetian galleys, and missionaries began to dream of carrying the faith to the Orient. In part, they were inspired by the legend of Prester John, a great priest king, ruler of a vast and wealthy territory. It appears now that this great monarch was first thought of as ruling Ethiopia. By the thirteenth century, thanks to a forged letter purporting to have been written by Prester John himself, ruler of the Three Indias, his kingdom was thought to be somewhere in Asia. Whatever the incentives to exploration may have been, the result was a widening of the geographical horizons of the man of the Middle Ages. Even Lhasa was reached by Friar Odoric in the fourteenth century, and in the next hundred years notable journeys were made to the Malay Archipelago and to the west coast of Africa.

As every schoolboy knows, the rise of the Turks, with the incidental capture of Constantinople, made it imperative that a new route be found to the Indies. By this time the geographical work of Ptolemy, the second-century Egyptian astronomer, had been rediscovered, and a new problem was created. The discoveries of men since Ptolemy's time had to be fitted into the world picture drawn by the ancients, and through the period of the great voyages of the end of the fifteenth century cartographers tried valiantly to do this. With the work of Mercator and Ortelius, however, a new era in map-making begins, and the maps included in Hakluyt's *Voyages* look almost familiar to us today. Hakluyt himself was an ardent proponent of the study of geography and cartography, and he especially advocated the study of geography in terms of the modern achievements of actual navigators instead of in terms of ancient Latin and Greek classics.

In the pages of Hakluyt are recorded the attempts to find a northeast passage to China, which led to trade with Russia instead, and the efforts of Frobisher and others to find a northwest passage to China, which led to the rediscovery of Labrador (the Vinland of the Vikings). Search for a northern passage continued through the seventeenth century, and Captain Cook in the eighteenth century, after exploring the Pacific, attempted the northwest passage in reverse from Alaska.

But Cook was principally concerned with another of the great objectives of maritime activity: the search for *Terra Australis,* the great southern continent supposed to surround the South Pole and to extend north into the tropics. Search for this great continent had led the Dutchman Torres to touch at the northern end of Australia and his compatriots Van Diemen and Tasman to make notable discoveries. It remained for Cook, however, to prove that New Zealand is an island, to explore the east coast of Australia effectively, and, on his second voyage, to carry his search for the mythical southern continent south of the Antarctic Circle.

By the close of the eighteenth century the world was mapped with some exactness, at least so far as the continental outlines were concerned. There were many blank spaces, however, in the interior of Australia, Arabia, India, and Africa, and although China had been mapped, Lhasa was not reliably known to have been reached since the journey of Friar Odoric in the fourteenth century. Much remained to be done in the nineteenth century, the great period of geographical exploration.

Ronald Latham (essay date 1958)

SOURCE: An introduction to *The Travels of Marco Polo,* translated by Ronald Latham, Penguin Books, 1958, pp. vii-xxix.

[*In the following excerpt, Latham examines Rustichello's contribution to Polo's book and asserts that, while Polo's observations in other fields tend to be conservative, his remarks on the "human geography" of the places he visited are outstanding.*]

The book most familiar to English readers as The Travels of Marco Polo was called in the prologue that introduced it to the reading public at the end of the thirteenth century a Description of the World (Divisament dou Monde). It was in fact a description of a surprisingly large part of the world—from the Polar Sea to Java, from Zanzibar to Japan—and a surprisingly large part of it from first-hand observation. The claim put forward in the Prologue, that its author had travelled more extensively than any man since the Creation, is a plain statement of fact, so far at least as it relates to anyone who has left a record of his travels. Even among the Arab globe-trotters he had no serious competitor till Ibn Batuta, two generations later. And to western Christendom the world he revealed was almost wholly unknown. Some stretches of the trail he blazed were trodden by no other European foot for over 600 years—not, perhaps, till the opening of the Burma Road during the last war. And the task of putting it on the map, in the most literal sense, is not yet complete.

The book can be enjoyed by the modern reader, as it was by the contemporary, for its own sake, as a vivid description of a fantastic world so remote from his own experience that it scarcely matters whether he thinks of it as fact or fiction. The enquirer who wishes to explore this world more thoroughly, in order to read the book with a just appraisal of its place in the development of human intercourse and knowledge, will find himself embarked on a journey potentially as long and varied as Polo's own. . . .

In 1298, according to the Prologue, Marco was a prisoner of war at Genoa. Ramusio says that he had been captured at the battle of Curzola (6 September 1298), when serving as 'gentleman commander' of a Venetian galley. But this again appears to be hearsay, if not mere conjecture. He was probably released under the terms of a peace treaty signed on 25 May 1299. At any rate, the captivity involved a period of enforced leisure, during which the restless wanderer had little to do but talk, and it is not surprising that his traveller's tales aroused the interest of his fellow prisoners. Among these was one Rustichello of Pisa, a romance-writer of some repute, who was interested in a more professional way. He had at one time enjoyed the patronage of Prince Edward of England, afterwards Edward I, and it is believed that, like the legate Tedaldo, he had travelled in his suite to Palestine. He may even have met the Polos there twenty-five years before, and must at least have known of their romantic mission. Now he was quick to perceive in Marco's narratives a new theme for his art, as picturesque as 'the matter of Britain' or 'the matter of Troy' or the legendary exploits of Alexander the Great—a theme that made up in novelty what it unfortunately lacked in love interest. Marco in his turn evidently cooperated by sending to Venice for his notes. And from this partnership of the merchant adventurer with the observant eye and retentive memory and the professional romancer with the all-too-fluent pen emerged one of the world's most remarkable books. We may regret that, with such incomparable material to work on, neither of the men was a literary genius—that Marco failed to impart, or Rustichello to elicit, a living drama of events and personalities, an image of the impact on a mind moulded by medieval Catholicism of a highly developed alien civilization. But genius of this order is rare. And the book the two collaborators actually produced, for which the literature of their day afforded no model, is sufficiently remarkable as it stands.

Rustichello's share in the joint venture has probably been underrated. Professor L. F. Benedetto, who produced the first critical edition of the Polo manuscripts in 1928, has clearly demonstrated, by comparison with his other writings, that Rustichello was responsible for the leisurely, conversational style of the oldest French manuscript, with its continual recapitulations and personal adjurations to the reader (*Que vos en diroie? Si vos die; Sachiez por voire,* etc.)—a seeming-artless style that reveals in fact the art of the story-teller in an age when stories were few and time was plentiful. He has also shown not only that the opening invocation to 'emperors and kings, dukes and marquises', etc. occurs verbatim in an Arthurian romance by Rustichello but that whole passages of narrative have been lifted with the minimum of adaptation from the same source. Thus the dramatic account of the welcome accorded to the Polos on their second visit to Kubilai and the commendation of the young Marco is closely modelled on Rustichello's previous description of the arrival of Tristan at King Arthur's court at Camelot—a description which already owed much to earlier writers and was of course in the central stream of romantic tradition. At the very outset a stock formula of knight errantry (*il ne trevent aventure que a mentovoir face*) is introduced into the report of a trade mission. With this clue to guide us we can safely see the hand of Rustichello in the conventional battle-pieces that largely fill the last chapter of the present work, with their monotonous harangues and their insistence on all the punctilio of 'Frankish' chivalry. It is tempting to go further. The sequence of the topographical survey is rather awkwardly broken by a series of digressions in which well-known legends of the Middle East—the miracle of the mountain, the tale of the Magi, the pretended paradise of Alamut—are related in the conventional romantic manner. Is it not possible that these stories, which could probably have been picked up by any visitor to the Holy Land, were inserted by Rustichello as a sop to his public, and that their attribution to Marco is a mere literary device? When we have travelled further east, outside the romancer's ken, such digressions become fewer and usually take the stock form of a battle-scene which may not owe more to Marco than a few names. There are other features of the book that are as likely to be due to Rustichello as to Marco, such as the tendency to glamorize the status of the Polos at the Tartar court, particularly their relation to the princesses entrusted to their care, the vein of facetiousness that often accompanies references to sexual customs, and the eagerness to acclaim every exotic novelty as a 'marvel' It is likely that without the aid of Rustichello Marco would never have written a best-seller. Conceivably he might have produced something not much more readable than Pegolotti's *Handbook.* More probably he would never have written a book at all.

As to Marco's own personality, apart from this book there are perhaps only two bits of evidence that throw any light on it at all. One is his will, dated 9 January 1323/4—a businesslike, unsentimental document by which he left the bulk of his possessions to be divided equally among his three daughters. The one human touch is the manumission of his Tartar slave Peter. The bequests of specified sums suggest a substantial but by no means colossal fortune. The second fact is his nickname of 'Million' (*Il Milione*), which appears in an official document of 1305; if this is really a tribute to his gift of 'talking big', it may well have been inspired by his book rather than by his conversation. He remains in fact a somewhat colourless personality, especially if we admit the possibility that such gleams of colour as appear in his book may be due to the refractive medium of the chronicler.

His travels are proof in themselves of enterprise, resource, and dogged endurance, and there can be no doubt that he travelled with his wits about him and his eyes open. Primarily they were the eyes of a practical traveller and a merchant, quick to notice the available sources of food and water along the route, the means of transport, and the obstacles interposed by nature or by man, and no less quick to observe the marketable products of every district, whether natural or manufactured, and the channels through which flowed the interlacing streams of export and import. Despite the ever-present risks of shipwreck, piracy, brigandage, extortion, and wild beasts, this was a world of highly organized commerce. And to Western merchants, who had hitherto known little more of it than its terminal points on the Mediterranean and the Black Sea, this inside information promised to be as useful as it was fascinating. The trade-routes followed by the Polos were mainly such as would quickly swallow the profits except on goods of very high value in proportion to their bulk. Hence in part that emphasis, to which the book owes much of its appeal, on precious gems and spices and gorgeous fabrics of silk and cloth of gold, as against the more humdrum commodities that formed the staple of medieval, as of modern, commerce. But we need not doubt that the cataloguing of these costly rarities gave pleasure to the author, as it has done to generations of readers.

From this practical standpoint, Marco judged town and countryside alike in terms of productivity: a 'fine' town is a thriving one, a 'fine' province a fertile one, and little use is made of more discriminating epithets. The descriptions of architecture and artefacts suggest a taste for efficiency, sound workmanship, costly materials, and bright colours rather than artistic sensibility. But there are hints of a feeling for natural scenery unusual in that age: the descriptions of the Pamirs and the Gobi reveal rather more than a recognition of the healthiness of the hill air and the desolation of the desert. The judgements passed on men and states show something of the same mercantile approach. The languages of medieval Europe had no word to express the concept civilization'; but Marco comes near to conveying the notion by his use of the word *domesce*; and he has a clear enough appreciation of its blessings. His 'good' men are hard-working, law-abiding folk who live by trade and industry *si come bone jens doient faire*; his 'bad' men are the indolent or unruly, the stuff that brigands and corsairs are made of. It is by a more chivalric standard, however, that he (or Rustichello) praises the prowess of the Tartar warriors or blames the climate of Lesser Armenia for the degeneracy of its inhabitants. His reference to the stinginess of the Kashgaris strikes a note of personal experience.

He is true to his age in classifying the people he encounters primarily on the basis of religion rather than of culture or colour. He does not, however, go much beyond the rudimentary classification into Christians, Jews, Saracens, and idolaters. While well aware that Nestorians, Jacobites, and Armenians are 'imperfect' Christians, he betrays no interest in doctrinal differences. Of the Jews, considering the part they played in international trade, he has surprisingly little to say. For Moslems, whom he persists in describing as 'worshippers of Mahomet', he has the traditional Christian hostility, embittered perhaps by commercial rivalry. It is in his attitude to 'idolaters', primarily Buddhists and Hindus, that he displays most clearly that tolerant attitude that we might expect from one who was in such a literal sense a man of the world. He admires the austerity of their holy men, even comparing the Buddha to a Christian saint, and acknowledges the efficacy of their humanitarian doctrines, though it cannot be said that he shows any insight into their philosophy of life. It has been suggested that he was deterred from speaking too openly on matters of religion by fear of ecclesiastical censure. It is even possible that the surviving manuscripts of his work have already undergone a certain process of censorship. Certainly, among those passages that are omitted by most of the manuscripts, there are several that might well have given offence to the church. Some of these betray just such an accommodating temper as we might expect to find in Marco himself; but others look more like the comments of some zealous churchman disgusted in a thoroughly orthodox manner by the lukewarmness of his fellow Christians.

In the field of natural history Marco's curiosity and powers of observation served him well. His descriptions of exotic plants, beasts, and especially birds are usually far more accurate and recognizable than those to be found in contemporary herbals and bestiaries. He was evidently a keen sportsman and shared that enthusiasm for falconry which was prevalent in his day among the aristocracies of Christendom, Islam, and the Far East alike. His curiosity, however, scarcely extended into the field of human history. Apart from echoes of Christian tradition and allusions to the Alexander legend, both of which may well be due to Rustichello, the horizon of his book barely extends beyond the rise of his Mongol patrons less than a century before. His accounts of the dynastic succession of the Khans and their mutual relationships are full of inaccuracies. . . . Even his narratives of contemporary campaigns are a disconcerting blend of fact and fable; and he gives little indication of the use of documentary sources. His distorted picture of earlier events is partly due to the role he assigns to 'Prester John'. It is possible that the original of this legendary priest-king was one of the Christian rulers of Abyssinia, whose successors were certainly identified with him in the fifteenth century. But in Polo's time his realm was generally believed to be somewhere in the Far East. As early as 1148 a disastrous defeat suffered by the Saracens in Turkestan was attributed to this mysterious champion of Christendom, though the actual victor was not in fact a Christian at all. Not long after this an unknown genius, possibly a Greek, had concocted a 'Letter of Prester John', purporting to be addressed to the two Christian Emperors and the Pope, which dwelt encouragingly on his power and benevolence towards the West and alluringly on the oriental splendour of his court. Thanks to this Letter, which soon became a best-seller, every European traveller in the East was on the look-out for Prester John, 'of whose great empire all the world speaks'. Some place clearly had to be found for him in Marco's narrative. He was actually identified (as he had been already by Roubrouck) with a Nestorian ruler of the Turkish Kerait clan named Togrul, known to the Chinese as Wang Khan, who played a prominent part in the early career of Chinghiz, at first as an ally, later as an enemy. His story is here romanticized in the Rustichello manner, and he is said to have passed on the title to a certain George, who is known from other sources as a Christian prince subject to Kubilai. Marco seems further to have confused the title Ung Khan, his version of Wang Khan, with Ung, which apparently denoted a tribe living near the Great Wall of China. This wall, which he never actually mentions, was called by Arab writers 'the Wall of Gog and Magog' and linked up with the legend that Alexander had cut off these barbarous tribes from the civilized world by a gigantic barrier. Marco's narrative had already located this barrier in a more traditional setting in the Caucasus; but the coincidence of the names Ung and Mungul (or Mongol) was too tempting; so Gog and Magog are perforce dragged in here. The whole passage exemplifies the sort of scholarly speculation from which the unscholarly Marco is on the whole singularly free.

The same freedom from speculation is a still more conspicuous quality of Marco Polo as a geographer. Apart from some confusion about the four rivers of Paradise he is scarcely ever influenced by those preconceptions about the shape and features of the earth that bedevil most medieval geographers, Christian, Moslem, and Chinese. A more learned writer might have avoided Polo's gaffe about travelling farther north than the Pole Star; but he would probably have been misled into more damaging errors. As a rule, Polo is content to plot the position and extent of countries, towns, and natural features according to a rough-and-ready framework of directions and distances that makes no exaggerated claims to precision. His favourite unit of distance, the 'day's journey', is obviously a highly elastic quantity, but no doubt sufficiently precise in its context for the traveller on a recognized caravan route. When he is reproducing hearsay evidence, as to the size of Java for instance or the trend of the Arabian coast, he is naturally liable to serious error. But his own

A portrait of Kublai Khan.

observations, with due allowance for copyists' slips, are mostly pretty accurate. It would not be easy to translate them into a map, though they were certainly used by some cartographers in the fourteenth century; but they contained the essential data for a fairly reliable itinerary. We know that he fired the imagination of Columbus, who treasured a well-thumbed manuscript of his work and scribbled notes in the margin; but the Venetian cannot be held responsible for that fortunate underestimate of the size of the earth which encouraged the aspiring Genoese to seek for Cathay across the Atlantic.

It is when we turn to the wider field of 'geography' as the term is commonly used today, with an emphasis on 'human geography', that Polo's outstanding excellence is mostly clearly perceived. Instead of the picturesque fables that liven the pages of *Sir John Mandeville* and of many more authentic travellers, he gives us no less picturesque facts, and facts in great abundance. In no previous Western writer since Strabo, thirteen centuries before, and in none again for at least another two centuries, do we find anything remotely comparable with Polo's panorama of the nations. Persians, Turks, Tartars, Chinese, Tibetans, Indians, and a score of others defile before us, not indeed revealed in their inner thoughts and feelings, but faithfully portrayed in all such particulars as might meet the eye of an observant traveller, from the oddities of their physical features or dress to the multiplicity of strange customs by which they regulated their lives from the cradle to the grave. Faced with this superb *tableau vivant,* the most captious critic cannot but agree with Marco's own view, as modestly expressed in the Prologue: 'It would be a great pity if he did not have a written record made of all the things that he had seen and heard by true report, so that those who have not seen them and do not know them may learn them from this book.'

Leonardo Olschki (essay date 1960)

SOURCE: "Politics and Religion in Marco Polo's Asia," in *Marco Polo's Asia: An Introduction to His "Description of the World" Called "Il milione,"* University of California Press, 1960, pp. 178-210.

[*In the following essay, Olschki analyzes the accuracy of Polo's observations regarding Asian religion and politics in the thirteenth century.*]

Marco Polo's intention of conferring upon his journey the character of a religious mission is immediately evident in the first part of his book. Ecclesiastical and pious motives abound, from the moment when the three Venetians procured some oil from the lamp of the Holy Sepulcher in Jerusalem and departed with the Pope's blessing (*benedictio finalis*); then in the description of the Christian sects in western Asia; in the narration of the miracles worked by the Faith in the struggle against the infidels; and in the account of the homage paid by the Magi to the Christ Child, which opens his description of Persia.

At the same time, our traveler notes the most striking manifestations of the Mohammedan faith, notably in his description of the end of the Abbasid caliphate, and in his still more dramatic account of the sect of the Assassins in Persia, which, in Marco's times, caused a stir throughout the Old World from China to Spain. Nor does he fail to mention the "fire-worshipers," the last followers of Zoroaster. Further on, in his description of the peoples of Asia, Marco's attention is everywhere directed toward what may be called a denominational topography of the Orient; and his is the most extensive and most nearly complete portrayal of it that is to be found anywhere in the geographical and ecclesiastical literature of the Middle Ages.

To a faithful, devout Catholic unconcerned with theological inquiry or metaphysical conflict the coexistence of so many religions and their sects in an empire ruled by a single and still secure dynasty must have appeared at first sight a disconcerting and incomprehensible spectacle. Addressing a Europe in which Catholic orthodoxy had been restored with patience and wisdom, and with violence too, and dictating his book at the end of a century agitated by bitter religious struggles, Marco begins one of his best versions by explaining to his readers a phenomenon that distinguishes the Asiatic world in its essence from the Christian community of the West. "These Tartars," he says, "do not care what god is worshiped in their lands. If only all are faithful to the lord Kaan and quite obedient and give therefore the appointed tribute, and justice is well kept, thou mayest do what pleaseth thee with thy soul. They will not that thou speak evil of their souls; nor fail thou to assist at their doings. But do thou what thou wilt with God and thy soul, whether thou art Jew or pagan or Saracen or Christian who dwellest among the Tartars. They confess indeed in Tartary that Christ is Lord, but say that he is a proud Lord because he will not be with other gods but will be God above all the others in the world. And so in some places they have a Christ of gold and silver and keep him hidden in some chest, and say that he is the great and supreme Lord of the Christians."

This adequate description of the religious situation in the Chinghizide empire at the time of Marco's stay in Asia could not have been composed by anyone but him. It sums up all his long and varied experience of this facet of Oriental civilization. This frank, unruffled judgment was undoubtedly suppressed in the current versions of the Milione because of its disturbing novelty; for, among other things, it clearly indicated the insurmountable barrier that divided both the Roman and Greek Orthodox churches, with their equally rigid, dogmatic pretensions, from the civilization of Asia, which was apparently indifferent to denominational and ecclesiastical questions.

When the three Polos left Venice for China in 1271, the fervor of the mendicant orders and enlightened Papal policy had certainly restored religious unity to Europe. Nevertheless, the struggle against the heretics was not yet at an end. As late as 1276, in near-by Verona, one hundred and fifty "Patarins" were imprisoned and many of them were burned alive, and new sects continued to spring up here and there until the death of Fra Dolcino, the tough rebel mentioned by Dante. All this kept the thought of contemporary heresies present in Marco's mind as he made note of the various religions of Asia.

To the weak, unsuccessful crusades of the Emperor Frederick II and King Louis IX of France, and the conquest of the Levant by force of arms, there had now succeeded the conquest of souls by means of missions and public religious disputations. The latter, indeed, represent one of the most characteristic manifestations of the civilization of that age, from Morocco to China. Eloquent symptoms of it are to be found even in a book like this, inspired by its author's lay sentiments and interests. Hence, it is to the "holy strife of disputatious men" that we must look for the expression of the passions and tendencies that then dominated the religious field, and that are reflected in Marco Polo's activity and feelings.

Two noteworthy examples help to illustrate the different attitudes assumed in religious controversy by those who best represent his age, respectively in the West and the East, and reveal the contrast between the two worlds, as well as Marco's ability to adapt himself without conflict to either. Joinville relates in his biography of King Louis that, on the occasion of a theological dispute between the monks of the abbey at Cluny and the learned "grand master" of the Jews in France, a knight who was present, on hearing Christ's divinity and Mary's virginity brought into question, put an end to the discussion by cracking the unbeliever's head. The abbot protested, whereupon King Louis replied that the best way for a Christian layman to defend his faith against those people was "to thrust his sword into their entrails, as far as it would go." Such sentiments were then permissible to a king, a saint, famous down the ages for his piety and justice.

Later on—precisely, on May 31, 1254,—when Friar William of Rubruck, who had been sent to Mongolia by this same king, St. Louis of France, allowed his feelings to get the better of him in a celebrated theological dispute with the representatives of the religions of Asia who had gathered for the occasion in Karakorum, he was called into the presence of the Great Kaan of the Tartars, who had already decreed his expulsion. This all-powerful sovereign, who was already making preparations for the conquest of southern China and the Mongol advance to the shores of the Mediterranean, expressed his displeasure to the kneeling friar at this attempt to disturb the religious peace of his empire, and gave him a lecture: "We Mongols," he said, "believe that there is only one God, by whom we live and by whom we die, and for whom we have an upright heart. . . . But as God gives us the different fingers of the hand, so he gives to men divers ways. . . . God gave you the Scriptures, and you do not abide by them; he gave us diviners, we do what they tell us, and we live in peace."

The sovereign's profession of faith is famous in Asiatic history and literature, and corresponds exactly to the attitude manifested by this brother of Kublai in all his religious policy. For the Chinghizide rulers from China to the Crimea, the Christian faith was only one religion among the many professed in their immense empire; as Marco justly observed in the passage quoted, even those who recognized Christ's divinity denied Him supremacy over the other divinities of Asia and the claims of His church to spiritual sovereignty over the whole world.

These sentiments were also expressed by Kublai when he discussed religious questions with the Polo brothers. "There are four prophets," he said, "that are adored and revered by the whole world. The Christians declare their God to have been Jesus Christ, the Saracens Mohammed, the Jews Moses, the idolaters [i.e., the Buddhists] Sagamoni Borcan [i.e., Sakyamuni, the Buddha], who was the first god among the idols; and I honor and revere all four; that is to say, the one who is greatest in heaven and most true, and I pray that he may help me."

The contrast between the attitude of the Christian rulers and that of the pagan emperors sets off the rigid intransigence of the former and the considerate tolerance of the latter. The toleration of various cults in the Chinghizide dominion follows from this idea of their metaphysical equivalence and their political value, which Marco clearly expressed in his simple style; as did also both of the Tartar emperors in their serenely figurative speech, which in a way foreshadows the parable of the three rings, inspired by Oriental tales and immortalized by Boccaccio.

Which of the four prophets of one and the same god was preferred by him, Kublai, wise and calculating, never revealed either to Marco or to anyone else, thereby leaving to the faithful of each sect the illusion of his secret inclination toward their preference and the certainty of his equable protection. Our Venetians were indeed under the impression that he considered "the Christian faith to be the most true"; whereas, in fact, at that moment his Buddhist subjects had even more valid grounds for thinking that Kublai was one of them. And the Mongol shamans must have been equally sure of this same imperial privilege; for in all the Chinghizide courts they still represented the pagan traditions of the Tartar tribes, which were never given up by the sovereigns and ruling classes of the empire.

It was to these traditions that there belonged the god "who is greatest in heaven and most true"—namely, that supreme impersonal divinity of whom, according to Kublai, Jesus, Mohammed, Moses, and Sakyamuni are emanations, incarnations, and prophets, and equally worthy of worship and respect. This paramount divinity, whom the Tartars designated with the Turkish and Mongol name *Möngke Tängri,* or "Eternal Heaven," corresponding to the *T'ien* of the Chinese, of whom the emperor was supposed to be the son, was always invoked in imperial seals and proclamations, in order to signify that the sovereign was his representative on earth and the executor of his will.

If the demotion of Jesus Christ to the rank of prophet, the equal of Moses, Buddha, and Mohammed, must have sounded blasphemous to Marco, a good Catholic, the idea of an impersonal supreme divinity, so characteristic of the peoples of the Far East, must certainly have remained quite incomprehensible to him, as indeed to all who had and have grown up in the atmosphere of Biblical revelation. This is, indeed, the insurmountable barrier between the Orient and the West, which was already recognized by Mohammed when, in a famous passage in the Koran, he made the distinction between the Biblical peoples (*Ahl al-Kit b*), who were more or less tolerated in Mohammedan communities, and the idolaters, who were to be either converted or exterminated.

This intransigence on the part of the Biblical peoples, which is in contrast with the tolerance of the Oriental pagans, is above all to be explained by the fact that only monotheistic religions can be, and always have been, exclusive and irreconcilable to the point of fanaticism, whereas the pagan Pantheon readily opens its doors to all concordant divinities, generally fusing them in a pantheism that is simultaneously tribal, national, eclectic, and universal, such as developed in the Roman Empire and, conformably to Chinese traditions, in Chinghizide Asia. In both these empires the sovereign was in constant communion with the universal, impersonal divinity, together with its other emanations and incarnations, which he himself could create and multiply through the exercise of his own will and inspiration.

The Chinghizide dynasty only made use of this privilege in order to deify itself when Kublai, for reasons of state, formally took up again the traditional imperial ceremonies in the ancient national temples of China, assuming with these the dynastic cult of his ancestors. At the same time, he associated all the other cults of the subject peoples, of which hitherto the various Turkish and Mongol tribes of Upper Asia had known nothing, with his traditional shamanistic animism of Turko-Mongol origin, which was characteristic of the nomads of the steppes. With his Mongols, who dominated the whole continent, he remained faithful to the practices of their shamans; for the Chinese, he revived the cult of their rural divinities; from the Tibetans, subjects or tributaries of his empire, he took over the Lamaist worship of the Buddha. And, while he exploited the ability and experience of the Mohammedans, who were both powerful and numerous in his dominions, either directly, or by means of his vassals in the West, he entered into friendly relations with the Papacy and other Christian powers, with a view to a common assault against Islam, which was an obstacle to further Mongol expansion in the Mediterranean.

Thus, religion in the Chinghizide empire took on a markedly political function that was completely foreign to the Chinese tradition and even opposed to it. With the suppression of the Confucian caste the new dynastic cult ceased to be what it had always been in China, namely, national and exclusive. Instead, it now became a manifestation of that universal sovereignty for which it considered itself to be destined from the times of its founder. Thus, Kublai added the elements of imperial Chinese worship to the Mongol ceremonial, fusing the two traditions in the spectacular "epiphanies" described by Marco Polo as gigantic bacchanalia.

By accepting the worship of one's ancestors and that of the native agrarian deities, Kublai intended to create in his Chinese subjects the same illusion as that of which Marco Polo was for a time a victim; for Marco, as a result of certain of the sovereign's apparent tributes of devotion to Christian symbols when the great ceremonies were held, nourished the hope that the emperor might one day be baptized, if not by him, at least by one of the many Nestorian priests attached to the court—the same who may have suggested the idea of obtaining the oil from the lamp of the Holy Sepulcher, which the Polos did, in fact, convey to Peking by order of the Kaan himself. This also left the three Venetians with the illusion that they would later be able to carry out the Papal mandate entrusted to them by inducing him to become an apostolic Roman Catholic.

The condition placed on his conversion by Kublai had been expressed by him in person to Maffeo and Niccolò Polo at the time of their first visit to his court, in 1265, little more than ten years after the last Franciscan mission to Tartary had, by order of King Louis, explored the probability of converting the Chinghizide rulers. As is well known to readers of the Milione, after the two Venetians had begun to say "a few words about the Christian faith" and asked the sovereign why, since he considered it the best, he did not "become a Christian," they received the reply that "the Christians who are in these parts are so ignorant that they do nothing and can do nothing," whereas "these idolaters do whatever they wish" and might kill him with their secret, superhuman powers if he should turn toward the faith of the inept. The emperor concluded that if the hundred men he had requested from the Pope, "in the presence of these idolaters, reprove them for their actions, and tell them that they, too, are able to do such things, but do not wish to because they are done by the help of diabolic art and evil spirits, and so constrain them [the idolaters] that they have not the power to do such things in their presence; then, when we see this, we shall reprove them and their law; and so, I shall be baptized, and, when I am baptized, all my barons and nobles will be baptized, and then their subjects will receive baptism, and so there will be more Christians here than there are in your parts."

This conclusion, which sounds like the epic finale of a *chanson de geste* or a joke played by the wily emperor, bears a touch of authenticity, and becomes a characteristic expression of the Asiatic civilization of that age, when considered within the framework of the continent's religious and political history and in relation to the expansion of the Chinghizide regime. The whole of Kublai's speech to the Venetians already reveals a preference, which is more practical than doctrinal, for Lamaist Buddhism; and this, in fact, was to prevail over every other religion during his reign and in the further development and decline of the dynasty. Moreover, he openly declares his conception of religion as the mere instrument of his political power, which evaluates its merits according to the practical results and occult forces mastered by the respective clergy.

The powerful emperor, as Marco relates, had the three Venetians sit in his hall with ten thousand other persons while the *bacsi* with their art made the goblets full of wine, fermented milk, and other beverages, rise from the floor, where they had been lined up in the Mongol fashion, and come to Kublai without anyone's touching them, and then return empty to their point of departure. Similarly, Marco was able to watch the feats of the representatives of Buddhistic Tantrism from Tibet and Kashmir. When the Great Kaan was at his summer residence, "by will power and by means of their spells, they would keep all clouds and bad weather away from the palace."

Marco and his older companions, who undoubtedly saw these tricks and were ingenuously amazed by them, could not imagine that behind them lay hidden not only a religious faith but also a farsighted cultural policy, formulated by a sovereign who had only just emerged from the barbaric practices of the steppes and the forests. This policy was served not only by the representatives of all the great religions of Asia but also by the Christians of the Oriental Nestorian sect. These latter, as opposed to the orthodox of the various Eastern churches and the few Roman Catholics residing in the empire, had for centuries past adapted themselves to the native religious practices and claims, renouncing, as Marco himself tells us, an effective supremacy of Christ over the other divinities revered by the Asiatic peoples. The supremacy to which the Nestorians at the imperial court truly aspired was that of their sect over every other Christian church, while they contented themselves with being treated as the equals of the other religious groups represented and recognized at the court of the Great Kaan.

Kublai's promise to receive baptism, though aleatory, was not so misleading as it may seem at first sight. Nor was it altogether absurd for him to suppose that, once he should be baptized, the whole hierarchy of his vassals, and perhaps even the peoples of his dominion, would be converted to the Christian faith. Indeed, a large part of the evangelization of central and eastern Asia, and at the same time the expansion of other foreign cults throughout the continent, had been accomplished for almost a thousand years by peaceful conquest of the courts and of the nomadic or sedentary aristocracy, though these but rarely showed any determined interest in imposing the new faith on those among their subjects who preferred to remain faithful to the superstitious practices of the religion they already had.

Buddhism was introduced into Tibet in the VIth century as a result of the conversion of King Srong Tsan Gampo, who was influenced by one of his Chinese consorts and by another from Nepal. The court followed his example, and from that time Tibet became, as is known, the center of a Buddhist sect which in the XIIIth century extended itself to the Mongol aristocracy and then gained preponderance in Kublai's religious and cultural policy at the time of Marco Polo. Moreover, already in the first centuries of the Christian era, the impetus to the diffusion of Buddhism in China had come from the rulers and their courts. Since the age of Chinghiz Khan, the infiltration of Lamaist Buddhism in the Mongol court and aristocracy had been a phenomenon essentially political in character and consequences, which, on the one hand, led to the submission of the Tibetan monastic theocracy to the Chinghizide power, and, on the other, determined the esoteric, temporal tendencies of their great Lamaist convents and the political power of their spiritual and administrative head. In the same way, and unmotivated by any practical reason, in the VIIIth century the *Khakhan,* or king, of the Khazars, a powerful Altaic tribe that had settled between the Volga and the Crimea (a region called Gazaria by Marco Polo and his contemporaries), embraced Hebraism as the state religion. Together with the governing classes of that people, he thus came to represent the last ethnic conquest registered by the Law of Moses in its millenary existence.

All these conversions were the work of missionaries of the respective faiths and, it would appear, the fruit of theological discussions, which, as we know, were more than ever active in Marco's age. Kublai's request to the Pope is in harmony with this long Asiatic tradition; hence our lay missionary was not completely wrong in charging against the Christians the failure to convert Kublai. Like Christopher Columbus some two centuries later, Marco certainly believed that Kublai's conversion, and that of all his vassals, would have been accomplished if the hundred clerics requested from the Supreme Pontiff had duly arrived at his court.

This claim does, indeed, appear less absurd if it is remembered that, at the beginning of the XIth century, Syrian merchants and Nestorian priests respectively instructed and baptized the king of the Keraits, a Mongol tribe which became, and remained, Christian, as well as a number of neighboring Naiman nobles, of the Turkestan Uigurs and the Öngüt, who had settled in the region of the upper reaches of the Yellow River, in Chinese territory, having infiltrated by marriage and their contacts with the nomadic life the aristocracy of the Mongol steppes, the Turkish and Tartar tribes, and then the Chinghizide dynasty itself. Mangu Kaan, the grandson of Chinghiz Khan and his third successor to the imperial throne, his brother Hulagu, the conqueror of Persia and first of the Ilkhans, and Kublai himself, all had a Christian mother and Christian wives.

Moreover, it was then asserted that Chagatai, the son of Chinghiz Khan, lord of Central Asia and one of the greatest figures of this powerful dynasty, had more or less openly adhered to the Nestorian Church, without, however, conferring any lasting prestige on this sect in his prevalently Mohammedan dominion. The Catholic Church registered only one success in those times which would make it possible in retrospect to confirm the hopes and forecasts of the three Venetians, who were then already homeward bound on their return journey. Two years after their departure from Khanbaliq, the Taidu of the Tartars with its Turkish name, this capital received its first Catholic bishop, Friar John of Montecorvino. In a short space of time he was successful in bringing into the bosom of the Roman Church King George, lord of the Öngüt, of ancient Nestorian stock, and, according to Marco, a descendant of "Prester John." This son-in-law and vassal of Kublai was evidently known to our Venetian prior to his Catholic baptism as a result of more than one stay in his country.

In accordance with ancient Asiatic usage, King George's immediate entourage and part of his people followed his example, arousing the wrath of the Nestorian clergy. A palace conspiracy inspired by the latter put an end to the life of this first and last Catholic sovereign of eastern Asia, and brought about the destruction of the splendid church built by him in the capital, while it restored to the Nestorian sect the dynasty, the court, and all the converts in the land. All this took place in Chinese territory in the year 1298, when Marco was dictating the Milione in the prison at Genoa.

The foregoing examples make it possible to connect the Polos' mission and Marco's activity with these traditions in the religious and political history of Asia—a history which, though it appeared relatively tranquil at the time of their stay in the Far East, nevertheless was not devoid of ferment and conflict, as the Milione itself indicates. Indeed, behind the apparent tolerance so well described by its author a vast religious drama was stirring, in which Marco's mission was only a minor though significant episode.

Contrary to what may appear at first sight, the relationship between politics and religion in the Chinghizide empire was a close and continuous one, jealously guarded by church and state, and dependent on events and tendencies which, though information on the subject is scant, may nevertheless be clearly made out. The Mongol conquests of that age were never inspired by religious aims or pretexts as the Mohammedan advance in Persia and India had been, from the VIIth century on, or the Crusades that extended far beyond the Holy Land with the French territorial conquests and the commercial ventures of the Genoese and Venetians. The abolition of the Caliphate, the destruction of the Ishmaelitic sect of the Assassins, and the degradation of the cult of Confucius by the Mongols were, from one end of Asia to the other, exclusively political acts, inspired by the peril that these spiritual organizations, whether aggressive or not, represented for the conquerors. On the other hand, the rulers were well aware of the political value that the religious groups could acquire, once they had been made a part of, and were controlled by, the dynastic and administrative system of the empire.

Moreover, this political centralization offered new scope to the missionary activities of the organized cults of Asia, which had never ceased to expand and develop in the age-old, relentless competition between the various churches and sects: Christian, Buddhist, Mohammedan, Hebraic, Manichaean, and Zoroastrian. To these must be added, within the vast confines of the Chinese empire, its most ancient national religions: Taoism and Confucianism. The last to participate in this sectarian contest was the Catholic Church, with its Franciscan and Dominican missions, from 1247 to 1368, and, in the interval between 1265 and 1292, its no less active lay missionaries: Niccolò, Maffeo, and Marco Polo from Venice.

Whereas the Chinghizide sovereigns sought to advantage themselves through each of these ecclesiastical and cultural groups, considering them on all occasions to be the instruments of their policy and upholders of their dynasty, so, too, the respective churches tended to avail themselves of both policy and rule as instruments for their own propaganda and support for their clerical, doctrinal, and monastic organizations. In other words, the churches attempted to secure privileges for themselves, especially those of a fiscal, protective, or apologetic sort; and the rulers, on the other hand, endeavored to absorb and exploit the churches, as the circumstances and the political and practical value of the various doctrines and communities might warrant. The administrative vigilance to which the faiths were subjected enabled their more important representatives to exert an influence, in turn, on the emperor and his government—not unlike that attempted by the Polos, as a reward for their services, in favor of Christianity.

This characteristic aspect of Marco Polo's Asia—an effect, as we have seen, of the dynastic if not always the administrative centralization of the continent—was originated by Chinghiz Khan, the founder of the empire and its first lawgiver, and was maintained with the participation of the clergy and laymen of all faiths until the end of the medieval Catholic missions in the Far East. From the very beginning the Mongols entrusted the more important civic offices to representatives of foreign religions. Thus, the first chancellor of the new empire and civilizer of the nomadic barbarians called to govern the world was a Turkish Uigur, probably a Christian, who was followed by the "prothonotary" Chingai, who died in 1251, a Nestorian like his successor, Bulgai, the prime minister and head of the political police at the time of Mangu Kaan, Kublai's brother and predecessor on the imperial throne.

It was from two Mohammedan dignitaries from Central Asia that Chinghiz Khan received instruction in the art of governing towns and cities, after he had destroyed forever, with unparalleled cruelty, the flourishing centers of Islamic culture in Khorasan, the inheritors of Hellenic civilization in those historic regions and the diffusers of scientific knowledge throughout the Mohammedan and Christian worlds. One of these luminaries, the great Nasiruddin, then appears at the court of Mangu Kaan, as his counselor, toward the middle of the century, at the time when the lamas of Tibet were beginning their successful task of Buddhistic penetration in the same circles at the capital, which led to the triumph of their practices and doctrines in the whole of Mongolia and, thence, in Kublai's China.

Meanwhile, the Chinese religious organizations had also entered the lists, after a thousand years of alternating vicissitudes in their own land. An episode famous both in the history of China and in the life story of Chinghiz Khan deals with the meeting between the great conqueror and the spiritual head of the Taoists, who, leaving his Chinese hermitage in 1221, joined Chinghiz in the Hindu Kush, in Afghan territory, to administer to him, not the drug of immortality, in which neither seriously believed, but the grave and subtle teachings of his sect. On this occasion he was able to insure for his followers not only a dominant position in Cathay but also fiscal and moral privileges never attained by his successors, down to our own times. As a result, the *tuini,* as they are called by William of Rubruck, and the *sensin* described in the Milione as the faithful of this religion, abounded at the court at Karakorum and Peking, until this sect was suppressed and its sacred books destroyed by order of Kublai, at the suggestion of Buddhists. Moreover, in the reign of Chinghiz Khan a host of Confucian scholars collaborated with their country's conqueror and rose high in the ranks of the Mongol administration and of the court hierarchy, where they finally prevailed, at least numerically, and made the court and native nobility familiar with the fundamental doctrines of their powerful, historic caste, which at last was dissolved by Kublai himself.

The Nestorian churches, the mosques, the Taoist, Lamaist, and Confucian temples, all rose up as near as possible to the imperial residences, both in the capitals and in the vast encampments of pavilions, tents, and chariots where the court spent a part of each year, as Marco describes at length. In this way the various sects, all committed to praying for the sovereign's health and longevity, continually reminded him of their presence, knowing that the prosperity of their institutions and the prestige of their doctrines depended on his good-will. Hence, when Friar John of Montecorvino, who arrived at Peking a short while after the Polos' departure, built there the first Catholic bishop's church in the empire, which was financed by the rich Italian merchant Pietro da Lucalongo, he desired it to be erected so near to the emperor's residence that the latter, as the Friar himself tells us, could hear not only its bells but also the divine office chanted by its parishioners. "Et hoc mirabile factum longe lateque divulgatum est inter gentes."

The result of all this was that at Karakorum, and then in the other residences, there beat upon the imperial ears, in a contest of sonority and propaganda, the chimes of the Catholics, the reverberation of the Nestorian tablets, the intonation of the muezzin, and the raucous sound of the powerful Lamaistic trumpets, not to mention the drums of the shamans, the gongs of the *tuins,* and, at Peking, perhaps even the shofar of the Jews. And each of these sects offered to the sovereign and his government the wealth of culture and experience accumulated in the course of their millenary traditions.

These were the circles in which the Polos moved when they found themselves at Kublai's court as representatives of the Pope and of Western civilization. They were present at the solemn ceremonies at which the emperor and "all his barons and nobles who attended" devoutly kissed "the book in which the four Gospels are." Year after year these ceremonies were followed, as the principal feast days came round, by acts of homage to the cults of "Saracens, Jews, and Idolaters," apparently in an even-handed manner, confirming the theoretical equivalence of all religions in the public life of the empire.

It will be noted that Marco lists only foreign cults, revealing, among other things, the existence in the capital of an organized Jewish community, which was granted official recognition. It is also certain that his "Idolaters" were not Chinese Buddhists of ancient tradition, in large part monks and scholars, but rather the representatives of the Tibetan Lamaist sect, which was already influential in Mongolia at the time of Mangu, and was now elevated by Kublai to the highest pinnacles of court and state. This preference is to be explained by the prestige enjoyed during the decisive years of his reign by the Tibetan Phags-pa, inventor of the official script of the empire and spiritual guide of its ruler, who, with his help, succeeded in extending Chinghizide sovereignty to Tibet, making it thenceforward a state subject to China.

This was the moment when Lamaist Buddhism contrived after age-long struggles to bring about suppression of the national Taoist religion of China, the sacred books of which were destroyed and the privileges annulled that had been granted by Chinghiz Khan. Hence the ancient and once popular sect, now in abject decline, is not expressly named by Marco as among those honored by Kublai and his court, from which the Confucian men of letters were excluded both as a sect and as a caste. While it is true that they were individually admitted to government office, they were nevertheless relegated as a group to the lowest classes of the social order of the empire.

As we see, the *tregua Dei* described by Marco was not so complete and secure as he would have us believe. The suppression of the Taoists and the humiliation of the Confucians were acts of government that were intended to deprive of their spiritual support the Chinese who were subject to the Mongol dynasty. Kublai himself, probably at the instigation of Buddhists and Christians at his court, forbade the Mohammedans of the empire their ritual practices for more than seven years and placed the whole sect in danger, after having learned of the Koran's precept to kill all polytheists who would not be converted to the Mohammedan faith. He only yielded to practical considerations—political, commercial, or fiscal—when the imperial coffers began to register the deleterious effects of these measures on the transcontinental trade by land and sea, which for centuries had been carried on exclusively by Mohammedan merchants and shipowners from Persia and China.

The most propitious occasion for giving his peoples a spectacular proof of his denominational policy presented itself to Kublai in the year 1288, when the most precious relics of the Buddha arrived in the capital. These were his miraculous bowl, two of his teeth, and a tuft of his hair, which hitherto had been preserved in a sanctuary on the island of Ceylon, an ancient center of his cult. Marco was present and gave a full description of this event, on which the emperor conferred a special solemnity by requiring the entire population of Peking and the representatives of all the religions to turn out for the processional entry of the relics into his capital.

This would seem to represent the triumph of Buddhism over the other religions of the empire. And such indeed it was, especially since the acquisition of the treasures, at a high price, as Marco points out, was undoubtedly inspired by the powerful lamas of the court after the suppression of Taoism. However, the Saracens, together with the Christians of the East, who were no less active in their propaganda, looked on them as relics of Adam, who was unknown to the Buddhists, and venerated them as of that origin not only in Ceylon and the rest of India, but—as Marco insinuates—also at Peking, although he entertained some doubts of their authenticity. However this may be, on this unique occasion the Biblical religionists agreed to associate with the "Idolaters" of the Chinese or Tibetan sect in worshiping these objects, which, taken with the oil from the lamp of the Holy Sepulcher, made manifest the religious unity of the empire while leaving to each worshiper the right, as noted by Marco, to interpret and venerate them in his own way.

The fact is all the more characteristic inasmuch as the transference of these relics is merely an episode in the Chinghizide policy of expansion, then aimed at the conquest of Indochina and Burma, and of Ceylon and other islands of the Indian Ocean, which in some degree were already tributaries of the Tartar empire. These universally revered relics became a vehicle for, and a symbol of, that centralization of spiritual and political power which Kublai claimed for himself and his dynasty in the sense of Chinghizide universalism rather than in accordance with the national traditions of ancient China.

In the years of Marco's stay in the Far East all the recognized religions passed under state control. A special commission was set up for each one, which supervised its activities and finances, and watched its leanings, without interfering in questions of doctrine. Freedom of worship was therefore limited, and even if, as Marco asserts, everyone could dispose of his soul in the manner he willed, the religious congregations not approved by the police ran grave risks and had to meet in the greatest secrecy.

Of the existence of these secret communities the Milione offers us a few examples, which are all the more valuable since the official Chinese sources of the period do not deal with religious questions except to record fiscal and administrative affairs. The first reference to the secret cults concludes Marco's observations on religious liberty in the Tartar empire, and concerns those Christians, probably of the Greek rite, who kept hidden in their places of worship crucifixes of gold and silver representing, as the text has it, "the supreme lord of Christianity." These precautions were due, not to the worth of the sacred objects, but rather to the well-known fact that the Nestorians, who were still influential in the empire, did not permit the use of crucifixes, either because the doctrines of the sect forbade it, or because they feared lest the horror and divine and human degradation of the Agony should appear repugnant and inauspicious to the pagans and therefore harmful to the prestige of their faith. Indeed, none of the numberless Christian crosses found in central and eastern Asia bears the figure of Christ, who, according to the Nestorian interpretation of the Passion, was crucified as man and not as God. And so great was the distaste of the pagans for this instrument of torture and death that the Emperor Kublai, although he respected and favored the Christian faith of every rite, nevertheless—as Marco tells us—"would in no wise suffer the Christians to carry the cross before them; this was because so great a man as Christ had been scourged and had died on it," words that clearly reveal the Nestorian conception of the Crucifixion and the authenticity of the text in which they are found.

The Nestorian clergy's jealousy of Catholic influence in Asia is confirmed by an event, related by Friar William of Rubruck, which is characteristic of the cold war waged by the various churches aspiring to supremacy, or at least to special privileges, in the circles of the Chinghizide court. When the French sculptor Guillaume Boucher made a crucifix for a high official of the imperial government, a Nestorian who was courted by different groups of Christians in the capital, the sacred object was stolen by the Nestorian clergy of the court and was never returned to the person for whom it was intended—who, by a stroke of irony, was also the head of the political police of the empire. Moreover, we may suppose that in the open struggle between Nestorians and Catholics at the court of Peking, during the reign of Kublai's successors to the Chinese throne, the crucifix played an important part as a symbol unworthy of Christ's divinity and an object detested by the ruling classes of the empire.

Marco Polo participated in this secret struggle between the religions and sects of Asia so far as he could do so both as a good Christian and as his sovereign's zealous servant. Thus, he once happened to discover a secret religious community in the city of Foochow, a populous

This portrait of Kublai Khan, made from a Chinese engraving, appeared in Sir Henry Yule's edition of Marco Polo's book.

commercial center of southern China, which with obvious joy he recognized to be a Christian congregation. It was, however, a Manichaean community, the residue of an ancient secret cult that according to tradition had been kept alive since the time when this dualistic religion, which in its various ramifications extended from China to Spain, had been dissolved and prohibited throughout China by the edict of Wu Tsung in the year 843 A.D.

Marco's mistake is to be explained not only by his zeal, but also by the fact that this sect, persecuted since its origins in every part of the world, associated its heretical cult of an impersonal and mythical Christ with doctrines and rites derived from Buddhism and various Zoroastrian sects connected with gnosis and with the Gospels and other sacred books of the East. According as their environment in the respective countries demanded, the Manichaeans concealed their practices beneath the more or less authentic appearances of the religions tolerated, now emphasizing the Christian element, and now, especially in their liturgical and symbolical iconography, bringing to the forefront the pagan aspects of their religion. Thus, in their isolated community at Foochow, they had managed to elude the vigilance both of the other denominations in this great city and of the political authorities, who were unaware of its existence until the arrival of Marco and his uncle Maffeo in the course of one of their journeys through those distant regions of the empire.

Once their attention had been drawn by a learned Saracen to this indeterminate religious group, the two Venetians began insistently to interrogate its members, who were terrified by this inquest, which, they felt, might deprive them of the practice of their faith and bring down upon them the sovereign's wrath. Their terror shows that they belonged to a prohibited sect, evidently Manichaean, which already on several occasions had been denounced to the authorities of the past régime of the Sung without the latter's having been able to suppress it entirely.

However, since they found a psalter among the books of this community, and had observed three images in one of its temples, which, according to Marco, represented three of the Apostles, the two Venetians thought they had discovered a Christian fellowship and advised its members to send two messengers to the Great Kaan in order to obtain his recognition and protection for their practices and beliefs. Marco's circumstantial account almost permits us to hear the debates between the head of the Christians and the leader of the Buddhists at court, who upheld in turn their arguments in favor of their respective confessions and jurisdictions.

These arguments can easily be reconstructed because the psalter, included in the sacred texts of the Manichaeans, belonged also to the traditional cult of Jesus (though this may have degenerated into a form blasphemously heretical), and so could testify in favor of the Christians. On the other hand, the fundamentally Buddhistic substance of their homiletic literature and the three images in their temple, interpreted as representing the three hypostases of the Buddha, which were common in his Chinese cult, argued for that faith. Driven to extremities by the emperor, who had intervened in these inconclusive discussions, the emissaries of the secret community at Foochow preferred, as Marco tells us, to make an official declaration that they belonged to the Christian faith, most probably in order to escape the vigilance of the powerful Buddhistic church, which had persecuted them for a long time past, and—as the Manichaeans had always done, at all times and in all places—in order to continue under false appearances the actual practices of their community and its ancient cult. This, indeed, maintained its secret existence until the XVIIth century in the same center, the last outpost of a universal faith that had reached its zenith in Europe in Marco Polo's age, in Central Asia at the time of the ephemeral Uiguric empire (IXth century), and in China in the golden age of the T'ang dynasty.

The authenticity of this account is beyond doubt. No one in those times, or for many centuries to come, could have possessed or invented such definite information of this congregation lost among the various religious communities of the populous Chinese city. Odoric of Pordenone, who visited Foochow in 1324, or thereabouts, admired its "cocks, the biggest in the world," and the "chickens white as snow," but found no trace of Christians or Manichees. Nor could anyone but Marco have been so well acquainted with the procedure of the imperial ministry of cults at the time of Kublai, who had set it up as part of the political organization of his empire.

Undoubtedly a pious exaggeration, however, is the Milione's total of Christian families—700,000—who were supposed to have settled in southern China. Even if we admit that the statistics of the Milione are nearly always inexact, and often differ in its various versions, we cannot possibly attribute this reckoning to Marco. If it is not due to the slip of a scribe's pen, it is perhaps a pious invention on the part of the compiler of this authoritative version, who, greatly interested in the religions of Asia, probably wished to rekindle the diminished fervor for the missions to the Orient.

Marco, indeed, was perfectly well aware of how small, among the general population, was the scattering of Christians in Chinghizide Asia. According to an approximate calculation, at the height of its power the whole Chinese empire did not number more than 100,000 Christians among its inhabitants. These included Nestorians or Christians of the Greek rite, and the Armenians, who were then a part of the Chinghizide empire, the numerous Alans of the imperial guard, the Catholics of the Franciscan missions, and the merchants with their families, who, it would seem, were for the most part Italians. The imperial ministry whose task it was to supervise their groups and cults was organized only in 1289, undoubtedly as a result of the influx of Christians into China and the increasing importance of the empire's relations with Byzantium and the Mediterranean world.

In fact, no trace remained of the ancient Nestorian colony founded at Hsinanfu in 635 by Christians from Syria and Persia, who had fled from the Arab invasion of their lands after their suppression in China, which occurred in September, 845. The first Christians to return were those who followed the Mongolian conquerors of the northern provinces of China, from the year 1215 onward. They were Turks of varied stock, who mainly came from the regions on the borders of northwestern China which were affiliated to the new Chinghizide empire. The Christian infiltration from western Asia was accomplished for the most part by individuals, if we except the Alans, who from the time of Chinghiz Khan represented, as we know, the élite of the imperial army.

In the same year in which he arrived at Peking (1275), two Nestorian monks, native-born residents of the capital and important figures in the history of Oriental Christianity of those times, moved in the opposite direction—toward the western regions of the Chinghizide empire bordering on the Christian lands of the Levant—on a politico-religious mission inspired by Kublai. The shrewd emperor wished to make his authority felt as head of the dynasty and protector of the Christians of Asia, since the great Baibars, the Mameluke sultan of Egypt, was harassing Kublai's vassals in Asia Minor, with the result that Abaqa, the Chinghizide sovereign of Persia, had determined to solicit an alliance with the Pope and the kings of France and England against the common Mohammedan enemy.

The imperial mission met with success. One of the two Turko-Chinese monks, Marc by name, arrived at Baghdad and, in 1281, was elected patriarch of the Nestorians there, with the name of Jaballaha III. His companion, Rabban Sauma, who wrote a fascinating account of his embassy, continued in 1287 his historic mission to the West, which led him to Rome, Genoa, and France, where he met Philip the Fair and Edward I of England—the two sovereigns who, on account of their avarice and pride, aroused the noble wrath of Dante Alighieri.

The age was that of the greatest expansion of Christianity in the Ancient World, when the contacts between the Asiatic sovereigns and the Papacy were most frequent, and the mendicant orders most active in creating new episcopal and suffragan seats in Central Asia and China, where they attracted to their churches and monasteries the heterodox elements of the Asian continent rather than individual followers of other doctrines. In Marco's times, that which united all Christians from the Yellow Sea to the Atlantic was more than anything else their common front against Islam, which likewise extended from one end to the other of the Ancient World; but as a practical measure it was a political solidarity, and therefore contingent and of short duration.

In the Levant the Mohammedans finally prevailed, when, upon Ghazan's conversion, the Mongol dynasty in Persia embraced the religion of Mohammed. In the Orient, Lamaist Buddhism gradually consolidated its strong position at the court of Kublai's successors. However, these dominant religious groups were less violent against the Christians than the Nestorians were against their Catholic and Greek brethren in the empire. Hopes of securing political, courtly, fiscal, and social privileges were always more decisive than doctrinal or denominational ambitions.

All the Catholics admitted at court or protected by the Chinghizide sovereigns had to suffer the resentment, jealousy, and persecution of the native Christians who were opposed to the propaganda of the Franciscan missionaries in China. As a layman, Marco was not directly affected, although even before his arrival in those far-off lands he represented with obvious pride not only his faith, but also that Christian civilization which, even when surrounded by the wonders of the Orient, he considered superior in its doctrines, moral worth, and practical realizations.

When, however, the official collaboration of the various faiths and laws came to an end in 1368 with the collapse of the dynasty and its rule, however nominal, over the whole of Asia, the weak Christian diaspora of Central Asia and the Far East was forced to yield to the pressure exerted by the native religions and national tendencies. Hence, when at the end of the XVIth century the first Jesuit missionaries visited these lands, the Christianity of the medieval Orient was but a vague memory.

Henry H. Hart (essay date 1967)

SOURCE: "Epilogue," in *Marco Polo, Venetian Adventurer,* University of Oklahoma Press, 1967, pp. 233-64.

[*In the following excerpt, Hart examines the impact of Polo's book on the sciences of geography and cartography.*]

Messer Marco Polo's reputation for veracity as an author suffered greatly during his lifetime, for his contemporaries (with very few exceptions) could not and did not accept his book seriously. Their ignorance and bigotry, their belief in and dependence on the ecclesiastical pseudogeography of the day, their preconceived ideas of the unvisited parts of the earth, as well as the inherited legends and utter nonsense to which the medieval mind clung with a blind persistence that is incomprehensible to modern man—all these factors combined to make it impossible to perceive or accept the truths contained in Marco's writings.

Jacopo d'Acqui, a contemporary of the traveler, records an anecdote which may be true. Marco's friends were evidently much concerned over the unfavorable reputation which he had gained by telling what were considered incredible exaggerations or downright lies. "And," noted Jacopo, "because [in Marco's book] there were to be found great things, things of mighty import, and, indeed almost unbelievable things, he was entreated by his friends when he was at the point of death to correct his book and to retract those things that he had written over and above the truth. To which he replied 'I have not written down the half of those things which I saw.'" Whether the incident as reported occurred or not, every page of his volume attests to the truth of his statement concerning what he had himself seen.

This attitude of unbelief persisted for a number of years. The Description of the World was viewed as a creation of the author's vivid imagination by most of its readers—and, indeed, the manuscript was often bound in with manuscripts of romances and was usually classified as one. The compilation or fictional book of *Travels* of Sir John Maundeville, a spurious work, was very evidently more popular than Polo's truths, for five times as many editions of Maundeville were published in the fifteenth century as of Marco Polo's volume.

Even as late as the end of the fourteenth century the veracity of the Description was often denied, doubted, or challenged. A Florentine manuscript of the work transcribed in 1392 is still preserved in the National Library of that city. Appended to it is the following curious note:

> Here ends the book of Messer Marco Polo of Venice, which I, Amelio Bonaguisi wrote with my own hand while Podestà of Cierreto Guidi to pass the time and [drive away] melancholy. The contents appear to me to be incredible things and his statements appear to me not lies but more likely miracles. And it may well be true that about which he tells; but I do not believe it, though none the less there are found throughout the world many very different things in one country and another. But this [book] seems to me, as I copied it for my pleasure to be [composed of] matters not to be believed or credited. At least, so I aver for myself. And I finished copying [it] in the aforementioned Cierreto Guidi on the 12th day of November in the year of the Lord 1392. And, the book being finished, we give thanks to Christ our Lord, Amen.

Bonaguisi's aspersions on Marco's veracity are not half so significant as is the revelation of the attitude of mind and lack of belief in his book by those living in his own century.

Marco Polo's ill fortune pursued him even after men had begun to accept his book as a real contribution to geography and the other sciences. All knowledge of the man himself was lost, neglected, or ignored to such an extent that one historical writer of sixteenth-century Spain (Mariana) referred to him as "one Marco Polo, a Florentine physician," and an English author of the early nineteenth century spoke of him as "a Venetian priest."

The demand of navigators for better maps finally resulted in the production of more accurate charts for the use of seafaring men. The first of these were the justly famous *portolani* made for practical navigation rather than for the general student. The *portolani* reached their highest point of excellence in the products of a family of Catalonian Jews who did their work on the island of Majorca at the end of the fourteenth century. The greatest of their atlases was that of 1375. It "differs from the ordinary Portolans in that it has been expanded into a sort of world map. Following the text of Marco Polo, it depicts eastern Asia, the Deccan Peninsula and the Indian Ocean far better than any of the earlier maps" [Erwin Raisz, *General Cartography,* 1938]. These charts were first made in the thirteenth century and were used through the sixteenth century by seamen. Before the compass came into general use, the names of the winds were used to designate directions. "Legends were often inserted referring to the products of the region bearing the legend, or to the character of the inhabitants of the same. Much of this information appears to have been derived from Pliny, Solinus, Isador (of Seville, in no way a reliable authority) or from travelers such as Marco Polo" [Edward L. Stevenson, *Portolan Charts,* 1911]. There is an unsubstantiated tradition that the world map of Marino Sanudo, made about 1320, was a copy of one brought from China by Marco Polo.

Gradually the map makers of Europe recognized the validity of the geographical findings of Messer Marco, and a hundred years after his death the results of his book began to appear in their work. The influence of the Venetian's contribution became ever greater, in spite of many manifest errors in his location of various regions. Errera, the Italian historian, speaks of the writings of Polo as "a reliable fountain of truth" accepted by the end of the fourteenth century. The leaders of the European advances in science and discovery in that century and during the age of the great discoveries were often close students of Marco Polo's book. Fra Mauro's wall map of 1459, now in the Marcian Library at Venice, though it employs the fallacious theory of the disklike shape of the earth, appears to have taken place names and features from the book of Marco.

In 1426 (or 1428) Prince Pedro, the elder brother of Prince Henry the Navigator, visited Venice. While he was there, he was presented by the Signoria a copy of Marco's book and, according to tradition, a map copied from one made by Polo of his travels in the East. Thus Marco Polo in all likelihood made a substantial contribution of valuable knowledge to the group of Portuguese geographers and navigators on the very eve of the discovery and exploration of a New World.

Contarini's map, published probably in Venice in 1506 (the earliest map known showing any part of America) contains names of places first mentioned by Marco Polo. Likewise the 1508 map of Johann Ruysch, published in Rome, contains for the first time the delineation of internal parts of East Asia, "no longer based on . . . Marinus of Tyre and Ptolemy . . . but on more modern reports, especially those of Marco Polo." The very important influence of Polo's book upon cartography need not be pursued further here, as later material is easily found in all histories of discovery, exploration, geography, or map making.

Marco Polo's contribution to his fellow men is not limited to his influence on the writings and maps of geographers. His prodigious memory, aided by the notes sent to him in his Genoese prison from his home in Venice, preserved aspects of the history, ethnology, sociology, physical geography, zoology, botany, economics, products, and politics of Asia such as have never been gathered into a single book by one man before or since. Even a short dissertation on each of the subjects discussed or mentioned by him would fill a small library. A list of the plants and animals named by him, excluding those which can no longer be identified from his descriptions, would fill pages. Yet carping critics complain that he has omitted much, instead of marveling that he has included so much precious information about the Asia of the thirteenth century which would otherwise have been irretrievably lost to the world.

Robert B. Downs on the impact of Marco Polo's travels on Christopher Columbus:

A momentous consequence of Marco Polo's travels was its influence on Christopher Columbus. As noted in Washington Irving's *Life of Columbus,* "the travels of Marco Polo furnish a key to many parts of the voyages and speculations of Columbus, without which it would hardly be comprehensible; it was evidently an oracular work with him." Marco's account was avidly studied by Columbus, who made marginal notes on his copy and carried it with him on his first voyage to the New World. The Orient could be reached, Columbus concluded, by traveling west across the Atlantic, as well as east by Marco Polo's route.

Robert B. Downs, in In Search of New Horizons: Epic Tales of Travel and Exploration, *American Library Association, 1978.*

Mary B. Campbell (essay date 1988)

SOURCE: "Merchant and Missionary Travels," in *The Witness and the Other World: Exotic European Travel Writing, 400-1600,* Cornell, 1988, pp. 87-121.

[*In the following excerpt, Campbell discusses methods of description and narration employed by Polo, suggesting that "the being" that Polo has given to the East in his book "is the body of the West's desire."*]

In the works of Marco Polo and the Franciscan friar William of Rubruck, the experiencing narrator born and bred in the pilgrimage accounts meets the fabulous and relatively unprescribed East of *Wonders* [*of the East*] and the Alexander romances. One might expect this encounter between the eyewitness and the factitious to be a meeting of matter and antimatter, in which explosion a host of images will perforce be smashed. But images are hardier than that:

> They have many wild elephants and they also have unicorns enough which are not at all by any means less than an elephant in size. And they are made like this, for they have the hair of the buffalo; it has the feet made like the feet of an elephant. It has one horn in the middle of the forehead very thick and large and black. . . . It has the top of the head made like a wild boar and always carriers its head bent towards the ground and stays very willingly amongst lakes and forests in the mud and in the mire like swine. It is a very ugly beast to see and unclean. And they are not so as we here say and describe, who say that it lets itself be caught in the lap by a virgin girl; but I tell you that it is quite the contrary of that which we believe that it was. [A. C. Moule and Paul Pelliot eds., Marco Polo: The Description of the World, 1938].

Marco Polo has brought the West its first authentic rhinoceros, under cover of the same old unicorn, and very much in the style of *Wonders*.

Of course his book is radically different from *Wonders,* but it is not exactly a corrective. Amazon, unicorn, and doghead live on, witnessed and verified. The trees are full of flour, the desert is full of ghouls, the mountain streams flow with diamonds. The strangeness of his East is a familiar strangeness, nearly as familiar to his readers as the Holy Land was to the readers of Egeria and Arculf. Marco Polo travels across a landscape half created in advance of him, and at the appropriate moments his scribe, Rusticello the romancer, speaks in the voice that has been largely responsible for that creation.

But whatever familiar features the landscape offers in isolated perspective, its position relative to Europe and Home has changed. To Marco Polo and Friar William it is neither central nor marginal, and its emphasized quality is neither sacred nor grotesque. The Tartar conquests are a serious political reality, and the East is becoming dangerously palpable. In this East, according to Matthew Paris, Alexander's famous wall has been broken down and the "unclean peoples" have spread all over Asia, even to the Danube: "Swarming like locusts over the face of the earth [the Tartari] have brought terrible devastation to the eastern parts [of Europe], laying it waste with fire and carnage . . . it seemed that God did not wish them to come out; nevertheless it is written in sacred history that they shall come out toward the end of the world, and shall make a great slaughter of men."

Although western Europe's initial terror of the Mongols dissipated rapidly, to be replaced by a desperate hope that a European-Mongol alliance might eliminate the Saracen menace, the Mongols' territory was no longer politically neutral, no longer a conveniently blank screen for imaginative projection. Friar William's journey to Karakorum was intended to open up at least a religious communication between the two civilizations, and the Polos hoped to open commercial relations. The two narratives belong then to a stupendous historical moment: in the second half of the thirteenth century the Eastern and Western limits of the *orbis terrarum* finally confronted each other in the flesh. The contact was not destined to last, but of course no one knew that.

Coming into European political history, the East was to some extent divested of its purely emblematic and psychological function: since the thirteenth century it has become both more and less than an eidolon. The images that comprised the merely legendary East survived, but the nature of the "lattice" in which they found their places altered significantly. For one thing, the actual population of the East became a matter of interest and commentary. Uninhabited territory was seen as exactly that: the absence of man and his products was a notable absence, and when encountered, neither marvel nor miracle was produced from the magician's empty hat. "When one leaves this province of Ghinghin talas of which I have told you above he goes riding continually ten days marches between sunrising and the Greek wind [i.e., east and northeast]. And in all this way there are no dwellings, or very few; and so there is nothing else which does to mention in our book". That "nothing" is precisely what Egeria, Arculf, and the author of *Wonders* filled their texts with, and those "dwellings" precisely what the early writers ignored.

At last the emphatic quality of the East has become its actualness, and the object to which its narrator would like to render himself transparent exists in the same way, along the same latitudes of the physical universe, as does the object Home. Many of the categories under which Home is describable are sensed as applicable to the East as well, and the objects and customs of Home enter the picture explicitly, not only in a fragmentation of similes but in analogies and comparisons:

> For you may know quite truly that all idols have their proper days dedicated to them, on which days they make solemnities and reverence & great feasts in their names every year, as our saints have on the special days [Marco Polo: The Description of the World]

> Wherever [these Iugar priests] go they are always in saffron coats, quite close-fitting and with a belt on top, just like Frenchmen, and they have a cloak on their left shoulder, hanging down in folds over the breast and back to their right side as the deacon wears a chausuble in Lent. [William of Rubruck's *Itinerarium*, translated in *Mission to Asia*, edited by Christopher Dawson].

Such analogies demonstrate a sense, novel for medieval Europe, that the two worlds are both different *and* susceptible of relation to one another. From this point on we will be particularly concerned with charting the progress of that relation as it is both controlled and expressed in the literary "relations" of European travelers.

In the real world of a merchant it is the quotidian that matters. Marco Polo describes political and military structures, imports, exports, and mediums of exchange, religious customs, the protocols of marriage and burial, birds, beasts and countryside, the layout and architecture of cities. The phenomenal world is the only one we see here. Even when dealing with topics that might lead into metaphysical realms, Marco's eye is focused on the outward, public surface of things: on religious rites, not religious ideas, the outcome of battles, not the war of ideologies, the behavior of a nation, not its mythology.

Despite its reduction to more or less "hard" facts, the East has not escaped the network of symbolic geography. The conceptual division of the world into West and East is too useful a category of thought to disappear. But as a vehicle for metaphor it is used more consciously now. We know and feel the difference between the "East" of Hesse's *Journey to the East* and the East to which we are about to export nuclear technology or from which we buy cheap clothing. The reading audiences of Marco Polo and Friar William were only just beginning to conceive of a bare and practical, mundane and geographical East—an East from which real soldiers could come and besiege their cities. That East, with all its implications for theology and natural philosophy, was mainly accessible through the manuscripts of these travelers. They had an important task in hand: the transformation of an imaginative entity, previously more useful as figure or fantasy, into a topic for geography and history. The plethora of facts contained in the accounts of Eastern travel in the thirteenth century is random enough to elude their authors' capacities to characterize and rich enough to offer a compelling opportunity to later writers as well as to European culture at large. What literary organization does appear in their works, however, will have a confining and shaping effect on imaginations to come. What did Marco Polo and William of Rubruck make of their burden of new knowledge in carrying it back to Europe? How did they adapt the available powers of the written word to the task of turning fable into geography and history?

Marco Polo's book was by far the more widely read and influential, although it is neither earlier nor indeed better than William's (and was preceded in Europe by three other firsthand accounts of the Tartar East). According to A. C. Moule, in the introduction to the Moule and Pelliot edition,

> The question of the true text of the book is a very curious and intricate one. . . . The book may have become popular, although Ramusio probably exaggerates when he says that "all Italy in few months was full of it." But this popularity resulted not in the preservation of it but in the destruction of the book in the form in which it left the author's hands, till there has survived no single known copy which can claim at all to be either complete or correct. . . . It was very long and not a little dull, the work of one who had, as has been said, "looked at everything and seen nothing"; it was written in an uncouth French much mingled with Italian which sometimes puzzled even contemporary interpreters; and so from the first each copyer omitted, abridged, paraphrased, made mistakes and mistranslations, as he saw fit, influenced naturally by his own point of view and immediate interests or purpose; and the result with which we have to deal is nearly 120 manuscripts of which, it is little exaggeration to say, no two are exactly alike.

In line with the variorum spirit of Moule and Pelliot's edition, we will consider as part of Marco's book anything that has been believed to be so by medieval and Renaissance translators and readers. The book was in a sense the collaborative effort of a whole culture, enacting by its means its discovery of the Orient, and it is particularly as such an effort that it interests me here.

Even the urtext, whatever and wherever it may be, was not the work of a single individual. The essential originality of Marco's book is amazing when one considers that, of all the possible conduits for his memory, he chose as his ghostwriter Rusticello of Pisa, a man who had been a professional writer of Arthurian romances for the court of Prince Edward of England. But Rusticello's immediate impact on the work appears to have been relatively superficial. He is responsible for the language of romance that suffuses the narratives of the Tartar wars at the end of the work and perhaps for the more thoroughly fictional of the stories that replace data in chapters on cities Marco did not visit. The structure of the work, the selection of its material, and most of all the conception of the act of telling it displays are all Marco's—or, as that name renders a rather problematic voice, are at any rate not the contributions of Rusticello's genre. Would a professional romancer have said this: "And after we had begun about the Greater Sea then we repented of it . . . , because many people know it clearly. And therefore we will leave it then, and will begin about other things"?

What is significant about the collaboration is not so much the degree to which the fiction writer adulterated the words of the documentarist, but the fact of the collaboration itself. To the extent that this autobiographical opportunity has not in the least been seen as such, we are still in the literary world of Egeria, whose "I" is only *an* "I," providing its text with little more than the brute context of eyewitnessing. In Marco's case, as in Egeria's, the only differentiating factor in the narrator's persona lies in the author's public identity. Marco is a merchant, and therefore he witnesses with the eye of a merchant, as Egeria had with the eye of a nun.

The similarities do not extend much further. For Marco's material is as open-ended and his topography as unlandscaped as Egeria's had been finite and prefabricated. Egeria had only to finger verbally the rosary beads of the already imaginatively tangible Holy Land. Marco had to turn into words a world that, for Europeans, was without a true history, a being. He had to do for the reality of Asia roughly what the Scriptures had done for Palestine.

No matter how undaunted his tone then, he must be aware that it is through him and the transcription of his experience that the East will receive its imprimatur. Unauthorized by God, unaided by a muse, politically and ecclesiastically uninvested, he must render the rest of the world in his own person, simply on the basis of his experience. Although William of Rubruck had come before him, the friar's account had been a letter to a king, and Marco's enterprise was a letter to Europe.

"There are two Armenies, one is called Armenie the Great and one Armenie the little". The void behind this bald statement is hard to realize. A voice that can substantively predicate the mere existence of something as vast as a country is a voice with primal responsibilities and which sees itself as such. ("In the beginning God created heaven, and earth"; "All Gaul is divided into three parts.") This of course is also the voice of the textbook, but what textbook for adults begins by announcing the existence of anything the size of Armenia? And in the heyday of scholasticism, what private secular man would undertake to so essentially declare the truth of things?

Yet that is the mode of Messer Marco's "narrative." It is in fact *not* a narrative. It is a *descriptio* of unprecedented scope, confident enough to present itself as the equivalent of knowledge. It is even less reportage than is Egeria's *Peregrinatio.* It is as declarative and impersonal in the majority of its sentences as *Wonders of the East,* although in its ostentatious basis in experience it places the ultimate source of authority firmly in the eyewitness.

The eyewitness cannot be just anyone, as Montaigne's speaker could have been—that would throw the emphasis of the work onto the nature and quality of the personal experience of travel (where in modern travel literature, and to some extent in Friar William's account, it mostly does lie). But this book is about "the different generations of men and the diversities of the different regions and lands of the world". So while the eyewitness is the absolute prerequisite for a book about that which can only be known to others by hearsay, the personal aspect of Marco's experience is of negligible importance and he must obtain the authority to speak from someplace beyond his private self. The voice of Rusticello resolves this problem in the opening of the prologue:

> And each one who shall read or hear this book must believe it fully, because all are most truthful things. For I make you know that since our Lord God fashioned Adam our first father & Eve with his hands until this moment never was Christian, Saracen, nor pagan nor Tartar nor Indian nor any man of any kind

> who saw & knew or inquired so much of the different parts of the world & of the great wonders so much as this said Master Marc Pol searched out and knows, nor had travelled through them. . . . And therefore he says to himself that it would be too great evil if he did not cause all the great wonders which he saw & which he heard for truth to be put in writing so that the other people who did not see them nor know may know them by this book.

Thus, while Marco's authority is indeed founded in his personal experience, that experience is in a way transpersonal as well. As the *first* man to see the whole world, he exists in the mythic-heroic sphere of first and founding gestures, *in illo tempore*. He is literally a living legend, and it is from that order of existence that he speaks, and because of that the reader can "believe it fully." We are reminded of the traveler's mythic nature at several other points in the book as well: at the end of the section on Cathay, before we turn to India, Rusticello says:

> Master Marc Pol stays there in Indie so long and went and came there so often and inquired and asked so much, that both by hearing and by sight he was able fully to learn and to see and knows so much of them, of their affairs and of their customs and of their trade, that there was scarcely a man who ever knew or saw so much of them, as he did, who would know better how to tell the truth about them.

And again, in the epilogue of a fourteenth-century manuscript, the opening formula is repeated:

> But I believe that our return was the pleasure of God, that the things which are in the world might be known. For, according as we have told at the beginning of the book in the first heading, there never was any man, neither Christian nor Saracen nor Tartar nor pagan, who has ever explored so much of the world as did Master Marc son of Master Nicolau Pol noble and great citizen of the city of Venice.
>
> Thank God Amen.

Like *Wonders of the East,* and for some of the same reasons, this work is, as I have said before, a group effort. The "I" (variously rendered throughout any one manuscript as "I," "he," "one," "we," and "you") is not the authentic "I" of a private and personal self but an image created by Marco Polo, Rusticello, and a host of translators, redactors, and editors over a period of centuries. The image is that of First Traveler, and the position it takes in relation to the World is the result of a consensus among literate men as to what that position must be. There is a real variety among the texts, not in structure but in what fills the space between the setting out and the final account of the Tartar wars. The book came to be seen as a sort of encyclopedia, to which later knowledge (or ignorance) and fuller detail from other sources could be added at will, sometimes in the middle of a sentence. What information the original manuscripts contained was frequently distorted and altered by translators and editors whose scant knowledge of the East did not equip them for their task. But Polo's authority is stamped on every version, and when a mapmaker drew from him, he did not worry about how close his manuscript was to an "original"—or to the truth. (This is of course a characteristic medieval approach to authorship: Moses, Aristotle, Albertus Magnus, any number of writers became posthumous fathers to work not their own, in an inversion of the equally characteristic practice of plagiarism. But it is interesting in light of Marco's unique claim to authority. Neither "ancient" nor ecclesiastic, he has become an umbrella figure on the basis merely of living in and moving around the physical world.)

The information contained in the manuscripts varies, but it is always handled in the same way, by a series of formulas and according to a system of priorities that give the book its ultimate integrity. The strict itinerary structure of the pilgrimage narrative is not so important here. The route is relatively arbitrary, as there are no stations of the cross to be followed across Asia. Nor is there any reason for us to follow so closely in this traveler's footsteps: it is not vicarious experience he means to offer, but knowledge in more or less raw form.

But while we do not follow Marco's exact itinerary, there is a route here (as opposed to the "concatenation" of *Wonders*) and it is based on Marco's experience—or on the rough map into which that experience has crystallized in his memory. We are explicitly kept in the dark about India in the earlier portion of the book, even though our route passes as close as Kashmir:

> We shall not go forward, because if we were to go forward twelve days marches further we should enter into Indie . . . and I do not wish to go in there at this point because on our return journey we shall tell you all the things of Indie in order in the third book. And so we will go back to our province towards Badascian, because by other road or in other directions we shall not be able to go.

There is no geographically logical reason not to talk about India after discussing Kashmir. The obstacle is that Marco himself did not discover the two places in that order. In his later discussion of the kingdom of Mangi, which "the Great Kaan has divided into nine parts", he tells us only about three of those parts (though we fully expected to hear about all nine):

> Of these three however we have told thus in order because Master Marc made his passage through them, for his way was directed hither. But of the other six also he heard and learned many things, and we should know well how to tell you of them; but because . . . he did not travel over them he would not have been able to tell so fully as about the others.

On the arrangement of his discussion of Cathay:

> Now you may know that . . . Master Marc Pol himself, the great lord sends him as a messenger towards sunsetting. And he set out from Cambulac and went quite four months of days journeys toward sunsetting,

> and therefore we shall tell you all that he saw on that road, going and coming.

This seems an odd sort of fidelity to an arbitrary order. Marco's experience was a temporal and contingent one, and the material of his book is laid out on a fixed and spatial grid. Why transfer the temporal order to what seems primarily a rendering of space, a verbal *mappa mundi?* The answer lies in the fact that Marco and Rusticello are consciously creating a book, not a map, a reading experience that exploits the linear and sequential path of the person who turns the pages, one after another, or of the person who listens to a story being told. Despite its encyclopedic breadth of topics, their book seems intended to be read straight through like a novel, rather than dipped into like a reference book (and the recent introduction of paper into Italy had made such private reading more common). More explicitly than Egeria, the authorial "I" is taking us on a journey (in which he frequently becomes "we"), a journey that has its own present and future tenses in addition to Egeria's simple and ultimately uninviting past.

"We shall now leave this district with out going any further . . . " "On our return journey we shall tell you all about India . . ." "If the traveler leaves Karakorum and Altai . . ." "Let us now continue our journey towards the East." "For this purpose the Great Khan leaves this palace and goes elsewhere. But before we follow him . . ." "So let us return to Zaiton and recommence our book from that point." "We told you earlier in the book about Hormuz and Kais and Kerman. Since we went out by another route, it is fitting that we should return to this point. But . . . we will not loiter here now." "But, now that we have embarked on this topic, we have had second thoughts about setting it down in writing . . ." Not only do we share with the authorial "I" a present-tense mental journey, complete with future possibilities and roads not chosen, but the author even allows us into the present tense of his dictation: the book itself, as well as the journey it creates, exists in time. "Now I will tell you" and "I have told you" occur on almost every page. "We have already told you," "we told you earlier about," and "now you have heard" are frequent. Particularly intimate are the spots where Marco changes direction in midparagraph. He begins to tell us about the Black Sea:

> On the mouth of the entry of the Greater Sea on the side of the sunsetting there is a mountain which is called the Far. And after we had begun about the Greater Sea then we repented of it . . . , because many people know it clearly. And therefore we will leave it.

> Now since we have told you of these Tartars of the Sunrising then we will leave them for you and will turn again to tell about the great Turquie so as you will be able to hear clearly. But it is truth that we have told you in the book above all the facts of the great Turquie . . . and so we have nothing more to tell of it. And so we will leave it.

Of course these passages sound like the sort of thing one might expect from a slavishly transcribed dictation. But, as noted earlier, Rusticello did not simply write down what Marco said. The work is thoroughly embellished with refining rhetorical touches and set pieces from chivalric romance. The opening and closing fanfares, already quoted, the fine speeches put in the mouths of Tartar "barons" during the account of their wars, Rusticello's occasional remarks of praise or wonder at the extent of Marco's travel or the breadth of his observation: all this betrays the scribe's editorial confidence and autonomy. That he did not choose to refine away these particular moments of hesitation suggests that they seemed appropriate to the work's intentions. Certainly they are not isolated from the effect of the whole.

There is something intricately artificial in all this. Despite the loud claims the text makes for the authenticity of its data and the plain veracity of its author, and despite Europe's serious need for information about the East and the Tartars, the experience it gives us is predominantly one of pleasure, and the pleasure is rooted in the work's overt manipulation of our imaginative faculties. We are to pretend we are on a journey. We are to pretend that we share in the identity of the narrator. We are finally and most exquisitely to pretend that our reading *is* a journey, that in some sense we are moving, embarking, loitering, passing on, as we sit still in our rooms turning the pages of a book.

Many refused to believe Marco Polo, and legend has it (according to Ramusio, his sixteenth-century Venetian editor and biographer) that at his deathbed friends begged him to retract his book. No doubt this was partly the effect of his subject matter, much of which is hard to credit even now (though most of it has been verified by later travelers). But the work bears about it as well the smell of fiction, for the first time in this previously documentary literature. It will not be long now before Mandeville erupts onto the scene, in a fictional work that ironically enough inherited much of its credibility from its likeness to the slightly suspicious book of Marco Polo.

It is not hard to see in this kind of transmission the rudiments of what Bakhtin calls, idiosyncratically, the novel—in contradistinction to the epic. Egeria's transmission of the Holy Land was the product of what Bakhtin would term "epic consciousness," in which

> both the singer and the listener, immanent in the epic as a genre, are located in the same time and on the same evaluative (hierarchical) plane, but the represented world of the heroes stands on an utterly different and inaccessible time-and-value plane, separated by epic distance. To portray an event on the same time-and-value plane as oneself and one's contemporaries (and an event that is therefore based on personal experience and thought) is to undertake a radical revolution, and to step out of the world of epic into the world of the novel [*Dialogic imagination*].

Of course Bakhtin is tracing the lineage of this genre at a level deeper than that of textural formalities. He is interested in the whole project of consciousness into which the novel as we usually think of it fits, and he thinks in terms of the *longue durée*. But when speaking of literary origins, one is always speaking of shift and expansion in a culture's imaginative relations with the world of which literature speaks. Both the novel and the modern travel book express a concern with personal, individual experience once almost entirely absent in Western literature. The story of its growing status in our literature brings the histories of the two genres closer together than critical tradition might indicate.

Bakhtin would place the roots of this "radical revolution" far earlier than Marco Polo. Because for him the novelistic consciousness is the product of "polyglossia," the "cultural interanimation, interaction of ideologies and [especially] languages," he traces it as far back as Xenophon's *Cyropaedia,* in which the hero (Cyrus the Great) is "foreign and barbaric." "The world has opened up; one's own monolithic and closed world (the world of the epic) has been replaced by the great world of one's own plus 'the others'".

Marco is certainly a latecomer to this consciousness produced by the interanimation of languages; most European countries have been bilingual (at least) for well over a millennium by his time, as well as in contact, however tentatively, with other cultures—Slavic and Islamic. But one might imagine that each new step toward the alien would be accompanied by a new flurry of novelistic activity, a sharper, deeper engagement with the contemporary world and the project of rendering it. Who could be more likely than such a traveler as Marco to reproduce, on a smaller scale, that great plunge into reverence for the present which first took place during the Hellenic confrontation with the otherness of Persia? Ctesias, often considered the first Western travel writer, fought in the same war that "opened up the world" to Xenophon, and Marco is his direct heir, another avatar of the First Traveler.

One of Bakhtin's criteria for the novel is the coexistence within a text of several metalanguages, the parodic or quasi-parodic use of voices from many genres to produce a single voice identified with none of them. In Marco's text we find at least three: the present tenses of the letter writer reflecting the time of writing ("we have already told you"); the narrative present tense that enacts the time of reading ("when the traveler leaves"); and the biblical, or textbook, present tense which, in Todorov's phrase, "institutes reality" and which has received its justification from Rusticello's valorizing of the traveler. The content of the East is transmitted in this last voice, in sentences that, like those of *Wonders,* declare the static and permanent existence of things.

This last and most purely discursive voice is what seems to separate Marco definitively from the genres of memoir, autobiography, and the novel. It functions to secure his claims to truth and operates by erasing the individual Marco of the "letter writer" (as well as the individual reader-"traveler" who "leaves," "embarks," "loiters," and so on). Marco remains admirably dense to the connotations of the things he chooses to transmit. He evaluates rarely and does not speak (as Friar William had, or as Odoric of Pordenone would a few years later) as a propagandist for the Western norm. He is interested in neither shattering nor protecting familiar visions of the East, as his depiction of the unicorn, quoted earlier, makes clear. Where the evidence of his senses confirms "our stories," he shows no disrespect for them, and where it does not he is scandalized at having been misinformed.

But for the most part Marco is not revising or replacing old images but filling in blanks where even blanks have not been previously imagined. The frequent baldness of the style, despite occasional rhapsodic passages (to which we will return later), further emphasizes the annunciative quality already noted in his sentence structure, where little beyond existence is predicted. Detail is repeatedly eschewed as tedious: "And I would well tell you how [the ships] were made, but because it would be too long a matter I will not mention it to you at this point." "and you may know that we do not tell you of all the cities of the kingdoms [of Mangi] because it would be too long a matter to mention".

Often satisfied with describing the parts of large territories by repeating a formula in which only the proper nouns change, his apparently fuller passages are really only finer articulations of the major pattern ("x exists"). Marco has divided the East into countries and territories that do or do not owe allegiance to the Great Kaan. These countries are usually further divided into cities and stretches of countryside through which "the traveler" passes. The cities are divided into buildings and markets, people, and products, while the countryside is divided into fauna, wild flora, agriculture, and mineral deposits. Countryside is characterized as "fine" or "desolate," depending on its productivity, and cities as beautiful or splendid. If the city is big or the countryside "fine" he will go on to subdivide it, filling in more blanks:

> Cobinan is a very great city. And the people of that country worship the abominable Mahomet. There is iron and steel and andanique enough, and many mirrors of the finest steel are made there very beautiful and large. And tutty is made there, which is not made elsewhere, which is very good for disease of the eyes. And with it spodium is made there also; which I saw made, and I will tell you how they are made.

> And again there is a beautiful plain in which there are cranes enough and pheasants and partridges enough and many other kinds of birds. . . . And there are found five kinds and manner of cranes in these regions, which I will describe to you. The one kind is all black like a raven with great wings and they are very large. The second kind is all white . . . [etc.].

The practical result of this tendency in the work has already been noted—the variations and distortions from manuscript to manuscript are limited almost entirely to the content of Marco's blanks and formulas, as if that content were somehow less sacrosanct than the syntax and the formulas that contain it. And why not? The differences between Boeach and Locac, southeast and southwest, one hundred *li* and one hundred miles, are of interest only to another merchant or to a prospective conqueror. Marco's book is formally addressed to "*all people* who wish to know"—not to specialists, not necessarily to those whose self-interest could be served by an exact knowledge of the East. Olschki calls its presentation of geographical data vague, conventional ("the various data . . . are nearly always generic, not specific, and are often blurred or arid"), and points out that even the commercial data it contains are nothing so systematic as the lists and instructions in Pegolotti's *Pratica della mercatura* (published fifty years after Marco's book; Olschki, *Marco Polo's Asia*).

The book is neither geography nor a merely mercantile itinerary. Neither is William of Rubruck's book, which is far more autobiographical and more finely detailed, and which suffered almost *no* textual distortions in the history of its dissemination. But William's book is specifically addressed to the missionary and military interests of the crusader king Louis IX. William is reporting, while Marco is excitedly establishing a matrix for existences.

The particular kind of entertainment the book offers is based on the reader's ability to believe that what he is hearing about and imagining is actual, but it does not matter too much *what* he is imagining. "Boeach" and "Locac" offer an identical pleasure, the pleasure of the exotic name. Real exotica are more titillating than the fabulous variety, and thus the book was more pleasurable to those who could believe it. Marco made it as believable as he could, in particular by means of its comprehensive scope and formulaic description, and as a result Europe altered its maps and its ideas of the *orbis terrarum* according to the book's new lattice. Later accounts of travel to the East would not be able to claim as their raison d'être the establishment of a palpable image of the East and would function as correctives, addenda, analyses, or memoirs. From Marco's time on, Europe had an East in its real geography—an East that it had yet to evaluate and respond to, but one through which it had ridden with eyes open, and soul asleep and dreaming.

So far we have been paying particular attention to the structural devices through which Il milione makes its claims to authority and historicity. Its successful and novel achievement of both qualities assured that its informing vision would become canonical as well as its data. The exuberant, even joyous, nature of that vision is separable from the scientific or journalistic truth value of the data that embody it, but was destined to control even scientific attempts to represent the East for centuries to come. It is time then to turn our attention to the purely imaginative and psychological satisfactions of Marco Polo's Elsewhere.

Marco's book is a tissue of compromises and cross-purposes in which the voices sometimes subvert each other's aims and strategies. His literary situation is a confusing one: he is producing a new kind of book about an old topic, based on an old mode of experience in a completely new world. Despite the originality of his practical orientation and attempted transparency, his book maintains the quality of wonder that had characterized the Western attitude toward the Orient, in one form or another, since before Ctesias. The definition of *wonder* has shifted a little, and its relative importance has dimmed, but the word appears twice in the first few sentences of Marco's prologue and frequently introduces a description. More than that, it is a quality of Marco's perception implicit throughout the work in the relation of certain types of phenomena.

A wonder is more than simply something we do not have at home. The travel memoirs of the twentieth century are full of exotica, but the climate of the times discourages the perception of wonders except in the stubbornly naïve. (Erik von Daneken and John Lilly pander to what is left of our capacity in this area.) A wonder partakes of another Nature—it cannot be crossbred with our fauna or wholly imported to our shores. And there is something essentially positive about it. No matter how ugly this crocodile is, one is expected to enjoy the fact of its existence:

> And the very great adders are bred in this province, and those great serpents which are so much beyond measure that all men who see them have great fear of them and must wonder at them. . . . And I will tell you how large and thick they are. For you may know for truth that there are some of them ten large paces long and some more and some less, which are quite as thick as a large butt, for they measure ten palms round; and these of this size are the largest. And they have two short legs in front near the head, which have no feet except that they have three claws, namely two small and one larger claw made sharp like a falcon's or a lion's. It has the head very large and the eyes such that they are larger than a large loaf of ours worth four dinars, all shining; the mouth is so large that it would well swallow a man or an ox at one time. It has very large and sharp teeth. And it is so very exceedingly hideous and great and fierce that there is no man nor woman nor beast in the world that does not fear to go near them, and has not dread of them.

(Characteristically, this ferocious monster's flesh "is very good to eat and they eat it very gladly," and his gall "is much prized because great medicine is made of it" which cures cancer, rabies, and the pangs of childbirth—an extension into the purely phenomenal sphere of the *bonus* and *malus* significances of the old allegorical *monstra.*)

Although the physical description of the crocodile is almost pedantically accurate and true to life, we have not so much been given an addition to our zoological knowledge as a tangible expression of the Other World. Unlike the fire-breathing serpents of *Wonders,* this monster has been verified by an eyewitness and its properties and powers do not exceed the bounds of easy belief. But like so many of the less practical tidbits in Marco's book, and contributing to a total effect that subverts the work's overtly familiarizing approach, it proclaims the fundamental difference of the world in which we are traveling.

This difference is presented at a much higher pitch of intensity in *Wonders* and founded on a much more obvious distinction in the sacramentalizing pilgrimage itineraries. And in fact Marco subdues his own sense of it in his book with his attention to what is or could be close kin to the normal and by the empiricism that continually pits the evidence of his senses against traditional fabulous lore. Strangeness is by no means a crucial criterion in his selection of data, as it had been for Arculf: towns that manufacture steel and plains full of pheasants are perfectly possible in Europe, and their presence in the East titillates more by their familiarity than by any alien qualities they may manifest.

But the undertone of otherness is there, and in its freedom from the cruder qualities of the supernatural emphasized by *Wonders* and the Alexander romances, the book renders more clearly the fundamental components of the East's imaginative appeal. Supernature is only one of the Natures from which we can feel alienated and to which we can be drawn for relief from our own. What Marco cannot quite refrain from dwelling on, despite his urgent objectivity (and despite the paganism and "barbarism" that so appalled Friar William, John of Plano Carpini, and Odoric of Pordenone), is the splendor, the power, the fecundity of the East. It will be remembered that even Egeria, the zealously idealist pilgrim, was stirred into an *occupatio* by the physical splendor of the churches of Jerusalem on Easter—the most enthusiastic plunge into physical description in her whole letter. Marco too is prodded into a more emotive discourse when opportunities arise for him to treat of the Khan's splendor and the splendor of his chief cities and palaces.

In some ways the Khan *is* the East—certainly all of it but India and Japan is in his power and pays him tribute, and thus its wealth and productivity reflect directly on him:

> Now I have told you the way and the reason why the great lord must have and has more treasure than any man of this world. . . . Moreover I will tell you a greater thing, that all the lords of the earth have not so great riches, treasures, and expenses as the great lord has alone.

After a description of the Khan's winter hunting parties:

> He stays there this term in the greatest enjoyment and in the greatest delight in the world, so that it is a wonder to tell, for there is not a man in the world who did not see it who could believe it, because it is much more, his grandeur and his business and his delight, than I should be able to tell you.

After a description of the Khan's feasts:

> And again I will tell you a thing which I had forgotten to relate, which seems a great wonder which is somewhat fit to relate in our book. For you may know that when the great Kaan makes feast and ceremony as I have said above, a great lion is brought before the great lord. And as soon as he sees him the lion throws himself down lying before him and makes signs [of] great humility, and seems to know him for lord. He is so tame that he stays thus before him with no chain and not tied at all, lying quietly at the king's feet like a dog; and it is indeed a thing which makes one wonder.

The long section of the book which treats explicitly and almost exclusively of the Khan's magnificence is introduced in these words:

> Kaan means to say in our language the great lord of lords, emperor, and this lord who now reigns indeed he really has this name . . . by right because everyone knows truly that this great Kaan is the most powerful man in people and in lands and in treasure that ever was in the world or that is now from the time of Adam our first father till this moment. . . . And this I shall show you quite clearly in the course of this our second book . . . so that each will be sure that he is . . . the greatest lord that ever was born in the world or that now is, and in the following chapters I shall show you the reason how.

The Khan has hereby been removed (with the same formula that transformed Marco himself in the prologue) from the sphere of the mundane. Not that he is made fabulous—the whole weight of Marco's account supports the notion of the actuality and palpability of his power, its present-tense and provable truth. But his valorization separates him from all the rest of "the lords of the earth" and reestablishes the old gulf between the Natures of the West and the East. It is not so much that the East is in all ways *better* than Europe ("Nevertheless," Marco remarks after one particular burst of enthusiasm, "there does exist I know not what uneasiness about the people of Cathay"), but that its possibilities are separate and alien from our own. It cannot ultimately be better because it is spiritually benighted, but in Marco's book it is confirmed as the location of all that an oppressively spiritualized culture dreams of most deeply and inchoately.

They do not grow on "berries 150 feet long," but gems are peculiarly plentiful:

> And do not believe that the good diamonds come into our Christian countries but the greater part & the most noble diamonds they go and are carried only to the great Kaan and to the kings and barons of these different regions and realms, for they have the great treasures of the world and buy all the dear stones for themselves. For those which come to our countries, nothing comes but their leavings.

Costliness is everywhere; even the peasants dress in embroidered silks and satins. It is a shiny world: it is not wealth simply as wealth that Marco so admires, but wealth as manifested in radiance and color.

Organic nature is hardly less splendid:

> There are in this kingdom many strange beasts different from all the others in the world. For I tell you that

there are black lions without any other colour or mark. And there are also parrots of several kinds more beautiful than those which are brought to us this side of the sea, for there are some parrots all white as snow and they have the feet and the beak red, and again there are some parrots red and some white and green which are the most beautiful thing in the world to see, and green ones also. There are some again very small which are likewise very beautiful. There are also peacocks much more beautiful and larger and of another sort and size than ours. And also they have hens very different from ours and better than ours. And what shall I tell you about it? They have all things different from ours, and they are more beautiful and better. For . . . they have no fruits like ours, nor any beasts nor any birds; and this comes to pass, they say, through the great heat which is the rule there.

The climatic theory of cultural differences referred to in the last sentence had usually in the past been called on to explain the inferior natural and human forms of alien places. Here it seems to explain the opposite. Not only is this paradise full of *more* beautiful birds and flowers than we have at home, but it is emphatically *full* of them. The lists of which Marco is so fond have the effect of stuffing our visual field, so that the beauties of the East appear to us only in the form of abundances. His method of description lends itself so naturally to the production of this effect that although he is rarely drawn to the description of savage or unpleasant places, he renders them with an equal sense of abundance:

And the men make fires like this to protect themselves and their animals from the fierce wild beasts of which there are so many throughout that country and throughout that land that it is a wonder. And it is because no people live there [Tibet, which "Mongu Kaan has destroyed by war"] that these wild beasts have so multiplied. . . . And with all this some lions come sometimes or some bears and some of the other wild beasts which do them harm; for there is very great plenty of them in the land.

Inside the town dare live no sinful woman . . . , these are the women who do service to men for money, but I tell you they all live outside in the suburbs. And you may know that there are so great a multitude of them for the foreigners that no man could believe it, for I dare tell you in truth that there are quite twenty thousand, . . . and they all find a living. . . . Then you can see if there is great abundance of people in Cambulac since the worldly women there are as many as I have told.

This is no country for old men. Marco gives us several accounts of tribes that practice willing cuckoldry to entertain foreign travelers and freely countenance adultery ("if the woman be willing") and polygamy. The Oriental potentates with their hundreds of wives seem to spawn sons like mackerel, and Marco relishes the statistics. After describing a tribe that values most highly as brides women who have been promiscuous before marriage, he says: "Now I have told you of this marriage [custom], which it does well to say the manner of it. And into that country the young gentlemen from sixteen years to 24 will do well to go".

The wonder of this East then does not lie in the isolated monstrosities of the fabulous literature, nor in that propensity for miracles characteristic of the Holy Land of pilgrimage accounts. In Marco's book it is an atmosphere, compounded of brightness, license, and plenitude, which is not supernatural but otherworldly in its manifestations. Crocodiles, parrots, ruby mines, artificial hills of lapus lazuli, golden birds that sing, trained leopards, postal systems, polygamy: none of this is in the least impossible. It is unlikely, *unheimlich,* but credible. What makes it so *poignantly* unlikely, and wondrous, is that while it is not characteristic of Marco's Europe, it is characteristic of European dreams. Marco's factual celebration of the East is the bright shadow of the West's own poverty and political factionalism, its famines and depopulation, its spiceless cookery and rigid sexual morality. The qualities he discovers in the East characterize as well the imagined other worlds of "dream visions," chivalric romances, troubador love poetry, the backgrounds of medieval religious paintings, the mineral splendor of altar decorations, the growing (and controversial) sensuality of church music.

But the undertone of envy and desire in Marco's account is curiously resigned. Roger Bacon's remark on the importance of geography does not suggest that places have changeable natures: "If [the longitude and latitude of every place] were known, man would be able to know the characteristics of all things in the world and their natures and qualities which they contract from the force of this location" (*Opus majus*). Europe is what it is; its latitude and climate are its destiny, and though we can bring home cinnamon and galingale, the Land of Spices will remain a synonym for desire.

Creation ex nihilo is humanly impossible. Despite Marco's valiantly clear-eyed effort to photograph the memory of his journey without prejudice or fabulation, to let us know, simply, "the things which are in the world," he has added another link to the long chain of visions which constitutes our Elsewhere. It is a new link, in its empirical basis and its novelistic awareness of the reader's experience, but it is a vision, not a photograph. The East as complement to the West will necessarily change as the West's self-image changes, but in Marco's hands it remains largely a complement, dependent for its significance and its conceivability on the nature of the West. The being Marco has given it, by means of his bald declarations and copious lists, is the body of the West's desire. Friar John's *Historia Mongolorum* is a more complete and accurate account of the Mongols; Friar William is a much better writer; and Odoric's account (twenty years later than Marco's) reflects more faithfully the conscious European attitude toward the politically and spiritually "barbarous" Oriental states. But Marco's is the book that lived and entered into history, because in him the real and reachable Orient and the country of the heart's desire were inseparably, if unevenly, joined.

FURTHER READING

Baker, J. N. L. "The Middle Ages." In *A History of Geographical Discovery and Exploration,* pp. 34-57. New York: Cooper Square Publishers, 1967.

Discusses the advances made by Polo, his father, and his uncle in the field of geographical exploration.

Brendon, J. A. "Marco Polo." In *Great Navigators & Discoverers,* pp. 29-38. Freeport, N.Y.: Books for Libraries Press, 1930.

Provides an overview of Polo's life and travels.

Clark, William R. "Explorers of Old." In *Explorers of the World,* pp. 10-39. London: Aldus Books, 1964.

Describes Polo's travels throughout Asia and discusses his association with Kublai Khan.

Cordier, Henri. *Ser Marco Polo.* London: John Murray, 1920, 161 p.

Provides—as supplementary material to Henry Yule's edition of Polo's work—"notes and addenda" which contain "the results of recent research and discovery."

Penzer, N. M. "Marco Polo: Parts I and II." *The Asiatic Review* XXIV, No. 80 (October, 1928): 657-67; XXV, No. 81 (January, 1929): 49-56.

Examines in detail the history of a number of versions of Polian manuscripts.

Severin, Tim. *Tracking Marco Polo.* New York: Peter Bedrick Books, 1964, 164 p.

An account of the author's journey and observations as he followed the overland routes through Asia traversed by Polo.

Thomas, Henry, and Thomas, Dana Lee. "Marco Polo." In their *Living Biographies of Famous Men,* pp. 17-34. Garden City, N.Y.: Blue Ribbon Books, 1946.

Summary of Polo's life and travels that includes a number of exerpts from his work.

Sordello

c. 1189-1200 - c. 1269

(Also referred to as Sordel) Italian troubadour.

INTRODUCTION

One of the most celebrated early Italian troubadours, Sordello gained a formidable reputation primarily through his noble characterization in Dante Alighieri's *Purgatorio,* which immortalized the poet as a symbol of patriotic pride. Sordello wrote in the tradition of the troubadours—creative lyric poets of the late eleventh to the late thirteenth centuries who hailed primarily from northern Italy, northern Spain, and southern France and produced poems in their vernacular tongues. He composed about forty poems on such subjects as love, chivalry, and morality and became a fairly significant figure in the development of Italian literature, attracting attention to his native land as his fame spread. Following his death, his reputation grew as legends emerged about events in his life; early Mantuan chroniclers, perhaps influenced by Dante's portrayal of Sordello, centered on and presumably embellished his public importance and his gallant adventures. Scholars have debated whether these early characterizations contributed to Sordello's appeal to poets Robert Browning and Ezra Pound, both of whom were inspired by the troubadour. In 1840, Browning composed a largely imaginative version of the troubadour's life in his full-length poem *Sordello,* a complex and highly idealized account of the development of the poet's spirit. Pound, one of the staunchest defenders of Browning's poem, echoed Sordello's lyrics in several of his *Cantos,* perhaps impressed, as scholars have suggested, by the troubadour's disdain for moral and political corruption as well as by his dedication to a plain style of composition.

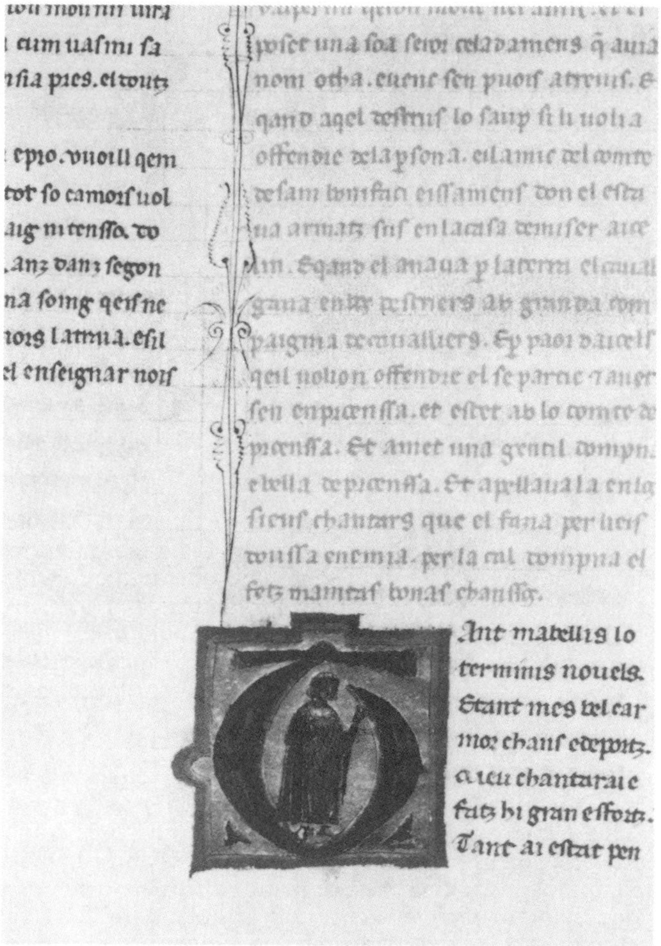

Biographical Information

Most existing accounts of Sordello's life are considered unreliable, coming from his songs; from *vidas,* factually questionable biographies whose authors are unknown but thought to have been other troubadours; and *razos,* prose explanations preceding the songs. It is generally acknowledged that he was active in politics, attaching himself to wealthy, pro-Empire clans, and that he was entangled at various times in scandalous activities that threatened his courtly duties. He was born in the city of Goito, near Mantua, sometime between 1189 and the turn of the thirteenth century. His family belonged to the minor nobility, and he spent his youth learning the art of being a courtier, which often involved the composition of music in the troubadour tradition of southern France. One of the first historical mentions of Sordello occurs in the mid-1220s and recounts his patronage at various courts of Lombardy in northern Italy, where he exchanged verses with fellow troubadours and began acquiring a reputation as a poet of merit. Sometime during the mid- to late-1220s he was involved in the abduction and possible seduction of Cunizza, wife of one of his hosts, Count Ricciardo di San Bonifacio, and sister of the notorious Lord Ezzelino da Romano. Allegedly, he then traveled to Onedes, where he secretly wedded Lady Otta di Strassi (or Otha di Strassi), arousing the fury of her brothers. In danger of becoming the target of revenge by the Strassi clan as well as by Bonifacio, Sordello ultimately fled in the late 1220s to Provence, the center of culture in western Europe and where he most actively pursued his vocation as a troubadour poet. By the 1230s he had secured the patronage of Raymond Bérenger IV, ruler of Provence, in whose powerful court he encountered such notable literary figures as the poet Peire Bremon Ricas Novas, who appears in several of Sordello's poems. In addition, he associated with influential heads of state, including Lord Blacatz of Aups, whose death around 1237 prompted Sordello's most famous poem, and he fell in love with a lady, perhaps

Berenger's daughter Beatrice, for whom he wrote numerous chansons addressed to the *dolza enemia* ("sweet enemy"). Following the count's death in 1245, Sordello served as friend and counsellor to his successor, the ambitious Charles I of Anjou, during whose reign the poet was taken prisoner while on a military campaign to Italy. Evidencing his public significance at the time was Pope Clement IV's intervention on his behalf, which prompted his release. The last mention of Sordello occurs in 1269, when historical records show that his feudal holdings, which Charles had granted him for his services, had been turned over to another Provençal knight. This transfer of property has led scholars to assume that either Sordello had died by this time or that he died in Provence a short time thereafter, possibly at the hands of one of his enemies.

Major Works

Sordello was the author of approximately forty poems of various styles and subjects, all of which were written in Provençal, the language spoken by courtly audiences in Spain, Italy, and France. His minor works include several love lyrics celebrating purity and chastity, most of which were written while he was in Italy and later, while he served under Charles I. Scholars emphasize that the significance of these works lies in the biographical information they provide rather than their artistic merit. Other of his minor works include his *tensos,* or *partimens* ("debate poems"), in which the poet holds discussions with such historical figures as Bertran d'Alamanon (it is not clear whether his subjects actually contributed their portions). In direct contrast with the idealized vision of his love poems, these debate poems reveal a pragmatic, and even cynical, side to the poet. Sordello's major works are predominantly *sirventes* (satiric poems) and *cansos* ("songs"), most of which he wrote from the 1230s to the early 1240s. His *cansos* form a more or less unified group and, although lacking the originality of his *sirventes,* are significant for their elegance and simplicity. Written in the style of *trobar pla* ("plain composition")—rather than *trobar clus* ("hermetic or closed composition"), customary among other troubadours—these lyrics, scholars believe, may have influenced later poets, including Dante, to abandon highly metaphoric and abstruse writing in favor of a clear and limpid style. In addition, Sordello's love poems, though often conventional in motif, are distinguished by their concentration on the theme of honor—regarded as the highest aspiration of a lover and the highest virtue of a lady. This focus marked a shift in troubadour poetry from an emphasis on the emotional, bereaved state of the dejected lover, to an examination of spiritual and moral questions. Sordello further explored this theme in his well-known didactic *sirvente Ensenhamen d'Onor* (*Instruction in Honor*), in which he contemplated the qualities that constitute honor. Characteristic of didactic poetry of the time, with its vague terminology and lack of heightened poetic feeling, *Instruction in Honor* offers a portrait of the morality of the period, when one's worth was measured not by intrinsic characteristics but by reputation. In his *sirventes,* Sordello both censures his country's moral and political climate and launches bitter assaults against his contemporaries; several of these attack his adversary Peire Bremon Ricas Novas, who accused him of imposture. Sordello's best-known, as well as his most successful, *sirvente* is the high-minded "Lament on Lord Blacatz" (c. 1237). In this *planh* ("funeral lament") the poet praises the courage and merits of his charitable patron and friend and criticizes the weaknesses of western European sovereigns, advising them to feed upon the subject's heart so that they too might become brave and generous. A political diatribe against decadent rulers, the work was imitated or parodied by at least two of Sordello's contemporaries. "Lament on Lord Blacatz" also inspired Dante; in cantos six through eight of his *Purgatorio,* the Florentine poet depicts an impressive Sordello who, in the Vale of Negligent Rulers, voices a severe invective against the princes of his time.

Textual History

None of Sordello's works composed in his native Tuscan, the standard literary dialect of Italian, survive. Scholars believe that his approximately thirty-four to forty works in Provençal may have been initially preserved through oral performance, as troubadour poems were often performed by either the composer or a *joglar* ("minstrel") before court audiences. This oral stage preceded or occurred simultaneously with the copying of his poems into manuscripts, possibly originally intended as memory prompts for the performer. By the mid-thirteenth century, scribes and perhaps even various troubadours themselves began a serious effort to record lyrics in collections of Old Provençal writings; several other collections followed in the thirteenth and fourteenth centuries. Modern editions of Sordello's writings have been undertaken by several German and French philologists. Most notable among these are the eighteenth-century Provençal authority Jean Baptiste de La Sainte-Palaye and the nineteenth-century Provençal scholar François Raynouard, who compiled the poet's writings in both *Choix de poésies originales des troubadours* (1816-21) and *Lexique roman* (1838-44). In the late 1800s Cesar de Lollis produced the authoritative Italian text *Vita e poesie di Sordello di Goito;* this work was followed in the mid-1950s by Marco Boni, whose *Sordello, le poesie* underwent revision by its editor more than fifteen years later. While many English translations of Sordello's individual works have been made since the nineteenth century, primarily for inclusion in anthologies of troubadour poetry, it was not until 1987 that James J. Wilhelm, an American medievalist and Pound scholar, produced the first complete critical edition, *The Poetry of Sordello.*

Critical Reception

During his lifetime Sordello was generally recognized as an influential and talented Provençal poet; as evidence of this, scholars point to the troubadour Americ de Peguillan of Toulouse, who declared in one of his poems that only Sordello could judge its merit. By the late nineteenth century, critics had begun to speculate that perhaps some of Sordello's best writings were not preserved, maintaining that his extant works comprise only a portion of his total work. Around the turn of the twentieth century, critical tide shifted toward the perception that his poetic talent exceeded that of other Provençal poets. Singling out his "Lament for Lord Blacatz" as one of his finest works, commentators praised its originality, with Eugene Benson claiming that it "stirred the troubadours of the day. It gave them a new suggestion, a new idea, and they tried to equal it, if not to surpass it." Early twentieth-century scholars had also probed the tales surrounding Sordello's life and attempted to separate historical fact from legend. This led to the theory of two Sordellos: one, the honorable, illustrious poet of Italy who defended his native Mantua against attackers; the other, a vagabond adventurer and lover of pleasure. While contemporary critics have attempted to resolve this issue by seeking additional biographical materials, modern debates have revolved more frequently around Dante's interest in the troubadour. Attempting to reconcile the stature granted him by Dante with Sordello's actual poetic output and personal history, some scholars have purported that Dante admired Sordello for recognizing the limitations of his own vernacular and adopting Provençal instead. Others have maintained that Sordello's main attractions for Dante were the variety, vigor, and political convictions with which his works are infused and which in turn inspired several passages of Dante's *Purgatorio.* Although Sordello's love poems have been viewed historically as lacking originality, some scholars have found that his ruminations on love do individualize his work. For example, as Sordello equates his lady with a captor and himself with a prisoner, he contemplates the psychological effects of unrequited love, thus marking a transition in troubadour poetry toward an increasingly moralistic tone.

PRINCIPAL ENGLISH TRANSLATIONS

**Anthology of Troubadour Lyric Poetry* (edited and translated by Alan R. Press) 1971

The Poetry of Sordello (edited and translated by James J. Wilhelm) 1987

*An anthology of troubadour material that includes translations of a number of Sordello's poems.

CRITICISM

Dante Alighieri (poem date c. 1307-20)

SOURCE: "Cantos VI-IX," in *Purgatorio,* translated by Allen Mandelbaum, University of California Press, 1982, pp. 48-80.

[*Dante is perhaps the most famous poet of the Middle Ages. An accomplished prose and verse stylist in both Latin and Italian, he was the first major author to compose literature in the Italian vernacular. His most famous work is the* Commedia *(c. 1320), later known as the* Divina Commedia, *which consists of three sections:* Inferno, Purgatorio, *and* Paridiso, *and details Dante's journey through the locales of medieval theology. In the following excerpt from the* Purgatorio *(c. 1307-20), Dante and Vergil experience a joyous encounter in the underworld with the Mantuan Sordello, who serves as their companion and guide, revealing to them the spirits of great rulers. Dante, who was significantly influenced by Sordello, links the troubadour with Roman history and extols him as a symbol of patriotic pride.*]

CANTO VI

". . . But see—beyond—a soul who is completely
apart, and seated, looking toward us; he
will show us where to climb most speedily."
We came to him. O Lombard soul, what pride
and what disdain were in your stance! Your eyes
moved with such dignity, such gravity!
He said no thing to us but let us pass,
his eyes intent upon us only as
a lion watches when it is at rest.
Yet Virgil made his way to him, appealing
to him to show us how we'd best ascend;
and he did not reply to that request,
but asked us what our country was and who
we were, at which my gentle guide began
"Mantua"—and that spirit, who had been
so solitary, rose from his position
saying: "O Mantuan, I am Sordello,
from your own land!" And each embraced the other.
Ah, abject Italy, you inn of sorrows,
you ship without a helmsman in harsh seas,
no queen of provinces but of bordellos!
That noble soul had such enthusiasm:
his city's sweet name was enough for him
to welcome—there—his fellow-citizen.
But those who are alive within you now
can't live without their warring—even those
whom one same wall and one same moat enclose
gnaw at each other. Squalid Italy,
search round your shores and then look inland—see
if any part of you delight in peace.
What use was there in a Justinian
mending your bridle, when the saddle's empty?
Indeed, were there no reins, your shame were less.
Ah you—who if you understood what God
ordained, would then attend to things devout
and in the saddle surely would allow
Caesar to sit—see how this beast turns fierce
because there are no spurs that would correct it,
since you have laid your hands upon the bit!
O German Albert, you who have abandoned
that steed become recalcitrant and savage,
you who should ride astride its saddlebows—
upon your blood may the just judgment of
the stars descend with signs so strange and plain

that your successor has to feel its terror!
For both you and your father, in your greed
for lands that lay more close at hand, allowed
the garden of the Empire to be gutted.
Come—you who pay no heed—do come and see
Montecchi, Cappelletti, sad already,
and, filled with fear, Monaldi, Filippeschi.
Come, cruel one, come see the tribulation
of your nobility and heal their hurts;
see how disconsolate is Santafior!
Come, see your Rome who, widowed and alone,
weeps bitterly; both day and night, she moans:
"My Caesar, why are you not at my side?"
Come, see how much your people love each other!
And if no pity for us moves you, may
shame for your own repute move you to act.
And if I am allowed, o highest Jove,
to ask: You who on earth were crucified
for us—have You turned elsewhere Your just eyes?
Or are You, in Your judgment's depth, devising
a good that we cannot foresee, completely
dissevered from our way of understanding?
For all the towns of Italy are full
of tyrants, and each townsman who becomes
a partisan is soon a new Marcellus.
My Florence, you indeed may be content
that this digression would leave you exempt:
your people's strivings spare you this lament.
Others have justice in their hearts, and thought
is slow to let it fly off from their bow;
but your folk keep it ready—on their lips.
Others refuse the weight of public service;
whereas your people—eagerly—respond,
even unasked, and shout: "I'll take it on."
You might be happy now, for you have cause!
You with your riches, peace, judiciousness!
If I speak truly, facts won't prove me wrong.
Compared to you, Athens and Lacedaemon,
though civil cities, with their ancient laws,
had merely sketched the life of righteousness;
for you devise provisions so ingenious—
whatever threads October sees you spin,
when mid-November comes, will be unspun.
How often, in the time you can remember,
have you changed laws and coinage, offices
and customs, and revised your citizens!
And if your memory has some clarity,
then you will see yourself like that sick woman
who finds no rest upon her feather-bed,
but, turning, tossing, tries to ease her pain.

CANTO VII

When glad and gracious welcomings had been
repeated three and four times, then Sordello
drew himself back and asked: "But who are you?"
"Before the spirits worthy of ascent
to God had been directed to this mountain,
my bones were buried by Octavian.
I am Virgil, and I am deprived of Heaven
for no fault other than my lack of faith."
This was the answer given by my guide.
Even like one who, suddenly, has seen
something before him and then, marveling,
does and does not believe, saying, "It is . . .
is not," so did Sordello seem, and then
he bent his brow, returned to Virgil humbly,
and clasped him where the lesser presence clasps.
He said: "O glory of the Latins, you
through whom our tongue revealed its power, you,
eternal honor of my native city,
what merit or what grace shows you to me?
If I deserve to hear your word, then answer:
tell me if you're from Hell and from what cloister."
"Through every circle of the sorry kingdom,"
he answered him, "I journeyed here; a power
from Heaven moved me, and with that, I come.
Not for the having—but not having—done,
I lost the sight that you desire, the Sun—
that high Sun I was late in recognizing.
There is a place below that only shadows—
not torments—have assigned to sadness; there,
lament is not an outcry, but a sigh.
There I am with the infant innocents,
those whom the teeth of death had seized before
they were set free from human sinfulness;
there I am with those souls who were not clothed
in the three holy virtues—but who knew
and followed after all the other virtues.
But if you know and you are able to,
would you point out the path that leads more quickly
to the true entry point of Purgatory?"
He answered: "No fixed place has been assigned
to us; I'm free to range about and climb;
as far as I may go, I'll be your guide.
But see now how the day declines; by night
we cannot climb; and therefore it is best
to find some pleasant place where we can rest.
Here to the right are spirits set apart;
if you allow me, I shall lead you to them;
and not without delight, you'll come to know them."
"How is that?" he was asked. "Is it that he
who tried to climb by night would be impeded
by others, or by his own lack of power?"
And good Sordello, as his finger traced
along the ground, said: "Once the sun has set,
then—look—even this line cannot be crossed.

And not that anything except the dark
of night prevents your climbing up; it is
the night itself that implicates your will.
Once darkness falls, one can indeed retreat
below and wander aimlessly about
the slopes, while the horizon has enclosed
the day." At which my lord, as if in wonder,
said: "Lead us then to there where, as you say,
we may derive delight from this night's stay."
We had not gone far off, when I perceived
that, just as valleys hollow mountains here
in our world, so that mountain there was hollowed.
That shade said: "It is there that we shall go—
to where the slope forms, of itself, a lap;
at that place we'll await the new day's coming."
There was a slanting path, now steep, now flat;
it led us to a point beside the valley,
just where its bordering edge had dropped by half.
Gold and fine silver, cochineal, white lead,
and Indian lychnite, highly polished, bright,
fresh emerald at the moment it is dampened,
if placed within that valley, all would be
defeated by the grass and flowers' colors,
just as the lesser gives way to the greater.
And nature there not only was a painter,
but from the sweetness of a thousand odors,
she had derived an unknown, mingled scent.
Upon the green grass and the flowers, I
saw seated spirits singing *"Salve, Regina";*
they were not visible from the outside.
"Before the meager sun seeks out its nest,"
began the Mantuan who led us here,
"do not ask me to guide you down among them.
From this bank, you'll be better able to
make out the acts and features of them all
than if you were to join them in the hollow.
He who is seated highest, with the look
of one too lax in what he undertook—
whose mouth, although the rest sing, does not move—
was Emperor Rudolph, one who could have healed
the wounds that were the death of Italy,
so that another, later, must restore her.
His neighbor, whose appearance comforts him,
governed the land in which are born the waters
the Moldau carries to the Elbe and
the Elbe to the sea: named Ottokar—
in swaddling-bands he was more valiant than
his son, the bearded Wenceslaus, who feeds
on wantonness and ease. That small-nosed man,
who seems so close in counsel with his kindly
friend, died in flight, deflowering the lily:
see how he beats his breast there! And you see
the other shade, who, as he sighs, would rest
his cheek upon his palm as on a bed.
Father and father-in-law of the pest
of France, they know his life—its filth, its vice;
out of that knowledge grows the grief that has
pierced them. That other, who seems so robust
and sings in time with him who has a nose
so manly, wore the cord of every virtue;
and if the young man seated there behind him
had only followed him as king, then valor
might have been poured from vessel unto vessel;
one cannot say this of his other heirs;
his kingdoms now belong to James and Frederick—
but they do not possess his best bequest.
How seldom human worth ascends from branch
to branch, and this is willed by Him who grants
that gift, that one may pray to Him for it!
My words suggest the large-nosed one no less
than they refer to Peter, singing with him,
whose heir brings Puglia and Provence distress:
the plant is lesser than its seed, just as
the man whom Beatrice and Margaret wed
is lesser than the husband Constance has.
You see the king who led the simple life
seated alone: Henry of England—he
has better fortune with his progeny.
He who is seated lowest on the ground,
and looking up, is William the Marquis—
for him, both Alexandria and its war
make Monferrato and Canavese mourn."

CANTO VIII

It was the hour that turns seafarers' longings
homeward—the hour that makes their hearts grow tender
upon the day they bid sweet friends farewell;
the hour that pierces the new traveler
with love when he has heard, far off, the bell
that seems to mourn the dying of the day;
when I began to let my hearing fade
and watched one of those souls who, having risen,
had signaled with his hand for our attention.
He joined his palms and, lifting them, he fixed
all his attention on the east, as if
to say to God: "I care for nothing else."
"Te lucis ante" issued from his lips
with such devotion and with notes so sweet
that I was moved to move beyond my mind.
And then the other spirits followed him—
devoutly, gently—through all of that hymn,
their eyes intent on the supernal spheres.
Here, reader, let your eyes look sharp at truth,

for now the veil has grown so very thin—
it is not difficult to pass within.
I saw that company of noble spirits,
silent and looking upward, pale and humble,
as if in expectation; and I saw,
emerging and descending from above,
two angels bearing flaming swords, of which
the blades were broken off, without their tips.
Their garments, just as green as newborn leaves,
were agitated, fanned by their green wings,
and trailed behind them; and one angel came
and stood somewhat above us, while the other
descended on the opposite embankment,
flanking that company of souls between them.
My eyes made out their blond heads clearly, but
my sight was dazzled by their faces—just
like any sense bewildered by excess.
"Both come from Mary's bosom," said Sordello,
"to serve as the custodians of the valley
against the serpent that will soon appear."
At this, not knowing where its path might be,
frozen with fear, I turned around, pressing
close to the trusty shoulders. And Sordello
continued: "Let us now descend among
the great shades in the valley; we shall speak
with them; and seeing you, they will be pleased."
I think that I had taken but three steps
to go below, when I saw one who watched
attentively, trying to recognize me.
The hour had now arrived when air grows dark,
but not so dark that it deprived my eyes
and his of what—before—they were denied.
He moved toward me, and I advanced toward him.
Noble Judge Nino—what delight was mine
when I saw you were not among the damned!
There was no gracious greeting we neglected
before he asked me: "When did you arrive,
across long seas, beneath this mountainside?"
I told him, "Oh, by way of the sad regions,
I came this morning; I am still within
the first life—although, by this journeying,
I earn the other." When they heard my answer,
Sordello and Judge Nino, just behind him,
drew back like people suddenly astonished.
One turned to Virgil, and the other turned
and called to one who sat there: "Up, Currado!
Come see what God, out of His grace, has willed!"
Then, when he turned to me: "By that especial
gratitude you owe to Him who hides
his primal aim so that no human mind
may find the ford to it, when you return
across the wide waves, ask my own Giovanna—
there where the pleas of innocents are answered—
to pray for me. I do not think her mother
still loves me: she gave up her white veils—surely,
poor woman, she will wish them back again.
Through her, one understands so easily
how brief, in woman, is love's fire—when not
rekindled frequently by eye or touch.
The serpent that assigns the Milanese
their camping place will not provide for her
a tomb as fair as would Gallura's rooster."
So Nino spoke; his bearing bore the seal
of that unswerving zeal which, though it flames
within the heart, maintains a sense of measure.
My avid eyes were steadfast, staring at
that portion of the sky where stars are slower,
even as spokes when they approach the axle.
And my guide: "Son, what are you staring at?"
And I replied: "I'm watching those three torches
with which this southern pole is all aflame."
Then he to me: "The four bright stars you saw
this morning now are low, beyond the pole,
and where those four stars were, these three now are."
Even as Virgil spoke, Sordello drew
my guide to him: "See there—our adversary!"
he said; and then he pointed with his finger.
At the unguarded edge of that small valley,
there was a serpent—similar, perhaps,
to that which offered Eve the bitter food.
Through grass and flowers the evil streak advanced;
from time to time it turned its head and licked
its back, like any beast that preens and sleeks.
I did not see—and therefore cannot say—
just how the hawks of heaven made their move,
but I indeed saw both of them in motion.
Hearing the green wings cleave the air, the serpent
fled, and the angels wheeled around as each
of them flew upward, back to his high station.
The shade who, when the judge had called, had drawn
closer to him, through all of that attack,
had not removed his eyes from me one moment.
"So may the lantern that leads you on high
discover in your will the wax one needs—
enough for reaching the enameled peak,"
that shade began, "if you have heard true tidings
of Val di Magra or the lands nearby,
tell them to me—for there I once was mighty.
Currado Malaspina was my name;
I'm not the old Currado, but I am
descended from him: to my own I bore
the love that here is purified." I answered:
"I never visited your lands; but can

there be a place in all of Europe where
they are not celebrated? Such renown
honors your house, acclaims your lords and lands—
even if one has yet to journey there.
And so may I complete my climb, I swear
to you: your honored house still claims the prize—
the glory of the purse and of the sword.
Custom and nature privilege it so
that, though the evil head contorts the world,
your kin alone walk straight and shun the path
of wickedness." And he: "Be sure of that.
The sun will not have rested seven times
within the bed that's covered and held fast
by all the Ram's four feet before this gracious
opinion's squarely nailed into your mind
with stouter nails than others' talk provides—
if the divine decree has not been stayed."

CANTO IX

Now she who shares the bed of old Tithonus,
abandoning the arms of her sweet lover,
grew white along the eastern balcony;
the heavens facing her were glittering
with gems set in the semblance of the chill
animal that assails men with its tail;
while night within the valley where we were
had moved across two of the steps it climbs,
and now the third step made night's wings incline;
when I, who bore something of Adam with me,
feeling the need for sleep, lay down upon
the grass where now all five of us were seated.
At that hour close to morning when the swallow
begins her melancholy songs, perhaps
in memory of her ancient sufferings,
when, free to wander farther from the flesh
and less held fast by cares, our intellect's
envisionings become almost divine—
in dream I seemed to see an eagle poised
with golden pinions, in the sky: its wings
were open; it was ready to swoop down.
And I seemed to be there where Ganymede
deserted his own family when he
was snatched up for the high consistory.
Within myself I thought: "This eagle may
be used to hunting only here; its claws
refuse to carry upward any prey
found elsewhere." Then it seemed to me that, wheeling
slightly and terrible as lightning, it
swooped, snatching me up to the fire's orbit.
And there it seemed that he and I were burning;
and this imagined conflagration scorched
me so—I was compelled to break my sleep.
Just like the waking of Achilles when
he started up, casting his eyes about him,
not knowing where he was (after his mother
had stolen him, asleep, away from Chiron
and in her arms had carried him to Skyros,
the isle the Greeks would—later—make him leave);
such was my starting up, as soon as sleep
had left my eyes, and I went pale, as will
a man who, terrified, turns cold as ice.
The only one beside me was my comfort;
by now the sun was more than two hours high;
it was the sea to which I turned my eyes.
My lord said: "Have no fear; be confident,
for we are well along our way; do not
restrain, but give free rein to, all your strength.
You have already come to Purgatory;
see there the rampart wall enclosing it;
see, where that wall is breached, the point of entry.
Before, at dawn that ushers in the day,
when soul was sleeping in your body, on
the flowers that adorn the ground below,
a lady came; she said: 'I am Lucia;
let me take hold of him who is asleep,
that I may help to speed him on his way.'
Sordello and the other noble spirits
stayed there; and she took you, and once the day
was bright, she climbed—I following behind.
And here she set you down, but first her lovely
eyes showed that open entryway to me;
then she and sleep together took their leave."
Just like a man in doubt who then grows sure,
exchanging fear for confidence, once truth
has been revealed to him, so was I changed;
and when my guide had seen that I was free
from hesitation, then he moved, with me
behind him, up the rocks and toward the heights.
Reader, you can see clearly how I lift
my matter; do not wonder, therefore, if
I have to call on more art to sustain it.
Now we were drawing closer; we had reached
the part from which—where first I'd seen a breach,
precisely like a gap that cleaves a wall—
I now made out a gate and, there below it,
three steps—their colors different—leading to it,
and a custodian who had not yet spoken.
As I looked more and more directly at him,
I saw him seated on the upper step—
his face so radiant, I could not bear it;
and in his hand he held a naked sword,
which so reflected rays toward us that I,
time and again, tried to sustain that sight
in vain. "Speak out from there; what are you seeking?"
so he began to speak. "Where is your escort?
Take care, lest you be harmed by climbing here."

My master answered him: "But just before,
a lady came from Heaven and, familiar
with these things, told us: 'That's the gate; go there.'"
"And may she speed you on your path of goodness!"
the gracious guardian of the gate began
again. "Come forward, therefore, to our stairs."
There we approached, and the first step was white
marble, so polished and so clear that I
was mirrored there as I appear in life.
The second step, made out of crumbling rock,
rough-textured, scorched, with cracks that ran across
its length and width, was darker than deep purple.
The third, resting above more massively,
appeared to me to be of porphyry,
as flaming red as blood that spurts from veins.
And on this upper step, God's angel—seated
upon the threshold, which appeared to me
to be of adamant—kept his feet planted.
My guide, with much good will, had me ascend
by way of these three steps, enjoining me:
"Do ask him humbly to unbolt the gate."
I threw myself devoutly at his holy
feet, asking him to open out of mercy;
but first I beat three times upon my breast.
Upon my forehead, he traced seven *P*'s
with his sword's point and said: "When you have entered
within, take care to wash away these wounds."
Ashes, or dry earth that has just been quarried,
would share one color with his robe, and from
beneath that robe he drew two keys; the one
was made of gold, the other was of silver;
first with the white, then with the yellow key,
he plied the gate so as to satisfy me.
"Whenever one of these keys fails, not turning
appropriately in the lock," he said
to us, "this gate of entry does not open.
One is more precious, but the other needs
much art and skill before it will unlock—
that is the key that must undo the knot.
These I received from Peter; and he taught me
rather to err in opening than in keeping
this portal shut—whenever souls pray humbly."
Then he pushed back the panels of the holy
gate, saying: "Enter; but I warn you—he
who would look back, returns—again—outside."
And when the panels of that sacred portal,
which are of massive and resounding metal,
turned in their hinges, then even Tarpeia
(when good Metellus was removed from it,
for which that rock was left impoverished)
did not roar so nor show itself so stubborn.
Hearing that gate resound, I turned, attentive;
I seemed to hear, inside, in words that mingled
with gentle music, *"Te Deum laudamus."*
And what I heard gave me the very same
impression one is used to getting when
one hears a song accompanied by organ,
and now the words are clear and now are lost.

From *The Vidas of the Troubadours* (c. late 1200s):

Sordel was from Mantoana, from a castle called Goito, and was a noble castellan. And he was a charming man in appearance, and was a good singer and a good inventor of poetry, and a great lover. But he was very treacherous toward ladies and toward the barons with whom he lived. And he loved Milady Cunizza, sister of Lord Ezzelino and of Lord Alberico de Romano, who was wife of the Count of San Bonifacio, with whom Sordel lived.

And under orders of Lord Ezzelino he stole Lady Cunizza, and took her away. And shortly thereafter, he went to Cenedes, to a castle of the Estras belonging to Lord Enrico and Lord Guglielmo and Lord Valpertino, who were his very good friends. And he secretly married one of their sisters, called Otta. And afterwards, he went to Treviso. And when the Lord of Estras learned this, he wished to harm him personally, as did the friends of the Count of San Bonifacio. So he stayed armed in the house of Milord Ezzelino. And when he travelled by land, he rode a good charger with a great escort of knights.

And out of fear of those who sought to harm him, he left and went to Provence. And he stayed with the Count of Provence. And he loved a noble and beautiful lady from Provence. And he called her "Doussa-Enemia" in the songs which he composed for her. For this lady he composed many good songs.

Margarita Egan, translator, in The Vidas of the Troubadours, *Garland Publishing, Inc., 1984.*

Caroline H. Dall (essay date 1872)

SOURCE: "Sordello, the Troubadour," in *Sordello: A History and a Poem,* Robert Brothers, 1886, pp. 5-11.

[*The following is an excerpt from an article by Dall first published in a periodical in 1872. She summarizes the disparate chronicles of Sordello's life and speculates that perhaps two interpretations of the troubadour's character existed: one as a singer only and the other as a warrior and thinker. Dall also assesses the poet's writings, finding that "the best of Sordello's verses show a dignity of composition and purity of taste which put him in the very front rank of the Provençals."*]

"Who wills has heard Sordello's story told," yet not without some hard work; some diving into old and musty chronicles, the best American collection of which perished when the library of the Canadian Parliament was burned.

It was the audacity of genius only that dared found a poem on a history so obscure that no two writers can be found who call its hero by the same family name. Had Sordello, on the contrary, been an historic personage, stark and startling as Wellington himself, the din of political turmoil, the smoke of war, intrigue, conflicting houses and interests into which he was born, might have sued for explanation at the poet's hand. It would even have helped a little had Browning only said, "Salinguerra and Taurello are the same man."

In Aliprando's fabulous "History of Milan" we find long stories of Sordello, borrowed, doubtless, from still older sources, and stealing out of his verses into the solemn Latin prose of Platina's "History of Mantua." There we are told that Sordello was born into the Visconti family, at Goïto, in Mantua, in 1189. A mere boy, he startled the world of letters by a poem called **"Trésor."** That of arms did not open to him till he was twenty-five, when he distinguished himself, not only by bravery and address, but by a dignity and grace of manner the first glimpse of his slight figure hardly promised.

He was conqueror in scores of tilts, and vanquished foreigners went back to France to proclaim his chivalry to that court.

Then Louis wanted him, and Sordello was hastening across the Alps, when Ecelin da Romano called him to Verona. Here his young life was made wretched by Beatrice, sister of Ecelin. Prayers, tears, and swoons, however, did not prevent him from seeking in Mantua a refuge from an intrigue unworthy of his honor. She followed him to Mantua, disguised as a page, and in the end became his wife. A few days after the wedding, to which it can hardly be said that he consented, the Troubadour very naturally remembered that King Louis needed him. Partly at court, and partly in the ancient French city of Troyes, his valor, his gallantry, and his sweet verses won all hearts. Louis made him a chevalier, and gave him three thousand francs and a golden falcon. On his return, the Italian cities met him, one after the other, with stately congratulation, the Mantuans coming in a crowd to greet him. In 1229 he joined his wife at Padua, and that city celebrated his return by a whole week of festivity. From 1250 to 1253 the brother of Beatrice, Ecelin da Romano, besieged Mantua. At last the unwilling husband led the people out, and in the fray that followed Ecelin perished.

But this graceful story could not have been true. At the time when it asserts that Sordello went into France there was no Louis—only a Philip Augustus—on the throne. The siege of Mantua did not begin till 1256, and Ecelin died in 1259. His sister's real name was Cuniza. Perhaps Sordello told some such story of himself in one of the dancing rhymes he sung by the camp-fire. Very soon did such songs turn into history.

Rolandino, a Latin historian, born at Padua, in the year 1200, and therefore a contemporary, mentions the matter differently.

"Cuniza, wife of Richard of St. Boniface, and sister of Ecelin da Romano, was *stolen* from her husband," he says, "by one Sordello, who was of *the same family.*" The ambiguity of this last phrase perplexed Tiraboschi, but would hardly deserve our attention if it had not furnished a hint for the modern poem. In Browning's hands, Sordello is no guilty troubadour, but the unwitting victim of political schemers, held as a hostage by his ambitious enemy, and that enemy a woman. Palma takes the place of Cuniza, but with no dishonor to her family. Rolandino adds that the pair took refuge with the father of Cuniza, who finally drove them forth in disgrace.

Dante, however, had something to say of Sordello which Browning has remembered.

At the entrance of Purgatory, in a spot where the impenitent mingle with those who have died a violent death, Virgil meets Sordello. "O Mantuan!" he cries; "I am Sordello, born in thy land." Dante here attributes to him "the lion's glance and port," and in his treatise "De Volgari Eloquentia" says that Sordello excelled in all kinds of composition, and that he helped to form the Tuscan tongue by some happy attempts which he made in the dialects of Cremona, Brescia, and Verona, cities not far removed from Mantua. He also speaks of a "Goïto Mantuan," who was the author of many good songs, and who left in every stanza an unmatched line which he called the key: and this singer Tiraboschi thinks is our Troubadour.

Benvenuto d'Imola, a commentator on Dante, of the fourteenth century, says, in a note to the sixth canto of the "Purgatory,"—"Sordello was a native of Mantua, an illustrious and skilful warrior, and an accomplished courtier. This chevalier lived in the time of Ecelin da Romano, whose sister conceived for him so violent a passion that she often had him brought to her apartments by a private way. Informed of this intrigue, Ecelin disguised himself as a servant, and surprised the unfortunate poet, who promised on his knees not to repeat the offence. But," continues Benvenuto in forcible Latin, "the cursed Cuniza dragged him anew into perdition. He was naturally grave, virtuous, and prudent. To withdraw himself from Ecelin he fled, but was pursued and assassinated."

Benvenuto attributes to Sordello a *Latin* work, **"Thesaurus Thesaurorum;"** and if such a work ever existed we understand the sympathy with which the Troubadour embraced the knees of Virgil,—"O Glory of the Latins!" etc. Dante, at all events, thought of him as a patriot, and his outburst over the meeting colors the modern poem. That his poems were more philosophical than amatory was a still further appeal to the sympathy of the Florentine.

While Benvenuto was indignantly cursing Cuniza, some sketches of the Troubadour were written in Provençal, which say: "Born in the Mantuan territory, of a poor knight named Elcorte, Sordello early began to write the songs and short satires called in the language of that day *Sirventes.* He was attached to the Count of St. Boniface, and the lover of his wife, and eloped with her under the protection of her brothers." At war with the count, these brothers seem to have been rather more anxious to do him an ill turn than to protect their family honor. "Then Sordello went into Provence, where they gave him a château, and he became honorably connected in marriage,"—Cuniza vanishing, we suppose, clean out of life, for she is named no more.

The lives of the Provençals, published by Nostradamus, in the sixteenth century, do not agree with the foregoing. They say Sordello was a Mantuan, who at the age of fifteen entered the service of Berenger, Count of Provence, and that his poetry was preferred to that of Folquet of Marseilles, Percival Doria, and all other Genoese and Tuscan troubadours. Beside writing philosophic songs, he wrote in Provençal an essay entitled **"The Progress and Power of the Kings of Arragon in the Comté of Provence."** Among his poems was one especially distinguished,—a satire,—in which, while lamenting the death of Blacas, he burst into a philippic against all Christian princes. He died soon after this, in 1281.

Giambattista d'Arco attributes to Sordello several historical translations out of the Latin into the "vulgar tongue," and an original treatise on **"The Defence of Walled Towns."**

The memoirs of the early Italian poets by Alessandro Tilioli are still unpublished, but the manuscript only repeats the fable of Platina.

Tiraboschi, who had access to a very large number of manuscripts, rejects most of these splendid stories. According to him, Sordello was a Mantuan, born at Goïto, at the very close of the twelfth century. He went into Provence, but not when a boy. He eloped with the wife of his friend, Count Boniface. He was of noble family, and a warrior; but never a captain-general nor a governor of Mantua. He died a violent death, about the middle of the thirteenth century; but in 1281 he would have been a hundred years old!

And this ends the story. As we work our way through the old chronicles, it would seem at times as if there must have been two men,—one a warrior and a thinker, the other a singer only,—whose lives have become inextricably blended, and whose characteristics have bewildered the chroniclers by turns. But the shadowy old Podestà of Mantua, whom Dante is supposed to have remembered with Ghibelline sympathy, eludes observation even more successfully than the troubadour. If he ever lived, he must consent in this day to transfer his "lion port," his "Latin tongue," and **"The Defence of Walled Towns"** he put before the Mantuan council, to the graceless head of the idle singer.

The conflicting tales are only worth recalling because each fragment of them has had more or less to do with Browning's poem.

None of the prose translations, nor any poems, written by Sordello in the Tuscan tongue survive. His verses in the Provençal are all that remain to vindicate his genius. Thirty-four pieces, for the most part gallant songs, challenge the statement of Nostradamus,—that he was devoted to philosophy. Two have been translated by Millot. The refrain of the first is,—

> "Alas! of what use to have eyes
> If they gaze not on her I desire?"

It is written in very pure taste. The second is a more ordinary affair. Three of the pieces are of the sort called "Tensons,"—that is, dialogues. One discusses the duty of a bereaved lover. The second compares the pursuit of knightly feats with the delights of love, and weighs the satisfactions of each. The third discusses "the bad faith of princes,"—a subject which he renews in an epistle addressed to St. Boniface. We should have but a poor opinion of his mettle were this epistle the only testimony to it; for he begs to be excused from joining the crusaders! He "is in no haste," he says, "to enter on eternal life." His other poems are *Sirventes*.

Many of them attack the troubadour Vidal. In these, threats mingled with insults, which become gross as soon as they are translated. Some, which relate to the moral and political aspects of his own time, merit our attention, and doubtless have furnished Browning with more than one pungent line. In one, the poet scoffs at those who, under pretext of extirpating heretical Albigenses, have banded together to despoil Raymond, Count of Toulouse. The Satire in which he entreats this prince not to submit to insult or rapine must have been written in 1228; because it speaks of the absolution just received by Raymond VII.

His best poem is his lament for Blacas, a Spanish troubadour of remarkable personal courage. It is a satire, and sovereign princes are urged to share between them the heart of the hero.

"Let the emperor eat first of it," says the song, "that he may recover what the Milanese have taken! Let the noble King of France eat of it, that he may regain Castile! but it must be when his mother is not looking!" etc.

This King of France was probably Louis IX., and the verses must have been written in the ten years preceding 1236.

The best of Sordello's verses show a dignity of composition and purity of taste which put him in the very front rank of the Provençals. His great hold on posterity consists in the fact that he *preceded Dante in the classic use of the vulgar tongue.*

Ida Farnell (essay date 1896)

SOURCE: "Sordello," in *The Lives of the Troubadours,* David Nutt, 1896, pp. 225-31.

[*In the following excerpt, Farnell attests to the significance of Sordello, citing the high esteem in which Dante held the poet as well as the energy and vitality of the poet's major works. Of these, the critic contends that "Lament for Lord Blacatz" demonstrates "originality and force."*]

The name of Sordel, or Sordello, is a household word among us, and the noble lines in Dante's *Purgatorio,* with the profound and complex character in Browning's poem, cannot but inspire one with a wish to know something of the Sordello of actual life. Yet, on turning to the scanty records, and to the poems left us of him, we are at first somewhat disconcerted. One of the biographies represents him as a false-hearted traitor, false both to the husband who gave him shelter, and to the wife whom he seduced. Some of his canzones are those of a skilful, but somewhat ironic and cynical rhymer, whose chief merit, as has been remarked, is that of saying agreeably what everyone already knows, and whose chief source of pride is the exceeding number of ladies whom he has won and betrayed. Nor should we greatly esteem his valour if we are to regard as a true expression of his sentiments—a poem, in which he begs his lord, the Count of Provence, to excuse him from accompanying him on the Crusade (of 1248), and confesses his fear of the perils to which the expedition would expose him.

Yet this same Sordello is the noble poet, whom Virgil and Dante find sitting in majestic solitude, and the recognition of whom causes them such joy. That his nobility of soul was a mere conception of Dante's we can in no way suppose, and one is therefore brought to the conclusion, that the sins and follies recorded of him were in after years atoned for, and also that the poems of his preserved to us were only a portion, perhaps the least worthy portion, of the work he accomplished. This latter conclusion is, indeed, borne out by Dante's declaring in his *De Vulgari Eloquio,* that Sordello was of great eloquence, in poetry as well as in speech.

[The] originality and force [of Sordello's poem on Blacatz] are in the most striking contrast to the elegant insipidity of some of the canzones, while the splendid audacity of its attack upon the great sovereigns of the age, is without parallel even among the troubadours.

—Ida Farnell

There are three poems, however, that even without Dante's praise of Sordello, would sufficiently testify to his power. The first, which Dante obviously refers to in the *Purgatorio,* where he makes Sordello the guide to the Dale of Kings is a 'complaint.' The second is a long didactic poem, the ***Ensegnamen d'Onor,*** or ***Lesson of Honour,*** a work of considerable interest, some learning, and at times much pithy vigour. It is full of the sentiment of noble pride and reason that inspired Dante in the Convito, and especially in the canzone that treats of true nobility. A third poem is on the death of his friend and rival Blacatz, and its originality and force are in the most striking contrast to the elegant insipidity of some of the canzones, while the splendid audacity of its attack upon the great sovereigns of the age, is without parallel even among the troubadours. Sordello has also left us various very bitter sirventes against individual contemporaries, amongst others, a series of poems against a rival troubadour, who, in his turn, speaks of Sordello as a man who "for his misdeeds had needs flee from Lombardy . . . a false, wanton jongleur, living on his jongleur tricks." We know Sordello on unimpeachable evidence as the friend and counsellor of Charles of Anjou, as a person of sufficient consequence for the Pope to insist upon his being promptly released from captivity. Of his death by violence tradition speaks; and Dante seems to confirm the report by the position he allots him in Purgatory. The Lady Cunizza (sister of Eccelin da Romano, the Ghibelline tyrant), whom Sordello carried off, is also noticed by Dante, and given a place in the Heaven of Venus (*Paradiso,* IX. 13).

"O anima lombarda,
Come ti stavi altera e disdegnosa,
E nel muover degli occhi onesta e tarda!
Ella non ci diceva alcuna cosa;
Ma lasciavane gir, solo guardando
A guisa di leon, quando si posa.
Pur Virgilio si trasse a lei pregando
Che ne mostrasse la miglior salita:
E quella non rispose al suo dimando;
Ma di nostro paese, e della vita
Ci chiese. E'l dolce Duca incominciava:
Mantova. E l'ombra, tutta in sè romita,
Surse vêr lui del luogo ove pria stava,
Dicendo: O mantovano, io son Sordello
Della tua terra. E l'un l'altro abbracciava."

Purgatorio, VI. 61-75.

(—"O Lombard soul,
How lofty and disdainful thou didst bear thee,
And grand and slow in moving of thine eyes,
Nothing whatever did it say to us,
But let us go our way, eyeing us only
After the manner of a couchant lion;
Still near to it Virgilius drew, entreating
That it would point us out the best ascent;
And it replied not unto his demand,
But of our native land and of our life
It questioned us; and the sweet guide began:
'Mantua,'—and the shade all in itself recluse,
Rose tow'rds him from the place where first it was,
Saying, 'O Mantuan, I am Sordello
Of thine own land,' and one embraced the other.")

Longfellow's translation.

An excerpt from Sordello's "Lament for Blacas"

I would lament Sir Blacatz in this simple melody, with sad and sorry heart, and I have indeed reason for it, since in him have I lost a lord and good friend, and all worthy qualities have with his death disappeared. So mortal is the loss that I have not the faintest hope that it might ever be made good, unless in this way: that his heart be cut out and the great nobles eat of it, who now live disheartened—then they'll have heart enough!

Let there first eat of it, because his need is great, the Emperor of Rome, if he wants to conquer the Milanese by force; for they deem him conquered, and he lives deprived of his heritage, in spite of his Germans. And straight after him let the French king eat of it, then he'll recover Castile which he's losing through his stupidity; but if it annoys his mother, he'll not eat of it at all, for it well appears, from his repute, that he does nothing which might annoy her. . . .

Sordello, in Anthology of Troubadour Lyric Poetry, *edited and translated by Alan R. Press, University of Texas Press, 1971.*

H. J. Chaytor (essay date 1902)

SOURCE: "Notes: Sordello," in *The Troubadours of Dante,* Oxford at the Clarendon Press, 1902, pp. 173-76.

[*In the following excerpt, Chaytor outlines Sordello's biographical history and explores Dante's significant inclusion of the poet in the* Purgatorio *and* De Vulgari Eloquentia, *finding that "there is no necessity whatever . . . to imagine that two separate Sordellos are mentioned."*]

There is much uncertainty concerning the facts of Sordello's life: he was born at Goito, near Mantua, and was of noble family. His name is not to be derived from *sordidus,* but from *Surdus,* a not uncommon patronymic in North Italy during the thirteenth century. Of his early years nothing is known: at some period of his youth he entered the court of count Ricciardo di San Bonifazio, the lord of Verona, where he fell in love with his master's wife, Cunizza da Romano (*Par.* ix. 32) and eloped with her. The details of this affair are entirely obscure; according to some commentators, it was the final outcome of a family feud, while others assert that the elopement took place with the connivance of Cunizza's brother, the notorious Ezzelino III (*Inf.* xii. 110): the date is approximately 1225. At any rate, Sordello and Cunizza betook themselves to Ezzelino's court. Then, according to the Provencal biography, follows his secret marriage with Otta, and his flight from Treviso, to escape the vengeance of the angry relatives. He thus left Italy about the year 1229, and retired to the South of France, where he visited the courts of Provence, Toulouse, Roussillon, penetrating also into Castile. A chief authority for these wanderings is the troubadour Peire Bremon Ricas Novas (see introd. to XLII), whose 'sirventes' speaks of him as being in Spain at the court of the king of Leon: this was Alfonso IX, who died in the year 1230. He also visited Portugal, but for this no date can be assigned. Allusions in his poems show that he was in Provence before 1235: about ten years later we find him at the court of the countess Beatrice (*Purg.* vii. 128), daughter of Raimond Berengar, count of Provence, and wife of Charles I of Anjou. Beatrice may have been the subject of several of his love poems: but the 'senhal' Restaur and Agradiva, which conceal the names possibly of more than one lady, cannot be identified. From 1252-1265 his name appears in several Angevin treaties and records, coupled with the names of other well-known nobles, and he would appear to have held a high place in Charles' esteem. It is uncertain whether he took part in the first crusade of S. Louis, in 1248-1251, at which Charles was present: but he followed Charles on his Italian expedition against Manfred in 1265, and seems to have been captured by the Ghibellines before reaching Naples. At any rate, we find him a prisoner at Novara in September 1266; pope Clement IV induced Charles to ransom him, and in 1269, as a recompense for his services, he received five castles in the Abruzzi, near the river Pescara: shortly afterwards he died. The circumstances of his death are unknown, but from the fact that he is placed by Dante among those who were cut off before they could repent it has been conjectured that he came to a violent end. He has left to us forty poems, including fragments and the ***Ensenhamen,*** and stands high above the Provencal-Italian school of his time. Dante mentions him twice—in the famous passage in the *Purgatorio* (vi. 58 *et seqq.*) and in the *De Vulgari Eloquentia* (i. 15). The question why Dante gave Sordello so honourable a place in his poem has been the cause of much controversy: on the one hand, it is said that Sordello's didactic poem, the ***Ensenhamen,*** with its high and pure morality, made a great impression upon Dante; whereas other critics consider the lament for Blacatz as the cause. The arguments are to be seen in detail in De Lollis' edition of Sordello, and O. Schultz, *Zeitschrift für Rom. Phil.* vii. 214. Two facts seem to tell against the ***Ensenhamen*** theory: first, that there were other Provencal didactic works extant, as good as or better than Sordello's poem, and probably no less accessible to Dante: we may instance 'The four cardinal virtues' of Daude de Pradas, and the 'Romans di mondana vida' of Folquet de Lunel. Further, the poetical value of the ***Ensenhamen*** seems small to us, and the sentiment commonplace compared with the chivalrous ideal of the *Vita Nuova,* though its theory agrees with that upheld in the *Convito.* On the other hand, the kings mentioned in the Blacatz lament are partly coincident with the series in the *Purgatorio*: the lament itself was a famous poem, was twice parodied by other troubadours, and must have been known to Dante. In fact, as has been often observed, the episode of the eaten heart at the outset of the *Vita Nuova* is probably drawn from this source.

The passage in the *De Vulg. El.* i. 15 has also been the subject of controversy: 'Dicimus ergo quod forte non male opinantur qui Bononienses asserunt pulcriori locutione loquentes, cum ab Imolensibus, Ferrariensibus et Mutinensibus circumstantibus aliquid proprio vulgari adsciscunt;

sicut facere quoslibet a finitimis suis conicimus, ut Sordellus de Mantua sua ostendit, Cremonae, Brixiae atque Veronae confini: qui tantus eloquentiae vir existens, non solum in poetando, sed quomodocunque loquendo patrium vulgare deseruit.' 'We say, then, that they are probably not far wrong who assert that the people of Bologna speak a more beautiful tongue (than other dialects), because they receive into their own speech some elements from their neighbours of Imola, Ferrara, and Modena; even as we have concluded that anybody (who writes poetry in his vulgar tongue) borrows from his neighbours, as Sordello shows in the case of his native Mantua, to which Cremona, Brescia and Verona are adjacent: and he, who was a man of such distinguished eloquence, not only in poetry, but in every other mode of expression, abandoned his native dialect.' 'Facere' is the 'verbum vicarium,' equivalent to 'aliquid . . . adsciscere,' and 'suis' refers to 'quoslibet.' Dante, then, in searching for the *Illustre vulgare,* speaks of the dialect of Bologna as being mixed: this might be an argument in its favour, inasmuch as he has already pointed out that all writers in their own tongue used a mixed dialect: for examples, see the previous chapters. He now adds a further instance, Sordello, who strengthens the argument in favour of mixed dialects, because so distinguished a man as he employed such a dialect. But, he adds, Sordello abandoned his dialect: that fact shows that it could not have been *curiale et illustre,* just as the defection of Guido Guinicelli and others from the dialect of Bologna is an argument fatal to the pretensions of that dialect, which is the present subject of discussion. In other words, the remark that Sordello abandoned his own dialect for Provencal is an anticipation of the argument employed towards the end of the chapter, whereby the pretensions of Bologna are quashed: if certain local dialects were *curialia et illustria,* poets would not abandon them as they do. The text, then, seems plain as it stands, and there is no necessity whatever to suppose lacunae, or to imagine that two separate Sordellos are mentioned in the *Purgatorio* and the *De Vulg. El.* respectively. If none of Sordello's early essays in his native dialect have come down to us, that is hardly a matter for surprise.

Eugene Benson (essay date 1903)

SOURCE: "Part V," in *Sordello and Cunizza,* J. M. Dent & Co., 1903, pp. 59-87.

[*In the following excerpt from his full-length study of the troubadour, Benson addresses the theory of two Sordellos: one a noble public figure and the other a reckless adventurer and lover. He suggests that Sordello's varied life might be understood as representative of one who abandons the passions of youth for the dignity of adulthood.*]

There are two brief and ancient Provençal documents concerning Sordello—the lives of the Provençal poets, transcribed in red, preceding the specimens of their poetry. One describes him as a Mantuan of the Castle of Goito, a courteous Captain, most attractive in his person, a great lover, but crafty and false to women, and to his hosts with whom he stayed—and states that he loved Cunizza, the sister of Ser Ezzelino and of Ser Alberico of Romano, and wife of Count San Bonifazio; and that he was a great personage who went about with a splendid suite of knights. The other MS. adds he was the son of a poor knight, Ser El Cort, etc.

The first is one of the treasures of the Vatican, the other of the *Bibl. Nationale de Paris.* Both agree as to his excellence as a poet, his flight with Cunizza, and they alike leave no doubt as to his adventurous career and self-exile from Italy, and refuge at the court of the Count of Provence, where he lived in honour.

"Gallant and Bard and Knight" he was, and praising him as such, the Mantuan chroniclers are supported by all that has been found of contemporary testimony concerning him, though we must reject the incidents and orations with which they illustrate and magnify his public life. There is no evidence that he was a Prince Visconti or Lord of Mantua. The oldest Mantuan chronicle (*Breve Chronicon Mantuanum ab anno* 1095-1299) does not mention his name. It was first stated that he was Prince of Mantua by Volteranno, and repeated by Leandro Albertus in his *Descrittione d'Lombardie;* following both, Ziloti, Equiciola, Maffei, Sacchi, Gionta, Sainte-Pelaye, and others to our day call him Prince Visconti, and Lord of Mantua. Pietro Lambechie, in his annotations to Platina's "History of Mantua," remarks that no contemporary mentions Sordello as Prince of Mantua. Sordello may have been Podestà, or Governor of the city at some time. Its form of government was republican, and doubtless he may have been elected Podestà, an office held but for six months at a time, without re-election. It is not improbable that he filled the office with honour, and his position then would account for Volteranno's expression when he called him *principe de Mantua.* That he returned from Provence and distinguished himself in the defence of the city when Ezzelino ravaged the land, may be true, but we lack historic evidence of it. Legend alone, generally based on truth, first presents him as the valiant defender of his mother city. It is only when he is associated with Charles of Anjou that we have historic data of his later military life and of his public importance. He is spoken of as *dominus Sordellus* in an act of the year 1259 when Charles Count of Anjou and of Provence receives as a part of his dominion the city of Cuneo. He is one of the eight witnesses of the deed, and his name appears with other personages who are present: he also appeared in an official character as a follower of Charles of Anjou in the city of Riez, in the Bishop's palace; as a witness, with other dignitaries, to attest the treaty between Guido Delfino of Albona and of Vienne, and Charles of Anjou in 1257. Sordello is one of the signers with other persons of importance; and, on the same day, and at the same place, another document is signed by sixteen witnesses, the Bishop of Frioul, and other personages of rank and merit, including "*il milite Sordello.*" That he was a man of consequence in the suite of Charles of Anjou is indisputable. The legend that so persistently associates his name with the time of Mantuan liberty, may stand as so much tribute to his fame—though of a later date. O. Schultze, whose researches have brought together some new facts concerning Sordello, refers to a notice by Bartholemy, from which it appears that Barral de Baux transmitted to Sordello, on the 15th of December 1255, fifty pounds, which were due to Sordello as part of the yearly pension paid to him by the commune of Marseilles. It is also apparent from Buffi, *Histoire de Marseilles,* referred to by O. Schultze, that Sordello lived at Marseilles at the Court of Barral, and later, that he served as witness in a matter between Anjou and the Bishop of Marseilles at San Remy in 1257.

Sordello's adventures, his losses at play—one satire in Provençal plainly charges him with being a desperate gambler—his love of good company, his disputes, in the fashion of his day, with rival wits and troubadours, and later, his professed distaste for military life, have so far compromised his name that there is question of *two* Sordellos, for some have found it difficult to reconcile the youth of Sordello, his early manhood even, with the impressive personality described by Dante—the lover and companion of Virgil in the Under World—the translator of Cæsar, the austere patriot, grieved and indignant at the condition of Italy. Several writers, who have attempted to tell Sordello's story, have resorted to this theory of two Sordellos, attributing to one an illustrious origin, the honours of the defence of Mantua, a grave and studious life, and the violent death of an Italian patriot of the thirteenth century, whom they call Prince Visconti, Podestà of Mantua; the other Sordello is the famous troubadour who went to Provence, to whom it pleased the early Italian chroniclers to attribute the heroic deeds and lost writings of the great Mantuan who was so admired by Dante. To confirm the theory of two Sordellos they cited Dante's treatise in prose, *de la volgare eloquenza* in which he speaks of a poet called Gotto, Mantovano, and elsewhere, in the same work alludes to Sordello of Mantua, in a passage which, if not taken in its obvious sense, is perplexing. Tiraboschi's conjecture that Dante's poet, called Gotto, Mantovano, is one and the same person as Sordello Mantovano, seems to be correct, and there are satisfactory reasons for thinking that the Sordello of the *Ante Purgatorio* is the Sordello alluded to in Dante's *Volgare eloquenza.* In that treatise, he says, Sordello is admirable in his language; not only in his poems, but in whatever fashion he expresses himself; for he abandoned the common speech or dialect. Dante does not say that Sordello wrote Provençal, but speaks of him as a poet, and we must infer that Sordello expressed himself in the *aulic* or courtly language, *il linguagio nobile.* Nothing of his Italian poetry but a conjectural piece attributed to him has reached us.

Benvenuto da Imola, who relates Sordello's adventurous love for Cunizza, affirms that Ezzelino drove him away and that his emissaries followed and assassinated him. The story no doubt was the popular version, for a long time accepted, to account for Sordello's disappearance from North Italy. Rolandino's expression concerning him has not escaped comment. In his account of Ezzelino, he says, *Sordellus de ipsius familia.* Did he mean that he was by birth of the same family, or merely that he was of the household, or in the service of the family of Romano? There is no other indication of a family tie. The Chronicle of Pietro Gerardo of Padua, purporting to have been written in the time of Ezzelino (but its geniuneness has since been questioned), mentions Sordello as a man faithful to Ezzelino. The fact that he carried off Ezzelino's sister from her husband at her own brother's instigation, indicates that he held close and trusted relations with the family of Romano. Rolandino's allusion to Sordello as of the family of Ezzelino, gives probability to Browning's representation of the famous troubadour in his youth living under the care of Adelaide, the Florentine wife of Ezzelino III. As we have pointed out, conjecture can lead us in no more alluring path, nor find a more interesting situation, than by following Sordello and Cunizza from the days of their childhood in one of the many castles of the Ezzelini, at the base of the Venetian Alps—at Bassano, or Verona,—to the time of her marriage with Count Richard, the hereditary foe of her family, and to her flight with Sordello two years later. That Sordello should have become notorious as a gallant by this adventure with the young wife of a prominent nobleman, is to say he bore himself like a knight who was bound to rescue and serve his lady; the law of honour of the time, made such service paramount to all other obligations. Whatever claims his host, the Count of Saint Boniface had in his absence upon Sordello, they were not sufficient to make him resist the wishes and the commands of the family of Romano urging him to assist Cunizza to escape from her husband's castle. As it is expressly stated that he took her away at the instigation of her brothers, it is not improbable that some tie of blood bound him to execute their wishes; some potency of association, some urgent necessity, enlisted him to act for them and for his lady. So much at least is suggested if not defined by Rolandino, who does not censure Sordello for his conduct in the affair—that is left to the older Provençal biographer. He rather seems to justify him, while he relates Cunizza's own adventures, and depicts her as an extravagant and restless spirit. The precise degree of family interest and personal passion, or the chivalric disinterestedness of his age, that gave impetus to Sordello's conduct at the castle of San Bonifazio, is hardly to be determined at this late hour, and we must accept it as we find it, an incident of mediæval private life. For thirty-five years the rival families of Romano and Bonifazio were battling with each other, now in the streets of Verona, now at Vicenza, Padua, Ferrara,—ravaging each other's lands and assaulting each other's castles. The whole Trevisian March, and part of Lombardy, followed the fortunes of one or the other of these leaders—the one Guelph, the other Ghibelline—Bonifazio, partisan of the Pope, Ezzelino, Vicar of the German Emperor, Frederic II. Both sought their own aggrandisement, and each other's destruction; for they were not less intent on public sway than private vengeance. Contemporary testimony tells us that Sordello was *pros e valens,* as he was called in a tenzon by Alberico of Romano, then Podestà of Treviso. But he was not a man to remain a mere partisan or but a man of action. Probably his sincerity, his sensibility, his imagination, made it impossible for him to give himself entirely to the personal animosities of his time. Be this as it may, his own humanising passion had compromised him with the two most potent lords of North Italy. On one side was his enemy Count Richard of San Bonifazio, allied with the great Lord of Este, on the other was Ezzelino, the Ghibelline, for the most part master of all between the Brenta and the Piave. Sordello had given mortal offence to both. He found himself in danger of sudden death at the hands of one, or both, united to drive him from Italy, or to destroy him. He seems to have gone first to the Court of Alberic of Romano, at the time at enmity with his brother Ezzelino. There, too, Cunizza went, for she also left Verona and her dreaded brother, to live under the roof of Alberic at Treviso. Before or later, Sordello went beyond, to Onigo, and perhaps to the Court of the Patriarch of Aquileia. According to the brief biography in the Provençal Codex, at the Vatican, he became involved in a love affair with Otta of Onigo. She was the sister of his hosts, two brothers, the lords of the land.

The immediate cause of Sordello's flight from Italy was not only the enmity of Count Bonifazio, but the nearer and more pressing one of the exasperation of the brothers—the lords of Strasso—whose sister, Otta, he had clandestinely married, after which we hear of him at Treviso, where, in spite of powerful protection, he was not secure. At any rate then and there was closed his experience in the *marca Treviziana.* He appears next in Provence, and there is evidence that he went to Spain and Portugal. De Lollis, who traces him step by step from his part in a tavern brawl at Florence on to the last historic record of his life in the suite of Charles of Anjou in the Kingdom of Naples, has left no fact unexamined concerning him. His deductions sometimes lower rather than enhance the historic figure of Sordello, who, like Dante, or King David, outgrew the sins of his youth—the rank dressing of his lusty years—nor did they prevent him from becoming, as we have seen, one of the most honoured and striking personalities of a great epoch. One modern critic censures his conduct both as regards Cunizza and Otta, and another would induce us to think that he gave a platonic love to Cunizza, but acquitted himself badly in eloping with Otta, whom he abandoned. How culpable he was towards one or both of his hosts is not for us to determine at this late date. But it is manifest that he was without defence. His situation was not only one of great peril, it meant certain destruction for him if he remained in Italy. And furthermore he probably had little sympathy for the ruthless purpose of either party who sought the headship of Italy to rule in the name of Pope or Emperor. He went into exile. He went to the most civilised court of Europe—to Provence, where his fame preceded him. He had already become known as a Provençal poet, and he was appealed to as a judge of good verse. Americ de Peguillan of Toulouse, who lived some time in Italy, concludes one of his own pieces of verse by saying that his messenger will carry it to Sordello, who will give a true verdict upon it according to his custom. This circumstance is cited as a proof that the Provençals themselves regarded him as a judge of Provençal poetry.

Sordello is best explained as one of those rich organisations more often met with perhaps in Italy, but which every man of genius in greater or less degree illustrates. His life reveals the difference which exists in such a man between his youth and age. We see he outlived the mob of his passions, and reached the dignity of a grand character. He became entirely delivered from what are called the sins of youth. They had their time of blossoming. It is correct to represent him as too finely organised, too much in advance of his time, to be willing to give himself wholly to the life of action, and as a fighting man and politician emulate or succeed to Salinguerra, or do the work of an Ezzelino. This is in strict conformity with the historic evidence concerning Sordello. He did indeed keep himself more or less apart from the bloody business of his time—till the last account of him in 1267, when Charles of Anjou sends him to Naples and he is referred to as Sordello of Godio. He was for many years in the service of one of the most implacable men of the age. Strange destiny, associated briefly, in his youth with the terrible Ezzelino, in his latest years with Anjou—the two greatest soldiers and tyrants of his time! But even Ezzelino was not always a horror to men. He comes to us splendid and pleasant, at a moment of knightly life, in an anecdote kept in the *Cento Novelle.*

Sordello's residence at the court of the Count of Provence lets us see him in the most brilliant and honoured conditions of his being, and knowing something of it at least adds to our sense of the *milieu* of his life at that time.

Provence is a country of fervid and dazzling skies, rivalling both Italy and Spain in colour, in light, and in form. The afterglow of Greece and Rome shone there, for Roman refinement survived longest between the Alps and the Pyrenees. From the eleventh to the thirteenth century a brilliant life and a new literature made the country a centre of cultivated interest. Its literature was formative even in Italy. It drew from Italy poets of great name. The three elements of what has been called artistic poetry, love of glory, enjoyment of life, and worship of woman, found the most remarkable expression in the poets of its refined and passionate people. Everything favoured their delicate and ardent imagination. Moorish influences from Spain enriched their life after Greek and Latin influences had been exhausted. Provence gave to the world what has been well called the courtly poetry, the poetry of a privileged class, of privileged lives; it was brilliant, exclusive, extravagant; an expression of studied art, of delicate sentiment. It was admired and praised by Dante. Its poets were princes, barons, knights; and yet in the crowd of courtly poets of rank were men of obscure origin and poor estate, lifted by their gifts and rewarded for their talents. Any man of merit and fame was sure of a welcome at the castle courts of the great lords of the South of France.

Sordello was fortunate in seeking this land of princes and poets. Count Raymond Berenger the Fifth was surrounded by men of distinction from all parts of Europe, and his court was perhaps the most splendid of all the great seigneurs of Provence. It was compared to King Arthur's.

It is affirmed that Sordello first went to Provence at the age of seventeen, called to the service of Count Berenger V. because of his excellence as a poet, and his "curious and learned inventions."

The family of the Count of Provence was of singular interest and high in fortune. His four daughters made illustrious marriages: each one became a queen. Marguerite was married to Louis, King of France; Eleanor to Henry III., King of England; Souci to Richard, Count of Cornwall; and the youngest daughter, Beatrice, became wife of Charles, Count of Anjou, in 1246, one year after the death of her father, and lived to be crowned Queen of Naples. Sordello remained attached to the fortunes of this princely family about forty years after the death, in 1245, of his protector, Count Raymond. It is not without interest to know that the tombs of his great patrons are in the church of St John at Aix in Provence, where you may still see the effigy of the old lover of a splendid and cultivated life. He holds in one hand his sword and in the other the Rose of Gold given by Innocent IV.; and there, also at his side, is the statue of Beatrice of Savoy, his wife.

There is but the barest indication of Sordello's presence at other courts in the South of France—at Marseilles, at Montpellier, at Toulouse. But to all the long period of his life in Provence we are guided by a few widely separated dates and the mention of a few cities.

When Sordello appeared in Provence a new life brightened again the land which but a few years before had been made a place of wailing by the merciless persecutions of Innocent III.; and it was in its liberated and awakened society that Sordello confirmed his fame as a Provençal poet. To this period of his life belong many of his poems. They emanated from a fearless spirit. In them he disputes, praises, or laments; or, in friendly contest with a rival poet, celebrates his lady. Sometimes he expresses the perfect submission of a Provençal lover; then in scornful terms he resents injurious comment on the cause of his flight from Lombardy. We learn from his verse the name of the Countess of Rhodes; of Agradiva; of Cunizza; great ladies whom he adored: and there is a mystery as to which one he calls his *bel restaurs,* which one he calls his *doussa enemia.* In these poems we find him, so to speak, in the full play of his spirit, all but a Provençal himself, rising to manly grandeur in the universally admired *Serventes* or *Planh* in which he sang his sorrow for the loss of Blacas. The grace of a perfect artist is shown in the turn he gives to his satire, which strikes to the quick the weakness or the vice it touches; but he does not leave with us the bitter sense of it, nor does he compromise himself, or appear as a mere railer. We feel his serene and amiable nature while he says that he is so hated by great barons because he openly tells the truth, yet turns to his Lady with: "Lady, beautiful restorer, dear as life, so long as I find you kind I care not who is unfriendly," and he leaves us with the thought of him as a tender and delicate soul. But in some of his poems he does not appear heroic, nor do they even express any elevation of mind.

It is perhaps best to be indulgent towards him concerning their significance. And in any case, we are not to take them as indicative of the temper and pitch of his character; for there is a point, a mood, when every man, no matter how great his genius, or how high his sentiment of life, is on the level of common things, and expresses them. A great dramatist, like Shakespeare, delivers himself of this vulgar mood in his comic characters. Shakespeare's Falstaff, his Sir Toby, his fools and clowns are at least so much of his mind, that we can say: so, at a given moment, he thought, saw life, used the stuff of his experience. A purely lyric genius has not this vicarious issue for his personal moods nor his commoner sympathies: he either keeps them voiceless, or, like Beaudelaire, compromises himself by confessing to the world what bad company he has met, and what reprehensible thoughts have possessed him.

Sismondi's sweeping conclusion about Provençal poetry, his censure of its scandalous element, is one that bears upon every literature of life. It is intemperate to press it exclusively against the Provençal poets; and Sismondi contradicts himself, and yet is nearer the truth when he says:—"Cependant c'est un merite de la poesie Provençale d'avoir rendu un culte a cette beauté cheveleresque, et d'avoir conservé au milieu des vices du siècle le respect de ce qui est honnête, et l'amour des sentiments élevés."

The exaggerated sentiments, the over-refined language, and constant interest in the springtime of life of the Provençal poets, and their worship of the lady, was an offset to mediæval invective *contro fœminis.* Before we object to it all, or repeat the usual phrase about the monotony and the immorality of the courtly poetry, we should consider how much more objectionable was the expression of the common or popular mind against women. The Provençal poets exalted "the Lady" as a true civiliser, they celebrated her as a purifying element of matter, while the clergy degraded woman as a provocation to "sin." Mediæval Latin abounds in gross invective, in ribald satire against women, because the ascetic mind of the time found in her, as in love, in marriage, and even in the family, not only its corrective, but its most potent adversary. All honour, then, to the Provençal poets who reacted against the darker mind of their age and broke through its restricting and false morality. Their sentiment of life was far more humanising and liberating than the teaching of the cloister and the practices of the cell. When Italy was traversed by thousands of flagellants grovelling and bleeding in pentitential abasement, or rushing wildly from city to city striving after the impossible, neither the Umbrian madman nor the Umbrian saint were justified. If we look then to Provence, or to the Marca Trevigiana, and to the last Provençal poets, we find something better, and Sordello in his disinterested worship of his lady appears nearer to us than the fanatics of his age. When he says he asks of love but consolation and honour he is like a modern man.

Though Sordello had early and frequent intercourse with the Provençals, he remained Italian in his spirit, and realistic rather than extravagant, like many of the poets of the South of France. He was a realist in love; he was not scholastic and metaphysic like Guido Guinecelli and Dante. He even said he would write for his lady simply, and things easily understood. Dante, though he developed the "philosophic" argument as it was not dreamed of by the Provençals, is in his most potent expression a true successor and imitator of Sordello—realistic in expression, ideal in sentiment, direct, vivid, personal. Italian poetry of the thirteenth century, while it derived much from the Provençal, embodied a new element—abstract and difficult for most readers. But Sordello, Italian as he was, did not illustrate nor express the new spirit, though it is claimed he shows a glimmering of it—of the *dolce stil nuovo*—of Dante and Cavalcante, which was developed after his work was done. Italian poetry of the *Vita Nuova,* the new life, the new love, was far more mystical than Sordello's, whose wit and charm and passion sought a more direct expression, more vigorous, and at once satiric and fervid. His satire is terse, vital, conclusive. His expression of sentiment has a certain passionate grace which confirms the report that he was the most irresistible troubadour of his time. He even boasts that no one could resist his advances; and, like D'Annunzio to-day, regarded himself in his youth as an "uomo fatale." This part of his story no doubt belongs to his reckless days. He reached a graver mind, a nobler fame.

Canello thought Sordello's lament for Blacas Pindaric in its force and fire. Perticare devoted himself to prove that it was so admired by Dante that he even adopted the primary image or conception of it, an image which seems barbarous and revolting to our taste, in the nineteenth century, and it is startling enough to arrest attention even now. A heart of flame, a heart pierced with seven swords, symbol of the seven sins, visible, represented in its proper form, carved or painted upon the breast of a Madonna, or of an image of Christ, either in Spain, Italy, or France, often shocks our Northern taste in these countries, and we quite forget the bloody and lurid rhetoric of our own hymns—

> "There is a fountain filled with blood
> Drawn from Emmanuel's veins."

All of which is kindred to the symbolism of fact—the image of a heart to be eaten—which I find in Sordello's famous poem, and also in Dante's *Vita Nuova*—

> *e d'este core ardendo*
> *Lei paventosa umilmento pascea.*

Sordello by a bold and sudden expression of his imagination recommends that a piece of the great heart of Blacas be given to each of the cowardly princes he names, that they may get courage by feeding upon it. With this strong metaphor he expresses his high sense of his friend's virtues and his scorn for the princes who lacked the courage for which Blacas was renowned. No funeral lament ever served better to express at the same time a sense of the worth of the dead and contempt for the living. The irony of it is unsurpassed. This celebrated poem, of which there have been several translations in Italian, stirred the troubadours of the day. It gave them a new suggestion, a new idea, and they tried to equal it, if not to surpass it, imitating Sordello's **"Lament."** It has been remarked that up to the time of its appearance the Provençal poets had produced funeral elegies which were "as monotonous as they were cold." Sordello distinguished himself by his originality, and there is something both new and felicitous in the *motif* and expression of this little piece; it would be difficult to say which is the most poignant, the terms of praise or of satire, that with so much energy and frankness are contrasted with each other. I am but quoting the language of Fauriel, commenting on Sordello's famous verse. I may add that it is plainly the expression of a living and indomitable mind, as remarkable for its proud and derisive spirit as for its freshness. Bertrand d'Allamanon and Peire Bremon both adopted Sordello's idea, one suggesting that Blacas' heart should be given to noble ladies as heavenly food; the other dividing his body between nations as a miracle-working substance.

With this strong metaphor [Sordello] expresses his high sense of his friend's virtues and his scorn for the princes who lacked the courage for which Blacas was renowned. No funeral lament ever served better to express at the same time a sense of the worth of the dead and contempt for the living. The irony of it is unsurpassed.

—Eugene Benson

I should leave the reader with an inadequate idea of Sordello's poetry by referring only to this often cited poem. It is said that there is more originality and talent shown in his satirical than in his love poems; and yet, several of these last are admitted to be both charming and graceful. Very interesting is Sordello's own admission that he affects two styles, one simple and easy to understand, the other a thing of great art. He says: "It gives me pleasure to compose a pleasant song to a gay air. The dearest lady of my choice to whom I give myself, does not enjoy verses written with studied art. Since it does not please her, henceforth I will only write songs easy to sing, pleasant to hear, plain in meaning; songs for her who likes what is artless."

In one of his most bitter *serventes* he replies to an attack by Peire Bremon, and says he will unmask the idiot who has accused him of imposture. It is in this piece that Sordello resents being called a *jongleur*—

> *Ben a gran tort car m'apella joglar*
> (Vatican *codice*).

and in a few lines the difference of social condition of a troubadour and a *jongleur,* is stated. Speaking of himself

Sordello says he does not follow others, but others follow him; that he takes nothing which can be made a reproach to him; that he is just and loyal, and lives upon his own revenues. After drawing the portrait of his slanderer, he declares that if he meets the gallant who libels him, he will assuredly give his wife occasion to wear mourning; vows to justify his threats if he catches him, and adds that all the gold of Montpellier will not save him from his blows. Another of his poems turns upon a question of chivalry and love. It is a debate with his friend Bertrand d'Allamanon. Sordello makes himself the exponent of the lover, Bertrand is the advocate of the knight. Sordello says it is a poor business to exchange the lover's delights for blows, and hunger, and cold, and heat. He expresses his aversion to the soldier's ideal. After boasting of his own preference for "the sovereign joys of love," he says, that he goes to the embrace of his lady while his friend Bertrand goes to battle, and if Bertrand has the esteem of the great French lords, he has the sweet kisses of his love, which are worth the finest stroke of lance in all the world. It is obvious that if we take this debate seriously Sordello represents himself as a "*lâche* Lombard." But doubtless only a man who had given well-known proofs of valour, and whose courage was beyond question would have ventured this kind of pleasantry. Very likely it was his extravagant way of playing a higher compliment to his mistress; for by declaring he holds glory less than her love, he for the moment shows himself the more extravagant in his love; the super-subtle Italian outdoes the Provençal in a contest at the Castle Court, to win the favour of his lady. He seems to have loved a noble lady who gave him by word no encouragement, but whose look bid him to hope. She is that lady of whose tender glance he tells us in one of his poems. He says that since the eyes have no power to deceive he will believe what they tell him. This lady is "full of honour and virtue," the object of his most delicate and passionate homage. The ideal is present in his love poems, and there is also grace and mockery in them; in others we find an exultant and boastful libertinage. In a spirit of Italian bravado he says that the whole world has made war upon him because of his amours, and that he is advised to change his ways; that everybody tells him of his dangers from jealous husbands. He says that they have indeed good cause to be jealous, but that he neither cares for their displeasure or hatred. He says no woman has ever resisted his "sweet solicitations." All this no doubt expresses an average Italian morality of the time, and it is now hardly amusing. He is redeemed by a better mood, one of true devotion and refined taste. His dispute with Bertrand shows his purely Italian spirit, at bottom practical, keen, calculating.

Sordello requests Charles of Anjou not to take him to the Crusades. He says he is in no hurry to go to Paradise; that the sea makes him sick, though it may be good for the health of other men. He recommends it to his old friend Bertrand. All this, with its mixture of license and good sense, and its very modern temper, is but the playfulness of a lively spirit, nor should it be taken so seriously as to discredit his courage and fidelity. And yet it has so far put him in question, that Emeric David refused to accept him as the same Sordello whom Dante admired. Even Fauriel could not reconcile the Sordello of the verse with the Sordello of Dante, and thought Dante must have ignored not only his poetry, but his real character,—using him wilfully as a type of his own patriotism.

Perticare, who is supported by Bartoli, is of the opinion that, on the contrary, Dante was so truly informed of, and filled with sympathy for the historic Sordello, and that he so well understood his mind, that his own famous expression of sorrow over Italy in the Seventh Canto of the *Purgatorio,* is wholly in the temper of Sordello himself, and that Dante absorbs, as it were, the genius of the Mantuan troubadour. The spirit is Sordello's, but the great monologue is Dante's.

Twice thus, by two poets, Sordello's spirit has been evoked, and his name has been used as the fit and noblest expression, the personal embodiment of their own sentiment of life. What Dante did, Browning has done in his own way, following Dante's example, giving to his thoughts the prestige of Sordello's name.

Like Dante, Sordello's intellect was first awakened by love. The years transformed an earthly passion, and he appears in a graver character. "A ceaseless round of study" led him, like our own Milton, "to the shady places of philosophy"; for it is as a writer of learned treatises that he is first mentioned after Dante. Nostredamus, citing the record of the monk of the island of Lerins, refers to his treatises on the gravest subjects in the library of the convent, and says that love is not the theme of his verse.

Sainte-Pelaye and Crescimbeni—the one in France, the other in Italy—were the first to correct this statement by mentioning that fifteen of his poems are devoted to love. But it was as the writer of the **"Thesaurus Thesaurum,"** of **"Summa Juris,"** and of **"Los progres e avansaments dei Res d'Aragon"** that he was held in esteem by his immediate successors. His satire on "the Great Barons" in the form of a funeral lament for his own great-hearted friend Blacas, is oftener mentioned and cited than his love poems. But he is the author of a remarkable expression concerning the sweet tyranny of a woman over the life of her lover. He calls her *dolza enemia*—sweet enemy, an expression which both Petrarch and Bramante have appropriated; and it appears again in the French verse of Du Bellay. Perhaps the most original of Sordello's terms of endearment is when he calls his lady *Belh Restaur*—beautiful restorer.

We have no data to determine Sordello's precise relations to the later political tragedies of his time. De Lollis thinks that he was at the battle of Benevento. He is but able to cite documents of 1269—after the victory of Charles of Anjou—wherein Sordello is endowed with feudal rights over five castles and adjacent land in the Abruzzi. These documents show that Sordello was honoured and trusted, and, in fact, his *grandia grato et accepta servitia* is recorded: *Sordellus de Godio delectus miles familiaris et fidelis.* And, citing the deed, Prof. de Lollis says that the two titles had a real and definite value; for that of *miles* was conferred only upon one who had been knighted by the king, with the usual ceremony; and the term *familiaris* implied rights and duties highly honourable at Court.

It was a sixteenth century legend that Sordello was buried at San Pietro, in Mantua—that city set by the Mincio, which there spreads its shining waters into twin lakes. The old town has a bridal look in spring-time, with its blossoming orchards and green meadows. So beautiful and broad a vision of fresh and limpid water gives to the lily city an enchanting aspect, and it could hardly ever have been obliterated from the mind of a poet. It is, perhaps, with a lasting sense of the hold of first impressions, and the dearness of one's native place, that Dante represented Sordello's watchful spirit suddenly surging out of silence at the mention of "Mother City." The brilliant figure of the splendid cavalier of the *Marca Treviziana,* the unrivalled poet of Provence in Italy, is supplanted by the graver personage of later life, the "good" Sordello with something majestic, something of what Aristotle called magnificence in his nature, alone, yet free to companion the greatest spirits—

un anima
Sola soletta, verso noi riguarda.

M. A. Dunne (essay date 1910)

SOURCE: "One of Dante's Troubadours," in *The American Catholic Quarterly Review,* Vol. XXXV, No. 140, October, 1910, pp. 606-24.

[*In the following essay, Dunne contrasts three views of the character of Sordello—as revealed by a Provençal chronicler, by Dante in his* Purgatorio, *and by Browning in his poem* Sordello—*proposing that "the real Sordello lives in no one of the three."*]

I.

THE SORDEL OF THE CHRONICLERS.

Sordel—a soft, uncertain, two syllabled cadence—we find the name on the illuminated pages of the Provença chroniclers; Sordello, stronger for the added vowel, we spell it out through the soft starlight of Dante's middle realm, and Sordello it remains through all the six cantos of Browning's marvelous unscrolling of the incidents in the development of a human soul. It was in the high suntide of the mediæval period that the historic Sordello first came into prominence. When he died it was sundown of the ages of faith. He was contemporary at birth with Albertus Magnus, Thomas Aquinas and Innocent III., and at death with Duns Scotus, Roger Bacon and the founders of the English House of Commons. The jongleurs have told his tale after their fashion, intermingling fact and fancy, presenting first-hand and second-hand information with the impartiality of a delightfully naïve credulity. The sad-eyed exile of Florence has taken up the theme and sketched it in his strong, simple way, illuminating the lines of truth and beauty and shrouding in merciful shadows the years of weakness, the hours of cowardice, the moments of shame. And finally Browning comes with his insistent "and you shall hear Sordello's story told," unfolding the development of the soul of the poet, inventing a brilliant episode, startling us by the boldness of an unforeseen conclusion. But the real Sordello lives in no one of the three. The chroniclers were simple and obvious; they failed. Dante was balanced perfectly between crass obviousness and the eerie-suggestiveness of the ultra-esoteric. He did not succeed. Browning wrote for the attentive reader in a style full of elisions and abrupt transitions. But Sordello's story remains untold. The mediæval gossips give us their legends; they are the hearsays of the period. Dante abridges these accounts for us, emphasizing the good and eliminating the evil. This is the idealization of a kindred spirit. Browning generalizes the incidents, so that what was the story of one man becomes the history of all mankind, the key to the tragedy of all idealism and the comedy of all realism.

There are three accounts concerning the birth of Sordello. According to an old Proven¸al manuscript in the Vatican he was the son of a poor knight named El Corte. Another version, based upon a line in Rolandino's chronicle, makes him a member of the family of Salinguerra. The third, Aliprando, in his rhyming history of Milan, avers that he was of noble birth, belonging to the house of the Visconti. All three agree that he was born in Goito, near Mantua, at the close of the twelfth century, probably between 1189 and 1194. On the highway between Brescia and Mantua one passes the little village of Goito, "tidy, white and quiet." A heap of ancient ruins, a wall of impressive thickness and a narrow door are all that remain of the famous castle, "the lodge of the Lady Adelaide." There is nothing of romantic charm, no leafy paths nor pebbly brooks nor wild ravines with unexpected heights and depths as described by Browning. Six hundred years ago it was much as it is to-day. Then, as now, swampy flats and shallow marshes stretched away on every side to meet monotonous sweeps of meadow broken at regular intervals by long rows of mulberry bushes. From the early days of sudden onslaught by fierce Gothic hordes to the latest encounters between Austrians and Piedmontese in 1848, Goito's fortunes have been linked with those of its important neighbor, Mantua. But after all the throb and tumult of its stirring history, it boasts but one claim to immortality, one association that insures perpetuation to its name—on its reedy plain was born Sordello, the mysterious, the most celebrated of the early Italian minstrels, one who wrote in the style of the earlier French troubadours and in their Provencal tongue.

It is to Aliprando's rhyming chronicle we must turn if we would find the source of the Sordellan legends recounted by the earlier biographers. Aliprando tells us of the boy Sordel, and how as a youth he astounded the world of letters by a wonderful poem, **"Le Trésor;"** how when he grew to manhood, arms proved more seductive than letters and challenge after challenge was accepted from overconfident knights; how the King of France, hearing of these deeds of valor, invited the brave bard to cross the Alps—of Sordello's preparations for the journey and how at the last moment he changed his mind at the earnest entreaty of Ezzelino da Romano, who urged him to come to reside with the Romano family at Verona; of his sojourn at Verona, and how when he found that Ezzelino's sister Beatrice was losing her heart to him, he fled to Mantua; how Beatrice followed him disguised as a page; of his marriage with Beatrice; of his visit to France, where his valor, gallantry and poetic talents were greatly admired; of the presents bestowed upon him by the King, three thousand francs and a golden falcon; how he returned to Italy, where he was received with great pomp as the first warrior of his time; how the Mantuans came out to greet him, but he refused to tarry until he reached Verona, where he was reunited with his bride; of his return with her to Mantua, where they were welcomed by eight days of public rejoicing. Then comes the story of Ezzelino's anger because of the marriage and of his attempt to take the city; of Sordello's defense of the walls and of Ezzelino's ignominious defeat. The narrative concludes with an account of the onset of the poet at the head of a band of Milanese against his crafty enemy. For the second time Sordello was the victor, slaying his opponent with his own hands.

The whole narrative is a sorry mixture of blind anachronism and blundering romance. Tiraboschi rejects most of it. And yet this chronicle is the storehouse from which the historical writers of the next century drew their stories of the Goitan troubadour and of the Lady Beatrice, who never existed. Tiraboschi had access to a large number of early manuscripts which he studied faithfully and transcribed with an almost Teutonic accuracy and patience. He says that Sordello was born near Mantua towards the close of the twelfth century; that he went to Provence when a boy; that he eloped with the wife of Count Richard, of Saint Boniface; that he was of noble birth and a famous warrior; that he died a violent death in the middle of the thirteenth century. Rolandino inserts in his version an ambiguous line, upon which Browning founds the relationship of Sordello and Salinguerra. "Cunizza, wife of Richard of Saint Boniface," Rolandino writes, "and sister of Ezzelino da Romano, was stolen from her husband by one Sordello, *who was of the same family.*" Benvenuto d'Imola's note to Canto VI. of the Purgatorio is not without interest. "Sordello was a native of Mantua," Benvenuto tells us, "an illustrious and skillful warrior and an accomplished courtier. This chevalier lived in the time of Ecelin da Romano, whose sister conceived for him a violent affection. Informed of this intrigue, Ecelin disguised himself as a servant and surprised the unfortunate pair. The poet promised on his knees not to repeat the offense. But the cursed Cunizza dragged him anew to perdition. He was naturally grave, virtuous and prudent. To withdraw himself from Ecelin he fled, but was pursued and assassinated."

Modern students of Provençal literature have spared no pains in their quest of the truth underlying this tissue of biographical fact and legendary fancy. The result has been an endless controversy, in which one faction loudly condemns, while the other heaps up superlative praises. De Lollis can see in Sordello only a time-serving adventurer, Guelph or Ghibelline as occasion demanded, a mediocre poet, a faithless lover and a betrayer of the confidence of his friend and patron, Richard of Saint Boniface. Torraca can see only the most celebrated of the Provençals, a poet of unusual vigor and fecundity, a noble patriot, a dauntless warrior. This diversity of opinion, based upon divergent historical accounts, has led to the theory that there were two Sordellos, contemporaries—the one a poet, student and philosopher; the other a vagabond soldier, a tramp—jongleur, a tavern-brawler, the hero of the many graceless episodes that have been erroneously associated with the name of the great Lombardy troubadour. Through the painstaking researches of Gitterman several documents have been brought to light that seem to point to the existence not only of two, but of three Sordellos, all living in Northern Italy in the early decades of the thirteenth century. To the third Sordello Gitterman attributes the adventure with Cunizza. There is much to be said in favor of the triumvirate. But it would seem that since all three are connected in the Provençal accounts with Ezzelino, and since all three are synchronal and synspatial, it is possible that they were also identical in personality. The high praise of Dante and the gossip of the Provençal tale-bearers, in all likelihood, refer to the same man. Perhaps Sordello, like his successor, Dante, found himself with life half spent, "all in a gloomy wood astray, gone from the path direct." Perhaps his youth was desecrated by leaps of overvaulting ambition, an inordinate love of self-aggrandizement and lawless pleasure-guests. But if he came at last to see the error of his ways; if in the end he followed the Light and abjured Darkness; if his later years were consecrated to truth-seeking and beauty-loving and the doing of good, we must judge him by his final choice, not by his early errors. It is the Master's way to be merciful. Our age, however, is too apt to speak of repentant sinners as if their sinning and repenting were something to their credit. The true penitent never sees sin in that light. By every deliberate choice of evil something is forever lost—lost for eternity. The Master pardoned Peter, but John was the disciple that He loved.

Besides, we must not forget that De Lollis and his school of critics find plenty of evidence to support their censures. Early in his twenties Sordello appears as a disturber of the peace in a tavern at Florence. A fight ensues and a wine flask is broken over the poet's head. Then there is the story of his cowardly refusal to accompany Saint Louis on a crusade because of his fear of rough waters. His apologists insist that this refusal was a mere pleasantry, one that would never have been indulged in except by a man whose reputation for bravery was too well established to be in any danger of question or suspicion. From all accounts he was a great traveler. He left Italy in 1229 and made a tour of the south of France, visiting the courts of Provence, Toulouse, Rousillon, Castile, Leon and Portugal. About ten years later we find him at the castle of the Countess Beatrice, daughter of Raymond Berenger, Count of Provence, and wife of Charles I. of Anjou. Charles took the wandering minstrel under his protection, and time and again proved himself a friend in need. The poet repaid him by complaints and ingratitude. "How can a man be cheerful," Sordello asks, "when he is poor, sick all the time and unfortunate in lord, love and lady?" To which Charles replied: "I have always cherished and honored him. I have given him substantial property and a wife of his own choosing. But he is a fool and a nuisance and would not be grateful if one gave him a county." For all this, some years later we find Charles bestowing five castles in the Abruzzi upon "his intimate and faithful friend Sordello," as a reward for services rendered in an expedition against Manfred. During this expedition the poet was taken prisoner at Novara by the Ghibellines. At first Charles received the news with indifference. But Pope Clement IV. interceded in behalf of the troubadour, asking that he be ransomed and recompensed for his sufferings. Charles' indifference was at once transformed into active interest, and the gift of the Abruzzi castles followed. And so Sordello returned to continue his programme of finding friends and losing them, of falling in love and promptly falling out again. Love, except of self, and friendship, except with a view to some personal advantage, he could not understand. And yet he wrote much of love and friendship. Such baseless vaporings coarsen the soul; they even leave an impression upon the body. And, in fact, our poet was not imposing in presence. His well-cut lips smiled too easily; his bold black eyes suggested recklessness and daring rather than courage. Such lips might say harsh words upon slight provocation; such eyes could never brighten save in selfish cunning or through some sordid joy or gain. For him duty consisted in getting what he wanted. In one of his poems he tells us:

> And whoso lacks the thing his heart desires
> Is worse than dead. He lives in woe and need.

In another he advocates the dual service of God and Mammon:

> Whoe'er considers life with care
> Will always find, so I declare,
> One thing enjoined by wisdom's rod,
> To please at once the world and God.

Shortly after Sordello received his castle-grant he disappeared. From the fact that Dante places him among those who died before they could repent, it is conjectured that he met a violent end. It ma be that he fell at the hand of Ezzelino, as Benvenuto d'Imola testifies. Ezzelino is held responsible for so many crimes that one more laid at his door can hardly make much difference. Villani says that "Ezzelino was the cruelest and most redoubtable tyrant that ever existed among Christians." And Symonds in "The Renaissance in Italy" portrays him thus: "Ezzelino, a small, pale, wiry man, with terror in his face and enthusiasm for evil in his heart, lived a foe to luxury, cold to the pathos of children, dead to every higher emotion. His one passion was the love of power. When he captured Friola he deprived all the citizens of their eyes, noses and legs, and then ordered the unfortunates to be exposed to the mercy of the elements. He expired in agony, wrenching from his wounds the dressings placed there by his enemies to keep him from dying." According to a sixteenth century legend, Sordello lies at San Pietro, in Mantua, near his beloved Mincio. Virgil celebrates "Mincius crowned with sea-green reeds;" Milton sings of "smooth-sliding Mincius circled with vocal reeds." There our poet sleeps. He is done with the mad rivalries and bitter animosities of the Italy of the thirteenth century; with the perpetual struggle between Pope and Emperor and the ever-recurring battles between commune and nobles. And yet these centuries were in no sense dark. Through all the clamor and confusion two ideals were growing steadily clearer and brighter—one was the chivalric ideal of love with all that it enjoins of sympathy with the weak and suffering and reverence for womanhood; the other was the glorification of utter selflessness by the triple vows of poverty, chastity and obedience. The knights and their various allied orders were the propagators of the first; the gentle saint of Assisi and his brothers were the champions of the second. Sordello in his youth had chosen, not the monk's, but the knight's part.

II.

THE SORDELLO OF DANTE.

Three of the principal characters in the Sordellan cycle appear in the Divine Comedy—Sordello himself, Cunizza and Ezzolino. Ezzolino is confined with the violent in the Seventh Circle of the Inferno. There, guarded by the Minotaur, runs a river of blood, wherein are tormented such as have committed acts of violence against their neighbors. Some are immersed to their eyebrows, others to their throats, according to the degree of their guilt. From the crimson flood loud shrieks arise as the unhappy sufferers forever renew their futile attempts to escape. The banks are patrolled by Centaurs armed with keen arrows. One of these monsters explains:

> These are the souls of tyrants who were given
> To dealing woe and death. They wail aloud
> Their merciless wrongs. Here Alexander dwells,
> And Dionysius fell, who many a year
> Of woe wrought for fair Sicily. That brow
> Whereon the hair so jetty clustering hangs
> Is Ezzolino; that with flaxen locks,
> Obizzo of Este, in the world destroyed
> By his foul stepson.

Cunizza circles in the Third Heaven of the Paradiso in the planet Venus. She describes to Dante the site of Romano, where she and her brother Ezzolino were born. She comments upon the fair fame won by the troubadour Folco, and regrets that no such fame is now sought by her countrymen of Venetia. Then, seeming no longer to heed Dante, she resumes her place on the wheel of light and continues her dance in the heavenly cosmos. Cunizza, like Sordello, must have found "the path direct" in her later years. Although placed in Paradise by the sternest of moralizers and the most uncompromising of all lovers of justice, she has not escaped veiled censures and even open reproach. The commentators heap up footnotes. They remind us that while William of Lucerne was declaring Cunizza beyond all other women in worth and beauty and threatening those who made war upon her reputation with a sword which would surely cut before it bent, Ugo de Saint Cyr was replying with a smile that an infinite number of wounds would not suffice to vindicate the honor of the Lady of Romano; that all the doctors in Salterno could not medicine her good name. Dante's exaltation of her has led to endless controversy and speculation. It may be that the Florentine's fervid Ghibelline faith scorned the slanderous stories circulated by Guelph chroniclers concerning the daughter of a champion of the Emperor. Or he may have been influenced by the so-called "document of emancipation" executed in 1265. This was a deed of manumission granting freedom to all the slaves and bondsmen of the house of Romano. It was signed by Cunizza in her extreme old age. Transfigured by her sorrow and delivered from the tumult of her youthful emotions, her declining years seem to have been serenely calm and even solemn. If in those later days she ever met Sordello, we have no record of the meeting. And yet their mutual tenderness and the bond of a common repentance may have brought them together for a brief moment at the end, perhaps to ask forgiveness and to say a last farewell. For years the aged penitent dwelt with the Cavalcanti, the family of Guido Cavalcanti, the poet-friend of Dante. There Dante must have known her in his childhood days. There he must have heard the whole sad story of her life. And after her death he must have heard of the penitential spirit of her closing years, of her edifying death and of the grateful prayers of the emancipated dependents who never wearied of rehearsing the virtues of the good Cunizza, the last Lady of Romano.

Sordello is consigned to the purifying flames of the Purgatorio. There, at the foot of the mount, in company with those who have come to sudden and untimely ends, he meets Dante and Virgil. The spirits press about the living poet and his guide, chanting:

> We all by violence died, and to our latest
> Were sinners, but then warmed by light from heaven;
> So that, repenting and forgiving, we
> Did issue out of life at peace with God,
> Who with desire to see Him fills our hearts.

After some converse with Giacopo del Cassero, a Ghibelline of note; Buonconte da Montefeltro, Dante's comrade-in-arms at the battle of Campaldino, and Pia, a lady of Sienna, who was murdered in secret by her husband, the two poets observe a solitary spirit that has not joined in the general press, standing apart from the crowd. Virgil speaks:

> But lo! a spirit there
> Stands solitary, and toward us looks:
> It will instruct us in the speediest way.

Dante continues:

> We soon approach'd it. Oh, thou Lombard spirit!
> How didst thou stand in high abstracted mood,
> Scarce moving with slow dignity thine eyes!
> It spoke not aught, but let us onward pass,
> Eyeing us as a lion on his watch.
> But Virgil with entreaty mild advanced,
> Requesting it to show the best ascent;
> It answer to his question none returned,
> But of our country and our kind of life
> Demanded. When my courteous guide began,
> "Mantua," the shadow in itself absorb'd,
> Rose towards us from the place in which it stood
> And cried: "Mantuan, I am thy countryman,
> Sordello." Each the other then embraced.

At the first mention of his native city Sordello is aroused. He becomes all alertness and attention. So it should be, Dante muses bitterly. Italy is worthy of such love, but her sons are recreant. He opens his heart in a long wail of mingled pity and scorn:

> Ah, slavish Italy! Thou inn of grief!
> Vessel without a pilot in loud storm!
> Lady no longer of fair provinces,
> But weedy wastes o'ergrown. This gentle spirit
> Even from the pleasant sound of his dear land
> Was prompt to greet a fellow-citizen
> With such glad cheer: while now thy living ones
> In thee abide not without war; and one
> Malicious gnaws another, ay, of those
> Whom the same wall and the same moat contains.
> Seek, wretched one, around thy sea-coast wide;
> Then homeward to thy bosom turn and mark,
> If any part of thee sweet peace enjoy.

Then follows a scathing arraignment of the factions in the various cities of Italy and of the callousness of the rulers who leave them to their fate. Florence is at first sarcastically omitted from the censorship; but the sarcasm soon dies away in a groan of despair when he recalls the depths to which the fair city by the Arno has fallen:

> My Florence. . . .
> How many times within my memory
> Customs and laws and coins and offices
> Have been by thee renewed and people changed.
> If thou remember'st well and canst see clear,
> Thou wilt perceive thyself like a sick wretch,
> Who finds no rest upon her down, but oft
> Shifting her side, short respite seeks from pain.

Sordello was overjoyed when he found that this shade from the dim corridors of the under-world was a Mantuan; but when, upon further questioning, he found that his guest was none other than Master Virgil, he fell upon his knees in loving reverence, exclaiming:

> Glory of Latium,
> In whom our tongue its utmost power displayed;
> Boast of my honored birthplace! What desert
> Of mine, what favor rather, undeserved,
> Shows thee to me? If I to hear that voice
> Am worthy, say if from below thou comest,
> And from what cloister's pale?

Virgil replies that he belongs in that part of the Inferno where "mourning's voice sounds not of anguish sharp, but breathes in sighs;" where souls abide who "the three holy virtues put not on, but understood the rest and without blame followed them all." Then he asks to be directed up the mountain-side. Sordello answers:

> Thou beholdest now how day declines;
> And upward to proceed by night, our power
> Excels. Therefore, it may be well to choose
> A place of pleasant sojourn. To the right
> Some spirits sit apart retired. If thou
> Consentest, I to these will lead thy steps,
> And thou wilt know them, not without delight.

In accordance with this plan the three poets ascend an eminence whence they behold a pleasant recess in the form of a flowery vale. Within the enclosure on the grass are the spirits of dead Kings and rulers chanting the Salve Regina. Sordello names and describes them as he points them out: The Emperor Rudolph, "who might have healed the wounds whereof fair Italy died;" Ottocar of Bohemia, "with kindly visage;" Philip III. of France, "that one with nose deprest;" Henry of Navarre, "him of gentle look, who flying expired, withering the lily's flower;" Charles I. of Anjou, "him of feature prominent;" Henry III., "the King of simple life and plain, Harry of England," and last, but not least, William, Marquis of Montferrat, "who sits lowest, yet his gaze directs aloft." The night descends, and with it two green-robed angels with emerald wings. "From Mary's bosom both are come," explains Sordello, "as a guard for the vale against him who hither tends, the Serpent." The poets enter the valley and Dante is speaking with Nino, the judge of Gallura, when the Serpent glides noiselessly in between the grass and flowers. But the "celestial falcons," the verdant-vested sentinels, swoop down and the ancient enemy of the human race disappears from view. The night advances; the eastern cliffs begin to glow. Dante, still burdened by his earthly frame, is forced to rest. He sinks upon the ground overcome by sleep. And while he sleeps Lucia comes and carries him up the mountain-side, where, awaking two hours later, he finds himself with Virgil at the gate of Purgatory. Sordello and the spirits of the vale of flowers have been left behind.

It is the general opinion of critics and commentators that this entire episode, with its famous Italian Jeremiad, was suggested to Dante by the Goitan bard's **"Lament for Blacas."** This elegy, written upon the death of Blacas, a Spanish troubadour of extra-ordinary personal courage, urges the craven-hearted rulers of the age to eat of the great heart of the dead Blacas, in the hope that they, too, may become brave and generous and honor-loving. "Why," asks Tommaseo in his "Nuovi Studi du Dante," "does Dante place Sordello as a guide through the flowery valley where Kings and rulers are found? Because in this place he meant to call together to himself as judge many of the most powerful princes of Italy and of Europe, and Sordello in a Provençal song did similar work and judged with lofty severity many great princes of his time."

The **"Lament"** is noteworthy and in the original may well have made a deep impression on Dante. The first stanza eulogizes the brave troubadour:

> I fain would mourn Blacas—let all the world
> attend!
> For sorrow, grief and pain my bosom justly
> rend;
> In him am I despoiled of master and of friend,
> And every noble trait hath met in him its end.
> So mortal is the blow, such fatal ills impend,
> We can but vainly hope the generous loss to
> mend,
> Unless his heart we take and through the nations
> send
> That cowardly lords may eat, for that will
> courage lend.

The succeeding stanzas arraign the Roman Emperor, Frederick II., against whom Milan had rebelled; Louis IX. of France, who, influenced by his mother, allowed his right to the throne of Castile to lapse; the English King, Henry III., who had lost territory to the French, and the Spanish King, Ferdinand III. of Castile, for allowing his mother to interfere in affairs of state. They are all invited to partake of the heart of the brave Blacas. No funeral dirge ever served better to express at the same time deep love and reverence for the dead and supreme contempt for the living. The irony is unsurpassed:

> The first of all to eat, since greatest is his need,
> Shall be the Roman Emperor, if he would
> succeed
> Against the Milanese, who count themselves
> freed;
> For he, despite his Germans, hath the worst
> indeed.
> The witless King of France shall next upon it
> feed,
> And then regain Castile, lost ere he gave it heed;
> But he will never taste it if his mother plead,
> For he would grieve her not—he well deserves
> his meed.
>
> Then let the King of England, timid as a hart,
> Eat bountifully thereof, and quickly will he start
> To win back the lands which France with lance
> and dart—
> Because she knows him well—hath taken for her
> part.
> But let the Spanish King eat doubly of the heart,
> Too weak for one good realm, while two are on
> his chart;
> But should he wish to eat it, let him go apart,
> For should his mother know, her stick would
> make him start.

Dante tells us in his *De Volgari Eloquia* that Sordello excelled in all kinds of composition and that he helped to form the Tuscan tongue by some happy attempts which he made in the dialects of Cremona, Brescia and Verona. Dante also speaks of a "Goito Mantuan" who was the author of many good songs and who left in every stanza an unmatched line which he called "the key." This singer, according to Tiraboschi, was our Lombardy minstrel. None of the Italian poems has come down to us; the Goito Lay, whatever may have been its theme or merit, is lost forever. Gone, too, are his **"History of the House of Aragon"** and his **"Defense of Walled Towns."** His extant poems, thirty-four in number, have been collected by Sainte-Pelaye, Fauriel, Raynouard, Diez, Mahn and de Lollis. They are all in Provençal and for the most part gallant songs. They are remarkable, Gismondi tells us, for "the harmony and sensibility of their verses" and for "the purity and delicacy of their sentiments."

But the poet-patriot of Dante is not the restless traveler and polished courtesan of the early biographers, nor the gay chanter in novel metre and faultless phrase of loves that wax and wane, as portrayed by some of the later critics, nor yet the severe ruler and judge, who, repenting of his youthful follies, has lost all that is human and engaging, degenerating into a mere bundle of sententiousness and self-complacency, as others would have us believe. The Sordello of Dante is an exalted nature, a man of his age, and yet a true contemplative with a turn for speculation and an ironical contempt for mere worldliness and its concomitants. Dante calls him "the good Sordello" and "the courteous Sordello." He must have left a noble record—a record lost in part to us—thus to have impressed so penetrating a student of human nature, so impartial a lover of righteousness. Like a recluse, we discern the shadowy form of the famous Goitan, moving majestically among the spirits of the mighty ones of former days. He is with them, but not of them.

> But lo! a spirit there
> Stands solitary, and towards us looks.

III.

THE POET-PHILOSOPHER OF BROWNING.

The Sordello of Browning is a poet, a troubadour, with a poet's sensitiveness to beauty and a troubadour's faith in the springtime of things, in fresh green leaves and the aspirations of youth and the love that lasts forever and forever. But he is more than a lover of the beautiful. "The poet, when he leans on truth, is a philosopher," Plato tells us. If not in the beginning, at least in the end, the Sordello of Browning loves truth as passionately as he loves beauty. And so we have Sordello, the poet-philosopher, as the hero of a poem which is a study of the proper service of the poet. Browning ascribes to the mediæval minstrel the thoughts, emotions and ideals of a Dante, makes him a modern who chooses unhesitatingly the side of the people, transforms Cunizza into Palma as the romantic factor in the story, and concludes with the dramatic incident in which Palma reveals the fact that Sordello is, in reality, Salinguerra's son. Of course, we know that the Lombardy minstrel was intensely Ghibelline in his sympathies, and therefore a partisan of the Emperor as against the people's party, which was championed by the Pope; we know that he loved Cunizza and not Palma, her elder sister, and we know that there is no historical basis for Palma's revelation, unless the ambiguous line in Rolandino's Chronicle can be conformed to some such supposition. Browning's version is founded upon the ancient Provençal record of Sordello's youth in the north of Italy; but in the long years of his tempestuous life our troubadour traveled over the greater part of Southern Europe. His youth in Northern Italy was not the third part of his life. He was over eighty when Charles of Anjou, King of Naples, gave him five castles in the Abruzzi. After that he disappeared—died, I suppose, as we all do in the end.

Browning intentionally ignores the mere facts. "The historical decoration," he writes, "was purposely of no more importance than a background requires; my stress lay on the incidents in the development of a soul. Little else is worth study." And so he attempts to body forth for us the soul of Sordello—the soul of a poet who would feign be a philosopher, too. Now there is an ancient feud between poetry and philosophy. Plato tells us so in the Republic when he decides that the verse-makers are to be forever banished from his ideal state. "For if we allow the honeyed muse to enter either in epic or lyric strains, not law and the reason of mankind, which by common consent have ever been deemed best, but pleasure and pain will be the rulers in our state," he explains. And truly the feud is an ancient one; there is none older. Feeling and thought have ever been at outs in the soul of man; there has never been a truce in the perpetual warfare waged between heart and head. And compromises are unendurable; we demand complete surrender from one side or the other and absolute perfection in the final adjustment. Browning is not so exacting. Perhaps, he argues, perfection is for eternity and approximations to perfection for time; perhaps ideal standards are not adapted to measuring the half-flights of our earth-life. But, he continues, if we must choose between the heart and the head, let it be the heart.

> Forget
> Vain ordinances. I have one appeal—
> I feel, am what I feel, know what I feel:
> So much is truth to me.

This is a sort of pragmatic emotionalism which accepts our feelings as deeper and truer than our thoughts. A profounder analysis reveals the synthesis of thought and feeling in action, the unity of truth and beauty in goodness. There is no conflict, no need of choosing between the two.

"Who will may hear Sordello's story told," the poet assures us at the opening of the poem; "who would has heard Sordello's story told" are his concluding words, the last line of the last book. The first two books describe Sordello's failure as a poet; the last four tell how near he came to failing as a man. And the story is easy to follow if one is familiar with the history of the period. The opening scene is set in Verona. The curtain rises with Palma, Sordello, Ezzelino, Salinguerra and all the various adherents of Pope and Emperor upon the stage. Guelphs and Ghibellines are locked in a death-struggle. But this is just a device to arouse interest and to focus attention upon the principal characters. The poet soon decides that it is best after all to begin at the beginning. The scene shifts from Verona to Goito. Sordello is a boy upon the hillsides there. The seasons come and go in a mist of white or green or russet. The child lives in a dream-world, because the real one is as yet inaccessible. But he is a poet and gives his heart unreservedly to all that is fair and lovely and of good report. And at first he is wholly absorbed in the exquisite beauty of the material universe—the simmering quiet of long summer afternoons sacred to the noiseless flight of azure damsel-flies or broken by the swift onset of palpitating lightning flashes alternating with rumbling thunder-rolls; the cold white calm of wintry nights with snow-shrouded forests gleaming under the moon's ensilvering pall. But externals cannot satisfy his soul for long. His sympathies widen. He becomes interested in man and man's work in the world; he comes to understand something of the beauty of the human soul, of the sweetness of its love and friendship, the austere heights of its sacrifices and renunciations, its capacity for illimitable happiness and immeasurable pain. He weaves all these experiences into his songs and sings because he cannot help singing. The love of nature leads him to the love of man. Perhaps his love for mankind will lead him to a love higher still. If he seeks unweariedly, he will find at last; if he knocks unceasingly, the golden door will be opened unto him. Browning outlines the process for us in advance:

Fresh births of beauty wake
Fresh homage; *every grade of love is past,*
With every mode of loveliness. Then cast
Inferior idols off their borrowed crown
Before a coming glory. Up and down
Runs arrowy fire, while *earthly forms combine*
To throb the secret forth, a touch divine—
And the scaled eyeball owns the mystic rod;
Visibly through his garden walketh GOD.

First nature, then man, and finally God: these are the successive objects of Sordello's love as his awakening soul grows out of the dream-life of his childhood into the verities of manhood. His love of nature is deep and genuine. There are the oaks and scarlet maples and lady-birches to shelter him from the hot sun; there are the shining depths of the Nuncio and its sandy banks overrun with slimy water-life; there are rings of vineyards circling the southern hillsides and pleasant pasture lands on the northern slopes; there are the wild creatures that creep timidly up out of the swampy defiles and morasses Mantuawards, and the tams, domestic ones that live about the lodge. And in the midst of all this natural beauty, shut in amongst the mountains, stands the castle of the Lady Adelaide. Without, it is a stately pile; within, it is a "maze of corridors contrived for sin," a labyrinth of dusk winding-stairs leading to inner chambers, and dim galleries girdling forbidden passageways. This is Sordello's home—all the home he has ever known. For his parents are dead, so they tell him, and the Lady Adelaide has been good enough to take him as her page. He is left quite to himself; he has no playmates. Sometimes he sits for hours in the evening in the maple-paneled room with the slim palm pillars; sometimes he visits the cumbrous font in the central vault and wonders at the patience of the Caryatides that stand, year after year, shoulder to shoulder, at the fountain's edge. Sometimes the statues seem to smile at him, or their look of weariness lessens as he assures them of his sympathy.

Calmly, then
About this secret lodge of Adelaide's
Glided his youth away; beyond the glades
Of the fir-forest border, and the rim
Of the low range of mountains, was for him
No other world: but this appeared his own
To wander through at pleasure and alone.

Thus he lives and dreams and plans a wondrous future. He will be satisfied with nothing short of perfection; he will be a poet. And Palma of the golden hair, the fair daughter of Agnes Ese and Ecelin. Palma will be his bride. The gossips about the castle say that she is betrothed to Count Richard of Saint Boniface; but there are also rumors to the effect that she has rejected his suit. As an adventurous spider that spins its web and flings it out from barbican to battlement, so our young architect of fate erects his visionary dome in the first white glory of the morning and sees it gleaming with rainbow-edged raindrops in the gold and purple majesty of the advancing day. And yet there is danger ahead. The world brushes cobwebs and dream-webs impatiently aside. But there can be no turning back now; nature can never again be all sufficient. He longs for real life in a real world of real men and women.

His opportunity comes sooner than he expects. A troubadour, Eglamor by name, a protegé of Count Richard, is to sing at a court of love. These courts are supposed to have been assemblies of ladies that met to hear the cases of recreant lovers. Chaucer refers to these courts, but they are never mentioned in the tensos of the troubadours. Raynouard, however, the compiler of the great collection of Proven¸al poetry, maintains that these courts actually existed and that their decisions were held as binding as those of any other court. The day comes and Sordello is present. Eglamor, smiling in conscious power, sings, to the accompaniment of his jongleur, Naddo, his song to the Lady Elys—el lys, the lily. The crowd applauds. But Sordello is disappointed. He steps forward on the impulse of the moment and takes up the same theme:

The true lay with the true end,
Taking the other's names and time and place
For his. On flew the song, a giddy race,
After the flying story; word made leap
Out word, rhyme, rhyme; the lay could barely
  keep
Pace with the action visibly rushing past.

The people fall back aghast. Then the air is rent with shouts of approval. And Palma is there. She has heard the song and has noted the matchless lines, the immortal part of the impromptu Goito lay:

Take Elys there,
Her head that's sharp and perfect like a pear,
So close and smooth are laid the few fine locks,
Colored like honey, oozed from topmost rocks,
Sun-blanched the livelong summer.

Sordello grows faint when he sees her. She unbinds a scarf from her neck and decorates him with it as a token of her favor. It is too much. He stammers something, anything, and the jongleurs bear him away. Eglamor accepts his defeat with touching gentleness—Eglamor, who had loved art better than life, who had not understood that to be a man is greater than to be a poet. He places his crown beneath that of his successful rival and lies down to die. Sordello recovers in time to go out to meet the funeral procession. They lay the vanquished minstrel to rest under a canopy of primeval pines in a covert of tender ferns and wild-wood flowers, while his successor speaks words of eulogy and prays that his fame may be everlasting. And the prayer is not fruitless. A tiny white flower is named for the dead bard. On its frail petals his name will be borne to succeeding generations.

A plant they have, yielding a three-leaved bell,
Which whitens at the heart ere noon, and ails
Till evening; evening gives it to her gales
To clear away with such forgotten things
As are an eyesore to the morn: this brings
Him to their mind and bears his name.
So much for Eglamor.

And so Sordello comes into his own. He is accepted of men, even of Palma. And at first he strives earnestly to perfect his work, for he is too true an artist not to be aware of his limitations. He is forever melting, welding, hammering out words in the hope of fashioning an armor worthy of his thoughts. He succeeds a little, but fails more, partly because of the distractions growing out of the plaudits of the mob. He begins to lose faith in art and to weary of a life devoted to pleasuring the populace. And so when Naddo comes requesting that he sing at a festival to be held in honor of Tanrello Salinguerra, he refuses flatly. He steals away to Goito to the home of his boyhood, and leaves the world to sing and feast and celebrate as best it can without him. He realizes that he has failed as a poet, or rather that poetry has failed in proving itself inadequate as an embodiment of the emotions and aspirations of life. His sojourn at Goito is in the nature of a spiritual retreat. The day of trial is coming. He will need all the strength he can gather from the sacred silence of the woody solitudes. A year passes and then a message from Palma. Eccelin's two sons have taken Guelph brides, Palma is once more betrothed to Saint Boniface. Palma desires that Sordello shall compose the marriage hymn. To Naddo's surprise Sordello consents to depart at once for Verona.

And now comes the rest. Palma and Sordello are alone together in a room of the palace at Verona. All is confusion and excitement outside. The promised peace that was to crown the Guelph-Ghibelline alliances seems farther off than ever. It is time some strong hand seize the reins. Palma looks to Sordello. He can control the situation if he will only stand with the Ghibellines—make the Kaiser's cause his own. She speaks deliberately and with feeling. She tells him how she has loved him ever since the day when she first saw him; how she has planned for him, and how, at last, the time has come when her dreams may be realized. Sordello listens in silence. He is a man of thought rather than a man of action. He sets out for Ferrara, where the strife is at its height, to make a calm study of the merits of the two parties, so that he may choose his side in the contest. But the rival claims are bewildering; good and bad are mingled in both camps. Guelph or Ghibelline matters not, he concludes after much meditating. Man's welfare depends on neither. A new Rome, free from the bitterness of party strife, a great free commonwealth with justice and righteousness as its watchwords—this is his dream. But before sunset his dream dissolves. He sees that the race progresses slowly; that out of the good and evil of to-day are evolved the perfection of to-morrow. He sees that the Guelphs, led by the Pope, represent the popular cause—the people's party. Therefore, he decides to stand with the Guelphs, to persuade Salinguerra to stand with them. He goes to him and makes his plea in the presence of Palma. Salinguerra in turn tries to convert Sordello to the Ghibelline side, and ends by solemnly investing the poet with his own badge—the symbol of supreme leadership among the followers of the Emperor. All three are aware of the significance of the act. If Sordello will he may be chief of the more powerful of the two parties, and with Palma as his bride, rule all Northern Italy. But the price is oppression of the people, the sacrifice of his most sacred convictions. How often our modern statesmen have been tested by a similar temptation and have weakly chosen the badge of Cæsar and trampled in the dust the banner of the Cross. The moment is a dramatic one, and a dramatic revelation crowns it. Palma has long known certain facts concerning the birth and parentage of Sordello, facts concealed by the dead Adelaide for reasons of her own. Sordello is Salinguerra's son, who did not perish in the fire at Vicenza, as had always been supposed. Surely now he will accept his mission, will stand with his father, with the Emperor. Sordello is aroused at last; Salinguerra is overcome. The girl leads the old warrior from the room. Sordello remains with the Emperor's badge upon his breast torn between conflicting emotions.

It is evening, and the moon is rising over the city. The badge gleams in the white light, burns into his very soul. He cannot think clearly; his head is hot. Palma had said something about his need of a determining outside influence to give coherence to his life, "some moon to control his spiritual sea-depths."

But years and years the sky above
Held none, and so, untasked of any love,
His sensitiveness ideal, now amort,
Alive now, and to sullenness or sport
Given wholly up, disposed itself anew
At every passing instigation, grew
And dwindled at caprice, in foam-showers spilt,
Wedge-like insisting, quivered now a gilt

Shield in the sunshine, now a blinding race
Of whitest ripples o'er the reef; found place
For much display, not gathered up and hurled
Right from the heart, encompassing the world.

Others with half his strength accomplish more, just because of the concrete definiteness of their working ideals. They are swayed by one, not many motives. He is strong and yet he needs external strength. Long ago he had discovered that he could not find that strength in nature; now he sees that he cannot find it in man. Even Palma's love is insufficient, for Palma's plans are for this world, and "there is a life beyond life." There is need of a power "utterly incomprehensible" and "out of all rivalry," a being at once human and divine, one who can love infinitely and be satisfied with a finite love in return. But this infinite being is none other than the Christ of the Christian Revelation. And those who would follow Him must love the Cross and wear the thorn-crown. The struggle is to the death, but Sordello is equal to it. He tears the badge from his breast and tramples it underfoot. Thus is his spiritual triumph complete. He has not failed as a man. But the physical strain is greater than he can bear. When Palma and Salinguerra return to receive his answer to their proposal, they find him dead. Palma kneels down to kiss his cold lips, and for a moment his heart beats audibly. But it is only for a moment. He is dead. Taurello and the Emperor must seek some other representative. Guelphs and Ghibellines must work out their salvation unaided by the dream-builder of a new Rome. As for the poet, his songs, as well as his life, are soon forgotten, all except the matchless description in the inspired Goito lay:

So, on a heathy brown and nameless hill
By sparkling Asolo, in mist and chill,
Morning just up, higher and higher runs
A child barefoot and rosy. . . .
Up and up goes he, singing all the while
Some unintelligible words to beat
The lark, God's poet, swooning at his feet,
So worsted is he at *"the few fine locks,*
Stained like pale honey, oozed from topmost
rocks,
Sun-blanched the livelong summer"—all that's
left
Of the Goito lay.

It is morning; the child sings and Sordello sleeps.

Ezra Pound (essay date 1913)

SOURCE: "Troubadours: Their Sorts and Conditions," in *Literary Essays of Ezra Pound,* edited by T. S. Eliot, New Directions, 1954, pp. 94-108.

[*Regarded as one of the twentieth-century's most influential American poets and critics, Pound is chiefly renowned for his ambitious poetry cycle, the* Cantos, *which he revised and enlarged throughout much of his life. These poems are significant for their lyrical intensity, metrical*

From Browning's *Sordello* (1840):

Who will, may hear Sordello's story
told:
His story? Who believes me shall behold
The man, pursue his fortunes to the
end,
Like me: for as the friendless-people's
friend
Spied from his hill-top once, despite the
din
And dust of multitudes, Pentapolin
Named o' the Naked Arm, I single out
Sordello, compassed murkily about
With ravage of six long sad hundred
years.
Only believe me. Ye believe?

Appears
Verona . . . Never, I should warn you
first,
Of my own choice had this, if not the
worst
Yet not the best expedient, served to
tell
A story I could body forth so well
By making speak, myself kept out of
view,
The very man as he was wont to do,
And leaving you to say the rest for him.
Since, though I might be proud to see
the dim
Abysmal Past divide its hateful surge,
Letting of all men this one man emerge
Because it pleased me, yet, that moment
past,
I should delight in watching first to last
His progress as you watch it, not a whit
More in the secret than yourselves who
sit
Fresh-chapleted to listen. But it seems
Your setters-forth of unexampled
themes,
Makers of quite new men, producing
them,
Would best chalk broadly on each
vesture's hem,
The wearer's quality; or take their
stand,
Motley on back and pointing-pole in hand,
Beside him. So, for once I face ye,
friends,
Summoned together from the world's
four ends,
Dropped down from heaven or cast up
from hell,
To hear the story I propose to tell. . . .

Robert Browning, in The Poems of Robert Browning, *Oxford University Press, 1932.*

experimentation, literary allusions, varied subject matter and verse forms, and incorporation of phrases from foreign languages. An avid student of politics and history, Pound was particularly interested in the poetry of Provence, translating Old Provençal verse and exploring the lives and songs of the troubadours. In the following essay, originally published in 1913 in The Quarterly Review, *he reveals the richness and variety of troubadour life as evidenced both in the poets' own* canzoni *(verse) and in the* razos *(prose chronicles). In addition, Pound documents the three aspects of style common to the later Provençal period: an emphasis on art and aesthetics, the use of elevated reflections on love, and the employment of satire.*]

The argument whether or no the troubadours are a subject worthy of study is an old and respectable one. If Guillaume, Count of Peiteus, grandfather of King Richard Coeur de Leon, had not been a man of many energies, there might have been little food for this discussion. He was, as the old book says of him, 'of the greatest counts in the world, and he had his way with women.' He made songs for either them or himself or for his more ribald companions. They say that his wife was Countess of Dia, 'fair lady and righteous', who fell in love with Raimbaut d'Aurenga and made him many a song. Count Guillaume brought composition in verse into court fashions, and gave it a social prestige which it held till the crusade of 1208 against the Albigenses. The mirth of Provencal song is at times anything but sunburnt, and the mood is often anything but idle. De Born advises the barons to pawn their castles before making war, thus if they won they could redeem them, if they lost the loss fell on the holder of the mortgage.

The forms of this poetry are highly artificial, and as artifice they have still for the serious craftsman an interest, less indeed than they had for Dante, but by no means inconsiderable. No student of the period can doubt that the involved forms, and the veiled meanings in the 'trobar clus', grew out of living conditions, and that these songs played a very real part in love intrigue and in the intrigue preceding warfare. The time had no press and no theatre. If you wish to make love to women in public, and out loud, you must resort to subterfuge; and Guillaume St Leider even went so far as to get the husband of his lady to do the seductive singing.

If a man of our time be so crotchety as to wish emotional, as well as intellectual, acquaintance with an age so out of fashion as the twelfth century, he may try in several ways to attain it. He may read the songs themselves from the old books—from the illuminated vellum—and he will learn what the troubadours meant to the folk of the century just after their own. He will learn a little about their costume from the illuminated capitals. Or he may try listening to the words with the music, for, thanks to Jean Beck and others, it is now possible to hear the old tunes. They are perhaps a little Oriental in feeling, and it is likely that the spirit of Sufism is not wholly absent from their content. Or, again, a man may walk the hill roads and river roads from Limoges and Charente to Dordogne and Narbonne and learn a little, or more than a little, of what the country meant to the wandering singers, he may learn, or think he learns, why so many canzos open with speech of the weather; or why such a man made war on such and such castles. Or he may learn the outlines of these events from the 'razos', or prose paragraphs of introduction, which are sometimes called 'lives of the troubadours'. And, if he have mind for these latter, he will find in the Bibliothèque Nationale at Paris the manuscript of Miquel de la Tour, written perhaps in the author's own handwriting; at least we read 'I Miquel de la Tour, scryven, do ye to wit'.

Miquel gives us to know that such and such ladies were courted with greater or less good fortune by such and such minstrels of various degree, for one man was a poor vavassour, and another was King Amfos of Aragon; and another, Vidal, was son of a furrier, and sang better than any man in the world; and Raimon de Miraval was a poor knight that had but part of a castle; and Uc Brunecs was a clerk and he had an understanding with a *borgesa* who had no mind to love him or to keep him, and who became mistress to the Count of Rodez. 'Voila l'estat divers d'entre eulx.'

The Piazza Sordello in Mantua. In his early years the poet resided at the palace on the right, which once housed the Gonzaga family, rulers of the city for nearly four hundred years.

The monk, Gaubertz de Poicebot, 'was a man of birth; he was of the bishopric of Limozin, son of the castellan of Poicebot. And he was made monk when he was a child in a monastery, which is called Sain Leonart. And he knew well letters, and well to sing and well *trobar* [a poetical composition, literally 'to find']. And for desire of woman he went forth from the monastery. And he came thence to the man to whom came all who for courtesy wished honour and good deeds—to Sir Savaric de Mauleon—and this man gave him the harness of a joglar and a horse and clothing; and then he went through the courts and composed and made good canzos. And he set his heart upon a donzella gentle and fair and made his songs of her, and she did not wish to love him unless he should get himself made a knight and take her to wife. And he told En Savaric how the girl had refused him, wherefore En Savaric made him a knight and gave him land and the income from it. And he married the girl and held her in great honour. And it happened that he went into Spain, leaving her behind him. And a knight out of England set his mind upon her and did so much and said so much that he led her with him, and he kept her long time his mistress and then let her go to the dogs (malamen anar). And En Gaubertz returned from Spain, and lodged himself one night in the city where she was. And he went out for desire of woman, and he entered the *alberc* of a poor woman; for they told him there was a fine woman within. And he found his wife. And when he saw her, and she him, great was the grief between them and great shame. And he stopped the night with her, and on the morrow he went forth with her to a nunnery where he had her enter. And for this grief he ceased to sing and to compose.' If you are minded, as Browning was in his *One Word More,* you may search out the song that En Gaubertz made, riding down the second time from Malleon, flushed with the unexpected knighthood.

Per amor del belh temps suau
E quar fin amor men somo.

[For love of the fair time and soft,
And because fine love calls me to it.]

'For love of the sweet time and soft' he beseeches this 'lady in whom joy and worth have shut themselves and all good in its completeness' to give him grace and the kisses due to him a year since. And he ends in envoi to Savaric.

Senher savaric larc e bo
Vos troba hom tota fazo
Quel vostre ric fag son prezan
El dig cortes e benestan.

[Milord Savaric, generous
To thy last bond, men find thee thus,
That thy rich acts are food for praise
And courtly are thy words and days.]

La Tour has given us seed of drama in the passage above rendered. He has left us also an epic in his straightforward prose. 'Piere de Maensac was of Alverne (Auvergne) a poor knight, and he had a brother named Austors de Maensac, and they both were troubadours and they both were in concord that one should take the castle and the other the *trobar*.' And presumably they tossed up a *marabotin* or some such obsolete coin, for we read, 'And the castle went to Austors and the poetry to Piere, and he sang of the wife of Bernart de Tierci. So much he sang of her and so much he honoured her that it befell that the lady let herself go gay (*furar a del*). And he took her to the castle of the Dalfin of Auvergne, and the husband, in the manner of the golden Menelaus, demanded her much, with the church to back him and with the great war that they made. But the Dalfin maintained him (Piere) so that he never gave her up. He (Piere) was a straight man (*dreitz om*) and good company, and he made charming songs, tunes and the words, and good coblas of pleasure.' And among them is one beginning

Longa saison ai estat vas amor
Humils e francs, y ai faich son coman.

[For a long time have I stood toward Love
Humble and frank, and have done his
commands.]

Dante and Browning have created so much interest in Sordello that it may not be amiss to give the brief account of him as it stands in a manuscript in the Ambrosian library at Milan. 'Lo Sordels *si fo di Mantovana.* Sordello was of Mantuan territory of Sirier (this would hardly seem to be Goito), son of a poor cavalier who had name Sier Escort (Browning's El Corte), and he delighted himself in chançons, to learn and to make them. And he mingled with the good men of the court. And he learned all that he could and he made coblas and sirventes. And he came thence to the court of the Count of St Bonifaci, and the Count honoured him much. And he fell in love with the wife of the Count, in the form of pleasure (*a forma de solatz*), and she with him. (The Palma of Browning's poem and the Cunizza of Dante's.) And it befell that the Count stood ill with her brothers. And thus he estranged himself from her and from Sier Sceillme and Sier Albrics. Thus her brothers caused her to be stolen from the Count by Sier Sordello and the latter came to stop with them. And he (Sordello) stayed a long time with them in great happiness, and then he went into Proenssa where he received great honours from all the good men and from the Count and from the Countess who gave him a good castle and a wife of gentle birth.' (Browning with perfect right alters this ending to suit his own purpose.)

The luck of the troubadours was as different as their ranks, and they were drawn from all social orders. We are led far from polite and polished society when we come to take note of that Gringoire, Guillem Figiera, 'son of a tailor; and he was a tailor; and when the French got hold of Toulouse he departed into Lombardy. And he knew well *trobar* and to sing, and he made himself *joglar* among the townsfolk (*ciutadins*). He was not a man who knew how to carry himself among the barons or among the better class, but much he got himself welcomed among harlots and slatterns and by innkeepers and taverners. And if he saw coming a good man of the court, there where he was, he was sorry and grieved at it, and he nearly split himself to take him down a peg (*et ades percussava de lui abaissar*).'

For one razo that shows an unusual character there are a dozen that say simply that such or such a man was of Manes, or of Cataloigna by Rossilon, or of elsewhere, 'a poor cavalier.' They made their way by favour at times, or by singing, or by some form of utility. Ademar of Gauvedan 'was of the castle Marvois, son of a poor knight. He was knighted by the lord of Marvois. He was a brave man but could not keep his estate as knight, and he became jongleur and was respected by all the best people. And later he went into orders at Gran Mon'. Elias Cairels 'was of Sarlat; ill he sang, ill he composed, ill he played the fiddle and worse he spoke, but he was good at writing out words and tunes. And he was a long time wandering, and when he quitted it, he returned to Sarlat and died there'. Perdigo was the son of a fisherman and made his fortune by his art. Peirol was a poor knight who was fitted out by the Dalfin of Auvergne and made love to Sail de Claustra; and all we know of Cercamon is that he made *vers* and *pastorelas* in the old way and that 'he went everywhere he could get to'. Pistoleta 'was a singer for Arnaut of Marvoil, and later he took to *trobar* and made songs with pleasing tunes and he was well received by the best people, although a man of little comfort and of poor endowment and of little stamina. And he took a wife at Marseilles and became a merchant and became rich and ceased going about the courts'. Guillems the skinny was a joglar of Manes, and the capital letter shows him throwing 3, 5, and 4, on a red dice board. 'Never had he on harness, and what he gained he lost *malamen,* to the taverns and the women. And he ended in a hospital in Spain.

The razos have in them the seeds of literary criticism. The speech is, however, laconic. Aimar lo Ners was a gentleman. 'He made such songs as he knew how to.' Aimeric de Sarlat, a joglar, became a troubadour, 'and yet he made but one song.' Piere Guillem of Toulouse 'Made good coblas, but he made too many'. Daude of Pradas made canzos 'per sen de trobar', which I think we may translate 'from a mental grasp of the craft'. 'But they did not move from love, wherefore they had not favour among folk. They were not sung'. We find also that the labour and skill were divided. One man played the viol most excellently, and another sang, and another spoke his songs to music, and another, Jaufre Rudel, Brebezieu's father-in-law, made 'good tunes with poor words to go with them'.

The troubadour's person comes in for as much free criticism as his performance. Elias fons Slada was a 'fair man verily, as to feature, a joglar, no good troubadour'. [Pound notes that "the 'joglar' was the player and singer, the 'troubadour' the 'finder' or composer of songs and words."] But Faidit, a joglar of Uzerche, 'was exceedingly greedy both to drink and to eat, and he became fat beyond measure. And he took to wife a public woman; very fair and well taught she was, but she became as big and fat as he was. And she was from a rich town Alest of the Mark of Provenca from the seignory of En Bernart d'Andussa.'

One of the noblest figures of the time, if we are to believe the chronicle, was Savaric de Mauleon, the rich baron of Peiteu, mentioned above, son of Sir Reios de Malleon; 'lord was he of Malleon and of Talarnom and of Fontenai, and of castle Aillon and of Boetand of Benaon and of St Miquel en Letz and of the isles of Ners and of the isle of Mues and of Nestrine and of Engollius and of many other good places.' As one may read in the continuation of this notice and verify from the razos of the other troubadours, 'he was of the most open-handed men in the world.' He seems to have left little verse save the tenzon with Faidit.

'Behold divers estate between them all!' Yet, despite the difference in conditions of life between the twelfth century and our own, these few citations should be enough to prove that the people were much the same, and if the preceding notes do not do this, there is one tale left that should succeed.

The Vicomte of St Antoni was of the bishopric of Caortz (Cahors), Lord and Vicomte of St Antoni; and he loved a noble lady who was wife of the seignor of Pena Dalbeges, of a rich castle and a strong. The lady was gentle and fair and valiant and highly prized and much honoured; and he very valiant and well trained and good at arms and charming, and a good trobaire, and had name Raimons Jordans; and the lady was called the Vicomtesse de Pena; and the love of these two was beyond all measure. And it befell that the Vicount went into a land of his enemies and was grievous wounded, so that report held him for dead. And at the news she in great grief went and gave candles at church for his recovery. And he recovered. And at this news also she had great grief.' And she fell a-moping, and that was the end of the affair with St Antoni, and 'thus was there more than one in deep distress'. 'Wherefore' Elis of Montfort, wife of William à-Gordon, daughter of the Viscount of Trozena, the glass of fashion and the mould of form, the pride of 'youth, beauty, courtesy', and presumably of justice, mercy, long-suffering, and so forth, made him overtures, and successfully. And the rest is a matter much as usual.

If humanity was much the same, it is equally certain that individuals were not any more like one another; and this may be better shown in the uncommunicative *canzoni* than in the razos. Thus we have a pastoral from the sensitive and little known Joios of Tolosa:

> Lautrier el dous temps de pascor
> En una ribeira,

which runs thus:

'The other day, in the sweet time of Easter, I went across a flat land of rivers hunting for new flowers, walking by the side of the path, and for delight in the greenness of things and because of the complete good faith and love which I bear for her who inspires me, I felt a melting about my heart and at the first flower I found, I burst into tears.

And I wept until, in a shady place, my eyes fell upon a shepherdess. Fresh was her colour, and she was white as a snow-drift, and she had doves' eyes,' . . .

In very different key we find the sardonic Count of Foix, in a song which begins mildly enough for a spring song:

Mas qui a flor si vol mesclar,

and turns swiftly enough to a livelier measure:

Ben deu gardar lo sieu baston
Car frances sabon grans colps dar
Et albirar ab lor bordon
E nous fizes in carcasses
Ni en genes ni en gascon.

Let no man lounge amid the flowers
Without a stout club of some kind.
Know ye the French are stiff in stour
And sing not all they have in mind,
So trust ye not in Carcason,
In Genovese, nor in Gascon.

My purpose in all this is to suggest to the casual reader that the Middle Ages did not exist in the tapestry alone, nor in the fourteenth-century romances, but that there was a life like our own, no mere sequence of citherns and citoles, nor a continuous stalking about in sendal and diaspre. Men were pressed for money. There was unspeakable boredom in the castles. The chivalric singing was devised to lighten the boredom; and this very singing became itself in due time, in the manner of all things, an ennui.

There has been so much written about the poetry of the best Provençal period, to wit the end of the twelfth century, that I shall say nothing of it here, but shall confine the latter part of this essay to a mention of three efforts, or three sorts of effort which were made to keep poetry alive after the crusade of 1208.

Any study of European poetry is unsound if it does not commence with a study of that art in Provence. The art of quantitative verse had been lost. This loss was due more to ignorance than to actual changes of language, from Latin, that is, into the younger tongues. It is open to doubt whether the Aeolic singing was ever comprehended fully even in Rome. When men began to write on tablets and ceased singing to the *barbitos,* a loss of some sort was unavoidable. Propertius may be cited as an exception, but Propertius writes only one meter. In any case the classic culture of the Renaissance was grafted on to medieval culture, a process which is excellently illustrated by Andreas Divus Iustinopolitanus's translation of the *Odyssey* into Latin. It is true that each century after the Renaissance has tried in its own way to come nearer the classic, but, if we are to understand that part of our civilization which is the art of verse, we must begin at the root, and that root is medieval. The poetic art of Provence paved the way for the poetic art of Tuscany; and to this Dante bears sufficient witness in the *De Vulgari Eloquio.* The heritage of art is one thing to the public and quite another to the succeeding artists. The artist's inheritance from other artists can be little more than certain enthusiasms, which usually spoil his first work; and a definite knowledge of the modes of expression, which knowledge contributes to perfecting his more mature performance. This is a matter of technique.

After the compositions of Vidal, Rudel, Ventadour, of Bornelh and Bertrans de Born and Arnaut Daniel, there seemed little chance of doing distinctive work in the 'canzon de l'amour courtois'. There was no way, or at least there was no man in Provence capable of finding a new way of saying in six closely rhymed strophes that a certain girl, matron or widow was like a certain set of things, and that the troubadour's virtues were like another set, and that all this was very sorrowful or otherwise, and that there was but one obvious remedy. Richard of Brebezieu had done his best for tired ears; he had made similes of beasts and of stars which got him a passing favour. He had compared himself to the fallen elephant and to the self-piercing pelican, and no one could go any further. Novelty is reasonably rare even in modes of decadence and revival. The three devices tried for poetic restoration in the early thirteenth century were the three usual devices. Certain men turned to talking art and aesthetics and attempted to dress up the folk-song. Certain men tried to make verse more engaging by stuffing it with an intellectual and argumentative content. Certain men turned to social satire. Roughly, we may divide the interesting work of the later provençal period into these three divisions. As all of these men had progeny in Tuscany, they are, from the historical point of view, worth a few moments' attention.

The first school is best represented in the work of Giraut Riquier of Narbonne. His most notable feat was the revival of the *Pastorela.* The Pastorela is a poem in which a knight tells of having met with a shepherdess or some woman of that class, and of what fortune and conversation befell him. The form had been used long before by Marcabrun, and is familiar to us in such poems as Guido Cavalcanti's *In un boschetto trovai pastorella,* or in Swinburne's *An Interlude.* Guido, who did all things well, whenever the fancy took him, has raised this form to a surpassing excellence in his poem *Era in pensier d'Amor, quand' io trovai.* Riquier is most amusing in his account of the inn-mistress at Sant Pos de Tomeiras, but even there he is less amusing than was Marcabrun when he sang of the shepherdess in *L'autrier iost' una sebissa.* Riquier has, however, his place in the apostolic succession; and there is no reason why Cavalcanti and Riquier should not have met while the former was on his journey to Campostella, although Riquier may as easily have not been in Spain at the time. At any rate the Florentine noble would have heard the *Pastorelas* of Giraut; and this may have set him to his *ballate,* which seem to date from the time of his meeting with Mandetta in Toulouse. Or it may have done nothing of the kind. The only more or less settled fact is that Riquier was then the best known living troubadour and near the end of his course.

The second, and to us the dullest of the schools, set to explaining the nature of love and its effects. The normal modern will probably slake all his curiosity for this sort of work in reading one such poem as the King of Navarre's *De Fine amour vient science e beautez*. 'Ingenium nobis ipsa puella fecit', as Propertius put it, or *anglice*:

Knowledge and beauty from true love are wrought,
And likewise love is born from this same pair;
These three are one to whomso hath true thought, etc.

There might be less strain if one sang it. This peculiar variety of flame was carried to the altars of Bologna, whence Guinicello sang:

Al cor gentil ripara sempre amore,
Come l'augello in selva alla verdura

And Cavalcanti wrote: 'A lady asks me, wherefore I wish to speak of an accident which is often cruel', and Dante, following in his elders' footsteps, the *Convito*.

The third school is the school of satire, and is the only one which gives us a contact with the normal life of the time. There had been Provençal satire before Piere Cardinal; but the sirventes of Sordello and De Born were directed for the most part against persons, while the Canon of Clermont drives rather against conditions. In so far as Dante is critic of morals, Cardinal must be held as his forerunner. Miquel writes of him as follows:

'Piere Cardinal was of Veillac of the city Pui Ma Donna, and he was of honourable lineage, son of a knight and a lady. And when he was little his father put him for canon in the *canonica major* of Puy; and he learnt letters, and he knew well how to read and to sing; and when he was come to man's estate he had high knowledge of the vanity of this world, for he felt himself gay and fair and young. And he made many fair arguments and fair songs. And he made canzos, but he made only a few of these, and sirventes; and he did best in the said sirventes where he set forth many fine arguments and fair examples for those who understand them; for much he rebuked the folly of this world and much he reproved the false clerks, as his sirventes show. And he went through the courts of kings and of noble barons and took with him his joglar who sang the sirventes. And much was he honoured and welcomed by my lord the good king of Aragon and by honourable barons. And I, master Miquel de la Tour, escriuan (scribe), do ye to wit that N. Piere Cardinal when he passed from this life was nearly a hundred. And I, the aforesaid Miquel, have written these sirventes in the city of Nemze (Nîmes) and here are written some of his sirventes.'

If the Vicomtesse de Pena reminds us of certain ladies whom we have met, these sirventes of Cardinal may well remind us that thoughtful men have in every age found almost the same set of things or at least the same sort of things to protest against; if it be not a corrupt press or some monopoly, it is always some sort of equivalent, some conspiracy of ignorance and interest. And thus he says, 'Li clerc si fan pastor.' The clerks pretend to be shepherds, but they are wolfish at heart.

If he can find a straight man, it is truly matter for song; and so we hear him say of the Duke of Narbonne, who was apparently, making a fight for honest administration:

Coms raymon duc de Narbona
Marques de proensa
Vostra valors es tan bona
Que tot lo mon gensa,
Quar de la mar de bayona
En tro a valenca
Agra gent falsae fellona
Lai ab vil temensa,
Mas vos tenetz vil lor
Q'n frances bevedor
Plus qua perditz austor
No vos fan temensa.

'Now is come from France what one did not ask for'—he is addressing the man who is standing against the North—

Count Raymon, Duke of Narbonne,
Marquis of Provence,
Your valour is sound enough
To make up for the cowardice of
All the rest of the gentry.
For from the sea at Bayonne,
Even to Valence,
Folk would have given in (sold out),
But you hold them in scorn,
[Or, reading 'l'aur', 'scorn the gold'.]
So that the drunken French
Alarm you no more
Than a partridge frightens a hawk.

Cardinal is not content to spend himself in mere abuse, like the little tailor Figeira, who rhymes Christ's 'mortal pena' with

Car voletz totzjors portar la borsa plena,

which is one way of saying 'Judas!' to the priests. He, Cardinal, sees that the technique of honesty is not always utterly simple.

Li postilh, legat elh cardinal
La cordon tug, y an fag establir
Que qui nos pot de traisson esdir,

which may mean, 'The pope and the legate and the cardinal have twisted such a cord that they have brought things to such a pass that no one can escape committing treachery.' As for the rich:

Li ric home an pietat tan gran
Del autre gen quon ac caym da bel.
Que mais volon tolre q lop no fan
E mais mentir que tozas de bordelh.

The rich men have such pity
For other folk—about as much as Cain had for Abel.
For they would like to leave less than the wolves do,
And to lie more than girls in a brothel.

Of the clergy, 'A tantas very baylia', 'So much the more do I see clerks coming into power that all the world will be theirs, whoever objects. For they'll have it with taking or with giving' (i.e. by granting land, belonging to one man, to someone else who will pay allegiance for it, as in the case of De Montfort), 'or with pardon or with hypocrisy; or by assault or by drinking and eating; or by prayers or by praising the worse; or with God or with devilry.' We find him putting the age-long query about profit in the following:

He may have enough harness
And sorrel horses and bays;
Tower, wall, and palace,
May he have
—the rich man denying his God.

The stanza runs very smoothly to the end

Si mortz no fos
Elh valgra per un cen

A hundred men he would be worth
Were there no death.

The modern Provençal enthusiast in raptures at the idea of chivalric love (a term which he usually misunderstands), and little concerned with the art of verse, has often failed to notice how finely the sound of Cardinal's poems is matched with their meaning. There is a lash and sting in his timbre and in his movement. Yet the old man is not always bitter; or, if he is bitter, it is with the bitterness of a torn heart and not a hard one. It is so we find him in the sirvente beginning:

As a man weeps for his son or for his father,
Or for his friend when death has taken him,
So do I mourn for the living who do their own ill,
False, disloyal, felon, and full of ill-fare,
Deceitful, breakers-of-pact,
Cowards, complainers,
Highwaymen, thieves-by-stealth, turn-coats,
Betrayers, and full of treachery,
Here where the devil reigns
And teaches them to act thus.

He is almost the only singer of his time to protest against the follies of war. As here:

Ready for war, as night is to follow the sun,
Readier for it than is the fool to be cuckold
When he has first plagued his wife!
And war is an ill thing to look upon,
And I know that there is not one man drawn into it
But his child, or his cousin or someone akin to him
Prays God that it be given over.

He says plainly, in another place, that the barons make war for their own profit, regardless of the peasants. 'Fai mal senher vas los sieu.' His sobriety is not to be fooled with sentiment either martial or otherwise. There is in him little of the fashion of feminolatry, and the gentle reader in search of trunk-hose and the light guitar had better go elsewhere. As for women: 'L'una fai drut.'

One turns leman for the sake of great possessions;
And another because poverty is killing her,
And one hasn't even a shift of coarse linen;
And another has two and does likewise.
And one gets an old man—and she is a young wench,
And the old woman gives the man an elixir.

As for justice, there is little now: 'If a rich man steal by chicanery, he will have right before Constantine (i.e. by legal circumambience) but the poor thief may go hang.' And after this there is a passage of pity and of irony fine-drawn as much of his work is, for he keeps the very formula that De Born had used in his praise of battle, 'Belh mes quan vey'; and, perhaps, in Sir Bertrans' time even the Provençal wars may have seemed more like a game, and may have appeared to have some element of sport and chance in them. But the twelfth century had gone, and the spirit of the people was weary, and the old canon's passage may well serve as a final epitaph on all that remained of silk thread and *cisclatons,* of viol and *gai saber.*

Never agin shall we see the Easter come in so fairly,
That was wont to come in with pleasure and with song,
No! but we see it arrayed with alarms and excursions,
Arrayed with war and dismay and fear,
Arrayed with troops and with cavalcades,
Oh, yes, it's a fine sight to see holder and shepherd
Going so wretched that they know not where they are

C. M. Bowra (essay date 1953)

SOURCE: "Dante and Sordello," in *Comparative Literature,* Vol. V, No. 1, Winter, 1953, pp. 1-15.

[*Bowra, an English critic and literary historian, was considered among the foremost classical scholars of the first half of the twentieth century. He also wrote extensively on modern literature, particularly modern European poetry, in studies noted for their erudition, lucidity, and straightforward style. In the following essay, he argues against the theory that Dante, by placing Sordello in Purgatory, characterized the troubadour as among the negligent rulers. Proposing that Sordello's placement in the poem resulted from his violent death and inability to repent, Bowra maintains that Dante had ample reason to respect the troubadour, citing in particular the political invective of the "Lament for Lord Blacatz," which Dante not only admired but imitated.*]

On the lowest slope of the Mount of Purgatory Dante and Virgil, seeing that night is coming on, decide to make enquiries about the best way of ascent. They mark a solitary figure looking towards them and approach:

> Venimmo a lei: O anima Lombarda,
> Come ti stavi altera e disdegnosa,
> E nel mover degli occhi onesta e tarda!
>
> Ella non ci diceva alcuna cosa;
> Ma lasciavane gir, solo sguardando
> A guisa di leon quando si posa.
> (*Purg.* VI, 61-66)

When questioned by Virgil about the way upward, this figure replies by asking about the strangers' country and life. On hearing the word "Mantua" he leaps up and embraces Virgil, and reveals that he is Sordello of the same city. At this dramatic point Dante suddenly breaks his narrative to devote seventy-six lines to a blistering denunciation of Italian discords and lawlessness. Then he picks up the tale and makes Sordello and Virgil exchange information about their respective places in the afterworld. Sordello then guides the two poets to the Valley of the Negligent Rulers, where he points out with appropriate comments the chief inmates and adds some hard words about their sons. When during the night Dante and Virgil are transported to Purgatory proper, Sordello remains behind:

> Sordel rimase, e l'altre gentil forme.
> (*Purg.* IX, 58)

He has played his part and is not mentioned again.

Sordello is an important and engaging figure of his time, at once poet and man of affairs. Born towards the beginning of the thirteenth century at Goito, near Mantua, he entered the court of Count Ricciardo di San Bonifazio, lord of Verona, where he fell in love with his master's wife, Cunizza da Romano, and about 1223 eloped with her to the court of her brother, the terrible Ezzelino, at Treviso. Soon afterwards he abandoned Cunizza and made a secret marriage with Otta di Strasso. This meant that he had to flee from Treviso and the fury of his wife's relatives, and no doubt explains why about 1229 he left Italy for the south of France, where in due course he visited the courts of Provence, Toulouse, Roussillon, and Castile. About 1245 we find him at the court of the Countess Beatrice, daughter of Raymond Berengar, count of Provence, and wife of Charles of Anjou. From 1252 to 1265 Sordello's name appears in several treaties and records, which show that Charles held him in high esteem and entrusted him with important tasks. He followed Charles on his Italian expedition against Manfred in 1265, but seems to have been captured by the Ghibellines before reaching Naples. At any rate, in September 1266 he was a prisoner at Novara; but Clement IV persuaded Charles to ransom him, and in 1269 he received as a recompense for his services five castles in the Abruzzi near the Pescara River. Nothing more is recorded of him; but, since in the same year the castles passed to other owners, the probability is that he died at this time, being by now an elderly man.

If Sordello is not in the highest rank of troubadours, he is certainly the most distinguished of those who came from Italy and sufficiently original and powerful to have attracted Dante's attention by his poetry.

—C. M. Bowra

Sordello was also a poet of distinction and renown. Of his poetry there survive twelve *chansons,* four *partimens,* two *tensons,* eight *sirventes,* fifteen *coblas,* and a long didactic poem in 1,327 lines called **"L'Ensegnamen d'Onor."** His shorter poems may lack the virile gaiety of Guillaume of Aquitaine or the accomplished grace of Bernart de Ventadour or the passion of Bertran de Born, but they have their own distinction. He is an accomplished metrist, who knows how to lace rhymes into elaborate patterns; a stylist, who avoids phrases which are too trite or too recondite; a man of the world, who relates his poetry to his own varied experience. We can understand that Dante might think well of him, since, unlike Arnaut Daniel, who combines protestations of ideal love with desires which are more earthy, he is a thorough Platonist. Whatever his actual conduct may have been, his poetry is consistently high-mined and idealistic. He tells his lady that he does not wish to taste of any fruit whose sweetness will turn to bitterness (xxi, 23-24), that no knight loves his lady unless he loves his own honor equally (xxv, 17-19), that he will never reveal to any honest woman his true feelings about her (xxiv, 49-50), that every loyal lover is sufficiently recompensed if he is honored in himself (xxvii, 1 ff.). He builds his cult of ideal love on personal honor and is quite consistent in his conclusions. It is not surprising that, in the interchange of verse between him and Peire Guillem, Peire says that he has never known anyone like Sordello; since he disdains what other men make it their ambition to win (xviii, 13 ff.). In Sordello's system the man of honor must love a woman as honorable as himself and be as sensitive for her reputation as for his own. If Sordello is not in the highest rank of troubadours, he is certainly the most distinguished of those who came from Italy and sufficiently original and powerful to have attracted Dante's attention by his poetry.

It has been claimed that Dante regards Sordello as himself a member of the class of negligent rulers and that this determines his place in Purgatory. So R. W. Church says [in *Dante and Other Essays*]: "He is placed among those who had great opportunities and great thoughts—the men of great chances and great failures." Something of the same kind seems to have been in Browning's mind when he wrote his remarkable poem about Sordello. For Browning he is an interesting failure, who might have been a true forerunner of Dante but through some defect of character or conviction failed to realize his proper destiny. It is true that Browning does not follow history very closely and that his Sordello is largely an imaginary figure; however, he too regards him as one who had great gifts and chances but failed to take advantage of them:

> one who was chiefly glad
> To have achieved the few real deeds he had,
> Because that way assured they were not worth
> Doing, so spared from doing them henceforth—
> A tree that covets fruitage and yet tastes
> Never itself, itself.

Church and Browning can hardly be right about Dante's treatment of Sordello. The only possible evidence that he is one of the negligent rulers is that Dante and Virgil leave him with them when they ascend to Purgatory proper, and that is by no means conclusive. On the other hand, there are good arguments against this view. First, if Sordello were himself one of this company, his language about its other members would be unsuitable, especially in Purgatory, for one who has himself been guilty of the same fault. Secondly, he was never himself in so exalted a position as the kings and princes whom he criticizes. He belonged to a section of society eminent enough in its own way but not charged with imperial or regal responsibilities, and Dante would hardly have classed him with the Emperor or the kings of France and England.

In fact, it is quite clear where Dante places Sordello, and his reasons for doing so are of some interest. When Dante and Virgil meet him, he is outside Purgatory proper and says of his position:

> "Loco certo non c'è posto:
> Licito m'è andar suso ed intorno;
> Per quanto ir posso, a guida mi t'accosto."
> (*Purg.* VII, 40-42)

Sordello's place indicates that he is one of the late repentant who have died violent deaths. Apparently Dante knew something about him which is not mentioned by the brief Provençal biographies. Nor is this surprising, since the biographies are very feeble affairs and draw most of their information from the poems. There is no difficulty about Dante knowing of an event which took place in 1269 and must have made a stir at the time, since Sordello was a man of some importance. The passage not only settles where Dante places Sordello but also indicates that he knew more of him than his poems. At the end of a varied life Sordello died a violent death, and to this Dante implicitly refers.

That Dante had various sources of information is clear from a passage in the *De vulgari eloquentia,* where in discussing the need for an *illustre vulgare* he considers the Bolognese dialect but, after admitting its merits, comes to the conclusion that it too is not fitted for the highest purposes of poetry. He illustrates his point from Sordello:

> Dicimus ergo quod forte non male opinantur qui Bononienses asserunt pulcriori locutione loquentes, cum ab Imolensibus, Ferrarensibus, et Mutinensibus circumstantibus aliquid proprio vulgari adsciscunt; sicut facere quoslibet a finitimis suis conicimus, ut Sordellus de Mantua sua ostendit, Cremonae, Brixiae, atque Veronae confini; qui tantus eloquentiae vir existens, non solum in poetando sed quomodocunque loquendo patrium vulgare deseruit. [1, 15]

> We say, then, that perhaps those are not far wrong who assert that the people of Bologna use a more beautiful speech, since they receive into their own dialect something borrowed from their neighbours of Imola, Ferrara, and Modena, just as we conjecture that all borrow from their neighbours, as Sordello showed with respect to his own Mantua, which is adjacent to Cremona, Brescia, and Verona; and he who was so distinguished by his eloquence, not only in poetry but in every other form of utterance forsook his native vulgar tongue.

The example supports Dante's contention that Italian dialects are not suited to the grand style; Sordello tried first to write in his own vernacular but abandoned it, presumably for Provençal. We know nothing of his work in Italian, since it is doubtful whether a poem claimed for him by Bertoni is his, but Dante not only knew his Italian poems but other works, presumably not in verse, or at least knew his reputation as a writer or a speaker. In this, as in other respects, Dante was better informed about Sordello than we are.

Concerning one matter Dante shows a remarkable restraint. He must have known about the elopement with Cunizza and is not likely to have approved of it. Of course, if he said nothing about it, no question would arise; but he comes near to referring to it in the *Paradiso,* when Cunizza, being placed in Venus, explains that she is rightly placed in the star of love and that her former sins no longer distress her:

> "Cunizza fui chiamata, e qui refulgo,
> Perchè mi vinse il lume d'esta stella;
>
> Ma lietamente a me medesma indulgo
> La cagion di mia sorte, e non mi noia;
> Che parria forse forte al vostro vulgo."
> (*Par.* IX, 32-36)

Here Dante is a little artful. He would know that any mention of Cunizza would stir his readers to expect some mention of Sordello, but he says nothing of him. Instead he rather tantalizingly makes Cunizza speak of her devotion to another troubadour, Folquet of Marseilles. Dante's silence on Sordello suggests that he has weighed his faults with his virtues and decided that the virtues win.

Yet, though Dante admired Sordello and surely approved of his love poetry, what he liked most seems to have been the courageous expression of political convictions in which Sordello more than once indulged. In the *Purgatorio* Sordello's first function is to provide a starting point for Dante's passionate outburst on the woes of Italy. The abrupt transition is surely dictated by Sordello's own views on such matters and especially by what he says in **"L'Ensegnamen d'Onor,"** where he sets out his notions of chivalrous behavior and his theory of *pretz,* or worth. It is by no means the only poem of its kind, nor the best. It is quite legitimate to prefer the "Romans di Mondana Vita" of Folquet de Lunel or the "Four Cardinal Virtues" of Daude de Pradas; and, of course, if Dante himself knew these other poems, he may well have thought them better. But that is no reason for arguing, as some have, that Dante would therefore pay no attention to Sordello's poem, still less that he did not know it. Since he seems to have been well acquainted with Sordello's writings, we can hardly doubt that he knew this piece. Once he decided to make use of Sordello in the *Divine Comedy,* he would naturally seize on relevant elements in his outlook and especially on those which were expressed at some length in **"L'Ensegnamen d'Onor."**

Though the chivalrous ideal set forth in this poem is commonplace in comparison with that of the *Vita Nuova* or even of the *Convito,* with which it has more in common, it certainly says much of which Dante would approve and very little of which he would disapprove. Just as in his shorter poems Sordello makes the ideal love of a woman an important part of his whole conception of honor, so here he bases his philosophy and especially his notions of *pretz* and *onor* on the inspiration and challenge which such a love gives. His course is somewhat sluggish and circuitous. He dilates on the love of God and the origin of evil before he reaches the rules of behavior. He does not at first say much about women or love, but that is because he keeps them in reserve. As he draws to his close, he expands upon the relations of women and their lovers and tells how they should bear themselves and what conversation they should hold. Then in the last paragraph he pays a tribute to his own lady, Agradiva, who inspires all that is best in his life. In this poem ideal love is a pivotal point in a system of worth and honor; and, though Sordello does not draw such bold conclusions as Dante would, he is a consistent apologist for the cult of love as a system of life.

In **"L'Ensegnamen d'Onor"** Sordello proves himself worthy of Dante's respect as a critic of life and politics, whose philosophy is of the kind which Dante himself held and developed. In this we may see Dante's reason for placing his outburst on Italy immediately after Virgil and Sordello have greeted each other as fellow Mantuans. This covers a deeper kinship between them, and Dante draws the moral:

> Quell'anima gentil fu così presta,
> Sol per lo dolce suon della sua terra,
> Di fare al cittadin suo quivi festa;
>
> E ora in te non stanno senza guerra
> Li vivi tuoi, e l'un l'altro si rode
> Di quei ch'un muro ed una fossa serra.
> (*Purg.* VI, 79-84)

Italy is equally dear to Virgil, to Dante, and to Sordello. From his knowledge of Sordello's work Dante advances from the friendly warmth of the greeting to a fierce denunciation, in which he not only says much with which Sordello would agree but even seems to follow with his own vivid variations certain topics with which Sordello deals in his poem.

If we compare Dante's outburst with Sordello's **"L'Ensegnamen d'Onor,"** we may notice several points of similarity, which suggest that Dante has a clear purpose in his abrupt change of subject. There is, it is true, a great difference of manner between the two poets. While Sordello is dry and abstract and theoretical, Dante is vivid and personal and illustrates individual issues with homely or colloquial phrases. But behind this difference there are considerable resemblances of thought and outlook; indeed each point made by Dante can be paralleled by something said by Sordello. Dante begins by denouncing the disobedience prevalent in Italy and proclaiming the need to let the Emperor rule; Sordello (lines 543 ff.) also lays down the need for an ideal of service and blames those who shun what is right or accept what is not. Dante then blames the German Albert for deserting his duty and calls down judgment from Heaven on him; Sordello (lines 589 ff.) says that a common failing of the great is to be interested in themselves instead of in those whom they rule. Dante ascribes imperial negligence to the avarice of Albert and his father; Sordello (lines 506 ff.) expatiates on the duties of wealth and the need for generosity. In his denunciation of Florence, Dante says that its people have no justice in their hearts, though its name is often on their lips; Sordello (lines 601 ff.) inveighs against those who condemn the faults of others and pay no attention to their own. Dante blames the Florentines for refusing public burdens; Sordello (lines 55 ff.) regards such service as owed to both God and man. Finally, Dante denounces the improvidence which means that what is spun in October does not reach to mid-November; Sordello (lines 489 ff.) regards forethought as the first duty of all rulers. Thus Dante's principles of government, as revealed in his outburst on Italy, may be illustrated almost line by line from Sordello's poem.

This does not mean that Dante necessarily had **"L'Ensegnamen d'Onor"** before him when he wrote this passage or even that he knew it so well that he was able to adapt its thoughts to his own. But it suggests at least that he knew it and agreed with it and saw in it sufficient justification for making the meeting with Sordello the occasion for a denunciation of Italy and its rulers. It is of course true that other poets expressed ideas very like Sordello's and that, if he had wished, Dante could have used them. But he does not, for a good reason. Sordello appealed to him on more than one account; the appeal of Mantua was in itself sufficient to give Sordello a priority over other politically minded poets and to provide the use of his own appearance for an outburst of Dante's own feelings. The passage is introduced with great skill, both formally and essentially. After the moving character of the meeting between the two Mantuans, what follows comes with an impressive shock of contrast; but the similarity between Sordello's views and Dante's justifies the introduction of a theme which might otherwise do undue violence to the narrative.

In this passage Dante agrees with Sordello on some general principles of politics, though he gives them a particular application, which Sordello does not. Later in the *Purgatorio,* when Dante is concerned with political personalities, he again chooses to follow a model from Sordello. In Canto VII, 83-136, Sordello points out various negligent rulers who are seated on the grass in the wonderful valley and comments on them and on others who are not present. Here, we can hardly doubt, Dante had in mind Sordello's most famous poem, the *planh* which he wrote on the death of Blacatz and which is so important that it must be quoted in full (from the Hill and Bergin *Anthology,* Yale Romanic Studies, No. XVII):

Planher vuelh en Blacatz en aquest leugier so
Ab cor trist e marrit, et ai en be razo,
Qu'en luy ai mescabat senhor et amic bo,
E quar tug l'ayp valent en sa mort perdut so:
Tant es mortals lo dans, qu'ieu noy ai sospeisso
Que jamais si revenha, s'en aital guiza no,
Qu'om li traga lo cor, e qu'en manjol baro
Que vivon descorat, pueys auran de cor pro.

Premiers manje del cor, per so que grans ops l'es,
L'emperaire de Roma, s'elh vol los Milanes
Per forsa conquistar, quar luy tenon conques,
E viu deseretatz, malgrat de sos Ties;
E deseguentre lui manj' en lo reys frances,
Pueys cobrara Castella, que pert per nescies;
Mas, si pez' a sa maire, elh no'n manjara ges,
Quar ben para son pretz qu'elh non fai ren quel pes.

Del rey engles me platz, quar es pauc coratjos,
Que manje pro del cor, pueys er valens e bos,
E cobrara la terra, per que viu de pretz blos,
Quel tol lo reys de Fransa quar lo sap nualhos;
E lo reys castelas tanh qu'en manje per dos,
Quar dos regismes ten, e per l'un non es pros;
Mas, s'elh en vol manjar, tanh qu'en manj' a rescos,
Que, sil mair' o sabia, batria l ab bastos.

Del rey d'Arago vuel del cor deja manjar,
Que aisso lo fara de l'anta descarguar
Que pren sai de Marcella e d'Amilau, qu'onrar
Nos pot estiers per ren que puesca dir ni far;
Et apres vuelh del cor don hom al rey navar,
Que valia mais coms que reys, so aug comtar:
Tortz es quan Dieus fai home en gran ricor pojar,
Pus sofracha de cor lo fai de pretz bayssar.

Al comte de Toloza a ops qu'en manje be,
Sil membra so que sol tener ni so que te,
Quar, si ab autre cor sa perda non reve,
Nom par que la revenha ab aquel qu'a en se.
El coms proensals tanh qu'en manje, sil sove
C'oms que deseretatz viu guaire non val re,
E, sitot ab esfors si defen nis chapte,
Ops l'es mange del cor pel greu fais qu'el soste.
Li baro m volran mal de so que ieu dic be,
Mas ben sapchan qu'ie'ls pretz aitan pauc quon ylhe me.

Belh Restaur, sol qu'ab vos puesca trobar merce,
A mon dan met quascun que per amic nom te.

Blacatz is dead. In this plain descant I intend
To weep for him, nor care a jot if I offend;
For in him I have lost my master and good friend,
And know that with his death all princely virtues end.
It is a mortal loss, which nought can ever mend,
In truth I so suspect, unless his heart we send
To the great lords to eat. To hearts they can't pretend!
But then they'll have enough of heart to make amend.

First let the Emperor eat. Great need of it is his,
If he would crush by force the rebel Milanese
And force his conquerors to do what he decrees;
Despite his German guards he has no fiefs or fees.
Then let the French king eat, and may-be he will seize
Castile again, which he lost by his idiocies.
But he'll refrain if his good mother disagrees;
Honor, we know, forbids that he should her displease.

I bid the English king, who is so ungallant,
Eat of the heart; then he'll be bold and valiant,
Win back the lands whose loss proclaims him recreant,
All that the French king took, knowing him indolent.
Next the Castilian king enough for two will want;
Two realms has he, but ev'n for one his heart's too scant.
If he would eat, let him be secret and not flaunt;
He'll feel his mother's stick if she learns of his vaunt.

Then of this heart must eat the king of Aragon;
So shall he wash away the shame which he has won
At Marseilles and Milhau; of his lost honor none
Can he recover now, whatever's said and done.
Then unto Navarre's king I bid this heart be shown,—
Better as count than king in my comparison,—
Great pity 'tis when God exalts dominion
For princes who then bid all name and fame be gone.

Next, the Count of Toulouse is in sore need of it,
If he recall what lands he has, of what he's quit,
To win his losses back a new heart he must fit,—
The heart that he has now will mend them not a bit.
Last, the Count of Provence will eat if he admit
That the disinherited are honored not a whit;
Yes, let him do his best himself to benefit;
So burdensome a load he bears that he must eat.

For all these well said words I'll win the great lords' hate,
But let them know I'll pay their knocks back with like weight.
Sweet Comfort, if I find your favor in the end,
I'm little vexed by those who scorn to call me friend.

This unusual poem shows the strength and originality of Sordello's art and makes it easier to understand why Dante forgave him his sins and gave him an honorable part in the *Divine Comedy.*

In the well-regulated world of Provençal poetry Sordello's *planh* has a peculiar place. It has precedents in such pieces as Cercamon's lament for Guillaume of Aquitaine in 1137, or Bertran de Born's for Henry II's son, the "young king," in 1183, or those of Jaucelm Faidit and Giraut de Borneil for Richard Cœur de Lion in 1199. The lament was an ancient form and followed conventional lines, in which the poets usually complain that with the passing of a great man chivalry, valor, and courtesy have vanished from the earth. They do not usually seize the occasion, as Sordello does, to say unpleasant things about the living. But historically he is justified in this, because the *planh* is closely related to the *sirventés,* which is what the Provençal poets use when they wish to criticize their lords and masters or to pass political judgments. Sordello must have known this, and his poem is close to such poems as that written by the younger Bertran de Born against King John in 1204, in which he mocks him for the loss of Poitou and Guyenne, accuses him of betraying his armies, and generally derides his failure. Sordello's originality lies in finding in Blacatz's death an opportunity to say what he feels about the rulers of Europe. If the form allowed some latitude, he took all that he could and made the most of it.

Blacatz, whose death Sordello laments, is not unknown to history. He was seigneur of Aups near Draguignan and is mentioned in several documents after 1194. Himself the author of ten surviving poems, he was also the friend and patron of poets and was praised for his generosity and goodness. Sordello seems to have come into contact with him at the court of Guida, daughter of Henry I, count of Rodez, before 1240. She has been thought to be the "Belh Restaurs" to whom he addresses several poems, including the *planh,* and she is associated with Sordello in the parody of it written by Bertrand d'Alamanon. Though in 1240 Sordello is known to have been at Montpellier, it looks as if he wrote the *planh* when he was back with Guida and addressed it to her because she too had been a friend of the dead man. The freedom with which he speaks sheds an interesting light on the conditions of the time, when a small court like that of Guida could flaunt its opposition to the great powers of Europe. Sordello throws his net wide. In turn he denounces the Emperor Frederick II, Louis IX of France, Henry III of England, Ferdinand III of Castile, James I of Aragon, Thibaut I of Navarre, Raymond VII of Toulouse, and Raymond Berengar V of Provence.

It is not impossible to fix an approximate date for the poem. The death of Blacatz seems to have coincided with a considerable crisis in western Europe. In 1242 Raymond VII of Toulouse formed a league of southern potentates in the hope of shaking off French suzerainty and received assurances of help from the kings of Castile and Aragon. At the same time Henry III of England set sail for France on May 9 with the ambition of regaining the lands lost by his father. On July 23 he was defeated by Louis IX at Saintes, and, though his army remained for some time in France, it had no hope of success. Despite this Raymond tried to make a treaty with Henry and eventually did so by the end of August. Then in October all went wrong. The count of Foix deserted; the kings of Castile and Aragon held aloof from action; and on October 20 Raymond submitted to Louis. It is a sorry tale, and Sordello takes full advantage of it.

Of his eight rulers five were involved in the revolt, and each is mocked for his failure—Henry III, quite accurately, for lands lost to the French king, not so much what John had already lost but Poitou and Saintonge as far as the Gironde; Ferdinand III for his cowardice in failing to help Raymond VII; James I for still not being master of Marseilles, which ought to have been his on the death of Raymond Berengar IV, and of Milhau, which once belonged to his house but was still in the hands of Toulouse with the connivance of Louis IX and the Pope; Raymond VII of Toulouse for his failure to regain lands lost earlier to Louis; and Raymond Berengar V of Provence for gaining nothing by making up his quarrel with Toulouse and being forced to accept a diminution of his domains. The outbreak of 1242 was largely an attempt to regain territories recently lost; when it failed, these remained with their recent owners and especially with Louis.

To this list Sordello adds three other names, Frederick II, Louis IX, and Thibaut I, who fall in rather a different category, since they were not on the defeated side in the revolt. Frederick could hardly be omitted from a list of living monarchs; and Sordello, who himself came from Lombardy, delights in his continued lack of success with the Milanese, whom he defeated at Cortenuova in 1237 but never subdued. Louis had indeed defeated his enemies in France, but Sordello condemns him for not making the most of his victory and taking Castile, to which he had a reasonable claim through his mother, especially since Ferdinand's mother, Berengaria, was declared not to have been married to his father, Alfonso X of Leon. Finally, since Thibaut of Navarre, formerly count of Champagne, is not known to have joined Raymond VII, Sordello probably derides him for his behavior in the recent crusade, when he retreated before the Saracens and took ship home. These three additional names complete Sordello's picture of western Europe governed by poltroons. Although his actual occasion seems to have been the war of 1242, he passes beyond it to a wider view and distributes his blows impartially on eight potentates.

Sordello's *planh* evidently made a considerable mark, since it was soon imitated or parodied by Peire Bremon Ricas Novas and by Bertran d'Alamanon. It also became known in due course to Dante, who was evidently taken by the image of eating the dead man's heart. To this there seems to be no parallel in mediaeval poetry except in poems obviously derived from Sordello. It is conceivable that it comes from folk song or folk tale, since the troubadours were not averse from drawing on such popular sources, but even for this the nearest parallel is no closer than a Greek [source] in which an eagle summons other birds to eat of its vitals. Dante's debt to the *planh* may first be seen in a poem in the *Vita Nuova,* where the figure of Love appears to him in a vision:

Allegro mi sembrava Amor, tenendo
Mio core in mano, e nelle braccia avea
Madonna, involta in un drappo, dormendo.

Poi la svegliava, e d'este core ardendo
Lei paventosa umilmente pascea;
Appresso gir ne lo vedea piangendo.

Dante does not use the image of eating the heart quite as Sordello does; while Sordello insists that it will give strength to the feeble, Dante suggests that his whole being is absorbed in that of his lady. None the less, the two poems are sufficiently similar to justify the conclusion that Dante has borrowed something from Sordello.

If this was the first impression which the *planh* made on Dante, it was not the only one. When he came to write the *Purgatorio,* he was interested not in the image of the heart but in the denunciation of European rulers. If Sordello's poem surveys these about 1242, the speech which Dante gives him covers some forty years of history as seen in retrospect from the ideal date of 1300. Dante uses the presence of the negligent rulers for two purposes, first to comment on those who belong to the class, then to say something, usually unpleasant, about their sons and successors. The negligent rulers named are the Emperor Rudolph, Ottocar of Bohemia, Philip III of France, Henry of Navarre, Peter III of Aragon, Charles I of Anjou, Henry III of England, and William of Montferrat. Only concerning two of these does Dante say enough to show why they are placed where they are. The Emperor Rudolph is guilty of negligence:

. . . fa sembianti
D'aver negletto ciò che far dovea.
(*Purg.* VII, 91-92)

In the previous canto he has been associated with his son Albert as being guilty of neglecting their own lands in their covetousness (*Purg.* VI, 97-105), and now Dante stresses the fruit of this policy in the condition of Italy, whose wounds Rudolph might have healed. Dante is also explicit about Philip III of France, who "died in flight, dishonoring the lily"—a reference to Philip's fatal defeat in 1285 by Roger di Loria, the admiral of Peter III of Aragon. However, Dante may have had more than this in mind, since Philip had tried to seize Aragon for his son, Charles of Valois, of whom Dante had a low opinion because of his interference in Florentine politics (*Purg.* XX, 71). So perhaps he here recalls that among Philip's other faults was favoritism to an unworthy son.

Though Dante does not explain why the other kings and princes are classed as negligent, there is no great difficulty. They have all in their own way failed, presumably through some weakness of character, and their failure has led to discord or defeat. Whatever their personal virtues and charms may have been, and Dante is generous enough about them, they have none the less failed in their first duty, which is to rule and keep order. Ottocar of Bohemia has divided the Empire in his struggle with Rudolph of Hapsburg. The policies of Charles of Anjou ended in disaster when he was driven out of Sicily after the Sicilian Vespers, but before that he had caused havoc in Italy (*Purg.* XX, 67 ff.; *Par.* VIII, 73 ff.). Henry III of England, the only figure who appears both in Sordello's poem and here, "il re della semplice vita," is another whose efforts to regain his lost lands have failed and have been followed by civil war. William of Montferrat tried to lead a league against Charles of Anjou, but could not control its members and was ruined when Alessandria rose against him; he was put in a cage where he was kept until his death. Neither Henry of Navarre nor Peter III of Aragon, despite many chivalrous qualities and the admiration of their contemporaries, were really successful kings. The company is well enough chosen and excites little comment. Indeed the only possible criticism of it is that we may feel surprise at Charles of Anjou being so well treated. Elsewhere Dante says of him:

Carlo venne in Italia, e, per vicenda,
Vittima fè di Corradino; e poi
Ripinse al ciel Tommaso, per ammenda.
(*Purg.* XX, 67-69)

The deaths of Conradin and Thomas Aquinas might seem to argue graver faults in Charles than negligence, but for some reason Dante condones them and sets Charles in reasonably good company.

In his choice of negligent rulers Dante follows very much the same principles as Sordello in his *planh*. Each condemns rulers for not ruling and suggests that it is due to a failure of character. With Sordello the failure is simply cowardice; with Dante it is something wider, a failure to sustain responsibility, or something like moral cowardice. He seems to have taken Sordello's idea and expanded it. If Sordello thinks that a king's first duty is to hold all the lands which belong to his house, Dante thinks that it is to govern well what lands he has and not to promote discord. If Sordello insists in the case of Thibaut that elevation to kingship is no reason for lapsing into idleness, Dante throughout implies that rulers have great responsibilities and that the higher their position the more it demands of them. If Sordello regards war as the test of a man's worth, Dante at least regards defeat as a sign of weakness. Finally, it is noteworthy that, while Sordello does not shrink from deriding St. Louis, Dante nowhere finds a place for him in the *Divine Comedy* or even mentions him by name. This king, who seems to us to embody so much that is best in the thirteenth century, evidently did not appeal to Dante. Though the two poets may differ in temperament, they judge rulers by much the same standards and have much the same ideas of what qualities rulers ought to possess.

If part of Sordello's speech is more generous than suits what we know of his character, that is no doubt because Dante wishes to be fair to men like Henry III, who was renowned for his piety, or Peter III, who was praised for his virtue and probity. But Dante was capable of scorn equal to Sordello's and was not afraid to show it when he thought it deserved. He ingeniously makes the sight of the negligent rulers an occasion to mention others who are not present, usually because they are still alive. Of these only two receive favorable comment, Edward I of England, who is a better man than his father, and the eldest son of Peter III of Aragon, who did not reign long enough to make his influence felt. The others mentioned are less worthy—Wenceslas I of Bohemia, Philip the Fair of France, James II of Aragon, his brother Frederick II of Sicily, and Charles II of Naples. If the fathers' faults are pardonable, those of the sons are not. They are men of Dante's own time, concerning whose characters and careers he is well informed and concerning whom he has usually something to say elsewhere in the *Divine Comedy*. So he speaks of Wenceslas:

> Che mai valor non conobbe, nè volle.
> (*Par.* XIX, 126)

Philip the Fair, "il mal di Francia," with his "vita viziata e lorda" is accused of abetting simony (*Inf.* XIX, 87), of ruining his country by debasing its coinage (*Par.* XXX, 118), and of being a new Pilate in his treatment of the Church (*Purg.* XX, 91). James II of Aragon is denounced for participating in the foul deeds of his uncle and brother and making cuckold their family and its two kingdoms (*Par.* XIX, 136-138). Frederick II of Sicily is attacked for avarice and baseness (*Par.* XIX, 130); and Charles II of Naples is associated with him, when Dante says that Sicily weeps because they are alive (*Par.* XX, 62), while the same Charles is blamed for selling his daughter (*Purg.* XX, 80). If the fathers were no worse than feeble and indolent, the sons are vicious and bring disaster by their evil behavior.

For this state of affairs Dante offers an explanation. It is, he makes Sordello say, usual for families to get worse as they continue:

> Rade volte risurge per li rami
> L'umana probitate: e questo vuole
> Quei che la dà, perchè da lui si chiami.
> (*Purg.* VII, 121-123)

In the *Paradiso* Dante reverts to the question of heredity and comes to a somewhat different conclusion, when Charles Martel explains that the fault lies rather with the assigning of tasks to men who are not naturally fitted for them:

> Ma voi torcete alla religione
> Tal che fia nato a cignersi la spada,
> E fate re di tal ch'è da sermone:
>
> Onde la traccia vostra è fuor di strada.
> (*Par.* VIII, 145-148)

An age which had known both Boniface VIII and Henry III might well grant the truth of these words, and they are probably nearer to Dante's own final conclusions than the doctrine of natural decline which he gives to Sordello in the *Purgatorio*. Indeed the doctrine may well have been given to Sordello because it suits his outlook and opinions. Sordello not only says that Louis IX and Ferdinand III are weaker than their mothers, but implies that all his kings and princes are worse than their forefathers, whose lands they are too feeble to hold. The theory of degeneration suits Sordello's critical temper and is aptly attributed to him. If later Dante passes beyond it, this is only another sign that Sordello's view was much to his taste, but that, with his usual gift for improving upon the lessons of his masters, he altered it and adapted it to another, more comprehensive view of history.

Peter Makin (essay date 1978)

SOURCE: "Sordello," in *Provence and Pound,* University of California Press, 1978, pp. 186-214.

[*Makin is an educator and Pound scholar. In the following excerpt, he discusses the content, style, and language of Sordello's poetry, and examines the influence of his life and works on Pound's early verse and his* Cantos.]

Pound's respect for both Browning and Dante gave him good reasons to be interested in Sordello. But in the early years of studying the troubadours he brushed over him; he tended to think of writing as either noble-and-difficult or easy-and-slick, and Sordello was easy.

But when Pound came back to the troubadours he followed Dante's lead even more carefully, and his opinion of Sordello improved. In 1937 he wrote, 'With Sordello the fusion of word, sound, movement is so simple one only understands his superiority to other troubadours after having studied Proven¸al and half-forgotten it, and come back to twenty years later' [quoted in *Letters,* to Katue Kitasono, 11 March 1937]. He explained further:

> Only after long domesticity with music did I, at any rate, see why Dante has mentioned Sordello, or has he even done so in *De Eloquio?*
>
> Above other troubadours, as I feel it *now,* Sordello's hand (or word) 'deceives the eye' honestly. The complete fluidity, the ease that comes only with mastery in strophes so simple in meaning that they leave nothing for the translator [quoted in *Guide to Kulchur,* 1938].

One might think that Arnaut Daniel is an acquired taste; but now Pound spoke of his 'merits that can be picked out, demonstrated, explained'; Sordello was for those who had 'direct perception of quality' [quoted in *Guide to Kulchur*]. Writing about his great praise in the early days for Arnaut, he now said 'A more mature judgment, or greater familiarity with Provencal idiom might lead one to prefer the limpid simplicity of some of Sordello's verses' [quoted in *The Spirit of Romance*].

So the history of Pound on Sordello is like the history of Pound on Bernart de Ventadorn: late appreciation of a mastery in music that can only be hinted at, not shown. The two troubadours also have a lot in common in their 'content'.

The first impression that Sordello's poetry gives is bland, not only in sound but in thought; there is rarely an idea or a phrase that has not been smoothed by use in another troubadour's work. Sordello himself says he belongs to the school of *trobar leu,* the easy style:

> I like to make, with easy words,
> a pleasing song and one with a light melody,
> because the finest lady one can choose,
> to whom I hand myself over and surrender and give myself,
> does not like and is not pleased by master-class poetry;
> and because it doesn't please her, from now on I'll make my singing
> easy to sing and agreeable to listen to,
> clear to understand and delicate, whoever has the delicacy to pick it out.
>
> **["Bel m'es ab motz leugiers a far"]**

Sordello does not include the striking nature-imagery that even Bernart de Ventadorn opened with; he sticks more or less closely to the casuistry of love. Sometimes he admits that he is interested in love-making, perhaps, obliquely, but everything is so surrounded with fear of doing the wrong thing it is difficult to know what Sordello is at:

> And if love makes me want anything
> you should not do,
> for pity's sake I wish to ask you
> that you should not do it;
> for I prefer to live in torments
> than that your worth [*pretz*] should be devalued,
> lady, for anything you might do for me;
> because I have enough from you, whom I desire,
> if only you sincerely permit me
> to love and serve you.
>
> **["Dompna, meillz qu'om pot pensar"]**

From Pound's *Canto II:*

> Hang it all, Robert Browning,
> there can be but the one "Sordello."
> But Sordello, and my Sordello?
> Lo Sordels si fo di Mantovana.
> So-shu churned in the sea.
> Seal sports in the spray-whited circles of cliff-wash,
> Sleek head, daughter of Lir,
> eyes of Picasso
> Under black fur-hood, lithe daughter of Ocean;
> And the wave runs in the beach-groove:
> "Eleanor . . . !"
> And poor old Homer blind, blind, as a bat,
> Ear, ear for the sea-surge, murmur of old men's voices:
> "Let her go back to the ships,
> Back among Grecian faces, lest evil come on our own,
> Evil and further evil, and a curse cursed on our children,
> Moves, yes she moves like a goddess
> And has the face of a god
> and the voice of Schoeney's daughters,
> And doom goes with her in walking,
> Let her go back to the ships,
> back among Grecian voices."
> And by the beach-run, Tyro,
> Twisted arms of the sea-god,
> Lithe sinews of water, gripping her, cross-hold,
> And the blue-gray glass of the wave tents them,
> Glare azure of water, cold-welter, close cover.
> Quiet sun-tawny sand-stretch,
> The gulls broad out their wings,
> nipping between the splay feathers;
> Snipe come for their bath,
> bend out their wing-joints,
> Spread wet wings to the sun-film,
> And by Scios,
> to left of the Naxos passage,
> Naviform rock overgrown,
> algæ cling to its edge,
> There is a wine-red glow in the shallows,
> a tin flash in the sun-dazzle. . . .

Ezra Pound, in The Cantos of Ezra Pound, *Faber and Faber, 1975.*

Sordello has aetherialised his lady into nothing but a source of moral worth, and when he meets someone who thinks of women as flesh and blood, they cannot even speak the same language. Montanhagol asks him which is best: that he should know his lady's heart, or that she should know his. Sordello answers:

> 'Montanhagol, it would please me
> a hundred times more
> that she for whom I die living
> should know . . .
> my heart, that she holds in torment,
> than that I should know hers;
> because if the truth should show to her
> how I am tormented for her,
> she would take pity on it,
> or all her heart would be
> hard as stone, cold as ice . . .'
>
> 'Sordello, it is truly much better
> that you should know the heart and the feelings
> of her whom you love truly
> —whether she loves you or is fooling you;
> because often under a fine appearance
> great falsity hides,
> and, if you find yourself being fooled,
> you will seem too mad
> if, after that, you love unloved . . .'
>
> 'Montanhagol, I don't take it
> as any trickery from her
> whom I love and serve loyally,
> even if it pleases her to kill me . . .'
>
> **["Senh' En Sordel, mandamen"]**

They are the adepts of two different faiths: Montanhagol of all the mediaeval beliefs that woman was a sink of iniquity, and Sordello of the religion of Courtly Love. It is difficult to say which is narrower.

The kind of casuistry that Sordello shared with Bernart de Ventadorn also brought a 'morality' into love. For them, moral value in the troubadour depends on the quality of lady he chooses and on his devotion; but moral value in the lady depends on the quality of man she deigns to accept and on her pity on his devotion. This is a little circular; did nobody start off with intrinsic value, inspiring devotion or acceptance from their partner? Hence the terms become somewhat vague, and both in their etymology and in their use there is a suggestion that words like *pretz* mean 'high reputation' or 'the fact that I, or people generally, esteem you'. The *reductio ad absurdum* would be something like this: 'I love you, and you have *valor,* so that it is unthinkable that you should refuse me, because a lady who has *valor* never refuses a knight who has *valor,* what though my only *valor* be this, that I have set my sights on a lady of such great *valor* as yourself.' Thus:

> . . . because I love what is uniquely estimable
> [*de bon pretz*],
> I prefer to love her uselessly
> rather than another who might deign to take me
> to her;
> but I don't serve her unrewarded,
> because a real lover never serves unrewarded
> when he serves with his heart in an honoured
> and valued [*prezan*] place;
> wherefore the honour is a reward to me for the
> fact
> that I don't seek the overplus, though I'd
> certainly accept it.
>
> **["Ben m'es ab motz leugiers a far"]**

Sordello is in Bernart de Ventadorn's prison, and he uses the same apparatus to lament it:

> I hate mirrors, for they are too harmful to me
> in relation to her who makes me languish in her
> prison,
> and when she looks at her body and her shapes,
> thinking what sort of person she is, she thinks
> little of my torment. . . .
>
> **["Atretan dei ben chantar finamen"]**

A large part of his verses is taken up with considering how little, when he thinks of the great worth of the lady who is the cause of his torments, he cares about his torments—he only regrets that when she has killed him there will be no one to sing her praises properly. We can see the beginning of the Petrarchan war games, with their glances as darts of love, their wounds, their sallies and retreats of spirits, at moments in Sordello. Sordello tells us how part of his fineness consists in not wanting the wrong thing, because he could not love her half so much, loved he not honour more; because of this fineness he should and sometimes does feel secure against all rivals, since she is bound to love the finest of her lovers. This concern with his own state is what really marks him out as a later troubadour, sharing the Gothicness of expression that Pound speaks of with Bernart and with Arnaut. We find in William IX of Aquitaine that he expresses a desire for a presence that he feels would transform his world, and he expresses his pain at its lack. It is we, the readers, who can see the effects of this want on him. But with the later troubadours we find them in 90 per cent of their verse expressing, not their desire or its unfulfilment, but their observations as to the effect of its unfulfilment, held as a permanent state, on themselves. It makes me, they observe endlessly, into an *amans fis,* a 'fine lover'—Sordello talks of his 'fine joy', of himself as one of the 'fine courtly men', of his 'fine heart' that she has stolen, and of handing himself over to her 'fine and true'.

Though there is much scope for fun at the expense of these contortions, they led Sordello to a very high development of his art. The prison of love was his 'subject'; it fitted his nature, as we can see; he refined the weapons of poetry to a point where he could use them on it with psychological exactitude. He invented an intricate causative logic which dominates the poem and expresses his entrapment. *Quar,* 'because', *per que,* 'wherefore', and their equivalents begin almost every clause. In a typical

Sordello stanza the reasoning that constitutes his prison builds up continuously in a complicated series of subordinations, weaving through the gentle rhythms and imposing its continuity on them with many enjambments, until it reaches a perfect stasis in the last line, often containing both a verbal and logical paradox and a highly developed cross-play of sounds. He is held in a languishing happiness:

> Now towards the time of May
> when I see leaf and flower appear
> to reach my duty
> I shall sing in the best manner in the world,
> worthy lady, since I cannot cease,
> since I turn back to see you, from singing,
> but because I don't see you my life seems death to me,
> and singing pain, and pleasure unhappiness
> [*e chanz dolors e plazers desconortz*].
> **["Er encontra l temps de mai"]**

Sordello only hits the gentle plaintive rhythm that is his 'voice' when he uses a line that is longer than that of most troubadour songs; most of his groups of lines that do not have or lead to this metric length are of little strength. He needs leisure to develop his peculiar soft ennui. When he hits this rhythm he begins to interweave his sounds and verbal contrasts to an extraordinary degree. The following stanza, for example, has an intense cross-play of verbal contrasts, which I have italicised:

> As the *ill* person who cannot *keep well*
> when he is *cured,* so that the *illness takes* him again
> and *makes* him *worse* in this *second sickening*
> than it *made* him before, so it has *taken* me and *takes* me
> with the *illness* of love with which I have *sickened again:*
> because I did not *keep* myself from it when I had got away,
> now I have such an *illness* as I will never be *cured* of
> if the beautiful one through whom I have it doesn't *cure* me.
> **["Si co l malaus qe no se sap gardar"]**

The way in which the verbal play fits into the ambulation of sounds can only be heard in the original:

> Si co l malaus qe no se sap gardar
> qan es garitz, per qe l mals lo repren
> e l fai trop peig en son recalivar
> qe non a faich, aisi m'es pres e m pren
> del mal d'amor dun sui recalivatz:
> qar no m gardei qan eu n'era escapatz,
> ar ai tal mal dun jamais non garai
> si no m garis la bella per cui l'ai.

The whole of Sordello's real content, that is the content in which he differentiates himself from other poets and makes us 'smell' his individuality, is this logic through which he points out to his beautiful captor one by one the interconnected reasons why it is through her that he is trapped. On rare occasions it focuses so sharply on the nature of the captor that it produces a most beautiful 'sympathetic parallel' to her in the nature-imagery that traditionally starts the Provencal poem:

> Atretan dei ben chantar finamen
> d'invern com faz d'estiu, segon rason,
> per c'ab lo freitz voill far gaia canson
> que s'en pascor de chantar cor mi pren,
> quar la rosa sembla lei de cui chan,
> aultresi es la neus del sieu senblan:
> per qu'en andos dei per s'amor chantar,
> tant fort mi fan la rosa e l neus menbrar.
> **[Atretan dei ben chantar finamen]**

We have seen Pound's attempt at this in Canto VI; he caught the obsessive repetitions, but it was beyond even his art to catch the sound of Sordello's invention, the winding syntax:

> I must sing as finely
> in winter as I do in summer, according to reason,
> for with the cold I want to make a gay song,
> since if the desire to sing takes me at Easter,
> because the rose resembles the lady I sing of,
> equally the snow is like her;
> so that in each season I must sing for her love;
> so much do the rose and the snow remind me.
> [quoted in *Cantos*]

SORDELLO AND CUNIZZA, HISTORICALLY

Pound did not dwell on the beauty of Sordello's work; it was the story of Cunizza, Sordello's sometime lady, that impressed him and made her one of the lights at the centre of his Paradise. One of the Provencal *vidas* sums up the story:

> Sordello was from Sirier in Mantuan country, the son of a poor knight who was called Sir El Cort. And he delighted himself in learning songs and in composing; and he stayed with the good courtiers, and learned all that he could; and made *coblas* and *sirventes.*
>
> And he came away to the court of the Count of San Bonifacio; and the Count honoured him greatly. And he fell in love with the wife of the Count, in the manner of pleasure, and she with him. And it happened that the Count did not get on with her brothers, and estranged himself from her. And Sir Ezzelino and Sir Alberico, her brothers, had Sordello abduct her from the Court; and he came away to stay with them; and he was with them a long time in great happiness.
>
> And then he went off to Provence, where he received great honour from all good men, and from the Count and the Countess, who gave him a good castle and a noble wife [quoted in *Biographies,* by Boutière and Schutz].

Though this story is suspiciously like the *vida* of Bernart de Ventadorn, we know a great deal more about Sordello. Like William IX of Aquitaine, he was a political figure, which both attracted public attention to his deeds and provided a different kind of documentation.

Sordello had made a poor start in his career—we know of it chiefly from his competitors, the troubadours who infested the courts of northern Italy around 1220. They accused him of being a gambler, and of being a *jongleur,* willing to sing anyone's songs for handouts. No doubt he had risen above these circles by the time he met Cunizza. Sordello had been at the court of Azzo VII d'Este, and from there he went to the court of Azzo's friend, Rizzardo di San Bonifacio, in Verona. At the beginning of the year 1222, the Da Romano and the San Bonifacio had concluded a peace in their lengthy and bitter struggle, and as a sign of trust had married off Cunizza da Romano to Rizzardo di San Bonifacio, while Zilia di San Bonifacio went in marriage to Ezzelino II da Romano. Cunizza is the lady to whom a love-judgement is referred in one of Sordello's songs, a *partimen* with another troubadour. The two houses were back at war by 1226, and the troubadours were soon spreading the news that Sordello had carried Cunizza off. The chronicler Rolandino, whom Pound uses extensively, relates that Ezzelino II

> In the sixth place begot the lady Cunizza, the order of whose life was thus:—At first she was given as wife to Count Rizzardo di San Bonifacio; but in a while, on the orders of Ezzelino her father, Sordello, a man from his retinue, took the lady away from her husband secretly, and with her it was said that he lay while she was staying at her father's court. And when Sordello had been driven out by Ezzelino, a certain knight, Bonio of Treviso by name, loved the lady, and took her away from her father's court secretly, and she, excessively in love with him, went around very many parts of the world with him, having much pleasure and spending a great deal. At last they both returned to Alberico da Romano, the brother of the lady, who ruled reigned in Treviso, against the will of Ezzelino her brother, as it was said and became apparent; and there this Bonius stayed with the said lady Cunizza, though the wife of Bonius was still living and staying in Treviso.

This was not the end of Cunizza's affairs:

> Bonius was finally killed by the sword on a certain Sunday, when Ezzelino apparently wanted to snatch the city of Treviso from the rule of his brother. When, after all this, the lady Cunizza had fallen as far as to her brother Ezzelino, he married her to Sir Aimeric, or Rainier, of Braganza, a nobleman. But afterwards, when war broke out in the Marca [Trevigiana], Ezzelino had his kinsman killed with certain noblemen of Braganza and elsewhere in the Marca. Yet again Cunizza, after the death of her brother Ezzelino, got married, in Verona.

Sordello also proceeded to other affairs. The other Proven¸al *vida,* which calls him 'very treacherous and false towards ladies and towards the barons with whom he stayed', says that after the liaison with Cunizza he secretly married one Otta di Strasso, and had to stay armed in Ezzelino da Romano's house to protect himself from her brother and from Cunizza's people. He then travelled westwards to Provence; a song by Uc de Saint-Circ describes his expertise in seducing his way through the courts. He stayed with the great patron Savaric de Mauléon, in Aquitaine, and visited St. James of Compostella. By 1241 he was with Raimon-Bérenger of Provence, beginning a new career in politics. His famous song of the 'three disinherited men' curses the Count of Toulouse, the King of Aragon, and the Count of Provence, each beaten in recent struggles. Another famous *sirventes* starts out as a lament on the death of Blacatz, a nobleman of Provence who was a patron of troubadours, and turns on the cowardly princes of Europe to tell them they need to eat the dead man's heart, for his courage. This poem immediately raised Sordello's status; his name began to appear among those of great vassals. But Raimon-Bérenger died in 1245, and Sordello transferred his loyalties to the new master of Provence, Charles of Anjou, and he began to appear in the acts of this prince as *miles,* 'knight'. When Charles of Anjou set off to conquer the kingdom of Sicily in 1265, Sordello probably went with the land army, but Charles seems to have ditched him, for we find his name in this surprising letter to Charles from Pope Clement IV:

> . . . many people presume that having subjected them to labours beyond their capacities, you are defrauding your Proven¸al men of their pay. . . . Your knight Sordello is languishing at Novara; even had he not deserved well of you, he ought to be bought out, and how much more should he be ransomed for his merits; and many others who have served you in Italy have returned naked and poor to their homes [quoted in Sordello, *Le Poesie,* edited by M. Boni].

Sordello was soon released and back in favour: Charles began to shower him with gifts. First came a castle; then after the battle of Tagliacozzo, that secured the Kingdom of Naples for Charles of Anjou, more fiefs; then more castles, and even, it seems, a cloth-works. Sordello was worth 200 ounces of gold per annum, and was a *familiaris* of one of the great princes of Europe. At the height of his prosperity he died, at some time around 1269.

As for Cunizza, one would have presumed that she was dead by the time that Sordello returned to Italy, were it not for an act which survives from that very year. Boni describes how Sordello 'returned, changed, to a changed Italy, where many of those he had known or at whose side he had lived had disappeared'. Rizzardo di San Bonifacio was dead. Ezzelino da Romano had died of wounds received at the battle of Cassano d'Adda; his brother Alberico had been betrayed to the Guelfs, who had butchered him, with his wife and children, at San Zeno. Only Cunizza still lived. When the Romano house fell, after her third marriage, she had found refuge in Tuscany with her relatives on her mother's side. On 1 April 1265, being a guest at the house of Cavalcante de' Cavalcanti, she signed an act of manumission freeing her brothers' slaves, violently execrating those who had handed over Alberico and his family to their deaths, and finally (as Boni does not say) freeing them also.

SORDELLO IN DANTE AND POUND: THE SCOURGE OF PRINCES

Most readers take their knowledge of Sordello from Dante, where in the *Purgatorio* (as Pound notes in *The Spirit of Romance*) Virgil says: '"But see there a soul, that stationed/entirely alone looks towards us. . . ."' Dante describes Sordello:

O Lombard soul,
how you were proud and disdainful,
and honest and slow in the moving of your
eyes!
It said nothing to us;
but let us go on, only watching
in the manner of a lion when it rests.
But Virgil went on towards it, asking
that it show us the best way up;
and it did not answer his question;
but questioned us
about our countries and our lives.

Sordello and Virgil, fellow-Mantuans, embrace, and on these implications of past glory Dante builds a great invective against modern Italy.

Pound picks up the tone of this famous picture of Sordello Mantuan, the lion in repose, when he describes Henry James:

And the great domed head, *con gli occhi onesti e tardi*

'with the honest and slow eyes'. Pound is thinking of Henry James the rebel, the teller of uncomfortable truths, whose club (with that of Browning) had beaten what little intelligence London possessed into its skull, and whose death, as Eliot said, would cement the new Anglo-American *entente,* in this comparison with Sordello. For Sordello appears 'before hell mouth' in Canto XVI, and Pound's Hell is London:

And in the west mountain, Il Fiorentino,
Seeing hell in his mirror,
and lo Sordels
Looking on it in his shield;
And Augustine, gazing toward the invisible
[quoted in *Cantos*].

Pound also takes Dante's Sordello to scourge the princes of Europe as described by Thomas Jefferson in 1822:

a guisa de leon
The cannibals of Europe are eating one another
again
quando si posa [quoted in *Cantos*].

The authority of Jefferson, observing from his retirement, is like that of Sordello: 'in the manner of a lion/ . . . when it rests.'

But Pound notes that 'Sordello's right to this lonely and high station above "the valley of the kings" has at times been questioned . . .' [quoted in *The Spirit of Romance*]. Sordello's right to his position in Purgatory depends not on his political importance, which has not been questioned, but on his moral stature; and it his been said that in his political songs the attacks are unjust and the themes hackneyed. We find it difficult to care about the cowardice of princes, but this is the constant theme of Sordello and other troubadours. The theme is a fusion of two currents of feeling: the first is that a prince's highest duty is to defend his patrimony, and the second, in the case of a great proportion of songs by Sordello's contemporaries, is that the expansionism of 'the Church and the French' is a usurpation. The princes in question would realise the hopes of their peoples simply by making good their claim to what belonged to them as of 'right', custom, or divine law. This vindication of territorial rights had been elevated, for example by Bertran de Born, into an equivalent of 'honour'. To us it seems a strange localisation of honour, but at least it was an ethical concept, and could be seen as embodying systems of personal values; for all these troubadours it was the one obstacle to mere greed, and in particular, at this time, the greed of the Church and the French, making itself felt most particularly in the Albigensian Crusade. Originality of theme and treatment was not something the troubadours saw in the same light as the twentieth century; what Sordello does in his Blacatz *sirventes* is to invest his polemic with the solemnity of mourning in these majestic hexameters with their heavy ending, tones no doubt picked up from Bertran de Born's lament for the Young King:

Planher vuelh en Blacatz en aquest leugier so
ab cor trist e marrit, et ai en be razo,
qu'en luy ai mescabat senhor et amic bo,
e quar tug l'ayp valent en sa mort perdut so. . . .
["Planher vuelh en Blacatz"]

I want to lament Sir Blacatz with this slight tune
with a sad and low heart—and I have good
reason,
for in him I've lost a good lord and friend,
and since in his death all ways worth anything
are lost. . . .

CUNIZZA IN PARADISE

Cunizza, of whom we know no more than the scraps I have related, is to be found in Dante's Paradise, where one might not particularly have expected her. She introduces herself:

In that part of the evil Italian land
that is between the Rialto [that is, Venice]
and the sources of Brenta and Piava
rises a hill, not very high,
from which once descended a spark [Ezzelino da
Romano]
that caused great destruction to the land.
From one root were born both I and it;
I was called Cunizza, and I shine here

because the light of this star [Venus] overcame
me.
But joyfully I pardon myself
the cause of my fate, and I don't lament,
which would probably seem strange to your
people.

It has indeed seemed strange to people here below that Cunizza should not lament the sins we know she committed. Thus Hauvette:

> Dante seems to have known nothing about the gallantries that marked the youth of Sordello; this impression is the stronger in that the poet has put Cunizza in Paradise, naturally in the heaven of Venus, but without any allusion either to Sordello or to the other lovers of this joyous lady. It seems therefore that Dante was passably ill-informed here [quoted in *France*].

In this strange reasoning it is natural that Cunizza should be in the heaven of Venus, but apparent that Dante knew nothing of her amours or her first lover's. Critics are quite aware that the heaven of Venus is the sphere of sensual love, but cannot admit any connection, since God is the very opposite of sensual love; one, for example, can only guess that Dante put her there because she freed her slaves.

But Dante's Cunizza after all has the authority of being in his Paradise, and she says specifically that she pardons herself 'the cause of my fate, and I don't lament.' She makes it quite clear that the 'cause' of her 'fate' is that

the light of this star [Venus] overcame me

and warns us that we will find this surprising. Pound gave the words of Dante's poem the attention they ask for. In *The Spirit of Romance* he connected this passage with the words of Folquet de Marseille:

> Here, in defiance of convention, we find Cunizza:
>
> Out of one root spring I with it; Cunizza was I called, and
> here I glow because the light of this star overcame me.
>
> In Canto IX, lines 103-106, [Folquet's]
>
> Yet here we not repent, but smile; not at the sin, which
> cometh not again to mind, but at the Worth that
> ordered and provided,
>
> we have matter for a philosophical treatise as long as the *Paradiso*.

The sin that Folquet speaks of is the ardour of his love, which he has described at length. We know quite a lot about the career of this man from troubadour to heretic-hunting bishop, and he seems to have been just as deep in the pleasures of love as Cunizza; his words, dismissing his sins, are almost identical with Cunizza's.

The early commentators on Dante could see that he had made Cunizza into Venus: 'Rightly the poet figures himself finding this lady in the sphere of Venus; for if the noble Cypriots dedicated their Venus and the Romans their Flora, each a most beautiful and splendid whore (*formosissimam & ditissimam meretricem*), how much more worthily and nobly could the Christian poet save Cunizza' [Benvenuto da Imola, quoted in Chabaneau, *Biographies*]. They had no doubt that she liked to have lovers: 'It is to be known that the said lady Cunizza is said to have been in love at all times of her life, and her love was of such generosity that she would have held it great ill-breeding to think of denying it to anyone who asked courteously' [Jacopo della Lana, quoted in Chabaneau, *Biographies*]. There is no doubt that they were right. Pound is no doubt also right in deducing from the evidences of her life a 'grace' of character:

> Cunizza, white-haired in the House of the Cavalcanti, Dante, small guttersnipe, or small boy hearing the talk in his father's kitchen or, later, from Guido, of beauty incarnate, or, if the beauty can by any possibility be brought into doubt, at least and with utter certainty, charm and imperial bearing, grace that stopped not an instant in sweeping over the most violent authority of her time and, from the known fact, that vigour which is a grace in itself. There was nothing in Crestien de Troyes' narratives, nothing in Rimini or in the tales of the ancients to surpass the facts of Cunizza, with, in her old age, great kindness, thought for her slaves [quoted in *Guide to Kulchur*].

Using his methods of argument by juxtaposition, Pound suggested that such grace was an influence which would propagate itself (as in Canto VI's line of descent), and that it was incompatible with any crudeness of cultural manifestation. This passage on Cunizza in the *Guide to Kulchur* is immediately followed by a whole string of examples of the mediaeval clarity and precision: Sordello's verse, the exactitude of mediaeval theology, the beauty of Romanesque architecture descended from Byzantium, and its relation to Moslem building and to certain buildings in Poitiers. All this amounts, Pound says, to an 'anti-usura paideuma'. The connection between Cunizza and these things is that a sharper awareness of emotional distinctions will lead one to sharper distinctions elsewhere. That is why Pound felt that the troubadours were 'raised' by their ladies; that is why Dante's Beatrice, who ultimately leads him to Paradise, was first worshipped for her material beauty.

Though each of the demigoddesses in the Cantos has her adequate worshipper, for whom she creates emotional clarity, each at some point causes destruction. In the Pisan Cantos Pound remarks:

and the greatest is charity
to be found among those who have not observed
regulations

Both clarity and chaos come into Sordello's Cantos XXIX and XXXVI.

Canto XXIX is about woman-born disorder and clarity. It begins with the chaos wrought by Pernella, the concubine of Aldobrando Orsini,

> Bringing war once more on Pitigliano

which rhymes with the chaos in the house of Este wrought by Parisina, a parallel to Eleanor of Aquitaine in Cantos VIII and XX. It notes the complaints of Sextus Propertius against his girl's infidelities, and then moves to the document whereby Cunizza freed her slaves:

> Liberans et vinculo ab omni liberatos
> ['freeing the freedmen from every chain']
> As who with four hands at the cross roads
> By king's hand or sacerdos'
> are given their freedom
> —Save who were at Castra San Zeno. . . .
>
> Cunizza for God's love, for remitting the soul of her father
> —May hell take the traitors of Zeno.

Pound interpolates two lines from Rolandino's chronicle:

> And fifth begat he Alberic
> And sixth the Lady Cunizza.

Then he returns to the document of emancipation:

> In the house of the Cavalcanti
> anno 1265:
> Free go they all as by full manumission
> All serfs of Eccelin my father da Romano
> Save those who were with Alberic at Castra San Zeno
> And let them go also
> The devils of hell in their body.

Finally he goes back to Rolandino's account, pausing only to put in the line from Dante's words by Cunizza in Paradise—'The light of this star o'ercame me':

> And sixth the lady Cunizza
> That was first given Richard St Boniface
> And Sordello subtracted her from that husband
> And lay with her in Tarviso
> Till he was driven out of Tarviso
> And she left with a soldier named Bonius
> nimium amorata in eum ['excessively in love with him']
> And went from one place to another
> 'The light of this star o'ercame me'
> Greatly enjoying herself
> And running up the most awful bills.
> And this Bonius was killed on a sunday
> and she had then a Lord from Braganza
> and later a house in Verona.

'This star' (Venus) predominates in this short life of Cunizza, and Pound makes it merge with the grace that freed her slaves. After the Cunizza passage, Canto XXIX shows examples of American suburban social life and the unsatisfying sexual *moeurs* of the Twenties young. Then comes a diatribe against woman:

> a chaos
> An octopus
> A biological process
> and we seek to fulfill. . . .
> TAN AIODAN, our desire, drift. . . .
> Ailas e que'm fau miey huelh
> Quar noi vezon so qu'ieu vuelh.

We 'seek to fulfill' 'our desire', like the cock parading his feathers and his noise, with all kinds of attractions, including song; the biological pull results ultimately in the scrap of Sordello's song that Pound quotes: 'Alas, and what are my eyes doing to me/for they do not see what I wish' [from **"Ailas, e que m fau miey huelh"**].

Canto XXXVI begins with Pound's final translation of the 'Philosophic Canzone' of Cavalcanti. Cavalcanti's neo-Platonism in this song puts a particular emphasis on Love's place in the memory:

> Where memory liveth,
> it takes its state
> Formed like a diafan from light on shade

Sordello, Cunizza his *mantram,* and Sordello's temporal affairs—as being part of Cunizza's sphere of influence—are placed with this Cavalcanti. After the canzone the Canto introduces Scotus Erigena, who gave Pound the idea of a material universe as lights radiated by God. It considers oppositions to him: the later Church which confused him with contemporary rationalist heretics; and Aquinas and Aristotle, 'greek-splitting' metaphysicians. Then there is the rite of coition, which is behind what Pound thought of as a continuous cultural stream that produced the balanced part of the Western 'paideuma', including both Erigena and the troubadours; and Sordello appears:

> Sacrum, sacrum, inluminatio coitu.
> Lo Sordels si fo di Mantovana
> of a castle named Goito.

'The rite, the rite, illumination in coition' is a Latin dictum of Pound's; 'Sordello was from Mantua country' is from the *vida.* Then Pound cites Sordello's dealings with Charles of Anjou: receiving castles, complaining about the things he has already received (including a cloth-works), and being helped out of prison by a letter to Charles from the Pope:

> 'Five castles!'
> 'Five castles!'
> (king giv' him five castles)
> 'And what the hell do I know about dye-works?!'

His Holiness has written a letter:
'CHARLES the Mangy of Anjou. . . .
. . way you treat your men is a scandal. . . .'

Pound quotes from the document giving various castles to Sordello, and notes that he sold them all soon afterwards (in fact they may have been sold after his death):

Dilectis miles familiaris . . . castra Montis Odorisii
Montis Sancti Silvestri pallete et pile. . . .
['Beloved knight of our retinue . . . the castles of
Monte Odorisio, / Monte San Silvestro, Paglieta and Pila. . . .']
In partibus Thetis ['In the district of Thetis']. . . .
vineland
land tilled
the land incult
pratis nemoribus pascuis
['meadows groves pastures']
with legal jurisdiction
his heirs of both sexes
. . . sold the damn lot six weeks later,
Sordellus de Godio.
Quan ben m'albir e mon ric pensamen.

The last line is the key: it is the interiorised icon, the troubadours' version of Love's place in the memory, the goddess that they preferred to any passing pleasure, from this stanza by Sordello:

When I consider well in my proud thoughts
[*Quan ben m'albir en mon ric pensamen*]
of her to whom I give myself up and surrender myself, what kind
she is,
I love her so much, because her worth is beyond that of the delightful
women that exist,
that in the matter of love I esteem each one as nothing,
and since I know no other in the world so worthy
of whom I might take pleasure lying kissing;
for I do not want to taste any fruit
through which the sweet should turn sour for me
["Atretan dei ben chantar finamen"]

Teodolinda Barolini (essay date 1979)

SOURCE: "Bertran de Born and Sordello: The Poetry of Politics in Dante's *Comedy*," in *PMLA*, Vol. 94, No. 3, May, 1979, pp. 395-405.

[*In the following essay, Barolini attempts to illuminate Sordello's stature in Dante's* Purgatorio *by comparing his position with that of another figure in the work, Provençal troubadour Bertran de Born.*]

The stature Dante grants Sordello in the *Comedy* has long puzzled critics, since it seems greater than warranted by the achievements of this Provençal poet. Not only does the meeting with Sordello, in the sixth canto of the *Purgatorio*, serve as the catalyst for the stirring invective against Italy that concludes the canto, but Sordello is assigned the important task of guiding Vergil and Dante to the valley of the princes and identifying for the two travelers its various royal inhabitants. This seems a large role for a poet who was—and is—best known as the author of a satirical lament with political overtones, the lament for Blacatz. Indeed, although there is a definite consonance between the tone of that lament and the hortatory tone of the character in the *Comedy*, Sordello's poetic oeuvre does not by itself convincingly account for his function in Dante's poem. In the absence of other explanations, however, critics have traditionally agreed that we must turn to Sordello's *planh* for an understanding of his position in the *Comedy*.

In this so-called lament Sordello violently satirizes the princes of Europe, whom he criticizes for their cowardice; in fact, the work is more a *sirventes* than a *planh*, more a diatribe against the living than a lament for the dead. The poem begins conventionally enough, bewailing the death of Blacatz and complaining, in the usual manner, that all virtue and bravery have died with him; it soon becomes apparent, however, that this death is more a pretext than a theme. Consequently, Blacatz is not mentioned after the first verse:

Planher vuelh en Blacatz en aquest leugier so,
ab cor trist e marrit; et ai en be razo,
qu'en luy ai mescabat senhor et amic bo,
e quar tug l'ayp valent en sa mort perdut so;
tant es mortals lo dans qu'ieu non ai sospeisso
que jamais si revenha, s'en aital guiza no;
qu'om li traga lo cor e que n manio l baro
que vivon descorat, pueys auran de cor pro.

Premiers manje del cor, per so que grans ops l'es
l'emperaire de Roma, s'elh vol los Milanes
per forsa conquistar . . .

I want to lament Sir Blacatz in this light melody, with a sad and afflicted heart; and I have good reason, for in him I have lost a lord and a good friend, and because all that is virtuous is lost in his death. This damage is so fatal that I have no hope that it can ever be remedied, if not in this way: let his heart be taken out and the barons eat of it who live without heart—then will they have heart.

Let the first to eat of the heart, because he has great need of it, be the Emperor of Rome, if he wants to conquer the Milanese by force . . .

Using throughout the poem the motif of Blacatz' heart as a necessary source of courage for the cowardly kings, Sordello pillories a different prince in each stanza. By the end he has indicted the emperor, Frederick II, as well as Louis IX of France, Henry III of England, Ferdinand III of Castile and León, James I of Aragon, Thibaut I of

The mountainous town of Aups in Provence, the seat of the subject of Sordello's often-quoted "Lament for Lord Blacatz."

Navarre, Raymond VII of Toulouse, and Raymond Bérenger IV of Provence—all for being too weak and spineless to fight for their rightful territories.

The Sordello of *Purgatorio* vii is also given to judging the behavior of rulers; here, too, he rebukes the princes for negligence and for failing to govern properly, much as he had done in his lament while on earth. There has been a shift, however, from the simple feudal attitude of the *planh,* in which the loss of land is considered a stain on the personal honor of the prince, to the lofty Dantesque concept of the sovereign's moral obligation to his subjects. Once this inevitable transposition has been taken into account, the correspondences between the historical Sordello and the Sordello of the *Comedy* are clear enough—and yet somehow inadequate, for the discrepancy between the poet's stature as a person and his stature as a character remains. Neither Sordello's poetry nor his Lombard origins (which permit him to greet Vergil with the famous verse "O Mantoano, io son Sordello / de la tua terra!" 'O Mantuan, I am Sordello of your land!') satisfactorily justify his prominence in the *Comedy*—justify it, that is, in a more than mechanical way.

It is this gap between the real and the fictional that has made Sordello the subject of so much critical debate, to the point of being labeled "l'enigma dantesco" by a scholar who believed that the character would remain a problem until biographical material was discovered to explain Dante's esteem for him [Vincenzo de Bartholomaeis, *Primordi della lirica d'arte in Italia, 1943*]. In this paper, however, I propose a reading for Sordello that requires no external data. I submit that there is an internal coherence to the Sordello episode, that there are internal reasons both for his role and for his stature. A comparison between Sordello and another of the *Comedy*'s poets, Bertran de Born, will, I believe, shed some light on Dante's underlying logic and intentions.

The analogy between Sordello and Bertran de Born is by no means self-evident. Indeed, Thomas Bergin [in "Dante's Provençal Gallery," *Speculum* 40 (1965)] sets up a quite different pattern, claiming that there is a trio of Provençal poets in the *Comedy,* composed of Bertran in the *Inferno,* Arnaut Daniel in the *Purgatorio,* and Folquet de Marselha in the *Paradiso.* "Of all Dante's triads," he writes, "the Provençal poets are most obviously and architectonically disposed, one for each *cantica,* each one clearly and prominently placed, varying only, I would say, in their degree of integration with their milieu." But Bergin is then left with the problem of a fourth poet who wrote in the *langue d'oc*—Sordello—and is forced to conclude that Dante did not intend Sordello "to 'count' as a Provençal figure. . . . Dante sees in Sordello not the

Provençal poet but the Italian-born patriot and judge of princes." This interpretation violates one sense of the episode, for Sordello's tribute to Vergil at the beginning of *Purgatorio* vii is clearly the tribute of one poet to another.

Without denying the validity of Bergin's Provençal trio, I would comment that, although Dante is a poet of symmetries, his symmetries are not necessarily straightforward or clear-cut. In fact, Dante tends to establish contradictory or, rather, counterbalancing symmetrical structures, such as the odd asymmetrical canticle of thirty-four cantos, which then creates a new symmetry by bringing the total number of cantos to one hundred. Similarly, the neat symmetrical relationship between the *Comedy*'s three Provençal poets is marred by the presence of a fourth, Sordello, and again the solution may be overlapping symmetries: the trio pointed to by Bergin and the duo that I am suggesting, which, significantly, includes as its pivotal figure precisely the poet excluded by the first arrangement. My claim that Sordello should be juxtaposed with Bertran de Born, as Cacciaguida is with Brunetto, or Cunizza with Francesca, is based on one simple but, I believe, telling observation: of all the lyric poets in the *Comedy* only Bertran and Sordello are not love poets. In other words, if we look, not at the restricted group of Provençal poets, but at the larger group of all lyric poets in the *Comedy*—Bertran de Born, Sordello, Bonagiunta da Lucca, Guido Guinizzelli, Arnaut Daniel, and Folquet de Marselha (in order of appearance)—the first two stand out as poets whose major poetic concerns are different from those of the others; indeed, Bertran and Sordello are revealed as the *Comedy*'s two "political" poets. Surely this identifying bond between them is sufficient basis for comparison.

Before examining these two poets as they are presented in the *Comedy,* I should like to say a word about the poetry of Bertran de Born. He, too, was celebrated for laments; the two traditionally attributed to him are both for Prince Henry, also called the Young King (because he was crowned during his father's lifetime, since Henry II of England hoped thus to ensure the succession), a prince with whom Bertran was presumably on intimate terms. These poems are the famous "Si tuit li dol e lh plor e lh marrimen" and the less well known "Mon chan fenisc ab dol et ab maltraire." It is worth noting that, unlike Sordello's *planh* for Blacatz, these are true laments. They follow the *planh*'s customary format of both praising the dead man and mourning his loss. The first stanza of "Si tuit li dol" is representative of the poem and of the genre:

Si tuit li dol e lh plor e lh marrimen
E las dolors e lh dan e lh chaitivier
Qu'om anc auzis en est segle dolen
Fossen ensems, sembleran tot leugier
Contra la mort del jove rei engles,
Don rema pretz e jovens doloros
E l mons oscurs e teintz e tenebros,
Sems de tot joi, ples de tristor e d'ira.

If all the sorrow, tears, anguish, pain, loss, and misery which man has heard of in this sorrowful life were heaped together, they would all seem light compared to the death of the young English king; for him worth and youth grieve, and the world is dark, covered over, and in shade, lacking all joy, full of sadness and spite. (*Die Lieder*)

The grief of the poet is echoed formally in the repetition of "marrimen" and "ira" at the end of the first and last lines of each stanza. The Young King ("jove rei engles") is also mentioned in each stanza, indeed always in the same place, at the end of the fifth line, thus constituting with "marrimen" and "ira" the obsessive poles about which the poem moves.

Bertran was also the author of numerous *sirventes* celebrating war, poems that take delight in describing the carnage of the battlefield in vivid detail:

Ie us dic que tan no m'a sabor
Manjar ni beure ni dormir
Com a, quan auch cridar: "A lor!"
D'ambas las partz et auch ennir
    Chavals vochs per l'ombratge,
Et auch cridar: "Aidatz! Aidatz!"
E vei chazer per los fossatz
    Paucs e grans per l'erbatge,
E vei los mortz que pels costatz
An los tronzos ab los cendatz.

I tell you that there is no such savor for me in eating or drinking or sleeping, as when I hear men shouting "At them!" from both sides, and hear the horses neighing in the shadows; and hear men cry "Help! Help!" and see small and great fall in the ditches, on the grass; and when I see the dead, who through their sides have the stumps of lances with silken pennants. (*Die Lieder*)

In these poems, Bertran constantly urges the barons on to battle, as does Sordello in his lament for Blacatz. Sordello, however, recommends war as an antidote for cowardly behavior, which he finds reprehensible in princes, and as a means of securing lost territory, whereas Bertran's reasons for warmongering are unabashedly mercenary and self-serving, and his only concern is loot. Therefore, even when Bertran and Sordello share similar social themes and a similar polemical bent, Bertran's verse completely lacks the didactic element that distinguishes the poetry of Sordello. Sordello, in his lament for Blacatz, as in his ***Ensenhamens d'onor,*** wants to instruct us in correct chivalric and princely conduct (this is explicit in the title of the longer work, ***The Teachings of Honor***). It is this aspect of Sordello's poetry and personality that must have initially appealed to Dante and provided him with the starting point for the character of the *Comedy.*

The canto in which the travelers first meet Sordello, the sixth of the *Purgatorio,* is known as one of the three "political" cantos of the *Comedy,* forming a triad with the sixth cantos of the *Inferno* and the *Paradiso* (in the *Inferno* Dante focuses on Florence, in the *Purgatorio* on Italy, and in the *Paradiso* on the empire). Although the political aspect of *Purgatorio* vi comes to the fore most clearly in the invective beginning "Ahi serva Italia, di dolore ostello" (l. 76), it is signaled from the line in which Dante apostrophizes a soul, as yet unidentified, by referring to the part of Italy from which it came: "o anima lombarda . . ." (l. 61). This soul turns out to be Sordello, whose Lombard origins immediately draw him to Vergil. The invective against Italy derives from the ironic contrast between Sordello's loving response to Vergil as a fellow Mantuan ("e l'un l'altro abbracciava" 'and one embraced the other' [*Purg*. vi.75]) and the discord characteristic of Italy, where fellow citizens "gnaw" rather than embrace each other ("e l'um l'altro si rode / di quei ch'un muro e una fossa serra" 'and one gnaws at the other, of those who are enclosed by one wall and one moat' [*Purg*. vi.83-84]). The appellation "anima lombarda" brings to mind another episode—also political—where an Italian place-name is used as a form of address; I refer to *Inferno* X, where Farinata degli Uberti calls out to Dante, "O Tosco che per la città del foco / vivo ten vai" 'O Tuscan, who through the city of fire go alive' (l. 22).

Many commentators have drawn the reader's attention to the similarities between Sordello and Farinata; Croce called Sordello the "Farinata del *Purgatorio*" [in *La poesia di Dante,* 1922]. Both appear in episodes dealing with the theme of love of one's native land, and there are deliberate correspondences in the presentations of the two characters, correspondences that are heightened by intentional verbal echoes. Both Farinata and Sordello are isolated and haughty: "guardommi un poco, e poi, quasi *sdegnoso"* 'he looked at me for a moment, and then, almost disdainful' (*Inf.* X.41; italics added here and in succeeding quotations); "come ti stavi altera e *disdegnosa"* 'how you were haughty and disdainful' (*Purg*. vi.62). In each encounter Vergil sees the soul first and points it out to Dante, using the same expression: *"Vedi là* Farinata che s'è dritto" 'See there Farinata, who has risen straight' (*Inf.* X.32); "Ma *vedi là* un'anima" 'But see there a soul' (*Purg*. vi.58). Each time the necessary password is a sound evoking the soul's native land: Farinata hears Dante's Tuscan accent, and Sordello reacts to the first word of Vergil's reply, "Mantüa . . ." (l. 72). Furthermore, in both episodes a conversation is interrupted, suspended, and suddenly resumed. Farinata and Dante are interrupted by Cavalcante de' Cavalcanti; they stop conversing until he disappears and then begin again as though he had not existed. Similarly, the conversation between Sordello and Vergil is interrupted by the apostrophe to Italy, which cuts in and continues to the end of the sixth canto. So abrupt is the break that when the conversation resumes at the beginning of the seventh canto, Sordello does not yet know who Vergil is. These devices serve rhetorically to underscore Sordello as a purgatorial corrective to Farinata. In Hell, love of one's native land is put into the context of "heresy" or divisiveness, so that Farinata is able to turn common Tuscan origins into barriers of family allegiance and party affiliation. In Purgatory, common Lombard origins become the reason for an embrace; Sordello's immediate reaction to the word "Mantüa" is part of a context that stresses unity, here the unity resulting from a shared birthplace.

Sordello, then, is related in three ways to the theme of politics in the *Comedy*. First, he is intrinsically connected by virtue of his historical identity as a poet concerned about the behavior of rulers in his day. Second, he is connected by his situation in the sixth, political, canto of the *Purgatorio,* where his embrace of Vergil, "a minute and touching demonstration of the unitive power of the political community," gives rise to the invective in which Dante deplores the lack of unity in Italy. Third, Sordello is the poetic refocusing of Farinata, the lens through which the theme of love of one's native land reappears on the slopes of Mount Purgatory.

The common denominator in these various aspects of the Dantesque Sordello is the concept of political unity, played against its contrary, discord and fragmentation. And here, it seems to me, there is a particular feature of Sordello's career that would have greatly interested Dante, enough to have determined Dante's development of Sordello's role. Sordello was that anomaly among poets—one who wrote in a language not his own. Although an Italian from Goito near Mantua, he wrote in Provençal. That Dante was intrigued by this is clear from what he has to say about Sordello in the *De Vulgari Eloquentia:* "[Sordellus] qui, tantus eloquentie vir existens, non solum in poetando, sed quomodocunque loquendo patrium vulgare deseruit." Dante finds it a particular sign of Sordello's "eloquentia" that Sordello should have abandoned his native tongue not just "in poetando" but in "quomodocunque loquendo," in any form of discourse whatsoever. Significantly, Dante does not cite any of Sordello's poetry in the *De Vulgari Eloquentia;* all that seems to interest him is the concept of linguistic internationalism that Sordello here embodies. The *De Vulgari Eloquentia* is, in part, a polemic against linguistic provincialism; the "vulgare illustre" as practiced by Dante and his friend Cino da Pistoia is conceived as the Italian that would be in common use if Italy were not divided into many warring city-states but were one united nation, an Italian strained of provincial and municipal impurities. Dante singles out Sordello for praise because Sordello too reacted against the limitations of his regional dialect and, although it was not for him to discover the Italian *vulgare illustre,* he did the next best thing: he turned to a *vulgare* that was already *illustre,* namely Provençal.

It is well known to what extent Dante associated language and politics. The story of the Tower of Babel as recounted at the beginning of the *De Vulgari Eloquentia* shows how the fragmentation of the original language into many new ones made it impossible for the builders to work together and thus ultimately led to their political division into different peoples: " . . . ut qui omnes *una eademque loquela* deserviebant ad opus, ab opere *multis diversificati loquelis* desinerent et nunquam ad idem commertium convenirent" (Bk. I, Ch. vii, par. 6; italics mine). They came to the work with "one same language," but they left it "estranged from one another by a multiplicity of languages." In the *Comedy* Sordello stands for the reversal of this trend, for the initiative that would ideally lead back to the same language for all, which in turn would spell political harmony. Viewed in this context, the words with which Sordello honors Vergil in *Purgatorio* vii become singularly appropriate:

"O gloria di *Latin,*" disse, "per cui
mostrò ciò che potea la lingua *nostra,*
o pregio etterno del loco ond' io fui,
qual merito o qual grazia mi ti mostra?"

"O glory of the Latins," he said, "through whom our tongue showed what it could do, o eternal honor of the place that I was from, what merit or what grace reveals you to me?" (*Purg.* vii.16-19; italics mine)

No one has a better right than Sordello to speak of "Latins" or of "our" tongue; in his crossing of linguistic boundaries he showed himself to be a true cosmopolitan, or "Latin," aware of the common heritage that underlies all the languages of "Romania" and makes them interchangeable, "ours" as it were. It is not because he is as great a poet as Vergil that Sordello is chosen to eulogize him but because he demonstrates in his own person the unity of a linguistic tradition that is rooted in Latin language and literature and that cannot be divorced from a political tradition rooted in the Roman Empire. As there is in fact one language, shared by a Roman poet and a Lombard troubadour, so should there be one empire. And thus we come back, by a slightly different route, to Sordello as an emblem of political unity in the *Comedy*. Because he thought nothing of crossing both the linguistic and the political boundaries of his day, Sordello stands in opposition to the emperor, who in the invective of Canto vi is accused of *not* crossing boundaries: by remaining in Germany, the emperor allowed Italy to disintegrate into a swarm of warring factions and permitted the inherent unity of the Holy Roman Empire to be destroyed.

As it happens, Bertran de Born is also mentioned in the *De Vulgari Eloquentia,* where he appears as the prototype of the poet of arms in a Romance language, a martial poet for whom Dante can find no equivalent in Italian literature. His poetic credentials in the treatise are excellent; he is in the company of Arnaut Daniel, who represents love poetry and whose Italian counterpart is Cino da Pistoia, and Giraut de Bornelh, who as the Provençal "poet of rectitude" is paired with Dante himself. The first verse of one of Bertran's *sirventes,* in which he rejoices in a forthcoming battle, is quoted in full (Bk. II, Ch. ii, par. 9). Moreover, unlike Sordello, Bertran appears in the *Convivio* as well; he is the only poet in a group of nobles being praised for their generosity. Yet, in the *Comedy* Bertran is in the ninth *bolgia* of the eighth circle of Hell, among the "sowers of scandal and of schism."

Since the *De Vulgari Eloquentia* is a work of criticism, its evaluations of poets must meet, or at least appear to meet, certain minimal standards of impartiality and objectivity. This respect for the "truth" is waived in the *Comedy,* where the history of a given poet (as indeed that of any other character) is often modified according to the part that the figure has been assigned to play in the *Comedy*'s overall scheme. As a result, Dante's treatment of a poet in the *De Vulgari Eloquentia* frequently differs from his treatment of the same poet in the *Comedy:* some figures, like Sordello, are "enlarged" in the latter work, whereas others, like Bertran, are "diminished." Still, there is always some basis in fact for Dante's distortions of history, for those aspects of an actual figure or situation that he chooses to develop out of proportion to all else.

We have seen how Dante focuses on certain aspects of the historical Sordello—his birthplace, political poetry, and language shift—to create the character of *Purgatorio* vi, vii, and viii. In his re-creation of the historical Bertran, Dante has as a starting point the amorality of Bertran's verse, as well as its sanguinary and bloodthirsty qualities, which Dante reproduces in the carnage of the ninth *bolgia.* But Dante's elaboration of Bertran does not rest primarily on his poetry. The key to the Dantesque character lies in the reports about Bertran that circulated in the Provençal *vidas.* The *vidas,* or biographies, exaggerate Bertran's already inflated notion of himself as Prince Henry's counselor; hence, we learn from them that Bertran was Henry's chief adviser, personally responsible for fanning the hostilities between the prince and his father. Moreover, and more important, the *vidas* specify that Bertran did this with his poetry:

Et era seigner, totas vez qan se volia, del rei Henric d'Englaterra e del fill de lui; mas totz temps volia qu'ill aguesson gerra ensems, lo paire e l fills e ill fraire, l'uns ab l'autre, e totz temps volc qe l reis de Franssa e l reis d'Englaterra agessen gerra ensems; e s'il avian patz ni treva, ades se penava e is percassava *ab sos sirventes* de desfar la patz e de mostrar cum chascuns era desonratz en la patz [italics mine].

And he was lord, whenever he wished, of King Henry of England and of his son. But he always wanted them to wage war against each other, the father and the son and the brother, the one against the other, and he always wanted the King of France and the King of England to wage war. And if they had peace or a truce, he would put himself to great pains and strive *with his sirventes* to undo the peace and to show how each one was dishonored by peace [quoted in *Le biografie trovadoriche,* edited by Guido Favati, 1961].

The sinners of the ninth *bolgia* are the sowers of discord; the wounds they display on their bodies correspond to the wounds that they inflicted on the social fabric during their lifetimes. Hence Bertran arrives carrying his head before him like a lantern; it is severed from his body to indicate that he served the son from the father. His account of his sin conforms closely to the *vida* (there are even similar turns of phrase; compare "lo paire e l fills e ill fraire, l'uns ab l'autre" with "il padre e 'l figlio in sé"):

"E perché tu di me novella porti,
sappi ch'i' son Bertram dal Bornio, quelli
che diedi al re giovane i ma' conforti.

Io feci il padre e 'l figlio in sé ribelli;
    Achitofèl non fé più d'Absalone
    e di Davìd coi malvagi punzelli.
Perch'io parti' così giunte persone,
    partito porto il mio cerebro, lasso!,
    dal suo principio ch'è in questo troncone.
Così s'osserva in me lo contrapasso."

"And so that you may carry news of me, know that I am Bertran de Born, the one who gave the evil counsels to the young king. I made the father and the son into rebels against each other; Ahithophel did no more for Absalom and David with his wicked incitements. Because I disjoined persons thus united, I carry my brain, alas! disjoined from its root in this trunk. So in me the *contrapasso* is observed." (*Inf.* xxviii.133-42)

The theme of *Inferno* xxviii, the sowing of discord, is fundamentally political. Bertran's sin was distinctly political; although the social unit he affected was technically the family, the family in question was a royal one, so that his actions necessarily had social and political consequences. In fact, not only Bertran's but all the sins of *Inferno* xxviii can be classified as social and political. Mohammed and Alì (and Fra Dolcino, who is mentioned by Mohammed) brought schism into the church; Pier da Medicina was a troublemaker in the courts of Romagna; Gaius Scribonius Curio indirectly started the civil wars by inciting Caesar to cross the Rubicon; Mosca de' Lamberti authorized the killing of Buondelmonte, thus giving rise to the Florentine factions and internecine fighting of Dante's day.

These souls are not developed as characters in any way; they are permitted only depersonalized existences under the label of "seminator di scandalo e di scisma" (l. 35). They have no significance for Dante other than as exempla of a particular sin. This is especially obvious in the depiction of Bertran de Born, as such treatment is unexpected; the *De Vulgari Eloquentia* and the *Convivio* attest to Dante's previous interest in (and respect for) Bertran both as poet and as personality. Yet here Bertran, too, is kept at a distance. He expounds the nature of his sin and its exact repercussions in Hell with mathematical clarity and precision; he presents one by one, as though filling out a dossier, his name, the sin for which he is in this *bolgia,* a biblical comparison (should the visitors need elucidation), and the correspondences between sin and punishment. It is no accident that he, of all the sinners in the *Inferno,* should be the one to enunciate the law of the *contrapasso*. The cold, clinical quality of his words is heightened by the pathetic interpolations "Oh me!" and "lasso!" (ll. 123, 140), so at variance with the tone of the rest of his speech. In a canto where all the figures are exemplary, Bertran de Born is served up as the last and supreme exemplum: his sin is the worst, his punishment the most gruesome.

All Dante's efforts in *Inferno* xxviii, in terms of the characters he presents and the way in which he presents them, are directed toward making a statement about schism, that is, toward making a political statement. This intention is reflected not only in the sins represented but in other, more subtle ways as well. The tone of the canto is set from the beginning by the fifteen-line comparison describing five battles that encompass the political history of southern Italy from Roman times to the takeover by Charles of Anjou in 1266 (ll. 7-21). The reference by name to Livy, historian of Rome, is noteworthy (it is the only time in the *Comedy* that he is mentioned), as is the bewildering array of proper names, which has the effect of battering the reader with historical and political data. Furthermore, it is certainly significant that *Inferno* xxviii contains clear reminiscences of other cantos in the *Inferno* where Dante airs his political beliefs, namely, *Inferno* vi, where he discusses Florence with Ciacco, and *Inferno* x, where he meets the great Ghibelline leader, Farinata.

In *Inferno* vi Dante questions Ciacco about the whereabouts of five well-known Florentines; one of these men, Mosca de' Lamberti, turns up in Canto xxviii among the sowers of discord. There the dialogue between Dante and Mosca is reminiscent of the dialogue between Dante and Farinata in Canto x; in both passages Dante retorts acrimoniously, saying something that causes the sinner even greater suffering. A last link between these cantos is the prophesying that occurs in all of them (politics being in some respects the art of successfully foretelling the future). In *Inferno* vi Ciacco hints at Dante's exile by predicting the overthrow of his party, the Bianchi; Farinata, in *Inferno* x, also alludes to Dante's exile, and then goes on to explain the nature of foresight in Hell. Therefore, it hardly seems coincidental that in *Inferno* xxviii "l'antiveder" 'foresight' (l. 78) is once more practiced, this time by Mohammed and Pier da Medicina. These correspondences are signposts marking the similar thematic concerns that underlie all three cantos.

As a canto that deals with a political theme—specifically, the "unmaking of peace," to borrow a phrase from the Provençal *vida*—*Inferno* xxviii stands in opposition to that canto of unity and peacemaking, *Purgatorio* vi. Stylistic points of comparison between the two cantos support this conclusion. In his reading of *Purgatorio* vi, Aurelio Roncaglia has drawn attention to the recurrence of expressions denoting separation; these expressions, like "nave sanza nocchiere" 'ship without helmsman,' "sella vota" 'empty saddle,' and "vedova Roma" 'widowed Rome,' are concentrated in the invective against Italy. Roncaglia's conclusion is that "La frequenza di questa sigla avulsiva rappresenta la tormentosa fissità d'uno stato sentimentale di lacerazione" 'the frequency of this rending motif represents the tormenting fixity of a sentimental state of laceration.' *Inferno* xxviii also displays a motif of laceration tied to a discourse on politics; as is typical of Hell, however, the laceration is expressed, not through mere metaphors of bereavement, but through physical wounds. Hence we find, to mention only two of the *bolgia*'s inhabitants, A'l "fesso nel volto dal mento al ciuffetto" 'with his face cleft from his chin to his forelock' (l. 33) and Pier da Medicina "che forata avea la gola / e tronco 'l naso infin sotto le ciglia, / e non avea mai ch'una orecchia sola" 'who had his throat pierced and his nose cut off up to his eyebrows and who had only one ear' (ll. 64-68). Another similarity is the massive use of proper names in both cantos, which serves to stress the historical, specific, and ephemeral nature of politics. For example, in *Inferno* xxviii, between lines 14 and 18, the following names occur: Ruberto Guiscardo, Ceperan, Pugliese, Tagliacozzo, and Alardo; in *Purgatorio* vi, in only two lines, we find Montecchi, Cappelletti, Monaldi, and Filippeschi.

Inferno xxviii, then, stands in opposition to *Purgatorio* vi, and in much the same way as did *Inferno* x. In the episodes of Farinata and Sordello the theme "division versus unity" is treated under the rubric, so to speak, of "love of one's native land." In the episodes of Bertran and Sordello, the same theme is treated under the rubric "poets who in their poetry fostered either divisiveness or unity." The Provençal *vida* specifically declares that Bertran strove to stir up trouble between father and son "ab sos sirventes" 'with his *sirventes';* there is perhaps an allusion to this in Dante's verse "quelli / che diedi al re giovane i ma' conforti" 'the one who gave the evil counsels to the young king,' where the nature of the "conforti" is not specified but certainly implied. Bertran is Sordello's poetic counterpart; this is confirmed and thrown into relief by their being the only two lyric poets in the *Comedy* who are not love poets. Bertran's political poetry fostered disunity and schism by encouraging the Young King to disobey his father. Sordello's political poetry, by criticizing the princes in a way that prefigures Dante's own critical stance in *Purgatorio* vi and vii, served the final goal of political unity. Their poetry thus becomes emblematic of everything that each comes to stand for in the *Comedy:* one for separating, disjoining, undoing, taking apart what ought to be united; the other for crossing over, bringing together, reuniting what has been torn asunder. The relationship between the two political poets is one more strand in the web of overlapping political themes that converge in the sixth and seventh cantos of the *Purgatorio*. . . .

In the *Comedy,* therefore, Dante uses Bertran and Sordello as exempla of the uses to which a poet can put his poetry in the service of the state. For Dante, a poet does not function in a vacuum; in fact, after the *stil novo* phase, in which he addressed himself to a small group of initiates, Dante kept on enlarging his audience until it included, in the *Comedy,* anyone capable of following him. One could almost say that the larger the audience, the greater the poet. Political poets by necessity address themselves to a larger audience than do love poets; hence theirs is a greater responsibility. As one would expect, the poet in Hell, Bertran, is the exemplum of the political poet who misused his position in life. By abetting disobedience and revolt, Bertran put his poetry to bad use, mishandling the responsibility that a poet has to his audience. Sordello, in Purgatory, is the counterexemplum: the political poet who behaved responsibly and put his poetry to good use.

We can now see why Sordello is treated far more sympathetically in the *Comedy* than his influence or position in life would lead us to expect. The historical Sordello has been absorbed by a Sordello whose function confers on him some signal honors and privileges not granted to any other lyric poet. For instance, only the epic poets are permitted to move in the *Comedy,* while the lyric poets remain fixed in their respective circles, terraces, or heavens. And yet Sordello moves. Although it is true that, since he cannot leave Ante-Purgatory, he cannot move "up" in the way that Vergil and Statius do, he is nonetheless the only lyric poet to move at all. (I do not refer to movement that is part of punishment or purgation, like Guinizzelli's motion through the flames.) Sordello's presence spans three cantos, from *Purgatorio* vi to viii (he is mentioned for the last time in *Purgatorio* ix.58: "Sordel rimase e l'altre genti forme" 'Sordello remained and the other noble souls'), thus holding the stage longer than any other lyric poet. He greets Vergil in a manner that foreshadows Statius' greeting of Vergil later on. Most important, he serves as a guide to the travelers, even saying "a guida mi t'accosto" 'I will take your side as guide' (*Purg.* vii.42), thus implicitly aligning himself with the other two poet-guides, Vergil and Statius. All in all, Sordello's preeminence among the lyric poets in the *Comedy* is quite out of keeping with his worldly fame; one could say that he enjoys quasi-epic status.

This status is underscored by the similarity between the valley of the princes and Limbo, the home of the classical poets; as Bergin points out [in "Dante's Provençal Gallery], "The garden of the princes is the 'amoenus locus' corresponding to the Limbo of the *Inferno*." Moreover, the word "onesto," etymologically related to the word "onore," which occurs eight times in various forms in *Inferno* iv and which is Limbo's verbal talisman, is twice used in connection with Sordello: "e nel mover de li occhi *onesta* e tarda" 'and in the movement of your eyes how dignified and slow' (*Purg.* vi.63); "Poscia che l'accoglienze *oneste* e liete" After the dignified and joyful greetings' (*Purg.* vii.1; my italics in both quotations). These efforts to link Sordello to the *Comedy*'s epic and classical poets also serve to separate and distinguish him from the *Comedy*'s lyric love poets.

By the time Dante came to write the *Comedy* he was incapable of an unalloyed aesthetic judgment; hence Sordello, owing to his role as a moral and political poet in the service of political unity, is given marks of distinction not accorded to other lyric poets, even though this group includes some whom we would consider poetically greater than he. For that matter, Bertran too is a greater poet than Sordello, objectively speaking, and we have seen how little this fact counts in the final judgment. Sordello's position depends entirely on the importance Dante attaches to political unity and peace as the basis, the sine qua non, of mankind's temporal well-being. Sordello's poetry does not have the educational value of epic poetry, nor does it speak to all humanity; Dante feels, however, that it comes closer to these ideals than does any other form of lyric poetry. Consequently, Dante deliberately links Sordello to the epic poets. he also takes care to make clear that, in this respect as well, Bertran is the exact opposite of Sordello. The description of Bertran in *Inferno* xxviii as one who carries his head like a lantern ("e 'l capo tronco tenea per le chiome, / pesol con mano a guisa di lanterna" 'and it was holding the truncated head by the hair, dangling in its hand like a lantern' [ll. 121-22]) and lights the way for himself by himself ("Di sé facea a sé stesso lucerna" 'Of itself it was making for itself a lamp' [l. 124]) cannot but call to mind Statius' tribute to Vergil in *Purgatorio* xxii: "Facesti come quei che va di notte, / che porta il lume dietro e sé non giova, / ma dopo sé fa le persone dotte" 'You did as one who goes by night, who carries the light behind him and helps not himself, but makes those who come after him wise' (ll. 67-69). Bertran is a grotesque inversion of Vergil: in one there is total severance, a self-sufficiency that is not strength but meaninglessness, whereas in the other there is a sharing, a passing on, and an illumination of others even at the expense of oneself.

To end, I should like to return briefly to the world outside the *Comedy*. As we have seen, a comparison of the poetry of Bertran and Sordello reveals how different their attitudes are. It is interesting that Dante's treatment of these figures parallels the actual disparity; he sets them up for comparison in order to reveal them as polar opposites. In some ways, however, Dante reverses the real-life situation. Sordello, who wrote a biting and savage poem (which, had it been acted on, would have resulted in fighting in every corner of Europe), is reincarnated as an emblem of unity; whereas Bertran, whose poems in fact had little political impact, becomes an emblem of schism. The point is that both these decisions, although justifiable, are not without their arbitrary features. Dante was not interested in finding for each character in his poem a niche to correspond exactly to the merits of that person as a historical figure; he is interested in creating ideal categories that will illuminate the structure of reality as he sees it. Into these categories he fits his characters. Only in this way could his poem avoid being an inventory of dead souls and become what he wanted it to be and what it is—an insight into the nature of things so compelling that it directs the wills of the living and obliges them, through a recognition of reality, to be saved.

So it is for souls in general, and so it is for poets. If Dante has two political poets, they must perforce have more than gossip value; they must illustrate more than the fate that each found on dying. The ideal categories would naturally have to do with the use or misuse of their poetry, and Dante would look for figures whose biographies and poetic output worked well within these categories, even if not slavishly corresponding in all details. Accordingly, in his treatment of Bertran de Born and Sordello we have a clear example of Dante's deliberate revision of history for didactic purposes, to impart a moral lesson concerning the ways we use our gifts vis-à-vis society, and an instance of the truth of Irma Brandeis' precept that "Dante in his *Comedy* never *serves* history; he uses it . . . ". Dante's handling of the poets Bertran and Sordello thus permits us a fascinating glimpse into the workings of his own creative and poetic strategies; to put it another way, we can learn from these episodes not only something about the poetry of politics but a little about the politics of poetry as well.

James J. Wilhelm (essay date 1987)

SOURCE: An introduction to *The Poetry of Sordello,* edited and translated by James J. Wilhelm, Garland Publishing, Inc., 1987, pp. xi-xxxi.

[*Wilhelm is an American medievalist and Pound scholar. In the following excerpt from his introduction to* The Poetry of Sordello, *he speculates that Dante was inspired by the vitality and variety he found in Sordello's works, as evidenced in the invective satire of the troubadour's* sirventes, *the political diatribe of his "Lament for Lord Blacatz," and the skepticism of his debate poems. Wilhelm also addresses the pronounced influence of Sordello on later poets, including Browning and Pound.*]

ARTISTIC ACHIEVEMENT

The poetry of Sordello seems to have been rated more highly by other poets than by critics. Dante, in his *De vulgari eloquentia,* singles out Sordello as a man who "had great eloquence, not only in the writing of poetry, but also in any number of other forms" (1.15.2), by which he must have meant prose works that did not survive. Dante also mentions that Sordello did not find his native Mantuan dialect conducive to the writing of great poetry, and so he abandoned it for Provençal.

Clearly the most influential work of Sordello was not any of his love poems, but his well-known **"Lament for Lord Blacatz"** (No. 26). Sordello was not the first person to write a dirge in Provençal; in fact, the first troubadour whose work survives, Duke William IX of Aquitaine, wrote a beautiful and compelling lament on his own future demise (*Pos de chantar m'es pres talenz;* ed. Bond). The genre of *planctus* in Latin (*planh* in Provençal) was already well established, existing as a secular counterpart to funeral services for great men; but the vigor that Sordello brought to this frequently clichéd kind of poem is obvious. Instead of indulging in mere repetitive praise, Sordello boldly turned his poem into a political diatribe in which he railed out against the decadent princes of the world. It was doubtlessly this zeal that won him the role as cicerone for the Vale of Negligent Rulers in Dante's *Purgatorio,* Canto 7, where Dante also put Charles of Anjou. But since the dirge is so different from Sordello's love poems, which imitate the standard patterns of earlier troubadours, it has always been rated higher.

The twelve surviving love poems of Sordello are, however, anything but trite. It is true that they employ rather fixed styles of expression that had been established in the tradition from the time of Duke William at the turn of the twelfth century onward. The male persona usually laments his bereaved condition, since he is not rewarded by his lady for his "fine love" (*fin 'amors*), and he almost seems to wallow in a state of masochistic pleasure. This is especially obvious in the third stanza of Poem 7:

> I'm killing myself in love and torturing myself
> with grief

For a joy that alienates me, and mercy doesn't help;
But I shouldn't complain at all on my behalf
Because, since I'm hers, she can, if she wants, do me in;
And if she kills me, she doesn't offend me one bit,
Because I'll take all the damages. . . .

This is the dying gasp of a rhetoric that was once vital, witty, and charged with a dialectic of love that contained much of the wit of Ovid. But by the thirteenth century, after the Albigensian Crusade had reduced the South to misery and servitude, the spirit and the liveliness had disappeared from most Provençal song. The fact that the music did not survive also weakens the case for originality. Still, many of the lines are extremely memorable, as in Poem 3, line 17: "When I think deeply in my rich meditations. . . . "Poem 1 has a lovely refrain for every stanza. Poem 2 contains the elaborate metaphor of the lady as a lodestar in stanza 3. Everywhere in this poetry, the diction is relaxed and the syntax uncluttered. We should not be searching for inventive metaphors or neologisms here, since Sordello wrote in the style of *trobar pla* (plain composition), not in the *trobar clus* (closed or hermetic composition) of Arnaut Daniel and Raimbaut of Orange. Ezra Pound, who was drawn at first to Arnaut, said in the revised edition of his *Spirit of Romance:* "A more mature judgment, or greater familiarity with Provençal idiom might lead one to prefer the limpid simplicity of some of Sordello's verses". But simplicity is often a difficult thing both to admire and to define.

From Dante's *De Vulgari Eloquentia:*

We feel that they are not far from the truth who declare that the Bolognese have the most attractive speech, since they add to their own language by borrowings from the people of Imola, Ferrara and Modena round about them. We conjecture that everyone borrows thus from his neighbour, as Sordello shows in the case of his own Mantua, that borders on Cremona, Brescia, and Verona; indeed, he, a man of great eloquence, deserted his native vernacular not only in writing his poetry but in his ordinary talk. . . .

Dante Alighieri, in Dante: Literature in the Vernacular (De Vulgari Eloquentia), *translated by Sally Purcell, Carcanet New Press Limited, 1981.*

Perhaps the most underrated parts of the Sordello corpus are his debate poems (*tensos, partimens*) in which other people supposedly speak (whether other people actually did contribute their parts of the stanzas is a moot point). No. 13, the already mentioned debate with Joan (John), is a hilarious exchange of insults in the jongleur tradition, recalling the patter of modern vaudeville; Joan accuses Sordello, in fact, of being a lowly performer, and Sordello only half-heartedly refutes this. No. 14 concerns the nature of love, in which Sordello takes the role of the hedonist (in direct contrast with the high idealization of his love songs). Similarly, in Poem 17, a debate with Bertran d'Alamanon, Sordello opts for pleasure in love over glory in arms. These poems, along with many of the fragments, offer a pragmatic, even a cynical side to Sordello's character that has to be balanced with the sometimes cloying idealization of the chansons. The dialectic, in short, was no longer in a single poem toward the end of the troubadour tradition, but had gravitated into different genres.

Another group of poems that may well have interested Dante are the *sirventes* (the moral and political satires). No. 19 is a stern moral warning to Sir Raymond (probably Berengar) to rule his state well. No. 20 is a **"Satire Against Three Disinherited Lords,"** which perpetuates the vigorous role of the secular moralist that had been established by Bertran de Born in the twelfth century. No. 21 extols the chivalric value of *mezura* (control, temperance), and ties in neatly with the long ***Ensenhamen d'onor*** (***Instruction in Honor***), as well as with Poem 39. No. 22, a diatribe against the evil rich, again sounds like Bertran or Marcabru, while Poems 23 to 25 are three vitriolic attacks on an erstwhile friend, Peire Bremon Ricas Novas, who almost seems to have stumbled into Sordello's disfavor. Here the invective is equal to any to be found in the great Roman satirists, such as Horace or Martial, who were probably as well known to Sordello as they were to Dante, and this bitterness is not at all unlike that to be found in the great Florentine himself.

In fact, if one considers the entire corpus of Sordello's work, it shows that Sordello shared many of the same interests with that later writer of epic: love, chivalry or ceremonious behavior, and morality. It is especially this last category that seems to form a bond. Despite the limited manuscript history of the ***Instruction in Honor,*** many people feel that Dante knew this poetic treatise which, like Brunetto Latini's *Tesoretto,* bridges the secular and religious worlds, just as Dante's *Divine Comedy* does. In conclusion, although many scholars have puzzled about why Dante should have found Sordello so interesting, if one reads the man's whole work, one sees that there was no one in the Italy of his day who was writing works in any language with such variety and vigor. If one then adds Brunetto's moral epic for the serious dimension sometimes lacking in Sordello, one can see two important foundations for Dante's own work. Sordello is in no way as profound as later poets such as Guido Cavalcanti or Guido Guinizelli, who allied the lyric with Neoplatonic or Aristotelian philosophy, but without Sordello and Brunetto before him, Dante would have found his career much more difficult to establish.

SOURCES AND INFLUENCES

The sources of Sordello are, as has been said, the whole preceding Provençal troubadour tradition. When Sordello began to write in the early thirteenth century, that tradition, which had flourished in the twelfth, was now on the wane—thanks to the natural attrition of all movements but more cogently because of the brutal Albigensian Crusade, which had been waged by Rome and Paris on the men of the Languedoc. As an Italian, Sordello did not necessarily feel out of place with a language and a tradition where the competition was now decidedly second-class. Instead of viewing him as part of this decadence, however, we should see him as a pivotal figure with respect to the blossoming literature of Italy, since he would be idolized as a local talent who excelled in what had been a foreign endeavor. It is clear that part of Dante's tribute to Sordello stemmed from the fact that the Mantuan had "put the Italians on the map."

Since Sordello elected to write in the "plain style" rather than the "closed style" of troubadour composition, he also helped to set a tone for the future. Following in the footsteps of Bernart de Ventadorn rather than Arnaut Daniel, Sordello must have eventually convinced Dante and his circle that more was to be gained by writing in a manner that was clear, limpid, and easily perceptible than in the difficult, abstruse manner that Dante flirted with in his Rock-Lady Sestina or Guido Cavalcanti in his *Donna mi prega*. Although some scholars have seen an indebtedness in Sordello to certain passages of Peire Vidal or to Bertran de Born or others, these are isolated and not always authoritatively established. Sordello was too good a poet to be merely imitative, the way Peire Bremon Ricas Novas and Bertran d'Alamanon were in copying his **"Dirge for Blacatz."**

The influence of Sordello is, in fact, much more interesting to study than are his sources. Obviously his most important influence was on Dante himself, and, through the Florentine, upon later generations of Italians who somehow took the Mantuan to be more important than he actually was, both historically and aesthetically. A prime reason for Sordello's expanded reputation is surely the dramatic way in which he is presented in the *Comedy*. Vergil and Dante are beginning to climb Mount Purgatory, when they see a shade up ahead who causes Vergil to say:

> "But look at that soul there, sitting
> All by himself, staring at us both:
> He will show us the quickest way."
> We walked over to him; O Lombard soul,
> Who sat there so high and mighty,
> And in the movement of your eyes so noble and slow!
> He did not say a word to us,
> But let us move up, only eying us
> The way a lion looks when it is crouching.
> Then Vergil drew forward to him,
> Asking him to show us the easiest passage up;
> And he did not respond to this demand,
> But asked him instead where we came from
> And how we were; and my beloved leader began,
> "Mantua . . ."—when the shade, drawn into himself,
> Arose from the place where he sat,
> Saying, "O Mantuan, I am Sordello,
> From your same country!" And the two embraced. (6.58-75)

In short, Dante makes Sordello an important link with the Roman past, and he also makes him a patriot of his native country. This identification would not be lost in the next century when one Aliprandi of Mantua would write a rhymed chronicle of his city in which Sordello would emerge as a kind of folk hero, far more a warrior like Ezzelino da Romano than a poet. Dante himself obviously appreciated Sordello's handling of language, as the reference in *De vulgari* shows, but the moral vigor of the man is what comes through most strongly in the literary portrait, especially since Sordello contrasts with the lazy, negligent rulers whom he points out in the Vale of Princes. As a result, later Mantuan chroniclers would make him more a man of action than a creator of works.

Aliprandi, for example, in his *Aliprandina* (ca. 1415) has him write a book in his youth called ***Thesaurus thesaurorum*** (***Treasure of Treasures***; obviously modeled after Brunetto Latini's *Tesoretto*), which may have been the ***Ensenhamen*** under a different name; but he goes on to involve Sordello, whom he sees as a member of the Visconti family, in exploits throughout Europe, has him fall in love with a certain Beatrice, sister of Ezzelino, and, after many exploits and escapades, he marries her and settles in Mantua. Then Platina in his *Historia urbis Mantuae* continued the same tradition, making Sordello the speaker of a famous patriotic address against the incursions of the Paduans. The notoriously fantastic-minded Jehan de Nostredame in his *Lives of the Most Famous and Ancient Provençal Poets* (1575) clung more closely to the corpus of Sordello's work, and, having his own roots in France, told a story that was much closer to the truth, although sloppy in its dating.

The legend of Sordello continued in the 1600s, but in the Age of Reason, a certain amount of skepticism crept in. The scholar Giovanni Tiraboschi in his *History of Italian Literature* (1788) complained about the discrepancies in the presentations of Aliprandi and Platina, and this led in the Romantic Era to Friedrich Diez's questioning the whole matter of Sordello's life as traditionally presented. His monumental *Leben und Werke der Troubadours* (2nd ed., 1882) presented an admirable portrait of Sordello that was far removed from fantasy.

Meanwhile, however, the legend was attracting authors as well as critics and historians. In 1840, the young Robert Browning published his *Sordello,* which, although it has its roots in Dante, is entirely a production of the imagination. This extremely difficult work, usually considered the most obscure in the Browning corpus, again offers a dashing courtier who is in love with a woman named Palma (a curious change from Cunizza) and who is deeply embroiled in the Guelph-Ghibelline politics of the thirteenth century. The poem is difficult not only because of its syntax but also because Browning, however he interpreted the confusing politics of Lombardy and Romany, did not succeed in making the issues clear to most readers.

Probably the staunchest defender of Browning's *Sordello* was Ezra Pound, who helped to revolutionize the poetic practices of the twentieth century. In his early correspondence, Pound repeatedly urged people to read Browning's poem, although he did not make the reasons for doing it clear. Pound's own Canto 2 of his *Cantos* opens with the line "Hang it all, Robert Browning, there can be but the one *Sordello!*" This is actually a rather playful vaunt, in which Pound asserts that his own reading of the man has to stand up against that of all other interpreters. What Pound admires Sordello for is exactly what excites Dante: the man's vigor, and, despite his amatory excesses, his dedication to a life of action.

Pound tries to capture the energy of Sordello's life in lines that close Canto 36, which consists largely of Pound's own translation of Cavalcanti's complex explanation of the nature of love, *Donna mi prega.* There is then a line in Latin: "Sacrum, sacrum, inluminatio coitu" (Sacred, sacred, the illumination in coitus), underscoring the importance of the sexual act, which Pound sees Sordello and Cavalcanti promoting. Then follow two lines from Vida B and a conflated paraphrase of Charles of Anjou's donation of land in the Abruzzi, followed by the line from Song 3, verse 17, that haunted Pound (in English: "When I think deeply in my rich meditations"):

Lo Sordels si fo di Mantovana
of a castle named Goito.
"Five castles!"
"Five castles!"
(king giv' him five castles)
"And what the hell do I know about dye-works?!"
His Holiness has written a letter:
"CHARLES the Mangy of Anjou. . . .
. . . way you treat your men is a scandal. . . ."
Dilectis miles familiaris . . . castra Montis Odorisii
Montis Sancti Silvestri pallete et pile
In partibus Thetis. . . . vineland

land tilled

the land incult

pratis nemoribus pascuis

with legal jurisdiction
his heirs of both sexes,
. . . sold the damn lot six weeks later,
Sordellus de Godio.
Quan ben m'albir e mon ric pensamen. (36)

Pound adds Cunizza to the troubadour in a passage that closes Canto 6, along with selections from and the names of witnesses to her famous will that freed some slaves. He opens by quoting Vida B and then closes this portrait with his own translation or free paraphrase of the first stanza of Poem 3, *Atretan deu ben chantar finamen*:

E lo Sordels si fo di Mantovana,
Son of a poor knight, Sier Escort,
And he delighted himself in chançons
And mixed with the men of the court
And went to the court of Richard Saint Boniface
And was there taken with love for his wife

Cunizza, da Romano,
That freed her slaves on a Wednesday
Masnatas et servos, witness
Picus de Farinatis
and Don Elinus and Don Lipus
sons of Farinato de'Farinati
"free of person, free of will
free to buy, witness, sell, testate."
A marito subtraxit ipsam . . .
dictum Sordellum concubuisse:
"Winter and Summer I sing of her grace,
As the rose is fair, so fair is her face,
Both Summer and Winter I sing of her,
The snow makyth me to remember her." (6)

To Pound, Cunizza's great act of generosity redeems a wayward life, just as Sordello's lines of poetry redeem him too.

It is doubtful that, without Dante, Sordello would have been so important to succeeding generations; but with that help, Sordello has become a recurrent factor in Western literature, and he promises to fascinate and inspire other generations in the future.

FURTHER READING

Brooke, Stopford A. "Browning and Sordello." In his *The Poetry of Robert Browning,* pp. 200-18. New York: AMS Press, 1965.

Draws various analogies between the two poets and their works, including the correlation between their social, political, and religious contexts, and the connection between Browning and the fictional Sordello.

Chaytor, H. J. *The Troubadours and England.* Cambridge at the University Press, 1923, 164 p.

Examines the influence of the Provençal troubadours on the Middle English lyric.

Church, R. W. "Sordello." In his *Dante and Other Essays,* pp. 221-60. London: Macmillan and Co., 1891.

Analyzes Browning's poem *Sordello,* acknowledging the obscure and complex nature of the work while emphasizing its underlaying "great and profound idea": contemplation of a failed, though noble spirit.

Egan, Margarita, trans. *The Vidas of the Troubadours.* New York: Garland Publishing, 1984, 124 p.

Provides translations of the *vidas,* the biographies of the troubadours, which were originally written in Old Provençal and which often served to introduce selections from the poets' lyrics.

Lindsay, Jack. *The Troubadours and Their World of the Twelfth and Thirteenth Centuries.* London: Frederick Muller, 1976, 306 p.

Offers verse and prose translations of troubadour poetry as well as descriptive passages detailing background on the poets' lives, and historical and cultural information about the period.

Su Shih

1036-1101

(Also known as Su Tung-p'o.) Chinese poet and essayist.

INTRODUCTION

Considered one of the greatest of the Sung dynasty (960-1279) poets, Su was a popular and prolific author who composed poetry, essays, satires, art criticism, political, philosophical, and medical treatises, and experimented in the traditional *shih* and *tz'u* genres. Many scholars have noted that Su was a supreme master of *fu,* or prose poetry, and, while his philosophical ideas and theories of landscape continue to interest twentieth-century critics, it is for his simple, lyrical expressions of friendship, the pleasures of drinking, and the pain of loneliness that he remains best known today.

Biographical Information

Su was born in Mei-shan, now Szechwan Province. His father, a civil servant, and his mother, a devout Buddhist whose faith early influenced her son, provided Su with a good education at a private school run by a Taoist priest. In 1056, like most well-educated young men in China at the time, Su took the government civil service exam and passed with distinction. He received a post as a supervisor of public works in 1061, but, always an unconventional and outspoken thinker, made political enemies when he caricatured the verse of some official censors and was exiled to Huang-chou from 1080 to 1084. Around this time, Su began calling himself Tung-p'o chu-shih, or "the Layman of Eastern Slope," a reference to the piece of land he farmed during this period; Su Tung-p'o has traditionally been used as the poet's literary name. Su experienced two more punishments during his government career: he was jailed in 1094 for some critical references to the government, and in 1097 he was banished to the island of Hainan for having spoken disrespectfully to the Emperor. In letters written to friends during this period Su often lamented the transient life he lived as a civil servant and the isolation he experienced while in exile. His contemporaries characterized him as a compassionate, humane official who did what he could to improve the lot of the poor farmers among whom he lived and who cultivated a warm relationship with the citizenry wherever he happened to be. In his official capacity, Su oversaw the building of dams and coordinated famine relief, but he also involved himself in caring for orphans and in the prevention of female infanticide. He also became interested in medicine (there is a book of medicinal recipes ascribed to him and a contemporary, Shen Kua) and developed his considerable skill as a painter and calligrapher. Having been restored to favor in 1000, Su died in 1101.

Major Works

While Su's political writings and philosophical commentaries partake of the Confucian tradition, his poetry exhibits Taoist, Buddhist, and Confucian influences, as well as that of earlier Chinese poets, from whom Su borrowed freely. His best-known poems—"The Red Cliff," "The Pavillion of Flying Cranes," "Bending Bamboos of Yun-Tang Valley," "Pine Wine of the Middle Mountains," and "The Pavillion of Glad Rain," for example—are noted for their simple, spontaneous outpouring of emotion, and their emphasis on self-knowledge and unity with nature. These aspects, critics have noted, also typify the classical movement in Chinese literature which was taking place between the eighth and twelfth centuries, and of which Su was one of the leaders. Scholars also credit Su with the revival of the *fu* genre, which had been neglected for several centuries by Chinese writers. The theme of unity with nature and the striving toward Taoist goals also figures prominently in Su's painting poems, compositions which explicate various paintings in philosophical and poetic terms.

Critical Reception

Of the vast number of poems and essays written by Su, approximately 2,400 survive in authentic texts; scholars are able to date the majority of his writings fairly accurately. Su's works have been extremely popular with readers from his own time onward, and, while they were banned right after his death because of his unorthodox political views, they were circulated widely and eventually restored to favor. Twentieth-century critics have continued to explore various aspects of Su's writings—for example, the imagery and poetic voice in his verse writings, his theory of art as expressed through his landscape and painting poems, and his views on his contemporaries and his society as seen in his prose works. Most scholars still agree with Herbert A. Giles's assessment of Su: "Under his hands, the language of which China is so proud may be said to have reached perfection of finish, of art concealed. [In] subtlety of reasoning, in the lucid expression of abstractions, such as in English too often eludes the faculty of the tongue, Su Tung P'o is an unrivalled master."

PRINCIPAL ENGLISH TRANSLATIONS

**Gems of Chinese Literature* (edited by Herbert A. Giles) 1923

Selections from the Works of Su Tung-P'o (translated by Cyril Drummond Le Gros Clark) 1931

Su Tung-P'o: Selections from a Sung Dynasty Poet (translated by Burton Watson) 1965

The Road to East Slope: The Development of Su Shi's Poetic Voice (translated by Michael Fuller) 1990

*Includes selections from the works of Su Shih.

CRITICISM

Cyril Drummond Le Gros Clark (essay date 1931)

SOURCE: An introduction to *Selections from the Works of Su Tung-p'o,* translated by Cyril Drummond Le Gros Clark, Jonathan Cape, 1931, pp. 23-33.

[*Clark is a scholar and translator of Chinese literature. Here, he describes the general tenor of Su's works, emphasizing that "permeating his writings is an unmistakable sympathy with his fellow beings, an understanding of their lives, a compassion for their troubles."*]

It has been said that Su Shih revived 'the plain speaking of the satirical odes.' Certain it is that as a satirist who never hesitated to censure or ridicule when he considered either necessary, Tung-p'o stands out most prominently amongst his contemporaries. A brilliant essayist and poet, he—like Ou-yang Hsiu—is regarded as an almost universal genius, but is even a greater favourite with the Chinese literary public. To quote Dr. H. A. Giles in his *Gems of Chinese Literature,* 'Under his hands, the language of which China is so proud may be said to have reached perfection of finish, of art concealed. In subtlety of reasoning, in the lucid expression of abstractions, such as in English too often elude the faculty of the tongue, Su Tung-p'o is an unrivalled master.'

His writings were voluminous, and numerous editions of his complete works, under the title of *Tung-p'o Ch'üan Chi,* have been published from the time of the Sung dynasty down to the present day. These works covered a great variety of subjects and were produced in many different styles, including letters, essays, records, memorials, epitaphs, prose-poems and verse.

A study of this literature gives the reader an insight into not only the times in which the author lived but also the character and temperament of the man himself. His extreme outspokenness, for instance, was continually getting him into trouble with the Throne, resulting in a series of banishments and dismissals from the posts he held, a process which continued intermittently throughout his life. Commencing with his opposition to Wang An-shih, the Innovator, and the poet's departure from the Capital to a subordinate post at Hangchow, he, shortly afterwards, lampooned in verse two of the Court Censors and, in 1072, was dismissed to Huangchow. Seven years later, on being transferred to Huchow, he presented a memorial returning thanks for this appointment. A Censor discovered allusions derogatory to the Government and Tung-p'o was thrown into prison. After several years of changing fortune during which he was summoned to return to Court, he was obliged once more to go into the provinces and, in 1094, was accused of having spoken disrespectfully of the late Emperor, and banished, first to Huichow in Kuangtung, and afterwards to the island of Hainan.

His experiences, however, had taught him in later life to be more careful in his political references, and we find few of them in his writings during his last years. Here and there occurs a vague allusion, but he appears rather to warn his friends against making similar mistakes. In a letter to his grand-nephew, Yüan Lao, he counsels him to be on his guard in all things while in the metropolis. He concludes his letter with the words—'And now, above all things be circumspect.' In another letter to the same relative he writes, 'I assure you I am anxious to compose the Epitaph and have no thought of drawing back, but, of late, anxieties and fears have crowded upon me thicker than ever. I can set about nothing nowadays without taking all sorts of precautions—eating, drinking, or talking, it is all the same. I fancy you will divine my meaning.'

Wherever he went and whatever post he held, Tung-p'o seemed to leave his mark in some practical manner, generally by digging wells. A train of wells marked his wanderings over the Empire, and he records in his writings his experiences in this line, notably in Ch'ien T'ang, in

Chekiang and in Kiungchow in Hainan. In this latter place he found two springs to the north-east of the city, a few feet apart, but with waters of different taste. We are credibly informed that the Chinese profess great faith in the quality of this well, known as Tung-p'o's Double Spring, 'nor is their belief much shaken by the fact that foreign analysis is in favour of a rival well.' He added largely to the architectural beauties of Hangchow; at Yinchow he carried on successfully the work of famine relief, and the Yellow River benefited by his engineering skill.

Many of his essays and poems contain passages of great beauty, such as ***The Red Cliff,*** and ***The Pavilion of Flying Cranes.*** To read, for instance, the **'Song of the Cranes'** in the original Chinese is a delight which only the sublime poetry of the Immortals can bring to one. Again, his powers of imagination are manifested in such lines as his description of Ts'ao Ts'ao's fleet sailing down towards the Red Cliff; the raging typhoon; Wang Hsün marching upon K'un Yang. Or his description of that night under the Stonebell Hill, when, accompanied by his son, Mai, he took a boat to investigate the uncanny sounds which came from its foot. 'The mighty rock rose to a height of a thousand feet, like an infuriate beast or strange monster about to pounce upon us. Falcons, perched upon the hills, rose in screaming fright to the clouds on hearing the sounds of men.

'There were noises too, like an old man coughing and cackling, in the gulleys of the hill—'

We find, too, passages of extreme tenderness, showing how deeply he felt the loss of a friend. His references to Wên Yü-k'o in the ***Bending Bamboos of Yün-Tang Valley*** are most touching in their sorrow, as for instance when he tells how, while drying his books and pictures, he picked up a painting done by his dead friend. 'I put away the volumes, and sobbed.' And his life-long correspondence with his brother Tzu-Yu, which displayed a brotherly love of unusual devotion. It was during their journey together to their respective places of banishment, when Tung-p'o was going to Hainan, that Tzu-Yu made a pathetic appeal to his elder brother to give up his too free indulgence in the wine-cup. Tung-p'o, we are informed, was repentant for the moment, but after throwing off a few lines to commemorate the occasion, and to record his formal renunciation of Bacchus, he crossed over to Hainan to lead anything but a teetotaler's life. 'Heaven,' he mused, 'was using him as its instrument to propagate the principles of the true doctrine in this outlandish corner of the earth; and, after all, the world was a mere delusion, man's home everywhere, and his best source of happiness a contented mind.' As he stepped on board the vessel for Hainan, he told Tzu-Yu that he 'was now floating out to sea on the Confucian raft and that the faith would have free course,' adapting thereby a quotation from the *Analects* to his own case.

We read in a letter written during his later years to Ch'êng Ch'üan-fu, a graduate, as follows:

> The Huichow wine you sent me is splendid. When at Huichow, I used to give the preference to the Mei brand, but this is far and away the better. The pleasure of wine-bibbing is, I assure you, no slight support in my solitude.

One need only read his ***Pine Wine of the Middle Mountains*** to realise that Tung-p'o was a tippler, but that, even in his cups, he could describe with so vivid a touch his drunken sensations. 'How much have I already drunk to-day? Ah! I feel I can escape now from the fetters of mortality!—I soar over the running deer in the mountain peaks, and join the leaping monkeys on the overhanging cliffs. Thence do I plunge into the billowing clouds of a vast ocean.—Heaven in tumult!'

What a genius was his! And yet, permeating his writings is an unmistakable sympathy with his fellow beings, an understanding of their lives, a compassion for their troubles. His description of the coming of rain after the great drought and the joy of the people, and the song which he wrote to commemorate the Pavilion which he raised, calling it **'The Pavilion to Glad Rain,'** are surely thoughts of a man deeply and personally in sympathy with not only his social companions and intimates but with the poorer farmers and labourers with whom his official duties would bring him into contact. Writing to a friend from Hainan, he said that he had adopted the local dress and cared not what other people thought, so long as the change made him more comfortable in his surroundings. He felt that he would be happy if he could only learn the native dialect. As one writer has said of him, 'His taste for natural scenery often led him away into unbeaten tracks, while his sympathy with his kind, the pleasure of society, and his love of hearing the traditional lore of a bygone age made him equally happy in the company of the scholar, the peasant, the aboriginal Li, the gossiping old woman, or the prattling little child. With the last he was a special favourite, and, "Here's old Su coming" was the greeting he received from the Tamchow youngster of the time.' His exhortation addressed to the people of Hainan to improve their agricultural methods may be taken as an outstanding example of his compassion. 'The Island,' he wrote, 'does not grow enough rice for its own consumption and its people have to fill their bellies with slops made of a mixture of sweet potatoes, taros, and rice. I have been moved to pity at their conditions.'—After encouraging them to 'clear away the jungle and mark out your land into cultivable areas,' he concludes by telling them that 'when the fall comes, and you gather in all round your full bins of the ripe grain, you can hold high revel at your harvest-home and imbibe unrestrainedly of the very best.' A delightful reminder to us of his love of the wine-cup! One calls to mind, too, the incident at Huichow when a subscription was being raised for the construction of a bridge. Tung-p'o was without money, but gave his belt, with its clasp of rhinoceros horn, to assist the fund.

Tung-p'o extended this sympathy to the lower animals, and his writings are full of references to the birds and beasts of his world. Who but a lover of horses could have written the description of the reluctant departure of the guests from the Inn, at the Sign of the Screeching Phoenix, with their horses looking back at the grooms and whinnying? Nor does he omit to mention his faithful Hainanese dog, Black-Mouth, whose only weakness was a liking for meat which occasionally got the better of his honesty, and who, when his master received news of his recall from banishment, wagged his tail with glee! To this dog Tung-p'o dedicated a special poem.

There are many references in his works to the flora and fauna of the various districts he visited; and the medicinal properties of herbs, a subject in which he was evidently well read, receive special emphasis. ***A Draught of Sesamum*** is only one of many of his prose essays which are devoted to this topic. His early training in Taoism, and his numerous quotations from the works of Chuang Tzu, are sufficient reasons for his deep interest in the materia medica of his time, founded upon the union of the Yang and the Yin. Referring to the ingredients of a drug he writes:

> It is Immortality, the Aim of Tao.
> The divine Elixir, like the Island of the Blest,
> Affords you shelter.

Tung-p'o was deeply affected by his adversities, more especially after the death of his constant companion, the fair Chao Yün, in Huichow. During his later years in banishment, we read of him repairing by daytime to 'a little lodge on the bluff overlooking the sea, where he watched the passing ships and wondered when the craft would come to take him homeward.' Again, when no vessels arrived from the north with rice, he would be overcome with despondency at his privations, and the weight of declining years. And yet, even in his despair, we find his saving sense of humour rising through the mists. Who could but smile, for instance, at his first effort to eat a betel-nut, a curiosity to his northern experience? The violent indigestion and sleepless night that followed his experiment resulted in an avowal of vengeance and condemnation of the offending nut in a number of verses!

Perhaps the best proof of his personal popularity, however, may be seen in the fact that, no matter where he went—whether in favour or disgrace—he succeeded in collecting around him a devoted band of admiring disciples attracted, one must think, rather by his genial good nature under adversity than by his brilliant genius. While he was in Hainan, some of these young men actually came all the way from Kiangsu, an astonishing fact when one considers the difficult means of communication in those days.

But it is as the merry wine-drinking poet that we like best to remember him, betaking himself with a few select intimates to some woodland retreat or high tower whence the world might be viewed impersonally, and the doctrines of Taoism tested with the magic aid of the best wine. ***The Tower of Tranquillity*** at Chiao-Hsi, whither he often went accompanied by friends, or the 'Wine Palace' at Tamchow erected by Tung-p'o and the two brothers Li for their convivial gatherings, were, after all, but repetitions of the famous hard-drinking coteries of the T'ang poets—the Six Idlers of the Bamboo Brook and the Eight Immortals of the Wine-cup of Li Po, or the Nine Old Gentlemen of Hsiang-Shan of Po Chü-i. 'How pleasant are these visits,' he would write with a contentment of mind which amazed his brother Tzu-Yu; for, he said, 'I wander beyond the confines of a material world.'

Ch'ien Chung-shu (essay date 1935)

SOURCE: A foreword to *The Prose-Poetry of Su Tung-P'o,* translated by Cyril Drummond Le Gros Clark, 1935. Reprint by Paragon Book Reprint Corp., 1964, xiii-xxii.

[*Ch'ien Chung-shu is one of China's most distinguished literary figures. A professor of English and Chinese at Kwang Hua University in Shanghai, he is the author of numerous essays, a significant body of literary criticism, and several short stories. He is probably best known for his novel* Wei Cheng *(1947;* Fortress Besieged, *1979), a satire regarded as one of the greatest Chinese literary works of the twentieth century. Below, he comments on Su's prose poems and adds that "the interest of Su Tung-p'o for us lies in the fact that he does not share the spirit of his age."*]

Of the Sung dynasty, it may be said, as Hazlitt said of himself in the words of Iago, that it is nothing if not critical. The Chinese people dropped something of their usual wise passiveness during the Sung dynasty, and "pondered, searched, probed, vexed, and criticised." This intellectual activity, however, is not to be compared with that of the Pre-Chin period, the heyday of Chinese philosophy. The men of the Sung dynasty were inquisitive rather than speculative, filled more with a sense of curiosity than with a sense of mystery. Hence, there is no sweep, no daring, no roominess or margin in their intellectualism. A prosaic and stuffy thing theirs is, on the whole. This critical spirit revealed itself in many directions, particularly in the full flourish of literary criticism and the rise of the *tao-hsüeh,* that *mélange adultère* of metaphysic, psychology, ethics and casuistry. . . .

The Chinese common reader often regards the men of the Sung dynasty as prigs. Their high seriousness and intellectual and moral squeamishness are at once irritating and amusing to the ordinary easy-going Chinese temperament. There is something paralysing and devitalising in their wire-drawn casuistry which induces hostile critics to attribute the collapse of the Sung dynasty to its philosophers. There is also a disingenuousness in their attempts at what may be called, for want of a better name, philosophical masquerade: to dress up Taoism or Buddhism as orthodox Confucianism. One need but look into *Sketches in a Villa* and *Causeries on Poetry in a Garden* to see what a good laugh those two coxcombs of letters, Chi Yüan and Yüan Mei have had at the expense of the Sung philosophers and critics respectively. Nevertheless one is compelled to admit that the Sung philosophers are unequalled in the study of mental chemistry. Never has human nature been subject to a more rigorous scrutiny before or since in the history of Chinese thought. For what strikes one most in the *tao-hsüeh* is the emphasis on self-knowledge. This constant preying upon itself of the mind is quite in the spirit of the age. The Sung philosophers are morbidly introspective, always feeling their moral pulses and floundering in their own streams of consciousness. To them, their mind verily "a kingdom is." They analyse and pulverise human nature. But for that moral bias, which Nietzsche thinks to be also the bane of German philosophy, their vivisection of the human soul would have contributed a good deal to what Santayana calls literary psychology.

The poetry of the Sung dynasty is also a case in point. It is a critical commonplace that the Sung poetry furnishes a striking contrast to the T'ang poetry. Chinese poetry, hitherto ethereal and delicate, seems in the Sung dynasty to take on flesh and becomes a solid, full-blooded thing. It is more weighted with the burden of thought. Of course, it still looks light and slight enough by the side of Western poetry. But the lightness of the Sung poetry is that of an aeroplane describing graceful curves, and no longer that of a moth fluttering in the mellow twilight. In the Sung poetry one finds very little of that suggestiveness, that charm of a beautiful thing imperfectly beheld, which foreigners think characteristic of Chinese poetry in general. Instead, one meets with a great deal of naked thinking and outright speaking. It may be called "Sentimental" in contradistinction to the T'ang poetry which is on the whole "Naïve," to adopt Schiller's useful antithesis. The Sung poets, however, make up for their loss in lisping naïveté and lyric glow by a finesse in feeling and observation. In their descriptive poetry, they have the knack of taking the thing to be described *sur le vif*—witness Lu Yu and Yang Wan-li. They have also a better perception of the nuances of emotion than the T'ang poets, as can be seen particularly in their *tz'u,* a species of song for which the Sung dynasty is justly famous. Small wonder that they are deliberate artists, considering the fact that they all have been critics in the off-hours of their inspiration. The most annoying thing about them is perhaps their erudition and allusiveness which make the enjoyment of them to a large extent the luxury of the initiated even among the Chinese.

The interest of Su Tung-p'o for us lies in the fact that he does not share the spirit of his age. He seems to be born out of his due time and is nonetheless an anachronism for being himself unaware of it. To begin with, he is not critical in the sense that his contemporaries are critical. In the excellent account of Su's philosophy of art, Mr. C. D. Le Gros Clark has shown that Su goes to the root of the matter; he turns from the work of art to the mind of the artist. A poet, according to Su, should "merge himself" with reality, and not content himself with the mere polishing of literary surfaces. Compared to this conception of the ontological affinity between the artist and Nature, the most meticulous studies of Su's contemporaries in diction and technique dwindle into mere fussiness of the near-sighted over details. Again, Su has a rooted antipathy against the spiritual pedantry of *tao-hsüeh,* that "unseasonable ostentation" of conscience and moral sense. He speaks disparagingly of the high talk about human nature and reason, and the inefficiency of those who model themselves upon Confucius and Mencius. He is also opposed to Ch'êng I, the leader of the *tao-hsüeh* party in politics, with a virulence almost incompatible with his otherwise genial and tolerant character. He is probably still in purgatory for these offences. Chu Hsi has condemned him several times in his writings—and, in a way, to be dispraised of Chu Hsi is no small praise! Finally, as a poet, he is comparatively the most "naïve" among his "sentimental" contemporaries. Though no "native woodnotes wild," his poetry smells more of the perfume of books, as the Chinese phrase goes, than of the lamp oil. His stylistic feats seem rather lucky accidents than the results of sweating toil. He is much more spontaneous and simple in the mode of feeling than (say) Huang T'ing-chien who, with Su, is the twin giant in the Sung poetry. Ling Ai-hsüan has put the contrast between Su and Huang in a nutshell, comparable to Johnson's epigram on the difference between Dryden and Pope: "Su's poetry is manly and walks in big strides, while Huang's is womanlike and walks in a mincing gait." Has not Su himself also said that simplicity and primitiveness should be the criteria of good art?

Su's strains are as profuse as his art is unpremeditated. He throws out his good things to the winds with the prodigality and careless opulence of Nature. Here's God's plenty indeed! As he says of his own style; "My style is like a spring of inexhaustible water which bubbles and over-flows where it lists, no matter where. Running its course through the plains, it may glide along at the speed of a thousand *li* a day. When it threads its way through cliffs and mountains, one never knows beforehand what shape it may assume to conform with these obstacles . . . . It flows where it must flow and stops where it must stop." Elsewhere he repeats almost *verbatim* what he says here with the additional metaphor that style should be like the floating cloud. It is significant that this simile of water with its association of fluidity and spontaneity recurs with slight variations in all criticisms of Su. To quote a few examples from his contemporaries will suffice: his brother Tzu-yu likens his style to a mountain stream young after rain; Huang T'ing-chien, to the sea, tractless and boundless, into which all rivers empty, Li Chi-ch'ing, to an impetuous flood; Hsü Kai, to a big river. Thus the abiding impression of Su's art is one of "spontaneous overflow." Ch'ien Ch'ien-i varies the metaphor by comparing Su's style to quicksilver and draws the conclusion that the Taoist and Buddhist Naturalism must have been the formative influence in Su's life and art—a conclusion Mr. Le Gros Clark arrives at independently four centuries later.

It is strange that this Naturalism, which exercises a liberating influence upon Su, should also form an important element in the harrowing, cut-and-dry Sung philosophy or *tao-hsüeh.* One is tempted to think that, whereas the Sung philosophers are only naturalistic in creed, Su is naturalistic in character. Su is a spirit apart indeed!

Famed in all great arts, Su is supreme in prose-poetry or

fu. In other species of writing, he only develops along the lines laid down by his immediate predecessors; but his prose-poetry is one of those surprises in the history of literature. Here is an art rediscovered that has been lost for several centuries. The whole T'ang dynasty is a blank as far as prose-poetry is concerned. The famous prose-poems by Han Yü and Liu Tsung-yüan are all stiff-jointed, imitative and second-rate. Ou-yang Hsiu first shows the way by his magnificent *Autumn Dirge,* and Su does the rest. In Su's hands, the *fu* becomes a new thing: he brings ease into what has hitherto been stately; he changes the measured, even-paced tread suggestive of the military drill into a swinging gait, and he dispenses altogether with that elaborate pageantry which old writers of *fu* are so fond of unrolling before the reader. He is by far the greatest *fu*-writer since Yü Sin. While Yü Sin shows how supple he can be in spite of the cramping antithetical style of the *fu,* Su succeeds in softening and thawing this rigid style, smoothing over its angularity and making the sharp points of the rhyming antitheses melt into one another. T'ang Tzu-hsi does not exaggerate when he says that in *fu* Su "beats all the ancients." . . . [This] is not the place for a detailed discussion of the literary qualities of Su's *fu*. Su's usual freakishness, buoyancy, humour, abundance of metaphor are all there. But critics, while noting these, have overlooked that which distinguishes his *fu* from his other writings . . . the difference in *tempo*. Su's normal style is "eminently rapid," as Arnold says of Homer; in his prose-poems, however, he often slackens down almost to the point of languidness as if he were caressing every word he speaks. Take for instance the section in ***Red Cliff,*** Part I, beginning with Su's question "Why is it so?" It moves with the deliberate slowness and ease of a slow-motion picture. What is said above does not apply, of course, to such sorry stuff as ***Modern Music in the Yen Ho Palace, On the Restoration of the Examination System,*** etc., which Mr. Le Gros Clark has also translated for the sake of having Su's prose-poems complete in English. They are written in the *style empesé,* being rhetorical exercises borrowed from "ambulant political experts," as Mr. Waley points out.

There is, therefore, no better proof of Mr. Le Gros Clark's deep knowledge of Chinese literature than his choice of Su's *fu* for translation. Throughout the whole translation he shows the scruples of a true scholar and the imaginative sympathy possible only to a genuine lover of Su. His notes and commentaries are particularly valuable, and so much more copious and learned than Lang Yeh's that even Chinese students will profit by them in reading Su's prose-poems in the original. If the English reader still cannot exchange smiles and salutes with Su across the great gulf of time so familiarly as the Chinese does, it is perhaps due to a difficulty inherent in the very nature of translation. It is certainly no fault of Su's accomplished translator.

Cyril Drummond Le Gros Clark (essay date 1935)

SOURCE: An introduction to *The Prose-Poetry of Su Tung-P' o,* translated by Cyril Drummond Le Gros Clark, 1935. Reprint by Paragon Book Reprint Corp., 1964, pp. 3-52.

[*In the following essay, Clark explores the elements of Su's philosophy of art, contending that he combined aspects of Confucianism, Taoism, and Buddhism into one unified vision of life and art.*]

Outside his own country Su Tung-p'o is, perhaps, best known as a satirist whose writings were continually getting him into trouble. Chinese commentators do not agree with this interpretation of Su's writings, and it is probable that satire is the exception, rather than the rule, in the poet's intention. When he was satirical, it must be remembered that he used this most subtle of weapons with a purpose and that, behind that purpose, there stood a man who possessed a remarkable philosophy.

A Confucian in his conduct of life and political attitude, he nevertheless continually draws upon the wells of Buddhism and Taoism for inspiration in his writings and his art. An analysis of his *fu,* for instance, will demonstrate that he did not hesitate to quote from the works of these three doctrines; of which, in fact, he possessed an intimate knowledge. How can this apparent divergence in his creed be reconciled?

Su Shih was an artist, and in Taoism and the Mah y na system of Buddhism he undoubtedly recognized media through which he could most satisfactorily interpret the rhythm of Nature in his art. He himself has recorded, in his role as art-critic, his opinion regarding the necessity of unity between the artist-creator and nature, and it is in his writings that we may find the answer to this riddle. Referring with admiration, as he often does, to Wên Yü-k'o, he writes: "When one totally merges oneself with things, then is one always able to find delight in them." He refers again and again to this 'oneness' of the creator with that which he would recreate. Writing of Li Lung-mien, he described him as one who "lived in the mountains and did not merge himself in one thing only. Thus he combined in his spirit all things (nature) and, with the force of his intellect, penetrated several different arts." Nevertheless, to the creator or artist, the presence of *Tao* was as essential as the possession of talent. "When one possesses *Tao* and no talent, one may perhaps have the mirage of a thing in the heart, but it cannot take upon itself form under the hand." Here he followed Chuang Tzu who, "overwhelmed by the consciousness of the Infinity of Nature, reconciled all diversity in the all-pervading unity." He considered that *Tao* was, in fact, as necessary to the artist in his creative work as was the ability to create; for *Tao* inspired, and the artist gave form to that inspiration through painting or poetry.

This inspiration, which he drew from *Tao,* Su credited equally to Buddhism, for he has recorded the debt owed to Buddhism by Li Lung-mien in the latter's painting of Buddhist figures, which Su regarded as having been created from the Idea lying behind them. "I once saw Buddhist figures by Li Lung-mien. They are all created from the Idea behind them—Buddhism. Thus, that which the

Buddha and Boddhisatva spake, and Li Lung-mien painted, are here produced in a single form." Inspiration could, in fact, emerge from actual spiritual experience.

Describing a painting of the Buddha by Wu Tao-yüan, for whom he had the greatest respect, Su wrote that "Wu's art of painting the Buddha was certainly the result of spiritual experience. In a dream he found himself transformed into a winged Buddhist Immortal; and, on awaking, his brush commenced to work without apparent control by himself. It seemed as though divine power had indeed entered into the fine hairs of the brush." The picture had been badly torn when Su first saw it. "Nevertheless," he adds, "though the material has rotted, yet is the divine afflatus still there."

Elsewhere Su explains in greater detail his theory of the co-ordination between the artist and *Tao*. In the ***Bending Bamboos of Yün-tang Valley,*** he quotes Wên Yü-k'o's opinion on this subject, which occupied an important place in the perception of the Bamboo-painters. "If you wish to paint bamboo, you must first visualise it in your mind's eye. With brush in hand, study for a long time your subject. Directly you see what you want to paint, quickly follow it up with strokes of the brush. Thus, by close pursuit you reach out after your conception. Just as when a hare rises, the falcon stoops; the slightest hesitation, and it has disappeared." Referring to his own inability to accomplish this—"impression and expression are not in harmony, and the mind and hand do not coordinate," Su likens the man "who fails thoroughly to grasp the vision in his mind to one who appears habitually to conceive, but at the moment of portrayal suddenly loses, that vision."

The conception of unity with Nature through *Tao* Su applied to all art, to poetry as well as to painting. "Surely", he continues, "this does not apply to bamboos alone? When Tzu-yu wrote a poem called *Bamboos painted in ink,* he presented it to Yü-k'o, saying 'The cook who carves the bullock and he who cultivates his soul both work on this principle.' . . . And now the Master has applied this tenet to the bamboo. Personally, I regard him as one who has found *Tao*." This 'nearness to nature,' which seems to be so inherent in Su Tung-p'o, has been well stated by Professor Ku Teng [in his "Su Tung-p'o als Kunstkritiker," *Ostasiatische Zeitschrift* (May-June, 1932)]: "Su is neither a Naturalist in the sense that the desire for physical nearness to Nature (*äusserlichen Naturnähe*) stifles his sensitiveness, nor an individualist for whom Nature is the means of expression. But he creates unconsciously, he creates naively, so to speak. These traits come out in his poems wherein he tells us that 'I did not search for the artistic, nor in my writing (of characters) for the strange, but I regarded primitive Naturalism as my Master'."

Su again uses this expression in another poem: "The School of subtile painting," he wrote, "first realised the simplicity of art." In the same poem, he compares poet and painter: "The painters of old, who were not conventional, agreed with the poets in their artistic expression," viz., primitive simplicity.

While he subordinated art to moral teaching, and while he regarded art as a means of learning Confucianism on the one hand, and Buddhism on the other, Su clearly intended to borrow from Taoism and Buddhism all that they could give him for the purposes of his art, for he realised also that these conceptions, and especially Taoism, would "act as a regulator which would preserve Confucianism from superficiality and utilitarianism."

As stated above, his conception of the true painter was also his opinion of the true poet. In fact, he regarded them as interchangeable terms. Referring to this opinion, he wrote that "Shao-ling's (Tu Fu) poems are paintings without form; Han Kan's paintings are poems without words. This is the summit of achievement in painting and poetry." . . . Elsewhere he records that "poetry and painting follow one rule only—simplicity and primitiveness." In like manner did he praise Wang Wei's poems for which he had the highest esteem. "When I study Wang Wei's poems," he writes, "I find in them something of painting. When I regard his paintings, they are like his poems."

This close comparison between the painter and poet is of great importance in an elucidation of Su Shih's philosophy of art, for the records he has left us as an art-critic leave no doubt regarding his inmost opinion of contemporary art.

He refers on many occasions to 'the School of Gentlemen-painters', an expression first used, incidentally, by the poet, and of which school he himself was a member. It is not my purpose to discuss in detail the objects or history of this branch of the Southern School which was formed in opposition to the Northern or professional school. It will suffice to mention here that, in the course of time, the gentlemen-painters turned towards naturalism for their self-expression, painting only when they felt themselves inspired to paint, and protested against the conventionalism of the professional painters. In the words of a poem by Su Shih . . . , "He who lays stress on 'form,' when criticising paintings, stands on the same level as a child."

Here we see Su Shih rebelling against the fetters of convention and form that had for so long bound painter and poet within certain narrow and artificial limits. He attempted to escape from those bonds by freedom of expression. "A caged bird remembers how to fly, a tethered horse to gallop," he wrote in one of his poems. But he went further, for he recognized in the rhythm of Nature to be found in Taoism that very inspiration for which he was searching. By identification of self with the subject, the painter could in truth interpret that subject. "Of Wên Yü-k'o," he wrote, "one can really say that he has succeeded in setting down the soul of bamboo, of stone, of old trees. . . . Thus, when a man is sensible to every characteristic, then is he in union with Nature. When he abhors artificiality, then does he dwell in the realm of the Gentlemen-painters."

In this same [piece], the poet speaks with contempt of those other schools of painting who stressed the outward form. "Craftsmen," he wrote, "can work out 'Form', can in fact achieve it. But only those possessing surpassing ability (the Gentlemen-painters) can fathom its Essence." By this latter expression Su referred to the law of its being. . . .

He aimed at freedom from mere objectivity in his work, a freedom which he could find only in this all-embracing unity with Nature; and he recognized in Wang Wei a man who had attained such freedom, "as that of an Immortal." Describing the terrifying effects of a typhoon, he marvels that we should be so alarmed by what is, in reality, but a transient phase of nature. "Surely," he asks, "the importance which we attach to mere volume can only be attributed to the contemptible fact that one's senses are entirely influenced by objective matter?" In another *fu,* Su expresses this view even more clearly, emphasising the necessity of subjectivity before *Tao* can be found. "You derive your knowledge from much book-learning. You search for *Tao,* but find it not. Instead of being subjective, you are entirely objective—the slave of circumstances. And so the gnawing of a rat disturbs you!"

Everywhere can Su find beauty, and his writings are filled with his impressions clothed in poetic language. He tells us how he saw the shadows of bamboos and cypresses floating as waterplants on the lake's surface. How, when walking through the Courtyards, with the moon as his sole companion,

> incense, heavy with moisture, warns me of the night's
> approach,
> and dancing flower-shadows seem to urge the coming of
> the Spring.

He describes the scenery from a favourite retreat, where

> Rushes and lotus are like a vast expanse of ocean,
> With here and there a small boat sailing.
> Truly a spot remote from all the world.

Or, again, he is on a house-boat on the lake:

> A gentle breeze blows softly on the rushes,
> And, through the open door, I see the rain and moonlit-lake.
> Boatman and waterfowl together sleep.
> A large fish turns with sudden splash like a fox in flight.
> When the night is deep, all nature is in harmony,
> And man and beast are one.
> Substance and shadow allied, alone I stand enchanted,
> Pitying the cold worms on islets born of secret tides.
> Framed in the sinking moon I watch a spider hanging from
> a willow-tree.
> Suddenly the world seems filled with sorrow,
> For beauty is but passing—has straightway fled.
> A cock crows; a bell resounds. A flock of birds takes wing
> And a drum replies in echo from the prow.

The spell was broken. But in that moment of time Su had captured all eternity, and in his poems we can recognize the poet's urge to become one with Nature. He could identify the shadows of the bamboos with waterplants; he could conceive the unity of all creation in the stillness of a night; he grasped greedily at a beauty which he felt was transient and yet eternal. "Birth, growth, change and decay," he wrote, "all is but a moment in time. But I know that all creation is but nothingness."

And so, as Ku Teng points out [in *Ostasiatische Zeitschrift,* November-December, 1932], we can imagine the mood in which he created his paintings of bamboos.

This identification of the artist with his subject, the merging of "self" in "All-things," is further exemplified by Su Shih in a poem on Han Kan, who, "when he painted a horse, became, in fact, a horse. And when I write a poem (about him), I visualise him painting."

Chu Hsi, in his *Philosophy of Human Nature,* has recorded the saying of a friend and pupil of Su Shih, Li Fang-shu: "To be one with all things in the universe," he said, "is Love".

In Su's opinion, this unity was essential in the true poet and painter. Without it the source of his inspiration failed, for the many varied moods of nature must be reflected in his soul, even as Su himself records, "the fulness of the moon and calmness of the river" was once reflected in himself.

He likened his creative work to a spring of inexhaustible water which pours down into the plains, its course conforming to the obstacles in its path. "As to the reason that it (the river) flows over cliffs and mountains, winding in conformity with these obstacles, this may not be known. What may be known is that always it flows where it must flow, and stops where it must stop." By which analogy the poet wished to show that, while inspiration was essential to the artist, interpretation of that inspiration must conform to certain incomprehensible laws.

He again uses the parable of a stream in his *fu,* ***Rock of Yen-yü***. The river

> . . . journeys from afar, and in its course
> Of many thousand *li*
> It overflows vast deserts, meets no curb.
> Boasting in its pride, no barrier avails.
> And suddenly the gorge encloses it,
> Swallowing its flood of water.
> . . . It struggles . . .
> In deafening and clamorous convulsion,
> Striving with all its raging might against the rock,
> . . . With the noise and rushing of a torrent

Bursts river into gorge, and thence flows
 peacefully,
Its wrath subsiding.

Su is here clearly comparing a river with his own inspiration and to the channels through which that inspiration must express itself. He is, however, lost in speculation as to the reason behind those laws, and he closes his *fu* by adjuring the reader not to attempt "to analyse my chain of thought. It will suffice that you conceive the Eternal Fitness of All things."

Su Shih's associations with the Sung School of Philosophy may be recalled by the knowledge that the philosophers of this School undoubtedly were indebted to both Buddhism and Taoism. In fact, as Richard Wilhelm has pointed out, the assimilation of Buddhism in China was only made possible by amalgamation with Confucianism and Taoism, an intellectual achievement that stands to the credit of Neo-Confucianism.

It should here be mentioned that Su Shih found himself in opposition to much of the teaching of this School. Rival Schools were formed, one of which was known as the Su School, founded by Su Hsün who was joined by his two sons, Su Shih and Su Chê.

Though united in their opposition to the reforms of Wang An-shih, these schools differed fundamentally in their interpretation of the Classics. It is of interest, therefore, to note that, as stated above, the representatives of the Sung School—notably Chu Hsi himself—were at one time or another devotees of Buddhism and Taoism. "While the springs of the Sung Philosophy are to be found in the Classics, the stream was fed by affluents of widely different origin," the very metaphor employed by Su to express the sources of his inspiration—an inexhaustible spring whose waters follow many courses. Indeed, the similarity of thought inherent in Su Shih and Chu Hsi included Chuang Tzu's unity of nature, "a doctrine which constitutes the very warp and woof of Chu Hsi's philosophy and that of his school. For them man and the universe are one."

This tendency of the different Schools of thought of this period to borrow from Taoism and Buddhism may seem surprising in view of the professed orthodoxy of their teaching. When it is remembered, however, that intellectual life was then mainly concentrated in the followers of Taoism and Buddhism, it will be understood why leaders of religious thought such as Chou Tun-i, a contemporary of Su Shih, turned naturally to those other Schools for their inspiration. It was, in fact, a revolt against tradition and literary pedantry, a revolt in which Su took his full share, and which he directed not only against the School of professional painters but also against the new emphasis on technique in the poetry of the Sung dynasty, which distinguished it from the purely natural beauty of T'ang poetry.

We may here give a short description of the views held by the Sung School of philosophers, and of Su's arguments with that School as expressed through the Su School.

The dualistic conception of the world reached maturity in the Sung dynasty. In this respect, it should be noted that both the Taoist and Sung systems of philosophy agreed on the question of cosmic evolution, *viz.,* Heaven, Earth and Man; and in both systems the terms "heaven" and "earth" were intimately associated with the terms "spirit" and "matter." There was, however, during this period a definite renaissance of philosophy and the sciences. Nevertheless, the Sung scholars cannot be said to have produced anything quite new. Rather they rejuvenated Confucianism and, in their speculations on the philosophy of Nature, they developed old ideas about the origin of the universe.

The *Book of Changes* played an important part in formulating and developing the ideas of the Sung Schools. The *Supreme Ultimate* and the *Two Modes* of the Sung Philosophy, for instance, had their origin in a passage from this ancient work, while the theory of the *Five Elements* also held a prominent place in the disquisitions of those Schools. We know, too, that the Sung philosophers believed in the destruction of the world followed by a reconstruction, a process which would be repeated at regular periods.

Now Su Shih held similar views in his conception of the universe. But he differed fundamentally from the Sung School in the interpretation of the Classics. The principle point of difference concerned the exact meaning of the terms "Nature" and "Decree". Influenced by Buddhist and Taoist theories, the Su School maintained that "Nature itself is pre-existent and eternal, an empty shell, as it were, to be received by man as the receptacle for those four ethical principles which become his own by a voluntary acceptance." The School differed, too, in the interpretation of Tzu Ssu's dictum in the *Doctrine of the Mean,* on which Chu Hsi's doctrine was, afterwards, largely based, *viz.,* "the Decree of Heaven is what is termed our Nature." This term [decree], the Su School argued, "was merely a name borrowed by the sages to represent a certain phase in the Evolution of the Nature which had no substantive existence in itself."

In his work, Chu Hsi accuses the Su School of falling into the erroneous teachings of the Buddhists, and exhorts them to examine more thoroughly the Classics, including the *Yi Ching,* the *Book of History,* the *Odes,* the *Doctrine of the Mean,* and *Mencius.*

It is not my intention to explore more deeply the philosophical controversies of this period, the devious channels of which the student may seek for himself in the works of Chu Hsi and of the later commentators, both Chinese and foreign, of the Sung Schools of Philosophy. Suffice it to say that the zest of appreciation for study, and the zeal for the past and for new interpretations of that past, were woven into the fabric of the spirit of the time.

The interest displayed in the bronzes of antiquity was

reflected in the interest of these men, like Su Shih, in painting, calligraphy, and poetry—appreciation of the accepted past tempered by an intent eagerness to interpret that past through study.

We have seen that Su was a rebel against the formal restrictions which played such an important part in the poetry of the Sung dynasty. He rebelled, too, against "form" in the art of painting, as we perceive in the theories expressed by him as an art-critic, and as an Ink-painter, the chief characteristic of which School was that it set itself above "form." "For the ink-painter, external form was an impediment to true artistic expression. . . . On the one hand, the ink-painter destroyed the established and usual forms, while, on the other, he built up a new and original world. He created, unusual and self-willed, and ranged himself against the phenomenal forms of the real world (Erscheinungsformen der realen Welt)." How is this revolt against convention manifested in Su's written works?

Waley has described his poetry as "almost wholly a patchwork of earlier poems," adding that "he hardly wrote a poem which does not contain a phrase (sometimes a whole line) borrowed from Po Chü-i, for whom in his critical writings he expresses boundless admiration" [in *170 Chinese Poems*].

A careful examination of the works of Su Tung-p'o—especially of his *fu*—will show that this statement is, to say the least, rather too sweeping in its condemnation. It would be idle to contend that the poet did not borrow from the Masters of the T'ang dynasty (he quotes often from the poetry of Tu Fu, Li T'ai-po and Han Yü, as well as of Po Chü-i), but should he be condemned for so doing? Rebel against convention though he was, he did not hesitate to employ the words or phrases of these poets whose works he admired. Su is too great a genius to be relegated to the position of a minor poet on this account, and his very genius prevented him from being too scrupulous in his grammar or his references, so that his quotations are not always accurate in their rendering. Nevertheless, he has created anew, and poetry becomes, in this Master's hands, a mosaic of beauty. The effect is flowing and harmonious. One is reminded of the saying of the Lord Krishna, "I am the thread that runs through all these different ideas, and each one is a pearl." The pearls were the thoughts gleaned from others; the thread the Master's touch. And the effect—a necklace of perfectly matched pearls, lovely to behold. Su Shih seems to recreate his borrowed phrases, giving them a new vitality and an added lustre.

If Su found himself fettered by convention in his poems, then perhaps he saw a means of escape in his *fu,* which did not bind him to so rigid a law of metre or of formal restrictions. Indeed, one feels that the poet recognized in the *fu* a channel through which inspiration could find its easiest expression, inspiration that welled from the spring of Nature herself.

Nor can this inspiration be said to have been derived wholly from the wine-cup. Su deliberately exaggerates the importance that wine played in his life, but he had his tongue in his cheek! The Ink-painters of the Sung dynasty were free from decadence, and Su was one of the foremost exponents of this School of painting. For, while it cannot be denied that he created when he had "taken of the wine," that state should not be confused with sordid drunkenness. "Wine," he writes, "is the Decree in the life of man." But he did not permit it to deaden his senses; always could he retain that clarity of mind that characterises all his writings. "Though inwardly I remain unblemished, outwardly I surrender to the fruit of the vine," for thus could he find *Tao*. He describes how that he would drink not more than five cups the whole day, how that no one drank so little as he did, but it pleased him to see others drinking. When a friend visited him, he would slowly raise his cup and drink; thus could he approach his friend in an exalted mood. He never drank to excess, though he tells how he would often set the cup to his lips. Sometimes, indeed, he fell asleep in his seat and his acquaintances imagined that he was drunk. But he emphasises the fact that his thoughts remained perfectly lucid.

"All my friends," he wrote, "encourage me to drink wine to excess, but I listen not. For who would be such a fool as to do so? Except perhaps the man who cannot realize that the attributes of a gentleman are not in keeping with a drunken stupor!" And yet Su obviously found wine an aid to his inspiration. For, like Ou-yang Hsiu, he regarded the source of his drunkenness "not in the wine that he drank, but among the mountains and streams." Wine was but the means to the attainment of joy in landscape which was the "work of the heart." Encouraged by it, he was able to soar to untold heights of poesy and imagination.

> How much have I already drunk to-day?
> Ah! I feel I can escape the fetters of mortality.
> I fling away my staff and rise.
> Away with all your cares and worries, lads!
> I soar over running deer on mountain peaks,
> And join the leaping monkeys on overhanging
> cliffs.
> Thence do I plunge into the billowing clouds of
> a vast ocean,
> Heaven in tumult!

In another *fu* he praises the wonderful properties of wine which could exalt him above the common-place things of the world,

> For now may I wash the cup and taste the wine,
> Ridding myself of the numb obstinacy
> Of my loins and legs.
> Forsooth! I feel I can swallow three rivers in
> one gulp,
> And gobble up the spirits and demons
> Of fish and dragon!
> In my drunken slumber, dreams come in riotous
> confusion.

Wine he compares to "a maid unsullied by the world." It is "pure as a babe that has not yet smiled."

At Prince Wang's court: Su Shih is second from left.

Like the warmth of spring is the abundance of its flavour,
Like the winds of autumn is the chill of its breadth. . . .
Just a little wine I sipped—only a drop,
And see how drunk I am!
I roam beyond the limits of mortality,
My eyes fixed in unseeing gaze.
To return once more to the realities of this world,
And lo! All things do themselves unfold!

Commenting on this trait in Su's character, Ku Teng says, "Su, where drink is concerned is no drunkard; but where enjoyment is concerned, then he is the drinker." For he recognized that through wine could perfection be attained, and therein was in agreement with Po Chü-i.

Su Shih was not merely an interested scholar searching into the truths of Buddhism and Taoism. He went further in his studies of these religions, for we know that he actually practised the art of the Taoist, and the many quotations he gives in his writings taken from Buddhist and Taoist works show a vast and intimate knowledge of those works.

In one poem he describes in beautiful language the inner contemplation as practised by a Buddhist devotee:

He closed his eyes in contemplation,
His mind becoming as a still deep pool.
And in the pool's reflection he could see
That all things were an empty dream.

His mistress, Chao Yün, a girl who was his companion for twenty-three years, died in the Buddhist faith. In a poem written on her death and that of her baby son, Su Shih refers to the *Small Conveyance* for her far journey across the Sānsara to the Shores of Nirvâna.

In his preface to this poem, he records her last words as she passed away, words taken from the *Diamond Sûtra*:

Like a dream, like a vision, like a bubble,
Like a shadow, like dew, like lightning.

Always does Su refer to the evanescence of creation, and elsewhere he asks his reader to remember that "life is but a bubble, a shadow," in which the years and scenes decay in the twinkling of an eye; fleeting "as a cherry which drops through the hand like a silken thread; or as the sun which crosses the vision like an arrow." It is transient as "the morning and evening of a day"; ephemeral as "a wave that is born only to die again."

And yet, "I believe in the Elixir of the Winged Immortals," he wrote, and he recognized that *Tao* could be found in all places, however strange; that, to the sincere seeker, indeed, the Truth may be near at hand, even as the Elixir of Life was found to have sprouted spontaneously within the walls of the palace of the Emperor Wu. In his poem, ***The Palace of the Grotto of Mists,*** Su reveals how he found the Secret Elixir hidden away amongst the mountains, an abode of beauty:

> And yet men search the Life Elixir
> To preserve with bitterness the looks of youth!

Again, in his *fu,* ***A Draught of Sesamum,*** the poet speaks of his search for this Elixir:

> It is Immortality, the Aim of *Tao.*
> The Divine Elixir, like the Islands of the Blest,
> Affords you shelter. . . .
> Perfect *Yang*—powerfully active,
> Springing from Earth;
> Perfect *Yin*—majestically passive,
> Ascending to Heaven.

Su Shih clearly saw that more roads than one led to his goal, and he did not hesitate to walk those roads. His comparison of himself (when exiled to Hainan in the year 1098) with an ant marooned on a grain floating in a bowl of water has been quoted in the notes to the ***Red Cliff*** in this book. Despairing of regaining dry land, he suddenly discovers that the water has dried up. "I thought," he wrote, "that I should never meet you again. How could I know that, in the winking of an eye, roads would thus open up in all directions? When I think of this, I can only laugh."

The roads he saw before him were those of Confucianism, Taoism, and Buddhism, the three life-conceptions (*Lebensauffassungen*) which he made into one whole, in which he found *Tao,* and through which his whole idea of life was centred in one art. To such a man and philosopher, calamity or poverty were negligible, were incidents of no real importance in life.

Through them and through self-denial, he wrote, "one may attain to perfect Love." "What is Poverty?" he asks elsewhere. "Life in this world is just the bending and the straightening of an elbow!" He regarded penury, in fact, as a necessary preparation for the creation of true poetry; for, only a poor man—a man who had no need of money—could find *Tao* in all creation. "Poetry does not impoverish man," he wrote; "but it takes a poor man to create a finished poem." Mere worldly fame was not, he considered, a subject worthy of discussion. But the study and undersanding of *Tao*—-this was a matter for deep satisfaction.

Su, indeed, may be called an artist in the truest sense of the word, for to him art was life and life was art. In them both was to be found the rhythm of Nature, and in Nature could be found the Truth; hidden perhaps from the dogmatist and bigot, but visible to him who sought for it "in the strange and lonely places."

"In my old age," he wrote in the year 1079, "I think I shall buy some land overlooking the waters of the river Ssu, so that I can gaze toward Ling Pi in the South and listen to the confused crowing of the cocks and the barking of the dogs. With my kerchief and my staff, and wearing my sandals, I shall visit Chang's garden at all times and seasons, and pass the hours in leisurely companionship with his children's children."

With Renan, Su Shih could say that "la Verité consiste dans les nuances."

Burton Watson (essay date 1965)

SOURCE: An Introduction to *Su Tung-P'o: Selections from a Sung Dynasty Poet,* translated by Burton Watson, Columbia University Press, 1965, pp. 3-16.

[*Watson is a scholar and translator of Chinese and Japanese literature whose numerous publications include* Early Chinese Literature *(1962) and* Great Historical Figures of Japan *(1978). Here, he presents an overview of Su's life and works, touching on his style and the Buddhist and Taoist influences in his poetry.*]

Culturally, the Sung period was one of the great ages of Chinese history. The dynasty, which lasted from 960 to 1279, faced powerful enemies abroad: the Liao, a Khitan state in the northeast; a Tangut state called Hsi-hsia in the northwest; and later the Jurchen Tungus and Mongols. Militarily too weak to overpower these menacing neighbors, it was forced to buy peace with heavy tribute, at the same time maintaining costly border defenses in case of duplicity. Internally this hardbought peace was put to good use. The empire was ruled by a strong central government whose elaborate bureaucracy functioned, at least until the fiscal strain of national defense became intolerable, with considerable efficiency. Cities grew in size, trade flourished, and education, encouraged by the civil service examination system and spread through government schools and private academies, reached a larger number of people than ever before. New philosophical systems evolved, voluminous histories and encyclopedias were compiled, and painting and porcelain reached their highest level of development.

In comparison with the preceding centuries, the Sung period was also strikingly modern in character. By Sung times the Chinese had gotten up off the floor and were sitting on chairs, contraptions that came in from the west with Buddhism and spread slowly throughout Chinese society; they were reading printed books, drinking tea, carrying on at least part of their monetary transactions with paper money, and experimenting with explosive weapons. Many of them lived in large cities—the main Sung capital, K'ai-feng, was almost certainly the largest city in the world at that time—and traveled freely about the empire by boat, horse, carriage, or palanquin over an elaborate system of roads and waterways. In their way of life, their values, and their interests, the Sung people were in many respects far closer to modern Western man than our European ancestors of the same period.

This perhaps explains why so much of their poetry reads like the product of our own time. Less intense and less brilliant than that of the T'ang, it is broader in scope and of greater philosophic depth and complexity. Whereas earlier poets had regarded certain themes as intrinsically outside the pale of poetry, the Sung poets tried their hand at every subject imaginable, from iron mines to body lice. Where T'ang poets were content to employ one perfect and profoundly suggestive metaphor, Sung poets piled up metaphors until they were satisfied they had said all they wanted to say—and, as the enormous volume of their work (estimated at several hundred thousand extant poems) suggests, they had a great deal to say. Poetry was for the Sung gentleman, even more than for his predecessor in the T'ang, a part of everyday life, a normal medium for expressing his thoughts and feelings on any subject he chose.

The work of Su Shih, the greatest of the Sung poets, more commonly known by his literary name, Su Tung-p'o, well illustrates these qualities. He was born in 1037 in Meishan, a town situated at the foot of Mount Omei in present-day Szechwan Province. His remote family background is uncertain, though there is reason to believe that his people were connected with the local weaving industry. His grandfather was illiterate, and his father, Su Hsün, did not begin serious literary studies until he was in his late twenties, though his father's older brother passed the civil service examination and became an official. His mother was from a prominent family, an educated woman and a devout Buddhist, and undoubtedly had a great influence upon her son's development. He had only one brother, Su Ch'e or Su Tzu-yu, three years younger than himself.

Su Tung-p'o and his brother were educated by their parents and at a private school in the neighborhood run by a Taoist priest, and by 1056 they felt confident enough to go to K'aifeng to take the government civil service examinations. Their father had taken them earlier and failed, but he accompanied his sons to the capital. The boys passed the first examination with distinction, and in the following year passed the second, receiving the *chin-shih* degree. At the same time Su Hsün won private recognition of his literary ability from prominent scholars in the capital.

Upon the death of their mother in 1057, the sons returned with their father to Szechwan to observe the customary three-year mourning period, actually a period of twenty-seven months. The three journeyed to the capital again in 1060, where Su Hsün received an official appointment and his sons, after passing the special examination the following year, were assigned to posts in the provinces. Thus the so-called Three sus, father and sons, were launched on the careers that would make their names famous in Chinese literary and political history.

I will not trace here all the moves in the subsequent career of the poet; it would be tedious and confusing. . . .

An excerpt from a letter from Su Shih to Shieh Minshih

I have looked over your poems and prose. In general, writing should be like sailing clouds and flowing water. It has no definite [required] form. It goes where it has to go and stops where it cannot but stop. One has thus a natural style, with all its wayward charms. Confucius said, "If a statement is not beautiful, it will not be read far and wide." Again he said, "In writing, all one asks is successful expression of an idea." One may think that if a statement merely aims at expressing one's thoughts, it will not be beautiful. That is not true. It is not easy to express exactly a fugitive idea or a passing thought. First of all, it is difficult to see and appreciate it in one's mind and heart—not one in a million can do it—and even harder to express it by writing or by word of mouth. When this is done, that thought or idea is given proper expression, and when one can do this, one can do anything with writing. Yang Shiung (53 B.C.-A.D. 18) loved to dress up his superficial ideas in archaic, abstruse language. For if he said clearly what he thought, it would be shown to be something everybody knew already. . . . These are examples of his superficiality. This is something about writing which can be spoken about only to those who really understand. I mention this merely in passing. Ouyang Shiu (1007-1072) said that writing is like gold or jade, with a definite market price for a certain quality. Literary reputation is not something which can be made or minimized by someone's expressed opinion.

Su Tungpo, in The Importance of Understanding: Translations from the Chinese, *by Lin Yutang, The World Publishing Company, 1960.*

Instead I will list the principal facts in outline:

1061-65 Su Tung-p'o served as assistant magistrate in Shensi.

1065 Returned to the capital.

1066 Su Hsün died. His sons accompanied the body home to Szechwan and observed the mourning period. This was their last trip home.

1068 The two brothers occupied posts in the capital.

1071-79 Out of favor with the ruling clique in the capital, Su Tung-p'o moved about in a series of provincial posts. In the seventh month of 1079, he was arrested on charges of slandering the emperor, imprisoned in the capital, released, and banished to Huang-chou.

The last entry demands explanation. The dynasty's administrative and fiscal system was functioning badly because of the heavy strain of tribute and defense expenditures, and most thinking men of the time, including Su Tung-p'o and his father, agreed that reforms were needed. Attempts along this line had been made earlier, and when a forceful new statesman named Wang An-shih (1021-86) came to prominence in 1069, he began, with the full support of the ruler, Emperor Shen-tsung, a vigorous reform program known as the "New Laws." Just what these new laws were need not concern us here, but they were sufficiently radical to offend the more conservative elements in the government and, perhaps more from faulty administration than from the provisions of the laws themselves, caused considerable hardship in the provinces. Su Tung-p'o, living in the provinces, could see the hardship at first hand, and became more and more outspoken in his criticisms, until his enemies in the capital could no longer tolerate him. Using statements in his own poems as evidence, they tried him on charges of slander and effected what amounted to banishment by assigning him an insignificant post in the region of Huang-chou on the north bank of the Yangtze in central China. I would like to note, however, that by this time Wang An-shih, to whom is usually assigned all the blame for the failures and abuses of the reform program, was out of political life and living in retirement at Nanking. However much Su may have disagreed with Wang's political opinions, he seems to have borne no grudge against Wang himself, but on the contrary exchanged poems with him and went out of his way to visit him in later years. Political feelings ran high, but these were highly civilized men. Under the Sung, Su Tung-p'o and those who thought like him suffered the inconvenience and disgrace of banishment. Under almost any earlier dynasty they would very likely have lost their heads.

1080-84 Exiled to Huang-chou.

1085 Returned to the capital and high political office after the overthrow of the "New Laws" party.

1086-93 Held various posts in the capital and the provinces.

1094 Banished a second time with the return of the "New Laws" party to power. Ordered to proceed to Hui-chou in Kwangtung, east of present-day Canton.

1097 Ordered even father south to the island of Hainan.

1100 Permitted to return to the mainland; restored to favor and office.

1101 Became ill and died at Ch'ang-chou in Chekiang.

Two facts about the poet's life will be apparent from this outline. One is that he spent his entire adult years moving about from place to place, from office to office, which is why so much of his poetry deals with journeys. This was the ordinary life of a Chinese bureaucrat. After a man had entered the administration, usually by way of the civil service examinations, he was assigned to a post, sometimes in the capital but more often in the provinces. In the Sung period it was usual for an official to remain at a particular provincial post no longer than three years—long enough to learn what he needed to know about the region, but not so long that he would begin to identify himself too closely with local interests. Hence a man like Su Tung-p'o was destined to pick up his family and move, say good-by to old friends and start out to make new ones, at least every three years and sometimes oftener. The life of a high provincial official was not particularly difficult, his duties were hardly taxing, and in normal times at least his income was sufficient; but he was never permitted to stay in one place long enough to put down roots. Rootless wandering is said to be a characteristic of present-day Americans, but it is hard to think of any group in America, except perhaps migratory laborers, who could match the old-style Chinese official on this score.

Second, if Su Tung-p'o had been inclined toward bitterness, he had plenty of cause for it. Not only was he obliged by the bureaucratic system to spend almost all his life in separation from his homeland and the one person he felt closest to, his brother Tzu-yu; he was twice forced by political shifts into exile, the second time at an advanced age and to the torrid southernmost extremity of the empire. These periods of banishment not only brought disgrace and the frustration of all his political ambitions, but often involved real physical hardship. The surprising thing is that if he felt bitter or sorry for himself he seldom shows it in his poems. He writes occasionally in a mood of depression or despair; the infrequency of meetings with his brother is a theme that always brings out a strain of sadness. But he seems to have possessed an irrepressible interest in life, an engagement with his fellow men and his surroundings that made it impossible for him to brood for long. Far from being bitter, he is actually one of the most cheerful of the great Chinese poets.

He was not only a first-class poet and prose writer, but a distinguished painter and calligrapher as well, and he saw with a painter's eye. His descriptive passages are not limited to the conventional props and landscapes of earlier poetry, but depict all kinds of scene down to the most commonplace; within the confines of Chinese verse form, they are masterpieces of precision and detail. He tells the reader exactly what flowers are blooming, exactly what crops are growing in the fields, just what the weather is like and what people are doing. When later Chinese critics sometimes complained that his poetry lacks suggestiveness, it was probably this very fullness and precision they were objecting to.

He was also, like most major Sung poets, a philosopher. Although he has left no systematic exposition of his ideas, repeatedly he breaks into the descriptive passages of his poems with philosophical meditation. By Sung times, the sea of faith that had been Chinese Buddhism at its height was receding, and native Confucian ways of thought, oriented about the family and the state and strongly rational and humanistic, were beginning to reassert themselves. Su's own philosophy represents a combination of Confucian and Buddhist ideas, with a large mixture of philosophical Taoism.

The Confucian side of his thinking is less apparent in his poetry than in his political papers and his life as a whole—his strong family devotion, the fact that he chose a career in politics, the fearlessness with which he spoke out against abuses in government, the numerous public works for the benefit of the local inhabitants that he undertook at his various provincial posts. In his poetry it is rather the Buddhist and Taoist aspects of his thinking that find expression. His mother, it will be recalled, was a devout Buddhist. He himself took considerable interest in Buddhist literature and doctrine, and spent much time visiting temples in the areas where he was assigned. After his dismissal from office and banishment to Huang-chou in 1080 this interest deepened; and the influence of Buddhist thought, particularly that of the Zen sect, the most active and intellectual of the Buddhist schools at this time, is apparent in his writings of this period. It was also at this time that he began to call himself Tung-p'o chü-shih or "The Layman of Eastern Slope," after the plot of land he farmed. From this title his literary name Tung-p'o derives.

The influence of Taoism is most clearly seen in his sensitivity to the natural world. He was fascinated by stories of immortal spirits, elixirs of long life, and other popular lore, and good-naturedly took part in prayers for rain and similar ceremonies of the folk religion, though the rational Confucian side of his nature told him there was no basis for such acts or beliefs. And yet he repeatedly refers to a supernatural force which he calls "The Creator," a word taken from the works of Chuang Tzu, and which he often describes in terms of a child. It is a force which moves throughout the natural world, childlike in its lack of thought or plan, yet capable of influencing the destinies of all beings in the universe. And when man learns to be equally free of willfulness and to join in the Creator's game, then everything in the natural world will become his toy. It is no accident that Su in his descriptions of nature makes far freer use of personification and pathetic fallacy than any of his predecessors.

Su experimented with nearly every form in traditional Chinese literature. . . . Most of the poems I have translated are in the *shih* form, the standard form of classical Chinese poetry, characterized generally by lines of equal length and, with rare exceptions, an even number of lines. Enjambment is rare; there is almost always a pause at the end of each line. Poems in this form fall into two groups: those in the so-called old style, which allows occasional lines of irregular length and does not require any set tonal pattern within the lines; and those in the "modern style," which demands lines of equal length and sometimes of fixed number, and requires an elaborate internal tonal pattern the rules of which are too complex to go into here. Both forms employ end rhyme; sometimes the same rhyme is used throughout a single poem, sometimes in longer poems it changes at points where the poem shifts direction. Su composed in both styles, in most cases using a 5-character or a 7-character line.

Poetry was part of the everyday social life of an educated man in China, and it was customary for friends and acquaintances to exchange poems on various occasions or to get together and compose poems on a particular theme. Sometimes they assigned rhymes to each other; sometimes they composed poems employing the same rhyme as that of a friend's poem to which they were responding, occasionally (a real tour de force) using not only the same rhyme, but the very same rhyme words in the same order as those of the original poem. Su mentions all these practices in the introductions to his poems; he even carried the game a step farther by composing poems to the same rhymes as those of a poet of the distant past, T'ao Yüan-ming (365-427).

Nearly all the poems [I have translated] are descriptions of actual occurrences in the poet's life or scenes he had encountered. A few, however, belong to a genre very popular among Chinese poets: that of the poem written to accompany a painting, describing not an actual landscape but a pictured one. Because of their artificial and secondhand nature such poems have seldom appealed to me, but Su, as so often with other forms, has succeeded in giving life even to this rather stilted genre, and I have therefore included several poems of this type.

The second poetic form represented in my selection is the *tz'u,* which employs lines of unequal length but follows a set line, rhyme, and tonal pattern. The *tz'u* were originally songwords written to accompany tunes that came in from Central Asia. It became the custom to write numerous lyrics to fit a single tune, so that in time a number of fixed metrical patterns were established, each known by the name of the tune it fitted. In late T'ang and Five Dynasties times, when the genre was new, these *tz'u* usually dealt with mildly erotic themes and were considered somewhat less respectable than the *shih,* but by Sung times the situation was changing. Su Tung-p'o, one of the acknowledged masters of the *tz'u* form, employed it to treat many of the same themes he treated in his *shih.* He thus opened up new areas of expression for the *tz'u,* though the people of his day, who did not always appreciate this fact, complained that his *tz'u* were actually *shih* in disguise. They also complained that his *tz'u* were difficult to sing, but since the tunes of the *tz'u* were lost long ago, we cannot tell just what they meant by this. . . .

The third poetic form is represented by Su's two famous *fu* or prose poems on the Red Cliff. The *fu* form is old in Chinese literature and before Sung times it was employed usually for lengthy descriptive pieces, often of a fantastic nature, or briefer evocations of emotional states. It is most often a mixture of prose passages and rhymed sections, the latter in strongly rhythmical patterns with elaborate use of parallelism. Su employs a variation of the form known as *wen fu* or "prose *fu,"* which is extremely loose in structure and makes only sparing use of rhyme and parallelism. Even so, it retains a sensuousness of language and rhythmical swing that set it off from pure prose.

Su wrote rapidly and, unlike many of his contemporaries, did not often go back to polish and rewrite. Some 2,400 poems of his have been preserved, about 90 percent of which can be dated. Many of them were printed and published during his lifetime, and though for political reasons his works were banned for a while after his death, the ban was later lifted and his writings circulated freely and widely. They have thus come down to us in excellent condition. . . .

The Chinese literary tradition, particularly in poetry, grew by feeding upon itself, and it is only natural that Su's poetry should contain echoes of earlier works, phrases and lines which he borrowed from his predecessors and adapted to his own use. Chinese commentators make it their job to point out such borrowings, and a glance at their notes on his poetry is apt to give the impression that his language is unduly bookish and derivative. This is not so. When he wrote, Chinese poetry already had a history of some fifteen hundred years, and he could hardly have avoided repeating the usages of the past without straining for novelty at every turn. A good poet was expected to draw aptly and skillfully upon the works of his predecessors, thereby adding a richness of association to his diction. But a great one had to have such complete mastery of the tradition that he could at the same time express his own thoughts freely and naturally, and could advance and enrich the tradition in some way, adding new depth and nuance. This Su Tung-p'o did. . . . It is an indication of Su's greatness. . . . that. . . . allusions and associations constitute only a minor part of the interest of his poetry, and that without any knowledge of them his works can still be read with enjoyment and profit. . . .

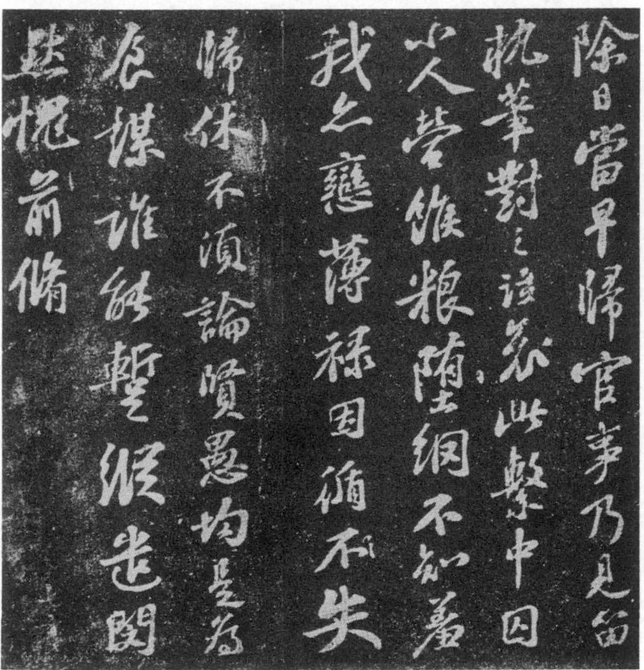

A Sung rubbing taken from a stone inscription of a poem Su Shih wrote on New Year's Eve, 1071.

Andrew L. March (essay date 1966)

SOURCE: "Self and Landscape in Su Shih," *Journal of the American Oriental Society,* Vol. 86, 1966, pp. 377-96.

[*March is a professor of geology, anthropology, and China humanities who has written many journal articles and* The Idea of China: Myth and Theory in Geographic Thought *(1974). In the following excerpt, he explores the connection between Su's concept of art, his understanding of landscape, and his striving to perfect himself according to the principles of the Tao.*]

Su Shih's Fertile and energetic mind was more poetic than discursive, and the weight of his ideas is often carried by images appealing to experience rather than by rational argument. Landscape images in particular form a coherent pattern in his writings, and the experience of landscape seems central to his artistic, ethical, and social conceptions of self.

By landscape I mean part of what we often call nature, but the trouble with nature is that the word has far too many other senses (as in human nature, God and nature, mother nature) and hence is uncontrollably suggestive and vague. Landscape, as in the terms landscape painting and landscape poetry, is somewhat sharper and more manageable. It means here not any class of objects which could be defined by enumeration, but, like certain geographical terms (resource, boundary, route), one kind of human interpretation of environment. This interpretation selects the parts of the world (on the scale of our ordinary perceptions) which are relatively unsocialized: where there is relatively little sign of man, and where occupance, especially by men in groups, is relatively sparse. The most prominent objects are non-human ones—rocks, trees, hills, streams. The strongest contrast is with the densely socialized space of cities, and cities have probably been a prerequisite for the emergence of landscape as a distinct category of experience.

There is no Chinese term quite like landscape. Typical expressions are "hills (mountains) and waters," "river and hill," "hills, streams, herbs, trees," or even "hills, streams, herbs, trees, birds, beasts, fish, reptiles, insects"—selective generic lists of landscape's most common elements. Though often not referring to any specific assemblage, these terms are concrete and give a sharp if composite image unlike that conveyed by the word nature. The key criterion, however, is still that of landscape: these things are non-human and are relatively undetermined by society.

Landscape, Su Shih felt, is not located and timed like social things, but is everywhere and always essentially the same. As the human mind experiences landscape, these qualities are translated into detachment and spontaneity; the social self, and the death that goes with it, appear superfluous and illusory. Su Shih casts these ideas especially, though not exclusively, in an elaborate symbolism of water, or fluid in general.

Landscape, and the experience of landscape, are placeless: they have no specific spatial focus or boundary. Describing a painting *Misty Yangtze and Folded Hills,* Su writes:

> Above the river, heavy on the heart, thousand-fold hills:
> Layers of green floating in the sky like mist.
> Mountains? clouds? too far away to tell
> Till clouds part, mist scatters, on mountains that remain.
> Then I see, in gorge cliffs, black-green clefts
> Where a hundred waterfalls leap from the sky,
> Threading woods, tangling rocks, lost and seen again,
> Falling to valley mouths to feed swift streams.
> Where the river broadens, mountains part, foothill forests end,
> A small bridge, a country store set against the slope:
> Now and then travelers pass beyond tall trees;
> A fishing boat—one speck where the river swallows the sky. . . .

As he describes it, the painting (evidently a horizontal scroll) creates a space without center or edge, through which in imagination the viewer can move freely, unhampered by scientific perspective, and can stop here and there to share in what is happening. Su continues, after the part quoted above, with a return in thought to real landscapes he has seen—the painting is something continuous with the real world, not abstracted from or opposed to it. Landscape itself goes on and on like an endless scroll and has no boundaries or regularly defined outlines:

> About painting, I have said that people, birds and animals, buildings, and vessels all have set shapes; as for hills, rocks, bamboos, trees, water, waves, mist, and clouds, although they have no set shapes, they do have set principles. Everyone knows when the set shape is missing, but even those versed in painting cannot all tell when the set principle is not there. So anyone who dishonestly makes a reputation in painting must do it in genres without set shapes. However, when a set shape is missed, that is all there is to it—the painting as a whole is not hurt. But if the set principles are not there, the whole thing is spoiled: since the shapes are not set, great care must be taken with the principles. There are artisans who can get the shapes exact, but as for the principles, only highly educated and gifted men can see them. . . .

As the mind, guided only by these "principles," expands into indefinite spaces, it seems to lose the sense of its own uniqueness among the landscape things.

> **"Crossing at Seven Li Shallows"**
>
> A boat, light as a leaf
> Two oars frighten wild geese.
> Water reflects the clear sky, lucid waves are smooth.
> Fish wriggle in the weedy mirror
> Herons dot misty spits.
> Across the sand brook, swift
> The frost brook, cold
> The moon brook, bright.
>
> Layer upon layer, like a painting
> Bend after bend, like a screen.
> Remember empty old Yen Ling long ago.
> 'Lord,' 'Minister'—a dream;
> Now, of old: vain fames.
> Only, the far hills are long
> The cloud hills tumbled
> The dawn hills green.

"Like a painting" this space is boundless (not infinite): "layer upon layer," "bend after bend," "far hills," "cloud hills"; and it is not centered so that anything would seem to point at the poet. Especially the last three lines of each stanza, with their various aspects of brook and hill, exclude any focus on a particular self or a particular spot. Vague horizons, and blurred focus connoting loss of the self's uniqueness are also in this poem (which has no "I" in the original):

> Drunk, abob in a light boat
> Letting it drift, into the thick of the flowers
> Fooled by the sensory world
> I hadn't meant to stop in here.
>
> Far misty water
> Thousand miles' slanted evening sunlight
> Numberless hills
> Riot of red like rain
> I don't remember how I came.

There is the same feeling of space in imagery expressing Su's experience as an official who never stayed more than a few years or months in one place, adrift like the unrooted duckweed:

> . . . Man's life goes everywhere, duckweed drifting. . . .
> . . . When will this life's floating and drifting cease?

Whatever other possibilities such a feeling of space may hold, to Su the point was that all landscapes, in experience, are essentially the same, and that therefore one need have no attachment to particular landscapes.

> Eighty some paces below Lin-kao House [where he was staying] is the Great River [Yangtze]. Half of it is meltwater from the snows of O-mei [near his birth-

> place in Szechuan], and I use it for cooking, drinking, and washing. What need to go back home? River and hill, wind and moon really have no set owner: the man of leisure owns them. . . .
>
> On the twelfth night of the tenth moon of the sixth year of Yuanfeng [1083], I had undressed and was going to bed, when the moonlight entered my door, and I got up, happy of heart. There was no one to share this happiness with me, so I walked over to the Changtien Temple to look for Huaimin. He, too, had not yet gone to bed, and we paced about in the garden. It looked like a transparent pool with the shadows of bamboos and pine trees cast by the moonlight. Isn't there a moon every night? And aren't there bamboos and pine trees everywhere? But there are few carefree [lit., leisurely] people like the two of us.

Like painted ones, real landscapes have "set principles"; if one can appreciate these, then the "set shapes" of particular places and circumstance do not matter. Places are interchangeable, and the self is not limited or determined by place.

> When I stayed at Chia-yu Temple in Hui-chou, once I was walking below Pine Wind House. My feet were tired, and had no strength; I longed to go to bed. I stopped to rest, looked up at the House which was still at treetop level, and said to myself, "How shall I ever get there?" After a time I exclaimed, "Why can't I rest right here?" Then I felt like a hooked fish who suddenly manages to get free. If a person has this insight, then even if two armies are joining in battle, drums sounding like thunder, where to go forward is to die at the hands of the enemy, to go back is to die in the hands of the law—even at a time like that, there is nothing to keep him from deeply resting.

As appears in this last essay, places come to stand for all external circumstances and particular things, a point that Su makes more explicit elsewhere:

> There is nothing that is not worth attending to in some respect; and if a thing is worth attending to it can give delight. There is no need for things to be rare or exceptional, luxurious or perfect. Common rice wine can make one drunk, and ordinary fruits and vegetables can fill one's hunger. Reasoning so, where can I go that I would not have delight? . . . [He argues that if external contingencies are rightly seen, our pleasure and pain need not depend on them. He tells of his transfer from a fine gay place to a poor dull one, and describes how even here he found much to delight him. He has built a terrace to which his brother has given the name "Elevation",] to show that I find delight wherever I go, as I move outside of [attachment to particular] things.

Thus the centerless, always equivalent space of landscape, as he experienced it in his official wanderings, meant to Su that one could and ought to feel unattached to particular places, and indeed independent of all external circumstances.

His landscape time resembles this space in several ways. Even more than the place, the time at which one lives is beyond one's control, and Su was capable of the conventional complaint that he was "born too late." But in the landscape, there is a blurring and an opening up of time as there is of space so that the present instant, like the immediate place, does not have unique importance. In the poem on the **"Misty Yangtze"** painting (above), it is clear that Su does not consider himself to be looking at an instantaneous image, like a photograph. In imagination, he is moving about in time as well as in space; he is wandering here and there as the scroll unwinds, and sharing in the continuing actions of the painted people. Again, in **"Crossing at Seven Li Shallows,"** the scene is not presented as an instantaneous cross-section of time. What is felt as present is present in experience, not necessarily in a given moment of external time. Landscape impressions which, if taken as simultaneous, call up slightly contradictory images, occur together in the poem: clear sky/cloud, mist; dawn/moon. In the second stanza, the expansion outward in space is joined by an expansion backward in a time, which, too, is not infinite but has no definite boundaries. And what is real turns out to be the landscape which does not change, being no different (in "set principles") now from in Yen Ling's day, whereas political concerns, contingent on the historical moment, are "a dream" and "vain" (empty). Landscape is the same at all times, as it is at all places; and if a man emphasizes the sides of himself that he associates with landscape, he can feel as detached from particular moments or periods as from particular places and things.

Landscape time is not empty or abstract, but events in it have a legendary, rather than historical, cast, and its activities are leisurely and spontaneous. We can approach these points through the Rip-van-Winklesque tale of Wang Chih, to which Su alludes in a poem. Wang Chih, who lived at Ch'ü-chou in Chekiang province in the mid Chin dynasty, went into the mountains to cut wood, and came upon a cave in which two young men were playing a game like checkers, or else making music and singing. Chih put down his ax and watched, and they gave him something like a datestone to put in his mouth which made him feel no hunger or thirst. They told him, "You have been here a long time; better go back." He picked up his ax and saw that the handle had all rotted away. Hurrying home, he found that decades (or centuries) had passed, and none of his relatives or friends were left. He went back to the mountains and got the Tao (became immortal); occasionally someone saw him there, and hence the mountain was called Rotten Ax Handle Mountain.

At the beginning of this story, Wang Chih appears as a historical figure in that we know where and when he lived, and there is nothing unusual about his going to cut wood. But when he is in the cave, time for him is not just historical time running at a different rate—it has a quite other quality, so that his trip back to his village and final return to the mountain can no longer be placed in any dynasty. "Long time," "decades," "centuries"—time has vaguely continued to pass, but as it were in a different direction, diverging from history. By calling such events in landscape time legendary, I mean to imply two things:

that they have a popular, little-tradition quality in that they are not precisely dated or verified; and that they do not fit into any continuing scheme of historical development with its plots of before and after, purpose and cause. Here is another example of legend in landscape:

"On the Red Cliff"

The waves of the mighty River flowing eastward
Have swept away the brilliant figures of a thousand
generations.
West of the old fortress,
So people say, is Lord Chou's Red Cliff of the time of
the Three States.
The tumbling rocks thrust into the air;
The roaring surges dash upon the shore,
Rolling into a thousand drifts of snow.
The River and the mountains make a vivid picture—
What a host of heroes once were!
It reminds me of the young Lord then,
When the fair Younger Ch'iao newly married him,
Whose valorous features were shown forth;
With a feather fan and a silken cap,
Amid talking and laughing, he put his enemy's ships
to ashes and smoke.
While my thoughts wander in the country of old,
Romantic persons might smile at my early grey hair.
Ah! life is but like a dream;
With a cup of wine, let me yet pour a libation to the
moon on the River.

The old battle is not seen as history with a plot or a lesson; in the poem, Su cares nothing about its rights and wrongs, or its causes, purposes, or effects. It is dated, but Su is unconcerned whether this is its actual site: "so people say"; "it reminds me"; elsewhere he says that he does not know whether the battle took place here (and in fact it did not).

Su Shih, of course, by no means always saw past events in this legendary light; he had a strong sense of historical time too, as we shall see farther on. Probably it was his very knowledge of history that gave him a realistic appreciation of time's immensity such that, even with the withdrawal of history's ordering scaffold of dynasties, reigns, and years, great depth was left in the landscape's present.

On the scale of immediate human activities, landscape time has a leisurely quality which is also illustrated in the story of Wang Chih. The young men's checkers or music, and Wang Chih's watching, are not an empty idleness, but chronology and duration are irrelevant to them: they are not directed from outside, nor are they controlled by a plan made in the past or a purpose reaching into the future, in contrast to Wang Chih's original intent to cut wood. That leisure is a prerequisite for appreciation of landscape appears in two of the pieces quoted earlier (**"Eighty some paces . . ."** and **"On the twelfth night . . ."**). This is also the time mode of spontaneity—it too is cut off from past and future, and complete in itself.

Landscape time in Su Shih is deeply colored by death. The timelessness of landscape makes an ironic contrast with man's temporary life. Landscape time is all quality, but man sees time also as duration, at the end of a certain quantity of which he must die. But if a person can associate himself with landscape to the point of becoming a part of it (like Wang Chih), perhaps its timelessness can be converted to something like an eternity of duration, and he can escape the death that ordinary social time would have brought him:

> . . . Now Ts'ao Ts'an was a famous official under the Han, and Mr. Ko was his teacher: an eminent man, surely. But the histories do not record his death. Was he not a Perfect Man of old, who got the Tao and did not die? Chiao-hsi on the east borders the sea; to the south it reaches to Chiu-hsien Mountain; in the north it goes to Lao Mountain. In this area there are many noble hermits. If they are heard of, they are not seen; if they are seen, you cannot make them come. For all I know, Mr. Ko comes and goes as one of them. But I am not worthy to have sight of him.
>
> Le-t'ien built a thatched hut on Lu-shan in order to refine the elixir. He had almost accomplished it when his stove and cauldron failed, and the next day a letter arrived appointing him Governor of Chung-chou. By this we may know the impossibility of living in the world and at the same time being free of worldly affairs. . . .

Actually, Su doubted that anyone had ever really become immortal:

> Ever since I reached the age of understanding, I have heard about what people call Taoists, who have the art of prolonging their years, such as Chao Pao-i, Hsü Teng, and Chang Yüan-meng, who all lived to be nearly a hundred. But in the end they died, just like ordinary people. When I came to Huang-chou I heard . . . of an outstanding Different [immortal] man called Chu Yüanching (?); very many high officials honored him as their teacher. But finally he too got sick, and died of a stroke and spasms. He really was an alchemist, though; he left behind some medicines and elixir gold, which were all taken over by the government. I do not know if there really are no Different men in the world, or if there are, but no one sees them; anyhow, these I have mentioned were not such. I wonder if what was anciently recorded of Different men is true or false. Probably they were much the same as these, and people with an interest in strange matters have embellished it.

All these themes—self, space, time, and death—coalesce for Su Shih in the symbol of water. Water fascinated him above all else in the landscape, and he saw it everywhere, in innumerable shapes and forms.

When I first came to the South Sea [to Hainan] and looked all around at the unbroken sky and water, I lamented sorrowfully, "When will I ever be able to depart from this island?" But when I think about it, heaven and earth are in the midst of the waters, the Nine Continents are in the Great Ying Ocean, China is in a smaller ocean—what lives that is not on an island?

This mountain is set in the air.
Milky water fills its stomach,
And where it finds a fissure, comes to view,
Always with its own same taste and smell.
Sometimes it is shallow, sometimes deep,
Square or round, depending on what holds it.
Sometimes it sounds and makes mist;
Sometimes it forms a broken thread.
In places it cries in empty caverns,
Zitherns and lutes amid chinking girdle-stones.
In places it runs in clefts of green rock,
With the writhing gait of dragons and
phoenixes. . . .

Mysterious interconnections and circulations link the earth's waters together in one vast system:

. . . Water travels underground, appearing and disappearing at distances of thousands of li, uninterrupted even by rivers and seas. . . .

Water is a primary and irreducible image, and a highly effective one. I can only add (less effectively) that it stands for something like an undifferentiated, timeless, and selfless essence of the landscape. The individual human self is simply a part of this essence, separated, until death, from the rest, temporarily and precariously *contained* in the body as in a stream channel, a boat, a well, or a jar. This is the meaning, in Su Shih, of the old image that compares man's life to a stream flowing eastwards across China to the sea. Thus he writes, eulogizing a Taoist,

. . . He is a riverful of vernal water flowing
east,
A mighty stream, emptying straight into the
wide sea,
Never flagging till it runs up onto P'eng-lai [the
island of the immortals in the Eastern Sea].

Of himself, he says:

My home is where the [Yangtze] River's water
has its
source;
In my official travels I have followed it right
down
to the sea. . . .

Again, a drifting boat—connoting also detachment from particular places—is a kind of container, holding man apart for a while:

Last year I visited New Hall
After spring wind had melted off the snow;
In the pond, half a punt-pole of water
Along the pond, a thousand feet of willows,
And lovely ladies like blooms of peach and
plum:
Butterflies came into the sleeves of their gowns.
Where is that landscape now? . . . (?)
The years and months cannot be grasped by
thought,
Speedy as a boat loose upon a current.
Pomp and circumstance truly are a dream,
Flourishings and failings go their quiet way.
Only the same old moon
Still shines on a cup of wine,
And must be sorry for one in the boat,
Sitting steady, oblivious of time.

The water-clock (or leak: *lou*), which I give as "time" in the last line, marks the passage of time by a small constant flow of water and so, like our sands of time in the hour-glass, is an image of the measure of human life: time runs out. Su hints that the man in the boat, borne on the waters of time, leaks like a water-clock; here as elsewhere, death means that the separation from the general waters of the world is not maintained, and the individual self is dissipated in their impersonal circulations. Man is more explicitly likened to a water-clock in the **"Inscription for the Lotus Clepsydra at Hsü-chou,"** and to a leaking jar in the **"Notice of 'Hall of Thought,'"** and I shall quote these two essays later in other contexts.

Accordingly, the earth's waters have in them something of men who have died and become as timeless and ubiquitous as the landscape they now belong to. Their presence can be focused anew at particular places and times, contained, here, as in a well or spring.

"Temple Inscription for Han Wen-kung at Ch'ao-chou"

[Han was banished to Ch'ao-chou. Su praises him, and points out that the people here still revere him and sacrifice to his spirit.]

. . . You might say, "He was ten thousand *li* from his country, in exile at Ch'ao-chou. He was here less than a year before he went back. If he has consciousness after his death, it is certain that he has no special regard for Ch'ao-chou." I say, Not so. His spirit is in the world as water is in the ground: there is nowhere one can go where it is not. But only the people of Ch'ao-chou believe in him deeply and think of him to the utmost, "vapors of death bringing sadness" [*Li Chi* 24/26] (?). Your view is as if one were to dig a well and having found water were to say, "Here is the only place that there is water." How could that be right?

"Inscription for Six One Spring"

When Ou-yang Wen-chung was getting old he called himself the Six One Retired Gentleman. When I was made Vice-Administrator at Ch'ien-t'ang, I saw him south of Ju-yin. He said, "Hui-ch'in, a monk of West Lake, is a highly educated man, and good at poetry.

Once I wrote 'Pleasure in the Mountains' in three parts as a present for him. When you have leisure from the affairs of the people, and are at a loss for company among the mountains and lakes, then go and spend some time with Ch'in!"

Three days after I had arrived at my post I visited Ch'in below Ku-shan. He clapped his hands and discussed personalities, and said, "He [Ou-yang] is a man of heaven [has the Tao]. People see him when he temporarily dwells among them, but they do not know that he mounts the clouds and rides the wind, crosses the Five Peaks and bestrides the wide sea. People in these parts are sorry that he never comes. But he has the ends of the earth at his beck and call; there is nowhere he does not reach. No one is fit to possess the beauties of river and mountain, but their rare and lovely, elegant and refined breath is something that good writers constantly use. Thus I say that West Lake is, as it were, just an object on Ou-yang's writing table." Although Ch'in's words were magical and strange, still the principle is quite true.

The next year Ou-yang died, and I wept for him at Ch'in's dwelling. After another eighteen years, I was made Magistrate of Ch'ien-t'ang. Ch'in too had long since undergone his metamorphosis. I visited his old place, and his disciple Erh Chung was there. He had made portraits of Ou-yang and Ch'in and served them as if they were alive. Below the dwelling there had previously been no spring, but a few months before I arrived a spring started behind the lecture hall at the foot of Ku-shan. It welled up and ran over, very clear and sweet. On its site the cliff had been cut away and stones set up to make a building. Erh-chung said to me, "The Teacher heard you were coming, and sent out the spring to ease your fatigue. Is it proper for you to make no answer?" Then I pondered deeply the meaning of the things Ch'in had said long ago, and I named it Six One Spring, and wrote this inscription for it:

"The spring emerged thousands of *li* from him, and eighteen years after his death, and yet it is named Six One. Is this not almost nonsensical? I say: The beneficent influence of a noble man surely does not just reach to five generations and then stop. In the proper hands; it should be able to extend to a hundred generations. I will try to climb Ku-shan with my sons, and look out over Wu and Yüeh, sing 'Pleasure in the Mountains,' and drink this water. Then the residual presence of his noble personality will also perhaps be manifested to them in this spring."

What has become of the problem of death, and the ironic contrast between mortal man and timeless landscape? Evidently the landscape does allow a certain immortality (at least for noble men), but it is of a bitter sort because, whatever residues may be tapped by those coming later, the body is dead and with it the individual self.

But if the fluids can be forced to stay in the body, in defiance of their natural tendency to escape, then, Su felt, the physical body and the separate self need not die at all. So it is argued in the following excerpts from two of his essays on Taoist theories of "nourishing life" (*yang-sheng*). The terminology is that of alchemy, but the elements are used to dramatize the motions of the soul in a manner roughly parallel to psychoanalysis. Dragon, mercury, and water are equivalent, as are tiger, lead, and fire.

"Discourse on Dragon and Tiger (Lead and Mercury)"

All the reasons for men's living and dying proceed from [the trigrams] *k'an* [water] and *li* [fire]. When *k'an* and *li* are joined, there is life; when they are separated, there is death;—this is an ineluctable principle. *Li* is the heart [and mind], *k'an* is the kidneys [and testicles]. What the heart assents to is always right. Even in Chieh [the wicked last emperor of Hsia] and Chih [an ancient bandit] this is so; the reason they behave as they do is simply that they make light of what is within themselves, and emphasize externals, and thus always do things to which the heart would not assent. When the kidneys are strong and overflow, then one has thoughts of desire. Even in Yao [the ancient sage-emperor] and Yen [a favorite disciple of Confucius] this is so; the reason they behave as they do is simply that they emphasize what is within themselves, and make light of externals, and thus always do things to which the heart assents. Seen in this light, the heart's nature is law-abiding and right, and the kidney's nature is lewd and wrong; these are certainly the properties of fire and water.

. . . The dragon is what is watery; it is semen and blood. It issues from the kidneys and is stored in the liver. Its sign is *k'an*. The tiger is what is fiery. It is lead, and breath, and strength. It issues from the heart and the lungs control it. Its sign is *li*. When the heart is moved, then the breath acts with it; when the kidneys overflow, then the semen and blood flow with them—and they are like fire's smoke and flame, which never return again to the firewood.

In people who do not study the Tao, the dragon always comes out with the water, hence the dragon flies and the mercury is light; and the tiger always comes out with the fire, hence the tiger runs away, and the lead is withered. This is the usual way of living men; those who obey it die—but those who rebel against it are immortal. Hence the True Man's words: "Acting in accordance, is man; acting in opposition, is Tao" [or: "obeying the Elements makes man, rebelling against the Elements makes Tao"]. And again:

"The art of reversing the Five Elements:
The dragon comes out of the fire.
Acting contrary to the Five Elements:
The tiger is born into the midst of the water."

[He describes the manipulation of breath and saliva, and the meditation, whereby these results can be obtained.]

. . . Now *li* is *li* [attached]: to show itself in attachment to things is the nature of fire. My eyes are drawn by color, my ears by sound, my mouth by taste, my nose by fragrance, and at once the fire follows along and attaches to the object. But if I am still, and not drawn by anything external, the fire has nothing to attach itself to. Then where will it go? It will necessarily tend to associate itself with its consort, water.

K'an is *hsien* [pit]: to receive things when they come is the nature of water, so of course it will receive its own mate. When water and fire are united, then the fire will not blaze up, and the water will rise of its own accord. Then you have "the dragon coming out of the fire." When the dragon comes out of the fire, then the dragon does not fly, and the mercury does not dry up. [More on technique.]

. . . This theory is curious yet comprehensible, marvellous yet simple, and deserves complete credence. But I have a great sorrow. All my life I have again and again expressed my ambition to practice this, but I have always gone wide of the mark and not been able to accomplish it. I think this Tao cannot be accomplished unless one spoils one's body following it, violently purifies one's mind to receive it, and spends one's whole life keeping it. [He tells of his recent very arduous efforts to practice it.] . . . I did not go for walks in the country, and except for seeing Taoists, I received no guests and did not drink with anyone. It was all to no avail—I greatly fear that with my easy-flowing nature I cannot follow out these prescriptions to the end. . . .

"On Nourishing Life" *(Continued)*

. . . What is meant by "lead"? all breath is called lead. It may run or hurry, inhale or exhale, grasp or strike—everything that moves is lead. The breath is expelled and taken in by the lungs: the lungs are metal and the white tiger, and so are called "lead" and "tiger". What is meant by "mercury"? all water is called mercury. Spit, tears, pus, blood, semen, sweat, excreta—everything wet is mercury. It is housed and stored in the liver: the liver is wood and the green dragon, and so is called "mercury" and "dragon". . . .

When the heart is not in charge, and the kidneys govern, sounds and colors entice from without, and wicked lust arises within, the watery quintessence flows down [as semen] to make a man, or to turn putrid—this is the mercury dragon coming out of the water. Liking, anger, grief, and joy are all things that come from the heart. Liking is followed by grasping and taking; anger, by fighting and hitting; grief, by beating the breast and leaping; joy, by tapping the time and dancing. The heart moves inside, and the breath responds to it outside. This is the lead tiger coming out of the fire. When mercury dragons come out of the water, and lead tigers come out of the fire, can any go back, once out? Thus it is said that these are both the ways of death. . . .

The fluid in the body is analyzed into two aspects, water and fire. In the ordinary course of life, the quintessential part of both escapes, drawn by sensual attractions and pushed by desire (water), or as gestures expressing emotions by which the heart (mind) is moved. Most men let this happen, and that is why they die. In a good man fire is dominant, and his conduct is right; in an evil man water is dominant, and his conduct is wicked. But both die. The Taoist struggles against death by allowing neither emotions nor sensual attractions to push or lure the fire and water out of his body. He turns his attention inward, cutting himself off from the outer worlds of landscape and of men, and forces the two elements to cancel each other's spontaneous outward flow: such is the road to immortality of body and self.

This discipline is a stubborn resistance to man's tendency to be like, or indeed part of, the landscape: "Acting in accordance, is man; acting in opposition, is Tao." The Taoist says, in effect, "I will not let myself be carried along like all other things; I am a man and different from them, and I will do all I can to maintain my separate self in man's here and now—my living body and my lifetime. I will not be cheated by the phantasm of an immortality without self in the timeless landscape, but I will have an immortality with self in human time—even if it means giving up all else that makes life worth while" for to "act in opposition" is immensely difficult and disagreeable, requiring that one do violence to body and mind.

> The space between heaven and earth
> Is mostly occupied by water.
> Man comes and man goes
> Like a pelican in a river.
> Going with the flow,
> He sails like a cloud, speeds like a bird;
> The water abets him,
> A thousand *li* are like a foot.
> But wading against the current,
> When it rises above his knees, he stops;
> The water opposes him,
> A foot is like a thousand *li*. . . .

Much easier is to ride with the current and accept the death of the body, like Su's admired friend Wu Fu-ku, a Taoist of another sort who considered "long life and immortality as irrelevancies, and breathing exercises and medicines as rubbish"; and at the same time to accept life in the ordinary sense, letting desires and emotions come out as they arise, as befitted what Su called his "easy-flowing" (*i liu*) nature.

If the death of the body is accepted, man is no longer in opposition to what the landscape stands for, and the comparison between man and landscape has lost its irony. To a friend regretting the brevity of life and envying the river and the moon that do not die, Su says,

> Do you know how it is with the water and the moon? The one flows on like this, but is never gone; the other waxes and wanes like that, but in the end has not shrunk or grown. If you consider their changefulness, then heaven and earth have never been still for an instant. If you consider their changelessness, then we with everything else have no end. What is there to be envious about?

Man is included again in a homogeneous world, so that if you fully understand the water and the moon, man's life and death are clear to you too. In the enduring flux of such a world, there is no place for a unique and continuing human self which would be different from all else. The conscious ego which the Taoist feared would die with his body can be regarded as an illusion even before his death.

> . . . Recently, Prefectural Supervisor Chu Yen studied Ch'an [Zen] for a long time. Suddenly in the *Surangama Sutra* he seemed to grasp something. He asked the teaching monk I-chiang, "After the body dies, where is the mind?" Chiang said, "Before the body dies, where is the mind?" . . .

The contained fluid which seems to be man's separate self is not really unique in the general flow of things, and in any case it is probably impossible to hold it in and escape death. How, then, should one let it out? The belief that man and landscape are ultimately identical provided Su Shih with an explanation and justification for much of his own behavior: what the landscape does is art, and art in turn is the standard of true human conduct, the way one should go about emptying the container. Su saw his own life in these terms.

In both process and product, art is the same as landscape. The sameness is neither formal nor static, but one of principle and motion.

> The excellence of writers of old was not that they could write, but that they could not help writing. Hills and streams have mists, plants have flowers and fruit, which when full and ripe appear outside—even if they wished not to have them, could they help it? Ever since youth we have heard our father discuss literature. He holds that it is a thing made by ancient sages when they had something that they could not stop themselves from writing. Hence although my brother Ch'e and I write a great deal, we have never ventured to write with premeditation.
>
> In the year *chi-hai* [1059] we accompanied [our father, Su Hsün] on a trip in the mid-Yangtze valley. . . . The elegance and beauty of landscapes, the simplicity and rudeness of customs, the mementos of sages and noble men, and all that our ears and eyes encountered, evoked various responses in us which we expressed in our verses. . . . These writings come from the midst of talk and laughter, and were not laboriously put together. . . .
>
> My writing is like a ten-thousand-gallon spring. It can issue from the ground anywhere at all. On smooth ground it rushes swiftly on and covers a thousand *li* in a single day without difficulty. When it twists and turns among mountains and rocks, it fits its form to the things it meets: unknowable. What can be known is, it always goes where it must go, always steps where it cannot help stopping—nothing else. More than that even I cannot know.

"At Kuo Hsiang-cheng's When I was Drunk, I Painted Bamboos and Rocks upon the Wall. . . "

> My empty guts get wine, and tips of sprouts appear,
> Liver and lungs fork and branch, bearing bamboos
> and rocks.
> Lushly they will be made, cannot be turned back.
> I spit them at the snow white walls, Sir, of your
> house.
> My whole life I have loved poems, long loved paintings
> too;
> I have met many angry words for scribbling and
> daubing on walls. . . .

> Alas! is it because Yü-k'o so loved beauty and rarity, or is it that "having no employment (in government) he acquired many arts?" [*Analects* IX/6, after Legge]. First I saw his poems and prose, then I had the opportunity of seeing his [calligraphy in the] running, draft, seal, and chancery [styles]. I thought this was all, but a year after he died I also saw his "flying white." What manifold beauties, as it shows all aspects of the myriad things! It moves in the air, like a thin cloud before the moon. It flutters, like a pennon curling in the long wind. It is supple, like floating gossamer wound round willow catkins. It is slender and graceful, like the stems of the floating-heart dancing in running water. Standing far apart, [the strokes] are distant but still relate to each other; standing near together, they are close but still do not crowd. His skill reached such heights as this, and I did not know it until now. So my knowledge of Yü-k'o was certainly very slight, and what I did not know about him must be beyond reckoning. Alas!
>
> The monk Huai-ch'u showed me two sutras written in the hand of Jo-k'uei. There are several chapters to a sutra, several hymns to a chapter, several verses to a hymn, several characters to a verse, several brushstrokes to a character. There is an unlimited number of strokes, yet the characters and strokes are everywhere one and equal. They have no high and low, light and heavy, great and small. And how can they all be one? Because the self is forgotten. If the self is not forgotten, there are already two phenomena present in a single stroke, to say nothing of many strokes. Like sand by the sea: no one polishes it, but it is naturally uniform, with no difference of coarse and fine. Like rain in the air: no one spreads it, but it scatters naturally, with no difference of sparse or dense. . . .
>
> . . . Although I sometimes still keep one [a pleasing painting or calligraphy], if someone takes it away, I do not regret it. They are like mists and clouds passing before one's eyes, like the many birds stirring one's ear—does one not welcome them with delight? yet one does not think of them again when they are gone. . . .

Describing art with this abundance of landscape images, Su imbues it with landscape's qualities. Place, or particular circumstances, are irrelevant to it: "it can issue from the ground anywhere at all" and "covers a thousand *li* in a single day." Works of art are interchangeable, like landscapes: "one does not think of them again when they are gone." Art has the same time as landscape, being independent of plan or forethought, memory or regret; it is an unpredictable unpremeditated local upwelling of the watery essence that man, beneath his conscious knowledge, has in common with landscape. Periodically, when a certain fullness is reached, it issues irresistably from the artist just as mists from hills and rivers, flowers and fruits from plants, water from springs, bamboo from the ground. Without conscious purpose, and unlimited by place or time, it shows no individuality or evidence of self: like sand and rain, Jo-k'uei's brushstrokes seem to arrange and assort themselves spontaneously.

This rhythm—gathering to fullness in the unknown dark of the body (underground), then emitting—is that of the release of various things from the body, especially excreta, semen, and progeny, and from one point of view Su undoubtedly read his own physiology into the landscape. I think the closest parallel is with male orgasm. This interpretation is born out by Su's implicit equating of art with desire (in **"Notice of 'Hall of Thought,'"** below), and by the short period of execution and the small scale of most of his own works. Such a male idea of art also is consonant with the opposition between art and *yang-sheng:* Su makes plain that "nourishing life" is modeled on the longer female rhythms of conception, gestation, and birth, and that the intent is to become one's own mother and pass one's individual self on to an immortal child.

Each of the various arts, as one would expect, represents an aspect of the fluid-like essence in the artist, and artistic expression is a little like decanting a pousse-café:

> Yü-k'o's prose is the lees of his virtue. Yü-k'o's poetry is the residue of his prose. What his poetry cannot exhaust overflows and is calligraphy, changes and is painting. Both are left over from the poetry. But fewer people love his prose and poetry [than love his painting and calligraphy]. Is there anyone to love his virtue as much as his painting? Alas!

Not only the arts, but virtue as well is made of this one same stuff, and Su's ideal man (Gentleman or Sage) is one whose whole conduct, whether specifically art or not, is informed with the qualities Su felt in the landscape. Such a man acts spontaneously, i.e. his behavior comes from within, and is unplanned and unforced; he does not thoughtfully apply preconceived standards of right and wrong, but reacts immediately and sensually to good or evil.

> **"Notice of 'Hall of Thought'"**
>
> Chang Chih-fu of Chien-an built a room west of the public office building and named it "Thought". He said, "I will come here morning and evening, and in everything I do, I will always think before I act. You write me a notice on it."
>
> Alas! I am the man in the empire most wanting in premeditative thought. When something comes up I speak out, and do not take time off to think. If I thought before I spoke, [the event] would [still] be incomplete; if I thought after having spoken, it would be too late [or: When something comes up, it happens all at once, and I do not take time to think. To think of it before it happens, I have not learned to do; to think of it after it happens, would be too late]. And so all my life I do not know what I would have "thought". Words arise in my mind, and rush into my mouth. If I spit them out it offends people, if I swallow them back it offends me; and thinking it better to offend other people, in the end I spit them out.
>
> The Gentleman reacts to good just as he loves a lovely color, toward evil just as he hates a hateful smell. How could it be that when he is confronted with a matter he thinks, calculating and deliberating its good and evil aspects, and only then rejects or espouses it? Hence if one, in a situation where righteousness is called for, thinks of advantage, the righteousness must come to nothing; in a situation where war is called for, if one thinks of life, the war will be feeble. Our failure and success, gain and loss, death and life, misfortune and good luck are matters of fate [and should be left to fate].
>
> When I was young I met a hermit who said, "Infants are close to the Tao—they have little thought and few desires." I said, "Then thought is on a par with desire?" He said, "It is worse than desire." In the yard were two jars for storing water. The hermit pointed to them and said, "This one has a tiny leak, from that one a quart is taken every day and thrown away. Which will be empty first?" I said, "It would have to be the one with the tiny leak." The way premeditative thought steals from a man is in small amounts but unceasingly. What the hermit said makes sense to me, and I act accordingly. Besides, the joys of not thinking are indescribable: one is empty yet enlightened, one yet universal, tranquil yet not slack, at rest without settling down in retirement, intoxicated without drinking wine, asleep without shutting an eye.
>
> Is it not a mistake to use all this as a notice for a Hall of Thought? Well, every one of these things has its place, and "all things develop together, but do not harm one another; their ways run along together, but do not infringe upon each other" [*The Mean* 30/3]. With Chih-fu's nobility of character, what he means by "thought" is surely not the vulgar kind of bustling premeditative thought. The *Book of Changes* says "without thought, without action." I should like to learn this. The *Book of Songs* says "thought without wrong." Chih-fu has this. . . .

Infants are near the Tao (immortality) because they lose from themselves almost nothing of the contained essence symbolized by water—without trying, they seem to carry out the theory of "nourishing life" which, as we have seen, Su Shih could not do. How should an adult like him empty the jug? Evidently not by the slow leak of "thought" (anxiety about the consequences of one's behavior): for all his "alas!" Su is proud of rejecting thought, as does his ideal Gentleman. If one cannot keep it in and live forever, one should let the water come out of itself, when and as it will, without calculation, like the landscape and like the artist who writes or paints when he cannot help it. This, in the hermit's parable, is desire: the expenditure is by whole quarts but not continuous. One will die, but not so soon as with thought, and meanwhile the path of desire brings joy, freedom from anxiety, and a sense of integrity; and one can be a true Gentleman.

For Su Shih, the function of art was expressed by this complex of images relating it to landscape on the one hand and to conduct on the other. The practice of the arts was a way of realizing in oneself the sagely state of mind, which could then be extended to include all one's conduct. After that, there is no longer any particular reason to practice the arts in the narrower sense.

> With Yü-k'o's ink bamboos, it used to be that when he saw fine boiled silk or good paper, he would start painting away enthusiastically—he could not help it. His guests would vie with each other for the pictures and take them away to keep, which Yü-k'o did not much mind. Later on when he saw someone laying out the brushes and inkstones he would recoil and go away. You could beg till the end of the year for a picture and not get one. On being asked the reason, Yü-k'o said, "I was studying the Tao and not reaching it. My purpose was frustrated, and having nowhere to direct it I uttered it all in ink bamboos. It was a sickness. Now I am well, so why should I act like that?"
>
> As I see it, Yü-k'o has not been able to keep his sickness for himself. But if he cannot contain it, will he not utter it? I will spy out the utterances and lay hold of them; and if he still thinks it sickness, I too will profit by it. The fact is, I am sick too. . . .

Art to Su was by no means amoral, nor was it just a vehicle or ornament of moral truth and external to it, as the Neo-Confucians and their forerunners considered: springing from the same source as virtue and described in the same images as sagely conduct, art was itself an aspect of the Tao. Actual arts such as painting and lute-playing were not themselves the Tao, but expressions of one's motion toward it (i.e., toward the more general Tao of truth or sageliness, not the immortality of the Taoists), they could, like the Buddhist sutras, be regarded as way-stations.

> . . . The Ch'ien-t'ang monk Ssu-ts'ung at the age of seven played the lute well. At twelve he gave up the lute and studied calligraphy. After he became skilled in calligraphy, in ten years he gave it up and studied poetry; in his poems there are extraordinary passages. Then he read the *Hua-yen Sutra,* and entered into the Realm of Reality and the Sea of Wisdom . . . I have heard that when one's thoughts are trained so they are reaching close to the Tao, the *Hua-yen,* the Realm of Reality, and the Sea of Wisdom are only way-stations; and this is even more true of calligraphy, poetry, and the lute. No matter how hard he tries, no student of the Tao achieves it if he starts from nothing . . . If Ts'ung does achieve it, his lute-playing and calligraphy, and above all his poetry, will have had something to do with it. Like water, Ts'ung will be able to reflect all things in one, and his calligraphy and poetry will become still more extraordinary. I will keep watch on them, and take them as indications of how profoundly Ts'ung achieves the Tao.

As artist, man acts like landscape, because his behavior is a limited expression of the very essence that actuates landscape. As sage, man acts artistically, emitting this same essence freely and spontaneously. Artist and sage have no self, and hence no guilt and no anxiety about death. But one could not be in society, let alone an official as Su was for most of his life, without a continuing self, a self that looked ahead, that willy-nilly had its place, that was held responsible for past and future acts. This self was still vulnerable to the leaks in the clock and jar, to "thought," guilt, and anxiety. History and society, the great tradition of Chinese civilization, created the conditions in which a distinct landscape experience was possible, but at the same time negated it.

Landscape is by definition asocial, and it will not have escaped the reader that Su's art and sageliness, associated as they were with landscape, had an asocial or even antisocial cast. These emissions from the body can be rude and repellent: he "spits" his paintings at the wall of his friend's house, and has "met many angry words for scribbling and daubing on walls"; if he spits his words out he offends other people, if he swallows them back he offends himself, "and thinking it better to offend other people, in the end I spit them out." Again, he writes,

> . . . By nature I am not careful of what I say. No matter who I am talking to, I always empty out my insides. If there is anything left, it is like eating something I cannot swallow—I have to spit it out and have done with it. But some people remember my rudeness and hold it against me. . . .

And in the hermit's image of the water-jar, Su chooses "desire" as preferable, in any event, to "thought." This desire is not only like landscape and like art and sageliness, it is also the very desire that gives rise to the antisocial behavior of the depraved emperor and the notorious bandit in the essays on the Dragon and Tiger; their heart-mind (organ of thought as well as of right moral sense) is subordinate to their kidneys-testicles (organ of desire). Art, and the sageliness modeled on it, are socially ambivalent, disconcerting, and unpredictable.

Carried over into political life, in the circumstances of the times, this was a dangerous attitude. "In any matter," Su Shih's brother wrote of him, "he had to be straight; he could not temporize and conform to the common view." From the time when Wang An-shih first came to court (1069), Su's frank speech and writings repeatedly evoked the enmity of one or another clique and he was harassed with onerous assignments, investigations, banishments, imprisonment, loss of rank, and the threat of execution. The Taoist notion that letting out (as opposed to bottling up) would shorten one's life was reinforced externally by the very real possibility that one would be harmed or killed by the antagonisms that political frankness aroused.

The relation in Su's thought between landscape and society can be approached through the self whose existence the asocial landscape excluded. This was the social self, a myth without which no society could function. In its various groups, from the family to the state, society attributes to its members, and they accept, unique selves (represented by proper names) which maintain an identity through time, can be expected to plan and remember, are susceptible to satisfaction or guilt for the past and anxiety or hope for the future, and are at least fairly predictable and responsible. As an official, Su was exposed to this myth in an extreme form: the political self.

The ordinary social self has meaning in respect to limited groups of family, friends, and colleagues, within a lifetime or a narrow string of ancestors and descendants. But the political self, especially for a prominent official such as Su became, was theoretically the self in respect to no particular group but vis-à-vis the whole country (mankind), all history (past and future), and the ultimate in political authority and legitimacy (the emperor). While "career-minded" or "abusive" bureaucrats might merely pay lip service to or even ignore such a universal self-concept, an "idealistic scholar-official" like Su insisted on swallowing it and trying to reconcile it with his other parts. This maximum conception of the political self was summed up a generation before Su Shih in Fan Chung-yen's description of the ideal official:

> . . . When they [virtuous men of old] held high office at the court, they were anxious for the people; when they were in banishment far among the rivers and lakes, they were anxious for their prince. Thus in favor they had cares, in disgrace they had them as well. When, then, were they joyous? The answer must necessarily be: they were the first in the empire to be sorrowful, the last in the empire to be joyous. Oh! were it not for such men, whom should I take as my model? . . .

By Su Shih's time the slow development of the government system had reached a point where such an elevated view of the ideal bureaucrat, combining broad sensibilities and subtle understanding with complete dedication to the state in the person of the emperor, could not be put into practice (if indeed it ever had been possible). Political centralization, whose growth had faltered during the late T'ang and the Five Dynasties, more than recouped its losses in the Northern Sung which had a smaller territory to administer, was under military pressure from several border peoples, and was eager to forestall a new emergency of local power such as had plagued China for two hundred years. In the capital, the authority of the emperor was intensified at the expense of the high officials, many of whose powers were either transferred to him or dispersed. Thus for example the emperor in T'ang apparently could only veto or put his seal to edicts written by the Prime Minister, while Sung Prime Ministers were restricted to submitting drafts or memoranda which the emperor then made into edicts himself. Local government was made more strictly dependent on the capital; like court officials, local officials retained a rank and a nominal post in the central government, and were considered to be on temporary assignment. Local revenues seem all to have been ascribed to the central government, instead of only in part as before. Thorough checks operated on officials at all levels—Prefectural Administrators, for example, were doubled with a concurrent Vice-Administrator whose signature was required before the Administrator's directives could take effect, and who memorialized directly to the capital. Even nepotism was formalized and exploited in a system of "controlled sponsorship" which made officials responsible for the future conduct of appointees they had brought into the government. Officials were subject to rapid promotion and demotion, and might be moved arbitrarily around the country, often staying only a few months in a given assignment, sometimes having their orders changed while they were en route. By Su Shih's time there was an excess of officials who had to compete with each other for positions, thereby (like Marx's industrial reserve army) weakening themselves vis-à-vis the central government. (Despite the concentration of power in their hands, however, the Northern Sung emperors did not themselves actually behave oppressively or despotically.)

In general, the measures taken by the fashioners of the Sung constitution to ensure that the country would not again suffer a fragmentation of the central power were successful, but only at the price of considerable confusion, ambiguity, and inefficiency in the bureaucracy, and the risk of disillusionment of idealistic scholar-bureaucrats like Su Shih who found themselves unable to devote their entire energies and loyalties to the emperor's service. The ideal political self became untenable through the operations of the antagonistic factions, succeeding each other in power, and using (at least in Su's case) the Censorate as their main instrument to suppress opposition.

Thus Su Shih during the greater part of his life was not his own man; where he went and what he did, in his official capacities, were matters beyond his control (though not always entirely beyond his influence). The emperor's power over his life was very much like fate, except that fate was inscrutable while state power, as exercised by the factions, was not. Superlatively creative and original in so much of his life, Su did not wholly succeed in adjusting his political ideas to this situation. Nor did the political thought of his day offer him a means of doing justice to his own conception of the ideal man as a selfless artist and sage who could be fully involved in political issues without denying what was represented by the landscape experience.

The ideal self of the Confucian tradition as current in Su's time was highly political, yet, in theory, harmonized also with man's place in the natural world. This self was defined and placed so as to be proof against travel, demotion, or death, but it was inadequate to the reality whose symbols Su read in the landscape.

Just as in real political space everything was centered on the capital, and the whereabouts of every official was known and controlled, so the Confucian conceptual space was oriented to, and a rationalization of, social man. Cosmology, epistemology, and ethics are integrated into this system, and the social self, first taking shape in the family, becomes a political, and indeed a cosmic one. Thus of the emperor Su writes:

The Sovereign of men takes the utmost integrity as his Way and the utmost compassion as his virtue. . . . What is utmost integrity? from the great ministers above to the little people below, from his family on the inside to the Four Barbarians without, to treat all with sincerity. . . . If one atom of falsity arises in his mind, then, as sickness shows first in the pulse and wine in the complexion, there will be some tiny sign in his voice or expression, and mistrust will spread to a thousand *li* and more. The strong will become his enemies and the weak will murmur against him. [Everywhere] within the Four Seas [people will think of him] with the hatred of bandits for the authorities, with the fear of game for the hunter. Then the Sovereign of men will stand alone and be in great peril. . . .

And from the viewpoint of a subject or official, Chang Tsai writes:

Heaven is my father and earth is my mother, and even such a small creature as I finds an intimate place in their midst.

Therefore that which extends throughout the universe I regard as my body and that which directs the universe I consider as my nature.

All people are my brothers and sisters, and all things are my companions.

The great ruler [the emperor] is the eldest son of my parents [Heaven and earth], and the great ministers are his stewards. . . .

Do nothing shameful even in the recesses of your own house and thus bring no dishonor to them [Heaven and earth]. . . .

A similar schema of the political self appears in the following Chinese box of sorites from the *Great Learning:*

The ancients who wished clearly to exemplify illustrious virtue throughout the world, first ordered well their own states. Wishing to order well their states, they first regulate their families. Wishing to regulate their families, they first cultivated their own persons. Wishing to cultivate their persons, they first rectified their minds. Wishing to rectify their minds, they first sought for absolute sincerity in their thoughts. Wishing for absolute sincerity in their thoughts, they first extended their knowledge. This extension of knowledge lay in the investigation of things.

Things being investigated, knowledge became complete. Their knowledge being complete, their thoughts became sincere. Their thoughts being sincere, their minds were then rectified. Their minds being rectified; their persons became cultivated. Their persons being cultivated, their families were regulated. Their families being regulated, their states were rightly governed. Their states being rightly governed, the world was at peace.

The ancients were concerned first with the world (or "empire"), treated as an extension of society; their persons, with mind, thoughts, knowledge, were only means. They were precisely located in the middle of a nested hierarchy of relations, none of which was in contradiction to another. The whole structure rested in the faith that nothing would turn up in the investigation of things which would lead a person to go contrary to family, state, or world. Since the argument begins and ends with the world, it has the effect of a command *not* to discover anything that might distract from the development of a strong political self. Everything hinges on the "extension of knowledge" by the "investigation of things."

It was asked whether the investigation of things required an investigation of them one by one, or whether one might simply investigate a single thing, and thereby come to a complete understanding of the Principles of all? The reply [of Ch'eng Yi] was: How can one expect to comprehend them all at once? Not even Master Yen [Confucius's disciple] would have dared to claim that by merely investigating a single thing one could comprehend the Principles of all. What is necessary is today to investigate one thing, and tomorrow to investigate another. Only after this has been practiced over a long period can one reach a free and automatic comprehension of all.

The solution to the problem is already contained in the method. "Today . . . tomorrow . . . long period"—it is a systematic and prolonged accumulation of knowledge, and hence takes for granted that man's continuing, planning, responsible self is no myth. Like the joy of Fan Chungyen's sages, spontaneity ("free and automatic comprehension") is indefinitely postponed.

The diametric contrast of these images with the centerless space of Su's landscape is evident. Equally great is the difference from his conception of knowledge, in which effortless spontaneity and delight are not afterthoughts but the very keys to the artist's and sage's understanding.

Someone said, the Recluse Lung-mien painted the picture *Mountain Home* in such a way that afterwards people going to the mountain could let their legs carry them where they would, they would naturally find out the roads and paths, as if they were seeing something they had dreamed, or remembered from a previous life. Without asking, they would know the names of the springs, rocks, grasses, and trees on the mountain; when they met fishermen, woodcutters, and hermits on the mountain, they would recognize them without being told their names. Is this not because [Lung-mien] made strenuous efforts of memory, and did not forget [these details when he painted the picture]?

I said, Not so. When people paint the sun, it often looks like a cookie, but this does not mean they have forgotten the sun. When you are drunk, you do not drink through your nose; in dreams, you do not grasp things with your toes: what comes naturally to you, you remember spontaneously, without effort. When the Recluse was on the mountain, he did not dwell upon any one thing, hence his spirit was linked to all things and his knowledge was that of all the artisans put together [each of which has intimate knowledge of only one kind of thing]. . . .

> . . . "When we have intelligence resulting from sincerity, this condition is to be ascribed to nature; when we have sincerity resulting from intelligence, this condition is to be ascribed to instruction. But given the sincerity, and there shall be the intelligence; given the intelligence, and there shall be the sincerity" [*The Mean* 21, Legge's translation].
>
> Now, what is sincerity? it means having delight. To have delight is to have spontaneous confidence, hence it is called sincerity. And what is intelligence? it means knowing. To know is to be wise, hence it is called intelligence. Sages are those who, before they know, already delight. . . . "The Master said: To know is not so good as to love; to love is not so good as to delight" [*Analects* VI/18]. Knowing, and delighting: this is the difference between the [mere] virtuous man and the sage. . . .

This emphasis on spontaneity and delight, rather than a calculated accumulation of knowledge, is at odds with the strong social time of the Chinese state as reflected in Su's own thought. The Confucian political self was exactly poised in the calendrical time of history between the edifying past and the judging future. The study of history was far from an immediate experience, in the landscape, of quasi-legendary past events. It was a guide to planned, reasoned, unspontaneous action; the deeds and fortunes of the men whose biographies made up history were to be taken as examples to follow or shun.

> If there was once someone who succeeded by doing this, I must do likewise; if there was once someone who failed by doing that, I must do the opposite. . . .

This is a far cry from loving good like a lovely color and hating evil like a hateful smell: it is the very "thought" that Su distrusted and disowned.

Death is experienced only vicariously and in social time, since a person's own death has no immediate meaning to him other than as symbol or forethought. The political self is strongly aware of being a historical personage who will die, and it is interested in its own biography and in the special kind of immortality which is the preservation of name and reputation in future ages. When Su shows concern with posthumous fame, it is almost invariably in respect to those of his writings he considered to belong to the great tradition in which history happens—his commentaries on the *Book of Changes* and the *Book of History,* and his ***Analysis of the Analects,*** rather than the less formal occasional pieces (poems, notices, letters, etc.) for which he is chiefly remembered and admired today. For example:

> . . . We anchored for the night out in the ocean. The sea and the sky met, and the sky was filled by the Milky Way. I got up, and sat looking to the four quarters, and sighed deeply. How unfortunate to take this risk! I made the crossing [from Hainan] to Hsü-wen and now I am in the same danger again. My youngest son Kuo was snoring away beside me; I called him but he did not answer. I had with me my commentaries on the *Book of History,* the *Book of Changes,* and the *Analects,* and there are no other copies in the world. I held them and exclaimed, "If heaven does not want these to be lost (?), we shall get safely ashore again!"—and so we did. . . .

The incompatibility of all this with Su's landscape ideas is clear. The contrast between the egoless self represented by landscape and the strong self presupposed by political life was a difference between two areas of his own experience, both of which he felt as valid and neither of which he was willing to suppress or anesthetize.

That the social self, with its imputed responsibility and guilt, was a myth, he came to realize fully on the occasion of his first banishment, at Huang-chou.

> In Yüan-feng 2 [1079-80], 12th month, I, as magistrate of Wu-hsing, committed offenses. The Emperor refrained from executing me, and made me Assistant Commandant of Militia at Huang-chou so that I might think on my errors and renew myself there. In the second month of the following year I arrived at Huang-chou.
>
> When I had more or less solved the problem of living quarters, and had some scant provision of food and clothing, I closed the door and made a clean start. I summoned my faculties and humbly reflected, seeking a way of renewing myself. I looked back on all my utterances and activities: they had all missed the Tao, not only the things by which I had given offense at present. Starting to reform one thing, I feared I was missing the others. I sought them out methodically, and some I regretted unendurably. So I sighed deeply, and said, "My Tao is not equal to controlling my energies; my character is not equal to mastering my habits. I am not digging at the roots, but merely pruning among the branches. Even if I reform now, I will surely act the same again later. Why not restore my integrity like a Buddhist monk (?), and seek to wash it all clean at once?"
>
> I found a monastery south of the town, called An-kuo Temple, with fine woods and tall bamboos, ponds and pavillions. Every two or three days I went there and burned incense and sat in silence, investigating myself deeply. And "things" and "self" forgot each other; my person and my mind were all emptiness. I sought whence the faults were first born, but could not find out. My whole consciousness was pure and clean, and the staining dirt fell away of itself. Inside and out, I was untrammeled and independent. Privately, I rejoiced in this. . . .

The political system assumed that a disgraced official was shamed, and should accept that shame by feeling guilt. Here Su deliberately seeks for the continuing self in which the unendurable guilt lay, and finds instead no guilt and no self. The political acceptability of his conduct could not be guaranteed by any identifiable inner standard which would accurately reflect the outer.

Why then go on acting as if the political self were true,

and continue to expose oneself to such vicissitudes and disillusionments? Undoubtedly in part simply from early indoctrination and habit, as witness this episode from Su's childhood:

> Once his mother was reading from the *Eastern Han History* and came to the biography of Fan P'ang [an official who voluntarily gave himself up to arrest and execution, with the approval of his mother who said that if he had a good name, why should he expect long life too?]. She sighed grievously. Su Shih was in attendance and said, "If I act as P'ang did, would my mother condone it?" She answered, "If you can be a Fan P'ang, can I not be a Fan P'ang's mother?"

But Su is quite capable of admiring the opposite extreme, an ignorant man completely disengaged from society:

> Shuai Tzu-lien was a farmer of Heng-shan. Ignorant, uncouth, and stubborn, he was generally known as Ox Shuai. In his old age he joined South Peak Monastery and became a Taoist. Seven *li* southwest of the monastery is Tzu-hsü Pavillion, a shrine of the former Wei Fu-jen. None of the Taoists would live there because of its desolation and solitude. Only Tzu-lien liked it; he simply sat erect and silent (?), and no one saw what he did. But he was quite addicted to wine. Sometimes when he was drunk he would lie among the mountains and woods, and even if a great storm came up he would not be aware of it; likewise tigers and wolves would pass before him and not molest him.
>
> The former Executive of the Ministry of Rites Wang Hu was sent to be magistrate of Ch'ang-sha, and he received an imperial command to conduct prayers to the South Peak. He visited the shrine of Wei Fu-jen, and there was Tzu-lien, too drunk to stand up. He looked straight at the magistrate and said, "Country Taoists love wine, but cannot always get it. When they do get it, they at once get drunk. Will the official excuse me?" The magistrate observed what an unusual man he was, and had him carried back with him. He stayed more than a month, withdrawn and not speaking, and was sent back to the mountain again. [The magistrate] said, "An old man like me cannot fathom the hidden light and inner splendor of the honored teacher.
>
> [Ox Shuai predicts the day of his death, and afterwards his grave is opened and his corpse found to be gone, showing that he had achieved the Tao.]
>
> . . . The Recluse of East Slope [Su Shih] says: If a man harbors something within himself, even some small knack, he is not quick to make it known; with a Perfect Man [Taoist immortal] this is even more true—you surely will not find out what he is. It is hard to find anyone who can recognize a Perfect Man. If Mr. Wang had not himself had the Tao, he would not have been able to know how extraordinary Ox Shuai was. . . .

Su, of course, could not uneducate himself, and the possibility of a life like Ox Shuai's was in any case diminished for him by his unsuccess with the techniques of Taoism. But more importantly it was the narrowness of such a life, excluding art and scholarship as well as direct participation in society, that made it just as unacceptable as an entire submergence in the political life. The breadth that could come only from learning and from preparing for public service was indispensable. Thus "only highly educated and gifted men can see" the all-important "principles" in landscape; Lung-mien's "knowledge was that of all the artisans put together"; and similarly, "in Chao Yün-tzu's paintings even where the brush has hardly touched it is clear what he means—artisan [painters] cannot do this." Without the education of a scholar-official, and the social sensibilities that went with it, one could not understand landscape or art or (therefore) true sageliness.

Moreover, the ideal political man, whether emperor or official, does not in fact set out to engage in politics or administration. His qualities are precisely those of the artist-sage—detachment, spontaneity, selflessness—except that he is ready, if necessary, to break his self-containment in response to the needs of society when something is amiss. Thus Su advised the Emperor Shen-tsung: "I wish you would wait quietly for things to come up, and then respond to them." One should not want to administer, and if all is well in society administration is superfluous. "The Noble Man," Su writes, "moves according to a reason; when the reason is gone, he stops. In response to a matter, he acts; when the matter is over, he leaves off"; and he goes on to praise an official who "was never angry, yet the people committed no crimes; he never held investigations, yet his staff did not cheat. With nothing to attend to from morning to night, all he did was whistle and sing." And Su himself professes to prefer retirement to government service (one also lives longer in retirement):

> . . . I have wanted to retire for the last ten years, and have begged for it earnestly and unceasingly, but the best I have got is provincial assignments. If things go well for a gentleman, and he is lucky, he can rise to the rank of minister as easily as turning over his hand; but it is retiring that has always been the hard thing. . . .
>
> I had read in Tzu-mei's poem *Temple of Six Accords* the lines: "Waiting for the goldfish at Pine Bridge/ Tarrying alone expectantly till evening" and had not understood them. When I was Vice-Administrator at Ch'ien-t'ang I learned that this fish, colored like gold, was in a pool behind the temple. Yesterday I myself went beside the pool and spent a long time dropping biscuit in. Finally he came out, just barely; he rejected the biscuit and went back, to be seen no more.
>
> Since it was over forty years ago that Tzu-mei wrote that poem, and he already speaks of "tarrying," this fish must have been chary of himself for a long time. If it were not for his reluctance to come forward and his readiness to retire, and his care about what he eats, how would he have ever lived so long?

But in service or out, the ideal is the same. The political self—that to which shame and glory would be relevant—distorts one's understanding and management of social matters, just as it falsifies one's perception of landscape.

"Inscription for the Lotus Clepsydra at Hsü-chou"

> . . . What people have faith in is their hands and feet, their eyes and ears. The eyes tell many and few, the hands know heavy and light. Yet no one takes measurements with his hands or makes calculations with his eyes; for this people always depend on measuring instruments and scales. Is this not mistrusting oneself and trusting instead to things? The reason is, people feel that because [these instruments] are without purposefulness and without self, they get at the truth about all things. Thus though heaven and earth are cold or hot, sun and moon are bright or dim, and the K'un-lun range stretches over more than 387,000 *li*, they cannot escape the three-foot indicator-rod and the five-quart vase [of the water-clock]; though with a clap of thunder day is darkened by wind, rain, and snow, still [the clock's] rate has a measurement which is not speeded or slowed.
>
> If every official, like the vase filling with water, would not exceed his capacity; like the water that floats the indicator-rod, would not depart from the level; and, like the rise and fall of the rod, would show the ups and downs of the times, and fall without counting it shame, rise without counting it glory—then the people would be docile and submit in their hearts, and trust their life and death to us.

The sage is not responsible for the ups and downs of the times; all he must do is be available to repair things if necessary, and if opportunity arises.

> . . . Master Su says: Although the Sages cannot make the times, still they do not miss the times. The times cannot be made by the Sages—all the Sages can do is not miss the times. . . .

The artist expends himself in art as part of his personal spiritual progress, because of internal needs or "sickness"; the more complete sage, adding social concern, expends himself also when something is wrong in society. If neither the person nor the society is sick, then there is no expenditure, and even the Taoist ideal of immortality through complete self-containment is realized effortlessly. But society, if not perhaps the person, is always sick, and hence there is social time, death, and history.

Such an idealized view of political man was, as we have seen, greatly at variance with Su's experience of politics in theory and practice. And in fact he did not believe the contradiction could be resolved within the state as he knew it; for the type of the harmonious society, he turns outside history to the quasi-legendary dawn of civilization, when the sage-kings first felt obliged to give the people rites (mores and institutions) and implements:

> Anciently, in their original state, the people were ignorant of implements with which to sustain life. Hitting, grabbing, yanking, tearing, they struggled with the birds and beasts for each day's survival. In constant anxiety, at morning they could make no provision for evening, and lived in mortal fear of running short. Hence there arose no trickery or deceit, and the people had no knowledge.
>
> But the Sages deplored the fact that they made no distinctions [among persons], and grieved that they had no [secure] livelihood. Therefore they devised and perfected all such things as pots, ploughs, bows and arrows, boats, carts, and nets, so that the people were happy and comfortable and became lords of nature, bending all things to their wishes. For the first time people had the means to satisfy the desires of their mouths, bellies, ears, and eyes. With implements and ease came trickery and deceit. Getting what they sought and following their desires, they wanted more and more. Then the Sages grieved at their cruelty, treachery, fickleness, and deceit, and at their unruliness. Therefore they established the rites to restore the original situation: the purpose of the rites is to restore the root and revert to the beginning. . . .
>
> The Sages had no intention of gaining empire. They were like the rivers and seas, into which all valleys lead. They were like the unicorn and phoenix, around which the birds and beasts congregate. Even if they wished to refuse, how could they? . . . These three Sages [Yü, T'ang, and Wu] tried to decline, but could not get rid of it; tried to escape, but could not avoid it. . . .

Only here, on the dreamlike horizon of time where landscape, history, legend, and art seem to converge in a single experience, did all contradictions disappear.

> . . . Since Ch'in united the empire and extinguished the Rites and Music, the *shao* has not been performed for 1313 years. If the instruments were preserved and the performers missing, the *shao* would be a mystery; so much the more when both instruments and performers' [skills] are gone and have not been handed down. But although the *shao* is lost, there is something that is not lost and is still preserved, for it is always with sun and moon, heat and cold, dark and light, wind and rain between heaven and earth. Nowadays . . . people's ears have never heard earth's music, still less can they hear heaven's [natural] music. But if one's ear does hear heaven's music, then everything that has shape and sound is his feathers and tail, shield and ax, pipes and stone chimes, gourds and strings [i.e., the antique paraphernalia of music and dance].
>
> . . . I have climbed up on Shao Rock, below Shun Peak, and looked out to Ts'ang-wu Mountain in the distance, and the Chiu-i Range. I attended to the spitting and swallowing of rivers and mountains, the swaying of the trees and herbs, the cries of the birds and animals, the breathing of all the apertures: and all these doings were harmonious song. There was no numbered measure, yet an even rhythm formed of itself. Is this not the *shao* in all its perfection? The limits established in heaven set the world in order. If man is in accord the Air [breath, energy] answers; if the Air answers, there is music. And then 'the nine melodies of the

shao, the coming of the phoenix, the dancing of the hundred beasts' all are there, spread out before him in glory. . . .

Kojiro Yoshikawa (essay date 1967)

SOURCE: "Late Period of the Northern Sung—1050-1100," in *An Introduction to Sung Poetry*, translated by Burton Watson, Cambridge, Mass.: Harvard University Press, 1967, pp. 85-133.

[*In the following excerpt, Yoshikawa presents a detailed discussion about the manner in which Su was able to "transcend sorrow by means of a philosophy that viewed the infinite variety of human life with a largeness of vision that was equally varied."*]

Su Tung-p'o's poetic works, in which he gives free and unrestrained expression to his rich and varied talent, are unmatched in stature by anything else in Sung poetry. First of all, he took over the interest in description that was already evident in the work of Ou-yang Hsiu and developed it to the fullest extent. As descriptions of objects we may note the series of poems written early in his career which he called **"Eight Sights of Feng-hsiang,"** particularly that entitled **"Song of the Stone Drums,"** while as descriptions of journeys or outings we should note his **"Visit to Gold Mountain Temple"** and **"Hundred Pace Rapids,"** both of them remarkable for their keenness of observation, imaginativeness and use of simile. Because both these are rather lengthy, I shall quote a poem written early in 1077 when the poet was on his way from Mi-chou in Shantung to the capital. It is in five-character old form and bears this heading: "I was detained by a heavy snow at Wei-chou on New Year's Eve, but on the morning of the first day it cleared and I resumed my journey. Along the way, it started to snow again."

New Year's Eve blizzard kept me from leaving;
On the first, clear skies see me off.
The east wind blows away last night's drunk;
On a lean horse, I nod in the remains of a
dream.
Dim and hazy, the dawn light breaks through;
Fluttering and turning, the last flakes fall.
I dismount and pour myself a drink in the
field—
Delicious—but who to share it with?
All at once evening clouds close down,
Tumbling flurries that show no break.
Flakes big as goose feathers hang from the
horse's mane
Till I think I'm riding a great white bird.
Three years' drought plaques the east;
Roofs sag on house rows, their owners fled.
The old farmer lays aside his plow and sighs,
Gulps tears that burn his starving guts.
Spring snow falls late this year
But spring wheat can still be planted.
Do I grumble at the trials of official travel?
To help you I'll sing a song of good harvest.

In his later years, Su's use of simile became freer than ever. When he was exiled to Hainan he described the journey which he made in a semicircle along the coast of the island, from Ch'iung-chou on the north shore to Tan-chou on the east shore, as being "like following the from of the crescent moon." Or, to turn to an example of simile applied to an intimate scene of daily life, he writes of his son thumping out of the rhythm of the poems he has memorized:

The little boy sits with book closed,
Reciting poems from memory as though striking
a lute.

But we should not let ourselves become too engrossed in the surface brilliance of Su's poetry; beneath this surface lies a deep and penetrating warmth of personality. Of the various tasks which the poet was able to accomplish, the most important was that of freeing Chinese poetry from the preoccupation with sorrow that had characterized it for so long.

. . . [One] of the important accomplishments of Sung poetry was to escape from that preoccupation. The escape first became a real possibility with the poetry of Su Tung-p'o. Ou-yang Hsiu himself was not fully conscious of that fact, and his method of escape was a negative one, seeking only to maintain a state of mental serenity.

In Su Tung-p'o's case, however, the escape was conscious and deliberate. He set about to transcend sorrow by means of a philosophy that viewed the infinite variety of human life with a largeness of vision that was equally varied. Moreover, he was able, because of the breadth and warmth of his personality, to expound his philosophy effectively in words. . . .

This new, broad-visioned philosophy of Su Tung-p'o is based upon the recognition that man's life does not consist of sorrow alone. Sorrow, to be sure, is to be found everywhere in life, and yet it is not the only element of which life is made. If there is sorrow, there is joy as well, the two intertwined like the strands of a rope. It is therefore foolish to become engrossed in the sorrowful side of life alone. Indeed, one should go a step further and examine whether those things which by ordinary standards are regarded as sorrows and misfortunes are really so or not. Looked at from the broader point of view, they may not be sorrows at all.

The following poem in five-character old form is an expression of this outlook. It was written shortly after the poet arrived in Huang-chou, his place of exile, and had moved from the quarters first assigned him to a slightly better house, the official lodge attached to the post station at a place called Lin-kao overlooking the Yangtze. The poem is called **"Moving to Lin-kao Pavilion."**

Between heaven and earth I live,
One ant on a giant grindstone,

Trying in my petty way to walk to the right
While the turning of the mill wheel takes me
endlessly left.
Though I go the way of benevolence and duty,
I can't escape from hunger and cold.
The sword-cooker—a perilous way to fix rice!
The mat of spikes—no restful sitting there!
But don't I have the beautiful hills and rivers?
I no sooner turn my eyes than wind and rain
bear them off.
A man doesn't have to be old to retire,
But how many have the daring to do it?
Fortunately I've been turned out and abandoned,
A weary horse with pack and saddle removed.
All my family here, we have the run of the river
post house.
When things looked blackest, Heaven poked a
hole for me.
Hunger and poverty now multiplied, now
divided,
I don't see that I deserve either condolence or
congratulation.
Peaceful and calm, I have no joy or sorrow;
My complaint has no reason to end with a *so*!

The term in line four translated as "mill wheel," literally, "wind wheel," derives from Buddhist literature and refers to the forces which move the world. In lines seven and eight, the poet refers to two types of side-show performers, the man who prepares rice for cooking while seated on the point of a sword, and the man who sits down on a mat of spikes, suggesting that his own position may be equally perilous and uncomfortable. After referring to the beauties of the natural world and the fickles with which they may be snatched from man's sight by storm and change, the poem takes a brighter turn. From the ordinary point of view, exile can only be considered a misfortune. And yet the poet, because he looks at life with a broader and more varied view, can speak of his exile as a fortunate occurrence. Perhaps his present situation is actually one of happiness, or at least will be the source from which some future happiness will spring. Or perhaps one should forget both sorrow and happiness and be content with a state of calm. The songs of the state of Ch'u in ancient times, most of them laments or complaints, employed an exclamatory particle pronounced so at the end of the lines to give the rhythm a raped and forceful beat. But the poet in his new-won state of peace and calm has no need for such exclamations in his song.

Such is the general meaning of the poem. The line "Hunger and poverty now multiplied, now divided," reflects a philosophy of cyclical change such as is expressed in the *Book of Changes*. The outlook which regards misfortune as fortune, or which transcends such relative distinctions and value judgments, is based upon the philosophy of Chuang Tzu, particularly as it is expressed in the second chapter of the work which bears his name, the *Ch'i-wu-lun*, or "Discussion on Making All Things Equal."

Chuang Tzu's doctrine of "making all things equal" is only briefly touched upon in the poem quoted above. In the poem which I shall quote next, it appears much more clearly. This poem was written in 1071, when the poet, aged thirty-six, was on his way from the capital to Hangchow to assume the post of vice-governor. As he traveled down the Grand Canal, he stopped at Ch'en-chou in Honan to visit his younger brother Su Tzu-yu, who had, like the poet himself, clashed with Wang An-shih and had been assigned to an insignificant post in Ch'en-chou, referred to in the poem as Wan-ch'iu. After they had visited for some time, Su Tzu-yu accompanied his brother as far as Ying-chou in Anhwei, where they parted. The poem, in five-character old-form, is the second of two entitled **"On Taking Leave of Tzu-yu at Ying-chou: Two Poems."** The first, which begins

The traveler's sails are spread in the west wind,
Tears of parting fall into the clear Ying. . .

is given up to a mood of sorrow. But the second poem introduces the philosophy of the "equalization of things" as a means of transcending sorrow.

Let the place be close by and parting faces
hardly change;
Let it be distant and tears wet our robes.
But a foot apart, if we cannot meet,
We might as well be parted a thousand miles.
And if in life there were no partings,
Who would know the gravity of love?
When I first came to Wan-ch'iu
The children danced and hung on my clothes.
You knew then this sorrow was coming
And begged me to stay till autumn winds pass.
By now autumn winds are gone,
But the sorrow of parting never ends.
You ask when I'll be coming back?
I answer, when the Year Star is in the east.
Since parting and meeting are an endless cycle,
Grief and joy must jostle each other.
As we talk about it, we give great sighs—
Our lives are like wind-blown tumbleweed.
But too much worry brings the grey hairs early.
Haven't you seen what it did to Master Six-one?

The poem begins at once with a breadth of vision that transcends the distinction of ordinary life. People are sorrowful when someone they love is going far away, but hardly disturbed at all if the destination is close by, though the fact of separation is exactly the same in both cases. To be consistent, therefore, we must either regard all partings as sorrowful, or admit that none of them really deserves to be lamented. Already the poet is seeking a broader view that will transcend sorrow. The couplet that follows is even more daring:

And if in life there were no partings,
Who could know the gravity of love?

Parting contains not only the negative element of sorrow, but a positive element as well; it serves to make us aware of the value of love. In this sense, should it not also be regarded as an occasion for happiness, or at least as a necessary step in the direction of future happiness? So far as I know, this view of the value of separation is original with Su Tung-p'o. I can recall nothing to match it in Chinese literature before him.

The breadth of vision with which the poem begins is not necessarily sustained throughout. In the central section the sadness of parting from his brother momentarily overwhelms the poet. The "Year Star" in line fourteen is the planet Jupiter, whose twelve-year cycle was used by the Chinese in measuring time. At the time when the poet was writing, Jupiter was in the northeast sector of the sky marked by the cyclical sign *hai.* Three years later, it would be dead east in the sector marked by the sign *yu,* and his term as vice-governor of Hangchow would be ended.

In the closing lines, the poet once more makes an effort to rise above his sorrow, this time by reference to the philosophy of cyclical change. His grief was in fact too strong in this case to be banished by the thought of future meetings and happiness, and led him to the simile of the wind-blown tumbleweed, which I shall have occasion to discuss later. But there is a final rallying of spirit in the last couplet, and the poem ends on a relatively light note with a reference to "Master Six-one," one of the names of Ou-yang Hsiu. Ou-yang Hsiu, the teacher of Su Tung-p'o had of course gone to call on him and pay his respects when he passed through Ying-chou. It was the last meeting between teacher and disciple; Ou-yang Hsiu died the following year.

Though the poet makes the bold assertion that it is separation alone that teaches us the real value of love, he is not wholly successful in driving away sorrow. It would almost appear, in fact, that his efforts to do so on occasion only lead him deeper into grief. And yet the underlying tenor of the poem is one of transcendence of sorrow through greater breadth of vision.

This, then, is the first stage of Su Tung-p'o's philosophy. As we have seen, the doctrines upon which it is based are not original with him, but derived partly from the *Chuang Tzu* and partly from the view of cyclical change expressed in the *Book of Changes.* What is new and original with Su, I believe, is the attitude which recognizes sorrow as a necessary and inescapable element of life, but considers an exclusive preoccupation with sorrow to be ridiculous.

It was always easy for Confucianism, with its strong element of idealism, to visualize a society without sorrow. The sadness and indignation expressed by the poets in the *Book of Odes* are the sadness and indignation of men who had hoped for better things, but whose hopes have been betrayed, and the same, I believe, may be said of the poetry of Tu Fu in the T'ang period. This was not true of Su Tung-p'o who asserted that sorrow, and the misfortunes that are the cause of sorrow, are omnipresent in human life and constitute one of its inescapable elements. As long as the possibility of conflict exists between the individual and society, or between desire and fate, he perceived that sorrow would always be a necessary part of human life.

As an illustration of Su's view of the omnipresence of sorrow, we may look at a poem written in 1079, eight years after the one quoted above, when the poet was transferred from the post of governor of Hsü-chou in Kiangsu to that of governor of Hu-chou in Chekiang. He had been a good governor, and when he prepared to leave Hsü-chou, the people flocked to see him off and even tried to prevent his departure. The poem, in five-character old form, is the first of five written at the time to be sent to his brother and bearing the title, **"I have left my post in Hsü-chou and am proceeding to Nan-ching; I am writing these on horseback to send to Tzu-yu."**

Clerks, townsmen, don't hang on me!
Songs, flutes, don't sob like that!
My life is made of sojourns only;
Is this the first time I've had to take leave?
Separation follows us everywhere;
Sadness and fret are bound up with love.
Since I have done you no favor,
For whose sake do you shed these tears?
Scrambling like mischievous children,
Trying to break my whip, to slash my stirrups—
By the roadside, that pair of stone men:
How many governors have they seen depart?
If they knew what has happening, how they'd laugh,
Clapping their hands till their hat strings snapped!

In the opening lines, the poet points out that since "My life is made of sojourns only," separation is inevitable, and the sorrow which separation occasions may be said to be an ever-present element in human life. But if "separation follows us everywhere," then it is not foolish to allow one's emotions to become so bound up with the occasion? In pointing out the omnipresence of sorrow, he urges a way to escape it. In the lines that follow he deliberately adopts a cold attitude, denying that he has done anything to win the affection of the people, scolding them for trying impetuously to prevent his departure by breaking his whip or attempting to cut his stirrups. In the closing lines he returns once more to the theme of the frequency of parting, pointing to the stone figures by the roadside and imagining how many times in the past they have witnessed such a scene of the departure of a governor. If they were aware of what went on around them, they would surely laugh uproariously at the foolishness of human beings in behaving in this fashion over something as frequent and inevitable as separation. The poet no doubt felt deep regret at leaving the people of Hsü-chou, among whom he had lived for over two years. But, at least on the surface of the poem, none of this appears; he merely points to the ubiquitous nature of sorrow, and advises us not to become preoccupied with it.

This is the second stage of Su's new, broad-visioned philosophy, by which he proposes to transcend sorrow. But the poem quoted above also reveals a very important mode of thinking which makes it representative of the third state of Su's philosophy. I am referring to the view which sees man's life as a thing of long duration. This outlook is revealed in the third line: "My life is made of sojourns only," which in the original is in simile form, literally, "My life is like sojourns only."

True, on the surface the line says nothing about life being long. The surface meaning is that life is a thing of doubt and uncertainty, like so many inn stops along a road. But beneath the surface there exists an awareness of the long time-span of human life. If there were no such awareness, then the following line, "Is this the first time I've had to take leave?" with its sense of almost endless succession of partings stretching out of the past and into the future, would be impossible to imagine.

If we look back now at the first two stages of Su's philosophy we will see that the view of cyclical change which appears in the first stage, and the recognition of the omnipresence of sorrow in human life which appears in the second stage, both imply a consciousness of the long duration of human life. But this consciousness is first clearly stated in the line, "My life is made of sojourns only."

This is not the only poem in which the poet employs this line; it is to be found in many places in his works, as is the similar line in the poem to his brother, quoted earlier: "Our lives are like wind-blown tumbleweed." These two similes, the brief sojourn and the wind-blown tumbleweed, in addition to expressing the uncertainty of life, often imply the unspoken premise that man's life is of long duration. For example, in the poem called **"Passing the Huai,"** which was written when the poet had been released from prison and was on his way to exile in Huang-chou, we find the following lines which imply that, because life is nothing but a long series of ups and downs, one's destination can never be fixed:

> My life is made of sojourns only,
> And I never get to choose the place I'm to go.

Or, in a poem written to the rhymes of a poem by his friend Wang Chin-ch'ing, in which the poet, after his return to political power, reminisces over his period of exile in Huang-chou, we read:

> My life is made of sojourns only;
> What is good luck, what is bad?
> Better to forget them both.
> Who can recapture last night's dream?

The view of cyclical change, the alternation of good luck and bad, demands a long period of time in order to be conceivable.

Another example is to be found in a poem written during his exile on Hainan Island and employing the same rhymes as T'ao Yüan-ming's poem entitled **"Imitating the Ancients"**:

> My life is made of sojourns only;
> What shall I point to and call my house?

Because life is of such long duration, one may come to realize that any place is home.

The last example I shall cite is from a poem written when the poet had left Hainan Island and passed through Yü-ku-t'ai in Kiangsi on his way north:

> My life is made of sojourns only;
> The peaks and the sea—those were pleasure trips too.

The "peaks and the sea" refer respectively to his place of exile in Hui-chou and Hainan Island. Looking back on it, the poet now sees that his exile too was only one small incident in a long life crowded with incident, just another "pleasure trip."

This view, which sees man's life as a period of long duration, is original with Su; or, if it is not actually original with him, he used it to create a new era of poetry, for such a view had never been common in the poetry of earlier times. Until Su's time, it had been customary, on the contrary, to emphasize the brevity and fleeting quality of man's life.

As evidence we may point to the fact that the sojourn simile is never used in earlier poetry in the way in which Su used it. The simile itself is by no means original with Su, but is very old in Chinese poetry. Before his time, however, it was employed rather to emphasize the brief duration of man's life and swiftness with which he moves toward death. It is found first in the twelfth of the anonymous "Nineteen Old Poems" which date from the first or second century A.D.

> Man's life is brief as a sojourn;
> His years lack the firmness of metal or stone.

Ts'ao P'i (188-226) used the simile in his poem in folk-style entitled *Shan-tsai-hsing,* again probably to emphasize the brevity of life:

> Man's life is like a sojourn;
> With so many sorrows, what can he do?

Chu Yi, a scholar of the Southern Sung, in the first *chüan* of his *Yi-chüeh-liao tsa-chi,* has noted the sources from which Su Tung-p'o took his allusions and figures of speech. On the Sojourn simile, he points to the following lines in a poem entitled "Thoughts on the Times" by Po Chü-i:

> How long is the life of man?
> He is in the world for a sojourn only.

and those in a poem by the same poet called "Autumn Mountain":

> Man's life lasts no time at all,

Like a sojourn between heaven and earth.

All of these examples obviously place emphasis upon the brevity of life.

But Su, while employing the same simile, invested it with a new meaning. What he did represents not only a shift in the meaning of the simile, but in the whole attitude toward human life. It is hardly necessary to add that the attitude which emphasizes the length of human life will be less productive of sorrow and despair, and more productive of hope, than one which emphasizes the brevity of life. True, Su sees life as a period which is full of ups and downs. But it is precisely because it is long that it is so marked by fluctuations. And when one is conscious of this lengthy and fluctuating character, it becomes more foolish than ever to allow oneself to think only of the sorrow which occurs during the low points. One must learn to put faith in the future.

We find this view of the length and changing quality of life clearly and logically stated in Su's works. But even where it is not explicitly stated, it seems always to underlie his poetry. We feel its presence, for example, in the famous poem in seven-character regulated verse written when the poet was en route by water from the capital to Hangchow. It bears the heading, "Passed the place where the Ying River enters the Huai, and for the first time saw the mountains along the Huai. Today we reached Shou-chou."

I travel day and night toward the Yangtze and
  the sea.
Maple leaves, reed flowers—fall has endless
  sights.
On the broad Huai I can't tell if the sky is near
  or far;
Green hills keep rising and falling with the
  boat.
Shou-chou—already I see the white stone
  pagoda,
Though short oars haven't brought us round
  Yellow Grass Hill.
Waves calm, wind mild—I look for the landing.
My friends have stood a long time in twilight
  mist.

Already in the opening lines we have a sense of life as a journey, as a thing of length and duration. In the lines that follow, the sky, whose distance it is impossible to discern, may be intended as a symbol of some aspect of man's life; the rising and falling of the green hills are surely meant to symbolize the up-and-down quality of life. After describing the circuitous course which the boat must take to reach its destination, the poet concludes on a note of expectation and quiet joy as he imagines how his friends, not yet in sight, have been standing waiting for him in the twilight mist.

Su Tung-p'o's philosophy for the transcendence of sorrow, the first three stages of which I have described above, reaches its culmination in the fourth stage. This culmination is to be found in the view that, if the outward process of life is characterized by a continuing series of ups and downs, then man's true inner life must lie in a continued resistance. This does not necessarily mean that one struggles against the ups and downs. The act of resignation may also be regarded as a kind of resistance exercised by the human will.

An early expression of this idea is to be found in the opening lines of **"Beginning of Autumn: A Poem to Send to Tzu-yu,"** which the poet wrote during his period of exile in Huang-chou:

The hundred rivers day and night flow on,
We and all things following:
Only the heart remains unmoved,
Clutching the past.

The same idea is clearly expressed in a poem written in 1097, during his second period of exile, when he was ordered to move from Hui-chou to the Island of Hainan. In five-character old form, it too is addressed to his brother Tzu-yu and begins as follows:

I've had a lot of trouble from the time I was
  young,
Dodging and threading my way through life.
A hundred years aren't easy to live out;
We must draw the strong bow inch by inch.
I'm old—what is left to say?
Honor and shame mean nothing now.
I face the single road to nirvana;
Wherever else I took, the way is blocked.

Here the term "hundred years" applied to man's life clearly describes the sense of life's duration, while the metaphor of drawing a stiff bow expresses the exertion and resistance with which life must be lived. In the lines that follow the poet's nerve seems to fail him, and he speaks somewhat despairingly. But later on in the poem, we once more find such lines as the following:

This parting, how's it worth talking about?
My life surely won't come to an end yet!

A final example is to be found in a poem written in the summer of 1101, just before the poet's death. In five-character regulated verse, it is the second of two poems entitled **"Following the Rhymes of Chiang Hui-shi."** It was written when he was traveling home along the Yangtze from his place of exile in the south.

Bell and drum on the south river bank:
Home! I wake startled from a dream.
Drifting clouds—so the world shifts;
Lone moon—such is the light of my mind.
Rain drenches down as from a title basin;
Poems flow out like water spilled.
The two rivers vie to send me off;
Beyond treetops I see the slant of a bridge.

In the opening couplet the poet wakes startled from a dream-a dream which in a larger sense is symbolic of the whole astonishing up-and-down course of his life. In the couplet that follows, in the contrast between the shifting clouds of the world and the steady brightness of the moon, he gives precise expression to the pride of a man who has resisted and overcome his environment. Wang Ying-lin, an eminent scholar of the end of the Southern Sung period, in his *K'un-hsüeh chi-wen,* comments upon this second couplet; "T'ung-p'o in his late years achieved great profundity." After a reference to the poet's unflagging creativity, the poem returns to a contemplation of the natural scene, ending with a delicate contrast between the rolling rivers and the static lines of the bridge seen above the tops of the trees.

I have attempted to outline the process by which Su Tung-p'o transcended sorrow. In the discussion of the line, "My life is a sojourn only," I have drawn gratefully upon the study by Yamamoto Kazuyoshi, "Some Remarks on the Poetry of Su Shih" [*Journal of Chinese Literature,* 13, October, 1960]. Certain aspects of my discussion may be based upon rather arbitrary judgments, but the correctness of my general conclusion is borne out, I believe, by the fact that, in spite of the extreme fluctuations of fortune to which the poet was subjected during his lifetime, his 2400 poems contain almost no works that are wholly sorrowful in tone. As case in point I will cite a poem written near the end of 1079 to say farewell to his brother. The poet was in prison under accusation of "slandering the Emperor," and fully expected to die. It is in seven-character regulated verse.

Under the heaven of our holy ruler, all things turn to spring,
But I in dark ignorance have destroyed myself.
Before my hundred years are past, I'm called to settle up;
My leaderless family, ten months, must be your worry now.
Bury me anywhere on the green hills
And another year in night rain grieve for me alone.
Let us be brothers in lives and lives to come,
Mending then the bonds that this world breaks.

The poem is one of great sorrow, not surprisingly in view of the circumstances under which it was composed. Even so, there is a suggestion of hope, though it must wait until the next world for fulfillment. And although the word "to grieve," so rare in Su's poetry, appears here, it is interesting to note that it is applied not to the poet himself but to his brother.

This mood of sorrow did not last, however, for shortly after the poem quoted above was written, on the 28th day of the 12th month, after a hundred days in prison, the poet was set free. The following poem celebrates his release in terms of outspoken boldness. . . . [It] is in the same form and follows the same rhymes as the poem of sorrow quoted above, a fact that lends emphasis to the dramatic change of mood.

A hundred days, free to go, and it's almost spring;
For the years left, pleasure will be my chief concern.
Out the gate, I do a dance, wind blows my face;
Our galloping horses race along as magpies cheer.
I face the wine cup and it's all a dream,
Pick up a poem brush, already inspired.
Why try to fix the blame for trouble past?
Years now I've stolen posts I never should have had.

For the purpose of comparison I shall quote here a poem written under circumstances rather similar to those of Su's prison poem above. It is by the T'ang poet Han Yü and was written when he was on his way into exile in 819 after incurring the imperial wrath because of his attack on Buddhism expressed in his famous "Memorial on the Buddha Bone." Like Su's poem, it is seven-character regulated verse. It bears the title "Written on my way into exile when I reached the Lan-t'ien Pass and shown to my brother's grandson Hsiang." Hsiang had accompanied the poet as far as the Lan-t'ien Pass, south of Ch'ang-an.

One document at dawn, submitted to the nine-tiered palace;
By evening, banished to Ch'ao-chou eight thousand li away.
For our holy ruler I longed to drive away the evil;
What thought for this old body, for the few years remaining?
Clouds blanket the Ch'in Range-which way is home?
Snow blocks the Lan Pass-my horse will not go on.
You must have some purpose, coming so far with me:
Be kind and gather up my bones from the shores of the fetid river.

Like Su, Han Yü had resigned himself to the thought of death, and his poem is given up to sadness. The clouds of the Ch'in Range, the snow in the Lan-t'ien Pass, everything that he sees, serves only to deepen his sorrow. But, unlike Su, who imagines himself being buried somewhere "on the green hills," Han Yü can only visualize his bones being left to rot by the malarial rivers of Ch'ao-chou far to the south and begs his kinsman to rescue them from the fate.

Su Tung-p'o did more than simply transcend his own personal sorrow; he initiated a new era in the history of Chinese poetry. The preoccupation with sorrow which had become a habit with the poets of earlier ages was brought to an end by his efforts, and poetry was led into the direction of a more hopeful view of life. Su's admirers in later centuries have loved him for his largeness and freedom of spirit, and his detractors have criticized him for the almost excessive ease with which his poetry flows along. But whatever they have thought of him, the poets who live after Su Tung-p'o gave far less space in their songs to the despair and sorrow of life than those who had lived before him, and this fact was the direct result of the revolution which he had brought about in the tenor of Chinese poetry.

Future historians of literature and philosophy will some day, it is to be hoped, make an exhaustive study of the epoch-making nature of Su Tung-p'o's literary works. When they do, they will have to give careful attention to one aspect of his personality in particular: the great breadth of his love. He was no political planner like Wang An-shih, but he had an innate love for the common people. It may be seen, for example, in the following poem written in 1071 when the poet was vice-governor of Hangchow. In five-character old form, it describes how the poet was kept late at his office on New Year's Eve by criminal cases. According to custom, cases involving the death penalty had to be settled before the New Year, which marked the beginning of spring.

New Year's Eve—you'd think I could go home early
But official business keeps me.
I hold the brush and face them with tears:
Pitiful convicts in chains,
Little men who tried to fill their bellies,
Fell into the law's net, don't understand disgrace.
And I? In love with a meager stipend
I hold on to my job and miss the chance to retire.
Do not ask who is foolish or wise;
All of us alike scheme for a meal.
The ancients would have freed them a while at New Year's-
Would I dare do likewise? I am silent with shame.

When the poet compares himself to the condemned prisoners and tell us, "Do not ask who is foolish or wise," he is not, I believe, speaking as a member of the ruling class who feels a certain tenderness toward his charges. He himself often denied that he belonged to the elite and expressed the desire to live the life of an ordinary citizen. When he was exiled to Huang-chou, he lived among farmers and actually became a farmer himself, working a plot of land at a place called Tung-p'o, or Eastern Slope. The following poem, the fifth of eight entitled **"Eastern Slope,"** gives a glimpse of his life at that time. It is five-character old form.

A good farmer hates to wear out the land;
I'm lucky this plot was ten years fallow.
It's too soon to count on mulberries;
My best bet is a crop of wheat.
I planted seed and within the month
Dirt on the rows was showing green.
An old farmer warned me,
Don't let seedlings shoot up too fast!
If you want plenty of dumpling flour
Turn a cow or sheep in here to graze.
Good advice—I bowed my thanks;
I won't forget you when my belly's full.

He hoped to become a farmer once more at the time of his second exile in Hainan Island, as may be seen in the following poem dating from that period, though he was unable to realize his desire. In five-character old poem form, it is called **"Buying Rice."** As the poet buys rice and other necessities in the market place, he images how happy he would be if he could have a plot of land and grow his own food.

I buy rice and bundles of firewood,
Each commodity at its proper stall.
But getting them like this without plowing or gathering,
Though I fill my belly, the flavor is thin.
Bowing twice, I'll beg the lord of the land
Please to let me have a plot of ground.
I know where I was wrong, I laugh at past dreams;
If I work for my food, I need feel no shame.
Spring seedlings—when will they bloom?
Summer barngrass—its seeds are ripe by now!
Fondly I will stroke the plow and share—
Who understands what it would mean to me?

The principal fault of Su Tung-p'o's poetry is that he often wrote with an ease and facility that bordered on carelessness. In [**"Following the Rhymes of Chiang Hui-shu"**] we have already encountered a description of the facility with which he composed: "Poems flow out like water spilled"; and in another poem he writes,

A new poem is like a crossbow pellet;
Once it's left the hand it never stops a moment.

He certainly did not belong to the painstaking, hard-working category of poets. His manner of composition was an expression of the freedom of his mind and of his talent. But although he himself was not the hard-working type, he could appreciate the worth of the man who was perhaps the hardest-working poet of the past, Tu Fu, and, along with Wang An-shih, strived to win for Tu Fu the recognition he deserved.

. . . Su Tung-p'o composed poems to the rhymes of all T'ao Yüan-ming's poems, completing the task during his years of exile in Hainan. This feat, too, is an expression of the overflow of energy and talent which characterized his work. I shall quote an example of T'ao Yüan-ming's poetry and the poem which Su wrote to match it. T'ao Yüan-ming's poem is the third of his twenty poems entitled "Drinking Wine," in five-character lines.

A thousand years the Way's been lost;
Men are stingy with their hearts.
They have wine but they're unwilling to drink;
They think of nothing but worldly fame.
What's so precious about this body of ours?
Is it not the fact that it's alive?
One life—how long does it last?
Swift as a bolt of lightning it passes.

Within the press of a hundred years,
What will you do with this fame of yours?

The following is Su's poem, which employs the same rhyme words. The "refined gentlemen south of the Yangtze" are T'ao Yüan-ming's contemporaries of the Eastern Chin dynasty, which had its capital at Nanking.

The Way is lost, and men have lost themselves;
Words spoken now are never from the heart.
The refined gentlemen south of the Yangtze
In the midst of drunkenness still sought fame.
Yüan-ming alone was pure and true,
Living his life in talk and laughter.
He was like a bamboo before the wind,
Swaying and bending, all its leaves tremble,
Some facing up, some down, each a different shape—
When he'd had his wine, the poems wrote themselves.

The last line probably refers less to T'ao Yüan-ming's way of writing poetry than it does to that of Su Tung-p'o himself.

Wang An-shih, in spite of his good intentions, was never popular with the common people of his time. Su Tung-p'o, by contrast, seems to have been loved by all who knew him. There must have been something very different in the manner of the two men. Su's poetic follower, the Buddhist priest Ts'an-liao, wrote the following poem after Su's death. In seven-character *chüeh-chü* form, it is entitled "Poem Written in Memory of My Teacher Tung-p'o."

When with tall hat and firm baton he stood in council,
The crowds were awed at the dignity of the statesman in him.
But when in cloth cap he strolled with cane and sandals,
He greeted little children with gentle smiles.

Ts'an-liao was also acquainted with Wang An-shih. For the sake of comparison, I shall quote a poem which he wrote on visiting the Ting-lin Temple where Wang An-shih, referred to here by his title Duke Ching, used to walk. In the same form as the poem above, it is called "Visiting the Ting-lin Temple and Paying My Respects to the Portrait of Duke Ching."

Old trees, green rattan, one trail winding through;
Our Duke in days past would wander here.
Under the lonely roof, I look at his portrait:
The hero's air, the noble pose, impressive still.

Yu-Shih Chen (essay date 1988)

SOURCE: "Su Shih: A Theory of Perception in Art," in *Images and Ideas in Chinese Classical Prose: Studies of Four Masters,* Stanford University Press, 1988, pp. 133-53.

[*Here, Yu-Shih Chen explores Su's intellectual and artistic development during the period of 1071 to 1085, characterizing him as an intuitive and unorthodox thinker.*]

Su Shih (1036-1101) was 30 years younger than his patron Ou-yang Hsiu, and so their careers and thoughts were not . . . closely intertwined. . . . Politically, Su Shih, like Ou-yang Hsiu in his later years, was part of the conservative opposition to the New Law Reform. In literary theory, they are frequently mentioned together in the context of the *ku-wen* revival of the early Sung. Although intellectually and artistically they were of different generations and differed in almost every essential aspect, . . . they have been perceived by critics and literary historians as the principal advocates of *ku-wen* in the Sung and as leading stylists who so perfected *ku-wen* and its theoretical basis that they determined its development for centuries to come.

The Impact of Political Exile

Like his father, Su Hsün (1009-66), and his younger brother, Su Ch'e (1039-1112), Su Shih commanded a formidable prose style, which won him a great reputation in the famous *chin-shih* examination of 1057, administered by Ou-yang Hsiu, and in a special examination of 1060, for which Ou-yang Hsiu sponsored him. He was promoted from the provinces to the capital in 1065, but his career there was interrupted at the outset by the compulsory mourning for his father, and he returned only in 1069, just as Wang An-shih was coming to power. Because of his outspoken opposition to Wang's administrative reforms, Su Shih was demoted in 1071 and served in a series of provincial posts until he was dismissed from office in 1079 and banished to Huang-chou (in modern Hopei). He returned to the capital in 1085, after the fall of the reform party, and briefly held high posts in the central government at various times in the following eight years. When the reformists regained power in 1094, they banished him to the extreme south, where he remained until shortly before his death.

Su Shih was thus only superficially involved in the great struggle between the conservative party of Han Ch'i and Ssu-ma Kuang and the radical reformist party of Wang An-shih; despite his early promise and ambition, he never quite attained sufficient eminence to become a central participant. Even when his party was in power, it denied him preferment during most of his career, distrusting his independence of mind. Su Shih, then, was unsuccessful in public life, and his preeminence in the eyes of posterity largely results from his prodigious literary talent.

As the twentieth-century scholar Kuo Shao-yü has noted, Su Shih was not primarily interested in literature for the sake of reviving the Confucian *tao,* or any *tao* for that matter. He was interested in the *art* of literature.

Bamboos, painted by Su Shih in 1094.

> The literary theories of Su [Hsün], Su [Shih], and Su [Ch'e] were basically different from those of Ou[-yang Hsiu] and Tseng [Kung, 1019-83]. The reason they were different was their different underlying attitude toward literature. . . . The Confucians Liu [K'ai], Mu [Hsiu], and Tseng [Kung] studied the literary works of the ancients with a view to seeking the *tao* embodied in those works. Although they did not necessarily find the *tao*, they never dared to announce boldly to the world, as Su Hsün did, that they were studying literature for literature's sake. . . . The Sus theorized only about the style of literature, not its content. . . . This is what was seminal about the literary theories of the three Sus. [Vol. 1]

It is important to note here that the relationship between *tao* and *wen* in Su Shih's thinking marked a decisive turn away from Han Yü's and Ou-yang Hsiu's idea of "literature as a vehicle for the *tao*." Su Shih's "way of literature" approximated the ancient concept of art or consummate skill in the *Chuang-tzu*. Therefore, in discussing his theory and practice of *ku-wen*, we must pay special attention to his distinctive tendency to equate *ku-wen* with *wen* in general and the *tao* of *ku-wen* with the *tao* of the arts in general. Reflecting his reorientation of *ku-wen* theory toward a general theory of art and letters, Su Shih explicitly included technique (*fa*) among the criteria for evaluating literature. This addition of *fa* to the theory of literature was unprecedented, and it marks the second significant departure in the Sung development of *ku-wen*, the first being Ou-yang Hsiu's introduction of the ideas of simplicity and universality.

Philosophically, Su Shih stood with the generation of Neo-Confucian thinkers that included Chou Tun-yi, Shao Yung, and Chang Tsai, rather than with his patron Ou-yang Hsiu; he shared his older Neo-Confucian contemporaries' fascination with the "ultimate" and with the metaphysics derived from the *Yi ching*. He was interested in Chou Tun-yi's attempt "to explain how the countless differentiated phenomena of existence derive from an original source which is itself . . . undifferentiated" [De Bary]. Shao Yung's theory of a numerical universe, of number as an essential concept for interpreting existence, influenced Su's thinking on the nature of change and its meaning for man's life. From Chang Tsai he borrowed the idea that the primal material force (*ch'i*) "is a constant process of change, integrating to form human beings and the other creatures of the world, disintegrating again to return to the state of the Great Vacuity. Man's task in the world is to comprehend this process of change and to harmonize his action with it."

In discussing Su Shih's intellectual and literary development, it is expedient to focus on the years 1071 to 1085, from his demotion to the provinces through his first banishment. It was during this time, especially during his exile at Huang-chou, that his ideas crystallized and matured and found expression in several of his greatest works. It is clear from his writings that in exile Su Shih relied heavily on Buddhism to forget his frustrations in the political sphere. Buddhism helped him to maintain his intellectual and emotional equilibrium—he did not indulge in the bitter rage and self-pity of Liu Tsung-yüan or the immoderate drinking of Ou-yang Hsiu—and in his works of this period, he arrived at a transcendent view of life in the general scheme of things that could be called positively optimistic.

Nature and the World of Art: Yi, Fa, and Kung

The reorientation of the literary ideal in the eleventh century from the extraordinary (*ch'i*) to the universal (*ch'ang*), as we now know, was related to a revised view of nature among Sung writers. Writers like Ou-yang Hsiu came to identify the universal in nature with a life-affirming and life-sustaining constant. Su Shih, by contrast, saw the universal as a process of dynamic fluctuation that is essentially inconclusive: dissolution succeeds growth, completion is followed by destruction. All things in nature dissolve in time, and in time they assume new forms and appearances. Thus, change, when viewed not as a finite phenomenon in human life but as an infinite succession of dissolution and growth flowing through time, becomes continuity. This new vision of an infinite process forming the content of the universal gave rise to an immensely productive idea in Su Shih's writings—the notion that dissolution and growth, change and continuity, death and life, are but two phases of a single and harmonious whole. The phenomenon of change and the impermanence of life merged in Su Shih's thought into a central concept, which I shall call the "two-oneness" of change and continuity in time. The concept is important because it offers a rare point of focus for discussing visible turning points in the Sung development of *ku-wen.*

Su Shih formulated his idea of continuity-in-change after his arrival at Huang-chou in 1080. Thereafter, he elaborated various aspects of the concept in his correspondence and in miscellaneous writings and applied these different aspects in his creative works. In the following, I first consider Su Shih's views after 1080 on the vicissitudes of nature as represented in the art of painting and refer to earlier remarks he made on literary style that contained germs of his mature conception of art in general. Then I examine his famous **"Rhymeprose on the Red Cliff"** (1082) as an illustration of how he used these ideas in his creative writings and of how they elucidate some difficult passages in that work.

The impressive transformation in Su Shih's writings after his arrival at Huang-chou was noted by his younger brother, Su Ch'e:

> Once he said to [me] Ch'e, "In my opinion, you are the only one among today's scholars who can compete with me." When he was demoted and banished to Huang-chou, he closed his door to the world and gave full rein to his brush and ink. His writings suddenly changed, becoming like [the rush of] a river in flood; and [I] Ch'e was left staring, never able to equal him again.

The simile of a river in flood suggests a considerable growth of vitality and resources, an expansion of vistas, and a proportionate loosening of set, conscious bounds. To appreciate what Su Ch'e meant by the simile in terms of Su Suih's literary style, it would be useful to examine some of the principles that had guided Su Shih's writings before the Huang-chou period.

The Preface to the *First Volume of the Journey South* (1059) contains a revealing passage:

> For the writers of former times, [literary] craft did not mean merely that one was able to write in this or that manner; craft meant that one could not but write in this or that manner. Like the clouds above mountains and rivers, like the flowers and fruits of plants and trees, it was the outward manifestation of [innate] fullness and luxuriance; even if they had wished not to have such a manifestation, would that have been possible?
> Ever since my youth, I have heard my father discourse on literature, remarking that the sages of ancient times composed because they could not but do so. [I] Shih and my younger brother, Ch'e, wrote a great deal, but never with the conscious intent [*yi*] to compose anything. In the year *chi-hai* [1059], we accompanied our father on a trip to Ch'u. There was nothing to do on the boat, because gambling, chess playing, and drinking are not what a family should enjoy together. The beauty of the scenery, the simplicity of the local customs, the historical associations of former worthies [with the region], and all that with which our senses came into contact stimulated our hearts and issued forth in lyrical verses. . . . These verses were done while we were talking and laughing together; they were not labored writings.

Su Shih was 24 years old when the preface was written. His distinction here between writings that are noted for their literary craft or artistry (*kung*) and writings that are distinguished for their level of conscious intent or conception (*yi*) is significant, as is his distinction between literary craft that stems from effort and literary craft that is spontaneous and free from human control. Of these two kinds of craft, Su Shih valued the latter more, and he seemed pleased that it informed most of his own writings at that time. Of writings distinguished for their level of conscious intent, he gives us no criterion of value judgment here except to hold up the compositions of the ancient sages as the ideal.

As Su Shih's critical thinking developed, the emphasis on *yi* over *kung* in evaluating a work became more pronounced. For example, although Su Shih did not dispute that novelty (*hsin*), extraordinariness (*ch'i*), loftiness (*kao*), and ornateness (*hua*) are characteristics of *kung,* he looked on them with distaste when the intent (*yi*) behind these skillful displays was nothing more than to gain conventional approval. By 1072, Su Shih had begun to emphasize change and to criticize the exaltation of the constant or universal (*ch'ang*), the cornerstone of Ou-yang Hsiu's critical theories, when it reflected man's conceptual manipulation of the natural course of events. In his Preface to the *Collected Poems of Shao Mao-ch'eng,* he wrote: "It is indeed difficult for human desires to coincide with the natural course. . . . How can [the coincidental] be universal? When such a coincidence occurs by chance, people then insist that it should be universal. This is why men are mostly discontented and lacking in understanding."

In Su Shih's mature reflections on art, after 1080, we find a consistent tendency to emphasize nature (*t'ien*) over man (*jen*) and a shift of focus from craft or artistry (*kung*) to intent or conception (*yi*); in Ch'ien Chung-shu's words, there was a propensity in Su Shih's thinking on art to "turn from the work of art to the mind of the artist." In contrast to Su's definition of literary craft quoted above, the basis of evaluating *kung* shifted from the criterion of spontaneity, which pertains to the stylistic quality of a literary *work,* to the writer's mode of *thought,* which reflects his philosophical thinking as well as his ethical outlook. For example, in contrasting nature and man, Su Shih ceased to identify *yi* with the writings of sages alone and began to link it with nature (*t'ien*). At this point, *yi* became an increasingly important critical concept in his literary theory. A given subject, when seen from the detached perspective of the natural course of events, assumes a form of expression and dictates a set of technical rules very different from those of the same subject seen from the perspective of individual human bias.

Much of Su Shih's critical discussion of *yi* dealt with the art of painting, and not by coincidence. Painting communicates and represents nature directly, and to Su Shih, an accomplished painter himself, it was the art of nature par excellence: the painter's art, insofar as it seeks to approximate that which naturally exists in the absence of human agency, mirrors the working of nature (*t'ien kung*) and its *yi* (*t'ien yi*). An examination of Su Shih's discussion of painting is illuminating not only because he obviously considered the arts of painting and poetry in unison but also because ideas concerning the two forms of art can generally be conveyed more vividly and more convincingly in terms of the visual art. Cyril Drummond Le Gros Clark deemed "the close comparison between the painter and the poet" to be "important to an elucidation of Su Shih's philosophy of art." However, what is crucial in Su Shih's association of the poet with the painter is not so much a comparison as a convergence of the painter's and the poet's minds on the conceptual level with regard to an understanding of the working of nature and an appraisal of the role of artistic expression in the total process of creating a work of art, whether verbal or pictorial.

Water, especially water in motion, is a favorite symbol in Su Shih's criticism of literature and art. It symbolizes spontaneity, freedom, change, continuity, and all aspects of nature in which man aspires to participate. In his **"Postscript to the Paintings of P'u Yung-sheng"** (ca. 1081), Su Shih commented:

> Most painters of water, ancient and modern, have painted it as extending far over a level surface with fine ripples. Those skilled at this technique can at best make it rise and fall in waves, so that people touch it with their hands, thinking it really three-dimensional; this they take to be the highest achievement. But in merit, these paintings hardly differ by a hair's breadth from the craftsmanship of representing water on block-print sheets.
>
> During the Kuang-ming era [880-81] of the T'ang dynasty, the private scholar Sun Wei first formulated an original conception [*hsin-yi*] [in painting water]. He painted [it in] dashing torrents and huge waves, turning and twisting with the mountains and rocks, taking its form from whatever things [*wu*] it encountered. He showed water in all its various aspects, and his work was pronounced "creative and preeminent" [*shen-yi*]. Later, two natives of Shu, Huang Ch'üan and Sun Chih-wei, mastered the technique [*fa*] of his brush strokes. . . . In recent years, P'u Yung-sheng of Ch'eng-tu . . . began to paint water in motion. He showed a grasp of the original conception [*yi*] of the two Suns.

In the postscript, Su Shih states that three things are to be considered in the painting of water: *yi, fa,* and *kung*—that is, the painter's conception of the subject, his technique, and his execution. Of the three, *yi* prescribes the technique and determines the merit of the execution. The character of water, when conceived in its essentially changeable nature, is expressed as "taking its form from whatever things it encountered" in the painting. But when conceived in its local appearances, it is generally represented as "extending far over a level surface with fine ripples." The difference between the two conceptions (*yi*) of water is reflected in the technique (*fa*), resulting in two methods of painting water. Sun Wei was able to realize the first conception of water, and so Su Shih describes his painting as "creative and preeminent." Sun Chih-wei mastered Sun Wei's technique and was able to execute the same effect, but because the original conception did not come from him, his painting is praised only for its forcefulness. P'u Yung-sheng recreated the *fa* and the *yi* of the two Suns in making water come alive in his painting, but it is hard to imagine that Su Shih regarded his accomplishment as anything more than skillful execution since neither the *yi* nor the *fa* of painting water in motion originated with him.

Su Shih, indirectly through a postscript that discussed three painters and their representations of water in motion, underlined the close and well-ordered relationship among *yi, fa,* and *kung* in a finished work of art. In his **"Discourse on Literature,"** he described his own style:

> My writing is like ten thousand barrels of spring water, gushing from the ground, choosing no specific outlet. On level ground, it floods and covers thousands of miles in a day without the least effort. Turning and twisting with the mountains and rocks, it takes its forms from whatever things it encounters, unpredictably. All that can be foretold is that it always goes where it should go, and it always stops where it cannot but stop. That is all. As for the rest, I myself am unable to tell.

And in his **"Letter in Answer to Hsieh Min-shih"** he said,

> I have perused the letters and verses and miscellaneous essays you sent me. On the whole, they are like moving clouds and flowing water, without any fixed quality, just going always where they should go and stopping always where they cannot but stop. Your style is natural, and it expresses itself exuberantly.

Critics are wont to quote these two passages as indicative of Su Shih's ideal of literary style. However, once the inherent relationship among *yi,* fa, and *kung* is clear, we can see that there is a qualitative difference between the two styles. Like the two painters of "living water" in the **"Postscript,"** the lack of an expressed source of being in Hsieh Min-shih's writing precludes the presence of a vital, productive *yi*. Su Shih's own writing, on the other hand, has a definite origin (gushing from a spring underground) and a well-formulated method of expression (taking its forms from whatever things it encounters). The spring is an admirable image of a great, abundant, and natural reservoir of vitality, accumulated over time (fed by constant practice, continued reflection, and vast learning) and the fountainhead of his literary output. Once above ground, its spontaneity in action is to be understood in the same sense as the lack of self-consciousness of the master carver in the *Chuang-tzu,* whose skill is already one with the *tao* and no longer needs the mediation or guidance of conscious method. Such spontaneous skill, as a natural expression of the artist's spiritual communion with the *tao,* is certainly not to be compared to the moving clouds in Hsieh Min-shih's case, which, to all appearance, have no real connection with the topography of the sky.

To attain such unconscious skill, which implies a direct communication between the *tao* and execution, it is imperative that the conceiving spirit (*shen*) be free of all emotional affect. In his **"Postscript to the Calligraphy of the Six T'ang Masters"** (1081), Su Shih pointed to the undesirable effect of emotional and moral bias in a work of art: "In the case of petty men, even if their calligraphic art is craftsmanlike (*kung*), it invariably carries an expression that is smug and ingratiating. The fact is that a man's feelings always show through with his thoughts. Is this not what Master Han said about the axe thief?"

When affected by emotion, the conceiving mind, the agent of direct communication between man and nature and between nature and art, becomes individualized and consequently carries the taint of a localized and unnatural form. How is a writer to attain a style of writing comparable to the category of creative and preeminent (*shen-yi*) in painting and be freed, so to speak, from the appearance of an axe thief?

In another passage of the letter to Hsieh Min-shih, Su Shih, elaborated on the concept of *tz'u-ta* ("language must communicate") as the ultimate achievement in literary skill, the stylistic equivalent of *shen-yi* in painting.

> Confucius said, "Language not in good style will not travel far." He also said, "It is sufficient if language communicates the meaning." However, language that merely communicates [the author's] intent [*yi*] is often suspected of being less than good style; this is greatly in error. To seek out the innermost mystery of things is like trying to tether the wind or capture a shadow. Not one man in thousands can have a perfect understanding [of the mystery] in his mind, much less be able to make it perfectly intelligible in speech or in writing. To be able to do this is what is meant by "language communicating the meaning." When language communicates, it is in more than sufficiently good style.

What language communicates, after all, is *yi*. And to make language communicate, a writer, according to Su Shih, must first have "the mystery of things" clearly conceived in his mind—that is, he must conceive his subject as a painter conceives nature, with his mind detached from personal emotions; his mind must also be free of moral bias, so that things will communicate by themselves in speech or in writing. One way to accomplish this is to see the subject in the way a painter sees water, through a series of external changes, because change is the the visible way in which things express themselves in nature: dashing torrents, huge waves, and gushing springs, all changing form at every encounter with things, express the nature of water.

The "Two-Oneness" of Change and Continuation in the **"Rhymeprose on the Red Cliff"**

Once this conception and expression of change in nature are transferred to the conception of change in the human world, man's life and history, with all their ups and downs and their monumental events, become one with the twists and turns of the torrents and waves. The **"Rhymeprose on the Red Cliff"** (1082) may be viewed as a literary recreation of this transference of perspective, the natural rhythm of change applied to the vicissitudes of human life and history; as the transient in man merges with the continual process of dissolution and growth in nature, the boundaries between finite mind and infinite nature dissolve. . . .

One question often raised about the **"Rhymeprose on the Red Cliff"** is whether the work is to be read as two pieces or one. In fact, the first part is much more often read than the second, which is not infrequently omitted from anthologies. This practice is based on a failure to appreciate the underlying unity of the two parts. Another question concerns the discrepancy between the single crane and the two feather-robed Taoist priests in the second part; this problem is closely related to the issue of whether the **"Rhymeprose on the Red Cliff"** is one work or two. The problem of the crane has elicited the interest of many scholars and created much discomfort among critics. A common solution has been textual emendation: "*two* Taoist priests" is changed to "*one* Taoist priest," and the discrepancy conveniently disappears, although some editions of Su Shih's collected works persist in printing "*two* Taoist priests." But this textual problem of two or one can probably best be solved by an examination of the themes of the rhymeprose and of the idea of two-oneness.

Part I of the prose poem opens with Su Shih and his guests riding in a boat under the Red Cliff by the light of the full moon in the seventh month of the year. They are in a convivial mood, drinking and chanting poetry. Presently one of the guests begins to play his flute. The plaintiveness of the music rouses Su Shih to ask why he plays so sadly. The guest replies that the scene has reminded him of a poem written below the Red Cliff by the great hero Ts'ao Ts'ao in his prime, nearly 900 years before. That reminder has caused him to reflect on his own mortality. He envies the river, which flows endlessly, and wishes that he could roam the heavens forever as a companion to the moon. But knowing that his wish is impossible, he can only express his sadness in music. Su Shih counters the guest's lament by pointing out that the river and the moon remain ever the same despite the appearance of continual change. There is no occasion for envy or sadness, Su Shih says, since from the standpoint of change, nothing ever endures, and nature cannot be possessed by the force of human desires and aspirations. All that man can do is to enjoy what is offered him in his encounters with nature. Thereupon, the guest takes heart, and all present continue their carousal till daybreak, when they are all drunk and pillowed on one another.

The first piece, then, is a statement on human mortality and freedom cast in the form of a dialogue between Su

Shih and his guest. The guest mourns the transience of man's life and fame and aspires to immortality. According to Su Shih, however, there is no such thing as mortality or immortality; these are merely human concepts prompted by human desires and aspirations. If one can contemplate the manifestations of mortality and transience in life and in history in the same way in which he contemplates the water and the moon in nature—detached from personal sentiments and desires—then he will see that there is no cause to mourn.

Part II of the rhymeprose recounts another visit to the Red Cliff three months later. The season and the mood are both quite different. It is again a clear, moonlit night, but in place of the soft breeze on the water, there is a heavy frost on the ground. The conviviality of the occasion is not so pronounced since food and drink are not ready at hand. Su Shih's conversation with his guests, which bears on the latter problem, is in sharp contrast to the earlier exalted discourse on the exploits of past heroes and the impermanence of life. There is again a boat ride, but the center of action shifts to the land.

Su Shih is seen walking with two guests through a winter landscape from his country retreat to his home. Presently, having obtained fish and wine, they are on their way to the Red Cliff. Su Shih then leaves his guests and climbs to the top of the cliff. The scene has changed beyond recognition since his last visit, and Su Shih is oppressed by its bleakness. High above the river, he sits alone and whistles to the wind; but it is too cold to stay there long, and he descends and returns to the boat. It is almost midnight. A solitary crane flies by. Shortly after, the guests leave and Su Shih goes home to sleep. In a dream, he encounters two Taoist priests, in feather robes, who inquire about his excursion that night. Suddenly realizing that the priests are the very crane that flew by his boat earlier, he awakes with a start. He looks out of his door, but there is no sign of the priests.

In comparison with the first part, the second is quite low-keyed. It is tempting to interpret its subdued tone in the same light as that in which some critics interpret the change in scenery and mood—that is, as a deliberate attempt to bring out by contrast the theme of change and transience in life. Such an interpretation, however, entails serious contradictions not only in the development of the two parts of the piece itself but also with regard to what we have already understood of Su Shih's appreciation of the phenomenon of change in nature. Within the rhymeprose itself, Master Su has already argued in the first part that there is no basis for melancholy over the passing of good moments in history and in life; he has offered the moon and the running water as two arresting images of how things can be seen from the dualistic perspective of change-continuity. The moon and the water are still present in the second part. Which of the two, then, are we to accept as representing the basic theme of the whole piece—the changing mood of Su Shih under two different circumstances or the consistently unchanging moon and water? This issue, a highly speculative one, is visibly projected in the one-crane two-priests enigma.

Before we examine the conception of change implied in the shift of number from one to two, let us consider the use of the dream in literature as a device for expressing speculative thought. One example that comes readily to mind is the dream in the second chapter of the *Chuang-tzu,* where, after a long discussion of dreams and their interpretation, it is said that Chuang Chou dreamt that he was a butterfly.

> Once Chuang Chou dreamt he was a butterfly, a butterfly flitting and fluttering around, happy with himself and doing as he pleased. He didn't know he was Chuang Chou. Suddenly he woke up and there he was, solid and unmistakable Chuang Chou. But he didn't know if he was Chuang Chou who had dreamt he was a butterfly, or butterfly dreaming he was Chuang Chou. Between Chuang Chou and a butterfly there must be *some* distinction! This is called the Transformation of Things.

The dream in the *Chuang-tzu,* as in the second part of Su Shih's rhymeprose, suggests a move away from reality toward meditation on what constitutes reality. The issue in question in the *Chuang-tzu* is not whether it is Chuang Chou dreaming or the butterfly dreaming. The dream is the framework in which the idea of the "transformation of things" is expressed. Poised between two possible modes of reality—Chuang Chou dreaming and the butterfly dreaming—but committed to neither, one is forced by the lack of resolution on a realistic level to take notice of the idea of "transformation," which presents a resolution on the speculative level; namely, the merging of the two differentiated states of being in time—Chuang Chou and the butterfly. This merging in time constitutes the formal structure of the idea of "transformation."

Similarly, the lack of a resolution between the apparently contradictory positions of Su Shih in Parts I and II forces one to seek a unifying standpoint on the speculative level—that is, through the idea of two-oneness as projected in the dream: the transformation of one crane into two Taoist priests. What the dream in the second part seeks to communicate is essentially the same speculation about change as that expressed in the dialogue between Master Su and his guest in the first part. But now there is an implicit exchange of positions: Su Shih assumes the position of the guest, and the dream speaks for his own previous position. In the dream, not only is emotional bias verbally excluded from the depiction of the coexistence of change and continuity, but differentiated time, the usual context of change, is eliminated as well. In terms of differentiated existence over time, one that approximates the numerically rational correspondences of nature seen in distinct, arrested moments, one crane should indeed "change" into one Taoist priest (or vice versa provided that that kind of change is considered more possible than changing into two). But if existence is seen in terms of undifferentiated continuity, the crane, on the speculative level, is at once itself and the Taoist priest, which makes two. The dream, therefore, is a poetic marker of this shift in modes of thought; it is the author's way of calling attention to the fact that what is under consideration is only a speculative idea—a theme, so to speak—which is not something that can be proved in realistic terms or be called true or false.

In an early controversy over the two-one problem, a Sung scholar remarked that the passage about the crane and two Taoist priests may contain an allusion to a story about the T'ang emperor Ming-huang. According to the story, the emperor Ming-huang went hunting on the Double Ninth and shot a solitary crane flying in the mountains. The crane flew away to the southwest with the arrow. Nearby was a temple that an itinerant Taoist priest was accustomed to visit three or four times every year. One day, the priest arrived with an arrow in his hand. He told the residents of the temple that the owner of the arrow would be there two years later and that they should return the arrow to him. Two years later, the emperor visited the temple. When he saw the arrow and the date inscribed on it, he realized that the crane he had shot on that ninth day of the ninth month was the very same itinerant Taoist priest.

The inference here is, of course, that Su Shih may have been alluding to the crane in the story of the emperor Ming-huang and translating the possibility of their being one and the same crane into the presence of two Taoist priests in the dream (for what more apt image could one use to express the idea of possibility?). Or, if one wants to be witty, the crane of the rhymeprose could merely have joined the crane of the story of the emperor Ming-huang, and both cranes continued their existence as priests. At any rate, "playing" with the allusion also collapses the chronology, making the Ming-huang crane a contemporary, in some way, of the rhymeprose crane. This collapse of time is achieved by the image of two priests walking together. One priest would constitute a simple allusion to the previous test. However, even if we grant this playfulness to the author, this is still a local solution, which explains the dream but does not elucidate the total unity of the two prose poems.

The **"Rhymeprose on the Red Cliff"** was, in my opinion, certainly conceived as one piece twice enacted in different moments of life. The theme is that of time and life as conceived from the two complementary viewpoints of change and continuity. From the first part to the second, there is a steady progression from the concrete to the abstract, from the human to the natural, and from change-in-time (historical moments such as Ts'ao Ts'ao's battle at the Red Cliff) to timeless becoming (the dream). The order of progression in the two parts strongly suggests that the abstract and timeless (one crane) encompasses the concrete and differentiated (two priests). This idea of "two-oneness" is at once the beginning and the origin of all successive changes in time.

L. E. J. Brouwer, the Dutch philosopher and mathematician, said the following about man's intuition of two-oneness as the origin of numbers:

> This neo-intuitionism considers the falling apart of moments of life into qualitatively different parts, to be reunited only while remaining separated by time, as the fundamental phenomenon of the intellect, passing by abstracting from its emotional content into the fundamental phenomenon of mathematical thinking, the intuition of two-oneness, the basal intuition of mathematics, creates not only the numbers one and two, but also all finite ordinal numbers, in as much as one of the elements of the two-oneness may be thought of as a new two-oneness, which process may be repeated indefinitely.

This pregnant passage can be seen as bringing Su Shih's fundamental insight on change and continuity to the highest level of abstraction, removing all specificity from every concrete phenomenon of change and grasping the absolute essentials of identity and difference. The abstraction of all emotional content contrasts well with Su Shih's similar demand for the less austere purpose of avoiding bias. But, of course, Su Shih's crane image is much more evocative than a simple mathematical concept. The crane suggests not only two-oneness but a whole process of change and continuity, a variation on a theme that takes on its own life and escapes abstraction.

Change, or transformation, need not be a tragic phenomenon; it may simply be the process of coming into being or passing from one state of being to another. Change may be the law governing not decline and death but the incessant process of generation, as in the *Yi ching;* it may be the law governing incipiency, birth, and the phenomenal world. In other words, death is tragic and the phenomenon of existence impermanent only if one insists on seeing them from the perspective of a single life-death succession (*sheng-ssu*). Su Shih, in his **"Rhymeprose on the Red Cliff,"** has eliminated the sense of the tragic view of life (which is not the same as eliminating the sense of the tragic in life) by broadening the span of life beyond the confines of one life-death succession to the life-[death]-life succession (*sheng-sheng*) of the *Yi ching* tradition. He has thereby escaped the law governing change as decline and death and has attained freedom from the necessity of the tragic, as Han Yü, Liu Tsung-yüan, and Ou-yang Hsiu did before him.

Han Yü attained freedom through identification with the orthodox Confucian tradition, thereby transcending time. Liu Tsung-yüan attained it through an affirmation of the necessity of moral good in man, thus transcending the necessity of physical law (*tzu-jan*) of nature and history. Ou-yang Hsiu liberated himself through a firm grasp of the irreducible facts in life, which comprehend different phases and levels of man's achievement and which make reality credible. Su Shih achieved the same end by dissolving the boundary between the real and the unreal, between the desirable and the undesirable, and finally between life and death. Because all four men ultimately derived the inspiration for their affirmation of life from the schools of thought of ancient times (*ku*) and because each produced a body of prose works expressing that affirmation, they are usually considered together as writers of the ancient-prose style (*ku-wen*). The fact that Su Shih articulated his most penetrating statement on *tao* and *wen* in rhymeprose—which is not purely a prose form—

need not prevent us from considering him within the framework of the *ku-wen* movement. The keynote of dissolution of the boundary between manifested (literary) forms in Su Shih's concept of literature and art is eminently present in this work of literary art. This dissolution of boundary in Su Shih's thinking about *wen* and *tao* (whether in terms of the *Yi ching* or Buddhism or Taoism) marks a second turn away from the norm established by Han Yü in his program for *ku-wen* writers, which insists on a pure integration of the ancient (Confucian) *tao* with established, classical literary forms.

As many of Su Shih's critics charged in his lifetime, he was an eclectic and unorthodox thinker. A central characteristic of his eclecticism is that he seems never to have followed any one line of thought to a definitive position; his conclusions were intuitive rather than formal. This eclecticism is probably the reason why he has never been accorded a conspicuous place in Chinese intellectual history, and why so few literary historians and critics have tried to place his works in their contemporary intellectual context. On the whole, when we look at the concepts of *ch'i* and *li* and the principle of generation (*sheng-sheng*) of the *Yi ching,* which informed his method (*fa*) of literary creation and art criticism, it is apparent that he was more a disciple of contemporary Neo-Confucian thinkers like Shao Yung (1011-77), Chang Tsai (1020-77), Ch'eng Yi (1033-1108), and Ch'eng Hao (1032-85) than of the T'ang *ku-wen* masters. Therefore, his *ku-wen* theory and practice must be understood not primarily in terms of what he had in common with his mentor Ou-yang Hsiu or his much-admired predecessors Han Yü and Liu Tsung-yüan but in terms of what was current, volatile, and revolutionary in the intellectual trends of his own time. Only then can we begin to appreciate the complexity of the process in the *ku-wen* movement that transformed T'ang classicism into Sung Neo-Confucianism.

FURTHER READING

Egan, Ronald C. "Poems on Paintings: Su Shih and Huang T'ing-chien." *Harvard Journal of Asiatic Studies* 43, No. 2 (December 1983): 413-51.

Studies Su's poems on paintings and concludes that, "ultimately, it is. . . familiarity with the art form that frees Su and Huang [the other poet whose works are discussed in this article] from any sense of obligation to dwell, in their poems, on the representation itself. They are at ease with the idea of depicting reality on silk and do not feel the need to reiterate, and hence to legitimize with words, what the painter has drawn with his brush. In this respect they remain true as poets to the anti-representational stance they take. . . ."

———. "Su Shih's 'Notes' as a Historical and Literary Source." *Harvard Journal of Asiatic Studies* 50, No. 2 (December 1990): 561-88.

Explores Su's "notes"—a genre of very short writings, usually on everyday subjects. Egan notes that they are significant because Su's notes "often provide insight into levels of mundane life that are seldom if ever illuminated in his more formal writings" and they "serve a larger purpose by helping to establish a context in which to read [Su's] poetry."

Fuller, Michael A. "Pursuing the Complete Bamboo in the Breast: Reflections on a Classical Chinese Image for Immediacy." *Harvard Journal of Asiatic Studies* 53, No. 1 (June 1993): 5-23.

Discusses Su's conception of the immediate and "the concepts and interpretive traditions supporting it."

Murck, Christian. "Su Shih's Reading of the *Chung yung*." In *Theories of the Arts in China*, edited by Susan Bush and Christian Murck, pp. 267-92. Princeton: Princeton University Press, 1983.

Examines Su's *Chung yung lun*, an essay on an important Confucian text, asserting that it "deepens our understanding of his aesthetics by helping situate artistic activity in the context of his personal approach to self-cultivation generally."

Pease, Jonathan. "Contour Plowing on East Slope: A New Reading of Su Shi." *Journal of the American Oriental Society* 112, No. 3 (July-September 1992): 470-77.

Generally favorable review of Michael A. Fuller's 1990 monograph, *The Road to East Slope: The Development of Su Shi's Poetic Voice.*

Sargent, Stuart H. "Colophons in Countermotion: Poems by Su Shih and Huang T'ing-chen." *Harvard Journal of Asiatic Studies* 52, No. 1 (June 1992): 263-302.

Discusses Su's poem paintings using the idea of "countermotion" as a heuristic aid. Sargent concludes that, "in the case of Su Shih, countermotion is to be found between the colophon [poem] and the painting as an object to be interpreted and placed within a wider literary or social context."

Yoshikawa, Koµjiroµ. "Late Period of the Northern Sung—1050-1100." In his *An Introduction to Sung Poetry*, translated by Burton Watson, pp. 85-133. Cambridge: Harvard University Press, 1967.

Overview of Su's life, works, style, and philosophy. The critic notes that Su's poetic works " are unmatched in stature by anything else in Sung poetry."

Yutang, Lin. *The Gay Genius: The Life and Times of Su Tungpo.* New York: John Day Co., 1947, 349 p.

Critical biography that also puts Su's life in the context of his era.

CLASSICAL AND MEDIEVAL LITERATURE CRITICISM

INDEXES

Literary Criticism Series
Cumulative Author Index

Literary Criticism Series
Cumulative Topic Index

CMLC Cumulative Nationality Index

CMLC Cumulative Title Index

CMLC Cumulative Critic Index

How to Use This Index

The main references

> **Calvino, Italo**
> **1923-1985.....CLC 5, 8, 11, 22, 33, 39, 73; SSC 3**

list all author entries in the following Gale Literary Criticism series:

BLC = *Black Literature Criticism*
CLC = *Contemporary Literary Criticism*
CLR = *Children's Literature Review*
CMLC = *Classical and Medieval Literature Criticism*
DA = *DISCovering Authors*
DC = *Drama Criticism*
HLC = *Hispanic Literature Criticism*
LC = *Literature Criticism from 1400 to 1800*
NCLC = *Nineteenth-Century Literature Criticism*
PC = *Poetry Criticism*
SSC = *Short Story Criticism*
TCLC = *Twentieth-Century Literary Criticism*
WLC = *World Literature Criticism, 1500 to the Present*

The cross-references

> See also CANR 23; CA 85-88;
> obituary CA 116

list all author entries in the following Gale biographical and literary sources:

AAYA = *Authors & Artists for Young Adults*
AITN = *Authors in the News*
BEST = *Bestsellers*
BW = *Black Writers*
CA = *Contemporary Authors*
CAAS = *Contemporary Authors Autobiography Series*
CABS = *Contemporary Authors Bibliographical Series*
CANR = *Contemporary Authors New Revision Series*
CAP = *Contemporary Authors Permanent Series*
CDALB = *Concise Dictionary of American Literary Biography*
CDBLB = *Concise Dictionary of British Literary Biography*
DLB = *Dictionary of Literary Biography*
DLBD = *Dictionary of Literary Biography Documentary Series*
DLBY = *Dictionary of Literary Biography Yearbook*
HW = *Hispanic Writers*
JRDA = *Junior DISCovering Authors*
MAICYA = *Major Authors and Illustrators for Children and Young Adults*
MTCW = *Major 20th-Century Writers*
NNAL = *Native North American Literature*
SAAS = *Something about the Author Autobiography Series*
SATA = *Something about the Author*
YABC = *Yesterday's Authors of Books for Children*

Literary Criticism Series Cumulative Author Index

Aldiss, Brian W(ilson) 1925- . . . . **CLC 5, 14, 40**
See also CA 5-8R; CAAS 2; CANR 5, 28; DLB 14; MTCW; SATA 34

Alegria, Claribel 1924- . . . . **CLC 75**
See also CA 131; CAAS 15; DLB 145; HW

Alegria, Fernando 1918- . . . . **CLC 57**
See also CA 9-12R; CANR 5, 32; HW

Aleichem, Sholom . . . . **TCLC 1, 35**
See also Rabinovitch, Sholem

Aleixandre, Vicente 1898-1984 . . . **CLC 9, 36**
See also CA 85-88; 114; CANR 26; DLB 108; HW; MTCW

Alepoudelis, Odysseus
See Elytis, Odysseus

Aleshkovsky, Joseph 1929-
See Aleshkovsky, Yuz
See also CA 121; 128

Aleshkovsky, Yuz . . . . **CLC 44**
See also Aleshkovsky, Joseph

Alexander, Lloyd (Chudley) 1924- . . **CLC 35**
See also AAYA 1; CA 1-4R; CANR 1, 24, 38; CLR 1, 5; DLB 52; JRDA; MAICYA; MTCW; SAAS 19; SATA 3, 49, 81

Alfau, Felipe 1902- . . . . **CLC 66**
See also CA 137

Alger, Horatio, Jr. 1832-1899 . . . . . **NCLC 8**
See also DLB 42; SATA 16

Algren, Nelson 1909-1981 . . . . **CLC 4, 10, 33**
See also CA 13-16R; 103; CANR 20; CDALB 1941-1968; DLB 9; DLBY 81, 82; MTCW

Ali, Ahmed 1910- . . . . **CLC 69**
See also CA 25-28R; CANR 15, 34

Alighieri, Dante 1265-1321 . . . . **CMLC 3**

Allan, John B.
See Westlake, Donald E(dwin)

Allen, Edward 1948- . . . . **CLC 59**

Allen, Paula Gunn 1939- . . . . **CLC 84**
See also CA 112; 143; NNAL

Allen, Roland
See Ayckbourn, Alan

Allen, Sarah A.
See Hopkins, Pauline Elizabeth

Allen, Woody 1935- . . . . **CLC 16, 52**
See also AAYA 10; CA 33-36R; CANR 27, 38; DLB 44; MTCW

Allende, Isabel 1942- . . . . **CLC 39, 57; HLC**
See also CA 125; 130; DLB 145; HW; MTCW

Alleyn, Ellen
See Rossetti, Christina (Georgina)

Allingham, Margery (Louise) 1904-1966 . . . . **CLC 19**
See also CA 5-8R; 25-28R; CANR 4; DLB 77; MTCW

Allingham, William 1824-1889 . . . **NCLC 25**
See also DLB 35

Allison, Dorothy E. 1949- . . . . **CLC 78**
See also CA 140

Allston, Washington 1779-1843 . . . . **NCLC 2**
See also DLB 1

Almedingen, E. M. . . . . **CLC 12**
See also Almedingen, Martha Edith von
See also SATA 3

Almedingen, Martha Edith von 1898-1971
See Almedingen, E. M.
See also CA 1-4R; CANR 1

Almqvist, Carl Jonas Love 1793-1866 . . . . **NCLC 42**

Alonso, Damaso 1898-1990 . . . . **CLC 14**
See also CA 110; 131; 130; DLB 108; HW

Alov
See Gogol, Nikolai (Vasilyevich)

Alta 1942- . . . . **CLC 19**
See also CA 57-60

Alter, Robert B(ernard) 1935- . . . . . . **CLC 34**
See also CA 49-52; CANR 1, 47

Alther, Lisa 1944- . . . . **CLC 7, 41**
See also CA 65-68; CANR 12, 30; MTCW

Altman, Robert 1925- . . . . **CLC 16**
See also CA 73-76; CANR 43

Alvarez, A(lfred) 1929- . . . . **CLC 5, 13**
See also CA 1-4R; CANR 3, 33; DLB 14, 40

Alvarez, Alejandro Rodriguez 1903-1965
See Casona, Alejandro
See also CA 131; 93-96; HW

Amado, Jorge 1912- . . . . . **CLC 13, 40; HLC**
See also CA 77-80; CANR 35; DLB 113; MTCW

Ambler, Eric 1909- . . . . **CLC 4, 6, 9**
See also CA 9-12R; CANR 7, 38; DLB 77; MTCW

Amichai, Yehuda 1924- . . . . . . **CLC 9, 22, 57**
See also CA 85-88; CANR 46; MTCW

Amiel, Henri Frederic 1821-1881 . . **NCLC 4**

Amis, Kingsley (William) 1922- . . **CLC 1, 2, 3, 5, 8, 13, 40, 44; DA**
See also AITN 2; CA 9-12R; CANR 8, 28; CDBLB 1945-1960; DLB 15, 27, 100, 139; MTCW

Amis, Martin (Louis) 1949- . . . . **CLC 4, 9, 38, 62**
See also BEST 90:3; CA 65-68; CANR 8, 27; DLB 14

Ammons, A(rchie) R(andolph) 1926- . . . . **CLC 2, 3, 5, 8, 9, 25, 57**
See also AITN 1; CA 9-12R; CANR 6, 36; DLB 5; MTCW

Amo, Tauraatua i
See Adams, Henry (Brooks)

Anand, Mulk Raj 1905- . . . . **CLC 23**
See also CA 65-68; CANR 32; MTCW

Anatol
See Schnitzler, Arthur

Anaya, Rudolfo A(lfonso) 1937- . . . . **CLC 23; HLC**
See also CA 45-48; CAAS 4; CANR 1, 32; DLB 82; HW 1; MTCW

Andersen, Hans Christian 1805-1875 . . **NCLC 7; DA; SSC 6; WLC**
See also CLR 6; MAICYA; YABC 1

Anderson, C. Farley
See Mencken, H(enry) L(ouis); Nathan, George Jean

Anderson, Jessica (Margaret) Queale . . . . **CLC 37**
See also CA 9-12R; CANR 4

Anderson, Jon (Victor) 1940- . . . . **CLC 9**
See also CA 25-28R; CANR 20

Anderson, Lindsay (Gordon) 1923-1994 . . . . **CLC 20**
See also CA 125; 128; 146

Anderson, Maxwell 1888-1959 . . . . . **TCLC 2**
See also CA 105; DLB 7

Anderson, Poul (William) 1926- . . . . **CLC 15**
See also AAYA 5; CA 1-4R; CAAS 2; CANR 2, 15, 34; DLB 8; MTCW; SATA-Brief 39

Anderson, Robert (Woodruff) 1917- . . . . **CLC 23**
See also AITN 1; CA 21-24R; CANR 32; DLB 7

Anderson, Sherwood 1876-1941 . . . . **TCLC 1, 10, 24; DA; SSC 1; WLC**
See also CA 104; 121; CDALB 1917-1929; DLB 4, 9, 86; DLBD 1; MTCW

Andouard
See Giraudoux, (Hippolyte) Jean

Andrade, Carlos Drummond de . . . . . . **CLC 18**
See also Drummond de Andrade, Carlos

Andrade, Mario de 1893-1945 . . . . . **TCLC 43**

Andreas-Salome, Lou 1861-1937 . . . **TCLC 56**
See also DLB 66

Andrewes, Lancelot 1555-1626 . . . . **LC 5**

Andrews, Cicily Fairfield
See West, Rebecca

Andrews, Elton V.
See Pohl, Frederik

Andreyev, Leonid (Nikolaevich) 1871-1919 . . . . **TCLC 3**
See also CA 104

Andric, Ivo 1892-1975 . . . . **CLC 8**
See also CA 81-84; 57-60; CANR 43; DLB 147; MTCW

Angelique, Pierre
See Bataille, Georges

Angell, Roger 1920- . . . . **CLC 26**
See also CA 57-60; CANR 13, 44

Angelou, Maya 1928- . . . . **CLC 12, 35, 64, 77; BLC; DA**
See also AAYA 7; BW 2; CA 65-68; CANR 19, 42; DLB 38; MTCW; SATA 49

Annensky, Innokenty Fyodorovich 1856-1909 . . . . **TCLC 14**
See also CA 110

Anon, Charles Robert
See Pessoa, Fernando (Antonio Nogueira)

Anouilh, Jean (Marie Lucien Pierre) 1910-1987 . . . . . . **CLC 1, 3, 8, 13, 40, 50**
See also CA 17-20R; 123; CANR 32; MTCW

Anthony, Florence
See Ai

Anthony, John
See Ciardi, John (Anthony)

Anthony, Peter
See Shaffer, Anthony (Joshua); Shaffer, Peter (Levin)

Anthony, Piers 1934- . . . . **CLC 35**
See also AAYA 11; CA 21-24R; CANR 28; DLB 8; MTCW

Antoine, Marc
See Proust, (Valentin-Louis-George-Eugene-) Marcel

Antoninus, Brother
See Everson, William (Oliver)

Antonioni, Michelangelo 1912- . . . . . **CLC 20**
See also CA 73-76; CANR 45

Antschel, Paul 1920-1970
See Celan, Paul
See also CA 85-88; CANR 33; MTCW

Anwar, Chairil 1922-1949 . . . . **TCLC 22**
See also CA 121

Apollinaire, Guillaume . . **TCLC 3, 8, 51; PC 7**
See also Kostrowitzki, Wilhelm Apollinaris de

Appelfeld, Aharon 1932- . . . . **CLC 23, 47**
See also CA 112; 133

Apple, Max (Isaac) 1941-. . . . . **CLC 9, 33**
See also CA 81-84; CANR 19; DLB 130

Appleman, Philip (Dean) 1926- . . . . . **CLC 51**
See also CA 13-16R; CAAS 18; CANR 6, 29

Appleton, Lawrence
See Lovecraft, H(oward) P(hillips)

Apteryx
See Eliot, T(homas) S(tearns)

Apuleius, (Lucius Madaurensis)
125(?)-175(?) . . . . **CMLC 1**

Aquin, Hubert 1929-1977. . . . . **CLC 15**
See also CA 105; DLB 53

Aragon, Louis 1897-1982 . . . . **CLC 3, 22**
See also CA 69-72; 108; CANR 28; DLB 72; MTCW

Arany, Janos 1817-1882. . . . . **NCLC 34**

Arbuthnot, John 1667-1735 . . . . **LC 1**
See also DLB 101

Archer, Herbert Winslow
See Mencken, H(enry) L(ouis)

Archer, Jeffrey (Howard) 1940- . . . . **CLC 28**
See also BEST 89:3; CA 77-80; CANR 22

Archer, Jules 1915- . . . . **CLC 12**
See also CA 9-12R; CANR 6; SAAS 5; SATA 4

Archer, Lee
See Ellison, Harlan (Jay)

Arden, John 1930- . . . . **CLC 6, 13, 15**
See also CA 13-16R; CAAS 4; CANR 31; DLB 13; MTCW

Arenas, Reinaldo
1943-1990 . . . . **CLC 41; HLC**
See also CA 124; 128; 133; DLB 145; HW

Arendt, Hannah 1906-1975 . . . . **CLC 66**
See also CA 17-20R; 61-64; CANR 26; MTCW

Aretino, Pietro 1492-1556 . . . . **LC 12**

Arghezi, Tudor. **CLC 80**
See also Theodorescu, Ion N.

Arguedas, Jose Maria
1911-1969 . . . . **CLC 10, 18**
See also CA 89-92; DLB 113; HW

Argueta, Manlio 1936- . . . . **CLC 31**
See also CA 131; DLB 145; HW

Ariosto, Ludovico 1474-1533 . . . . **LC 6**

Aristides
See Epstein, Joseph

Aristophanes
450B.C.-385B.C. . . . **CMLC 4; DA; DC 2**

Arlt, Roberto (Godofredo Christophersen)
1900-1942 . . . . **TCLC 29; HLC**
See also CA 123; 131; HW

Armah, Ayi Kwei 1939- . . . . **CLC 5, 33; BLC**
See also BW 1; CA 61-64; CANR 21; DLB 117; MTCW

Armatrading, Joan 1950- . . . . **CLC 17**
See also CA 114

Arnette, Robert
See Silverberg, Robert

Arnim, Achim von (Ludwig Joachim von Arnim) 1781-1831 . . . . **NCLC 5**
See also DLB 90

Arnim, Bettina von 1785-1859. . . . **NCLC 38**
See also DLB 90

Arnold, Matthew
1822-1888 . . . . . **NCLC 6, 29; DA; PC 5; WLC**
See also CDBLB 1832-1890; DLB 32, 57

Arnold, Thomas 1795-1842 . . . . . . **NCLC 18**
See also DLB 55

Arnow, Harriette (Louisa) Simpson
1908-1986 . . . . **CLC 2, 7, 18**
See also CA 9-12R; 118; CANR 14; DLB 6; MTCW; SATA 42; SATA-Obit 47

Arp, Hans
See Arp, Jean

Arp, Jean 1887-1966. . . . . **CLC 5**
See also CA 81-84; 25-28R; CANR 42

Arrabal
See Arrabal, Fernando

Arrabal, Fernando 1932- . . . **CLC 2, 9, 18, 58**
See also CA 9-12R; CANR 15

Arrick, Fran. . . . . **CLC 30**

Artaud, Antonin 1896-1948 . . . . . **TCLC 3, 36**
See also CA 104

Arthur, Ruth M(abel) 1905-1979. . . . **CLC 12**
See also CA 9-12R; 85-88; CANR 4; SATA 7, 26

Artsybashev, Mikhail (Petrovich)
1878-1927 . . . . **TCLC 31**

Arundel, Honor (Morfydd)
1919-1973 . . . . **CLC 17**
See also CA 21-22; 41-44R; CAP 2; CLR 35; SATA 4; SATA-Obit 24

Asch, Sholem 1880-1957 . . . . **TCLC 3**
See also CA 105

Ash, Shalom
See Asch, Sholem

Ashbery, John (Lawrence)
1927- . . . . . . **CLC 2, 3, 4, 6, 9, 13, 15, 25, 41, 77**
See also CA 5-8R; CANR 9, 37; DLB 5; DLBY 81; MTCW

Ashdown, Clifford
See Freeman, R(ichard) Austin

Ashe, Gordon
See Creasey, John

Ashton-Warner, Sylvia (Constance)
1908-1984 . . . . **CLC 19**
See also CA 69-72; 112; CANR 29; MTCW

Asimov, Isaac
1920-1992 . . . . . . **CLC 1, 3, 9, 19, 26, 76**
See also AAYA 13; BEST 90:2; CA 1-4R; 137; CANR 2, 19, 36; CLR 12; DLB 8; DLBY 92; JRDA; MAICYA; MTCW; SATA 1, 26, 74

Astley, Thea (Beatrice May)
1925- . . . . **CLC 41**
See also CA 65-68; CANR 11, 43

Aston, James
See White, T(erence) H(anbury)

Asturias, Miguel Angel
1899-1974 . . . . **CLC 3, 8, 13; HLC**
See also CA 25-28; 49-52; CANR 32; CAP 2; DLB 113; HW; MTCW

Atares, Carlos Saura
See Saura (Atares), Carlos

Atheling, William
See Pound, Ezra (Weston Loomis)

Atheling, William, Jr.
See Blish, James (Benjamin)

Atherton, Gertrude (Franklin Horn)
1857-1948 . . . . **TCLC 2**
See also CA 104; DLB 9, 78

Atherton, Lucius
See Masters, Edgar Lee

Atkins, Jack
See Harris, Mark

Atticus
See Fleming, Ian (Lancaster)

Atwood, Margaret (Eleanor)
1939- . . . . . **CLC 2, 3, 4, 8, 13, 15, 25, 44, 84; DA; PC 8; SSC 2; WLC**
See also AAYA 12; BEST 89:2; CA 49-52; CANR 3, 24, 33; DLB 53; MTCW; SATA 50

Aubigny, Pierre d'
See Mencken, H(enry) L(ouis)

Aubin, Penelope 1685-1731(?) . . . . **LC 9**
See also DLB 39

Auchincloss, Louis (Stanton)
1917- . . . . **CLC 4, 6, 9, 18, 45**
See also CA 1-4R; CANR 6, 29; DLB 2; DLBY 80; MTCW

Auden, W(ystan) H(ugh)
1907-1973 . . . . . . **CLC 1, 2, 3, 4, 6, 9, 11, 14, 43; DA; PC 1; WLC**
See also CA 9-12R; 45-48; CANR 5; CDBLB 1914-1945; DLB 10, 20; MTCW

Audiberti, Jacques 1900-1965 . . . . . . **CLC 38**
See also CA 25-28R

Audubon, John James
1785-1851 . . . . **NCLC 47**

Auel, Jean M(arie) 1936-. . . . . **CLC 31**
See also AAYA 7; BEST 90:4; CA 103; CANR 21

Auerbach, Erich 1892-1957 . . . . **TCLC 43**
See also CA 118

Bertolucci, Bernardo 1940- .... **CLC 16**
See also CA 106

Bertrand, Aloysius 1807-1841 .... **NCLC 31**

Bertran de Born c. 1140-1215 ..... **CMLC 5**

Besant, Annie (Wood) 1847-1933 ... **TCLC 9**
See also CA 105

Bessie, Alvah 1904-1985........... **CLC 23**
See also CA 5-8R; 116; CANR 2; DLB 26

Bethlen, T. D.
See Silverberg, Robert

Beti, Mongo................. **CLC 27; BLC**
See also Biyidi, Alexandre

Betjeman, John
1906-1984 .... **CLC 2, 6, 10, 34, 43**
See also CA 9-12R; 112; CANR 33; CDBLB 1945-1960; DLB 20; DLBY 84; MTCW

Bettelheim, Bruno 1903-1990 ...... **CLC 79**
See also CA 81-84; 131; CANR 23; MTCW

Betti, Ugo 1892-1953 .... **TCLC 5**
See also CA 104

Betts, Doris (Waugh) 1932-.... **CLC 3, 6, 28**
See also CA 13-16R; CANR 9; DLBY 82

Bevan, Alistair
See Roberts, Keith (John Kingston)

Bialik, Chaim Nachman
1873-1934 .... **TCLC 25**

Bickerstaff, Isaac
See Swift, Jonathan

Bidart, Frank 1939- .... **CLC 33**
See also CA 140

Bienek, Horst 1930-............ **CLC 7, 11**
See also CA 73-76; DLB 75

Bierce, Ambrose (Gwinett)
1842-1914(?) .... **TCLC 1, 7, 44; DA; SSC 9; WLC**
See also CA 104; 139; CDALB 1865-1917; DLB 11, 12, 23, 71, 74

Billings, Josh
See Shaw, Henry Wheeler

Billington, (Lady) Rachel (Mary)
1942- .... **CLC 43**
See also AITN 2; CA 33-36R; CANR 44

Binyon, T(imothy) J(ohn) 1936- .... **CLC 34**
See also CA 111; CANR 28

Bioy Casares, Adolfo
1914- ...... **CLC 4, 8, 13; HLC; SSC 17**
See also CA 29-32R; CANR 19, 43; DLB 113; HW; MTCW

Bird, Cordwainer
See Ellison, Harlan (Jay)

Bird, Robert Montgomery
1806-1854 .... **NCLC 1**

Birney, (Alfred) Earle
1904- .... **CLC 1, 4, 6, 11**
See also CA 1-4R; CANR 5, 20; DLB 88; MTCW

Bishop, Elizabeth
1911-1979 ...... **CLC 1, 4, 9, 13, 15, 32; DA; PC 3**
See also CA 5-8R; 89-92; CABS 2; CANR 26; CDALB 1968-1988; DLB 5; MTCW; SATA-Obit 24

Bishop, John 1935-............... **CLC 10**
See also CA 105

Bissett, Bill 1939-................ **CLC 18**
See also CA 69-72; CAAS 19; CANR 15; DLB 53; MTCW

Bitov, Andrei (Georgievich) 1937-... **CLC 57**
See also CA 142

Biyidi, Alexandre 1932-
See Beti, Mongo
See also BW 1; CA 114; 124; MTCW

Bjarme, Brynjolf
See Ibsen, Henrik (Johan)

Bjornson, Bjornstjerne (Martinius)
1832-1910 .... **TCLC 7, 37**
See also CA 104

Black, Robert
See Holdstock, Robert P.

Blackburn, Paul 1926-1971 ...... **CLC 9, 43**
See also CA 81-84; 33-36R; CANR 34; DLB 16; DLBY 81

Black Elk 1863-1950 .... **TCLC 33**
See also CA 144; NNAL

Black Hobart
See Sanders, (James) Ed(ward)

Blacklin, Malcolm
See Chambers, Aidan

Blackmore, R(ichard) D(oddridge)
1825-1900 .... **TCLC 27**
See also CA 120; DLB 18

Blackmur, R(ichard) P(almer)
1904-1965 .... **CLC 2, 24**
See also CA 11-12; 25-28R; CAP 1; DLB 63

Black Tarantula, The
See Acker, Kathy

Blackwood, Algernon (Henry)
1869-1951 .... **TCLC 5**
See also CA 105

Blackwood, Caroline 1931- .... **CLC 6, 9**
See also CA 85-88; CANR 32; DLB 14; MTCW

Blade, Alexander
See Hamilton, Edmond; Silverberg, Robert

Blaga, Lucian 1895-1961 .... **CLC 75**

Blair, Eric (Arthur) 1903-1950
See Orwell, George
See also CA 104; 132; DA; MTCW; SATA 29

Blais, Marie-Claire
1939- .... **CLC 2, 4, 6, 13, 22**
See also CA 21-24R; CAAS 4; CANR 38; DLB 53; MTCW

Blaise, Clark 1940-............... **CLC 29**
See also AITN 2; CA 53-56; CAAS 3; CANR 5; DLB 53

Blake, Nicholas
See Day Lewis, C(ecil)
See also DLB 77

Blake, William
1757-1827 .... **NCLC 13, 37; DA; PC 12; WLC**
See also CDBLB 1789-1832; DLB 93; MAICYA; SATA 30

Blasco Ibanez, Vicente
1867-1928 .... **TCLC 12**
See also CA 110; 131; HW; MTCW

Blatty, William Peter 1928-......... **CLC 2**
See also CA 5-8R; CANR 9

Bleeck, Oliver
See Thomas, Ross (Elmore)

Blessing, Lee 1949-............... **CLC 54**

Blish, James (Benjamin)
1921-1975 .... **CLC 14**
See also CA 1-4R; 57-60; CANR 3; DLB 8; MTCW; SATA 66

Bliss, Reginald
See Wells, H(erbert) G(eorge)

Blixen, Karen (Christentze Dinesen)
1885-1962
See Dinesen, Isak
See also CA 25-28; CANR 22; CAP 2; MTCW; SATA 44

Bloch, Robert (Albert) 1917-1994... **CLC 33**
See also CA 5-8R; 146; CAAS 20; CANR 5; DLB 44; SATA 12

Blok, Alexander (Alexandrovich)
1880-1921 .... **TCLC 5**
See also CA 104

Blom, Jan
See Breytenbach, Breyten

Bloom, Harold 1930- .... **CLC 24**
See also CA 13-16R; CANR 39; DLB 67

Bloomfield, Aurelius
See Bourne, Randolph S(illiman)

Blount, Roy (Alton), Jr. 1941- ..... **CLC 38**
See also CA 53-56; CANR 10, 28; MTCW

Bloy, Leon 1846-1917............ **TCLC 22**
See also CA 121; DLB 123

Blume, Judy (Sussman) 1938-... **CLC 12, 30**
See also AAYA 3; CA 29-32R; CANR 13, 37; CLR 2, 15; DLB 52; JRDA; MAICYA; MTCW; SATA 2, 31, 79

Blunden, Edmund (Charles)
1896-1974 .... **CLC 2, 56**
See also CA 17-18; 45-48; CAP 2; DLB 20, 100; MTCW

Bly, Robert (Elwood)
1926- .... **CLC 1, 2, 5, 10, 15, 38**
See also CA 5-8R; CANR 41; DLB 5; MTCW

Boas, Franz 1858-1942........... **TCLC 56**
See also CA 115

Bobette
See Simenon, Georges (Jacques Christian)

Boccaccio, Giovanni
1313-1375 .... **CMLC 13; SSC 10**

Bochco, Steven 1943-............. **CLC 35**
See also AAYA 11; CA 124; 138

Bodenheim, Maxwell 1892-1954 ... **TCLC 44**
See also CA 110; DLB 9, 45

Bodker, Cecil 1927- .... **CLC 21**
See also CA 73-76; CANR 13, 44; CLR 23; MAICYA; SATA 14

Boell, Heinrich (Theodor)
1917-1985 .... **CLC 2, 3, 6, 9, 11, 15, 27, 32, 72; DA; WLC**
See also CA 21-24R; 116; CANR 24; DLB 69; DLBY 85; MTCW

Boerne, Alfred
See Doeblin, Alfred

Branley, Franklyn M(ansfield) 1915- . . . . **CLC 21**
See also CA 33-36R; CANR 14, 39; CLR 13; MAICYA; SAAS 16; SATA 4, 68

Brathwaite, Edward Kamau 1930-. . . **CLC 11**
See also BW 2; CA 25-28R; CANR 11, 26, 47; DLB 125

Brautigan, Richard (Gary) 1935-1984 . . . . **CLC 1, 3, 5, 9, 12, 34, 42**
See also CA 53-56; 113; CANR 34; DLB 2, 5; DLBY 80, 84; MTCW; SATA 56

Braverman, Kate 1950- . . . . **CLC 67**
See also CA 89-92

Brecht, Bertolt 1898-1956 . . . . . . **TCLC 1, 6, 13, 35; DA; DC 3; WLC**
See also CA 104; 133; DLB 56, 124; MTCW

Brecht, Eugen Berthold Friedrich
See Brecht, Bertolt

Bremer, Fredrika 1801-1865 . . . . . **NCLC 11**

Brennan, Christopher John 1870-1932 . . . . **TCLC 17**
See also CA 117

Brennan, Maeve 1917-. . . . . **CLC 5**
See also CA 81-84

Brentano, Clemens (Maria) 1778-1842 . . . . **NCLC 1**
See also DLB 90

Brent of Bin Bin
See Franklin, (Stella Maraia Sarah) Miles

Brenton, Howard 1942-. . . . . **CLC 31**
See also CA 69-72; CANR 33; DLB 13; MTCW

Breslin, James 1930-
See Breslin, Jimmy
See also CA 73-76; CANR 31; MTCW

Breslin, Jimmy . . . . **CLC 4, 43**
See also Breslin, James
See also AITN 1

Bresson, Robert 1907-. . . . . **CLC 16**
See also CA 110

Breton, Andre 1896-1966. . . **CLC 2, 9, 15, 54**
See also CA 19-20; 25-28R; CANR 40; CAP 2; DLB 65; MTCW

Breytenbach, Breyten 1939(?)- . . **CLC 23, 37**
See also CA 113; 129

Bridgers, Sue Ellen 1942- . . . . **CLC 26**
See also AAYA 8; CA 65-68; CANR 11, 36; CLR 18; DLB 52; JRDA; MAICYA; SAAS 1; SATA 22

Bridges, Robert (Seymour) 1844-1930 . . . . **TCLC 1**
See also CA 104; CDBLB 1890-1914; DLB 19, 98

Bridie, James. **TCLC 3**
See also Mavor, Osborne Henry
See also DLB 10

Brin, David 1950-. . . . . **CLC 34**
See also CA 102; CANR 24; SATA 65

Brink, Andre (Philippus) 1935- . . . . **CLC 18, 36**
See also CA 104; CANR 39; MTCW

Brinsmead, H(esba) F(ay) 1922- . . . . **CLC 21**
See also CA 21-24R; CANR 10; MAICYA; SAAS 5; SATA 18, 78

Brittain, Vera (Mary) 1893(?)-1970 . . . . **CLC 23**
See also CA 13-16; 25-28R; CAP 1; MTCW

Broch, Hermann 1886-1951 . . . . **TCLC 20**
See also CA 117; DLB 85, 124

Brock, Rose
See Hansen, Joseph

Brodkey, Harold 1930-. . . . . **CLC 56**
See also CA 111; DLB 130

Brodsky, Iosif Alexandrovich 1940-
See Brodsky, Joseph
See also AITN 1; CA 41-44R; CANR 37; MTCW

Brodsky, Joseph . . **CLC 4, 6, 13, 36, 50; PC 9**
See also Brodsky, Iosif Alexandrovich

Brodsky, Michael Mark 1948- . . . . . **CLC 19**
See also CA 102; CANR 18, 41

Bromell, Henry 1947-. . . . . **CLC 5**
See also CA 53-56; CANR 9

Bromfield, Louis (Brucker) 1896-1956 . . . . **TCLC 11**
See also CA 107; DLB 4, 9, 86

Broner, E(sther) M(asserman) 1930- . . . . **CLC 19**
See also CA 17-20R; CANR 8, 25; DLB 28

Bronk, William 1918-. . . . . **CLC 10**
See also CA 89-92; CANR 23

Bronstein, Lev Davidovich
See Trotsky, Leon

Bronte, Anne 1820-1849. . . . . **NCLC 4**
See also DLB 21

Bronte, Charlotte 1816-1855 . . . **NCLC 3, 8, 33; DA; WLC**
See also CDBLB 1832-1890; DLB 21

Bronte, (Jane) Emily 1818-1848 . . . . **NCLC 16, 35; DA; PC 8; WLC**
See also CDBLB 1832-1890; DLB 21, 32

Brooke, Frances 1724-1789 . . . . **LC 6**
See also DLB 39, 99

Brooke, Henry 1703(?)-1783 . . . . **LC 1**
See also DLB 39

Brooke, Rupert (Chawner) 1887-1915 . . . . **TCLC 2, 7; DA; WLC**
See also CA 104; 132; CDBLB 1914-1945; DLB 19; MTCW

Brooke-Haven, P.
See Wodehouse, P(elham) G(renville)

Brooke-Rose, Christine 1926- . . . . . . **CLC 40**
See also CA 13-16R; DLB 14

Brookner, Anita 1928- . . . . . . **CLC 32, 34, 51**
See also CA 114; 120; CANR 37; DLBY 87; MTCW

Brooks, Cleanth 1906-1994 . . . . . **CLC 24, 86**
See also CA 17-20R; 145; CANR 33, 35; DLB 63; MTCW

Brooks, George
See Baum, L(yman) Frank

Brooks, Gwendolyn 1917- . . . . . . **CLC 1, 2, 4, 5, 15, 49; BLC; DA; PC 7; WLC**
See also AITN 1; BW 2; CA 1-4R; CANR 1, 27; CDALB 1941-1968; CLR 27; DLB 5, 76; MTCW; SATA 6

Brooks, Mel. . . . . **CLC 12**
See also Kaminsky, Melvin
See also AAYA 13; DLB 26

Brooks, Peter 1938- . . . . **CLC 34**
See also CA 45-48; CANR 1

Brooks, Van Wyck 1886-1963 . . . . . . **CLC 29**
See also CA 1-4R; CANR 6; DLB 45, 63, 103

Brophy, Brigid (Antonia) 1929- . . . . **CLC 6, 11, 29**
See also CA 5-8R; CAAS 4; CANR 25; DLB 14; MTCW

Brosman, Catharine Savage 1934-. . . . **CLC 9**
See also CA 61-64; CANR 21, 46

Brother Antoninus
See Everson, William (Oliver)

Broughton, T(homas) Alan 1936- . . . **CLC 19**
See also CA 45-48; CANR 2, 23

Broumas, Olga 1949- . . . . **CLC 10, 73**
See also CA 85-88; CANR 20

Brown, Charles Brockden 1771-1810 . . . . **NCLC 22**
See also CDALB 1640-1865; DLB 37, 59, 73

Brown, Christy 1932-1981 . . . . **CLC 63**
See also CA 105; 104; DLB 14

Brown, Claude 1937- . . . . **CLC 30; BLC**
See also AAYA 7; BW 1; CA 73-76

Brown, Dee (Alexander) 1908- . . **CLC 18, 47**
See also CA 13-16R; CAAS 6; CANR 11, 45; DLBY 80; MTCW; SATA 5

Brown, George
See Wertmueller, Lina

Brown, George Douglas 1869-1902 . . . . **TCLC 28**

Brown, George Mackay 1921-. . . . **CLC 5, 48**
See also CA 21-24R; CAAS 6; CANR 12, 37; DLB 14, 27, 139; MTCW; SATA 35

Brown, (William) Larry 1951-. . . . . . **CLC 73**
See also CA 130; 134

Brown, Moses
See Barrett, William (Christopher)

Brown, Rita Mae 1944- . . . . . **CLC 18, 43, 79**
See also CA 45-48; CANR 2, 11, 35; MTCW

Brown, Roderick (Langmere) Haig-
See Haig-Brown, Roderick (Langmere)

Brown, Rosellen 1939-. . . . . **CLC 32**
See also CA 77-80; CAAS 10; CANR 14, 44

Brown, Sterling Allen 1901-1989 . . . . **CLC 1, 23, 59; BLC**
See also BW 1; CA 85-88; 127; CANR 26; DLB 48, 51, 63; MTCW

Brown, Will
See Ainsworth, William Harrison

Brown, William Wells 1813-1884 . . . . **NCLC 2; BLC; DC 1**
See also DLB 3, 50

Browne, (Clyde) Jackson 1948(?)- . . . **CLC 21**
See also CA 120

Browning, Elizabeth Barrett
1806-1861 . . . . . **NCLC 1, 16; DA; PC 6; WLC**
See also CDBLB 1832-1890; DLB 32

Browning, Robert
1812-1889 . . . . **NCLC 19; DA; PC 2**
See also CDBLB 1832-1890; DLB 32; YABC 1

Browning, Tod 1882-1962 . . . . **CLC 16**
See also CA 141; 117

Bruccoli, Matthew J(oseph) 1931- . . **CLC 34**
See also CA 9-12R; CANR 7; DLB 103

Bruce, Lenny . . . . **CLC 21**
See also Schneider, Leonard Alfred

Bruin, John
See Brutus, Dennis

Brulard, Henri
See Stendhal

Brulls, Christian
See Simenon, Georges (Jacques Christian)

Brunner, John (Kilian Houston)
1934- . . . . **CLC 8, 10**
See also CA 1-4R; CAAS 8; CANR 2, 37; MTCW

Bruno, Giordano 1548-1600 . . . . **LC 27**

Brutus, Dennis 1924- . . . . **CLC 43; BLC**
See also BW 2; CA 49-52; CAAS 14; CANR 2, 27, 42; DLB 117

Bryan, C(ourtlandt) D(ixon) B(arnes)
1936- . . . . **CLC 29**
See also CA 73-76; CANR 13

Bryan, Michael
See Moore, Brian

Bryant, William Cullen
1794-1878 . . . . **NCLC 6, 46; DA**
See also CDALB 1640-1865; DLB 3, 43, 59

Bryusov, Valery Yakovlevich
1873-1924 . . . . **TCLC 10**
See also CA 107

Buchan, John 1875-1940 . . . . **TCLC 41**
See also CA 108; 145; DLB 34, 70; YABC 2

Buchanan, George 1506-1582 . . . . **LC 4**

Buchheim, Lothar-Guenther 1918- . . . **CLC 6**
See also CA 85-88

Buchner, (Karl) Georg
1813-1837 . . . . **NCLC 26**

Buchwald, Art(hur) 1925- . . . . **CLC 33**
See also AITN 1; CA 5-8R; CANR 21; MTCW; SATA 10

Buck, Pearl S(ydenstricker)
1892-1973 . . . . **CLC 7, 11, 18; DA**
See also AITN 1; CA 1-4R; 41-44R; CANR 1, 34; DLB 9, 102; MTCW; SATA 1, 25

Buckler, Ernest 1908-1984 . . . . **CLC 13**
See also CA 11-12; 114; CAP 1; DLB 68; SATA 47

Buckley, Vincent (Thomas)
1925-1988 . . . . **CLC 57**
See also CA 101

Buckley, William F(rank), Jr.
1925- . . . . **CLC 7, 18, 37**
See also AITN 1; CA 1-4R; CANR 1, 24; DLB 137; DLBY 80; MTCW

Buechner, (Carl) Frederick
1926- . . . . **CLC 2, 4, 6, 9**
See also CA 13-16R; CANR 11, 39; DLBY 80; MTCW

Buell, John (Edward) 1927- . . . . **CLC 10**
See also CA 1-4R; DLB 53

Buero Vallejo, Antonio 1916- . . . **CLC 15, 46**
See also CA 106; CANR 24; HW; MTCW

Bufalino, Gesualdo 1920(?)- . . . . **CLC 74**

Bugayev, Boris Nikolayevich 1880-1934
See Bely, Andrey
See also CA 104

Bukowski, Charles
1920-1994 . . . . **CLC 2, 5, 9, 41, 82**
See also CA 17-20R; 144; CANR 40; DLB 5, 130; MTCW

Bulgakov, Mikhail (Afanas'evich)
1891-1940 . . . . **TCLC 2, 16; SSC 18**
See also CA 105

Bulgya, Alexander Alexandrovich
1901-1956 . . . . **TCLC 53**
See also Fadeyev, Alexander
See also CA 117

Bullins, Ed 1935- . . . . **CLC 1, 5, 7; BLC**
See also BW 2; CA 49-52; CAAS 16; CANR 24, 46; DLB 7, 38; MTCW

Bulwer-Lytton, Edward (George Earle Lytton)
1803-1873 . . . . **NCLC 1, 45**
See also DLB 21

Bunin, Ivan Alexeyevich
1870-1953 . . . . **TCLC 6; SSC 5**
See also CA 104

Bunting, Basil 1900-1985 . . . . **CLC 10, 39, 47**
See also CA 53-56; 115; CANR 7; DLB 20

Bunuel, Luis 1900-1983 . . **CLC 16, 80; HLC**
See also CA 101; 110; CANR 32; HW

Bunyan, John 1628-1688 . . **LC 4; DA; WLC**
See also CDBLB 1660-1789; DLB 39

Burckhardt, Jacob (Christoph)
1818-1897 . . . . **NCLC 49**

Burford, Eleanor
See Hibbert, Eleanor Alice Burford

Burgess, Anthony
. **CLC 1, 2, 4, 5, 8, 10, 13, 15, 22, 40, 62, 81**
See also Wilson, John (Anthony) Burgess
See also AITN 1; CDBLB 1960 to Present; DLB 14

Burke, Edmund
1729(?)-1797 . . . . **LC 7; DA; WLC**
See also DLB 104

Burke, Kenneth (Duva)
1897-1993 . . . . **CLC 2, 24**
See also CA 5-8R; 143; CANR 39; DLB 45, 63; MTCW

Burke, Leda
See Garnett, David

Burke, Ralph
See Silverberg, Robert

Burney, Fanny 1752-1840 . . . . **NCLC 12**
See also DLB 39

Burns, Robert
1759-1796 . . . . . . **LC 3; DA; PC 6; WLC**
See also CDBLB 1789-1832; DLB 109

Burns, Tex
See L'Amour, Louis (Dearborn)

Burnshaw, Stanley 1906- . . . . . **CLC 3, 13, 44**
See also CA 9-12R; DLB 48

Burr, Anne 1937- . . . . **CLC 6**
See also CA 25-28R

Burroughs, Edgar Rice
1875-1950 . . . . **TCLC 2, 32**
See also AAYA 11; CA 104; 132; DLB 8; MTCW; SATA 41

Burroughs, William S(eward)
1914- . . . . **CLC 1, 2, 5, 15, 22, 42, 75; DA; WLC**
See also AITN 2; CA 9-12R; CANR 20; DLB 2, 8, 16; DLBY 81; MTCW

Burton, Richard F. 1821-1890 . . . . **NCLC 42**
See also DLB 55

Busch, Frederick 1941- . . . **CLC 7, 10, 18, 47**
See also CA 33-36R; CAAS 1; CANR 45; DLB 6

Bush, Ronald 1946- . . . . **CLC 34**
See also CA 136

Bustos, F(rancisco)
See Borges, Jorge Luis

Bustos Domecq, H(onorio)
See Bioy Casares, Adolfo; Borges, Jorge Luis

Butler, Octavia E(stelle) 1947- . . . . . **CLC 38**
See also BW 2; CA 73-76; CANR 12, 24, 38; DLB 33; MTCW

Butler, Robert Olen (Jr.) 1945- . . . . . **CLC 81**
See also CA 112

Butler, Samuel 1612-1680 . . . . **LC 16**
See also DLB 101, 126

Butler, Samuel
1835-1902 . . . . . . **TCLC 1, 33; DA; WLC**
See also CA 143; CDBLB 1890-1914; DLB 18, 57

Butler, Walter C.
See Faust, Frederick (Schiller)

Butor, Michel (Marie Francois)
1926- . . . . **CLC 1, 3, 8, 11, 15**
See also CA 9-12R; CANR 33; DLB 83; MTCW

Buzo, Alexander (John) 1944- . . . . . . **CLC 61**
See also CA 97-100; CANR 17, 39

Buzzati, Dino 1906-1972 . . . . **CLC 36**
See also CA 33-36R

Byars, Betsy (Cromer) 1928- . . . . **CLC 35**
See also CA 33-36R; CANR 18, 36; CLR 1, 16; DLB 52; JRDA; MAICYA; MTCW; SAAS 1; SATA 4, 46, 80

Byatt, A(ntonia) S(usan Drabble)
1936- . . . . **CLC 19, 65**
See also CA 13-16R; CANR 13, 33; DLB 14; MTCW

Byrne, David 1952- . . . . **CLC 26**
See also CA 127

Byrne, John Keyes 1926-
See Leonard, Hugh
See also CA 102

Carter, Angela (Olive) 1940-1992 ...... **CLC 5, 41, 76; SSC 13**
See also CA 53-56; 136; CANR 12, 36; DLB 14; MTCW; SATA 66; SATA-Obit 70

Carter, Nick
See Smith, Martin Cruz

Carver, Raymond 1938-1988 ... **CLC 22, 36, 53, 55; SSC 8**
See also CA 33-36R; 126; CANR 17, 34; DLB 130; DLBY 84, 88; MTCW

Cary, (Arthur) Joyce (Lunel) 1888-1957 .... **TCLC 1, 29**
See also CA 104; CDBLB 1914-1945; DLB 15, 100

Casanova de Seingalt, Giovanni Jacopo 1725-1798 .... **LC 13**

Casares, Adolfo Bioy
See Bioy Casares, Adolfo

Casely-Hayford, J(oseph) E(phraim) 1866-1930 .... **TCLC 24; BLC**
See also BW 2; CA 123

Casey, John (Dudley) 1939-........ **CLC 59**
See also BEST 90:2; CA 69-72; CANR 23

Casey, Michael 1947-.............. **CLC 2**
See also CA 65-68; DLB 5

Casey, Patrick
See Thurman, Wallace (Henry)

Casey, Warren (Peter) 1935-1988 ... **CLC 12**
See also CA 101; 127

Casona, Alejandro .... **CLC 49**
See also Alvarez, Alejandro Rodriguez

Cassavetes, John 1929-1989........ **CLC 20**
See also CA 85-88; 127

Cassill, R(onald) V(erlin) 1919-... **CLC 4, 23**
See also CA 9-12R; CAAS 1; CANR 7, 45; DLB 6

Cassity, (Allen) Turner 1929- .... **CLC 6, 42**
See also CA 17-20R; CAAS 8; CANR 11; DLB 105

Castaneda, Carlos 1931(?)-......... **CLC 12**
See also CA 25-28R; CANR 32; HW; MTCW

Castedo, Elena 1937- .... **CLC 65**
See also CA 132

Castedo-Ellerman, Elena
See Castedo, Elena

Castellanos, Rosario 1925-1974 .... **CLC 66; HLC**
See also CA 131; 53-56; DLB 113; HW

Castelvetro, Lodovico 1505-1571..... **LC 12**

Castiglione, Baldassare 1478-1529 ... **LC 12**

Castle, Robert
See Hamilton, Edmond

Castro, Guillen de 1569-1631........ **LC 19**

Castro, Rosalia de 1837-1885 ..... **NCLC 3**

Cather, Willa
See Cather, Willa Sibert

Cather, Willa Sibert 1873-1947 .... **TCLC 1, 11, 31; DA; SSC 2; WLC**
See also CA 104; 128; CDALB 1865-1917; DLB 9, 54, 78; DLBD 1; MTCW; SATA 30

Catton, (Charles) Bruce 1899-1978 .... **CLC 35**
See also AITN 1; CA 5-8R; 81-84; CANR 7; DLB 17; SATA 2; SATA-Obit 24

Cauldwell, Frank
See King, Francis (Henry)

Caunitz, William J. 1933- .... **CLC 34**
See also BEST 89:3; CA 125; 130

Causley, Charles (Stanley) 1917-..... **CLC 7**
See also CA 9-12R; CANR 5, 35; CLR 30; DLB 27; MTCW; SATA 3, 66

Caute, David 1936-............... **CLC 29**
See also CA 1-4R; CAAS 4; CANR 1, 33; DLB 14

Cavafy, C(onstantine) P(eter)...... **TCLC 2, 7**
See also Kavafis, Konstantinos Petrou

Cavallo, Evelyn
See Spark, Muriel (Sarah)

Cavanna, Betty .... **CLC 12**
See also Harrison, Elizabeth Cavanna
See also JRDA; MAICYA; SAAS 4; SATA 1, 30

Caxton, William 1421(?)-1491(?)..... **LC 17**

Cayrol, Jean 1911-............... **CLC 11**
See also CA 89-92; DLB 83

Cela, Camilo Jose 1916- .... **CLC 4, 13, 59; HLC**
See also BEST 90:2; CA 21-24R; CAAS 10; CANR 21, 32; DLBY 89; HW; MTCW

Celan, Paul ...... **CLC 10, 19, 53, 82; PC 10**
See also Antschel, Paul
See also DLB 69

Celine, Louis-Ferdinand .... **CLC 1, 3, 4, 7, 9, 15, 47**
See also Destouches, Louis-Ferdinand
See also DLB 72

Cellini, Benvenuto 1500-1571 .... **LC 7**

Cendrars, Blaise
See Sauser-Hall, Frederic

Cernuda (y Bidon), Luis 1902-1963 .... **CLC 54**
See also CA 131; 89-92; DLB 134; HW

Cervantes (Saavedra), Miguel de 1547-1616 ...... **LC 6, 23; DA; SSC 12; WLC**

Cesaire, Aime (Fernand) 1913- .... **CLC 19, 32; BLC**
See also BW 2; CA 65-68; CANR 24, 43; MTCW

Chabon, Michael 1965(?)- .... **CLC 55**
See also CA 139

Chabrol, Claude 1930- .... **CLC 16**
See also CA 110

Challans, Mary 1905-1983
See Renault, Mary
See also CA 81-84; 111; SATA 23; SATA-Obit 36

Challis, George
See Faust, Frederick (Schiller)

Chambers, Aidan 1934- .... **CLC 35**
See also CA 25-28R; CANR 12, 31; JRDA; MAICYA; SAAS 12; SATA 1, 69

Chambers, James 1948-
See Cliff, Jimmy
See also CA 124

Chambers, Jessie
See Lawrence, D(avid) H(erbert Richards)

Chambers, Robert W. 1865-1933... **TCLC 41**

Chandler, Raymond (Thornton) 1888-1959 .... **TCLC 1, 7**
See also CA 104; 129; CDALB 1929-1941; DLBD 6; MTCW

Chang, Jung 1952- .... **CLC 71**
See also CA 142

Channing, William Ellery 1780-1842 .... **NCLC 17**
See also DLB 1, 59

Chaplin, Charles Spencer 1889-1977 .... **CLC 16**
See also Chaplin, Charlie
See also CA 81-84; 73-76

Chaplin, Charlie
See Chaplin, Charles Spencer
See also DLB 44

Chapman, George 1559(?)-1634...... **LC 22**
See also DLB 62, 121

Chapman, Graham 1941-1989 ...... **CLC 21**
See also Monty Python
See also CA 116; 129; CANR 35

Chapman, John Jay 1862-1933 ..... **TCLC 7**
See also CA 104

Chapman, Walker
See Silverberg, Robert

Chappell, Fred (Davis) 1936-.... **CLC 40, 78**
See also CA 5-8R; CAAS 4; CANR 8, 33; DLB 6, 105

Char, Rene(-Emile) 1907-1988 .... **CLC 9, 11, 14, 55**
See also CA 13-16R; 124; CANR 32; MTCW

Charby, Jay
See Ellison, Harlan (Jay)

Chardin, Pierre Teilhard de
See Teilhard de Chardin, (Marie Joseph) Pierre

Charles I 1600-1649 .... **LC 13**

Charyn, Jerome 1937- .... **CLC 5, 8, 18**
See also CA 5-8R; CAAS 1; CANR 7; DLBY 83; MTCW

Chase, Mary (Coyle) 1907-1981 ...... **DC 1**
See also CA 77-80; 105; SATA 17; SATA-Obit 29

Chase, Mary Ellen 1887-1973....... **CLC 2**
See also CA 13-16; 41-44R; CAP 1; SATA 10

Chase, Nicholas
See Hyde, Anthony

Chateaubriand, Francois Rene de 1768-1848 .... **NCLC 3**
See also DLB 119

Chatterje, Sarat Chandra 1876-1936(?)
See Chatterji, Saratchandra
See also CA 109

Chatterji, Bankim Chandra 1838-1894 .... **NCLC 19**

Chatterji, Saratchandra .... **TCLC 13**
See also Chatterje, Sarat Chandra

Chatterton, Thomas 1752-1770 .... **LC 3**
See also DLB 109

Chatwin, (Charles) Bruce
1940-1989 .... **CLC 28, 57, 59**
See also AAYA 4; BEST 90:1; CA 85-88; 127

Chaucer, Daniel
See Ford, Ford Madox

Chaucer, Geoffrey
1340(?)-1400 .... **LC 17; DA**
See also CDBLB Before 1660; DLB 146

Chaviaras, Strates 1935-
See Haviaras, Stratis
See also CA 105

Chayefsky, Paddy .... **CLC 23**
See also Chayefsky, Sidney
See also DLB 7, 44; DLBY 81

Chayefsky, Sidney 1923-1981
See Chayefsky, Paddy
See also CA 9-12R; 104; CANR 18

Chedid, Andree 1920-............. **CLC 47**
See also CA 145

Cheever, John
1912-1982 ...... **CLC 3, 7, 8, 11, 15, 25, 64; DA; SSC 1; WLC**
See also CA 5-8R; 106; CABS 1; CANR 5, 27; CDALB 1941-1968; DLB 2, 102; DLBY 80, 82; MTCW

Cheever, Susan 1943-.......... **CLC 18, 48**
See also CA 103; CANR 27; DLBY 82

Chekhonte, Antosha
See Chekhov, Anton (Pavlovich)

Chekhov, Anton (Pavlovich)
1860-1904 ..... **TCLC 3, 10, 31, 55; DA; SSC 2; WLC**
See also CA 104; 124

Chernyshevsky, Nikolay Gavrilovich
1828-1889 .... **NCLC 1**

Cherry, Carolyn Janice 1942-
See Cherryh, C. J.
See also CA 65-68; CANR 10

Cherryh, C. J. .... **CLC 35**
See also Cherry, Carolyn Janice
See also DLBY 80

Chesnutt, Charles W(addell)
1858-1932 .... **TCLC 5, 39; BLC; SSC 7**
See also BW 1; CA 106; 125; DLB 12, 50, 78; MTCW

Chester, Alfred 1929(?)-1971 .... **CLC 49**
See also CA 33-36R; DLB 130

Chesterton, G(ilbert) K(eith)
1874-1936 .... **TCLC 1, 6; SSC 1**
See also CA 104; 132; CDBLB 1914-1945; DLB 10, 19, 34, 70, 98; MTCW; SATA 27

Chiang Pin-chin 1904-1986
See Ding Ling
See also CA 118

Ch'ien Chung-shu 1910-........... **CLC 22**
See also CA 130; MTCW

Child, L. Maria
See Child, Lydia Maria

Child, Lydia Maria 1802-1880 .... **NCLC 6**
See also DLB 1, 74; SATA 67

Child, Mrs.
See Child, Lydia Maria

Child, Philip 1898-1978 .... **CLC 19, 68**
See also CA 13-14; CAP 1; SATA 47

Childress, Alice
1920-1994 .. **CLC 12, 15, 86; BLC; DC 4**
See also AAYA 8; BW 2; CA 45-48; 146; CANR 3, 27; CLR 14; DLB 7, 38; JRDA; MAICYA; MTCW; SATA 7, 48, 81

Chislett, (Margaret) Anne 1943-.... **CLC 34**

Chitty, Thomas Willes 1926-....... **CLC 11**
See also Hinde, Thomas
See also CA 5-8R

Chivers, Thomas Holley
1809-1858 .... **NCLC 49**
See also DLB 3

Chomette, Rene Lucien 1898-1981
See Clair, Rene
See also CA 103

Chopin, Kate .... **TCLC 5, 14; DA; SSC 8**
See also Chopin, Katherine
See also CDALB 1865-1917; DLB 12, 78

Chopin, Katherine 1851-1904
See Chopin, Kate
See also CA 104; 122

Chretien de Troyes
c. 12th cent. - .... **CMLC 10**

Christie
See Ichikawa, Kon

Christie, Agatha (Mary Clarissa)
1890-1976 ...... **CLC 1, 6, 8, 12, 39, 48**
See also AAYA 9; AITN 1, 2; CA 17-20R; 61-64; CANR 10, 37; CDBLB 1914-1945; DLB 13, 77; MTCW; SATA 36

Christie, (Ann) Philippa
See Pearce, Philippa
See also CA 5-8R; CANR 4

Christine de Pizan 1365(?)-1431(?) .... **LC 9**

Chubb, Elmer
See Masters, Edgar Lee

Chulkov, Mikhail Dmitrievich
1743-1792 .... **LC 2**

Churchill, Caryl 1938-... **CLC 31, 55; DC 5**
See also CA 102; CANR 22, 46; DLB 13; MTCW

Churchill, Charles 1731-1764......... **LC 3**
See also DLB 109

Chute, Carolyn 1947-............. **CLC 39**
See also CA 123

Ciardi, John (Anthony)
1916-1986 .... **CLC 10, 40, 44**
See also CA 5-8R; 118; CAAS 2; CANR 5, 33; CLR 19; DLB 5; DLBY 86; MAICYA; MTCW; SATA 1, 65; SATA-Obit 46

Cicero, Marcus Tullius
106B.C.-43B.C. .... **CMLC 3**

Cimino, Michael 1943-............ **CLC 16**
See also CA 105

Cioran, E(mil) M. 1911-........... **CLC 64**
See also CA 25-28R

Cisneros, Sandra 1954-...... **CLC 69; HLC**
See also AAYA 9; CA 131; DLB 122; HW

Clair, Rene....................... **CLC 20**
See also Chomette, Rene Lucien

Clampitt, Amy 1920-1994 .... **CLC 32**
See also CA 110; 146; CANR 29; DLB 105

Clancy, Thomas L., Jr. 1947-
See Clancy, Tom
See also CA 125; 131; MTCW

Clancy, Tom...................... **CLC 45**
See also Clancy, Thomas L., Jr.
See also AAYA 9; BEST 89:1, 90:1

Clare, John 1793-1864 .... **NCLC 9**
See also DLB 55, 96

Clarin
See Alas (y Urena), Leopoldo (Enrique Garcia)

Clark, Al C.
See Goines, Donald

Clark, (Robert) Brian 1932-........ **CLC 29**
See also CA 41-44R

Clark, Curt
See Westlake, Donald E(dwin)

Clark, Eleanor 1913- .... **CLC 5, 19**
See also CA 9-12R; CANR 41; DLB 6

Clark, J. P.
See Clark, John Pepper
See also DLB 117

Clark, John Pepper
1935- .... **CLC 38; BLC; DC 5**
See also Clark, J. P.
See also BW 1; CA 65-68; CANR 16

Clark, M. R.
See Clark, Mavis Thorpe

Clark, Mavis Thorpe 1909-........ **CLC 12**
See also CA 57-60; CANR 8, 37; CLR 30; MAICYA; SAAS 5; SATA 8, 74

Clark, Walter Van Tilburg
1909-1971 .... **CLC 28**
See also CA 9-12R; 33-36R; DLB 9; SATA 8

Clarke, Arthur C(harles)
1917- ...... **CLC 1, 4, 13, 18, 35; SSC 3**
See also AAYA 4; CA 1-4R; CANR 2, 28; JRDA; MAICYA; MTCW; SATA 13, 70

Clarke, Austin 1896-1974......... **CLC 6, 9**
See also CA 29-32; 49-52; CAP 2; DLB 10, 20

Clarke, Austin C(hesterfield)
1934- .... **CLC 8, 53; BLC**
See also BW 1; CA 25-28R; CAAS 16; CANR 14, 32; DLB 53, 125

Clarke, Gillian 1937- .... **CLC 61**
See also CA 106; DLB 40

Clarke, Marcus (Andrew Hislop)
1846-1881 .... **NCLC 19**

Clarke, Shirley 1925-............. **CLC 16**

Clash, The
See Headon, (Nicky) Topper; Jones, Mick; Simonon, Paul; Strummer, Joe

Claudel, Paul (Louis Charles Marie)
1868-1955 .... **TCLC 2, 10**
See also CA 104

Clavell, James (duMaresq) 1925-1994 . . . . **CLC 6, 25, 87**
See also CA 25-28R; 146; CANR 26; MTCW

Cleaver, (Leroy) Eldridge 1935- . . . . **CLC 30; BLC**
See also BW 1; CA 21-24R; CANR 16

Cleese, John (Marwood) 1939- . . . . . **CLC 21**
See also Monty Python
See also CA 112; 116; CANR 35; MTCW

Cleishbotham, Jebediah
See Scott, Walter

Cleland, John 1710-1789 . . . . **LC 2**
See also DLB 39

Clemens, Samuel Langhorne 1835-1910
See Twain, Mark
See also CA 104; 135; CDALB 1865-1917; DA; DLB 11, 12, 23, 64, 74; JRDA; MAICYA; YABC 2

Cleophil
See Congreve, William

Clerihew, E.
See Bentley, E(dmund) C(lerihew)

Clerk, N. W.
See Lewis, C(live) S(taples)

Cliff, Jimmy . . . . **CLC 21**
See also Chambers, James

Clifton, (Thelma) Lucille 1936- . . . . **CLC 19, 66; BLC**
See also BW 2; CA 49-52; CANR 2, 24, 42; CLR 5; DLB 5, 41; MAICYA; MTCW; SATA 20, 69

Clinton, Dirk
See Silverberg, Robert

Clough, Arthur Hugh 1819-1861. . **NCLC 27**
See also DLB 32

Clutha, Janet Paterson Frame 1924-
See Frame, Janet
See also CA 1-4R; CANR 2, 36; MTCW

Clyne, Terence
See Blatty, William Peter

Cobalt, Martin
See Mayne, William (James Carter)

Cobbett, William 1763-1835 . . . . . **NCLC 49**
See also DLB 43, 107

Coburn, D(onald) L(ee) 1938- . . . . . . **CLC 10**
See also CA 89-92

Cocteau, Jean (Maurice Eugene Clement) 1889-1963 . . . . **CLC 1, 8, 15, 16, 43; DA; WLC**
See also CA 25-28; CANR 40; CAP 2; DLB 65; MTCW

Codrescu, Andrei 1946- . . . . **CLC 46**
See also CA 33-36R; CAAS 19; CANR 13, 34

Coe, Max
See Bourne, Randolph S(illiman)

Coe, Tucker
See Westlake, Donald E(dwin)

Coetzee, J(ohn) M(ichael) 1940- . . . . **CLC 23, 33, 66**
See also CA 77-80; CANR 41; MTCW

Coffey, Brian
See Koontz, Dean R(ay)

Cohen, Arthur A(llen) 1928-1986 . . . . **CLC 7, 31**
See also CA 1-4R; 120; CANR 1, 17, 42; DLB 28

Cohen, Leonard (Norman) 1934- . . . . **CLC 3, 38**
See also CA 21-24R; CANR 14; DLB 53; MTCW

Cohen, Matt 1942- . . . . **CLC 19**
See also CA 61-64; CAAS 18; CANR 40; DLB 53

Cohen-Solal, Annie 19(?)- . . . . **CLC 50**

Colegate, Isabel 1931- . . . . **CLC 36**
See also CA 17-20R; CANR 8, 22; DLB 14; MTCW

Coleman, Emmett
See Reed, Ishmael

Coleridge, Samuel Taylor 1772-1834 . . **NCLC 9; DA; PC 11; WLC**
See also CDBLB 1789-1832; DLB 93, 107

Coleridge, Sara 1802-1852. . . . . . . **NCLC 31**

Coles, Don 1928- . . . . **CLC 46**
See also CA 115; CANR 38

Colette, (Sidonie-Gabrielle) 1873-1954 . . . . . . **TCLC 1, 5, 16; SSC 10**
See also CA 104; 131; DLB 65; MTCW

Collett, (Jacobine) Camilla (Wergeland) 1813-1895 . . . . **NCLC 22**

Collier, Christopher 1930- . . . . **CLC 30**
See also AAYA 13; CA 33-36R; CANR 13, 33; JRDA; MAICYA; SATA 16, 70

Collier, James L(incoln) 1928- . . . . . **CLC 30**
See also AAYA 13; CA 9-12R; CANR 4, 33; CLR 3; JRDA; MAICYA; SATA 8, 70

Collier, Jeremy 1650-1726. . . . . **LC 6**

Collins, Hunt
See Hunter, Evan

Collins, Linda 1931-. . . . . **CLC 44**
See also CA 125

Collins, (William) Wilkie 1824-1889 . . . . **NCLC 1, 18**
See also CDBLB 1832-1890; DLB 18, 70

Collins, William 1721-1759 . . . . **LC 4**
See also DLB 109

Colman, George
See Glassco, John

Colt, Winchester Remington
See Hubbard, L(afayette) Ron(ald)

Colter, Cyrus 1910- . . . . **CLC 58**
See also BW 1; CA 65-68; CANR 10; DLB 33

Colton, James
See Hansen, Joseph

Colum, Padraic 1881-1972. . . . . **CLC 28**
See also CA 73-76; 33-36R; CANR 35; CLR 36; MAICYA; MTCW; SATA 15

Colvin, James
See Moorcock, Michael (John)

Colwin, Laurie (E.) 1944-1992 . . . . **CLC 5, 13, 23, 84**
See also CA 89-92; 139; CANR 20, 46; DLBY 80; MTCW

Comfort, Alex(ander) 1920-. . . . . **CLC 7**
See also CA 1-4R; CANR 1, 45

Comfort, Montgomery
See Campbell, (John) Ramsey

Compton-Burnett, I(vy) 1884(?)-1969 . . . . . . **CLC 1, 3, 10, 15, 34**
See also CA 1-4R; 25-28R; CANR 4; DLB 36; MTCW

Comstock, Anthony 1844-1915 . . . . **TCLC 13**
See also CA 110

Conan Doyle, Arthur
See Doyle, Arthur Conan

Conde, Maryse 1937-. . . . . **CLC 52**
See also Boucolon, Maryse
See also BW 2

Condillac, Etienne Bonnot de 1714-1780 . . . . **LC 26**

Condon, Richard (Thomas) 1915- . . . . **CLC 4, 6, 8, 10, 45**
See also BEST 90:3; CA 1-4R; CAAS 1; CANR 2, 23; MTCW

Congreve, William 1670-1729 . . . **LC 5, 21; DA; DC 2; WLC**
See also CDBLB 1660-1789; DLB 39, 84

Connell, Evan S(helby), Jr. 1924- . . . . **CLC 4, 6, 45**
See also AAYA 7; CA 1-4R; CAAS 2; CANR 2, 39; DLB 2; DLBY 81; MTCW

Connelly, Marc(us Cook) 1890-1980 . . . . **CLC 7**
See also CA 85-88; 102; CANR 30; DLB 7; DLBY 80; SATA-Obit 25

Connor, Ralph . . . . **TCLC 31**
See also Gordon, Charles William
See also DLB 92

Conrad, Joseph 1857-1924 . . . . **TCLC 1, 6, 13, 25, 43, 57; DA; SSC 9; WLC**
See also CA 104; 131; CDBLB 1890-1914; DLB 10, 34, 98; MTCW; SATA 27

Conrad, Robert Arnold
See Hart, Moss

Conroy, Pat 1945-. . . . . **CLC 30, 74**
See also AAYA 8; AITN 1; CA 85-88; CANR 24; DLB 6; MTCW

Constant (de Rebecque), (Henri) Benjamin 1767-1830 . . . . **NCLC 6**
See also DLB 119

Conybeare, Charles Augustus
See Eliot, T(homas) S(tearns)

Cook, Michael 1933- . . . . **CLC 58**
See also CA 93-96; DLB 53

Cook, Robin 1940- . . . . **CLC 14**
See also BEST 90:2; CA 108; 111; CANR 41

Cook, Roy
See Silverberg, Robert

Cooke, Elizabeth 1948- . . . . **CLC 55**
See also CA 129

Cooke, John Esten 1830-1886 . . . . . **NCLC 5**
See also DLB 3

Cooke, John Estes
See Baum, L(yman) Frank

Cooke, M. E.
See Creasey, John

Cooke, Margaret
See Creasey, John

Cooney, Ray .... **CLC 62**

Cooper, Douglas 1960-.......... **CLC 86**

Cooper, Henry St. John
See Creasey, John

Cooper, J. California.......... **CLC 56**
See also AAYA 12; BW 1; CA 125

Cooper, James Fenimore
1789-1851 .... **NCLC 1, 27**
See also CDALB 1640-1865; DLB 3; SATA 19

Coover, Robert (Lowell)
1932- .. **CLC 3, 7, 15, 32, 46, 87; SSC 15**
See also CA 45-48; CANR 3, 37; DLB 2; DLBY 81; MTCW

Copeland, Stewart (Armstrong)
1952- .... **CLC 26**

Coppard, A(lfred) E(dgar)
1878-1957 .... **TCLC 5**
See also CA 114; YABC 1

Coppee, Francois 1842-1908 ...... **TCLC 25**

Coppola, Francis Ford 1939-....... **CLC 16**
See also CA 77-80; CANR 40; DLB 44

Corbiere, Tristan 1845-1875 ..... **NCLC 43**

Corcoran, Barbara 1911-.......... **CLC 17**
See also AAYA 14; CA 21-24R; CAAS 2; CANR 11, 28; DLB 52; JRDA; SATA 3, 77

Cordelier, Maurice
See Giraudoux, (Hippolyte) Jean

Corelli, Marie 1855-1924......... **TCLC 51**
See also Mackay, Mary
See also DLB 34

Corman, Cid.......... **CLC 9**
See also Corman, Sidney
See also CAAS 2; DLB 5

Corman, Sidney 1924-
See Corman, Cid
See also CA 85-88; CANR 44

Cormier, Robert (Edmund)
1925- .... **CLC 12, 30; DA**
See also AAYA 3; CA 1-4R; CANR 5, 23; CDALB 1968-1988; CLR 12; DLB 52; JRDA; MAICYA; MTCW; SATA 10, 45

Corn, Alfred (DeWitt III) 1943-.... **CLC 33**
See also CA 104; CANR 44; DLB 120; DLBY 80

Corneille, Pierre 1606-1684......... **LC 28**

Cornwell, David (John Moore)
1931- .... **CLC 9, 15**
See also le Carre, John
See also CA 5-8R; CANR 13, 33; MTCW

Corso, (Nunzio) Gregory 1930-... **CLC 1, 11**
See also CA 5-8R; CANR 41; DLB 5, 16; MTCW

Cortazar, Julio
1914-1984 ...... **CLC 2, 3, 5, 10, 13, 15, 33, 34; HLC; SSC 7**
See also CA 21-24R; CANR 12, 32; DLB 113; HW; MTCW

Corwin, Cecil
See Kornbluth, C(yril) M.

Cosic, Dobrica 1921-.......... **CLC 14**
See also CA 122; 138

Costain, Thomas B(ertram)
1885-1965 .... **CLC 30**
See also CA 5-8R; 25-28R; DLB 9

Costantini, Humberto
1924(?)-1987 .... **CLC 49**
See also CA 131; 122; HW

Costello, Elvis 1955-.......... **CLC 21**

Cotter, Joseph Seamon Sr.
1861-1949 .... **TCLC 28; BLC**
See also BW 1; CA 124; DLB 50

Couch, Arthur Thomas Quiller
See Quiller-Couch, Arthur Thomas

Coulton, James
See Hansen, Joseph

Couperus, Louis (Marie Anne)
1863-1923 .... **TCLC 15**
See also CA 115

Coupland, Douglas 1961-.......... **CLC 85**
See also CA 142

Court, Wesli
See Turco, Lewis (Putnam)

Courtenay, Bryce 1933-.......... **CLC 59**
See also CA 138

Courtney, Robert
See Ellison, Harlan (Jay)

Cousteau, Jacques-Yves 1910-...... **CLC 30**
See also CA 65-68; CANR 15; MTCW; SATA 38

Coward, Noel (Peirce)
1899-1973 .... **CLC 1, 9, 29, 51**
See also AITN 1; CA 17-18; 41-44R; CANR 35; CAP 2; CDBLB 1914-1945; DLB 10; MTCW

Cowley, Malcolm 1898-1989 .... **CLC 39**
See also CA 5-8R; 128; CANR 3; DLB 4, 48; DLBY 81, 89; MTCW

Cowper, William 1731-1800....... **NCLC 8**
See also DLB 104, 109

Cox, William Trevor 1928- ... **CLC 9, 14, 71**
See also Trevor, William
See also CA 9-12R; CANR 4, 37; DLB 14; MTCW

Coyne, P. J.
See Masters, Hilary

Cozzens, James Gould
1903-1978 .... **CLC 1, 4, 11**
See also CA 9-12R; 81-84; CANR 19; CDALB 1941-1968; DLB 9; DLBD 2; DLBY 84; MTCW

Crabbe, George 1754-1832....... **NCLC 26**
See also DLB 93

Craig, A. A.
See Anderson, Poul (William)

Craik, Dinah Maria (Mulock)
1826-1887 .... **NCLC 38**
See also DLB 35; MAICYA; SATA 34

Cram, Ralph Adams 1863-1942.... **TCLC 45**

Crane, (Harold) Hart
1899-1932 .... **TCLC 2, 5; DA; PC 3; WLC**
See also CA 104; 127; CDALB 1917-1929; DLB 4, 48; MTCW

Crane, R(onald) S(almon)
1886-1967 .... **CLC 27**
See also CA 85-88; DLB 63

Crane, Stephen (Townley)
1871-1900 .... **TCLC 11, 17, 32; DA; SSC 7; WLC**
See also CA 109; 140; CDALB 1865-1917; DLB 12, 54, 78; YABC 2

Crase, Douglas 1944-.......... **CLC 58**
See also CA 106

Crashaw, Richard 1612(?)-1649...... **LC 24**
See also DLB 126

Craven, Margaret 1901-1980....... **CLC 17**
See also CA 103

Crawford, F(rancis) Marion
1854-1909 .... **TCLC 10**
See also CA 107; DLB 71

Crawford, Isabella Valancy
1850-1887 .... **NCLC 12**
See also DLB 92

Crayon, Geoffrey
See Irving, Washington

Creasey, John 1908-1973.......... **CLC 11**
See also CA 5-8R; 41-44R; CANR 8; DLB 77; MTCW

Crebillon, Claude Prosper Jolyot de (fils)
1707-1777 .... **LC 28**

Credo
See Creasey, John

Creeley, Robert (White)
1926- ..... **CLC 1, 2, 4, 8, 11, 15, 36, 78**
See also CA 1-4R; CAAS 10; CANR 23, 43; DLB 5, 16; MTCW

Crews, Harry (Eugene)
1935- .... **CLC 6, 23, 49**
See also AITN 1; CA 25-28R; CANR 20; DLB 6, 143; MTCW

Crichton, (John) Michael
1942- .... **CLC 2, 6, 54**
See also AAYA 10; AITN 2; CA 25-28R; CANR 13, 40; DLBY 81; JRDA; MTCW; SATA 9

Crispin, Edmund.......... **CLC 22**
See also Montgomery, (Robert) Bruce
See also DLB 87

Cristofer, Michael 1945(?)-........ **CLC 28**
See also CA 110; DLB 7

Croce, Benedetto 1866-1952 ...... **TCLC 37**
See also CA 120

Crockett, David 1786-1836 .... **NCLC 8**
See also DLB 3, 11

Crockett, Davy
See Crockett, David

Crofts, Freeman Wills
1879-1957 .... **TCLC 55**
See also CA 115; DLB 77

Croker, John Wilson 1780-1857 .. **NCLC 10**
See also DLB 110

Crommelynck, Fernand 1885-1970 .. **CLC 75**
See also CA 89-92

Cronin, A(rchibald) J(oseph)
1896-1981 .... **CLC 32**
See also CA 1-4R; 102; CANR 5; SATA 47; SATA-Obit 25

Author Index

Cross, Amanda
See Heilbrun, Carolyn G(old)

Crothers, Rachel 1878(?)-1958..... **TCLC 19**
See also CA 113; DLB 7

Croves, Hal
See Traven, B.

Crowfield, Christopher
See Stowe, Harriet (Elizabeth) Beecher

Crowley, Aleister.................. **TCLC 7**
See also Crowley, Edward Alexander

Crowley, Edward Alexander 1875-1947
See Crowley, Aleister
See also CA 104

Crowley, John 1942-.............. **CLC 57**
See also CA 61-64; CANR 43; DLBY 82; SATA 65

Crud
See Crumb, R(obert)

Crumarums
See Crumb, R(obert)

Crumb, R(obert) 1943-............ **CLC 17**
See also CA 106

Crumbum
See Crumb, R(obert)

Crumski
See Crumb, R(obert)

Crum the Bum
See Crumb, R(obert)

Crunk
See Crumb, R(obert)

Crustt
See Crumb, R(obert)

Cryer, Gretchen (Kiger) 1935-...... **CLC 21**
See also CA 114; 123

Csath, Geza 1887-1919........... **TCLC 13**
See also CA 111

Cudlip, David 1933-.............. **CLC 34**

Cullen, Countee
1903-1946 ...... **TCLC 4, 37; BLC; DA**
See also BW 1; CA 108; 124; CDALB 1917-1929; DLB 4, 48, 51; MTCW; SATA 18

Cum, R.
See Crumb, R(obert)

Cummings, Bruce F(rederick) 1889-1919
See Barbellion, W. N. P.
See also CA 123

Cummings, E(dward) E(stlin)
1894-1962 ...... **CLC 1, 3, 8, 12, 15, 68; DA; PC 5; WLC 2**
See also CA 73-76; CANR 31; CDALB 1929-1941; DLB 4, 48; MTCW

Cunha, Euclides (Rodrigues Pimenta) da
1866-1909 .... **TCLC 24**
See also CA 123

Cunningham, E. V.
See Fast, Howard (Melvin)

Cunningham, J(ames) V(incent)
1911-1985 .... **CLC 3, 31**
See also CA 1-4R; 115; CANR 1; DLB 5

Cunningham, Julia (Woolfolk)
1916- .... **CLC 12**
See also CA 9-12R; CANR 4, 19, 36; JRDA; MAICYA; SAAS 2; SATA 1, 26

Cunningham, Michael 1952- .... **CLC 34**
See also CA 136

Cunninghame Graham, R(obert) B(ontine)
1852-1936 .... **TCLC 19**
See also Graham, R(obert) B(ontine) Cunninghame
See also CA 119; DLB 98

Currie, Ellen 19(?)-............... **CLC 44**

Curtin, Philip
See Lowndes, Marie Adelaide (Belloc)

Curtis, Price
See Ellison, Harlan (Jay)

Cutrate, Joe
See Spiegelman, Art

Czaczkes, Shmuel Yosef
See Agnon, S(hmuel) Y(osef Halevi)

Dabrowska, Maria (Szumska)
1889-1965 .... **CLC 15**
See also CA 106

Dabydeen, David 1955- .... **CLC 34**
See also BW 1; CA 125

Dacey, Philip 1939- .... **CLC 51**
See also CA 37-40R; CAAS 17; CANR 14, 32; DLB 105

Dagerman, Stig (Halvard)
1923-1954 .... **TCLC 17**
See also CA 117

Dahl, Roald 1916-1990..... **CLC 1, 6, 18, 79**
See also CA 1-4R; 133; CANR 6, 32, 37; CLR 1, 7; DLB 139; JRDA; MAICYA; MTCW; SATA 1, 26, 73; SATA-Obit 65

Dahlberg, Edward 1900-1977... **CLC 1, 7, 14**
See also CA 9-12R; 69-72; CANR 31; DLB 48; MTCW

Dale, Colin...................... **TCLC 18**
See also Lawrence, T(homas) E(dward)

Dale, George E.
See Asimov, Isaac

Daly, Elizabeth 1878-1967......... **CLC 52**
See also CA 23-24; 25-28R; CAP 2

Daly, Maureen 1921-............. **CLC 17**
See also AAYA 5; CANR 37; JRDA; MAICYA; SAAS 1; SATA 2

Damas, Leon-Gontran 1912-1978 ... **CLC 84**
See also BW 1; CA 125; 73-76

Daniel, Samuel 1562(?)-1619........ **LC 24**
See also DLB 62

Daniels, Brett
See Adler, Renata

Dannay, Frederic 1905-1982 .... **CLC 11**
See also Queen, Ellery
See also CA 1-4R; 107; CANR 1, 39; DLB 137; MTCW

D'Annunzio, Gabriele
1863-1938 .... **TCLC 6, 40**
See also CA 104

d'Antibes, Germain
See Simenon, Georges (Jacques Christian)

Danvers, Dennis 1947-............ **CLC 70**

Danziger, Paula 1944- .... **CLC 21**
See also AAYA 4; CA 112; 115; CANR 37; CLR 20; JRDA; MAICYA; SATA 36, 63; SATA-Brief 30

Dario, Ruben 1867-1916 .... **TCLC 4; HLC**
See also CA 131; HW; MTCW

Darley, George 1795-1846........ **NCLC 2**
See also DLB 96

Daryush, Elizabeth 1887-1977.... **CLC 6, 19**
See also CA 49-52; CANR 3; DLB 20

Daudet, (Louis Marie) Alphonse
1840-1897 .... **NCLC 1**
See also DLB 123

Daumal, Rene 1908-1944......... **TCLC 14**
See also CA 114

Davenport, Guy (Mattison, Jr.)
1927- .... **CLC 6, 14, 38; SSC 16**
See also CA 33-36R; CANR 23; DLB 130

Davidson, Avram 1923-
See Queen, Ellery
See also CA 101; CANR 26; DLB 8

Davidson, Donald (Grady)
1893-1968 .... **CLC 2, 13, 19**
See also CA 5-8R; 25-28R; CANR 4; DLB 45

Davidson, Hugh
See Hamilton, Edmond

Davidson, John 1857-1909........ **TCLC 24**
See also CA 118; DLB 19

Davidson, Sara 1943-.............. **CLC 9**
See also CA 81-84; CANR 44

Davie, Donald (Alfred)
1922- .... **CLC 5, 8, 10, 31**
See also CA 1-4R; CAAS 3; CANR 1, 44; DLB 27; MTCW

Davies, Ray(mond Douglas) 1944- .. **CLC 21**
See also CA 116

Davies, Rhys 1903-1978........... **CLC 23**
See also CA 9-12R; 81-84; CANR 4; DLB 139

Davies, (William) Robertson
1913- ..... **CLC 2, 7, 13, 25, 42, 75; DA; WLC**
See also BEST 89:2; CA 33-36R; CANR 17, 42; DLB 68; MTCW

Davies, W(illiam) H(enry)
1871-1940 .... **TCLC 5**
See also CA 104; DLB 19

Davies, Walter C.
See Kornbluth, C(yril) M.

Davis, Angela (Yvonne) 1944-...... **CLC 77**
See also BW 2; CA 57-60; CANR 10

Davis, B. Lynch
See Bioy Casares, Adolfo; Borges, Jorge Luis

Davis, Gordon
See Hunt, E(verette) Howard, (Jr.)

Davis, Harold Lenoir 1896-1960.... **CLC 49**
See also CA 89-92; DLB 9

Davis, Rebecca (Blaine) Harding
1831-1910 .... **TCLC 6**
See also CA 104; DLB 74

Davis, Richard Harding
1864-1916 .... **TCLC 24**
See also CA 114; DLB 12, 23, 78, 79

Davison, Frank Dalby 1893-1970 ... **CLC 15**
See also CA 116

Davison, Lawrence H.
See Lawrence, D(avid) H(erbert Richards)

Davison, Peter (Hubert) 1928- . . . . . **CLC 28**
See also CA 9-12R; CAAS 4; CANR 3, 43; DLB 5

Davys, Mary 1674-1732. . . . . **LC 1**
See also DLB 39

Dawson, Fielding 1930- . . . . **CLC 6**
See also CA 85-88; DLB 130

Dawson, Peter
See Faust, Frederick (Schiller)

Day, Clarence (Shepard, Jr.) 1874-1935 . . . . **TCLC 25**
See also CA 108; DLB 11

Day, Thomas 1748-1789. . . . . **LC 1**
See also DLB 39; YABC 1

Day Lewis, C(ecil) 1904-1972 . . . . **CLC 1, 6, 10; PC 11**
See also Blake, Nicholas
See also CA 13-16; 33-36R; CANR 34; CAP 1; DLB 15, 20; MTCW

Dazai, Osamu . . . . **TCLC 11**
See also Tsushima, Shuji

de Andrade, Carlos Drummond
See Drummond de Andrade, Carlos

Deane, Norman
See Creasey, John

de Beauvoir, Simone (Lucie Ernestine Marie Bertrand)
See Beauvoir, Simone (Lucie Ernestine Marie Bertrand) de

de Brissac, Malcolm
See Dickinson, Peter (Malcolm)

de Chardin, Pierre Teilhard
See Teilhard de Chardin, (Marie Joseph) Pierre

Dee, John 1527-1608 . . . . **LC 20**

Deer, Sandra 1940-. . . . . **CLC 45**

De Ferrari, Gabriella . . . . **CLC 65**

Defoe, Daniel 1660(?)-1731 . . . . **LC 1; DA; WLC**
See also CDBLB 1660-1789; DLB 39, 95, 101; JRDA; MAICYA; SATA 22

de Gourmont, Remy
See Gourmont, Remy de

de Hartog, Jan 1914-. . . . . **CLC 19**
See also CA 1-4R; CANR 1

de Hostos, E. M.
See Hostos (y Bonilla), Eugenio Maria de

de Hostos, Eugenio M.
See Hostos (y Bonilla), Eugenio Maria de

Deighton, Len . . . . **CLC 4, 7, 22, 46**
See also Deighton, Leonard Cyril
See also AAYA 6; BEST 89:2; CDBLB 1960 to Present; DLB 87

Deighton, Leonard Cyril 1929-
See Deighton, Len
See also CA 9-12R; CANR 19, 33; MTCW

Dekker, Thomas 1572(?)-1632. . . . . . . **LC 22**
See also CDBLB Before 1660; DLB 62

de la Mare, Walter (John) 1873-1956 . . **TCLC 4, 53; SSC 14; WLC**
See also CDBLB 1914-1945; CLR 23; DLB 19; SATA 16

Delaney, Franey
See O'Hara, John (Henry)

Delaney, Shelagh 1939- . . . . **CLC 29**
See also CA 17-20R; CANR 30; CDBLB 1960 to Present; DLB 13; MTCW

Delany, Mary (Granville Pendarves) 1700-1788 . . . . **LC 12**

Delany, Samuel R(ay, Jr.) 1942- . . . . **CLC 8, 14, 38; BLC**
See also BW 2; CA 81-84; CANR 27, 43; DLB 8, 33; MTCW

De La Ramee, (Marie) Louise 1839-1908
See Ouida
See also SATA 20

de la Roche, Mazo 1879-1961 . . . . . . **CLC 14**
See also CA 85-88; CANR 30; DLB 68; SATA 64

Delbanco, Nicholas (Franklin) 1942- . . . . **CLC 6, 13**
See also CA 17-20R; CAAS 2; CANR 29; DLB 6

del Castillo, Michel 1933- . . . . **CLC 38**
See also CA 109

Deledda, Grazia (Cosima) 1875(?)-1936 . . . . **TCLC 23**
See also CA 123

Delibes, Miguel . . . . **CLC 8, 18**
See also Delibes Setien, Miguel

Delibes Setien, Miguel 1920-
See Delibes, Miguel
See also CA 45-48; CANR 1, 32; HW; MTCW

DeLillo, Don 1936- . . . . . **CLC 8, 10, 13, 27, 39, 54, 76**
See also BEST 89:1; CA 81-84; CANR 21; DLB 6; MTCW

de Lisser, H. G.
See De Lisser, Herbert George
See also DLB 117

De Lisser, Herbert George 1878-1944 . . . . **TCLC 12**
See also de Lisser, H. G.
See also BW 2; CA 109

Deloria, Vine (Victor), Jr. 1933-. . . . **CLC 21**
See also CA 53-56; CANR 5, 20; MTCW; NNAL; SATA 21

Del Vecchio, John M(ichael) 1947- . . . . **CLC 29**
See also CA 110; DLBD 9

de Man, Paul (Adolph Michel) 1919-1983 . . . . **CLC 55**
See also CA 128; 111; DLB 67; MTCW

De Marinis, Rick 1934- . . . . **CLC 54**
See also CA 57-60; CANR 9, 25

Demby, William 1922- . . . . **CLC 53; BLC**
See also BW 1; CA 81-84; DLB 33

Demijohn, Thom
See Disch, Thomas M(ichael)

de Montherlant, Henry (Milon)
See Montherlant, Henry (Milon) de

Demosthenes 384B.C.-322B.C. . . . **CMLC 13**

de Natale, Francine
See Malzberg, Barry N(athaniel)

Denby, Edwin (Orr) 1903-1983 . . . . . **CLC 48**
See also CA 138; 110

Denis, Julio
See Cortazar, Julio

Denmark, Harrison
See Zelazny, Roger (Joseph)

Dennis, John 1658-1734. . . . . **LC 11**
See also DLB 101

Dennis, Nigel (Forbes) 1912-1989 . . . . **CLC 8**
See also CA 25-28R; 129; DLB 13, 15; MTCW

De Palma, Brian (Russell) 1940-. . . . **CLC 20**
See also CA 109

De Quincey, Thomas 1785-1859 . . . **NCLC 4**
See also CDBLB 1789-1832; DLB 110; 144

Deren, Eleanora 1908(?)-1961
See Deren, Maya
See also CA 111

Deren, Maya . . . . **CLC 16**
See also Deren, Eleanora

Derleth, August (William) 1909-1971 . . . . **CLC 31**
See also CA 1-4R; 29-32R; CANR 4; DLB 9; SATA 5

Der Nister 1884-1950. . . . . **TCLC 56**

de Routisie, Albert
See Aragon, Louis

Derrida, Jacques 1930-. . . . . **CLC 24, 87**
See also CA 124; 127

Derry Down Derry
See Lear, Edward

Dersonnes, Jacques
See Simenon, Georges (Jacques Christian)

Desai, Anita 1937- . . . . **CLC 19, 37**
See also CA 81-84; CANR 33; MTCW; SATA 63

de Saint-Luc, Jean
See Glassco, John

de Saint Roman, Arnaud
See Aragon, Louis

Descartes, Rene 1596-1650 . . . . **LC 20**

De Sica, Vittorio 1901(?)-1974 . . . . . **CLC 20**
See also CA 117

Desnos, Robert 1900-1945 . . . . **TCLC 22**
See also CA 121

Destouches, Louis-Ferdinand 1894-1961 . . . . **CLC 9, 15**
See also Celine, Louis-Ferdinand
See also CA 85-88; CANR 28; MTCW

Deutsch, Babette 1895-1982 . . . . **CLC 18**
See also CA 1-4R; 108; CANR 4; DLB 45; SATA 1; SATA-Obit 33

Devenant, William 1606-1649 . . . . **LC 13**

Devkota, Laxmiprasad 1909-1959 . . . . **TCLC 23**
See also CA 123

De Voto, Bernard (Augustine) 1897-1955 . . . . **TCLC 29**
See also CA 113; DLB 9

De Vries, Peter 1910-1993 . . . . **CLC 1, 2, 3, 7, 10, 28, 46**
See also CA 17-20R; 142; CANR 41; DLB 6; DLBY 82; MTCW

Author Index

Dexter, Martin
See Faust, Frederick (Schiller)

Dexter, Pete 1943- . . . . **CLC 34, 55**
See also BEST 89:2; CA 127; 131; MTCW

Diamano, Silmang
See Senghor, Leopold Sedar

Diamond, Neil 1941- . . . . **CLC 30**
See also CA 108

di Bassetto, Corno
See Shaw, George Bernard

Dick, Philip K(indred)
1928-1982 . . . . **CLC 10, 30, 72**
See also CA 49-52; 106; CANR 2, 16; DLB 8; MTCW

Dickens, Charles (John Huffam)
1812-1870 . . . . . . **NCLC 3, 8, 18, 26, 37; DA; SSC 17; WLC**
See also CDBLB 1832-1890; DLB 21, 55, 70; JRDA; MAICYA; SATA 15

Dickey, James (Lafayette)
1923- . . . . **CLC 1, 2, 4, 7, 10, 15, 47**
See also AITN 1, 2; CA 9-12R; CABS 2; CANR 10; CDALB 1968-1988; DLB 5; DLBD 7; DLBY 82, 93; MTCW

Dickey, William 1928-1994 . . . . . . **CLC 3, 28**
See also CA 9-12R; 145; CANR 24; DLB 5

Dickinson, Charles 1951- . . . . **CLC 49**
See also CA 128

Dickinson, Emily (Elizabeth)
1830-1886 . . **NCLC 21; DA; PC 1; WLC**
See also CDALB 1865-1917; DLB 1; SATA 29

Dickinson, Peter (Malcolm)
1927- . . . . **CLC 12, 35**
See also AAYA 9; CA 41-44R; CANR 31; CLR 29; DLB 87; JRDA; MAICYA; SATA 5, 62

Dickson, Carr
See Carr, John Dickson

Dickson, Carter
See Carr, John Dickson

Diderot, Denis 1713-1784 . . . . **LC 26**

Didion, Joan 1934- . . . . . **CLC 1, 3, 8, 14, 32**
See also AITN 1; CA 5-8R; CANR 14; CDALB 1968-1988; DLB 2; DLBY 81, 86; MTCW

Dietrich, Robert
See Hunt, E(verette) Howard, (Jr.)

Dillard, Annie 1945- . . . . **CLC 9, 60**
See also AAYA 6; CA 49-52; CANR 3, 43; DLBY 80; MTCW; SATA 10

Dillard, R(ichard) H(enry) W(ilde)
1937- . . . . **CLC 5**
See also CA 21-24R; CAAS 7; CANR 10; DLB 5

Dillon, Eilis 1920- . . . . **CLC 17**
See also CA 9-12R; CAAS 3; CANR 4, 38; CLR 26; MAICYA; SATA 2, 74

Dimont, Penelope
See Mortimer, Penelope (Ruth)

Dinesen, Isak . . . . **CLC 10, 29; SSC 7**
See also Blixen, Karen (Christentze Dinesen)

Ding Ling . . . . **CLC 68**
See also Chiang Pin-chin

Disch, Thomas M(ichael) 1940- . . . **CLC 7, 36**
See also CA 21-24R; CAAS 4; CANR 17, 36; CLR 18; DLB 8; MAICYA; MTCW; SAAS 15; SATA 54

Disch, Tom
See Disch, Thomas M(ichael)

d'Isly, Georges
See Simenon, Georges (Jacques Christian)

Disraeli, Benjamin 1804-1881 . . **NCLC 2, 39**
See also DLB 21, 55

Ditcum, Steve
See Crumb, R(obert)

Dixon, Paige
See Corcoran, Barbara

Dixon, Stephen 1936- . . . . . **CLC 52; SSC 16**
See also CA 89-92; CANR 17, 40; DLB 130

Dobell, Sydney Thompson
1824-1874 . . . . **NCLC 43**
See also DLB 32

Doblin, Alfred . . . . **TCLC 13**
See also Doeblin, Alfred

Dobrolyubov, Nikolai Alexandrovich
1836-1861 . . . . **NCLC 5**

Dobyns, Stephen 1941- . . . . **CLC 37**
See also CA 45-48; CANR 2, 18

Doctorow, E(dgar) L(aurence)
1931- . . . . . **CLC 6, 11, 15, 18, 37, 44, 65**
See also AITN 2; BEST 89:3; CA 45-48; CANR 2, 33; CDALB 1968-1988; DLB 2, 28; DLBY 80; MTCW

Dodgson, Charles Lutwidge 1832-1898
See Carroll, Lewis
See also CLR 2; DA; MAICYA; YABC 2

Dodson, Owen (Vincent)
1914-1983 . . . . **CLC 79; BLC**
See also BW 1; CA 65-68; 110; CANR 24; DLB 76

Doeblin, Alfred 1878-1957 . . . . **TCLC 13**
See also Doblin, Alfred
See also CA 110; 141; DLB 66

Doerr, Harriet 1910- . . . . **CLC 34**
See also CA 117; 122; CANR 47

Domecq, H(onorio) Bustos
See Bioy Casares, Adolfo; Borges, Jorge Luis

Domini, Rey
See Lorde, Audre (Geraldine)

Dominique
See Proust, (Valentin-Louis-George-Eugene-) Marcel

Don, A
See Stephen, Leslie

Donaldson, Stephen R. 1947- . . . . **CLC 46**
See also CA 89-92; CANR 13

Donleavy, J(ames) P(atrick)
1926- . . . . **CLC 1, 4, 6, 10, 45**
See also AITN 2; CA 9-12R; CANR 24; DLB 6; MTCW

Donne, John
1572-1631 . . . . **LC 10, 24; DA; PC 1**
See also CDBLB Before 1660; DLB 121

Donnell, David 1939(?)- . . . . **CLC 34**

Donoghue, P. S.
See Hunt, E(verette) Howard, (Jr.)

Donoso (Yanez), Jose
1924- . . . . **CLC 4, 8, 11, 32; HLC**
See also CA 81-84; CANR 32; DLB 113; HW; MTCW

Donovan, John 1928-1992 . . . . **CLC 35**
See also CA 97-100; 137; CLR 3; MAICYA; SATA 72; SATA-Brief 29

Don Roberto
See Cunninghame Graham, R(obert) B(ontine)

Doolittle, Hilda
1886-1961 . . . . . **CLC 3, 8, 14, 31, 34, 73; DA; PC 5; WLC**
See also H. D.
See also CA 97-100; CANR 35; DLB 4, 45; MTCW

Dorfman, Ariel 1942- . . . . **CLC 48, 77; HLC**
See also CA 124; 130; HW

Dorn, Edward (Merton) 1929- . . . **CLC 10, 18**
See also CA 93-96; CANR 42; DLB 5

Dorsan, Luc
See Simenon, Georges (Jacques Christian)

Dorsange, Jean
See Simenon, Georges (Jacques Christian)

Dos Passos, John (Roderigo)
1896-1970 . . . . . . **CLC 1, 4, 8, 11, 15, 25, 34, 82; DA; WLC**
See also CA 1-4R; 29-32R; CANR 3; CDALB 1929-1941; DLB 4, 9; DLBD 1; MTCW

Dossage, Jean
See Simenon, Georges (Jacques Christian)

Dostoevsky, Fedor Mikhailovich
1821-1881 . . . . . . **NCLC 2, 7, 21, 33, 43; DA; SSC 2; WLC**

Doughty, Charles M(ontagu)
1843-1926 . . . . **TCLC 27**
See also CA 115; DLB 19, 57

Douglas, Ellen . . . . **CLC 73**
See also Haxton, Josephine Ayres; Williamson, Ellen Douglas

Douglas, Gavin 1475(?)-1522 . . . . **LC 20**

Douglas, Keith 1920-1944 . . . . **TCLC 40**
See also DLB 27

Douglas, Leonard
See Bradbury, Ray (Douglas)

Douglas, Michael
See Crichton, (John) Michael

Douglass, Frederick
1817(?)-1895 . . . . **NCLC 7; BLC; DA; WLC**
See also CDALB 1640-1865; DLB 1, 43, 50, 79; SATA 29

Dourado, (Waldomiro Freitas) Autran
1926- . . . . **CLC 23, 60**
See also CA 25-28R; CANR 34

Dourado, Waldomiro Autran
See Dourado, (Waldomiro Freitas) Autran

Dove, Rita (Frances)
1952- . . . . **CLC 50, 81; PC 6**
See also BW 2; CA 109; CAAS 19; CANR 27, 42; DLB 120

Dowell, Coleman 1925-1985 . . . . **CLC 60**
See also CA 25-28R; 117; CANR 10; DLB 130

Dowson, Ernest Christopher 1867-1900 . . . . **TCLC 4**
See also CA 105; DLB 19, 135

Doyle, A. Conan
See Doyle, Arthur Conan

Doyle, Arthur Conan 1859-1930 . . . . **TCLC 7; DA; SSC 12; WLC**
See also AAYA 14; CA 104; 122; CDBLB 1890-1914; DLB 18, 70; MTCW; SATA 24

Doyle, Conan
See Doyle, Arthur Conan

Doyle, John
See Graves, Robert (von Ranke)

Doyle, Roddy 1958(?)- . . . . **CLC 81**
See also AAYA 14; CA 143

Doyle, Sir A. Conan
See Doyle, Arthur Conan

Doyle, Sir Arthur Conan
See Doyle, Arthur Conan

Dr. A
See Asimov, Isaac; Silverstein, Alvin

Drabble, Margaret 1939- . . . . **CLC 2, 3, 5, 8, 10, 22, 53**
See also CA 13-16R; CANR 18, 35; CDBLB 1960 to Present; DLB 14; MTCW; SATA 48

Drapier, M. B.
See Swift, Jonathan

Drayham, James
See Mencken, H(enry) L(ouis)

Drayton, Michael 1563-1631 . . . . **LC 8**

Dreadstone, Carl
See Campbell, (John) Ramsey

Dreiser, Theodore (Herman Albert) 1871-1945 . . . . **TCLC 10, 18, 35; DA; WLC**
See also CA 106; 132; CDALB 1865-1917; DLB 9, 12, 102, 137; DLBD 1; MTCW

Drexler, Rosalyn 1926- . . . . **CLC 2, 6**
See also CA 81-84

Dreyer, Carl Theodor 1889-1968. . . . **CLC 16**
See also CA 116

Drieu la Rochelle, Pierre(-Eugene) 1893-1945 . . . . **TCLC 21**
See also CA 117; DLB 72

Drinkwater, John 1882-1937 . . . . . . **TCLC 57**
See also CA 109; DLB 10, 19

Drop Shot
See Cable, George Washington

Droste-Hulshoff, Annette Freiin von 1797-1848 . . . . **NCLC 3**
See also DLB 133

Drummond, Walter
See Silverberg, Robert

Drummond, William Henry 1854-1907 . . . . **TCLC 25**
See also DLB 92

Drummond de Andrade, Carlos 1902-1987 . . . . **CLC 18**
See also Andrade, Carlos Drummond de
See also CA 132; 123

Drury, Allen (Stuart) 1918- . . . . **CLC 37**
See also CA 57-60; CANR 18

Dryden, John 1631-1700 . . . **LC 3, 21; DA; DC 3; WLC**
See also CDBLB 1660-1789; DLB 80, 101, 131

Duberman, Martin 1930- . . . . **CLC 8**
See also CA 1-4R; CANR 2

Dubie, Norman (Evans) 1945- . . . . . . **CLC 36**
See also CA 69-72; CANR 12; DLB 120

Du Bois, W(illiam) E(dward) B(urghardt) 1868-1963 . . . . . . **CLC 1, 2, 13, 64; BLC; DA; WLC**
See also BW 1; CA 85-88; CANR 34; CDALB 1865-1917; DLB 47, 50, 91; MTCW; SATA 42

Dubus, Andre 1936- . . . **CLC 13, 36; SSC 15**
See also CA 21-24R; CANR 17; DLB 130

Duca Minimo
See D'Annunzio, Gabriele

Ducharme, Rejean 1941- . . . . **CLC 74**
See also DLB 60

Duclos, Charles Pinot 1704-1772 . . . . . **LC 1**

Dudek, Louis 1918- . . . . **CLC 11, 19**
See also CA 45-48; CAAS 14; CANR 1; DLB 88

Duerrenmatt, Friedrich 1921-1990 . . . . . . **CLC 1, 4, 8, 11, 15, 43**
See also CA 17-20R; CANR 33; DLB 69, 124; MTCW

Duffy, Bruce (?)- . . . . **CLC 50**

Duffy, Maureen 1933- . . . . **CLC 37**
See also CA 25-28R; CANR 33; DLB 14; MTCW

Dugan, Alan 1923- . . . . **CLC 2, 6**
See also CA 81-84; DLB 5

du Gard, Roger Martin
See Martin du Gard, Roger

Duhamel, Georges 1884-1966 . . . . **CLC 8**
See also CA 81-84; 25-28R; CANR 35; DLB 65; MTCW

Dujardin, Edouard (Emile Louis) 1861-1949 . . . . **TCLC 13**
See also CA 109; DLB 123

Dumas, Alexandre (Davy de la Pailleterie) 1802-1870 . . . . **NCLC 11; DA; WLC**
See also DLB 119; SATA 18

Dumas, Alexandre 1824-1895 . . . . **NCLC 9; DC 1**

Dumas, Claudine
See Malzberg, Barry N(athaniel)

Dumas, Henry L. 1934-1968 . . . . . **CLC 6, 62**
See also BW 1; CA 85-88; DLB 41

du Maurier, Daphne 1907-1989 . . . . . . **CLC 6, 11, 59; SSC 18**
See also CA 5-8R; 128; CANR 6; MTCW; SATA 27; SATA-Obit 60

Dunbar, Paul Laurence 1872-1906 . . . . . . **TCLC 2, 12; BLC; DA; PC 5; SSC 8; WLC**
See also BW 1; CA 104; 124; CDALB 1865-1917; DLB 50, 54, 78; SATA 34

Dunbar, William 1460(?)-1530(?) . . . . **LC 20**
See also DLB 132, 146

Duncan, Lois 1934- . . . . **CLC 26**
See also AAYA 4; CA 1-4R; CANR 2, 23, 36; CLR 29; JRDA; MAICYA; SAAS 2; SATA 1, 36, 75

Duncan, Robert (Edward) 1919-1988 . . . . **CLC 1, 2, 4, 7, 15, 41, 55; PC 2**
See also CA 9-12R; 124; CANR 28; DLB 5, 16; MTCW

Dunlap, William 1766-1839 . . . . **NCLC 2**
See also DLB 30, 37, 59

Dunn, Douglas (Eaglesham) 1942- . . . . **CLC 6, 40**
See also CA 45-48; CANR 2, 33; DLB 40; MTCW

Dunn, Katherine (Karen) 1945- . . . . . **CLC 71**
See also CA 33-36R

Dunn, Stephen 1939- . . . . **CLC 36**
See also CA 33-36R; CANR 12; DLB 105

Dunne, Finley Peter 1867-1936. . . . **TCLC 28**
See also CA 108; DLB 11, 23

Dunne, John Gregory 1932- . . . . **CLC 28**
See also CA 25-28R; CANR 14; DLBY 80

Dunsany, Edward John Moreton Drax Plunkett 1878-1957
See Dunsany, Lord
See also CA 104; DLB 10

Dunsany, Lord . . . . **TCLC 2, 59**
See also Dunsany, Edward John Moreton Drax Plunkett
See also DLB 77

du Perry, Jean
See Simenon, Georges (Jacques Christian)

Durang, Christopher (Ferdinand) 1949- . . . . **CLC 27, 38**
See also CA 105

Duras, Marguerite 1914- . . . . . . **CLC 3, 6, 11, 20, 34, 40, 68**
See also CA 25-28R; DLB 83; MTCW

Durban, (Rosa) Pam 1947- . . . . **CLC 39**
See also CA 123

Durcan, Paul 1944- . . . . **CLC 43, 70**
See also CA 134

Durkheim, Emile 1858-1917 . . . . . . **TCLC 55**

Durrell, Lawrence (George) 1912-1990 . . . . **CLC 1, 4, 6, 8, 13, 27, 41**
See also CA 9-12R; 132; CANR 40; CDBLB 1945-1960; DLB 15, 27; DLBY 90; MTCW

Durrenmatt, Friedrich
See Duerrenmatt, Friedrich

Dutt, Toru 1856-1877 . . . . **NCLC 29**

Dwight, Timothy 1752-1817 . . . . . . **NCLC 13**
See also DLB 37

Dworkin, Andrea 1946- . . . . **CLC 43**
See also CA 77-80; CANR 16, 39; MTCW

Dwyer, Deanna
See Koontz, Dean R(ay)

Dwyer, K. R.
See Koontz, Dean R(ay)

Dylan, Bob 1941- . . . . . . **CLC 3, 4, 6, 12, 77**
See also CA 41-44R; DLB 16

Eagleton, Terence (Francis) 1943-
See Eagleton, Terry
See also CA 57-60; CANR 7, 23; MTCW

Eagleton, Terry . . . . **CLC 63**
See also Eagleton, Terence (Francis)

Early, Jack
See Scoppettone, Sandra

East, Michael
See West, Morris L(anglo)

Eastaway, Edward
See Thomas, (Philip) Edward

Eastlake, William (Derry) 1917- . . . . . **CLC 8**
See also CA 5-8R; CAAS 1; CANR 5; DLB 6

Eastman, Charles A(lexander)
1858-1939 . . . . **TCLC 55**
See also NNAL; YABC 1

Eberhart, Richard (Ghormley)
1904- . . . . **CLC 3, 11, 19, 56**
See also CA 1-4R; CANR 2; CDALB 1941-1968; DLB 48; MTCW

Eberstadt, Fernanda 1960- . . . . **CLC 39**
See also CA 136

Echegaray (y Eizaguirre), Jose (Maria Waldo)
1832-1916 . . . . **TCLC 4**
See also CA 104; CANR 32; HW; MTCW

Echeverria, (Jose) Esteban (Antonino)
1805-1851 . . . . **NCLC 18**

Echo
See Proust, (Valentin-Louis-George-Eugene-) Marcel

Eckert, Allan W. 1931- . . . . **CLC 17**
See also CA 13-16R; CANR 14, 45; SATA 29; SATA-Brief 27

Eckhart, Meister 1260(?)-1328(?) . . **CMLC 9**
See also DLB 115

Eckmar, F. R.
See de Hartog, Jan

Eco, Umberto 1932- . . . . **CLC 28, 60**
See also BEST 90:1; CA 77-80; CANR 12, 33; MTCW

Eddison, E(ric) R(ucker)
1882-1945 . . . . **TCLC 15**
See also CA 109

Edel, (Joseph) Leon 1907- . . . . . . **CLC 29, 34**
See also CA 1-4R; CANR 1, 22; DLB 103

Eden, Emily 1797-1869 . . . . **NCLC 10**

Edgar, David 1948- . . . . **CLC 42**
See also CA 57-60; CANR 12; DLB 13; MTCW

Edgerton, Clyde (Carlyle) 1944- . . . . **CLC 39**
See also CA 118; 134

Edgeworth, Maria 1767-1849 . . . . . . **NCLC 1**
See also DLB 116; SATA 21

Edmonds, Paul
See Kuttner, Henry

Edmonds, Walter D(umaux) 1903- . . **CLC 35**
See also CA 5-8R; CANR 2; DLB 9; MAICYA; SAAS 4; SATA 1, 27

Edmondson, Wallace
See Ellison, Harlan (Jay)

Edson, Russell . . . . **CLC 13**
See also CA 33-36R

Edwards, Bronwen Elizabeth
See Rose, Wendy

Edwards, G(erald) B(asil)
1899-1976 . . . . **CLC 25**
See also CA 110

Edwards, Gus 1939- . . . . **CLC 43**
See also CA 108

Edwards, Jonathan 1703-1758 . . . . **LC 7; DA**
See also DLB 24

Efron, Marina Ivanovna Tsvetaeva
See Tsvetaeva (Efron), Marina (Ivanovna)

Ehle, John (Marsden, Jr.) 1925- . . . . **CLC 27**
See also CA 9-12R

Ehrenbourg, Ilya (Grigoryevich)
See Ehrenburg, Ilya (Grigoryevich)

Ehrenburg, Ilya (Grigoryevich)
1891-1967 . . . . **CLC 18, 34, 62**
See also CA 102; 25-28R

Ehrenburg, Ilyo (Grigoryevich)
See Ehrenburg, Ilya (Grigoryevich)

Eich, Guenter 1907-1972 . . . . **CLC 15**
See also CA 111; 93-96; DLB 69, 124

Eichendorff, Joseph Freiherr von
1788-1857 . . . . **NCLC 8**
See also DLB 90

Eigner, Larry . . . . **CLC 9**
See also Eigner, Laurence (Joel)
See also DLB 5

Eigner, Laurence (Joel) 1927-
See Eigner, Larry
See also CA 9-12R; CANR 6

Eiseley, Loren Corey 1907-1977 . . . . . **CLC 7**
See also AAYA 5; CA 1-4R; 73-76; CANR 6

Eisenstadt, Jill 1963- . . . . **CLC 50**
See also CA 140

Eisenstein, Sergei (Mikhailovich)
1898-1948 . . . . **TCLC 57**
See also CA 114

Eisner, Simon
See Kornbluth, C(yril) M.

Ekeloef, (Bengt) Gunnar
1907-1968 . . . . **CLC 27**
See also CA 123; 25-28R

Ekelof, (Bengt) Gunnar
See Ekeloef, (Bengt) Gunnar

Ekwensi, C. O. D.
See Ekwensi, Cyprian (Odiatu Duaka)

Ekwensi, Cyprian (Odiatu Duaka)
1921- . . . . **CLC 4; BLC**
See also BW 2; CA 29-32R; CANR 18, 42; DLB 117; MTCW; SATA 66

Elaine . . . . **TCLC 18**
See also Leverson, Ada

El Crummo
See Crumb, R(obert)

Elia
See Lamb, Charles

Eliade, Mircea 1907-1986 . . . . **CLC 19**
See also CA 65-68; 119; CANR 30; MTCW

Eliot, A. D.
See Jewett, (Theodora) Sarah Orne

Eliot, Alice
See Jewett, (Theodora) Sarah Orne

Eliot, Dan
See Silverberg, Robert

Eliot, George
1819-1880 . . . . . **NCLC 4, 13, 23, 41, 49; DA; WLC**
See also CDBLB 1832-1890; DLB 21, 35, 55

Eliot, John 1604-1690 . . . . **LC 5**
See also DLB 24

Eliot, T(homas) S(tearns)
1888-1965 . . . . . **CLC 1, 2, 3, 6, 9, 10, 13, 15, 24, 34, 41, 55, 57; DA; PC 5; WLC 2**
See also CA 5-8R; 25-28R; CANR 41; CDALB 1929-1941; DLB 7, 10, 45, 63; DLBY 88; MTCW

Elizabeth 1866-1941 . . . . **TCLC 41**

Elkin, Stanley L(awrence)
1930- . . . **CLC 4, 6, 9, 14, 27, 51; SSC 12**
See also CA 9-12R; CANR 8, 46; DLB 2, 28; DLBY 80; MTCW

Elledge, Scott . . . . **CLC 34**

Elliott, Don
See Silverberg, Robert

Elliott, George P(aul) 1918-1980 . . . . . **CLC 2**
See also CA 1-4R; 97-100; CANR 2

Elliott, Janice 1931- . . . . **CLC 47**
See also CA 13-16R; CANR 8, 29; DLB 14

Elliott, Sumner Locke 1917-1991 . . . **CLC 38**
See also CA 5-8R; 134; CANR 2, 21

Elliott, William
See Bradbury, Ray (Douglas)

Ellis, A. E. . . . . **CLC 7**

Ellis, Alice Thomas . . . . **CLC 40**
See also Haycraft, Anna

Ellis, Bret Easton 1964- . . . . **CLC 39, 71**
See also AAYA 2; CA 118; 123

Ellis, (Henry) Havelock
1859-1939 . . . . **TCLC 14**
See also CA 109

Ellis, Landon
See Ellison, Harlan (Jay)

Ellis, Trey 1962- . . . . **CLC 55**

Ellison, Harlan (Jay)
1934- . . . . **CLC 1, 13, 42; SSC 14**
See also CA 5-8R; CANR 5, 46; DLB 8; MTCW

Ellison, Ralph (Waldo)
1914-1994 . . . . **CLC 1, 3, 11, 54, 86; BLC; DA; WLC**
See also BW 1; CA 9-12R; 145; CANR 24; CDALB 1941-1968; DLB 2, 76; MTCW

Ellmann, Lucy (Elizabeth) 1956- . . . . **CLC 61**
See also CA 128

Ellmann, Richard (David)
1918-1987 . . . . **CLC 50**
See also BEST 89:2; CA 1-4R; 122; CANR 2, 28; DLB 103; DLBY 87; MTCW

Elman, Richard 1934- . . . . **CLC 19**
See also CA 17-20R; CAAS 3; CANR 47

Elron
See Hubbard, L(afayette) Ron(ald)

Eluard, Paul . . . . **TCLC 7, 41**
See also Grindel, Eugene

Elyot, Sir Thomas 1490(?)-1546 . . . . . **LC 11**

Elytis, Odysseus 1911- . . . . **CLC 15, 49**
See also CA 102; MTCW

Emecheta, (Florence Onye) Buchi 1944- . . . . **CLC 14, 48; BLC**
See also BW 2; CA 81-84; CANR 27; DLB 117; MTCW; SATA 66

Emerson, Ralph Waldo 1803-1882 . . . . . . **NCLC 1, 38; DA; WLC**
See also CDALB 1640-1865; DLB 1, 59, 73

Eminescu, Mihail 1850-1889 . . . . . **NCLC 33**

Empson, William 1906-1984 . . . . **CLC 3, 8, 19, 33, 34**
See also CA 17-20R; 112; CANR 31; DLB 20; MTCW

Enchi Fumiko (Ueda) 1905-1986. . . . **CLC 31**
See also CA 129; 121

Ende, Michael (Andreas Helmuth) 1929- . . . . **CLC 31**
See also CA 118; 124; CANR 36; CLR 14; DLB 75; MAICYA; SATA 61; SATA-Brief 42

Endo, Shusaku 1923- . . . . . **CLC 7, 14, 19, 54**
See also CA 29-32R; CANR 21; MTCW

Engel, Marian 1933-1985. . . . . **CLC 36**
See also CA 25-28R; CANR 12; DLB 53

Engelhardt, Frederick
See Hubbard, L(afayette) Ron(ald)

Enright, D(ennis) J(oseph) 1920- . . . . **CLC 4, 8, 31**
See also CA 1-4R; CANR 1, 42; DLB 27; SATA 25

Enzensberger, Hans Magnus 1929- . . . . **CLC 43**
See also CA 116; 119

Ephron, Nora 1941- . . . . **CLC 17, 31**
See also AITN 2; CA 65-68; CANR 12, 39

Epsilon
See Betjeman, John

Epstein, Daniel Mark 1948- . . . . **CLC 7**
See also CA 49-52; CANR 2

Epstein, Jacob 1956- . . . . **CLC 19**
See also CA 114

Epstein, Joseph 1937-. . . . . **CLC 39**
See also CA 112; 119

Epstein, Leslie 1938- . . . . **CLC 27**
See also CA 73-76; CAAS 12; CANR 23

Equiano, Olaudah 1745(?)-1797 . . . . **LC 16; BLC**
See also DLB 37, 50

Erasmus, Desiderius 1469(?)-1536. . . . **LC 16**

Erdman, Paul E(mil) 1932- . . . . **CLC 25**
See also AITN 1; CA 61-64; CANR 13, 43

Erdrich, Louise 1954-. . . . . **CLC 39, 54**
See also AAYA 10; BEST 89:1; CA 114; CANR 41; MTCW; NNAL

Erenburg, Ilya (Grigoryevich)
See Ehrenburg, Ilya (Grigoryevich)

Erickson, Stephen Michael 1950-
See Erickson, Steve
See also CA 129

Erickson, Steve . . . . **CLC 64**
See also Erickson, Stephen Michael

Ericson, Walter
See Fast, Howard (Melvin)

Eriksson, Buntel
See Bergman, (Ernst) Ingmar

Eschenbach, Wolfram von
See Wolfram von Eschenbach

Eseki, Bruno
See Mphahlele, Ezekiel

Esenin, Sergei (Alexandrovich) 1895-1925 . . . . **TCLC 4**
See also CA 104

Eshleman, Clayton 1935- . . . . **CLC 7**
See also CA 33-36R; CAAS 6; DLB 5

Espriella, Don Manuel Alvarez
See Southey, Robert

Espriu, Salvador 1913-1985. . . . . **CLC 9**
See also CA 115; DLB 134

Espronceda, Jose de 1808-1842. . . **NCLC 39**

Esse, James
See Stephens, James

Esterbrook, Tom
See Hubbard, L(afayette) Ron(ald)

Estleman, Loren D. 1952- . . . . **CLC 48**
See also CA 85-88; CANR 27; MTCW

Eugenides, Jeffrey 1960(?)- . . . . **CLC 81**
See also CA 144

Euripides c. 485B.C.-406B.C. . . . . **DC 4**
See also DA

Evan, Evin
See Faust, Frederick (Schiller)

Evans, Evan
See Faust, Frederick (Schiller)

Evans, Marian
See Eliot, George

Evans, Mary Ann
See Eliot, George

Evarts, Esther
See Benson, Sally

Everett, Percival L. 1956- . . . . **CLC 57**
See also BW 2; CA 129

Everson, R(onald) G(ilmour) 1903- . . . . **CLC 27**
See also CA 17-20R; DLB 88

Everson, William (Oliver) 1912-1994 . . . . **CLC 1, 5, 14**
See also CA 9-12R; 145; CANR 20; DLB 5, 16; MTCW

Evtushenko, Evgenii Aleksandrovich
See Yevtushenko, Yevgeny (Alexandrovich)

Ewart, Gavin (Buchanan) 1916- . . . . **CLC 13, 46**
See also CA 89-92; CANR 17, 46; DLB 40; MTCW

Ewers, Hanns Heinz 1871-1943 . . . **TCLC 12**
See also CA 109

Ewing, Frederick R.
See Sturgeon, Theodore (Hamilton)

Exley, Frederick (Earl) 1929-1992 . . . . **CLC 6, 11**
See also AITN 2; CA 81-84; 138; DLB 143; DLBY 81

Eynhardt, Guillermo
See Quiroga, Horacio (Sylvestre)

Ezekiel, Nissim 1924-. . . . . **CLC 61**
See also CA 61-64

Ezekiel, Tish O'Dowd 1943- . . . . **CLC 34**
See also CA 129

Fadeyev, A.
See Bulgya, Alexander Alexandrovich

Fadeyev, Alexander. . . . . **TCLC 53**
See also Bulgya, Alexander Alexandrovich

Fagen, Donald 1948-. . . . . **CLC 26**

Fainzilberg, Ilya Arnoldovich 1897-1937
See Ilf, Ilya
See also CA 120

Fair, Ronald L. 1932-. . . . . **CLC 18**
See also BW 1; CA 69-72; CANR 25; DLB 33

Fairbairns, Zoe (Ann) 1948- . . . . **CLC 32**
See also CA 103; CANR 21

Falco, Gian
See Papini, Giovanni

Falconer, James
See Kirkup, James

Falconer, Kenneth
See Kornbluth, C(yril) M.

Falkland, Samuel
See Heijermans, Herman

Fallaci, Oriana 1930- . . . . **CLC 11**
See also CA 77-80; CANR 15; MTCW

Faludy, George 1913- . . . . **CLC 42**
See also CA 21-24R

Faludy, Gyoergy
See Faludy, George

Fanon, Frantz 1925-1961 . . . . . **CLC 74; BLC**
See also BW 1; CA 116; 89-92

Fanshawe, Ann 1625-1680 . . . . **LC 11**

Fante, John (Thomas) 1911-1983 . . . **CLC 60**
See also CA 69-72; 109; CANR 23; DLB 130; DLBY 83

Farah, Nuruddin 1945-. . . . . . . **CLC 53; BLC**
See also BW 2; CA 106; DLB 125

Fargue, Leon-Paul 1876(?)-1947 . . . **TCLC 11**
See also CA 109

Farigoule, Louis
See Romains, Jules

Farina, Richard 1936(?)-1966 . . . . **CLC 9**
See also CA 81-84; 25-28R

Farley, Walter (Lorimer) 1915-1989 . . . . **CLC 17**
See also CA 17-20R; CANR 8, 29; DLB 22; JRDA; MAICYA; SATA 2, 43

Farmer, Philip Jose 1918- . . . . **CLC 1, 19**
See also CA 1-4R; CANR 4, 35; DLB 8; MTCW

Farquhar, George 1677-1707 . . . . **LC 21**
See also DLB 84

Farrell, J(ames) G(ordon) 1935-1979 . . . . **CLC 6**
See also CA 73-76; 89-92; CANR 36; DLB 14; MTCW

Farrell, James T(homas) 1904-1979 . . . . **CLC 1, 4, 8, 11, 66**
See also CA 5-8R; 89-92; CANR 9; DLB 4, 9, 86; DLBD 2; MTCW

Farren, Richard J.
See Betjeman, John

Folke, Will
See Bloch, Robert (Albert)

Follett, Ken(neth Martin) 1949- .... **CLC 18**
See also AAYA 6; BEST 89:4; CA 81-84; CANR 13, 33; DLB 87; DLBY 81; MTCW

Fontane, Theodor 1819-1898 ..... **NCLC 26**
See also DLB 129

Foote, Horton 1916- .... **CLC 51**
See also CA 73-76; CANR 34; DLB 26

Foote, Shelby 1916- .... **CLC 75**
See also CA 5-8R; CANR 3, 45; DLB 2, 17

Forbes, Esther 1891-1967.......... **CLC 12**
See also CA 13-14; 25-28R; CAP 1; CLR 27; DLB 22; JRDA; MAICYA; SATA 2

Forche, Carolyn (Louise)
1950- .... **CLC 25, 83, 86; PC 10**
See also CA 109; 117; DLB 5

Ford, Elbur
See Hibbert, Eleanor Alice Burford

Ford, Ford Madox
1873-1939 .... **TCLC 1, 15, 39, 57**
See also CA 104; 132; CDBLB 1914-1945; DLB 34, 98; MTCW

Ford, John 1895-1973............. **CLC 16**
See also CA 45-48

Ford, Richard 1944- .... **CLC 46**
See also CA 69-72; CANR 11, 47

Ford, Webster
See Masters, Edgar Lee

Foreman, Richard 1937-........... **CLC 50**
See also CA 65-68; CANR 32

Forester, C(ecil) S(cott)
1899-1966 .... **CLC 35**
See also CA 73-76; 25-28R; SATA 13

Forez
See Mauriac, Francois (Charles)

Forman, James Douglas 1932-...... **CLC 21**
See also CA 9-12R; CANR 4, 19, 42; JRDA; MAICYA; SATA 8, 70

Fornes, Maria Irene 1930-...... **CLC 39, 61**
See also CA 25-28R; CANR 28; DLB 7; HW; MTCW

Forrest, Leon 1937- .... **CLC 4**
See also BW 2; CA 89-92; CAAS 7; CANR 25; DLB 33

Forster, E(dward) M(organ)
1879-1970 ..... **CLC 1, 2, 3, 4, 9, 10, 13, 15, 22, 45, 77; DA; WLC**
See also AAYA 2; CA 13-14; 25-28R; CANR 45; CAP 1; CDBLB 1914-1945; DLB 34, 98; DLBD 10; MTCW; SATA 57

Forster, John 1812-1876 .... **NCLC 11**
See also DLB 144

Forsyth, Frederick 1938-...... **CLC 2, 5, 36**
See also BEST 89:4; CA 85-88; CANR 38; DLB 87; MTCW

Forten, Charlotte L. .... **TCLC 16; BLC**
See also Grimke, Charlotte L(ottie) Forten
See also DLB 50

Foscolo, Ugo 1778-1827.......... **NCLC 8**

Fosse, Bob .... **CLC 20**
See also Fosse, Robert Louis

Fosse, Robert Louis 1927-1987
See Fosse, Bob
See also CA 110; 123

Foster, Stephen Collins
1826-1864 .... **NCLC 26**

Foucault, Michel
1926-1984 .... **CLC 31, 34, 69**
See also CA 105; 113; CANR 34; MTCW

Fouque, Friedrich (Heinrich Karl) de la Motte
1777-1843 .... **NCLC 2**
See also DLB 90

Fournier, Henri Alban 1886-1914
See Alain-Fournier
See also CA 104

Fournier, Pierre 1916- .... **CLC 11**
See also Gascar, Pierre
See also CA 89-92; CANR 16, 40

Fowles, John
1926- ...... **CLC 1, 2, 3, 4, 6, 9, 10, 15, 33, 87**
See also CA 5-8R; CANR 25; CDBLB 1960 to Present; DLB 14, 139; MTCW; SATA 22

Fox, Paula 1923-................ **CLC 2, 8**
See also AAYA 3; CA 73-76; CANR 20, 36; CLR 1; DLB 52; JRDA; MAICYA; MTCW; SATA 17, 60

Fox, William Price (Jr.) 1926- ..... **CLC 22**
See also CA 17-20R; CAAS 19; CANR 11; DLB 2; DLBY 81

Foxe, John 1516(?)-1587 .... **LC 14**

Frame, Janet .... **CLC 2, 3, 6, 22, 66**
See also Clutha, Janet Paterson Frame

France, Anatole.................. **TCLC 9**
See also Thibault, Jacques Anatole Francois
See also DLB 123

Francis, Claude 19(?)- .... **CLC 50**

Francis, Dick 1920- .... **CLC 2, 22, 42**
See also AAYA 5; BEST 89:3; CA 5-8R; CANR 9, 42; CDBLB 1960 to Present; DLB 87; MTCW

Francis, Robert (Churchill)
1901-1987 .... **CLC 15**
See also CA 1-4R; 123; CANR 1

Frank, Anne(lies Marie)
1929-1945 .... **TCLC 17; DA; WLC**
See also AAYA 12; CA 113; 133; MTCW; SATA-Brief 42

Frank, Elizabeth 1945-............ **CLC 39**
See also CA 121; 126

Franklin, Benjamin
See Hasek, Jaroslav (Matej Frantisek)

Franklin, Benjamin 1706-1790... **LC 25; DA**
See also CDALB 1640-1865; DLB 24, 43, 73

Franklin, (Stella Maraia Sarah) Miles
1879-1954 .... **TCLC 7**
See also CA 104

Fraser, (Lady) Antonia (Pakenham)
1932- .... **CLC 32**
See also CA 85-88; CANR 44; MTCW; SATA-Brief 32

Fraser, George MacDonald 1925-.... **CLC 7**
See also CA 45-48; CANR 2

Fraser, Sylvia 1935-.............. **CLC 64**
See also CA 45-48; CANR 1, 16

Frayn, Michael 1933-...... **CLC 3, 7, 31, 47**
See also CA 5-8R; CANR 30; DLB 13, 14; MTCW

Fraze, Candida (Merrill) 1945-..... **CLC 50**
See also CA 126

Frazer, J(ames) G(eorge)
1854-1941 .... **TCLC 32**
See also CA 118

Frazer, Robert Caine
See Creasey, John

Frazer, Sir James George
See Frazer, J(ames) G(eorge)

Frazier, Ian 1951-................ **CLC 46**
See also CA 130

Frederic, Harold 1856-1898...... **NCLC 10**
See also DLB 12, 23

Frederick, John
See Faust, Frederick (Schiller)

Frederick the Great 1712-1786 ...... **LC 14**

Fredro, Aleksander 1793-1876..... **NCLC 8**

Freeling, Nicolas 1927- .... **CLC 38**
See also CA 49-52; CAAS 12; CANR 1, 17; DLB 87

Freeman, Douglas Southall
1886-1953 .... **TCLC 11**
See also CA 109; DLB 17

Freeman, Judith 1946-............ **CLC 55**

Freeman, Mary Eleanor Wilkins
1852-1930 .... **TCLC 9; SSC 1**
See also CA 106; DLB 12, 78

Freeman, R(ichard) Austin
1862-1943 .... **TCLC 21**
See also CA 113; DLB 70

French, Albert 1943- .... **CLC 86**

French, Marilyn 1929-...... **CLC 10, 18, 60**
See also CA 69-72; CANR 3, 31; MTCW

French, Paul
See Asimov, Isaac

Freneau, Philip Morin 1752-1832.. **NCLC 1**
See also DLB 37, 43

Freud, Sigmund 1856-1939 .... **TCLC 52**
See also CA 115; 133; MTCW

Friedan, Betty (Naomi) 1921-...... **CLC 74**
See also CA 65-68; CANR 18, 45; MTCW

Friedman, B(ernard) H(arper)
1926- .... **CLC 7**
See also CA 1-4R; CANR 3

Friedman, Bruce Jay 1930-.... **CLC 3, 5, 56**
See also CA 9-12R; CANR 25; DLB 2, 28

Friel, Brian 1929-........... **CLC 5, 42, 59**
See also CA 21-24R; CANR 33; DLB 13; MTCW

Friis-Baastad, Babbis Ellinor
1921-1970 .... **CLC 12**
See also CA 17-20R; 134; SATA 7

Frisch, Max (Rudolf)
1911-1991 ..... **CLC 3, 9, 14, 18, 32, 44**
See also CA 85-88; 134; CANR 32; DLB 69, 124; MTCW

Fromentin, Eugene (Samuel Auguste) 1820-1876 . . . . **NCLC 10**
See also DLB 123

Frost, Frederick
See Faust, Frederick (Schiller)

Frost, Robert (Lee) 1874-1963 . . . . **CLC 1, 3, 4, 9, 10, 13, 15, 26, 34, 44; DA; PC 1; WLC**
See also CA 89-92; CANR 33; CDALB 1917-1929; DLB 54; DLBD 7; MTCW; SATA 14

Froude, James Anthony 1818-1894 . . . . **NCLC 43**
See also DLB 18, 57, 144

Froy, Herald
See Waterhouse, Keith (Spencer)

Fry, Christopher 1907- . . . . **CLC 2, 10, 14**
See also CA 17-20R; CANR 9, 30; DLB 13; MTCW; SATA 66

Frye, (Herman) Northrop 1912-1991 . . . . **CLC 24, 70**
See also CA 5-8R; 133; CANR 8, 37; DLB 67, 68; MTCW

Fuchs, Daniel 1909-1993 . . . . **CLC 8, 22**
See also CA 81-84; 142; CAAS 5; CANR 40; DLB 9, 26, 28; DLBY 93

Fuchs, Daniel 1934- . . . . **CLC 34**
See also CA 37-40R; CANR 14

Fuentes, Carlos 1928- . . . . . . **CLC 3, 8, 10, 13, 22, 41, 60; DA; HLC; WLC**
See also AAYA 4; AITN 2; CA 69-72; CANR 10, 32; DLB 113; HW; MTCW

Fuentes, Gregorio Lopez y
See Lopez y Fuentes, Gregorio

Fugard, (Harold) Athol 1932- . . . . **CLC 5, 9, 14, 25, 40, 80; DC 3**
See also CA 85-88; CANR 32; MTCW

Fugard, Sheila 1932- . . . . **CLC 48**
See also CA 125

Fuller, Charles (H., Jr.) 1939- . . . . **CLC 25; BLC; DC 1**
See also BW 2; CA 108; 112; DLB 38; MTCW

Fuller, John (Leopold) 1937- . . . . **CLC 62**
See also CA 21-24R; CANR 9, 44; DLB 40

Fuller, Margaret . . . . **NCLC 5**
See also Ossoli, Sarah Margaret (Fuller marchesa d')

Fuller, Roy (Broadbent) 1912-1991 . . . . **CLC 4, 28**
See also CA 5-8R; 135; CAAS 10; DLB 15, 20

Fulton, Alice 1952- . . . . **CLC 52**
See also CA 116

Furphy, Joseph 1843-1912 . . . . **TCLC 25**

Fussell, Paul 1924- . . . . **CLC 74**
See also BEST 90:1; CA 17-20R; CANR 8, 21, 35; MTCW

Futabatei, Shimei 1864-1909 . . . . . . **TCLC 44**

Futrelle, Jacques 1875-1912 . . . . . . **TCLC 19**
See also CA 113

Gaboriau, Emile 1835-1873 . . . . . . **NCLC 14**

Gadda, Carlo Emilio 1893-1973 . . . . **CLC 11**
See also CA 89-92

Gaddis, William 1922- . . . . . **CLC 1, 3, 6, 8, 10, 19, 43, 86**
See also CA 17-20R; CANR 21; DLB 2; MTCW

Gaines, Ernest J(ames) 1933- . . . . **CLC 3, 11, 18, 86; BLC**
See also AITN 1; BW 2; CA 9-12R; CANR 6, 24, 42; CDALB 1968-1988; DLB 2, 33; DLBY 80; MTCW

Gaitskill, Mary 1954- . . . . **CLC 69**
See also CA 128

Galdos, Benito Perez
See Perez Galdos, Benito

Gale, Zona 1874-1938 . . . . **TCLC 7**
See also CA 105; DLB 9, 78

Galeano, Eduardo (Hughes) 1940- . . . **CLC 72**
See also CA 29-32R; CANR 13, 32; HW

Galiano, Juan Valera y Alcala
See Valera y Alcala-Galiano, Juan

Gallagher, Tess 1943- . . . . **CLC 18, 63; PC 9**
See also CA 106; DLB 120

Gallant, Mavis 1922- . . . . **CLC 7, 18, 38; SSC 5**
See also CA 69-72; CANR 29; DLB 53; MTCW

Gallant, Roy A(rthur) 1924- . . . . **CLC 17**
See also CA 5-8R; CANR 4, 29; CLR 30; MAICYA; SATA 4, 68

Gallico, Paul (William) 1897-1976 . . . **CLC 2**
See also AITN 1; CA 5-8R; 69-72; CANR 23; DLB 9; MAICYA; SATA 13

Gallup, Ralph
See Whitemore, Hugh (John)

Galsworthy, John 1867-1933 . . . . **TCLC 1, 45; DA; WLC 2**
See also CA 104; 141; CDBLB 1890-1914; DLB 10, 34, 98

Galt, John 1779-1839 . . . . **NCLC 1**
See also DLB 99, 116

Galvin, James 1951- . . . . **CLC 38**
See also CA 108; CANR 26

Gamboa, Federico 1864-1939 . . . . . . **TCLC 36**

Gandhi, M. K.
See Gandhi, Mohandas Karamchand

Gandhi, Mahatma
See Gandhi, Mohandas Karamchand

Gandhi, Mohandas Karamchand 1869-1948 . . . . **TCLC 59**
See also CA 121; 132; MTCW

Gann, Ernest Kellogg 1910-1991 . . . . **CLC 23**
See also AITN 1; CA 1-4R; 136; CANR 1

Garcia, Cristina 1958- . . . . **CLC 76**
See also CA 141

Garcia Lorca, Federico 1898-1936 . . . . **TCLC 1, 7, 49; DA; DC 2; HLC; PC 3; WLC**
See also CA 104; 131; DLB 108; HW; MTCW

Garcia Marquez, Gabriel (Jose) 1928- . . . . **CLC 2, 3, 8, 10, 15, 27, 47, 55, 68; DA; HLC; SSC 8; WLC**
See also AAYA 3; BEST 89:1, 90:4; CA 33-36R; CANR 10, 28; DLB 113; HW; MTCW

Gard, Janice
See Latham, Jean Lee

Gard, Roger Martin du
See Martin du Gard, Roger

Gardam, Jane 1928- . . . . **CLC 43**
See also CA 49-52; CANR 2, 18, 33; CLR 12; DLB 14; MAICYA; MTCW; SAAS 9; SATA 39, 76; SATA-Brief 28

Gardner, Herb . . . . **CLC 44**

Gardner, John (Champlin), Jr. 1933-1982 . . . . . **CLC 2, 3, 5, 7, 8, 10, 18, 28, 34; SSC 7**
See also AITN 1; CA 65-68; 107; CANR 33; DLB 2; DLBY 82; MTCW; SATA 40; SATA-Obit 31

Gardner, John (Edmund) 1926- . . . . . **CLC 30**
See also CA 103; CANR 15; MTCW

Gardner, Noel
See Kuttner, Henry

Gardons, S. S.
See Snodgrass, W(illiam) D(e Witt)

Garfield, Leon 1921- . . . . **CLC 12**
See also AAYA 8; CA 17-20R; CANR 38, 41; CLR 21; JRDA; MAICYA; SATA 1, 32, 76

Garland, (Hannibal) Hamlin 1860-1940 . . . . **TCLC 3; SSC 18**
See also CA 104; DLB 12, 71, 78

Garneau, (Hector de) Saint-Denys 1912-1943 . . . . **TCLC 13**
See also CA 111; DLB 88

Garner, Alan 1934- . . . . **CLC 17**
See also CA 73-76; CANR 15; CLR 20; MAICYA; MTCW; SATA 18, 69

Garner, Hugh 1913-1979 . . . . **CLC 13**
See also CA 69-72; CANR 31; DLB 68

Garnett, David 1892-1981 . . . . **CLC 3**
See also CA 5-8R; 103; CANR 17; DLB 34

Garos, Stephanie
See Katz, Steve

Garrett, George (Palmer) 1929- . . . . **CLC 3, 11, 51**
See also CA 1-4R; CAAS 5; CANR 1, 42; DLB 2, 5, 130; DLBY 83

Garrick, David 1717-1779 . . . . **LC 15**
See also DLB 84

Garrigue, Jean 1914-1972 . . . . **CLC 2, 8**
See also CA 5-8R; 37-40R; CANR 20

Garrison, Frederick
See Sinclair, Upton (Beall)

Garth, Will
See Hamilton, Edmond; Kuttner, Henry

Garvey, Marcus (Moziah, Jr.) 1887-1940 . . . . **TCLC 41; BLC**
See also BW 1; CA 120; 124

Gary, Romain . . . . **CLC 25**
See also Kacew, Romain
See also DLB 83

Gascar, Pierre . . . . **CLC 11**
See also Fournier, Pierre

Gascoyne, David (Emery) 1916- . . . . **CLC 45**
See also CA 65-68; CANR 10, 28; DLB 20; MTCW

Gaskell, Elizabeth Cleghorn 1810-1865 .... **NCLC 5**
See also CDBLB 1832-1890; DLB 21, 144

Gass, William H(oward) 1924- ... **CLC 1, 2, 8, 11, 15, 39; SSC 12**
See also CA 17-20R; CANR 30; DLB 2; MTCW

Gasset, Jose Ortega y
See Ortega y Gasset, Jose

Gates, Henry Louis, Jr. 1950-...... **CLC 65**
See also BW 2; CA 109; CANR 25; DLB 67

Gautier, Theophile 1811-1872 ..... **NCLC 1**
See also DLB 119

Gawsworth, John
See Bates, H(erbert) E(rnest)

Gaye, Marvin (Penze) 1939-1984 ... **CLC 26**
See also CA 112

Gebler, Carlo (Ernest) 1954-....... **CLC 39**
See also CA 119; 133

Gee, Maggie (Mary) 1948-......... **CLC 57**
See also CA 130

Gee, Maurice (Gough) 1931-....... **CLC 29**
See also CA 97-100; SATA 46

Gelbart, Larry (Simon) 1923- ... **CLC 21, 61**
See also CA 73-76; CANR 45

Gelber, Jack 1932-........ **CLC 1, 6, 14, 79**
See also CA 1-4R; CANR 2; DLB 7

Gellhorn, Martha (Ellis) 1908- .. **CLC 14, 60**
See also CA 77-80; CANR 44; DLBY 82

Genet, Jean 1910-1986 ... **CLC 1, 2, 5, 10, 14, 44, 46**
See also CA 13-16R; CANR 18; DLB 72; DLBY 86; MTCW

Gent, Peter 1942-................ **CLC 29**
See also AITN 1; CA 89-92; DLBY 82

Gentlewoman in New England, A
See Bradstreet, Anne

Gentlewoman in Those Parts, A
See Bradstreet, Anne

George, Jean Craighead 1919-...... **CLC 35**
See also AAYA 8; CA 5-8R; CANR 25; CLR 1; DLB 52; JRDA; MAICYA; SATA 2, 68

George, Stefan (Anton) 1868-1933 .... **TCLC 2, 14**
See also CA 104

Georges, Georges Martin
See Simenon, Georges (Jacques Christian)

Gerhardi, William Alexander
See Gerhardie, William Alexander

Gerhardie, William Alexander 1895-1977 .... **CLC 5**
See also CA 25-28R; 73-76; CANR 18; DLB 36

Gerstler, Amy 1956-.............. **CLC 70**

Gertler, T......................... **CLC 34**
See also CA 116; 121

Ghalib 1797-1869 .... **NCLC 39**

Ghelderode, Michel de 1898-1962 .... **CLC 6, 11**
See also CA 85-88; CANR 40

Ghiselin, Brewster 1903-.......... **CLC 23**
See also CA 13-16R; CAAS 10; CANR 13

Ghose, Zulfikar 1935-............. **CLC 42**
See also CA 65-68

Ghosh, Amitav 1956- .... **CLC 44**

Giacosa, Giuseppe 1847-1906 ...... **TCLC 7**
See also CA 104

Gibb, Lee
See Waterhouse, Keith (Spencer)

Gibbon, Lewis Grassic .... **TCLC 4**
See also Mitchell, James Leslie

Gibbons, Kaye 1960- .... **CLC 50**

Gibran, Kahlil 1883-1931 .... **TCLC 1, 9; PC 9**
See also CA 104

Gibson, William 1914-........ **CLC 23; DA**
See also CA 9-12R; CANR 9, 42; DLB 7; SATA 66

Gibson, William (Ford) 1948- ... **CLC 39, 63**
See also AAYA 12; CA 126; 133

Gide, Andre (Paul Guillaume) 1869-1951 .... **TCLC 5, 12, 36; DA; SSC 13; WLC**
See also CA 104; 124; DLB 65; MTCW

Gifford, Barry (Colby) 1946-....... **CLC 34**
See also CA 65-68; CANR 9, 30, 40

Gilbert, W(illiam) S(chwenck) 1836-1911 .... **TCLC 3**
See also CA 104; SATA 36

Gilbreth, Frank B., Jr. 1911-....... **CLC 17**
See also CA 9-12R; SATA 2

Gilchrist, Ellen 1935-.. **CLC 34, 48; SSC 14**
See also CA 113; 116; CANR 41; DLB 130; MTCW

Giles, Molly 1942- .... **CLC 39**
See also CA 126

Gill, Patrick
See Creasey, John

Gilliam, Terry (Vance) 1940-....... **CLC 21**
See also Monty Python
See also CA 108; 113; CANR 35

Gillian, Jerry
See Gilliam, Terry (Vance)

Gilliatt, Penelope (Ann Douglass) 1932-1993 .... **CLC 2, 10, 13, 53**
See also AITN 2; CA 13-16R; 141; DLB 14

Gilman, Charlotte (Anna) Perkins (Stetson) 1860-1935 .... **TCLC 9, 37; SSC 13**
See also CA 106

Gilmour, David 1949-............. **CLC 35**
See also CA 138

Gilpin, William 1724-1804....... **NCLC 30**

Gilray, J. D.
See Mencken, H(enry) L(ouis)

Gilroy, Frank D(aniel) 1925-........ **CLC 2**
See also CA 81-84; CANR 32; DLB 7

Ginsberg, Allen 1926- ...... **CLC 1, 2, 3, 4, 6, 13, 36, 69; DA; PC 4; WLC 3**
See also AITN 1; CA 1-4R; CANR 2, 41; CDALB 1941-1968; DLB 5, 16; MTCW

Ginzburg, Natalia 1916-1991 .... **CLC 5, 11, 54, 70**
See also CA 85-88; 135; CANR 33; MTCW

Giono, Jean 1895-1970.......... **CLC 4, 11**
See also CA 45-48; 29-32R; CANR 2, 35; DLB 72; MTCW

Giovanni, Nikki 1943- ...... **CLC 2, 4, 19, 64; BLC; DA**
See also AITN 1; BW 2; CA 29-32R; CAAS 6; CANR 18, 41; CLR 6; DLB 5, 41; MAICYA; MTCW; SATA 24

Giovene, Andrea 1904-............. **CLC 7**
See also CA 85-88

Gippius, Zinaida (Nikolayevna) 1869-1945
See Hippius, Zinaida
See also CA 106

Giraudoux, (Hippolyte) Jean 1882-1944 .... **TCLC 2, 7**
See also CA 104; DLB 65

Gironella, Jose Maria 1917- .... **CLC 11**
See also CA 101

Gissing, George (Robert) 1857-1903 .... **TCLC 3, 24, 47**
See also CA 105; DLB 18, 135

Giurlani, Aldo
See Palazzeschi, Aldo

Gladkov, Fyodor (Vasilyevich) 1883-1958 .... **TCLC 27**

Glanville, Brian (Lester) 1931- ...... **CLC 6**
See also CA 5-8R; CAAS 9; CANR 3; DLB 15, 139; SATA 42

Glasgow, Ellen (Anderson Gholson) 1873(?)-1945 .... **TCLC 2, 7**
See also CA 104; DLB 9, 12

Glaspell, Susan (Keating) 1882(?)-1948 .... **TCLC 55**
See also CA 110; DLB 7, 9, 78; YABC 2

Glassco, John 1909-1981 .... **CLC 9**
See also CA 13-16R; 102; CANR 15; DLB 68

Glasscock, Amnesia
See Steinbeck, John (Ernst)

Glasser, Ronald J. 1940(?)- .... **CLC 37**

Glassman, Joyce
See Johnson, Joyce

Glendinning, Victoria 1937-........ **CLC 50**
See also CA 120; 127

Glissant, Edouard 1928-........ **CLC 10, 68**

Gloag, Julian 1930- .... **CLC 40**
See also AITN 1; CA 65-68; CANR 10

Glowacki, Aleksander
See Prus, Boleslaw

Glueck, Louise (Elisabeth) 1943- .... **CLC 7, 22, 44, 81**
See also CA 33-36R; CANR 40; DLB 5

Gobineau, Joseph Arthur (Comte) de 1816-1882 .... **NCLC 17**
See also DLB 123

Godard, Jean-Luc 1930-........... **CLC 20**
See also CA 93-96

Godden, (Margaret) Rumer 1907-... **CLC 53**
See also AAYA 6; CA 5-8R; CANR 4, 27, 36; CLR 20; MAICYA; SAAS 12; SATA 3, 36

Godoy Alcayaga, Lucila 1889-1957
See Mistral, Gabriela
See also BW 2; CA 104; 131; HW; MTCW

Godwin, Gail (Kathleen)
1937- . . . . **CLC 5, 8, 22, 31, 69**
See also CA 29-32R; CANR 15, 43; DLB 6; MTCW

Godwin, William 1756-1836. . . . . . **NCLC 14**
See also CDBLB 1789-1832; DLB 39, 104, 142

Goethe, Johann Wolfgang von
1749-1832 . . . . **NCLC 4, 22, 34; DA; PC 5; WLC 3**
See also DLB 94

Gogarty, Oliver St. John
1878-1957 . . . . **TCLC 15**
See also CA 109; DLB 15, 19

Gogol, Nikolai (Vasilyevich)
1809-1852 . . . . **NCLC 5, 15, 31; DA; DC 1; SSC 4; WLC**

Goines, Donald
1937(?)-1974 . . . . **CLC 80; BLC**
See also AITN 1; BW 1; CA 124; 114; DLB 33

Gold, Herbert 1924- . . . . **CLC 4, 7, 14, 42**
See also CA 9-12R; CANR 17, 45; DLB 2; DLBY 81

Goldbarth, Albert 1948- . . . . **CLC 5, 38**
See also CA 53-56; CANR 6, 40; DLB 120

Goldberg, Anatol 1910-1982 . . . . **CLC 34**
See also CA 131; 117

Goldemberg, Isaac 1945- . . . . **CLC 52**
See also CA 69-72; CAAS 12; CANR 11, 32; HW

Golding, William (Gerald)
1911-1993 . . . . **CLC 1, 2, 3, 8, 10, 17, 27, 58, 81; DA; WLC**
See also AAYA 5; CA 5-8R; 141; CANR 13, 33; CDBLB 1945-1960; DLB 15, 100; MTCW

Goldman, Emma 1869-1940. . . . . . . **TCLC 13**
See also CA 110

Goldman, Francisco 1955- . . . . **CLC 76**

Goldman, William (W.) 1931- . . . . **CLC 1, 48**
See also CA 9-12R; CANR 29; DLB 44

Goldmann, Lucien 1913-1970 . . . . . . **CLC 24**
See also CA 25-28; CAP 2

Goldoni, Carlo 1707-1793 . . . . **LC 4**

Goldsberry, Steven 1949- . . . . **CLC 34**
See also CA 131

Goldsmith, Oliver
1728-1774 . . . . **LC 2; DA; WLC**
See also CDBLB 1660-1789; DLB 39, 89, 104, 109, 142; SATA 26

Goldsmith, Peter
See Priestley, J(ohn) B(oynton)

Gombrowicz, Witold
1904-1969 . . . . **CLC 4, 7, 11, 49**
See also CA 19-20; 25-28R; CAP 2

Gomez de la Serna, Ramon
1888-1963 . . . . **CLC 9**
See also CA 116; HW

Goncharov, Ivan Alexandrovich
1812-1891 . . . . **NCLC 1**

Goncourt, Edmond (Louis Antoine Huot) de
1822-1896 . . . . **NCLC 7**
See also DLB 123

Goncourt, Jules (Alfred Huot) de
1830-1870 . . . . **NCLC 7**
See also DLB 123

Gontier, Fernande 19(?)- . . . . **CLC 50**

Goodman, Paul 1911-1972. . . . **CLC 1, 2, 4, 7**
See also CA 19-20; 37-40R; CANR 34; CAP 2; DLB 130; MTCW

Gordimer, Nadine
1923- . . . . **CLC 3, 5, 7, 10, 18, 33, 51, 70; DA; SSC 17**
See also CA 5-8R; CANR 3, 28; MTCW

Gordon, Adam Lindsay
1833-1870 . . . . **NCLC 21**

Gordon, Caroline
1895-1981 . . . **CLC 6, 13, 29, 83; SSC 15**
See also CA 11-12; 103; CANR 36; CAP 1; DLB 4, 9, 102; DLBY 81; MTCW

Gordon, Charles William 1860-1937
See Connor, Ralph
See also CA 109

Gordon, Mary (Catherine)
1949- . . . . **CLC 13, 22**
See also CA 102; CANR 44; DLB 6; DLBY 81; MTCW

Gordon, Sol 1923- . . . . **CLC 26**
See also CA 53-56; CANR 4; SATA 11

Gordone, Charles 1925- . . . . **CLC 1, 4**
See also BW 1; CA 93-96; DLB 7; MTCW

Gorenko, Anna Andreevna
See Akhmatova, Anna

Gorky, Maxim . . . . **TCLC 8; WLC**
See also Peshkov, Alexei Maximovich

Goryan, Sirak
See Saroyan, William

Gosse, Edmund (William)
1849-1928 . . . . **TCLC 28**
See also CA 117; DLB 57, 144

Gotlieb, Phyllis Fay (Bloom)
1926- . . . . **CLC 18**
See also CA 13-16R; CANR 7; DLB 88

Gottesman, S. D.
See Kornbluth, C(yril) M.; Pohl, Frederik

Gottfried von Strassburg
fl. c. 1210- . . . . **CMLC 10**
See also DLB 138

Gould, Lois . . . . **CLC 4, 10**
See also CA 77-80; CANR 29; MTCW

Gourmont, Remy de 1858-1915. . . . **TCLC 17**
See also CA 109

Govier, Katherine 1948- . . . . **CLC 51**
See also CA 101; CANR 18, 40

Goyen, (Charles) William
1915-1983 . . . . **CLC 5, 8, 14, 40**
See also AITN 2; CA 5-8R; 110; CANR 6; DLB 2; DLBY 83

Goytisolo, Juan
1931- . . . . **CLC 5, 10, 23; HLC**
See also CA 85-88; CANR 32; HW; MTCW

Gozzano, Guido 1883-1916 . . . . **PC 10**
See also DLB 114

Gozzi, (Conte) Carlo 1720-1806 . . **NCLC 23**

Grabbe, Christian Dietrich
1801-1836 . . . . **NCLC 2**
See also DLB 133

Grace, Patricia 1937- . . . . **CLC 56**

Gracian y Morales, Baltasar
1601-1658 . . . . **LC 15**

Gracq, Julien . . . . **CLC 11, 48**
See also Poirier, Louis
See also DLB 83

Grade, Chaim 1910-1982 . . . . **CLC 10**
See also CA 93-96; 107

Graduate of Oxford, A
See Ruskin, John

Graham, John
See Phillips, David Graham

Graham, Jorie 1951- . . . . **CLC 48**
See also CA 111; DLB 120

Graham, R(obert) B(ontine) Cunninghame
See Cunninghame Graham, R(obert) B(ontine)
See also DLB 98, 135

Graham, Robert
See Haldeman, Joe (William)

Graham, Tom
See Lewis, (Harry) Sinclair

Graham, W(illiam) S(ydney)
1918-1986 . . . . **CLC 29**
See also CA 73-76; 118; DLB 20

Graham, Winston (Mawdsley)
1910- . . . . **CLC 23**
See also CA 49-52; CANR 2, 22, 45; DLB 77

Grant, Skeeter
See Spiegelman, Art

Granville-Barker, Harley
1877-1946 . . . . **TCLC 2**
See also Barker, Harley Granville
See also CA 104

Grass, Guenter (Wilhelm)
1927- . . . . . **CLC 1, 2, 4, 6, 11, 15, 22, 32, 49; DA; WLC**
See also CA 13-16R; CANR 20; DLB 75, 124; MTCW

Gratton, Thomas
See Hulme, T(homas) E(rnest)

Grau, Shirley Ann
1929- . . . . **CLC 4, 9; SSC 15**
See also CA 89-92; CANR 22; DLB 2; MTCW

Gravel, Fern
See Hall, James Norman

Graver, Elizabeth 1964- . . . . **CLC 70**
See also CA 135

Graves, Richard Perceval 1945- . . . . **CLC 44**
See also CA 65-68; CANR 9, 26

Graves, Robert (von Ranke)
1895-1985 . . . . . . **CLC 1, 2, 6, 11, 39, 44, 45; PC 6**
See also CA 5-8R; 117; CANR 5, 36; CDBLB 1914-1945; DLB 20, 100; DLBY 85; MTCW; SATA 45

Gray, Alasdair (James) 1934- . . . . . . **CLC 41**
See also CA 126; CANR 47; MTCW

Gray, Amlin 1946- . . . . **CLC 29**
See also CA 138

Gray, Francine du Plessix 1930-. . . . **CLC 22**
See also BEST 90:3; CA 61-64; CAAS 2; CANR 11, 33; MTCW

Gray, John (Henry) 1866-1934 .... **TCLC 19**
See also CA 119

Gray, Simon (James Holliday) 1936- .... **CLC 9, 14, 36**
See also AITN 1; CA 21-24R; CAAS 3; CANR 32; DLB 13; MTCW

Gray, Spalding 1941- .... **CLC 49**
See also CA 128

Gray, Thomas 1716-1771 ...... **LC 4; DA; PC 2; WLC**
See also CDBLB 1660-1789; DLB 109

Grayson, David
See Baker, Ray Stannard

Grayson, Richard (A.) 1951- .... **CLC 38**
See also CA 85-88; CANR 14, 31

Greeley, Andrew M(oran) 1928- .... **CLC 28**
See also CA 5-8R; CAAS 7; CANR 7, 43; MTCW

Green, Brian
See Card, Orson Scott

Green, Hannah
See Greenberg, Joanne (Goldenberg)

Green, Hannah .... **CLC 3**
See also CA 73-76

Green, Henry .... **CLC 2, 13**
See also Yorke, Henry Vincent
See also DLB 15

Green, Julian (Hartridge) 1900-
See Green, Julien
See also CA 21-24R; CANR 33; DLB 4, 72; MTCW

Green, Julien .... **CLC 3, 11, 77**
See also Green, Julian (Hartridge)

Green, Paul (Eliot) 1894-1981...... **CLC 25**
See also AITN 1; CA 5-8R; 103; CANR 3; DLB 7, 9; DLBY 81

Greenberg, Ivan 1908-1973
See Rahv, Philip
See also CA 85-88

Greenberg, Joanne (Goldenberg) 1932- .... **CLC 7, 30**
See also AAYA 12; CA 5-8R; CANR 14, 32; SATA 25

Greenberg, Richard 1959(?)- .... **CLC 57**
See also CA 138

Greene, Bette 1934- .... **CLC 30**
See also AAYA 7; CA 53-56; CANR 4; CLR 2; JRDA; MAICYA; SAAS 16; SATA 8

Greene, Gael .... **CLC 8**
See also CA 13-16R; CANR 10

Greene, Graham 1904-1991 .... **CLC 1, 3, 6, 9, 14, 18, 27, 37, 70, 72; DA; WLC**
See also AITN 2; CA 13-16R; 133; CANR 35; CDBLB 1945-1960; DLB 13, 15, 77, 100; DLBY 91; MTCW; SATA 20

Greer, Richard
See Silverberg, Robert

Greer, Richard
See Silverberg, Robert

Gregor, Arthur 1923- .... **CLC 9**
See also CA 25-28R; CAAS 10; CANR 11; SATA 36

Gregor, Lee
See Pohl, Frederik

Gregory, Isabella Augusta (Persse) 1852-1932 .... **TCLC 1**
See also CA 104; DLB 10

Gregory, J. Dennis
See Williams, John A(lfred)

Grendon, Stephen
See Derleth, August (William)

Grenville, Kate 1950- .... **CLC 61**
See also CA 118

Grenville, Pelham
See Wodehouse, P(elham) G(renville)

Greve, Felix Paul (Berthold Friedrich) 1879-1948
See Grove, Frederick Philip
See also CA 104; 141

Grey, Zane 1872-1939 .... **TCLC 6**
See also CA 104; 132; DLB 9; MTCW

Grieg, (Johan) Nordahl (Brun) 1902-1943 .... **TCLC 10**
See also CA 107

Grieve, C(hristopher) M(urray) 1892-1978 .... **CLC 11, 19**
See also MacDiarmid, Hugh
See also CA 5-8R; 85-88; CANR 33; MTCW

Griffin, Gerald 1803-1840 .... **NCLC 7**

Griffin, John Howard 1920-1980.... **CLC 68**
See also AITN 1; CA 1-4R; 101; CANR 2

Griffin, Peter 1942- .... **CLC 39**
See also CA 136

Griffiths, Trevor 1935- .... **CLC 13, 52**
See also CA 97-100; CANR 45; DLB 13

Grigson, Geoffrey (Edward Harvey) 1905-1985 .... **CLC 7, 39**
See also CA 25-28R; 118; CANR 20, 33; DLB 27; MTCW

Grillparzer, Franz 1791-1872...... **NCLC 1**
See also DLB 133

Grimble, Reverend Charles James
See Eliot, T(homas) S(tearns)

Grimke, Charlotte L(ottie) Forten 1837(?)-1914
See Forten, Charlotte L.
See also BW 1; CA 117; 124

Grimm, Jacob Ludwig Karl 1785-1863 .... **NCLC 3**
See also DLB 90; MAICYA; SATA 22

Grimm, Wilhelm Karl 1786-1859 .. **NCLC 3**
See also DLB 90; MAICYA; SATA 22

Grimmelshausen, Johann Jakob Christoffel von 1621-1676 .... **LC 6**

Grindel, Eugene 1895-1952
See Eluard, Paul
See also CA 104

Grisham, John 1955- .... **CLC 84**
See also AAYA 14; CA 138; CANR 47

Grossman, David 1954- .... **CLC 67**
See also CA 138

Grossman, Vasily (Semenovich) 1905-1964 .... **CLC 41**
See also CA 124; 130; MTCW

Grove, Frederick Philip .... **TCLC 4**
See also Greve, Felix Paul (Berthold Friedrich)
See also DLB 92

Grubb
See Crumb, R(obert)

Grumbach, Doris (Isaac) 1918- .... **CLC 13, 22, 64**
See also CA 5-8R; CAAS 2; CANR 9, 42

Grundtvig, Nicolai Frederik Severin 1783-1872 .... **NCLC 1**

Grunge
See Crumb, R(obert)

Grunwald, Lisa 1959- .... **CLC 44**
See also CA 120

Guare, John 1938- .... **CLC 8, 14, 29, 67**
See also CA 73-76; CANR 21; DLB 7; MTCW

Gudjonsson, Halldor Kiljan 1902-
See Laxness, Halldor
See also CA 103

Guenter, Erich
See Eich, Guenter

Guest, Barbara 1920- .... **CLC 34**
See also CA 25-28R; CANR 11, 44; DLB 5

Guest, Judith (Ann) 1936- .... **CLC 8, 30**
See also AAYA 7; CA 77-80; CANR 15; MTCW

Guevara, Che .... **CLC 87; HLC**
See also Guevara (Serna), Ernesto

Guevara (Serna), Ernesto 1928-1967
See Guevara, Che
See also CA 127; 111; HW

Guild, Nicholas M. 1944- .... **CLC 33**
See also CA 93-96

Guillemin, Jacques
See Sartre, Jean-Paul

Guillen, Jorge 1893-1984.......... **CLC 11**
See also CA 89-92; 112; DLB 108; HW

Guillen (y Batista), Nicolas (Cristobal) 1902-1989 ..... **CLC 48, 79; BLC; HLC**
See also BW 2; CA 116; 125; 129; HW

Guillevic, (Eugene) 1907- .... **CLC 33**
See also CA 93-96

Guillois
See Desnos, Robert

Guiney, Louise Imogen 1861-1920 .... **TCLC 41**
See also DLB 54

Guiraldes, Ricardo (Guillermo) 1886-1927 .... **TCLC 39**
See also CA 131; HW; MTCW

Gunn, Bill .... **CLC 5**
See also Gunn, William Harrison
See also DLB 38

Gunn, Thom(son William) 1929- .... **CLC 3, 6, 18, 32, 81**
See also CA 17-20R; CANR 9, 33; CDBLB 1960 to Present; DLB 27; MTCW

Gunn, William Harrison 1934(?)-1989
See Gunn, Bill
See also AITN 1; BW 1; CA 13-16R; 128; CANR 12, 25

Gunnars, Kristjana 1948- . . . . **CLC 69**
See also CA 113; DLB 60

Gurganus, Allan 1947- . . . . **CLC 70**
See also BEST 90:1; CA 135

Gurney, A(lbert) R(amsdell), Jr. 1930- . . . . **CLC 32, 50, 54**
See also CA 77-80; CANR 32

Gurney, Ivor (Bertie) 1890-1937 . . . **TCLC 33**

Gurney, Peter
See Gurney, A(lbert) R(amsdell), Jr.

Guro, Elena 1877-1913 . . . . **TCLC 56**

Gustafson, Ralph (Barker) 1909- . . . . **CLC 36**
See also CA 21-24R; CANR 8, 45; DLB 88

Gut, Gom
See Simenon, Georges (Jacques Christian)

Guthrie, A(lfred) B(ertram), Jr. 1901-1991 . . . . **CLC 23**
See also CA 57-60; 134; CANR 24; DLB 6; SATA 62; SATA-Obit 67

Guthrie, Isobel
See Grieve, C(hristopher) M(urray)

Guthrie, Woodrow Wilson 1912-1967
See Guthrie, Woody
See also CA 113; 93-96

Guthrie, Woody . . . . **CLC 35**
See also Guthrie, Woodrow Wilson

Guy, Rosa (Cuthbert) 1928- . . . . **CLC 26**
See also AAYA 4; BW 2; CA 17-20R; CANR 14, 34; CLR 13; DLB 33; JRDA; MAICYA; SATA 14, 62

Gwendolyn
See Bennett, (Enoch) Arnold

H. D. . . . . **CLC 3, 8, 14, 31, 34, 73; PC 5**
See also Doolittle, Hilda

H. de V.
See Buchan, John

Haavikko, Paavo Juhani 1931- . . . . **CLC 18, 34**
See also CA 106

Habbema, Koos
See Heijermans, Herman

Hacker, Marilyn 1942- . . . . **CLC 5, 9, 23, 72**
See also CA 77-80; DLB 120

Haggard, H(enry) Rider 1856-1925 . . . . **TCLC 11**
See also CA 108; DLB 70; SATA 16

Haig, Fenil
See Ford, Ford Madox

Haig-Brown, Roderick (Langmere) 1908-1976 . . . . **CLC 21**
See also CA 5-8R; 69-72; CANR 4, 38; CLR 31; DLB 88; MAICYA; SATA 12

Hailey, Arthur 1920- . . . . **CLC 5**
See also AITN 2; BEST 90:3; CA 1-4R; CANR 2, 36; DLB 88; DLBY 82; MTCW

Hailey, Elizabeth Forsythe 1938- . . . **CLC 40**
See also CA 93-96; CAAS 1; CANR 15

Haines, John (Meade) 1924- . . . . **CLC 58**
See also CA 17-20R; CANR 13, 34; DLB 5

Haldeman, Joe (William) 1943- . . . . . **CLC 61**
See also CA 53-56; CANR 6; DLB 8

Haley, Alex(ander Murray Palmer) 1921-1992 . . . . **CLC 8, 12, 76; BLC; DA**
See also BW 2; CA 77-80; 136; DLB 38; MTCW

Haliburton, Thomas Chandler 1796-1865 . . . . **NCLC 15**
See also DLB 11, 99

Hall, Donald (Andrew, Jr.) 1928- . . . . **CLC 1, 13, 37, 59**
See also CA 5-8R; CAAS 7; CANR 2, 44; DLB 5; SATA 23

Hall, Frederic Sauser
See Sauser-Hall, Frederic

Hall, James
See Kuttner, Henry

Hall, James Norman 1887-1951 . . . **TCLC 23**
See also CA 123; SATA 21

Hall, (Marguerite) Radclyffe 1886(?)-1943 . . . . **TCLC 12**
See also CA 110

Hall, Rodney 1935- . . . . **CLC 51**
See also CA 109

Halleck, Fitz-Greene 1790-1867 . . **NCLC 47**
See also DLB 3

Halliday, Michael
See Creasey, John

Halpern, Daniel 1945- . . . . **CLC 14**
See also CA 33-36R

Hamburger, Michael (Peter Leopold) 1924- . . . . **CLC 5, 14**
See also CA 5-8R; CAAS 4; CANR 2, 47; DLB 27

Hamill, Pete 1935- . . . . **CLC 10**
See also CA 25-28R; CANR 18

Hamilton, Alexander 1755(?)-1804 . . . . **NCLC 49**
See also DLB 37

Hamilton, Clive
See Lewis, C(live) S(taples)

Hamilton, Edmond 1904-1977 . . . . **CLC 1**
See also CA 1-4R; CANR 3; DLB 8

Hamilton, Eugene (Jacob) Lee
See Lee-Hamilton, Eugene (Jacob)

Hamilton, Franklin
See Silverberg, Robert

Hamilton, Gail
See Corcoran, Barbara

Hamilton, Mollie
See Kaye, M(ary) M(argaret)

Hamilton, (Anthony Walter) Patrick 1904-1962 . . . . **CLC 51**
See also CA 113; DLB 10

Hamilton, Virginia 1936- . . . . **CLC 26**
See also AAYA 2; BW 2; CA 25-28R; CANR 20, 37; CLR 1, 11; DLB 33, 52; JRDA; MAICYA; MTCW; SATA 4, 56, 79

Hammett, (Samuel) Dashiell 1894-1961 . . . . **CLC 3, 5, 10, 19, 47; SSC 17**
See also AITN 1; CA 81-84; CANR 42; CDALB 1929-1941; DLBD 6; MTCW

Hammon, Jupiter 1711(?)-1800(?) . . . . **NCLC 5; BLC**
See also DLB 31, 50

Hammond, Keith
See Kuttner, Henry

Hamner, Earl (Henry), Jr. 1923- . . . **CLC 12**
See also AITN 2; CA 73-76; DLB 6

Hampton, Christopher (James) 1946- . . . . **CLC 4**
See also CA 25-28R; DLB 13; MTCW

Hamsun, Knut . . . . **TCLC 2, 14, 49**
See also Pedersen, Knut

Handke, Peter 1942- . . **CLC 5, 8, 10, 15, 38**
See also CA 77-80; CANR 33; DLB 85, 124; MTCW

Hanley, James 1901-1985 . . . **CLC 3, 5, 8, 13**
See also CA 73-76; 117; CANR 36; MTCW

Hannah, Barry 1942- . . . . **CLC 23, 38**
See also CA 108; 110; CANR 43; DLB 6; MTCW

Hannon, Ezra
See Hunter, Evan

Hansberry, Lorraine (Vivian) 1930-1965 . . . . . . **CLC 17, 62; BLC; DA; DC 2**
See also BW 1; CA 109; 25-28R; CABS 3; CDALB 1941-1968; DLB 7, 38; MTCW

Hansen, Joseph 1923- . . . . **CLC 38**
See also CA 29-32R; CAAS 17; CANR 16, 44

Hansen, Martin A. 1909-1955 . . . . . **TCLC 32**

Hanson, Kenneth O(stlin) 1922- . . . . **CLC 13**
See also CA 53-56; CANR 7

Hardwick, Elizabeth 1916- . . . . **CLC 13**
See also CA 5-8R; CANR 3, 32; DLB 6; MTCW

Hardy, Thomas 1840-1928 . . . . . . **TCLC 4, 10, 18, 32, 48, 53; DA; PC 8; SSC 2; WLC**
See also CA 104; 123; CDBLB 1890-1914; DLB 18, 19, 135; MTCW

Hare, David 1947- . . . . **CLC 29, 58**
See also CA 97-100; CANR 39; DLB 13; MTCW

Harford, Henry
See Hudson, W(illiam) H(enry)

Hargrave, Leonie
See Disch, Thomas M(ichael)

Harjo, Joy 1951- . . . . **CLC 83**
See also CA 114; CANR 35; DLB 120; NNAL

Harlan, Louis R(udolph) 1922- . . . . . **CLC 34**
See also CA 21-24R; CANR 25

Harling, Robert 1951(?)- . . . . **CLC 53**

Harmon, William (Ruth) 1938- . . . . . **CLC 38**
See also CA 33-36R; CANR 14, 32, 35; SATA 65

Harper, F. E. W.
See Harper, Frances Ellen Watkins

Harper, Frances E. W.
See Harper, Frances Ellen Watkins

Harper, Frances E. Watkins
See Harper, Frances Ellen Watkins

Harper, Frances Ellen
See Harper, Frances Ellen Watkins

Harper, Frances Ellen Watkins 1825-1911 .... **TCLC 14; BLC**
See also BW 1; CA 111; 125; DLB 50

Harper, Michael S(teven) 1938- .. **CLC 7, 22**
See also BW 1; CA 33-36R; CANR 24; DLB 41

Harper, Mrs. F. E. W.
See Harper, Frances Ellen Watkins

Harris, Christie (Lucy) Irwin 1907- .... **CLC 12**
See also CA 5-8R; CANR 6; DLB 88; JRDA; MAICYA; SAAS 10; SATA 6, 74

Harris, Frank 1856(?)-1931 .... **TCLC 24**
See also CA 109

Harris, George Washington 1814-1869 .... **NCLC 23**
See also DLB 3, 11

Harris, Joel Chandler 1848-1908 ... **TCLC 2**
See also CA 104; 137; DLB 11, 23, 42, 78, 91; MAICYA; YABC 1

Harris, John (Wyndham Parkes Lucas) Beynon 1903-1969
See Wyndham, John
See also CA 102; 89-92

Harris, MacDonald .... **CLC 9**
See also Heiney, Donald (William)

Harris, Mark 1922- .... **CLC 19**
See also CA 5-8R; CAAS 3; CANR 2; DLB 2; DLBY 80

Harris, (Theodore) Wilson 1921-.... **CLC 25**
See also BW 2; CA 65-68; CAAS 16; CANR 11, 27; DLB 117; MTCW

Harrison, Elizabeth Cavanna 1909-
See Cavanna, Betty
See also CA 9-12R; CANR 6, 27

Harrison, Harry (Max) 1925-...... **CLC 42**
See also CA 1-4R; CANR 5, 21; DLB 8; SATA 4

Harrison, James (Thomas) 1937- .... **CLC 6, 14, 33, 66**
See also CA 13-16R; CANR 8; DLBY 82

Harrison, Jim
See Harrison, James (Thomas)

Harrison, Kathryn 1961- .... **CLC 70**
See also CA 144

Harrison, Tony 1937-............. **CLC 43**
See also CA 65-68; CANR 44; DLB 40; MTCW

Harriss, Will(ard Irvin) 1922-...... **CLC 34**
See also CA 111

Harson, Sley
See Ellison, Harlan (Jay)

Hart, Ellis
See Ellison, Harlan (Jay)

Hart, Josephine 1942(?)- .... **CLC 70**
See also CA 138

Hart, Moss 1904-1961 .... **CLC 66**
See also CA 109; 89-92; DLB 7

Harte, (Francis) Bret(t) 1836(?)-1902 .... **TCLC 1, 25; DA; SSC 8; WLC**
See also CA 104; 140; CDALB 1865-1917; DLB 12, 64, 74, 79; SATA 26

Hartley, L(eslie) P(oles) 1895-1972 .... **CLC 2, 22**
See also CA 45-48; 37-40R; CANR 33; DLB 15, 139; MTCW

Hartman, Geoffrey H. 1929-....... **CLC 27**
See also CA 117; 125; DLB 67

Haruf, Kent 19(?)- .... **CLC 34**

Harwood, Ronald 1934-........... **CLC 32**
See also CA 1-4R; CANR 4; DLB 13

Hasek, Jaroslav (Matej Frantisek) 1883-1923 .... **TCLC 4**
See also CA 104; 129; MTCW

Hass, Robert 1941-............ **CLC 18, 39**
See also CA 111; CANR 30; DLB 105

Hastings, Hudson
See Kuttner, Henry

Hastings, Selina .... **CLC 44**

Hatteras, Amelia
See Mencken, H(enry) L(ouis)

Hatteras, Owen .... **TCLC 18**
See also Mencken, H(enry) L(ouis); Nathan, George Jean

Hauptmann, Gerhart (Johann Robert) 1862-1946 .... **TCLC 4**
See also CA 104; DLB 66, 118

Havel, Vaclav 1936-........ **CLC 25, 58, 65**
See also CA 104; CANR 36; MTCW

Haviaras, Stratis .... **CLC 33**
See also Chaviaras, Strates

Hawes, Stephen 1475(?)-1523(?) ..... **LC 17**

Hawkes, John (Clendennin Burne, Jr.) 1925- ...... **CLC 1, 2, 3, 4, 7, 9, 14, 15, 27, 49**
See also CA 1-4R; CANR 2, 47; DLB 2, 7; DLBY 80; MTCW

Hawking, S. W.
See Hawking, Stephen W(illiam)

Hawking, Stephen W(illiam) 1942- .... **CLC 63**
See also AAYA 13; BEST 89:1; CA 126; 129

Hawthorne, Julian 1846-1934 ..... **TCLC 25**

Hawthorne, Nathaniel 1804-1864 ...... **NCLC 39; DA; SSC 3; WLC**
See also CDALB 1640-1865; DLB 1, 74; YABC 2

Haxton, Josephine Ayres 1921-
See Douglas, Ellen
See also CA 115; CANR 41

Hayaseca y Eizaguirre, Jorge
See Echegaray (y Eizaguirre), Jose (Maria Waldo)

Hayashi Fumiko 1904-1951....... **TCLC 27**

Haycraft, Anna
See Ellis, Alice Thomas
See also CA 122

Hayden, Robert E(arl) 1913-1980 ...... **CLC 5, 9, 14, 37; BLC; DA; PC 6**
See also BW 1; CA 69-72; 97-100; CABS 2; CANR 24; CDALB 1941-1968; DLB 5, 76; MTCW; SATA 19; SATA-Obit 26

Hayford, J(oseph) E(phraim) Casely
See Casely-Hayford, J(oseph) E(phraim)

Hayman, Ronald 1932-........... **CLC 44**
See also CA 25-28R; CANR 18

Haywood, Eliza (Fowler) 1693(?)-1756 .... **LC 1**

Hazlitt, William 1778-1830 ...... **NCLC 29**
See also DLB 110

Hazzard, Shirley 1931- .... **CLC 18**
See also CA 9-12R; CANR 4; DLBY 82; MTCW

Head, Bessie 1937-1986... **CLC 25, 67; BLC**
See also BW 2; CA 29-32R; 119; CANR 25; DLB 117; MTCW

Headon, (Nicky) Topper 1956(?)- ... **CLC 30**

Heaney, Seamus (Justin) 1939- .... **CLC 5, 7, 14, 25, 37, 74**
See also CA 85-88; CANR 25; CDBLB 1960 to Present; DLB 40; MTCW

Hearn, (Patricio) Lafcadio (Tessima Carlos) 1850-1904 .... **TCLC 9**
See also CA 105; DLB 12, 78

Hearne, Vicki 1946-.............. **CLC 56**
See also CA 139

Hearon, Shelby 1931-............. **CLC 63**
See also AITN 2; CA 25-28R; CANR 18

Heat-Moon, William Least.......... **CLC 29**
See also Trogdon, William (Lewis)
See also AAYA 9

Hebbel, Friedrich 1813-1863..... **NCLC 43**
See also DLB 129

Hebert, Anne 1916- .... **CLC 4, 13, 29**
See also CA 85-88; DLB 68; MTCW

Hecht, Anthony (Evan) 1923- .... **CLC 8, 13, 19**
See also CA 9-12R; CANR 6; DLB 5

Hecht, Ben 1894-1964 .... **CLC 8**
See also CA 85-88; DLB 7, 9, 25, 26, 28, 86

Hedayat, Sadeq 1903-1951........ **TCLC 21**
See also CA 120

Hegel, Georg Wilhelm Friedrich 1770-1831 .... **NCLC 46**
See also DLB 90

Heidegger, Martin 1889-1976 ...... **CLC 24**
See also CA 81-84; 65-68; CANR 34; MTCW

Heidenstam, (Carl Gustaf) Verner von 1859-1940 .... **TCLC 5**
See also CA 104

Heifner, Jack 1946-.............. **CLC 11**
See also CA 105; CANR 47

Heijermans, Herman 1864-1924 ... **TCLC 24**
See also CA 123

Heilbrun, Carolyn G(old) 1926-..... **CLC 25**
See also CA 45-48; CANR 1, 28

Heine, Heinrich 1797-1856 .... **NCLC 4**
See also DLB 90

Heinemann, Larry (Curtiss) 1944- .. **CLC 50**
See also CA 110; CANR 31; DLBD 9

Heiney, Donald (William) 1921-1993
See Harris, MacDonald
See also CA 1-4R; 142; CANR 3

Heinlein, Robert A(nson) 1907-1988 ...... **CLC 1, 3, 8, 14, 26, 55**
See also CA 1-4R; 125; CANR 1, 20; DLB 8; JRDA; MAICYA; MTCW; SATA 9, 69; SATA-Obit 56

Helforth, John
See Doolittle, Hilda

Hellenhofferu, Vojtech Kapristian z
See Hasek, Jaroslav (Matej Frantisek)

Heller, Joseph 1923- .... **CLC 1, 3, 5, 8, 11, 36, 63; DA; WLC**
See also AITN 1; CA 5-8R; CABS 1; CANR 8, 42; DLB 2, 28; DLBY 80; MTCW

Hellman, Lillian (Florence) 1906-1984 ...... **CLC 2, 4, 8, 14, 18, 34, 44, 52; DC 1**
See also AITN 1, 2; CA 13-16R; 112; CANR 33; DLB 7; DLBY 84; MTCW

Helprin, Mark 1947- ..... **CLC 7, 10, 22, 32**
See also CA 81-84; CANR 47; DLBY 85; MTCW

Helvetius, Claude-Adrien 1715-1771 .... **LC 26**

Helyar, Jane Penelope Josephine 1933-
See Poole, Josephine
See also CA 21-24R; CANR 10, 26

Hemans, Felicia 1793-1835 ...... **NCLC 29**
See also DLB 96

Hemingway, Ernest (Miller) 1899-1961 .... **CLC 1, 3, 6, 8, 10, 13, 19, 30, 34, 39, 41, 44, 50, 61, 80; DA; SSC 1; WLC**
See also CA 77-80; CANR 34; CDALB 1917-1929; DLB 4, 9, 102; DLBD 1; DLBY 81, 87; MTCW

Hempel, Amy 1951- .... **CLC 39**
See also CA 118; 137

Henderson, F. C.
See Mencken, H(enry) L(ouis)

Henderson, Sylvia
See Ashton-Warner, Sylvia (Constance)

Henley, Beth .... **CLC 23**
See also Henley, Elizabeth Becker
See also CABS 3; DLBY 86

Henley, Elizabeth Becker 1952-
See Henley, Beth
See also CA 107; CANR 32; MTCW

Henley, William Ernest 1849-1903 .... **TCLC 8**
See also CA 105; DLB 19

Hennissart, Martha
See Lathen, Emma
See also CA 85-88

Henry, O. .... **TCLC 1, 19; SSC 5; WLC**
See also Porter, William Sydney

Henry, Patrick 1736- .... **LC 25**
See also CA 145

Henryson, Robert 1430(?)-1506(?).... **LC 20**
See also DLB 146

Henry VIII 1491-1547 .... **LC 10**

Henschke, Alfred
See Klabund

Hentoff, Nat(han Irving) 1925- ..... **CLC 26**
See also AAYA 4; CA 1-4R; CAAS 6; CANR 5, 25; CLR 1; JRDA; MAICYA; SATA 42, 69; SATA-Brief 27

Heppenstall, (John) Rayner 1911-1981 .... **CLC 10**
See also CA 1-4R; 103; CANR 29

Herbert, Frank (Patrick) 1920-1986 ...... **CLC 12, 23, 35, 44, 85**
See also CA 53-56; 118; CANR 5, 43; DLB 8; MTCW; SATA 9, 37; SATA-Obit 47

Herbert, George 1593-1633 .... **LC 24; PC 4**
See also CDBLB Before 1660; DLB 126

Herbert, Zbigniew 1924- .... **CLC 9, 43**
See also CA 89-92; CANR 36; MTCW

Herbst, Josephine (Frey) 1897-1969 .... **CLC 34**
See also CA 5-8R; 25-28R; DLB 9

Hergesheimer, Joseph 1880-1954 .... **TCLC 11**
See also CA 109; DLB 102, 9

Herlihy, James Leo 1927-1993 ...... **CLC 6**
See also CA 1-4R; 143; CANR 2

Hermogenes fl. c. 175- .... **CMLC 6**

Hernandez, Jose 1834-1886...... **NCLC 17**

Herrick, Robert 1591-1674 .... **LC 13; DA; PC 9**
See also DLB 126

Herring, Guilles
See Somerville, Edith

Herriot, James 1916- .... **CLC 12**
See also Wight, James Alfred
See also AAYA 1; CANR 40

Herrmann, Dorothy 1941- .... **CLC 44**
See also CA 107

Herrmann, Taffy
See Herrmann, Dorothy

Hersey, John (Richard) 1914-1993 .... **CLC 1, 2, 7, 9, 40, 81**
See also CA 17-20R; 140; CANR 33; DLB 6; MTCW; SATA 25; SATA-Obit 76

Herzen, Aleksandr Ivanovich 1812-1870 .... **NCLC 10**

Herzl, Theodor 1860-1904 .... **TCLC 36**

Herzog, Werner 1942- .... **CLC 16**
See also CA 89-92

Hesiod c. 8th cent. B.C.- .... **CMLC 5**

Hesse, Hermann 1877-1962 .... **CLC 1, 2, 3, 6, 11, 17, 25, 69; DA; SSC 9; WLC**
See also CA 17-18; CAP 2; DLB 66; MTCW; SATA 50

Hewes, Cady
See De Voto, Bernard (Augustine)

Heyen, William 1940- .... **CLC 13, 18**
See also CA 33-36R; CAAS 9; DLB 5

Heyerdahl, Thor 1914- .... **CLC 26**
See also CA 5-8R; CANR 5, 22; MTCW; SATA 2, 52

Heym, Georg (Theodor Franz Arthur) 1887-1912 .... **TCLC 9**
See also CA 106

Heym, Stefan 1913- .... **CLC 41**
See also CA 9-12R; CANR 4; DLB 69

Heyse, Paul (Johann Ludwig von) 1830-1914 .... **TCLC 8**
See also CA 104; DLB 129

Heyward, (Edwin) DuBose 1885-1940 .... **TCLC 59**
See also CA 108; DLB 7, 9, 45; SATA 21

Hibbert, Eleanor Alice Burford 1906-1993 .... **CLC 7**
See also BEST 90:4; CA 17-20R; 140; CANR 9, 28; SATA 2; SATA-Obit 74

Higgins, George V(incent) 1939- .... **CLC 4, 7, 10, 18**
See also CA 77-80; CAAS 5; CANR 17; DLB 2; DLBY 81; MTCW

Higginson, Thomas Wentworth 1823-1911 .... **TCLC 36**
See also DLB 1, 64

Highet, Helen
See MacInnes, Helen (Clark)

Highsmith, (Mary) Patricia 1921- .... **CLC 2, 4, 14, 42**
See also CA 1-4R; CANR 1, 20; MTCW

Highwater, Jamake (Mamake) 1942(?)- .... **CLC 12**
See also AAYA 7; CA 65-68; CAAS 7; CANR 10, 34; CLR 17; DLB 52; DLBY 85; JRDA; MAICYA; SATA 32, 69; SATA-Brief 30

Higuchi, Ichiyo 1872-1896....... **NCLC 49**

Hijuelos, Oscar 1951- ...... **CLC 65; HLC**
See also BEST 90:1; CA 123; DLB 145; HW

Hikmet, Nazim 1902(?)-1963....... **CLC 40**
See also CA 141; 93-96

Hildesheimer, Wolfgang 1916-1991 .... **CLC 49**
See also CA 101; 135; DLB 69, 124

Hill, Geoffrey (William) 1932- .... **CLC 5, 8, 18, 45**
See also CA 81-84; CANR 21; CDBLB 1960 to Present; DLB 40; MTCW

Hill, George Roy 1921- .... **CLC 26**
See also CA 110; 122

Hill, John
See Koontz, Dean R(ay)

Hill, Susan (Elizabeth) 1942- .... **CLC 4**
See also CA 33-36R; CANR 29; DLB 14, 139; MTCW

Hillerman, Tony 1925- .... **CLC 62**
See also AAYA 6; BEST 89:1; CA 29-32R; CANR 21, 42; SATA 6

Hillesum, Etty 1914-1943 .... **TCLC 49**
See also CA 137

Hilliard, Noel (Harvey) 1929- ...... **CLC 15**
See also CA 9-12R; CANR 7

Hillis, Rick 1956- .... **CLC 66**
See also CA 134

Hilton, James 1900-1954 .... **TCLC 21**
See also CA 108; DLB 34, 77; SATA 34

Himes, Chester (Bomar) 1909-1984 .... **CLC 2, 4, 7, 18, 58; BLC**
See also BW 2; CA 25-28R; 114; CANR 22; DLB 2, 76, 143; MTCW

Hinde, Thomas .... **CLC 6, 11**
See also Chitty, Thomas Willes

Hindin, Nathan
See Bloch, Robert (Albert)

Hine, (William) Daryl 1936- .... **CLC 15**
See also CA 1-4R; CAAS 15; CANR 1, 20; DLB 60

Hinkson, Katharine Tynan
See Tynan, Katharine

Hinton, S(usan) E(loise) 1950- .... **CLC 30; DA**
See also AAYA 2; CA 81-84; CANR 32; CLR 3, 23; JRDA; MAICYA; MTCW; SATA 19, 58

Hippius, Zinaida .... **TCLC 9**
See also Gippius, Zinaida (Nikolayevna)

Hiraoka, Kimitake 1925-1970
See Mishima, Yukio
See also CA 97-100; 29-32R; MTCW

Hirsch, E(ric) D(onald), Jr. 1928-... **CLC 79**
See also CA 25-28R; CANR 27; DLB 67; MTCW

Hirsch, Edward 1950- .... **CLC 31, 50**
See also CA 104; CANR 20, 42; DLB 120

Hitchcock, Alfred (Joseph) 1899-1980 .... **CLC 16**
See also CA 97-100; SATA 27; SATA-Obit 24

Hitler, Adolf 1889-1945.......... **TCLC 53**
See also CA 117

Hoagland, Edward 1932- .... **CLC 28**
See also CA 1-4R; CANR 2, 31; DLB 6; SATA 51

Hoban, Russell (Conwell) 1925- .. **CLC 7, 25**
See also CA 5-8R; CANR 23, 37; CLR 3; DLB 52; MAICYA; MTCW; SATA 1, 40, 78

Hobbs, Perry
See Blackmur, R(ichard) P(almer)

Hobson, Laura Z(ametkin) 1900-1986 .... **CLC 7, 25**
See also CA 17-20R; 118; DLB 28; SATA 52

Hochhuth, Rolf 1931-........ **CLC 4, 11, 18**
See also CA 5-8R; CANR 33; DLB 124; MTCW

Hochman, Sandra 1936-.......... **CLC 3, 8**
See also CA 5-8R; DLB 5

Hochwaelder, Fritz 1911-1986...... **CLC 36**
See also CA 29-32R; 120; CANR 42; MTCW

Hochwalder, Fritz
See Hochwaelder, Fritz

Hocking, Mary (Eunice) 1921- ..... **CLC 13**
See also CA 101; CANR 18, 40

Hodgins, Jack 1938-.............. **CLC 23**
See also CA 93-96; DLB 60

Hodgson, William Hope 1877(?)-1918 .... **TCLC 13**
See also CA 111; DLB 70

Hoffman, Alice 1952-............. **CLC 51**
See also CA 77-80; CANR 34; MTCW

Hoffman, Daniel (Gerard) 1923- .... **CLC 6, 13, 23**
See also CA 1-4R; CANR 4; DLB 5

Hoffman, Stanley 1944-............ **CLC 5**
See also CA 77-80

Hoffman, William M(oses) 1939- ... **CLC 40**
See also CA 57-60; CANR 11

Hoffmann, E(rnst) T(heodor) A(madeus) 1776-1822 .... **NCLC 2; SSC 13**
See also DLB 90; SATA 27

Hofmann, Gert 1931-............. **CLC 54**
See also CA 128

Hofmannsthal, Hugo von 1874-1929 .... **TCLC 11; DC 4**
See also CA 106; DLB 81, 118

Hogan, Linda 1947- .... **CLC 73**
See also CA 120; CANR 45; NNAL

Hogarth, Charles
See Creasey, John

Hogg, James 1770-1835.......... **NCLC 4**
See also DLB 93, 116

Holbach, Paul Henri Thiry Baron 1723-1789 .... **LC 14**

Holberg, Ludvig 1684-1754 .... **LC 6**

Holden, Ursula 1921-............. **CLC 18**
See also CA 101; CAAS 8; CANR 22

Holderlin, (Johann Christian) Friedrich 1770-1843 .... **NCLC 16; PC 4**

Holdstock, Robert
See Holdstock, Robert P.

Holdstock, Robert P. 1948-........ **CLC 39**
See also CA 131

Holland, Isabelle 1920- .... **CLC 21**
See also AAYA 11; CA 21-24R; CANR 10, 25, 47; JRDA; MAICYA; SATA 8, 70

Holland, Marcus
See Caldwell, (Janet Miriam) Taylor (Holland)

Hollander, John 1929-...... **CLC 2, 5, 8, 14**
See also CA 1-4R; CANR 1; DLB 5; SATA 13

Hollander, Paul
See Silverberg, Robert

Holleran, Andrew 1943(?)-......... **CLC 38**
See also CA 144

Hollinghurst, Alan 1954-.......... **CLC 55**
See also CA 114

Hollis, Jim
See Summers, Hollis (Spurgeon, Jr.)

Holmes, John
See Souster, (Holmes) Raymond

Holmes, John Clellon 1926-1988.... **CLC 56**
See also CA 9-12R; 125; CANR 4; DLB 16

Holmes, Oliver Wendell 1809-1894 .... **NCLC 14**
See also CDALB 1640-1865; DLB 1; SATA 34

Holmes, Raymond
See Souster, (Holmes) Raymond

Holt, Victoria
See Hibbert, Eleanor Alice Burford

Holub, Miroslav 1923-............. **CLC 4**
See also CA 21-24R; CANR 10

Homer c. 8th cent. B.C.- ..... **CMLC 1; DA**

Honig, Edwin 1919- .... **CLC 33**
See also CA 5-8R; CAAS 8; CANR 4, 45; DLB 5

Hood, Hugh (John Blagdon) 1928- .... **CLC 15, 28**
See also CA 49-52; CAAS 17; CANR 1, 33; DLB 53

Hood, Thomas 1799-1845........ **NCLC 16**
See also DLB 96

Hooker, (Peter) Jeremy 1941-...... **CLC 43**
See also CA 77-80; CANR 22; DLB 40

Hope, A(lec) D(erwent) 1907- .... **CLC 3, 51**
See also CA 21-24R; CANR 33; MTCW

Hope, Brian
See Creasey, John

Hope, Christopher (David Tully) 1944- .... **CLC 52**
See also CA 106; CANR 47; SATA 62

Hopkins, Gerard Manley 1844-1889 .... **NCLC 17; DA; WLC**
See also CDBLB 1890-1914; DLB 35, 57

Hopkins, John (Richard) 1931-...... **CLC 4**
See also CA 85-88

Hopkins, Pauline Elizabeth 1859-1930 .... **TCLC 28; BLC**
See also BW 2; CA 141; DLB 50

Hopkinson, Francis 1737-1791 ...... **LC 25**
See also DLB 31

Hopley-Woolrich, Cornell George 1903-1968
See Woolrich, Cornell
See also CA 13-14; CAP 1

Horatio
See Proust, (Valentin-Louis-George-Eugene-) Marcel

Horgan, Paul 1903- .... **CLC 9, 53**
See also CA 13-16R; CANR 9, 35; DLB 102; DLBY 85; MTCW; SATA 13

Horn, Peter
See Kuttner, Henry

Hornem, Horace Esq.
See Byron, George Gordon (Noel)

Hornung, E(rnest) W(illiam) 1866-1921 .... **TCLC 59**
See also CA 108; DLB 70

Horovitz, Israel (Arthur) 1939-..... **CLC 56**
See also CA 33-36R; CANR 46; DLB 7

Horvath, Odon von
See Horvath, Oedoen von
See also DLB 85, 124

Horvath, Oedoen von 1901-1938... **TCLC 45**
See also Horvath, Odon von
See also CA 118

Horwitz, Julius 1920-1986......... **CLC 14**
See also CA 9-12R; 119; CANR 12

Hospital, Janette Turner 1942-..... **CLC 42**
See also CA 108

Hostos, E. M. de
See Hostos (y Bonilla), Eugenio Maria de

Hostos, Eugenio M. de
See Hostos (y Bonilla), Eugenio Maria de

Hostos, Eugenio Maria
See Hostos (y Bonilla), Eugenio Maria de

Hostos (y Bonilla), Eugenio Maria de 1839-1903 .... **TCLC 24**
See also CA 123; 131; HW

Houdini
See Lovecraft, H(oward) P(hillips)

Hougan, Carolyn 1943- .... **CLC 34**
See also CA 139

Household, Geoffrey (Edward West) 1900-1988 .... **CLC 11**
See also CA 77-80; 126; DLB 87; SATA 14; SATA-Obit 59

Housman, A(lfred) E(dward) 1859-1936 ...... **TCLC 1, 10; DA; PC 2**
See also CA 104; 125; DLB 19; MTCW

Housman, Laurence 1865-1959 ..... **TCLC 7**
See also CA 106; DLB 10; SATA 25

Howard, Elizabeth Jane 1923- ... **CLC 7, 29**
See also CA 5-8R; CANR 8

Howard, Maureen 1930- ..... **CLC 5, 14, 46**
See also CA 53-56; CANR 31; DLBY 83; MTCW

Howard, Richard 1929- ...... **CLC 7, 10, 47**
See also AITN 1; CA 85-88; CANR 25; DLB 5

Howard, Robert Ervin 1906-1936 ... **TCLC 8**
See also CA 105

Howard, Warren F.
See Pohl, Frederik

Howe, Fanny 1940- .... **CLC 47**
See also CA 117; SATA-Brief 52

Howe, Irving 1920-1993........... **CLC 85**
See also CA 9-12R; 141; CANR 21; DLB 67; MTCW

Howe, Julia Ward 1819-1910 ..... **TCLC 21**
See also CA 117; DLB 1

Howe, Susan 1937-............... **CLC 72**
See also DLB 120

Howe, Tina 1937-................ **CLC 48**
See also CA 109

Howell, James 1594(?)-1666 .... **LC 13**

Howells, W. D.
See Howells, William Dean

Howells, William D.
See Howells, William Dean

Howells, William Dean 1837-1920 .... **TCLC 7, 17, 41**
See also CA 104; 134; CDALB 1865-1917; DLB 12, 64, 74, 79

Howes, Barbara 1914- .... **CLC 15**
See also CA 9-12R; CAAS 3; SATA 5

Hrabal, Bohumil 1914-......... **CLC 13, 67**
See also CA 106; CAAS 12

Hsun, Lu .... **TCLC 3**
See also Shu-Jen, Chou

Hubbard, L(afayette) Ron(ald) 1911-1986 .... **CLC 43**
See also CA 77-80; 118; CANR 22

Huch, Ricarda (Octavia) 1864-1947 .... **TCLC 13**
See also CA 111; DLB 66

Huddle, David 1942- .... **CLC 49**
See also CA 57-60; CAAS 20; DLB 130

Hudson, Jeffrey
See Crichton, (John) Michael

Hudson, W(illiam) H(enry) 1841-1922 .... **TCLC 29**
See also CA 115; DLB 98; SATA 35

Hueffer, Ford Madox
See Ford, Ford Madox

Hughart, Barry 1934-............. **CLC 39**
See also CA 137

Hughes, Colin
See Creasey, John

Hughes, David (John) 1930- .... **CLC 48**
See also CA 116; 129; DLB 14

Hughes, (James) Langston 1902-1967 ..... **CLC 1, 5, 10, 15, 35, 44; BLC; DA; DC 3; PC 1; SSC 6; WLC**
See also AAYA 12; BW 1; CA 1-4R; 25-28R; CANR 1, 34; CDALB 1929-1941; CLR 17; DLB 4, 7, 48, 51, 86; JRDA; MAICYA; MTCW; SATA 4, 33

Hughes, Richard (Arthur Warren) 1900-1976 .... **CLC 1, 11**
See also CA 5-8R; 65-68; CANR 4; DLB 15; MTCW; SATA 8; SATA-Obit 25

Hughes, Ted 1930- .... **CLC 2, 4, 9, 14, 37; PC 7**
See also CA 1-4R; CANR 1, 33; CLR 3; DLB 40; MAICYA; MTCW; SATA 49; SATA-Brief 27

Hugo, Richard F(ranklin) 1923-1982 .... **CLC 6, 18, 32**
See also CA 49-52; 108; CANR 3; DLB 5

Hugo, Victor (Marie) 1802-1885 .. **NCLC 3, 10, 21; DA; WLC**
See also DLB 119; SATA 47

Huidobro, Vicente
See Huidobro Fernandez, Vicente Garcia

Huidobro Fernandez, Vicente Garcia 1893-1948 .... **TCLC 31**
See also CA 131; HW

Hulme, Keri 1947- .... **CLC 39**
See also CA 125

Hulme, T(homas) E(rnest) 1883-1917 .... **TCLC 21**
See also CA 117; DLB 19

Hume, David 1711-1776............. **LC 7**
See also DLB 104

Humphrey, William 1924- .... **CLC 45**
See also CA 77-80; DLB 6

Humphreys, Emyr Owen 1919-..... **CLC 47**
See also CA 5-8R; CANR 3, 24; DLB 15

Humphreys, Josephine 1945-.... **CLC 34, 57**
See also CA 121; 127

Hungerford, Pixie
See Brinsmead, H(esba) F(ay)

Hunt, E(verette) Howard, (Jr.) 1918- .... **CLC 3**
See also AITN 1; CA 45-48; CANR 2, 47

Hunt, Kyle
See Creasey, John

Hunt, (James Henry) Leigh 1784-1859 .... **NCLC 1**

Hunt, Marsha 1946-.............. **CLC 70**
See also BW 2; CA 143

Hunt, Violet 1866-1942 .... **TCLC 53**

Hunter, E. Waldo
See Sturgeon, Theodore (Hamilton)

Hunter, Evan 1926- .... **CLC 11, 31**
See also CA 5-8R; CANR 5, 38; DLBY 82; MTCW; SATA 25

Hunter, Kristin (Eggleston) 1931-... **CLC 35**
See also AITN 1; BW 1; CA 13-16R; CANR 13; CLR 3; DLB 33; MAICYA; SAAS 10; SATA 12

Hunter, Mollie 1922-............. **CLC 21**
See also McIlwraith, Maureen Mollie Hunter
See also AAYA 13; CANR 37; CLR 25; JRDA; MAICYA; SAAS 7; SATA 54

Hunter, Robert (?)-1734............. **LC 7**

Hurston, Zora Neale 1903-1960 .... **CLC 7, 30, 61; BLC; DA; SSC 4**
See also BW 1; CA 85-88; DLB 51, 86; MTCW

Huston, John (Marcellus) 1906-1987 .... **CLC 20**
See also CA 73-76; 123; CANR 34; DLB 26

Hustvedt, Siri 1955-............... **CLC 76**
See also CA 137

Hutten, Ulrich von 1488-1523....... **LC 16**

Huxley, Aldous (Leonard) 1894-1963 ..... **CLC 1, 3, 4, 5, 8, 11, 18, 35, 79; DA; WLC**
See also AAYA 11; CA 85-88; CANR 44; CDBLB 1914-1945; DLB 36, 100; MTCW; SATA 63

Huysmans, Charles Marie Georges 1848-1907
See Huysmans, Joris-Karl
See also CA 104

Huysmans, Joris-Karl.............. **TCLC 7**
See also Huysmans, Charles Marie Georges
See also DLB 123

Hwang, David Henry 1957- .... **CLC 55; DC 4**
See also CA 127; 132

Hyde, Anthony 1946-............. **CLC 42**
See also CA 136

Hyde, Margaret O(ldroyd) 1917- ... **CLC 21**
See also CA 1-4R; CANR 1, 36; CLR 23; JRDA; MAICYA; SAAS 8; SATA 1, 42, 76

Hynes, James 1956(?)-............ **CLC 65**

Ian, Janis 1951- .... **CLC 21**
See also CA 105

Ibanez, Vicente Blasco
See Blasco Ibanez, Vicente

Ibarguengoitia, Jorge 1928-1983.... **CLC 37**
See also CA 124; 113; HW

Ibsen, Henrik (Johan) 1828-1906 .... **TCLC 2, 8, 16, 37, 52; DA; DC 2; WLC**
See also CA 104; 141

Ibuse Masuji 1898-1993........... **CLC 22**
See also CA 127; 141

Ichikawa, Kon 1915-.............. **CLC 20**
See also CA 121

Idle, Eric 1943- . . . . **CLC 21**
See also Monty Python
See also CA 116; CANR 35

Ignatow, David 1914- . . . . . . **CLC 4, 7, 14, 40**
See also CA 9-12R; CAAS 3; CANR 31; DLB 5

Ihimaera, Witi 1944- . . . . **CLC 46**
See also CA 77-80

Ilf, Ilya . . . . **TCLC 21**
See also Fainzilberg, Ilya Arnoldovich

Immermann, Karl (Lebrecht)
1796-1840 . . . . **NCLC 4, 49**
See also DLB 133

Inclan, Ramon (Maria) del Valle
See Valle-Inclan, Ramon (Maria) del

Infante, G(uillermo) Cabrera
See Cabrera Infante, G(uillermo)

Ingalls, Rachel (Holmes) 1940- . . . . . **CLC 42**
See also CA 123; 127

Ingamells, Rex 1913-1955 . . . . **TCLC 35**

Inge, William Motter
1913-1973 . . . . **CLC 1, 8, 19**
See also CA 9-12R; CDALB 1941-1968; DLB 7; MTCW

Ingelow, Jean 1820-1897 . . . . **NCLC 39**
See also DLB 35; SATA 33

Ingram, Willis J.
See Harris, Mark

Innaurato, Albert (F.) 1948(?)- . . **CLC 21, 60**
See also CA 115; 122

Innes, Michael
See Stewart, J(ohn) I(nnes) M(ackintosh)

Ionesco, Eugene
1909-1994 . . . . **CLC 1, 4, 6, 9, 11, 15, 41, 86; DA; WLC**
See also CA 9-12R; 144; MTCW; SATA 7; SATA-Obit 79

Iqbal, Muhammad 1873-1938 . . . . . **TCLC 28**

Ireland, Patrick
See O'Doherty, Brian

Iron, Ralph
See Schreiner, Olive (Emilie Albertina)

Irving, John (Winslow)
1942- . . . . **CLC 13, 23, 38**
See also AAYA 8; BEST 89:3; CA 25-28R; CANR 28; DLB 6; DLBY 82; MTCW

Irving, Washington
1783-1859 . . . . **NCLC 2, 19; DA; SSC 2; WLC**
See also CDALB 1640-1865; DLB 3, 11, 30, 59, 73, 74; YABC 2

Irwin, P. K.
See Page, P(atricia) K(athleen)

Isaacs, Susan 1943- . . . . **CLC 32**
See also BEST 89:1; CA 89-92; CANR 20, 41; MTCW

Isherwood, Christopher (William Bradshaw)
1904-1986 . . . . **CLC 1, 9, 11, 14, 44**
See also CA 13-16R; 117; CANR 35; DLB 15; DLBY 86; MTCW

Ishiguro, Kazuo 1954- . . . . . . **CLC 27, 56, 59**
See also BEST 90:2; CA 120; MTCW

Ishikawa Takuboku
1886(?)-1912 . . . . **TCLC 15; PC 10**
See also CA 113

Iskander, Fazil 1929- . . . . **CLC 47**
See also CA 102

Ivan IV 1530-1584 . . . . **LC 17**

Ivanov, Vyacheslav Ivanovich
1866-1949 . . . . **TCLC 33**
See also CA 122

Ivask, Ivar Vidrik 1927-1992 . . . . **CLC 14**
See also CA 37-40R; 139; CANR 24

Jackson, Daniel
See Wingrove, David (John)

Jackson, Jesse 1908-1983 . . . . **CLC 12**
See also BW 1; CA 25-28R; 109; CANR 27; CLR 28; MAICYA; SATA 2, 29; SATA-Obit 48

Jackson, Laura (Riding) 1901-1991
See Riding, Laura
See also CA 65-68; 135; CANR 28; DLB 48

Jackson, Sam
See Trumbo, Dalton

Jackson, Sara
See Wingrove, David (John)

Jackson, Shirley
1919-1965 . . . . **CLC 11, 60, 87; DA; SSC 9; WLC**
See also AAYA 9; CA 1-4R; 25-28R; CANR 4; CDALB 1941-1968; DLB 6; SATA 2

Jacob, (Cyprien-)Max 1876-1944 . . . **TCLC 6**
See also CA 104

Jacobs, Jim 1942- . . . . **CLC 12**
See also CA 97-100

Jacobs, W(illiam) W(ymark)
1863-1943 . . . . **TCLC 22**
See also CA 121; DLB 135

Jacobsen, Jens Peter 1847-1885 . . **NCLC 34**

Jacobsen, Josephine 1908- . . . . **CLC 48**
See also CA 33-36R; CAAS 18; CANR 23

Jacobson, Dan 1929- . . . . **CLC 4, 14**
See also CA 1-4R; CANR 2, 25; DLB 14; MTCW

Jacqueline
See Carpentier (y Valmont), Alejo

Jagger, Mick 1944- . . . . **CLC 17**

Jakes, John (William) 1932- . . . . **CLC 29**
See also BEST 89:4; CA 57-60; CANR 10, 43; DLBY 83; MTCW; SATA 62

James, Andrew
See Kirkup, James

James, C(yril) L(ionel) R(obert)
1901-1989 . . . . **CLC 33**
See also BW 2; CA 117; 125; 128; DLB 125; MTCW

James, Daniel (Lewis) 1911-1988
See Santiago, Danny
See also CA 125

James, Dynely
See Mayne, William (James Carter)

James, Henry
1843-1916 . . . . . . **TCLC 2, 11, 24, 40, 47; DA; SSC 8; WLC**
See also CA 104; 132; CDALB 1865-1917; DLB 12, 71, 74; MTCW

James, M. R.
See James, Montague (Rhodes)

James, Montague (Rhodes)
1862-1936 . . . . **TCLC 6; SSC 16**
See also CA 104

James, P. D. . . . . **CLC 18, 46**
See also White, Phyllis Dorothy James
See also BEST 90:2; CDBLB 1960 to Present; DLB 87

James, Philip
See Moorcock, Michael (John)

James, William 1842-1910 . . . . . **TCLC 15, 32**
See also CA 109

James I 1394-1437 . . . . **LC 20**

Jameson, Anna 1794-1860 . . . . **NCLC 43**
See also DLB 99

Jami, Nur al-Din 'Abd al-Rahman
1414-1492 . . . . **LC 9**

Jandl, Ernst 1925- . . . . **CLC 34**

Janowitz, Tama 1957- . . . . **CLC 43**
See also CA 106

Jarrell, Randall
1914-1965 . . . . **CLC 1, 2, 6, 9, 13, 49**
See also CA 5-8R; 25-28R; CABS 2; CANR 6, 34; CDALB 1941-1968; CLR 6; DLB 48, 52; MAICYA; MTCW; SATA 7

Jarry, Alfred 1873-1907 . . . . **TCLC 2, 14**
See also CA 104

Jarvis, E. K.
See Bloch, Robert (Albert); Ellison, Harlan (Jay); Silverberg, Robert

Jeake, Samuel, Jr.
See Aiken, Conrad (Potter)

Jean Paul 1763-1825 . . . . **NCLC 7**

Jefferies, (John) Richard
1848-1887 . . . . **NCLC 47**
See also DLB 98, 141; SATA 16

Jeffers, (John) Robinson
1887-1962 . . . . **CLC 2, 3, 11, 15, 54; DA; WLC**
See also CA 85-88; CANR 35; CDALB 1917-1929; DLB 45; MTCW

Jefferson, Janet
See Mencken, H(enry) L(ouis)

Jefferson, Thomas 1743-1826 . . . . **NCLC 11**
See also CDALB 1640-1865; DLB 31

Jeffrey, Francis 1773-1850 . . . . **NCLC 33**
See also DLB 107

Jelakowitch, Ivan
See Heijermans, Herman

Jellicoe, (Patricia) Ann 1927- . . . . . . **CLC 27**
See also CA 85-88; DLB 13

Jen, Gish . . . . **CLC 70**
See also Jen, Lillian

Jen, Lillian 1956(?)-
See Jen, Gish
See also CA 135

Jenkins, (John) Robin 1912- . . . . **CLC 52**
See also CA 1-4R; CANR 1; DLB 14

Kadohata, Cynthia . . . . **CLC 59**
See also CA 140

Kafka, Franz 1883-1924 . . . . **TCLC 2, 6, 13, 29, 47, 53; DA; SSC 5; WLC**
See also CA 105; 126; DLB 81; MTCW

Kahanovitsch, Pinkhes
See Der Nister

Kahn, Roger 1927- . . . . **CLC 30**
See also CA 25-28R; CANR 44; SATA 37

Kain, Saul
See Sassoon, Siegfried (Lorraine)

Kaiser, Georg 1878-1945 . . . . **TCLC 9**
See also CA 106; DLB 124

Kaletski, Alexander 1946- . . . . **CLC 39**
See also CA 118; 143

Kalidasa fl. c. 400- . . . . **CMLC 9**

Kallman, Chester (Simon) 1921-1975 . . . . **CLC 2**
See also CA 45-48; 53-56; CANR 3

Kaminsky, Melvin 1926-
See Brooks, Mel
See also CA 65-68; CANR 16

Kaminsky, Stuart M(elvin) 1934- . . . **CLC 59**
See also CA 73-76; CANR 29

Kane, Paul
See Simon, Paul

Kane, Wilson
See Bloch, Robert (Albert)

Kanin, Garson 1912-. . . . . **CLC 22**
See also AITN 1; CA 5-8R; CANR 7; DLB 7

Kaniuk, Yoram 1930- . . . . **CLC 19**
See also CA 134

Kant, Immanuel 1724-1804 . . . . . . **NCLC 27**
See also DLB 94

Kantor, MacKinlay 1904-1977 . . . . . . **CLC 7**
See also CA 61-64; 73-76; DLB 9, 102

Kaplan, David Michael 1946- . . . . . . **CLC 50**

Kaplan, James 1951- . . . . **CLC 59**
See also CA 135

Karageorge, Michael
See Anderson, Poul (William)

Karamzin, Nikolai Mikhailovich 1766-1826 . . . . **NCLC 3**

Karapanou, Margarita 1946- . . . . **CLC 13**
See also CA 101

Karinthy, Frigyes 1887-1938 . . . . . . **TCLC 47**

Karl, Frederick R(obert) 1927- . . . . . **CLC 34**
See also CA 5-8R; CANR 3, 44

Kastel, Warren
See Silverberg, Robert

Kataev, Evgeny Petrovich 1903-1942
See Petrov, Evgeny
See also CA 120

Kataphusin
See Ruskin, John

Katz, Steve 1935- . . . . **CLC 47**
See also CA 25-28R; CAAS 14; CANR 12; DLBY 83

Kauffman, Janet 1945- . . . . **CLC 42**
See also CA 117; CANR 43; DLBY 86

Kaufman, Bob (Garnell) 1925-1986 . . . . **CLC 49**
See also BW 1; CA 41-44R; 118; CANR 22; DLB 16, 41

Kaufman, George S. 1889-1961 . . . . . **CLC 38**
See also CA 108; 93-96; DLB 7

Kaufman, Sue . . . . **CLC 3, 8**
See also Barondess, Sue K(aufman)

Kavafis, Konstantinos Petrou 1863-1933
See Cavafy, C(onstantine) P(eter)
See also CA 104

Kavan, Anna 1901-1968 . . . . . . **CLC 5, 13, 82**
See also CA 5-8R; CANR 6; MTCW

Kavanagh, Dan
See Barnes, Julian

Kavanagh, Patrick (Joseph) 1904-1967 . . . . **CLC 22**
See also CA 123; 25-28R; DLB 15, 20; MTCW

Kawabata, Yasunari 1899-1972 . . . . . **CLC 2, 5, 9, 18; SSC 17**
See also CA 93-96; 33-36R

Kaye, M(ary) M(argaret) 1909- . . . . . **CLC 28**
See also CA 89-92; CANR 24; MTCW; SATA 62

Kaye, Mollie
See Kaye, M(ary) M(argaret)

Kaye-Smith, Sheila 1887-1956. . . . . **TCLC 20**
See also CA 118; DLB 36

Kaymor, Patrice Maguilene
See Senghor, Leopold Sedar

Kazan, Elia 1909- . . . . **CLC 6, 16, 63**
See also CA 21-24R; CANR 32

Kazantzakis, Nikos 1883(?)-1957 . . . . **TCLC 2, 5, 33**
See also CA 105; 132; MTCW

Kazin, Alfred 1915- . . . . **CLC 34, 38**
See also CA 1-4R; CAAS 7; CANR 1, 45; DLB 67

Keane, Mary Nesta (Skrine) 1904-
See Keane, Molly
See also CA 108; 114

Keane, Molly . . . . **CLC 31**
See also Keane, Mary Nesta (Skrine)

Keates, Jonathan 19(?)- . . . . **CLC 34**

Keaton, Buster 1895-1966 . . . . **CLC 20**

Keats, John 1795-1821 . . . **NCLC 8; DA; PC 1; WLC**
See also CDBLB 1789-1832; DLB 96, 110

Keene, Donald 1922- . . . . **CLC 34**
See also CA 1-4R; CANR 5

Keillor, Garrison . . . . **CLC 40**
See also Keillor, Gary (Edward)
See also AAYA 2; BEST 89:3; DLBY 87; SATA 58

Keillor, Gary (Edward) 1942-
See Keillor, Garrison
See also CA 111; 117; CANR 36; MTCW

Keith, Michael
See Hubbard, L(afayette) Ron(ald)

Keller, Gottfried 1819-1890. . . . . . . **NCLC 2**
See also DLB 129

Kellerman, Jonathan 1949- . . . . **CLC 44**
See also BEST 90:1; CA 106; CANR 29

Kelley, William Melvin 1937- . . . . . . **CLC 22**
See also BW 1; CA 77-80; CANR 27; DLB 33

Kellogg, Marjorie 1922- . . . . **CLC 2**
See also CA 81-84

Kellow, Kathleen
See Hibbert, Eleanor Alice Burford

Kelly, M(ilton) T(erry) 1947- . . . . **CLC 55**
See also CA 97-100; CANR 19, 43

Kelman, James 1946- . . . . **CLC 58, 86**

Kemal, Yashar 1923- . . . . **CLC 14, 29**
See also CA 89-92; CANR 44

Kemble, Fanny 1809-1893 . . . . **NCLC 18**
See also DLB 32

Kemelman, Harry 1908- . . . . **CLC 2**
See also AITN 1; CA 9-12R; CANR 6; DLB 28

Kempe, Margery 1373(?)-1440(?) . . . . . **LC 6**
See also DLB 146

Kempis, Thomas a 1380-1471 . . . . **LC 11**

Kendall, Henry 1839-1882. . . . . . . **NCLC 12**

Keneally, Thomas (Michael) 1935- . . . . . . **CLC 5, 8, 10, 14, 19, 27, 43**
See also CA 85-88; CANR 10; MTCW

Kennedy, Adrienne (Lita) 1931- . . . . **CLC 66; BLC; DC 5**
See also BW 2; CA 103; CAAS 20; CABS 3; CANR 26; DLB 38

Kennedy, John Pendleton 1795-1870 . . . . **NCLC 2**
See also DLB 3

Kennedy, Joseph Charles 1929-
See Kennedy, X. J.
See also CA 1-4R; CANR 4, 30, 40; SATA 14

Kennedy, William 1928- . . . **CLC 6, 28, 34, 53**
See also AAYA 1; CA 85-88; CANR 14, 31; DLB 143; DLBY 85; MTCW; SATA 57

Kennedy, X. J. . . . . **CLC 8, 42**
See also Kennedy, Joseph Charles
See also CAAS 9; CLR 27; DLB 5

Kenny, Maurice (Francis) 1929- . . . . **CLC 87**
See also CA 144; NNAL

Kent, Kelvin
See Kuttner, Henry

Kenton, Maxwell
See Southern, Terry

Kenyon, Robert O.
See Kuttner, Henry

Kerouac, Jack . . . . . **CLC 1, 2, 3, 5, 14, 29, 61**
See also Kerouac, Jean-Louis Lebris de
See also CDALB 1941-1968; DLB 2, 16; DLBD 3

Kerouac, Jean-Louis Lebris de 1922-1969
See Kerouac, Jack
See also AITN 1; CA 5-8R; 25-28R; CANR 26; DA; MTCW; WLC

Kerr, Jean 1923- . . . . **CLC 22**
See also CA 5-8R; CANR 7

Kerr, M. E. . . . . **CLC 12, 35**
See also Meaker, Marijane (Agnes)
See also AAYA 2; CLR 29; SAAS 1

Kerr, Robert . . . . **CLC 55**

Kerrigan, (Thomas) Anthony 1918- . . . . **CLC 4, 6**
See also CA 49-52; CAAS 11; CANR 4

Kerry, Lois
See Duncan, Lois

Kesey, Ken (Elton) 1935- . . . . . . **CLC 1, 3, 6, 11, 46, 64; DA; WLC**
See also CA 1-4R; CANR 22, 38; CDALB 1968-1988; DLB 2, 16; MTCW; SATA 66

Kesselring, Joseph (Otto) 1902-1967 . . . . **CLC 45**

Kessler, Jascha (Frederick) 1929- . . . . **CLC 4**
See also CA 17-20R; CANR 8

Kettelkamp, Larry (Dale) 1933- . . . . **CLC 12**
See also CA 29-32R; CANR 16; SAAS 3; SATA 2

Keyber, Conny
See Fielding, Henry

Keyes, Daniel 1927- . . . . **CLC 80; DA**
See also CA 17-20R; CANR 10, 26; SATA 37

Khanshendel, Chiron
See Rose, Wendy

Khayyam, Omar 1048-1131 . . . . **CMLC 11; PC 8**

Kherdian, David 1931- . . . . **CLC 6, 9**
See also CA 21-24R; CAAS 2; CANR 39; CLR 24; JRDA; MAICYA; SATA 16, 74

Khlebnikov, Velimir . . . . **TCLC 20**
See also Khlebnikov, Viktor Vladimirovich

Khlebnikov, Viktor Vladimirovich 1885-1922
See Khlebnikov, Velimir
See also CA 117

Khodasevich, Vladislav (Felitsianovich) 1886-1939 . . . . **TCLC 15**
See also CA 115

Kielland, Alexander Lange 1849-1906 . . . . **TCLC 5**
See also CA 104

Kiely, Benedict 1919- . . . . **CLC 23, 43**
See also CA 1-4R; CANR 2; DLB 15

Kienzle, William X(avier) 1928- . . . . **CLC 25**
See also CA 93-96; CAAS 1; CANR 9, 31; MTCW

Kierkegaard, Soren 1813-1855 . . . . **NCLC 34**

Killens, John Oliver 1916-1987 . . . . . **CLC 10**
See also BW 2; CA 77-80; 123; CAAS 2; CANR 26; DLB 33

Killigrew, Anne 1660-1685 . . . . **LC 4**
See also DLB 131

Kim
See Simenon, Georges (Jacques Christian)

Kincaid, Jamaica 1949- . . . **CLC 43, 68; BLC**
See also AAYA 13; BW 2; CA 125; CANR 47

King, Francis (Henry) 1923- . . . . . **CLC 8, 53**
See also CA 1-4R; CANR 1, 33; DLB 15, 139; MTCW

King, Martin Luther, Jr. 1929-1968 . . . . **CLC 83; BLC; DA**
See also BW 2; CA 25-28; CANR 27, 44; CAP 2; MTCW; SATA 14

King, Stephen (Edwin) 1947- . . . . . . **CLC 12, 26, 37, 61; SSC 17**
See also AAYA 1; BEST 90:1; CA 61-64; CANR 1, 30; DLB 143; DLBY 80; JRDA; MTCW; SATA 9, 55

King, Steve
See King, Stephen (Edwin)

Kingman, Lee . . . . **CLC 17**
See also Natti, (Mary) Lee
See also SAAS 3; SATA 1, 67

Kingsley, Charles 1819-1875 . . . . . **NCLC 35**
See also DLB 21, 32; YABC 2

Kingsley, Sidney 1906- . . . . **CLC 44**
See also CA 85-88; DLB 7

Kingsolver, Barbara 1955- . . . . . . **CLC 55, 81**
See also CA 129; 134

Kingston, Maxine (Ting Ting) Hong 1940- . . . . **CLC 12, 19, 58**
See also AAYA 8; CA 69-72; CANR 13, 38; DLBY 80; MTCW; SATA 53

Kinnell, Galway 1927- . . . . **CLC 1, 2, 3, 5, 13, 29**
See also CA 9-12R; CANR 10, 34; DLB 5; DLBY 87; MTCW

Kinsella, Thomas 1928- . . . . **CLC 4, 19**
See also CA 17-20R; CANR 15; DLB 27; MTCW

Kinsella, W(illiam) P(atrick) 1935- . . . . **CLC 27, 43**
See also AAYA 7; CA 97-100; CAAS 7; CANR 21, 35; MTCW

Kipling, (Joseph) Rudyard 1865-1936 . . . . . . **TCLC 8, 17; DA; PC 3; SSC 5; WLC**
See also CA 105; 120; CANR 33; CDBLB 1890-1914; DLB 19, 34, 141; MAICYA; MTCW; YABC 2

Kirkup, James 1918- . . . . **CLC 1**
See also CA 1-4R; CAAS 4; CANR 2; DLB 27; SATA 12

Kirkwood, James 1930(?)-1989 . . . . . . **CLC 9**
See also AITN 2; CA 1-4R; 128; CANR 6, 40

Kis, Danilo 1935-1989 . . . . **CLC 57**
See also CA 109; 118; 129; MTCW

Kivi, Aleksis 1834-1872 . . . . **NCLC 30**

Kizer, Carolyn (Ashley) 1925- . . . . **CLC 15, 39, 80**
See also CA 65-68; CAAS 5; CANR 24; DLB 5

Klabund 1890-1928 . . . . **TCLC 44**
See also DLB 66

Klappert, Peter 1942- . . . . **CLC 57**
See also CA 33-36R; DLB 5

Klein, A(braham) M(oses) 1909-1972 . . . . **CLC 19**
See also CA 101; 37-40R; DLB 68

Klein, Norma 1938-1989 . . . . **CLC 30**
See also AAYA 2; CA 41-44R; 128; CANR 15, 37; CLR 2, 19; JRDA; MAICYA; SAAS 1; SATA 7, 57

Klein, T(heodore) E(ibon) D(onald) 1947- . . . . **CLC 34**
See also CA 119; CANR 44

Kleist, Heinrich von 1777-1811 . . . . **NCLC 2, 37**
See also DLB 90

Klima, Ivan 1931- . . . . **CLC 56**
See also CA 25-28R; CANR 17

Klimentov, Andrei Platonovich 1899-1951
See Platonov, Andrei
See also CA 108

Klinger, Friedrich Maximilian von 1752-1831 . . . . **NCLC 1**
See also DLB 94

Klopstock, Friedrich Gottlieb 1724-1803 . . . . **NCLC 11**
See also DLB 97

Knebel, Fletcher 1911-1993 . . . . **CLC 14**
See also AITN 1; CA 1-4R; 140; CAAS 3; CANR 1, 36; SATA 36; SATA-Obit 75

Knickerbocker, Diedrich
See Irving, Washington

Knight, Etheridge 1931-1991 . . . . **CLC 40; BLC**
See also BW 1; CA 21-24R; 133; CANR 23; DLB 41

Knight, Sarah Kemble 1666-1727 . . . . . **LC 7**
See also DLB 24

Knister, Raymond 1899-1932 . . . . . . **TCLC 56**
See also DLB 68

Knowles, John 1926- . . . . **CLC 1, 4, 10, 26; DA**
See also AAYA 10; CA 17-20R; CANR 40; CDALB 1968-1988; DLB 6; MTCW; SATA 8

Knox, Calvin M.
See Silverberg, Robert

Knye, Cassandra
See Disch, Thomas M(ichael)

Koch, C(hristopher) J(ohn) 1932- . . . **CLC 42**
See also CA 127

Koch, Christopher
See Koch, C(hristopher) J(ohn)

Koch, Kenneth 1925- . . . . **CLC 5, 8, 44**
See also CA 1-4R; CANR 6, 36; DLB 5; SATA 65

Kochanowski, Jan 1530-1584 . . . . **LC 10**

Kock, Charles Paul de 1794-1871 . . . . **NCLC 16**

Koda Shigeyuki 1867-1947
See Rohan, Koda
See also CA 121

Koestler, Arthur 1905-1983 . . . . **CLC 1, 3, 6, 8, 15, 33**
See also CA 1-4R; 109; CANR 1, 33; CDBLB 1945-1960; DLBY 83; MTCW

Kogawa, Joy Nozomi 1935- . . . . **CLC 78**
See also CA 101; CANR 19

Kohout, Pavel 1928- . . . . **CLC 13**
See also CA 45-48; CANR 3

Koizumi, Yakumo
See Hearn, (Patricio) Lafcadio (Tessima Carlos)

Kolmar, Gertrud 1894-1943 . . . . **TCLC 40**

Komunyakaa, Yusef 1947- . . . . **CLC 86**
See also DLB 120

Konrad, George
See Konrad, Gyoergy

Konrad, Gyoergy 1933- ...... **CLC 4, 10, 73**
See also CA 85-88

Konwicki, Tadeusz 1926-..... **CLC 8, 28, 54**
See also CA 101; CAAS 9; CANR 39; MTCW

Koontz, Dean R(ay) 1945-......... **CLC 78**
See also AAYA 9; BEST 89:3, 90:2; CA 108; CANR 19, 36; MTCW

Kopit, Arthur (Lee) 1937- .... **CLC 1, 18, 33**
See also AITN 1; CA 81-84; CABS 3; DLB 7; MTCW

Kops, Bernard 1926-.............. **CLC 4**
See also CA 5-8R; DLB 13

Kornbluth, C(yril) M. 1923-1958.... **TCLC 8**
See also CA 105; DLB 8

Korolenko, V. G.
See Korolenko, Vladimir Galaktionovich

Korolenko, Vladimir
See Korolenko, Vladimir Galaktionovich

Korolenko, Vladimir G.
See Korolenko, Vladimir Galaktionovich

Korolenko, Vladimir Galaktionovich 1853-1921 .... **TCLC 22**
See also CA 121

Kosinski, Jerzy (Nikodem) 1933-1991 .... **CLC 1, 2, 3, 6, 10, 15, 53, 70**
See also CA 17-20R; 134; CANR 9, 46; DLB 2; DLBY 82; MTCW

Kostelanetz, Richard (Cory) 1940- .. **CLC 28**
See also CA 13-16R; CAAS 8; CANR 38

Kostrowitzki, Wilhelm Apollinaris de 1880-1918
See Apollinaire, Guillaume
See also CA 104

Kotlowitz, Robert 1924-............ **CLC 4**
See also CA 33-36R; CANR 36

Kotzebue, August (Friedrich Ferdinand) von 1761-1819 .... **NCLC 25**
See also DLB 94

Kotzwinkle, William 1938- ... **CLC 5, 14, 35**
See also CA 45-48; CANR 3, 44; CLR 6; MAICYA; SATA 24, 70

Kozol, Jonathan 1936-............ **CLC 17**
See also CA 61-64; CANR 16, 45

Kozoll, Michael 1940(?)- .... **CLC 35**

Kramer, Kathryn 19(?)- .... **CLC 34**

Kramer, Larry 1935- .... **CLC 42**
See also CA 124; 126

Krasicki, Ignacy 1735-1801 .... **NCLC 8**

Krasinski, Zygmunt 1812-1859 .... **NCLC 4**

Kraus, Karl 1874-1936............ **TCLC 5**
See also CA 104; DLB 118

Kreve (Mickevicius), Vincas 1882-1954 .... **TCLC 27**

Kristeva, Julia 1941- .... **CLC 77**

Kristofferson, Kris 1936- .... **CLC 26**
See also CA 104

Krizanc, John 1956-.............. **CLC 57**

Krleza, Miroslav 1893-1981......... **CLC 8**
See also CA 97-100; 105; DLB 147

Kroetsch, Robert 1927- ...... **CLC 5, 23, 57**
See also CA 17-20R; CANR 8, 38; DLB 53; MTCW

Kroetz, Franz
See Kroetz, Franz Xaver

Kroetz, Franz Xaver 1946- .... **CLC 41**
See also CA 130

Kroker, Arthur 1945-............. **CLC 77**

Kropotkin, Peter (Aleksieevich) 1842-1921 .... **TCLC 36**
See also CA 119

Krotkov, Yuri 1917-.............. **CLC 19**
See also CA 102

Krumb
See Crumb, R(obert)

Krumgold, Joseph (Quincy) 1908-1980 .... **CLC 12**
See also CA 9-12R; 101; CANR 7; MAICYA; SATA 1, 48; SATA-Obit 23

Krumwitz
See Crumb, R(obert)

Krutch, Joseph Wood 1893-1970.... **CLC 24**
See also CA 1-4R; 25-28R; CANR 4; DLB 63

Krutzch, Gus
See Eliot, T(homas) S(tearns)

Krylov, Ivan Andreevich 1768(?)-1844 .... **NCLC 1**

Kubin, Alfred 1877-1959 .... **TCLC 23**
See also CA 112; DLB 81

Kubrick, Stanley 1928-............ **CLC 16**
See also CA 81-84; CANR 33; DLB 26

Kumin, Maxine (Winokur) 1925- .... **CLC 5, 13, 28**
See also AITN 2; CA 1-4R; CAAS 8; CANR 1, 21; DLB 5; MTCW; SATA 12

Kundera, Milan 1929- .... **CLC 4, 9, 19, 32, 68**
See also AAYA 2; CA 85-88; CANR 19; MTCW

Kunene, Mazisi (Raymond) 1930-... **CLC 85**
See also BW 1; CA 125; DLB 117

Kunitz, Stanley (Jasspon) 1905- .... **CLC 6, 11, 14**
See also CA 41-44R; CANR 26; DLB 48; MTCW

Kunze, Reiner 1933-.............. **CLC 10**
See also CA 93-96; DLB 75

Kuprin, Aleksandr Ivanovich 1870-1938 .... **TCLC 5**
See also CA 104

Kureishi, Hanif 1954(?)-........... **CLC 64**
See also CA 139

Kurosawa, Akira 1910-............ **CLC 16**
See also AAYA 11; CA 101; CANR 46

Kushner, Tony 1957(?)- .... **CLC 81**
See also CA 144

Kuttner, Henry 1915-1958........ **TCLC 10**
See also CA 107; DLB 8

Kuzma, Greg 1944-................ **CLC 7**
See also CA 33-36R

Kuzmin, Mikhail 1872(?)-1936 .... **TCLC 40**

Kyd, Thomas 1558-1594....... **LC 22; DC 3**
See also DLB 62

Kyprianos, Iossif
See Samarakis, Antonis

La Bruyere, Jean de 1645-1696...... **LC 17**

Lacan, Jacques (Marie Emile) 1901-1981 .... **CLC 75**
See also CA 121; 104

Laclos, Pierre Ambroise Francois Choderlos de 1741-1803 .... **NCLC 4**

Lacolere, Francois
See Aragon, Louis

La Colere, Francois
See Aragon, Louis

La Deshabilleuse
See Simenon, Georges (Jacques Christian)

Lady Gregory
See Gregory, Isabella Augusta (Persse)

Lady of Quality, A
See Bagnold, Enid

La Fayette, Marie (Madelaine Pioche de la Vergne Comtes 1634-1693....... **LC 2**

Lafayette, Rene
See Hubbard, L(afayette) Ron(ald)

Laforgue, Jules 1860-1887........ **NCLC 5**

Lagerkvist, Paer (Fabian) 1891-1974 .... **CLC 7, 10, 13, 54**
See also Lagerkvist, Par
See also CA 85-88; 49-52; MTCW

Lagerkvist, Par
See Lagerkvist, Paer (Fabian)
See also SSC 12

Lagerloef, Selma (Ottiliana Lovisa) 1858-1940 .... **TCLC 4, 36**
See also Lagerlof, Selma (Ottiliana Lovisa)
See also CA 108; SATA 15

Lagerlof, Selma (Ottiliana Lovisa)
See Lagerloef, Selma (Ottiliana Lovisa)
See also CLR 7; SATA 15

La Guma, (Justin) Alex(ander) 1925-1985 .... **CLC 19**
See also BW 1; CA 49-52; 118; CANR 25; DLB 117; MTCW

Laidlaw, A. K.
See Grieve, C(hristopher) M(urray)

Lainez, Manuel Mujica
See Mujica Lainez, Manuel
See also HW

Lamartine, Alphonse (Marie Louis Prat) de 1790-1869 .... **NCLC 11**

Lamb, Charles 1775-1834 .... **NCLC 10; DA; WLC**
See also CDBLB 1789-1832; DLB 93, 107; SATA 17

Lamb, Lady Caroline 1785-1828.. **NCLC 38**
See also DLB 116

Lamming, George (William) 1927- .... **CLC 2, 4, 66; BLC**
See also BW 2; CA 85-88; CANR 26; DLB 125; MTCW

L'Amour, Louis (Dearborn) 1908-1988 .... **CLC 25, 55**
See also AITN 2; BEST 89:2; CA 1-4R; 125; CANR 3, 25, 40; DLBY 80; MTCW

Lampedusa, Giuseppe (Tomasi) di ... **TCLC 13**
See also Tomasi di Lampedusa, Giuseppe

Lampman, Archibald 1861-1899 .. **NCLC 25**
See also DLB 92

Lancaster, Bruce 1896-1963........ **CLC 36**
See also CA 9-10; CAP 1; SATA 9

Landau, Mark Alexandrovich
See Aldanov, Mark (Alexandrovich)

Landau-Aldanov, Mark Alexandrovich
See Aldanov, Mark (Alexandrovich)

Landis, John 1950-............... **CLC 26**
See also CA 112; 122

Landolfi, Tommaso 1908-1979... **CLC 11, 49**
See also CA 127; 117

Landon, Letitia Elizabeth
1802-1838 .... **NCLC 15**
See also DLB 96

Landor, Walter Savage
1775-1864 .... **NCLC 14**
See also DLB 93, 107

Landwirth, Heinz 1927-
See Lind, Jakov
See also CA 9-12R; CANR 7

Lane, Patrick 1939- .... **CLC 25**
See also CA 97-100; DLB 53

Lang, Andrew 1844-1912 .... **TCLC 16**
See also CA 114; 137; DLB 98, 141; MAICYA; SATA 16

Lang, Fritz 1890-1976 .... **CLC 20**
See also CA 77-80; 69-72; CANR 30

Lange, John
See Crichton, (John) Michael

Langer, Elinor 1939- .... **CLC 34**
See also CA 121

Langland, William
1330(?)-1400(?) .... **LC 19; DA**
See also DLB 146

Langstaff, Launcelot
See Irving, Washington

Lanier, Sidney 1842-1881 .... **NCLC 6**
See also DLB 64; MAICYA; SATA 18

Lanyer, Aemilia 1569-1645 .... **LC 10**

Lao Tzu .... **CMLC 7**

Lapine, James (Elliot) 1949-....... **CLC 39**
See also CA 123; 130

Larbaud, Valery (Nicolas)
1881-1957 .... **TCLC 9**
See also CA 106

Lardner, Ring
See Lardner, Ring(gold) W(ilmer)

Lardner, Ring W., Jr.
See Lardner, Ring(gold) W(ilmer)

Lardner, Ring(gold) W(ilmer)
1885-1933 .... **TCLC 2, 14**
See also CA 104; 131; CDALB 1917-1929; DLB 11, 25, 86; MTCW

Laredo, Betty
See Codrescu, Andrei

Larkin, Maia
See Wojciechowska, Maia (Teresa)

Larkin, Philip (Arthur)
1922-1985 .... **CLC 3, 5, 8, 9, 13, 18, 33, 39, 64**
See also CA 5-8R; 117; CANR 24; CDBLB 1960 to Present; DLB 27; MTCW

Larra (y Sanchez de Castro), Mariano Jose de
1809-1837 .... **NCLC 17**

Larsen, Eric 1941- .... **CLC 55**
See also CA 132

Larsen, Nella 1891-1964 ..... **CLC 37; BLC**
See also BW 1; CA 125; DLB 51

Larson, Charles R(aymond) 1938-... **CLC 31**
See also CA 53-56; CANR 4

Lasker-Schueler, Else 1869-1945 .. **TCLC 57**
See also DLB 66, 124

Latham, Jean Lee 1902-........... **CLC 12**
See also AITN 1; CA 5-8R; CANR 7; MAICYA; SATA 2, 68

Latham, Mavis
See Clark, Mavis Thorpe

Lathen, Emma .... **CLC 2**
See also Hennissart, Martha; Latsis, Mary J(ane)

Lathrop, Francis
See Leiber, Fritz (Reuter, Jr.)

Latsis, Mary J(ane)
See Lathen, Emma
See also CA 85-88

Lattimore, Richmond (Alexander)
1906-1984 .... **CLC 3**
See also CA 1-4R; 112; CANR 1

Laughlin, James 1914-............ **CLC 49**
See also CA 21-24R; CANR 9, 45; DLB 48

Laurence, (Jean) Margaret (Wemyss)
1926-1987 .. **CLC 3, 6, 13, 50, 62; SSC 7**
See also CA 5-8R; 121; CANR 33; DLB 53; MTCW; SATA-Obit 50

Laurent, Antoine 1952- .... **CLC 50**

Lauscher, Hermann
See Hesse, Hermann

Lautreamont, Comte de
1846-1870 .... **NCLC 12; SSC 14**

Laverty, Donald
See Blish, James (Benjamin)

Lavin, Mary 1912-...... **CLC 4, 18; SSC 4**
See also CA 9-12R; CANR 33; DLB 15; MTCW

Lavond, Paul Dennis
See Kornbluth, C(yril) M.; Pohl, Frederik

Lawler, Raymond Evenor 1922- .... **CLC 58**
See also CA 103

Lawrence, D(avid) H(erbert Richards)
1885-1930 .... **TCLC 2, 9, 16, 33, 48; DA; SSC 4; WLC**
See also CA 104; 121; CDBLB 1914-1945; DLB 10, 19, 36, 98; MTCW

Lawrence, T(homas) E(dward)
1888-1935 .... **TCLC 18**
See also Dale, Colin
See also CA 115

Lawrence of Arabia
See Lawrence, T(homas) E(dward)

Lawson, Henry (Archibald Hertzberg)
1867-1922 .... **TCLC 27; SSC 18**
See also CA 120

Lawton, Dennis
See Faust, Frederick (Schiller)

Laxness, Halldor .... **CLC 25**
See also Gudjonsson, Halldor Kiljan

Layamon fl. c. 1200-............ **CMLC 10**
See also DLB 146

Laye, Camara 1928-1980 ... **CLC 4, 38; BLC**
See also BW 1; CA 85-88; 97-100; CANR 25; MTCW

Layton, Irving (Peter) 1912-..... **CLC 2, 15**
See also CA 1-4R; CANR 2, 33, 43; DLB 88; MTCW

Lazarus, Emma 1849-1887........ **NCLC 8**

Lazarus, Felix
See Cable, George Washington

Lazarus, Henry
See Slavitt, David R(ytman)

Lea, Joan
See Neufeld, John (Arthur)

Leacock, Stephen (Butler)
1869-1944 .... **TCLC 2**
See also CA 104; 141; DLB 92

Lear, Edward 1812-1888 .... **NCLC 3**
See also CLR 1; DLB 32; MAICYA; SATA 18

Lear, Norman (Milton) 1922- ...... **CLC 12**
See also CA 73-76

Leavis, F(rank) R(aymond)
1895-1978 .... **CLC 24**
See also CA 21-24R; 77-80; CANR 44; MTCW

Leavitt, David 1961-.............. **CLC 34**
See also CA 116; 122; DLB 130

Leblanc, Maurice (Marie Emile)
1864-1941 .... **TCLC 49**
See also CA 110

Lebowitz, Fran(ces Ann)
1951(?)-.................. **CLC 11, 36**
See also CA 81-84; CANR 14; MTCW

Lebrecht, Peter
See Tieck, (Johann) Ludwig

le Carre, John .... **CLC 3, 5, 9, 15, 28**
See also Cornwell, David (John Moore)
See also BEST 89:4; CDBLB 1960 to Present; DLB 87

Le Clezio, J(ean) M(arie) G(ustave)
1940- .... **CLC 31**
See also CA 116; 128; DLB 83

Leconte de Lisle, Charles-Marie-Rene
1818-1894 .... **NCLC 29**

Le Coq, Monsieur
See Simenon, Georges (Jacques Christian)

Leduc, Violette 1907-1972......... **CLC 22**
See also CA 13-14; 33-36R; CAP 1

Ledwidge, Francis 1887(?)-1917 ... **TCLC 23**
See also CA 123; DLB 20

Lee, Andrea 1953- .... **CLC 36; BLC**
See also BW 1; CA 125

Lee, Andrew
See Auchincloss, Louis (Stanton)

Lee, Don L. .... **CLC 2**
See also Madhubuti, Haki R.

Lee, George W(ashington)
1894-1976 .... **CLC 52; BLC**
See also BW 1; CA 125; DLB 51

Lewis, Janet 1899- . . . . **CLC 41**
See also Winters, Janet Lewis
See also CA 9-12R; CANR 29; CAP 1; DLBY 87

Lewis, Matthew Gregory 1775-1818 . . . . **NCLC 11**
See also DLB 39

Lewis, (Harry) Sinclair 1885-1951 . . . . . **TCLC 4, 13, 23, 39; DA; WLC**
See also CA 104; 133; CDALB 1917-1929; DLB 9, 102; DLBD 1; MTCW

Lewis, (Percy) Wyndham 1884(?)-1957 . . . . **TCLC 2, 9**
See also CA 104; DLB 15

Lewisohn, Ludwig 1883-1955. . . . . . **TCLC 19**
See also CA 107; DLB 4, 9, 28, 102

Lezama Lima, Jose 1910-1976 . . . **CLC 4, 10**
See also CA 77-80; DLB 113; HW

L'Heureux, John (Clarke) 1934- . . . . **CLC 52**
See also CA 13-16R; CANR 23, 45

Liddell, C. H.
See Kuttner, Henry

Lie, Jonas (Lauritz Idemil) 1833-1908(?) . . . . **TCLC 5**
See also CA 115

Lieber, Joel 1937-1971 . . . . **CLC 6**
See also CA 73-76; 29-32R

Lieber, Stanley Martin
See Lee, Stan

Lieberman, Laurence (James) 1935- . . . . **CLC 4, 36**
See also CA 17-20R; CANR 8, 36

Lieksman, Anders
See Haavikko, Paavo Juhani

Li Fei-kan 1904-
See Pa Chin
See also CA 105

Lifton, Robert Jay 1926- . . . . **CLC 67**
See also CA 17-20R; CANR 27; SATA 66

Lightfoot, Gordon 1938- . . . . **CLC 26**
See also CA 109

Lightman, Alan P. 1948- . . . . **CLC 81**
See also CA 141

Ligotti, Thomas 1953- . . . . **CLC 44; SSC 16**
See also CA 123

Liliencron, (Friedrich Adolf Axel) Detlev von 1844-1909 . . . . **TCLC 18**
See also CA 117

Lilly, William 1602-1681 . . . . **LC 27**

Lima, Jose Lezama
See Lezama Lima, Jose

Lima Barreto, Afonso Henrique de 1881-1922 . . . . **TCLC 23**
See also CA 117

Limonov, Eduard . . . . **CLC 67**

Lin, Frank
See Atherton, Gertrude (Franklin Horn)

Lincoln, Abraham 1809-1865. . . . . **NCLC 18**

Lind, Jakov . . . . **CLC 1, 2, 4, 27, 82**
See also Landwirth, Heinz
See also CAAS 4

Lindbergh, Anne (Spencer) Morrow 1906- . . . . **CLC 82**
See also CA 17-20R; CANR 16; MTCW; SATA 33

Lindsay, David 1878-1945 . . . . **TCLC 15**
See also CA 113

Lindsay, (Nicholas) Vachel 1879-1931 . . . . **TCLC 17; DA; WLC**
See also CA 114; 135; CDALB 1865-1917; DLB 54; SATA 40

Linke-Poot
See Doeblin, Alfred

Linney, Romulus 1930- . . . . **CLC 51**
See also CA 1-4R; CANR 40, 44

Linton, Eliza Lynn 1822-1898 . . . . **NCLC 41**
See also DLB 18

Li Po 701-763 . . . . **CMLC 2**

Lipsius, Justus 1547-1606 . . . . **LC 16**

Lipsyte, Robert (Michael) 1938- . . . . **CLC 21; DA**
See also AAYA 7; CA 17-20R; CANR 8; CLR 23; JRDA; MAICYA; SATA 5, 68

Lish, Gordon (Jay) 1934- . . **CLC 45; SSC 18**
See also CA 113; 117; DLB 130

Lispector, Clarice 1925-1977 . . . . **CLC 43**
See also CA 139; 116; DLB 113

Littell, Robert 1935(?)- . . . . **CLC 42**
See also CA 109; 112

Little, Malcolm 1925-1965
See Malcolm X
See also BW 1; CA 125; 111; DA; MTCW

Littlewit, Humphrey Gent.
See Lovecraft, H(oward) P(hillips)

Litwos
See Sienkiewicz, Henryk (Adam Alexander Pius)

Liu E 1857-1909 . . . . **TCLC 15**
See also CA 115

Lively, Penelope (Margaret) 1933- . . . . **CLC 32, 50**
See also CA 41-44R; CANR 29; CLR 7; DLB 14; JRDA; MAICYA; MTCW; SATA 7, 60

Livesay, Dorothy (Kathleen) 1909- . . . . **CLC 4, 15, 79**
See also AITN 2; CA 25-28R; CAAS 8; CANR 36; DLB 68; MTCW

Livy c. 59B.C.-c. 17 . . . . **CMLC 11**

Lizardi, Jose Joaquin Fernandez de 1776-1827 . . . . **NCLC 30**

Llewellyn, Richard
See Llewellyn Lloyd, Richard Dafydd Vivian
See also DLB 15

Llewellyn Lloyd, Richard Dafydd Vivian 1906-1983 . . . . **CLC 7, 80**
See also Llewellyn, Richard
See also CA 53-56; 111; CANR 7; SATA 11; SATA-Obit 37

Llosa, (Jorge) Mario (Pedro) Vargas
See Vargas Llosa, (Jorge) Mario (Pedro)

Lloyd Webber, Andrew 1948-
See Webber, Andrew Lloyd
See also AAYA 1; CA 116; SATA 56

Llull, Ramon c. 1235-c. 1316. . . . . **CMLC 12**

Locke, Alain (Le Roy) 1886-1954 . . . . **TCLC 43**
See also BW 1; CA 106; 124; DLB 51

Locke, John 1632-1704 . . . . **LC 7**
See also DLB 101

Locke-Elliott, Sumner
See Elliott, Sumner Locke

Lockhart, John Gibson 1794-1854 . . . . **NCLC 6**
See also DLB 110, 116, 144

Lodge, David (John) 1935- . . . . **CLC 36**
See also BEST 90:1; CA 17-20R; CANR 19; DLB 14; MTCW

Loennbohm, Armas Eino Leopold 1878-1926
See Leino, Eino
See also CA 123

Loewinsohn, Ron(ald William) 1937- . . . . **CLC 52**
See also CA 25-28R

Logan, Jake
See Smith, Martin Cruz

Logan, John (Burton) 1923-1987. . . . . **CLC 5**
See also CA 77-80; 124; CANR 45; DLB 5

Lo Kuan-chung 1330(?)-1400(?). . . . . . **LC 12**

Lombard, Nap
See Johnson, Pamela Hansford

London, Jack . . **TCLC 9, 15, 39; SSC 4; WLC**
See also London, John Griffith
See also AAYA 13; AITN 2; CDALB 1865-1917; DLB 8, 12, 78; SATA 18

London, John Griffith 1876-1916
See London, Jack
See also CA 110; 119; DA; JRDA; MAICYA; MTCW

Long, Emmett
See Leonard, Elmore (John, Jr.)

Longbaugh, Harry
See Goldman, William (W.)

Longfellow, Henry Wadsworth 1807-1882 . . . . **NCLC 2, 45; DA**
See also CDALB 1640-1865; DLB 1, 59; SATA 19

Longley, Michael 1939- . . . . **CLC 29**
See also CA 102; DLB 40

Longus fl. c. 2nd cent. - . . . . **CMLC 7**

Longway, A. Hugh
See Lang, Andrew

Lopate, Phillip 1943- . . . . **CLC 29**
See also CA 97-100; DLBY 80

Lopez Portillo (y Pacheco), Jose 1920- . . . . **CLC 46**
See also CA 129; HW

Lopez y Fuentes, Gregorio 1897(?)-1966 . . . . **CLC 32**
See also CA 131; HW

Lorca, Federico Garcia
See Garcia Lorca, Federico

Lord, Bette Bao 1938- . . . . **CLC 23**
See also BEST 90:3; CA 107; CANR 41; SATA 58

Lord Auch
See Bataille, Georges

Lord Byron
See Byron, George Gordon (Noel)

Lorde, Audre (Geraldine) 1934-1992 .... **CLC 18, 71; BLC; PC 12**
See also BW 1; CA 25-28R; 142; CANR 16, 26, 46; DLB 41; MTCW

Lord Jeffrey
See Jeffrey, Francis

Lorenzo, Heberto Padilla
See Padilla (Lorenzo), Heberto

Loris
See Hofmannsthal, Hugo von

Loti, Pierre .... **TCLC 11**
See also Viaud, (Louis Marie) Julien
See also DLB 123

Louie, David Wong 1954- .... **CLC 70**
See also CA 139

Louis, Father M.
See Merton, Thomas

Lovecraft, H(oward) P(hillips) 1890-1937 .... **TCLC 4, 22; SSC 3**
See also AAYA 14; CA 104; 133; MTCW

Lovelace, Earl 1935-.............. **CLC 51**
See also BW 2; CA 77-80; CANR 41; DLB 125; MTCW

Lovelace, Richard 1618-1657........ **LC 24**
See also DLB 131

Lowell, Amy 1874-1925 .... **TCLC 1, 8**
See also CA 104; DLB 54, 140

Lowell, James Russell 1819-1891 .. **NCLC 2**
See also CDALB 1640-1865; DLB 1, 11, 64, 79

Lowell, Robert (Traill Spence, Jr.) 1917-1977 ... **CLC 1, 2, 3, 4, 5, 8, 9, 11, 15, 37; DA; PC 3; WLC**
See also CA 9-12R; 73-76; CABS 2; CANR 26; DLB 5; MTCW

Lowndes, Marie Adelaide (Belloc) 1868-1947 .... **TCLC 12**
See also CA 107; DLB 70

Lowry, (Clarence) Malcolm 1909-1957 .... **TCLC 6, 40**
See also CA 105; 131; CDBLB 1945-1960; DLB 15; MTCW

Lowry, Mina Gertrude 1882-1966
See Loy, Mina
See also CA 113

Loxsmith, John
See Brunner, John (Kilian Houston)

Loy, Mina .... **CLC 28**
See also Lowry, Mina Gertrude
See also DLB 4, 54

Loyson-Bridet
See Schwob, (Mayer Andre) Marcel

Lucas, Craig 1951-................ **CLC 64**
See also CA 137

Lucas, George 1944-.............. **CLC 16**
See also AAYA 1; CA 77-80; CANR 30; SATA 56

Lucas, Hans
See Godard, Jean-Luc

Lucas, Victoria
See Plath, Sylvia

Ludlam, Charles 1943-1987 ..... **CLC 46, 50**
See also CA 85-88; 122

Ludlum, Robert 1927- .... **CLC 22, 43**
See also AAYA 10; BEST 89:1, 90:3; CA 33-36R; CANR 25, 41; DLBY 82; MTCW

Ludwig, Ken..................... **CLC 60**

Ludwig, Otto 1813-1865.......... **NCLC 4**
See also DLB 129

Lugones, Leopoldo 1874-1938 ..... **TCLC 15**
See also CA 116; 131; HW

Lu Hsun 1881-1936 .... **TCLC 3**

Lukacs, George .... **CLC 24**
See also Lukacs, Gyorgy (Szegeny von)

Lukacs, Gyorgy (Szegeny von) 1885-1971
See Lukacs, George
See also CA 101; 29-32R

Luke, Peter (Ambrose Cyprian) 1919- .... **CLC 38**
See also CA 81-84; DLB 13

Lunar, Dennis
See Mungo, Raymond

Lurie, Alison 1926-........ **CLC 4, 5, 18, 39**
See also CA 1-4R; CANR 2, 17; DLB 2; MTCW; SATA 46

Lustig, Arnost 1926-.............. **CLC 56**
See also AAYA 3; CA 69-72; CANR 47; SATA 56

Luther, Martin 1483-1546 .... **LC 9**

Luzi, Mario 1914-................ **CLC 13**
See also CA 61-64; CANR 9; DLB 128

Lynch, B. Suarez
See Bioy Casares, Adolfo; Borges, Jorge Luis

Lynch, David (K.) 1946-........... **CLC 66**
See also CA 124; 129

Lynch, James
See Andreyev, Leonid (Nikolaevich)

Lynch Davis, B.
See Bioy Casares, Adolfo; Borges, Jorge Luis

Lyndsay, Sir David 1490-1555 ...... **LC 20**

Lynn, Kenneth S(chuyler) 1923-.... **CLC 50**
See also CA 1-4R; CANR 3, 27

Lynx
See West, Rebecca

Lyons, Marcus
See Blish, James (Benjamin)

Lyre, Pinchbeck
See Sassoon, Siegfried (Lorraine)

Lytle, Andrew (Nelson) 1902-...... **CLC 22**
See also CA 9-12R; DLB 6

Lyttelton, George 1709-1773........ **LC 10**

Maas, Peter 1929- .... **CLC 29**
See also CA 93-96

Macaulay, Rose 1881-1958 ..... **TCLC 7, 44**
See also CA 104; DLB 36

Macaulay, Thomas Babington 1800-1859 .... **NCLC 42**
See also CDBLB 1832-1890; DLB 32, 55

MacBeth, George (Mann) 1932-1992 .... **CLC 2, 5, 9**
See also CA 25-28R; 136; DLB 40; MTCW; SATA 4; SATA-Obit 70

MacCaig, Norman (Alexander) 1910- .... **CLC 36**
See also CA 9-12R; CANR 3, 34; DLB 27

MacCarthy, (Sir Charles Otto) Desmond 1877-1952 .... **TCLC 36**

MacDiarmid, Hugh .... **CLC 2, 4, 11, 19, 63; PC 9**
See also Grieve, C(hristopher) M(urray)
See also CDBLB 1945-1960; DLB 20

MacDonald, Anson
See Heinlein, Robert A(nson)

Macdonald, Cynthia 1928-...... **CLC 13, 19**
See also CA 49-52; CANR 4, 44; DLB 105

MacDonald, George 1824-1905..... **TCLC 9**
See also CA 106; 137; DLB 18; MAICYA; SATA 33

Macdonald, John
See Millar, Kenneth

MacDonald, John D(ann) 1916-1986 .... **CLC 3, 27, 44**
See also CA 1-4R; 121; CANR 1, 19; DLB 8; DLBY 86; MTCW

Macdonald, John Ross
See Millar, Kenneth

Macdonald, Ross..... **CLC 1, 2, 3, 14, 34, 41**
See also Millar, Kenneth
See also DLBD 6

MacDougal, John
See Blish, James (Benjamin)

MacEwen, Gwendolyn (Margaret) 1941-1987 .... **CLC 13, 55**
See also CA 9-12R; 124; CANR 7, 22; DLB 53; SATA 50; SATA-Obit 55

Macha, Karel Hynek 1810-1846 .. **NCLC 46**

Machado (y Ruiz), Antonio 1875-1939 .... **TCLC 3**
See also CA 104; DLB 108

Machado de Assis, Joaquim Maria 1839-1908 .... **TCLC 10; BLC**
See also CA 107

Machen, Arthur................... **TCLC 4**
See also Jones, Arthur Llewellyn
See also DLB 36

Machiavelli, Niccolo 1469-1527 .. **LC 8; DA**

MacInnes, Colin 1914-1976...... **CLC 4, 23**
See also CA 69-72; 65-68; CANR 21; DLB 14; MTCW

MacInnes, Helen (Clark) 1907-1985 .... **CLC 27, 39**
See also CA 1-4R; 117; CANR 1, 28; DLB 87; MTCW; SATA 22; SATA-Obit 44

Mackay, Mary 1855-1924
See Corelli, Marie
See also CA 118

Mackenzie, Compton (Edward Montague) 1883-1972 .... **CLC 18**
See also CA 21-22; 37-40R; CAP 2; DLB 34, 100

Mackenzie, Henry 1745-1831 .... **NCLC 41**
See also DLB 39

Mackintosh, Elizabeth 1896(?)-1952
See Tey, Josephine
See also CA 110

MacLaren, James
See Grieve, C(hristopher) M(urray)

Mac Laverty, Bernard 1942- . . . . **CLC 31**
See also CA 116; 118; CANR 43

MacLean, Alistair (Stuart)
1922-1987 . . . . **CLC 3, 13, 50, 63**
See also CA 57-60; 121; CANR 28; MTCW; SATA 23; SATA-Obit 50

Maclean, Norman (Fitzroy)
1902-1990 . . . . **CLC 78; SSC 13**
See also CA 102; 132

MacLeish, Archibald
1892-1982 . . . . **CLC 3, 8, 14, 68**
See also CA 9-12R; 106; CANR 33; DLB 4, 7, 45; DLBY 82; MTCW

MacLennan, (John) Hugh
1907-1990 . . . . **CLC 2, 14**
See also CA 5-8R; 142; CANR 33; DLB 68; MTCW

MacLeod, Alistair 1936- . . . . **CLC 56**
See also CA 123; DLB 60

MacNeice, (Frederick) Louis
1907-1963 . . . . **CLC 1, 4, 10, 53**
See also CA 85-88; DLB 10, 20; MTCW

MacNeill, Dand
See Fraser, George MacDonald

Macpherson, (Jean) Jay 1931- . . . . . . **CLC 14**
See also CA 5-8R; DLB 53

MacShane, Frank 1927- . . . . **CLC 39**
See also CA 9-12R; CANR 3, 33; DLB 111

Macumber, Mari
See Sandoz, Mari(e Susette)

Madach, Imre 1823-1864 . . . . **NCLC 19**

Madden, (Jerry) David 1933- . . . . **CLC 5, 15**
See also CA 1-4R; CAAS 3; CANR 4, 45; DLB 6; MTCW

Maddern, Al(an)
See Ellison, Harlan (Jay)

Madhubuti, Haki R.
1942- . . . . **CLC 6, 73; BLC; PC 5**
See also Lee, Don L.
See also BW 2; CA 73-76; CANR 24; DLB 5, 41; DLBD 8

Maepenn, Hugh
See Kuttner, Henry

Maepenn, K. H.
See Kuttner, Henry

Maeterlinck, Maurice 1862-1949 . . . **TCLC 3**
See also CA 104; 136; SATA 66

Maginn, William 1794-1842 . . . . **NCLC 8**
See also DLB 110

Mahapatra, Jayanta 1928- . . . . **CLC 33**
See also CA 73-76; CAAS 9; CANR 15, 33

Mahfouz, Naguib (Abdel Aziz Al-Sabilgi)
1911(?)-
See Mahfuz, Najib
See also BEST 89:2; CA 128; MTCW

Mahfuz, Najib . . . . **CLC 52, 55**
See also Mahfouz, Naguib (Abdel Aziz Al-Sabilgi)
See also DLBY 88

Mahon, Derek 1941- . . . . **CLC 27**
See also CA 113; 128; DLB 40

Mailer, Norman
1923- . . . . . . **CLC 1, 2, 3, 4, 5, 8, 11, 14, 28, 39, 74; DA**
See also AITN 2; CA 9-12R; CABS 1; CANR 28; CDALB 1968-1988; DLB 2, 16, 28; DLBD 3; DLBY 80, 83; MTCW

Maillet, Antonine 1929- . . . . **CLC 54**
See also CA 115; 120; CANR 46; DLB 60

Mais, Roger 1905-1955 . . . . **TCLC 8**
See also BW 1; CA 105; 124; DLB 125; MTCW

Maistre, Joseph de 1753-1821 . . . . **NCLC 37**

Maitland, Sara (Louise) 1950- . . . . . . **CLC 49**
See also CA 69-72; CANR 13

Major, Clarence
1936- . . . . **CLC 3, 19, 48; BLC**
See also BW 2; CA 21-24R; CAAS 6; CANR 13, 25; DLB 33

Major, Kevin (Gerald) 1949- . . . . **CLC 26**
See also CA 97-100; CANR 21, 38; CLR 11; DLB 60; JRDA; MAICYA; SATA 32

Maki, James
See Ozu, Yasujiro

Malabaila, Damiano
See Levi, Primo

Malamud, Bernard
1914-1986 . . . . . . **CLC 1, 2, 3, 5, 8, 9, 11, 18, 27, 44, 78, 85; DA; SSC 15; WLC**
See also CA 5-8R; 118; CABS 1; CANR 28; CDALB 1941-1968; DLB 2, 28; DLBY 80, 86; MTCW

Malaparte, Curzio 1898-1957 . . . . . **TCLC 52**

Malcolm, Dan
See Silverberg, Robert

Malcolm X . . . . **CLC 82; BLC**
See also Little, Malcolm

Malherbe, Francois de 1555-1628 . . . . . **LC 5**

Mallarme, Stephane
1842-1898 . . . . **NCLC 4, 41; PC 4**

Mallet-Joris, Francoise 1930- . . . . . . **CLC 11**
See also CA 65-68; CANR 17; DLB 83

Malley, Ern
See McAuley, James Phillip

Mallowan, Agatha Christie
See Christie, Agatha (Mary Clarissa)

Maloff, Saul 1922- . . . . **CLC 5**
See also CA 33-36R

Malone, Louis
See MacNeice, (Frederick) Louis

Malone, Michael (Christopher)
1942- . . . . **CLC 43**
See also CA 77-80; CANR 14, 32

Malory, (Sir) Thomas
1410(?)-1471(?) . . . . **LC 11; DA**
See also CDBLB Before 1660; DLB 146; SATA 59; SATA-Brief 33

Malouf, (George Joseph) David
1934- . . . . **CLC 28, 86**
See also CA 124

Malraux, (Georges-)Andre
1901-1976 . . . . . . **CLC 1, 4, 9, 13, 15, 57**
See also CA 21-22; 69-72; CANR 34; CAP 2; DLB 72; MTCW

Malzberg, Barry N(athaniel) 1939- . . . **CLC 7**
See also CA 61-64; CAAS 4; CANR 16; DLB 8

Mamet, David (Alan)
1947- . . . . **CLC 9, 15, 34, 46; DC 4**
See also AAYA 3; CA 81-84; CABS 3; CANR 15, 41; DLB 7; MTCW

Mamoulian, Rouben (Zachary)
1897-1987 . . . . **CLC 16**
See also CA 25-28R; 124

Mandelstam, Osip (Emilievich)
1891(?)-1938(?) . . . . **TCLC 2, 6**
See also CA 104

Mander, (Mary) Jane 1877-1949 . . . **TCLC 31**

Mandiargues, Andre Pieyre de . . . . **CLC 41**
See also Pieyre de Mandiargues, Andre
See also DLB 83

Mandrake, Ethel Belle
See Thurman, Wallace (Henry)

Mangan, James Clarence
1803-1849 . . . . **NCLC 27**

Maniere, J.-E.
See Giraudoux, (Hippolyte) Jean

Manley, (Mary) Delariviere
1672(?)-1724 . . . . **LC 1**
See also DLB 39, 80

Mann, Abel
See Creasey, John

Mann, (Luiz) Heinrich 1871-1950 . . . **TCLC 9**
See also CA 106; DLB 66

Mann, (Paul) Thomas
1875-1955 . . . . **TCLC 2, 8, 14, 21, 35, 44; DA; SSC 5; WLC**
See also CA 104; 128; DLB 66; MTCW

Manning, David
See Faust, Frederick (Schiller)

Manning, Frederic 1887(?)-1935 . . . **TCLC 25**
See also CA 124

Manning, Olivia 1915-1980 . . . . . . **CLC 5, 19**
See also CA 5-8R; 101; CANR 29; MTCW

Mano, D. Keith 1942- . . . . **CLC 2, 10**
See also CA 25-28R; CAAS 6; CANR 26; DLB 6

Mansfield, Katherine
. . . . **TCLC 2, 8, 39; SSC 9; WLC**
See also Beauchamp, Kathleen Mansfield

Manso, Peter 1940- . . . . **CLC 39**
See also CA 29-32R; CANR 44

Mantecon, Juan Jimenez
See Jimenez (Mantecon), Juan Ramon

Manton, Peter
See Creasey, John

Man Without a Spleen, A
See Chekhov, Anton (Pavlovich)

Manzoni, Alessandro 1785-1873 . . **NCLC 29**

Mapu, Abraham (ben Jekutiel)
1808-1867 . . . . **NCLC 18**

Mara, Sally
See Queneau, Raymond

Marat, Jean Paul 1743-1793 . . . . **LC 10**

Marcel, Gabriel Honore 1889-1973 .... **CLC 15**
See also CA 102; 45-48; MTCW

Marchbanks, Samuel
See Davies, (William) Robertson

Marchi, Giacomo
See Bassani, Giorgio

Margulies, Donald .... **CLC 76**

Marie de France c. 12th cent. -.... **CMLC 8**

Marie de l'Incarnation 1599-1672.... **LC 10**

Mariner, Scott
See Pohl, Frederik

Marinetti, Filippo Tommaso 1876-1944 .... **TCLC 10**
See also CA 107; DLB 114

Marivaux, Pierre Carlet de Chamblain de 1688-1763 .... **LC 4**

Markandaya, Kamala .... **CLC 8, 38**
See also Taylor, Kamala (Purnaiya)

Markfield, Wallace 1926-........... **CLC 8**
See also CA 69-72; CAAS 3; DLB 2, 28

Markham, Edwin 1852-1940 ...... **TCLC 47**
See also DLB 54

Markham, Robert
See Amis, Kingsley (William)

Marks, J
See Highwater, Jamake (Mamake)

Marks-Highwater, J
See Highwater, Jamake (Mamake)

Markson, David M(errill) 1927- .... **CLC 67**
See also CA 49-52; CANR 1

Marley, Bob .... **CLC 17**
See also Marley, Robert Nesta

Marley, Robert Nesta 1945-1981
See Marley, Bob
See also CA 107; 103

Marlowe, Christopher 1564-1593 ..... **LC 22; DA; DC 1; WLC**
See also CDBLB Before 1660; DLB 62

Marmontel, Jean-Francois 1723-1799 .... **LC 2**

Marquand, John P(hillips) 1893-1960 .... **CLC 2, 10**
See also CA 85-88; DLB 9, 102

Marquez, Gabriel (Jose) Garcia
See Garcia Marquez, Gabriel (Jose)

Marquis, Don(ald Robert Perry) 1878-1937 .... **TCLC 7**
See also CA 104; DLB 11, 25

Marric, J. J.
See Creasey, John

Marrow, Bernard
See Moore, Brian

Marryat, Frederick 1792-1848 .... **NCLC 3**
See also DLB 21

Marsden, James
See Creasey, John

Marsh, (Edith) Ngaio 1899-1982 .... **CLC 7, 53**
See also CA 9-12R; CANR 6; DLB 77; MTCW

Marshall, Garry 1934- .... **CLC 17**
See also AAYA 3; CA 111; SATA 60

Marshall, Paule 1929- .... **CLC 27, 72; BLC; SSC 3**
See also BW 2; CA 77-80; CANR 25; DLB 33; MTCW

Marsten, Richard
See Hunter, Evan

Martha, Henry
See Harris, Mark

Martial c. 40-c. 104 .... **PC 10**

Martin, Ken
See Hubbard, L(afayette) Ron(ald)

Martin, Richard
See Creasey, John

Martin, Steve 1945- .... **CLC 30**
See also CA 97-100; CANR 30; MTCW

Martin, Violet Florence 1862-1915 .... **TCLC 51**

Martin, Webber
See Silverberg, Robert

Martindale, Patrick Victor
See White, Patrick (Victor Martindale)

Martin du Gard, Roger 1881-1958 .... **TCLC 24**
See also CA 118; DLB 65

Martineau, Harriet 1802-1876.... **NCLC 26**
See also DLB 21, 55; YABC 2

Martines, Julia
See O'Faolain, Julia

Martinez, Jacinto Benavente y
See Benavente (y Martinez), Jacinto

Martinez Ruiz, Jose 1873-1967
See Azorin; Ruiz, Jose Martinez
See also CA 93-96; HW

Martinez Sierra, Gregorio 1881-1947 .... **TCLC 6**
See also CA 115

Martinez Sierra, Maria (de la O'LeJarraga) 1874-1974 .... **TCLC 6**
See also CA 115

Martinsen, Martin
See Follett, Ken(neth Martin)

Martinson, Harry (Edmund) 1904-1978 .... **CLC 14**
See also CA 77-80; CANR 34

Marut, Ret
See Traven, B.

Marut, Robert
See Traven, B.

Marvell, Andrew 1621-1678 ..... **LC 4; DA; PC 10; WLC**
See also CDBLB 1660-1789; DLB 131

Marx, Karl (Heinrich) 1818-1883 .... **NCLC 17**
See also DLB 129

Masaoka Shiki .... **TCLC 18**
See also Masaoka Tsunenori

Masaoka Tsunenori 1867-1902
See Masaoka Shiki
See also CA 117

Masefield, John (Edward) 1878-1967 .... **CLC 11, 47**
See also CA 19-20; 25-28R; CANR 33; CAP 2; CDBLB 1890-1914; DLB 10, 19; MTCW; SATA 19

Maso, Carole 19(?)- .... **CLC 44**

Mason, Bobbie Ann 1940- .... **CLC 28, 43, 82; SSC 4**
See also AAYA 5; CA 53-56; CANR 11, 31; DLBY 87; MTCW

Mason, Ernst
See Pohl, Frederik

Mason, Lee W.
See Malzberg, Barry N(athaniel)

Mason, Nick 1945- .... **CLC 35**

Mason, Tally
See Derleth, August (William)

Mass, William
See Gibson, William

Masters, Edgar Lee 1868-1950 ...... **TCLC 2, 25; DA; PC 1**
See also CA 104; 133; CDALB 1865-1917; DLB 54; MTCW

Masters, Hilary 1928- .... **CLC 48**
See also CA 25-28R; CANR 13, 47

Mastrosimone, William 19(?)- ...... **CLC 36**

Mathe, Albert
See Camus, Albert

Matheson, Richard Burton 1926- ... **CLC 37**
See also CA 97-100; DLB 8, 44

Mathews, Harry 1930- .... **CLC 6, 52**
See also CA 21-24R; CAAS 6; CANR 18, 40

Mathews, John Joseph 1894-1979... **CLC 84**
See also CA 19-20; 142; CANR 45; CAP 2; NNAL

Mathias, Roland (Glyn) 1915- ...... **CLC 45**
See also CA 97-100; CANR 19, 41; DLB 27

Matsuo Basho 1644-1694............ **PC 3**

Mattheson, Rodney
See Creasey, John

Matthews, Greg 1949- .... **CLC 45**
See also CA 135

Matthews, William 1942- .... **CLC 40**
See also CA 29-32R; CAAS 18; CANR 12; DLB 5

Matthias, John (Edward) 1941- ...... **CLC 9**
See also CA 33-36R

Matthiessen, Peter 1927- .... **CLC 5, 7, 11, 32, 64**
See also AAYA 6; BEST 90:4; CA 9-12R; CANR 21; DLB 6; MTCW; SATA 27

Maturin, Charles Robert 1780(?)-1824 .... **NCLC 6**

Matute (Ausejo), Ana Maria 1925- .... **CLC 11**
See also CA 89-92; MTCW

Maugham, W. S.
See Maugham, W(illiam) Somerset

Maugham, W(illiam) Somerset 1874-1965 ...... **CLC 1, 11, 15, 67; DA; SSC 8; WLC**
See also CA 5-8R; 25-28R; CANR 40; CDBLB 1914-1945; DLB 10, 36, 77, 100; MTCW; SATA 54

Maugham, William Somerset
See Maugham, W(illiam) Somerset

Maupassant, (Henri Rene Albert) Guy de 1850-1893 .... **NCLC 1, 42; DA; SSC 1; WLC**
See also DLB 123

Maurhut, Richard
See Traven, B.

Mauriac, Claude 1914- .... **CLC 9**
See also CA 89-92; DLB 83

Mauriac, Francois (Charles) 1885-1970 .... **CLC 4, 9, 56**
See also CA 25-28; CAP 2; DLB 65; MTCW

Mavor, Osborne Henry 1888-1951
See Bridie, James
See also CA 104

Maxwell, William (Keepers, Jr.) 1908- .... **CLC 19**
See also CA 93-96; DLBY 80

May, Elaine 1932- .... **CLC 16**
See also CA 124; 142; DLB 44

Mayakovski, Vladimir (Vladimirovich) 1893-1930 .... **TCLC 4, 18**
See also CA 104

Mayhew, Henry 1812-1887 ...... **NCLC 31**
See also DLB 18, 55

Maynard, Joyce 1953- .... **CLC 23**
See also CA 111; 129

Mayne, William (James Carter) 1928- .... **CLC 12**
See also CA 9-12R; CANR 37; CLR 25; JRDA; MAICYA; SAAS 11; SATA 6, 68

Mayo, Jim
See L'Amour, Louis (Dearborn)

Maysles, Albert 1926- .... **CLC 16**
See also CA 29-32R

Maysles, David 1932- .... **CLC 16**

Mazer, Norma Fox 1931- .... **CLC 26**
See also AAYA 5; CA 69-72; CANR 12, 32; CLR 23; JRDA; MAICYA; SAAS 1; SATA 24, 67

Mazzini, Guiseppe 1805-1872 .... **NCLC 34**

McAuley, James Phillip 1917-1976 .... **CLC 45**
See also CA 97-100

McBain, Ed
See Hunter, Evan

McBrien, William Augustine 1930- .... **CLC 44**
See also CA 107

McCaffrey, Anne (Inez) 1926- ...... **CLC 17**
See also AAYA 6; AITN 2; BEST 89:2; CA 25-28R; CANR 15, 35; DLB 8; JRDA; MAICYA; MTCW; SAAS 11; SATA 8, 70

McCall, Nathan 1955(?)- .... **CLC 86**
See also CA 146

McCann, Arthur
See Campbell, John W(ood, Jr.)

McCann, Edson
See Pohl, Frederik

McCarthy, Charles, Jr. 1933-
See McCarthy, Cormac
See also CANR 42

McCarthy, Cormac 1933- ..... **CLC 4, 57, 59**
See also McCarthy, Charles, Jr.
See also DLB 6, 143

McCarthy, Mary (Therese) 1912-1989 ... **CLC 1, 3, 5, 14, 24, 39, 59**
See also CA 5-8R; 129; CANR 16; DLB 2; DLBY 81; MTCW

McCartney, (James) Paul 1942- .... **CLC 12, 35**

McCauley, Stephen (D.) 1955- ..... **CLC 50**
See also CA 141

McClure, Michael (Thomas) 1932- .... **CLC 6, 10**
See also CA 21-24R; CANR 17, 46; DLB 16

McCorkle, Jill (Collins) 1958- ...... **CLC 51**
See also CA 121; DLBY 87

McCourt, James 1941- .... **CLC 5**
See also CA 57-60

McCoy, Horace (Stanley) 1897-1955 .... **TCLC 28**
See also CA 108; DLB 9

McCrae, John 1872-1918 .... **TCLC 12**
See also CA 109; DLB 92

McCreigh, James
See Pohl, Frederik

McCullers, (Lula) Carson (Smith) 1917-1967 .... **CLC 1, 4, 10, 12, 48; DA; SSC 9; WLC**
See also CA 5-8R; 25-28R; CABS 1, 3; CANR 18; CDALB 1941-1968; DLB 2, 7; MTCW; SATA 27

McCulloch, John Tyler
See Burroughs, Edgar Rice

McCullough, Colleen 1938(?)- ...... **CLC 27**
See also CA 81-84; CANR 17, 46; MTCW

McElroy, Joseph 1930- .... **CLC 5, 47**
See also CA 17-20R

McEwan, Ian (Russell) 1948- ... **CLC 13, 66**
See also BEST 90:4; CA 61-64; CANR 14, 41; DLB 14; MTCW

McFadden, David 1940- .... **CLC 48**
See also CA 104; DLB 60

McFarland, Dennis 1950- .... **CLC 65**

McGahern, John 1934- .... **CLC 5, 9, 48; SSC 17**
See also CA 17-20R; CANR 29; DLB 14; MTCW

McGinley, Patrick (Anthony) 1937- .... **CLC 41**
See also CA 120; 127

McGinley, Phyllis 1905-1978 ...... **CLC 14**
See also CA 9-12R; 77-80; CANR 19; DLB 11, 48; SATA 2, 44; SATA-Obit 24

McGinniss, Joe 1942- .... **CLC 32**
See also AITN 2; BEST 89:2; CA 25-28R; CANR 26

McGivern, Maureen Daly
See Daly, Maureen

McGrath, Patrick 1950- .... **CLC 55**
See also CA 136

McGrath, Thomas (Matthew) 1916-1990 .... **CLC 28, 59**
See also CA 9-12R; 132; CANR 6, 33; MTCW; SATA 41; SATA-Obit 66

McGuane, Thomas (Francis III) 1939- .... **CLC 3, 7, 18, 45**
See also AITN 2; CA 49-52; CANR 5, 24; DLB 2; DLBY 80; MTCW

McGuckian, Medbh 1950- .... **CLC 48**
See also CA 143; DLB 40

McHale, Tom 1942(?)-1982 .... **CLC 3, 5**
See also AITN 1; CA 77-80; 106

McIlvanney, William 1936- .... **CLC 42**
See also CA 25-28R; DLB 14

McIlwraith, Maureen Mollie Hunter
See Hunter, Mollie
See also SATA 2

McInerney, Jay 1955- .... **CLC 34**
See also CA 116; 123; CANR 45

McIntyre, Vonda N(eel) 1948- ..... **CLC 18**
See also CA 81-84; CANR 17, 34; MTCW

McKay, Claude ..... **TCLC 7, 41; BLC; PC 2**
See also McKay, Festus Claudius
See also DLB 4, 45, 51, 117

McKay, Festus Claudius 1889-1948
See McKay, Claude
See also BW 1; CA 104; 124; DA; MTCW; WLC

McKuen, Rod 1933- .... **CLC 1, 3**
See also AITN 1; CA 41-44R; CANR 40

McLoughlin, R. B.
See Mencken, H(enry) L(ouis)

McLuhan, (Herbert) Marshall 1911-1980 .... **CLC 37, 83**
See also CA 9-12R; 102; CANR 12, 34; DLB 88; MTCW

McMillan, Terry (L.) 1951- ..... **CLC 50, 61**
See also BW 2; CA 140

McMurtry, Larry (Jeff) 1936- .... **CLC 2, 3, 7, 11, 27, 44**
See also AITN 2; BEST 89:2; CA 5-8R; CANR 19, 43; CDALB 1968-1988; DLB 2, 143; DLBY 80, 87; MTCW

McNally, T. M. 1961- .... **CLC 82**

McNally, Terrence 1939- ...... **CLC 4, 7, 41**
See also CA 45-48; CANR 2; DLB 7

McNamer, Deirdre 1950- .... **CLC 70**

McNeile, Herman Cyril 1888-1937
See Sapper
See also DLB 77

McPhee, John (Angus) 1931- ...... **CLC 36**
See also BEST 90:1; CA 65-68; CANR 20, 46; MTCW

McPherson, James Alan 1943- .... **CLC 19, 77**
See also BW 1; CA 25-28R; CAAS 17; CANR 24; DLB 38; MTCW

McPherson, William (Alexander) 1933- .... **CLC 34**
See also CA 69-72; CANR 28

Mead, Margaret 1901-1978 .... **CLC 37**
See also AITN 1; CA 1-4R; 81-84; CANR 4; MTCW; SATA-Obit 20

Meaker, Marijane (Agnes) 1927-
See Kerr, M. E.
See also CA 107; CANR 37; JRDA; MAICYA; MTCW; SATA 20, 61

Medoff, Mark (Howard) 1940- . . . **CLC 6, 23**
See also AITN 1; CA 53-56; CANR 5; DLB 7

Medvedev, P. N.
See Bakhtin, Mikhail Mikhailovich

Meged, Aharon
See Megged, Aharon

Meged, Aron
See Megged, Aharon

Megged, Aharon 1920- . . . . **CLC 9**
See also CA 49-52; CAAS 13; CANR 1

Mehta, Ved (Parkash) 1934- . . . . **CLC 37**
See also CA 1-4R; CANR 2, 23; MTCW

Melanter
See Blackmore, R(ichard) D(oddridge)

Melikow, Loris
See Hofmannsthal, Hugo von

Melmoth, Sebastian
See Wilde, Oscar (Fingal O'Flahertie Wills)

Meltzer, Milton 1915- . . . . **CLC 26**
See also AAYA 8; CA 13-16R; CANR 38; CLR 13; DLB 61; JRDA; MAICYA; SAAS 1; SATA 1, 50, 80

Melville, Herman
1819-1891 . . . . . **NCLC 3, 12, 29, 45, 49; DA; SSC 1, 17; WLC**
See also CDALB 1640-1865; DLB 3, 74; SATA 59

Menander
c. 342B.C.-c. 292B.C. . . . **CMLC 9; DC 3**

Mencken, H(enry) L(ouis)
1880-1956 . . . . **TCLC 13**
See also CA 105; 125; CDALB 1917-1929; DLB 11, 29, 63, 137; MTCW

Mercer, David 1928-1980. . . . . **CLC 5**
See also CA 9-12R; 102; CANR 23; DLB 13; MTCW

Merchant, Paul
See Ellison, Harlan (Jay)

Meredith, George 1828-1909 . . . **TCLC 17, 43**
See also CA 117; CDBLB 1832-1890; DLB 18, 35, 57

Meredith, William (Morris)
1919- . . . . **CLC 4, 13, 22, 55**
See also CA 9-12R; CAAS 14; CANR 6, 40; DLB 5

Merezhkovsky, Dmitry Sergeyevich
1865-1941 . . . . **TCLC 29**

Merimee, Prosper
1803-1870 . . . . **NCLC 6; SSC 7**
See also DLB 119

Merkin, Daphne 1954- . . . . **CLC 44**
See also CA 123

Merlin, Arthur
See Blish, James (Benjamin)

Merrill, James (Ingram)
1926- . . . . **CLC 2, 3, 6, 8, 13, 18, 34**
See also CA 13-16R; CANR 10; DLB 5; DLBY 85; MTCW

Merriman, Alex
See Silverberg, Robert

Merritt, E. B.
See Waddington, Miriam

Merton, Thomas
1915-1968 . . **CLC 1, 3, 11, 34, 83; PC 10**
See also CA 5-8R; 25-28R; CANR 22; DLB 48; DLBY 81; MTCW

Merwin, W(illiam) S(tanley)
1927- . . . . . . **CLC 1, 2, 3, 5, 8, 13, 18, 45**
See also CA 13-16R; CANR 15; DLB 5; MTCW

Metcalf, John 1938- . . . . **CLC 37**
See also CA 113; DLB 60

Metcalf, Suzanne
See Baum, L(yman) Frank

Mew, Charlotte (Mary)
1870-1928 . . . . **TCLC 8**
See also CA 105; DLB 19, 135

Mewshaw, Michael 1943- . . . . **CLC 9**
See also CA 53-56; CANR 7, 47; DLBY 80

Meyer, June
See Jordan, June

Meyer, Lynn
See Slavitt, David R(ytman)

Meyer-Meyrink, Gustav 1868-1932
See Meyrink, Gustav
See also CA 117

Meyers, Jeffrey 1939- . . . . **CLC 39**
See also CA 73-76; DLB 111

Meynell, Alice (Christina Gertrude Thompson)
1847-1922 . . . . **TCLC 6**
See also CA 104; DLB 19, 98

Meyrink, Gustav . . . . **TCLC 21**
See also Meyer-Meyrink, Gustav
See also DLB 81

Michaels, Leonard
1933- . . . . **CLC 6, 25; SSC 16**
See also CA 61-64; CANR 21; DLB 130; MTCW

Michaux, Henri 1899-1984 . . . . . . **CLC 8, 19**
See also CA 85-88; 114

Michelangelo 1475-1564. . . . . **LC 12**

Michelet, Jules 1798-1874 . . . . **NCLC 31**

Michener, James A(lbert)
1907(?)- . . . . **CLC 1, 5, 11, 29, 60**
See also AITN 1; BEST 90:1; CA 5-8R; CANR 21, 45; DLB 6; MTCW

Mickiewicz, Adam 1798-1855 . . . . . **NCLC 3**

Middleton, Christopher 1926- . . . . . . **CLC 13**
See also CA 13-16R; CANR 29; DLB 40

Middleton, Richard (Barham)
1882-1911 . . . . **TCLC 56**

Middleton, Stanley 1919- . . . . **CLC 7, 38**
See also CA 25-28R; CANR 21, 46; DLB 14

Middleton, Thomas 1580-1627. . . . . **DC 5**
See also DLB 58

Migueis, Jose Rodrigues 1901- . . . . . **CLC 10**

Mikszath, Kalman 1847-1910 . . . . . **TCLC 31**

Miles, Josephine
1911-1985 . . . . **CLC 1, 2, 14, 34, 39**
See also CA 1-4R; 116; CANR 2; DLB 48

Militant
See Sandburg, Carl (August)

Mill, John Stuart 1806-1873 . . . . . **NCLC 11**
See also CDBLB 1832-1890; DLB 55

Millar, Kenneth 1915-1983 . . . . **CLC 14**
See also Macdonald, Ross
See also CA 9-12R; 110; CANR 16; DLB 2; DLBD 6; DLBY 83; MTCW

Millay, E. Vincent
See Millay, Edna St. Vincent

Millay, Edna St. Vincent
1892-1950 . . . . . . **TCLC 4, 49; DA; PC 6**
See also CA 104; 130; CDALB 1917-1929; DLB 45; MTCW

Miller, Arthur
1915- . . . . **CLC 1, 2, 6, 10, 15, 26, 47, 78; DA; DC 1; WLC**
See also AITN 1; CA 1-4R; CABS 3; CANR 2, 30; CDALB 1941-1968; DLB 7; MTCW

Miller, Henry (Valentine)
1891-1980 . . . . **CLC 1, 2, 4, 9, 14, 43, 84; DA; WLC**
See also CA 9-12R; 97-100; CANR 33; CDALB 1929-1941; DLB 4, 9; DLBY 80; MTCW

Miller, Jason 1939(?)- . . . . **CLC 2**
See also AITN 1; CA 73-76; DLB 7

Miller, Sue 1943- . . . . **CLC 44**
See also BEST 90:3; CA 139; DLB 143

Miller, Walter M(ichael, Jr.)
1923- . . . . **CLC 4, 30**
See also CA 85-88; DLB 8

Millett, Kate 1934- . . . . **CLC 67**
See also AITN 1; CA 73-76; CANR 32; MTCW

Millhauser, Steven 1943- . . . . **CLC 21, 54**
See also CA 110; 111; DLB 2

Millin, Sarah Gertrude 1889-1968 . . **CLC 49**
See also CA 102; 93-96

Milne, A(lan) A(lexander)
1882-1956 . . . . **TCLC 6**
See also CA 104; 133; CLR 1, 26; DLB 10, 77, 100; MAICYA; MTCW; YABC 1

Milner, Ron(ald) 1938- . . . . **CLC 56; BLC**
See also AITN 1; BW 1; CA 73-76; CANR 24; DLB 38; MTCW

Milosz, Czeslaw
1911- . . . **CLC 5, 11, 22, 31, 56, 82; PC 8**
See also CA 81-84; CANR 23; MTCW

Milton, John 1608-1674 . . . **LC 9; DA; WLC**
See also CDBLB 1660-1789; DLB 131

Min, Anchee 1957- . . . . **CLC 86**

Minehaha, Cornelius
See Wedekind, (Benjamin) Frank(lin)

Miner, Valerie 1947- . . . . **CLC 40**
See also CA 97-100

Minimo, Duca
See D'Annunzio, Gabriele

Minot, Susan 1956- . . . . **CLC 44**
See also CA 134

Minus, Ed 1938- . . . . **CLC 39**

Miranda, Javier
See Bioy Casares, Adolfo

Mirbeau, Octave 1848-1917 . . . . **TCLC 55**
See also DLB 123

Miro (Ferrer), Gabriel (Francisco Victor)
1879-1930 . . . . **TCLC 5**
See also CA 104

Mishima, Yukio .... **CLC 2, 4, 6, 9, 27; DC 1; SSC 4**
See also Hiraoka, Kimitake

Mistral, Frederic 1830-1914 ...... **TCLC 51**
See also CA 122

Mistral, Gabriela............ **TCLC 2; HLC**
See also Godoy Alcayaga, Lucila

Mistry, Rohinton 1952-........... **CLC 71**
See also CA 141

Mitchell, Clyde
See Ellison, Harlan (Jay); Silverberg, Robert

Mitchell, James Leslie 1901-1935
See Gibbon, Lewis Grassic
See also CA 104; DLB 15

Mitchell, Joni 1943-.............. **CLC 12**
See also CA 112

Mitchell, Margaret (Munnerlyn) 1900-1949 .... **TCLC 11**
See also CA 109; 125; DLB 9; MTCW

Mitchell, Peggy
See Mitchell, Margaret (Munnerlyn)

Mitchell, S(ilas) Weir 1829-1914 .. **TCLC 36**

Mitchell, W(illiam) O(rmond) 1914- .... **CLC 25**
See also CA 77-80; CANR 15, 43; DLB 88

Mitford, Mary Russell 1787-1855.. **NCLC 4**
See also DLB 110, 116

Mitford, Nancy 1904-1973......... **CLC 44**
See also CA 9-12R

Miyamoto, Yuriko 1899-1951 ..... **TCLC 37**

Mo, Timothy (Peter) 1950(?)- ...... **CLC 46**
See also CA 117; MTCW

Modarressi, Taghi (M.) 1931- ...... **CLC 44**
See also CA 121; 134

Modiano, Patrick (Jean) 1945- ..... **CLC 18**
See also CA 85-88; CANR 17, 40; DLB 83

Moerck, Paal
See Roelvaag, O(le) E(dvart)

Mofolo, Thomas (Mokopu) 1875(?)-1948 .... **TCLC 22; BLC**
See also CA 121

Mohr, Nicholasa 1935-...... **CLC 12; HLC**
See also AAYA 8; CA 49-52; CANR 1, 32; CLR 22; DLB 145; HW; JRDA; SAAS 8; SATA 8

Mojtabai, A(nn) G(race) 1938- .... **CLC 5, 9, 15, 29**
See also CA 85-88

Moliere 1622-1673 .... **LC 28; DA; WLC**

Molin, Charles
See Mayne, William (James Carter)

Molnar, Ferenc 1878-1952........ **TCLC 20**
See also CA 109

Momaday, N(avarre) Scott 1934- .... **CLC 2, 19, 85; DA**
See also AAYA 11; CA 25-28R; CANR 14, 34; DLB 143; MTCW; NNAL; SATA 48; SATA-Brief 30

Monette, Paul 1945-.............. **CLC 82**
See also CA 139

Monroe, Harriet 1860-1936....... **TCLC 12**
See also CA 109; DLB 54, 91

Monroe, Lyle
See Heinlein, Robert A(nson)

Montagu, Elizabeth 1917-........ **NCLC 7**
See also CA 9-12R

Montagu, Mary (Pierrepont) Wortley 1689-1762 .... **LC 9**
See also DLB 95, 101

Montagu, W. H.
See Coleridge, Samuel Taylor

Montague, John (Patrick) 1929- .... **CLC 13, 46**
See also CA 9-12R; CANR 9; DLB 40; MTCW

Montaigne, Michel (Eyquem) de 1533-1592 .... **LC 8; DA; WLC**

Montale, Eugenio 1896-1981... **CLC 7, 9, 18**
See also CA 17-20R; 104; CANR 30; DLB 114; MTCW

Montesquieu, Charles-Louis de Secondat 1689-1755 .... **LC 7**

Montgomery, (Robert) Bruce 1921-1978
See Crispin, Edmund
See also CA 104

Montgomery, L(ucy) M(aud) 1874-1942 .... **TCLC 51**
See also AAYA 12; CA 108; 137; CLR 8; DLB 92; JRDA; MAICYA; YABC 1

Montgomery, Marion H., Jr. 1925- .. **CLC 7**
See also AITN 1; CA 1-4R; CANR 3; DLB 6

Montgomery, Max
See Davenport, Guy (Mattison, Jr.)

Montherlant, Henry (Milon) de 1896-1972 .... **CLC 8, 19**
See also CA 85-88; 37-40R; DLB 72; MTCW

Monty Python
See Chapman, Graham; Cleese, John (Marwood); Gilliam, Terry (Vance); Idle, Eric; Jones, Terence Graham Parry; Palin, Michael (Edward)
See also AAYA 7

Moodie, Susanna (Strickland) 1803-1885 .... **NCLC 14**
See also DLB 99

Mooney, Edward 1951-
See Mooney, Ted
See also CA 130

Mooney, Ted .... **CLC 25**
See also Mooney, Edward

Moorcock, Michael (John) 1939- .... **CLC 5, 27, 58**
See also CA 45-48; CAAS 5; CANR 2, 17, 38; DLB 14; MTCW

Moore, Brian 1921- .... **CLC 1, 3, 5, 7, 8, 19, 32**
See also CA 1-4R; CANR 1, 25, 42; MTCW

Moore, Edward
See Muir, Edwin

Moore, George Augustus 1852-1933 .... **TCLC 7**
See also CA 104; DLB 10, 18, 57, 135

Moore, Lorrie .... **CLC 39, 45, 68**
See also Moore, Marie Lorena

Moore, Marianne (Craig) 1887-1972 .... **CLC 1, 2, 4, 8, 10, 13, 19, 47; DA; PC 4**
See also CA 1-4R; 33-36R; CANR 3; CDALB 1929-1941; DLB 45; DLBD 7; MTCW; SATA 20

Moore, Marie Lorena 1957-
See Moore, Lorrie
See also CA 116; CANR 39

Moore, Thomas 1779-1852........ **NCLC 6**
See also DLB 96, 144

Morand, Paul 1888-1976 .... **CLC 41**
See also CA 69-72; DLB 65

Morante, Elsa 1918-1985........ **CLC 8, 47**
See also CA 85-88; 117; CANR 35; MTCW

Moravia, Alberto....... **CLC 2, 7, 11, 27, 46**
See also Pincherle, Alberto

More, Hannah 1745-1833 .... **NCLC 27**
See also DLB 107, 109, 116

More, Henry 1614-1687............. **LC 9**
See also DLB 126

More, Sir Thomas 1478-1535 .... **LC 10**

Moreas, Jean.................... **TCLC 18**
See also Papadiamantopoulos, Johannes

Morgan, Berry 1919-.............. **CLC 6**
See also CA 49-52; DLB 6

Morgan, Claire
See Highsmith, (Mary) Patricia

Morgan, Edwin (George) 1920-..... **CLC 31**
See also CA 5-8R; CANR 3, 43; DLB 27

Morgan, (George) Frederick 1922- .... **CLC 23**
See also CA 17-20R; CANR 21

Morgan, Harriet
See Mencken, H(enry) L(ouis)

Morgan, Jane
See Cooper, James Fenimore

Morgan, Janet 1945- .... **CLC 39**
See also CA 65-68

Morgan, Lady 1776(?)-1859...... **NCLC 29**
See also DLB 116

Morgan, Robin 1941-.............. **CLC 2**
See also CA 69-72; CANR 29; MTCW; SATA 80

Morgan, Scott
See Kuttner, Henry

Morgan, Seth 1949(?)-1990 .... **CLC 65**
See also CA 132

Morgenstern, Christian 1871-1914 .... **TCLC 8**
See also CA 105

Morgenstern, S.
See Goldman, William (W.)

Moricz, Zsigmond 1879-1942 ..... **TCLC 33**

Morike, Eduard (Friedrich) 1804-1875 .... **NCLC 10**
See also DLB 133

Mori Ogai .... **TCLC 14**
See also Mori Rintaro

Mori Rintaro 1862-1922
See Mori Ogai
See also CA 110

Moritz, Karl Philipp 1756-1793 ...... **LC 2**
See also DLB 94

Morland, Peter Henry
See Faust, Frederick (Schiller)

Morren, Theophil
See Hofmannsthal, Hugo von

Morris, Bill 1952-................ **CLC 76**

Morris, Julian
See West, Morris L(anglo)

Morris, Steveland Judkins 1950(?)-
See Wonder, Stevie
See also CA 111

Morris, William 1834-1896 .... **NCLC 4**
See also CDBLB 1832-1890; DLB 18, 35, 57

Morris, Wright 1910-... **CLC 1, 3, 7, 18, 37**
See also CA 9-12R; CANR 21; DLB 2; DLBY 81; MTCW

Morrison, Chloe Anthony Wofford
See Morrison, Toni

Morrison, James Douglas 1943-1971
See Morrison, Jim
See also CA 73-76; CANR 40

Morrison, Jim .... **CLC 17**
See also Morrison, James Douglas

Morrison, Toni
1931- .... **CLC 4, 10, 22, 55, 81, 87; BLC; DA**
See also AAYA 1; BW 2; CA 29-32R; CANR 27, 42; CDALB 1968-1988; DLB 6, 33, 143; DLBY 81; MTCW; SATA 57

Morrison, Van 1945- .... **CLC 21**
See also CA 116

Mortimer, John (Clifford)
1923- .... **CLC 28, 43**
See also CA 13-16R; CANR 21; CDBLB 1960 to Present; DLB 13; MTCW

Mortimer, Penelope (Ruth) 1918-.... **CLC 5**
See also CA 57-60; CANR 45

Morton, Anthony
See Creasey, John

Mosher, Howard Frank 1943-...... **CLC 62**
See also CA 139

Mosley, Nicholas 1923-........ **CLC 43, 70**
See also CA 69-72; CANR 41; DLB 14

Moss, Howard
1922-1987 .... **CLC 7, 14, 45, 50**
See also CA 1-4R; 123; CANR 1, 44; DLB 5

Mossgiel, Rab
See Burns, Robert

Motion, Andrew 1952-............ **CLC 47**
See also DLB 40

Motley, Willard (Francis)
1909-1965 .... **CLC 18**
See also BW 1; CA 117; 106; DLB 76, 143

Motoori, Norinaga 1730-1801 .... **NCLC 45**

Mott, Michael (Charles Alston)
1930- .... **CLC 15, 34**
See also CA 5-8R; CAAS 7; CANR 7, 29

Mowat, Farley (McGill) 1921- ..... **CLC 26**
See also AAYA 1; CA 1-4R; CANR 4, 24, 42; CLR 20; DLB 68; JRDA; MAICYA; MTCW; SATA 3, 55

Moyers, Bill 1934- .... **CLC 74**
See also AITN 2; CA 61-64; CANR 31

Mphahlele, Es'kia
See Mphahlele, Ezekiel
See also DLB 125

Mphahlele, Ezekiel 1919-..... **CLC 25; BLC**
See also Mphahlele, Es'kia
See also BW 2; CA 81-84; CANR 26

Mqhayi, S(amuel) E(dward) K(rune Loliwe)
1875-1945 .... **TCLC 25; BLC**

Mr. Martin
See Burroughs, William S(eward)

Mrozek, Slawomir 1930-........ **CLC 3, 13**
See also CA 13-16R; CAAS 10; CANR 29; MTCW

Mrs. Belloc-Lowndes
See Lowndes, Marie Adelaide (Belloc)

Mtwa, Percy (?)-................. **CLC 47**

Mueller, Lisel 1924-........... **CLC 13, 51**
See also CA 93-96; DLB 105

Muir, Edwin 1887-1959 .... **TCLC 2**
See also CA 104; DLB 20, 100

Muir, John 1838-1914 .... **TCLC 28**

Mujica Lainez, Manuel
1910-1984 .... **CLC 31**
See also Lainez, Manuel Mujica
See also CA 81-84; 112; CANR 32; HW

Mukherjee, Bharati 1940- .... **CLC 53**
See also BEST 89:2; CA 107; CANR 45; DLB 60; MTCW

Muldoon, Paul 1951- .... **CLC 32, 72**
See also CA 113; 129; DLB 40

Mulisch, Harry 1927-............. **CLC 42**
See also CA 9-12R; CANR 6, 26

Mull, Martin 1943-............... **CLC 17**
See also CA 105

Mulock, Dinah Maria
See Craik, Dinah Maria (Mulock)

Munford, Robert 1737(?)-1783 .... **LC 5**
See also DLB 31

Mungo, Raymond 1946-........... **CLC 72**
See also CA 49-52; CANR 2

Munro, Alice
1931- .... **CLC 6, 10, 19, 50; SSC 3**
See also AITN 2; CA 33-36R; CANR 33; DLB 53; MTCW; SATA 29

Munro, H(ector) H(ugh) 1870-1916
See Saki
See also CA 104; 130; CDBLB 1890-1914; DA; DLB 34; MTCW; WLC

Murasaki, Lady .... **CMLC 1**

Murdoch, (Jean) Iris
1919- ...... **CLC 1, 2, 3, 4, 6, 8, 11, 15, 22, 31, 51**
See also CA 13-16R; CANR 8, 43; CDBLB 1960 to Present; DLB 14; MTCW

Murnau, Friedrich Wilhelm
See Plumpe, Friedrich Wilhelm

Murphy, Richard 1927- .... **CLC 41**
See also CA 29-32R; DLB 40

Murphy, Sylvia 1937-............. **CLC 34**
See also CA 121

Murphy, Thomas (Bernard) 1935-... **CLC 51**
See also CA 101

Murray, Albert L. 1916- .... **CLC 73**
See also BW 2; CA 49-52; CANR 26; DLB 38

Murray, Les(lie) A(llan) 1938- ..... **CLC 40**
See also CA 21-24R; CANR 11, 27

Murry, J. Middleton
See Murry, John Middleton

Murry, John Middleton
1889-1957 .... **TCLC 16**
See also CA 118

Musgrave, Susan 1951- .... **CLC 13, 54**
See also CA 69-72; CANR 45

Musil, Robert (Edler von)
1880-1942 .... **TCLC 12; SSC 18**
See also CA 109; DLB 81, 124

Musset, (Louis Charles) Alfred de
1810-1857 .... **NCLC 7**

My Brother's Brother
See Chekhov, Anton (Pavlovich)

Myers, L. H. 1881-1944.......... **TCLC 59**
See also DLB 15

Myers, Walter Dean 1937- ... **CLC 35; BLC**
See also AAYA 4; BW 2; CA 33-36R; CANR 20, 42; CLR 4, 16, 35; DLB 33; JRDA; MAICYA; SAAS 2; SATA 41, 71; SATA-Brief 27

Myers, Walter M.
See Myers, Walter Dean

Myles, Symon
See Follett, Ken(neth Martin)

Nabokov, Vladimir (Vladimirovich)
1899-1977 ..... **CLC 1, 2, 3, 6, 8, 11, 15, 23, 44, 46, 64; DA; SSC 11; WLC**
See also CA 5-8R; 69-72; CANR 20; CDALB 1941-1968; DLB 2; DLBD 3; DLBY 80, 91; MTCW

Nagai Kafu...................... **TCLC 51**
See also Nagai Sokichi

Nagai Sokichi 1879-1959
See Nagai Kafu
See also CA 117

Nagy, Laszlo 1925-1978............ **CLC 7**
See also CA 129; 112

Naipaul, Shiva(dhar Srinivasa)
1945-1985 .... **CLC 32, 39**
See also CA 110; 112; 116; CANR 33; DLBY 85; MTCW

Naipaul, V(idiadhar) S(urajprasad)
1932- .... **CLC 4, 7, 9, 13, 18, 37**
See also CA 1-4R; CANR 1, 33; CDBLB 1960 to Present; DLB 125; DLBY 85; MTCW

Nakos, Lilika 1899(?)-............ **CLC 29**

Narayan, R(asipuram) K(rishnaswami)
1906- .... **CLC 7, 28, 47**
See also CA 81-84; CANR 33; MTCW; SATA 62

Nash, (Fredric) Ogden 1902-1971 .. **CLC 23**
See also CA 13-14; 29-32R; CANR 34; CAP 1; DLB 11; MAICYA; MTCW; SATA 2, 46

Nathan, Daniel
See Dannay, Frederic

Nathan, George Jean 1882-1958 ... **TCLC 18**
See also Hatteras, Owen
See also CA 114; DLB 137

Natsume, Kinnosuke 1867-1916
See Natsume, Soseki
See also CA 104

Natsume, Soseki .... **TCLC 2, 10**
See also Natsume, Kinnosuke

Natti, (Mary) Lee 1919-
See Kingman, Lee
See also CA 5-8R; CANR 2

Naylor, Gloria
1950- .... **CLC 28, 52; BLC; DA**
See also AAYA 6; BW 2; CA 107; CANR 27; MTCW

Neihardt, John Gneisenau
1881-1973 .... **CLC 32**
See also CA 13-14; CAP 1; DLB 9, 54

Nekrasov, Nikolai Alekseevich
1821-1878 .... **NCLC 11**

Nelligan, Emile 1879-1941........ **TCLC 14**
See also CA 114; DLB 92

Nelson, Willie 1933-.............. **CLC 17**
See also CA 107

Nemerov, Howard (Stanley)
1920-1991 .... **CLC 2, 6, 9, 36**
See also CA 1-4R; 134; CABS 2; CANR 1, 27; DLB 6; DLBY 83; MTCW

Neruda, Pablo
1904-1973 ..... **CLC 1, 2, 5, 7, 9, 28, 62; DA; HLC; PC 4; WLC**
See also CA 19-20; 45-48; CAP 2; HW; MTCW

Nerval, Gerard de
1808-1855 .... **NCLC 1; SSC 18**

Nervo, (Jose) Amado (Ruiz de)
1870-1919 .... **TCLC 11**
See also CA 109; 131; HW

Nessi, Pio Baroja y
See Baroja (y Nessi), Pio

Nestroy, Johann 1801-1862...... **NCLC 42**
See also DLB 133

Neufeld, John (Arthur) 1938- ...... **CLC 17**
See also AAYA 11; CA 25-28R; CANR 11, 37; MAICYA; SAAS 3; SATA 6, 81

Neville, Emily Cheney 1919-....... **CLC 12**
See also CA 5-8R; CANR 3, 37; JRDA; MAICYA; SAAS 2; SATA 1

Newbound, Bernard Slade 1930-
See Slade, Bernard
See also CA 81-84

Newby, P(ercy) H(oward)
1918- .... **CLC 2, 13**
See also CA 5-8R; CANR 32; DLB 15; MTCW

Newlove, Donald 1928- .... **CLC 6**
See also CA 29-32R; CANR 25

Newlove, John (Herbert) 1938-..... **CLC 14**
See also CA 21-24R; CANR 9, 25

Newman, Charles 1938-.......... **CLC 2, 8**
See also CA 21-24R

Newman, Edwin (Harold) 1919- .... **CLC 14**
See also AITN 1; CA 69-72; CANR 5

Newman, John Henry
1801-1890 .... **NCLC 38**
See also DLB 18, 32, 55

Newton, Suzanne 1936- .... **CLC 35**
See also CA 41-44R; CANR 14; JRDA; SATA 5, 77

Nexo, Martin Andersen
1869-1954 .... **TCLC 43**

Nezval, Vitezslav 1900-1958 ...... **TCLC 44**
See also CA 123

Ng, Fae Myenne 1957(?)-.......... **CLC 81**

Ngema, Mbongeni 1955- .... **CLC 57**
See also BW 2; CA 143

Ngugi, James T(hiong'o)........ **CLC 3, 7, 13**
See also Ngugi wa Thiong'o

Ngugi wa Thiong'o 1938-..... **CLC 36; BLC**
See also Ngugi, James T(hiong'o)
See also BW 2; CA 81-84; CANR 27; DLB 125; MTCW

Nichol, B(arrie) P(hillip)
1944-1988 .... **CLC 18**
See also CA 53-56; DLB 53; SATA 66

Nichols, John (Treadwell) 1940- .... **CLC 38**
See also CA 9-12R; CAAS 2; CANR 6; DLBY 82

Nichols, Leigh
See Koontz, Dean R(ay)

Nichols, Peter (Richard)
1927- .... **CLC 5, 36, 65**
See also CA 104; CANR 33; DLB 13; MTCW

Nicolas, F. R. E.
See Freeling, Nicolas

Niedecker, Lorine 1903-1970.... **CLC 10, 42**
See also CA 25-28; CAP 2; DLB 48

Nietzsche, Friedrich (Wilhelm)
1844-1900 .... **TCLC 10, 18, 55**
See also CA 107; 121; DLB 129

Nievo, Ippolito 1831-1861 .... **NCLC 22**

Nightingale, Anne Redmon 1943-
See Redmon, Anne
See also CA 103

Nik. T. O.
See Annensky, Innokenty Fyodorovich

Nin, Anais
1903-1977 ...... **CLC 1, 4, 8, 11, 14, 60; SSC 10**
See also AITN 2; CA 13-16R; 69-72; CANR 22; DLB 2, 4; MTCW

Nissenson, Hugh 1933-.......... **CLC 4, 9**
See also CA 17-20R; CANR 27; DLB 28

Niven, Larry .... **CLC 8**
See also Niven, Laurence Van Cott
See also DLB 8

Niven, Laurence Van Cott 1938-
See Niven, Larry
See also CA 21-24R; CAAS 12; CANR 14, 44; MTCW

Nixon, Agnes Eckhardt 1927-...... **CLC 21**
See also CA 110

Nizan, Paul 1905-1940........... **TCLC 40**
See also DLB 72

Nkosi, Lewis 1936-.......... **CLC 45; BLC**
See also BW 1; CA 65-68; CANR 27

Nodier, (Jean) Charles (Emmanuel)
1780-1844 .... **NCLC 19**
See also DLB 119

Nolan, Christopher 1965-.......... **CLC 58**
See also CA 111

Norden, Charles
See Durrell, Lawrence (George)

Nordhoff, Charles (Bernard)
1887-1947 .... **TCLC 23**
See also CA 108; DLB 9; SATA 23

Norfolk, Lawrence 1963-.......... **CLC 76**
See also CA 144

Norman, Marsha 1947- .... **CLC 28**
See also CA 105; CABS 3; CANR 41; DLBY 84

Norris, Benjamin Franklin, Jr.
1870-1902 .... **TCLC 24**
See also Norris, Frank
See also CA 110

Norris, Frank
See Norris, Benjamin Franklin, Jr.
See also CDALB 1865-1917; DLB 12, 71

Norris, Leslie 1921- .... **CLC 14**
See also CA 11-12; CANR 14; CAP 1; DLB 27

North, Andrew
See Norton, Andre

North, Anthony
See Koontz, Dean R(ay)

North, Captain George
See Stevenson, Robert Louis (Balfour)

North, Milou
See Erdrich, Louise

Northrup, B. A.
See Hubbard, L(afayette) Ron(ald)

North Staffs
See Hulme, T(homas) E(rnest)

Norton, Alice Mary
See Norton, Andre
See also MAICYA; SATA 1, 43

Norton, Andre 1912- .... **CLC 12**
See also Norton, Alice Mary
See also AAYA 14; CA 1-4R; CANR 2, 31; DLB 8, 52; JRDA; MTCW

Norton, Caroline 1808-1877...... **NCLC 47**
See also DLB 21

Norway, Nevil Shute 1899-1960
See Shute, Nevil
See also CA 102; 93-96

Norwid, Cyprian Kamil
1821-1883 .... **NCLC 17**

Nosille, Nabrah
See Ellison, Harlan (Jay)

Nossack, Hans Erich 1901-1978..... **CLC 6**
See also CA 93-96; 85-88; DLB 69

Nostradamus 1503-1566............ **LC 27**

Nosu, Chuji
See Ozu, Yasujiro

Notenburg, Eleanora (Genrikhovna) von
See Guro, Elena

Osborne, George
See Silverberg, Robert

Osborne, John (James)
1929- . . . . **CLC 1, 2, 5, 11, 45; DA; WLC**
See also CA 13-16R; CANR 21; CDBLB 1945-1960; DLB 13; MTCW

Osborne, Lawrence 1958- . . . . **CLC 50**

Oshima, Nagisa 1932- . . . . **CLC 20**
See also CA 116; 121

Oskison, John Milton
1874-1947 . . . . **TCLC 35**
See also CA 144; NNAL

Ossoli, Sarah Margaret (Fuller marchesa d')
1810-1850
See Fuller, Margaret
See also SATA 25

Ostrovsky, Alexander
1823-1886 . . . . **NCLC 30**

Otero, Blas de 1916-1979. . . . . **CLC 11**
See also CA 89-92; DLB 134

Otto, Whitney 1955-. . . . . **CLC 70**
See also CA 140

Ouida . . . . **TCLC 43**
See also De La Ramee, (Marie) Louise
See also DLB 18

Ousmane, Sembene 1923- . . . . **CLC 66; BLC**
See also BW 1; CA 117; 125; MTCW

Ovid 43B.C.-18(?). . . . . **CMLC 7; PC 2**

Owen, Hugh
See Faust, Frederick (Schiller)

Owen, Wilfred (Edward Salter)
1893-1918 . . . . . . **TCLC 5, 27; DA; WLC**
See also CA 104; 141; CDBLB 1914-1945; DLB 20

Owens, Rochelle 1936-. . . . . **CLC 8**
See also CA 17-20R; CAAS 2; CANR 39

Oz, Amos 1939- . . . **CLC 5, 8, 11, 27, 33, 54**
See also CA 53-56; CANR 27, 47; MTCW

Ozick, Cynthia
1928- . . . . **CLC 3, 7, 28, 62; SSC 15**
See also BEST 90:1; CA 17-20R; CANR 23; DLB 28; DLBY 82; MTCW

Ozu, Yasujiro 1903-1963 . . . . **CLC 16**
See also CA 112

Pacheco, C.
See Pessoa, Fernando (Antonio Nogueira)

Pa Chin . . . . **CLC 18**
See also Li Fei-kan

Pack, Robert 1929-. . . . . **CLC 13**
See also CA 1-4R; CANR 3, 44; DLB 5

Padgett, Lewis
See Kuttner, Henry

Padilla (Lorenzo), Heberto 1932- . . . **CLC 38**
See also AITN 1; CA 123; 131; HW

Page, Jimmy 1944-. . . . . **CLC 12**

Page, Louise 1955-. . . . . **CLC 40**
See also CA 140

Page, P(atricia) K(athleen)
1916- . . . . **CLC 7, 18; PC 12**
See also CA 53-56; CANR 4, 22; DLB 68; MTCW

Paget, Violet 1856-1935
See Lee, Vernon
See also CA 104

Paget-Lowe, Henry
See Lovecraft, H(oward) P(hillips)

Paglia, Camille (Anna) 1947-. . . . . . . **CLC 68**
See also CA 140

Paige, Richard
See Koontz, Dean R(ay)

Pakenham, Antonia
See Fraser, (Lady) Antonia (Pakenham)

Palamas, Kostes 1859-1943 . . . . **TCLC 5**
See also CA 105

Palazzeschi, Aldo 1885-1974 . . . . **CLC 11**
See also CA 89-92; 53-56; DLB 114

Paley, Grace 1922-. . . . **CLC 4, 6, 37; SSC 8**
See also CA 25-28R; CANR 13, 46; DLB 28; MTCW

Palin, Michael (Edward) 1943- . . . . . **CLC 21**
See also Monty Python
See also CA 107; CANR 35; SATA 67

Palliser, Charles 1947-. . . . . **CLC 65**
See also CA 136

Palma, Ricardo 1833-1919. . . . . **TCLC 29**

Pancake, Breece Dexter 1952-1979
See Pancake, Breece D'J
See also CA 123; 109

Pancake, Breece D'J. . . . . **CLC 29**
See also Pancake, Breece Dexter
See also DLB 130

Panko, Rudy
See Gogol, Nikolai (Vasilyevich)

Papadiamantis, Alexandros
1851-1911 . . . . **TCLC 29**

Papadiamantopoulos, Johannes 1856-1910
See Moreas, Jean
See also CA 117

Papini, Giovanni 1881-1956. . . . . . . **TCLC 22**
See also CA 121

Paracelsus 1493-1541 . . . . **LC 14**

Parasol, Peter
See Stevens, Wallace

Parfenie, Maria
See Codrescu, Andrei

Parini, Jay (Lee) 1948- . . . . **CLC 54**
See also CA 97-100; CAAS 16; CANR 32

Park, Jordan
See Kornbluth, C(yril) M.; Pohl, Frederik

Parker, Bert
See Ellison, Harlan (Jay)

Parker, Dorothy (Rothschild)
1893-1967 . . . . **CLC 15, 68; SSC 2**
See also CA 19-20; 25-28R; CAP 2; DLB 11, 45, 86; MTCW

Parker, Robert B(rown) 1932-. . . . . . **CLC 27**
See also BEST 89:4; CA 49-52; CANR 1, 26; MTCW

Parkin, Frank 1940-. . . . . **CLC 43**

Parkman, Francis, Jr.
1823-1893 . . . . **NCLC 12**
See also DLB 1, 30

Parks, Gordon (Alexander Buchanan)
1912- . . . . **CLC 1, 16; BLC**
See also AITN 2; BW 2; CA 41-44R; CANR 26; DLB 33; SATA 8

Parnell, Thomas 1679-1718 . . . . **LC 3**
See also DLB 94

Parra, Nicanor 1914- . . . . **CLC 2; HLC**
See also CA 85-88; CANR 32; HW; MTCW

Parrish, Mary Frances
See Fisher, M(ary) F(rances) K(ennedy)

Parson
See Coleridge, Samuel Taylor

Parson Lot
See Kingsley, Charles

Partridge, Anthony
See Oppenheim, E(dward) Phillips

Pascoli, Giovanni 1855-1912 . . . . . . **TCLC 45**

Pasolini, Pier Paolo
1922-1975 . . . . **CLC 20, 37**
See also CA 93-96; 61-64; DLB 128; MTCW

Pasquini
See Silone, Ignazio

Pastan, Linda (Olenik) 1932- . . . . . . **CLC 27**
See also CA 61-64; CANR 18, 40; DLB 5

Pasternak, Boris (Leonidovich)
1890-1960 . . . . . . **CLC 7, 10, 18, 63; DA; PC 6; WLC**
See also CA 127; 116; MTCW

Patchen, Kenneth 1911-1972 . . . **CLC 1, 2, 18**
See also CA 1-4R; 33-36R; CANR 3, 35; DLB 16, 48; MTCW

Pater, Walter (Horatio)
1839-1894 . . . . **NCLC 7**
See also CDBLB 1832-1890; DLB 57

Paterson, A(ndrew) B(arton)
1864-1941 . . . . **TCLC 32**

Paterson, Katherine (Womeldorf)
1932- . . . . **CLC 12, 30**
See also AAYA 1; CA 21-24R; CANR 28; CLR 7; DLB 52; JRDA; MAICYA; MTCW; SATA 13, 53

Patmore, Coventry Kersey Dighton
1823-1896 . . . . **NCLC 9**
See also DLB 35, 98

Paton, Alan (Stewart)
1903-1988 . . . . . . **CLC 4, 10, 25, 55; DA; WLC**
See also CA 13-16; 125; CANR 22; CAP 1; MTCW; SATA 11; SATA-Obit 56

Paton Walsh, Gillian 1937-
See Walsh, Jill Paton
See also CANR 38; JRDA; MAICYA; SAAS 3; SATA 4, 72

Paulding, James Kirke 1778-1860. . **NCLC 2**
See also DLB 3, 59, 74

Paulin, Thomas Neilson 1949-
See Paulin, Tom
See also CA 123; 128

Paulin, Tom . . . . **CLC 37**
See also Paulin, Thomas Neilson
See also DLB 40

Paustovsky, Konstantin (Georgievich)
1892-1968 . . . . **CLC 40**
See also CA 93-96; 25-28R

Pavese, Cesare 1908-1950 . . . . **TCLC 3**
See also CA 104; DLB 128

Pavic, Milorad 1929- . . . . **CLC 60**
See also CA 136

Pritchard, William H(arrison) 1932- . . . . **CLC 34**
See also CA 65-68; CANR 23; DLB 111

Pritchett, V(ictor) S(awdon) 1900- . . . . **CLC 5, 13, 15, 41; SSC 14**
See also CA 61-64; CANR 31; DLB 15, 139; MTCW

Private 19022
See Manning, Frederic

Probst, Mark 1925- . . . . **CLC 59**
See also CA 130

Prokosch, Frederic 1908-1989 . . . . **CLC 4, 48**
See also CA 73-76; 128; DLB 48

Prophet, The
See Dreiser, Theodore (Herman Albert)

Prose, Francine 1947- . . . . **CLC 45**
See also CA 109; 112; CANR 46

Proudhon
See Cunha, Euclides (Rodrigues Pimenta) da

Proulx, E. Annie 1935- . . . . **CLC 81**

Proust, (Valentin-Louis-George-Eugene-) Marcel 1871-1922 . . . **TCLC 7, 13, 33; DA; WLC**
See also CA 104; 120; DLB 65; MTCW

Prowler, Harley
See Masters, Edgar Lee

Prus, Boleslaw 1845-1912 . . . . **TCLC 48**

Pryor, Richard (Franklin Lenox Thomas) 1940- . . . . **CLC 26**
See also CA 122

Przybyszewski, Stanislaw 1868-1927 . . . . **TCLC 36**
See also DLB 66

Pteleon
See Grieve, C(hristopher) M(urray)

Puckett, Lute
See Masters, Edgar Lee

Puig, Manuel 1932-1990 . . . **CLC 3, 5, 10, 28, 65; HLC**
See also CA 45-48; CANR 2, 32; DLB 113; HW; MTCW

Purdy, Al(fred Wellington) 1918- . . . . **CLC 3, 6, 14, 50**
See also CA 81-84; CAAS 17; CANR 42; DLB 88

Purdy, James (Amos) 1923- . . . . **CLC 2, 4, 10, 28, 52**
See also CA 33-36R; CAAS 1; CANR 19; DLB 2; MTCW

Pure, Simon
See Swinnerton, Frank Arthur

Pushkin, Alexander (Sergeyevich) 1799-1837 . . . . **NCLC 3, 27; DA; PC 10; WLC**
See also SATA 61

P'u Sung-ling 1640-1715 . . . . **LC 3**

Putnam, Arthur Lee
See Alger, Horatio, Jr.

Puzo, Mario 1920- . . . . **CLC 1, 2, 6, 36**
See also CA 65-68; CANR 4, 42; DLB 6; MTCW

Pym, Barbara (Mary Crampton) 1913-1980 . . . . **CLC 13, 19, 37**
See also CA 13-14; 97-100; CANR 13, 34; CAP 1; DLB 14; DLBY 87; MTCW

Pynchon, Thomas (Ruggles, Jr.) 1937- . . . . . **CLC 2, 3, 6, 9, 11, 18, 33, 62, 72; DA; SSC 14; WLC**
See also BEST 90:2; CA 17-20R; CANR 22, 46; DLB 2; MTCW

Qian Zhongshu
See Ch'ien Chung-shu

Qroll
See Dagerman, Stig (Halvard)

Quarrington, Paul (Lewis) 1953- . . . . **CLC 65**
See also CA 129

Quasimodo, Salvatore 1901-1968 . . . **CLC 10**
See also CA 13-16; 25-28R; CAP 1; DLB 114; MTCW

Queen, Ellery . . . . **CLC 3, 11**
See also Dannay, Frederic; Davidson, Avram; Lee, Manfred B(ennington); Sturgeon, Theodore (Hamilton); Vance, John Holbrook

Queen, Ellery, Jr.
See Dannay, Frederic; Lee, Manfred B(ennington)

Queneau, Raymond 1903-1976 . . . . **CLC 2, 5, 10, 42**
See also CA 77-80; 69-72; CANR 32; DLB 72; MTCW

Quevedo, Francisco de 1580-1645 . . . . **LC 23**

Quiller-Couch, Arthur Thomas 1863-1944 . . . . **TCLC 53**
See also CA 118; DLB 135

Quin, Ann (Marie) 1936-1973 . . . . **CLC 6**
See also CA 9-12R; 45-48; DLB 14

Quinn, Martin
See Smith, Martin Cruz

Quinn, Simon
See Smith, Martin Cruz

Quiroga, Horacio (Sylvestre) 1878-1937 . . . . **TCLC 20; HLC**
See also CA 117; 131; HW; MTCW

Quoirez, Francoise 1935- . . . . **CLC 9**
See also Sagan, Francoise
See also CA 49-52; CANR 6, 39; MTCW

Raabe, Wilhelm 1831-1910 . . . . **TCLC 45**
See also DLB 129

Rabe, David (William) 1940- . . . **CLC 4, 8, 33**
See also CA 85-88; CABS 3; DLB 7

Rabelais, Francois 1483-1553 . . . . **LC 5; DA; WLC**

Rabinovitch, Sholem 1859-1916
See Aleichem, Sholom
See also CA 104

Racine, Jean 1639-1699 . . . . **LC 28**

Radcliffe, Ann (Ward) 1764-1823 . . **NCLC 6**
See also DLB 39

Radiguet, Raymond 1903-1923 . . . . **TCLC 29**
See also DLB 65

Radnoti, Miklos 1909-1944 . . . . **TCLC 16**
See also CA 118

Rado, James 1939- . . . . **CLC 17**
See also CA 105

Radvanyi, Netty 1900-1983
See Seghers, Anna
See also CA 85-88; 110

Rae, Ben
See Griffiths, Trevor

Raeburn, John (Hay) 1941- . . . . **CLC 34**
See also CA 57-60

Ragni, Gerome 1942-1991 . . . . **CLC 17**
See also CA 105; 134

Rahv, Philip 1908-1973 . . . . **CLC 24**
See also Greenberg, Ivan
See also DLB 137

Raine, Craig 1944- . . . . **CLC 32**
See also CA 108; CANR 29; DLB 40

Raine, Kathleen (Jessie) 1908- . . . **CLC 7, 45**
See also CA 85-88; CANR 46; DLB 20; MTCW

Rainis, Janis 1865-1929 . . . . **TCLC 29**

Rakosi, Carl . . . . **CLC 47**
See also Rawley, Callman
See also CAAS 5

Raleigh, Richard
See Lovecraft, H(oward) P(hillips)

Rallentando, H. P.
See Sayers, Dorothy L(eigh)

Ramal, Walter
See de la Mare, Walter (John)

Ramon, Juan
See Jimenez (Mantecon), Juan Ramon

Ramos, Graciliano 1892-1953 . . . . . **TCLC 32**

Rampersad, Arnold 1941- . . . . **CLC 44**
See also BW 2; CA 127; 133; DLB 111

Rampling, Anne
See Rice, Anne

Ramuz, Charles-Ferdinand 1878-1947 . . . . **TCLC 33**

Rand, Ayn 1905-1982 . . . . . . **CLC 3, 30, 44, 79; DA; WLC**
See also AAYA 10; CA 13-16R; 105; CANR 27; MTCW

Randall, Dudley (Felker) 1914- . . . . **CLC 1; BLC**
See also BW 1; CA 25-28R; CANR 23; DLB 41

Randall, Robert
See Silverberg, Robert

Ranger, Ken
See Creasey, John

Ransom, John Crowe 1888-1974 . . . . **CLC 2, 4, 5, 11, 24**
See also CA 5-8R; 49-52; CANR 6, 34; DLB 45, 63; MTCW

Rao, Raja 1909- . . . . **CLC 25, 56**
See also CA 73-76; MTCW

Raphael, Frederic (Michael) 1931- . . . . **CLC 2, 14**
See also CA 1-4R; CANR 1; DLB 14

Ratcliffe, James P.
See Mencken, H(enry) L(ouis)

Rathbone, Julian 1935- . . . . **CLC 41**
See also CA 101; CANR 34

Rattigan, Terence (Mervyn) 1911-1977 .... **CLC 7**
See also CA 85-88; 73-76; CDBLB 1945-1960; DLB 13; MTCW

Ratushinskaya, Irina 1954- .... **CLC 54**
See also CA 129

Raven, Simon (Arthur Noel) 1927- .... **CLC 14**
See also CA 81-84

Rawley, Callman 1903-
See Rakosi, Carl
See also CA 21-24R; CANR 12, 32

Rawlings, Marjorie Kinnan 1896-1953 .... **TCLC 4**
See also CA 104; 137; DLB 9, 22, 102; JRDA; MAICYA; YABC 1

Ray, Satyajit 1921-1992........ **CLC 16, 76**
See also CA 114; 137

Read, Herbert Edward 1893-1968.... **CLC 4**
See also CA 85-88; 25-28R; DLB 20

Read, Piers Paul 1941- ...... **CLC 4, 10, 25**
See also CA 21-24R; CANR 38; DLB 14; SATA 21

Reade, Charles 1814-1884 .... **NCLC 2**
See also DLB 21

Reade, Hamish
See Gray, Simon (James Holliday)

Reading, Peter 1946- .... **CLC 47**
See also CA 103; CANR 46; DLB 40

Reaney, James 1926- .... **CLC 13**
See also CA 41-44R; CAAS 15; CANR 42; DLB 68; SATA 43

Rebreanu, Liviu 1885-1944 .... **TCLC 28**

Rechy, John (Francisco) 1934- .... **CLC 1, 7, 14, 18; HLC**
See also CA 5-8R; CAAS 4; CANR 6, 32; DLB 122; DLBY 82; HW

Redcam, Tom 1870-1933 .... **TCLC 25**

Reddin, Keith..................... **CLC 67**

Redgrove, Peter (William) 1932- .... **CLC 6, 41**
See also CA 1-4R; CANR 3, 39; DLB 40

Redmon, Anne.................... **CLC 22**
See also Nightingale, Anne Redmon
See also DLBY 86

Reed, Eliot
See Ambler, Eric

Reed, Ishmael 1938- ... **CLC 2, 3, 5, 6, 13, 32, 60; BLC**
See also BW 2; CA 21-24R; CANR 25; DLB 2, 5, 33; DLBD 8; MTCW

Reed, John (Silas) 1887-1920 ...... **TCLC 9**
See also CA 106

Reed, Lou....................... **CLC 21**
See also Firbank, Louis

Reeve, Clara 1729-1807 .... **NCLC 19**
See also DLB 39

Reich, Wilhelm 1897-1957........ **TCLC 57**

Reid, Christopher (John) 1949-..... **CLC 33**
See also CA 140; DLB 40

Reid, Desmond
See Moorcock, Michael (John)

Reid Banks, Lynne 1929-
See Banks, Lynne Reid
See also CA 1-4R; CANR 6, 22, 38; CLR 24; JRDA; MAICYA; SATA 22, 75

Reilly, William K.
See Creasey, John

Reiner, Max
See Caldwell, (Janet Miriam) Taylor (Holland)

Reis, Ricardo
See Pessoa, Fernando (Antonio Nogueira)

Remarque, Erich Maria 1898-1970 .... **CLC 21; DA**
See also CA 77-80; 29-32R; DLB 56; MTCW

Remizov, A.
See Remizov, Aleksei (Mikhailovich)

Remizov, A. M.
See Remizov, Aleksei (Mikhailovich)

Remizov, Aleksei (Mikhailovich) 1877-1957 .... **TCLC 27**
See also CA 125; 133

Renan, Joseph Ernest 1823-1892 .... **NCLC 26**

Renard, Jules 1864-1910 .... **TCLC 17**
See also CA 117

Renault, Mary............... **CLC 3, 11, 17**
See also Challans, Mary
See also DLBY 83

Rendell, Ruth (Barbara) 1930- .. **CLC 28, 48**
See also Vine, Barbara
See also CA 109; CANR 32; DLB 87; MTCW

Renoir, Jean 1894-1979 .... **CLC 20**
See also CA 129; 85-88

Resnais, Alain 1922-.............. **CLC 16**

Reverdy, Pierre 1889-1960 .... **CLC 53**
See also CA 97-100; 89-92

Rexroth, Kenneth 1905-1982 ...... **CLC 1, 2, 6, 11, 22, 49**
See also CA 5-8R; 107; CANR 14, 34; CDALB 1941-1968; DLB 16, 48; DLBY 82; MTCW

Reyes, Alfonso 1889-1959 .... **TCLC 33**
See also CA 131; HW

Reyes y Basoalto, Ricardo Eliecer Neftali
See Neruda, Pablo

Reymont, Wladyslaw (Stanislaw) 1868(?)-1925 .... **TCLC 5**
See also CA 104

Reynolds, Jonathan 1942- .... **CLC 6, 38**
See also CA 65-68; CANR 28

Reynolds, Joshua 1723-1792 .... **LC 15**
See also DLB 104

Reynolds, Michael Shane 1937- .... **CLC 44**
See also CA 65-68; CANR 9

Reznikoff, Charles 1894-1976 .... **CLC 9**
See also CA 33-36; 61-64; CAP 2; DLB 28, 45

Rezzori (d'Arezzo), Gregor von 1914- .... **CLC 25**
See also CA 122; 136

Rhine, Richard
See Silverstein, Alvin

Rhodes, Eugene Manlove 1869-1934 .... **TCLC 53**

R'hoone
See Balzac, Honore de

Rhys, Jean 1890(?)-1979 .... **CLC 2, 4, 6, 14, 19, 51**
See also CA 25-28R; 85-88; CANR 35; CDBLB 1945-1960; DLB 36, 117; MTCW

Ribeiro, Darcy 1922- .... **CLC 34**
See also CA 33-36R

Ribeiro, Joao Ubaldo (Osorio Pimentel) 1941- .... **CLC 10, 67**
See also CA 81-84

Ribman, Ronald (Burt) 1932- .... **CLC 7**
See also CA 21-24R; CANR 46

Ricci, Nino 1959- .... **CLC 70**
See also CA 137

Rice, Anne 1941- .... **CLC 41**
See also AAYA 9; BEST 89:2; CA 65-68; CANR 12, 36

Rice, Elmer (Leopold) 1892-1967 .... **CLC 7, 49**
See also CA 21-22; 25-28R; CAP 2; DLB 4, 7; MTCW

Rice, Tim(othy Miles Bindon) 1944- .... **CLC 21**
See also CA 103; CANR 46

Rich, Adrienne (Cecile) 1929- .... **CLC 3, 6, 7, 11, 18, 36, 73, 76; PC 5**
See also CA 9-12R; CANR 20; DLB 5, 67; MTCW

Rich, Barbara
See Graves, Robert (von Ranke)

Rich, Robert
See Trumbo, Dalton

Richards, David Adams 1950-...... **CLC 59**
See also CA 93-96; DLB 53

Richards, I(vor) A(rmstrong) 1893-1979 .... **CLC 14, 24**
See also CA 41-44R; 89-92; CANR 34; DLB 27

Richardson, Anne
See Roiphe, Anne (Richardson)

Richardson, Dorothy Miller 1873-1957 .... **TCLC 3**
See also CA 104; DLB 36

Richardson, Ethel Florence (Lindesay) 1870-1946
See Richardson, Henry Handel
See also CA 105

Richardson, Henry Handel.......... **TCLC 4**
See also Richardson, Ethel Florence (Lindesay)

Richardson, Samuel 1689-1761 .... **LC 1; DA; WLC**
See also CDBLB 1660-1789; DLB 39

Richler, Mordecai 1931- .... **CLC 3, 5, 9, 13, 18, 46, 70**
See also AITN 1; CA 65-68; CANR 31; CLR 17; DLB 53; MAICYA; MTCW; SATA 44; SATA-Brief 27

Richter, Conrad (Michael) 1890-1968 .... **CLC 30**
See also CA 5-8R; 25-28R; CANR 23; DLB 9; MTCW; SATA 3

Riddell, J. H. 1832-1906 .... **TCLC 40**

Riding, Laura .... **CLC 3, 7**
See also Jackson, Laura (Riding)

Riefenstahl, Berta Helene Amalia 1902-
See Riefenstahl, Leni
See also CA 108

Riefenstahl, Leni .... **CLC 16**
See also Riefenstahl, Berta Helene Amalia

Riffe, Ernest
See Bergman, (Ernst) Ingmar

Riggs, (Rolla) Lynn 1899-1954 .... **TCLC 56**
See also CA 144; NNAL

Riley, James Whitcomb 1849-1916 .... **TCLC 51**
See also CA 118; 137; MAICYA; SATA 17

Riley, Tex
See Creasey, John

Rilke, Rainer Maria 1875-1926 .... **TCLC 1, 6, 19; PC 2**
See also CA 104; 132; DLB 81; MTCW

Rimbaud, (Jean Nicolas) Arthur 1854-1891 ..... **NCLC 4, 35; DA; PC 3; WLC**

Rinehart, Mary Roberts 1876-1958 .... **TCLC 52**
See also CA 108

Ringmaster, The
See Mencken, H(enry) L(ouis)

Ringwood, Gwen(dolyn Margaret) Pharis 1910-1984 .... **CLC 48**
See also CA 112; DLB 88

Rio, Michel 19(?)- .... **CLC 43**

Ritsos, Giannes
See Ritsos, Yannis

Ritsos, Yannis 1909-1990..... **CLC 6, 13, 31**
See also CA 77-80; 133; CANR 39; MTCW

Ritter, Erika 1948(?)- .... **CLC 52**

Rivera, Jose Eustasio 1889-1928... **TCLC 35**
See also HW

Rivers, Conrad Kent 1933-1968...... **CLC 1**
See also BW 1; CA 85-88; DLB 41

Rivers, Elfrida
See Bradley, Marion Zimmer

Riverside, John
See Heinlein, Robert A(nson)

Rizal, Jose 1861-1896........... **NCLC 27**

Roa Bastos, Augusto (Antonio) 1917- .... **CLC 45; HLC**
See also CA 131; DLB 113; HW

Robbe-Grillet, Alain 1922- ...... **CLC 1, 2, 4, 6, 8, 10, 14, 43**
See also CA 9-12R; CANR 33; DLB 83; MTCW

Robbins, Harold 1916- .... **CLC 5**
See also CA 73-76; CANR 26; MTCW

Robbins, Thomas Eugene 1936-
See Robbins, Tom
See also CA 81-84; CANR 29; MTCW

Robbins, Tom .... **CLC 9, 32, 64**
See also Robbins, Thomas Eugene
See also BEST 90:3; DLBY 80

Robbins, Trina 1938- .... **CLC 21**
See also CA 128

Roberts, Charles G(eorge) D(ouglas) 1860-1943 .... **TCLC 8**
See also CA 105; CLR 33; DLB 92; SATA-Brief 29

Roberts, Kate 1891-1985 .... **CLC 15**
See also CA 107; 116

Roberts, Keith (John Kingston) 1935- .... **CLC 14**
See also CA 25-28R; CANR 46

Roberts, Kenneth (Lewis) 1885-1957 .... **TCLC 23**
See also CA 109; DLB 9

Roberts, Michele (B.) 1949- .... **CLC 48**
See also CA 115

Robertson, Ellis
See Ellison, Harlan (Jay); Silverberg, Robert

Robertson, Thomas William 1829-1871 .... **NCLC 35**

Robinson, Edwin Arlington 1869-1935 .... **TCLC 5; DA; PC 1**
See also CA 104; 133; CDALB 1865-1917; DLB 54; MTCW

Robinson, Henry Crabb 1775-1867 .... **NCLC 15**
See also DLB 107

Robinson, Jill 1936- .... **CLC 10**
See also CA 102

Robinson, Kim Stanley 1952- ...... **CLC 34**
See also CA 126

Robinson, Lloyd
See Silverberg, Robert

Robinson, Marilynne 1944- .... **CLC 25**
See also CA 116

Robinson, Smokey .... **CLC 21**
See also Robinson, William, Jr.

Robinson, William, Jr. 1940-
See Robinson, Smokey
See also CA 116

Robison, Mary 1949- .... **CLC 42**
See also CA 113; 116; DLB 130

Rod, Edouard 1857-1910 .... **TCLC 52**

Roddenberry, Eugene Wesley 1921-1991
See Roddenberry, Gene
See also CA 110; 135; CANR 37; SATA 45; SATA-Obit 69

Roddenberry, Gene .... **CLC 17**
See also Roddenberry, Eugene Wesley
See also AAYA 5; SATA-Obit 69

Rodgers, Mary 1931- .... **CLC 12**
See also CA 49-52; CANR 8; CLR 20; JRDA; MAICYA; SATA 8

Rodgers, W(illiam) R(obert) 1909-1969 .... **CLC 7**
See also CA 85-88; DLB 20

Rodman, Eric
See Silverberg, Robert

Rodman, Howard 1920(?)-1985 ..... **CLC 65**
See also CA 118

Rodman, Maia
See Wojciechowska, Maia (Teresa)

Rodriguez, Claudio 1934- .... **CLC 10**
See also DLB 134

Roelvaag, O(le) E(dvart) 1876-1931 .... **TCLC 17**
See also CA 117; DLB 9

Roethke, Theodore (Huebner) 1908-1963 ...... **CLC 1, 3, 8, 11, 19, 46**
See also CA 81-84; CABS 2; CDALB 1941-1968; DLB 5; MTCW

Rogers, Thomas Hunton 1927- ..... **CLC 57**
See also CA 89-92

Rogers, Will(iam Penn Adair) 1879-1935 .... **TCLC 8**
See also CA 105; 144; DLB 11; NNAL

Rogin, Gilbert 1929- .... **CLC 18**
See also CA 65-68; CANR 15

Rohan, Koda .... **TCLC 22**
See also Koda Shigeyuki

Rohmer, Eric .... **CLC 16**
See also Scherer, Jean-Marie Maurice

Rohmer, Sax .... **TCLC 28**
See also Ward, Arthur Henry Sarsfield
See also DLB 70

Roiphe, Anne (Richardson) 1935- .... **CLC 3, 9**
See also CA 89-92; CANR 45; DLBY 80

Rojas, Fernando de 1465-1541 ...... **LC 23**

Rolfe, Frederick (William Serafino Austin Lewis Mary) 1860-1913...... **TCLC 12**
See also CA 107; DLB 34

Rolland, Romain 1866-1944....... **TCLC 23**
See also CA 118; DLB 65

Rolvaag, O(le) E(dvart)
See Roelvaag, O(le) E(dvart)

Romain Arnaud, Saint
See Aragon, Louis

Romains, Jules 1885-1972 .... **CLC 7**
See also CA 85-88; CANR 34; DLB 65; MTCW

Romero, Jose Ruben 1890-1952 ... **TCLC 14**
See also CA 114; 131; HW

Ronsard, Pierre de 1524-1585 .... **LC 6; PC 11**

Rooke, Leon 1934- .... **CLC 25, 34**
See also CA 25-28R; CANR 23

Roper, William 1498-1578 .... **LC 10**

Roquelaure, A. N.
See Rice, Anne

Rosa, Joao Guimaraes 1908-1967 ... **CLC 23**
See also CA 89-92; DLB 113

Rose, Wendy 1948- .... **CLC 85**
See also CA 53-56; CANR 5; NNAL; SATA 12

Rosen, Richard (Dean) 1949- .... **CLC 39**
See also CA 77-80

Rosenberg, Isaac 1890-1918....... **TCLC 12**
See also CA 107; DLB 20

Rosenblatt, Joe .... **CLC 15**
See also Rosenblatt, Joseph

Rosenblatt, Joseph 1933-
See Rosenblatt, Joe
See also CA 89-92

Rosenfeld, Samuel 1896-1963
See Tzara, Tristan
See also CA 89-92

Rosenthal, M(acha) L(ouis) 1917- . . . **CLC 28**
See also CA 1-4R; CAAS 6; CANR 4; DLB 5; SATA 59

Ross, Barnaby
See Dannay, Frederic

Ross, Bernard L.
See Follett, Ken(neth Martin)

Ross, J. H.
See Lawrence, T(homas) E(dward)

Ross, Martin
See Martin, Violet Florence
See also DLB 135

Ross, (James) Sinclair 1908- . . . . **CLC 13**
See also CA 73-76; DLB 88

Rossetti, Christina (Georgina) 1830-1894 . . . **NCLC 2; DA; PC 7; WLC**
See also DLB 35; MAICYA; SATA 20

Rossetti, Dante Gabriel 1828-1882 . . . . **NCLC 4; DA; WLC**
See also CDBLB 1832-1890; DLB 35

Rossner, Judith (Perelman) 1935- . . . . **CLC 6, 9, 29**
See also AITN 2; BEST 90:3; CA 17-20R; CANR 18; DLB 6; MTCW

Rostand, Edmond (Eugene Alexis) 1868-1918 . . . . **TCLC 6, 37; DA**
See also CA 104; 126; MTCW

Roth, Henry 1906- . . . . **CLC 2, 6, 11**
See also CA 11-12; CANR 38; CAP 1; DLB 28; MTCW

Roth, Joseph 1894-1939 . . . . **TCLC 33**
See also DLB 85

Roth, Philip (Milton) 1933- . . . . . . **CLC 1, 2, 3, 4, 6, 9, 15, 22, 31, 47, 66, 86; DA; WLC**
See also BEST 90:3; CA 1-4R; CANR 1, 22, 36; CDALB 1968-1988; DLB 2, 28; DLBY 82; MTCW

Rothenberg, Jerome 1931- . . . . **CLC 6, 57**
See also CA 45-48; CANR 1; DLB 5

Roumain, Jacques (Jean Baptiste) 1907-1944 . . . . **TCLC 19; BLC**
See also BW 1; CA 117; 125

Rourke, Constance (Mayfield) 1885-1941 . . . . **TCLC 12**
See also CA 107; YABC 1

Rousseau, Jean-Baptiste 1671-1741 . . . **LC 9**

Rousseau, Jean-Jacques 1712-1778 . . . . **LC 14; DA; WLC**

Roussel, Raymond 1877-1933 . . . . . **TCLC 20**
See also CA 117

Rovit, Earl (Herbert) 1927- . . . . **CLC 7**
See also CA 5-8R; CANR 12

Rowe, Nicholas 1674-1718 . . . . **LC 8**
See also DLB 84

Rowley, Ames Dorrance
See Lovecraft, H(oward) P(hillips)

Rowson, Susanna Haswell 1762(?)-1824 . . . . **NCLC 5**
See also DLB 37

Roy, Gabrielle 1909-1983 . . . . **CLC 10, 14**
See also CA 53-56; 110; CANR 5; DLB 68; MTCW

Rozewicz, Tadeusz 1921- . . . . **CLC 9, 23**
See also CA 108; CANR 36; MTCW

Ruark, Gibbons 1941- . . . . **CLC 3**
See also CA 33-36R; CANR 14, 31; DLB 120

Rubens, Bernice (Ruth) 1923- . . . **CLC 19, 31**
See also CA 25-28R; CANR 33; DLB 14; MTCW

Rudkin, (James) David 1936- . . . . . . **CLC 14**
See also CA 89-92; DLB 13

Rudnik, Raphael 1933- . . . . **CLC 7**
See also CA 29-32R

Ruffian, M.
See Hasek, Jaroslav (Matej Frantisek)

Ruiz, Jose Martinez . . . . **CLC 11**
See also Martinez Ruiz, Jose

Rukeyser, Muriel 1913-1980 . . . . **CLC 6, 10, 15, 27; PC 12**
See also CA 5-8R; 93-96; CANR 26; DLB 48; MTCW; SATA-Obit 22

Rule, Jane (Vance) 1931- . . . . **CLC 27**
See also CA 25-28R; CAAS 18; CANR 12; DLB 60

Rulfo, Juan 1918-1986 . . . . **CLC 8, 80; HLC**
See also CA 85-88; 118; CANR 26; DLB 113; HW; MTCW

Runeberg, Johan 1804-1877 . . . . . . **NCLC 41**

Runyon, (Alfred) Damon 1884(?)-1946 . . . . **TCLC 10**
See also CA 107; DLB 11, 86

Rush, Norman 1933- . . . . **CLC 44**
See also CA 121; 126

Rushdie, (Ahmed) Salman 1947- . . . . **CLC 23, 31, 55**
See also BEST 89:3; CA 108; 111; CANR 33; MTCW

Rushforth, Peter (Scott) 1945- . . . . . **CLC 19**
See also CA 101

Ruskin, John 1819-1900 . . . . **TCLC 20**
See also CA 114; 129; CDBLB 1832-1890; DLB 55; SATA 24

Russ, Joanna 1937- . . . . **CLC 15**
See also CA 25-28R; CANR 11, 31; DLB 8; MTCW

Russell, (Henry) Ken(neth Alfred) 1927- . . . . **CLC 16**
See also CA 105

Russell, Willy 1947- . . . . **CLC 60**

Rutherford, Mark . . . . **TCLC 25**
See also White, William Hale
See also DLB 18

Ryan, Cornelius (John) 1920-1974 . . . **CLC 7**
See also CA 69-72; 53-56; CANR 38

Ryan, Michael 1946- . . . . **CLC 65**
See also CA 49-52; DLBY 82

Rybakov, Anatoli (Naumovich) 1911- . . . . **CLC 23, 53**
See also CA 126; 135; SATA 79

Ryder, Jonathan
See Ludlum, Robert

Ryga, George 1932-1987 . . . . **CLC 14**
See also CA 101; 124; CANR 43; DLB 60

S. S.
See Sassoon, Siegfried (Lorraine)

Saba, Umberto 1883-1957 . . . . **TCLC 33**
See also CA 144; DLB 114

Sabatini, Rafael 1875-1950 . . . . **TCLC 47**

Sabato, Ernesto (R.) 1911- . . . . **CLC 10, 23; HLC**
See also CA 97-100; CANR 32; DLB 145; HW; MTCW

Sacastru, Martin
See Bioy Casares, Adolfo

Sacher-Masoch, Leopold von 1836(?)-1895 . . . . **NCLC 31**

Sachs, Marilyn (Stickle) 1927- . . . . . **CLC 35**
See also AAYA 2; CA 17-20R; CANR 13, 47; CLR 2; JRDA; MAICYA; SAAS 2; SATA 3, 68

Sachs, Nelly 1891-1970 . . . . **CLC 14**
See also CA 17-18; 25-28R; CAP 2

Sackler, Howard (Oliver) 1929-1982 . . . . **CLC 14**
See also CA 61-64; 108; CANR 30; DLB 7

Sacks, Oliver (Wolf) 1933- . . . . **CLC 67**
See also CA 53-56; CANR 28; MTCW

Sade, Donatien Alphonse Francois Comte 1740-1814 . . . . **NCLC 47**

Sadoff, Ira 1945- . . . . **CLC 9**
See also CA 53-56; CANR 5, 21; DLB 120

Saetone
See Camus, Albert

Safire, William 1929- . . . . **CLC 10**
See also CA 17-20R; CANR 31

Sagan, Carl (Edward) 1934- . . . . **CLC 30**
See also AAYA 2; CA 25-28R; CANR 11, 36; MTCW; SATA 58

Sagan, Francoise . . . . **CLC 3, 6, 9, 17, 36**
See also Quoirez, Francoise
See also DLB 83

Sahgal, Nayantara (Pandit) 1927- . . . **CLC 41**
See also CA 9-12R; CANR 11

Saint, H(arry) F. 1941- . . . . **CLC 50**
See also CA 127

St. Aubin de Teran, Lisa 1953-
See Teran, Lisa St. Aubin de
See also CA 118; 126

Sainte-Beuve, Charles Augustin 1804-1869 . . . . **NCLC 5**

Saint-Exupery, Antoine (Jean Baptiste Marie Roger) de 1900-1944 . . . . **TCLC 2, 56; WLC**
See also CA 108; 132; CLR 10; DLB 72; MAICYA; MTCW; SATA 20

St. John, David
See Hunt, E(verette) Howard, (Jr.)

Saint-John Perse
See Leger, (Marie-Rene Auguste) Alexis Saint-Leger

Saintsbury, George (Edward Bateman) 1845-1933 . . . . **TCLC 31**
See also DLB 57

Shacochis, Robert G. 1951-
See Shacochis, Bob
See also CA 119; 124

Shaffer, Anthony (Joshua) 1926-.... **CLC 19**
See also CA 110; 116; DLB 13

Shaffer, Peter (Levin)
1926- .... **CLC 5, 14, 18, 37, 60**
See also CA 25-28R; CANR 25, 47; CDBLB 1960 to Present; DLB 13; MTCW

Shakey, Bernard
See Young, Neil

Shalamov, Varlam (Tikhonovich)
1907(?)-1982 .... **CLC 18**
See also CA 129; 105

Shamlu, Ahmad 1925- .... **CLC 10**

Shammas, Anton 1951-............ **CLC 55**

Shange, Ntozake
1948- .... **CLC 8, 25, 38, 74; BLC; DC 3**
See also AAYA 9; BW 2; CA 85-88; CABS 3; CANR 27; DLB 38; MTCW

Shanley, John Patrick 1950-....... **CLC 75**
See also CA 128; 133

Shapcott, Thomas William 1935- ... **CLC 38**
See also CA 69-72

Shapiro, Jane..................... **CLC 76**

Shapiro, Karl (Jay) 1913- .. **CLC 4, 8, 15, 53**
See also CA 1-4R; CAAS 6; CANR 1, 36; DLB 48; MTCW

Sharp, William 1855-1905 .... **TCLC 39**

Sharpe, Thomas Ridley 1928-
See Sharpe, Tom
See also CA 114; 122

Sharpe, Tom..................... **CLC 36**
See also Sharpe, Thomas Ridley
See also DLB 14

Shaw, Bernard.................. **TCLC 45**
See also Shaw, George Bernard
See also BW 1

Shaw, G. Bernard
See Shaw, George Bernard

Shaw, George Bernard
1856-1950 .... **TCLC 3, 9, 21; DA; WLC**
See also Shaw, Bernard
See also CA 104; 128; CDBLB 1914-1945; DLB 10, 57; MTCW

Shaw, Henry Wheeler
1818-1885 .... **NCLC 15**
See also DLB 11

Shaw, Irwin 1913-1984....... **CLC 7, 23, 34**
See also AITN 1; CA 13-16R; 112; CANR 21; CDALB 1941-1968; DLB 6, 102; DLBY 84; MTCW

Shaw, Robert 1927-1978 .... **CLC 5**
See also AITN 1; CA 1-4R; 81-84; CANR 4; DLB 13, 14

Shaw, T. E.
See Lawrence, T(homas) E(dward)

Shawn, Wallace 1943- .... **CLC 41**
See also CA 112

Shea, Lisa 1953-................. **CLC 86**

Sheed, Wilfrid (John Joseph)
1930- .... **CLC 2, 4, 10, 53**
See also CA 65-68; CANR 30; DLB 6; MTCW

Sheldon, Alice Hastings Bradley
1915(?)-1987
See Tiptree, James, Jr.
See also CA 108; 122; CANR 34; MTCW

Sheldon, John
See Bloch, Robert (Albert)

Shelley, Mary Wollstonecraft (Godwin)
1797-1851 .... **NCLC 14; DA; WLC**
See also CDBLB 1789-1832; DLB 110, 116; SATA 29

Shelley, Percy Bysshe
1792-1822 .... **NCLC 18; DA; WLC**
See also CDBLB 1789-1832; DLB 96, 110

Shepard, Jim 1956-............... **CLC 36**
See also CA 137

Shepard, Lucius 1947- .... **CLC 34**
See also CA 128; 141

Shepard, Sam
1943- .... **CLC 4, 6, 17, 34, 41, 44; DC 5**
See also AAYA 1; CA 69-72; CABS 3; CANR 22; DLB 7; MTCW

Shepherd, Michael
See Ludlum, Robert

Sherburne, Zoa (Morin) 1912-...... **CLC 30**
See also AAYA 13; CA 1-4R; CANR 3, 37; MAICYA; SAAS 18; SATA 3

Sheridan, Frances 1724-1766......... **LC 7**
See also DLB 39, 84

Sheridan, Richard Brinsley
1751-1816 ... **NCLC 5; DA; DC 1; WLC**
See also CDBLB 1660-1789; DLB 89

Sherman, Jonathan Marc........... **CLC 55**

Sherman, Martin 1941(?)- .... **CLC 19**
See also CA 116; 123

Sherwin, Judith Johnson 1936-... **CLC 7, 15**
See also CA 25-28R; CANR 34

Sherwood, Frances 1940-.......... **CLC 81**

Sherwood, Robert E(mmet)
1896-1955 .... **TCLC 3**
See also CA 104; DLB 7, 26

Shestov, Lev 1866-1938 .... **TCLC 56**

Shiel, M(atthew) P(hipps)
1865-1947 .... **TCLC 8**
See also CA 106

Shiga, Naoya 1883-1971........... **CLC 33**
See also CA 101; 33-36R

Shih, Su 1036-1101............ **CMLC 15:**

Shilts, Randy 1951-1994 .... **CLC 85**
See also CA 115; 127; 144; CANR 45

Shimazaki Haruki 1872-1943
See Shimazaki Toson
See also CA 105; 134

Shimazaki Toson.................. **TCLC 5**
See also Shimazaki Haruki

Sholokhov, Mikhail (Aleksandrovich)
1905-1984 .... **CLC 7, 15**
See also CA 101; 112; MTCW; SATA-Obit 36

Shone, Patric
See Hanley, James

Shreve, Susan Richards 1939-...... **CLC 23**
See also CA 49-52; CAAS 5; CANR 5, 38; MAICYA; SATA 46; SATA-Brief 41

Shue, Larry 1946-1985............ **CLC 52**
See also CA 145; 117

Shu-Jen, Chou 1881-1936
See Hsun, Lu
See also CA 104

Shulman, Alix Kates 1932- ...... **CLC 2, 10**
See also CA 29-32R; CANR 43; SATA 7

Shuster, Joe 1914- .... **CLC 21**

Shute, Nevil...................... **CLC 30**
See also Norway, Nevil Shute

Shuttle, Penelope (Diane) 1947- ..... **CLC 7**
See also CA 93-96; CANR 39; DLB 14, 40

Sidney, Mary 1561-1621 .... **LC 19**

Sidney, Sir Philip 1554-1586.... **LC 19; DA**
See also CDBLB Before 1660

Siegel, Jerome 1914- .... **CLC 21**
See also CA 116

Siegel, Jerry
See Siegel, Jerome

Sienkiewicz, Henryk (Adam Alexander Pius)
1846-1916 .... **TCLC 3**
See also CA 104; 134

Sierra, Gregorio Martinez
See Martinez Sierra, Gregorio

Sierra, Maria (de la O'LeJarraga) Martinez
See Martinez Sierra, Maria (de la O'LeJarraga)

Sigal, Clancy 1926-................ **CLC 7**
See also CA 1-4R

Sigourney, Lydia Howard (Huntley)
1791-1865 .... **NCLC 21**
See also DLB 1, 42, 73

Siguenza y Gongora, Carlos de
1645-1700 .... **LC 8**

Sigurjonsson, Johann 1880-1919... **TCLC 27**

Sikelianos, Angelos 1884-1951 .... **TCLC 39**

Silkin, Jon 1930- .... **CLC 2, 6, 43**
See also CA 5-8R; CAAS 5; DLB 27

Silko, Leslie (Marmon)
1948- .... **CLC 23, 74; DA**
See also AAYA 14; CA 115; 122; CANR 45; DLB 143; NNAL

Sillanpaa, Frans Eemil 1888-1964... **CLC 19**
See also CA 129; 93-96; MTCW

Sillitoe, Alan
1928- .... **CLC 1, 3, 6, 10, 19, 57**
See also AITN 1; CA 9-12R; CAAS 2; CANR 8, 26; CDBLB 1960 to Present; DLB 14, 139; MTCW; SATA 61

Silone, Ignazio 1900-1978 .... **CLC 4**
See also CA 25-28; 81-84; CANR 34; CAP 2; MTCW

Silver, Joan Micklin 1935- .... **CLC 20**
See also CA 114; 121

Silver, Nicholas
See Faust, Frederick (Schiller)

Silverberg, Robert 1935- .... **CLC 7**
See also CA 1-4R; CAAS 3; CANR 1, 20, 36; DLB 8; MAICYA; MTCW; SATA 13

Smith, Wilbur (Addison) 1933- ..... **CLC 33**
See also CA 13-16R; CANR 7, 46; MTCW

Smith, William Jay 1918- .... **CLC 6**
See also CA 5-8R; CANR 44; DLB 5; MAICYA; SATA 2, 68

Smith, Woodrow Wilson
See Kuttner, Henry

Smolenskin, Peretz 1842-1885.... **NCLC 30**

Smollett, Tobias (George) 1721-1771 .. **LC 2**
See also CDBLB 1660-1789; DLB 39, 104

Snodgrass, W(illiam) D(e Witt)
1926- .... **CLC 2, 6, 10, 18, 68**
See also CA 1-4R; CANR 6, 36; DLB 5; MTCW

Snow, C(harles) P(ercy)
1905-1980 .... **CLC 1, 4, 6, 9, 13, 19**
See also CA 5-8R; 101; CANR 28; CDBLB 1945-1960; DLB 15, 77; MTCW

Snow, Frances Compton
See Adams, Henry (Brooks)

Snyder, Gary (Sherman)
1930- .... **CLC 1, 2, 5, 9, 32**
See also CA 17-20R; CANR 30; DLB 5, 16

Snyder, Zilpha Keatley 1927- ...... **CLC 17**
See also CA 9-12R; CANR 38; CLR 31; JRDA; MAICYA; SAAS 2; SATA 1, 28, 75

Soares, Bernardo
See Pessoa, Fernando (Antonio Nogueira)

Sobh, A.
See Shamlu, Ahmad

Sobol, Joshua..................... **CLC 60**

Soderberg, Hjalmar 1869-1941 .... **TCLC 39**

Sodergran, Edith (Irene)
See Soedergran, Edith (Irene)

Soedergran, Edith (Irene)
1892-1923 .... **TCLC 31**

Softly, Edgar
See Lovecraft, H(oward) P(hillips)

Softly, Edward
See Lovecraft, H(oward) P(hillips)

Sokolov, Raymond 1941- .... **CLC 7**
See also CA 85-88

Solo, Jay
See Ellison, Harlan (Jay)

Sologub, Fyodor .... **TCLC 9**
See also Teternikov, Fyodor Kuzmich

Solomons, Ikey Esquir
See Thackeray, William Makepeace

Solomos, Dionysios 1798-1857 ... **NCLC 15**

Solwoska, Mara
See French, Marilyn

Solzhenitsyn, Aleksandr I(sayevich)
1918- ...... **CLC 1, 2, 4, 7, 9, 10, 18, 26, 34, 78; DA; WLC**
See also AITN 1; CA 69-72; CANR 40; MTCW

Somers, Jane
See Lessing, Doris (May)

Somerville, Edith 1858-1949 ...... **TCLC 51**
See also DLB 135

Somerville & Ross
See Martin, Violet Florence; Somerville, Edith

Sommer, Scott 1951- .... **CLC 25**
See also CA 106

Sondheim, Stephen (Joshua)
1930- .... **CLC 30, 39**
See also AAYA 11; CA 103; CANR 47

Sontag, Susan 1933- ... **CLC 1, 2, 10, 13, 31**
See also CA 17-20R; CANR 25; DLB 2, 67; MTCW

Sophocles
496(?)B.C.-406(?)B.C..... **CMLC 2; DA; DC 1**

Sordello 1189-1269........... **CMLC 15:**

Sorel, Julia
See Drexler, Rosalyn

Sorrentino, Gilbert
1929- .... **CLC 3, 7, 14, 22, 40**
See also CA 77-80; CANR 14, 33; DLB 5; DLBY 80

Soto, Gary 1952-........ **CLC 32, 80; HLC**
See also AAYA 10; CA 119; 125; DLB 82; HW; JRDA; SATA 80

Soupault, Philippe 1897-1990 ...... **CLC 68**
See also CA 116; 131

Souster, (Holmes) Raymond
1921- .... **CLC 5, 14**
See also CA 13-16R; CAAS 14; CANR 13, 29; DLB 88; SATA 63

Southern, Terry 1926- .... **CLC 7**
See also CA 1-4R; CANR 1; DLB 2

Southey, Robert 1774-1843 .... **NCLC 8**
See also DLB 93, 107, 142; SATA 54

Southworth, Emma Dorothy Eliza Nevitte
1819-1899 .... **NCLC 26**

Souza, Ernest
See Scott, Evelyn

Soyinka, Wole
1934- .... **CLC 3, 5, 14, 36, 44; BLC; DA; DC 2; WLC**
See also BW 2; CA 13-16R; CANR 27, 39; DLB 125; MTCW

Spackman, W(illiam) M(ode)
1905-1990 .... **CLC 46**
See also CA 81-84; 132

Spacks, Barry 1931-............. **CLC 14**
See also CA 29-32R; CANR 33; DLB 105

Spanidou, Irini 1946- .... **CLC 44**

Spark, Muriel (Sarah)
1918- .... **CLC 2, 3, 5, 8, 13, 18, 40; SSC 10**
See also CA 5-8R; CANR 12, 36; CDBLB 1945-1960; DLB 15, 139; MTCW

Spaulding, Douglas
See Bradbury, Ray (Douglas)

Spaulding, Leonard
See Bradbury, Ray (Douglas)

Spence, J. A. D.
See Eliot, T(homas) S(tearns)

Spencer, Elizabeth 1921- .... **CLC 22**
See also CA 13-16R; CANR 32; DLB 6; MTCW; SATA 14

Spencer, Leonard G.
See Silverberg, Robert

Spencer, Scott 1945-.............. **CLC 30**
See also CA 113; DLBY 86

Spender, Stephen (Harold)
1909- .... **CLC 1, 2, 5, 10, 41**
See also CA 9-12R; CANR 31; CDBLB 1945-1960; DLB 20; MTCW

Spengler, Oswald (Arnold Gottfried)
1880-1936 .... **TCLC 25**
See also CA 118

Spenser, Edmund
1552(?)-1599 .... **LC 5; DA; PC 8; WLC**
See also CDBLB Before 1660

Spicer, Jack 1925-1965 ...... **CLC 8, 18, 72**
See also CA 85-88; DLB 5, 16

Spiegelman, Art 1948- .... **CLC 76**
See also AAYA 10; CA 125; CANR 41

Spielberg, Peter 1929- .... **CLC 6**
See also CA 5-8R; CANR 4; DLBY 81

Spielberg, Steven 1947- .... **CLC 20**
See also AAYA 8; CA 77-80; CANR 32; SATA 32

Spillane, Frank Morrison 1918-
See Spillane, Mickey
See also CA 25-28R; CANR 28; MTCW; SATA 66

Spillane, Mickey .... **CLC 3, 13**
See also Spillane, Frank Morrison

Spinoza, Benedictus de 1632-1677 .... **LC 9**

Spinrad, Norman (Richard) 1940- ... **CLC 46**
See also CA 37-40R; CAAS 19; CANR 20; DLB 8

Spitteler, Carl (Friedrich Georg)
1845-1924 .... **TCLC 12**
See also CA 109; DLB 129

Spivack, Kathleen (Romola Drucker)
1938- .... **CLC 6**
See also CA 49-52

Spoto, Donald 1941-.............. **CLC 39**
See also CA 65-68; CANR 11

Springsteen, Bruce (F.) 1949- ...... **CLC 17**
See also CA 111

Spurling, Hilary 1940-............ **CLC 34**
See also CA 104; CANR 25

Spyker, John Howland
See Elman, Richard

Squires, (James) Radcliffe
1917-1993 .... **CLC 51**
See also CA 1-4R; 140; CANR 6, 21

Srivastava, Dhanpat Rai 1880(?)-1936
See Premchand
See also CA 118

Stacy, Donald
See Pohl, Frederik

Stael, Germaine de
See Stael-Holstein, Anne Louise Germaine Necker Baronn
See also DLB 119

Stael-Holstein, Anne Louise Germaine Necker Baronn 1766-1817 .... **NCLC 3**
See also Stael, Germaine de

Stafford, Jean 1915-1979 . . . **CLC 4, 7, 19, 68**
See also CA 1-4R; 85-88; CANR 3; DLB 2; MTCW; SATA-Obit 22

Stafford, William (Edgar) 1914-1993 . . . . **CLC 4, 7, 29**
See also CA 5-8R; 142; CAAS 3; CANR 5, 22; DLB 5

Staines, Trevor
See Brunner, John (Kilian Houston)

Stairs, Gordon
See Austin, Mary (Hunter)

Stannard, Martin 1947- . . . . **CLC 44**
See also CA 142

Stanton, Maura 1946- . . . . **CLC 9**
See also CA 89-92; CANR 15; DLB 120

Stanton, Schuyler
See Baum, L(yman) Frank

Stapledon, (William) Olaf 1886-1950 . . . . **TCLC 22**
See also CA 111; DLB 15

Starbuck, George (Edwin) 1931- . . . . **CLC 53**
See also CA 21-24R; CANR 23

Stark, Richard
See Westlake, Donald E(dwin)

Staunton, Schuyler
See Baum, L(yman) Frank

Stead, Christina (Ellen) 1902-1983 . . . . **CLC 2, 5, 8, 32, 80**
See also CA 13-16R; 109; CANR 33, 40; MTCW

Stead, William Thomas 1849-1912 . . . . **TCLC 48**

Steele, Richard 1672-1729 . . . . **LC 18**
See also CDBLB 1660-1789; DLB 84, 101

Steele, Timothy (Reid) 1948- . . . . **CLC 45**
See also CA 93-96; CANR 16; DLB 120

Steffens, (Joseph) Lincoln 1866-1936 . . . . **TCLC 20**
See also CA 117

Stegner, Wallace (Earle) 1909-1993 . . . . **CLC 9, 49, 81**
See also AITN 1; BEST 90:3; CA 1-4R; 141; CAAS 9; CANR 1, 21, 46; DLB 9; DLBY 93; MTCW

Stein, Gertrude 1874-1946 . . . . . . **TCLC 1, 6, 28, 48; DA; WLC**
See also CA 104; 132; CDALB 1917-1929; DLB 4, 54, 86; MTCW

Steinbeck, John (Ernst) 1902-1968 . . . . . . **CLC 1, 5, 9, 13, 21, 34, 45, 75; DA; SSC 11; WLC**
See also AAYA 12; CA 1-4R; 25-28R; CANR 1, 35; CDALB 1929-1941; DLB 7, 9; DLBD 2; MTCW; SATA 9

Steinem, Gloria 1934- . . . . **CLC 63**
See also CA 53-56; CANR 28; MTCW

Steiner, George 1929- . . . . **CLC 24**
See also CA 73-76; CANR 31; DLB 67; MTCW; SATA 62

Steiner, K. Leslie
See Delany, Samuel R(ay, Jr.)

Steiner, Rudolf 1861-1925 . . . . **TCLC 13**
See also CA 107

Stendhal 1783-1842 . . . . . **NCLC 23, 46; DA; WLC**
See also DLB 119

Stephen, Leslie 1832-1904 . . . . **TCLC 23**
See also CA 123; DLB 57, 144

Stephen, Sir Leslie
See Stephen, Leslie

Stephen, Virginia
See Woolf, (Adeline) Virginia

Stephens, James 1882(?)-1950 . . . . . . **TCLC 4**
See also CA 104; DLB 19

Stephens, Reed
See Donaldson, Stephen R.

Steptoe, Lydia
See Barnes, Djuna

Sterchi, Beat 1949- . . . . **CLC 65**

Sterling, Brett
See Bradbury, Ray (Douglas); Hamilton, Edmond

Sterling, Bruce 1954- . . . . **CLC 72**
See also CA 119; CANR 44

Sterling, George 1869-1926 . . . . **TCLC 20**
See also CA 117; DLB 54

Stern, Gerald 1925- . . . . **CLC 40**
See also CA 81-84; CANR 28; DLB 105

Stern, Richard (Gustave) 1928- . . . **CLC 4, 39**
See also CA 1-4R; CANR 1, 25; DLBY 87

Sternberg, Josef von 1894-1969. . . . . **CLC 20**
See also CA 81-84

Sterne, Laurence 1713-1768 . . . . **LC 2; DA; WLC**
See also CDBLB 1660-1789; DLB 39

Sternheim, (William Adolf) Carl 1878-1942 . . . . **TCLC 8**
See also CA 105; DLB 56, 118

Stevens, Mark 1951- . . . . **CLC 34**
See also CA 122

Stevens, Wallace 1879-1955 . . . . **TCLC 3, 12, 45; DA; PC 6; WLC**
See also CA 104; 124; CDALB 1929-1941; DLB 54; MTCW

Stevenson, Anne (Katharine) 1933- . . . . **CLC 7, 33**
See also CA 17-20R; CAAS 9; CANR 9, 33; DLB 40; MTCW

Stevenson, Robert Louis (Balfour) 1850-1894 . . . . **NCLC 5, 14; DA; SSC 11; WLC**
See also CDBLB 1890-1914; CLR 10, 11; DLB 18, 57, 141; JRDA; MAICYA; YABC 2

Stewart, J(ohn) I(nnes) M(ackintosh) 1906- . . . . **CLC 7, 14, 32**
See also CA 85-88; CAAS 3; CANR 47; MTCW

Stewart, Mary (Florence Elinor) 1916- . . . . **CLC 7, 35**
See also CA 1-4R; CANR 1; SATA 12

Stewart, Mary Rainbow
See Stewart, Mary (Florence Elinor)

Stifle, June
See Campbell, Maria

Stifter, Adalbert 1805-1868 . . . . . . **NCLC 41**
See also DLB 133

Still, James 1906- . . . . **CLC 49**
See also CA 65-68; CAAS 17; CANR 10, 26; DLB 9; SATA 29

Sting
See Sumner, Gordon Matthew

Stirling, Arthur
See Sinclair, Upton (Beall)

Stitt, Milan 1941- . . . . **CLC 29**
See also CA 69-72

Stockton, Francis Richard 1834-1902
See Stockton, Frank R.
See also CA 108; 137; MAICYA; SATA 44

Stockton, Frank R. . . . . **TCLC 47**
See also Stockton, Francis Richard
See also DLB 42, 74; SATA-Brief 32

Stoddard, Charles
See Kuttner, Henry

Stoker, Abraham 1847-1912
See Stoker, Bram
See also CA 105; DA; SATA 29

Stoker, Bram . . . . **TCLC 8; WLC**
See also Stoker, Abraham
See also CDBLB 1890-1914; DLB 36, 70

Stolz, Mary (Slattery) 1920- . . . . **CLC 12**
See also AAYA 8; AITN 1; CA 5-8R; CANR 13, 41; JRDA; MAICYA; SAAS 3; SATA 10, 71

Stone, Irving 1903-1989 . . . . **CLC 7**
See also AITN 1; CA 1-4R; 129; CAAS 3; CANR 1, 23; MTCW; SATA 3; SATA-Obit 64

Stone, Oliver 1946- . . . . **CLC 73**
See also CA 110

Stone, Robert (Anthony) 1937- . . . . **CLC 5, 23, 42**
See also CA 85-88; CANR 23; MTCW

Stone, Zachary
See Follett, Ken(neth Martin)

Stoppard, Tom 1937- . . . . . . **CLC 1, 3, 4, 5, 8, 15, 29, 34, 63; DA; WLC**
See also CA 81-84; CANR 39; CDBLB 1960 to Present; DLB 13; DLBY 85; MTCW

Storey, David (Malcolm) 1933- . . . . **CLC 2, 4, 5, 8**
See also CA 81-84; CANR 36; DLB 13, 14; MTCW

Storm, Hyemeyohsts 1935- . . . . **CLC 3**
See also CA 81-84; CANR 45; NNAL

Storm, (Hans) Theodor (Woldsen) 1817-1888 . . . . **NCLC 1**

Storni, Alfonsina 1892-1938 . . . . **TCLC 5; HLC**
See also CA 104; 131; HW

Stout, Rex (Todhunter) 1886-1975 . . . **CLC 3**
See also AITN 2; CA 61-64

Stow, (Julian) Randolph 1935- . . **CLC 23, 48**
See also CA 13-16R; CANR 33; MTCW

Stowe, Harriet (Elizabeth) Beecher 1811-1896 . . . . **NCLC 3; DA; WLC**
See also CDALB 1865-1917; DLB 1, 12, 42, 74; JRDA; MAICYA; YABC 1

Strachey, (Giles) Lytton 1880-1932 .... **TCLC 12**
See also CA 110; DLBD 10

Strand, Mark 1934- ...... **CLC 6, 18, 41, 71**
See also CA 21-24R; CANR 40; DLB 5; SATA 41

Straub, Peter (Francis) 1943- ...... **CLC 28**
See also BEST 89:1; CA 85-88; CANR 28; DLBY 84; MTCW

Strauss, Botho 1944- .... **CLC 22**
See also DLB 124

Streatfeild, (Mary) Noel 1895(?)-1986 .... **CLC 21**
See also CA 81-84; 120; CANR 31; CLR 17; MAICYA; SATA 20; SATA-Obit 48

Stribling, T(homas) S(igismund) 1881-1965 .... **CLC 23**
See also CA 107; DLB 9

Strindberg, (Johan) August 1849-1912 ...... **TCLC 1, 8, 21, 47; DA; WLC**
See also CA 104; 135

Stringer, Arthur 1874-1950 .... **TCLC 37**
See also DLB 92

Stringer, David
See Roberts, Keith (John Kingston)

Strugatskii, Arkadii (Natanovich) 1925-1991 .... **CLC 27**
See also CA 106; 135

Strugatskii, Boris (Natanovich) 1933- .... **CLC 27**
See also CA 106

Strummer, Joe 1953(?)- .... **CLC 30**

Stuart, Don A.
See Campbell, John W(ood, Jr.)

Stuart, Ian
See MacLean, Alistair (Stuart)

Stuart, Jesse (Hilton) 1906-1984 .... **CLC 1, 8, 11, 14, 34**
See also CA 5-8R; 112; CANR 31; DLB 9, 48, 102; DLBY 84; SATA 2; SATA-Obit 36

Sturgeon, Theodore (Hamilton) 1918-1985 .... **CLC 22, 39**
See also Queen, Ellery
See also CA 81-84; 116; CANR 32; DLB 8; DLBY 85; MTCW

Sturges, Preston 1898-1959 .... **TCLC 48**
See also CA 114; DLB 26

Styron, William 1925- .... **CLC 1, 3, 5, 11, 15, 60**
See also BEST 90:4; CA 5-8R; CANR 6, 33; CDALB 1968-1988; DLB 2, 143; DLBY 80; MTCW

Suarez Lynch, B.
See Bioy Casares, Adolfo; Borges, Jorge Luis

Su Chien 1884-1918
See Su Man-shu
See also CA 123

Suckow, Ruth 1892-1960
See also CA 113; DLB 9, 102; SSC 18

Sudermann, Hermann 1857-1928 .. **TCLC 15**
See also CA 107; DLB 118

Sue, Eugene 1804-1857 .... **NCLC 1**
See also DLB 119

Sueskind, Patrick 1949- .... **CLC 44**
See also Suskind, Patrick

Sukenick, Ronald 1932- ..... **CLC 3, 4, 6, 48**
See also CA 25-28R; CAAS 8; CANR 32; DLBY 81

Suknaski, Andrew 1942- .... **CLC 19**
See also CA 101; DLB 53

Sullivan, Vernon
See Vian, Boris

Sully Prudhomme 1839-1907 ...... **TCLC 31**

Su Man-shu .... **TCLC 24**
See also Su Chien

Summerforest, Ivy B.
See Kirkup, James

Summers, Andrew James 1942- ..... **CLC 26**

Summers, Andy
See Summers, Andrew James

Summers, Hollis (Spurgeon, Jr.) 1916- .... **CLC 10**
See also CA 5-8R; CANR 3; DLB 6

Summers, (Alphonsus Joseph-Mary Augustus) Montague 1880-1948 .... **TCLC 16**
See also CA 118

Sumner, Gordon Matthew 1951- .... **CLC 26**

Surtees, Robert Smith 1803-1864 .... **NCLC 14**
See also DLB 21

Susann, Jacqueline 1921-1974 .... **CLC 3**
See also AITN 1; CA 65-68; 53-56; MTCW

Suskind, Patrick
See Sueskind, Patrick
See also CA 145

Sutcliff, Rosemary 1920-1992 ...... **CLC 26**
See also AAYA 10; CA 5-8R; 139; CANR 37; CLR 1; JRDA; MAICYA; SATA 6, 44, 78; SATA-Obit 73

Sutro, Alfred 1863-1933 .... **TCLC 6**
See also CA 105; DLB 10

Sutton, Henry
See Slavitt, David R(ytman)

Svevo, Italo .... **TCLC 2, 35**
See also Schmitz, Aron Hector

Swados, Elizabeth 1951- .... **CLC 12**
See also CA 97-100

Swados, Harvey 1920-1972 .... **CLC 5**
See also CA 5-8R; 37-40R; CANR 6; DLB 2

Swan, Gladys 1934- .... **CLC 69**
See also CA 101; CANR 17, 39

Swarthout, Glendon (Fred) 1918-1992 .... **CLC 35**
See also CA 1-4R; 139; CANR 1, 47; SATA 26

Sweet, Sarah C.
See Jewett, (Theodora) Sarah Orne

Swenson, May 1919-1989 .... **CLC 4, 14, 61; DA**
See also CA 5-8R; 130; CANR 36; DLB 5; MTCW; SATA 15

Swift, Augustus
See Lovecraft, H(oward) P(hillips)

Swift, Graham (Colin) 1949- .... **CLC 41**
See also CA 117; 122; CANR 46

Swift, Jonathan 1667-1745 ...... **LC 1; DA; PC 9; WLC**
See also CDBLB 1660-1789; DLB 39, 95, 101; SATA 19

Swinburne, Algernon Charles 1837-1909 ...... **TCLC 8, 36; DA; WLC**
See also CA 105; 140; CDBLB 1832-1890; DLB 35, 57

Swinfen, Ann .... **CLC 34**

Swinnerton, Frank Arthur 1884-1982 .... **CLC 31**
See also CA 108; DLB 34

Swithen, John
See King, Stephen (Edwin)

Sylvia
See Ashton-Warner, Sylvia (Constance)

Symmes, Robert Edward
See Duncan, Robert (Edward)

Symonds, John Addington 1840-1893 .... **NCLC 34**
See also DLB 57, 144

Symons, Arthur 1865-1945 .... **TCLC 11**
See also CA 107; DLB 19, 57

Symons, Julian (Gustave) 1912- .... **CLC 2, 14, 32**
See also CA 49-52; CAAS 3; CANR 3, 33; DLB 87; DLBY 92; MTCW

Synge, (Edmund) J(ohn) M(illington) 1871-1909 .... **TCLC 6, 37; DC 2**
See also CA 104; 141; CDBLB 1890-1914; DLB 10, 19

Syruc, J.
See Milosz, Czeslaw

Szirtes, George 1948- .... **CLC 46**
See also CA 109; CANR 27

Tabori, George 1914- .... **CLC 19**
See also CA 49-52; CANR 4

Tagore, Rabindranath 1861-1941 .... **TCLC 3, 53; PC 8**
See also CA 104; 120; MTCW

Taine, Hippolyte Adolphe 1828-1893 .... **NCLC 15**

Talese, Gay 1932- .... **CLC 37**
See also AITN 1; CA 1-4R; CANR 9; MTCW

Tallent, Elizabeth (Ann) 1954- ..... **CLC 45**
See also CA 117; DLB 130

Tally, Ted 1952- .... **CLC 42**
See also CA 120; 124

Tamayo y Baus, Manuel 1829-1898 .... **NCLC 1**

Tammsaare, A(nton) H(ansen) 1878-1940 .... **TCLC 27**

Tan, Amy 1952- .... **CLC 59**
See also AAYA 9; BEST 89:3; CA 136; SATA 75

Tandem, Felix
See Spitteler, Carl (Friedrich Georg)

Tanizaki, Jun'ichiro 1886-1965 .... **CLC 8, 14, 28**
See also CA 93-96; 25-28R

Tanner, William
See Amis, Kingsley (William)

Tao Lao
See Storni, Alfonsina

Tarassoff, Lev
See Troyat, Henri

Tarbell, Ida M(inerva) 1857-1944 .... **TCLC 40**
See also CA 122; DLB 47

Tarkington, (Newton) Booth 1869-1946 .... **TCLC 9**
See also CA 110; 143; DLB 9, 102; SATA 17

Tarkovsky, Andrei (Arsenyevich) 1932-1986 .... **CLC 75**
See also CA 127

Tartt, Donna 1964(?)-............. **CLC 76**
See also CA 142

Tasso, Torquato 1544-1595 .... **LC 5**

Tate, (John Orley) Allen 1899-1979 .... **CLC 2, 4, 6, 9, 11, 14, 24**
See also CA 5-8R; 85-88; CANR 32; DLB 4, 45, 63; MTCW

Tate, Ellalice
See Hibbert, Eleanor Alice Burford

Tate, James (Vincent) 1943- ... **CLC 2, 6, 25**
See also CA 21-24R; CANR 29; DLB 5

Tavel, Ronald 1940-............... **CLC 6**
See also CA 21-24R; CANR 33

Taylor, C(ecil) P(hilip) 1929-1981... **CLC 27**
See also CA 25-28R; 105; CANR 47

Taylor, Edward 1642(?)-1729.... **LC 11; DA**
See also DLB 24

Taylor, Eleanor Ross 1920-......... **CLC 5**
See also CA 81-84

Taylor, Elizabeth 1912-1975 ... **CLC 2, 4, 29**
See also CA 13-16R; CANR 9; DLB 139; MTCW; SATA 13

Taylor, Henry (Splawn) 1942-...... **CLC 44**
See also CA 33-36R; CAAS 7; CANR 31; DLB 5

Taylor, Kamala (Purnaiya) 1924-
See Markandaya, Kamala
See also CA 77-80

Taylor, Mildred D. .... **CLC 21**
See also AAYA 10; BW 1; CA 85-88; CANR 25; CLR 9; DLB 52; JRDA; MAICYA; SAAS 5; SATA 15, 70

Taylor, Peter (Hillsman) 1917- ...... **CLC 1, 4, 18, 37, 44, 50, 71; SSC 10**
See also CA 13-16R; CANR 9; DLBY 81; MTCW

Taylor, Robert Lewis 1912-........ **CLC 14**
See also CA 1-4R; CANR 3; SATA 10

Tchekhov, Anton
See Chekhov, Anton (Pavlovich)

Teasdale, Sara 1884-1933.......... **TCLC 4**
See also CA 104; DLB 45; SATA 32

Tegner, Esaias 1782-1846......... **NCLC 2**

Teilhard de Chardin, (Marie Joseph) Pierre 1881-1955 .... **TCLC 9**
See also CA 105

Temple, Ann
See Mortimer, Penelope (Ruth)

Tennant, Emma (Christina) 1937- .... **CLC 13, 52**
See also CA 65-68; CAAS 9; CANR 10, 38; DLB 14

Tenneshaw, S. M.
See Silverberg, Robert

Tennyson, Alfred 1809-1892 .. **NCLC 30; DA; PC 6; WLC**
See also CDBLB 1832-1890; DLB 32

Teran, Lisa St. Aubin de .... **CLC 36**
See also St. Aubin de Teran, Lisa

Terence 195(?)B.C.-159B.C....... **CMLC 14**

Teresa de Jesus, St. 1515-1582...... **LC 18**

Terkel, Louis 1912-
See Terkel, Studs
See also CA 57-60; CANR 18, 45; MTCW

Terkel, Studs .... **CLC 38**
See also Terkel, Louis
See also AITN 1

Terry, C. V.
See Slaughter, Frank G(ill)

Terry, Megan 1932-.............. **CLC 19**
See also CA 77-80; CABS 3; CANR 43; DLB 7

Tertz, Abram
See Sinyavsky, Andrei (Donatevich)

Tesich, Steve 1943(?)-.......... **CLC 40, 69**
See also CA 105; DLBY 83

Teternikov, Fyodor Kuzmich 1863-1927
See Sologub, Fyodor
See also CA 104

Tevis, Walter 1928-1984 .... **CLC 42**
See also CA 113

Tey, Josephine................... **TCLC 14**
See also Mackintosh, Elizabeth
See also DLB 77

Thackeray, William Makepeace 1811-1863 .... **NCLC 5, 14, 22, 43; DA; WLC**
See also CDBLB 1832-1890; DLB 21, 55; SATA 23

Thakura, Ravindranatha
See Tagore, Rabindranath

Tharoor, Shashi 1956- .... **CLC 70**
See also CA 141

Thelwell, Michael Miles 1939- ..... **CLC 22**
See also BW 2; CA 101

Theobald, Lewis, Jr.
See Lovecraft, H(oward) P(hillips)

Theodorescu, Ion N. 1880-1967
See Arghezi, Tudor
See also CA 116

Theriault, Yves 1915-1983......... **CLC 79**
See also CA 102; DLB 88

Theroux, Alexander (Louis) 1939- .... **CLC 2, 25**
See also CA 85-88; CANR 20

Theroux, Paul (Edward) 1941- .... **CLC 5, 8, 11, 15, 28, 46**
See also BEST 89:4; CA 33-36R; CANR 20, 45; DLB 2; MTCW; SATA 44

Thesen, Sharon 1946-............. **CLC 56**

Thevenin, Denis
See Duhamel, Georges

Thibault, Jacques Anatole Francois 1844-1924
See France, Anatole
See also CA 106; 127; MTCW

Thiele, Colin (Milton) 1920- .... **CLC 17**
See also CA 29-32R; CANR 12, 28; CLR 27; MAICYA; SAAS 2; SATA 14, 72

Thomas, Audrey (Callahan) 1935- .... **CLC 7, 13, 37**
See also AITN 2; CA 21-24R; CAAS 19; CANR 36; DLB 60; MTCW

Thomas, D(onald) M(ichael) 1935- .... **CLC 13, 22, 31**
See also CA 61-64; CAAS 11; CANR 17, 45; CDBLB 1960 to Present; DLB 40; MTCW

Thomas, Dylan (Marlais) 1914-1953 ... **TCLC 1, 8, 45; DA; PC 2; SSC 3; WLC**
See also CA 104; 120; CDBLB 1945-1960; DLB 13, 20, 139; MTCW; SATA 60

Thomas, (Philip) Edward 1878-1917 .... **TCLC 10**
See also CA 106; DLB 19

Thomas, Joyce Carol 1938-........ **CLC 35**
See also AAYA 12; BW 2; CA 113; 116; CLR 19; DLB 33; JRDA; MAICYA; MTCW; SAAS 7; SATA 40, 78

Thomas, Lewis 1913-1993 .... **CLC 35**
See also CA 85-88; 143; CANR 38; MTCW

Thomas, Paul
See Mann, (Paul) Thomas

Thomas, Piri 1928-............... **CLC 17**
See also CA 73-76; HW

Thomas, R(onald) S(tuart) 1913- .... **CLC 6, 13, 48**
See also CA 89-92; CAAS 4; CANR 30; CDBLB 1960 to Present; DLB 27; MTCW

Thomas, Ross (Elmore) 1926- ...... **CLC 39**
See also CA 33-36R; CANR 22

Thompson, Francis Clegg
See Mencken, H(enry) L(ouis)

Thompson, Francis Joseph 1859-1907 .... **TCLC 4**
See also CA 104; CDBLB 1890-1914; DLB 19

Thompson, Hunter S(tockton) 1939- .... **CLC 9, 17, 40**
See also BEST 89:1; CA 17-20R; CANR 23, 46; MTCW

Thompson, James Myers
See Thompson, Jim (Myers)

Thompson, Jim (Myers) 1906-1977(?) .... **CLC 69**
See also CA 140

Thompson, Judith .... **CLC 39**

Thomson, James 1700-1748 .... **LC 16**
See also DLB 95

Thomson, James 1834-1882...... **NCLC 18**
See also DLB 35

Thoreau, Henry David
1817-1862 ...... **NCLC 7, 21; DA; WLC**
See also CDALB 1640-1865; DLB 1

Thornton, Hall
See Silverberg, Robert

Thurber, James (Grover)
1894-1961 ... **CLC 5, 11, 25; DA; SSC 1**
See also CA 73-76; CANR 17, 39; CDALB 1929-1941; DLB 4, 11, 22, 102; MAICYA; MTCW; SATA 13

Thurman, Wallace (Henry)
1902-1934 .... **TCLC 6; BLC**
See also BW 1; CA 104; 124; DLB 51

Ticheburn, Cheviot
See Ainsworth, William Harrison

Tieck, (Johann) Ludwig
1773-1853 .... **NCLC 5, 46**
See also DLB 90

Tiger, Derry
See Ellison, Harlan (Jay)

Tilghman, Christopher 1948(?)-..... **CLC 65**

Tillinghast, Richard (Williford)
1940- .... **CLC 29**
See also CA 29-32R; CANR 26

Timrod, Henry 1828-1867 .... **NCLC 25**
See also DLB 3

Tindall, Gillian 1938-.............. **CLC 7**
See also CA 21-24R; CANR 11

Tiptree, James, Jr. .... **CLC 48, 50**
See also Sheldon, Alice Hastings Bradley
See also DLB 8

Titmarsh, Michael Angelo
See Thackeray, William Makepeace

Tocqueville, Alexis (Charles Henri Maurice Clerel Comte) 1805-1859..... **NCLC 7**

Tolkien, J(ohn) R(onald) R(euel)
1892-1973 .... **CLC 1, 2, 3, 8, 12, 38; DA; WLC**
See also AAYA 10; AITN 1; CA 17-18; 45-48; CANR 36; CAP 2; CDBLB 1914-1945; DLB 15; JRDA; MAICYA; MTCW; SATA 2, 32; SATA-Obit 24

Toller, Ernst 1893-1939 .... **TCLC 10**
See also CA 107; DLB 124

Tolson, M. B.
See Tolson, Melvin B(eaunorus)

Tolson, Melvin B(eaunorus)
1898(?)-1966 .... **CLC 36; BLC**
See also BW 1; CA 124; 89-92; DLB 48, 76

Tolstoi, Aleksei Nikolaevich
See Tolstoy, Alexey Nikolaevich

Tolstoy, Alexey Nikolaevich
1882-1945 .... **TCLC 18**
See also CA 107

Tolstoy, Count Leo
See Tolstoy, Leo (Nikolaevich)

Tolstoy, Leo (Nikolaevich)
1828-1910 ...... **TCLC 4, 11, 17, 28, 44; DA; SSC 9; WLC**
See also CA 104; 123; SATA 26

Tomasi di Lampedusa, Giuseppe 1896-1957
See Lampedusa, Giuseppe (Tomasi) di
See also CA 111

Tomlin, Lily .... **CLC 17**
See also Tomlin, Mary Jean

Tomlin, Mary Jean 1939(?)-
See Tomlin, Lily
See also CA 117

Tomlinson, (Alfred) Charles
1927- .... **CLC 2, 4, 6, 13, 45**
See also CA 5-8R; CANR 33; DLB 40

Tonson, Jacob
See Bennett, (Enoch) Arnold

Toole, John Kennedy
1937-1969 .... **CLC 19, 64**
See also CA 104; DLBY 81

Toomer, Jean
1894-1967 ...... **CLC 1, 4, 13, 22; BLC; PC 7; SSC 1**
See also BW 1; CA 85-88; CDALB 1917-1929; DLB 45, 51; MTCW

Torley, Luke
See Blish, James (Benjamin)

Tornimparte, Alessandra
See Ginzburg, Natalia

Torre, Raoul della
See Mencken, H(enry) L(ouis)

Torrey, E(dwin) Fuller 1937-....... **CLC 34**
See also CA 119

Torsvan, Ben Traven
See Traven, B.

Torsvan, Benno Traven
See Traven, B.

Torsvan, Berick Traven
See Traven, B.

Torsvan, Berwick Traven
See Traven, B.

Torsvan, Bruno Traven
See Traven, B.

Torsvan, Traven
See Traven, B.

Tournier, Michel (Edouard)
1924- .... **CLC 6, 23, 36**
See also CA 49-52; CANR 3, 36; DLB 83; MTCW; SATA 23

Tournimparte, Alessandra
See Ginzburg, Natalia

Towers, Ivar
See Kornbluth, C(yril) M.

Towne, Robert (Burton) 1936(?)-.... **CLC 87**
See also CA 108; DLB 44

Townsend, Sue 1946- .... **CLC 61**
See also CA 119; 127; MTCW; SATA 55; SATA-Brief 48

Townshend, Peter (Dennis Blandford)
1945- .... **CLC 17, 42**
See also CA 107

Tozzi, Federigo 1883-1920........ **TCLC 31**

Traill, Catharine Parr
1802-1899 .... **NCLC 31**
See also DLB 99

Trakl, Georg 1887-1914........... **TCLC 5**
See also CA 104

Transtroemer, Tomas (Goesta)
1931- .... **CLC 52, 65**
See also CA 117; 129; CAAS 17

Transtromer, Tomas Gosta
See Transtroemer, Tomas (Goesta)

Traven, B. (?)-1969............. **CLC 8, 11**
See also CA 19-20; 25-28R; CAP 2; DLB 9, 56; MTCW

Treitel, Jonathan 1959- .... **CLC 70**

Tremain, Rose 1943-.............. **CLC 42**
See also CA 97-100; CANR 44; DLB 14

Tremblay, Michel 1942-........... **CLC 29**
See also CA 116; 128; DLB 60; MTCW

Trevanian .... **CLC 29**
See also Whitaker, Rod(ney)

Trevor, Glen
See Hilton, James

Trevor, William
1928- .... **CLC 7, 9, 14, 25, 71**
See also Cox, William Trevor
See also DLB 14, 139

Trifonov, Yuri (Valentinovich)
1925-1981 .... **CLC 45**
See also CA 126; 103; MTCW

Trilling, Lionel 1905-1975 .... **CLC 9, 11, 24**
See also CA 9-12R; 61-64; CANR 10; DLB 28, 63; MTCW

Trimball, W. H.
See Mencken, H(enry) L(ouis)

Tristan
See Gomez de la Serna, Ramon

Tristram
See Housman, A(lfred) E(dward)

Trogdon, William (Lewis) 1939-
See Heat-Moon, William Least
See also CA 115; 119; CANR 47

Trollope, Anthony
1815-1882 ...... **NCLC 6, 33; DA; WLC**
See also CDBLB 1832-1890; DLB 21, 57; SATA 22

Trollope, Frances 1779-1863 ..... **NCLC 30**
See also DLB 21

Trotsky, Leon 1879-1940......... **TCLC 22**
See also CA 118

Trotter (Cockburn), Catharine
1679-1749 .... **LC 8**
See also DLB 84

Trout, Kilgore
See Farmer, Philip Jose

Trow, George W. S. 1943-......... **CLC 52**
See also CA 126

Troyat, Henri 1911-.............. **CLC 23**
See also CA 45-48; CANR 2, 33; MTCW

Trudeau, G(arretson) B(eekman) 1948-
See Trudeau, Garry B.
See also CA 81-84; CANR 31; SATA 35

Trudeau, Garry B.................. **CLC 12**
See also Trudeau, G(arretson) B(eekman)
See also AAYA 10; AITN 2

Truffaut, Francois 1932-1984....... **CLC 20**
See also CA 81-84; 113; CANR 34

Trumbo, Dalton 1905-1976 .... **CLC 19**
See also CA 21-24R; 69-72; CANR 10; DLB 26

Trumbull, John 1750-1831....... **NCLC 30**
See also DLB 31

Trundlett, Helen B.
See Eliot, T(homas) S(tearns)

Tryon, Thomas 1926-1991 .... **CLC 3, 11**
See also AITN 1; CA 29-32R; 135; CANR 32; MTCW

Tryon, Tom
See Tryon, Thomas

Ts'ao Hsueh-ch'in 1715(?)-1763....... **LC 1**

Tsushima, Shuji 1909-1948
See Dazai, Osamu
See also CA 107

Tsvetaeva (Efron), Marina (Ivanovna)
1892-1941 .... **TCLC 7, 35**
See also CA 104; 128; MTCW

Tuck, Lily 1938-................. **CLC 70**
See also CA 139

Tu Fu 712-770..................... **PC 9**

Tunis, John R(oberts) 1889-1975 ... **CLC 12**
See also CA 61-64; DLB 22; JRDA; MAICYA; SATA 37; SATA-Brief 30

Tuohy, Frank..................... **CLC 37**
See also Tuohy, John Francis
See also DLB 14, 139

Tuohy, John Francis 1925-
See Tuohy, Frank
See also CA 5-8R; CANR 3, 47

Turco, Lewis (Putnam) 1934- ... **CLC 11, 63**
See also CA 13-16R; CANR 24; DLBY 84

Turgenev, Ivan
1818-1883 ...... **NCLC 21; DA; SSC 7; WLC**

Turgot, Anne-Robert-Jacques
1727-1781 .... **LC 26**

Turner, Frederick 1943-........... **CLC 48**
See also CA 73-76; CAAS 10; CANR 12, 30; DLB 40

Tutu, Desmond M(pilo)
1931- .... **CLC 80; BLC**
See also BW 1; CA 125

Tutuola, Amos 1920- ... **CLC 5, 14, 29; BLC**
See also BW 2; CA 9-12R; CANR 27; DLB 125; MTCW

Twain, Mark
..... **TCLC 6, 12, 19, 36, 48, 59; SSC 6; WLC**
See also Clemens, Samuel Langhorne
See also DLB 11, 12, 23, 64, 74

Tyler, Anne
1941- .... **CLC 7, 11, 18, 28, 44, 59**
See also BEST 89:1; CA 9-12R; CANR 11, 33; DLB 6, 143; DLBY 82; MTCW; SATA 7

Tyler, Royall 1757-1826.......... **NCLC 3**
See also DLB 37

Tynan, Katharine 1861-1931 .... **TCLC 3**
See also CA 104

Tyutchev, Fyodor 1803-1873 ..... **NCLC 34**

Tzara, Tristan .... **CLC 47**
See also Rosenfeld, Samuel

Uhry, Alfred 1936-............... **CLC 55**
See also CA 127; 133

Ulf, Haerved
See Strindberg, (Johan) August

Ulf, Harved
See Strindberg, (Johan) August

Ulibarri, Sabine R(eyes) 1919- ..... **CLC 83**
See also CA 131; DLB 82; HW

Unamuno (y Jugo), Miguel de
1864-1936 .... **TCLC 2, 9; HLC; SSC 11**
See also CA 104; 131; DLB 108; HW; MTCW

Undercliffe, Errol
See Campbell, (John) Ramsey

Underwood, Miles
See Glassco, John

Undset, Sigrid
1882-1949 .... **TCLC 3; DA; WLC**
See also CA 104; 129; MTCW

Ungaretti, Giuseppe
1888-1970 .... **CLC 7, 11, 15**
See also CA 19-20; 25-28R; CAP 2; DLB 114

Unger, Douglas 1952-............. **CLC 34**
See also CA 130

Unsworth, Barry (Forster) 1930-.... **CLC 76**
See also CA 25-28R; CANR 30

Updike, John (Hoyer)
1932- ...... **CLC 1, 2, 3, 5, 7, 9, 13, 15, 23, 34, 43, 70; DA; SSC 13; WLC**
See also CA 1-4R; CABS 1; CANR 4, 33; CDALB 1968-1988; DLB 2, 5, 143; DLBD 3; DLBY 80, 82; MTCW

Upshaw, Margaret Mitchell
See Mitchell, Margaret (Munnerlyn)

Upton, Mark
See Sanders, Lawrence

Urdang, Constance (Henriette)
1922- .... **CLC 47**
See also CA 21-24R; CANR 9, 24

Uriel, Henry
See Faust, Frederick (Schiller)

Uris, Leon (Marcus) 1924-....... **CLC 7, 32**
See also AITN 1, 2; BEST 89:2; CA 1-4R; CANR 1, 40; MTCW; SATA 49

Urmuz
See Codrescu, Andrei

Ustinov, Peter (Alexander) 1921- .... **CLC 1**
See also AITN 1; CA 13-16R; CANR 25; DLB 13

Vaculik, Ludvik 1926- .... **CLC 7**
See also CA 53-56

Valdez, Luis (Miguel)
1940- .... **CLC 84; HLC**
See also CA 101; CANR 32; DLB 122; HW

Valenzuela, Luisa 1938-... **CLC 31; SSC 14**
See also CA 101; CANR 32; DLB 113; HW

Valera y Alcala-Galiano, Juan
1824-1905 .... **TCLC 10**
See also CA 106

Valery, (Ambroise) Paul (Toussaint Jules)
1871-1945 .... **TCLC 4, 15; PC 9**
See also CA 104; 122; MTCW

Valle-Inclan, Ramon (Maria) del
1866-1936 .... **TCLC 5; HLC**
See also CA 106; DLB 134

Vallejo, Antonio Buero
See Buero Vallejo, Antonio

Vallejo, Cesar (Abraham)
1892-1938 .... **TCLC 3, 56; HLC**
See also CA 105; HW

Valle Y Pena, Ramon del
See Valle-Inclan, Ramon (Maria) del

Van Ash, Cay 1918-.............. **CLC 34**

Vanbrugh, Sir John 1664-1726 ...... **LC 21**
See also DLB 80

Van Campen, Karl
See Campbell, John W(ood, Jr.)

Vance, Gerald
See Silverberg, Robert

Vance, Jack...................... **CLC 35**
See also Vance, John Holbrook
See also DLB 8

Vance, John Holbrook 1916-
See Queen, Ellery; Vance, Jack
See also CA 29-32R; CANR 17; MTCW

Van Den Bogarde, Derek Jules Gaspard Ulric Niven 1921-
See Bogarde, Dirk
See also CA 77-80

Vandenburgh, Jane .... **CLC 59**

Vanderhaeghe, Guy 1951- .... **CLC 41**
See also CA 113

van der Post, Laurens (Jan) 1906- ... **CLC 5**
See also CA 5-8R; CANR 35

van de Wetering, Janwillem 1931- .. **CLC 47**
See also CA 49-52; CANR 4

Van Dine, S. S................... **TCLC 23**
See also Wright, Willard Huntington

Van Doren, Carl (Clinton)
1885-1950 .... **TCLC 18**
See also CA 111

Van Doren, Mark 1894-1972..... **CLC 6, 10**
See also CA 1-4R; 37-40R; CANR 3; DLB 45; MTCW

Van Druten, John (William)
1901-1957 .... **TCLC 2**
See also CA 104; DLB 10

Van Duyn, Mona (Jane)
1921- .... **CLC 3, 7, 63**
See also CA 9-12R; CANR 7, 38; DLB 5

Van Dyne, Edith
See Baum, L(yman) Frank

van Itallie, Jean-Claude 1936-....... **CLC 3**
See also CA 45-48; CAAS 2; CANR 1; DLB 7

van Ostaijen, Paul 1896-1928 ..... **TCLC 33**

Van Peebles, Melvin 1932- ...... **CLC 2, 20**
See also BW 2; CA 85-88; CANR 27

Vansittart, Peter 1920-............ **CLC 42**
See also CA 1-4R; CANR 3

Van Vechten, Carl 1880-1964 ...... **CLC 33**
See also CA 89-92; DLB 4, 9, 51

Van Vogt, A(lfred) E(lton) 1912-..... **CLC 1**
See also CA 21-24R; CANR 28; DLB 8; SATA 14

Varda, Agnes 1928- .... **CLC 16**
See also CA 116; 122

Walker, Alice (Malsenior) 1944- .... **CLC 5, 6, 9, 19, 27, 46, 58; BLC; DA; SSC 5**
See also AAYA 3; BEST 89:4; BW 2; CA 37-40R; CANR 9, 27; CDALB 1968-1988; DLB 6, 33, 143; MTCW; SATA 31

Walker, David Harry 1911-1992.... **CLC 14**
See also CA 1-4R; 137; CANR 1; SATA 8; SATA-Obit 71

Walker, Edward Joseph 1934-
See Walker, Ted
See also CA 21-24R; CANR 12, 28

Walker, George F. 1947- .... **CLC 44, 61**
See also CA 103; CANR 21, 43; DLB 60

Walker, Joseph A. 1935- .... **CLC 19**
See also BW 1; CA 89-92; CANR 26; DLB 38

Walker, Margaret (Abigail) 1915- .... **CLC 1, 6; BLC**
See also BW 2; CA 73-76; CANR 26; DLB 76; MTCW

Walker, Ted .... **CLC 13**
See also Walker, Edward Joseph
See also DLB 40

Wallace, David Foster 1962- .... **CLC 50**
See also CA 132

Wallace, Dexter
See Masters, Edgar Lee

Wallace, (Richard Horatio) Edgar 1875-1932 .... **TCLC 57**
See also CA 115; DLB 70

Wallace, Irving 1916-1990....... **CLC 7, 13**
See also AITN 1; CA 1-4R; 132; CAAS 1; CANR 1, 27; MTCW

Wallant, Edward Lewis 1926-1962 .... **CLC 5, 10**
See also CA 1-4R; CANR 22; DLB 2, 28, 143; MTCW

Walpole, Horace 1717-1797.......... **LC 2**
See also DLB 39, 104

Walpole, Hugh (Seymour) 1884-1941 .... **TCLC 5**
See also CA 104; DLB 34

Walser, Martin 1927- .... **CLC 27**
See also CA 57-60; CANR 8, 46; DLB 75, 124

Walser, Robert 1878-1956........ **TCLC 18**
See also CA 118; DLB 66

Walsh, Jill Paton .... **CLC 35**
See also Paton Walsh, Gillian
See also AAYA 11; CLR 2; SAAS 3

Walter, Villiam Christian
See Andersen, Hans Christian

Wambaugh, Joseph (Aloysius, Jr.) 1937- .... **CLC 3, 18**
See also AITN 1; BEST 89:3; CA 33-36R; CANR 42; DLB 6; DLBY 83; MTCW

Ward, Arthur Henry Sarsfield 1883-1959
See Rohmer, Sax
See also CA 108

Ward, Douglas Turner 1930- .... **CLC 19**
See also BW 1; CA 81-84; CANR 27; DLB 7, 38

Ward, Mary Augusta
See Ward, Mrs. Humphry

Ward, Mrs. Humphry 1851-1920 .... **TCLC 55**
See also DLB 18

Ward, Peter
See Faust, Frederick (Schiller)

Warhol, Andy 1928(?)-1987........ **CLC 20**
See also AAYA 12; BEST 89:4; CA 89-92; 121; CANR 34

Warner, Francis (Robert le Plastrier) 1937- .... **CLC 14**
See also CA 53-56; CANR 11

Warner, Marina 1946- .... **CLC 59**
See also CA 65-68; CANR 21

Warner, Rex (Ernest) 1905-1986.... **CLC 45**
See also CA 89-92; 119; DLB 15

Warner, Susan (Bogert) 1819-1885 .... **NCLC 31**
See also DLB 3, 42

Warner, Sylvia (Constance) Ashton
See Ashton-Warner, Sylvia (Constance)

Warner, Sylvia Townsend 1893-1978 .... **CLC 7, 19**
See also CA 61-64; 77-80; CANR 16; DLB 34, 139; MTCW

Warren, Mercy Otis 1728-1814... **NCLC 13**
See also DLB 31

Warren, Robert Penn 1905-1989 .... **CLC 1, 4, 6, 8, 10, 13, 18, 39, 53, 59; DA; SSC 4; WLC**
See also AITN 1; CA 13-16R; 129; CANR 10, 47; CDALB 1968-1988; DLB 2, 48; DLBY 80, 89; MTCW; SATA 46; SATA-Obit 63

Warshofsky, Isaac
See Singer, Isaac Bashevis

Warton, Thomas 1728-1790......... **LC 15**
See also DLB 104, 109

Waruk, Kona
See Harris, (Theodore) Wilson

Warung, Price 1855-1911......... **TCLC 45**

Warwick, Jarvis
See Garner, Hugh

Washington, Alex
See Harris, Mark

Washington, Booker T(aliaferro) 1856-1915 .... **TCLC 10; BLC**
See also BW 1; CA 114; 125; SATA 28

Washington, George 1732-1799...... **LC 25**
See also DLB 31

Wassermann, (Karl) Jakob 1873-1934 .... **TCLC 6**
See also CA 104; DLB 66

Wasserstein, Wendy 1950- .... **CLC 32, 59; DC 4**
See also CA 121; 129; CABS 3

Waterhouse, Keith (Spencer) 1929- .... **CLC 47**
See also CA 5-8R; CANR 38; DLB 13, 15; MTCW

Waters, Roger 1944- .... **CLC 35**

Watkins, Frances Ellen
See Harper, Frances Ellen Watkins

Watkins, Gerrold
See Malzberg, Barry N(athaniel)

Watkins, Paul 1964- .... **CLC 55**
See also CA 132

Watkins, Vernon Phillips 1906-1967 .... **CLC 43**
See also CA 9-10; 25-28R; CAP 1; DLB 20

Watson, Irving S.
See Mencken, H(enry) L(ouis)

Watson, John H.
See Farmer, Philip Jose

Watson, Richard F.
See Silverberg, Robert

Waugh, Auberon (Alexander) 1939- .. **CLC 7**
See also CA 45-48; CANR 6, 22; DLB 14

Waugh, Evelyn (Arthur St. John) 1903-1966 ...... **CLC 1, 3, 8, 13, 19, 27, 44; DA; WLC**
See also CA 85-88; 25-28R; CANR 22; CDBLB 1914-1945; DLB 15; MTCW

Waugh, Harriet 1944- .... **CLC 6**
See also CA 85-88; CANR 22

Ways, C. R.
See Blount, Roy (Alton), Jr.

Waystaff, Simon
See Swift, Jonathan

Webb, (Martha) Beatrice (Potter) 1858-1943 .... **TCLC 22**
See also Potter, Beatrice
See also CA 117

Webb, Charles (Richard) 1939- ...... **CLC 7**
See also CA 25-28R

Webb, James H(enry), Jr. 1946- .... **CLC 22**
See also CA 81-84

Webb, Mary (Gladys Meredith) 1881-1927 .... **TCLC 24**
See also CA 123; DLB 34

Webb, Mrs. Sidney
See Webb, (Martha) Beatrice (Potter)

Webb, Phyllis 1927- .... **CLC 18**
See also CA 104; CANR 23; DLB 53

Webb, Sidney (James) 1859-1947 .... **TCLC 22**
See also CA 117

Webber, Andrew Lloyd .... **CLC 21**
See also Lloyd Webber, Andrew

Weber, Lenora Mattingly 1895-1971 .... **CLC 12**
See also CA 19-20; 29-32R; CAP 1; SATA 2; SATA-Obit 26

Webster, John 1579(?)-1634(?) .... **DC 2**
See also CDBLB Before 1660; DA; DLB 58; WLC

Webster, Noah 1758-1843 .... **NCLC 30**

Wedekind, (Benjamin) Frank(lin) 1864-1918 .... **TCLC 7**
See also CA 104; DLB 118

Weidman, Jerome 1913- .... **CLC 7**
See also AITN 2; CA 1-4R; CANR 1; DLB 28

Weil, Simone (Adolphine) 1909-1943 .... **TCLC 23**
See also CA 117

Weinstein, Nathan
See West, Nathanael

Weinstein, Nathan von Wallenstein
See West, Nathanael

Weir, Peter (Lindsay) 1944- . . . . **CLC 20**
See also CA 113; 123

Weiss, Peter (Ulrich)
1916-1982 . . . . **CLC 3, 15, 51**
See also CA 45-48; 106; CANR 3; DLB 69, 124

Weiss, Theodore (Russell)
1916- . . . . **CLC 3, 8, 14**
See also CA 9-12R; CAAS 2; CANR 46; DLB 5

Welch, (Maurice) Denton
1915-1948 . . . . **TCLC 22**
See also CA 121

Welch, James 1940- . . . . **CLC 6, 14, 52**
See also CA 85-88; CANR 42; NNAL

Weldon, Fay
1933- . . . . **CLC 6, 9, 11, 19, 36, 59**
See also CA 21-24R; CANR 16, 46; CDBLB 1960 to Present; DLB 14; MTCW

Wellek, Rene 1903- . . . . **CLC 28**
See also CA 5-8R; CAAS 7; CANR 8; DLB 63

Weller, Michael 1942- . . . . **CLC 10, 53**
See also CA 85-88

Weller, Paul 1958- . . . . **CLC 26**

Wellershoff, Dieter 1925- . . . . **CLC 46**
See also CA 89-92; CANR 16, 37

Welles, (George) Orson
1915-1985 . . . . **CLC 20, 80**
See also CA 93-96; 117

Wellman, Mac 1945- . . . . **CLC 65**

Wellman, Manly Wade 1903-1986 . . **CLC 49**
See also CA 1-4R; 118; CANR 6, 16, 44; SATA 6; SATA-Obit 47

Wells, Carolyn 1869(?)-1942 . . . . . . **TCLC 35**
See also CA 113; DLB 11

Wells, H(erbert) G(eorge)
1866-1946 . . . . **TCLC 6, 12, 19; DA; SSC 6; WLC**
See also CA 110; 121; CDBLB 1914-1945; DLB 34, 70; MTCW; SATA 20

Wells, Rosemary 1943- . . . . **CLC 12**
See also AAYA 13; CA 85-88; CLR 16; MAICYA; SAAS 1; SATA 18, 69

Welty, Eudora
1909- . . . . . . **CLC 1, 2, 5, 14, 22, 33; DA; SSC 1; WLC**
See also CA 9-12R; CABS 1; CANR 32; CDALB 1941-1968; DLB 2, 102, 143; DLBD 12; DLBY 87; MTCW

Wen I-to 1899-1946 . . . . **TCLC 28**

Wentworth, Robert
See Hamilton, Edmond

Werfel, Franz (V.) 1890-1945 . . . . . . **TCLC 8**
See also CA 104; DLB 81, 124

Wergeland, Henrik Arnold
1808-1845 . . . . **NCLC 5**

Wersba, Barbara 1932- . . . . **CLC 30**
See also AAYA 2; CA 29-32R; CANR 16, 38; CLR 3; DLB 52; JRDA; MAICYA; SAAS 2; SATA 1, 58

Wertmueller, Lina 1928- . . . . **CLC 16**
See also CA 97-100; CANR 39

Wescott, Glenway 1901-1987 . . . . **CLC 13**
See also CA 13-16R; 121; CANR 23; DLB 4, 9, 102

Wesker, Arnold 1932- . . . . **CLC 3, 5, 42**
See also CA 1-4R; CAAS 7; CANR 1, 33; CDBLB 1960 to Present; DLB 13; MTCW

Wesley, Richard (Errol) 1945- . . . . **CLC 7**
See also BW 1; CA 57-60; CANR 27; DLB 38

Wessel, Johan Herman 1742-1785 . . . . **LC 7**

West, Anthony (Panther)
1914-1987 . . . . **CLC 50**
See also CA 45-48; 124; CANR 3, 19; DLB 15

West, C. P.
See Wodehouse, P(elham) G(renville)

West, (Mary) Jessamyn
1902-1984 . . . . **CLC 7, 17**
See also CA 9-12R; 112; CANR 27; DLB 6; DLBY 84; MTCW; SATA-Obit 37

West, Morris L(anglo) 1916- . . . . . **CLC 6, 33**
See also CA 5-8R; CANR 24; MTCW

West, Nathanael
1903-1940 . . . . . **TCLC 1, 14, 44; SSC 16**
See also CA 104; 125; CDALB 1929-1941; DLB 4, 9, 28; MTCW

West, Owen
See Koontz, Dean R(ay)

West, Paul 1930- . . . . **CLC 7, 14**
See also CA 13-16R; CAAS 7; CANR 22; DLB 14

West, Rebecca 1892-1983 . . **CLC 7, 9, 31, 50**
See also CA 5-8R; 109; CANR 19; DLB 36; DLBY 83; MTCW

Westall, Robert (Atkinson)
1929-1993 . . . . **CLC 17**
See also AAYA 12; CA 69-72; 141; CANR 18; CLR 13; JRDA; MAICYA; SAAS 2; SATA 23, 69; SATA-Obit 75

Westlake, Donald E(dwin)
1933- . . . . **CLC 7, 33**
See also CA 17-20R; CAAS 13; CANR 16, 44

Westmacott, Mary
See Christie, Agatha (Mary Clarissa)

Weston, Allen
See Norton, Andre

Wetcheek, J. L.
See Feuchtwanger, Lion

Wetering, Janwillem van de
See van de Wetering, Janwillem

Wetherell, Elizabeth
See Warner, Susan (Bogert)

Whalen, Philip 1923- . . . . **CLC 6, 29**
See also CA 9-12R; CANR 5, 39; DLB 16

Wharton, Edith (Newbold Jones)
1862-1937 . . . . . . **TCLC 3, 9, 27, 53; DA; SSC 6; WLC**
See also CA 104; 132; CDALB 1865-1917; DLB 4, 9, 12, 78; MTCW

Wharton, James
See Mencken, H(enry) L(ouis)

Wharton, William (a pseudonym)
. . . . **CLC 18, 37**
See also CA 93-96; DLBY 80

Wheatley (Peters), Phillis
1754(?)-1784 . . . . **LC 3; BLC; DA; PC 3; WLC**
See also CDALB 1640-1865; DLB 31, 50

Wheelock, John Hall 1886-1978 . . . . **CLC 14**
See also CA 13-16R; 77-80; CANR 14; DLB 45

White, E(lwyn) B(rooks)
1899-1985 . . . . **CLC 10, 34, 39**
See also AITN 2; CA 13-16R; 116; CANR 16, 37; CLR 1, 21; DLB 11, 22; MAICYA; MTCW; SATA 2, 29; SATA-Obit 44

White, Edmund (Valentine III)
1940- . . . . **CLC 27**
See also AAYA 7; CA 45-48; CANR 3, 19, 36; MTCW

White, Patrick (Victor Martindale)
1912-1990 . . **CLC 3, 4, 5, 7, 9, 18, 65, 69**
See also CA 81-84; 132; CANR 43; MTCW

White, Phyllis Dorothy James 1920-
See James, P. D.
See also CA 21-24R; CANR 17, 43; MTCW

White, T(erence) H(anbury)
1906-1964 . . . . **CLC 30**
See also CA 73-76; CANR 37; JRDA; MAICYA; SATA 12

White, Terence de Vere
1912-1994 . . . . **CLC 49**
See also CA 49-52; 145; CANR 3

White, Walter F(rancis)
1893-1955 . . . . **TCLC 15**
See also White, Walter
See also BW 1; CA 115; 124; DLB 51

White, William Hale 1831-1913
See Rutherford, Mark
See also CA 121

Whitehead, E(dward) A(nthony)
1933- . . . . **CLC 5**
See also CA 65-68

Whitemore, Hugh (John) 1936- . . . . . **CLC 37**
See also CA 132

Whitman, Sarah Helen (Power)
1803-1878 . . . . **NCLC 19**
See also DLB 1

Whitman, Walt(er)
1819-1892 . . . . . **NCLC 4, 31; DA; PC 3; WLC**
See also CDALB 1640-1865; DLB 3, 64; SATA 20

Whitney, Phyllis A(yame) 1903- . . . . **CLC 42**
See also AITN 2; BEST 90:3; CA 1-4R; CANR 3, 25, 38; JRDA; MAICYA; SATA 1, 30

Winters, Janet Lewis .... **CLC 41**
See also Lewis, Janet
See also DLBY 87

Winters, (Arthur) Yvor 1900-1968 .... **CLC 4, 8, 32**
See also CA 11-12; 25-28R; CAP 1; DLB 48; MTCW

Winterson, Jeanette 1959- .... **CLC 64**
See also CA 136

Wiseman, Frederick 1930- .... **CLC 20**

Wister, Owen 1860-1938 .... **TCLC 21**
See also CA 108; DLB 9, 78; SATA 62

Witkacy
See Witkiewicz, Stanislaw Ignacy

Witkiewicz, Stanislaw Ignacy 1885-1939 .... **TCLC 8**
See also CA 105

Wittgenstein, Ludwig (Josef Johann) 1889-1951 .... **TCLC 59**
See also CA 113

Wittig, Monique 1935(?)- .... **CLC 22**
See also CA 116; 135; DLB 83

Wittlin, Jozef 1896-1976 .... **CLC 25**
See also CA 49-52; 65-68; CANR 3

Wodehouse, P(elham) G(renville) 1881-1975 ... **CLC 1, 2, 5, 10, 22; SSC 2**
See also AITN 2; CA 45-48; 57-60; CANR 3, 33; CDBLB 1914-1945; DLB 34; MTCW; SATA 22

Woiwode, L.
See Woiwode, Larry (Alfred)

Woiwode, Larry (Alfred) 1941- ... **CLC 6, 10**
See also CA 73-76; CANR 16; DLB 6

Wojciechowska, Maia (Teresa) 1927- .... **CLC 26**
See also AAYA 8; CA 9-12R; CANR 4, 41; CLR 1; JRDA; MAICYA; SAAS 1; SATA 1, 28

Wolf, Christa 1929- .... **CLC 14, 29, 58**
See also CA 85-88; CANR 45; DLB 75; MTCW

Wolfe, Gene (Rodman) 1931- .... **CLC 25**
See also CA 57-60; CAAS 9; CANR 6, 32; DLB 8

Wolfe, George C. 1954- .... **CLC 49**

Wolfe, Thomas (Clayton) 1900-1938 ... **TCLC 4, 13, 29; DA; WLC**
See also CA 104; 132; CDALB 1929-1941; DLB 9, 102; DLBD 2; DLBY 85; MTCW

Wolfe, Thomas Kennerly, Jr. 1931-
See Wolfe, Tom
See also CA 13-16R; CANR 9, 33; MTCW

Wolfe, Tom .... **CLC 1, 2, 9, 15, 35, 51**
See also Wolfe, Thomas Kennerly, Jr.
See also AAYA 8; AITN 2; BEST 89:1

Wolff, Geoffrey (Ansell) 1937- ..... **CLC 41**
See also CA 29-32R; CANR 29, 43

Wolff, Sonia
See Levitin, Sonia (Wolff)

Wolff, Tobias (Jonathan Ansell) 1945- .... **CLC 39, 64**
See also BEST 90:2; CA 114; 117; DLB 130

Wolfram von Eschenbach c. 1170-c. 1220 .... **CMLC 5**
See also DLB 138

Wolitzer, Hilma 1930- .... **CLC 17**
See also CA 65-68; CANR 18, 40; SATA 31

Wollstonecraft, Mary 1759-1797 ...... **LC 5**
See also CDBLB 1789-1832; DLB 39, 104

Wonder, Stevie .... **CLC 12**
See also Morris, Steveland Judkins

Wong, Jade Snow 1922- .... **CLC 17**
See also CA 109

Woodcott, Keith
See Brunner, John (Kilian Houston)

Woodruff, Robert W.
See Mencken, H(enry) L(ouis)

Woolf, (Adeline) Virginia 1882-1941 .... **TCLC 1, 5, 20, 43, 56; DA; SSC 7; WLC**
See also CA 104; 130; CDBLB 1914-1945; DLB 36, 100; DLBD 10; MTCW

Woollcott, Alexander (Humphreys) 1887-1943 .... **TCLC 5**
See also CA 105; DLB 29

Woolrich, Cornell 1903-1968 .... **CLC 77**
See also Hopley-Woolrich, Cornell George

Wordsworth, Dorothy 1771-1855 .... **NCLC 25**
See also DLB 107

Wordsworth, William 1770-1850 .... **NCLC 12, 38; DA; PC 4; WLC**
See also CDBLB 1789-1832; DLB 93, 107

Wouk, Herman 1915- .... **CLC 1, 9, 38**
See also CA 5-8R; CANR 6, 33; DLBY 82; MTCW

Wright, Charles (Penzel, Jr.) 1935- .... **CLC 6, 13, 28**
See also CA 29-32R; CAAS 7; CANR 23, 36; DLBY 82; MTCW

Wright, Charles Stevenson 1932- .... **CLC 49; BLC 3**
See also BW 1; CA 9-12R; CANR 26; DLB 33

Wright, Jack R.
See Harris, Mark

Wright, James (Arlington) 1927-1980 .... **CLC 3, 5, 10, 28**
See also AITN 2; CA 49-52; 97-100; CANR 4, 34; DLB 5; MTCW

Wright, Judith (Arandell) 1915- .... **CLC 11, 53**
See also CA 13-16R; CANR 31; MTCW; SATA 14

Wright, L(aurali) R. 1939- .... **CLC 44**
See also CA 138

Wright, Richard (Nathaniel) 1908-1960 .... **CLC 1, 3, 4, 9, 14, 21, 48, 74; BLC; DA; SSC 2; WLC**
See also AAYA 5; BW 1; CA 108; CDALB 1929-1941; DLB 76, 102; DLBD 2; MTCW

Wright, Richard B(ruce) 1937- ...... **CLC 6**
See also CA 85-88; DLB 53

Wright, Rick 1945- .... **CLC 35**

Wright, Rowland
See Wells, Carolyn

Wright, Stephen Caldwell 1946- .... **CLC 33**
See also BW 2

Wright, Willard Huntington 1888-1939
See Van Dine, S. S.
See also CA 115

Wright, William 1930- .... **CLC 44**
See also CA 53-56; CANR 7, 23

Wu Ch'eng-en 1500(?)-1582(?) .... **LC 7**

Wu Ching-tzu 1701-1754 .... **LC 2**

Wurlitzer, Rudolph 1938(?)- ... **CLC 2, 4, 15**
See also CA 85-88

Wycherley, William 1641-1715 .... **LC 8, 21**
See also CDBLB 1660-1789; DLB 80

Wylie, Elinor (Morton Hoyt) 1885-1928 .... **TCLC 8**
See also CA 105; DLB 9, 45

Wylie, Philip (Gordon) 1902-1971 ... **CLC 43**
See also CA 21-22; 33-36R; CAP 2; DLB 9

Wyndham, John .... **CLC 19**
See also Harris, John (Wyndham Parkes Lucas) Beynon

Wyss, Johann David Von 1743-1818 .... **NCLC 10**
See also JRDA; MAICYA; SATA 29; SATA-Brief 27

Yakumo Koizumi
See Hearn, (Patricio) Lafcadio (Tessima Carlos)

Yanez, Jose Donoso
See Donoso (Yanez), Jose

Yanovsky, Basile S.
See Yanovsky, V(assily) S(emenovich)

Yanovsky, V(assily) S(emenovich) 1906-1989 .... **CLC 2, 18**
See also CA 97-100; 129

Yates, Richard 1926-1992 ..... **CLC 7, 8, 23**
See also CA 5-8R; 139; CANR 10, 43; DLB 2; DLBY 81, 92

Yeats, W. B.
See Yeats, William Butler

Yeats, William Butler 1865-1939 ..... **TCLC 1, 11, 18, 31; DA; WLC**
See also CA 104; 127; CANR 45; CDBLB 1890-1914; DLB 10, 19, 98; MTCW

Yehoshua, A(braham) B. 1936- .... **CLC 13, 31**
See also CA 33-36R; CANR 43

Yep, Laurence Michael 1948- ...... **CLC 35**
See also AAYA 5; CA 49-52; CANR 1, 46; CLR 3, 17; DLB 52; JRDA; MAICYA; SATA 7, 69

Yerby, Frank G(arvin) 1916-1991 .... **CLC 1, 7, 22; BLC**
See also BW 1; CA 9-12R; 136; CANR 16; DLB 76; MTCW

Yesenin, Sergei Alexandrovich
See Esenin, Sergei (Alexandrovich)

Yevtushenko, Yevgeny (Alexandrovich) 1933- .... **CLC 1, 3, 13, 26, 51**
See also CA 81-84; CANR 33; MTCW

Yezierska, Anzia 1885(?)-1970 ..... **CLC 46**
See also CA 126; 89-92; DLB 28; MTCW

Yglesias, Helen 1915- .... **CLC 7, 22**
See also CA 37-40R; CAAS 20; CANR 15; MTCW

Yokomitsu Riichi 1898-1947 . . . . . . **TCLC 47**

Yonge, Charlotte (Mary)
1823-1901 . . . . **TCLC 48**
See also CA 109; DLB 18; SATA 17

York, Jeremy
See Creasey, John

York, Simon
See Heinlein, Robert A(nson)

Yorke, Henry Vincent 1905-1974 . . . **CLC 13**
See also Green, Henry
See also CA 85-88; 49-52

Yosano Akiko 1878-1942 . . **TCLC 59; PC 11**

Yoshimoto, Banana . . . . **CLC 84**
See also Yoshimoto, Mahoko

Yoshimoto, Mahoko 1964-
See Yoshimoto, Banana
See also CA 144

Young, Al(bert James)
1939- . . . . **CLC 19; BLC**
See also BW 2; CA 29-32R; CANR 26; DLB 33

Young, Andrew (John) 1885-1971 . . . . **CLC 5**
See also CA 5-8R; CANR 7, 29

Young, Collier
See Bloch, Robert (Albert)

Young, Edward 1683-1765 . . . . **LC 3**
See also DLB 95

Young, Marguerite 1909- . . . . **CLC 82**
See also CA 13-16; CAP 1

Young, Neil 1945- . . . . **CLC 17**
See also CA 110

Yourcenar, Marguerite
1903-1987 . . . . **CLC 19, 38, 50, 87**
See also CA 69-72; CANR 23; DLB 72; DLBY 88; MTCW

Yurick, Sol 1925- . . . . **CLC 6**
See also CA 13-16R; CANR 25

Zabolotskii, Nikolai Alekseevich
1903-1958 . . . . **TCLC 52**
See also CA 116

Zamiatin, Yevgenii
See Zamyatin, Evgeny Ivanovich

Zamyatin, Evgeny Ivanovich
1884-1937 . . . . **TCLC 8, 37**
See also CA 105

Zangwill, Israel 1864-1926 . . . . **TCLC 16**
See also CA 109; DLB 10, 135

Zappa, Francis Vincent, Jr. 1940-1993
See Zappa, Frank
See also CA 108; 143

Zappa, Frank . . . . **CLC 17**
See also Zappa, Francis Vincent, Jr.

Zaturenska, Marya 1902-1982 . . . . **CLC 6, 11**
See also CA 13-16R; 105; CANR 22

Zelazny, Roger (Joseph) 1937- . . . . . **CLC 21**
See also AAYA 7; CA 21-24R; CANR 26; DLB 8; MTCW; SATA 57; SATA-Brief 39

Zhdanov, Andrei A(lexandrovich)
1896-1948 . . . . **TCLC 18**
See also CA 117

Zhukovsky, Vasily 1783-1852 . . . . **NCLC 35**

Ziegenhagen, Eric . . . . **CLC 55**

Zimmer, Jill Schary
See Robinson, Jill

Zimmerman, Robert
See Dylan, Bob

Zindel, Paul 1936- . . . **CLC 6, 26; DA; DC 5**
See also AAYA 2; CA 73-76; CANR 31; CLR 3; DLB 7, 52; JRDA; MAICYA; MTCW; SATA 16, 58

Zinov'Ev, A. A.
See Zinoviev, Alexander (Aleksandrovich)

Zinoviev, Alexander (Aleksandrovich)
1922- . . . . **CLC 19**
See also CA 116; 133; CAAS 10

Zoilus
See Lovecraft, H(oward) P(hillips)

Zola, Emile (Edouard Charles Antoine)
1840-1902 . . . . . . **TCLC 1, 6, 21, 41; DA; WLC**
See also CA 104; 138; DLB 123

Zoline, Pamela 1941- . . . . **CLC 62**

Zorrilla y Moral, Jose 1817-1893 . . **NCLC 6**

Zoshchenko, Mikhail (Mikhailovich)
1895-1958 . . . . **TCLC 15; SSC 15**
See also CA 115

Zuckmayer, Carl 1896-1977 . . . . **CLC 18**
See also CA 69-72; DLB 56, 124

Zuk, Georges
See Skelton, Robin

Zukofsky, Louis
1904-1978 . . . . **CLC 1, 2, 4, 7, 11, 18; PC 11**
See also CA 9-12R; 77-80; CANR 39; DLB 5; MTCW

Zweig, Paul 1935-1984 . . . . **CLC 34, 42**
See also CA 85-88; 113

Zweig, Stefan 1881-1942 . . . . **TCLC 17**
See also CA 112; DLB 81, 118

Literary Criticism Series Cumulative Topic Index

This index lists all topic entries in the Gale Literary Criticism Series *Classical and Medieval Literature Criticism, Contemporary Literary Criticism, Literature Criticism from 1400 to 1800, Nineteenth-Century Literature Criticism,* and *Twentieth-Century Literary Criticism.*

Topic Index

CMLC Cumulative Nationality Index

CMLC Cumulative Title Index

Title Index

Title Index

Title Index

Title Index

CMLC Cumulative Critic Index

Critic Index

Critic Index

Apuleius **1**:13
Gibbs, Marion E.
Wolfram von Eshcenbach **5**:347, 429

Gifford, William
Juvenal **8**:6

Gilson, Etienne
Abelard **11**:17
Augustine, St. **6**:44
Averro s **7**:18, 26
Bacon, Roger **14**:86
Meister Eckhart **9**:42, 60

Gilula, Dwora
Terence **14**:389

Girard, René
The Book of Job **14**:191
Sophocles **2**:408

Gladstone, W. E.
Iliad **1**:297

Godwin, William
Poem of the Cid **4**:225

Goethe, Johann Wolfgang von
K lid sa **9**:130
Longus **7**:217
Menander **9**:227
Sophocles **2**:303

Goldberg, Sander M.
Menander **9**:276
Terence **14**:372

Goldin, Frederick
The Song of Roland **1**:251

Golding, Arthur
Ovid **7**:287

Goldsmith, Margaret E.
Beowulf **1**:134

Gollancz, I.
Sir Gawain and the Green Knight **2**:186

Göller, Karl Heinz
Morte Arthure **10**:418

Gombrowicz, Witold
Inferno **3**:131

Gomme, A. W.
Menander **9**:259

Good, Edwin M.
The Book of Job **14**:206

Goodell, Thomas Dwight
Aeschylus **11**:112

Goodheart, Eugene
The Book of Job **14**:171

Goodrich, Norma Lorre
Arthurian Legend **10**:100, 108

Gordis, Robert
The Book of Job **14**:175

Gordon, E. V.
Hrafnkel's Saga **2**:86

Gosse, Edmund
Beowulf **1**:73

Gottfried von Strassburg
Gottfried von Strassburg **10**:246, 249, 258
Wolfram von Eschenbach **5**:291

Gradon, Pamela
Beowulf **1**:138

Grahn, Judy
Sappho **3**:494

Grane, Leifn
Abelard **11**:25

Granrud, John E.
Cicero, Marcus Tullius **3**:205

Gransden, Antonia
Anglo-Saxon Chronicle **4**:21

Grant, Michael
Aeschylus **11**:175
Apuleius **1**:26
Cicero, Marcus Tullius **3**:285, 291
Josephus, Flavius **13**:240
Livy **11**:367
Ovid **7**:405

Graves, Robert
Aeneid **9**:394
Apuleius **1**:20
Iliad **1**:361
Menander **9**:236
Terence **14**:341

Gray, Wallace
Iliad **1**:405

Green, D. H.
Hartmann von Aue **15**:206
Wolfram von Eschenbach **5**:391

Green, Peter
Juvenal **8**:68
Ovid **7**:419
Sappho **3**:438

Greenberg, Moshe
The Book of Job **14**:196

Greene, Thomas
Aeneid **9**:399

Greenfield, Stanley B.
Beowulf **1**:119
The Dream of the Rood **14**:243

Gregory, Eileen
Sappho **3**:495

Grene, David
Aeschylus **11**:220

Grierson, Herbert J. C.
Beowulf **1**:90

Griffin, Jasper
Iliad **1**:392

Grigson, Geoffrey
Sei Shonagon **6**:300

Grimm, Charles
Chrétien de Troyes **10**:141

Groden, Suzy Q.
Sappho **3**:436

Groos, Arthur
Wolfram von Eschenbach **5**:423

Grossman, Judith
Arabian Nights **2**:57

Grossvogel, Steven
Boccaccio, Giovanni **13**:114

Grube, G. M. A.
Aristophanes **4**:136
Cicero, Marcus Tullius **3**:258

Gruffydd, W. J.
Mabinogion **9**:159

Grunmann-Gaudet, Minnette
The Song of Roland **1**:248

Guardini, Romano
Augustine, St. **6**:95
The Book of Psalms **4**:414

Guarino, Guido A.
Boccaccio, Giovanni **13**:52

Gudzy, N. K.
The Igor Tale **1**:485

Gunkel, Hermann
The Book of Psalms **4**:379

Gunn, Alan M. F.
Romance of the Rose **8**:402

Guthrie, W. K. C.
Plato **8**:321, 360

Hackett, Jeremiah M. G.
Bacon, Roger **14**:99, 110

Hadas, Moses
Aeschylus **11**:150
Apuleius **1**:23
Aristophanes **4**:121
Hesiod **5**:98
Juvenal **8**:45
Plato **8**:304
Sappho **3**:417
Seneca, Lucius Annaeus **6**:378, 385

Hägg, Tomas
Longus **7**:262

Haight, Elizabeth Hazelton
Apuleius **1**:18

Haines, C. R.
Sappho **3**:397

Haley, Lucille
Ovid **7**:310

Hallam, Henry
Bacon, Roger **14**:16
Poem of the Cid **4**:225

Hallberg, Peter
Hrafnkel's Saga **2**:124
Njáls saga **13**:339

Hallett, Judith P.
Sappho **3**:465

Halleux, Pierre
Hrafnkel's Saga **2**:99, 102

Halverson, John
Beowulf **1**:131

Hamilton, Edith
Aeschylus **11**:128
Aristophanes **4**:109
Sophocles **2**:328
Terence **14**:322

Hamori, Andras
Arabian Nights **2**:51

Handley, E. W.
Menander **9**:243, 276

Hanning, Robert
Marie de France **8**:158

Hanson-Smith, Elizabeth
Mabinogion **9**:192

Hardison, O. B., Jr.
Mystery of Adam **4**:203

Hardy, E. G.
Juvenal **8**:17

Hardy, Lucy
Boccaccio, Giovanni **13**:30

Harris, Charles
K lid sa **9**:81

Harrison, Ann Tukey
The Song of Roland **1**:261

Harrison, Robert
The Song of Roland **1**:220

Harsh, Philip Whaley
Menander **9**:216

Hart, Henry H.
Polo, Marco **15**:309

Hart, Thomas R.
Poem of the Cid **4**:306

Hartley, L. P.
Murasaki, Lady **1**:422

Hastings, R.
Boccaccio, Giovanni **13**:59

Hatto, A. T.
Gottfried von Strassburg **10**:259

Critic Index

Critic Index